MEMORIES OF A LOST WORLD

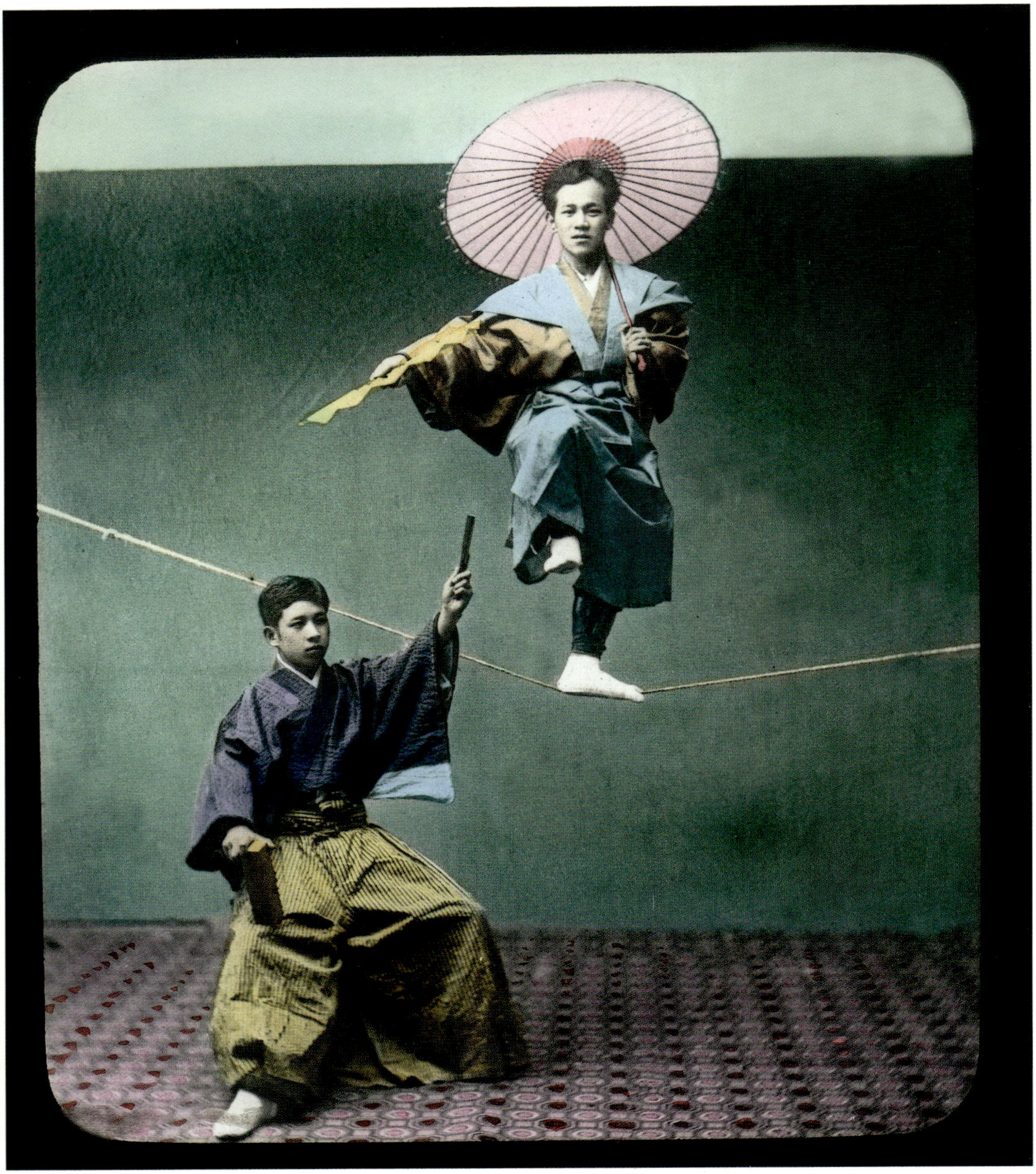

Charlotte Fiell

Memories of a Lost World

Travels through the Magic Lantern

with additional introductory text
by James R. Ryan

FIELL

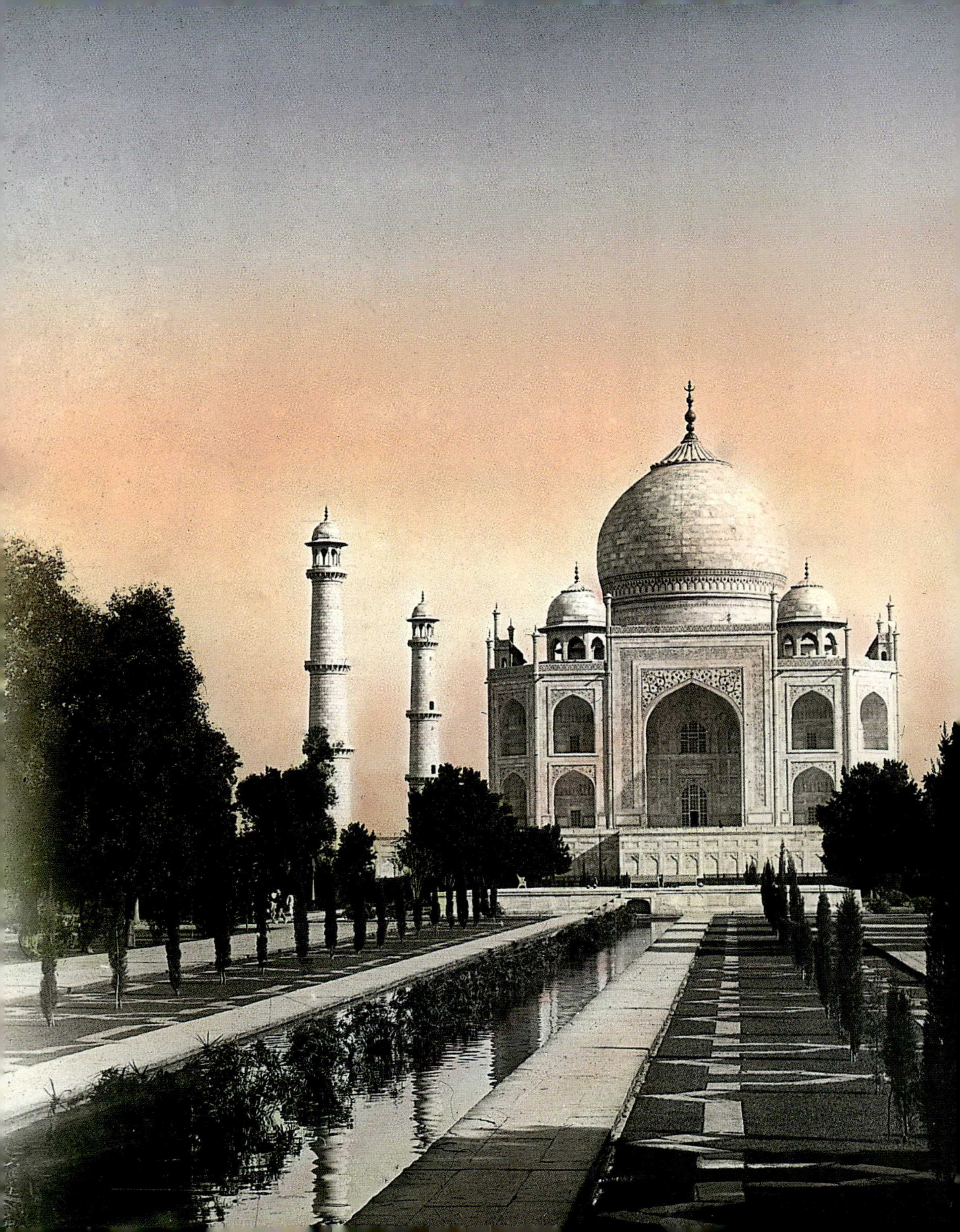

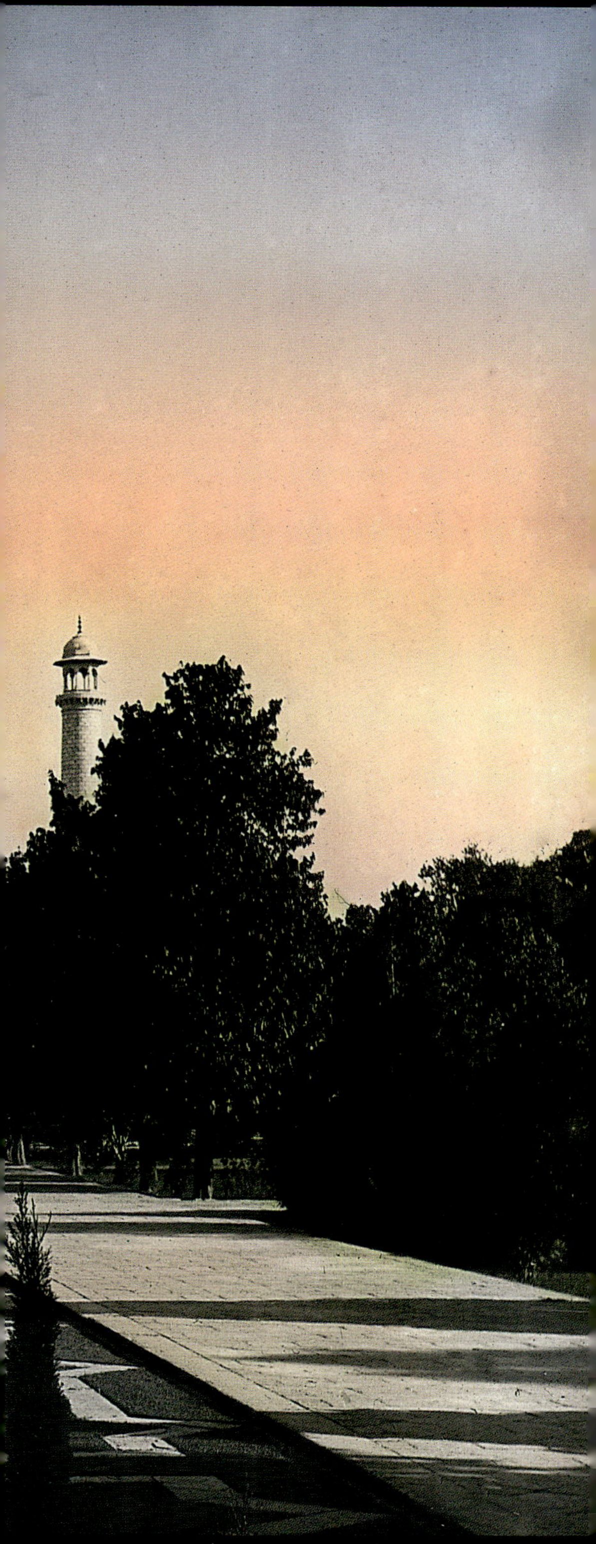

CONTENTS

The Middle East

Southern Asia

Eastern Asia

South Eastern Asia

Oceania

Antarctica

South America

Central America

United States of America

Canada

Alaska

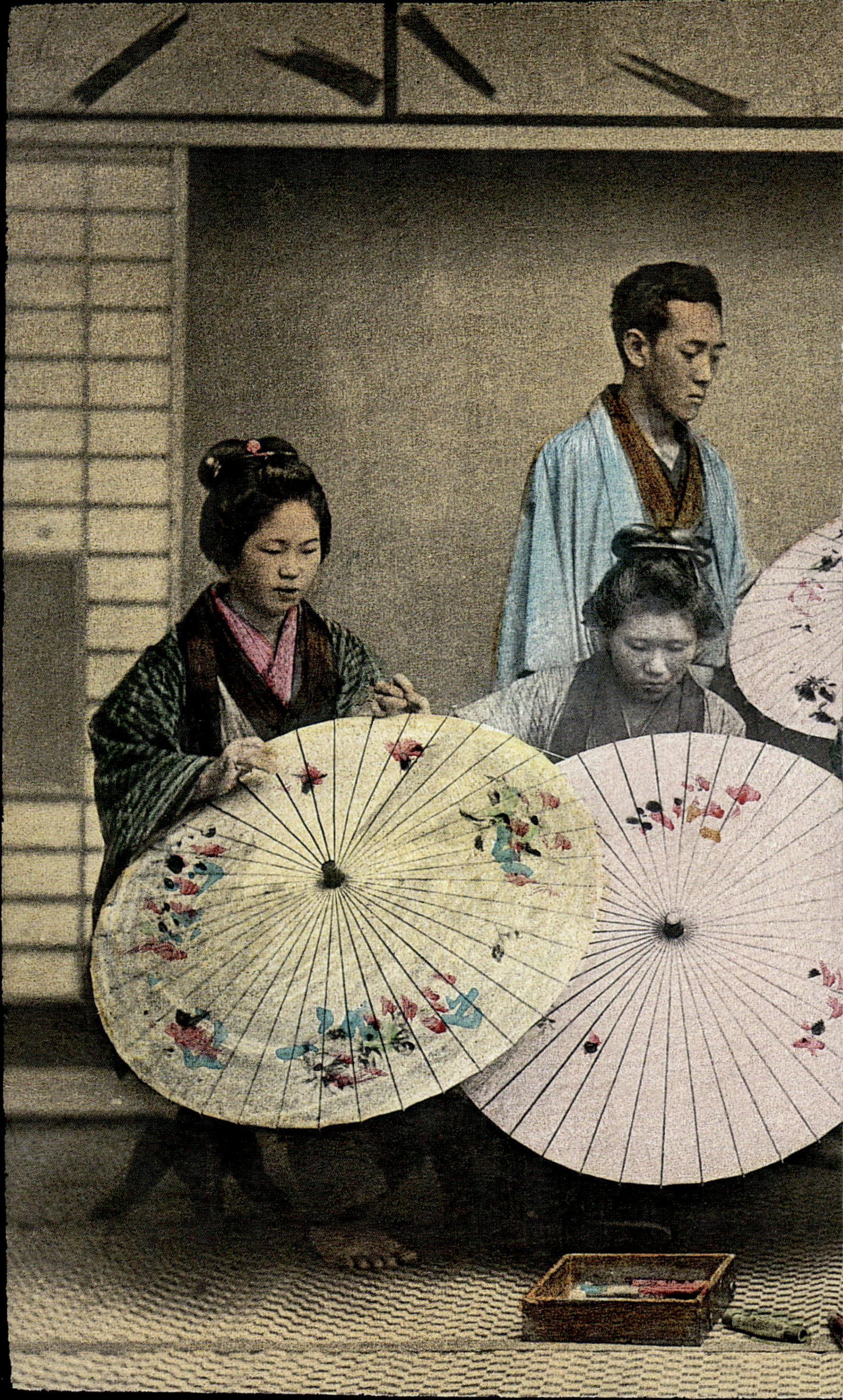

2 Young women manufacturing parasols, Japan, 1870s

2 Junge Frauen fertigen Sonnenschirme, Japan, 1870er Jahre

2 Jeunes femmes Faisant des parasols, Japon, années 1870

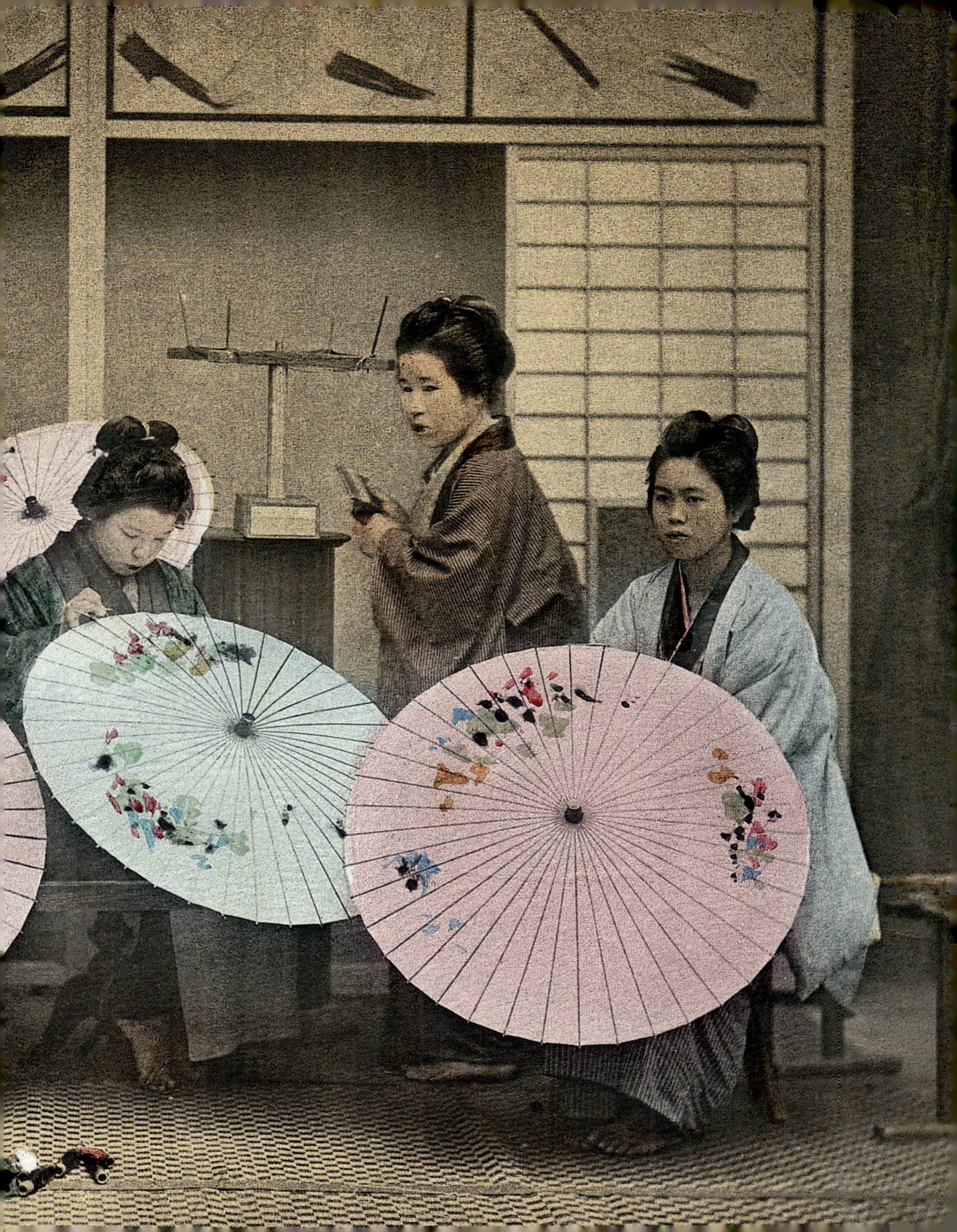

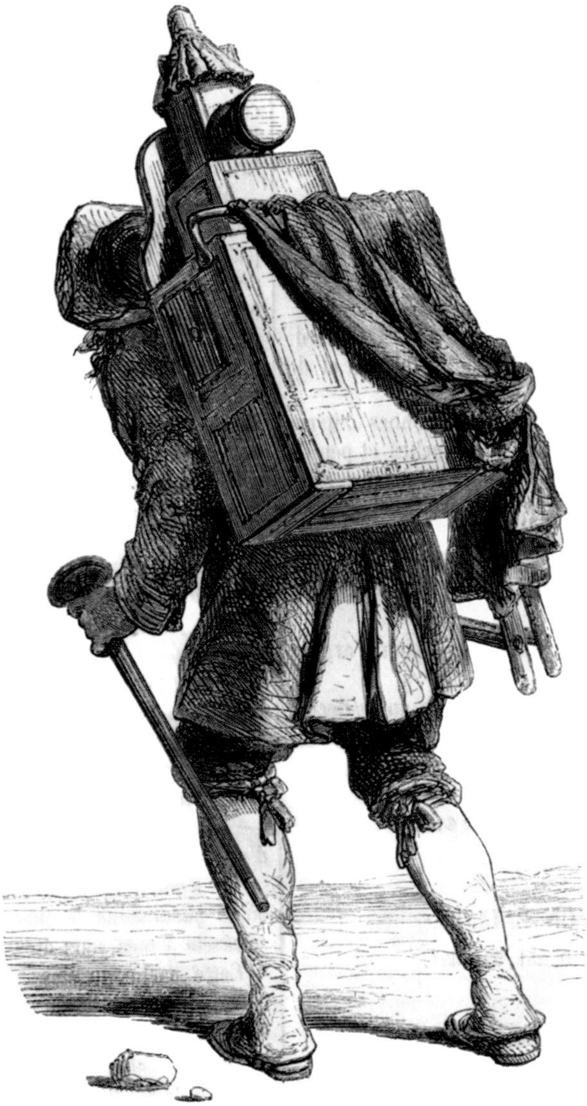

"Travelling Lanternist" engraving by A. Mouilleron after Poisson, 1774

"Reisender Laternist", Kupferstich von A. Mouilleron nach Poisson, 1774

Lanterniste ambulant. Gravure de A. Mouilleron, d'après Poisson, 1774

MEMORIES OF A LOST WORLD

CHARLOTTE FIELL

Before movies or television, or indeed mass travel, magic lantern slides were an important means by which people learnt about the world – its diverse landscapes, cultures and peoples. These early slide shows were multi-media presentations, often accompanied by readings and music. They were hugely popular, allowing audiences to travel up the Nile, across Asia, or into Africa – thereby opening a window onto a previously impenetrable world. Collected over a number of years, this comprehensive collection of slide images provides not only a cornucopia of poignant photographic memories, but also offers us a range of unique and fascinating historical insights into national characteristics and cultural practices ... a global tour of a lost world.

THE ORIGINS OF THE MAGIC LANTERN

The story of the 'magic lantern' projector stretches back two hundred years before the advent of photography. The first magic lantern slide projector is believed to have been invented by a Dutch mathematician and astronomer, Christiaan Huygens, in the late 1650s. However, the German Jesuit scholar Athanasius Kircher is sometimes misattributed with the device's invention after he outlined the principles of the device in his 1646 volume, *Ars Magna Lucis et Umbrae (The Great Art of Light and Shadow)*. The actual term 'magic lantern' was also coined during the mid-seventeenth century, referring to relatively primitive projectors lit by candles or oil lamps that were used in conjunction with hand-painted glass slides. In 1665, a London-based optician, John Reeves, began manufacturing lanterns for sale. The English diarist Samuel Pepys was one of his earliest customers, writing in August 1666, 'Comes by agreement Mr Reeves, bringing me a lanthorn [sic], with pictures on glass, to make strange things appear on a wall, very pretty'.

From the beginning of the eighteenth century onwards, numerous inventors became involved in the further development of the magic lantern, using various mirrors and lenses and better light sources to improve the projecting quality of the apparatus. These developments promoted the wider accessibility of lanterns, and significantly improved the clarity of projections. This, in turn, enabled lanternists to organize shows that could be enjoyed by larger audiences, thereby making these activities more financially viable.

OPTICAL MAGIC IN A PRE-PHOTOGRAPHIC AGE

The earliest lantern slides were mounted in wooden frames and often featured beautifully painted Romantic-style landscapes. They could also be used to project spookily frightening images of spectres and spirits in popular shows known as 'phantas-magoria' — which meant 'a gathering of ghosts'. For these early ghoulish spectaculars, the slides were often projected behind a gauze screen, so that projector and projectionist were invisible to the audience, thereby heightening the mystification of the seemingly terrifying apparitions appearing on the screen. Today, it is difficult for us to imagine the entrancing yet shocking impact that this optical magic had on people who had never witnessed anything comparable. In fact, these gothic supernatural shows – conjuring up raised spirits, horned demons and macabre skeletons – were the equivalent of today's most extreme horror films. Indeed charlatans used magic lantern shows to dupe the unsuspecting into believing they had indeed conjured up spirits from the dead, and exploited their gullibility for ill-gotten gain.

In the early nineteenth century these early projectors were not only used for phastamagoria shows, but for other popular entertainments, with lanternists going from town to town as itinerant showmen literally carrying their apparatus on their backs. In Britain, many of these touring lanternists were from Italy, and they become know as 'Savoyards' or 'Galantees'. The latter name is believed to derive from their cry: 'Galantee So!' – the Italian word '*galante*' meaning 'gallant', and 'so' being their heavily accented mispronunciation of 'show', and the combination meaning 'fine performance'. An organ-grinding assistant often accompanied these strolling lanternists giving their shows an added sensory dimension, and it was often the job of these assistants to provide a running commentary too.

Magic lantern slides were also widely used for educative purposes, such as the teaching of astronomy or botany. They also appear to have been extensively used as an instructional tool for the telling of Biblical stories – even the temperance movement used them to help spread its worthy message. And, of course, they were a wonderful form of entertainment for children, with numerous 'slide sets' manufactured from nursery rhymes, popular songs, amusing or moralising stories and, of course, traditional fairy tales. They were the children's cartoons of a pre-cinematic age. The first theatre devised specifically for magic lantern presentations was opened in 1848 at the Polytechnic Institution in London's fashionable Regent Street, and instantly became a major attraction offering well-attended spectaculars combining arresting images with sound, music and lectures. Indeed, it even boasted a team of people for sound effects who were hidden out of sight behind the screen. The Polytechnic's theatre (now part of the University of Westminster) had a capacity of 1,500 people and, apart from staging numerous magic lantern shows, it also hosted the famous optical projections of ghosts by the Victorian popular scientist and showman 'Professor' John Henry Pepper.

By the mid-nineteenth century, slide shows had also began to feature movement, with two or three sheets of glass being incorporated into each slide. These glass sheets were designed to move over each other, constituting rudimentary sequences of animated images and providing an optical illusion of motion. Many of these slides were humorous, with visual jokes of nose-growing, eye-crossing, head-bashing, hat-doffing, skeleton-dancing, pig-riding and so on. Others featured landscape scenes showing the passing of the day from early sunrise to moonlit night, or ships moving sedately across a horizon. Another type of moveable slide that made

"The Magic Lantern" drawn by H.G. Hine, The Illustrated London News, December 1858

"The Magic Lantern", Zeichnung von H.G. Hine, The Illustrated London News, Dezember 1858

"La lanterne magique", dessin de H.G. Hine, The Illustrated London News, décembre 1858

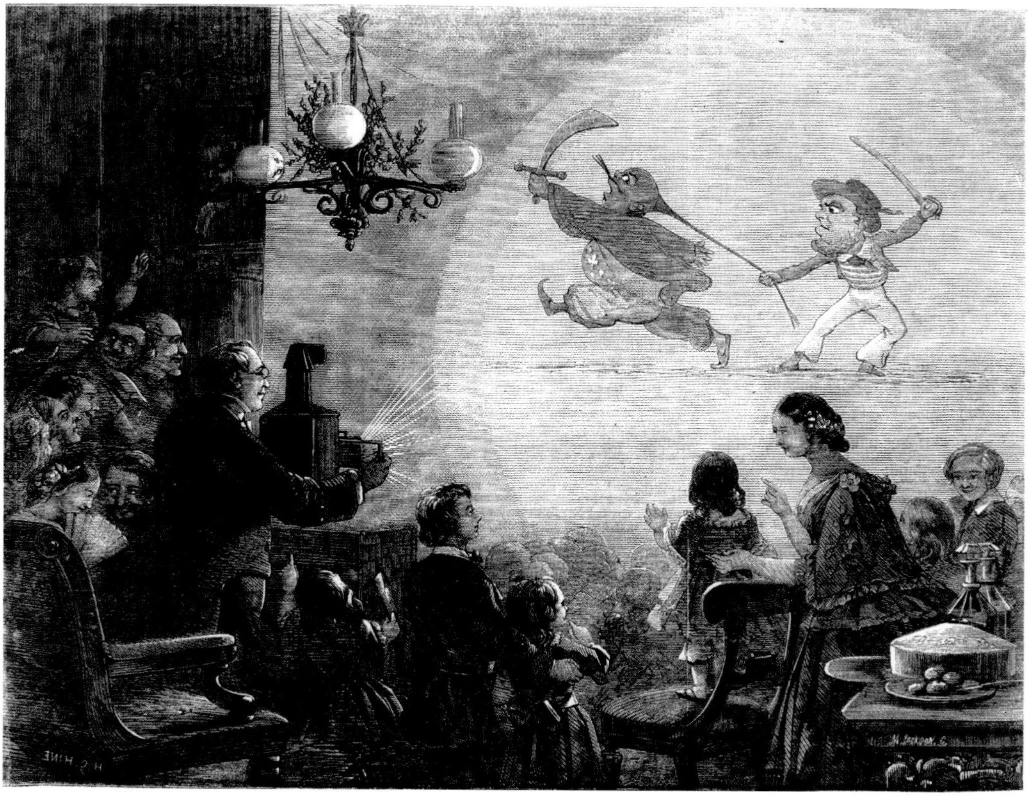

a great impact was the 'chromotrope' (introduced in the 1820s), which was a type of projected kaleidoscope of coloured geometric patterns that had a mesmerizing effect as its handle was mechanically cranked to rotate one piece of glass over another. Indeed these almost hypnotic slides were nicknamed 'artificial fireworks' by Victorian children revelling in their extraordinary explosions of light and colour.

Until the early nineteenth century, magic lantern slides had been drawn and coloured by hand before being mounted in sturdy wooden frames which made them safer to handle and protected the slides' painted surfaces from scratches. This relatively laborious process meant that early non-photographic slides were made using a system of serial production rather than true mass production. It was soon realized, however, that it was far more convenient for the lantern projector to have an in-built carrier into which slides could be dropped, and this of course necessitated a standard size of slide. In Britain a square format was adopted (83 mm × 83 mm), while in continental Europe and American slightly larger, landscape formats were selected (93 mm × 83 mm and 102 mm × 83 mm respectively). The introduction of a slide carrier also required the use of an extra slip of glass to protect the image from being scratched – the square of glass with the photographic image fixed to it was bonded to this additional glass layer using gummed tape. The image was also frequently framed within an

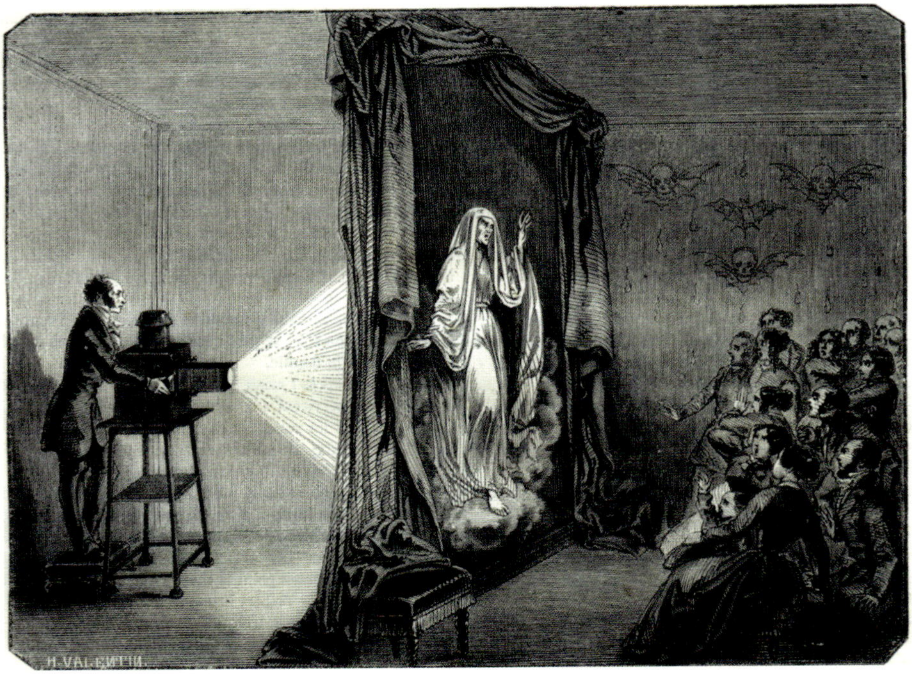

opaque paper border known as a mask, and many of the commercially-made slides were labelled with printed or written information identifying their subject matter.

Other technical innovations also facilitated the viable mass production of slides in the mid-nineteenth century, most notably the introduction of lithographic printing, which allowed images to be transferred and replicated exactly. By this stage, the quality of projectors had also progressed hugely, thanks not least to the availability of better illuminates. Intense white limelight became widely used in the 1870s, and later in the 1890s dazzling electric arc light was adopted. Quite simply, the stronger the light source encased within the projector, the better the image quality on the screen. During the mid-nineteenth century, the heyday of magic lantern performances, some of the projectors – generally known as 'Magic Lanterns' or 'Stereopticons' – were magnificent objects in their own right, and some of the finest examples featured cabinets made of richly toned mahogany and boasted up to three different lenses encased in gleaming brass. The models that comprised these multiple lenses were used to dissolve one image into another to provide the illusion of changing day into night, summer into winter or setting a ship or building on fire. It was, however, the advent of photographic slides in the mid-1800s that was to change the nature of magic lantern shows forever.

THE ADVENT OF PHOTOGRAPHIC SLIDES

Although the process for making daguerreotypes had been introduced by Louis Daguerre in January 1839, this early photographic process had no influence on the manufacture of lantern slides. Despite being the first large-scale and commercial photographic process, there was a significant drawback: daguerreotype images were fixed on

A scene showing a phantasmagoria projection, engraving after Gustave Moreau, 1849

Vorführung einer Phantasmagorie, Kupferstich nach Gustave Moreau, 1849

Projection fantasmagorique. Gravure d'après Gustave Moreau, 1849

copper plates that were coated with a light-sensitive silver compound, which meant that light could not pass through them. Moreover, they could not be reproduced and were therefore unique one-offs. In the early 1840s, calotypes were introduced by William Henry Fox Talbot, who is rightly regarded as the founder of modern photography. However this process, which used paper coated in light-sensitive silver iodide, shared the same drawback of incompatibility with the commercial replication of captured images.

The breakthrough finally came with the introduction of a new negative process developed by Abel Niépce de Saint-Victor known as 'niépceotype' that used egg albumen to bind the silver iodide salts onto glass plates. Particularly suited for landscape and architectural subjects, the process produced precise, almost grainless images. This method was further improved by the Philadelphia photographers Friedrich and Wilhelm Langenheim, who managed to create positive rather than negative images on sheets of glass. The first lantern slides using this process were produced in 1849, and the following year the brothers' 'hyalotype' method was patented. Although the Langenheims had initially conceived their slides as a form of entertainment in fee-paying picture shows, their photographic lantern slides soon gained a much wider remit, especially within the realms of education and home entertainment.

During the 1860s, albumen continued to be used for the production of magic lantern slides because it still offered excellent image resolution – a crucial consideration when projecting a photographic image onto a screen. However, other processes, including the use of collodian and gelatin emulsions, were also employed in the production of photographic slides. Many slides were coloured by hand using transparent dyes, sometimes in a very skilful manner and at other times rather more crudely. This hand tinting of slides gave the impression of full colour photography, decades before it had actually been invented. By the late nineteenth century, lantern slides were being commercially produced in their tens of thousands by a variety of companies. In London alone, there were twenty-eight different firms manufacturing slides during the 1880s and 1890s. During this period, and in order to meet the public's insatiable desire for new subject matter, intrepid photographers travelled to the four corners of the globe to record unfamiliar and exotic lands, peoples and cultures.

THE GOLDEN AGE OF THE PHOTOGRAPHIC MAGIC LANTERN IMAGE

As lantern shows became an increasingly popular way of seeing the wider world, slides began to be sold or rented out in boxed sets with accompanying booklets so that running commentaries could be delivered throughout the shows. For example, the Victor Animatograph Company of Davenport, Iowa, produced a set of sixty slides entitled, *Egypt, The Land of Romance*. The commentary had a distinctly dramatic quality: 'Since the dawn of history the ancient land of Egypt has been wrapt [sic] in a veil of mystery and romance, yet, as the mists of the centuries have been lifted, we find there the cradle of much of our modern civilization...But, before embarking upon our present trip up the Nile...'

And so it continues. It was also common for public performances to be accompanied by appropriate music further to heighten the drama.

In addition, magic lantern shows were increasingly being used as home entertainment, and cheaper toy projectors for children became extremely popular. Between the 1870s and the 1930s, firms such as Newton & Company and Bamforth & Company in England, or Underwood & Underwood and the Keystone View Company in the USA, produced impressive catalogues of photographic travelogues, many of which you will find represented over the following pages. Some amateur photographers also made lantern slides from their own negatives, and because these images were not produced in large industrialized quantities they are often remarkable for their careful and precise hand tinting. The subjects captured by these recreational photographers are also frequently more candid, showing intimate vignettes of family life or personal trips overseas. A further type of lantern slide included in this survey, and significant in terms of geographic and photographic history, are the images documenting exploration, such as Roald Amundsen's South Pole expedition (1910–1912). Of perhaps equal historical importance are the images with a socio-anthropological remit, including those that recorded indigenous peoples, such as a tribe of pygmies living in New Guinea.

Lantern slides were also important teaching aids, and were used not only by school boards, but also by missionary societies, who found they were an excellent way of showing peoples living in 'heathen lands' (as the Church of England's Zenana Missionary Society put it) who needed to be or who had already been converted to the joys of Christianity. Perhaps some of the most beautiful and poignant lantern slides, however, are those from Japan, many of which appear to capture scenes of everyday customs and rituals, but which in reality were taken in photographers' studios on a relatively staged set. This, of course, begs the question of whether they were overtly choreographed for the European market, with its voracious appetite for exotic orientalism, or whether they can be seen as true representations of Japanese life. Other slides that have an extraordinarily evocative resonance are those from Egypt – such as images of the Sphinx in its still unexcavated state, or the slide of Cleopatra's Needle before the obelisk made its long journey overseas. As with the study of all images, it is important to bear in the mind the historical, social and political contexts that may have influenced their composition. This is especially the case with lantern slides, because they were used to educate people in a period of high imperialism and colonialism – for instance, India was still under British rule, and European nations were scrambling to divide up the African continent.

The golden period of photographic magic lantern slides – from the 1870s to the 1930s – also coincided with the rise of Romanticism that nostalgically sought to trace national and cultural roots in the face of rapid industrialization. This further informed the choice of subjects and the ways in which they were depicted. This increasing mechanization and growing urbanization of these years in the West was also captured and celebrated through lantern images, from Peter Behren's AEG turbine hall in Berlin (a proto-Modern architectural masterpiece) to the early skyscrapers of Chicago. Above all, this collection of lantern images gives a world view of life before mass travel and mass communications, and as such reveals an age where national characteristics were less blurred by the culturally homogenizing influence of globalization.

With the introduction of cinema in 1895, when the Lumière brothers showed their first moving photographic pictures, it might have seemed that magic lantern shows had been rendered obsolete. This was not, however, the case. In spite of the fact that the magic lantern is often mistakenly identified as a pre-cinema phenomenon, slide shows remained a popular form of entertainment into the 1930s. It was, in fact, Kodak's introduction of thirty-five-millimetre Kodachrome slide film in 1936 that truly marked the end of the magic lantern. Those beautiful squares of sandwiched glass that offered such a tantalizing window into foreign lands, intriguing customs and different peoples became a thing of the past. In their time, they had been an optical wonder, exploring and communicating the natural and man-made worlds, and revealing the multi-faceted nature of mankind. And, as a lanternist would say, it is now time to embark on a fascinating journey back through time to the bustling streets of London, the ancient monuments of Egypt, the extraordinary customs of Japan and the majestic landscapes of the Americas... *Bon Voyage!*

TRAVELS THROUGH THE MAGIC LANTERN

JAMES R. RYAN

In its heyday in the late nineteenth century, the magic lantern show was a hugely popular form of spectacle both designed to educate and entertain large audiences. In theatres, schools, scientific societies and church halls throughout Britain, as well as further afield in Britain's colonies, continental Europe and North America, audiences thrilled to lantern slide shows on a wide variety of themes and topics. These ranged from sentimental tales designed to impart a lesson in morality, to stories of national heroes of the age, to lessons in science and discovery. Lantern slide shows also catered to an increasing hunger for photographic views of distant lands and new peoples fast being encountered in an age of empire, mass communication and modernity. It is this expanding geographical horizon that provides the backdrop to the lantern slides of around the world in this remarkable collection.

The lantern slides in this extensive collection have their origins in a diverse range of sources, from amateur makers to professional studios, all catering in some way to the taste amongst Western audiences in the nineteenth and early twentieth century for photographs of sites and scenes of travel from around the world. Recreating the precise routes through which each slide has survived and ended up fortuitously in this particular collection is an almost impossible task. Yet it is surely important that we acknowledge at the outset that such collections represent the tip of a visual iceberg, much which has long since melted away as lantern slides have been overlooked, discarded and destroyed in the decades since they lost their currency against moving images and 35 mm slides in the twentieth century. How comprehensive or representative surviving collections are is not always easy to ascertain; the less attractive imagery or interesting subject matter invariably fare less well in this process.

The popularity of lantern slides, like other technologies of printing, publishing and photography, was part and parcel of an unprecedented expansion in the circulation and viewing of printed words and images of all kinds in the nineteenth century. The growth of the middle classes and urban dwellers prompted a surge in demand for visual cultural forms that satisfied their interests and achievements. The growth of tourism, advertising, news and propaganda all stimulated the market for quantities of cheap, mass-produced ephemera. Improvements in education and the expansion of commerce and leisure time, fuelled further demand for technologies of visual instruction with which to inform, educate and entertain popular and specialist audiences.

The lantern slides in this collection are global in scope. Yet the imaginative geography lesson that they present tends to be one designed from the point of view of an exclusively white, Western and middle class audience. They could almost be a set of picture postcards compiled by an early twentieth century well-to-do tourist during a world tour. This is apparent both from the predominance of particular places in the collection as well as the motifs that structure views of landscape and portraits of people from particular places.

Take for example the lantern slides of Britain. The country is pictured along the lines of a tourist's itinerary, with the grandeur of London at its core. The photographs transport us virtually on a tourist's itinerary of the capital city's famous sites: the Houses of Parliament; Tower Bridge; the Crown Jewels (even pictured just as the tourist would view them - through railings and glass); London Zoo; St Paul's Cathedral; London Guildhall; Trafalgar Square and Victoria embankment – the latter with a Thames coloured an unlikely Prussian blue. Scenes of Ludgate Circus and The Strand show bustling crowds and traffic. Most interior scenes of landmark buildings, such as Westminster Abbey, as well as a good number of exterior views of landmarks such as Trafalgar Square are, by contrast, devoid of people, reflecting perhaps their making by commercial photographers seeking a clear, depopulated and more marketable view of key landmarks.

The British countryside, it would seem from these views, is populated by happy, colourful farmers and other rural folk tending contentedly to their fields and livestock. Well-dressed Edwardian children play against a backdrop of Shakespeare's England, replete with tudor cottages and country gardens. Churches nestle comfortably in rolling landscapes and across the great span of Britain's countryside, from picturesque glimpses of ruined abbeys and Cornish harbours to dramatic vistas in the Lake District, there are no signs of industrial modernity to be seen.

In offering a kind of virtual travel, lantern slides were aimed at equivalent audiences to the mass-produced, photographically-illustrated books published in the late nineteenth century such as *The Queen's Empire* (1897) that presented popular visual surveys of Britain and her empire. Such works presented a similar portrait of Britain, dominated by famous cities and landmark buildings and inhabited by a contented, loyal population characterised by locally based traditions. Lantern slides were seen as a particularly effective means to project a singular set of images and values to large audiences. Indeed, in 1902 the Colonial Office set up a Committee of Visual Instruction to coordinate the making of sets of photographic lantern slides with which to instruct school children of their role as imperial citizens. Lantern slides of Britain, structured much along the lines noted above, but with more emphasis on imperial defence and industrial power, were dispatched all over the empire to teach children of the empire about the mother country.

British colonial territories, including Australia and Canada, also used lantern slide shows, together with postcards, international exhibitions and fairs to project an image of their landscape within a familiar English aesthetic and to promote themselves for investment, immigration and tourism. Hence the photographs of such places tend to be projected and understood in terms of British colonial relationships and understood through a limited number of iconic themes. Australia is thus represented through photographs of marsupials, and sheep farming, while Canada is frequently made familiar to British audiences through views of Victorian colonial architecture, such as the

3 Bamum tribesman and children, Cameroon, c.1900

3 Stammesangehörige des Bamum-Volkes, Kamerun, um 1900

3 Membres de la tribu Bamoun, Cameroun, vers 1900

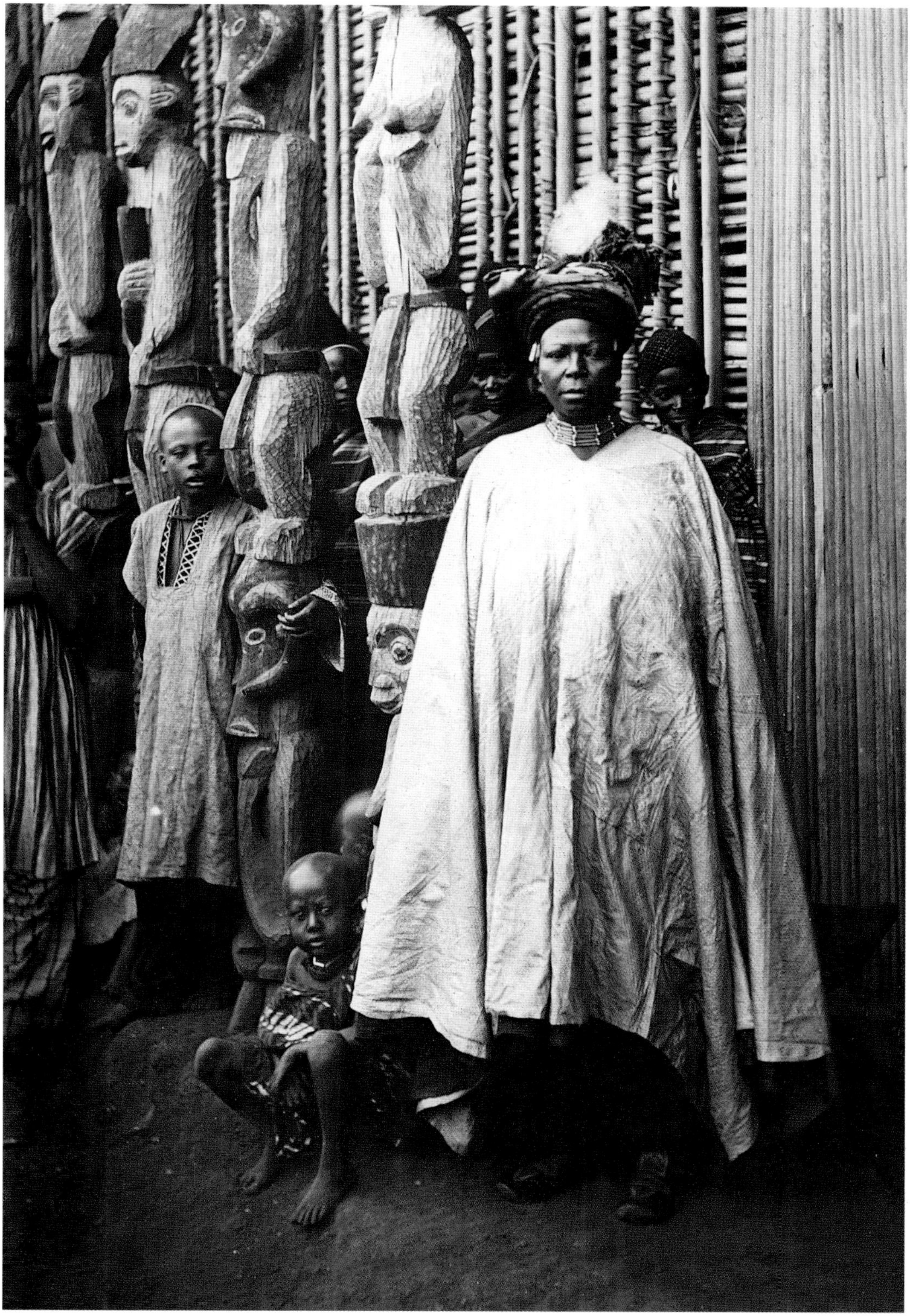

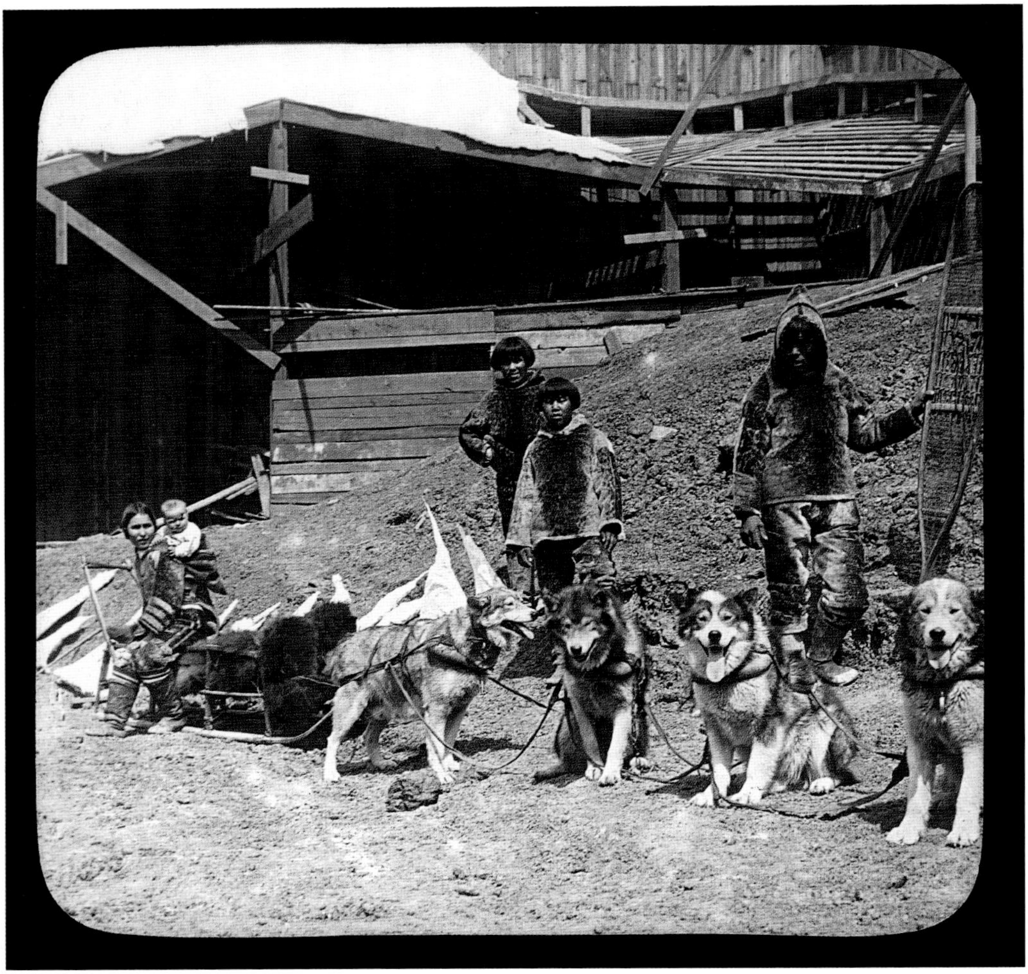

Parliament Buildings in Ottawa, and railways opening up new colonial territory.

The lantern slides of continental Europe in this collection, like those of Britain, tend to portray a tourist's view of highlights of particular countries. Rural peasants, clad in colourful costumes, and rural scenes of family units making a living from the land are a common theme, from grape picking in France to cleaning and sacking beans in Sicily. The scenes of Eastern Europe present a notable contrast between the modernity of government buildings, post offices and urban infrastructure and the very traditional lives of rural peasantry on display. The photographs of Germany in the slides present one of the few glimpses of industrial modernity, with scenes of blast furnaces and canals around the river Rhein.

The views of France, Switzerland and Italy are most consistently constructed as marketable scenes for tourist visitors. The views of Paris made

4 Eskimo Dog Team and Sledge, World's Fair, St. Louis, USA, 1904

4 Eskimos mit Schlittenhundegespann, Weltausstellung, St. Louis, USA, 1904

4 Chiens esquimaux et traîneau, Exposition Universelle, St. Louis, USA, 1904

by Beseler Lantern Slide Company of New York at the time of the Exposition Universelle in 1900 present a particularly attractive view of the grand boulevards, landmarks and promenades of the capital designed to appeal to the millions of visitors to the Exposition. The Grand Tour iconography continues through Monte Carlo, the Swiss Alps and though Italy and Greece, where the scenes focus on ancient monuments in Rome, Florence, Venice and Athens. Italians and Greeks appear occasionally in street scenes, in isolated portraits dressed in traditional costumes, or undertaking traditional rural pursuits; they are however a visual after-thought compared to the European heritage framed in the many photographs of ancient Roman and Greek monuments.

A few of the lantern slides of people in this collection fall into the category of genre photography. That is to say they are staged in order to enact a sentimental narrative or morality tale, rather than to document human experience according to conventions of realism. Portraits of 'quaint dairymaids', 'laughing farmers' or other rural workers posed in traditional costume tend, like genre paintings of mid-Victorian Britain, to present an idealised image of rural existence for an increasingly urbanised audience. Some of these lantern slides, for example of a mother praying with her two daughters, hark back to earlier Victorian lantern shows that combined popular sentiment with a social message. Victorian charities, temperance societies and non-conformist churches were active in performing lantern slide shows to illustrate social problems of drunkenness, poverty and idleness. Commercial studios such as James Bamforth of Holmfirth in Yorkshire produced a range of slides and scripts in the 1880s and 90s catering to the Victorian combination of sentiment and social conscience.

Other portraits of people are much more naturalistic in their composition. Views of rural labourers at work in South East Asia, cleaning and sacking beans in Sicily, or tilling the soil in Egypt are posed in a way to educate the viewer about the scene, rather than merely to provoke sentiment. Companies such as Keystone View Company, one of the largest makers and distributors of stereoscopic views and lantern slides, often included printed factual information about the scene depicted (for example on the reverse of stereo views) in order to make views marketable for educational and entertainment purposes. Indeed by the early twentieth century lantern slides had become an essential part of the equipment of school classrooms, particularly in the teaching of geography, and a sizeable market had developed in the sale and hire of lantern slides sets to schools for educational purposes.

Photographic portraits of non-white men, women and children made by Westerners in this period tend often to be framed, both consciously and unconsciously, by the visual conventions of physical anthropology where scrutiny and even measurement of the human body was regarded as a key marker of difference. This is evident in the lantern slides of people from Africa, particularly Central and Southern Africa, as well as India, the Middle East and the Pacific, where people are photographed in order to best display their physical form (for example, a side profile upper body view) and are characterized in the visual language of ethnographic 'types' (from 'water carriers' to 'fakirs'). While some portraits are obviously posed against unconvincing painted studio backdrops, catering to a colonial tourist demand for picturesque ethnographic 'types', others seem to have been made more spontaneously and naturalistically. The logic of much colonial tourist photography of this type however, whether studio made or not, is to cast particular non-white 'races' variously as uncivilized and exotic 'others'.

The colonial context of many of the views of Africa and India is apparent in signs of colonial economies, from ivory shipping in Mombassa to sisal plantations in Uganda, as well as the occasional view of pith-helmeted white men with uniformed African soldiers. In South Africa signs of colonial administration are more apparent still, with government buildings and urban infrastructure. However the influence that particular colonial relationships had in directly shaping photographic representations of different places is not always easy to determine. Many of the themes of colonial representation captured by military officers and explorers in colonial territories, such as natural resources, territorial conquest and ethnographic survey, are also prominent in the work of commercial photographers working further afield. Since commercial photographers were catering to Western image buyers they tended also to emphasise the civilizing influence of Western powers, through cultural infrastructure, architecture and commercial development. Hence photographs of the United States of America in this collection have their own colonial logic, depicting the process of Westward expansion and territorial acquisition from native Americans. Views of rows of oil wells in the landscape, or carcasses on the production line, attest to the march of progress and industry, while views of America's great cities such as New York represent the apogee of this process of modernity.

Photography of China in the nineteenth century was limited mostly to the few treaty ports that were open to foreign trade along the coast and Hong Kong, which was under British control, and included French, British, American, German as well as Chinese photographers. By the late 1890s Chinese commercial studios dominated the market, but continued to present Western views for a Western market. Hence photographs of China in this collection of lantern slides present a very conventional picture of everyday scenes, for example of street traders and barbers, and topography, notably of architectural signs of Western architecture and Chinese monuments.

Rather different in emphasis are the photographs of Japan. Views of Japan were amongst the most popular of tourist photographs in the early twentieth century, as is evidenced by the many beautifully coloured studio portraits of Japanese men and women in this collection. The European and American fashion for Japonese culture – Japonisme – in the nineteenth century ensured a strong demand from Western audiences for stereotypical views of geishas, maidens wearing beautiful kimonos and samurai warriors, as well as temples and views of Mount Fuji. Although some portraits of Japan conformed to Western stereotyped fantasies of 'oriental types', Japan was not a colonial territory and the Japanese had considerable influence over how they were depicted. Most importantly, by the late nineteenth century Japanese photographs were, unlike tourist views of other parts of the non-Western world, made by Japanese photographers who drew upon a pre-existing and pre-photographic iconography of Japanese identity and culture, marketing it successfully to Westerners.

The lantern slides in this remarkable collection present a compelling and complex picture of different places and peoples. In their origin the photographs are extraordinarily diverse, being drawn from official and private, professional and amateur sources; each has its own biography with both intended and unintended meanings. As lantern slides, these images have in common the fact that someone around a century ago deemed them suitable and significant enough to be transformed into a lantern slide, arranged in some kind of set and projected to an audience, probably with an accompanying textual narrative. Exactly who that audience was and what they made of the picture or its narrative interpretation is rarely documented and not straightforward to reconstruct. The geography lessons imparted by these lantern slides are informed in various ways by several dominant themes of the age, including empire, travel and modernity. It is no accident that the popularity of lantern slides mirrored the growth of late nineteenth and early twentieth century tourism and Western colonial power. In the magic of a lantern slide show all kinds of new realities could be presented to audiences hungry for sites and sensations of undiscovered worlds, from Africa to Antarctica. But there is an inequality in such narratives of discovery and exposure: while Western tourists are shown enjoying the view, gazing at the

5 Photographers at work, c.1910

5 Fotografen bei der Arbeit, um 1910

5 Photographes à l'œuvre, vers 1910

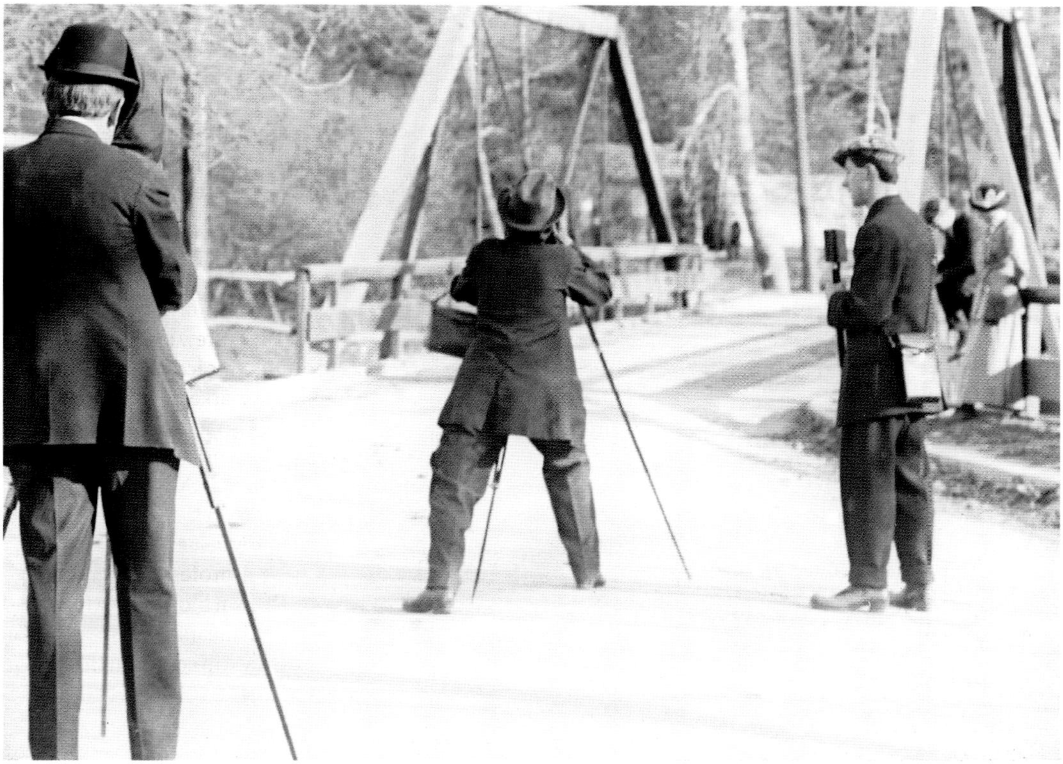

wilderness of North America, the Pyramids in Egypt or the English Lake District and able to rove around the globe imaginatively, non-Westerners are more usually depicted as the object of that same gaze, fixed in place and tradition. By the time that non-Western photographers were showing their full ability to control and project their own images of their worlds, lantern slides were in terminal decline as a form of popular entertainment, though their radical uses were not totally exhausted for several decades.

It is not always easy for viewers today to appreciate the popularity and sensorial impact that such lantern shows had on mass audiences in the late nineteenth century and early twentieth century. The accompanying music and spoken narrative have rarely survived alongside original slides, so recreating lantern shows in their full complexity is also difficult. It is clearly even harder in a printed book such as this, where original images need to be reordered to new interpretative logic. However, that should not stop collectors and admirers of lantern slides seeking to place these compelling images in some kind of wider cultural context and historical setting in order to better appreciate their attractions and attendant meanings.

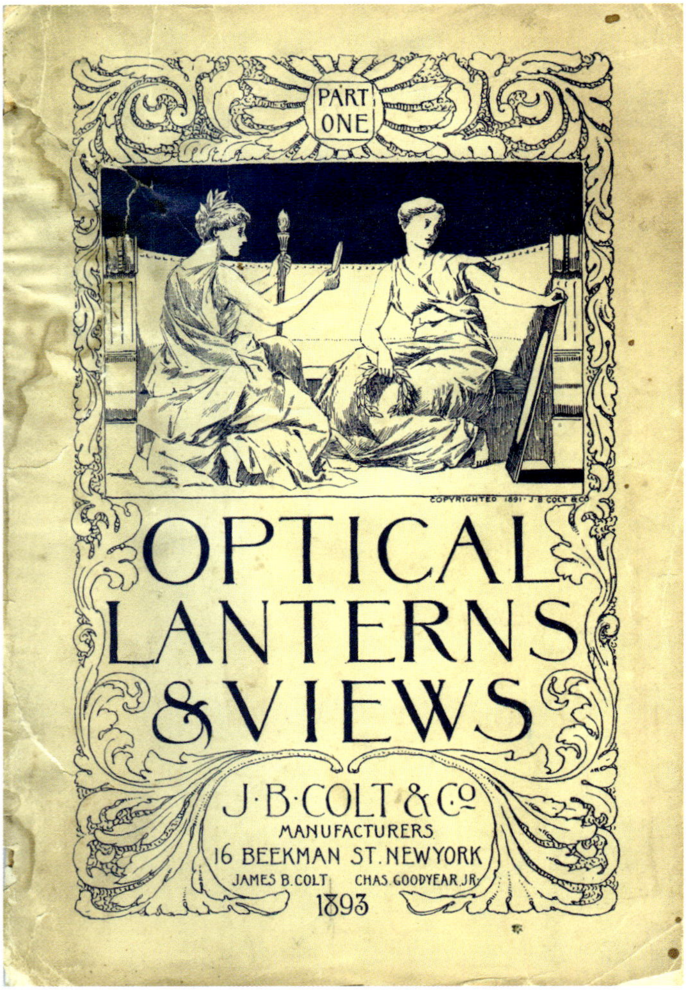

J.B. Colt & Co. catalogue, 1893

Katalog von J.B. Colt & Co., 1893

Catalogue J.B. Colt & Co. 1893

ERINNERUNGEN AN EINE VERLOREN GEGANGENE WELT

CHARLOTTE FIELL

Lange vor Film, Fernsehen oder gar Massentourismus bildeten die Diapositive, die mit der Laterna Magica projiziert wurden, ein wichtiges Medium, Menschen die Welt mit ihren verschiedenen Landschaften, Kulturen und Völkern nahezubringen. Die frühen Vorführungen waren multimediale Präsentationen, die oft von Lesungen und Musik begleitet wurden. Sie waren ungemein populär und ermöglichten es dem Publikum, den Nil aufwärts zu bereisen, Asien zu durchqueren oder ins Innere Afrikas vorzudringen, und so öffneten sie ein Fenster auf eine bis dahin verschlossene Welt. Die hier abgebildete, über viele Jahre entstandene umfassende Sammlung von Diamotiven bietet nicht nur eine Fülle ergreifender fotografischer Erinnerungen, sondern gewährt zudem einzigartige, facettenreiche und faszinierende historische Einblicke in nationale Eigenheiten und kulturelle Gebräuche – eine Zeitreise zurück in eine verloren gegangene Welt.

DIE ANFÄNGE DER LATERNA MAGICA

Die Geschichte der Projektion mit der ‚Zauberlaterne' nimmt ihren Anfang zweihundert Jahre vor dem Aufkommen der Fotografie. Man vermutet, dass die erste Laterna Magica Ende der 1650er Jahre vom niederländischen Mathematiker und Astronomen Christiaan Huygens ersonnen wurde. Fälschlicherweise wird die Erfindung bisweilen dem deutschen Gelehrten und Jesuitenpater Athanasius Kircher zugeschrieben, da Kircher das Prinzip des Projektionsapparates 1646 in seinem Werk *Ars Magna Lucis et Umbrae (Die Große Kunst des Lichts und des Schattens)* darlegt. Der Begriff ‚Zauberlaterne' oder ‚Laterna Magica' wurde ebenfalls Mitte des siebzehnten Jahrhunderts geprägt und bezog sich auf relativ primitive Projektionsgeräte, für die als Lichtquelle Kerzen oder Öllämpchen benutzt und handgemalte Glasplättchen verwendet wurden. 1665 begann der in London ansässige Optiker John Reeves mit der Herstellung und dem Verkauf von Laternen. Der englische Tagebuchautor Samuel Pepys war einer seiner ersten Kunden und schrieb im August 1666: „Vereinbarungsgemäß kommt Mr. Reeves und bringt mir eine Laterne mit Bildern hinter Glas, um sonderbare Dinge auf der Wand erscheinen zu lassen, sehr hübsch."

Seit dem frühen 18. Jahrhundert haben zahlreiche Erfinder die Weiterentwicklung der Laterna Magica vorangetrieben, indem sie verschiedene Hohlspiegel, Linsen und andere Lichtquellen einsetzten, um die Projektionsqualität des Apparates zu verbessern. Diese Fortschritte förderten die weitere Verbreitung der Laterna Magica und sorgten für eine größere Schärfe der Abbildungen. Das hinwiederum erlaubte es den Vorführern, Darbietungen zur Unterhaltung eines wachsenden Publikums zu organisieren und diese Veranstaltungen somit auch rentabler zu machen.

OPTISCHER ZAUBER IN EINEM VORFOTOGRAFISCHEN ZEITALTER

Die frühesten Dias für die Laterna Magica waren in Holzrahmen gefasst und zeigten oftmals wundervoll gemalte romantische Landschaften. Sie wurden auch genutzt, um spukhafte, Furcht erregende Bilder von Gespenstern oder Geistern in den äußerst beliebten ‚Phantasmagorien', den ‚Versammlungen der Geister', zu erzeugen. Bei diesen frühen makabren Spektakeln wurden die Bilder häufig hinter einem Tüllschirm projiziert, sodass Apparat und Vorführer für die Zuschauer unsichtbar blieben, wodurch der geheimnisvolle Effekt der scheinbar Angst einflößenden Erscheinungen auf der Leinwand noch erhöht wurde. Heute ist es nur schwer vorstellbar, welch trancehafte und zugleich erschütternde Wirkung dieser optische Zauber auf Menschen hatte, die nie zuvor etwas Ähnliches gesehen hatten. Diese schaurigen, übernatürlichen Präsentationen – das Beschwören von Geistern, gehörnten Dämonen und gruseligen Skeletten – waren die Vorläufer heutiger besonders grauenvoller Horrorfilme. Scharlatane veranstalteten Aufführungen mit der Laterna Magica, um Ahnungslosen vorzuspiegeln, sie hätten tatsächlich Geister von den Toten heraufbeschworen – und so nutzten sie Leichtgläubigkeit für schmählichen Gewinn aus.

Anfang des 19. Jahrhunderts wurden diese Projektionsgeräte nicht nur für Phantasmagorien verwendet, sondern auch für andere populäre Unterhaltungsformen, die Laternisten zum Besten gaben, die als fahrende Schausteller von Stadt zu Stadt zogen und ihren Apparat sprichwörtlich auf dem Rücken trugen. In England kamen viele dieser Wandervorführer aus Italien und wurden bekannt als ‚Savoyarden' oder ‚Galantees'. Man nimmt an, dass letztere Bezeichnung von ihrem Ruf „Galantee So!" herrührt – italienisch ‚galante' bedeutet ‚galant' und ‚so' war das mit mächtigem Akzent fehlerhaft ausgesprochene Wort für ‚show', die Kombination beider meinte eine ‚vorzügliche Vorstellung'. Oft hatte der umherziehende Schausteller einen Assistenten mit einem Leierkasten an seiner Seite, um dem Auftritt noch einen zusätzlichen Sinneseindruck zu verleihen. Dieser Helfer hatte vielfach zudem die Aufgabe, die Aufführung mit Kommentaren zu begleiten.

Die Bilder der Laterna Magica dienten in hohem Maße auch erzieherischen Zwecken, etwa Unterweisungen in Astronomie oder Botanik. Sie wurden darüber hinaus offenbar ausgiebig als Unterrichtsmittel eingesetzt, um biblische Geschichten zu erzählen – selbst die Temperenzbewegung machte sie sich zu Eigen, um ihre erbauliche Botschaft zu verbreiten. Und natürlich waren sie eine wunderbare Form, um Kindern ein Vergnügen zu bereiten, zum Beispiel mit ‚Diasätzen', die in Anlehnung an Kinderlieder, beliebte Melodien, amüsante oder moralisierende Geschichten und schließlich klassische Märchen hergestellt wurden. Es waren die Kindercartoons der Vor-Kino-Ära. Das erste Theater, das speziell für Vorführungen mit der Laterna Magica entstand, wurde 1848 an der Royal Polytechnic Institution in Londons eleganter Regent Street eröffnet. Es wurde schon bald zu einer großen Attraktion und bot gut besuchte Spektakel, die fesselnde Bilder mit Geräuschen, Musik und Lesungen kombinierten. Es konnte sich eines Teams von Geräuschemachern rühmen, die außer Sicht hinter der Leinwand verborgen waren. Das Theater an der Polytechnic Institution (heute Teil der Universität von Westminster) hatte ein Fassungsvermögen von 1.500 Zuschauern und war nicht nur die Bühne für zahllose Laterna-Magica-Vorstellungen, sondern auch der Ort, wo die berühmten optischen Geisterprojektionen des populären viktorianischen Wissenschaftlers und Schaustellers ‚Professor' John Henry Pepper stattfanden.

Um die Mitte des 19. Jahrhunderts wurde in den Darbietungen das ‚bewegte Bild' neu ins Repertoire aufgenommen. In einem Rahmen wurden zu diesem Zweck zwei oder drei Glasplättchen zusammengefügt, die derart geformt waren, dass sie übereinander geschoben werden konnten und so rudimentäre Sequenzen lebendiger Bilder erzeugten, die die optische Illusion einer Bewegung hervorriefen. Viele dieser Motive waren humoristisch und zeigten witzige Momente, etwa eine sich verlängernde Nase, Schielaugen, das Lüften eines Hutes, tanzende Skelette, Schweinereiten und dergleichen mehr. Andere präsentierten Landschaftsszenen im Übergang vom Tag zur Nacht oder Schiffe, die gemächlich am Horizont kreuzten. Ein zweiter Typ bewegter Bilder war das ‚Chromatrop' (eingeführt in den 1820er Jahren), das eine große Wirkung besaß. Es handelte sich um eine Art projiziertes Kaleidoskop bunter geometrischer Muster, die einen hypnotisierenden Effekt hatten, wenn die Glasplatten durch einen Kurbelmechanismus gegenläufig gedreht wurden. Diese Glasscheiben wurden in viktorianischer Zeit von Kindern scherzhaft ‚künstliches Feuerwerk' getauft, wodurch sie ihre Freude an den außergewöhnlichen Explosionen von Licht und Farbe bekundeten.

Die Bilder für die Laterna Magica wurden bis ins frühe 19. Jahrhundert von Hand gezeichnet und koloriert, bevor sie in stabile Holzrahmen eingepasst wurden, um sie sicher handhaben zu können und die gemalten Oberflächen vor Kratzern zu schützen. Dieser relativ mühsame Prozess bedeutete, dass die frühen nicht-fotografischen Bilder zwar durch ein System serieller Produktion, aber keineswegs echter Massenfertigung entstanden. Schon bald erkannte man, dass es für den Vorführer wesentlich einfacher wäre, wenn es einen eingebauten Träger gäbe, in den die Abbildungen gesteckt werden könnten, was aber natürlich eine Standardisierung der Bilder erforderte. In England entschied man sich für ein quadratisches Format (83 mm × 83 mm), auf dem Kontinent und in Amerika hingegen wurde ein etwas größeres rechteckiges Format gewählt (93 mm × 83 mm und 102 mm × 83 mm). Die Einführung des Trägers machte ein weiteres Glasplättchen notwendig, um das Bild vor Verkratzungen zu bewahren. Das Rechteck aus Glas mit der fotografischen Darstellung wurde an das zusätzliche Glasplättchen mittels eines Klebebands befestigt. Das Bild war oft von einem opaken Papierrahmen begrenzt, der Maske, und viele der kommerziell gefertigten Bilder wurden gekennzeichnet mit bedruckten oder beschriebenen Informationen, die das Thema skizzierten.

Technische Neuerungen erleichterten die rentable Massenproduktion von Bildern in der Mitte des 19. Jahrhunderts, allen voran die Einführung des lithografischen Drucks, der es erlaubte, Bilder zu übertragen und exakt zu replizieren. Die Qualität der Projektionsgeräte war zu diesem Zeitpunkt ebenfalls enorm fortgeschritten, nicht zuletzt wegen der Verfügbarkeit besserer Lichtquellen. Intensives weißes Kalklicht war in den 1870er Jahren weithin in Gebrauch und später, in den 1890er Jahren, kam grelles Bogenlicht zum Einsatz. Das Prinzip war ganz einfach: Je stärker die Lichtquelle im Projektionsapparat, desto besser die Bildqualität auf der Leinwand. In der Mitte des 19. Jahrhunderts, der Blütezeit von Aufführungen mit der Laterna Magica, waren einige Projektionsgeräte – im Allgemeinen als ‚Zauberlaterne' oder ‚Stereoptikon' bekannt – für sich allein genommen schon großartige Objekte. Einige der besonders herausragenden Beispiele hatten Gehäuse aus prächtig getöntem Mahagoniholz und verfügten über bis zu drei verschiedene Linsen, die in schimmerndem Messing gefasst waren. Die Modelle, die mehrere Linsen besaßen, benutzte man, um ein Bild mit einem anderen zu überblenden, wenn man die Illusion des Übergangs von Tag zu Nacht oder Sommer zu Winter oder die eines brennenden Schiffs oder Gebäudes erwecken wollte. Das Aufkommen der fotografischen Diapositive in der Mitte des 19. Jahrhunderts veränderte allerdings das Wesen der Vorführungen mit der Laterna Magica von Grund auf.

DAS AUFKOMMEN FOTOGRAFISCHER DIAPOSITIVE

Wenngleich die Herstellungsweise für Daguerreotypien bereits im Januar 1839 durch Louis Daguerre eingeführt worden war, so hatte dieser frühe fotografische Prozess keinen Einfluss auf die Fertigung von Laternenbildern. Auch wenn es sich um das erste fotografische Verfahren in größerem und kommerziellem Maßstab handelte, so gab es doch einen entscheidenden Nachteil: Die daguerreotypische Abbildung wurde auf einer Kupferplatte fixiert, die mit einer lichtempfindlichen Silberverbindung beschichtet war, sodass kein Licht durch sie hindurchgehen konnte. Darüber hinaus konnte eine Daguerreotypie nicht vervielfältigt werden und war damit ein Unikat. Anfang der 1840er Jahre brachte William Henry Fox Talbot dann die Kalotypien heraus und seitdem wird er als Begründer der modernen Fotografie angesehen. Auch diese Methode, bei der Papier mit beschichtetem lichtempfindlichem Silberjodid Anwendung fand, wies das Problem der Unvereinbarkeit mit der kommerziellen Replikation einer Aufnahme auf.

Der Durchbruch kam schließlich durch ein neues Negativverfahren, das Abel Niépce de Saint-Victor entwickelt hatte und als ‚Niépceotypie' bezeichnet wird. Niépce bediente sich Eialbumins, um die Silberjodidsalze auf den Glasplatten zu binden. Dieser Prozess, der besonders für Landschafts- und Architektursujets geeignet ist, führte zu exakten, fast kornfreien Abbildungen. Friedrich und Wilhelm Langenheim, zwei Fotografen aus Philadelphia, verbesserten diese Technik, sodass es nun möglich wurde, Positiv- statt Negativbilder auf Glasplättchen zu erzeugen. Die ersten Abbildungen für die Laterna Magica wurden 1849 auf diese Art produziert. Im Jahr darauf ließen sich die beiden Brüder das Verfahren als ‚Hyalotypie' patentieren. Ursprünglich hatten die Brüder Langenheim ihre Diapositive als eine Form der Unterhaltung für Bildpräsentationen gegen Eintrittsgeld konzipiert, schon bald aber gingen die Aufträge für fotografische Diapositive weit darüber hinaus, vor allem durch die Nachfrage im Bereich der Erziehung und der privaten Nutzung.

Während der 1860er Jahre blieb Albumin das Material für die Anfertigung von Dias für die Laterna Magica, lieferte es doch eine ausgezeichnete Bildauflösung, die ausschlaggebend ist, wenn eine fotografische Abbildung auf eine Leinwand projiziert werden soll. Diapositive wurden aber auch mit anderen Substanzen hergestellt, etwa Kollodium- oder Gelatineemulsion. Viele Bilder wurden mit farbigen Lasuren von Hand koloriert, manchmal auf sehr kunstvolle Art, dann aber auch eher roh. Diese Handkolorierungen ließen den Eindruck von Farbfotografien Jahrzehnte vor deren tatsächlicher Erfindung entstehen. Am Ende des 19. Jahrhunderts wurden Diapositive für die Laterna Magica zu Zehntausenden kommerziell von einer Reihe verschiedener Firmen produziert. Allein in London gab es zwischen den 1880er und 1890er Jahren achtundzwanzig Betriebe. Während dieser Zeit bereisten furchtlose Fotografen jeden Winkel der Erde, um unbekannte und exotische Länder, Völker und Kulturen mit der Kamera festzuhalten und so das unstillbare Verlangen der Menschen nach neuen Themen zu befriedigen.

DAS GOLDENE ZEITALTER DER FOTOGRAFISCHEN LATERNENBILDER

Da die Vorführungen mit der Laterna Magica sich einer immer größeren Beliebtheit erfreuten,

Advertisement for Criterion Magic Lanterns, 1898

Anzeige für Magische Laternen von Criterion, 1898

Réclame pour les lanternes magiques Criterion, 1898

um die weite Welt kennenzulernen, wurden die Diapositive in verpackten Sets, denen Broschüren mit begleitenden Kommentaren beigelegt wurden, verkauft oder vermietet. Die Victor Animatograph Company in Davenport, Iowa, lieferte beispielsweise ein Set mit sechzig Dias unter dem Titel *Egypt. The Land of Romance*. Der Kommentar dazu besaß eine ausgesprochen dramatische Qualität: „Seit den Urzeiten der Geschichte war das alte Land Ägypten von einem Schleier des Geheimnisvollen und Romantischen verhüllt, als sich aber die Nebel der Jahrhunderte lichteten, da haben wir dort die Wiege vieler Dinge unserer modernen Zivilisation gefunden ... Bevor wir aber für unsere Reise den Nil aufwärts an Bord gehen...“

Und in diesem Stil ging es dann weiter. Es war bei öffentlichen Vorstellungen allgemein üblich, dass die Präsentationen von Musik begleitet wurden, um die Dramatik zu erhöhen.

Darüber hinaus wuchs die Zahl der Laterna-Magica-Aufführungen, die der Unterhaltung zu Hause dienten, enorm an, und preiswertere Spielzeugprojektoren für Kinder waren äußerst populär. Firmen wie Newton & Company und Bamforth & Company in England oder Underwood & Underwood und Keystone View Company in den Vereinigten Staaten brachten zwischen den 1870er und 1930er Jahren beeindruckende Kataloge mit fotografischen Reiseberichten heraus, von denen viele auf den folgenden Seiten abgebildet sind. Einige Amateurfotografen stellten von ihren eigenen Negativen Diapositive für die Laterna Magica her, und da diese Bilder nicht in großen industriellen Stückzahlen gefertigt wurden, sind sie oft bemerkenswert wegen ihrer exakten Handkolorierungen. Die Themen, die diese Hobbyfotografen mit ihren Kameras einfingen, wirken vielfach auch natürlicher und ungestellter, wenn etwa intime Vignetten familiären Lebens oder persönliche Reisen ins Ausland dargestellt werden. Eine weitere Art von Diapositiven für die Laterna Magica, die dieses Buch präsentiert und die bedeutsam sind im Hinblick auf die Geschichte der Geografie und Fotografie, sind Bilder, die

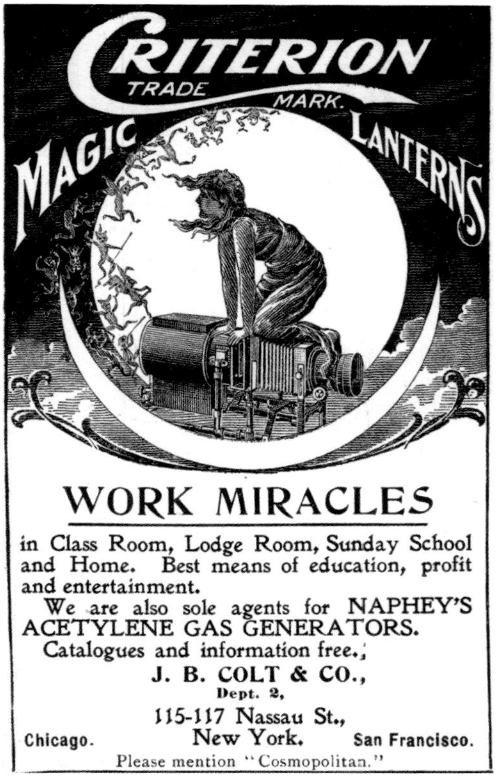

eine Forschungsreise dokumentieren, etwa Roald Amundsens Südpolexpedition (1910–1912). Historisch gesehen vermutlich ebenso wichtig sind Motive mit sozio-anthropologischem Hintergrund, unter anderem auch die, die Naturvölker zeigen, wie zum Beispiel die Pygmäen auf Neuguinea.

Diapositive für die Laterna Magica spielten auch als Lehrmittel eine ganz wesentliche Rolle. Sie wurden nicht nur zur Volksbildung, sondern auch von missionarischen Gesellschaften eingesetzt, die die Diapositive für einen vorzüglichen Weg hielten, um Menschen ‚in heidnischen Ländern' vorzuführen (wie es die Zenana-Missionsgesellschaft der Kirche von England ausdrückte), die entweder noch zu den Freuden des Christentums bekehrt werden mussten oder den Schritt bereits getan hatten.

Einige der vielleicht schönsten und ergreifendsten Aufnahmen sind die aus Japan, die scheinbar Szenen alltäglicher Bräuche und Rituale festhalten, tatsächlich aber in Studios von Fotografen inszeniert wurden. Das wirft natürlich die Frage auf, ob diese Bilder unverhohlen für den europäischen Markt mit seinem unstillbaren Appetit nach allem Exotischen aus Fernost choreografiert wurden oder ob sie als der Wirklichkeit entsprechende Darstellungen des Lebens in Japan gelten können. Andere Diapositive, die eine außergewöhnlich packende Wirkung hervorgerufen haben, sind die aus Ägypten, zum Beispiel die Abbildungen der damals noch immer nicht vollständig freigelegten Sphinx oder das Dia von ‚Kleopatras Nadel', bevor der Obelisk seine lange Reise übers Meer antrat. (Er steht heute an der Themse.) Die Beschäftigung mit Bildern sollte immer unter dem Gesichtspunkt erfolgen, dass historische, soziale oder politische Zusammenhänge deren Komposition beeinflusst haben könnten. Dies gilt ganz besonders für Laternendias, war ihr Zweck doch die Erziehung von Menschen zu Zeiten des Hochimperialismus und Kolonialismus – Indien stand schließlich noch unter britischer Herrschaft und die europäischen Nationen stritten miteinander um die Aufteilung des afrikanischen Kontinents.

Das goldene Zeitalter der fotografischen Diapositive für die Laterna Magica zwischen den 1870er und 1930er Jahren fiel zusammen mit dem Aufstieg des Romantizismus, der sich auf die nostalgische Spurensuche nach nationalen und kulturellen Wurzeln angesichts einer rasanten Industrialisierung begeben hatte. Dies beeinflusste ferner die Auswahl der Themen und die Art ihrer Wiedergabe. Die zunehmende Mechanisierung und wachsende Urbanisierung während dieser Jahre in der westlichen Welt wurde gleichfalls von den Bildern der Laterna Magica gespiegelt und gefeiert, der Bogen spannte sich von Peter Behrens' AEG-Turbinenhalle (ein protomodernes, architektonisches Meisterwerk) bis zu den Wolkenkratzern Chicagos. Die in diesem Band versammelten Laternenbilder vermitteln einen Eindruck des Lebens auf der Welt vor Massentourismus und Massenkommunikation und enthüllen dadurch eine Epoche, in der nationale Eigenheiten weniger durch den kulturell homogenisierenden Einfluss der Globalisierung verdeckt waren.

Das Jahr 1895 markiert die Aufführung der ersten bewegten fotografischen Bilder durch die Brüder Lumière und damit den Beginn des Kinozeitalters. Angesichts dieser Tatsache liegt die Vermutung nahe, dass dies das Ende der Darbietungen mit der Laterna Magica einläutete. Das war aber keineswegs der Fall. Obwohl die Laterna Magica häufig irrtümlich als Vorläufer der Kinoprojektoren gesehen wird, blieben Diapräsentationen eine beliebte Unterhaltungsform bis in die 1930er Jahre hinein. Es waren die Kodachrome-35-Millimeter-Diafilme, die Kodak 1936 auf den Markt brachte, die das Aus für die Laterna Magica bedeuteten. Die wundervollen Quadrate zusammengepresster Glasplättchen, die einen solch erregenden Ausblick auf fremde Länder, faszinierende Gebräuche und verschiedene Völker gewährten, wurden nun zu einem Ding der Vergangenheit – zu ihrer Zeit waren sie optische Wunder: Sie erforschten und vermittelten natürliche und von Menschenhand geschaffene Welten und offenbarten die vielen Facetten der menschlichen Existenz. Und nun, wie ein Vorführer der Laterna Magica erklären würde, ist es an der Zeit, sich auf eine Reise zurück in die geschäftigen Straßen Londons, zu den antiken Stätten Ägyptens, den ungewöhnlichen Sitten Japans und den majestätischen Landschaften des amerikanischen Kontinents vorzubereiten. Bon voyage!

REISEN MIT DER LATERNA MAGICA

JAMES R. RYAN

Vorführungen mit der Laterna Magica waren auf ihrem Höhepunkt Ende des 19. Jahrhunderts eine ungeheuer populäre Art von Spektakel, das ein großes Publikum sowohl erziehen als auch unterhalten wollte. In ganz England, aber auch weiter entfernt in Englands Kolonien, in Kontinentaleuropa oder Nordamerika verfolgten Zuschauer in Theatern, Schulen, wissenschaftlichen Gesellschaften und Gemeindesälen gebannt die Diapräsentationen mit der Laterna Magica über eine breite Vielfalt unterschiedlicher Themen und Inhalte. Der Bogen spannte sich von sentimentalen Erzählungen, die eine Lektion in Moral erteilen wollten, über Geschichten von Nationalhelden der Zeit bis hin zu Vorträgen über die Wissenschaften und Entdeckungen. Die Diashows befriedigten zudem den wachsenden Hunger auf fotografische Ansichten ferner Länder und neuer Völker, auf die man im Zeitalter der Weltreiche, der Massenkommunikation und der Modernität rasch gestoßen wurde. Es ist dieser sich erweiternde geografische Horizont, der die Kulisse für die Laternenbilder aus aller Welt dieses Buches bildet.

Die umfangreiche Sammlung Laternendias dieses Bandes stammt aus den verschiedensten Quellen und reicht von Amateurfotografen bis hin zu professionellen Studios, aber alle Bilder bedienen auf ihre Weise den Geschmack eines westlichen Publikums im 19. und frühen 20. Jahrhundert für Fotografien mit Schauplätzen und Reiseszenen rund um den Globus. Es ist eine nahezu unmögliche Aufgabe, die genauen Wege zu rekonstruieren, die jedes Dia genommen hat, um bewahrt zu bleiben und zufällig in dieser Sammlung zu enden. Wir sollten uns daher von vornherein der Tatsache bewusst sein, dass solche Sammlungen nur die Spitze eines visuellen Eisbergs darstellen, von dem Vieles bereits abgeschmolzen ist, da Laternendias im Laufe all der Jahrzehnte übersehen, weggeworfen und zerstört wurden, nachdem sie ihre Aktualität gegenüber ‚bewegten Bildern' und den 35-Millimeter-Dias im 20. Jahrhundert eingebüßt hatten. Wie umfangreich und repräsentativ erhaltene Diasammlungen sind, ist nicht immer einfach einzuschätzen – eher unattraktives Bildmaterial oder uninteressante Inhalte schneiden in diesem

Prozess der Bewertung stets weniger gut ab.

Die Beliebtheit von Laternenbildern war wie auch andere Technologien des Drucks, der Veröffentlichung oder Fotografie im 19. Jahrhundert einer beispiellosen Entwicklung in der Verbreitung und Rezeption des gedruckten Worts und von Abbildungen jeder Art geschuldet. Eine prosperierende Mittelklasse und eine zunehmende städtische Bevölkerung sorgten für eine schnell ansteigende Nachfrage nach visuellen kulturellen Formen, die ihren Interessen und Aktivitäten gerecht wurden. Das Anwachsen von Tourismus, Werbung, Nachrichten und Reklamen kurbelte den Markt für große Mengen preiswerter und massenproduzierter so genannter Ephemera an (kurzlebige Papiererzeugnisse). Fortschritte im Erziehungsbereich, die Expansion des Handels und die Ausweitung der Freizeit förderten zusätzlich den Bedarf an Technologien für den visuellen Unterricht, der der Information, der Erziehung und der Unterhaltung einer allgemeinen Zuschauerschaft, aber auch eines Fachpublikums diente.

Die hier gezeigten Laternendias sind ihrer Natur nach global. Die imaginäre Geografiestunde, die sie präsentieren, zielt allerdings ausschließlich auf ein weißes, westliches und der Mittelklasse angehörendes Publikum ab. Sie könnten fast ein Satz Bildpostkarten sein, den ein gut situierter Tourist des frühen 20. Jahrhunderts während einer Weltreise zusammengetragen hat. Dies wird ersichtlich am Übergewicht bestimmter Stätten in der Sammlung, aber auch an den Motiven, die die Landschaftsansichten und menschlichen Porträts an solchen Orten strukturieren.

Die Laternendias Englands sind dafür ein gutes Beispiel. Das Land wird entlang der Reiseroute eines Touristen illustriert, im Zentrum Londons Großartigkeit. Die Fotografien führen uns zu den touristischen Höhepunkten der Hauptstadt: dem Parlamentsgebäude, der Tower Bridge, den Kronjuwelen (so abgelichtet wie es ein Tourist getan hätte – durch Gitter und Glas hindurch), dem Londoner Zoo, St. Paul's Cathedral, der Guildhall, Trafalgar Square und Victoria Embankment – letztere Abbildung mit einer in unrealistischem Preußischblau kolorierten Themse. Szenen von Ludgate Circus oder der Strand zeigen geschäftige Menschenmengen und Verkehr. Die meisten Innenansichten bedeutender Wahrzeichen wie Westminster Abbey, aber auch eine ganze Anzahl von Außenaufnahmen zentraler Plätze, etwa Trafalgar Square, sind dagegen komplett entvölkert, möglicherweise weil sie von professionellen Fotografen gemacht wurden, die einen unverstellten, menschenleeren und besser vermarktbaren Blick auf solche Hauptattraktionen liefern wollten.

Die ländlichen Regionen Englands, dieser Eindruck entsteht jedenfalls durch die Bilder, scheinen von glücklichen, farbenprächtig gewandeten Bauern und anderem Landvolk besiedelt zu sein – sie alle kümmern sich zufrieden um Felder und Vieh. Gut gekleidete edwardianische Kinder spielen vor der Hintergrundszenerie von Shakespeares England, die reichlich mit Häusern und Landgärten aus der Tudorzeit bestückt ist. Kirchen schmiegen sich gemütlich in hügeligen Landschaften ein, und über die ganze Fläche der englischen ländlichen Gebiete, die von pittoresken Klosterruinen, kornischen Häfen oder dramatischen Ansichten des Lake District durchzogen ist, findet sich kein einziges Anzeichen industrieller Modernität.

Laternendias, die eine Art virtueller Reise anboten, wandten sich an dieselbe Zielgruppe wie die in Massen produzierten und mit Fotografien ausgestatteten Bücher im späten 19. Jahrhundert wie *The Queen's Empire* (1897), das einen populären Überblick über England und das Empire gewährte. Solche Publikationen zeichneten ein ähnliches Gemälde von England wie die Dias – eins, das von berühmten Städten und Meilensteinen der Architektur beherrscht war und eine glückliche, loyale Bevölkerung evozierte, die auf lokalen Traditionen fußte. Die Laternendias wurden insbesondere als geeignetes Medium betrachtet, um einer großen Zuschauerschaft ein ganz bestimmtes Bündel an Bildern und Werten zu vermitteln. 1902 gründete das Kolonialministerium ein Komitee für Anschauungsunterricht, das die Herstellung von fotografischen Sätzen für Laternenbilder koordinieren sollte, um Schulkinder auf ihre Rolle als Bürger des Empire vorzubereiten. Laternendias über England, die gemäß der oben skizzierten Inhalte gefertigt wurden, aber die Verteidigung des Empire und dessen Wirtschaftsmacht stärker betonten, wurden über das gesamte Empire verteilt, um Kinder innerhalb des britischen Herrschaftsgebiets über das Mutterland zu unterrichten.

In den britischen Kolonialgebieten wurden Laternendia-Shows zusammen mit Postkarten, internationalen Ausstellungen und Messen eingesetzt, um ein Porträt der jeweiligen Region im Rahmen der bekannten englischen Ästhetik zu schaffen und um für Investitionen, Einwanderung und Tourismus zu werben. Die zu diesem Zweck entstandenen Fotografien solcher Landstriche wurden im Kontext der britischen kolonialen Beziehungen kreiert und interpretiert, und die Motive konzentrierten sich auf eine begrenzte Anzahl typischer Themen. Australien wird daher durch Aufnahmen von Beuteltieren und Schafzucht charakterisiert, Kanada hingegen wird einem britischen Publikum bekannt gemacht durch Ansichten viktorianischer Kolonialarchitektur, etwa das Parlamentsgebäude in Ottawa, oder Eisenbahnen, mit denen neue koloniale Gebiete erschlossen werden.

Die Laternendias über Kontinentaleuropa in diesem Buch lassen wie die über England die Tendenz erkennen, die Attraktionen eines bestimmten Lands aus der Perspektive eines Touristen zu zeigen. Bauern vom Land in farbenprächtigen Trachten und ländliche Familien, die sich von der Feldarbeit ernähren, sind geläufige Themen, beispielsweise die Weintraubenernte in Frankreich oder das Säubern und Einsacken von Bohnen auf Sizilien. Die Szenen aus Osteuropa sind von einem bemerkenswerten Gegensatz zwischen der Modernität der Regierungs- oder Postgebäude sowie der städtischen Infrastruktur auf der einen und den sehr traditionellen ländlichen Lebensformen auf der anderen Seite geprägt. Die Abbildungen aus Deutschland mit Hochöfen und Kanälen entlang des Rheins gehören zu den wenigen Aufnahmen, die den industriellen Fortschritt dokumentieren.

Die Fotografien über Frankreich, die Schweiz und Italien sind am konsequentesten als vermarktbare Bilder für Touristen inszeniert. Die Ansichten von Paris, die die Beseler Lantern Slide Company aus New York zur Zeit der Weltausstellung 1900 gemacht hat, rücken die großen Boulevards, die Wahrzeichen und Promenaden der Hauptstadt in ein besonders vorteilhaftes Licht, um bei den Millionen von Besuchern der Weltausstellung Gefallen zu finden. Die Bildungsreise per Bild führt weiter nach Monte Carlo über die Schweizer Alpen nach Italien und Griechenland, im Zentrum stehen die antiken und klassischen Stätten in Rom, Florenz, Venedig und Athen. Italiener und Griechen tauchen ab und zu in Straßenszenen auf, einzeln in landestypischen Gewändern auf Porträts oder bei der Verrichtung traditioneller ländlicher Arbeiten – sie wirken allerdings wie eine visuelle Nachbetrachtung im Vergleich zum europäischen Kulturerbe, das sich zwischen den Rahmen der vielen Fotografien antiker römischer und griechischer Monumente in den Vordergrund drängt.

Einige wenige Laternendias in diesem Band mit Bildnissen von Personen fallen in die Kategorie der Genrefotografie. Diese inszenierten Darstellungen erzählen eine gefühlvolle oder moralische Geschichte statt menschliche Erfahrungen auf realistische Weise zu dokumentieren. Die Porträts ‚reizender Milchmädchen', ‚lachender Bauern' oder anderer Landarbeiter in typischer Tracht sollen wie die englische Genremalerei um 1870 einem immer größer werdenden städtischen Publikum ein idealisiertes Bild des Landlebens vorführen. Einige dieser Laternendias, beispielsweise die Mutter mit zwei Kindern im Gebet, weisen zurück auf frühere viktorianische Veranstaltungen mit der Laterna Magica, in denen Sentimentalität mit einer sozialen Botschaft verknüpft wurde. Viktorianische Wohltätigkeitsvereine, die Temperenzbewegung

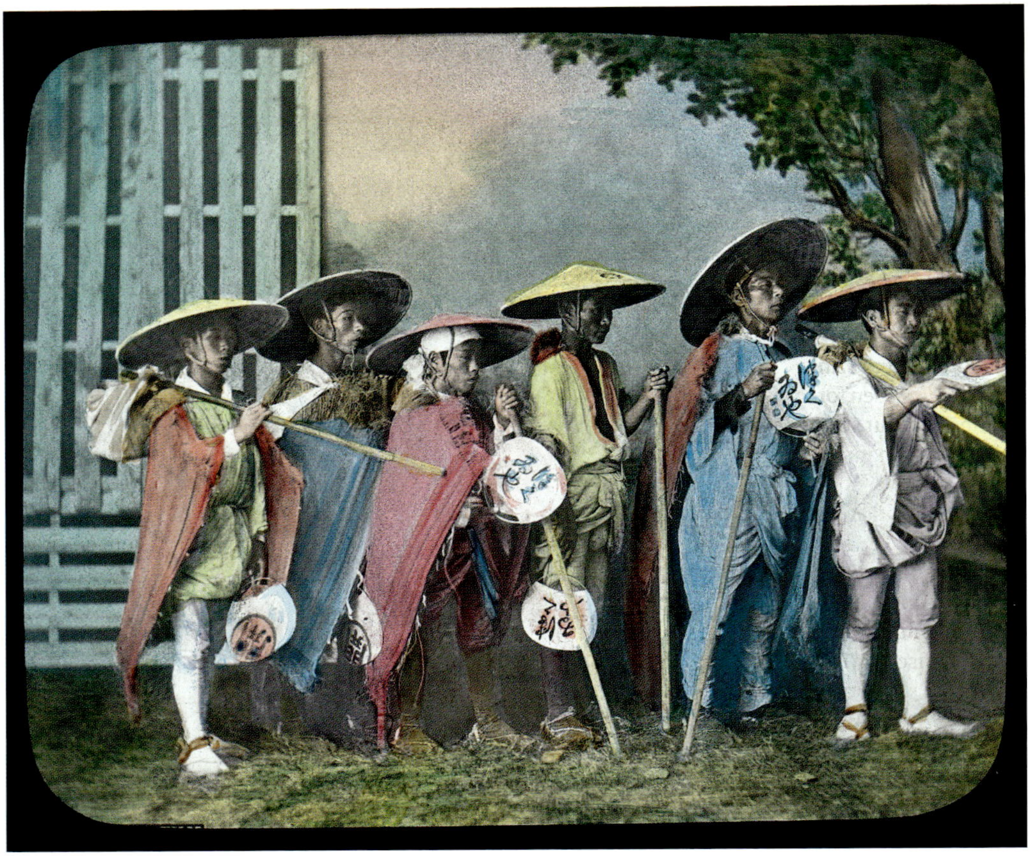

und die nonkonformistischen Kirchen bedienten sich ausgiebig der Dia-Aufführungen, um soziale Probleme des Alkoholismus, der Armut und des Müßiggangs zu illustrieren. Kommerzielle Studios wie James Bamforth in Holmfirth (Yorkshire) stellten während der 1880er und 1890er Jahre eine große Auswahl an Dias und Schriften her, die die Verbindung von Gefühl und sozialem Bewusstsein dieser Zeit widerspiegelten.

Andere Porträts hingegen sind in ihrer Komposition viel naturalistischer. Landarbeiter, die in Südostasien ihrer Tätigkeit nachgehen, auf Sizilien Bohnen säubern und einsacken oder in Ägypten den Boden bestellen, werden auf den Abbildungen so dargestellt, dass der Betrachter eher etwas über die Szene erfährt, als dass nur Emotionen geweckt werden. Firmen wie Keystone View Company, einem der größten Produzenten und Vertreiber von stereoskopischen Bildern und Laternendias, lieferten häufig gedruckte sachliche Informationen zu einem Schauplatz (beispielsweise auf der Rückseite einer stereoskopischen Ansicht), um Aufnahmen für erzieherische wie auch unterhaltsame Zwecke vermarkten zu können. Anfang des 20. Jahrhunderts gehörten Laternendias zur unerlässlichen Ausstattung von Klassenräumen, vor allem für den Geografieunterricht, und so hatte sich ein beträchtlicher Markt für den Verkauf oder

6 "Pilgrims on the march", Japan, 1890s

6 „Pilger unterwegs", Japan, 1890er Jahre

6 Pèlerins en marche, Japon, années 1890

die Ausleihe von Laternendiasätzen an Schulen entwickelt.

Porträts nicht-weißer Männer, Frauen und Kinder, die in dieser Zeit von westlichen Fotografen gemacht wurden, unterliegen zumeist bewusst oder unbewusst den eingrenzenden visuellen Konventionen der physischen Anthropologie, die die genaue Prüfung, ja sogar Messung des menschlichen Körpers als ein Schlüsselmerkmal von Unterschieden erachtete. Dies wird deutlich an den Dias von Menschen aus Afrika, insbesondere Zentral- und Südafrika, aus Indien, dem Nahen Osten und dem Pazifikraum. Die Einwohner dieser Regionen wurden fotografiert, um ihre Körperform bestmöglich zur Schau zu stellen (zum Beispiel als Ansicht des Oberkörpers im Seitenprofil) und um sie in der visuellen Sprache der ethnografischen ‚Typen' zu charakterisieren (von ‚Wasserträgern' bis zu ‚Fakiren'). Einige Porträts wurden offensichtlich vor wenig überzeugenden gemalten Studiokulissen aufgenommen, um die Erwartungshaltung eines kolonialen Touristen nach pittoresken, ethnografischen ‚Typen' zu erfüllen, andere jedoch scheinen viel spontaner und lebensnaher entstanden zu sein. Die Logik vieler kolonial-touristischer Fotografien dieser Art, egal ob Studioinszenierung oder nicht, besteht darin, bestimmte nicht-weiße ‚Rassen' in verschiedener Form als unzivilisiert und exotisch ‚anders' ins Bild zu setzen.

Der koloniale Kontext vieler Ansichten Afrikas oder Indiens wird erkennbar an den Zeichen kolonialer Wirtschaftsprozesse, etwa der Verschiffung von Elfenbein in Mombasa oder den Sisalplantagen in Uganda, aber auch an den gelegentlichen Fotos von weißen Männern mit Tropenhelmen und uniformierten afrikanischen Soldaten. In Südafrika sind die Anzeichen kolonialer Administration durch die Verwaltungsgebäude und die urbane Infrastruktur noch deutlicher. Der Einfluss, den bestimmte koloniale Zusammenhänge unmittelbar auf die fotografische Präsentation verschiedener Schauplätze hatten, ist nicht immer einfach festzulegen. Viele der Themen kolonialer Darstellungen, die von Offizieren oder Forschern in Kolonialgebieten etwa über natürliche Ressourcen, Gebietserweiterungen oder ethnografische Sachverhalte angefertigt wurden, figurieren prominent in den Arbeiten kommerzieller Fotografen, die vor Ort tätig waren. Da kommerzielle Fotografen den westlichen Bildkäufer im Blick hatten, neigten sie dazu, die zivilisatorische Bedeutung westlicher Stärke durch kulturelle Infrastruktur, Architektur und wirtschaftliche Entwicklung zu betonen. Die Fotografien der Vereinigten Staaten von Amerika innerhalb dieses Bandes, die den Fortgang der Westausdehnung und der Aneignung der Indianergebiete zum Inhalt haben, besitzen daher ihre ganz eigene koloniale Logik. Die Abbildungen von aneinandergereihten Ölquellen oder von Fließbändern dokumentieren den Siegeszug von Fortschritt und Industrie, Dias von Großstädten wie New York reflektieren den Gipfel dieses Prozesses der Modernität.

Aufnahmen aus China im 19. Jahrhundert waren nahezu ausschließlich auf die wenigen Vertragshäfen beschränkt, die für den Außenhandel entlang der Küste und Hongkongs, das unter britischer Herrschaft stand, geöffnet waren. Sie stammen von französischen, britischen, amerikanischen, deutschen und auch chinesischen Fotografen. Ende der 1890er Jahre beherrschten kommerzielle chinesische Studios den Markt, die aber weiterhin westliche Motive für einen westlichen Markt produzierten. Die Fotografien aus China in dieser Publikation zeichnen ein sehr konventionelles Bild alltäglicher Szenen, etwa von Straßenhändlern und Barbieren, aber auch der Topografie, die vor allem von den Wahrzeichen westlicher und chinesischer Architektur gekennzeichnet ist.

Einen ziemlich anderen Schwerpunkt lassen die Dias über Japan erkennen. Ansichten Japans zählten zu den beliebtesten touristischen Fotos im frühen 20. Jahrhundert, wovon die vielen, außergewöhnlich schön kolorierten Studioporträts japanischer Männer und Frauen in diesem Buch Zeugnis ablegen. Die europäische und amerikanische Modewelle im 19. Jahrhundert für alles

Japanische (Japonismus) sorgte für eine starke Nachfrage eines westlichen Publikums nach stereotypen Darstellungen von Geishas, jungen Frauen in wundervollen Kimonos und Samuraikriegern, aber auch nach Tempeln und Bildern des Berges Fuji. Wenn einige Japanporträts auch den stereotypisierten westlichen Fantasien ‚orientalischer Typen' entsprachen, so war Japan kein Kolonialgebiet und die Japaner hatten einen beträchtlichen Einfluss darauf, wie sie repräsentiert werden wollten. Besonders wichtig ist die Tatsache, dass japanische Fotografien Ende des 19. Jahrhunderts anders als touristische Aufnahmen aus anderen Teilen der nicht-westlichen Welt von japanischen Fotografen gemacht wurden, die auf eine bereits existierende und vorfotografische Ikonografie japanischer Identität und Kultur zurückgriffen und diese erfolgreich im Westen vermarkteten.

Die Laternendias, wie sie hier auf bemerkenswerte Weise zusammengestellt sind, bieten ein faszinierendes und vielfältiges Panorama von Schauplätzen und Menschen. Die Fotografien stammen aus äußerst unterschiedlichen Quellen, kommen sie doch von offiziellen Stellen ebenso wie aus Privathand und sind sie doch professioneller wie auch amateurhafter Natur. Jedes Dia hat seine eigene Biografie mit gewollter oder ungewollter Bedeutung. Alle Aufnahmen haben gemeinsam, dass vor rund einhundert Jahren Menschen sie für geeignet und signifikant genug hielten, um aus ihnen Laternendias herzustellen, sie in irgendeinem Diasatz zusammenzubringen und einem Publikum vorzuführen, möglicherweise begleitet von einem Erzähltext. Wer genau diese Zuschauer waren und wie sie ein Bild und dessen Kommentierung aufnahmen, ist kaum dokumentiert und nicht einfach zu rekonstruieren. Die Geografiestunden, die diese Laternendias vermittelten, wurden auf unterschiedliche Weise von einer Reihe aktueller Themen der Epoche geprägt, zum Beispiel dem Empire, Reisen und Modernität. Es ist kein Zufall, dass die Popularität von Laternendias den zunehmenden Tourismus im ausgehenden 19. und frühen 20. Jahrhundert sowie die westliche Kolonialherrschaft widerspiegelte. Der Zauber, der während einer Diashow mit der Laterna Magica entstand, ermöglichte die Präsentation aller erdenklichen neuen Fakten über Afrika bis hin zur Antarktis, die ein nach Schauplätzen und Sensationen aus unentdeckten Welten hungriges Publikum begierig aufsog. Es besteht jedoch ein Ungleichgewicht in solchen Erzählungen über Entdeckungen und deren Preisgabe: westliche Touristen werden gezeigt, wie sie den Anblick genießen, wenn sie die Wildnis Nordamerikas, die Pyramiden Ägyptens oder den englischen Lake District betrachten und fantasievoll rund um den Globus umherschweifen können, die nicht dem westlichen Kulturkreis angehörenden abgebildeten Menschen fungieren statt dessen aber als Objekt derselben Szene, gebunden an Ort und Tradition. Als nicht-westliche Fotografen ihre Fähigkeit demonstrierten, ganz und gar die Bilder ihrer Welt zu kontrollieren und zu entwerfen, da waren die Laternendias als Form populärer Unterhaltung bereits im finalen Niedergang.

Heutige Betrachter werden die Beliebtheit und sinnliche Qualität der Diavorführungen von Laternenbildern nicht immer leicht nachvollziehen können, die sie auf ein Massenpublikum im späten 19. und frühen 20. Jahrhundert ausübten. Die Musik und die gesprochenen Texte, die die Darbietungen begleiteten, sind nur selten zusammen mit den Dias erhalten geblieben, sodass die Wiederherstellung von Diashows in ihrer ganzen Komplexität ebenfalls schwierig ist. Dies gilt umso mehr für ein gedrucktes Buch wie das vorliegende, für das die Originalabbildungen einer anderen interpretatorischen Logik gehorchend neu geordnet werden müssen. Dennoch sollte dies Sammler und Liebhaber von Laternendias nicht abhalten, diese fesselnden Bilder in einem größeren kulturellen und historischen Zusammenhang zu platzieren, um ihre Anziehungskraft und die damit verbundenen Deutungen besser einschätzen zu können.

7 A Buddhist priest, Japan, 1880s

7 Buddhistischer Priester, Japan, 1880er Jahre

7 Prêtre bouddhiste, années 1880

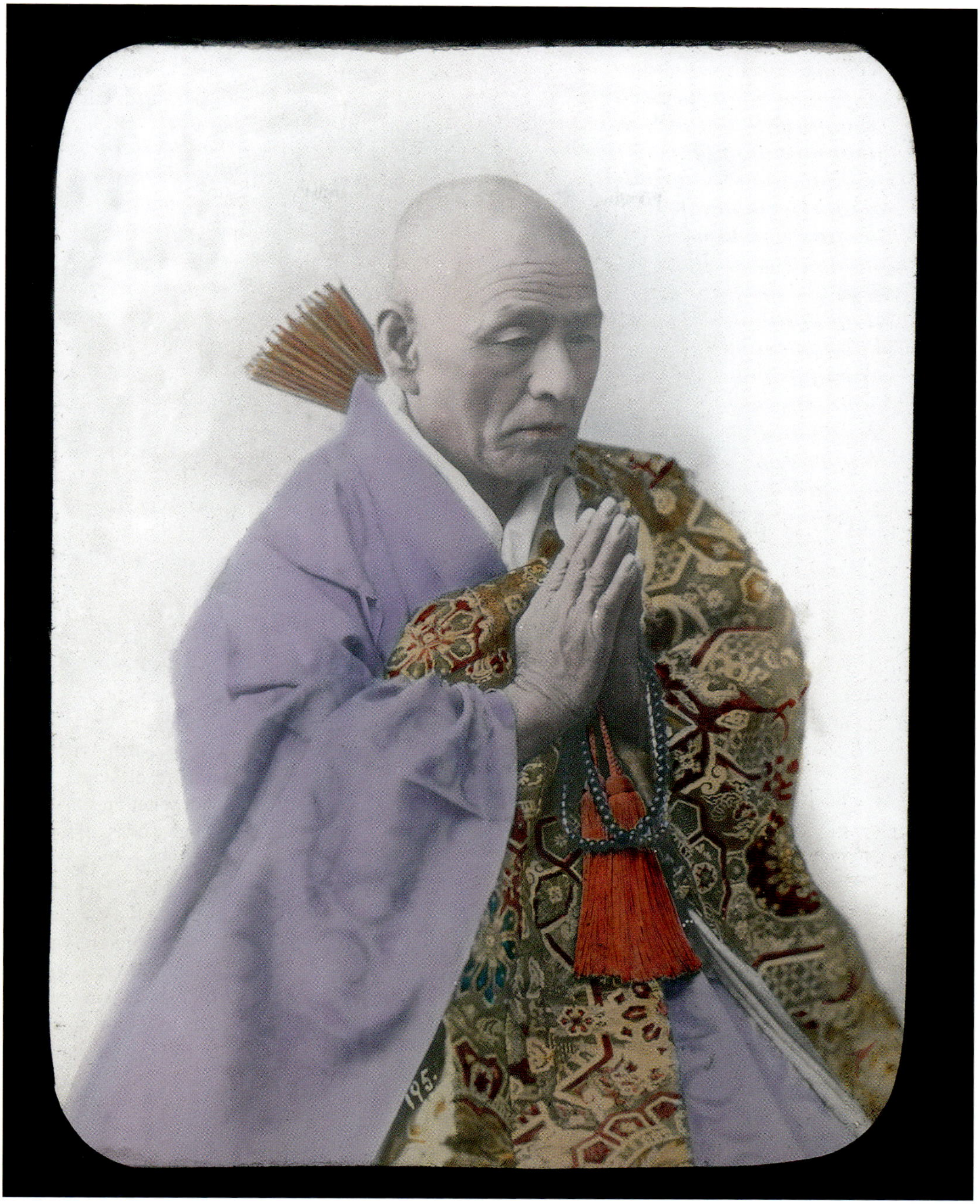
195.

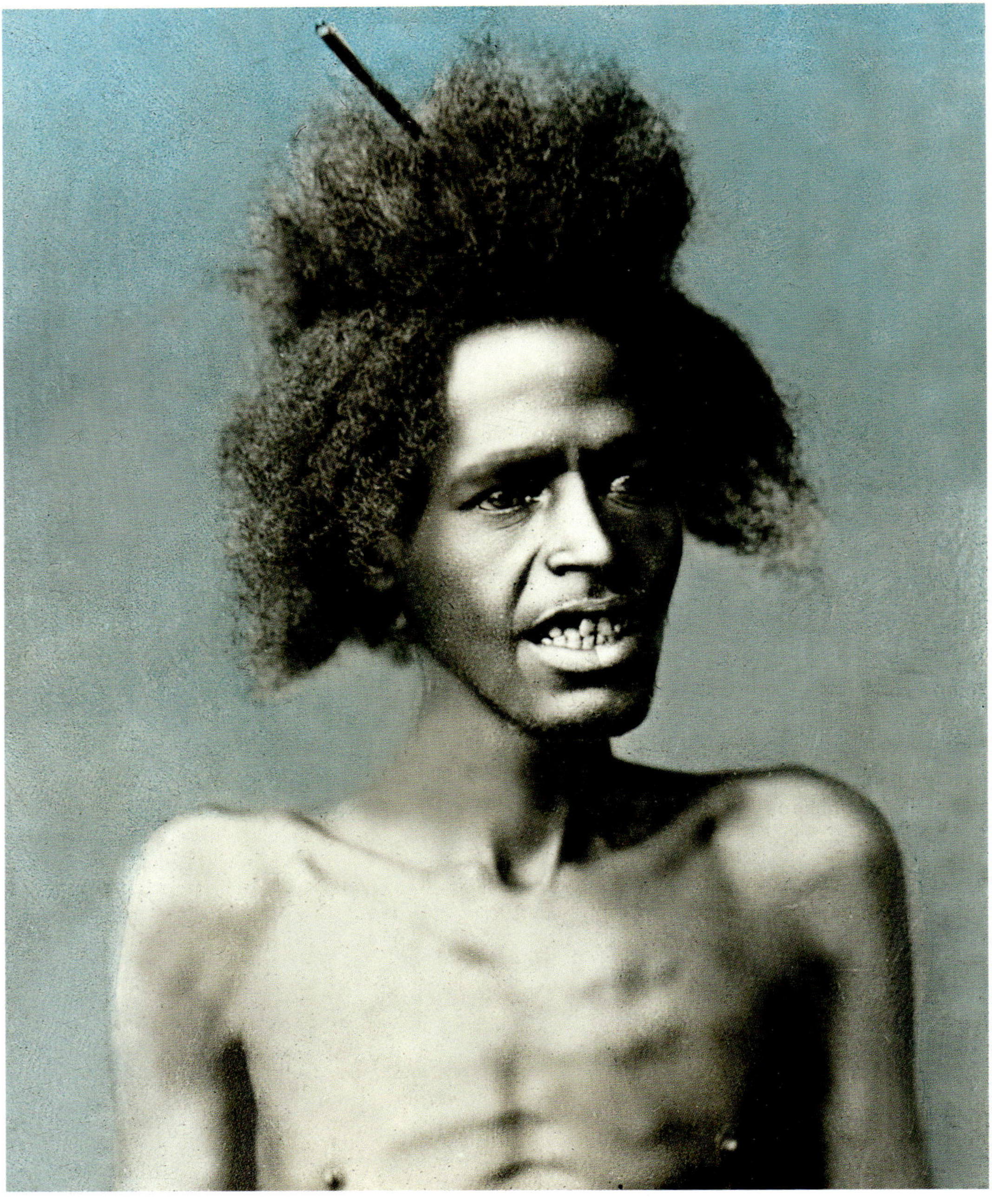

8 Tribesman, Africa, 1890s

8 Stammesangehöriger, Afrika, 1890er Jahre

8 Membre d'une tribu, Afrique, années 1890

MÉMOIRES D'UN MONDE PERDU

CHARLOTTE FIELL

Avant la télévision et le cinéma, ou même le tourisme de masse, la lanterne magique était pour les gens un moyen prisé pour découvrir le monde et ses divers paysages, cultures et peuples. Les projections des plaques en verre, souvent accompagnées de lectures et de musique, étaient les ancêtres des présentations multimédia. Elles étaient immensément populaires et donnaient au public l'impression de voyager sur le Nil, de traverser l'Afrique ou l'Asie, ouvrant ainsi une fenêtre sur un monde jusqu'alors impénétrable. Réuni au prix d'années de recherches, cet ensemble exhaustif de plaques pour lanternes magiques est non seulement une abondante et poignante mémoire photographique, mais il nous offre aussi un aperçu historique unique et fascinant sur des caractéristiques nationales et des pratiques culturelles. Un périple autour d'un monde perdu...

LES ORIGINES DE LA LANTERNE MAGIQUE

L'histoire de la lanterne magique remonte à plus de deux siècles avant l'avènement de la photographie. Le premier projecteur fut sans doute inventé par le mathématicien et astronome hollandais Christiaan Huygens à la fin des années 1650. L'invention est cependant attribuée par erreur à l'érudit jésuite allemand Athanasius Kircher, après qu'il en eut esquissé les principes dans son ouvrage *Ars Magna Lucis et Umbrae*, «Le grand Art de la Lumière et de l'Ombre» publié en 1646. L'actuel terme « lanterne magique » apparut au milieu du XVIIe siècle se rapportait à un projecteur relativement primitif, équipé de bougies ou de lampes à huile placées derrière la plaque en verre peinte à la main. En 1665, un opticien londonien, John Reeves, fabriqua des lanternes qu'il mit en vente. L'auteur intimiste Samuel Pepys, qui fut l'un de ses premiers clients, écrivit en août 1666 : « Comme convenu, Mr Reeves, apportez-moi une lanthorn (sic) avec des images sur verre, afin de faire apparaître d'étranges choses sur un mur, très jolies. »

Du début du XVIIIe siècle et par la suite, de nombreux inventeurs participèrent au développement de la lanterne magique, l'équipant de divers miroirs et lentilles, et de sources de lumière qui améliorèrent la qualité de la projection. Ces progrès favorisèrent l'accessibilité aux lanternes et améliorèrent considérablement la clarté des projections. Ils permirent aux lanternistes d'organiser des spectacles visant un public plus nombreux, rendant cette activité financièrement viable.

LA MAGIE OPTIQUE DE L'ÂGE PRÉ-PHOTOGRAPHIQUE

Les premières plaques étaient montées dans des cadres en bois et représentaient souvent de beaux paysages de style romantique. Elles servaient aussi à projeter des images effrayantes de spectres et d'esprits lors de spectacles populaires appelés « fantasmagories », étymologiquement, « des fantômes en place publique ». Pour ces spectaculaires effets fantomatiques, le projecteur et l'opérateur étaient souvent cachés derrière un voile de gaze afin de ne pas être visible du public, ce qui augmentait la mystification et rendait les apparitions à l'écran encore plus terrifiantes. Il est difficile, aujourd'hui, d'imaginer l'enchantement et l'impact de cette magie optique sur des gens qui n'avaient jamais rien vu de semblable. En fait, ces spectacles gothiques surnaturels, invoquant esprits, démons cornus et macabres squelettes, étaient l'équivalent de nos films d'horreur les plus extrêmes. Des charlatans se servirent même de lanternes magiques pour duper les gens peu méfiants en leur faisant croire qu'ils avaient véritablement invoqué les esprits des morts, exploitant ainsi leur crédulité pour leur soutirer de l'argent.

Au début du XIXe siècle, les projecteurs étaient utilisés non seulement pour les fantasmagories, mais aussi pour d'autres divertissements populaires. Les lanternistes allaient de ville en ville, comme des saltimbanques itinérants, portant leur matériel sur leur dos. En Grande-Bretagne, beaucoup venaient d'Italie et étaient appelés « Savoyards » ou « Galantees ». Ce surnom leur venait de leur cri, « Galantee So ! », de l'italien *galante*, « galant » et *so*, qui était la prononciation avec un épouvantable accent de *show*, « spectacle ». Les deux termes signifiaient « belle représentation ». Un joueur d'orgue de Barbarie accompagnait souvent le lanterniste vagabond, donnant ainsi une autre dimension au spectacle. C'est lui aussi qui disait les commentaires.

Les plaques pour lanternes magiques furent aussi largement utilisées à des fins éducatives, afin d'enseigner notamment l'astronomie ou la botanique. Il semble qu'elles furent aussi abondamment utilisées pour raconter des histoires bibliques. Même les ligues antialcooliques s'en servirent pour diffuser leurs messages d'intérêt public. Et bien sûr, il existait quantité de magnifiques images pour les enfants, de nombreux lots de plaques étant manufacturés tout exprès pour eux sur le thème des comptines, des chansons populaires, des histoires amusantes ou moralisatrices et aussi des contes de fée traditionnels. Ils étaient les dessins animés de l'âge précinématographique. La première salle expressément conçue pour les représentations de lanterne magique ouvrit ses portes en 1848 à l'Institut Polytechnique de Londres, dans la prestigieuse Regent Street. Elle devint rapidement une attraction majeure très courue où sons, musique et lectures se mêlaient à des images saisissantes. Des bruiteurs cachés derrière l'écran produisaient les effets sonores. Cette salle, qui fait maintenant partie de l'université de Westminster, pouvait recevoir jusqu'à 1 500 personnes et, en plus des nombreux spectacles de lanterne magique, elle hébergeait aussi les célèbres projections optiques de fantômes par le populaire homme de science et forain, le « professeur » John Henry Pepper.

Vers le milieu du XIXe siècle, du mouvement fut introduit dans les projections grâce à la superposition de deux ou trois plaques dans un même châssis. Elles étaient conçues pour coulisser les unes par rapport aux autres, produisant des séquences rudimentaires d'images animées donnant une illusion de mouvement. Beaucoup de ces plaques étaient humoristiques, avec des nez qui s'allongent, des yeux qui louchent, des coups sur la tête, des chapeaux ôtés, des squelettes dansants, des cochons que l'on chevauche, etc. D'autres représentaient

Advertisement for J.B. Colt & Co. magic lanterns, c.1895

Anzeige für Magische Laternen von J.B. Colt & Co., um 1895

Réclame pour les lanternes magiques J.B. Colt & Co., vers 1895

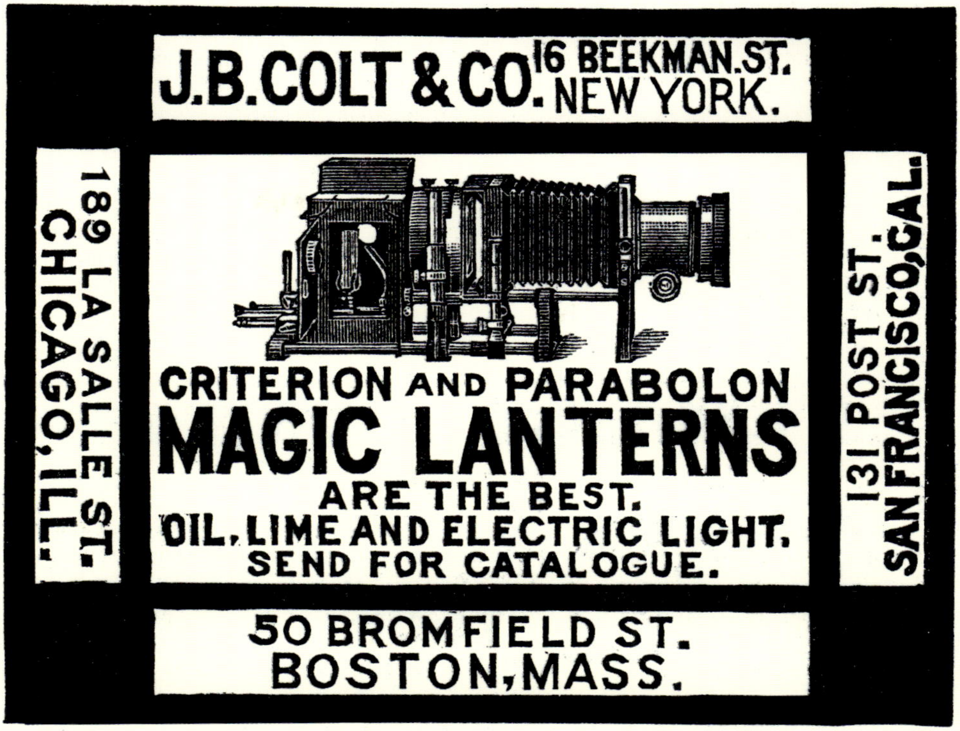

des paysages dont la lumière changeait au cours de la journée, passant de l'aube à la nuit éclairée de lune, ou encore des navires passant mollement à l'horizon. Un autre type de plaque animée qui étonna les foules fut le « chromotrope ». Inventé en 1820, c'était une sorte de fascinant kaléidoscope dont les motifs géométriques colorés qui étaient projetés variaient chaque fois que l'on pivotait le mécanisme d'un cran pour modifier la position d'une petite pièce en verre par rapport à une autre. Ces plaques aux effets hypnotiques étaient surnommées « feux d'artifices artificiels » par les enfants de l'époque victorienne qui raffolaient de leurs extraordinaires explosions de lumière et de couleurs.

Jusqu'au début du XIXe siècle, les plaques pour lanternes magiques étaient dessinées et coloriées à la main avant d'être montées dans de solides cadres en bois qui rendaient leur manipulation plus sûre et protégeait la surface peinte des rayures. En raison de ce procédé relativement laborieux, les premières plaques non photographiques étaient réalisées en petites séries, et non en quantité. Il apparut rapidement qu'il serait beaucoup plus commode d'équiper la lanterne magique d'un porte-plaque dans lequel les plaques pourraient être insérées. Ce dispositif supposait bien sûr une standardisation de leurs dimensions. En Grande-Bretagne, le format carré de 83 mm de côté fut adopté. Mais en Europe et en Amérique du Nord, de plus grandes tailles (93 mm × 83 mm et 102 mm × 83 mm) ont été utilisés. L'adoption du porte-plaque nécessita l'ajout d'un verre de protection supplémentaire afin de protéger l'image des abrasions. Il était maintenu contre la plaque par un ruban caout-

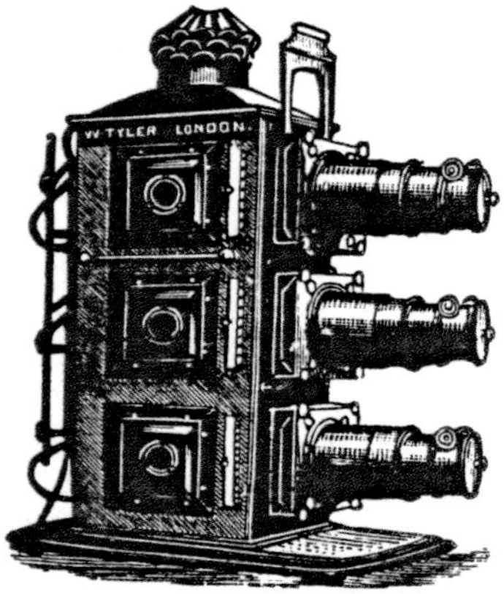

chouté. L'image était souvent entourée d'un papier opaque, le masque, et beaucoup de plaques vendues dans le commerce comportaient une étiquette ou une inscription décrivant leur sujet.

D'autres innovations facilitèrent la viabilité de la production en masse des plaques, au milieu du XIXe siècle, notamment l'apparition des presses lithographiques permettant le transfert et la réplication des images à l'identique. À cette époque, la qualité des projecteurs avait fait d'immenses progrès, grâce notamment à la disponibilité de meilleurs illuminants. Les intenses éclairages blancs à la chaux furent largement utilisés dans les années 1870 et plus tard, dans les années 1890, l'éblouissant arc électrique fut adopté. Plus la source lumineuse enfermée dans le projecteur était puissante, meilleure était la qualité de l'image à l'écran. Au milieu du XIXe siècle, qui fut l'âge d'or des lanternes magiques, certaines d'entre elles, de marque « Magic Lantern » ou « Stereopticons » étaient de beaux objets dont les plus précieux arboraient une ébénisterie en acajou, et jusqu'à trois objectifs sertis dans un fût de laiton brillant. Les modèles à plusieurs objectifs permettaient de réaliser des fondus-enchaînés donnant l'impression que la nuit succède au jour, l'hiver à l'été, ou qu'un édifice ou un navire prend feu. Mais c'est l'avènement des plaques d'après des photographies, à cette même époque, qui changea définitivement la nature de la lanterne magique.

L'AVÈNEMENT DES PLAQUES D'APRÈS PHOTO

Bien que le procédé du daguerréotype inventé par Louis Daguerre existât dès 1839, il n'eut cependant aucune influence sur la fabrication des plaques pour lanternes magiques. En dépit de son immense succès commercial, le daguerréotype présentait un inconvénient majeur : l'image était fixée sur une plaque de cuivre recouverte d'un composé argentique photosensible. La lumière ne pouvait donc pas le traverser. De plus, il était impossible de le dupliquer : chaque daguerréotype était unique. Au début des années 1840 apparurent les calotypes de William Henry Fox Talbot, considéré à juste titre comme le fondateur des techniques photographiques modernes. Mais ce procédé à base de papier imbibé d'une solution photosensible d'iodure d'argent présentait le même inconvénient quant à la réplication de la photo.

La grande avancée se produisit avec l'apparition d'un nouveau procédé de développement inventé par Abel Niepce de Saint-Victor. Une plaque de verre était recouverte d'une émulsion d'albumine d'œuf et de sels d'iodure d'argent. Particulièrement approprié pour les paysages et l'architecture, le procédé produisait une image précise, presque sans grain. Cette technique fut par la suite améliorée par deux photographes de Philadelphie, Friedrich et Wilhelm Langenheim, qui s'efforcèrent d'obtenir une image positive sur la plaque de verre, plutôt qu'une image négative. Les premières plaques pour lanternes magiques utilisant ce procédé furent produites en 1849, et l'année suivante, les deux frères brevetèrent le procédé sous le nom de « hyalotype ». Bien qu'ils aient d'abord conçu leurs plaques pour des projections publiques divertissantes et payantes, elles investirent rapidement d'autres domaines, notamment l'éducation et les projections à domicile.

Magic lantern slide showing triunial projector (three lenses), c.1870s

Projektor mit drei Linsen auf einem Dia für die Laterna Magica, um die 1870er Jahre

Plaque de lanterne magique représentant un projecteur à trois objectifs, vers les années 1870

Au cours des années 1860, l'albumine continua d'être utilisée pour la production de plaques pour lanternes magiques, car la résolution de l'image était excellente, ce qui était crucial pour les projections sur un écran. Mais d'autres procédés à base de collodion et de gélatine servirent à créer des plaques d'après photographie. Beaucoup étaient coloriées à la main avec des colorants transparents, parfois avec beaucoup de méticulosité, parfois plus grossièrement. Ce coloriage à la main donnait une illusion de photographie en couleur des décennies avant l'invention de cette dernière. À la fin du XIXe siècle, les plaques pour lanternes magiques furent produites par dizaines de milliers par diverses sociétés. Rien qu'à Londres, il y en avait vingt-huit entre les années 1880 et 1890. Au cours de cette période, pour répondre à l'insatiable désir de nouveautés du public, d'intrépides photographes sillonnèrent le globe pour ramener des images de pays, de peuples et de cultures exotiques peu connus.

L'ÂGE D'OR DES PLAQUES PHOTOGRAPHIQUES POUR LANTERNES MAGIQUES

Les spectacles de lanterne magique étant devenus un moyen extrêmement populaire de voir le vaste monde, les plaques commencèrent à être vendues ou louées, présentées dans des écrins avec un livret contenant le commentaire qui pouvait être dit pendant la projection. Par exemple, la compagnie Victor Animatograph de Davenport, dans l'Iowa, produisit un lot de soixante plaques intitulé *Égypte, pays de la romance*. Le commentaire était grandiloquent : « Dès le commencement de l'Histoire, l'antique terre d'Égypte fut enveloppée (sic) d'un voile de mystère et de romance mais, les brumes des siècles s'étant dissipées, nous y découvrons le berceau d'une grande partie de notre civilisation moderne (...) Cependant, avant d'entreprendre le présent voyage sur le Nil... » et cela continue ainsi. Il n'était pas rare que le spectacle public soit accompagné par une musique adéquate pour mieux mettre dans l'ambiance.

Les lanternes magiques étaient aussi largement utilisées à la maison. Les projecteurs bon marché pour les enfants furent très populaires. Entre les années 1870 et 1930, des sociétés comme Newton & Company et Bamforth & Company, en Angleterre, ou encore Underwood & Underwood ainsi que la Keystone View Company, aux États-Unis, produisirent d'impressionnants catalogues de carnets de route photographiques, dont beaucoup de clichés illustrent les pages de ce livre. Des amateurs confectionnèrent des plaques pour lanternes magiques à partir de leurs propres négatifs. Et comme ces images n'étaient pas produites industriellement en grande quantité, elles sont souvent remarquables par leur mise en couleur soignée et précise. Les sujets de ces photographes occasionnels sont souvent des scènes familiales prises sur le vif ou posées, ou des photos de voyages lointains. Un autre type de plaques pour lanternes magiques évoqué dans cette étude, important du point de vue historique et photographique, sont les images documentaires rapportées par des explorateurs,

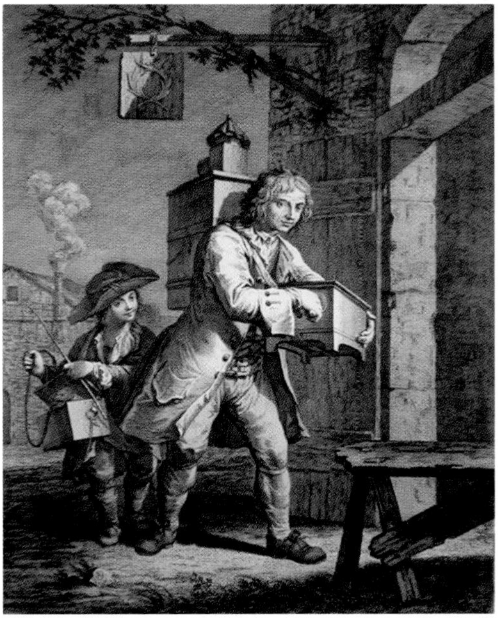

"Savoia colla lanterna magica" by Francesco Maggiotto, showing travelling lanternist, 18th century

„Savoia colla lanterna magica" von Francesco Maggiotto, reisender Laternist, 18. Jahrhundert

"Savoia colla lanterna magica" par Francesco Maggiotto, lanterniste ambulant, XVIIIe siècle

comme celles témoignant de l'expédition de Roald Amundsen au Pôle sud (1910–1912). Tout aussi importantes sont les images à caractère socio-anthropologique, comme celles montrant des peuples indigènes, les tribus de pygmées de Nouvelle-Guinée par exemple.

Les lanternes magiques furent aussi d'importants outils d'aide à l'enseignement. Elles furent non seulement utilisées dans les écoles, mais aussi par des sociétés de missionnaires qui estimaient qu'elles étaient un excellent moyen de monter « les pays païens » – pour reprendre l'expression de la Zenana Missionary Society de l'Église d'Angleterre –, qui devaient être convertis ou qui venaient d'être convertis aux joies du christianisme. Les plaques pour lanternes magiques les plus poignantes sont toutefois celle du Japon. Beaucoup représentent des coutumes et des rituels quotidiens, mais elles furent en réalité prises en studio et plus ou moins mises en scène. Ceci pose la question de savoir si les photographies d'origine ont été ouvertement chorégraphiées pour le marché européen dont le vorace appétit pour l'exotisme oriental est insatiable, ou s'il faut les considérer comme des représentations véridiques de la vie japonaise. D'autres plaques à l'extraordinaire résonnance évocatrice montrent l'Égypte, notamment le Sphinx avant son dessablement, ou l'Aiguille de Cléopâtre avant son long voyage au-delà des mers. Lorsqu'on regarde ces images, il est important de garder à l'esprit le contexte historique, social et politique susceptible d'avoir influencé leur réalisation. Ceci est notamment vrai des plaques pour lanternes magiques, car elles furent utilisées pour l'éducation à une ère d'impérialisme et de colonialisme triomphants. L'Inde était sous la domination britannique et les nations européennes luttaient pour se partager le continent africain.

La période faste des plaques pour lanternes magiques à partir de photographies, des années 1870 à 1930, coïncida avec la montée d'un romantisme qui cherchait nostalgiquement à retrouver les racines nationales et culturelles face à la rapide industrialisation. Ceci eut une incidence sur le choix des sujets et leur représentation. La mécanisation et l'urbanisation grandissantes des pays occidentaux, au cours de ces années, furent immortalisées et célébrées par les lanternes magiques, du hall des turbines de la firme AEG à Berlin – un chef d'œuvre de l'architecture proto-moderne – aux premiers gratte-ciels de Chicago. Mais par-dessus tout, cette collection d'images pour lanternes magiques ressuscite la vie dans le monde d'avant le tourisme de masse et les communications, et révèle par là-même un âge au cours duquel les caractères nationaux étaient moins estompés qu'aujourd'hui par l'homogénéisation culturelle engendrée par la globalisation.

Avec l'apparition du cinéma en 1895, lorsque les frères Lumière présentèrent leur premier film, l'on aurait pu penser que la lanterne magique tomberait en désuétude. Ce ne fut pourtant pas le cas. Bien qu'elle fût souvent présentée de manière erronée comme un phénomène précinématographique, elle resta un divertissement populaire jusqu'aux années 1930. C'est l'introduction de la pellicule Kodachrome 24 × 36 par Kodak qui sonna véritablement le glas de la lanterne magique. Leurs magnifiques carrés de verre qui avaient ouvert tant d'étonnantes fenêtres sur les pays lointains, les curieuses coutumes et les peuples si différents, furent relégués parmi les vestiges du passé. En leur temps, les lanternes magiques furent des merveilles d'optique qui donnaient à voir le monde de la nature et des hommes, révélant la diversité de l'humanité. Comme l'aurait dit un lanterniste, « le moment est maintenant venu d'embarquer pour un fascinant voyage dans le temps à travers les rues animées de Londres, les anciens monuments d'Égypte, les extraordinaires coutumes du Japon et les majestueux paysages de l'Amérique. Bon voyage! »

VOYAGES À TRAVERS LA LANTERNE MAGIQUE

JAMES R. RYAN

À leur âge d'or vers la fin du XIXe siècle, les spectacles de lanterne magique étaient immensément populaires, conçus aussi bien pour éduquer un large public que pour le divertir. Dans les théâtres, les écoles, les sociétés savantes et les salles paroissiales de toute la Grande-Bretagne, et même au delà dans les colonies britanniques, en Europe continentale et en Amérique du Nord, le public s'extasiait sur des plaques pour lanternes magiques exposant une grande variété de thèmes et de sujets. Ces derniers allaient des histoires romanesques moralisatrices jusqu'aux histoires de héros nationaux à travers les âges, en passant par les sciences et les découvertes. Les spectacles de lanterne magique assouvissaient également une demande croissante, sous l'empire britannique, de photographies montrant des terres lointaines et des peuples inconnus. Ils répondaient aussi à un désir de communication de masse et de modernité. L'expansion de cet horizon géographique est la toile de fond de toutes les plaques montrant le monde entier, appartenant à cette remarquable collection.

Ces plaques très diverses proviennent d'un vaste éventail de sources, des photographes amateurs aux studios professionnels, qui tous satisfaisaient d'une certaine manière les goûts du public occidental, au XIXe siècle et au début du XXe siècle, pour les photographies de sites et de scènes du monde entier. Reconstituer le cheminement précis que chacune d'elles a suivi pour terminer fortuitement dans cette collection en particulier est une tâche quasiment impossible. Il est cependant important de savoir que ces collections ne sont que la partie émergée d'un iceberg visuel dont une grande partie a depuis longtemps disparu, à cause de la négligence dont furent victimes les plaques pour lanternes. Au XXe siècle, elles furent abandonnées puis détruites lorsque leur valeur marchande périclita face à la concurrence du cinéma et de la pellicule 24 × 36. Il n'est pas toujours facile de déterminer jusqu'à quel point les collections qui nous sont parvenues sont complètes ou représentatives. L'imagerie ou les sujets les moins intéressants ont inévitablement été les premières victimes de cette désaffection.

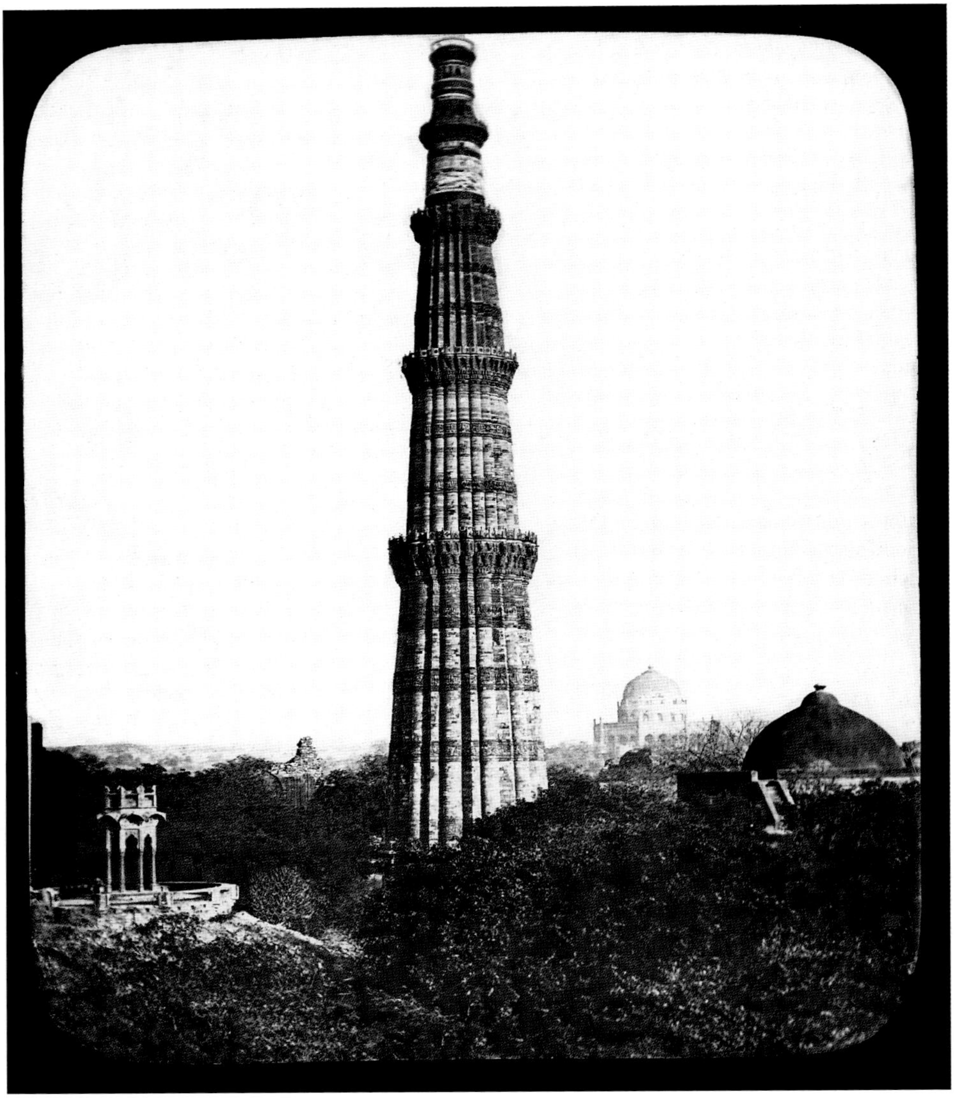

À l'instar des autres techniques d'impression, de publication et photographiques, la popularité des lanternes magiques fut, au XIXe siècle, un moteur essentiel d'une diffusion sans précédent de récits et d'images de toute nature. Le développement de la classe moyenne et d'une population citadine suscita une forte demande pour des formes de produits culturels visuels satisfaisant leurs intérêts et leur réalisation. L'expansion du tourisme, de la publicité, des journaux et de la propagande stimula le marché pour quantité de produits éphémères pas chers, produits en masse. Les progrès de

9 Qutb Minar, Delhi, 1870s

9 Qutb Minar, Delhi, 1870er Jahre

9 Qutb Minar, Delhi, années 1870

l'éducation, l'expansion du commerce et du temps de loisir alimentèrent également un désir d'instruction fondé sur le visuel, qui informerait, éduquerait et divertirait des publics aussi bien populaires que spécialisés.

Les plaques pour lanternes magiques de la présente collection couvrent le monde entier. La leçon de géographie innovatrice qu'elles représentent s'adressait à une audience exclusivement blanche, occidentale et appartenant à la classe moyenne. Elles auraient pu être des cartes postales illustrées rapportées d'un tour du monde par un touriste fortuné, au début du XXe siècle, comme il apparaît à la fois par la prédominance de certains lieux que par les motifs qui structurent les vues des paysages et des portraits dans des lieux particuliers.

Prenons par exemple les plaques pour lanternes magiques montrant la Grande-Bretagne. Le pays est dépeint selon un itinéraire touristique axé sur la grandeur de Londres. Les photographies nous entraînent virtuellement dans un circuit à travers les sites les plus célèbres de la capitale anglaise : le Parlement, le pont de Londres, les joyaux de la Reine – montrés tels que le touriste les voit : à travers des vitres grillagées –, le zoo de Londres, la cathédrale Saint-Paul, le Guildhall, Trafalgar Square et Victoria Embankment, avec la Tamise coloriée d'un improbable bleu de Prusse. Des images montrent la circulation animée à Ludgate Circus et dans Fleet Street. La plupart des scènes d'intérieur dans des édifices remarquables, comme l'abbaye de Westminster, ainsi que bon nombre parmi les extérieurs touristiques, comme Trafalgar Square, sont en revanche désertes, reflétant peut-être le choix des photographes professionnels de prendre des vues claires, sans personne et donc plus facilement commercialisables.

D'après ces vues, la campagne anglaise est peuplée de cultivateurs heureux, hauts en couleurs, et d'autres ruraux qui montrent avec contentement leurs champs et leur bétail. Des enfants de la Belle Époque, endimanchés, jouent sur fond d'Angleterre shakespearienne agrémenté de cottages élisabéthains et de jardins campagnards. Qu'il s'agisse d'églises douillettement nichées dans des paysages vallonnés et dans de vastes campagnes, de points de vue sur des abbayes en ruine, de ports cornouaillais ou de spectaculaires vues du Lake District, aucun signe de modernité industrielle n'est visible.

Destinées à offrir des voyages virtuels, les plaques pour lanternes magiques s'adressaient à la même audience que les ouvrages à gros tirages illustrés de photographies de la fin du XIXe siècle, comme *The Queen's Empire* (1897) qui publiait des documents visuels sur la Grande-Bretagne et son empire. Ils présentaient un portrait d'une Angleterre dominée par ses cités célèbres, des édifices monumentaux, et habitée par une population loyale et satisfaite, caractérisée par ses traditions locales. Les plaques étaient considérées comme un moyen particulièrement efficace pour projeter un lot singulier d'images et communiquer des valeurs à un large public. C'est pourquoi, en 1902, le Colonial Office instaura un Comité pour l'Instruction Visuelle chargé de coordonner la réalisation des jeux de plaques d'après photographies, dans le but d'instruire les enfants des écoles sur leur rôle de citoyens impériaux. Des plaques montrant la Grande-Bretagne, réalisées selon les directives citées précédemment, mais mettant l'accent sur la défense impériale et la puissance industrielle, furent expédiées partout dans l'Empire afin de montrer aux enfants le visage de la mère patrie.

Les territoires coloniaux britanniques, dont l'Australie et le Canada, recouraient eux aussi aux spectacles de lanterne magique, conjointement aux cartes postales, aux expositions internationales et aux foires, pour véhiculer une image de leurs paysages conforme à une esthétique anglaise familière, et promouvoir les investissements, l'immigration et le tourisme. Les photographies de ces pays visaient à être perçues en termes de relation coloniale britannique, et à n'être comprises qu'au travers d'un nombre réduit de thèmes emblématiques. L'Australie était ainsi représentée par des photographies de marsupiaux et des élevages de mouton, tandis que le Canada se faisait connaître du public par l'immeuble du Parlement à Ottawa et des voies ferrées désenclavant de nouveaux territoires coloniaux.

Dans cette collection, à l'instar des plaques britanniques, celles montrant l'Europe continentale présentent une vision très touristique des haut-lieux et des particularités des différents pays. Des paysans vêtus de costumes bigarrés, des scènes rurales de familles vivant sur leurs terres sont des thèmes courants, depuis les vendanges en France jusqu'au nettoyage et à l'emballage des haricots en Sicile. Les scènes d'Europe de l'ouest présentent un net contraste entre d'une part la modernité des édifices gouvernementaux, les bureaux de poste et l'infrastructure urbaine, et d'autre part le mode vie encore très traditionnel de la paysannerie. Les photographies de l'Allemagne sont les seules, parmi toutes les plaques, à montrer quelques aperçus de la modernité industrielle, avec des scènes de hauts-fourneaux et de canaux près du Rhin.

Les vues de la France, de la Suisse et de l'Italie sont les plus cohérentes car construites sous la forme de scènes commercialisables pour promouvoir le tourisme. Celles de Paris, confectionnées par la Beseler Lantern Slide Company de New York au moment de l'Exposition Universelle de 1900, présentent une vision particulièrement attractive des grands boulevards, ainsi que des lieux touristiques et des promenades dans la capitale. Elles furent conçues pour attirer des millions de visiteurs vers la grande exposition. Le périple iconographique se poursuit à travers Monte Carlo, les Alpes suisses, puis l'Italie et la Grèce où les scènes se focalisent sur les monuments anciens de Rome, Florence, Venise et Athènes. Les italiens et les grecs apparaissent occasionnellement dans des scènes de rues, sur des portraits, vêtus en costume national traditionnel, ou dans des activités traditionnelles en milieu rural. Des arrière-pensées par rapport à l'héritage européen ne sont toutefois pas absentes parmi les nombreuses photographies de la Rome antique et des monuments grecs.

Dans cette collection, quelques plaques montrant des gens appartiennent à la catégorie de la photographie de genre. Elles sont mises en scène dans le but de former une narration romanesque ou un conte moral, plutôt que d'exposer des modes de vie conformément aux conventions du réalisme. Des portraits de « mignonnes laitières », de « riants fermiers » et autres travailleurs ruraux posant en costume traditionnel tendaient, à l'instar des tableaux de l'Angleterre de l'époque mi-victorienne, à représenter une image idéalisée de la vie paysanne auprès d'un public de plus en plus urbanisé. Certaines de ces plaques, comme celle d'une mère priant avec ses deux filles, ramènent aux spectacles de lanterne magique victoriens où le sentiment populaire s'accompagnait d'un message social. Les œuvres de charité, les ligues antialcooliques et les églises non conformistes recourraient activement aux spectacles de lanterne magique pour illustrer les problèmes sociaux liés à l'alcoolisme, à la pauvreté et à l'oisiveté. Des studios commerciaux comme celui de James Bamforth, à Holmfirth dans le Yorkshire, produisirent un éventail de plaques et de récits dans les années 1880 et 90, satisfaisant ainsi l'alliance victorienne du sentiment et de la conscience sociale.

D'autres portraits sont plus naturalistes de par leur composition. Des vues de laboureurs dans le sud-est asiatique, le nettoyage et l'emballage des haricots en Sicile, ou le travail du sol en Égypte sont posées de manière à instruire le spectateur, plutôt que de se contenter de susciter un sentiment. Des sociétés comme la Keystone View Company, l'un des plus grands fabricants et distributeurs de vues stéréoscopiques et de plaques pour lanternes magiques, incluaient souvent dans leurs produits des informations factuelles sur les scènes représentées, au dos d'une vue stéréoscopique par exemple, afin de faciliter leur commercialisation en tant que produit éducatif ou de divertissement. Dès le début du XIXe siècle, les plaques devinrent ainsi un élément essentiel de l'équipement des salles de classe, notamment pour l'enseignement de la géographie. Un marché assez important se développa, axé sur la vente et la location de jeux de plaques éducatives destinées aux écoles.

À cette époque, les portraits photographiques d'hommes, de femmes et d'enfants non blancs réalisés par les occidentaux avaient souvent tendance à être dévalorisants, à la fois consciemment et inconsciemment. Les conventions visuelles de l'anthropologie physique étaient méticuleusement appliquées, et même la taille du corps humain était considérée comme un important élément de différenciation. Ceci est particulièrement évident sur les plaques montrant des africains, notamment d'Afrique centrale et du sud, mais aussi sur celles des Indes, du Moyen-Orient ou du Pacifique, où les peuples étaient photographiés de manière à exposer au mieux leur particularités physiques, par exemple, en buste et de profil. Ils étaient caractérisés en « types » ethnographiques : « porteurs d'eau », « fakirs », etc. Bien que certains portraits aient manifestement été posés en studio contre des toiles de fond peu convaincantes, afin d'approvisionner un tourisme colonial friand de « types » ethnographiques pittoresques, d'autres semblent avoir été pris de façon plus spontanée et plus naturelle. Pour beaucoup de photographies de tourisme colonial de ce type, prises en studio ou non, il s'agissait notamment de désigner tour à tour les « races » non blanches comme non civilisées ou exotiquement « autres ».

Le contexte colonial de beaucoup de vues d'Afrique et des Indes est apparent dans les représentations des économies coloniales, de l'embarquement de l'ivoire à Mombasa aux plantations de sisal en Ouganda, de même que dans les apparitions occasionnelles d'hommes blancs à casque colonial parmi des soldats africains en uniforme. En Afrique du Sud, les signes de l'administration coloniale sont encore plus apparents au travers des immeubles gouvernementaux et de l'infrastructure urbaine. L'influence que cette relation coloniale particulière exerçait sur la mise en forme des représentations photographiques dans les différents lieux n'est toutefois pas toujours facile à déterminer. Beaucoup de thèmes liés à la représentation coloniale, photographiés par les officiers militaires et les explorateurs dans les territoires coloniaux – comme les ressources naturelles, les conquêtes territoriales et les études ethnographiques –, sont saillants dans les travaux des photographes professionnels œuvrant dans les contrées reculées. Comme leur clientèle était occidentale, ils s'efforçaient de mettre en valeur l'influence civilisatrice des puissances occidentales au travers de leurs infrastructures coloniales, de l'architecture et du développement commercial. De ce fait, les photographies des États-Unis d'Amérique, dans la présente collection, souscrivent à leur propre logique coloniale lorsqu'elles décrivent l'expansion vers l'Ouest ainsi que les acquisitions territoriales aux dépends des amérindiens. Les vues de rangées de puits de pétrole dans le paysage, ou de carcasses sur des lignes de production, attestent de la marche du progrès et de l'industrie, tandis que des vues de grandes villes comme New York représentent l'apogée de ce processus de modernité.

Au XIXe siècle, la photographie en Chine se limitait essentiellement aux prises de vues dans les quelques ports ouverts au commerce avec les étrangers, le long de la côte, et à Hong Kong qui était sous la souveraineté britannique, où photographes français, britanniques, américains, allemands et chinois pouvaient s'installer. À la fin des années 1890, les studios professionnels chinois dominaient le marché, mais continuaient à présenter des vues à l'occidentale à destination du marché occidental. C'est pourquoi les photographies de la Chine, dans cette collection de plaques pour lanternes magiques, présentent une vision très conventionnelle des scènes quotidiennes – marchands ambulants, barbiers... –, de la topographie, notamment des caractéristiques de l'architecture occidentale et des monuments chinois.

Plutôt différentes sont les photographies du Japon, qui mettent l'accent sur d'autres éléments. Les vues de ce pays étaient parmi les plus prisées des photos touristiques au début du XXe siècle, comme le révèlent dans cette collection les nombreux portraits coloriés, réalisés en studio, de femmes et d'hommes japonais. L'engouement des européens et des américains pour la culture nippone au XIXe siècle – le japonisme –suscita une forte demande de vues stéréotypées de geishas, de jeunes filles vêtues de magnifiques kimonos et de guerriers samouraïs, ainsi que de photos de temples et des vues du mont Fuji. Bien que certains portraits japonais se conformaient aux fantaisies stéréotypées des occidentaux sur le « type oriental », le Japon n'était pas une colonie et les japonais avaient leur mot à dire sur la manière de les dépeindre. Mais surtout, à la fin du XIXe siècle, et contrairement aux vues touristiques prises ailleurs dans le monde non occidental, les photographies japonaises étaient réalisées par des photographes japonais qui s'appuyaient sur une iconographie préexistante et pré-photographique de la culture et de l'identité nippones. Ceci assura le succès de leur production auprès des occidentaux.

L'on trouve dans les plaques pour lanternes magiques de cette exceptionnelle collection des images complexes et captivantes de différents lieux et peuples. Ces photographies proviennent de sources extraordinairement diversifiées, officielles et privées, professionnelles et amateures. Chaque plaque a sa propre histoire, avec ses significations à la fois intentionnelles et non-intentionnelles. Elles partagent le fait que quelqu'un, voici un siècle, estima qu'elles étaient suffisamment adéquates et significatives pour devenir des plaques pour lanternes magiques formant un tout, et être ensuite projetées à un public, probablement accompagnée d'un texte. Savoir qui était exactement ce public, et connaître l'impression que leur laissèrent ces images ainsi que la narration a rarement été établi, et reconstituer tout cela n'est pas évident. Les leçons de géographie dispensées par ces plaques pour lanternes magiques sont influencées par plusieurs thèmes dominants de l'époque, comme l'Empire britannique, le voyage et la modernité. Ce n'est pas par hasard si la popularité de ces plaques se fit l'écho de l'expansion du tourisme et de la puissance coloniale occidentale à la fin du XIXe siècle et au début du XXe. La magie du spectacle révélait toutes sortes de réalités nouvelles à un public avide de sites et de l'impression d'un monde à découvrir, de l'Afrique à l'Antarctique. Mais ces récits de découvertes et ces présentations recelaient une inégalité car, tandis que les touristes occidentaux sont représentés en train de profiter du spectacle, contemplant les déserts d'Amérique du Nord, les pyramides d'Égypte ou Lake District en Angleterre, et capables de parcourir le monde de façon inventive, les non-occidentaux sont plus fréquemment dépeints comme des objets sur lesquels se porte le regard, fixés sur place et immobilisés par la tradition. À l'époque où les photographes non occidentaux démontrèrent leurs capacités à contrôler et projeter leurs propres images du monde, les plaques pour lanternes magiques arrivaient au terme de leur déclin en tant que divertissement populaire, bien que leurs usages dans les autres domaines n'aient pas été complètement épuisés pour un certain temps encore.

Il n'est pas toujours facile pour le spectateur d'aujourd'hui de mesurer la popularité et l'impact sensoriel des lanternes magiques sur le grand public à la fin du XIXe siècle et au début du XXe. La musique d'accompagnement et la narration récitée ont rarement survécu aux plaques. C'est pourquoi la reconstitution d'un spectacle de lanterne magique dans toute sa complexité est difficile. Elle l'est plus encore dans un ouvrage imprimé comme celui-ci, dans lequel l'ordre des images a dû être révisé afin de correspondre à une nouvelle logique interprétative. Ceci ne devrait toutefois pas empêcher les collectionneurs et les admirateurs des lanternes magiques de replacer ces images captivantes dans un contexte culturel et un cadre historique plus vastes afin de mieux apprécier leurs attraits ainsi que leurs significations concomitantes.

10 View of pilgrims at prayer, Mecca, part of Ottoman Empire (now Saudi Arabia), 1900s

10 Pilger beim Gebet, Mekka, Teil des Osmanischen Reichs (heute Saudi-Arabien), 1900er Jahre

10 Pèlerins priant à La Mecque, Empire ottoman (aujourd'hui en Arabie Saoudite), années 1900

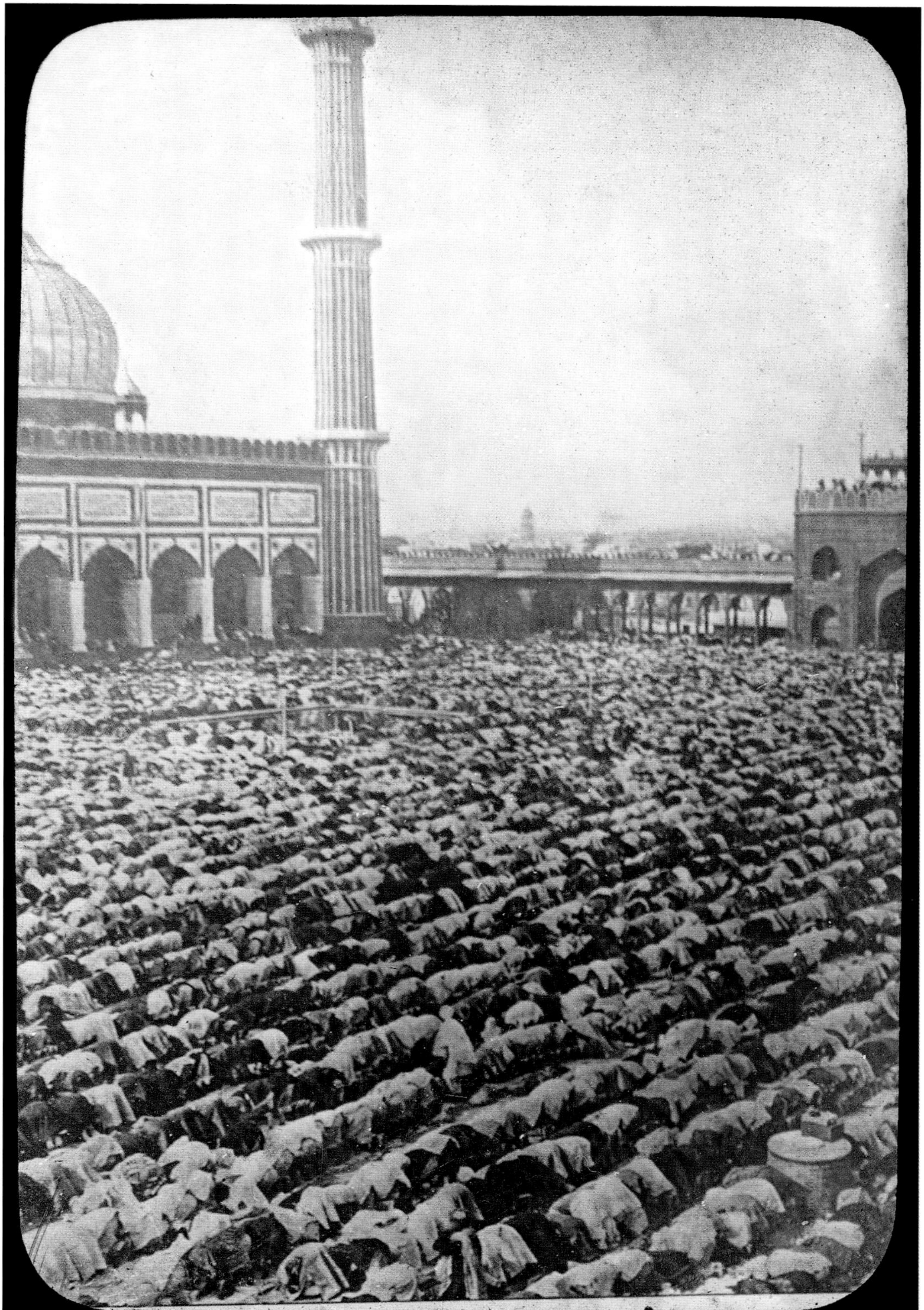

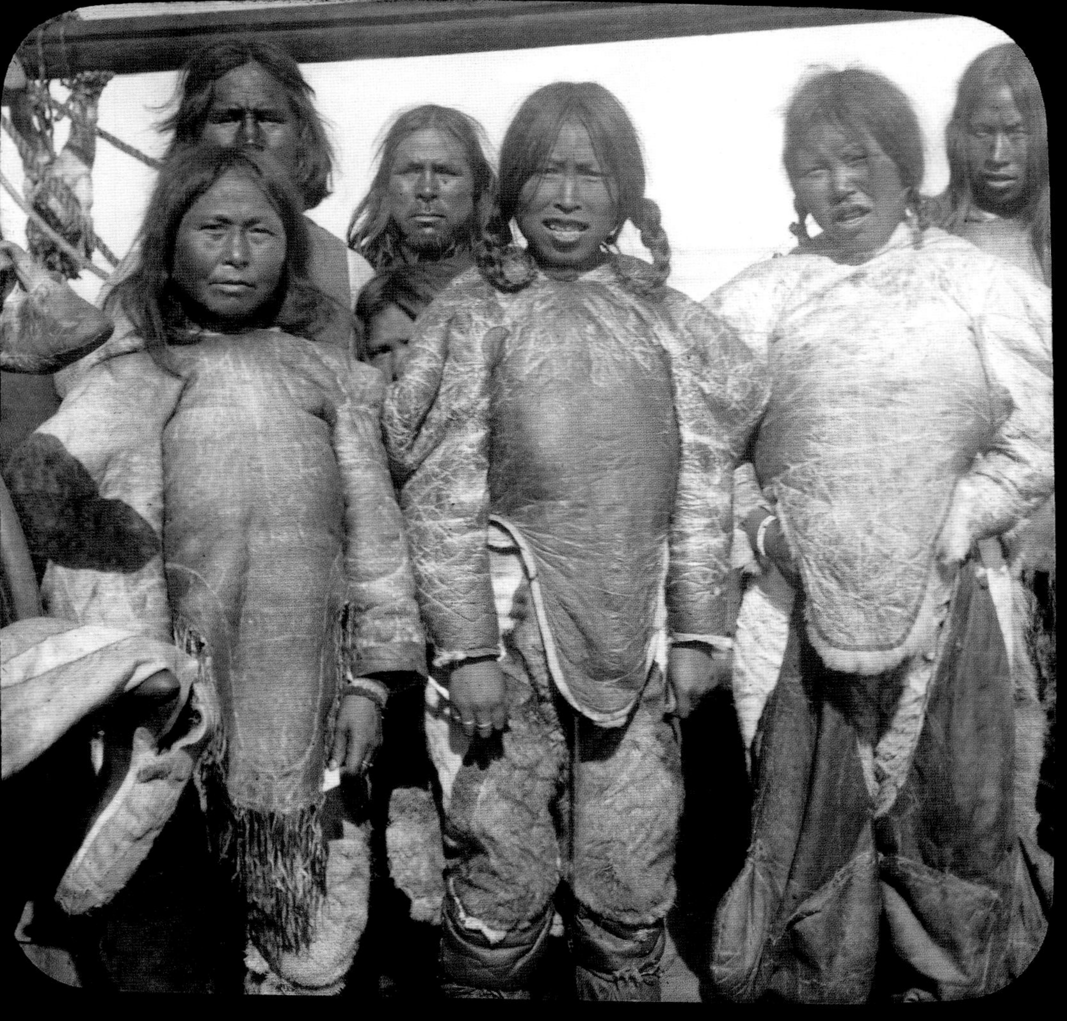

11 "Esquimaux Belles", Cape York, Greenland, c.1900
12 "Sea of icebergs", coast off Greenland, c.1900

11 "Esquimaux Belles", Kap York, Grönland, um 1900
12 „Meer der Eisberge", grönländische Küste, um 1900

11 Beautés esquimaudes, cap York, Groenland, vers 1900
12 Mer d'icebergs au large du Groenland, vers 1900

NORTHERN EUROPE

NORDEUROPA · EUROPE DU NORD

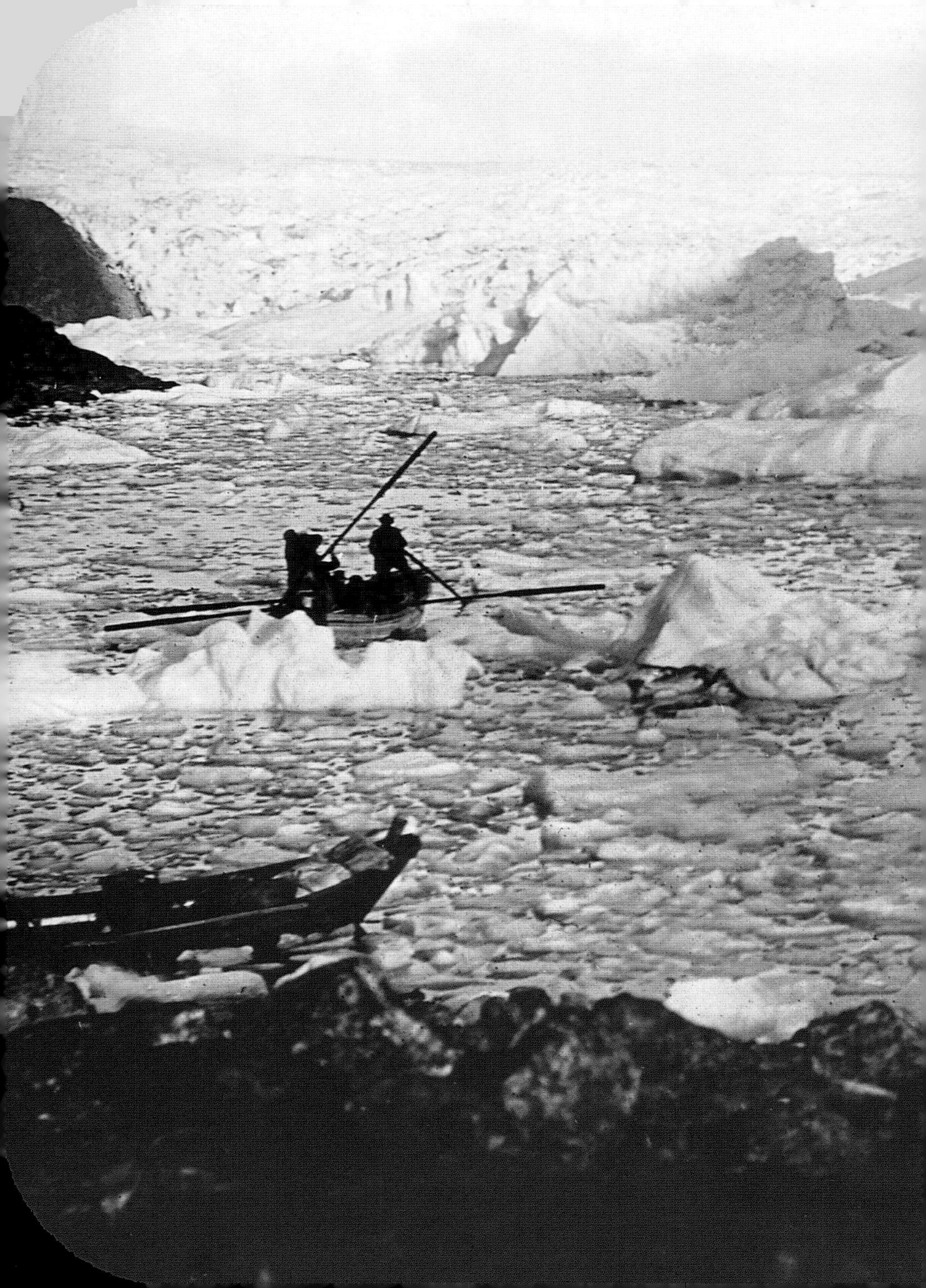

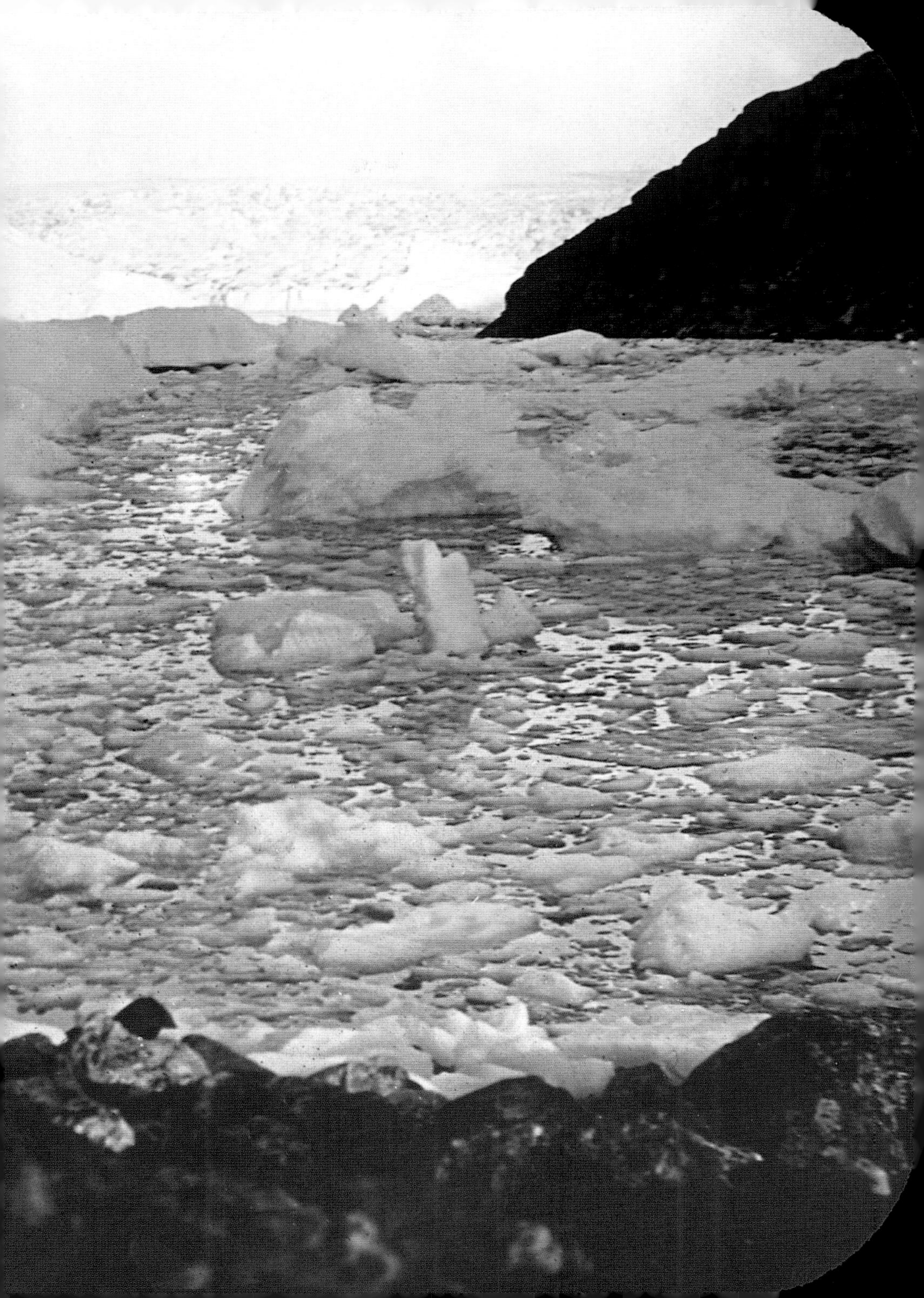

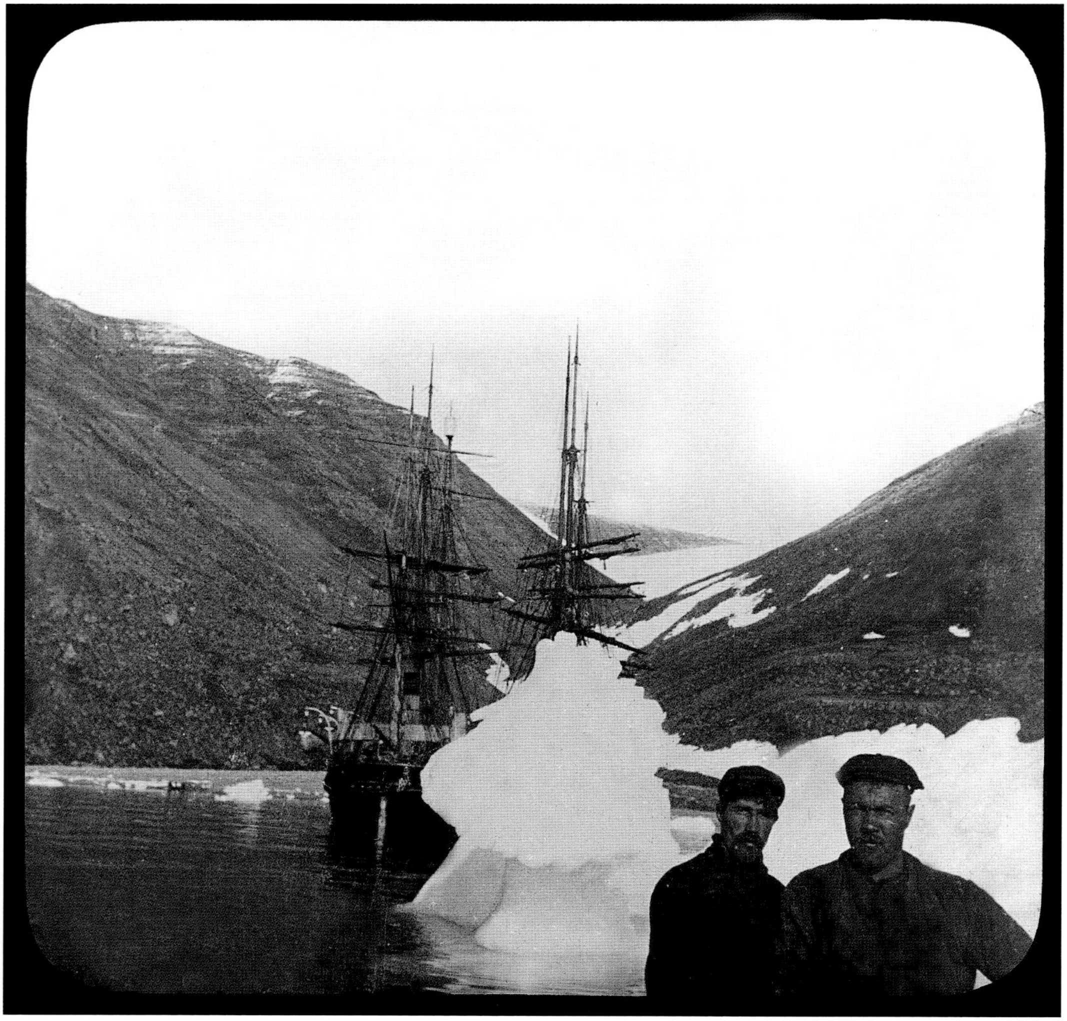

13 Two unidentified crew members in front of the "Windward" and "Eric" ships, Peary Expedition to Greenland, 1901

13 Zwei unbekannte Crewmitglieder vor den Schiffen „Windward" und „Eric", Peary-Expedition nach Grönland, 1901

13 Deux marins non identifiés devant les vaisseaux "Windward" et "Eric". Expédition de Peary au Groenland, vers 1901

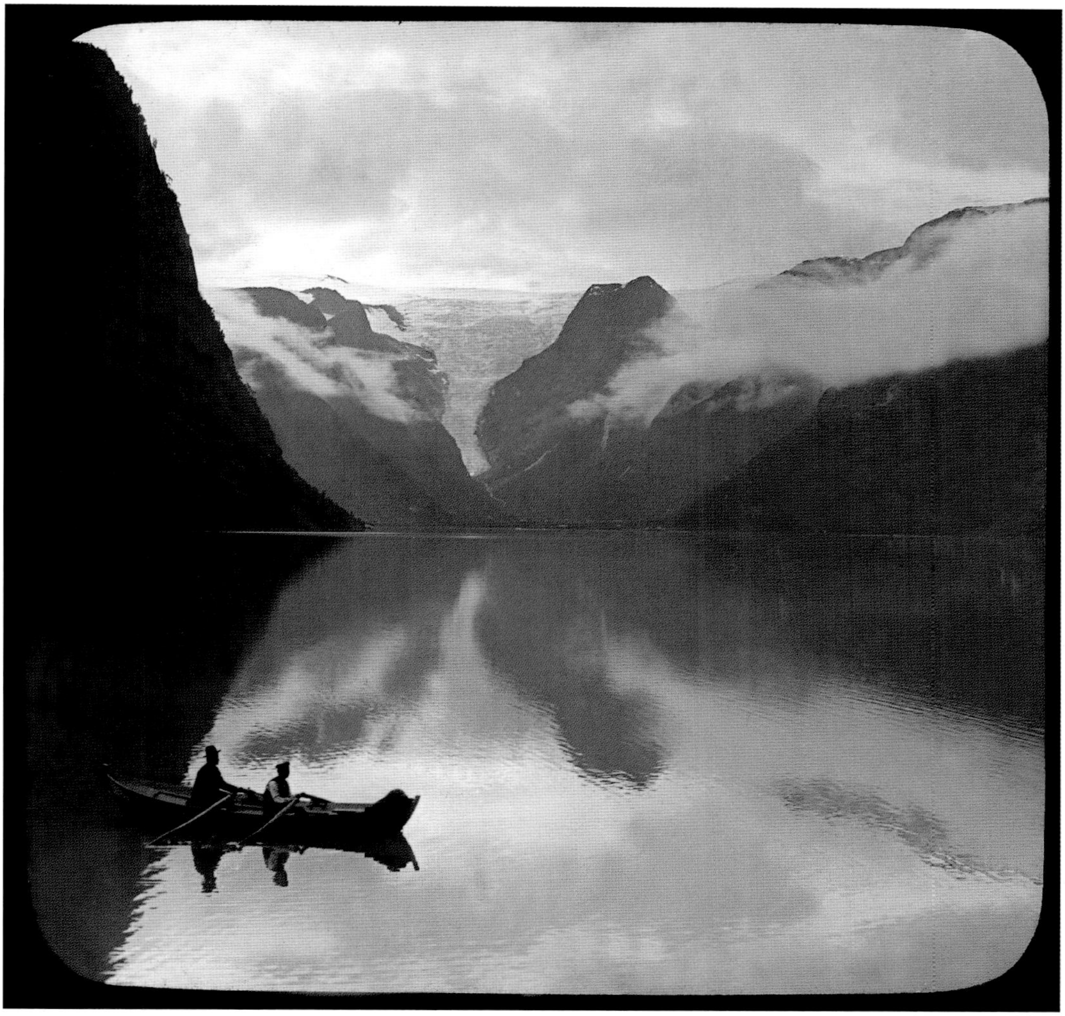

14 Lake Olden with Melkevoll Glacier in the distance, Norway, c.1900

14 Der Oldensee mit dem Melkevoll-Gletscher im Hintergrund, Norwegen, um 1900

14 Le lac Olden et au loin, le glacier Melkevoll. Norvège, vers 1900

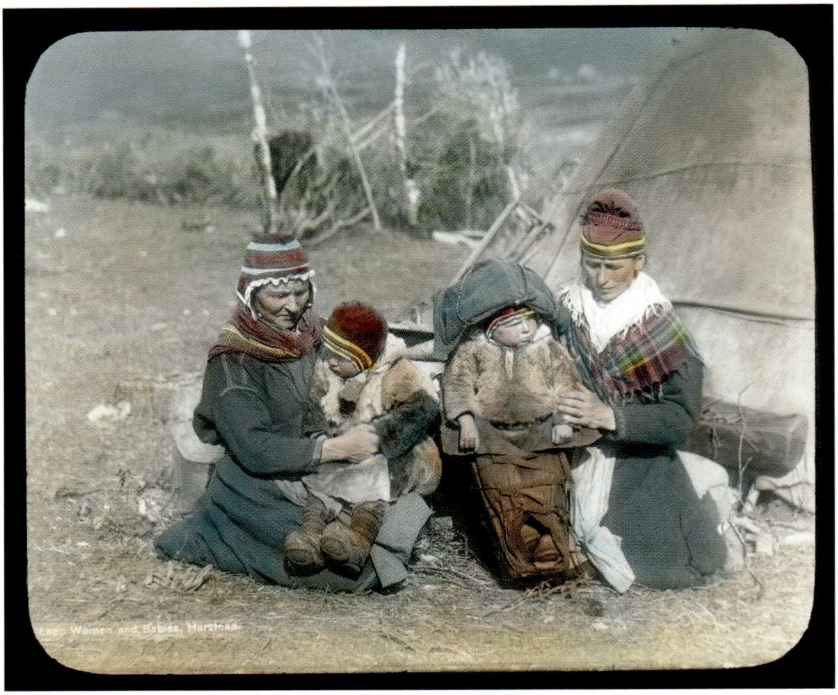

15 Lapp women and babies, Harstad, Norway, 1880s

15 Samische Frauen mit Kleinkindern, Harstad, Norwegen, 1880er Jahre

15 Femmes lapones et leurs bébés, Harstad, Norvège, années 1880

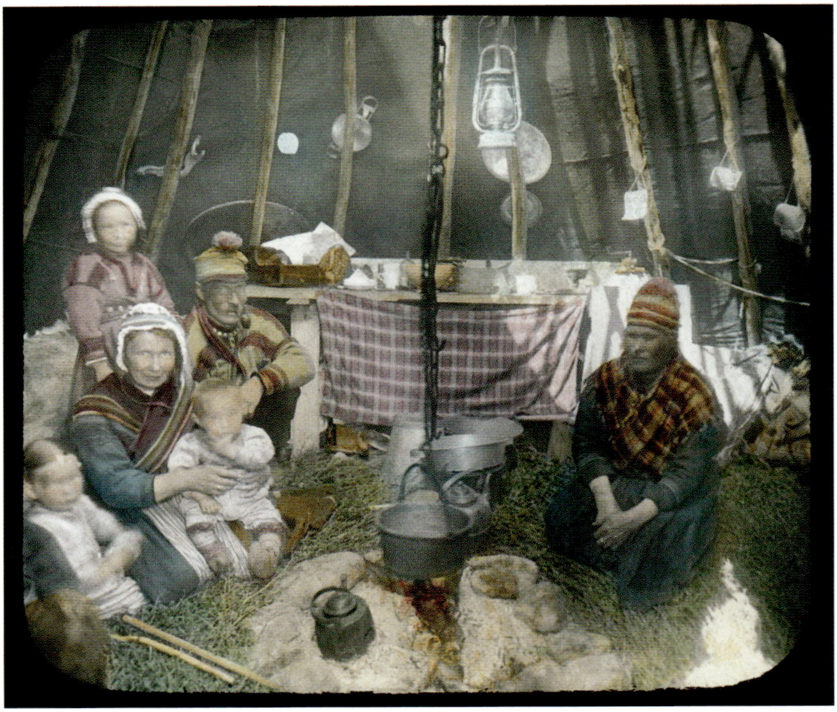

16 Lapp family living in a traditional kota (Lapp tepee), Harstad, Norway, 1880s

16 Samenfamilie in einer traditionellen Kota (samisches Tipi), Harstad, Norwegen, 1880er Jahre

16 Famille lapone dans le kota traditionnel (tipi lapon) ; Harstad, Norvège, années 1880

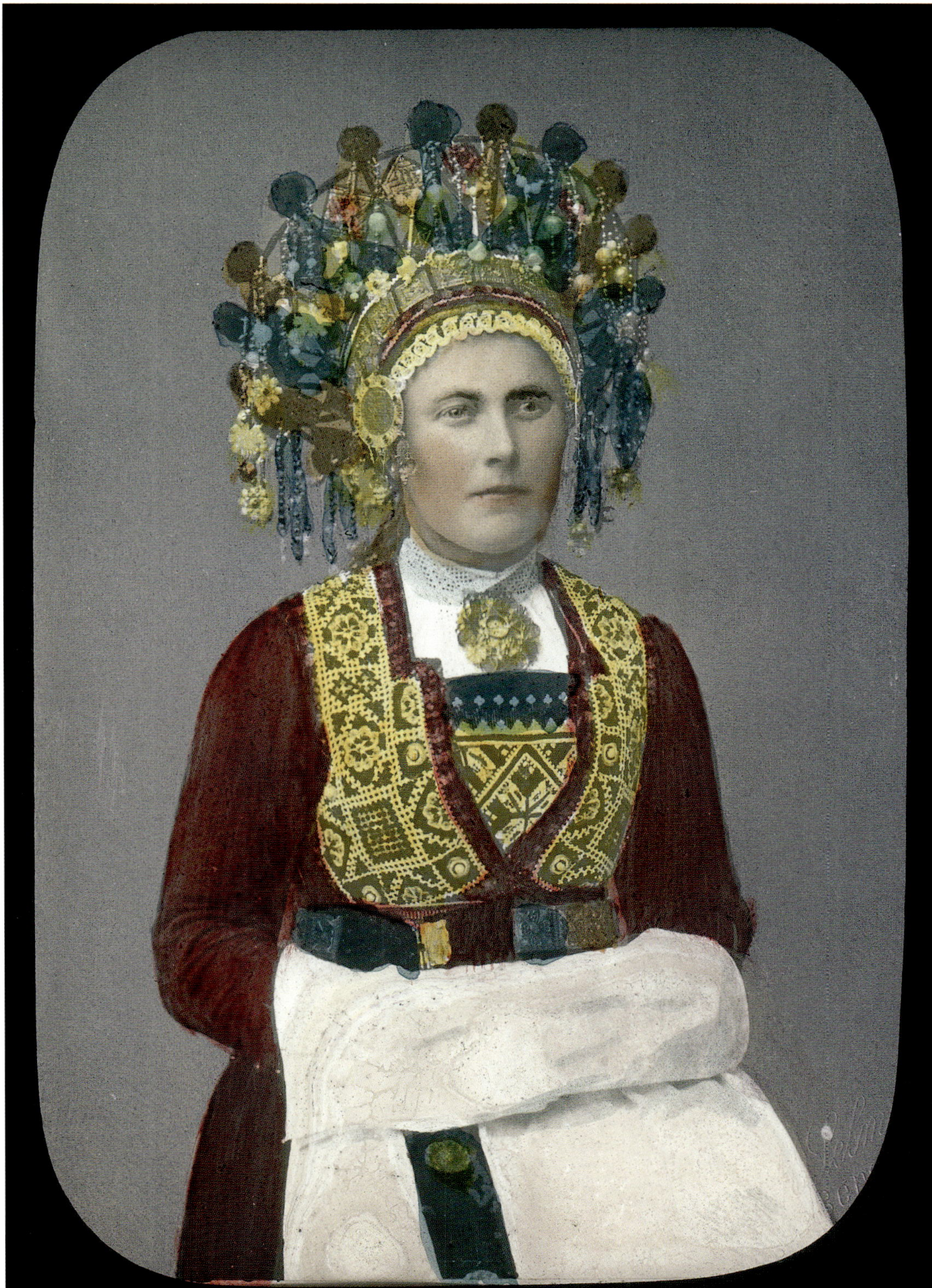

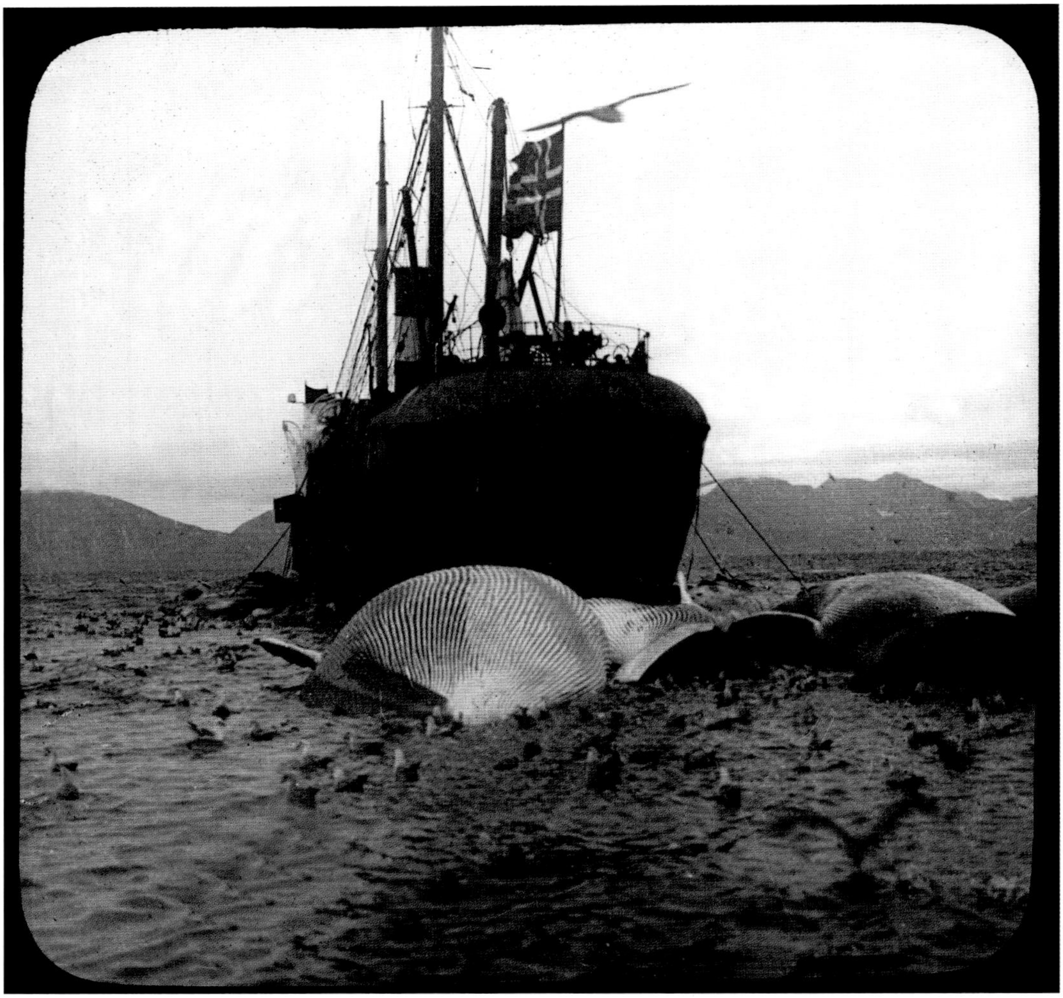

17 Woman dressed in traditional folk costume, Norway, 1880s
18 Floating Whale Station, Spitzenbergen, Lapland, c.1900 (now part of Norway)

17 Frau in traditioneller Volkstracht, Norwegen, 1880er Jahre
18 Schwimmende Walstation, Spitzbergen, Lappland, um 1900 (heute Teil Norwegens)

17 Femme en costume folklorique traditionnel, Norvège, années 1880
18 Baleinier usine, Spitzenbergen, Laponie (auj. à la Norvège), vers 1900

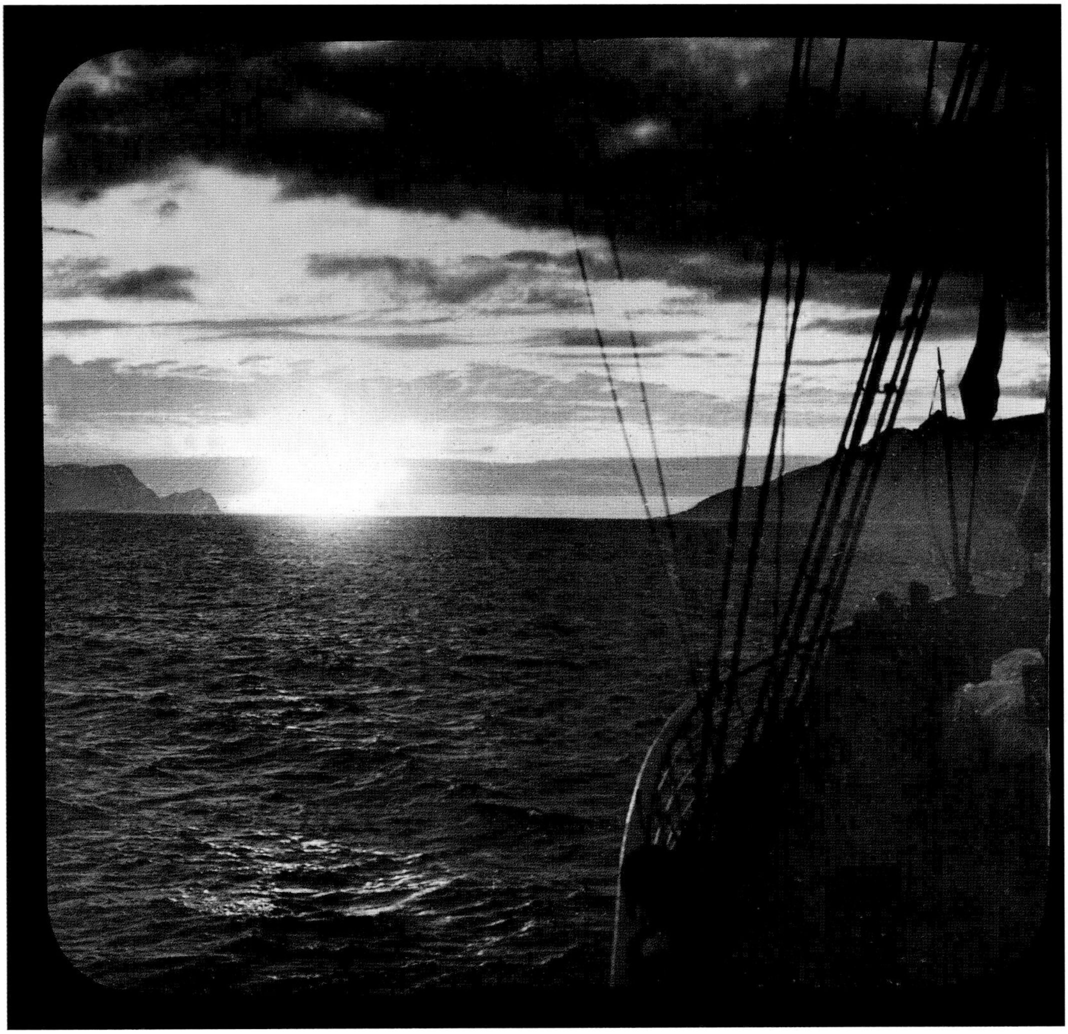

19 Midnight Sun, North Cape, Norway, c.1900

19 Mitternachtssonne, Nordkap, Norwegen, um 1900

19 Soleil de minuit, cap Nord, Norvège, vers 1900

20 Icelanders standing outside traditional turfed houses, Iceland, 1890s

20 Isländer vor traditionell mit Grassoden bedeckten Häusern, Island, 1890er Jahre

20 Villageois posant devant leurs maisons traditionnelles en tourbe, Islande, années 1890

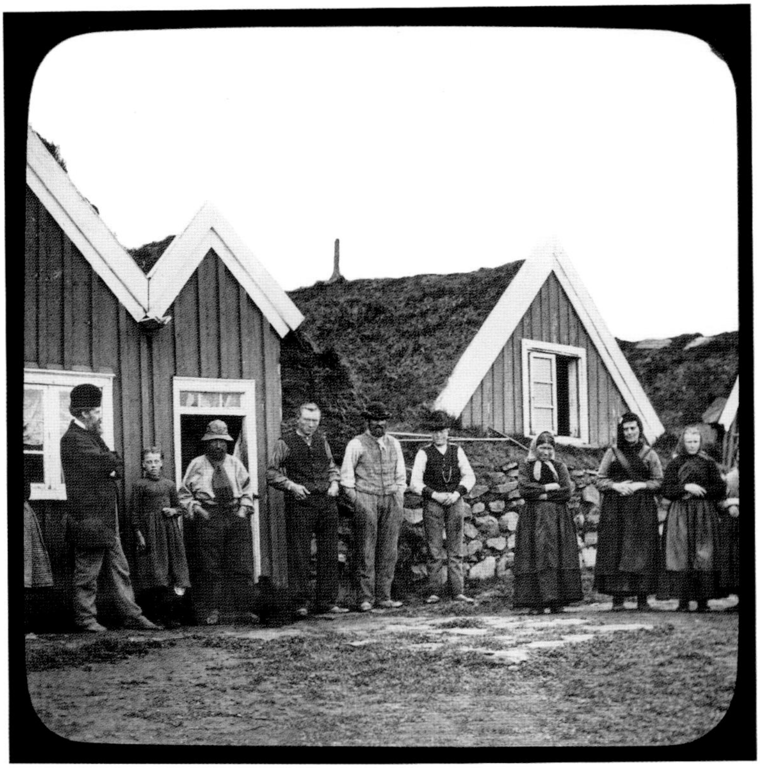

21 Grinding wood pulp, Norway, 1890s

21 Holzblöcke werden abgeschält, Norwegen, 1890er Jahre

21 Broyage de la pulpe de bois. Norvège, années 1890

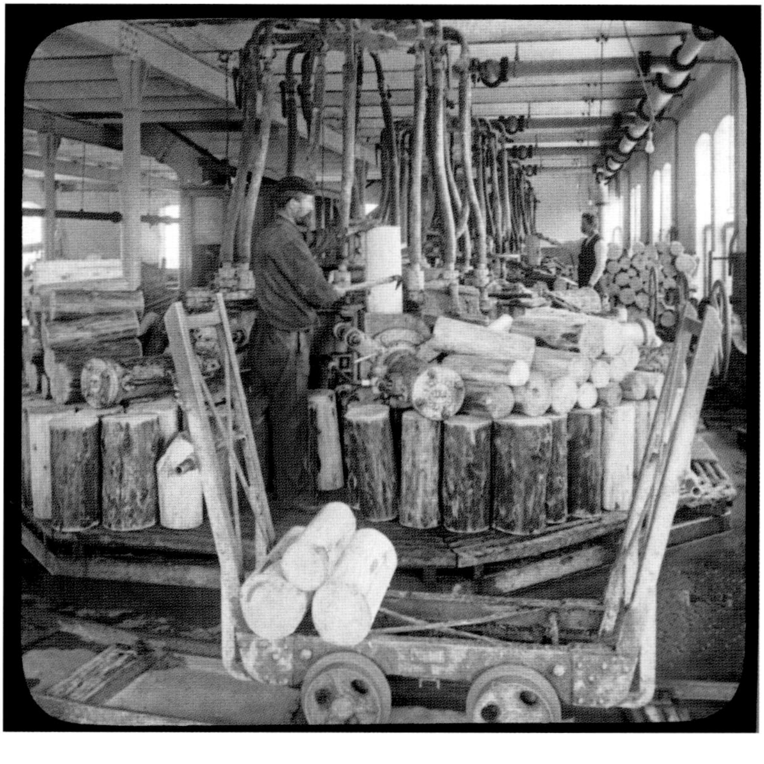

22 Making flat-bread, Norway, 1890s

22 Die Herstellung von Fladenbrot, Norwegen, 1890er Jahre

22 Confection du pain plat. Norvège, années 1890

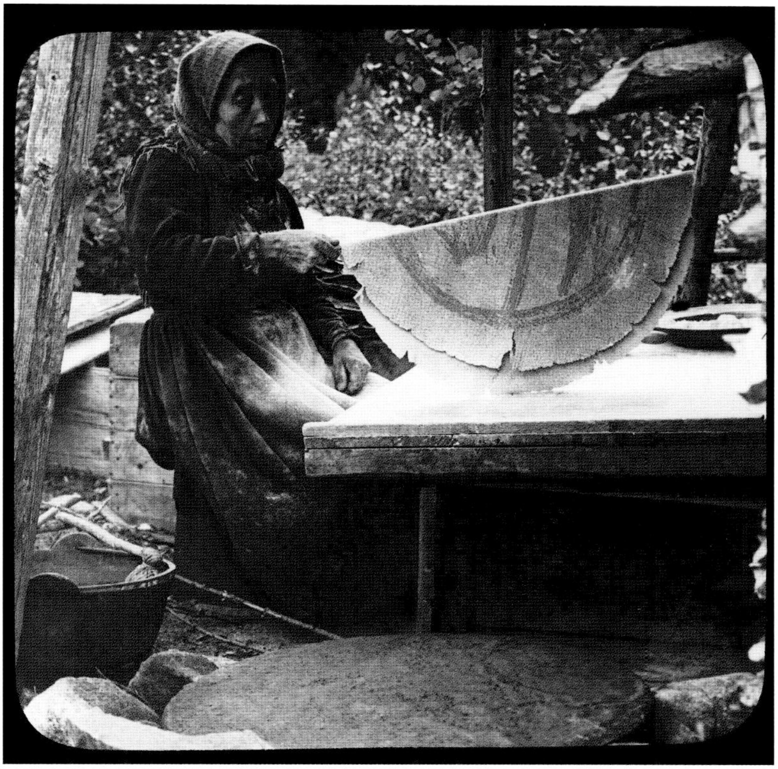

23 Milking goats, Norway, 1890s

23 Das Melken von Ziegen, Norwegen, 1890er Jahre

23 Traite des chèvres, Norvège, années 1890

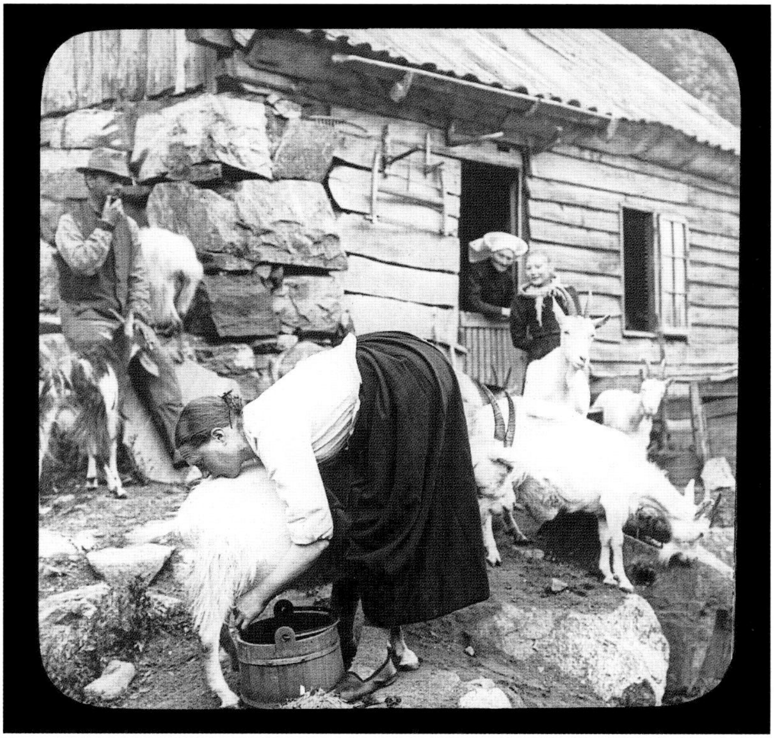

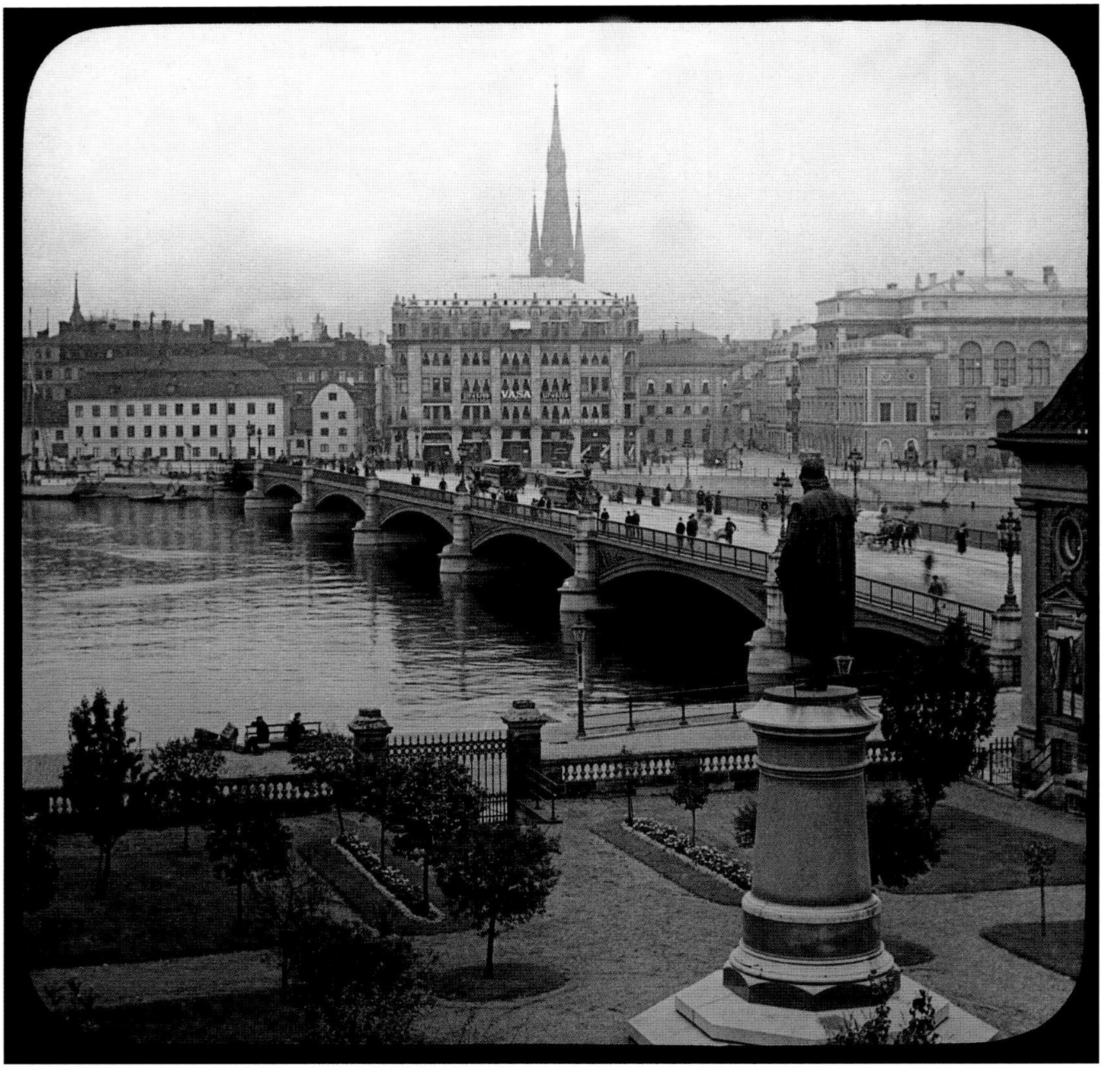

24 The Vasa Bridge, Stockholm, Sweden, 1900s
25 Dalecarlian maidens on a hillside overlooking Rattvik, Sweden, 1900s

24 Die Wasabrücke, Stockholm, Schweden, 1900er Jahre
25 Junge Mädchen aus Dalarna auf einem Hügel mit Blick auf Rättvik, Schweden, 1900er Jahre

24 Le pont Vasa à Stockholm, Suède, années1900
25 Jeunes femmes dalécarliennes sur une hauteur dominant Rattvik, Suède, années 1900

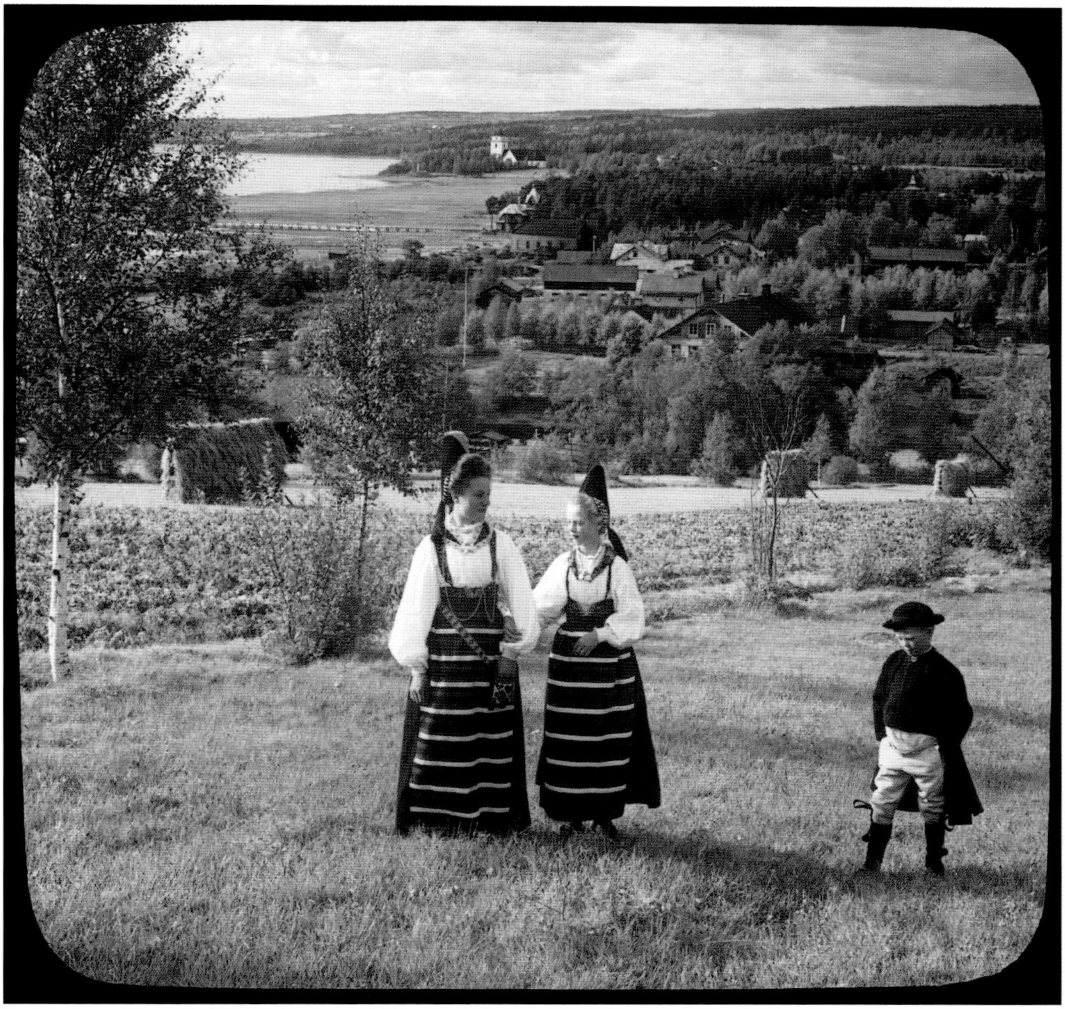

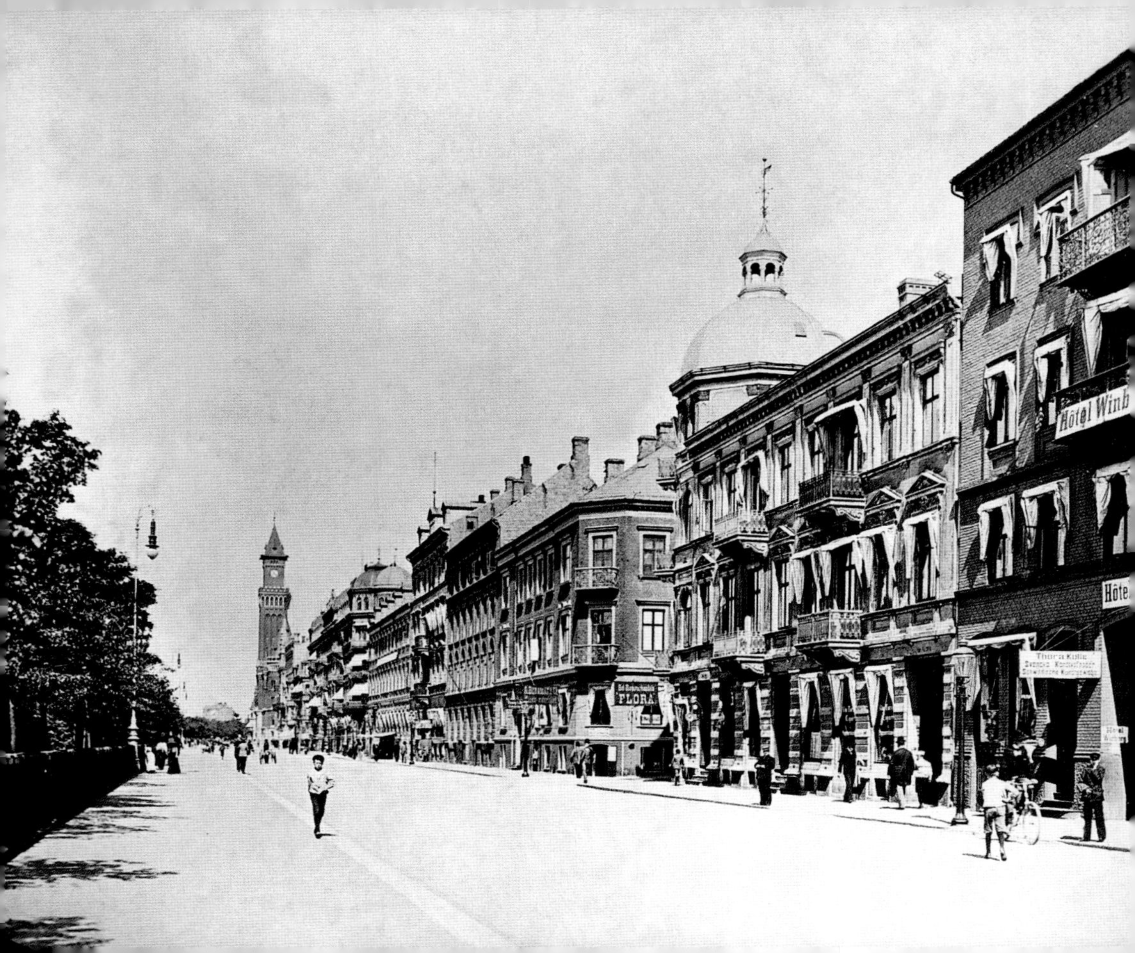
Hôtel Winb
FLORA

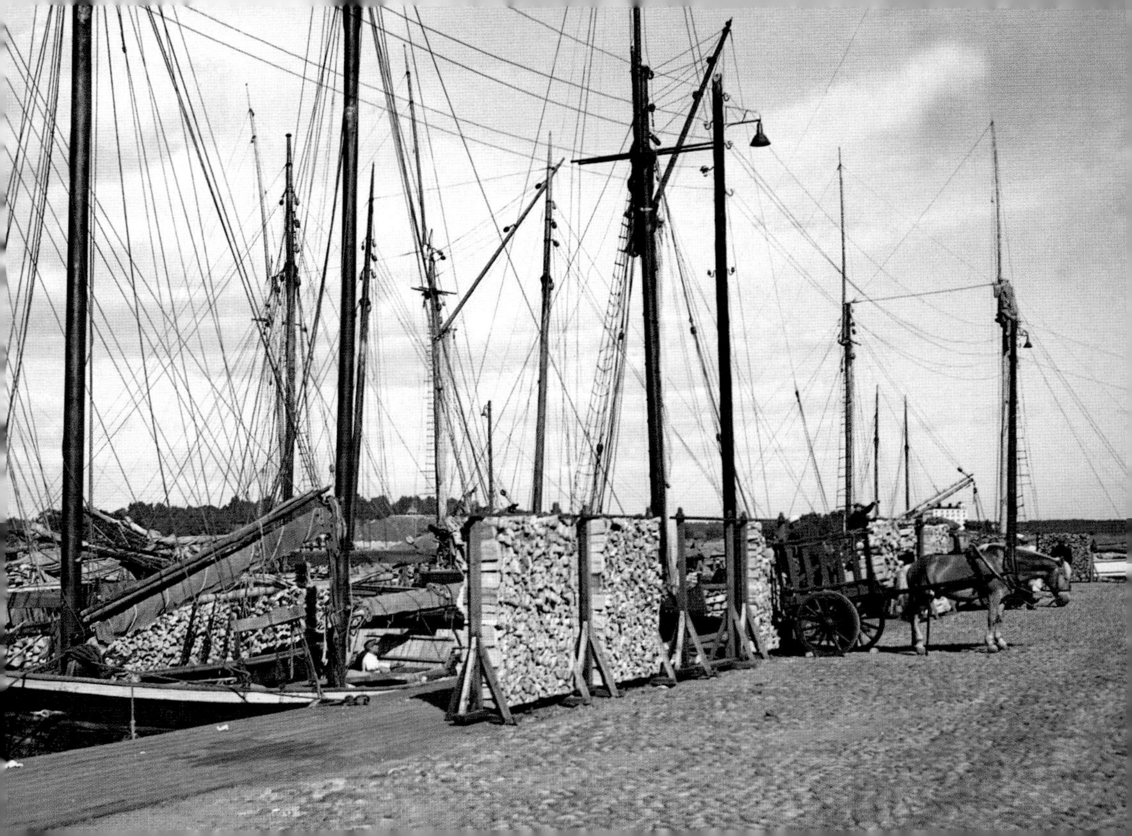

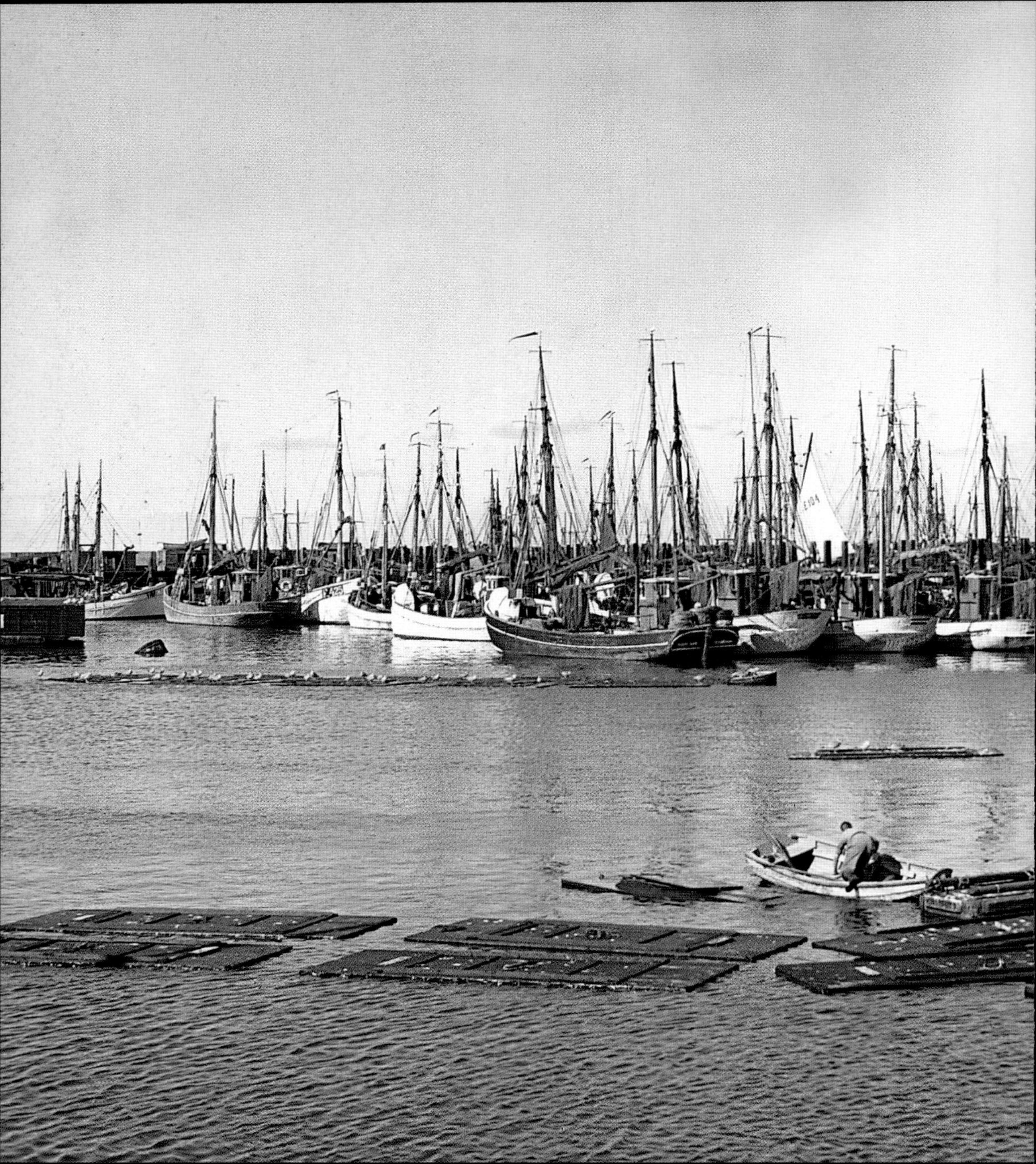

28 Fishing Fleet, Esbjerg, Denmark, 1937

28 Fischfangflotte, Esbjerg, Dänemark, 1937

28 Flotille de pêche, Esbjerg, Danemark, 1937

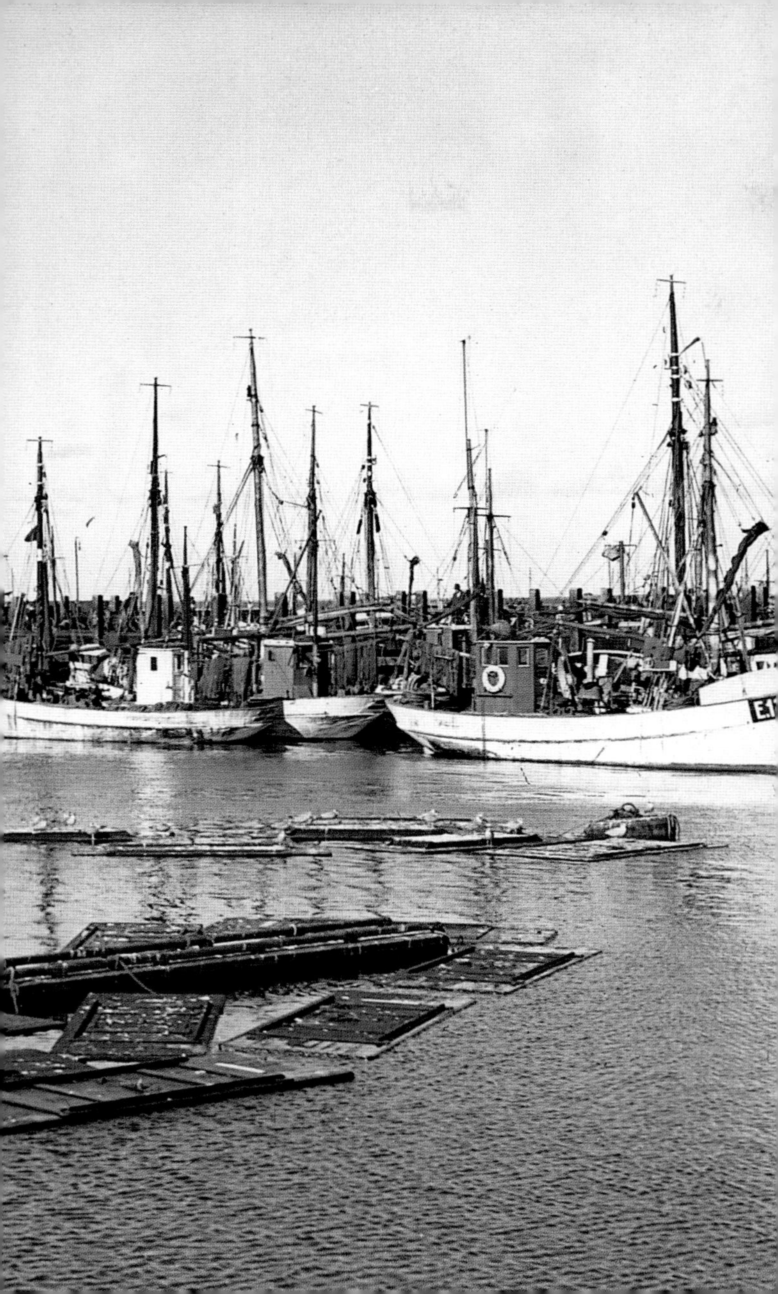

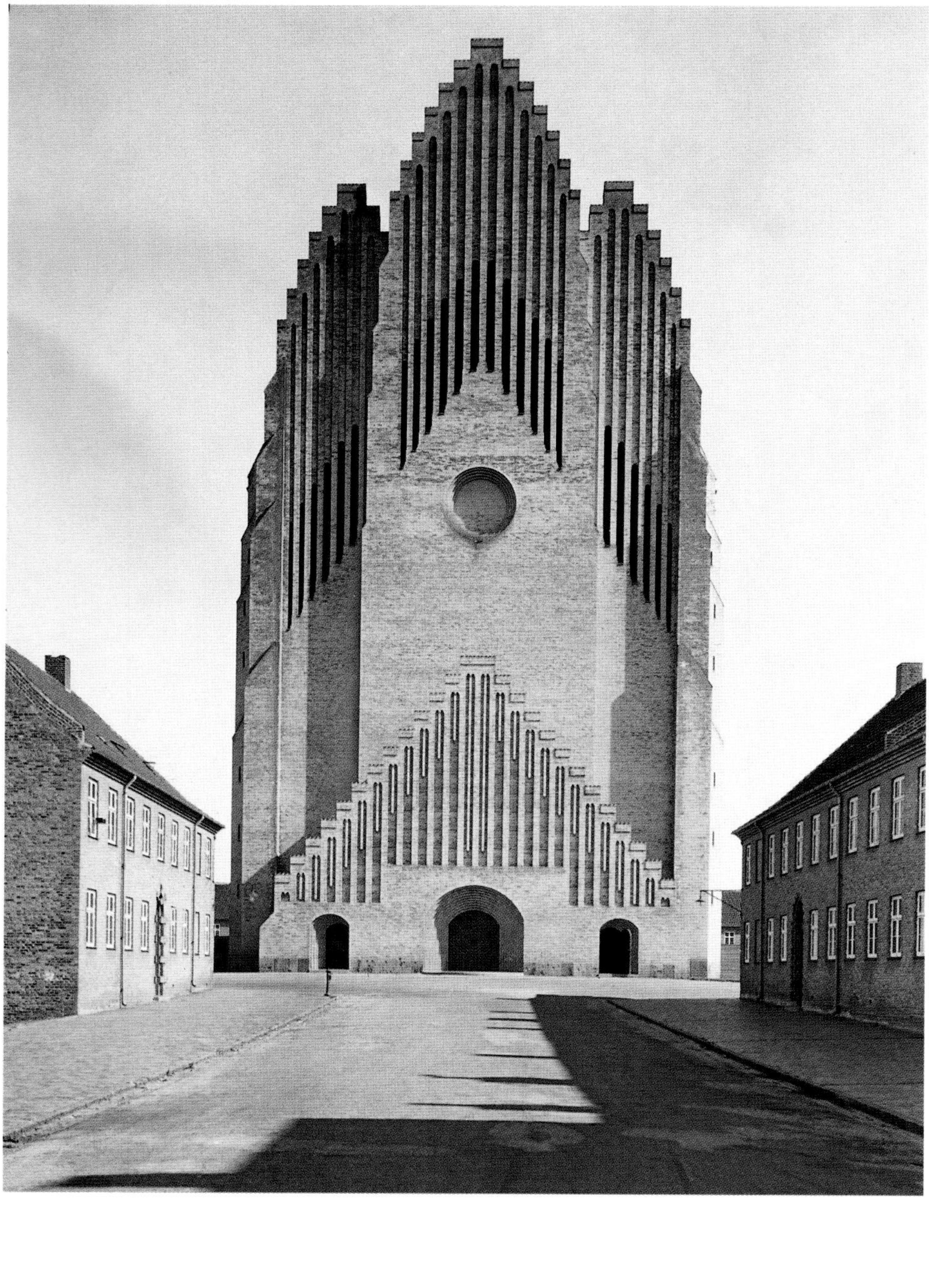

29 Grundtvig Church (designed by P.V.J. Klint), Copenhagen, Denmark, 1929

29 Die Grundtvigskirche (entworfen von P.V.J. Klint), Kopenhagen, Dänemark, 1929

29 Eglise Grundtvig (dessinée par P.V.J. Klint), Copenhagen, Danemark, 1929

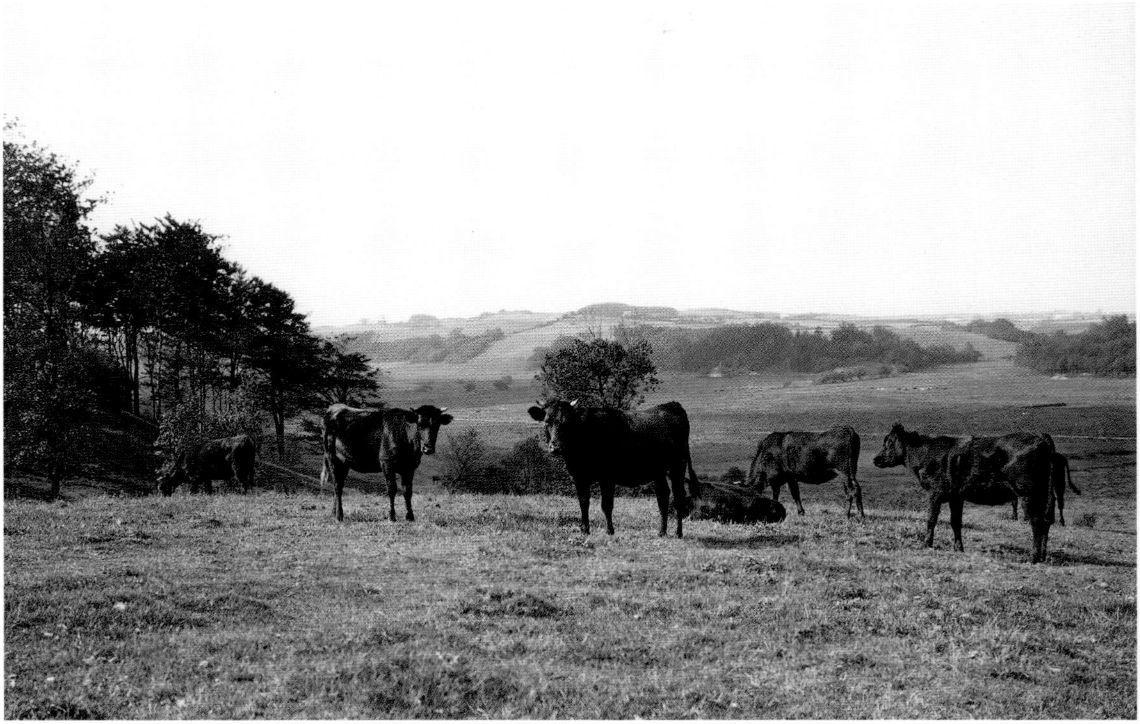

30 Grazing cattle and rolling countryside near Fredericia, Denmark, 1929

30 Weidende Rinder und Hügellandschaft nahe Fredericia, Dänemark, 1929

30 Troupeau au pâturage et collines près de Fredericia, Danemark, 1929

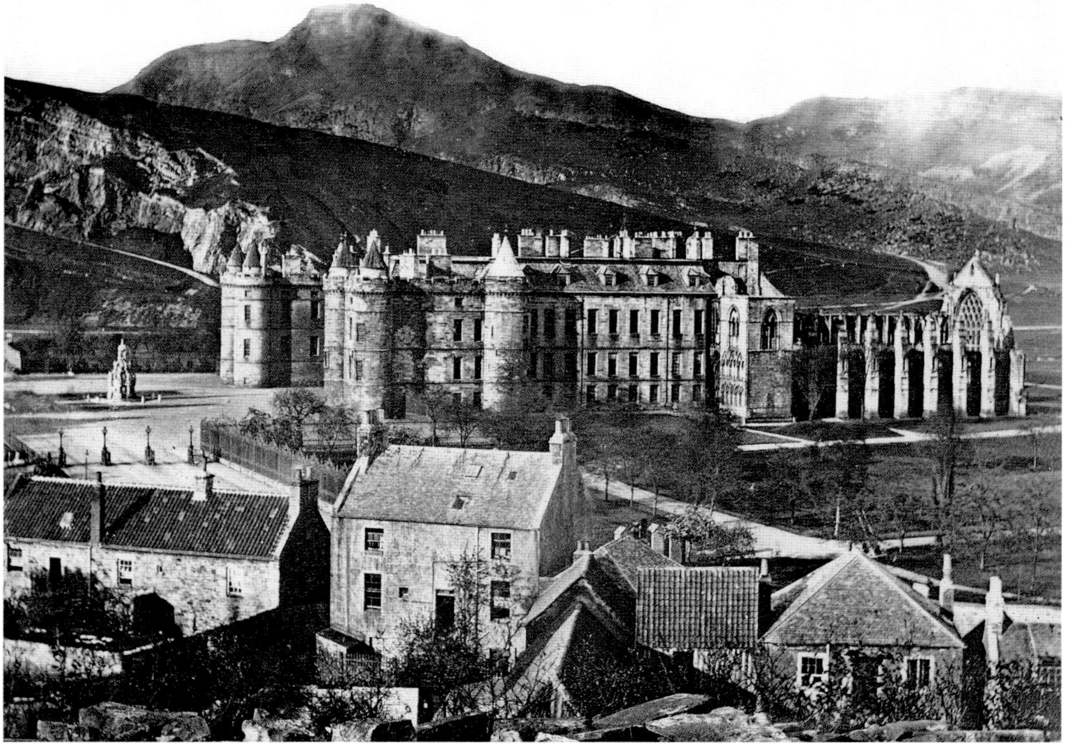

31 Palace of Holyroodhouse (Holyrood Palace), Scotland, 1870s
32 Crofter's Dwelling, Island of Skye, Scotland, 1880s

31 Der Holyroodhouse-Palast (Holyrood Palace), Schottland, 1870er Jahre
32 Behausung eines Kleinbauern, Isle of Skye, Schottland, 1880er Jahre

31 Palais de Holyroodhouse (Holyrood Palace), Écosse, années 1870
32 Habitat de modeste fermier, Île de Skye, Écosse, années 1880

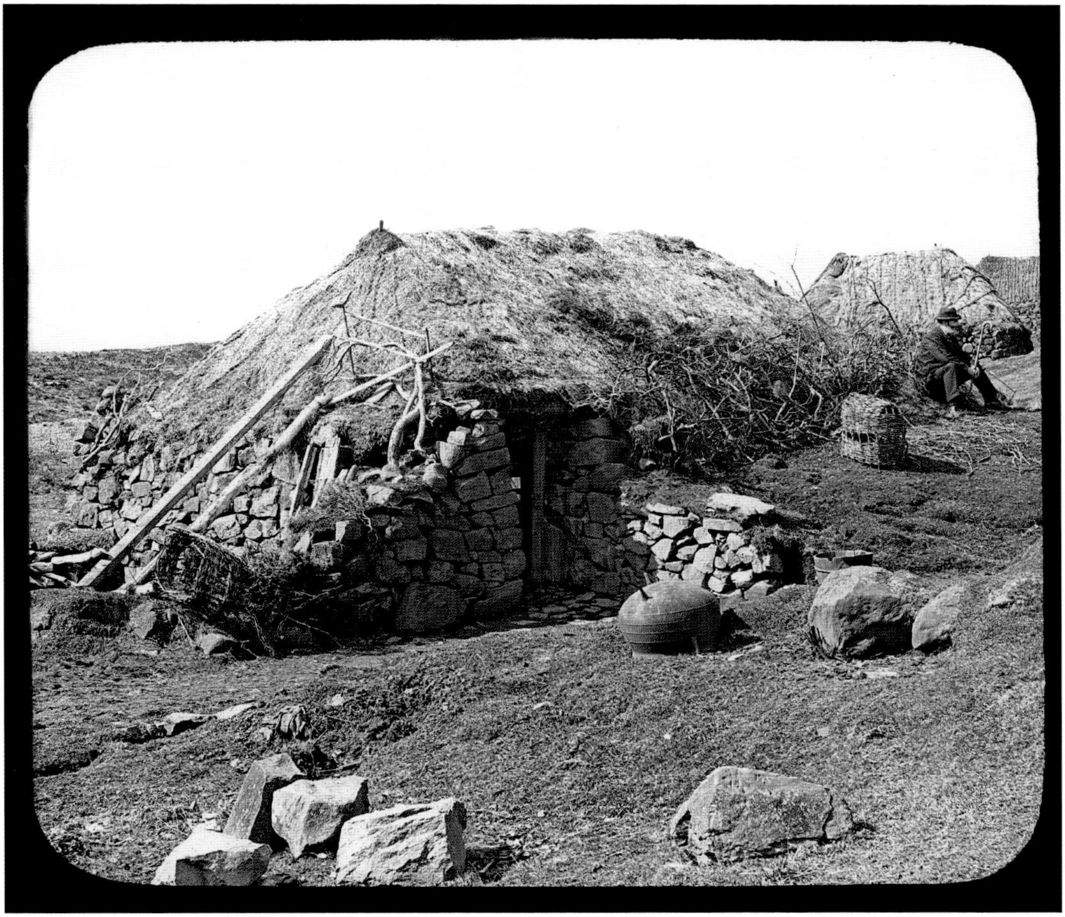

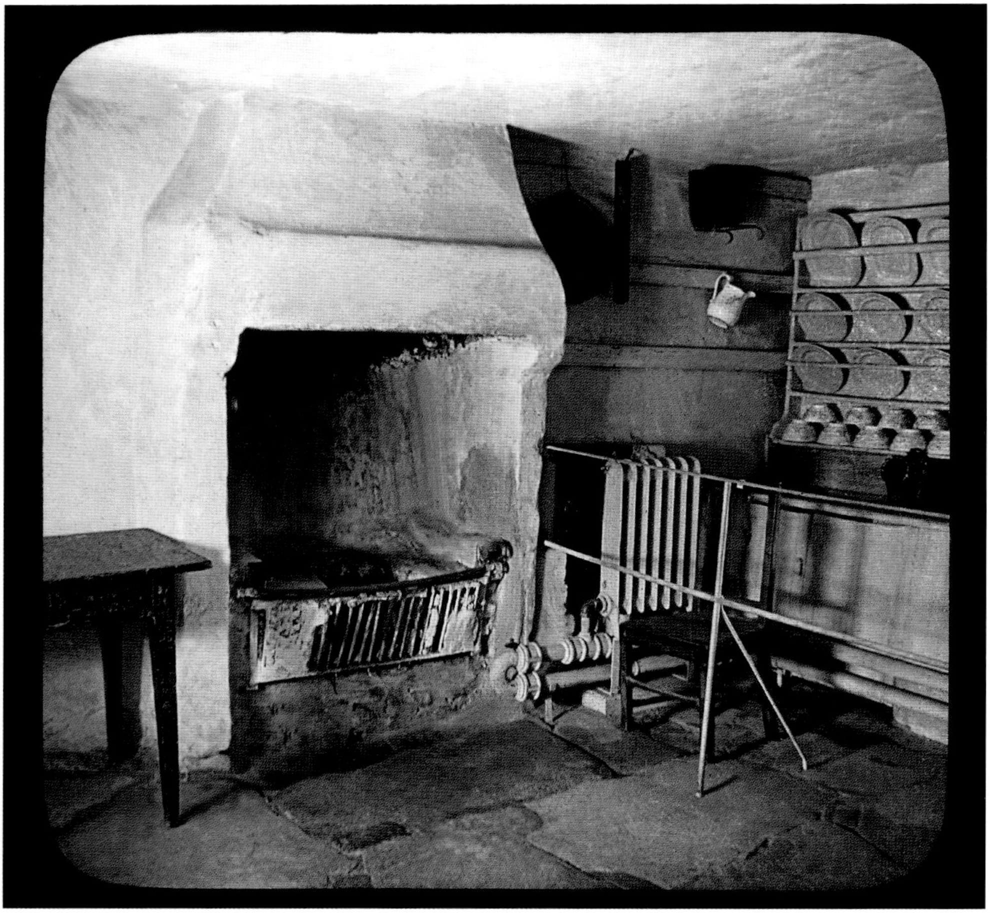

33 Burns Cottage, Ayr, Scotland, c.1900, the birthplace of the poet, Robert “Rabbie” Burns
34 Tossing the hammer, Inverness, Scotland, 1880s

33 Das Burns Cottage, Ayr, Schottland, um 1900, Geburtshaus des Dichters Robert „Rabbie“ Burns
34 Hammerwerfen, Inverness, Schottland, 1880er Jahre

33 Burns Cottage, Ayr, Écosse, vers 1900. Lieu de naissance du poète Robert “Rabbie” Burns
34 Lancer du marteau, Inverness, Écosse, années 1880

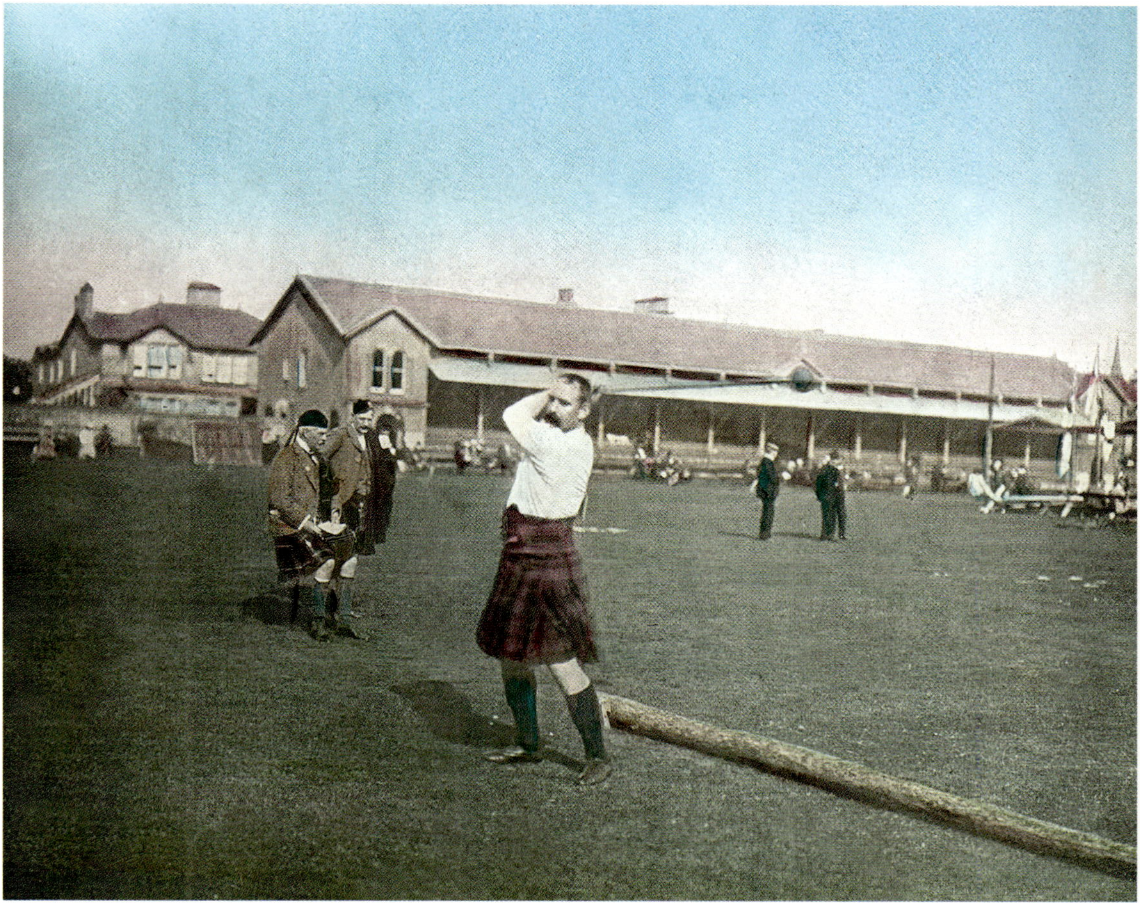

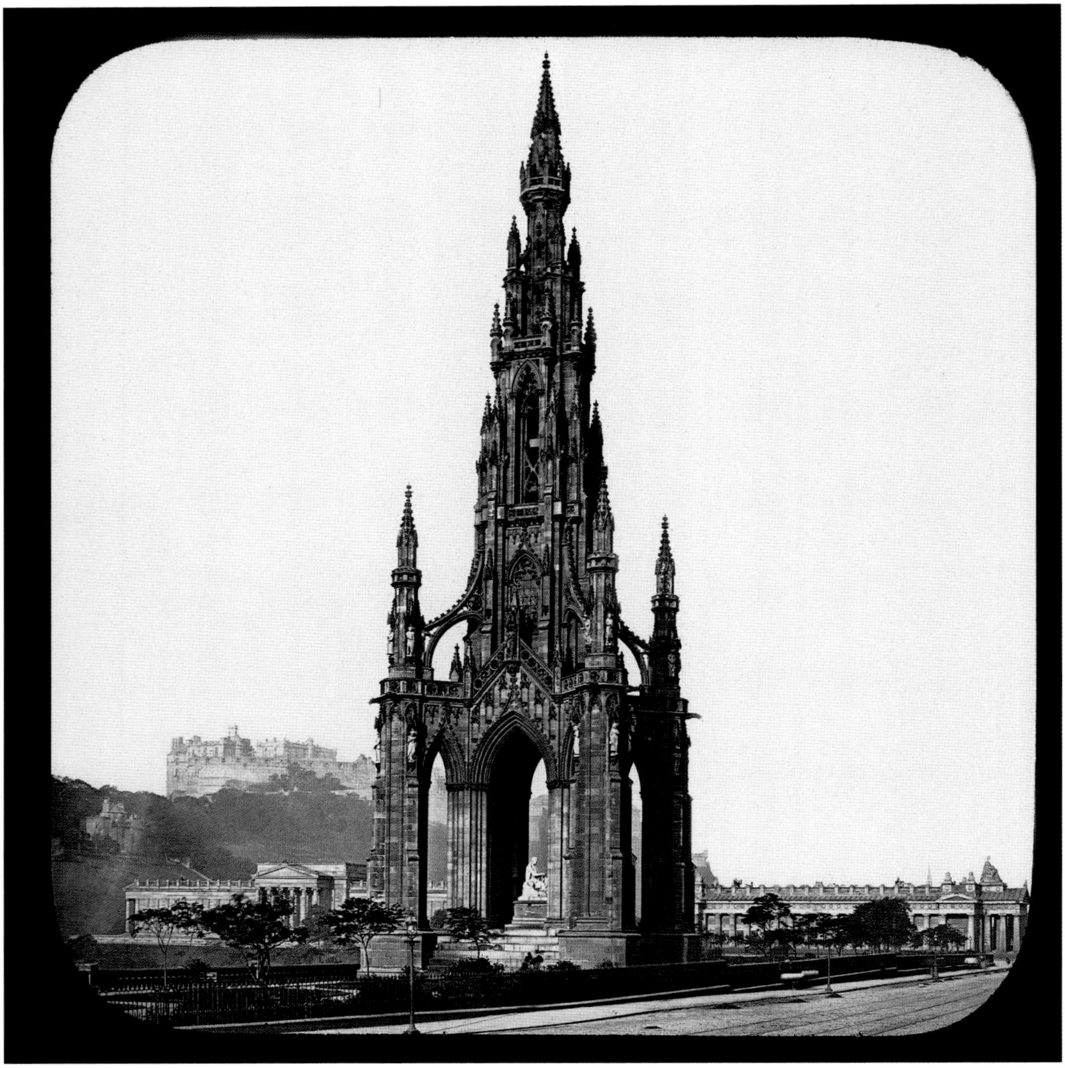

35 The Scott Monument (in tribute to the Scottish author, Sir Walter Scott), Edinburgh, Scotland, 1890s
36 Forth Bridge, Scotland, 1880s

35 Das Scott-Denkmal (zu Ehren des schottischen Schriftstellers Sir Walter Scott), Edinburgh, Schottland, 1890er Jahre
36 Die Forth-Brücke, Schottland, 1880er Jahre

35 Le monument Scott (en hommage à l'auteur écossais Sir Walter Scott), Edimbourg, Écosse, années 1890
36 Le pont de Forth, Écosse, années 1880

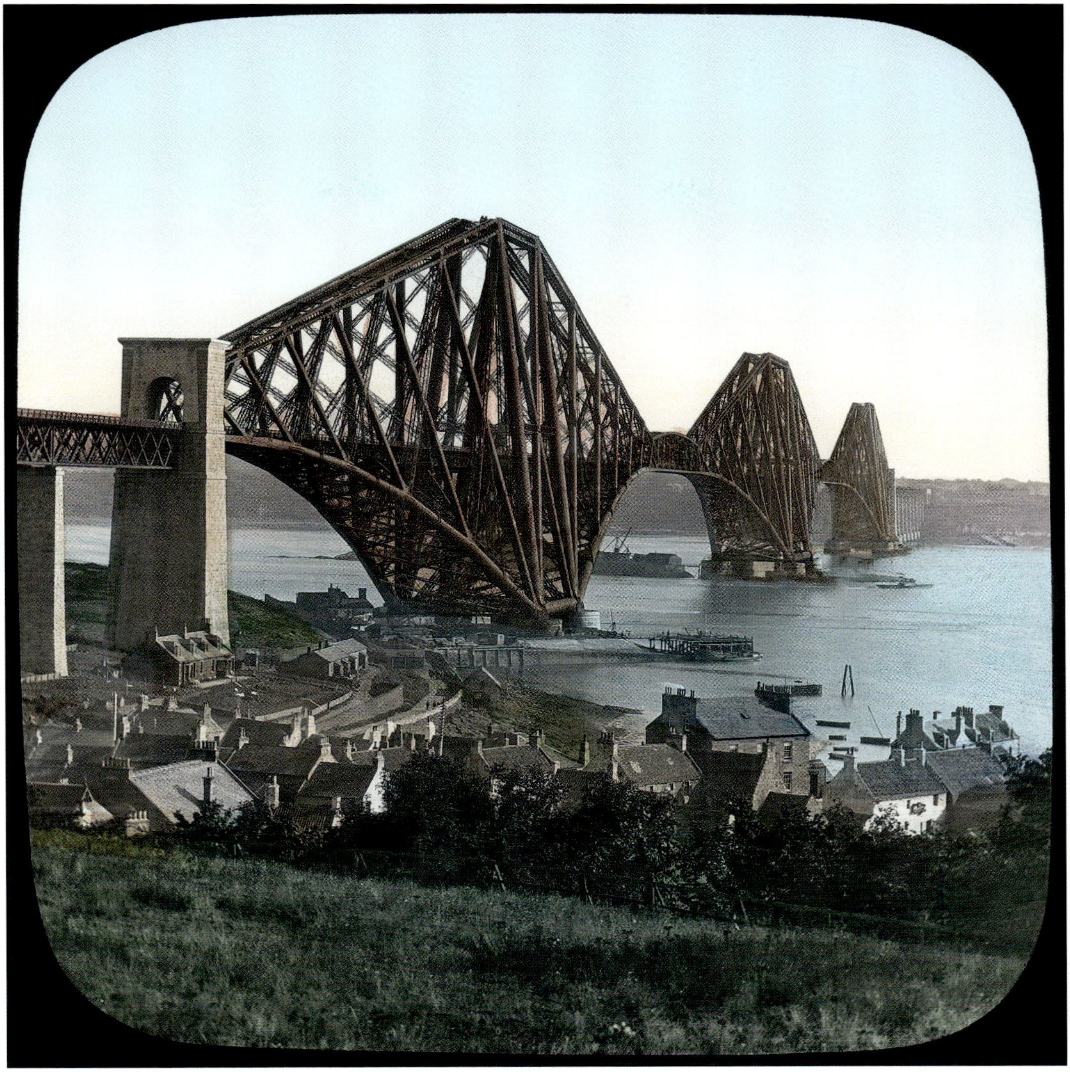

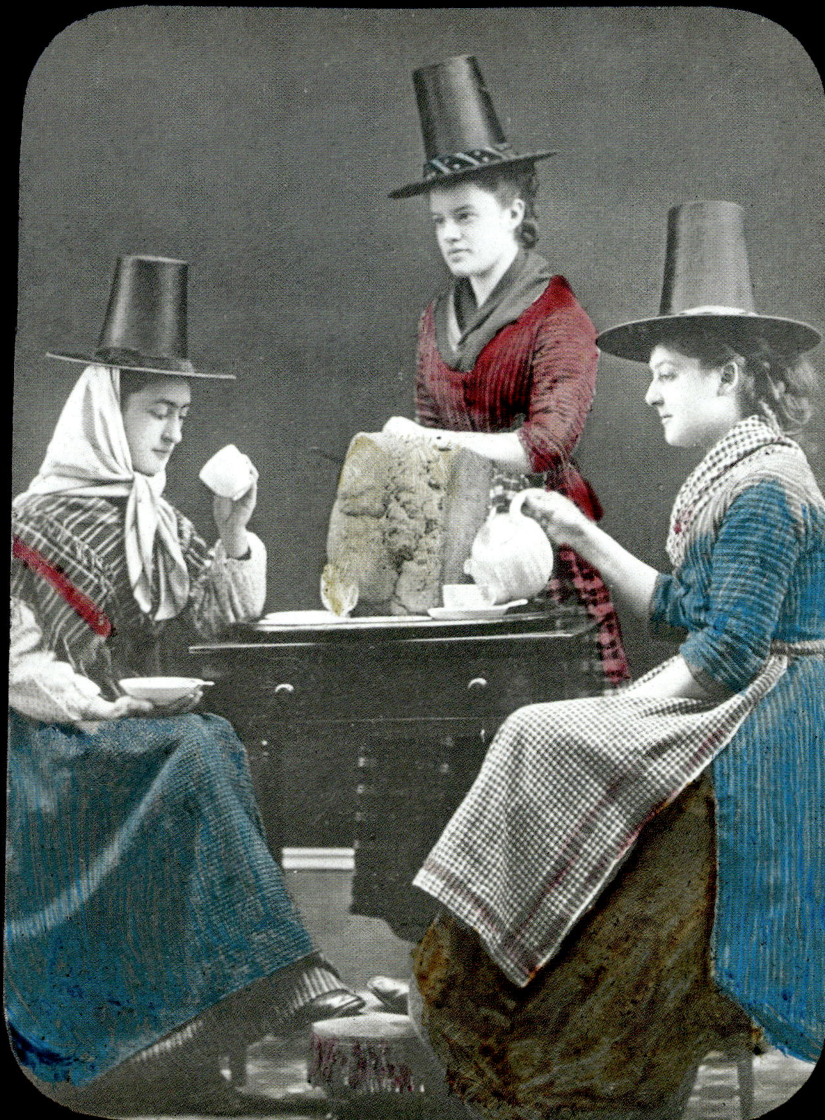

37 Women having tea and wearing traditional costume, Wales, Great Britain, 1890s

37 Frauen in traditioneller Tracht beim Teetrinken, Wales, 1890er Jahre

37 Femme en costume traditionnel, prenant le thé, Pays de Galles, Grande-Bretagne, années 1890

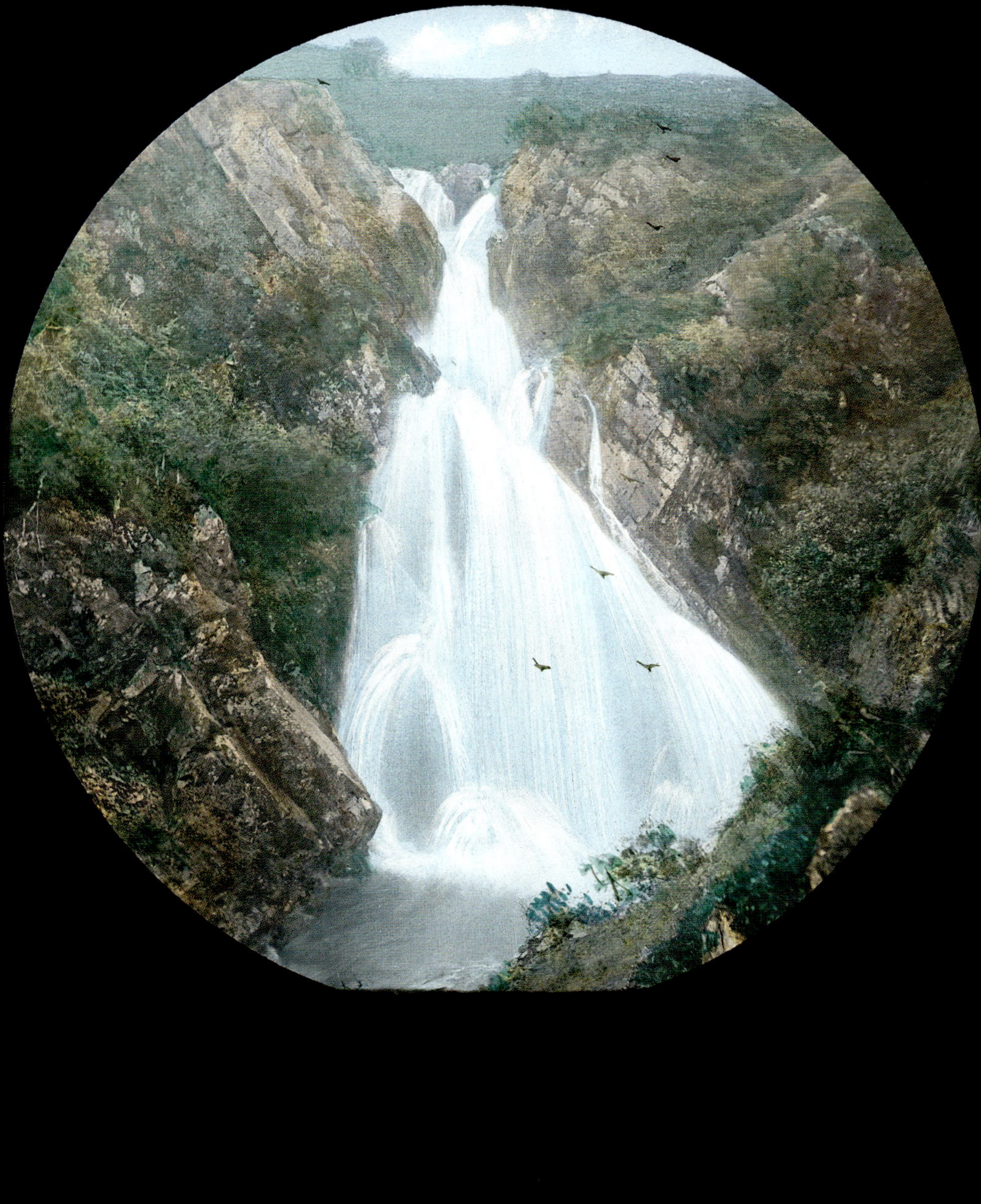

38 Llanberis Waterfall, Wales, 1880s

38 Wasserfall in Llanberis, Wales, 1880er Jahre

38 Chutes de Llanberis, Pays de Galles, années 1880

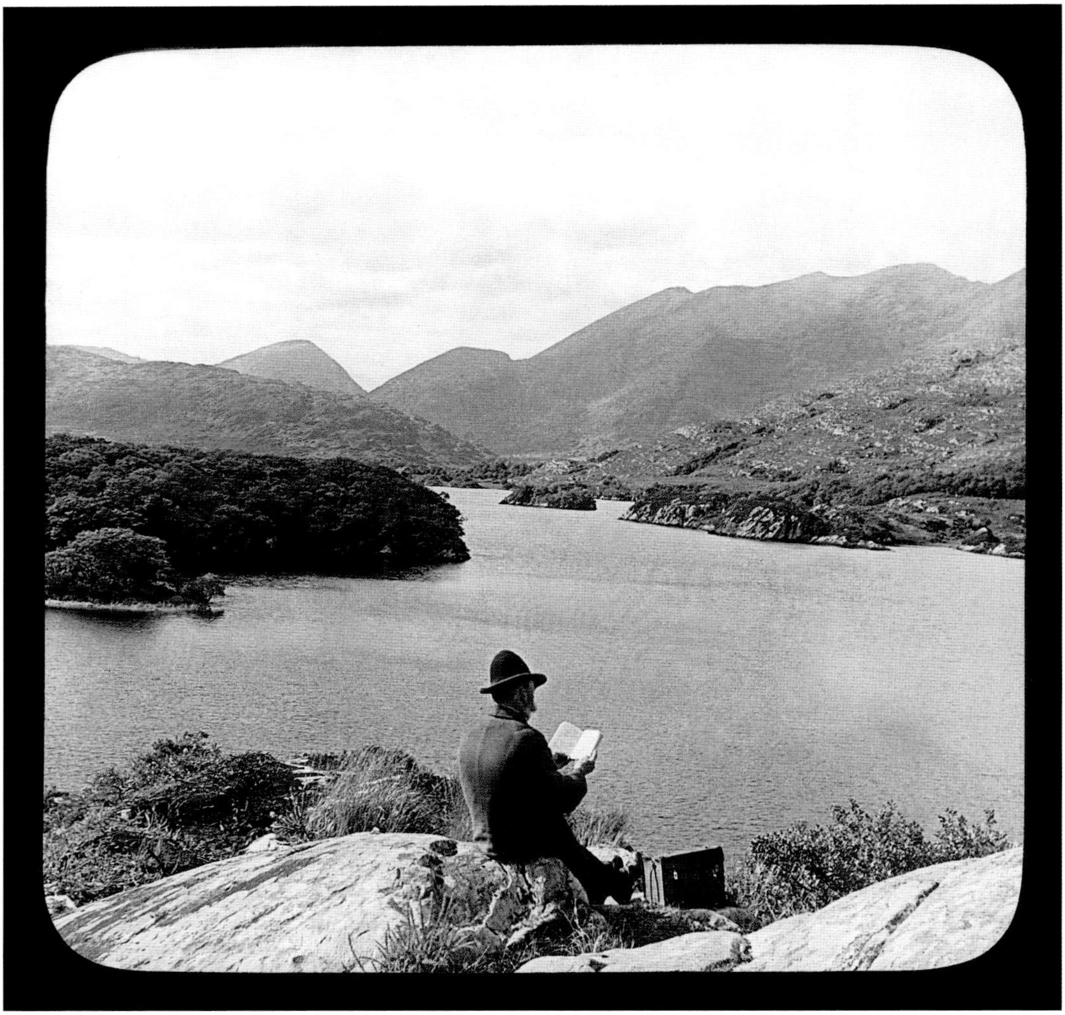

39 Lakes of Killarney,
Ireland, c.1900
40 Giant's Causeway,
Northern Ireland, c.1900

39 Die Seen von Killarney,
Irland, um 1900
40 Giant's Causeway,
Nordirland, um 1900

39 Lacs de Killarney,
Irlande, vers 1900
40 Chaussée des Géants,
Irlande du Nord, vers 1900

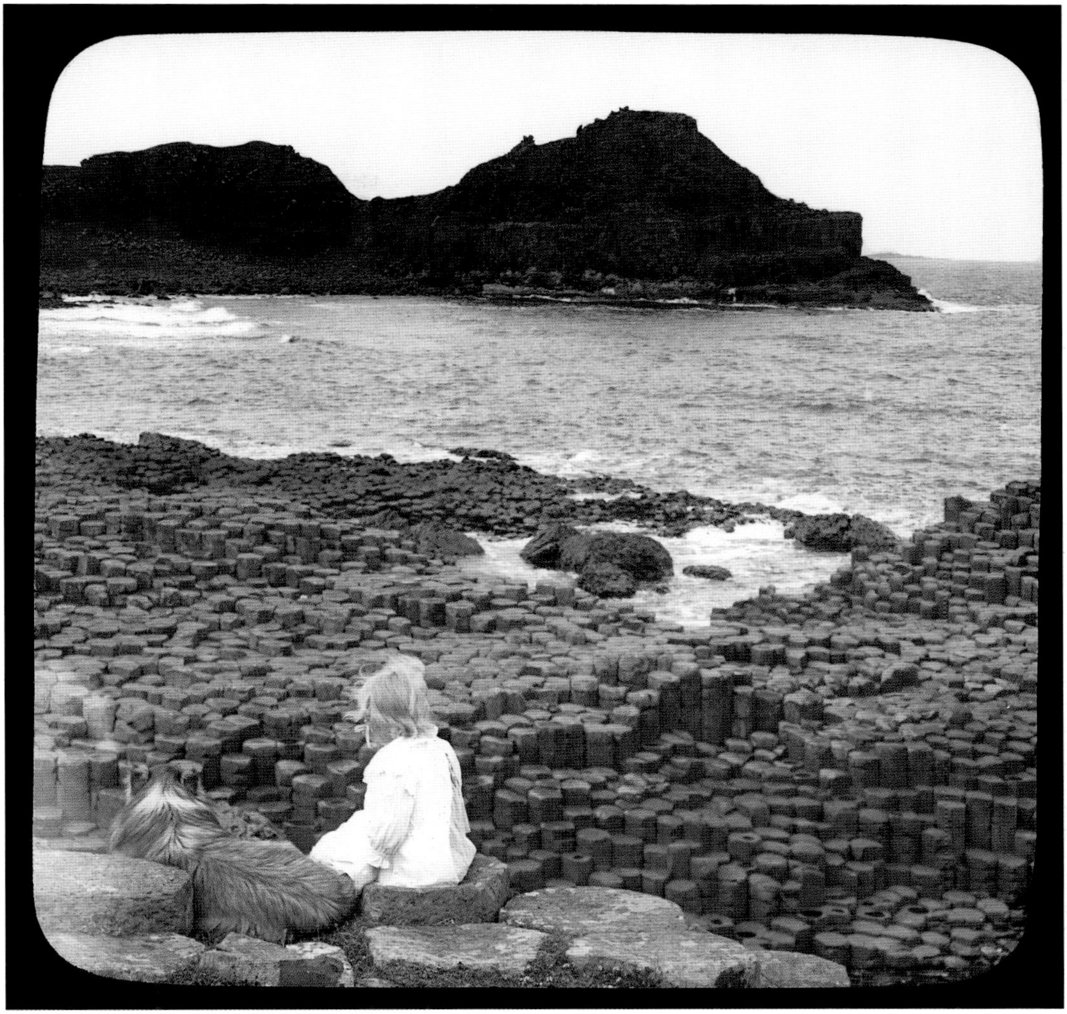

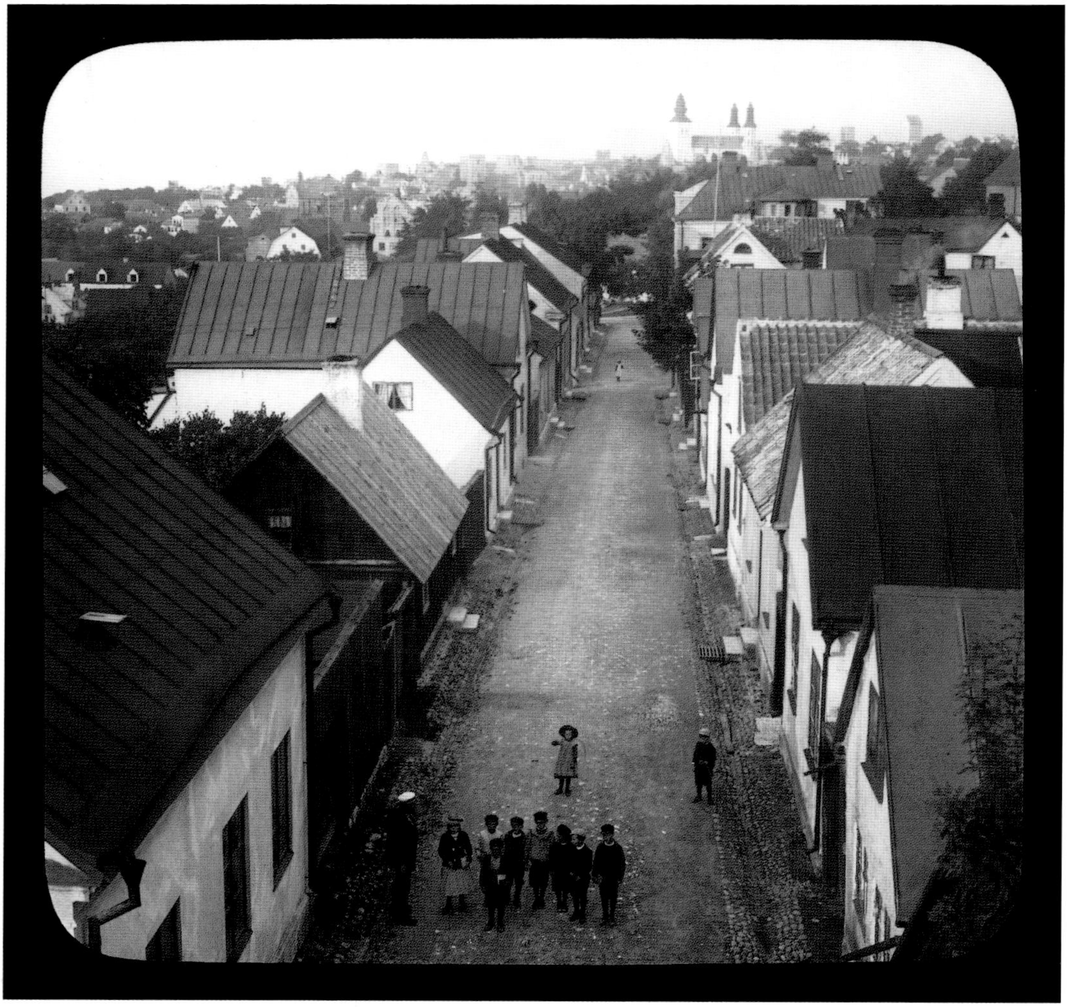

41 Looking North from the old city wall, Wisby, Ireland, c.1900
42 Royal Avenue, Belfast, Ireland, 1900s

41 Blick nach Norden von der alten Stadtmauer in Wisby, Irland, um 1900
42 Die Royal Avenue, Belfast, Nordirland, 1900er Jahre

41 Coup d'œil vers le nord depuis l'enceinte de la ville ancienne, Wisby, Irlande, vers 1900
42 Royal Avenue, Belfast, Irlande, années 1900

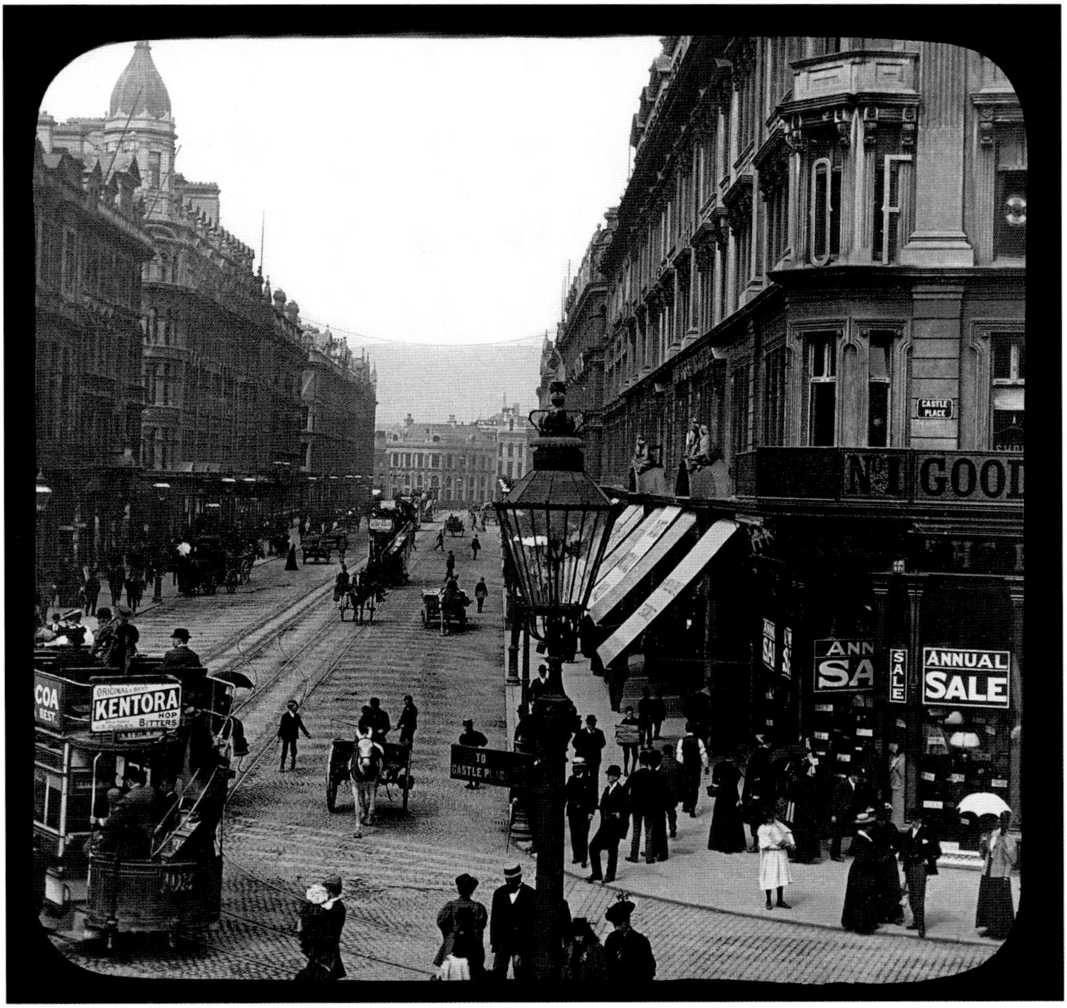
ORIGINAL & BEST
KENTORA
HOP
BITTERS
TO
CASTLE PLACE
CASTLE
PLACE
ANNUAL
SALE
SALE

43 An Irish jaunting car (cart), Ireland, 1880s

43 Irischer Jaunting-Car, Irland, 1880er Jahre

43 Promenade en carriole, Irlande, années 1880

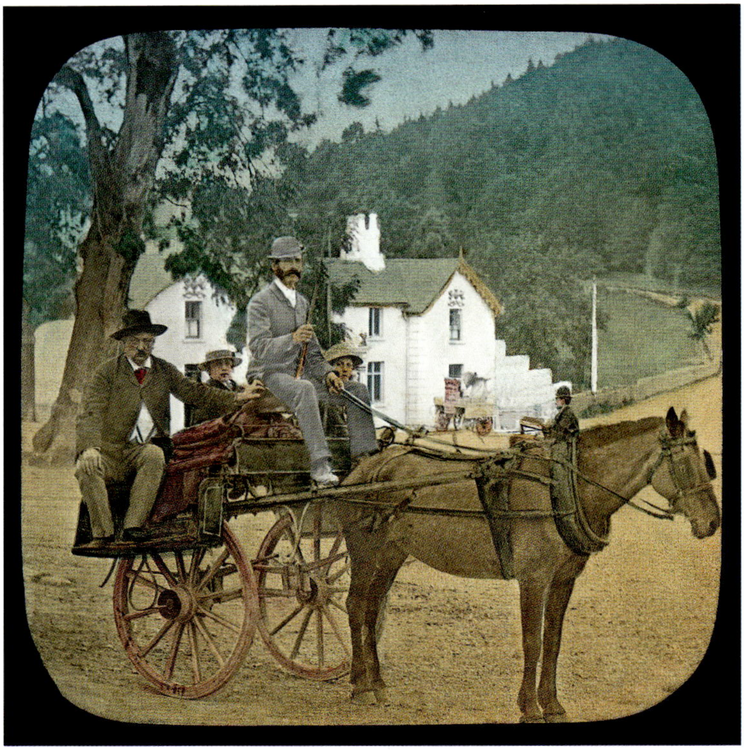

44 Sackville Street (O'Connell Street), Dublin, Ireland, 1880s

44 Die Sackville Street (O'Connell Street), Dublin, Irland, 1880er Jahre

44 Sackville Street (O'Connell Street), Dublin, Irlande, années 1880

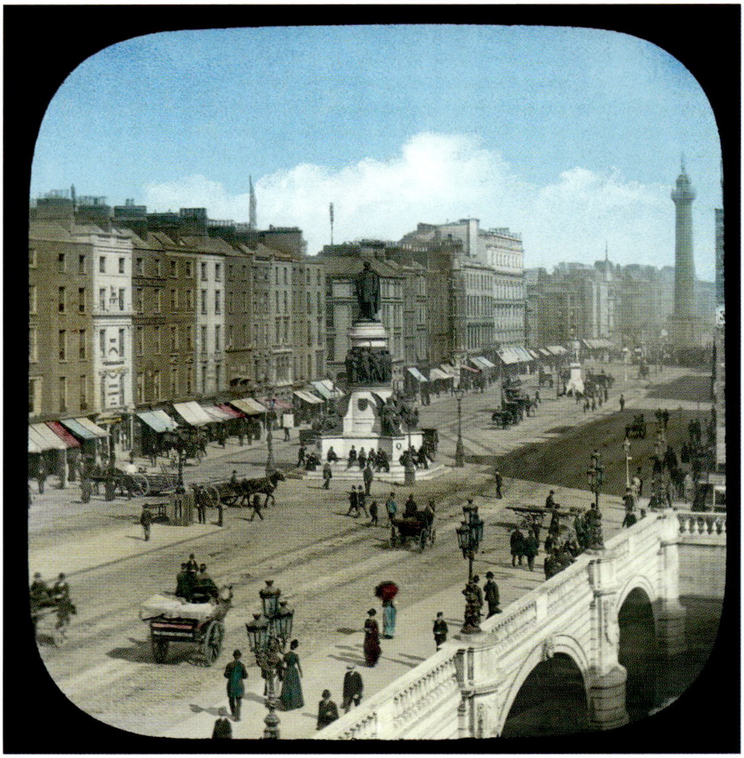

45 Killiney and the Vale of Shauganagh, County Dublin, Ireland, 1880s

45 Killiney und das Tal von Shauganagh, Grafschaft Dublin, Irland, 1880er Jahre

45 Killiney et la vallée de Shanganagh, comté de Dublin, Irlande, années 1880

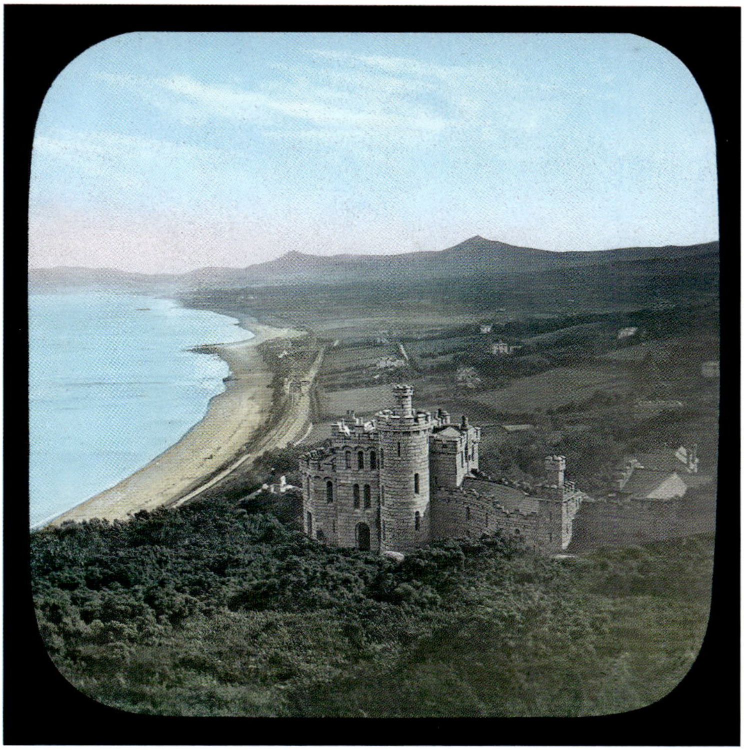

46 Lismore Castle, County Waterford, Ireland, 1880s

46 Schloss Lismore, Grafschaft Waterford, Irland, 1880er Jahre

46 Château de Lismore, comté de Waterford, Irlande, années 1880

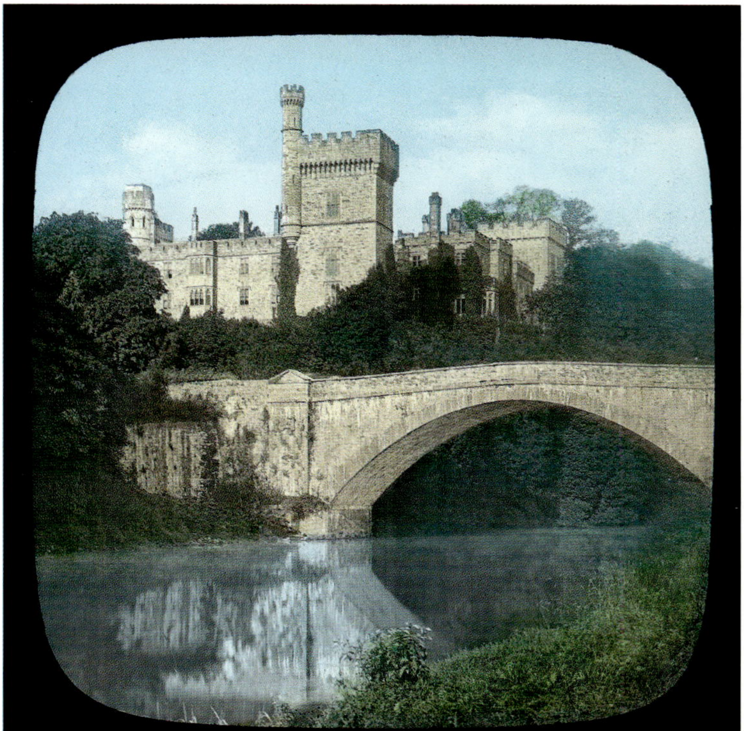

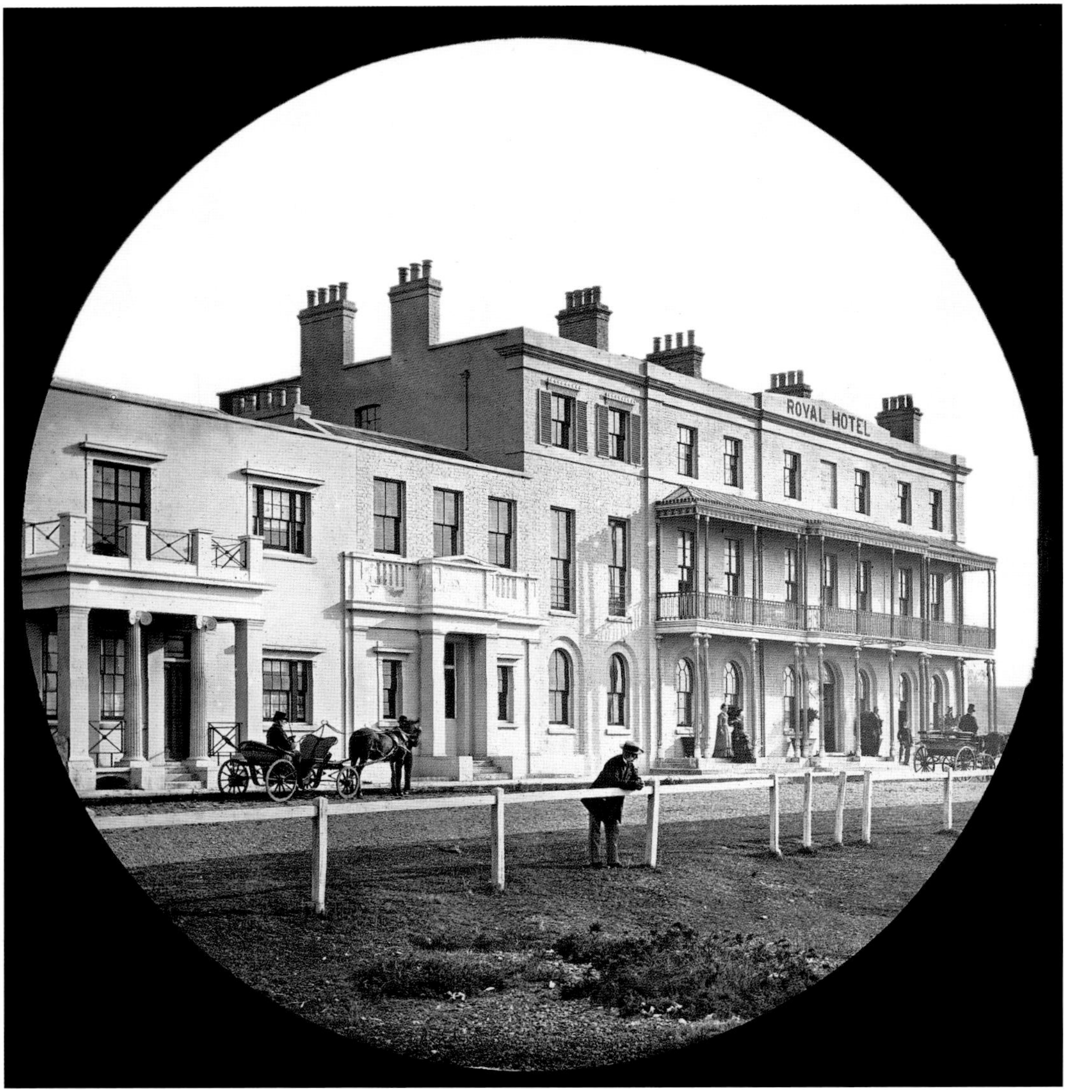

47 Royal Hotel, Hayling Island, British Isles, 1870s
48 Needle Rock, Plemont, Jersey, Channel Islands, 1880s

47 Das Royal Hotel, Insel Hayling, Britische Inseln, 1870er Jahre
48 Der Needle Rock, Plemont, Jersey, Kanalinseln, 1880er Jahre

47 Royal Hotel, île de Hayling, îles britanniques, années 1870
48 L'Aiguille, Plemont, Jersey, îles anglo-normandes, années 1880

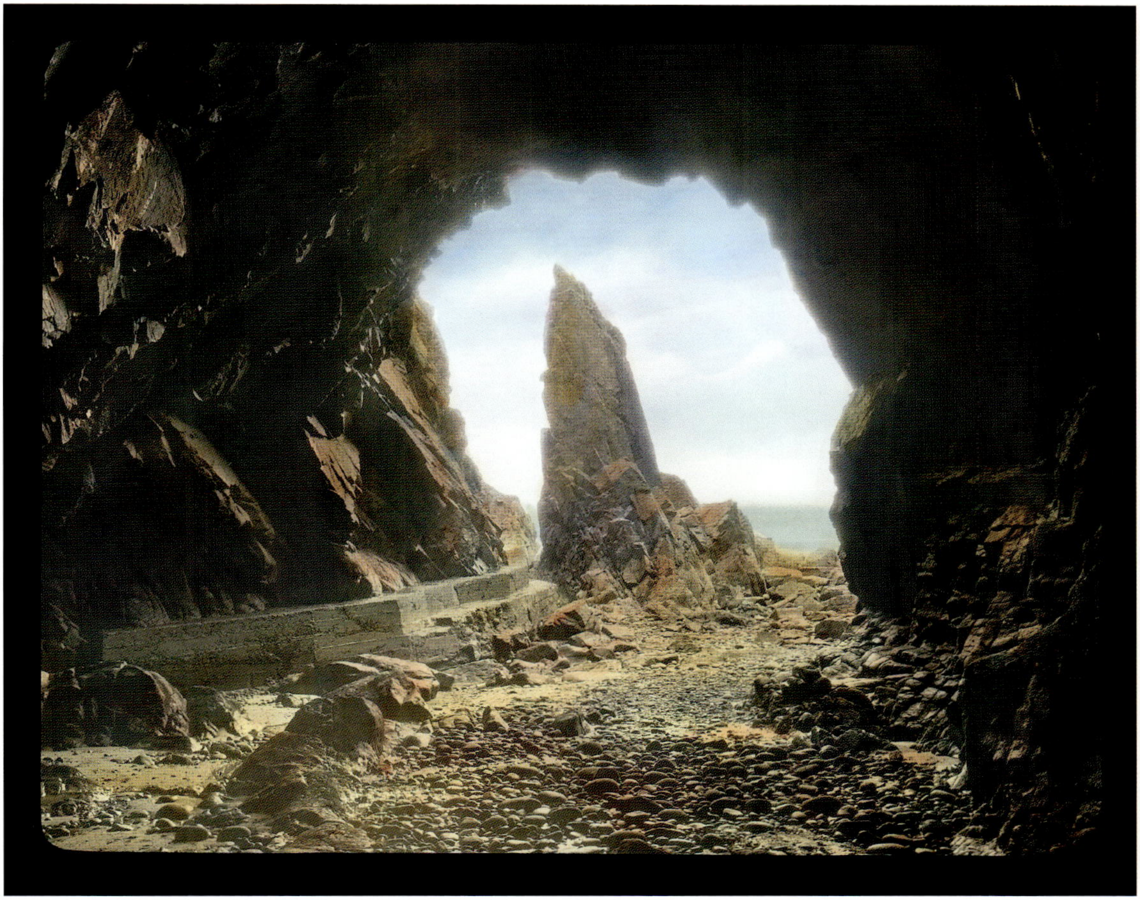

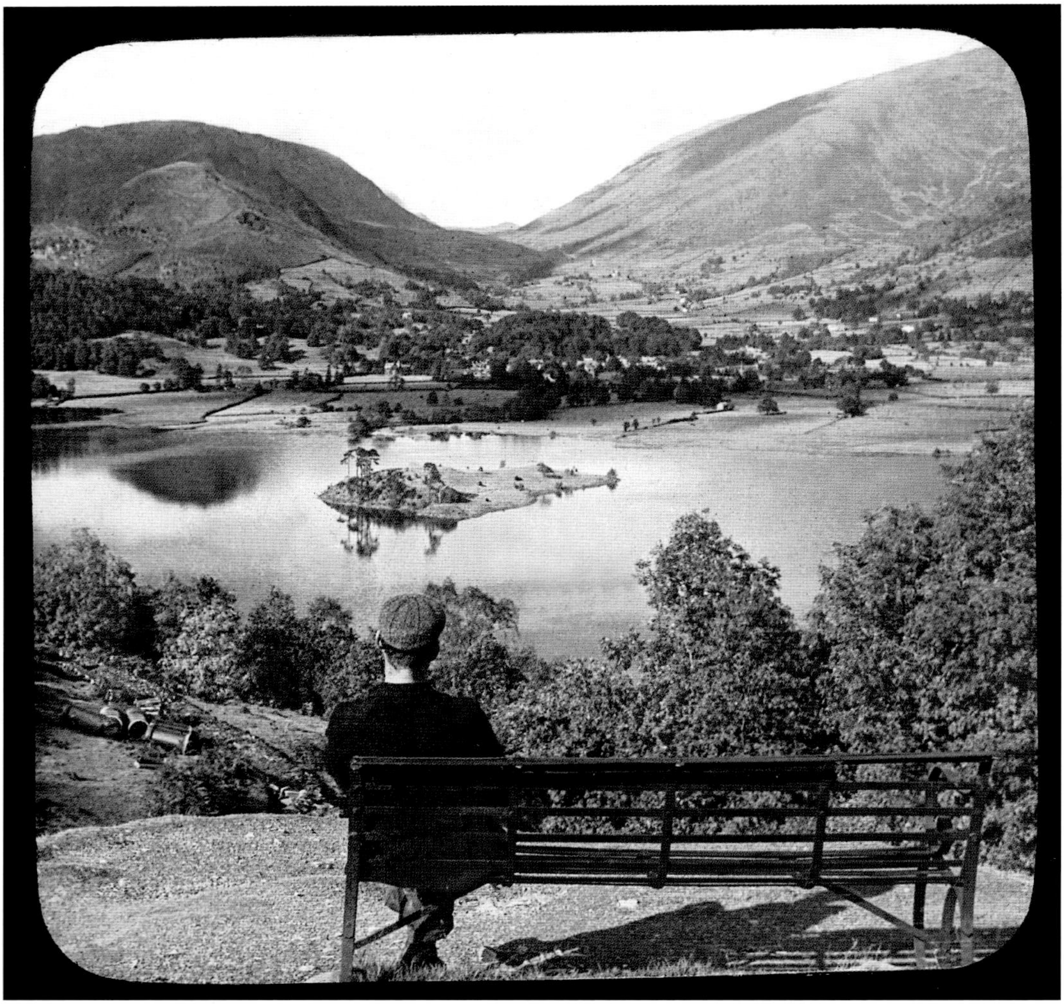

49 Lake Grasmere, England, 1900s
50 Children outside Anne Hathaway's Cottage, Shottery, near Stratford-upon-Avon, England, 1890s

49 Der Grasmere-See, England, 1900er Jahre
50 Kinder vor dem Anne Hathaway Cottage, Shottery, nahe Stratford-upon-Avon, England, 1890er Jahre

49 Lac Grasmere, Angleterre, années 1900
50 Enfants devant le cottage d'Anne Hathaway, Shottery, près de Stratford-upon-Avon, Angleterre, années 1890

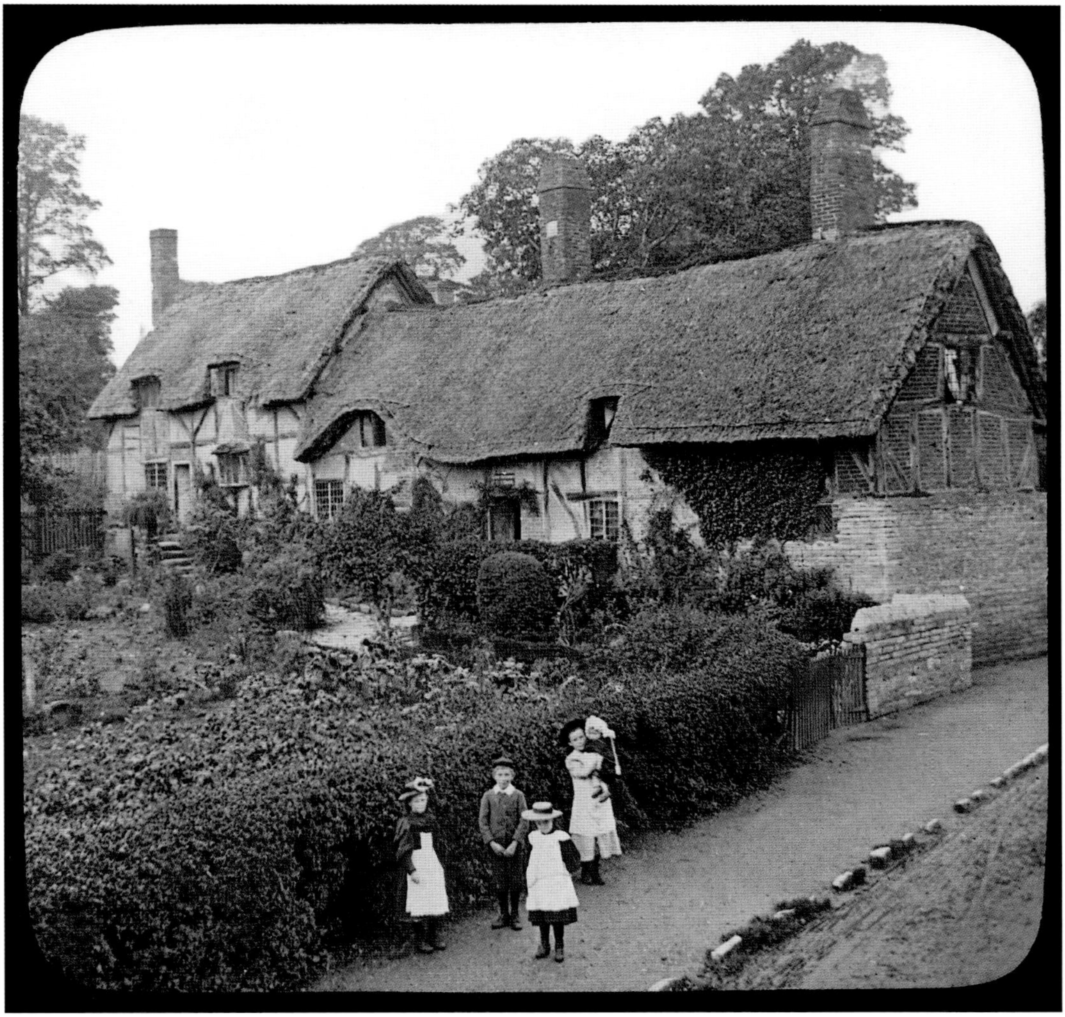

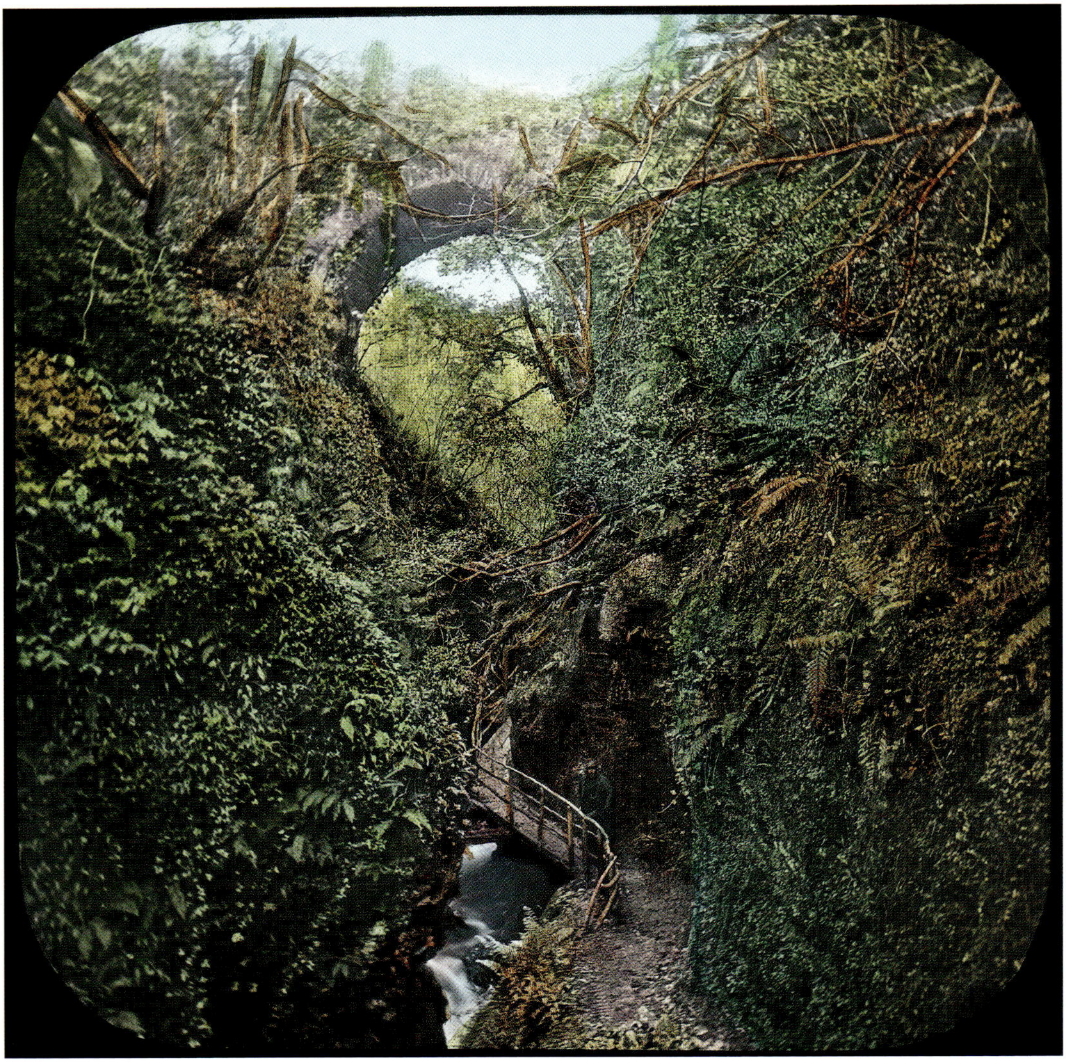

51 River scene, England, 1880s
52 Fountains Abbey, near Aldfield, North Yorkshire, England, 1880s

51 Flussszene, England, 1880er Jahre
52 Fountains Abbey, nahe Aldfield, North Yorkshire, England, 1880er Jahre

51 Torrent en Angleterre, années 1880
52 Fountains Abbey, près de Aldfield, North Yorkshire, Angleterre, années 1880

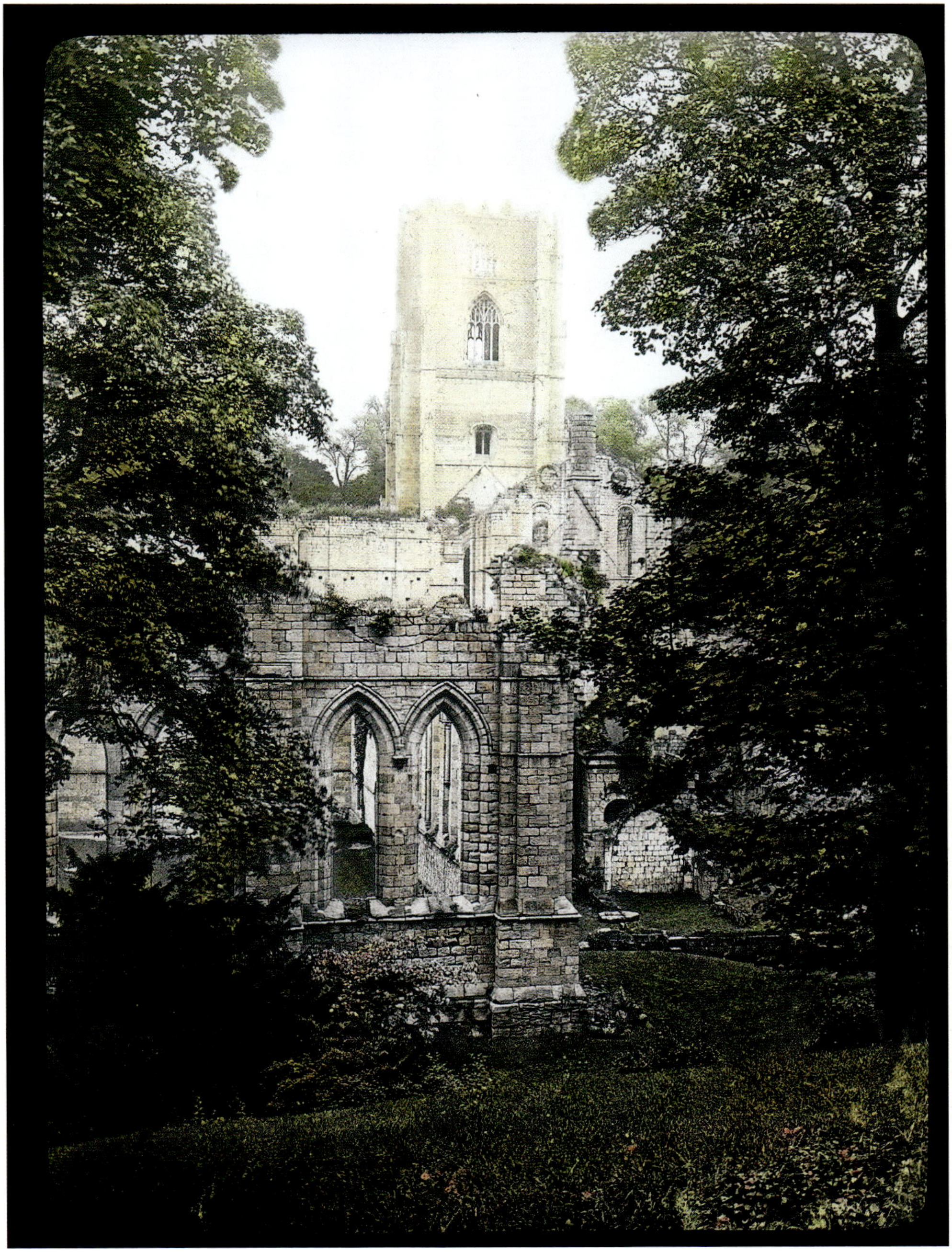

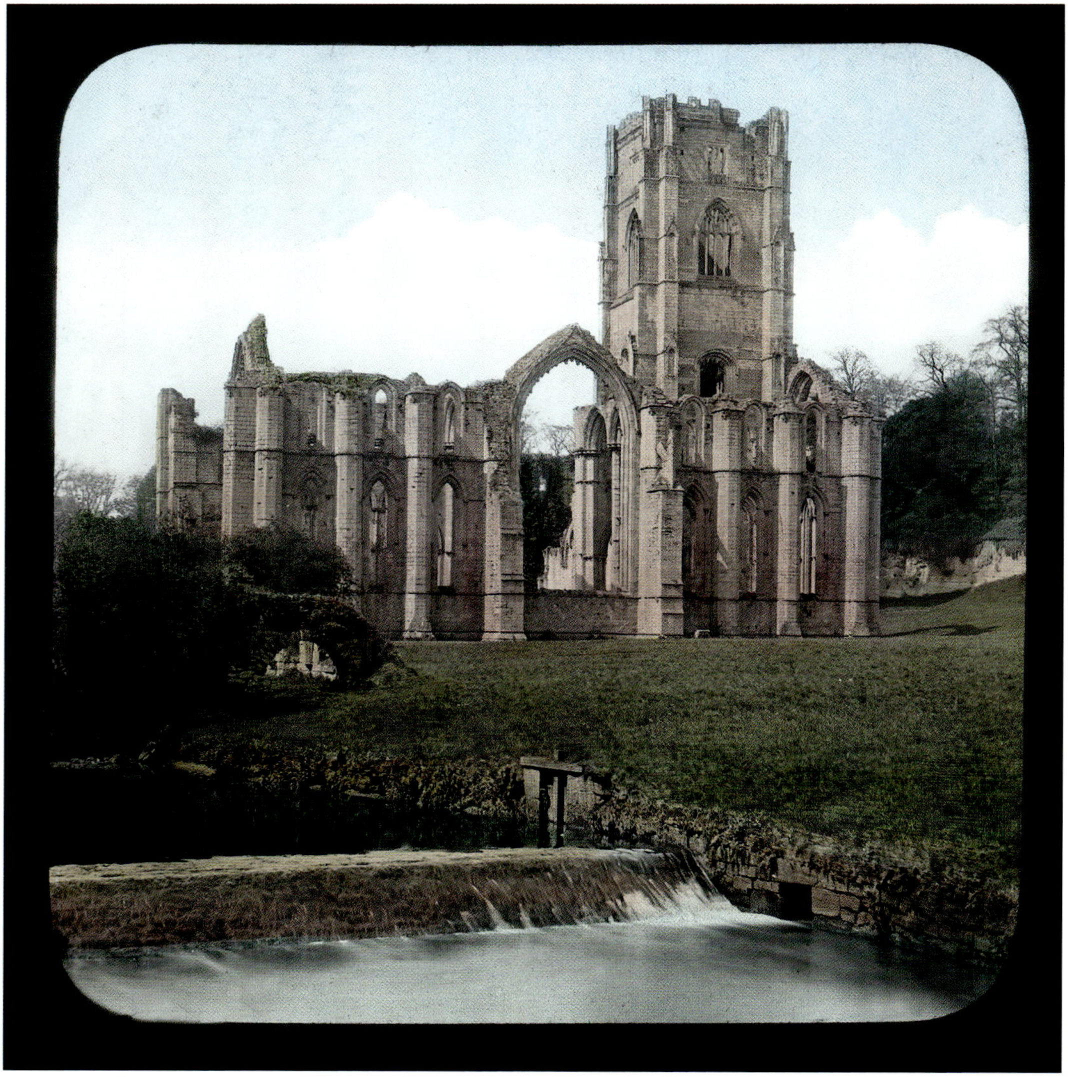

53 Fountains Abbey, nr. Aldfield, North Yorkshire, England, 1880s
54 St. Mary's Church, Ambleside, Lake District, England, 1880s

53 Fountains Abbey, nahe Aldfield, North Yorkshire, England, 1880er Jahre
54 Die St. Mary's Church, Ambleside, Lake District, England, 1880er Jahre

53 Fountains Abbey, près de Aldfield, North Yorkshire, Angleterre, années 1880
54 Église St. Mary, Ambleside, Lake District, Angleterre, années 1880

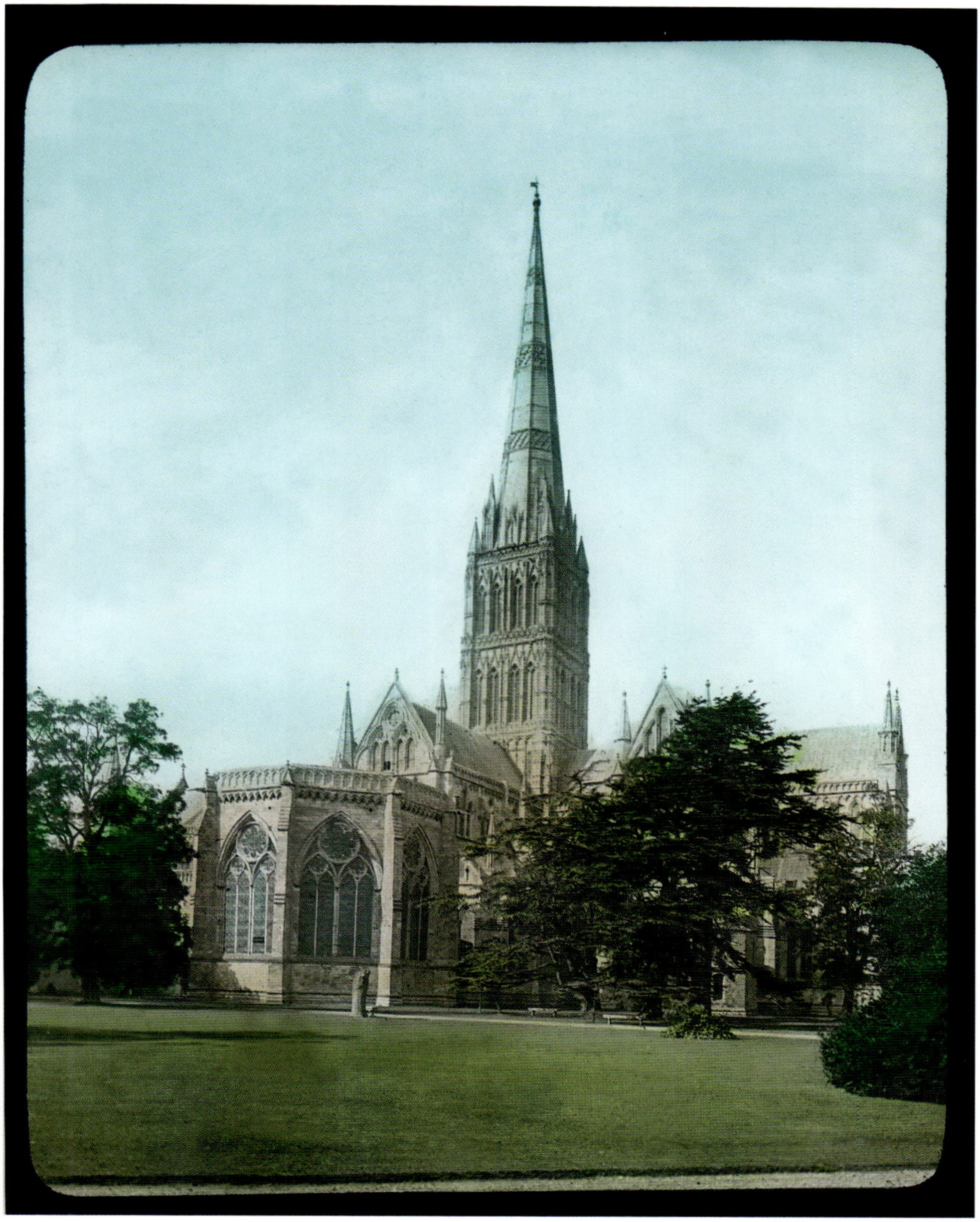

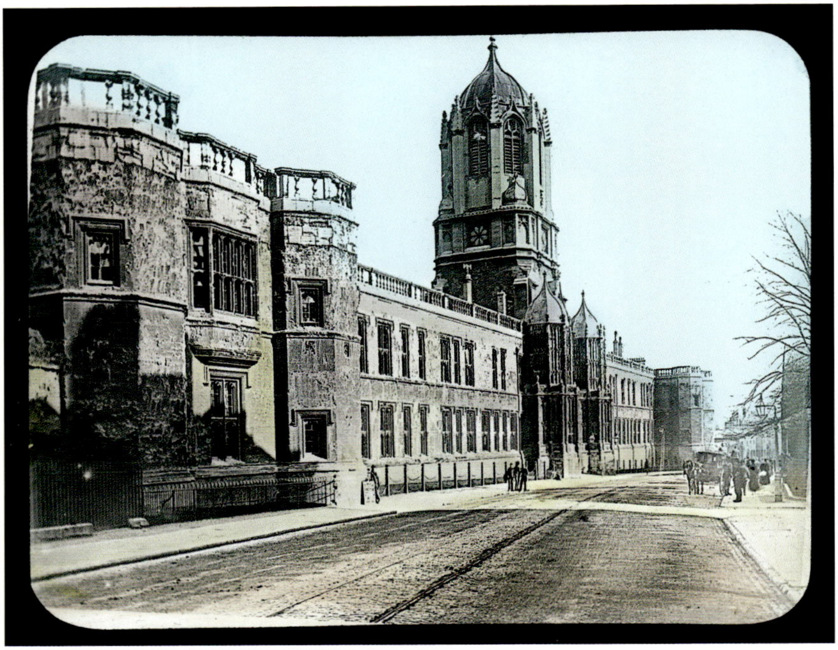

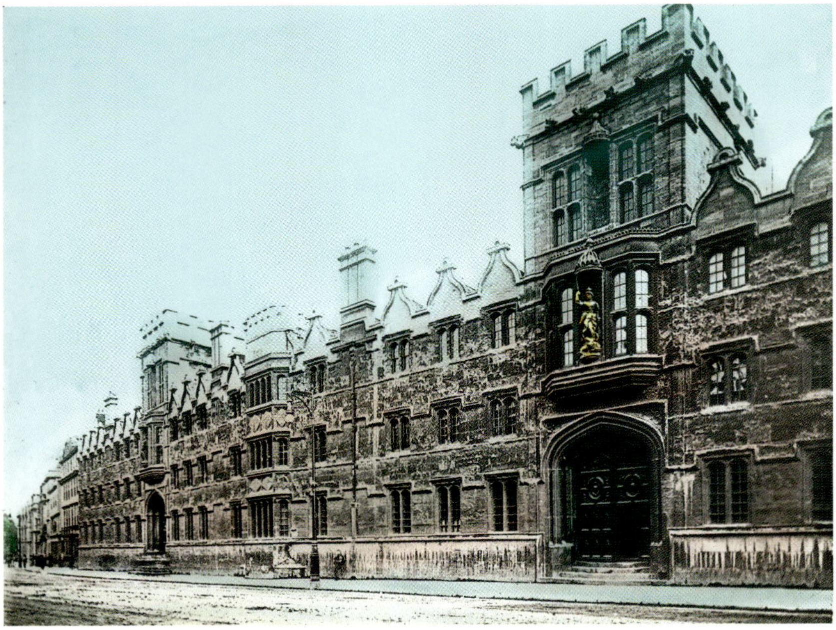

55–56 Christ Church and University College, Oxford, England, 1880s
57 Laughing farmer, England, 1890s

55–56 Die Christ Church und das University College, Oxford, England, 1880er Jahre
57 Lachender Bauer, England, 1890er Jahre

55–56 Église du Christ et University College, Oxford, Angleterre, années 1880
57 Fermier rigolard, Angleterre, années 1890

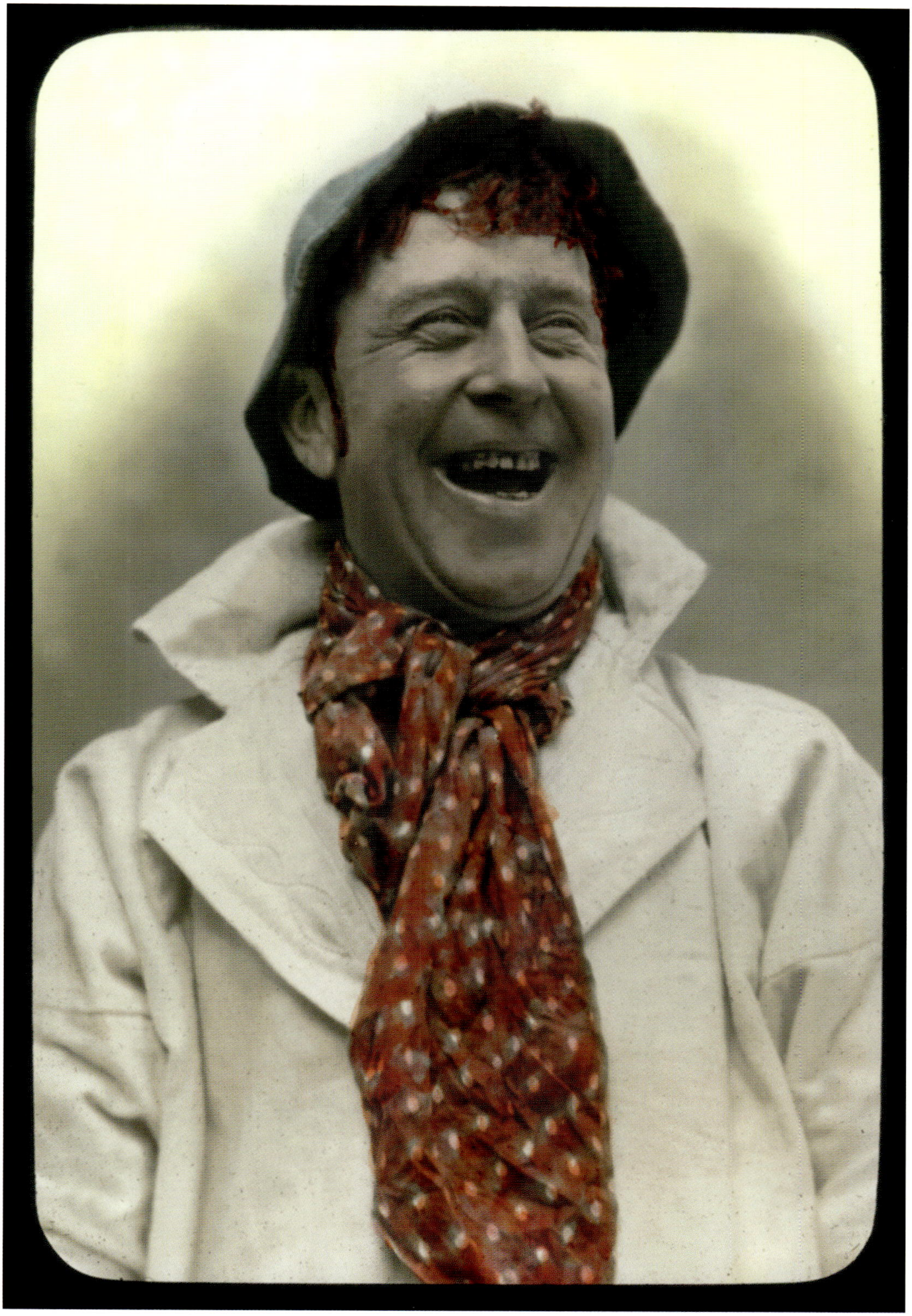

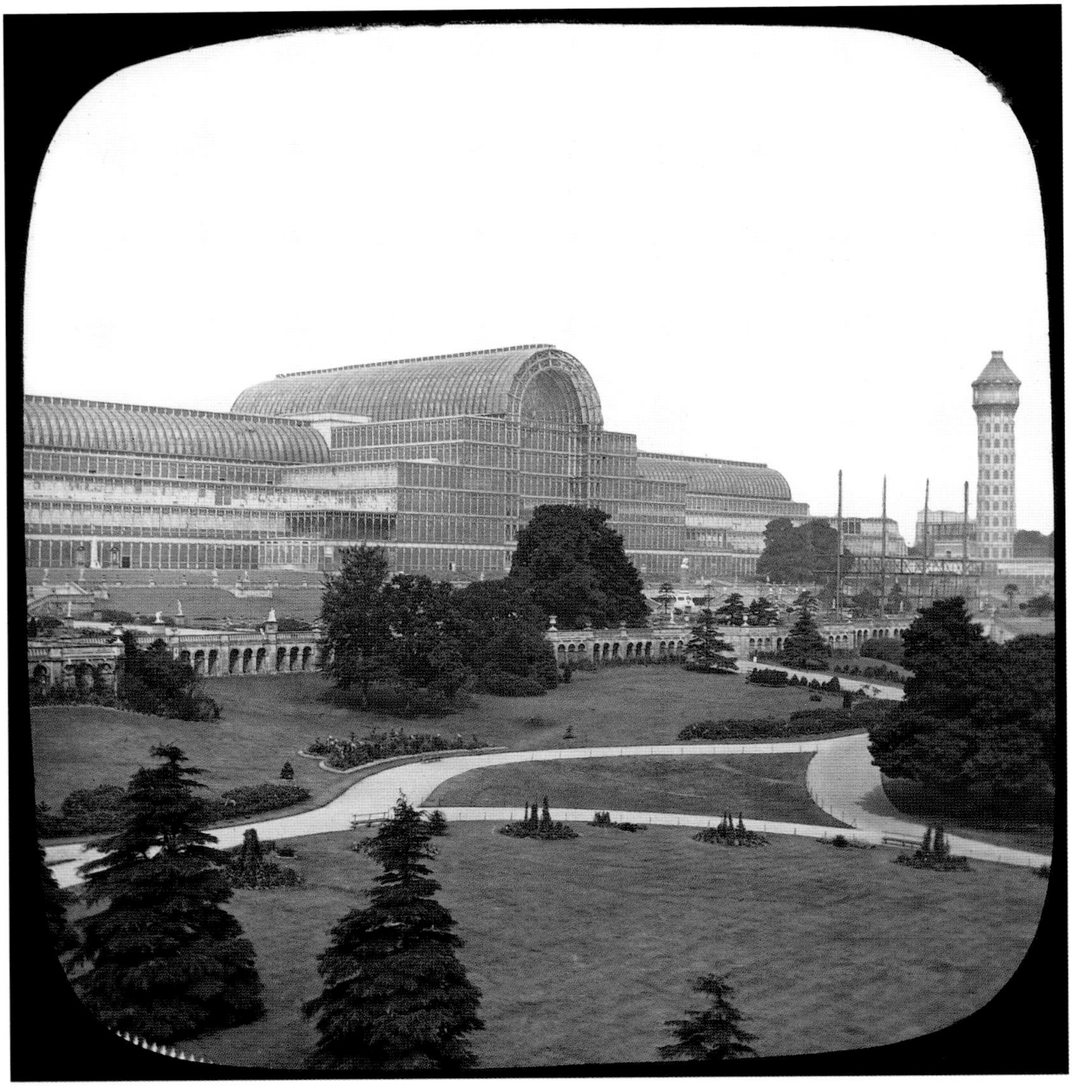

58 North Water Tower and Transept of The Crystal Palace having been moved to Sydenham Hill, South London, England, 1870s

58 Der North Water Tower und das Querhaus des Kristallpalastes nach seiner Wiederrichtung in Sydenham Hill, Süd-London, England, 1870er Jahre

58 Le château d'eau nord et le transept du Crystal Palace ont été transférés à Sydenham Hill, au sud de Londres. Angleterre, années 1870

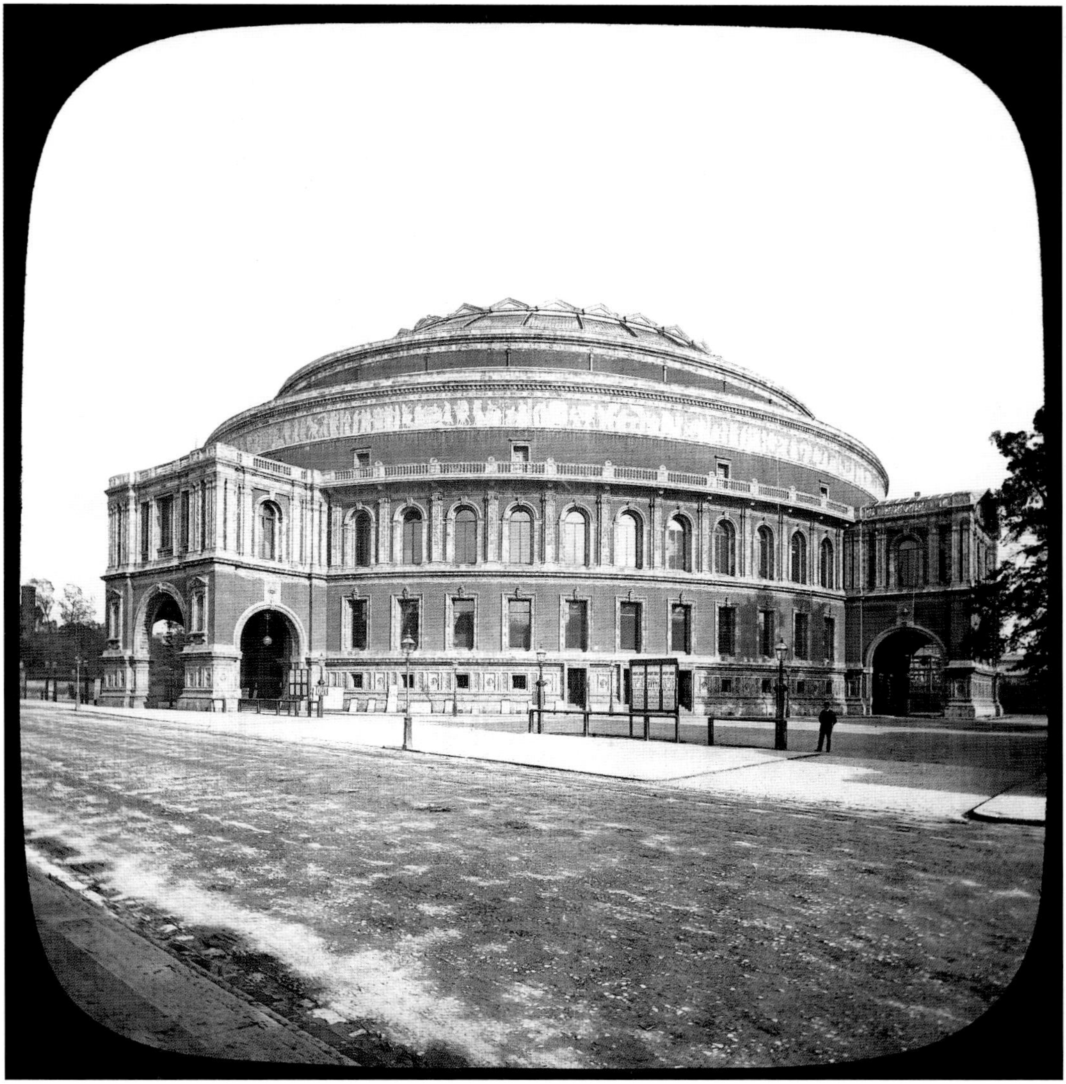

59 The Royal Albert Hall of Arts and Sciences, London, England, 1870s

59 Die Royal Albert Hall of Arts and Sciences, London, England, 1870er Jahre

59 The Royal Albert Hall of Arts and Sciences, Londres, Angleterre, années 1870

60 "Jumbo the Elephant" at London Zoo, 1880s

60 „Jumbo der Elefant" im Londoner Zoo, London, England, 1880er Jahre

60 "Jumbo l'éléphant" au zoo de Londres, années 1880

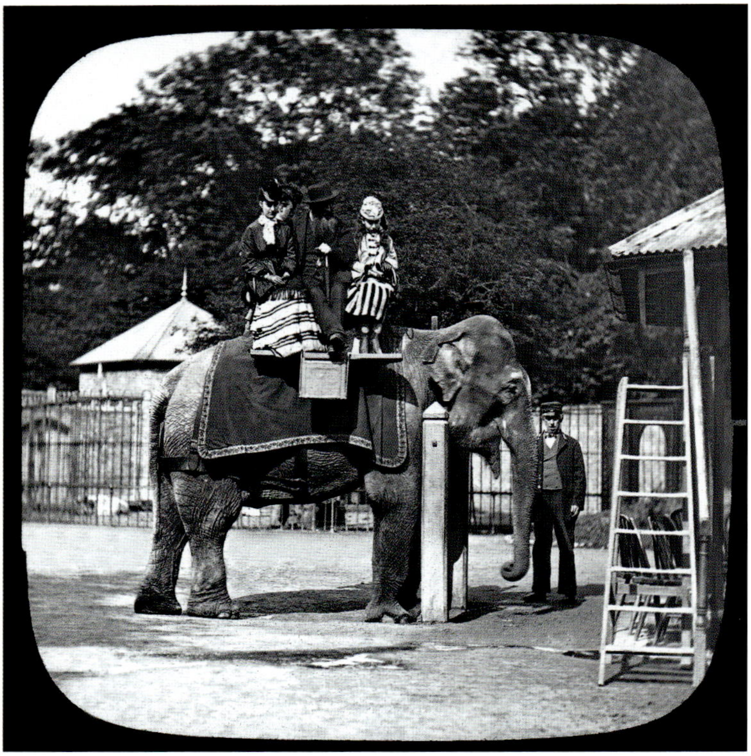

61 Riding the camel at London Zoo, London, England, 1880s

61 Kamelreiten im Londoner Zoo, London, England, 1880er Jahre

61 Promenade à dos de chameau au zoo de Londres. Angleterre, années 1880

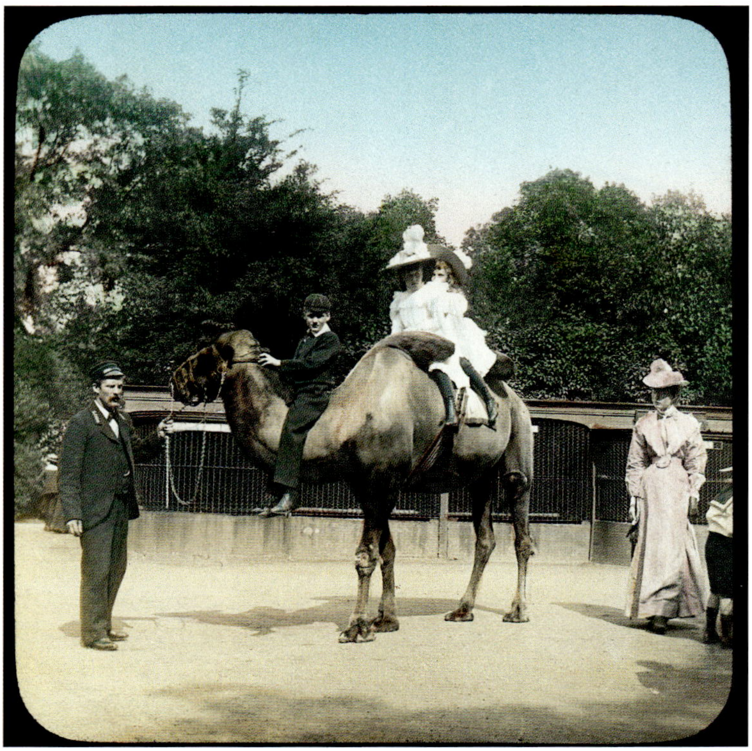

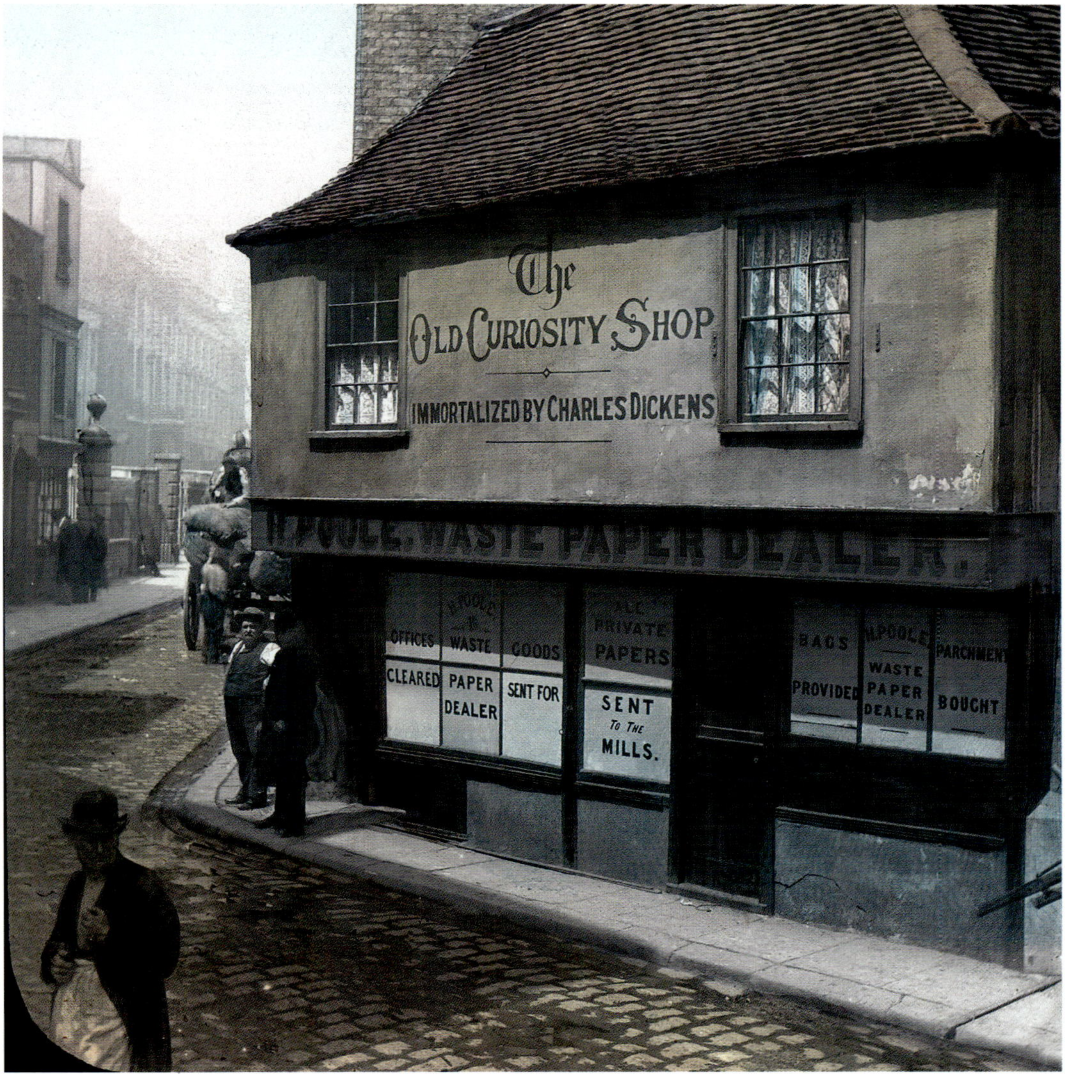

62 The Old Curiosity Shop, London, England, 1880s

62 The Old Curiosity Shop Der Raritätenladen, London, England, 1880er Jahre

62 The Old Curiosity Shop, Londres, Angleterre, années 1880

63 Victoria Embankment, London, England, 1880s

63 Victoria Embankment, London, England, 1880er Jahre

63 Victoria Embankment, Londres, Angleterre, années 1880

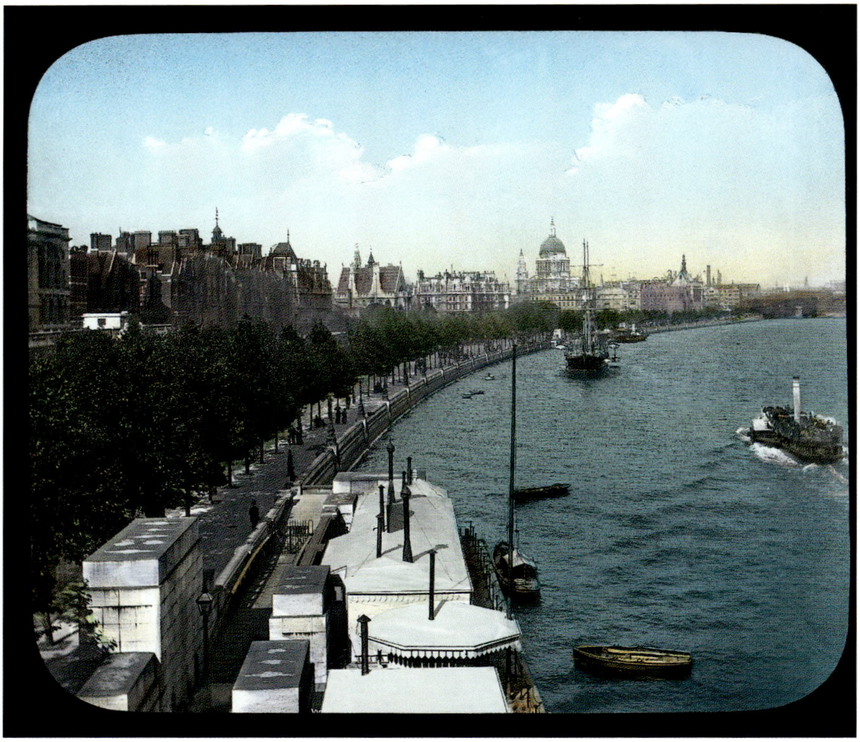

64 Westminster Abbey, London, England, 1880s

64 Westminster Abbey, London, England, 1880er Jahre

64 Abbaye de Westminster, Londres, Angleterre, années 1880

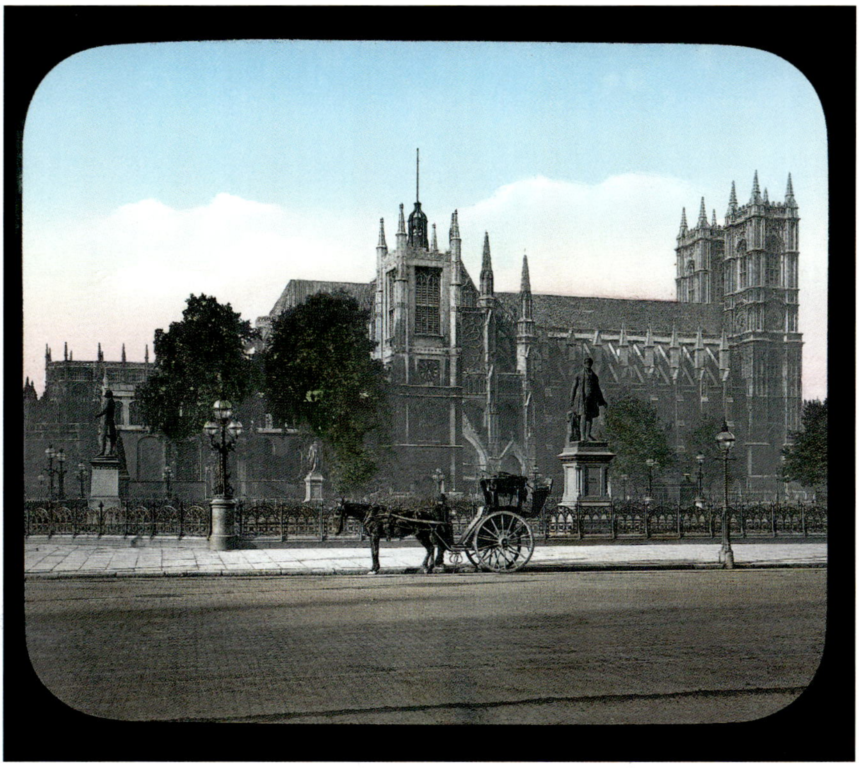

65 National Gallery, Trafalgar Square, London, England, 1880s

65 Die Nationalgalerie, Trafalgar Square, London, England, 1880er Jahre

65 National Gallery, Trafalgar Square, Londres, Angleterre, années 1880

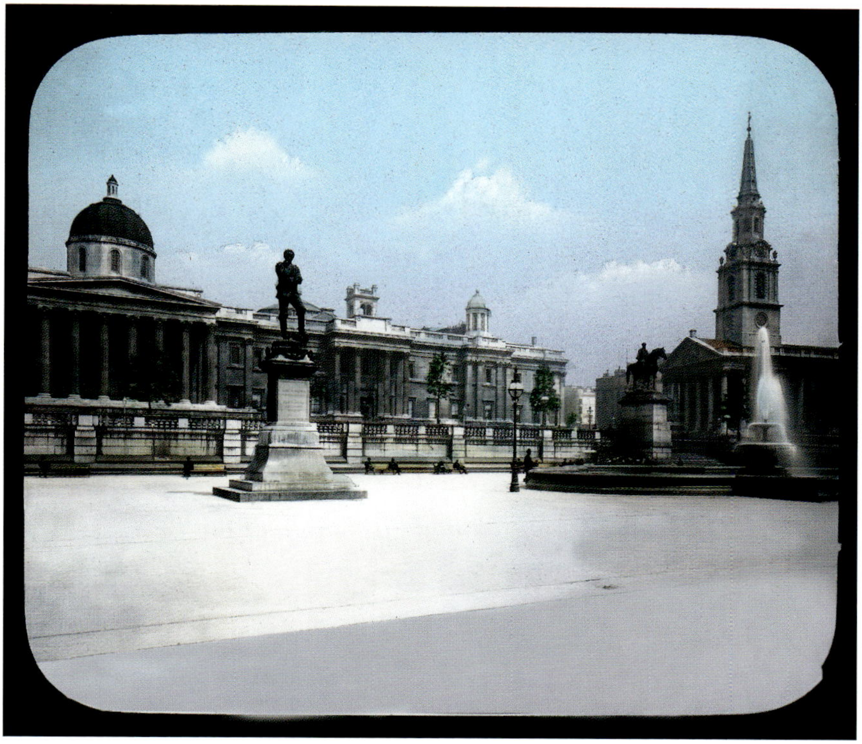

66 Burlington House (The Royal Academy) and Piccadilly, London, England, 1880s

66 Burlington House (The Royal Academy) und Piccadilly, London, England, 1880er Jahre

66 Burlington House (l'Académie Royale) et Piccadilly, Londres, Angleterre, années 1880

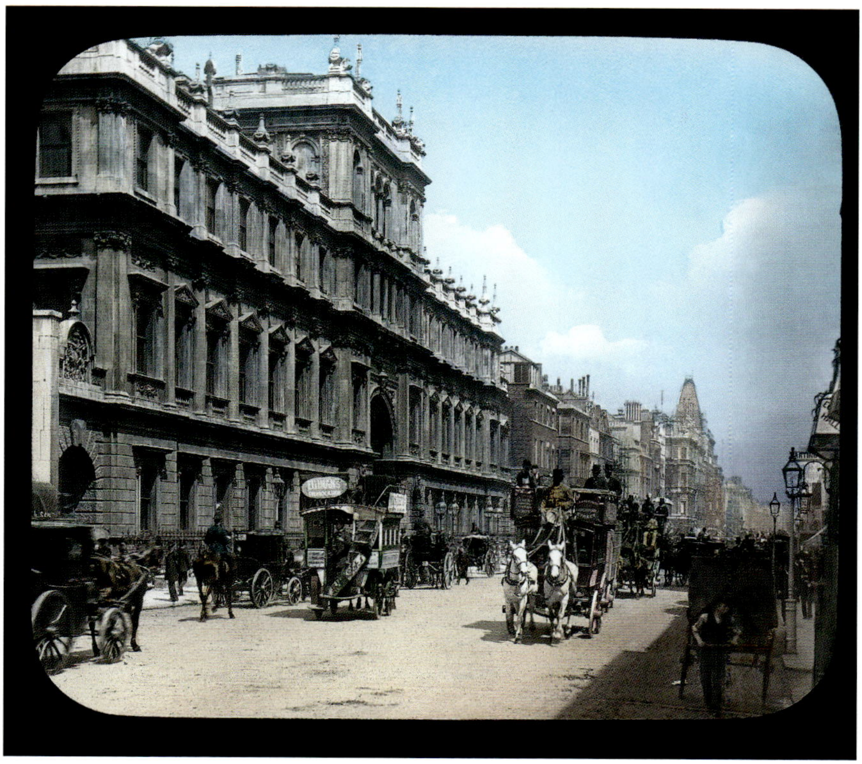

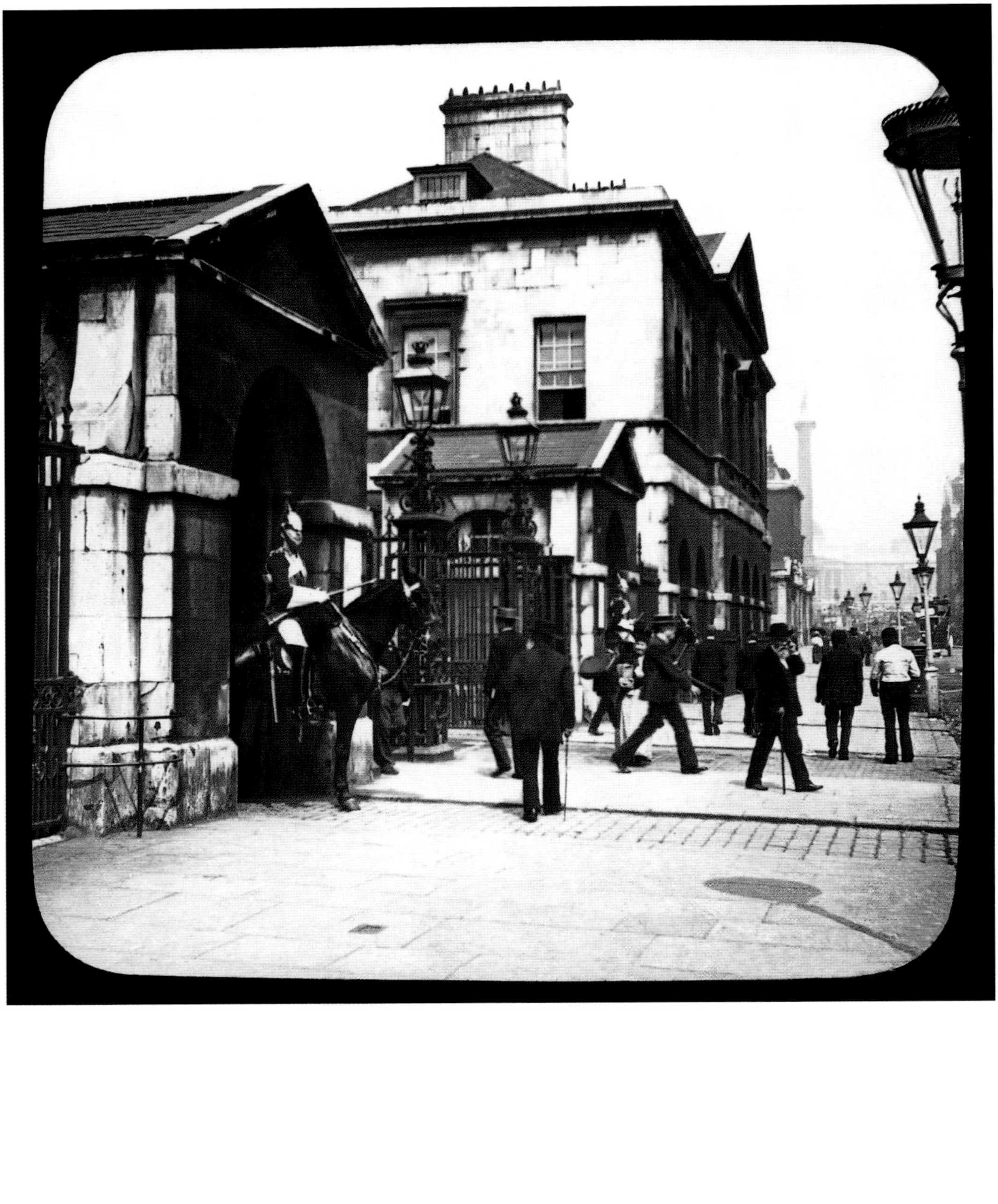

67 A mounted horse guard, London, England, 1910s
68 Empire Theatre, Leicester Square, London, England, 1912

67 Königlicher Gardist zu Pferde, London, England, 1910er Jahre
68 Das Empire Theatre, Leicester Square, London, England, 1912

67 Horse guard à cheval, Londres, Angleterre, années 1910
68 Théâtre de l'Empire, Leicester Square, Londres, Angleterre, 1912

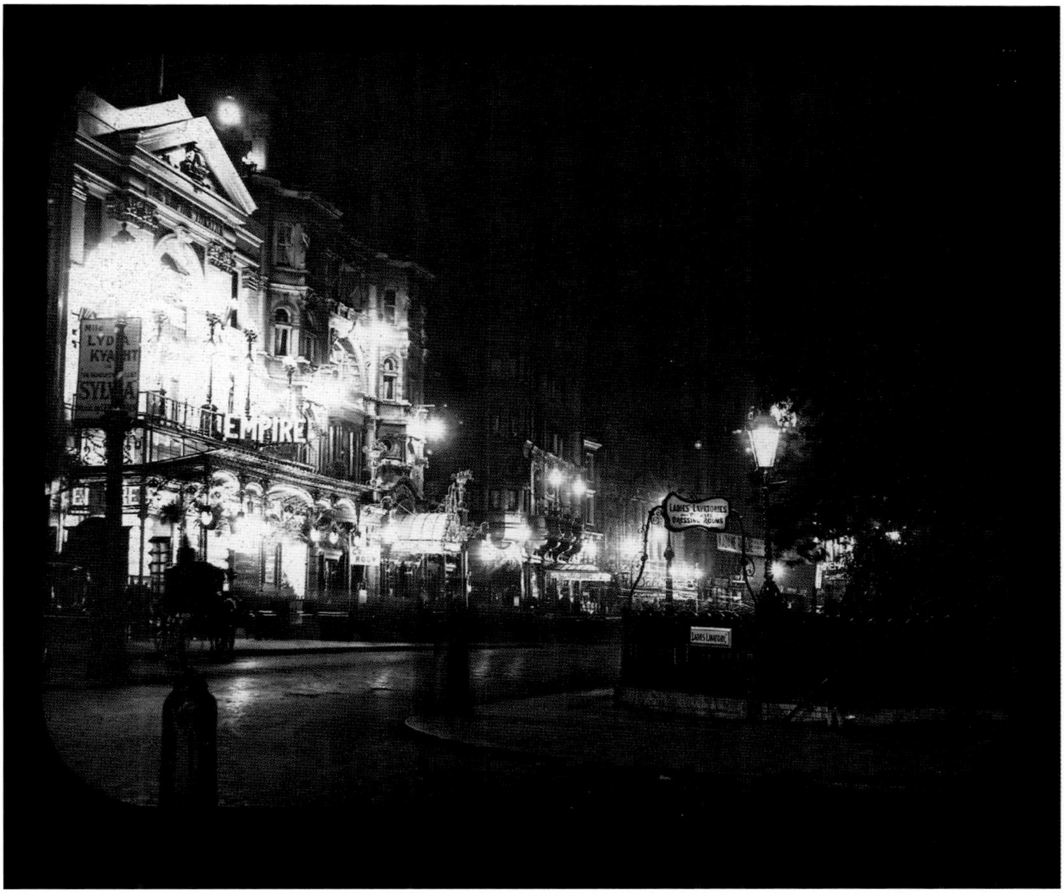
EMPIRE
LADIES' LAVATORIES
DRESSING ROOMS

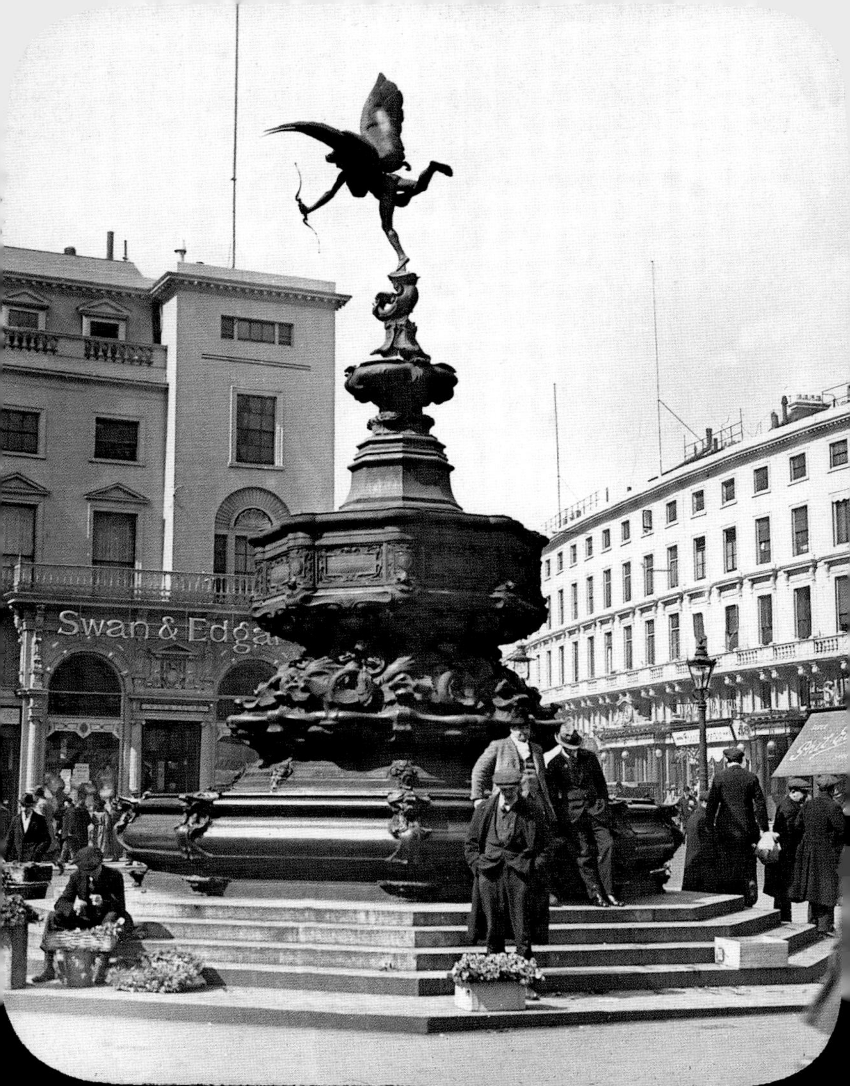

69 The Shaftesbury Memorial Fountain in Piccadilly Circus, London, England, 1910s
70 The Strand, London, England, 1880s

69 Der Shaftesbury-Gedenkbrunnen auf dem Piccadilly Circus, London, England, 1910er Jahre
70 The Strand, London, England, 1880er Jahre

69 La fontaine du Shaftesbury Memorial à Piccadilly Circus, Londres, Angleterre, années 1910
70 The Strand, Londres, Angleterre, années 1880

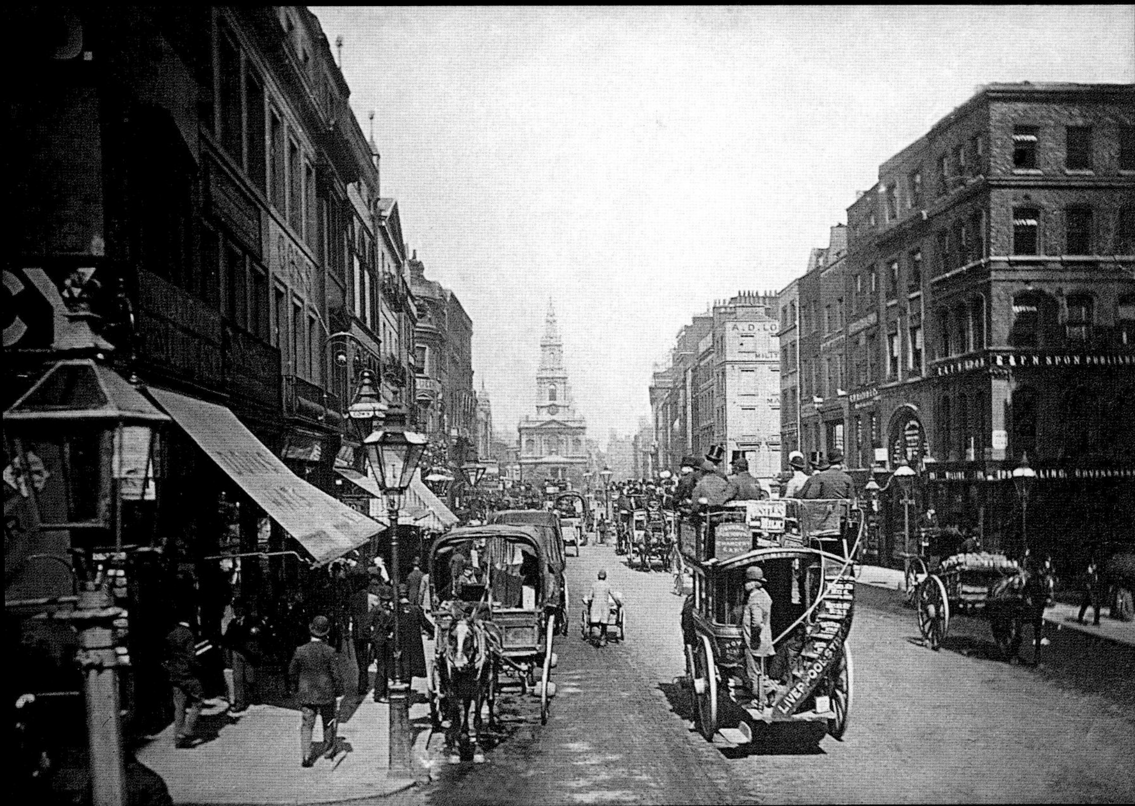

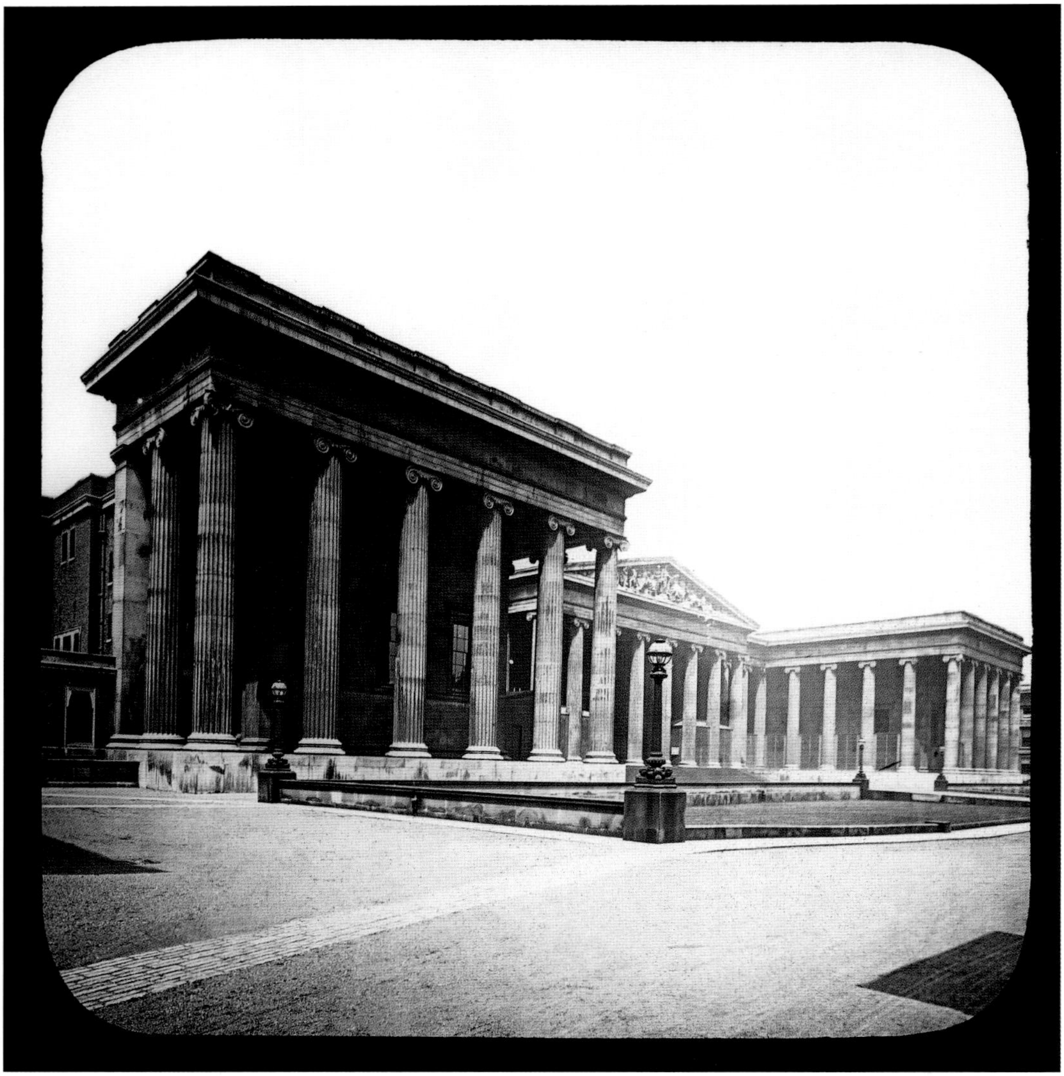

71 British Museum,
London, England, 1880s
72 Covent Garden Market,
London, England, 1880s

71 Das British Museum,
London, England,
1880er Jahre
72 Covent Garden
Market, London, England,
1880er Jahre

71 British Museum,
Londres, Angleterre,
années 1880
72 Marché de Covent
Garden, Londres,
Angleterre, années 1880

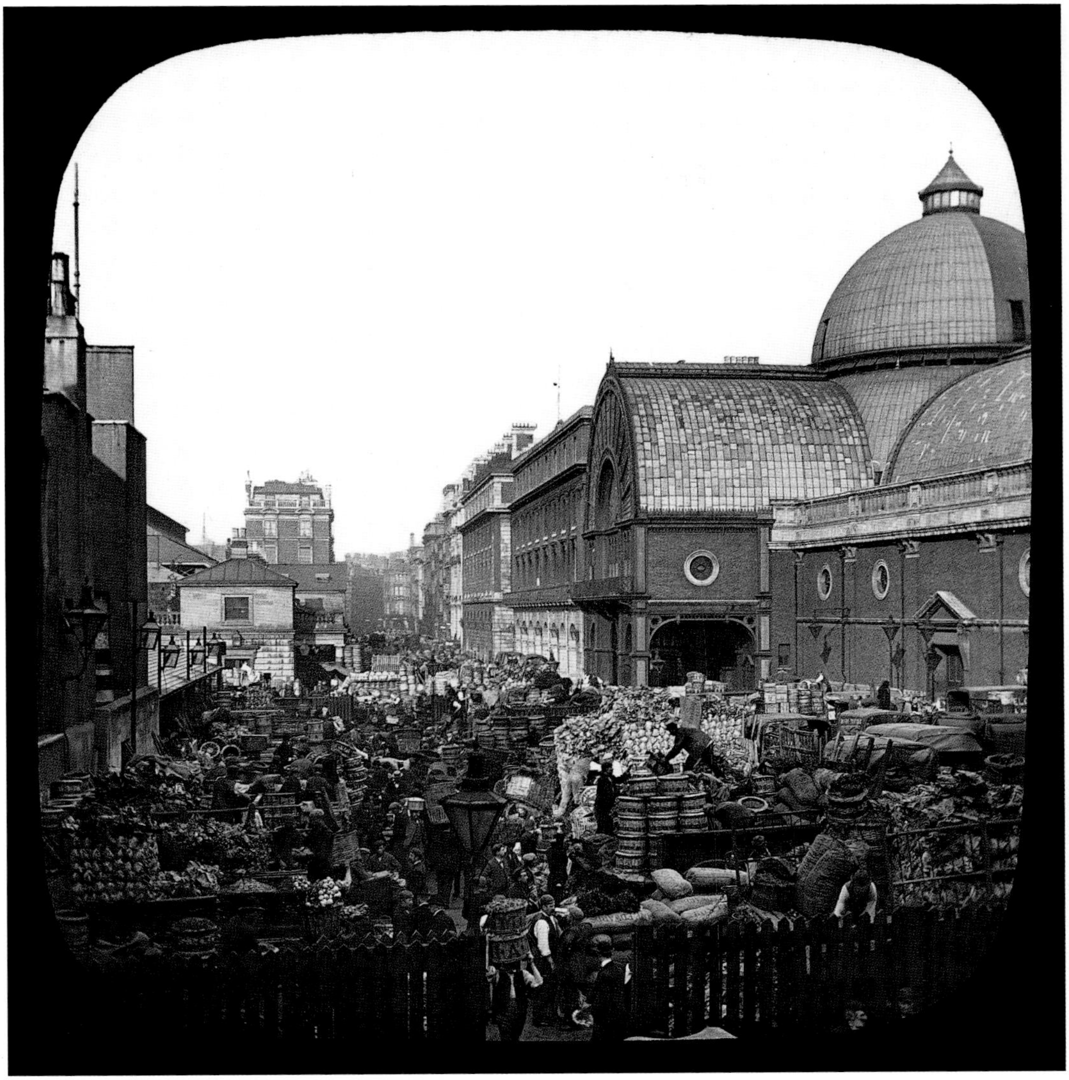

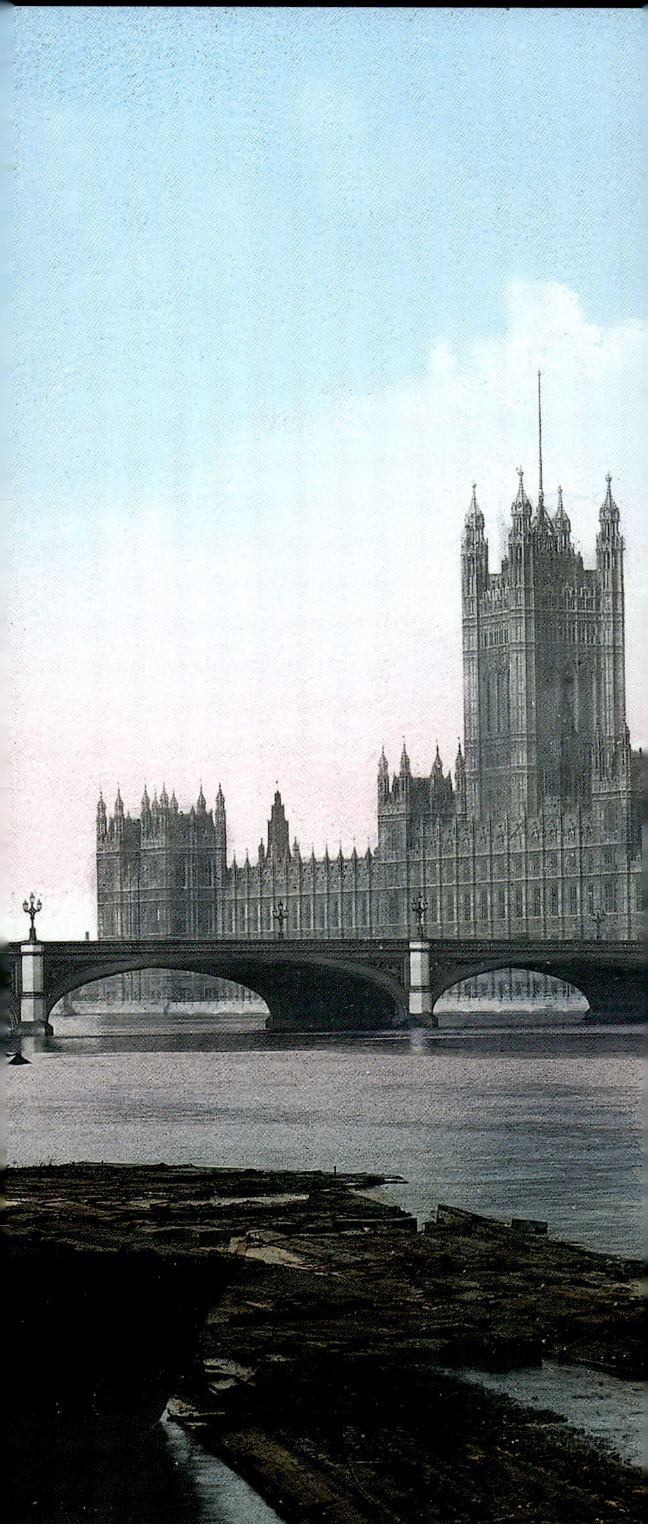

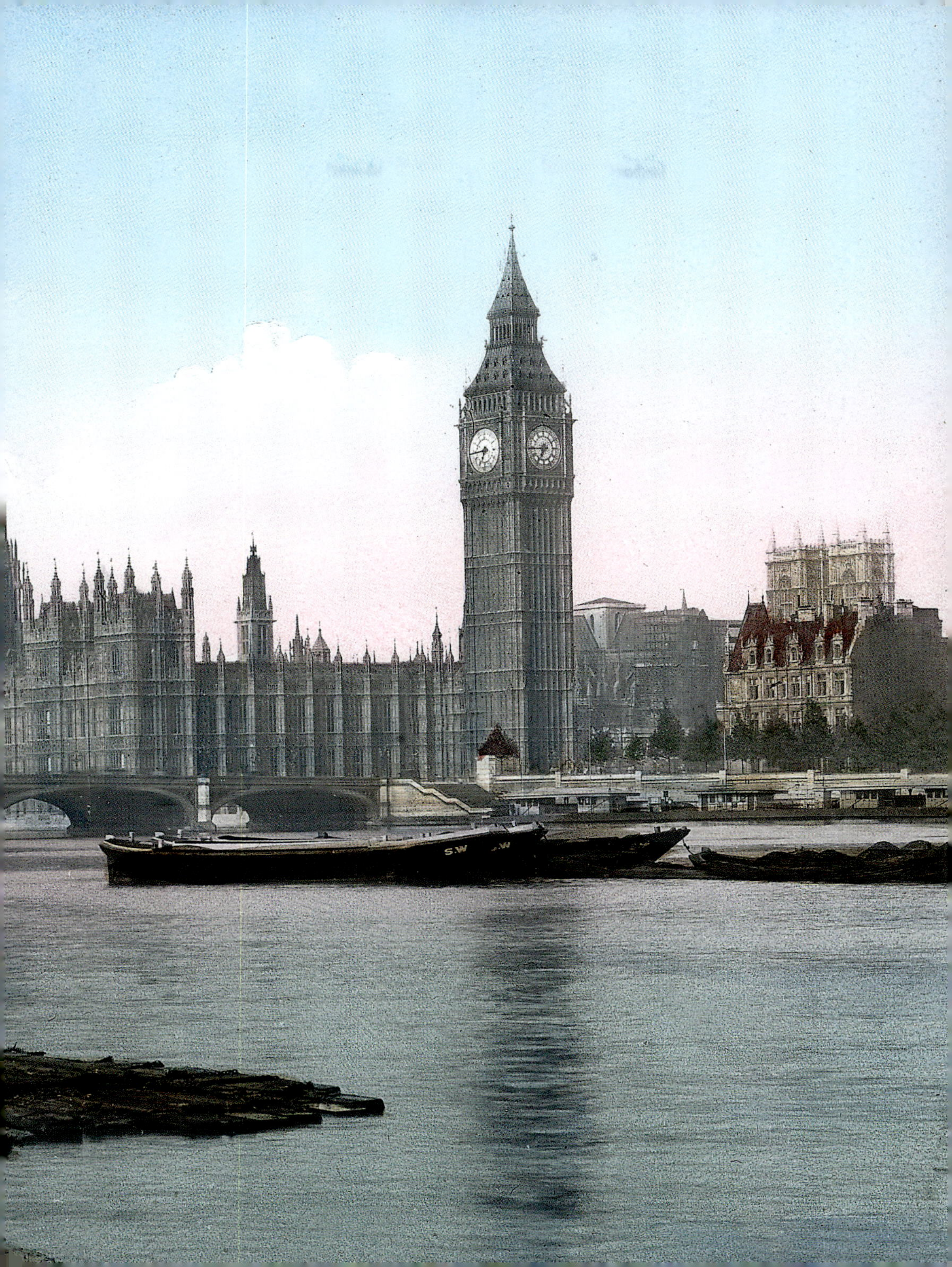
S.W

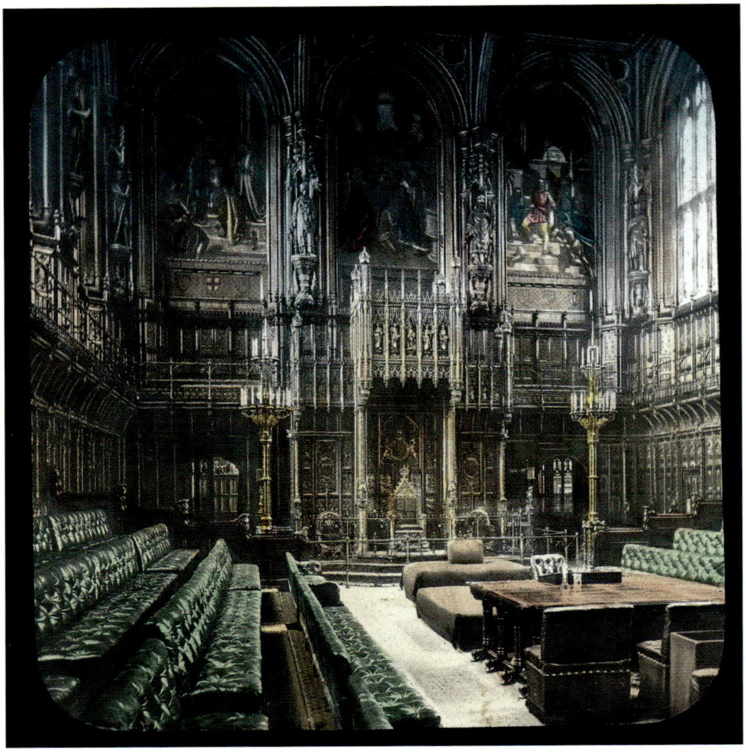

74 Chamber of the House of Lords, Houses of Parliament, London, 1880s

74 Der Sitzungssaal des Oberhauses, Parlamentsgebäude, London, England, 1880er Jahre

74 Chambre des Lords, Chambres du Parlement, Londres, années 1880

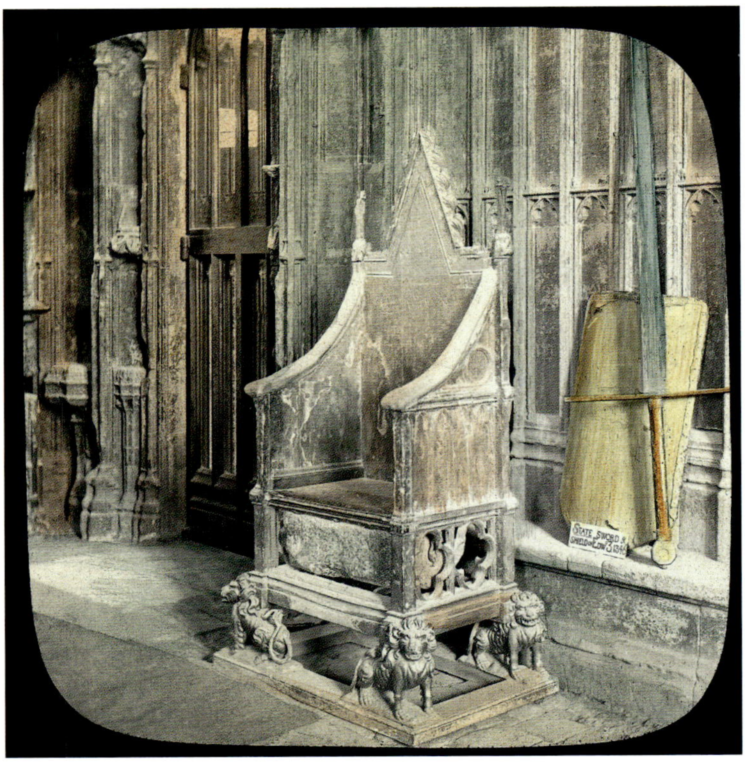

75 Coronation Throne (King Edward's Chair), Westminster Abbey, London, 1880s

75 Krönungsthron (König Edwards Stuhl), Westminster Abbey, London, England, 1880er Jahre

75 Trône du Couronnement (cathèdre du roi Édouard), abbaye de Westminster, Londres, années 1880

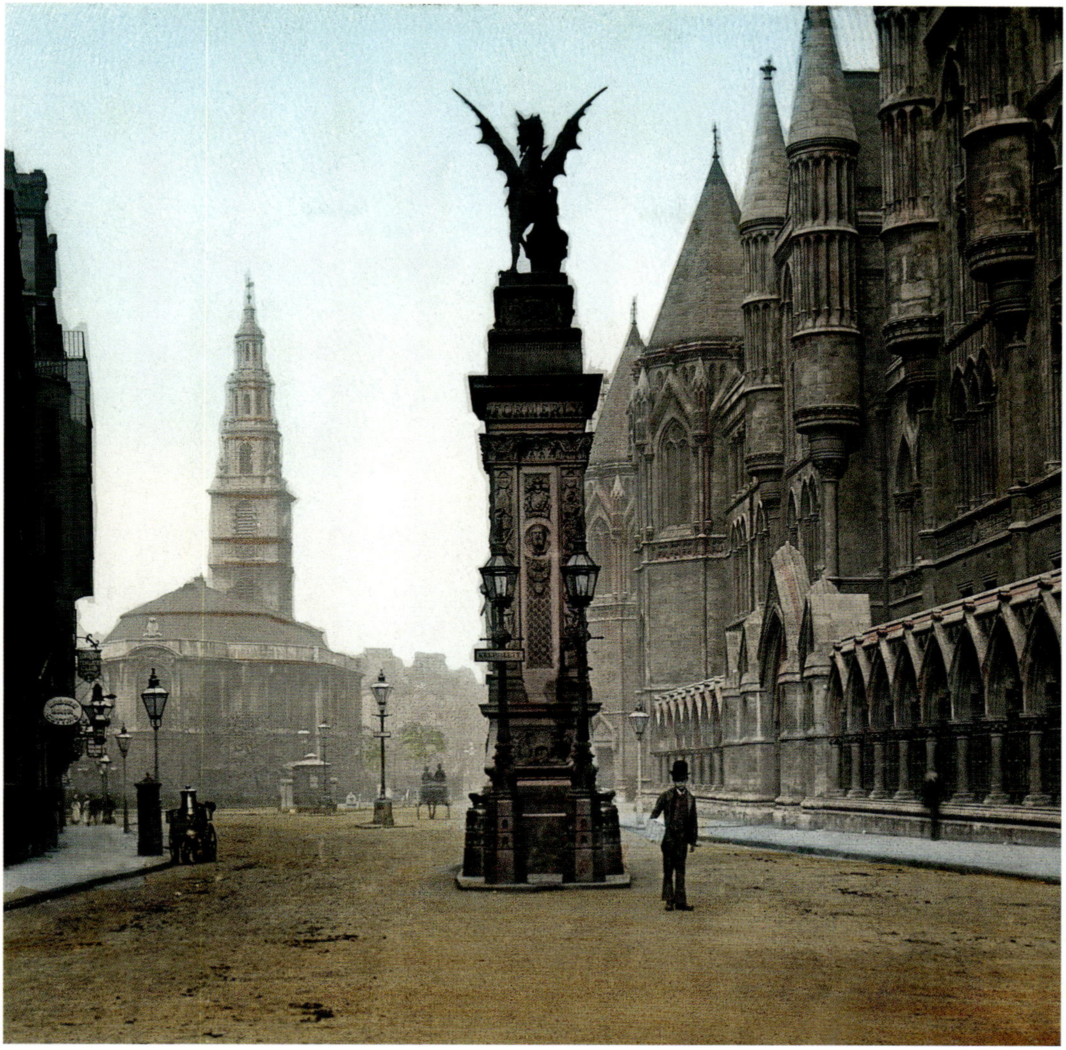

76 The Griffin (the site of Sir Christopher Wren's Temple Bar and the entrance to the City of London from Westminster), London, England, 1880s

76 Der Greif (Standort von Sir Christopher Wrens Temple Bar und Eingang zur City of London von Westminster aus), London, England, 1880er Jahre

76 Le Griffon (l'emplacement du Temple Bar de Sir Christopher Wren et l'entrée de la ville de Londres par Westminster), Londres, Angleterre, années 1880

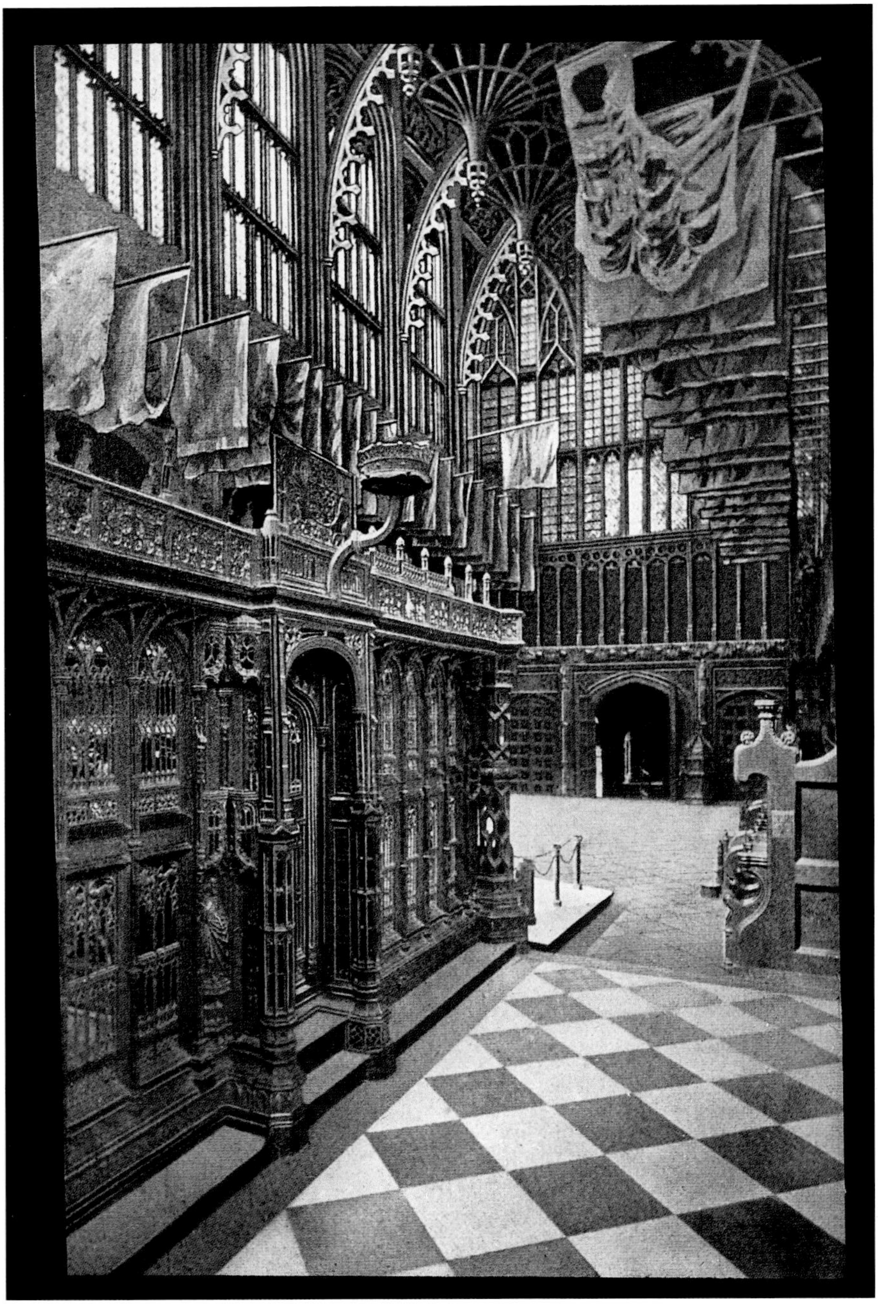

77 Henry the Seventh's Chapel, Westminster Abbey, London, 1880s

77 Die Kapelle Heinrichs VII., Westminster Abbey, London, England, 1880er Jahre

77 Chapelle de Henry VII, abbaye de Westminster, Londres, années 1880

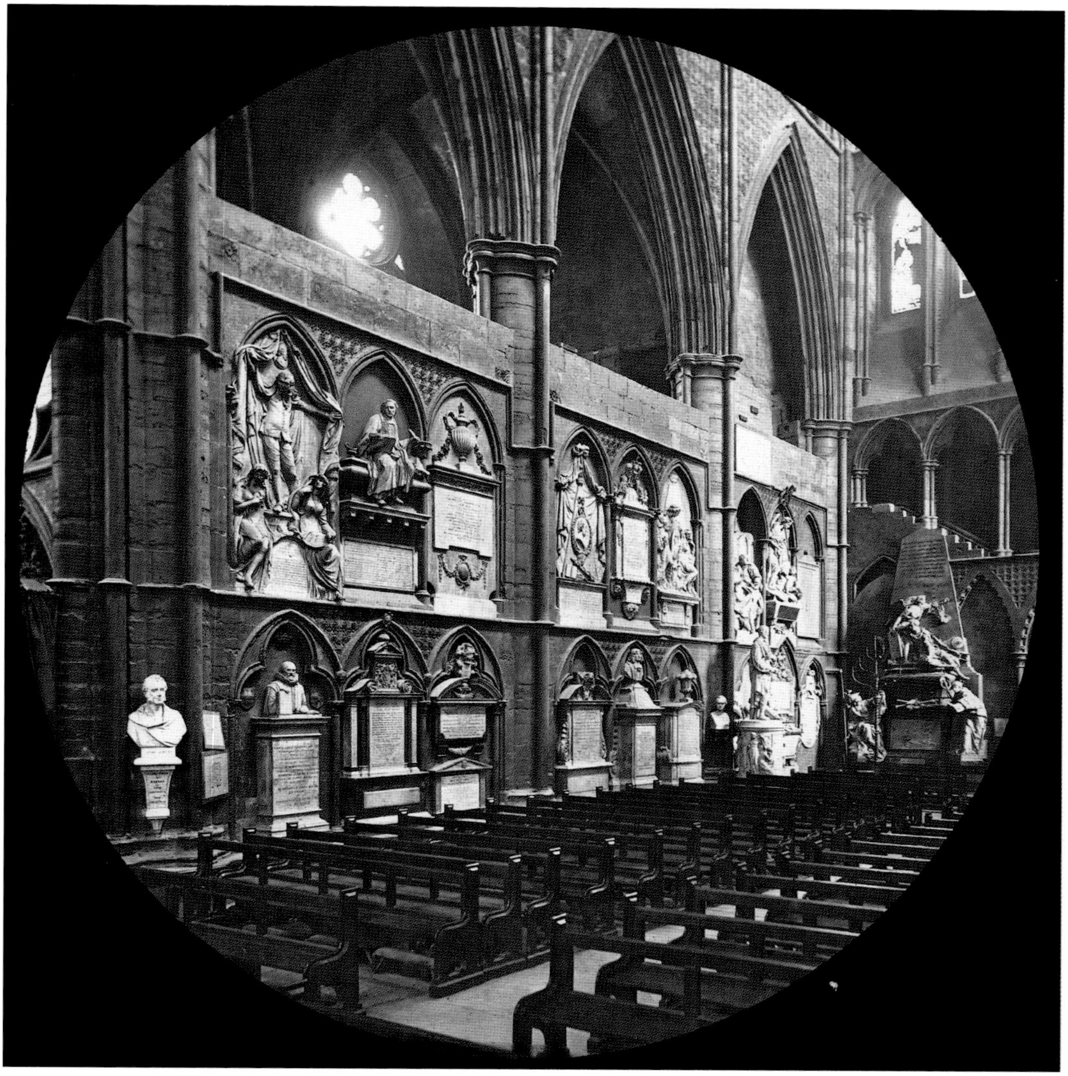

78 Poets' Corner,
Westminster Abbey,
London, England, 1870s

78 Die Dichterecke,
Westminster Abbey,
London, England,
1870er Jahre

78 Le Coin des Poètes,
Abbaye de Westminster,
Londres, Angleterre,
années 1870

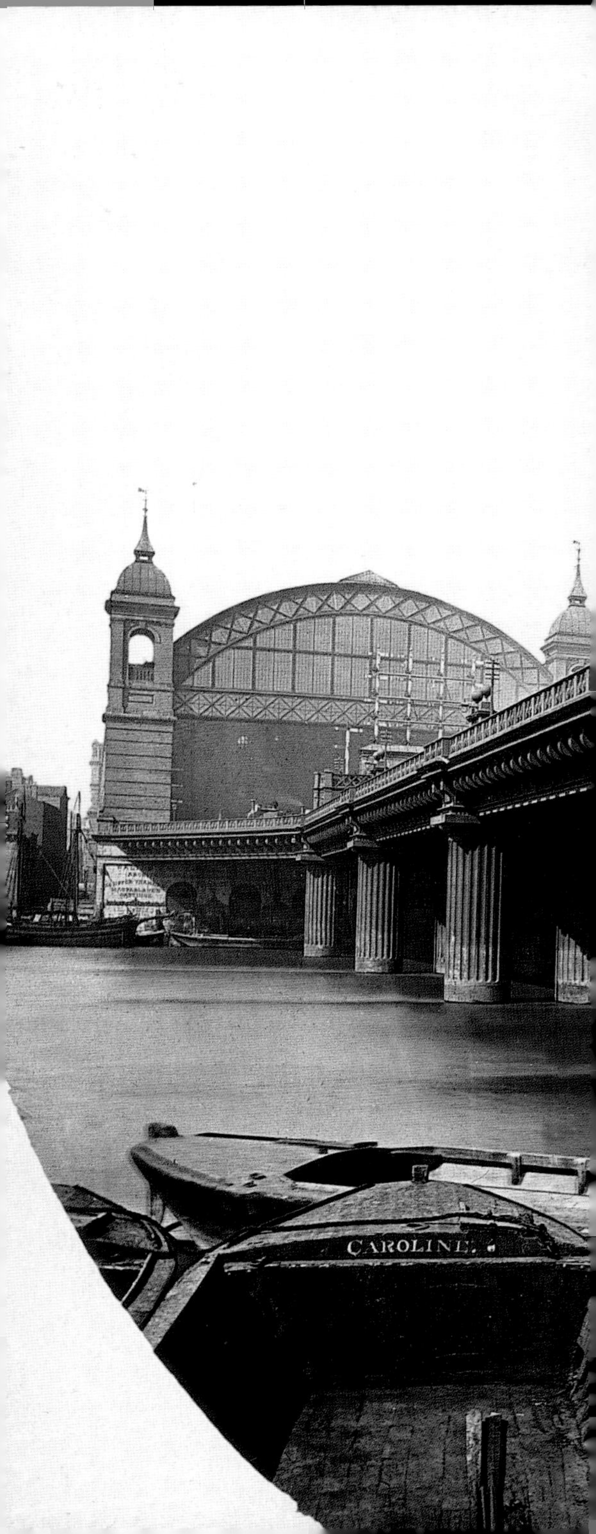
CAROLINE.

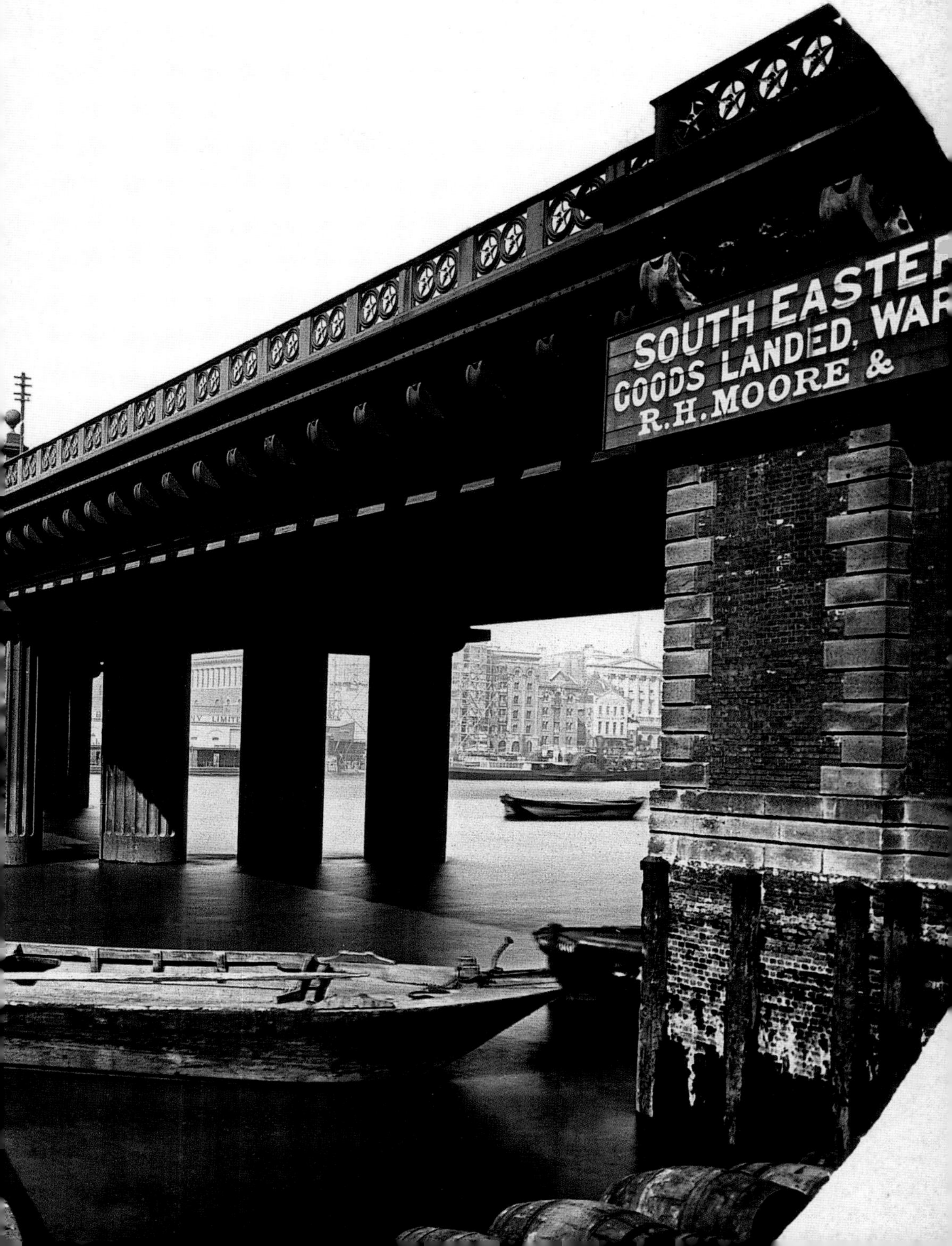
SOUTH EASTER
GOODS LANDED, WAR
R.H. MOORE &

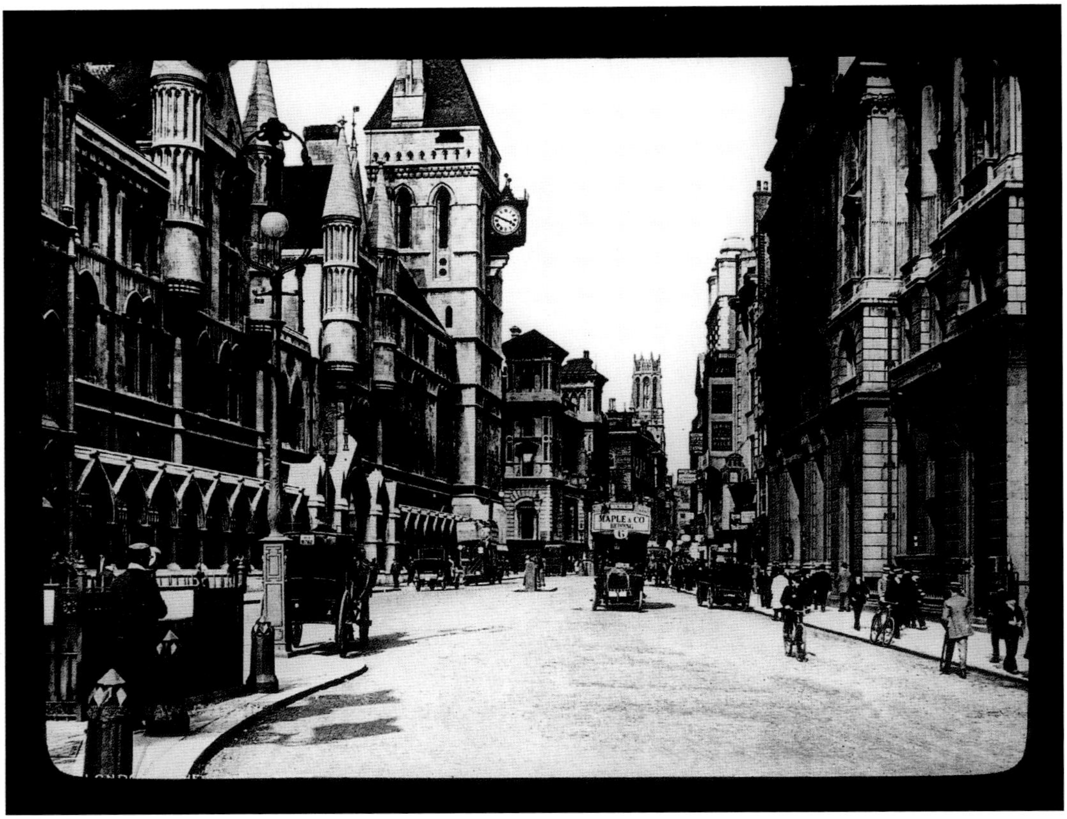

80 New Law Courts, The Strand, London, England, c.1910
81, 83 The Bank of England, London, England, c.1900
82 Ludgate Circus, London, England, 1890s

80 Die New Law Courts, The Strand, London, England, um 1910
81, 83 Die Bank von England, London, England, um 1900
82 Ludgate Circus, London, England, 1890er Jahre

80 New Law Courts, The Strand, Londres, Angleterre, vers 1910
81, 83 La Banque d'Angleterre, Londres, Angleterre, vers 1900
82 Ludgate Circus, Londres, Angleterre, années 1890

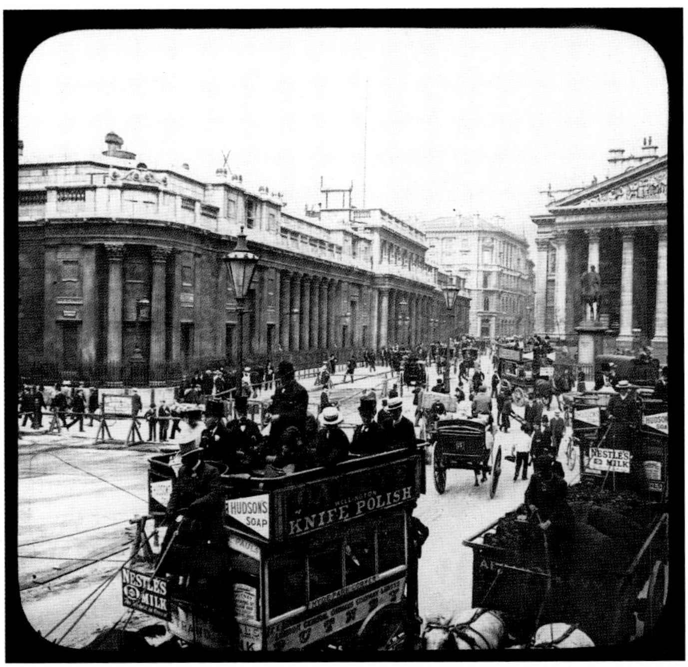

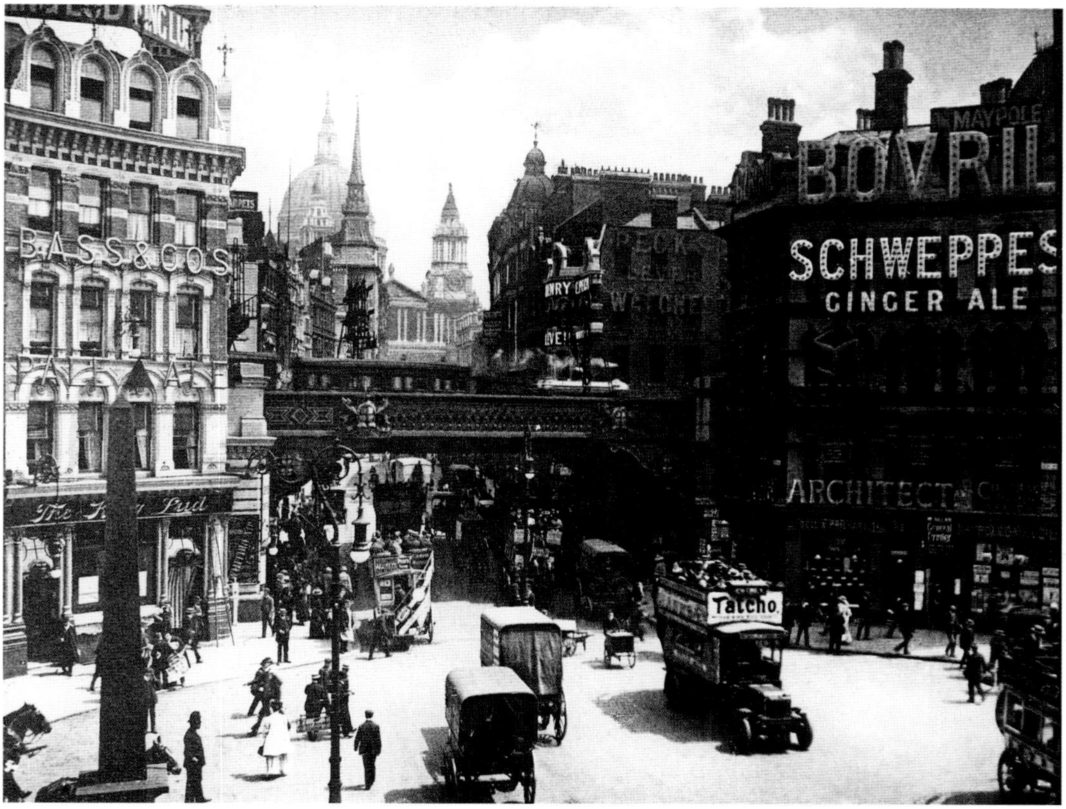
BASS&CO'S
MAYPOLE
BOVRIL
SCHWEPPES
GINGER ALE
Tatcho

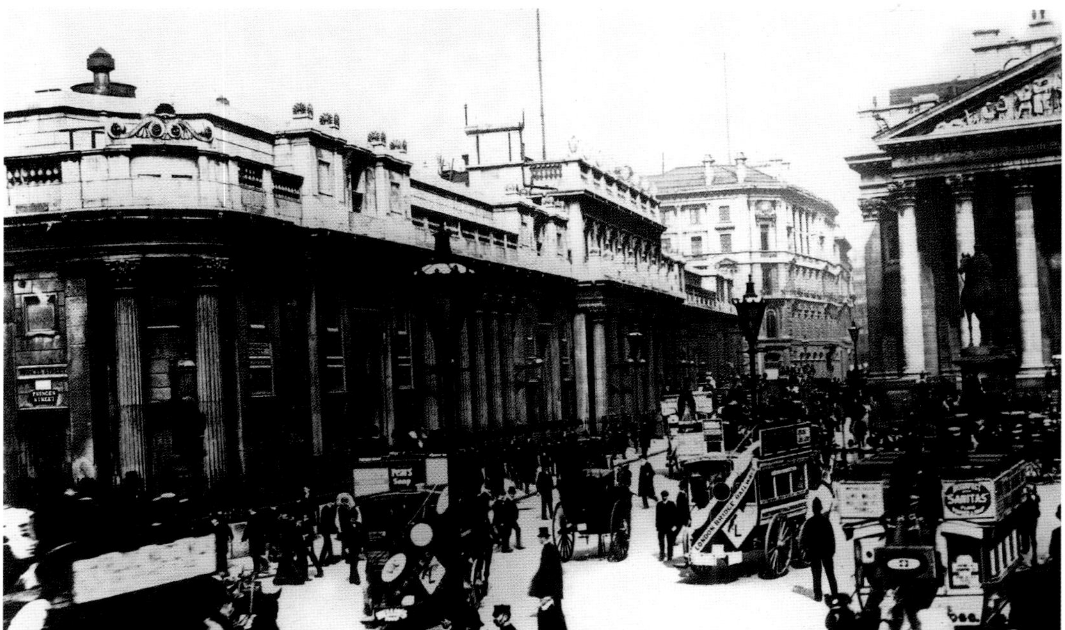
SANITAS

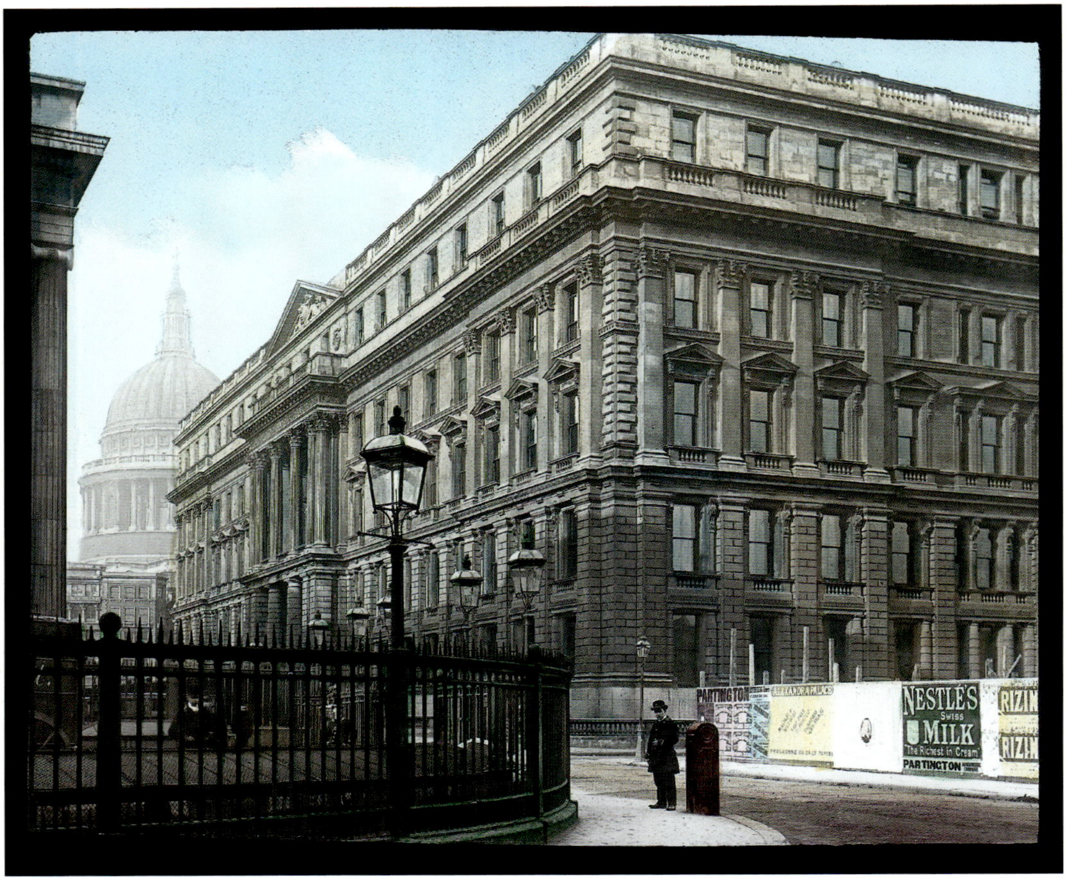

84 General Post Office, St. Martins-le-Grand, London, England, 1880s
85 The Guildhall, London, England, 1880s

84 Das Hauptpostamt, St. Martins-le-Grand, London, England, 1880er Jahre
85 Guildhall, London, England, 1880er Jahre

84 General Post Office, St. Martins-le-Grand, Londres, Angleterre, années 1880
85 The Guildhall, Londres, Angleterre, années 1880

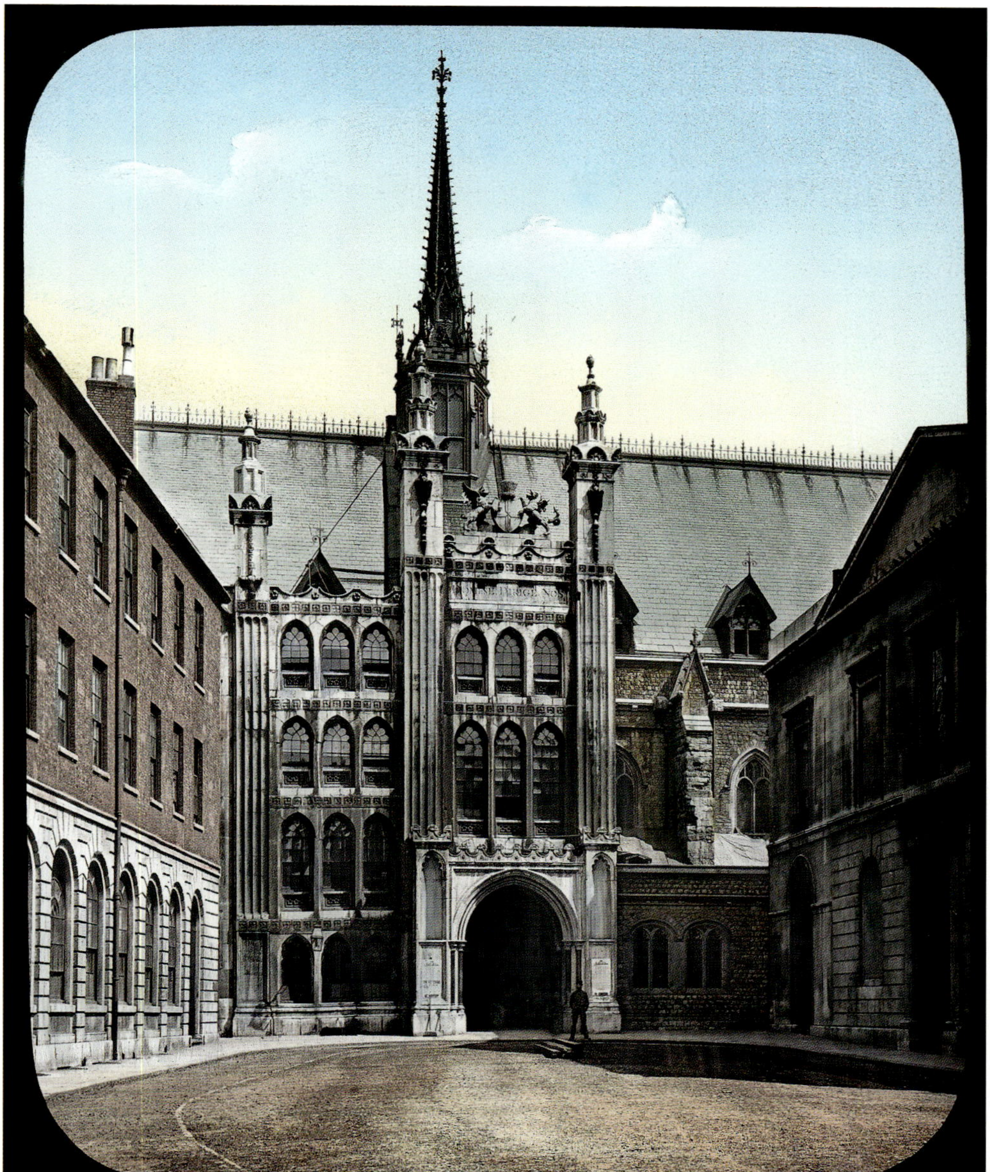

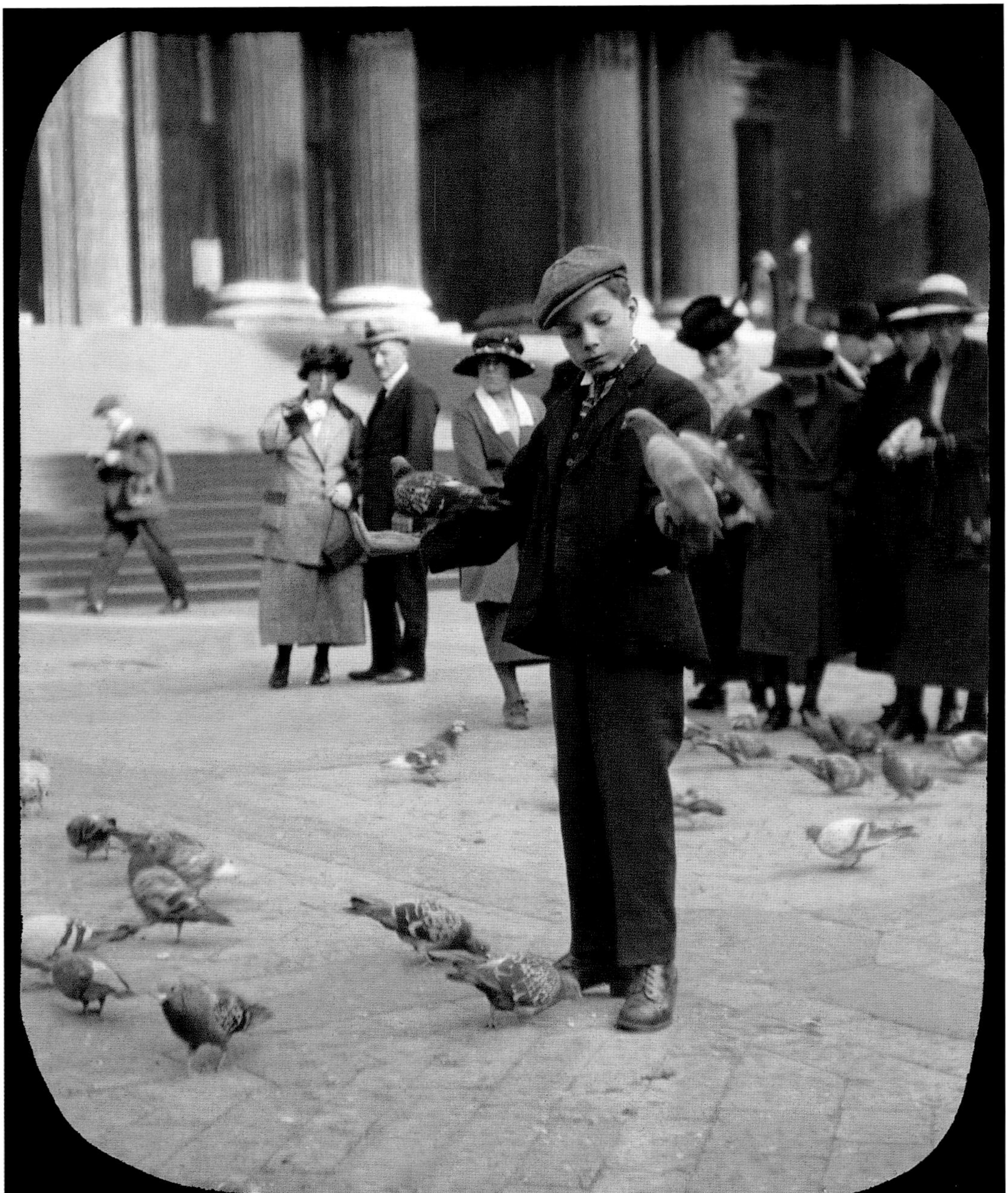

86 Feeding pigeons outside St. Paul's Cathedral, London, England, 1920s
87 St. Paul's Cathedral, London, England, c.1900

86 Taubenfüttern vor der St. Paul's-Kathedrale, London, England, 1920er Jahre
87 Die St. Paul's-Kathedrale, London, England, um 1900

86 Nourriture des pigeons près de la cathédrale St. Paul, Londres, Angleterre, années 1920
87 Cathédrale St. Paul, Londres, Angvers 1900

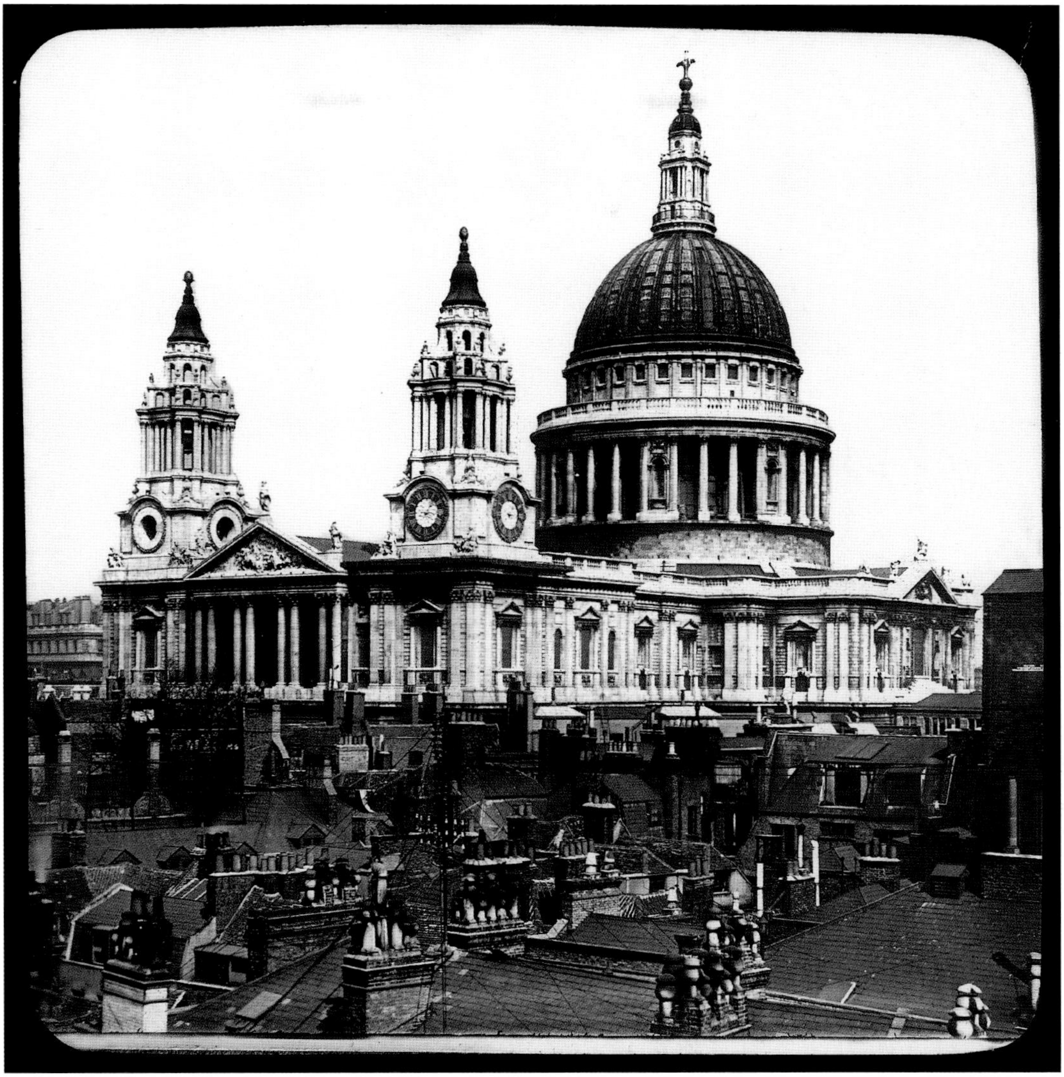

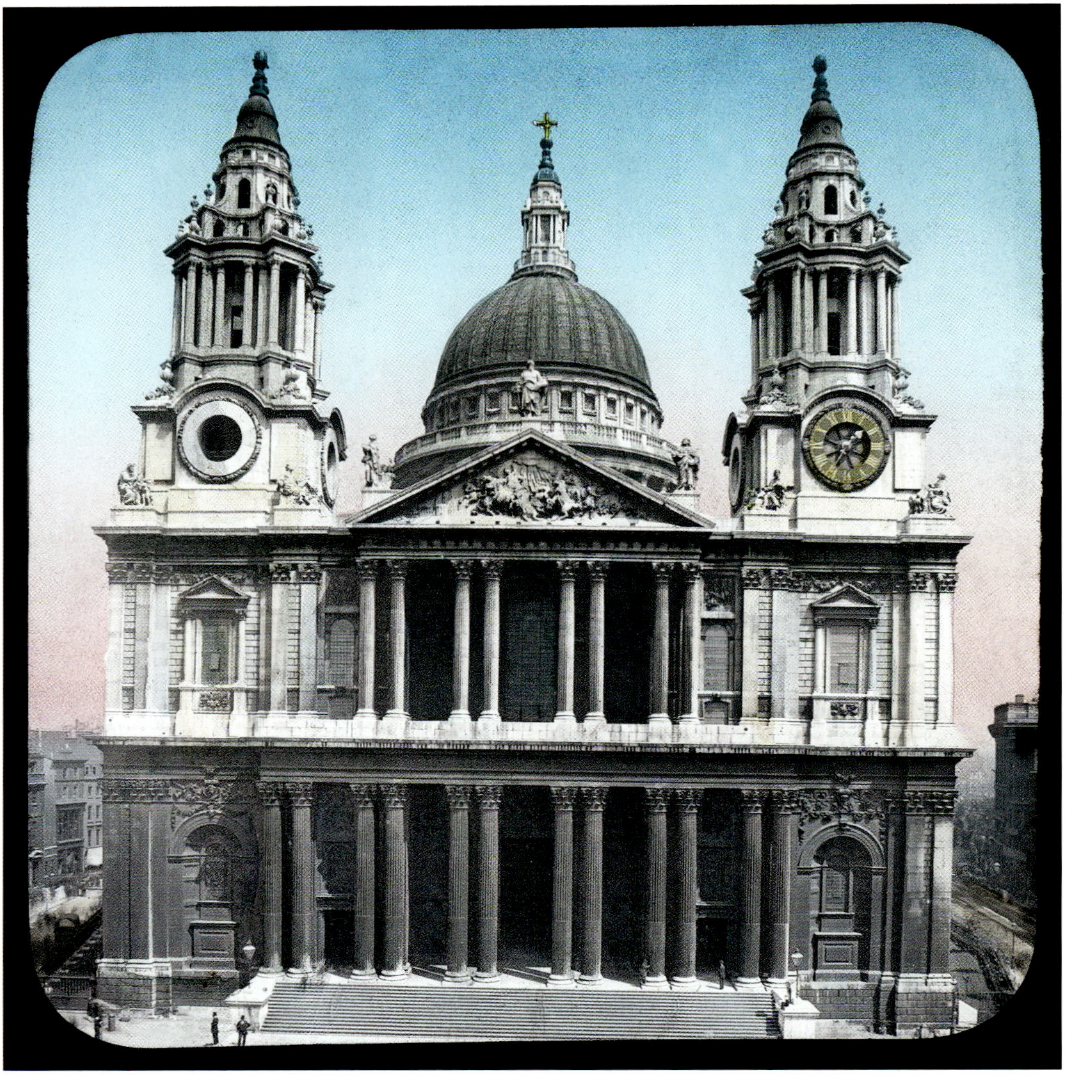

88 St. Paul's Cathedral (West Front), London, England, 1890s

88 Die St. Paul's-Kathedrale (Westfassade), London, England, 1890er Jahre

88 Cathédrale St. Paul (façade ouest), Londres, Angleterre, années 1890

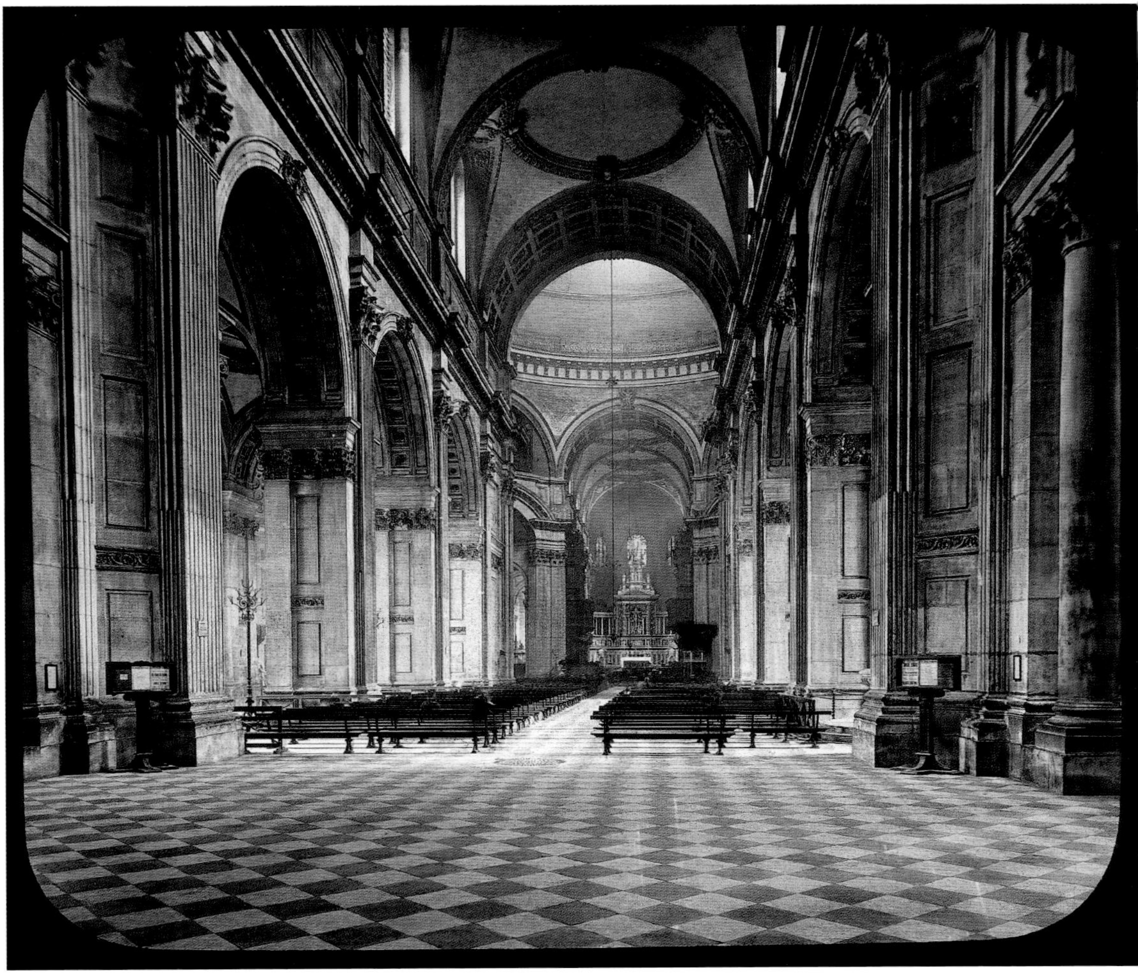

89 Nave (looking East), St. Paul's Cathedral, London, England, 1880s

89 Kirchenschiff (nach Osten), St. Paul's-Kathedrale, London, England, 1880er Jahre

89 Nef (direction ouest) de la cathédrale St. Paul, Londres, Angleterre, années 1880

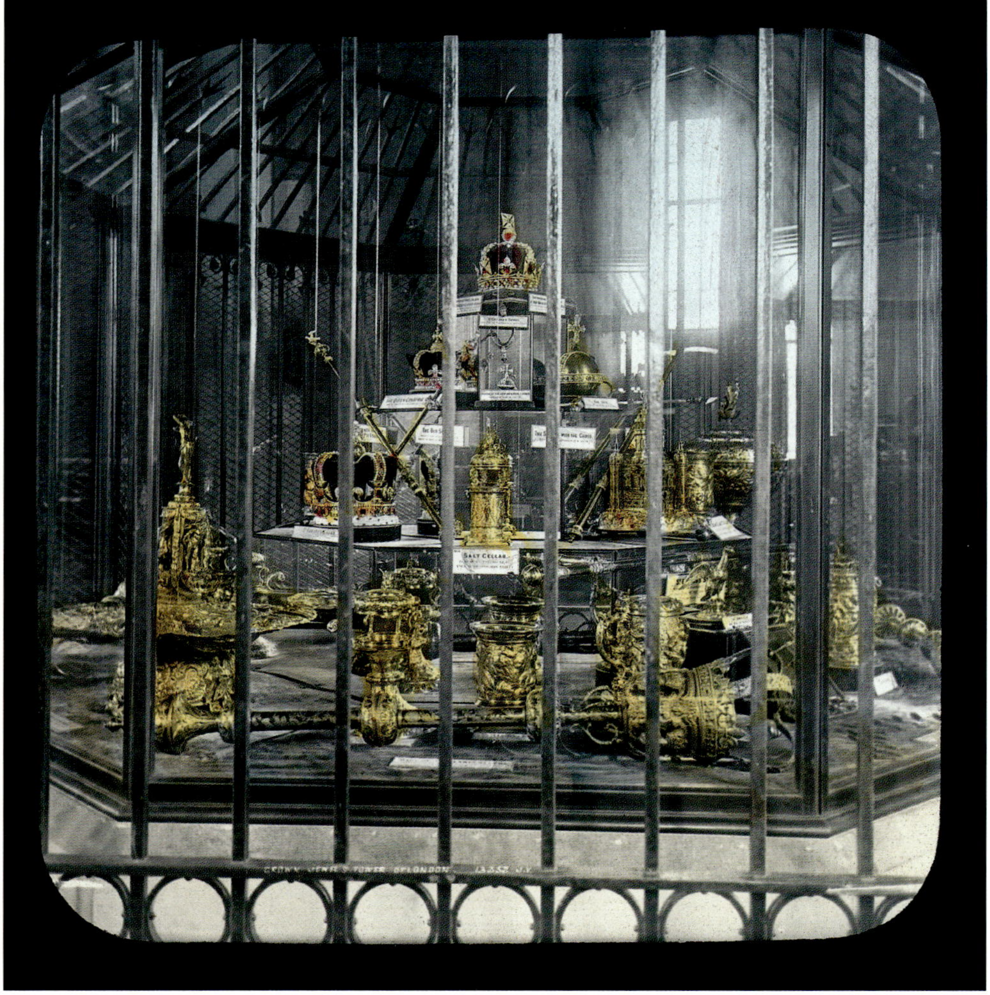

90 The Crown Jewels, The Tower of London, London, England, 1880s

90 Die Kronjuwelen, Der Tower von London, London, England, 1880er Jahre

90 Les joyaux de la Couronne, Tour de Londres, Angleterre, années 1880

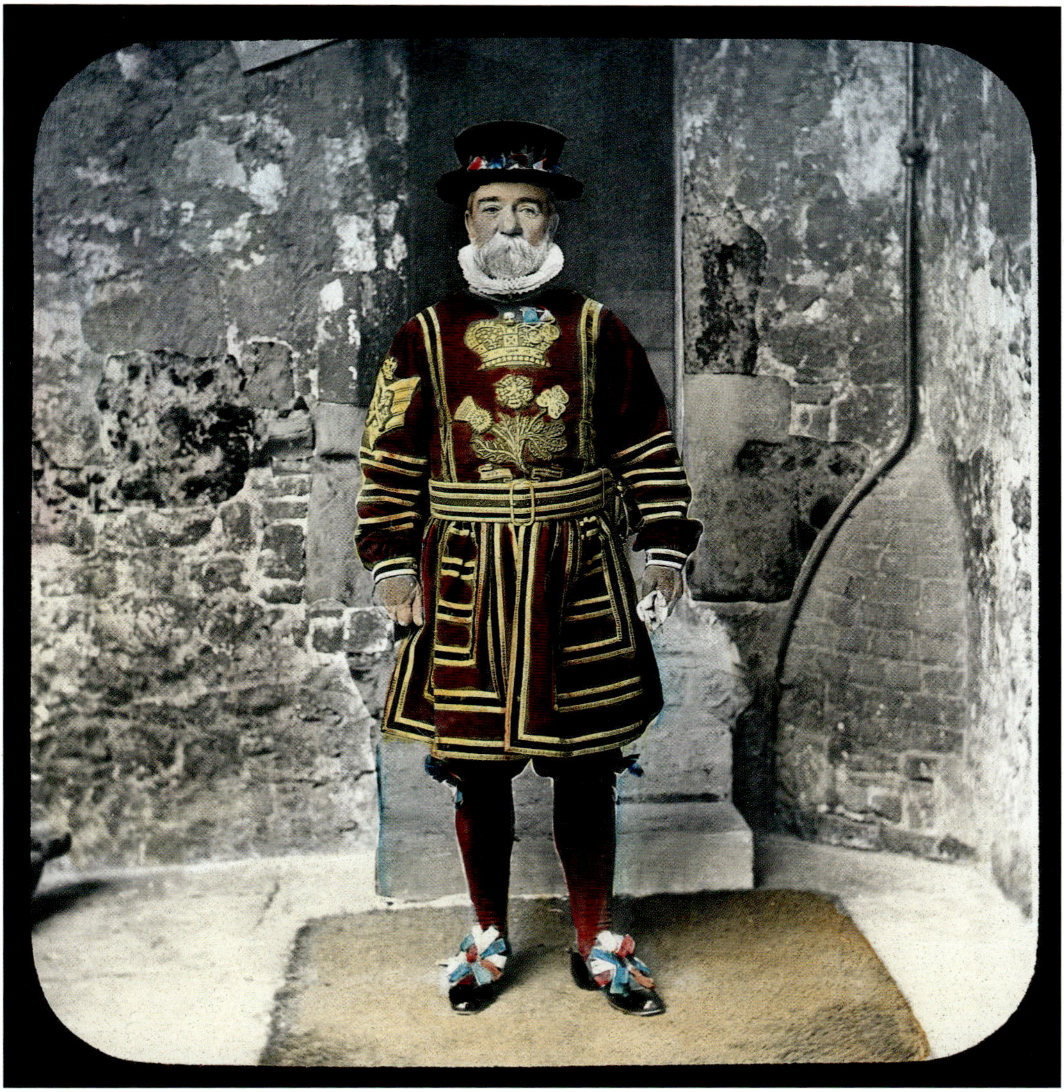

91 Beefeater (Yeoman Porter, Byward Tower), The Tower of London, London, England, 1880s

91 Beefeater (Yeoman Warder, Torwächter), Der Tower von London, London, England, 1880er Jahre

91 Beefeater (gardien Yeoman à la tour Byward), Tour de Londres, Angleterre, années 1880

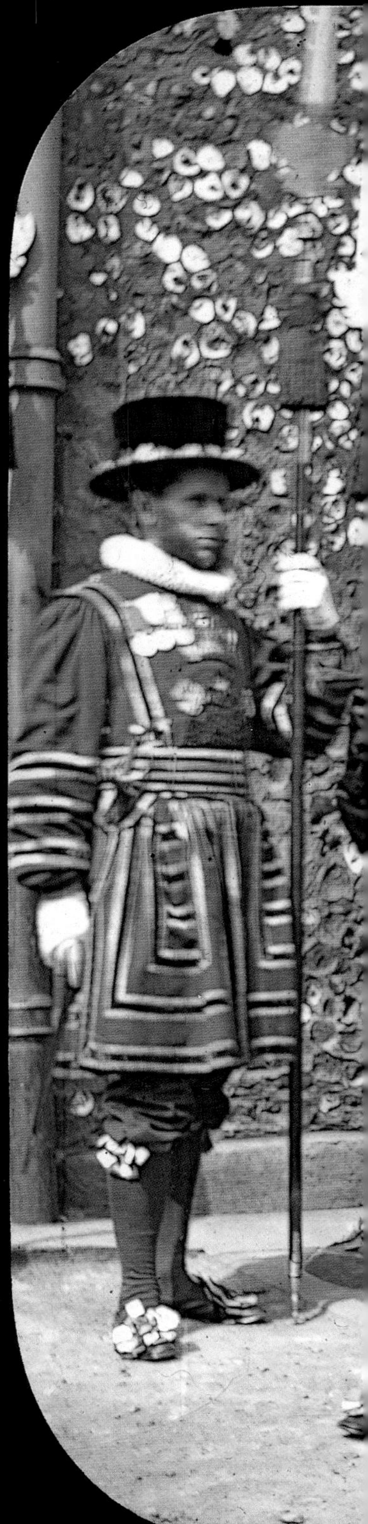

92 Yeomen Warders (Beefeaters) at the Tower of London, London, England, 1870s

92 Torwächter (Beefeaters, Yeoman Warders) am Tower von London, London, England, 1870er Jahre

92 Gardes Yeomen (Beefeaters) à la Tour de Londres, Angleterre, années 1870

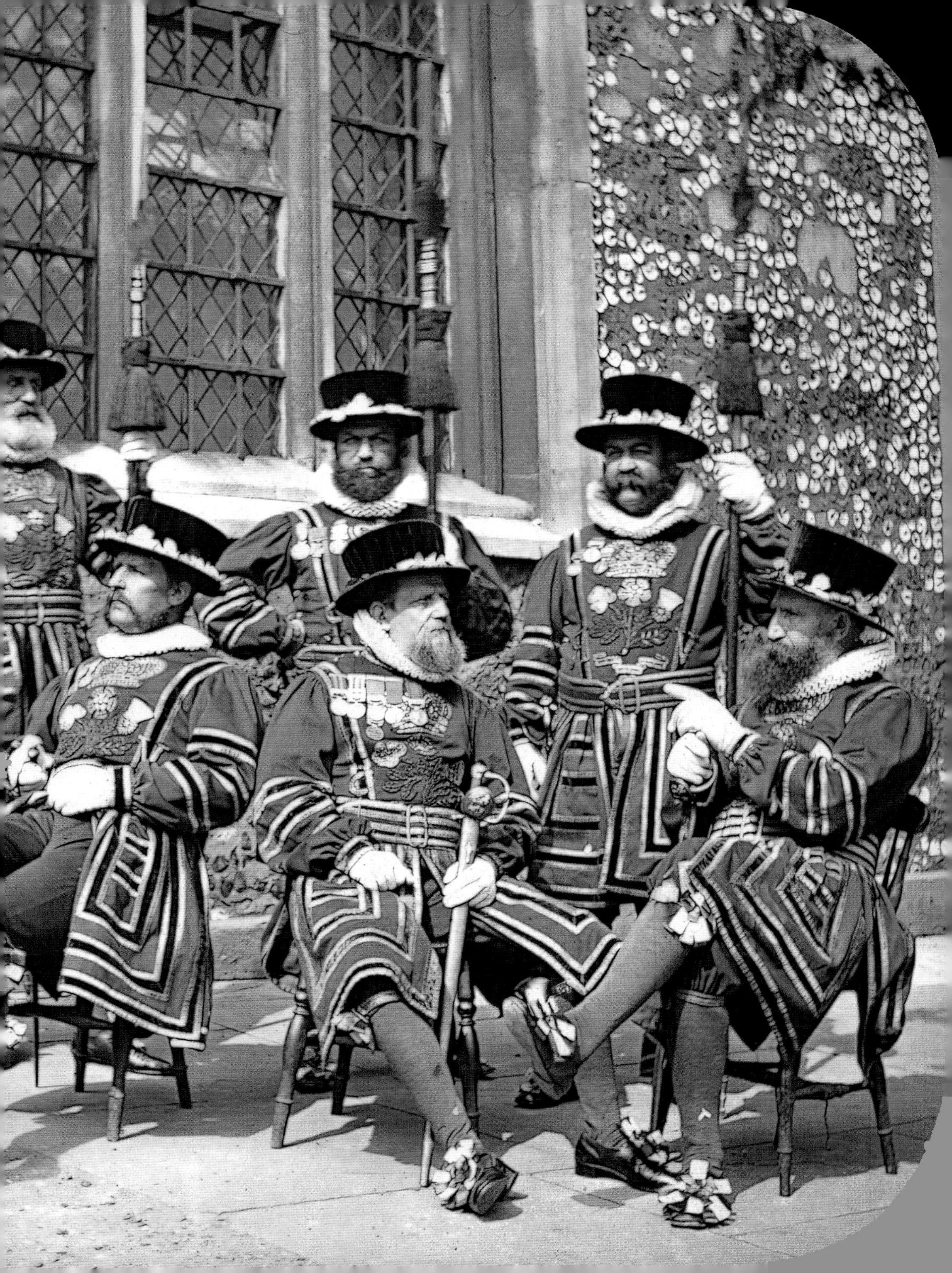

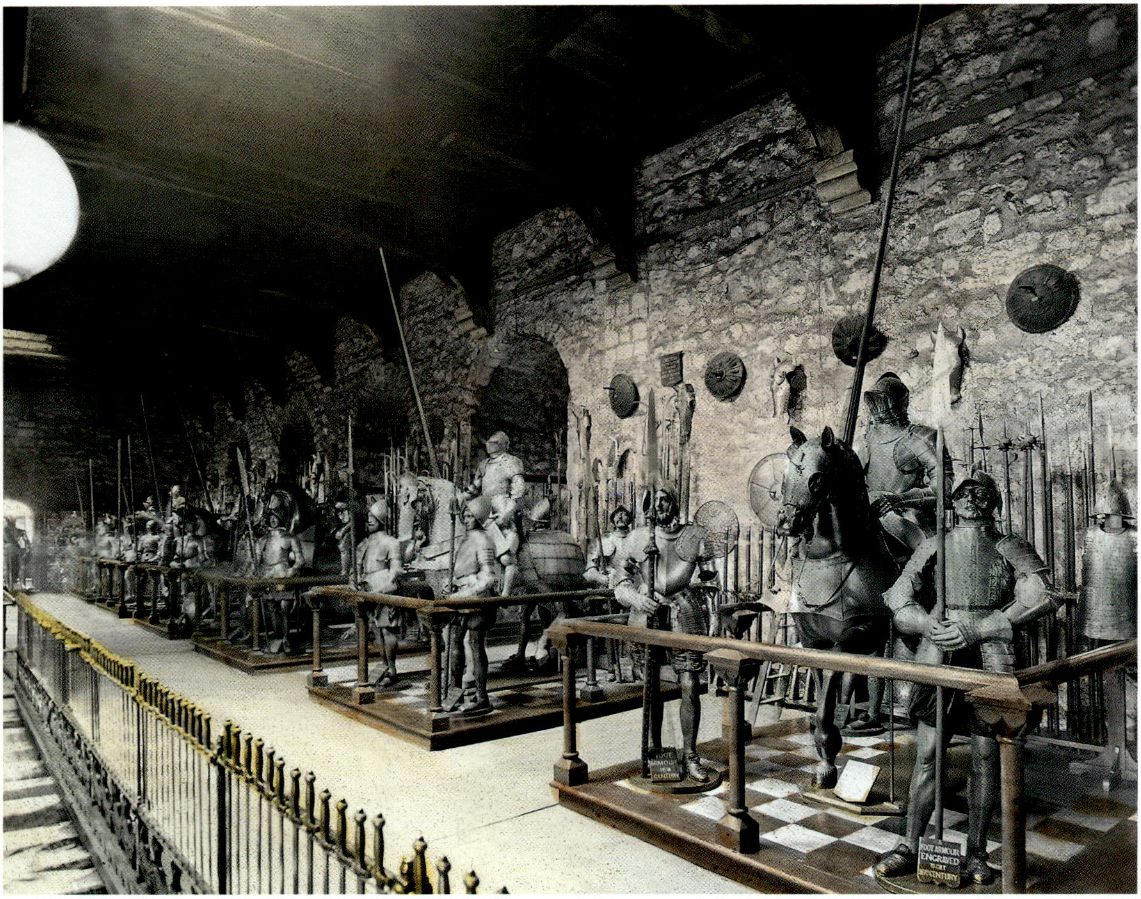

93 Horse Armoury, Tower of London, London, England, 1880s

93 Pferderüstungen, Der Tower von London, London, England, 1880er Jahre

93 Armures équestres, Tour de Londres, Angleterre, années 1880

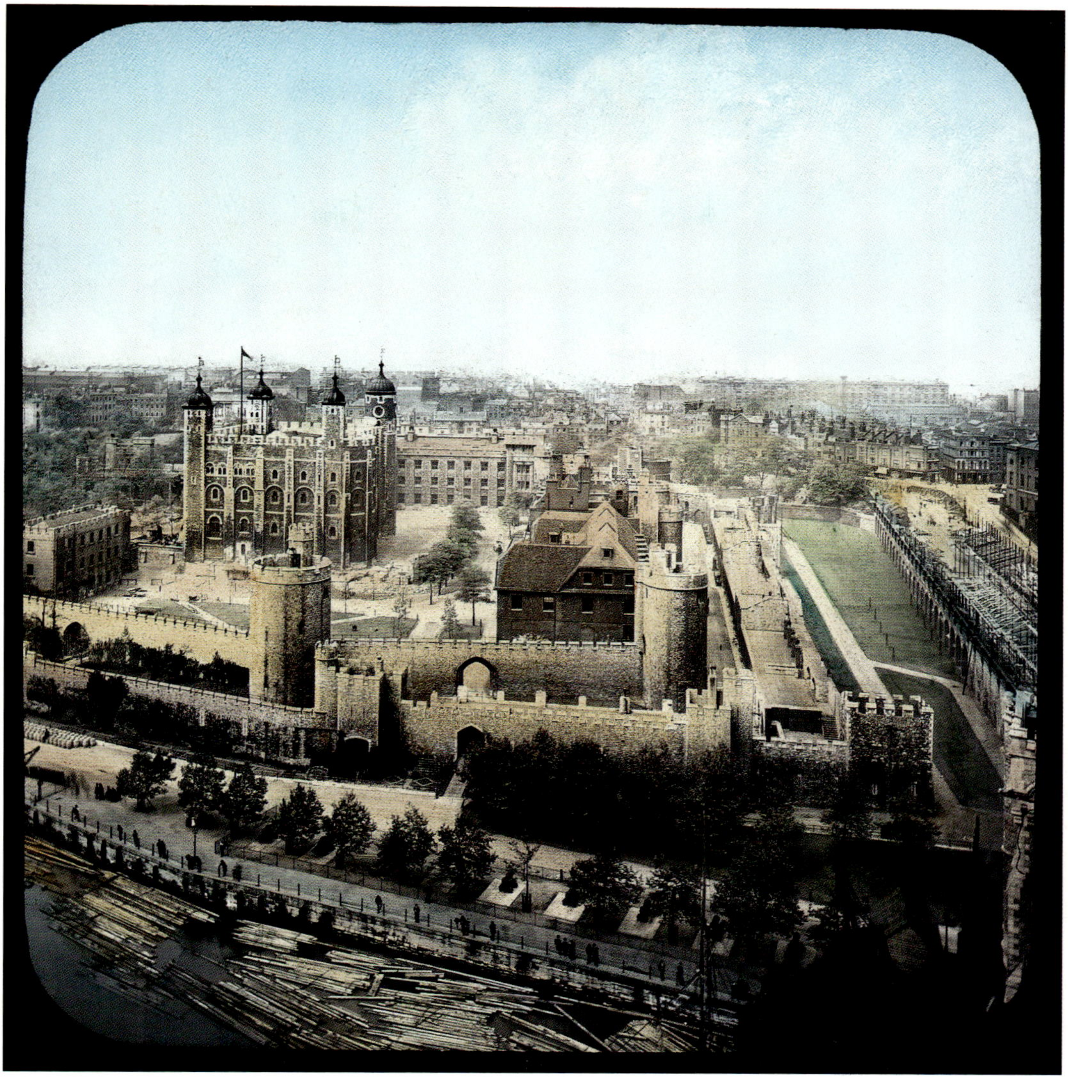

94 The Tower of London viewed from Tower Bridge, London, England, 1870s

94 Der Tower von London von der Tower-Brücke aus gesehen, London, England, 1870er Jahre

94 La Tour de Londres vue du Tower Bridge, Londres, Angleterre, années 1870

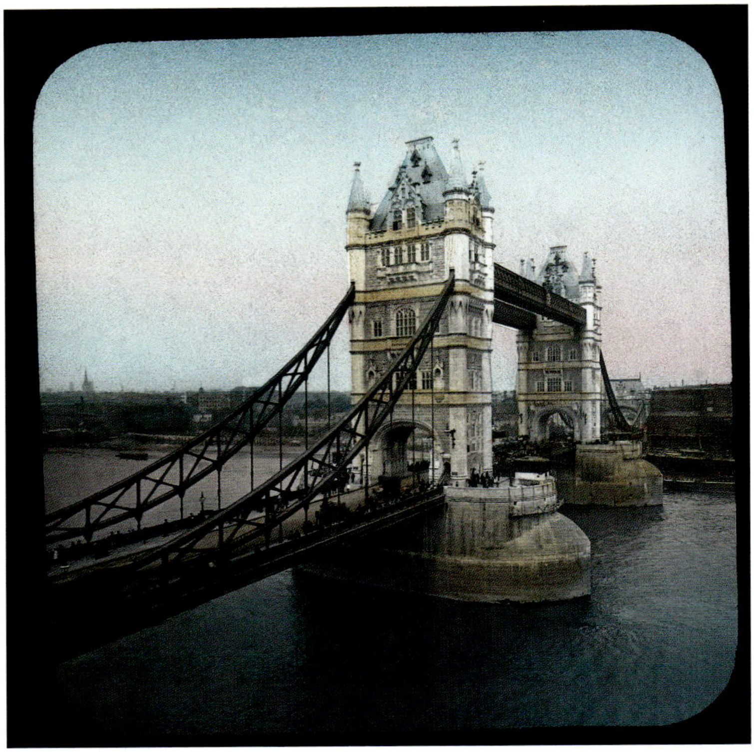

95 Opening Day, Tower Bridge, London, England, 1894

95 Der Tag der Eröffnung, Tower-Brücke, London, England, 1894

95 Le jour de l'inauguration du Tower Bridge, Londres, Angleterre, 1894

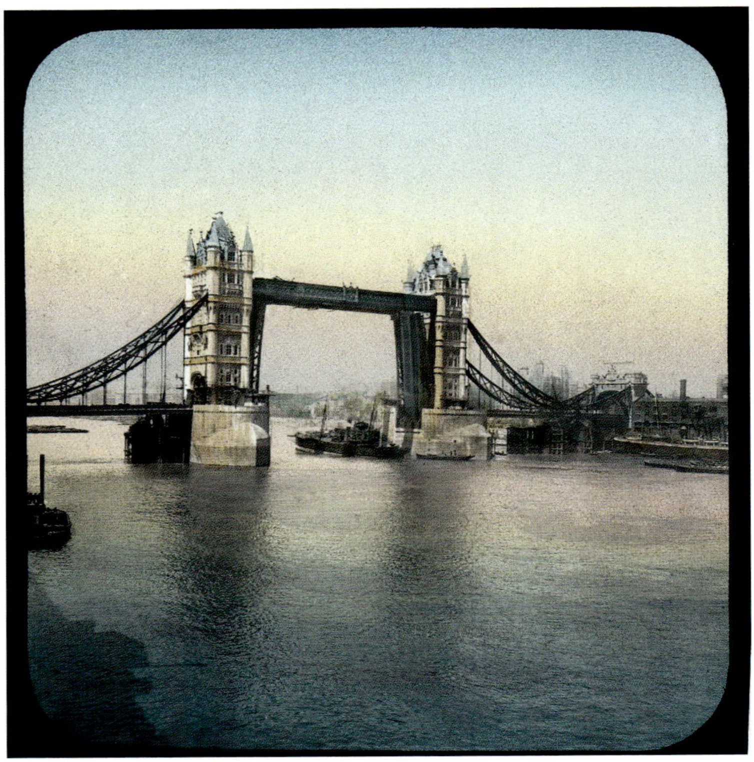

96 Opening Day, Tower Bridge, London, England, 1894

96 Der Tag der Eröffnung, Tower-Brücke, London, England, 1894

96 Le jour de l'inauguration du Tower Bridge, Londres, Angleterre, 1894

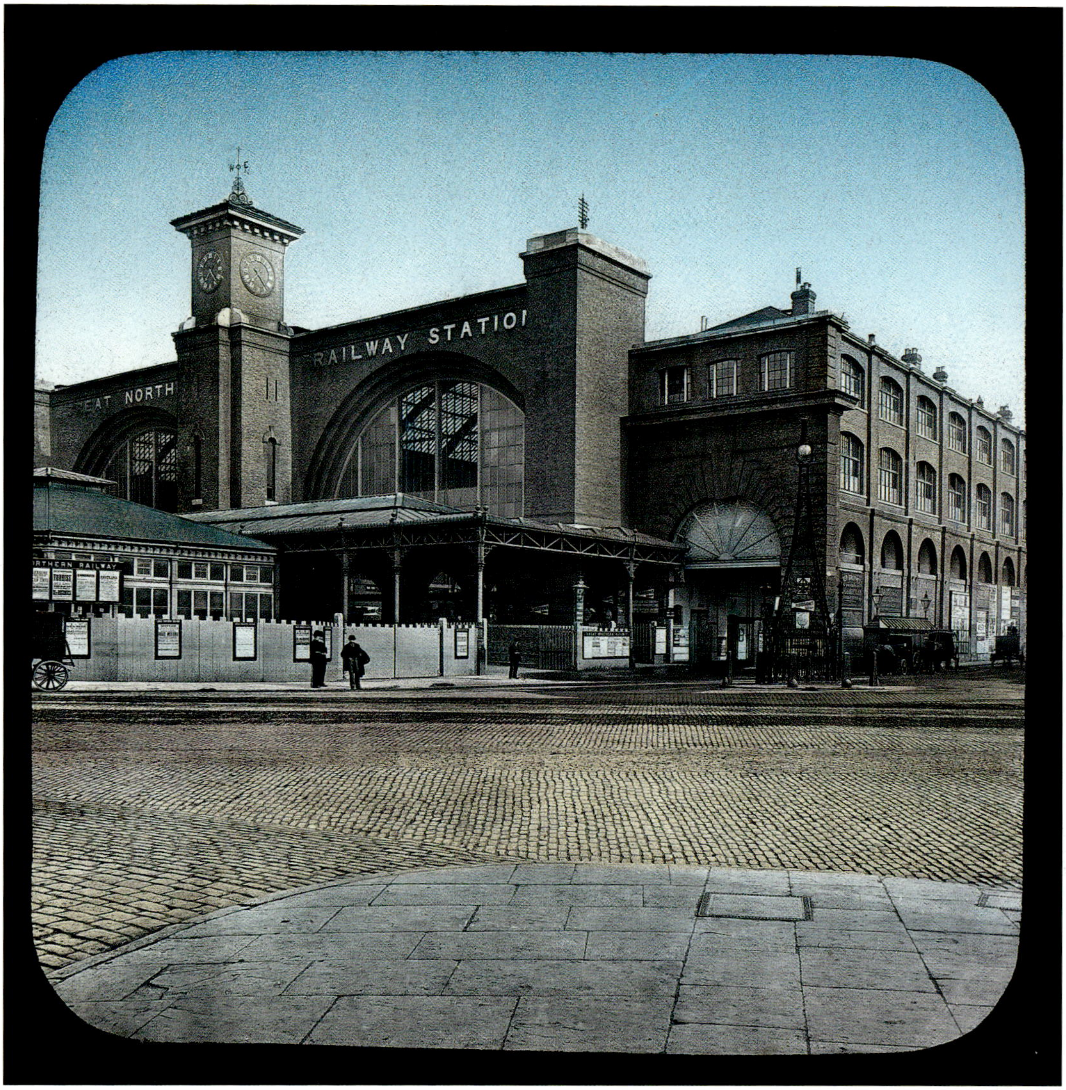

97 King's Cross Station, London, England, 1890s

97 Der King's Cross-Bahnhof, London, England, 1890er Jahre

97 Gare de King's Cross, Londres, Angleterre, années 1890

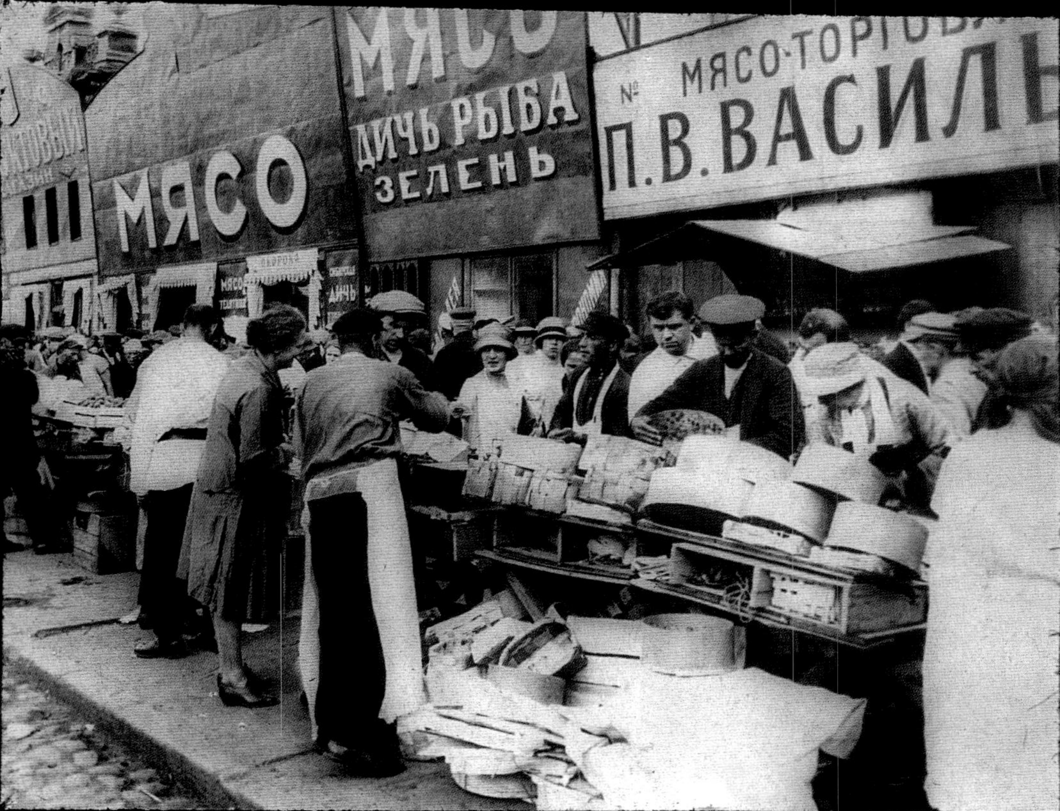

98 Small market,
Moscow, Russia, 1920s

98 Straßenmarkt,
Moskau, Russland,
1920er Jahre

98 Marché de rue,
Moscou, Russie,
années 1920

EASTERN EUROPE

OSTEUROPA · EUROPE DE L'EST

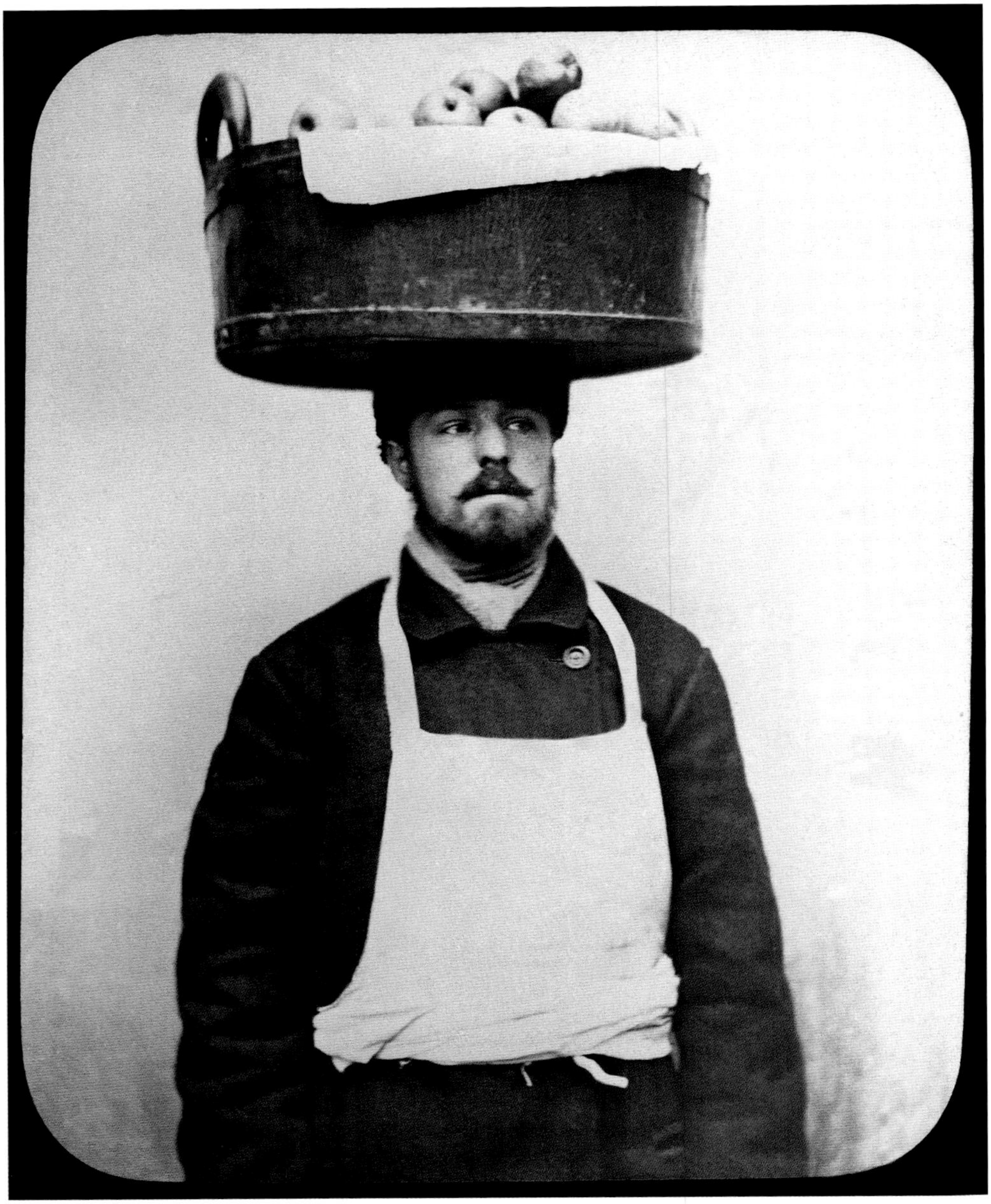

99 Street seller of apples, St. Petersburg, Russia, 1880s
100 "Ambulatory Seller of Trousers", St Petersburg, Russia, 1880s

99 Straßenverkäufer mit Äpfeln, St. Petersburg, Russland, 1880er Jahre
100 „Fahrender Hosenverkäufer", St. Petersburg, Russland, 1880er Jahre

99 Vendeur de pommes ambulant, Saint-Petersbourg, Russie, années 1880
100 Vendeur de pantalons ambulant, St Petersbourg, Russie, années 1880

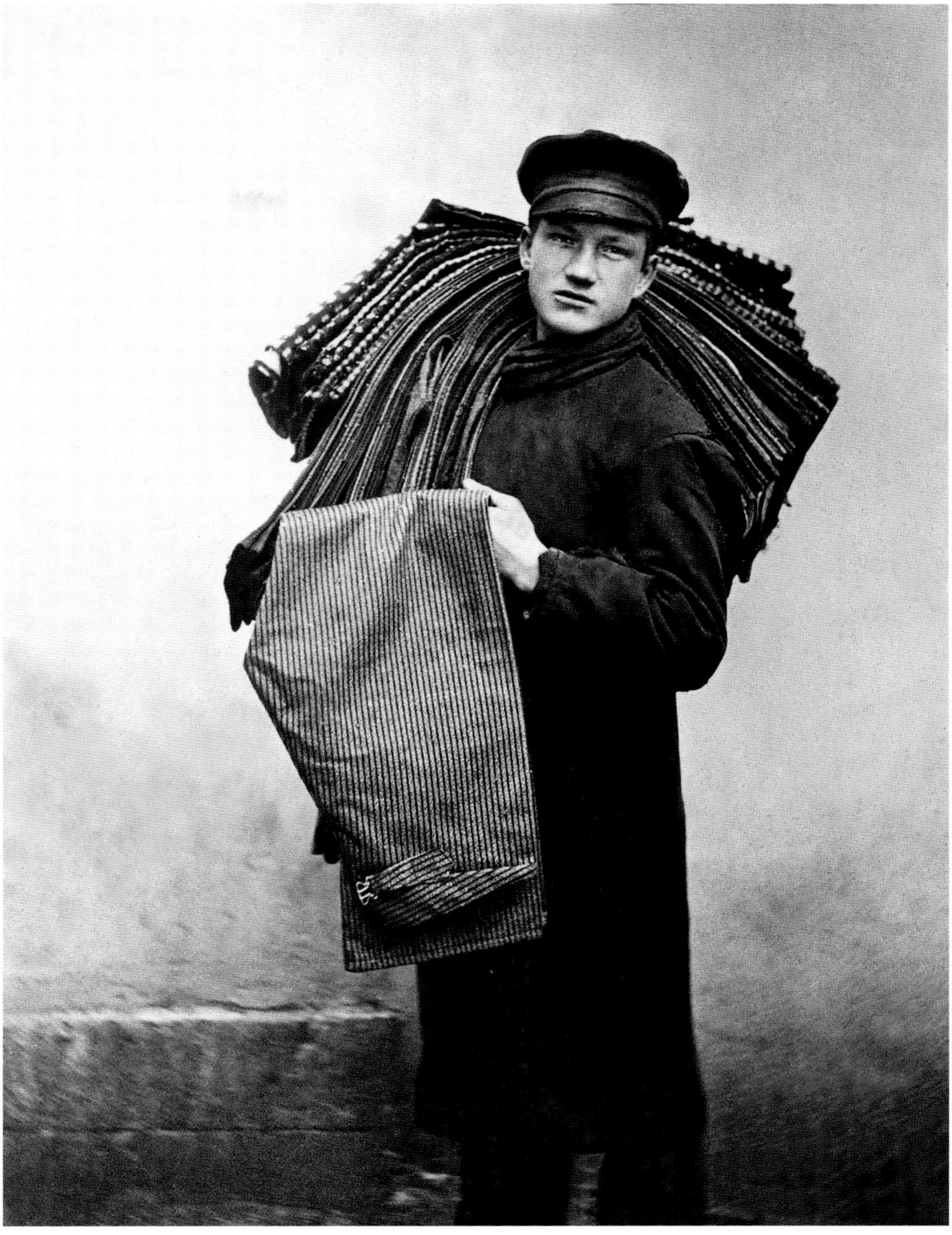

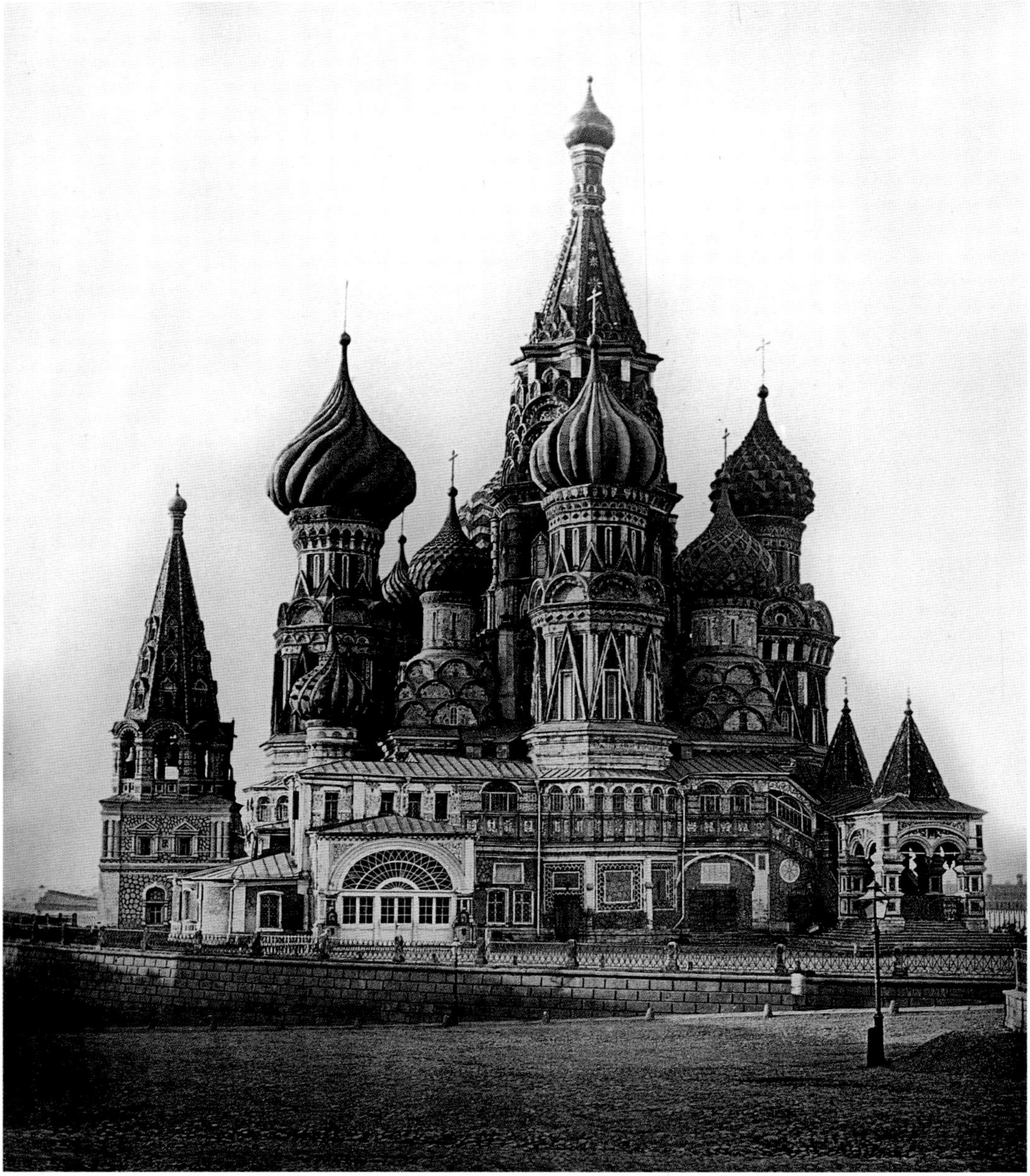

101 St. Basil's Cathedral, Moscow, Russia, 1870s

101 Die Basilius-Kathedrale, Moskau, Russland, 1870er Jahre

101 Cathédrale Saint-Basile, Moscou, Russie, années 1870

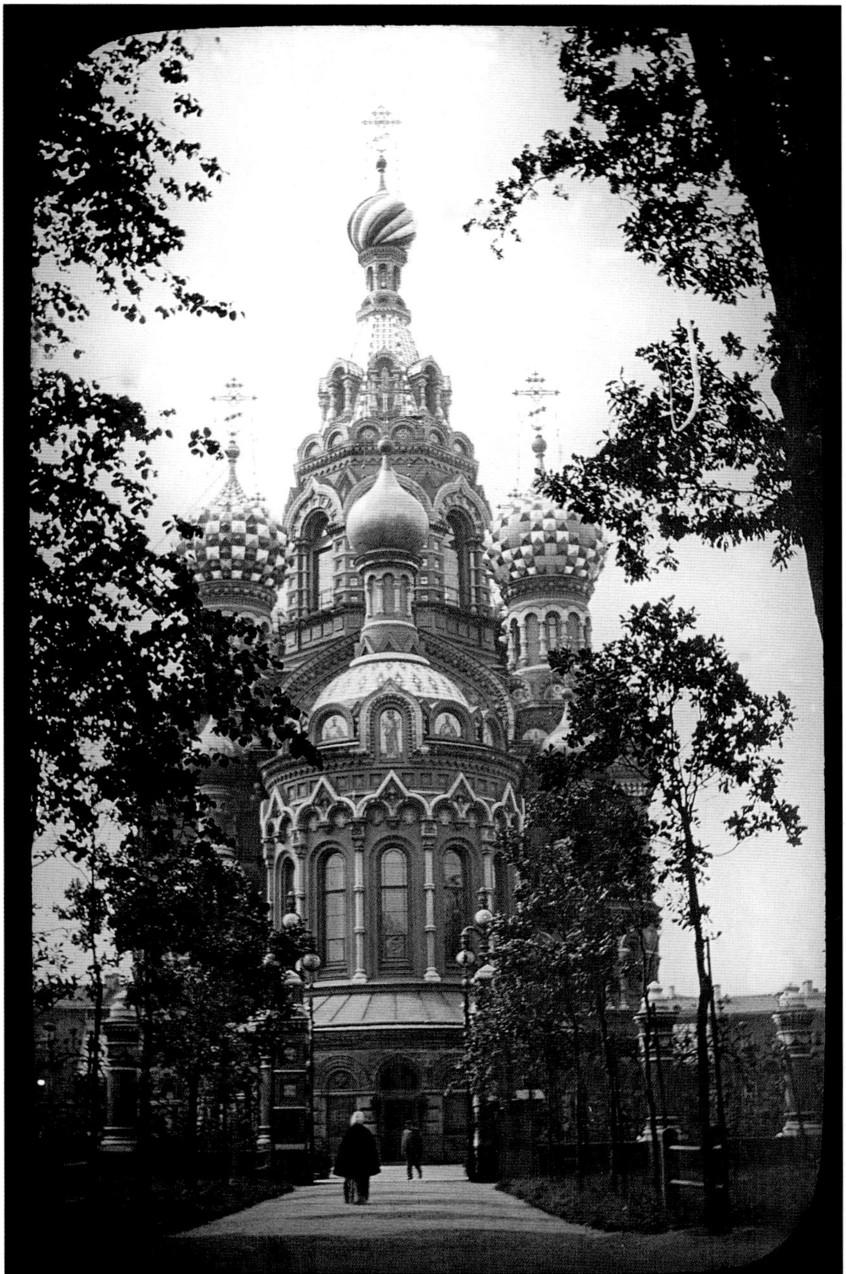

102 Church of the Resurrection (also known as the Church of The Saviour on the Spilled Blood), St. Petersburg, Russia, c.1907

102 Die Auferstehungskirche (auch bekannt als Bluterlöserkirche), St. Petersburg, Russland, um 1907

102 Église de la Résurrection (aussi appelée église du Sauveur-sur-le-sang-versé), Saint-Petersbourg, Russie, vers 1907

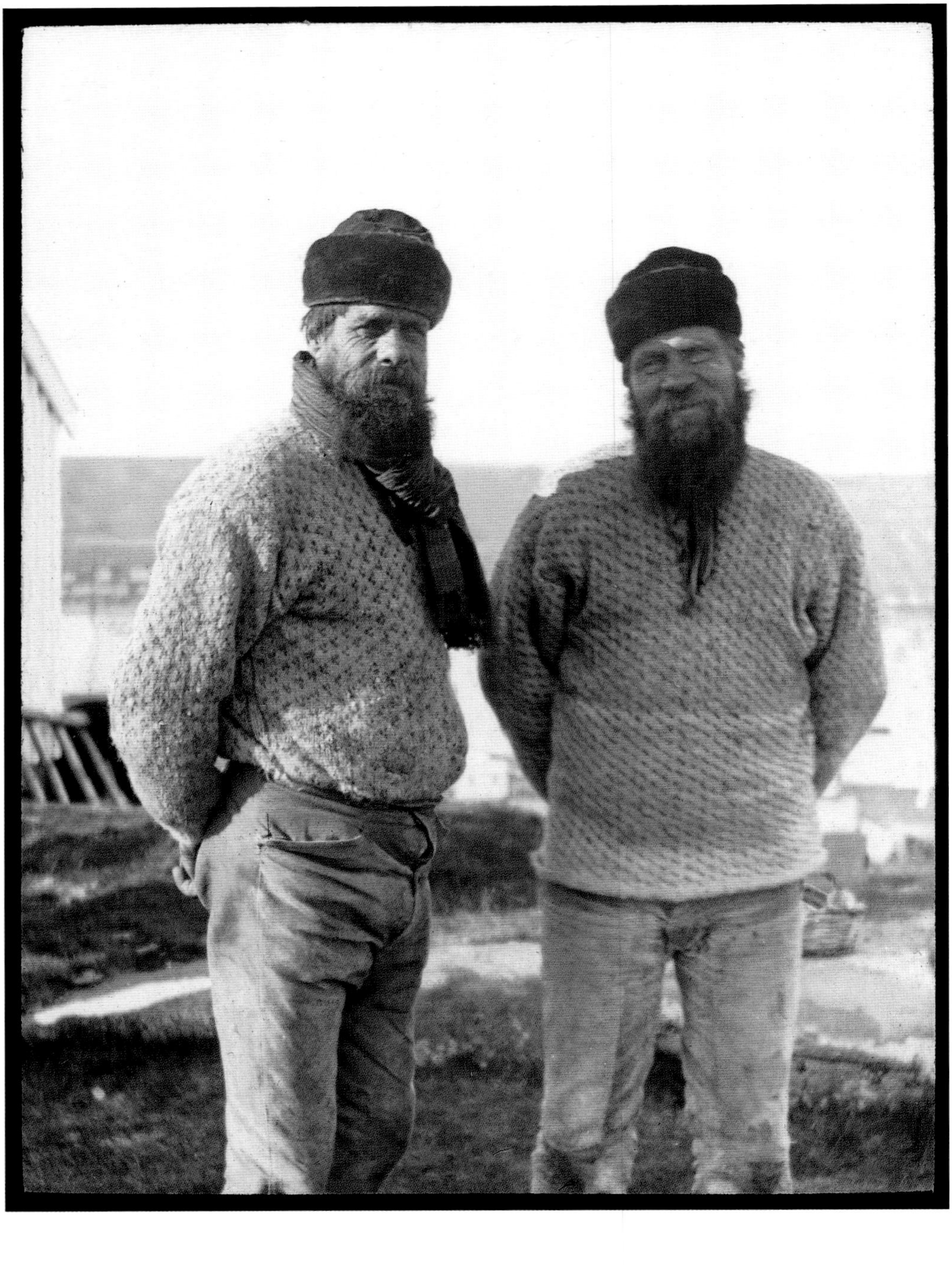

103 Russian sailors,
Russia, 1880s

103 Russische Seeleute,
Russland, 1880er Jahre

103 Marins russes, Russie,
années 1880

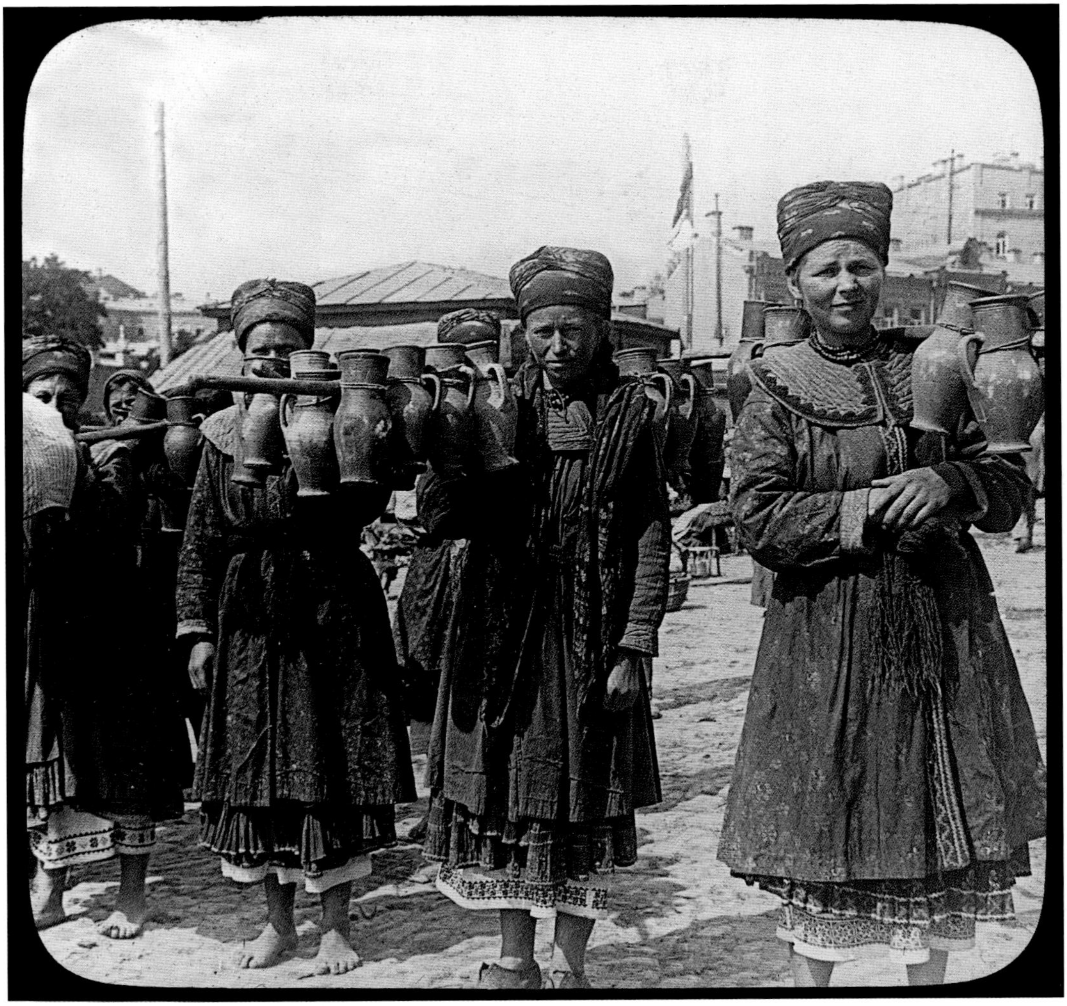

104 “Quaint dairy maids delivering milk in earthernware jars suspended on poles”, Kief (now Kiev), Russia (now Ukraine), 1890s

104 „Eigenwillig anmutende Milchmädchen liefern Milch in Tonkrügen an Stäben ab“, Kiew, Russland (heute Ukraine), 1890er Jahre

104 Pittoresques laitières livrant le lait dans des jarres en terre suspendues à un bâton, Kief (auj. Kiev), Russie (auj. Ukraine), années 1890

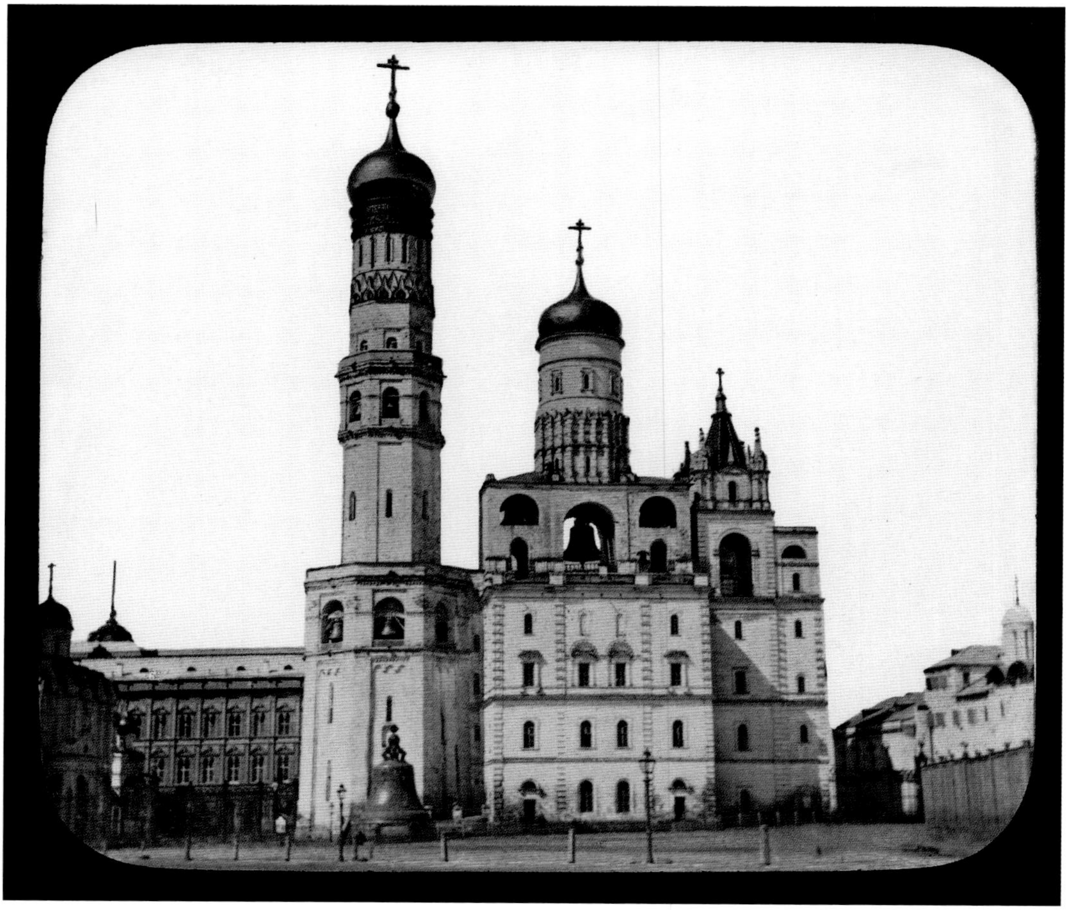

105 Ivan The Great Bell Tower and the Tsar Bell, Moscow, Russia, 1880s

105 Der Glockenturm Iwan der Große und die Zarenglocke, Moskau, Russland, 1880er Jahre

105 La tour-clocher d'Ivan-le-Grand et la cloche-tsar, Moscou, Russie, années 1880

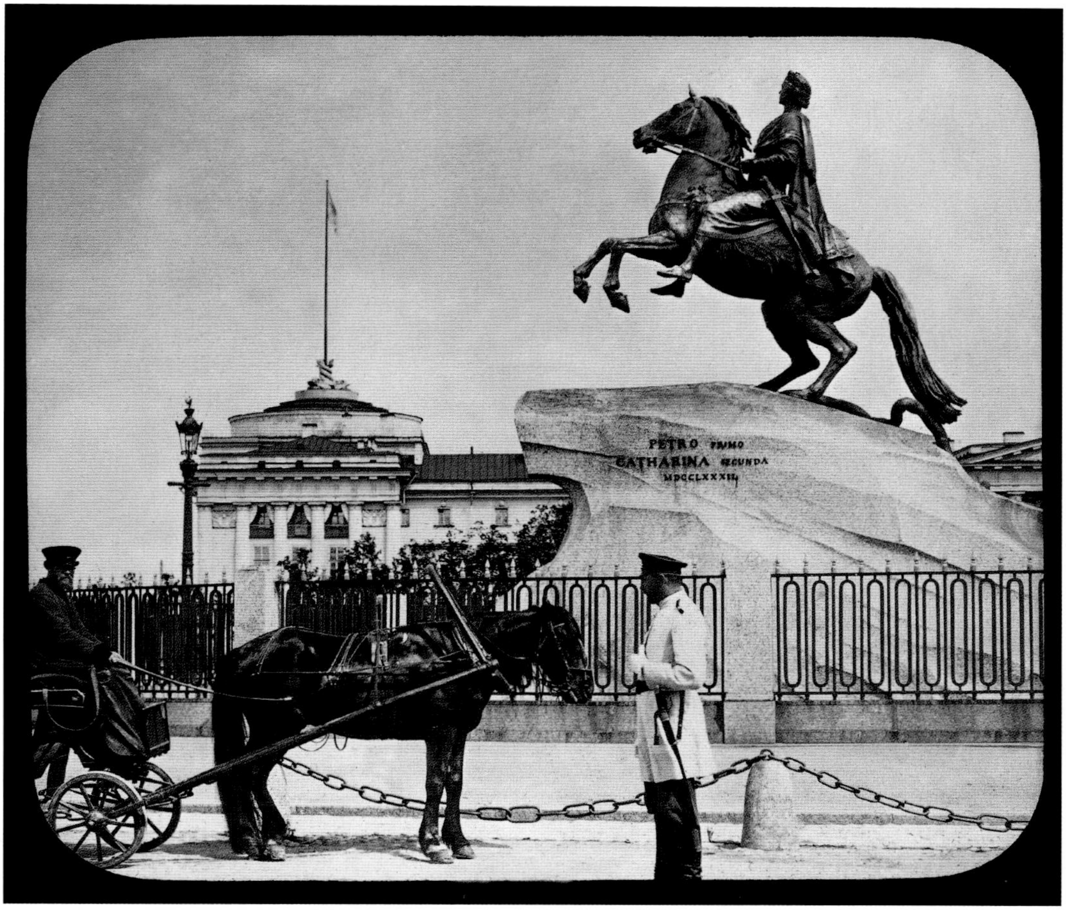

106 Statue of Peter the Great, St Petersburg, Russia, c.1900

106 Das Reiterstandbild Peters des Großen, St. Petersburg, Russland, um 1900

106 Statue de Pierre-le-Grand, Saint-Pétersbourg, Russie, vers 1900

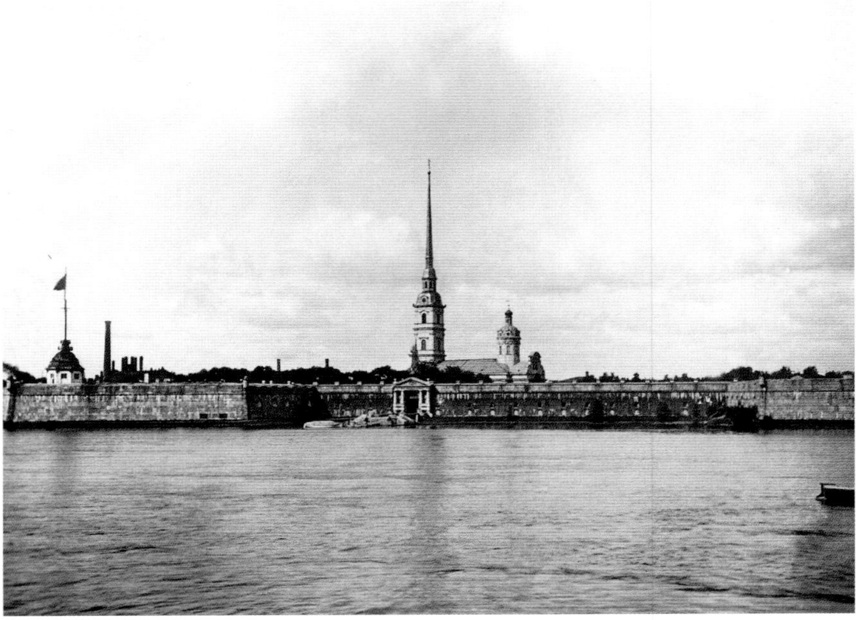

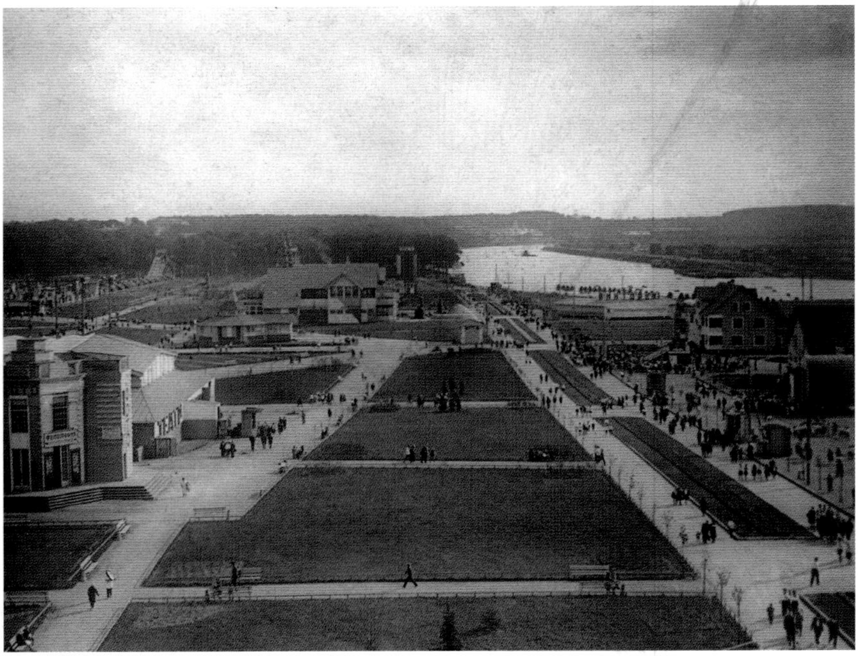

107 St. Peter and St. Paul's Fortess, St Petersburg, Russia, c.1900
108 Recreation Park, Moscow, Russia, 1920s

107 Die Peter-und-Paul-Festung, St. Petersburg, Russland, um 1900
108 Erholungspark, Moskau, Russland, 1920er Jahre

107 Forteresse Pierre-et-Paul, Saint-Pétersbourg, Russie, vers 1900
108 Parc public, Moscou, Russie, années 1920

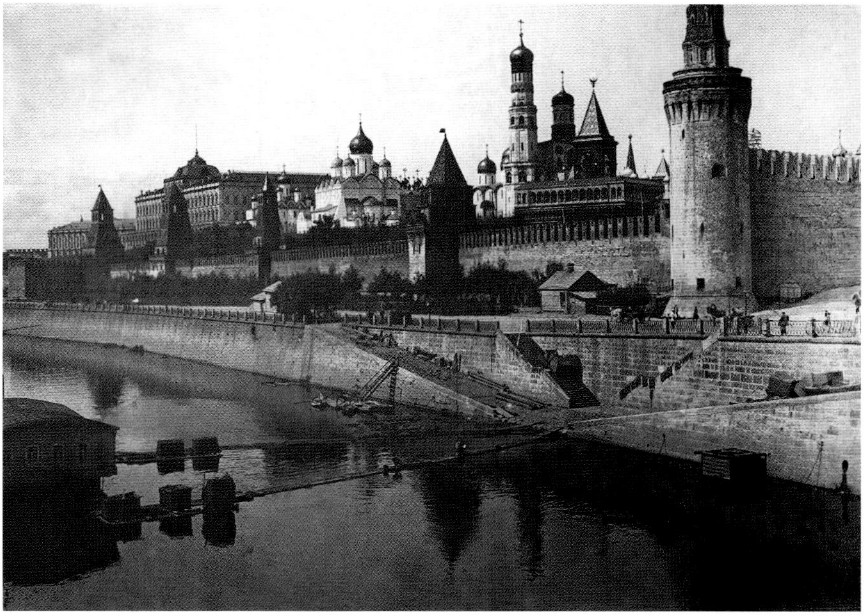

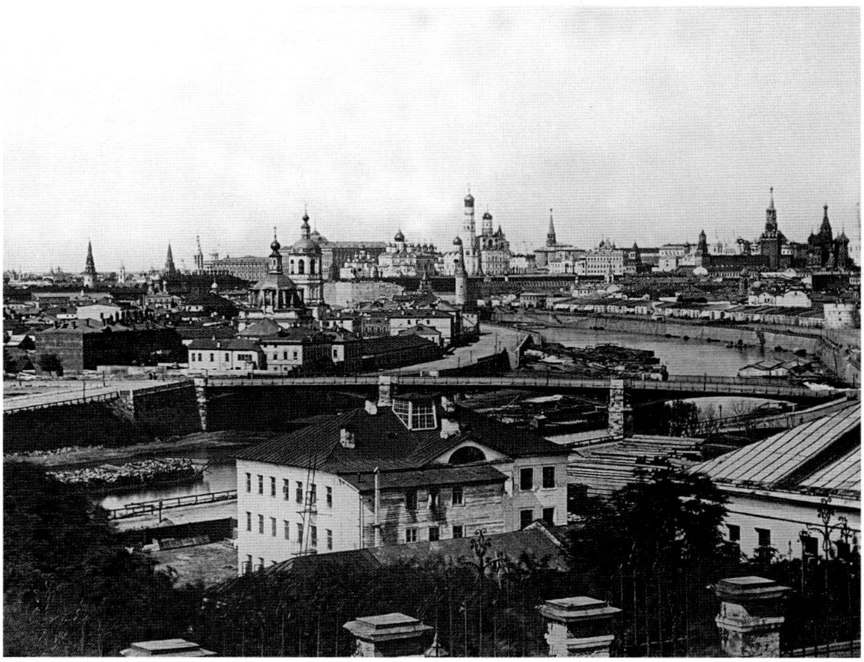

109 The Kremlin, Moscow, Russia, 1880s
110 View from the East to the Kremlin and inner city, Moscow, Russia, 1880s

109 Der Kreml, Moskau, Russland, 1880er Jahre
110 Blick von Osten auf den Kreml und die Innenstadt, Moskau, Russland, 1880er Jahre

109 Le Kremlin, Moscou, Russie, années 1880
110 Vues de l'est du Kremlin et de la ville, Moscou, Russie, années 1880

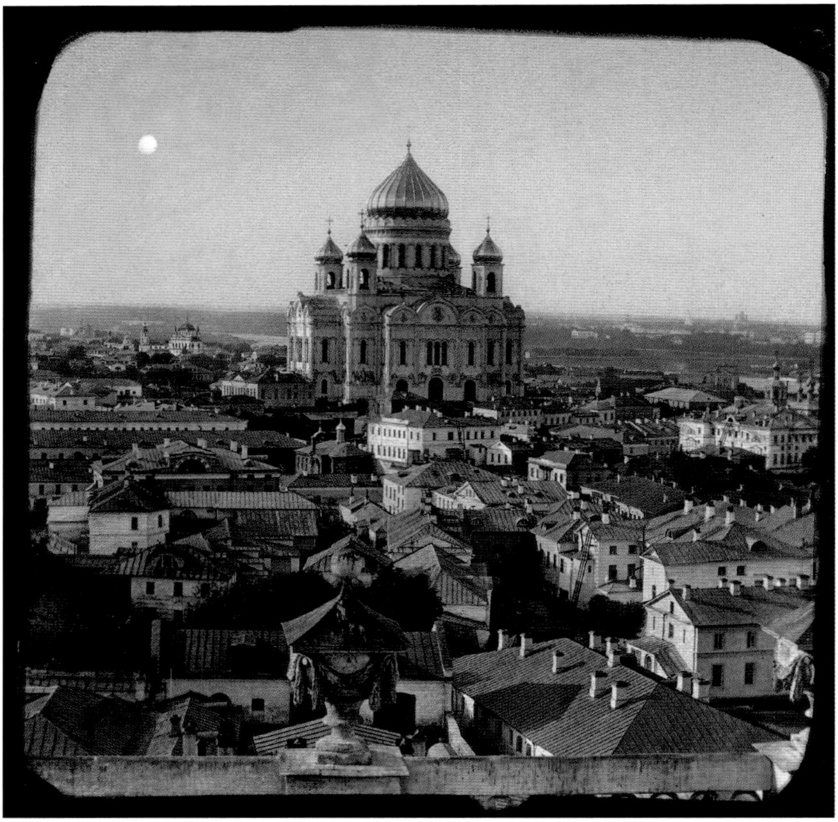

111 View of city (from the museum) overlooking the Cathedral of Christ the Saviour, Moscow, Russia, 1880s

111 Ansicht des Stadtzentrums (vom Museum aus) mit Blick auf die Christ-Erlöser-Kathedrale, Moskau, Russland, 1880er Jahre

111 Vue de la ville (depuis le musée) et de la cathédrale du Christ Sauveur, Moscou, Russie, années 1880

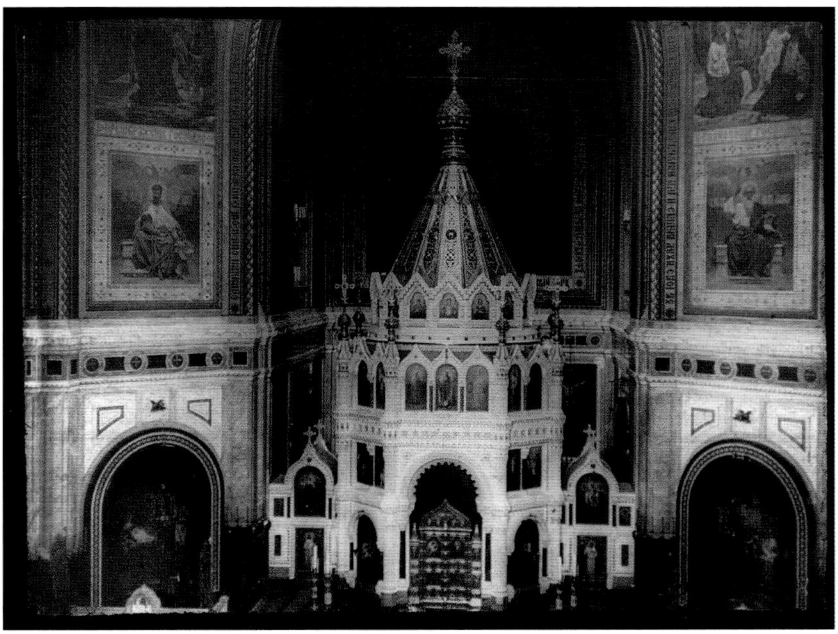

112 Cathedral of Christ the Saviour, Moscow, Russia, 1920s

112 Die Christ-Erlöser-Kathedrale, Moskau, Russland, 1920er Jahre

112 Cathédrale du Christ Sauveur, Moscou, Russie, années 1920

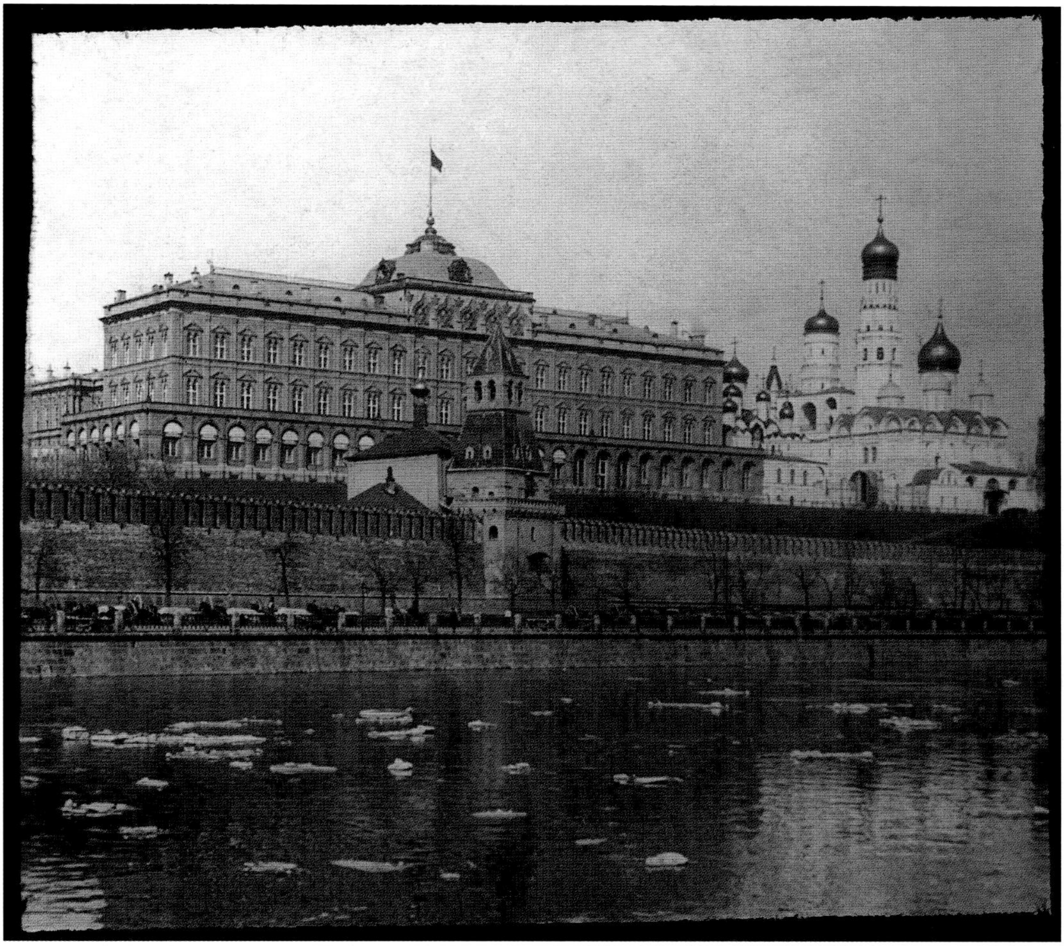

113 The Great Kremlin Palace, Moscow, Russia, 1920s

113 Der Große Kremlpalast, Moskau, Russland, 1920er Jahre

113 Le Grand palais du Kremlin, Moscou, Russie, années 1920

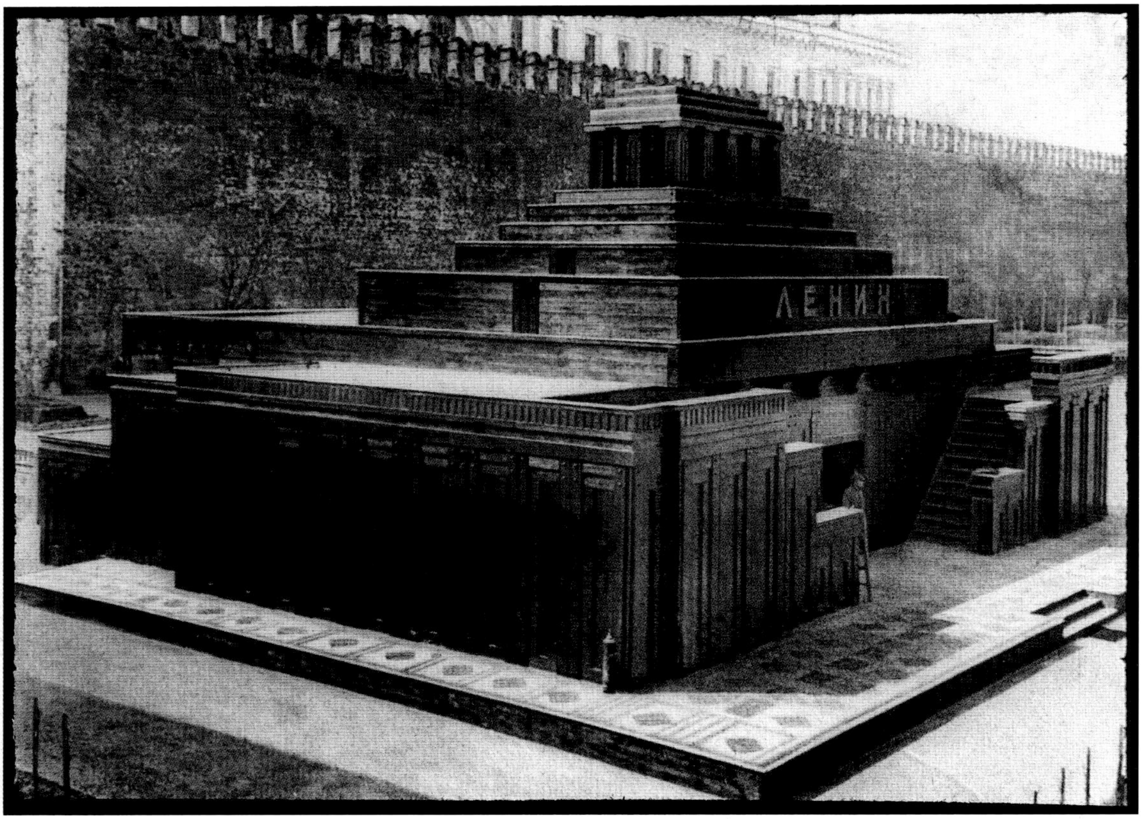

114 Lenin's Mausoleum (Lenin's Tomb), Red Square, Moscow, Russia, 1920s

114 Das Lenin-Mausoleum (Lenins Grabstätte), Roter Platz, Moskau, Russland, 1920er Jahre

114 Mausolée de Lénine (tombeau de Lénine), place Rouge, Moscou, Russie, années 1920

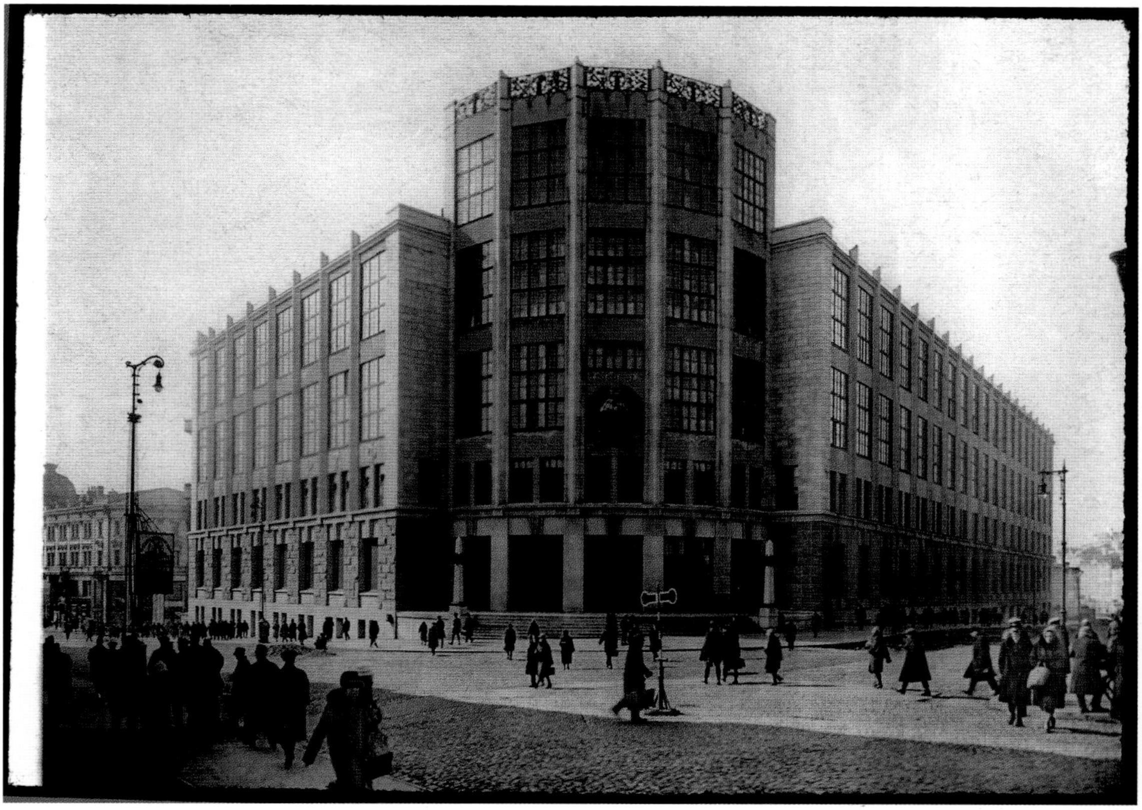

115 The Post Office building on Tverskaya, Moscow, Russia, 1920s

115 Das Post- und Telegrafenamt auf der Twerskaya, Moskau, Russland, 1920er Jahre

115 Immeuble de la poste de l'avenue Tverskaya, Moscou, Russie, années 1920

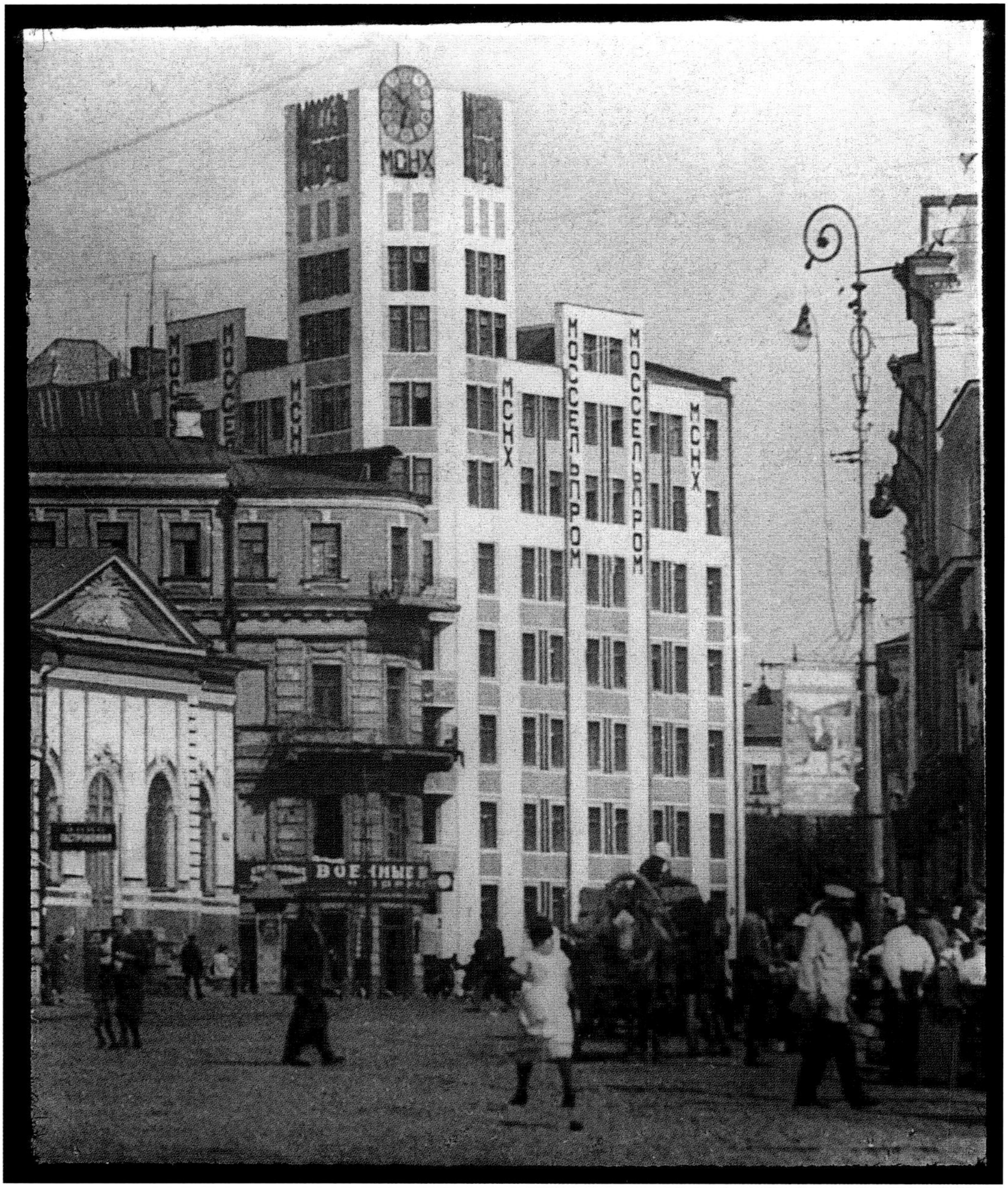

116 Mosselprom Department Store, Moscow, Russia, 1920s
117 Voskresensky (Resurrection) Gate, Red Square, Moscow, Russia, 1920s

116 Das Mosselprom-Kaufhaus, Moskau, Russland, 1920er Jahre
117 Das Auferstehungstor (Woskresenskije Worota), Roter Platz, Moskau, Russland, 1920er Jahre

116 Les grands magasins Mosselprom, Moscou, Russie, années 1920
117 Porte Voskresensky (de la Résurrection), place Rouge, Moscou, Russie, années 1920

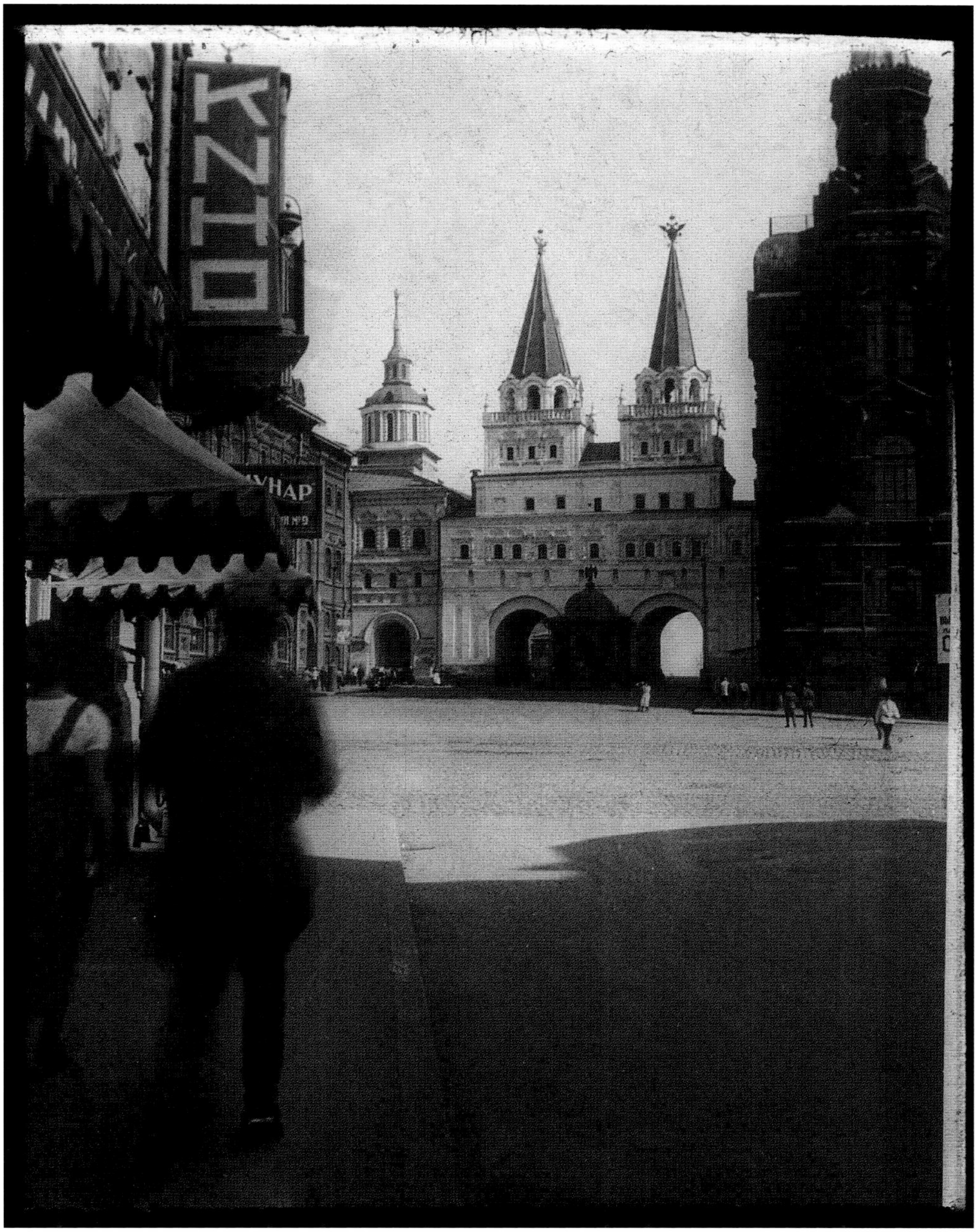
КИНО

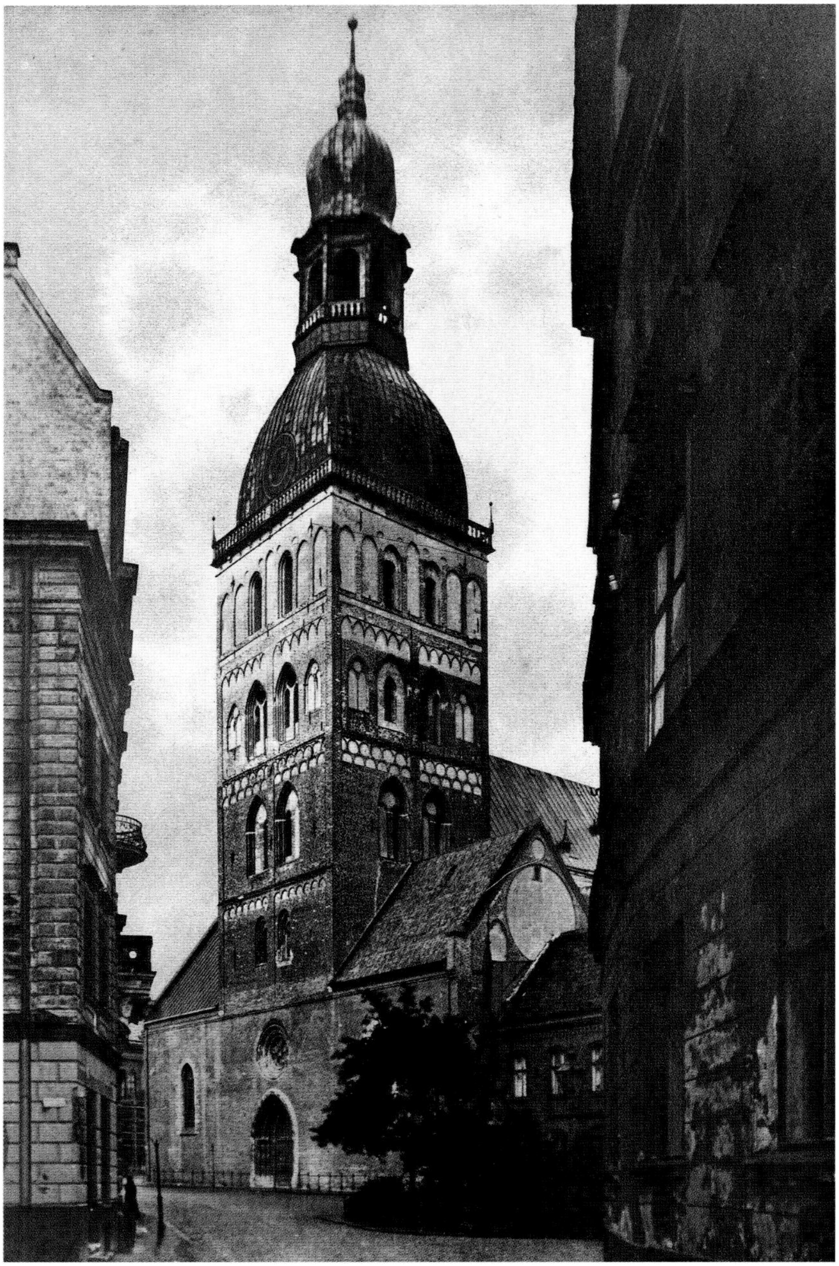

118 Rīgas Doms (Cathedral), Riga, Latvia, 1880s

118 Rīgas Doms (Dom), Riga, Lettland, 1880er Jahre

118 Dom (cathédrale) de Riga, Lettonie, années 1880

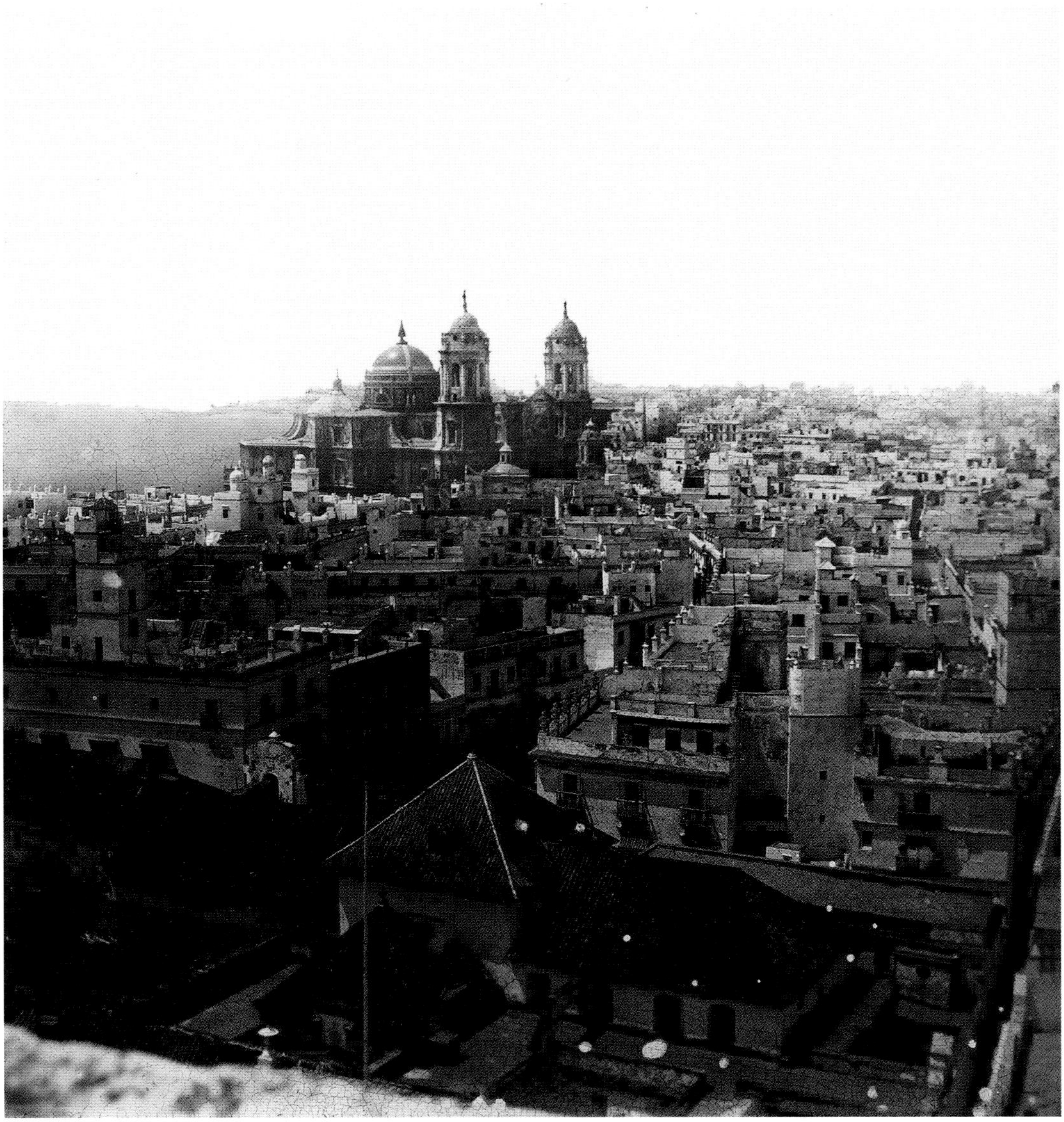

119 Panorama of Prague, Bohemia, Austria-Hungary (now Czech Republic), 1880s

119 Panoramablick über Prag, Böhmen, Österreich-Ungarn (heute Tschechische Republik), 1880er Jahre

119 Panorama de Prague, Bohême Autriche-Hongrie (auj. Rép. tchèque), années 1880

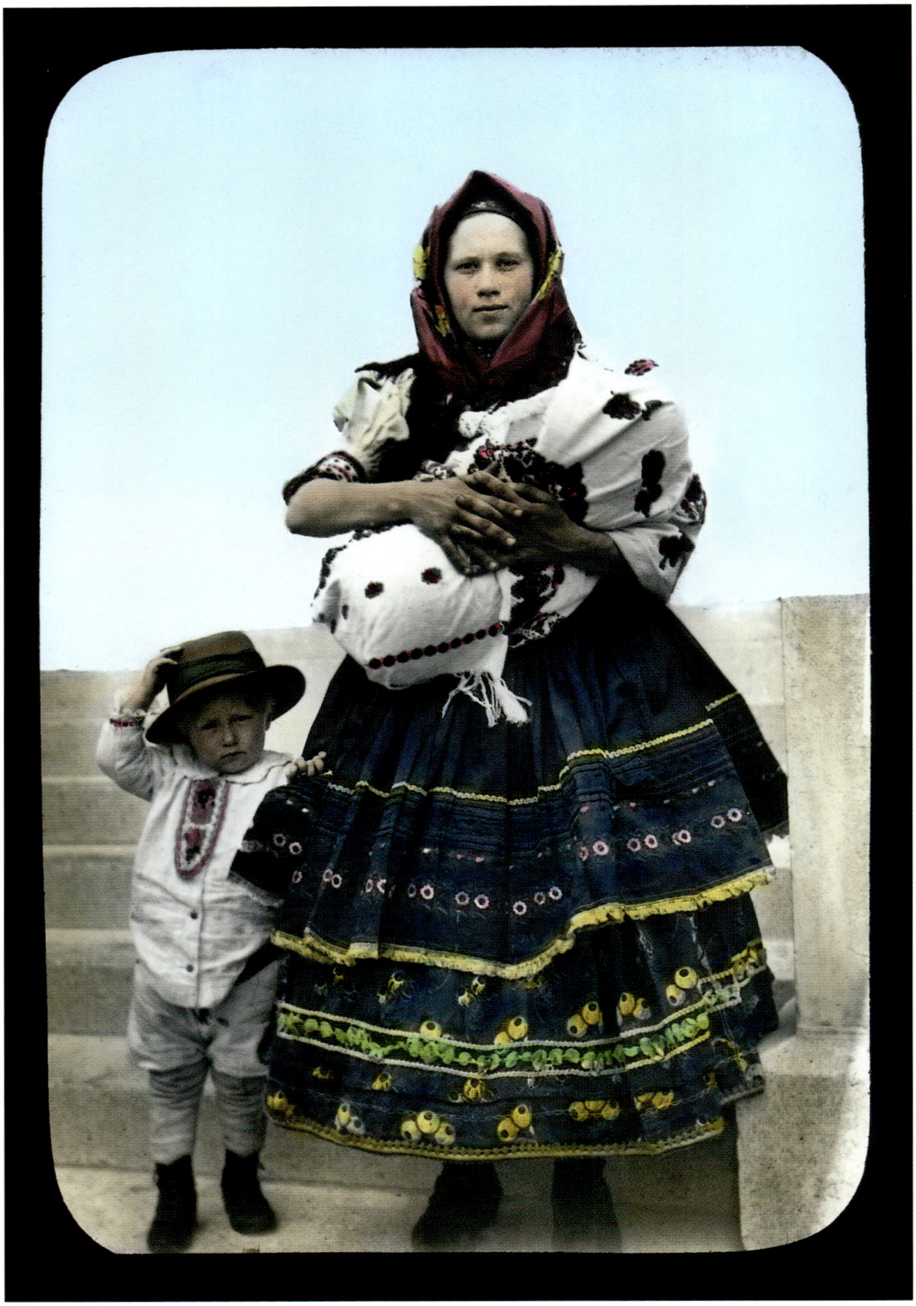

120 Woman with baby and child in national costume, Lithuania, 1890s
121 Family of gypsies, Hungary, c.1900

120 Frau mit Baby und Kind in Nationaltracht, Litauen, 1890er Jahre
121 Zigeunerfamilie, Ungarn, um 1900

120 Femme avec son bébé et son enfant, en costume national, Lithuanie, années 1890
121 Famille de tziganes, Hongrie, vers 1900

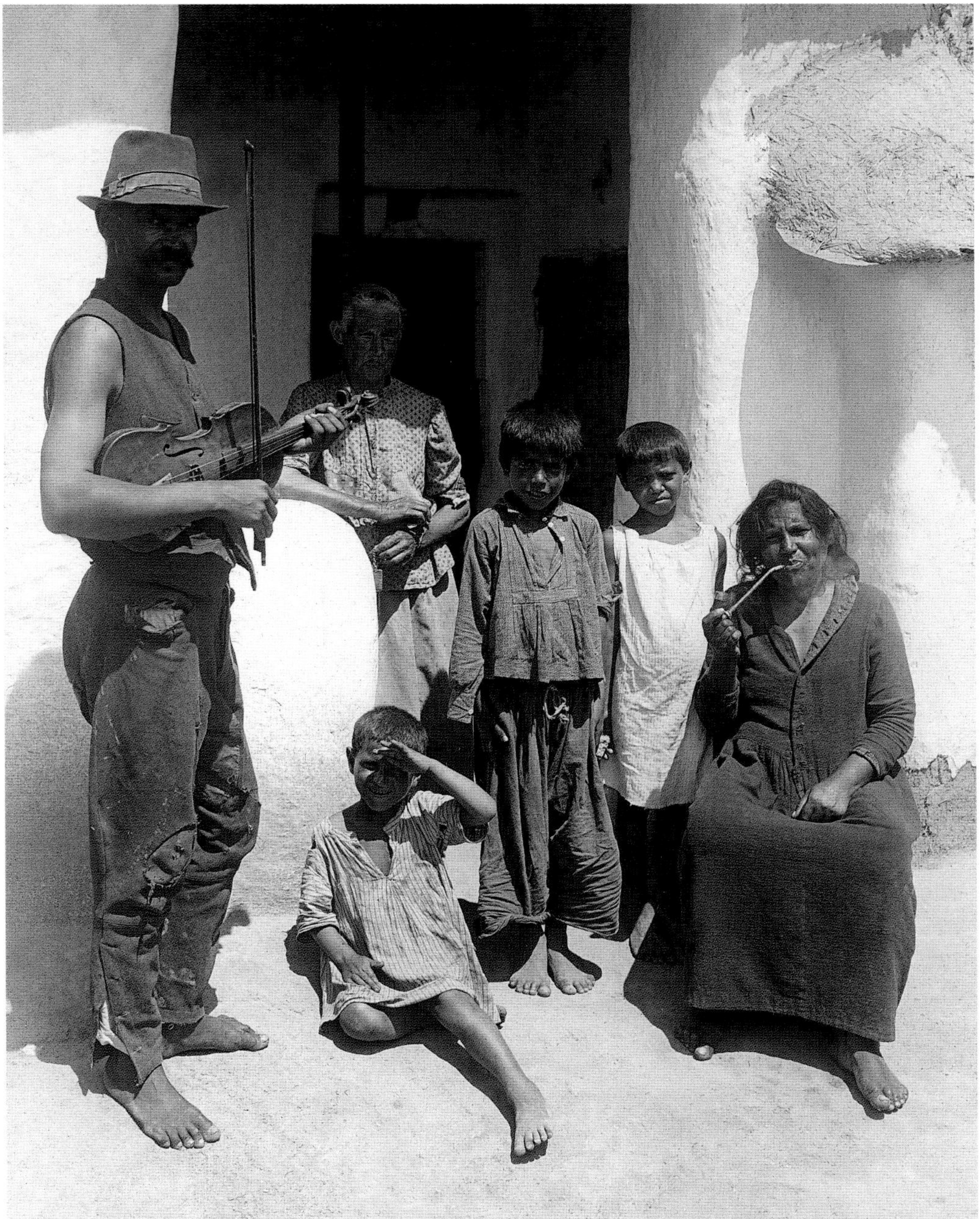

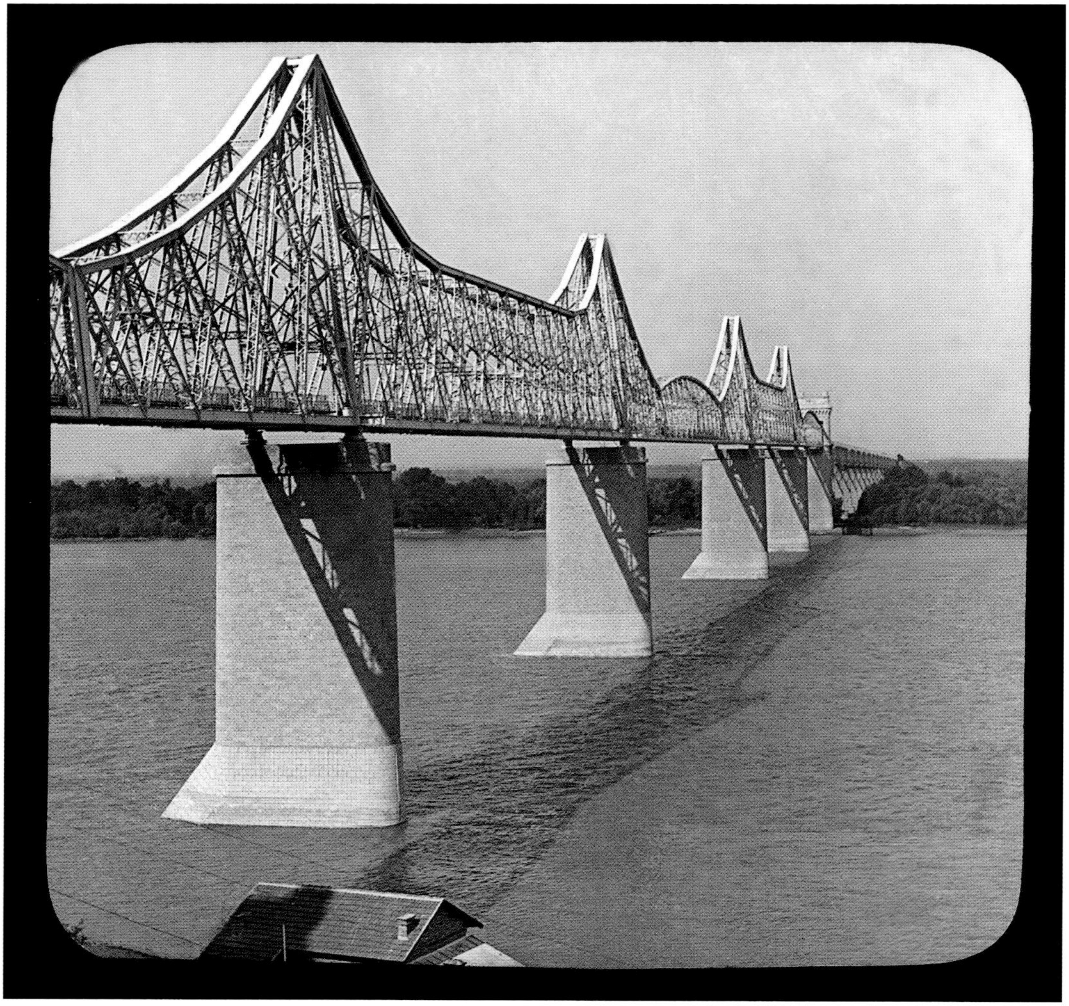

122 Railway Bridge over the River Danube, Czernavoda (Cernavodă), Romania, 1900s

122 Eisenbahnbrücke über die Donau, Czernavoda (Cernavodă), Rumänien, 1900er Jahre

122 Viaduc ferroviaire sur le Danube, Czernavoda (Cernavodă), Roumanie, années 1900

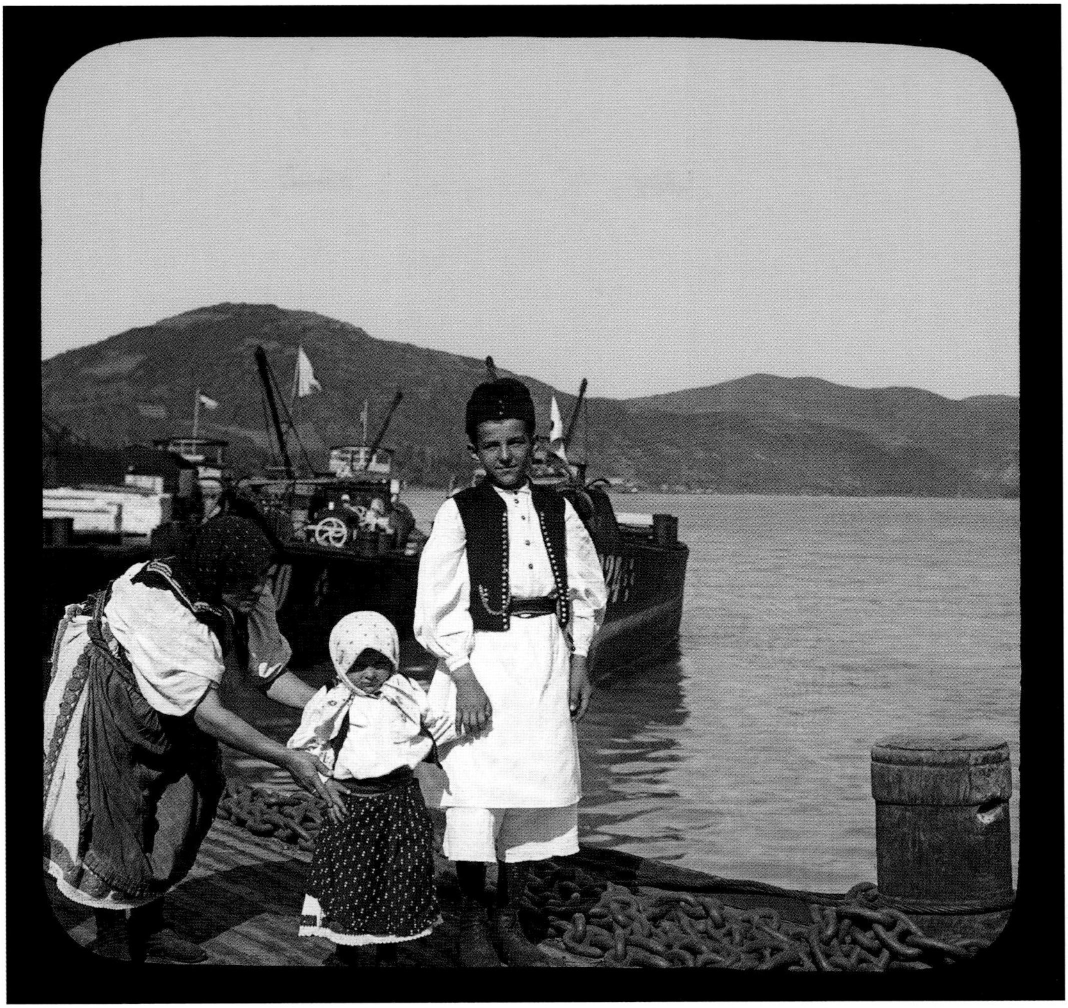

123 Romanian mother and children on the banks of the River Danube, Romania, 1900s

123 Rumänische Mutter und ihre Kinder am Ufer der Donau, Rumänien, 1900er Jahre

123 Mère roumaine et ses enfants sur une rive du Danube, Roumanie, années 1900

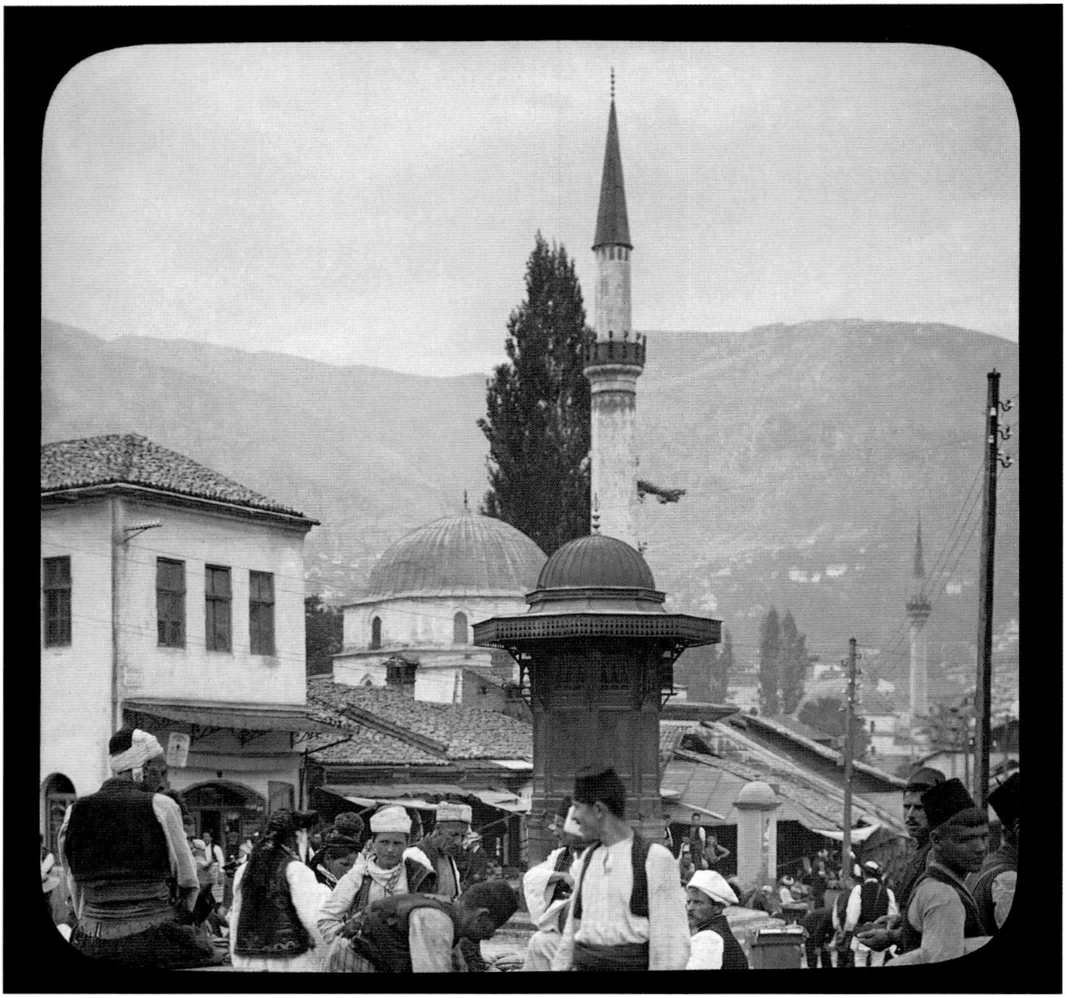

124 People wearing traditional costumes in the marketplace beside the Alipasina Mosque, Sarajevo, Bosnia, 1900s

124 Menschen in traditionellen Trachten auf dem Marktplatz neben der Alipasina-Moschee, Sarajewo, Bosnien, 1900er Jahre

124 Habitants en costume traditionnel sur la place du marché près de la mosquée Alipasina, Sarajevo, Bosnie, années 1900

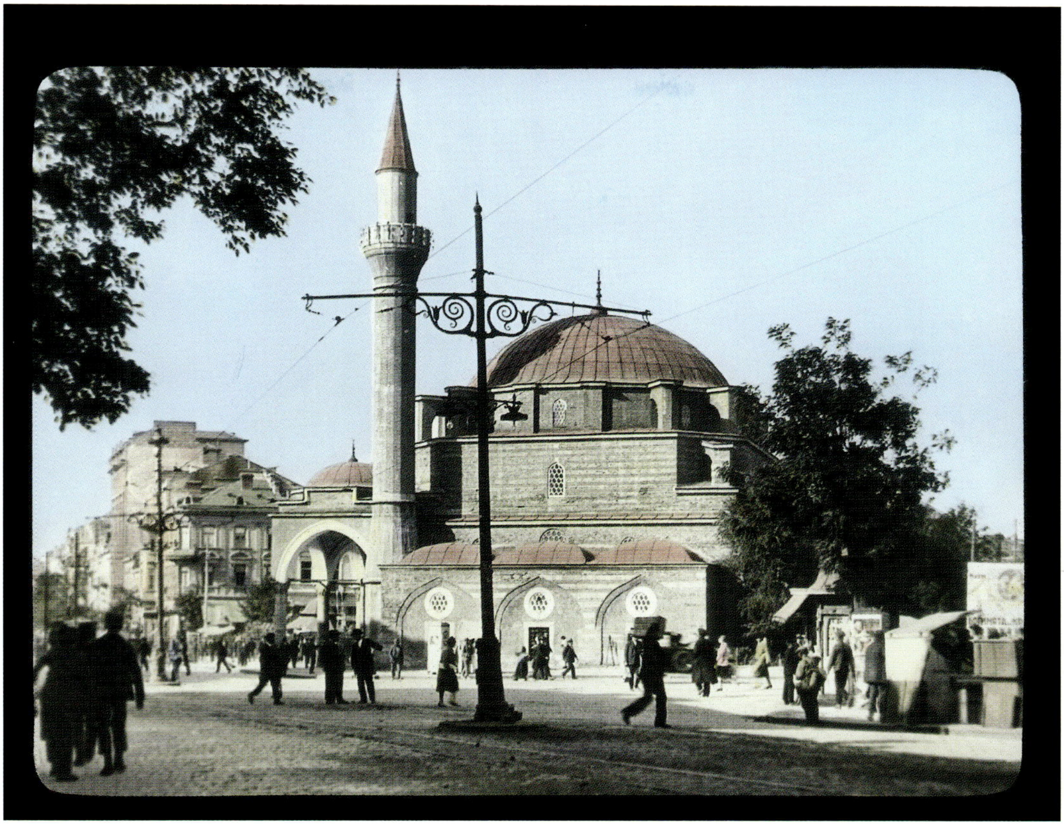

125 Banya Bashi Mosque in Sofia, Bulgaria, 1910s

125 Die Banja-Baschi-Moschee, Sofia, Bulgarien, 1910er Jahre

125 Mosquée Banya Bashi à Sofia, Bulgarie, années 1910

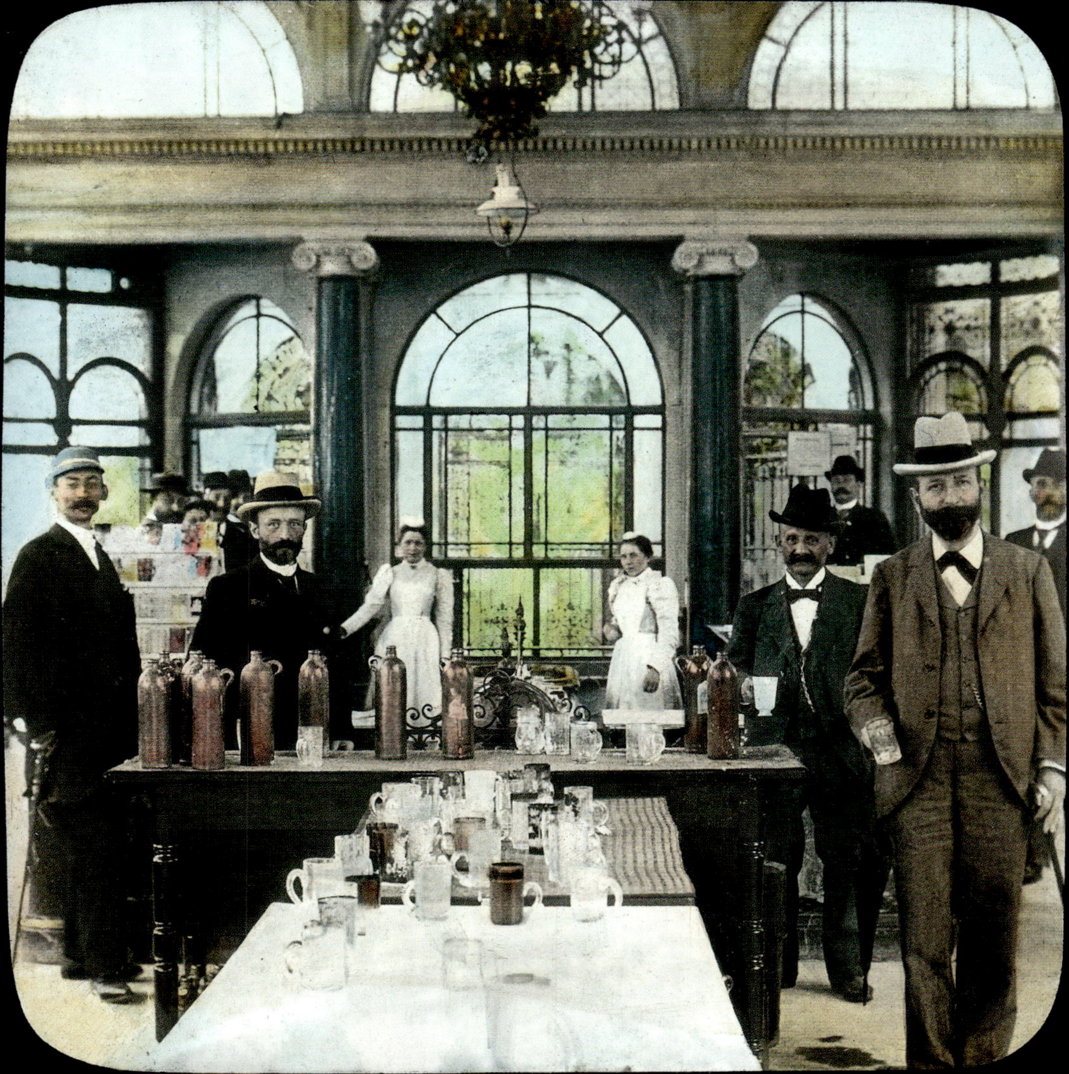

126 Springs in Kochbrunnen, Wiesbaden, Germany, 1880s

126 Der Kochbrunnen (eine Thermalquelle), Wiesbaden, Deutschland, 1880er Jahre

126 Sources à Kochbrunnen, Wiesbaden, Allemagne, années 1880

WESTERN EUROPE

WESTEUROPA · EUROPE DE L'OUEST

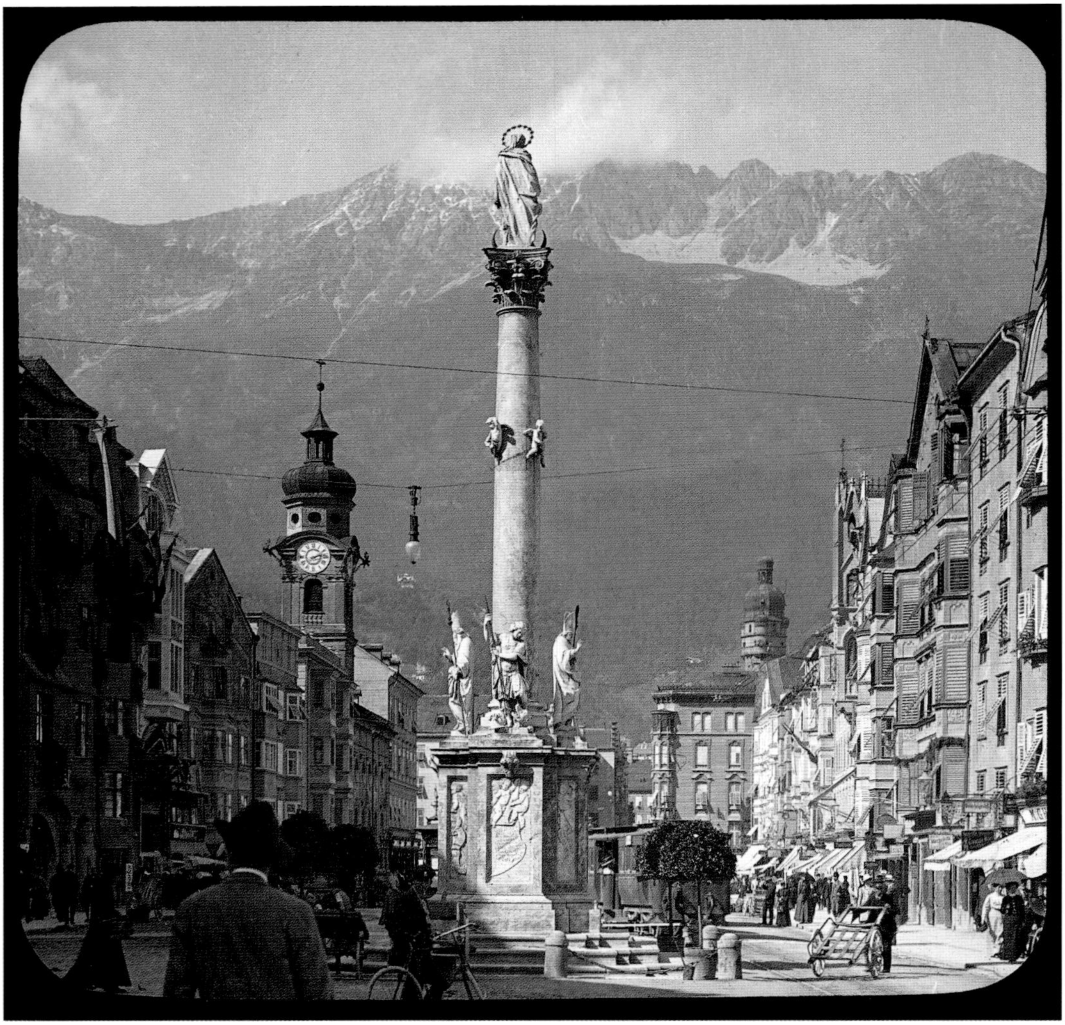

127 Marie Theresa Platz,
Innsbruck, Austria, 1900s

127 Die Maria-Theresien-Straße (Annasäule),
Innsbruck, Österreich,
1900er Jahre

127 Place Marie Theresa,
Innsbruck, Autriche,
années 1900

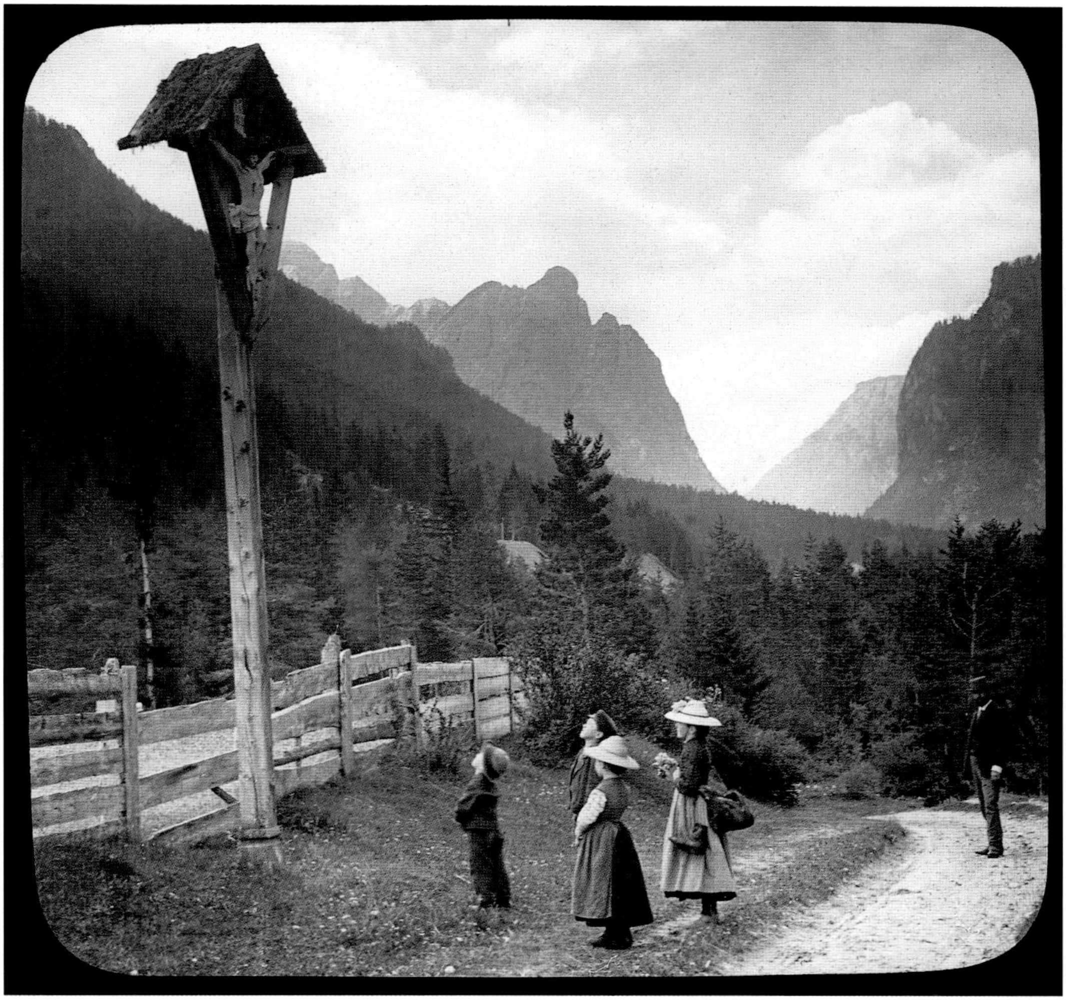

128 School children's morning devotion, Val Ampezzo, Austria, 1900s

128 Schulkinder bei der Morgenandacht, Val Ampezzo, Österreich, 1900er Jahre

128 Prière matinale des écoliers, Val Ampezzo, Autriche, années 1900

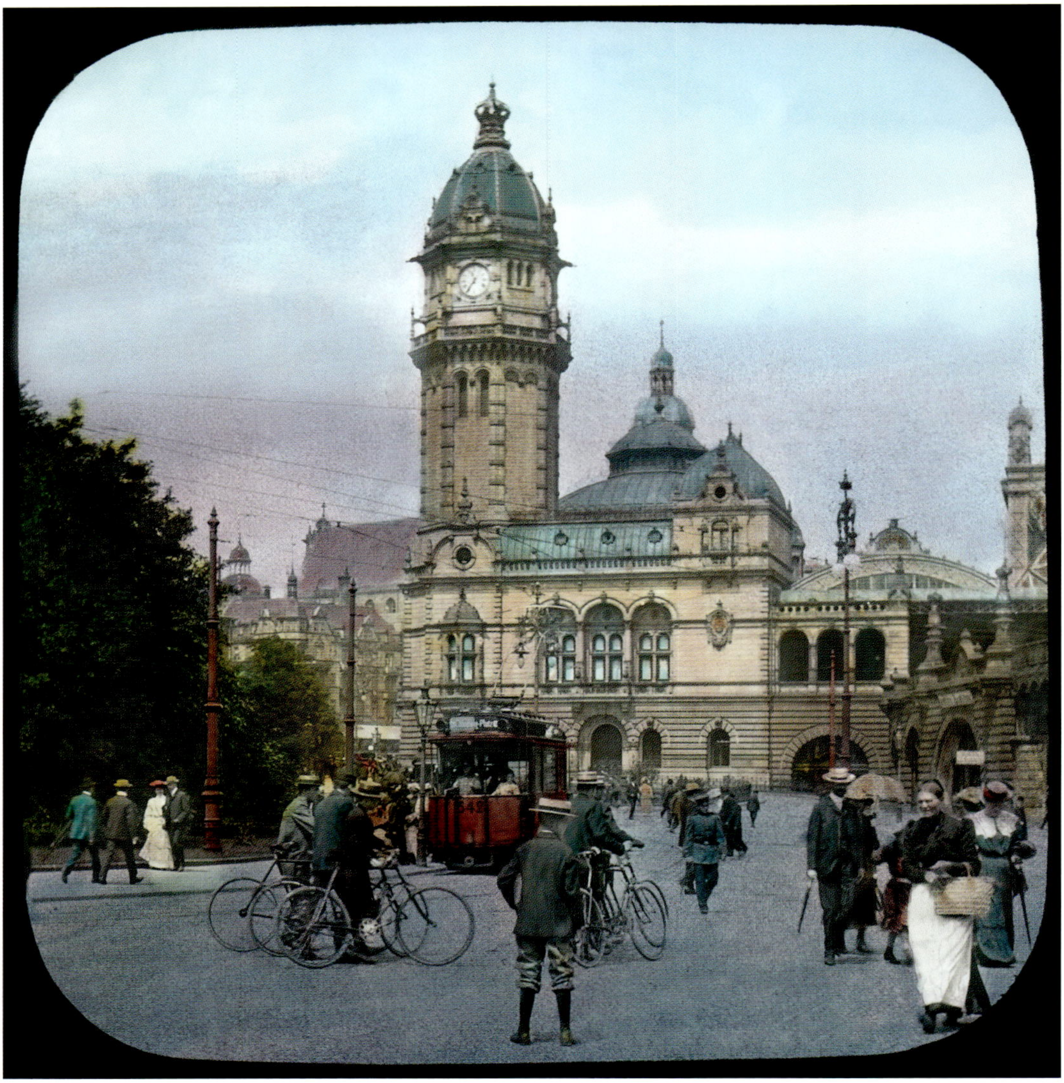

129 Railway station, Cologne, Germany, 1890s
130 Public gardens, Düsseldorf, Germany, 1890s

129 Der Hauptbahnhof, Köln, Deutschland, 1890er Jahre
130 Der Hofgarten, Düsseldorf, Deutschland, 1890er Jahre

129 Gare de chemin de fer, Cologne, Allemagne, années 1890
130 Jardin public, Düsseldorf, Allemagne, années 1890

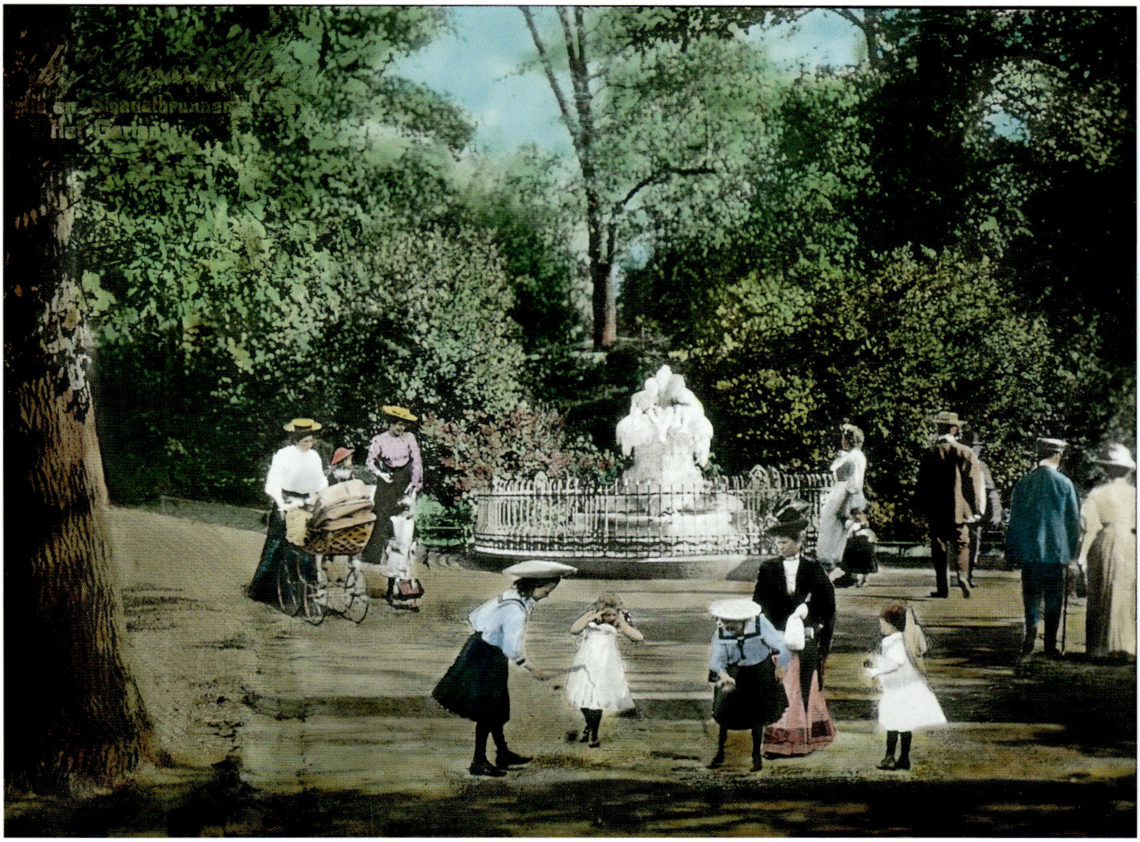

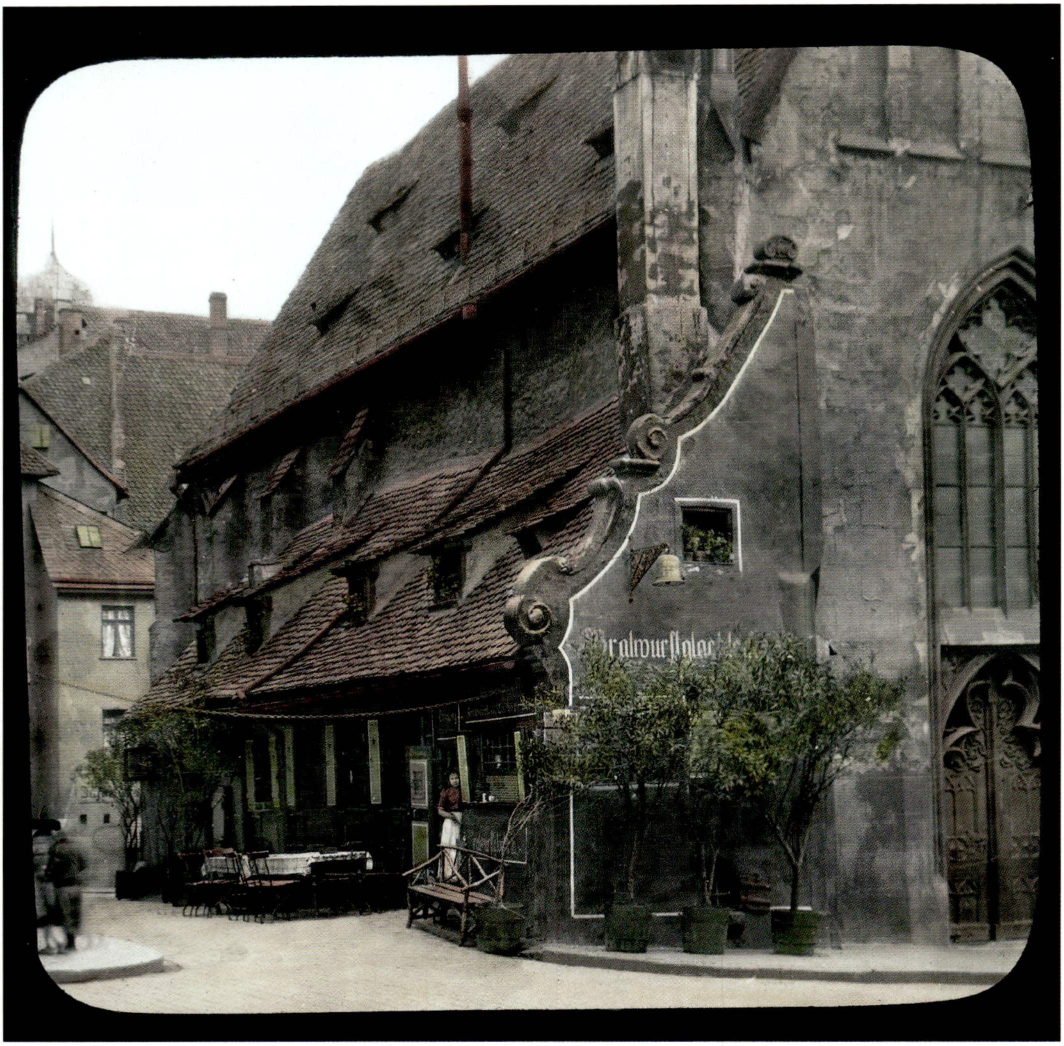

131 Bratwurst Glöcklein, Nuremberg, Germany, 1880s

131 Das Bratwurstglöcklein, Nürnberg, Deutschland, 1880er Jahre

131 Bratwurst Glöcklein, Nuremberg, Allemagne, années 1880

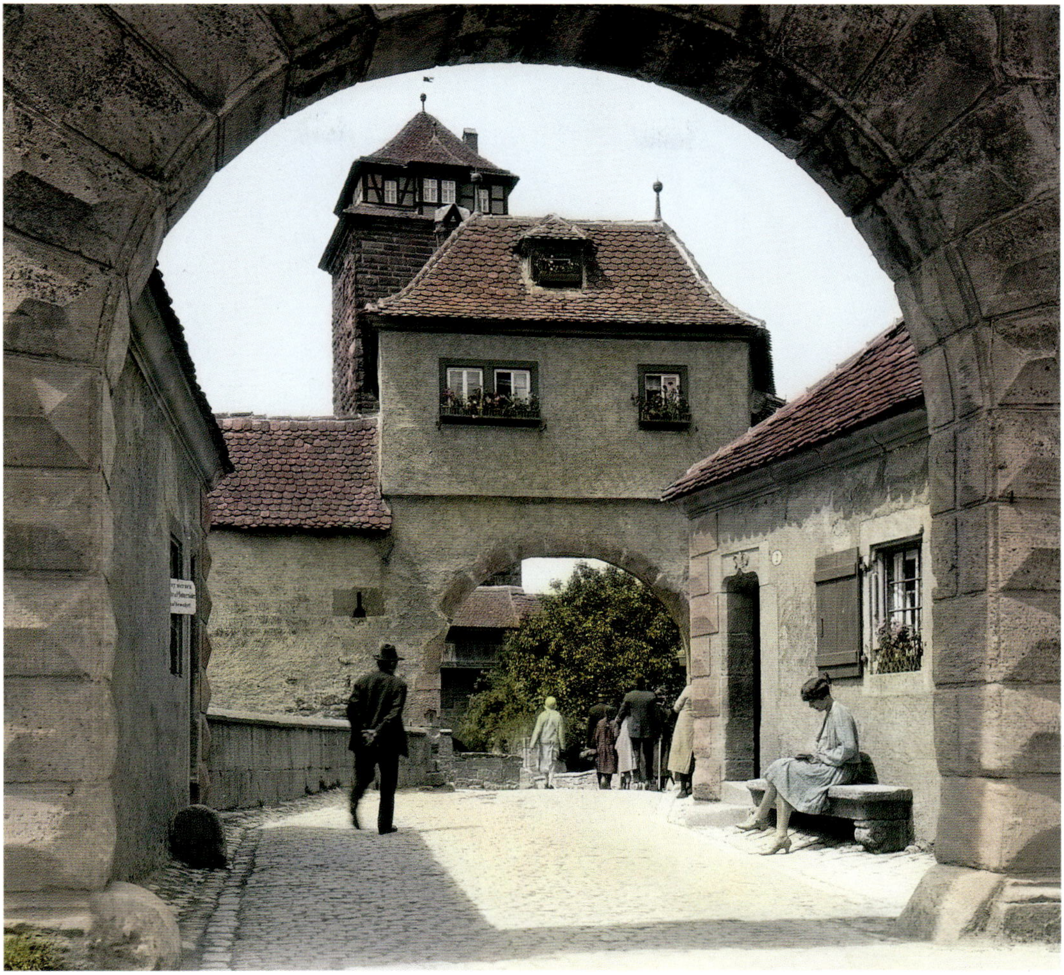

132 Gatehouse showing typical German architecture, Germany, 1920s

132 Torhaus in typischer deutscher Bauweise, Deutschland, 1920er Jahre

132 Porte à l'architecture typiquement germanique, Allemagne, années 1920

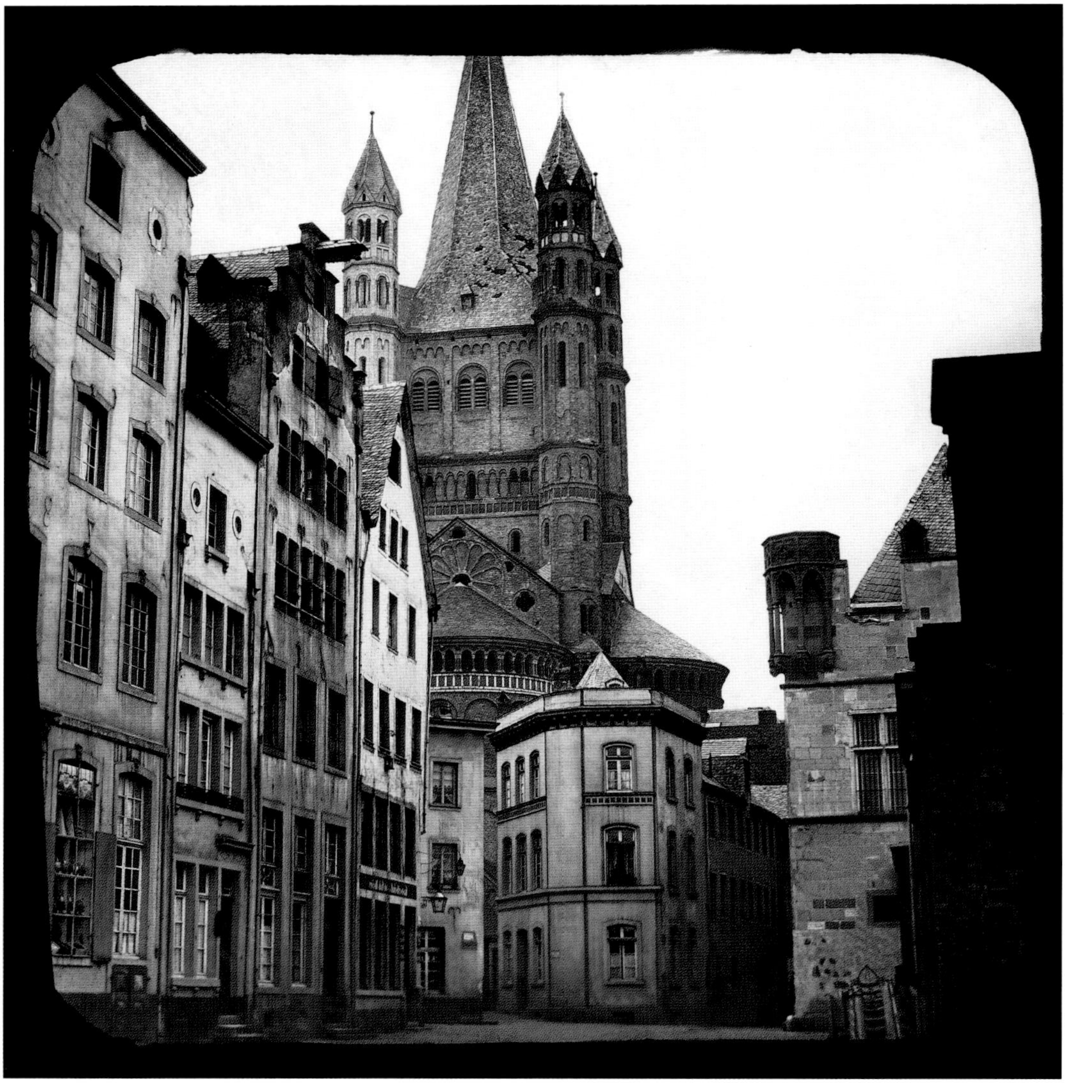

133 Groß St. Martin (Great St. Martin's Church), Cologne, Germany, 1870s
134 The Dom (Cathedral), Cologne, Germany, 1880s

133 Groß St. Martin, Köln, Deutschland, 1870er Jahre
134 Der Dom, Köln, Deutschland, 1880er Jahre

133 Groß St. Martin (église du Grand Saint-Martin), Cologne, Allemagne, années 1870
134 Dom (cathédrale) de Cologne, Allemagne, années 1880

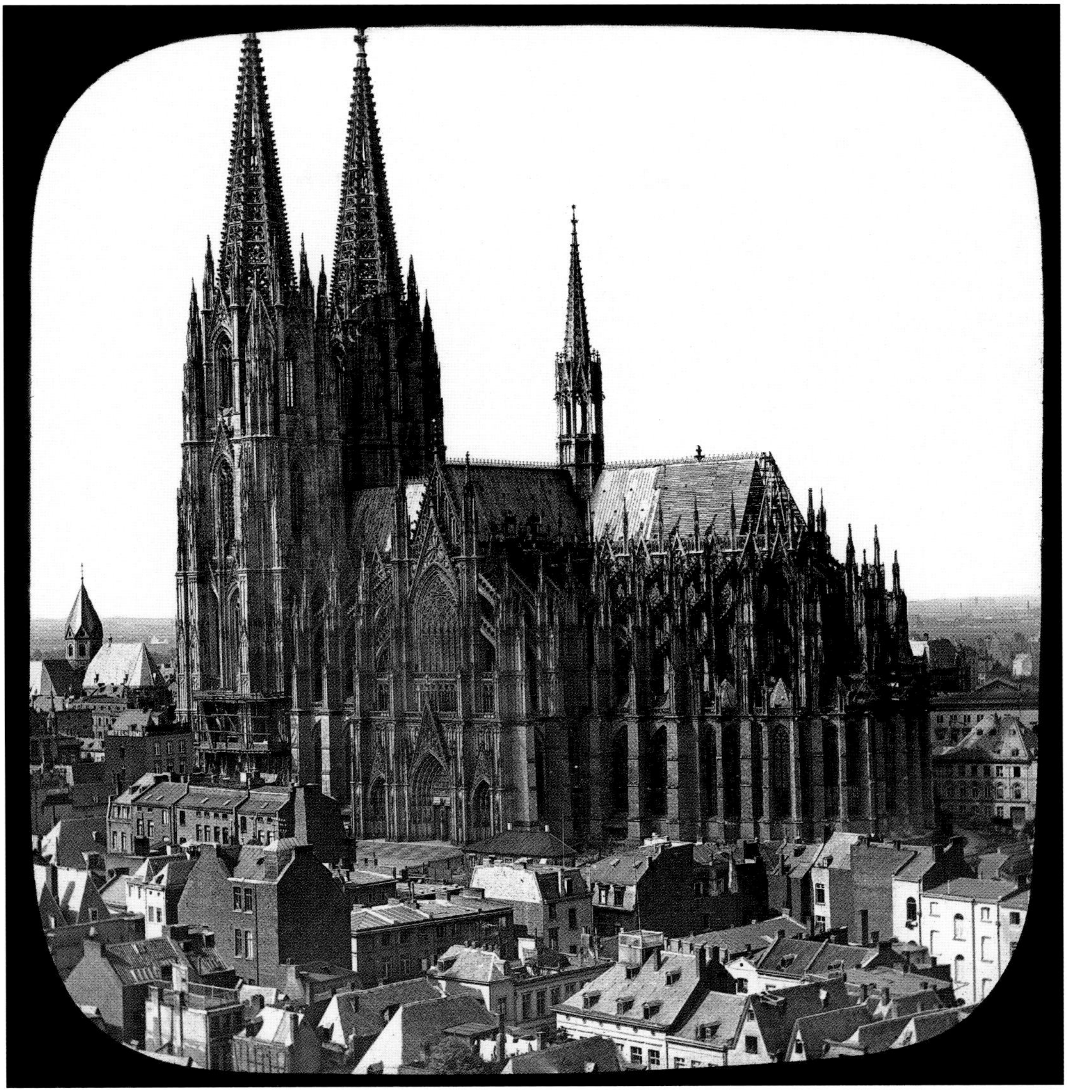

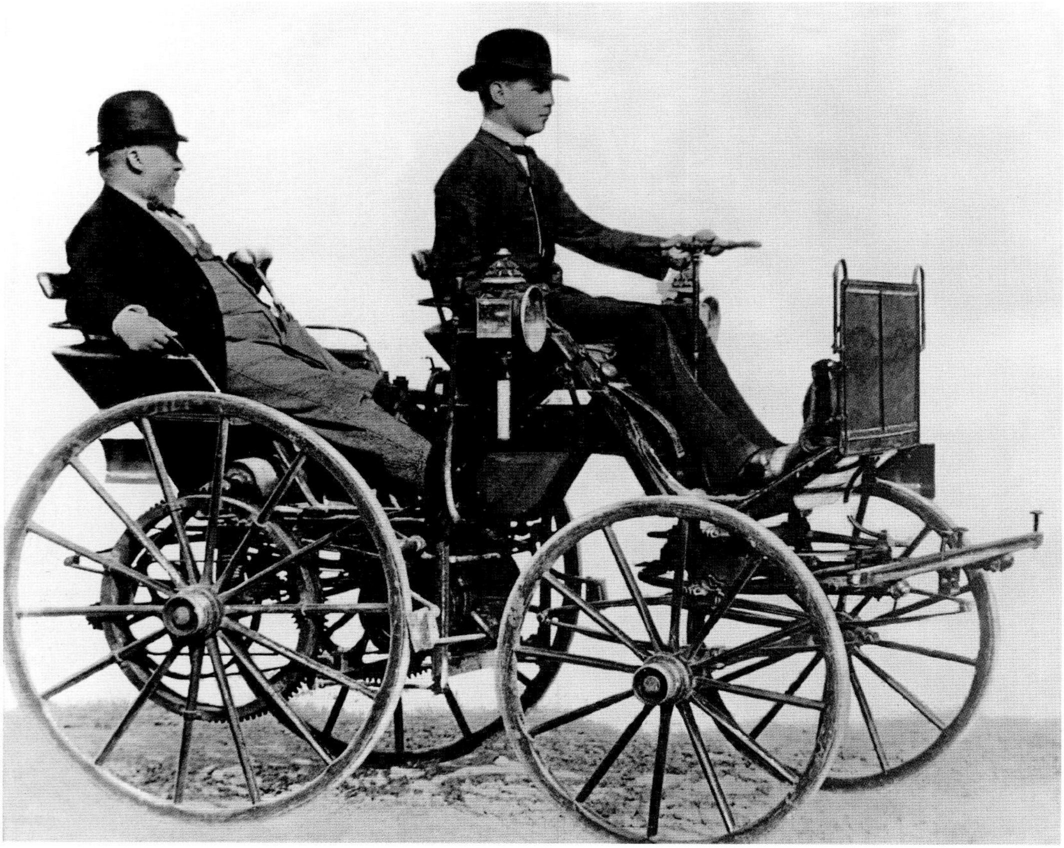

135 Gottlieb Daimler being driven by his son, Wilhelm in his Daimler-Wagen prototype (the world's first four-wheeled automobile), Germany, 1886

135 Gottlieb Daimler wird von seinem Sohn Wilhelm im Prototyp seiner Motorkutsche chauffiert (das erste Vierradauto der Welt), Deutschland, 1886

135 Gottlieb Daimler conduit par son fils Guillaume dans un prototype de véhicule Daimler (la première automobile à quatre roues du monde), Allemagne, 1886

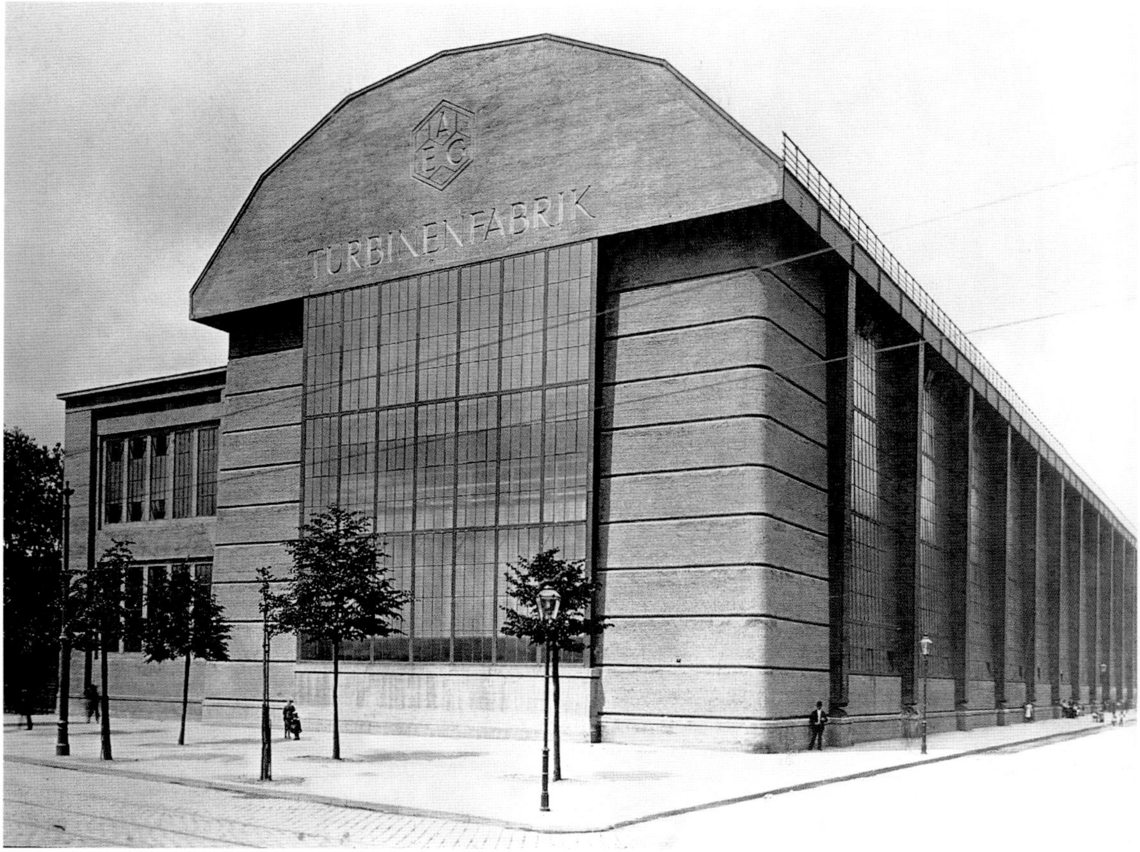

136 AEG turbine hall (designed by Peter Behrens), Berlin, Germany, 1909

136 Die AEG-Turbinenhalle (entworfen von Peter Behrens), Berlin, Deutschland, 1909

136 L'usine de turbines AEG (dessinée par Peter Behrens), Berlin, Allemagne, 1909

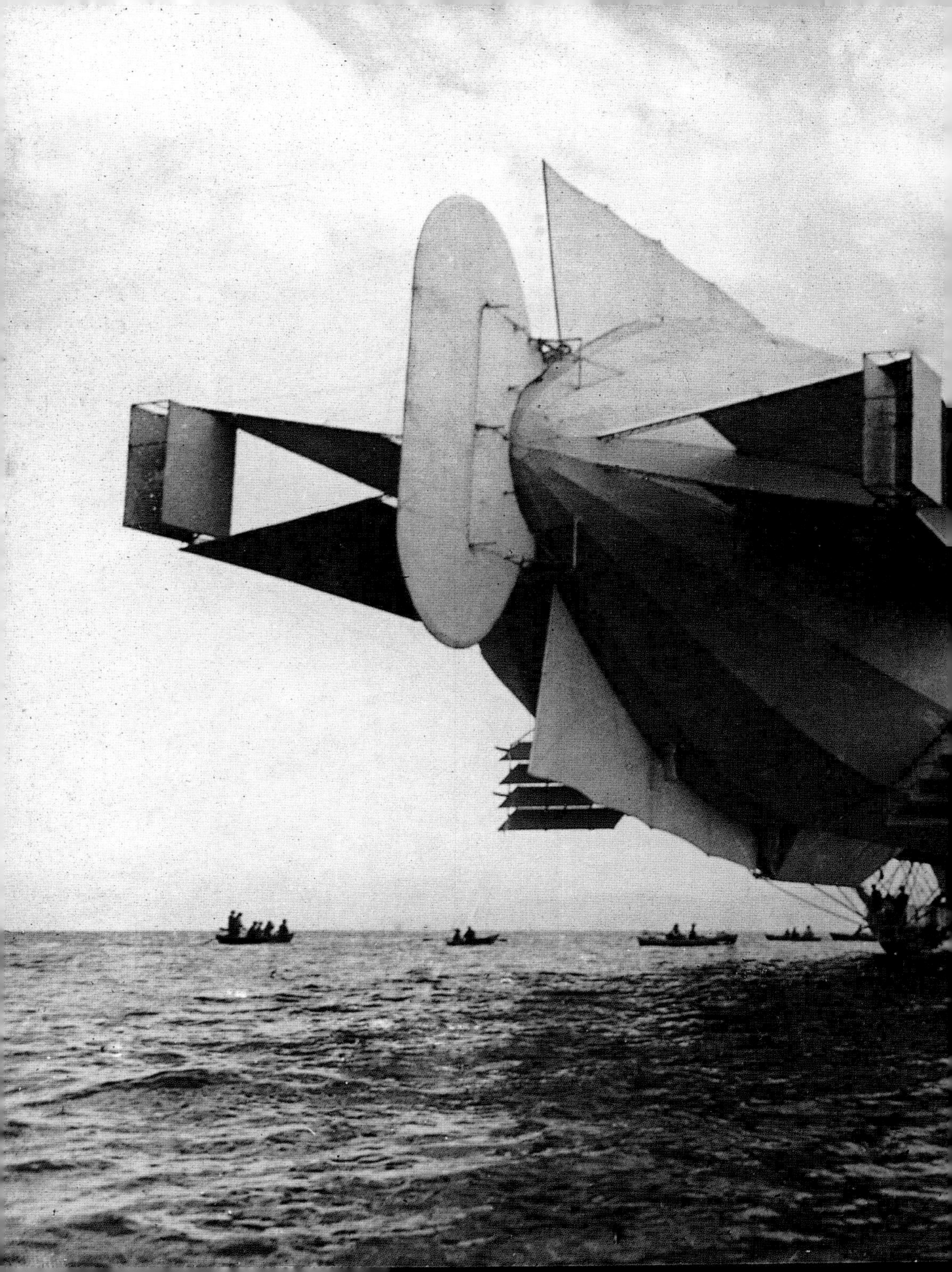

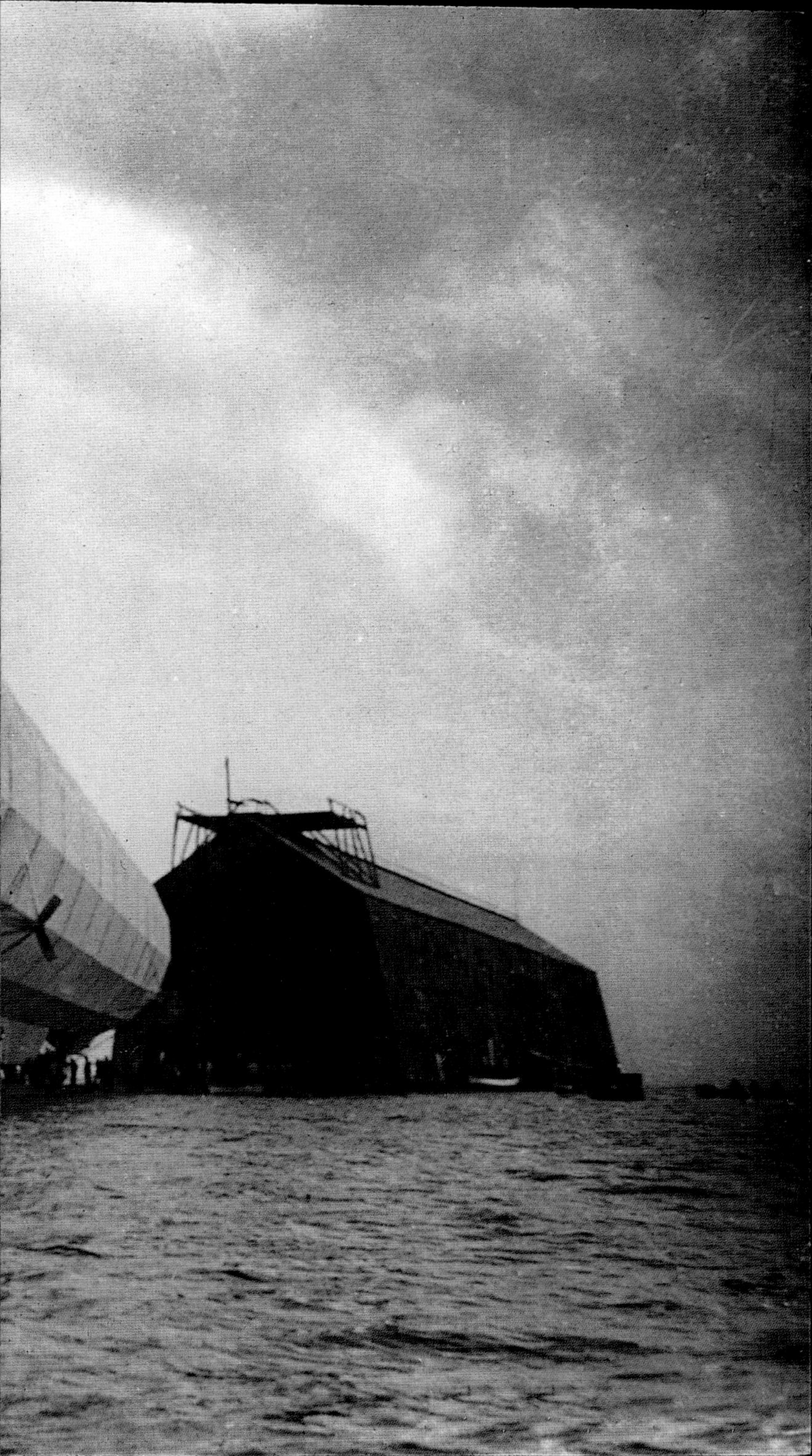

137 Zeppelin Model LZ3 Airship entering hangar on Lake Constance, Friedrichshafen, Germany, 1908

137 Das Luftschiff Zeppelin LZ3 wird in den Hangar auf dem Bodensee verbracht, Friedrichshafen, Deutschland, 1908

137 Un dirigeable Zeppelin modèle LZ3 entre dans un hangar sur le lac de Constance. Friedrichshafen, Allemagne, 1908

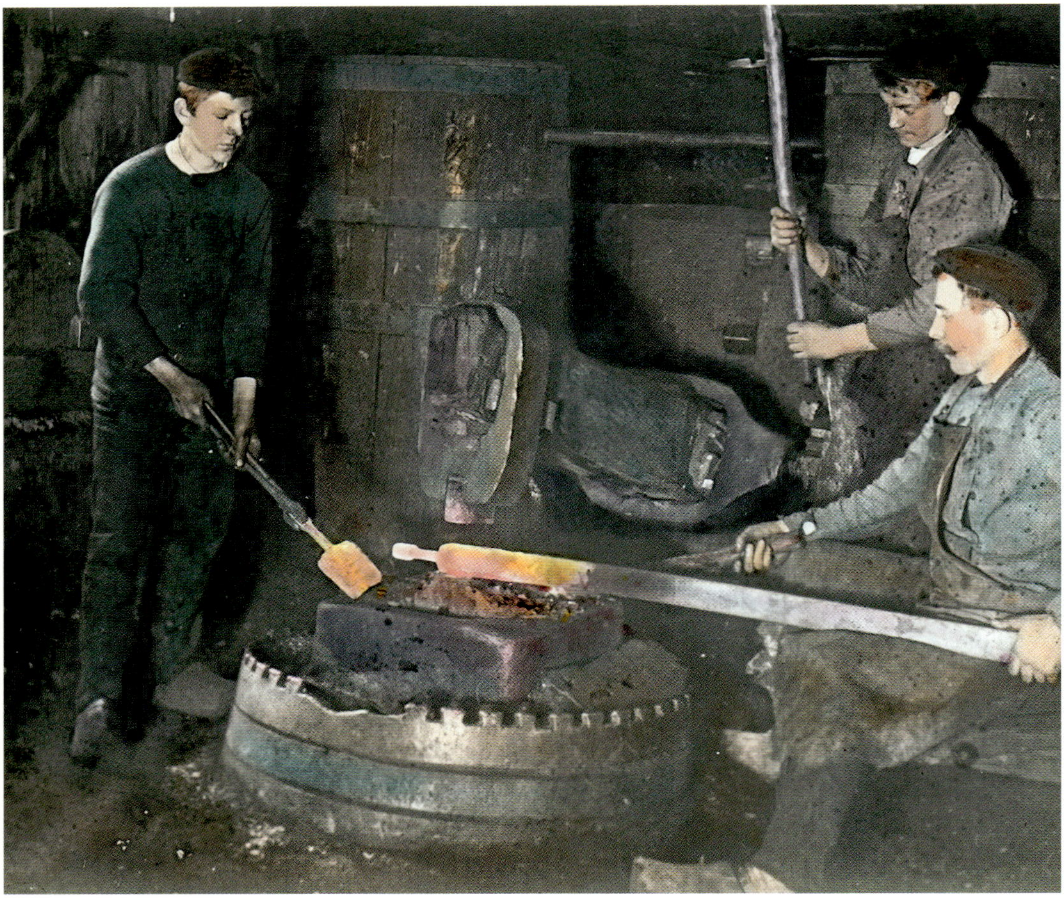

138 Ironworks, Germany, 1880s
139 "Union" blast furnace, Dortmund, Germany,1880s

138 Schmiedearbeiten, Deutschland, 1880er Jahre
139 Hochofen der „Dortmunder Union", Dortmund, Deutschland, 1880er Jahre

138 Ferronnerie. Allemagne, années 1880
139 Haut-fourneau "Union" à Dortmund, Allemagne, années 1880

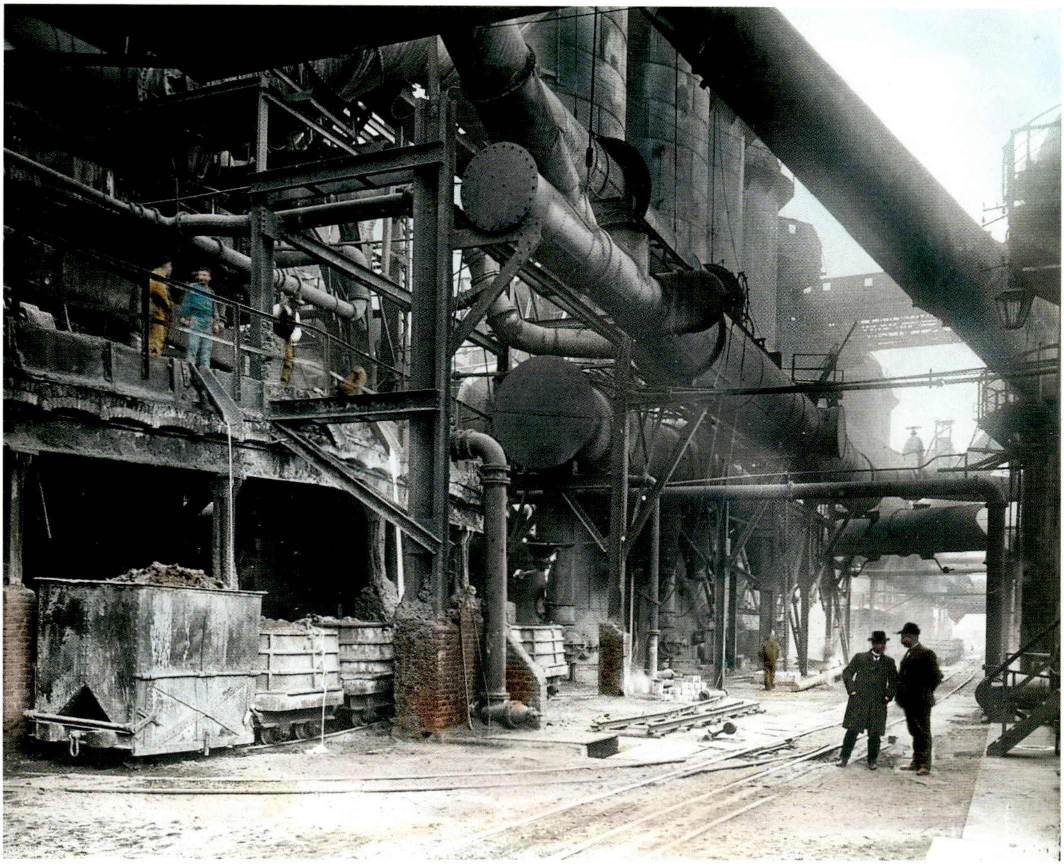

140 The Rhein-Ems Canal with the Prosper colliery in Bottrop, Germany, 1880s

140 Der Dortmund-Ems-Kanal mit dem Bergwerk Prosper-Haniel, Bottrop, Deutschland, 1880er Jahre

140 Le canal du Rhin à l'Ems et les houillères Prosper à Bottrop. Allemagne, années 1880

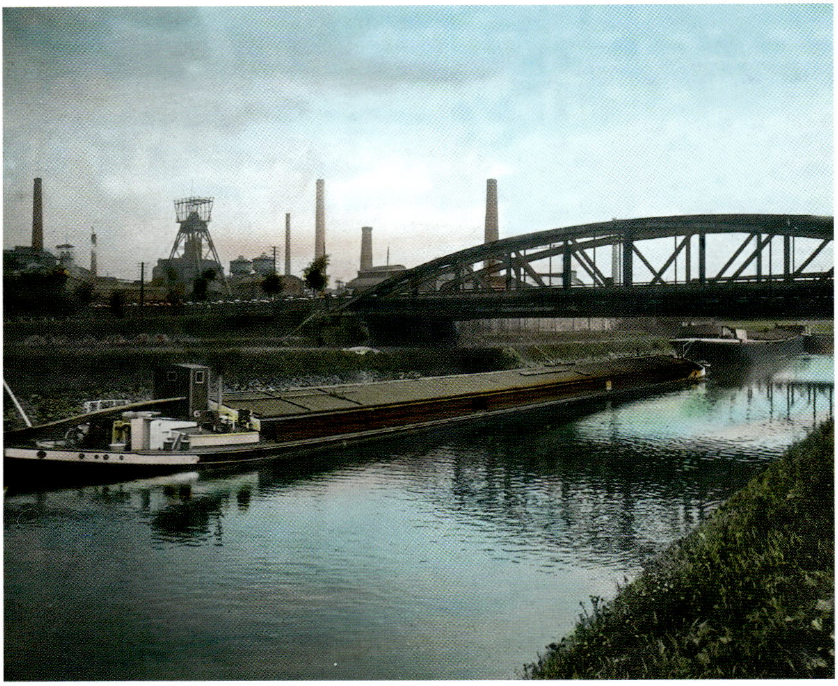

141 Wire factory, Hamm, Germany, 1880s

141 Drahtfabrik, Hamm, Deutschland, 1880er Jahre

141 Usine de câbles à Hamm, Allemagne, années 1880

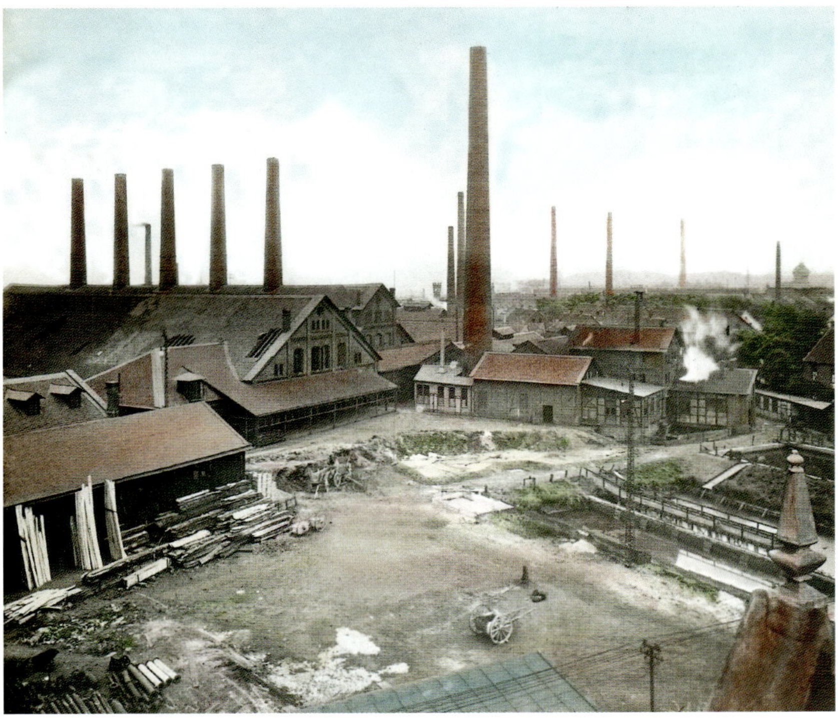

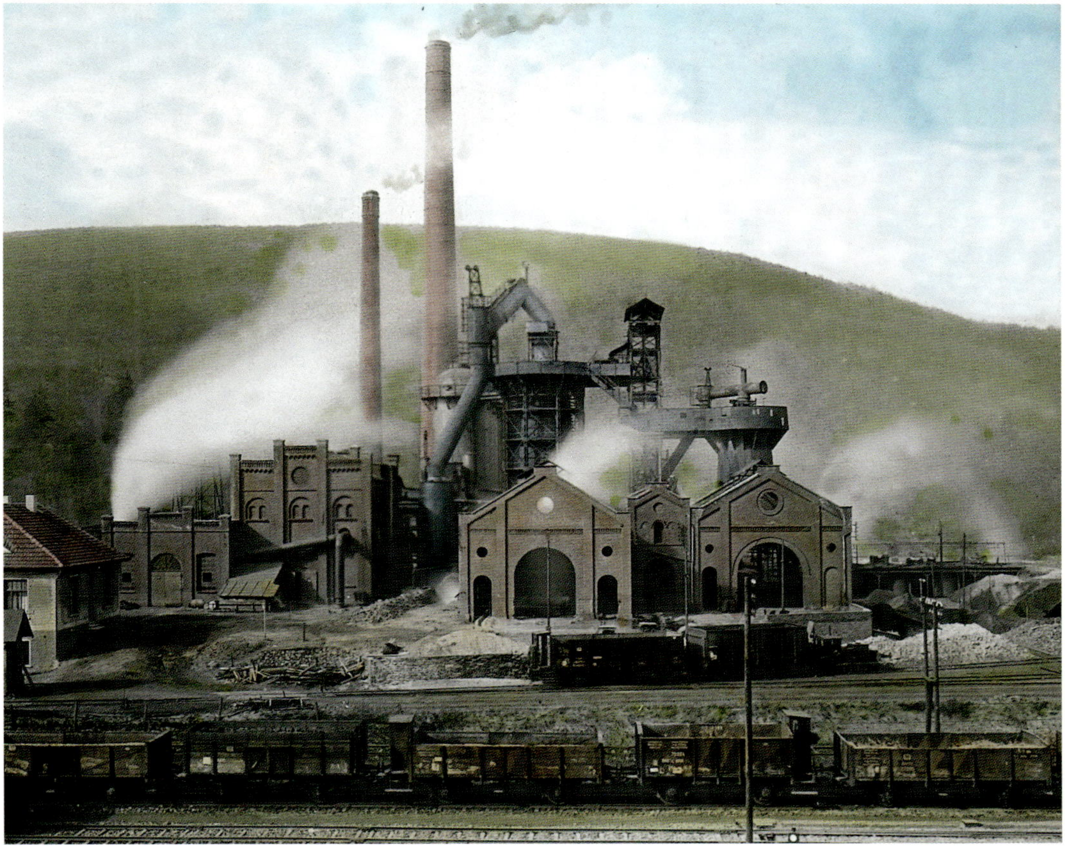

142 Marienhütte ironworks at Eiserfeld, Germany, 1880s

142 Die Marienhütte, Eiserfeld, Deutschland, 1880er Jahre

142 Aciéries Marienhütte à Eiserfeld, Allemagne, années 1880

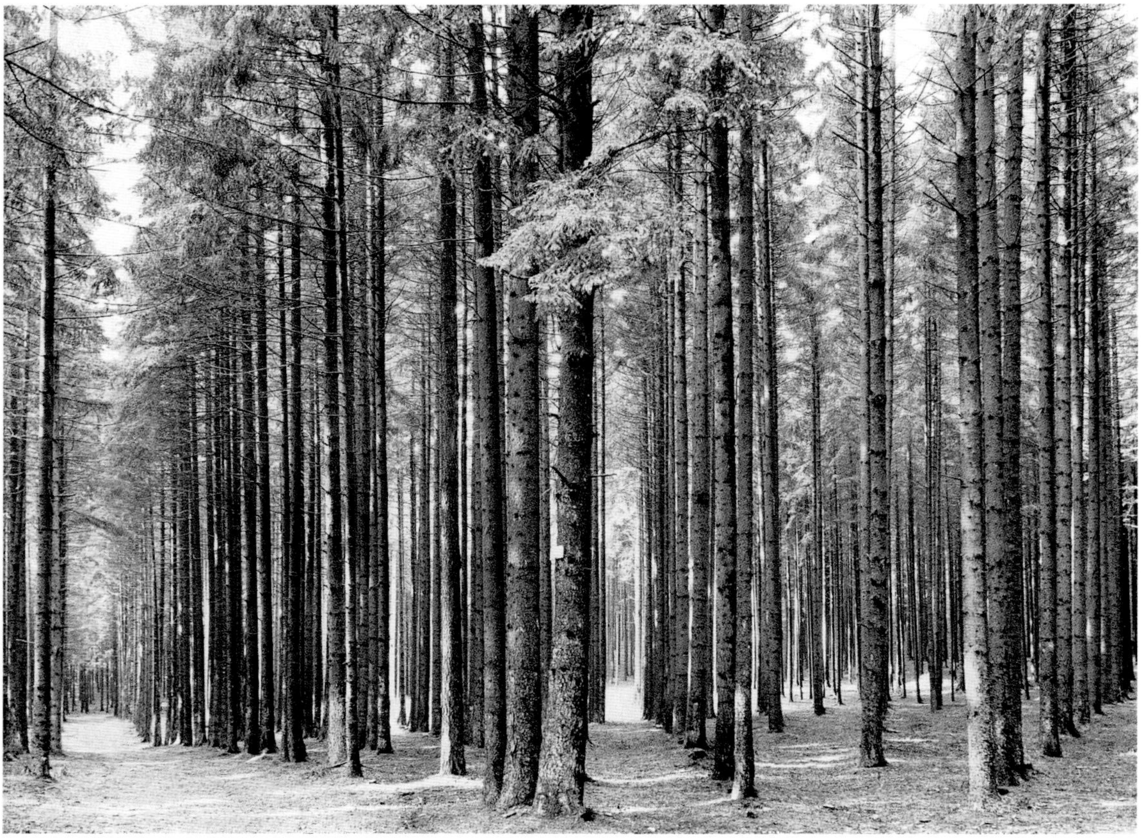

143 Forest plantation of spruce with roads radiating out from a common centre, near Eisenach in the Thuringian Forest, Germany, 1904

143 Fichtenschonung mit Wegen, die von einer gemeinsamen Mitte strahlenförmig abzweigen, Thüringer Wald nahe Eisenach, Deutschland, 1904

143 Allées radiales dans une plantation d'épicéas près d'Eisenach, dans la forêt thuringienne. Allemagne, 1904

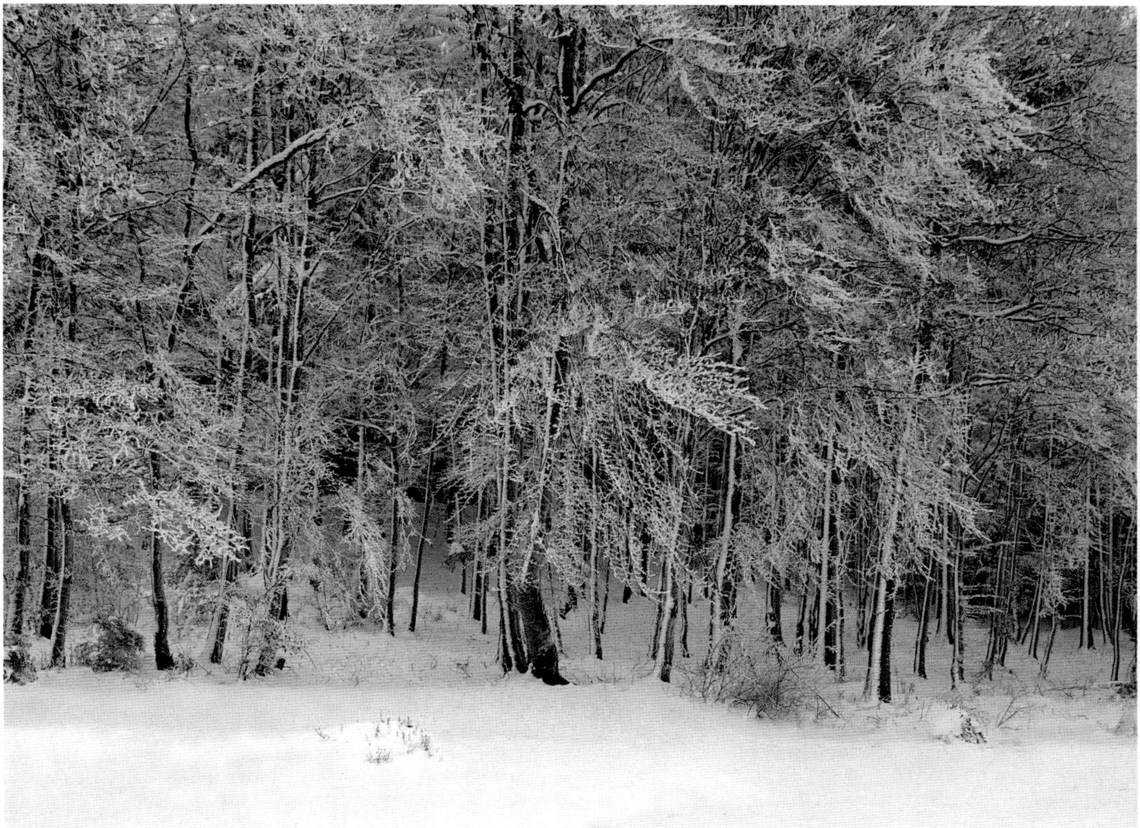

144 Trees covered with frost, near Starnberger-See, Bavaria, Germany, c.1900

144 Mit Raureif bedeckte Bäume, nahe Starnberger See, Bayern, Deutschland, um 1900

144 Arbres recouverts de givre près du lac de Starnberg, en Bavière. Allemagne, vers 1900

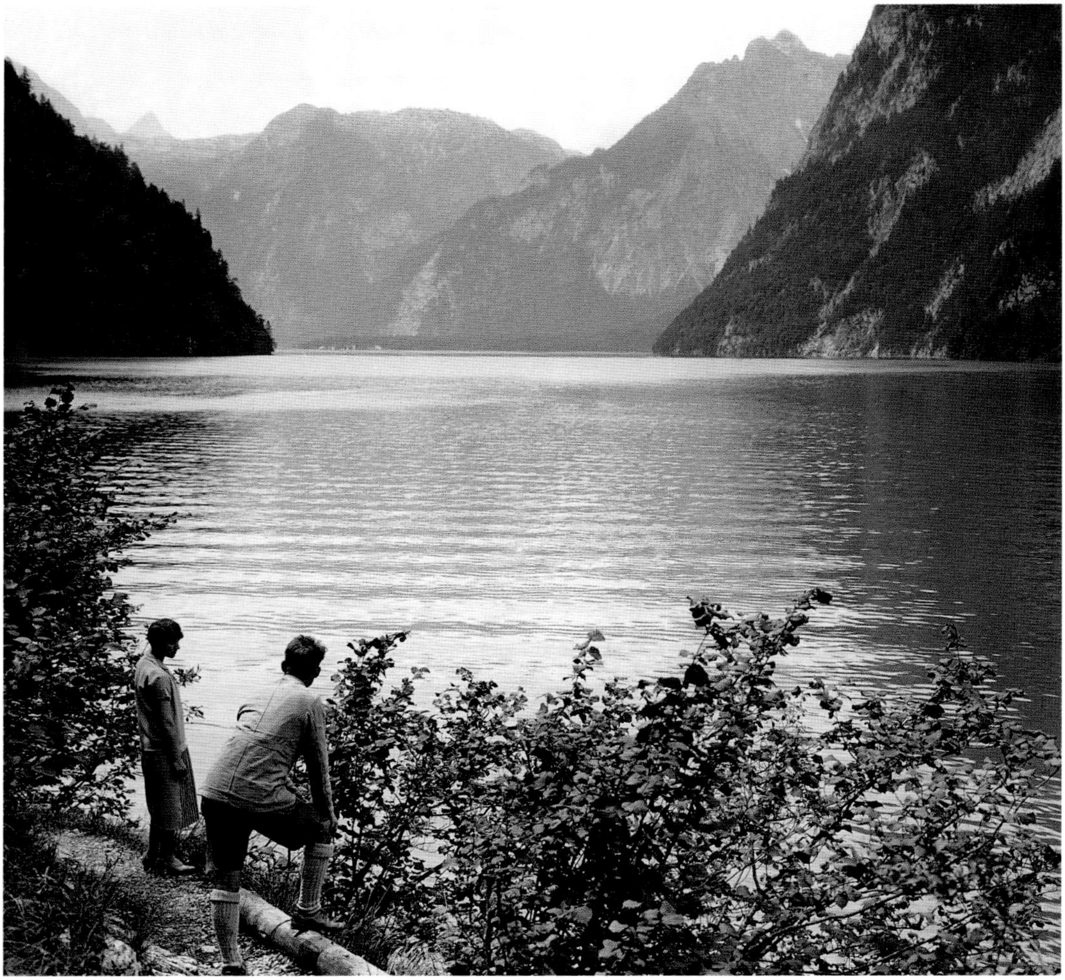

145 Mountains rising from Lake, Konigsee, Bavaria, Germany, 1927

145 Berge, die sich aus dem See erheben, Königssee, Bayern, Deutschland, 1927

145 Montagnes dominant les eaux du Königsee. Bavière, Allemagne, 1927

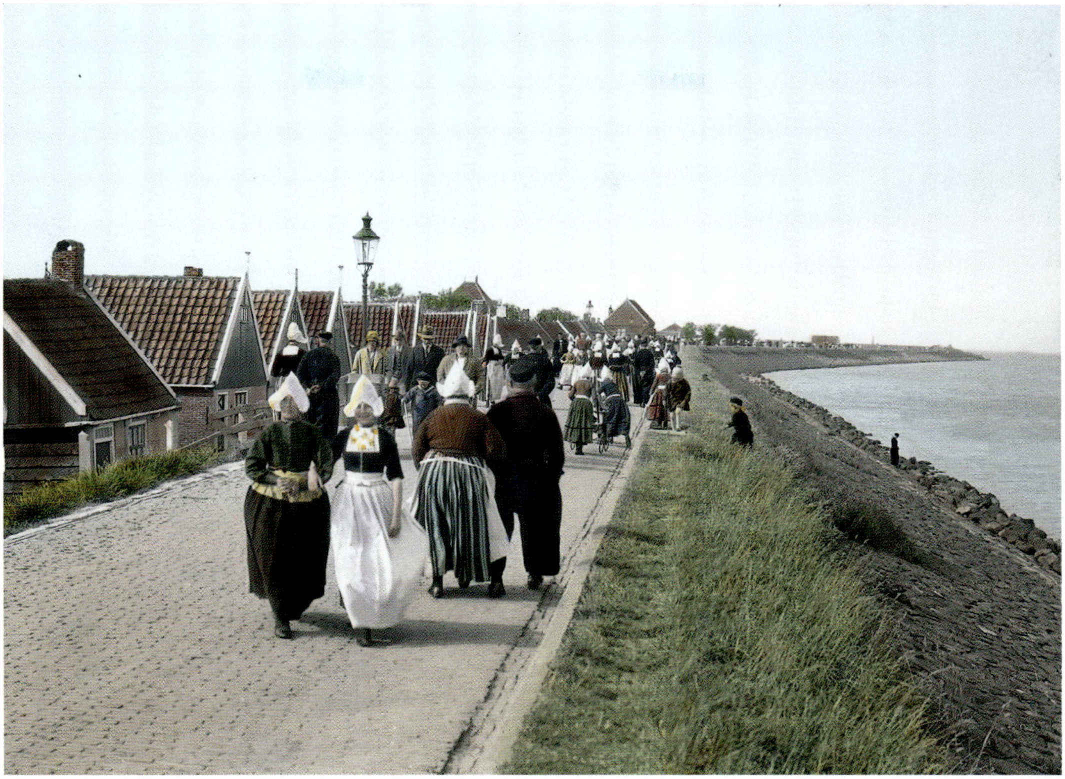

146 Promenading along the dyke (with houses built below the dyke), Volendam, Holland, 1928

146 Spaziergänger auf dem Deich (die Häuser sind unterhalb des Deichs errichtet), Volendam, Niederlande, 1928

146 Promenade sur la digue (et maisons en contre-bas), Volendam, Hollande, 1928

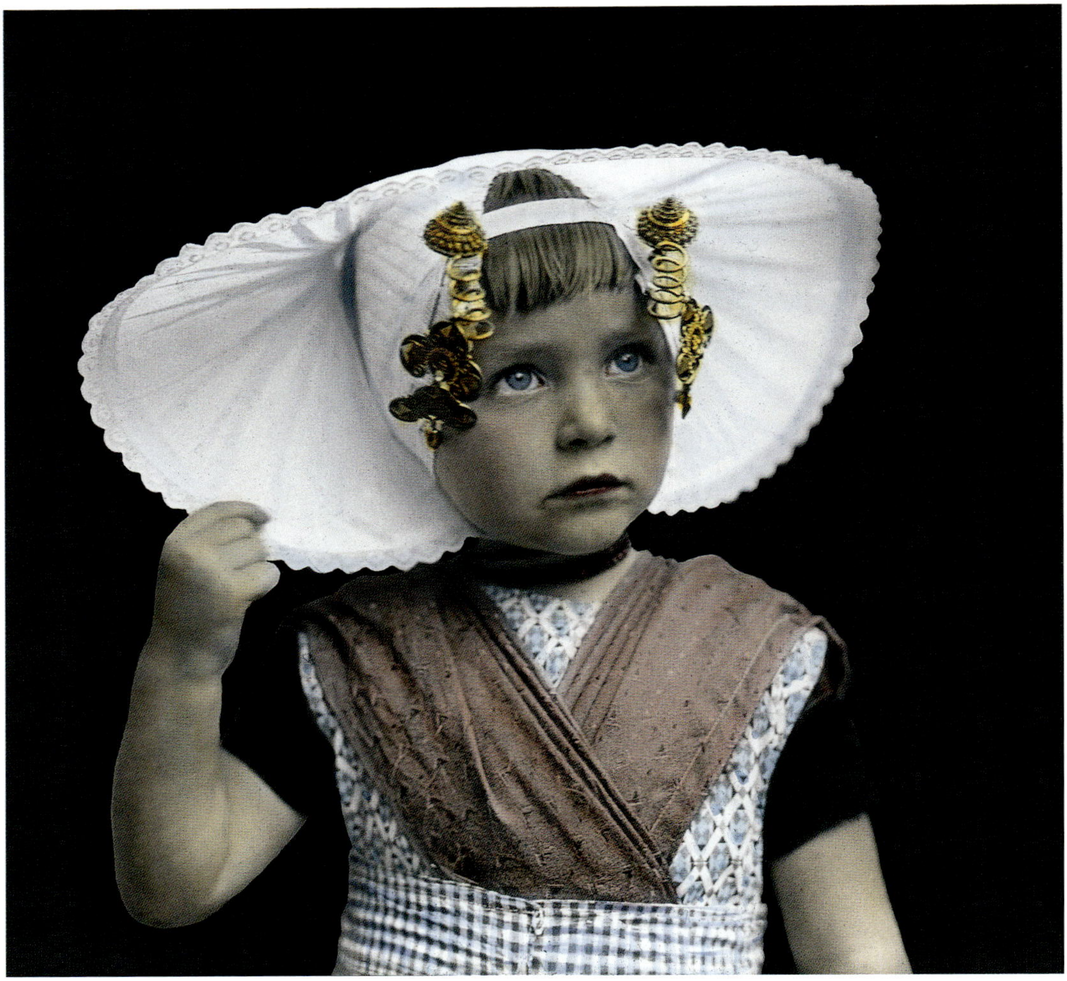

147 Girl wearing a Stiff Cap with Ornaments, Middleburg, The Netherlands, 1900s
148 Dutch girl, Holland, c.1900

147 Mädchen mit steifer Haube und Verzierungen, Middelburg, Niederlande, 1900er Jahre
148 Holländisches Mädchen, Niederlande, um 1900

147 Fillette portant une coiffe rigide ornementée, Middleburg, Pays-Bas, années 1900
148 Jeune fille, Hollande, vers 1900

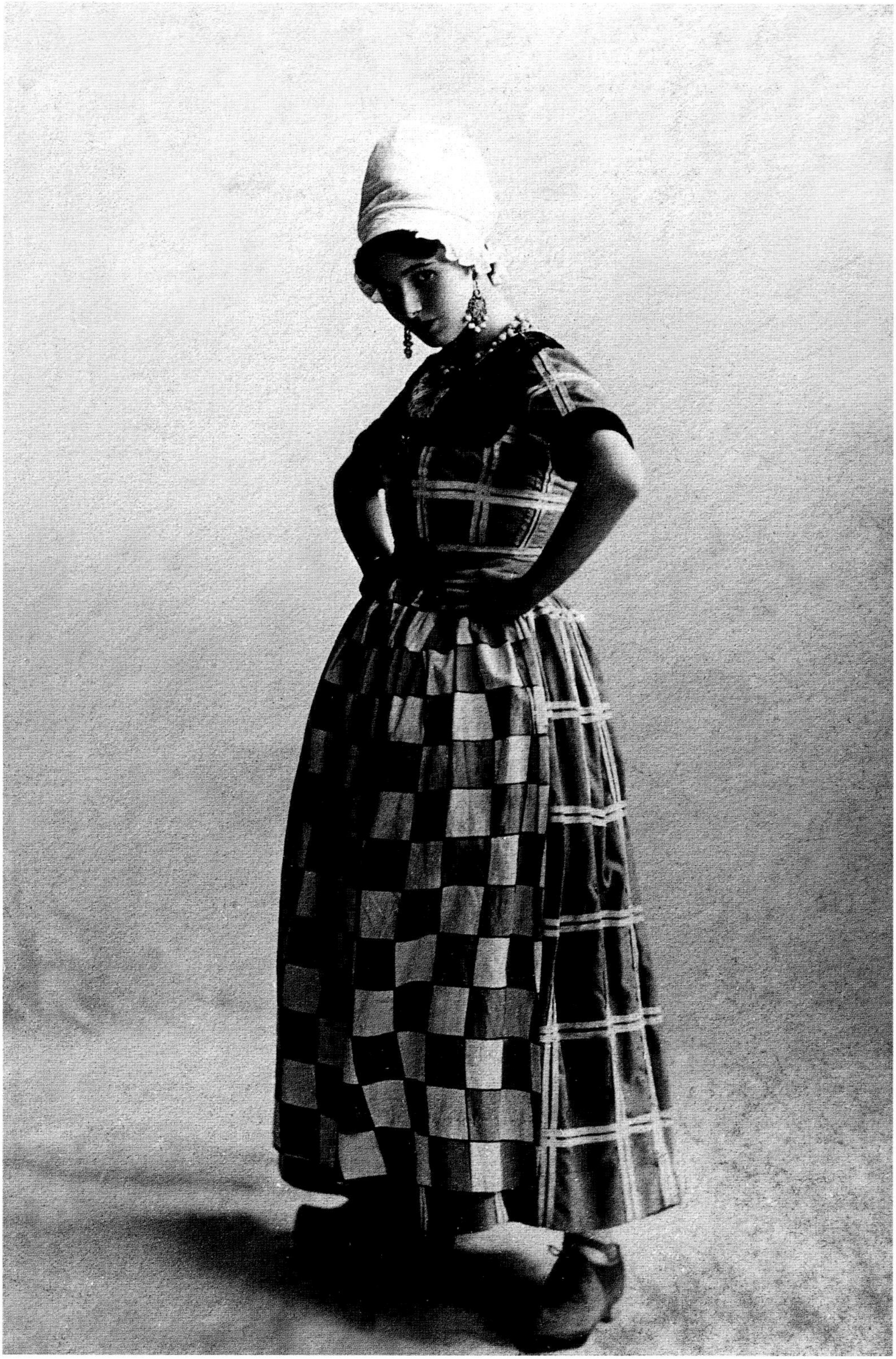

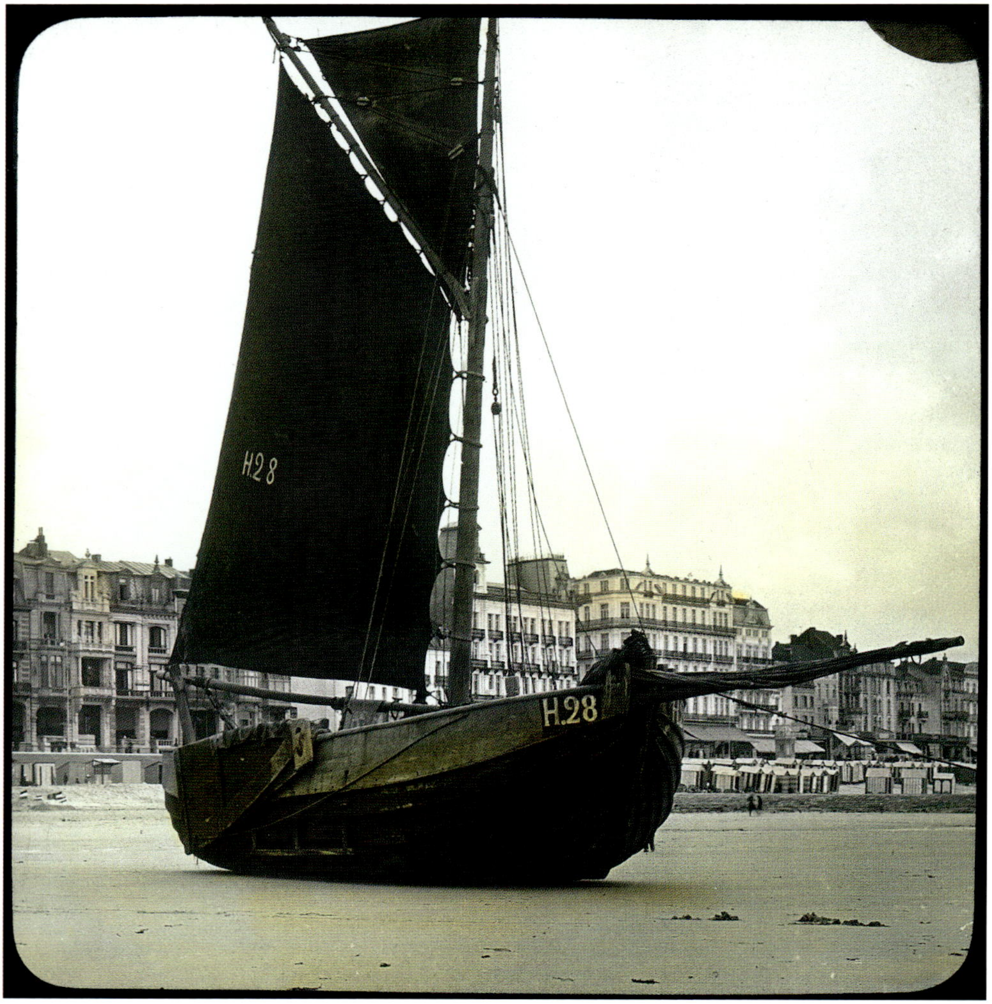

149 Heyst (Heist-aan-Zee), Holland, 1880s
150 Water Street, Zaandam, Holland, c.1900

149 Heist-aan-Zee, Belgien, 1880er Jahre
150 Wasserweg, Zaandam, Niederlande, um 1900

149 Heyst (Heist-aan-Zee), Hollande, années 1880
150 Canal à Zaandam, Hollande, vers 1900

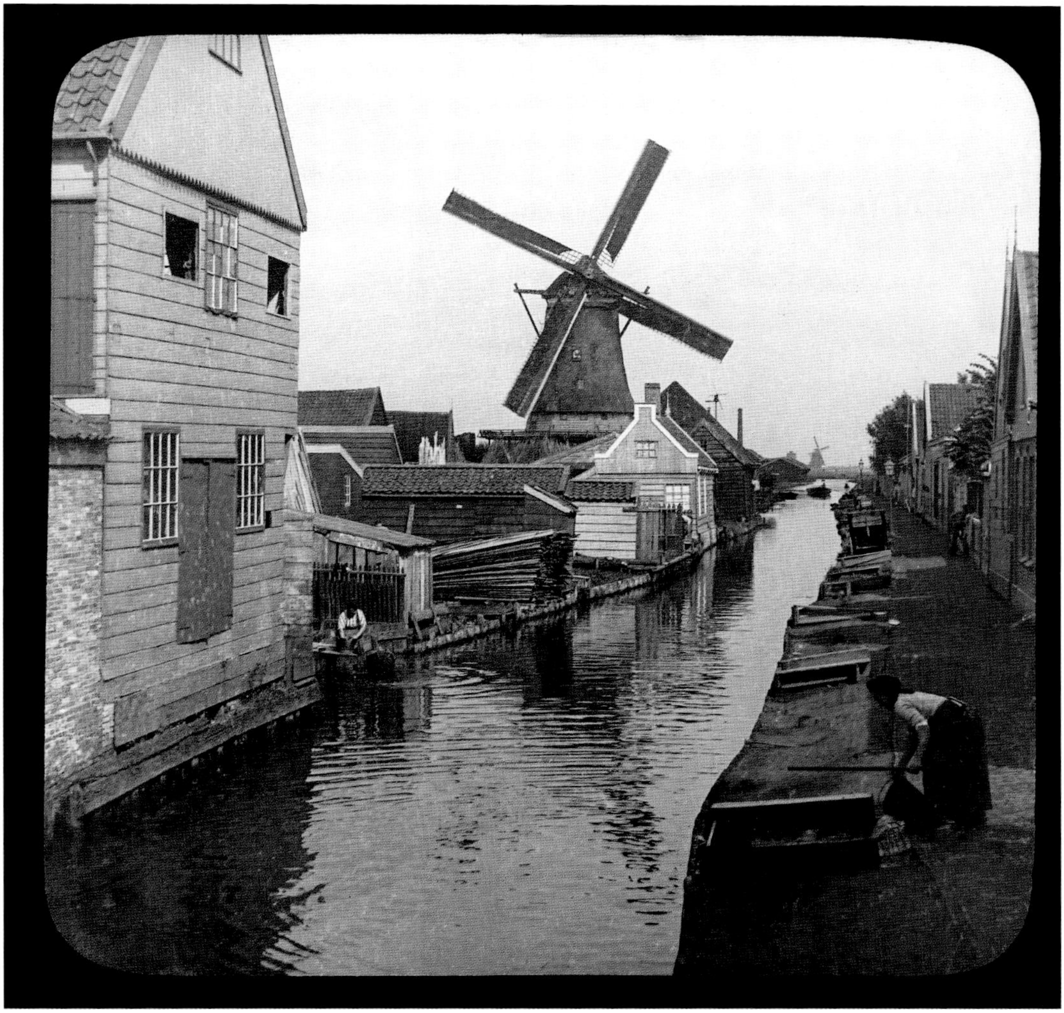

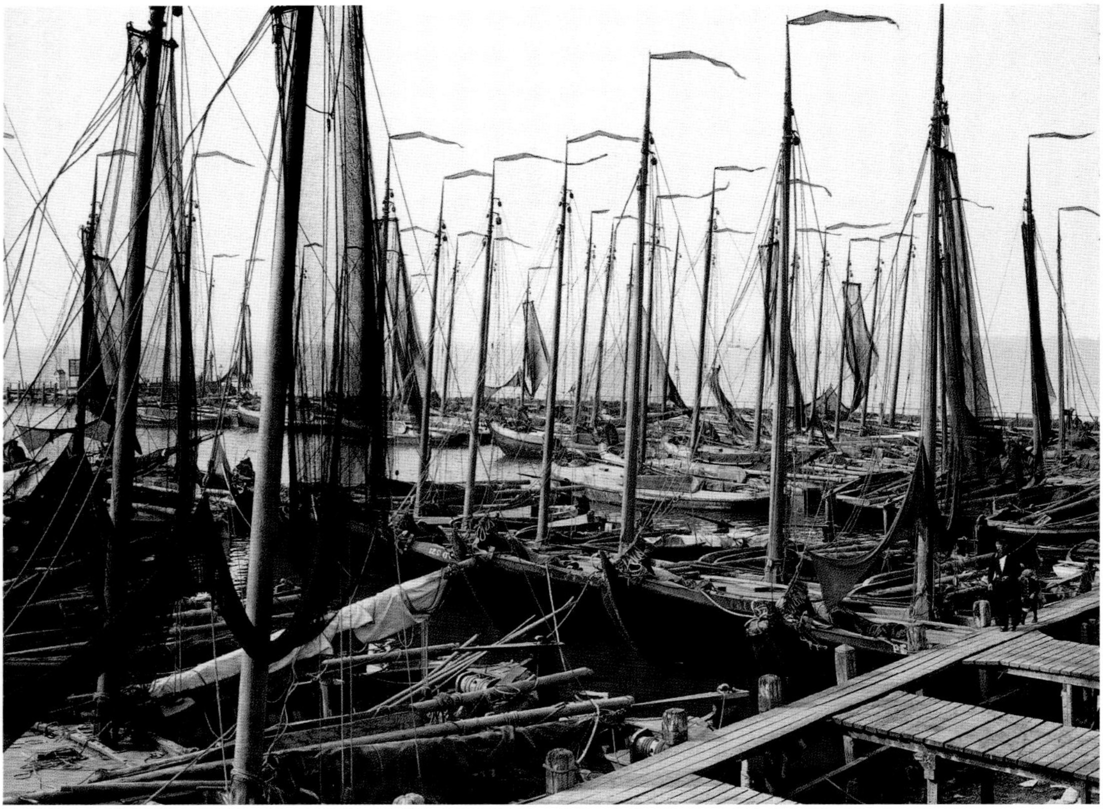

151 Harbour with fishing boats, Volendam (view South East into Zuider Zee), Holland, 1928

151 Hafen mit Fischerbooten, Volendam (Ansicht von Südost auf die Zuiderzee), Niederlande, 1928

151 Bateaux de pêche à Volendam (direction sud-est, vers le Zuider Zee), Hollande, 1928

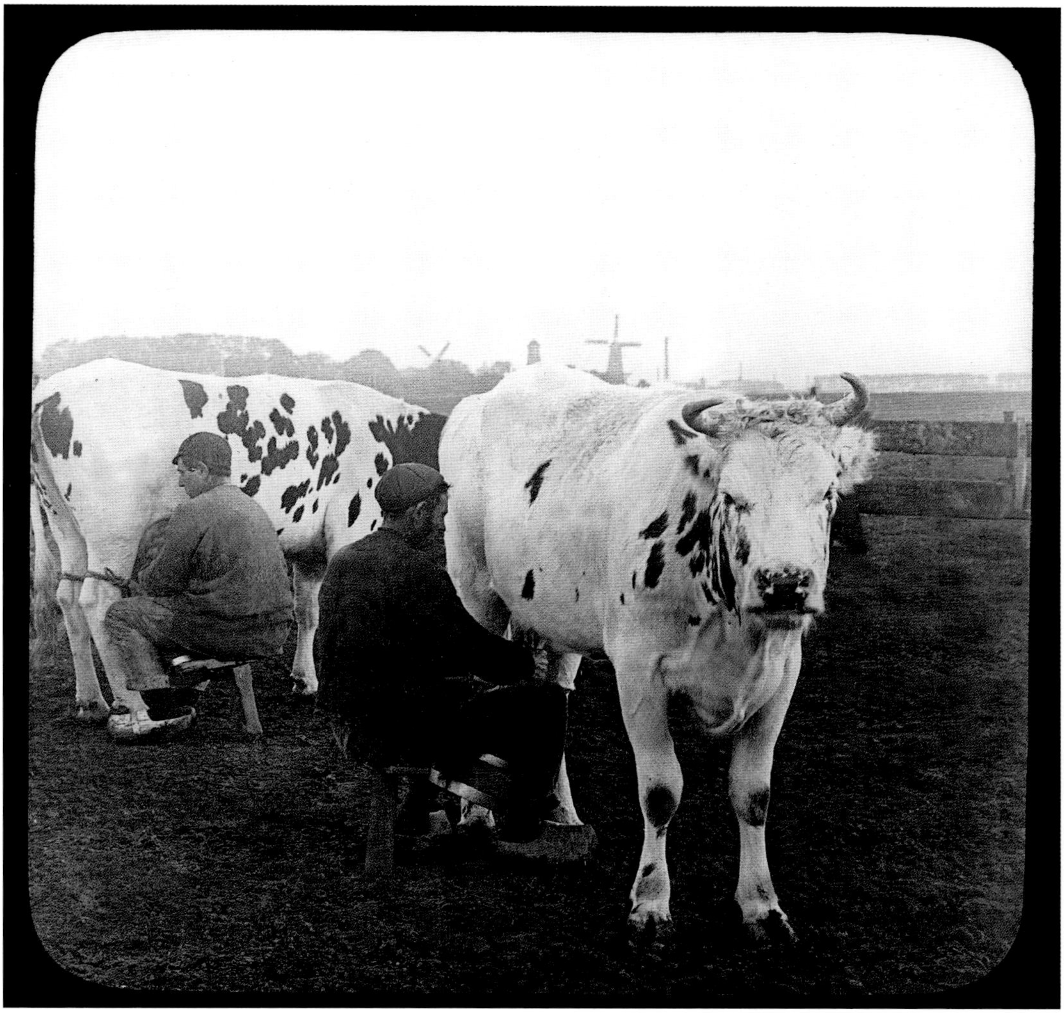

152 Farm hands milking Holstein-Fresian cattle, Rotterdam, Netherlands, 1880s

152 Knechte melken Kühe der Rasse Holstein-Friesian, Rotterdam, Niederlande, 1880er Jahre

152 Traite des vaches de race Holstein-Frisonne, Rotterdam, Pays-Bas, années 1880

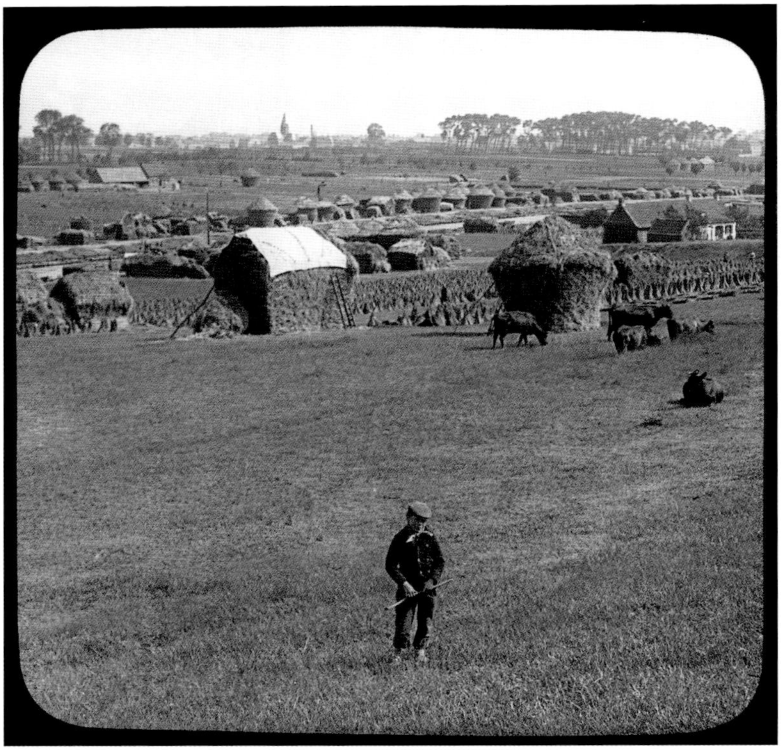

153 Flax curing in the fields near Courtrai, Belgium, 1880s

153 Flachstrocknung auf den Feldern nahe Kortrijk, Belgien, 1880er Jahre

153 Traitement du lin près de Courtrai, Belgique, années 1880

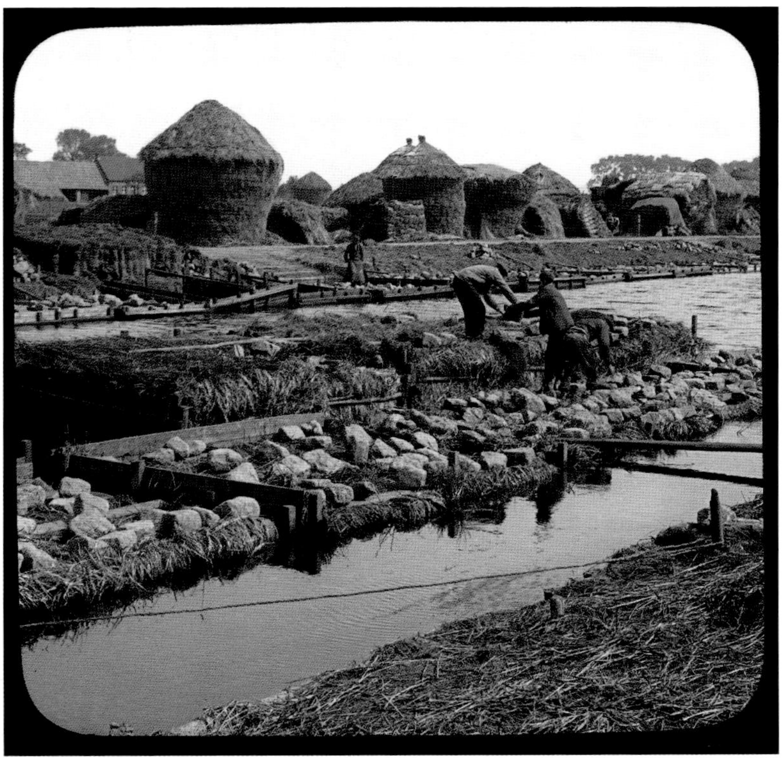

154 Flax soaked in River Lys, Courtrai, Belgium, 1880s

154 Flachsröstung im Fluss Leie, Kortrijk, Belgien, 1880er Jahre

154 Trempage du lin dans la rivière Lys. Courtrai, Belgique, années 1880

155 Palais de Justice (Palace of Justice), Brussels, Belgium, 1900s

155 Der Palais de Justice (Justizpalast), Brüssel, Belgien, 1900er Jahre

155 Palais de Justice, Bruxelles, Belgique, années 1900

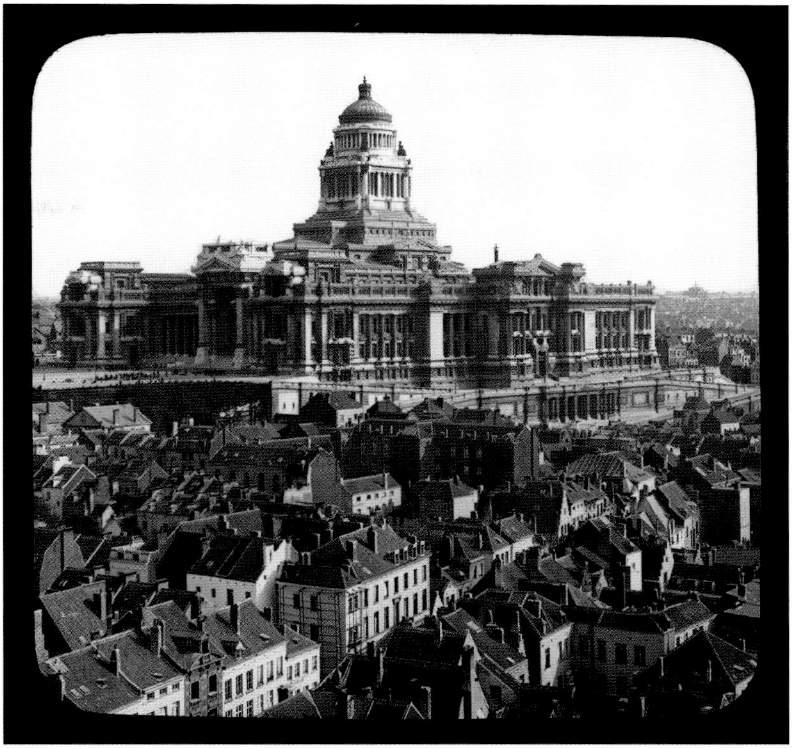

156 Belgian draft horses, Belgium, 1900s

156 Belgische Zugpferde, Belgien, 1900er Jahre

156 Chevaux de trait, Belgique, années 1900

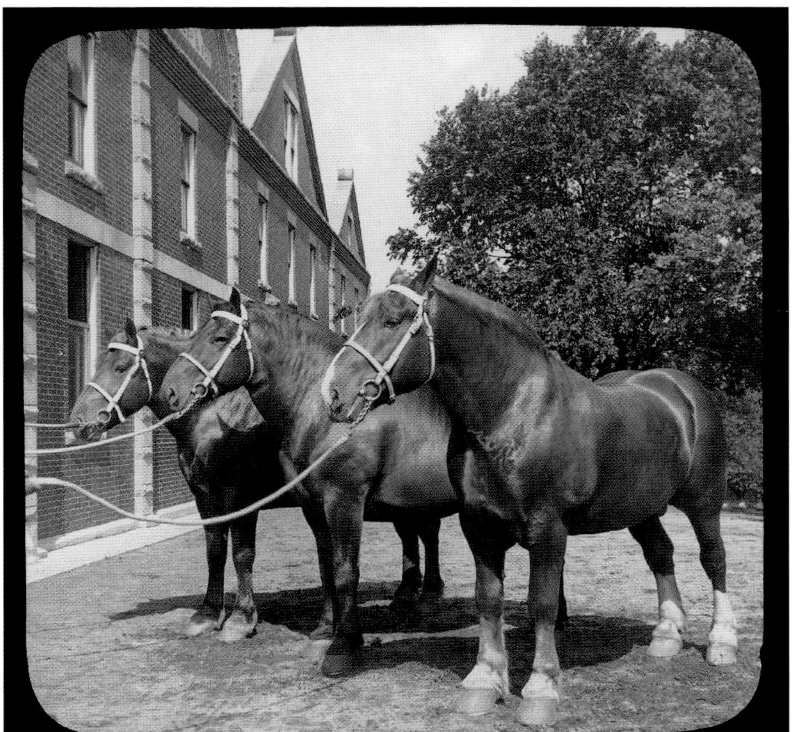

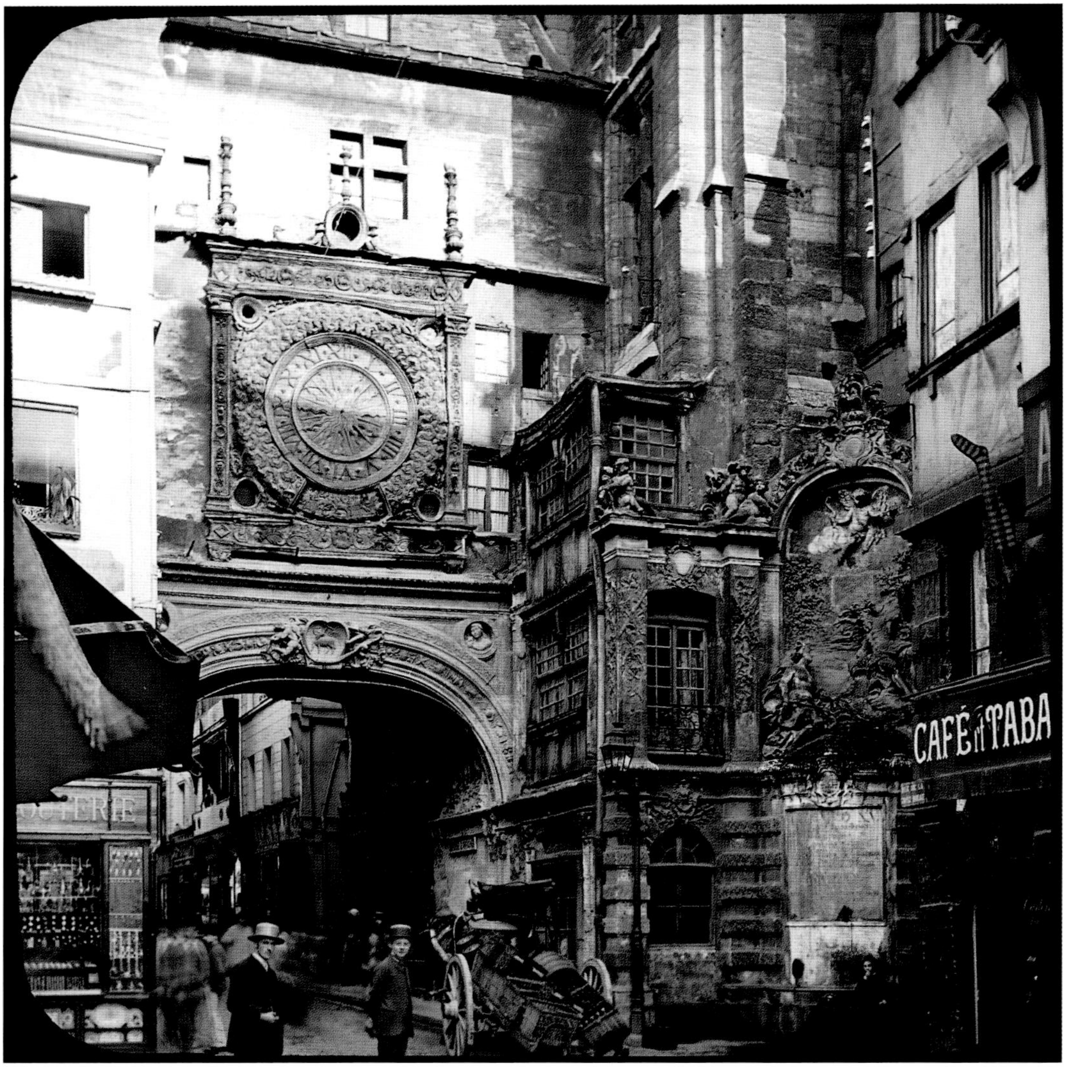

157 Le Gros-Horloge (City clock tower), Rouen, France, 1870s
158 Bonnet sellers, France, 1880s

157 Le Gros-Horloge (Die Große Turmuhr), Rouen, Frankreich, 1870er Jahre
158 Haubenverkäuferinnen, Frankreich, 1880er Jahre

157 Le Gros-Horloge de Rouen, France, années 1870
158 Vendeuses de bonnets, France, années 1880

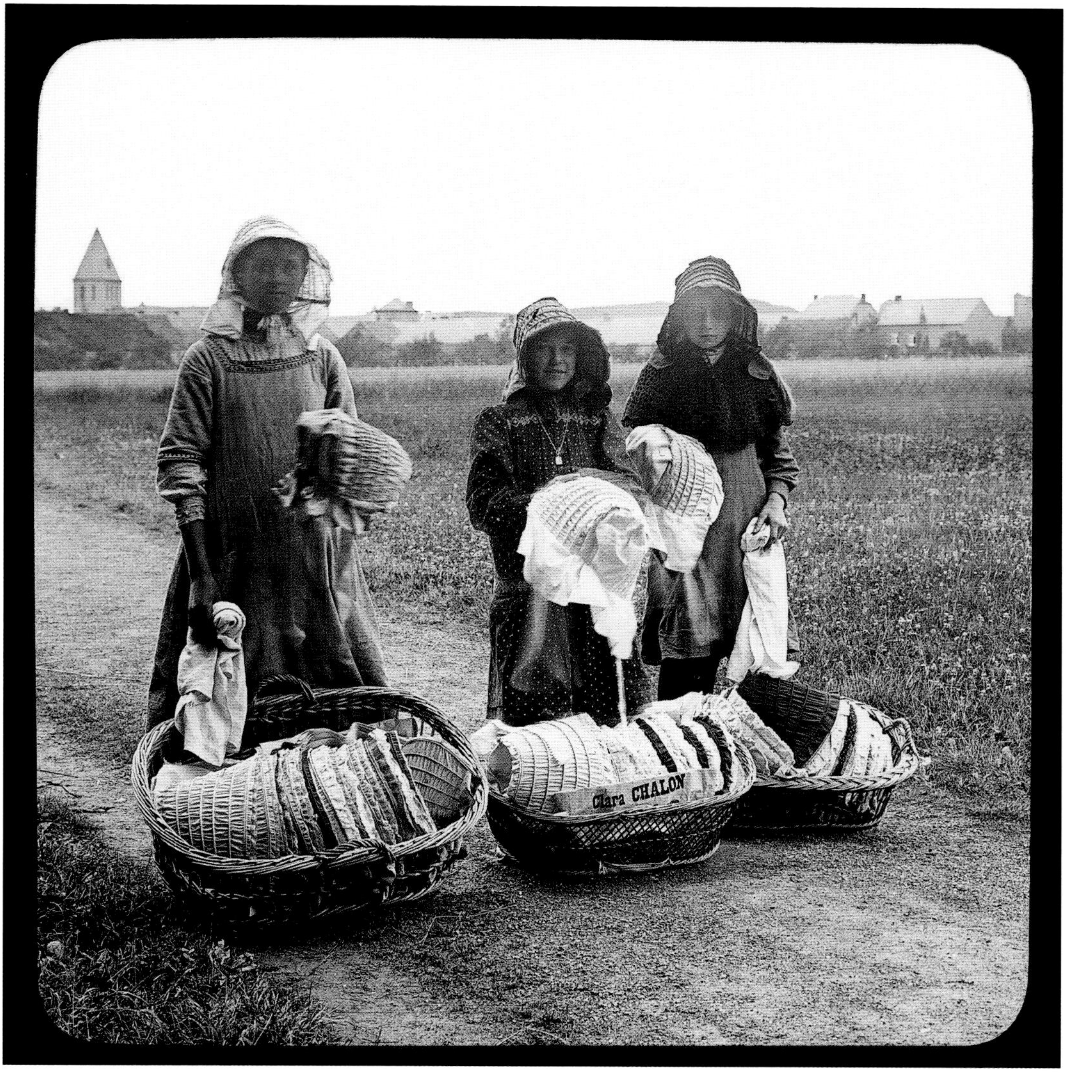
Clara CHALON

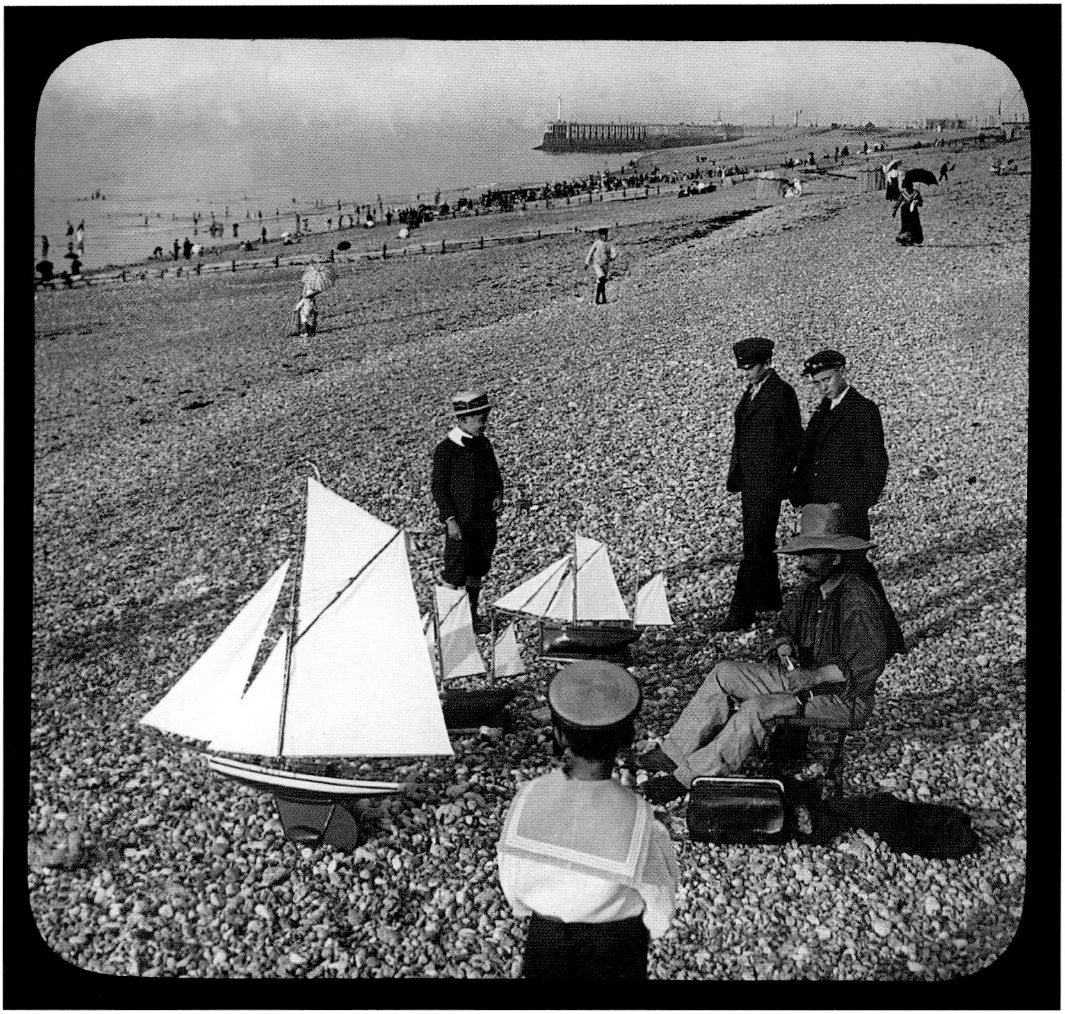

159 Children buying toy boats at the beach, France, c.1900
160 Breton children in traditional costume, France, c.1900

159 Kinder kaufen Spielzeugboote am Strand, Frankreich, um 1900
160 Bretonische Kinder in Trachtenkleidung, Frankreich, um 1900

159 Enfants achetant des petits bateaux. France, vers 1900
160 Enfants bretons en costume traditionnel. France, vers 1900

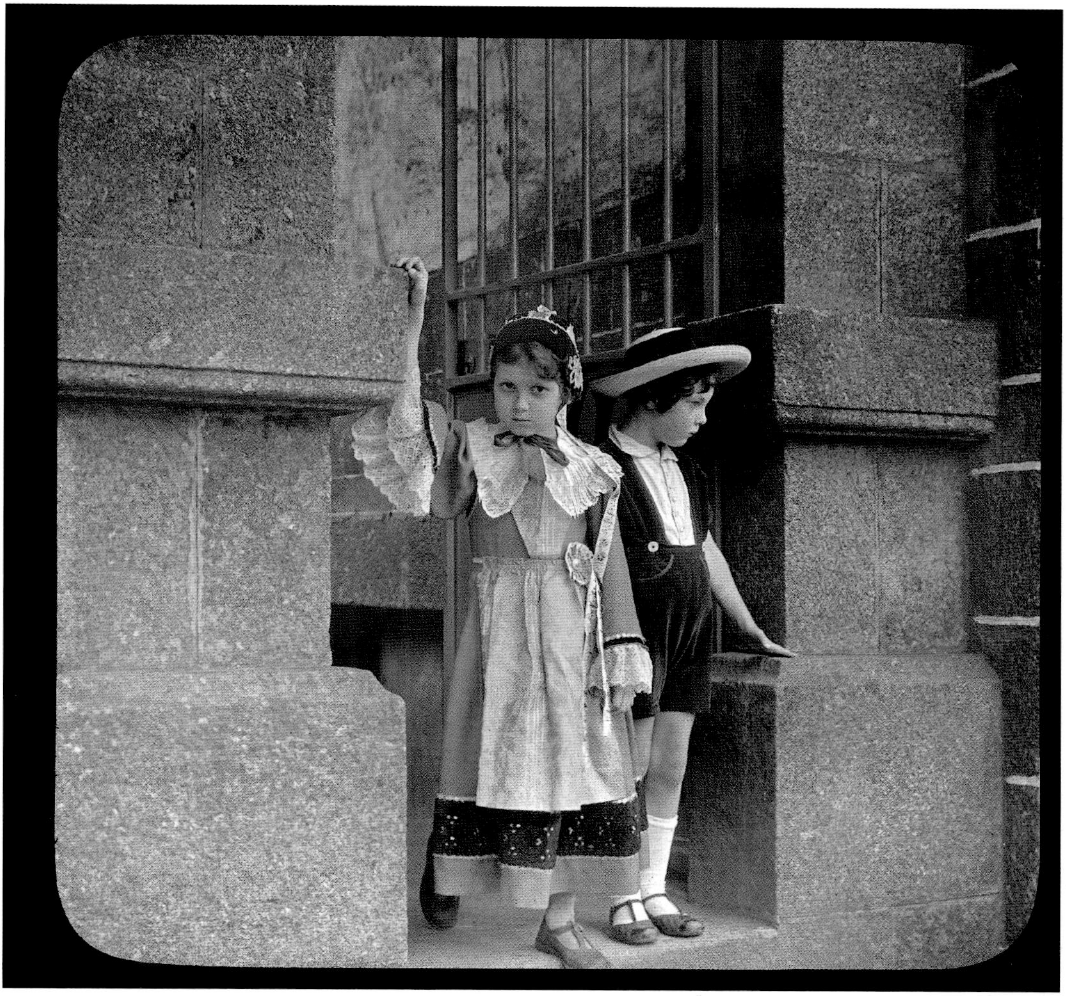

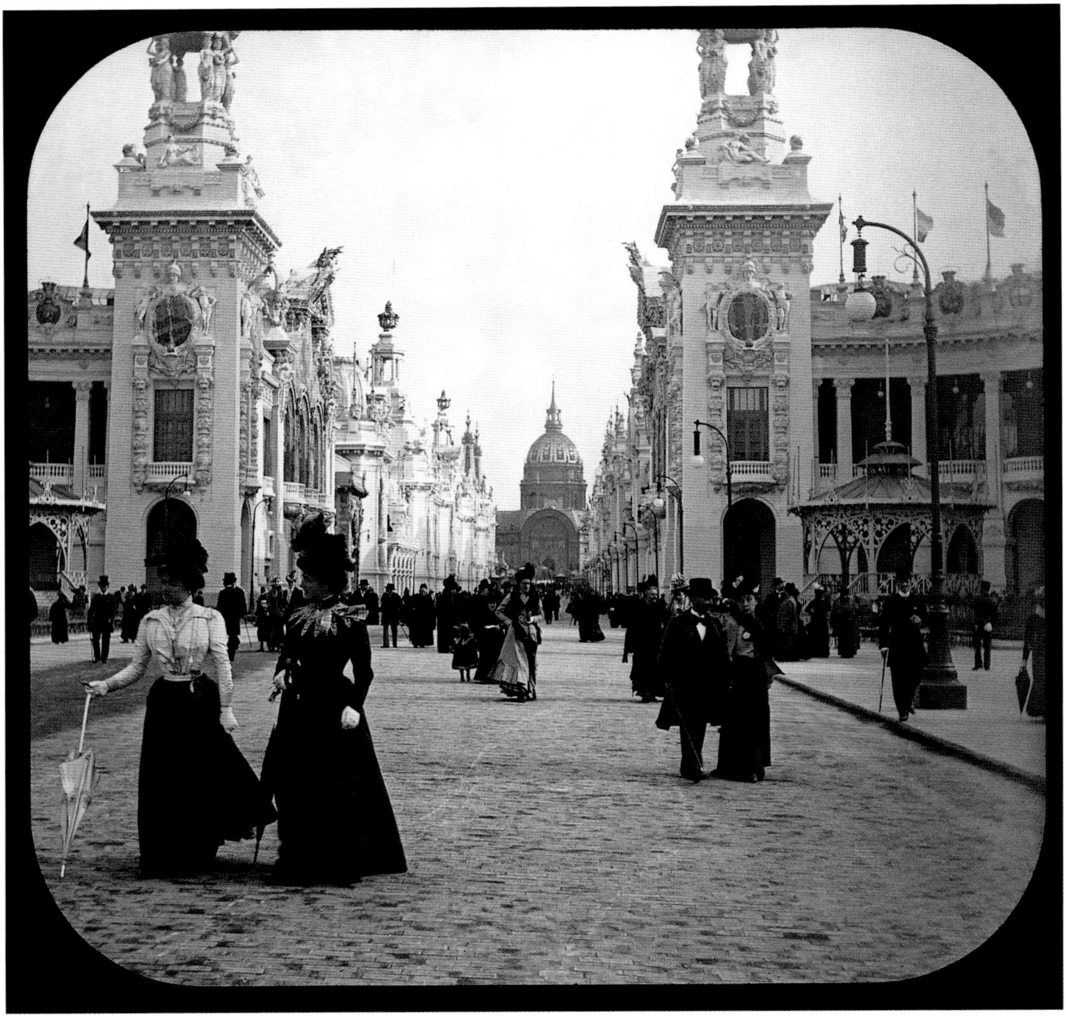

161 View of Esplanade des Invalides from the Ponte Alexandre III, Exposition Universelle, Paris, France, 1900

161 Blick auf die Esplanade des Invalides vom Pont Alexandre III aus, Weltausstellung, Paris, Frankreich, 1900

161 L'esplanade des Invalides vue du pont Alexandre III, Exposition Universelle, Paris, France, 1900

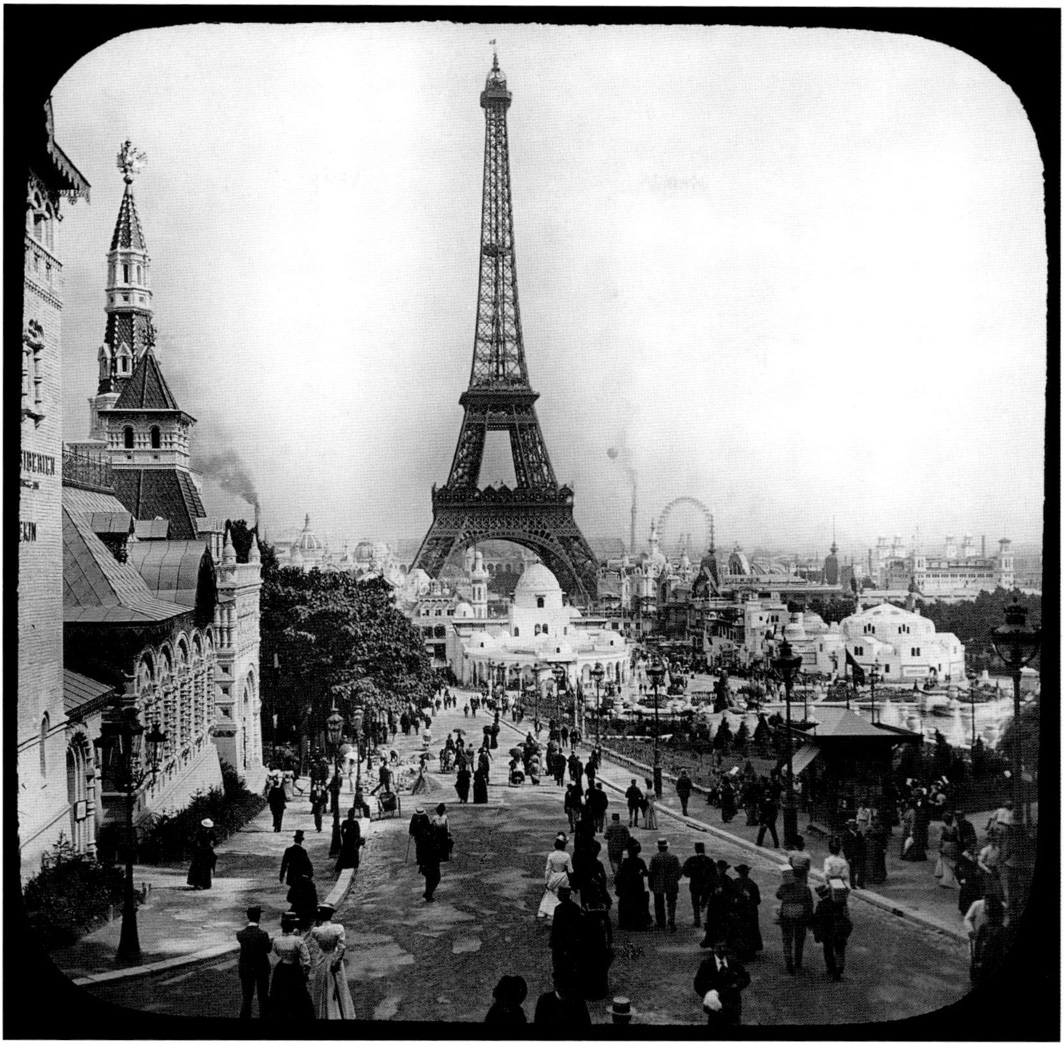

162 General view,
Exposition Universelle,
Paris, France, 1900

162 Gesamtansicht,
Weltausstellung, Paris,
Frankreich, 1900

162 Vue générale de
l'Exposition Universelle.
Paris, France, 1900

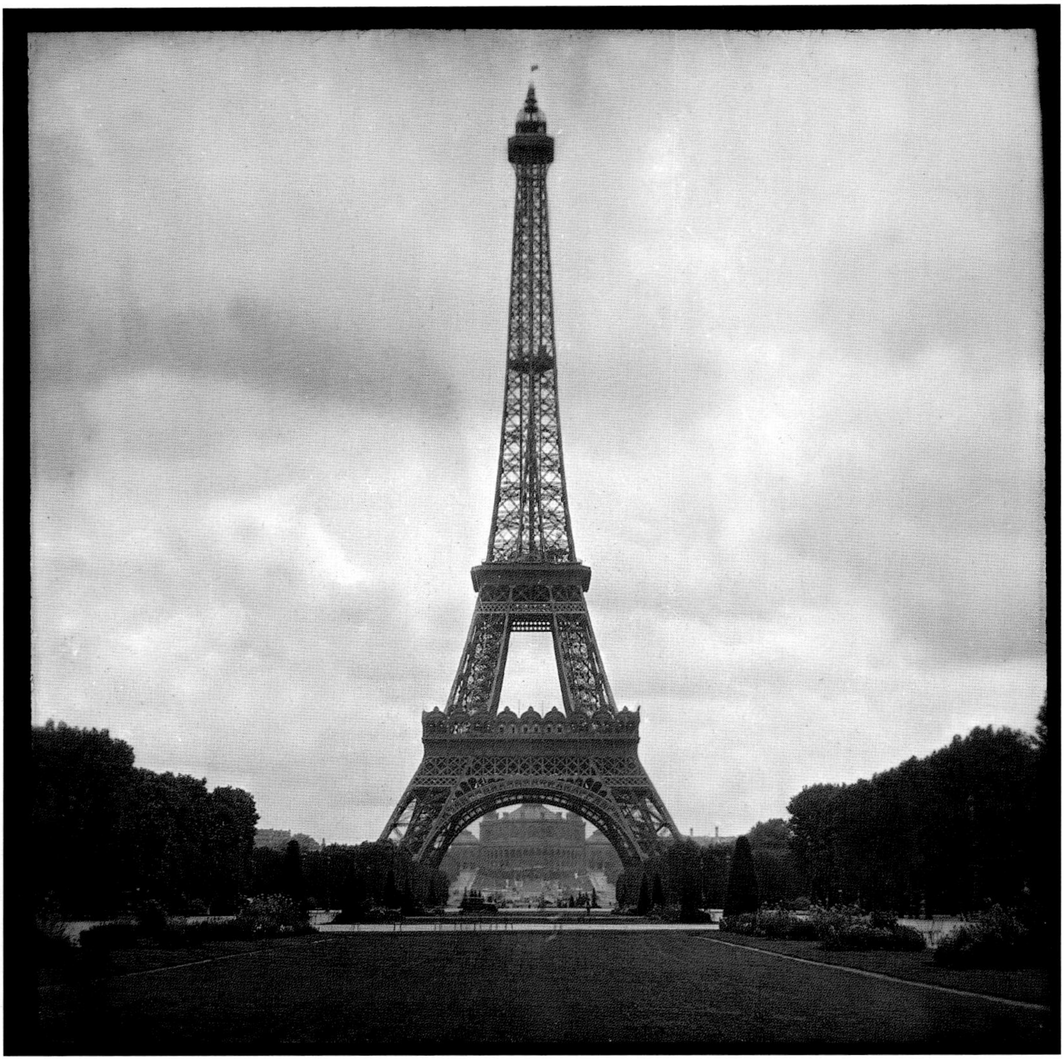

163 Eiffel Tower, Paris, France, c.1900
164 Le Pont d'Iéna spanning the River Seine, with the Trocadéro in the distance, Paris, 1900

163 Der Eiffelturm, Paris, Frankreich, um 1900
164 Der Pont d'Iéna, der die Seine überspannt, im Hintergrund der Trocadéro-Palast, Paris, Frankreich, 1900

163 Tour Eiffel, Paris, France, vers 1900
164 Le pont d'Iéna franchissant la Seine et, au fond, le Trocadéro. Paris, 1900

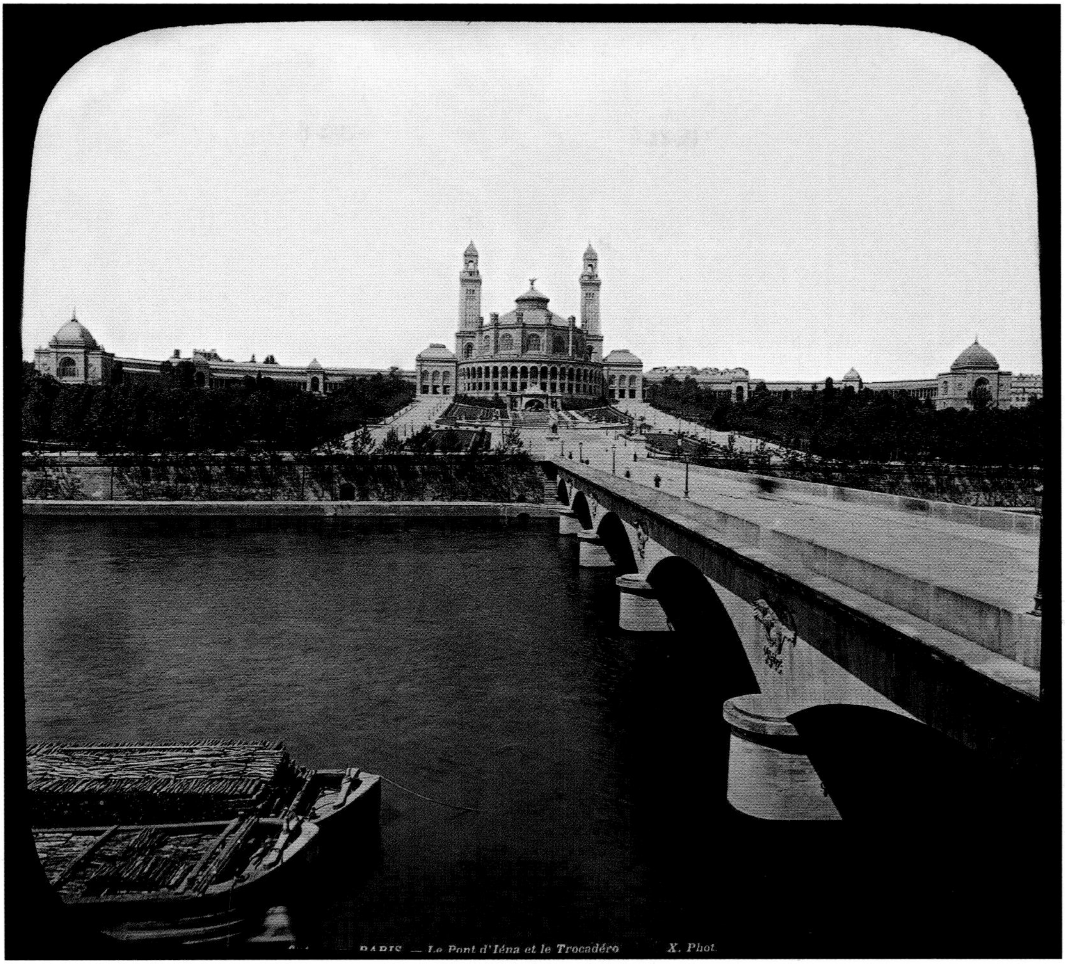
PARIS — Le Pont d'Iéna et le Trocadéro
X. Phot.

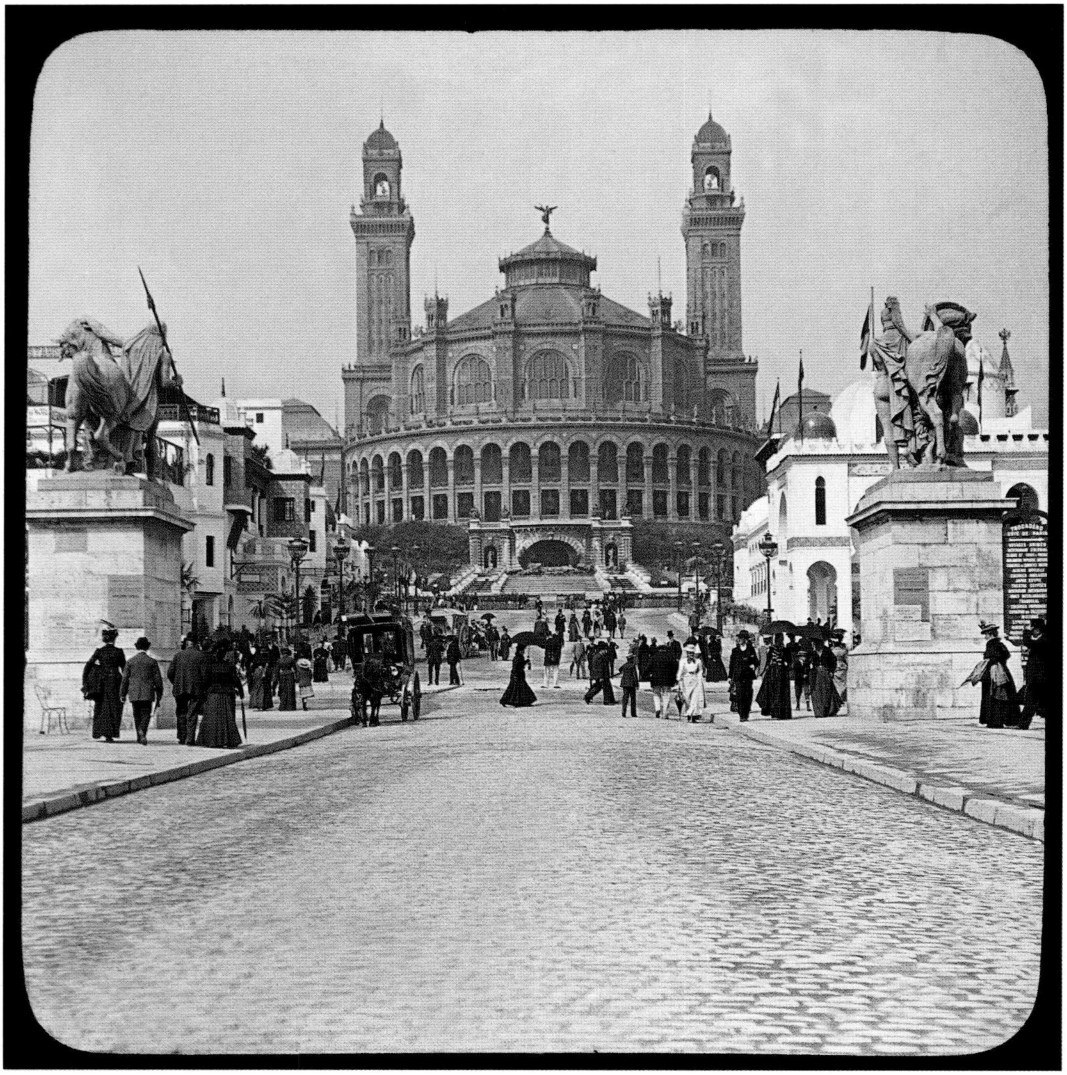

165 Palais du Trocadéro, Exposition Universelle, Paris, 1900
166 Bronze Huntress and Marble Bacchus, Exposition Universelle, Paris, 1900

165 Der Trocadéro-Palast, Weltausstellung, Paris, Frankreich, 1900
166 Bronzefigur Jägerin und Marmorskulptur Bacchus, Weltausstellung, Paris, Frankreich, 1900

165 Palais du Trocadéro, Exposition Universelle, Paris 1900
166 Chasseresse en bronze et Bacchus de marbre, Exposition Universelle, Paris 1900

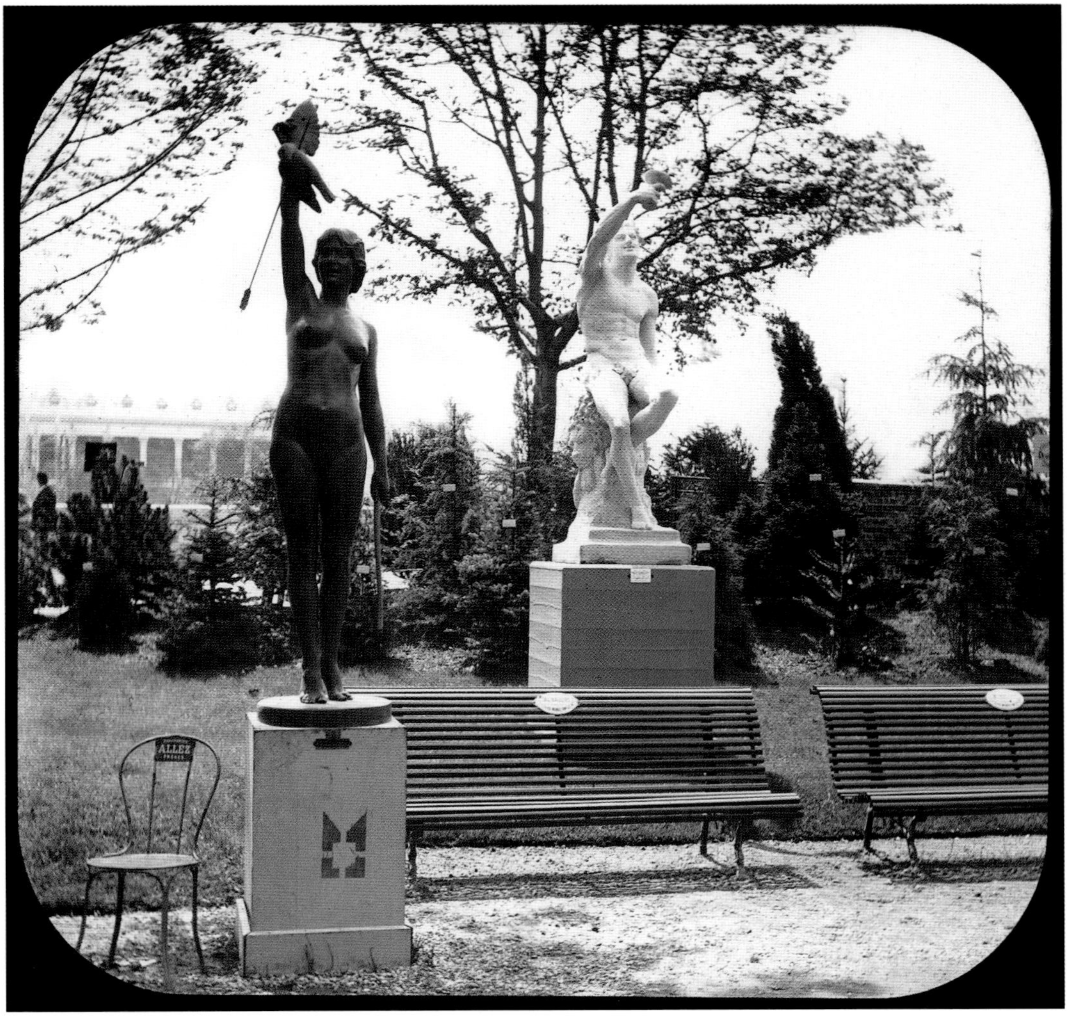
ALLEZ

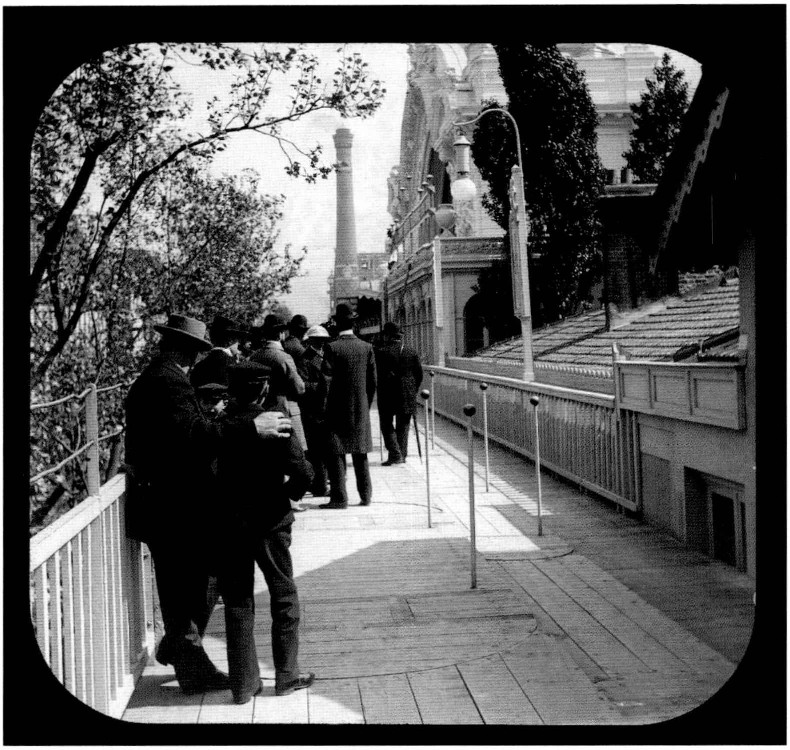

167 Moving platform near Agricultural Building, Exposition Universelle, Paris, France, 1900

167 Laufsteg nahe des Landwirtschaftsgebäudes, Weltausstellung, Paris, Frankreich, 1900

167 Trottoir roulant près du pavillon de l'agriculture. Exposition Universelle, Paris, France, 1900

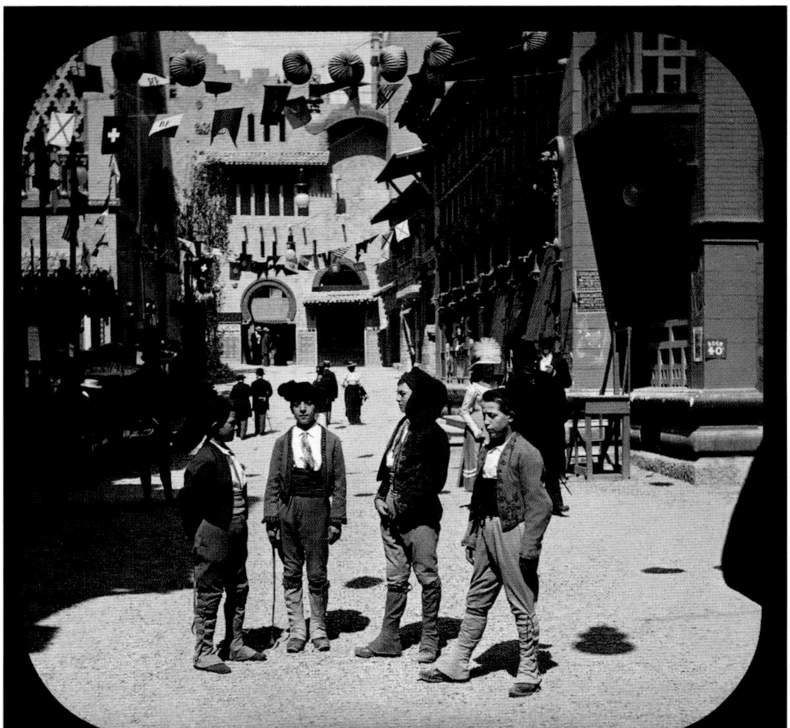

168 Group of Spanish boys from Andalusia, Exposition Universelle, Paris, France, 1900

168 Gruppe spanischer Jungen aus Andalusien, Weltausstellung, Paris, Frankreich, 1900

168 Groupe de jeunes andalous, Exposition Universelle, Paris, France, 1900

169 Street in Swiss Village, Exposition Universelle, Paris, France, 1900

169 Straße im Schweizer Dorf, Weltausstellung, Paris, Frankreich, 1900

169 Une rue du Village Suisse, Exposition Universelle, Paris, France, 1900

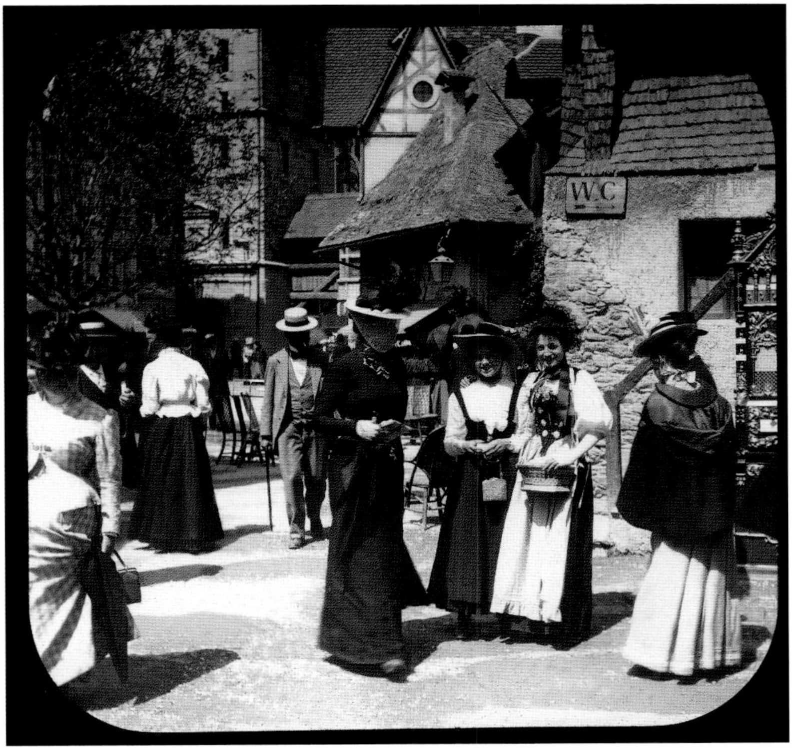

170 Flower market on Pont Saint-Michel, Paris, France, 1890s

170 Blumenmarkt auf der Pont Saint-Michel, Paris, Frankreich, 1890er Jahre

170 Le marché aux fleurs sur le pont Saint-Michel, Paris, France, années 1890

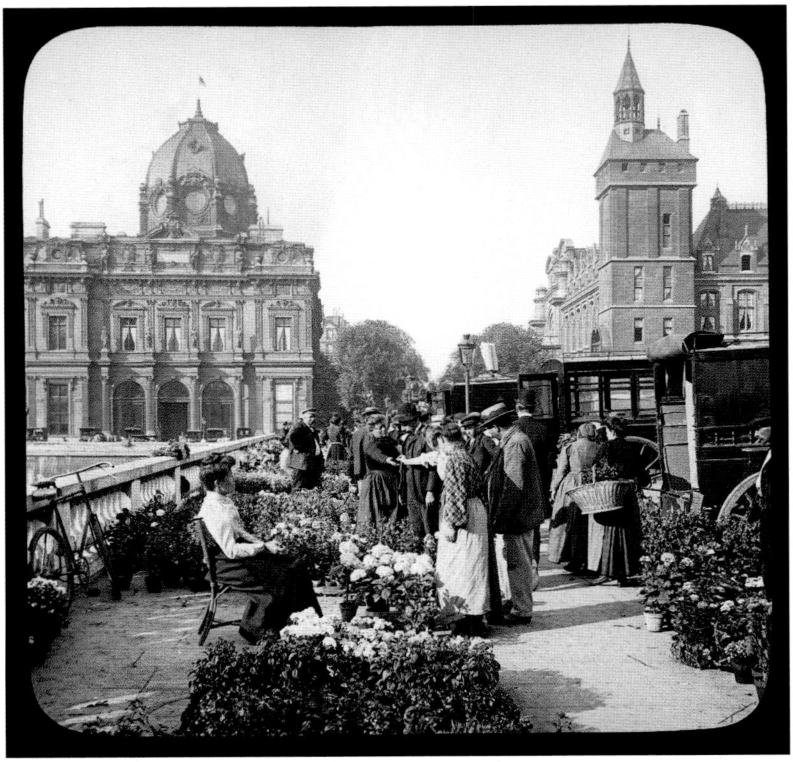

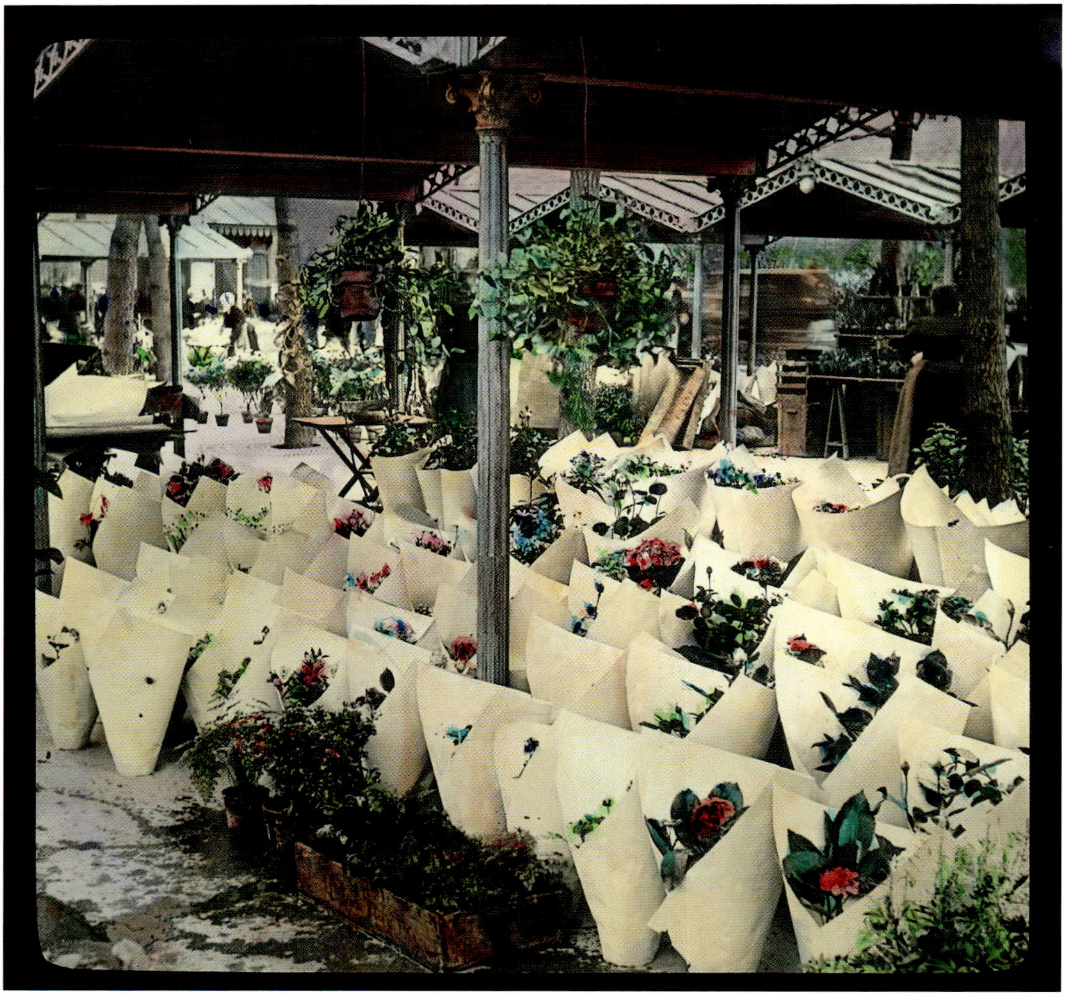

171 Flower market, Paris, France, 1880s
172 Jardin du Luxembourg, Paris, France, 1880s

171 Blumenmarkt, Paris, Frankreich, 1880er Jahre
172 Der Jardin du Luxembourg, Paris, Frankreich, 1880er Jahre

171 Marché aux fleurs, Paris, France, années 1880
172 Jardin du Luxembourg, Paris, France, années 1880

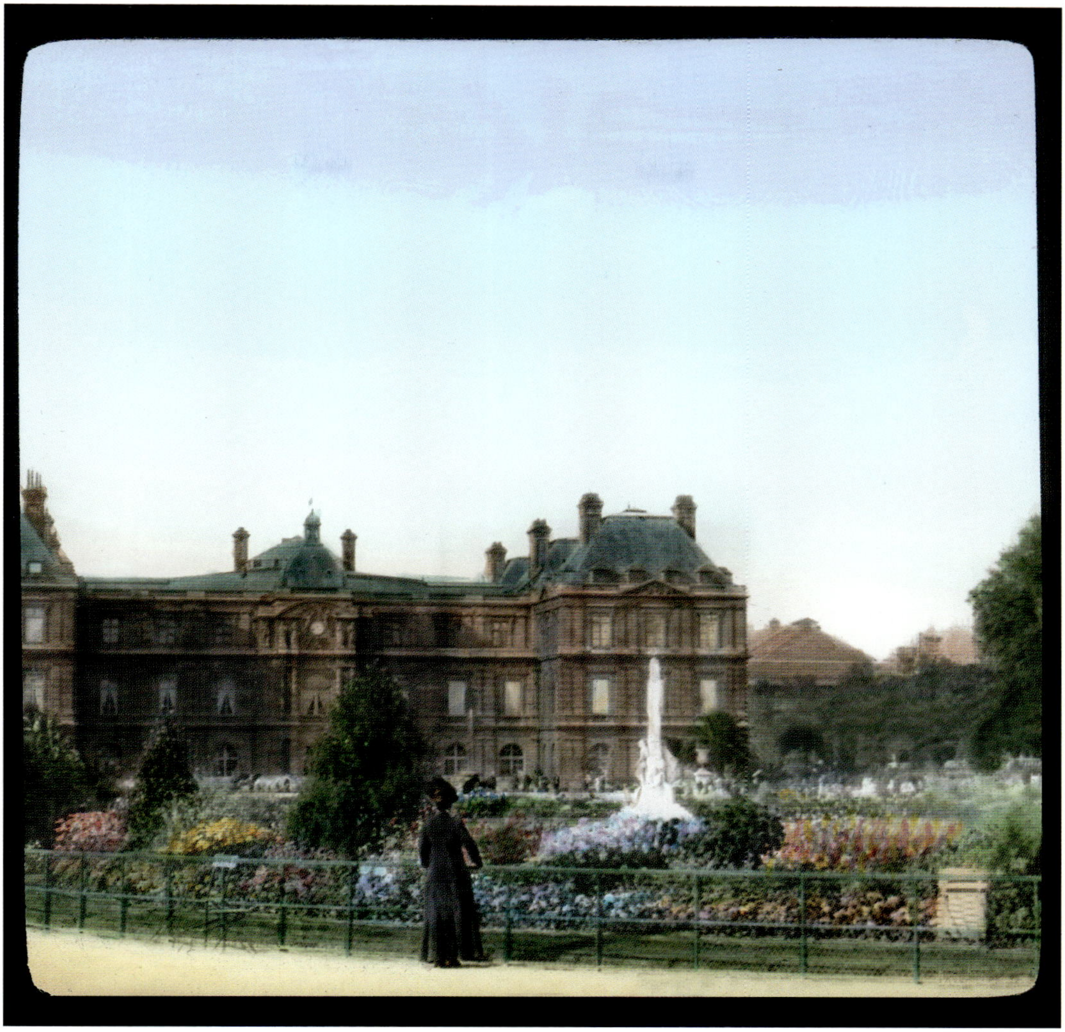

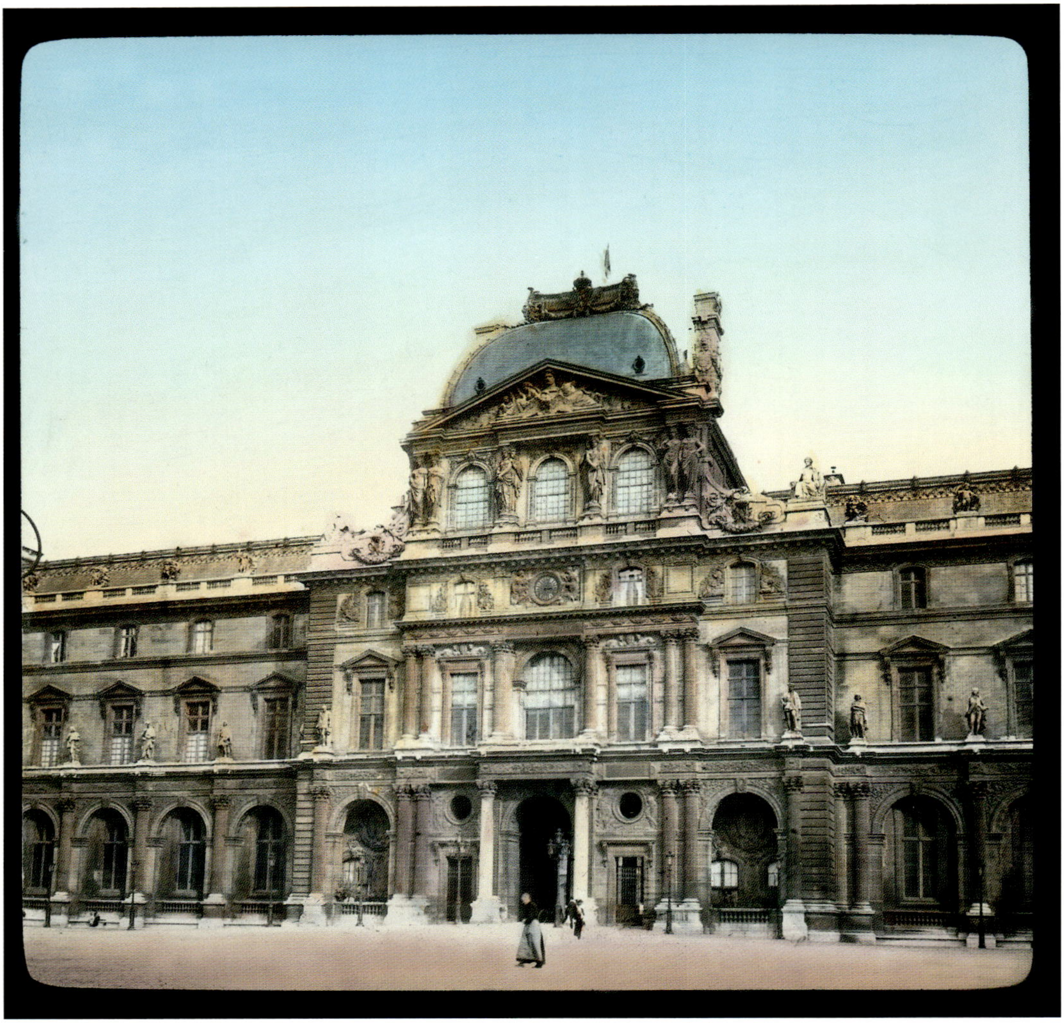

173 The Louvre, Paris, France, c.1900
174 Place de l'Opera, Paris, France, 1920s

173 Der Louvre, Paris, Frankreich, um 1900
174 Die Place de l'Opéra, Paris, Frankreich, 1920er Jahre

173 Le Louvre, Paris, France, vers 1900
174 Place de l'Opéra, Paris, France, années 1920

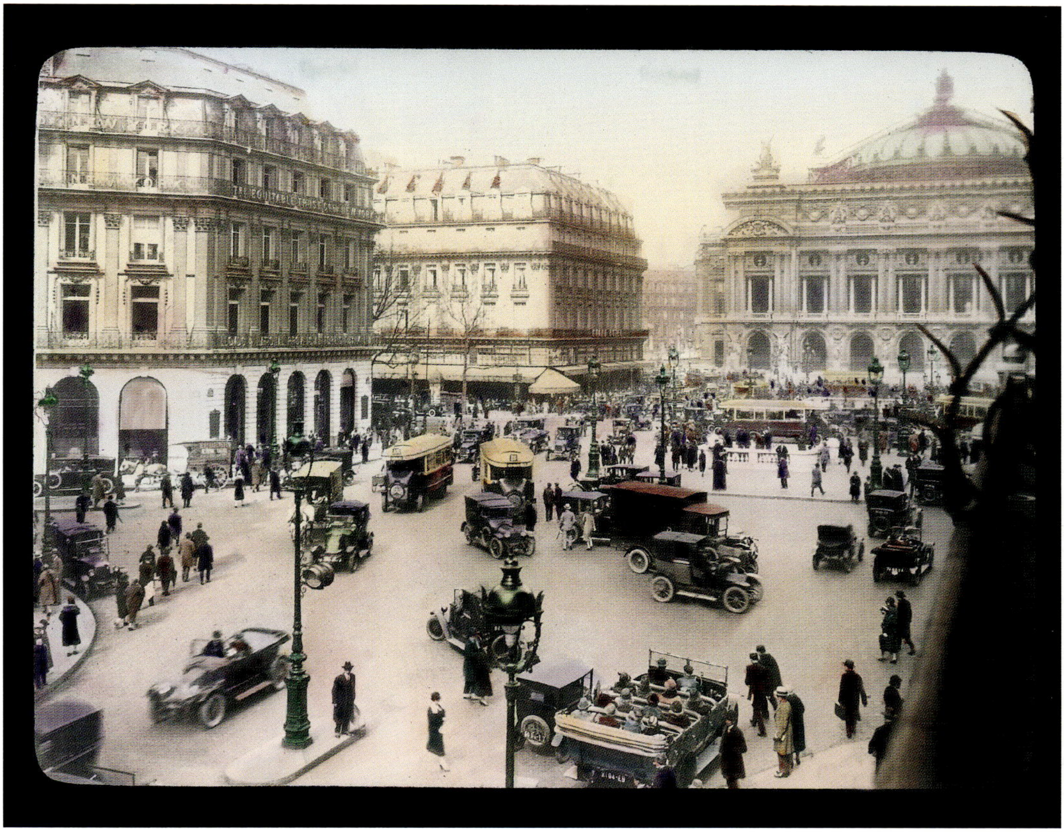

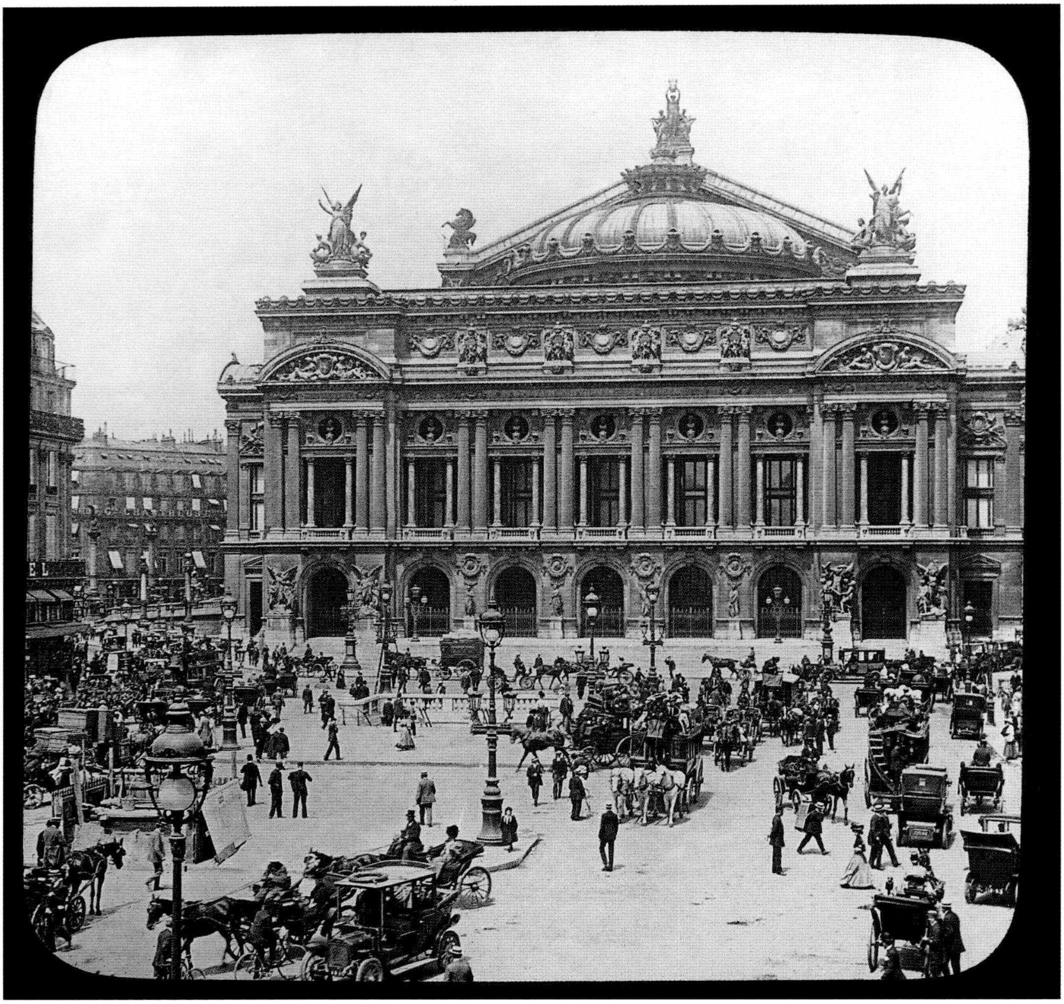

175 The Grand Opera, Paris, France, 1900s
176 Foyer of The Grand Opera, Paris, 1900s

175 Das Opernhaus, Paris, Frankreich, 1900er Jahre
176 Das Foyer des Opernhauses, Paris, Frankreich, 1900er Jahre

175 Opéra Garnier, Paris, France, années 1900
176 Foyer de l'Opéra Garnier, Paris, années 1900

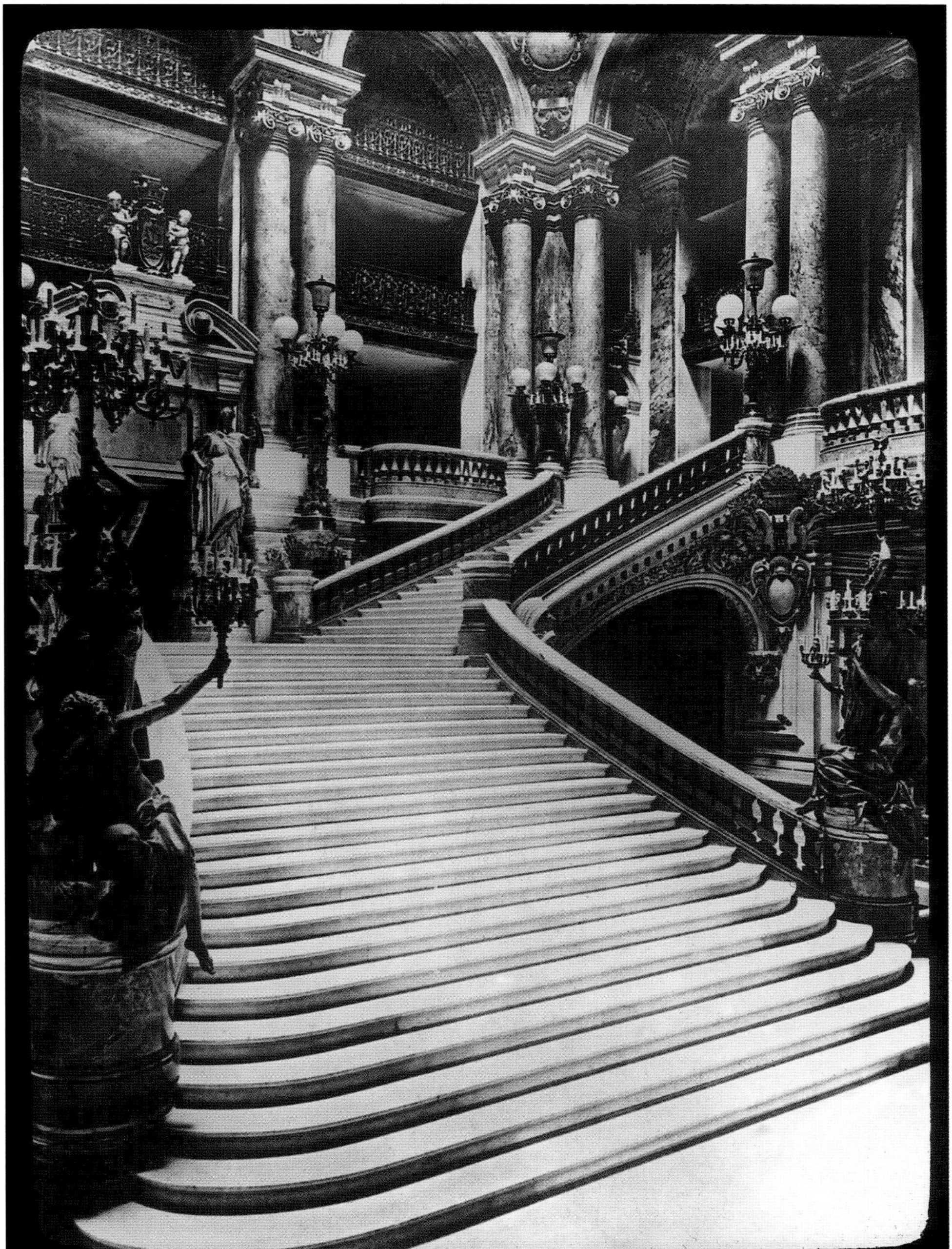

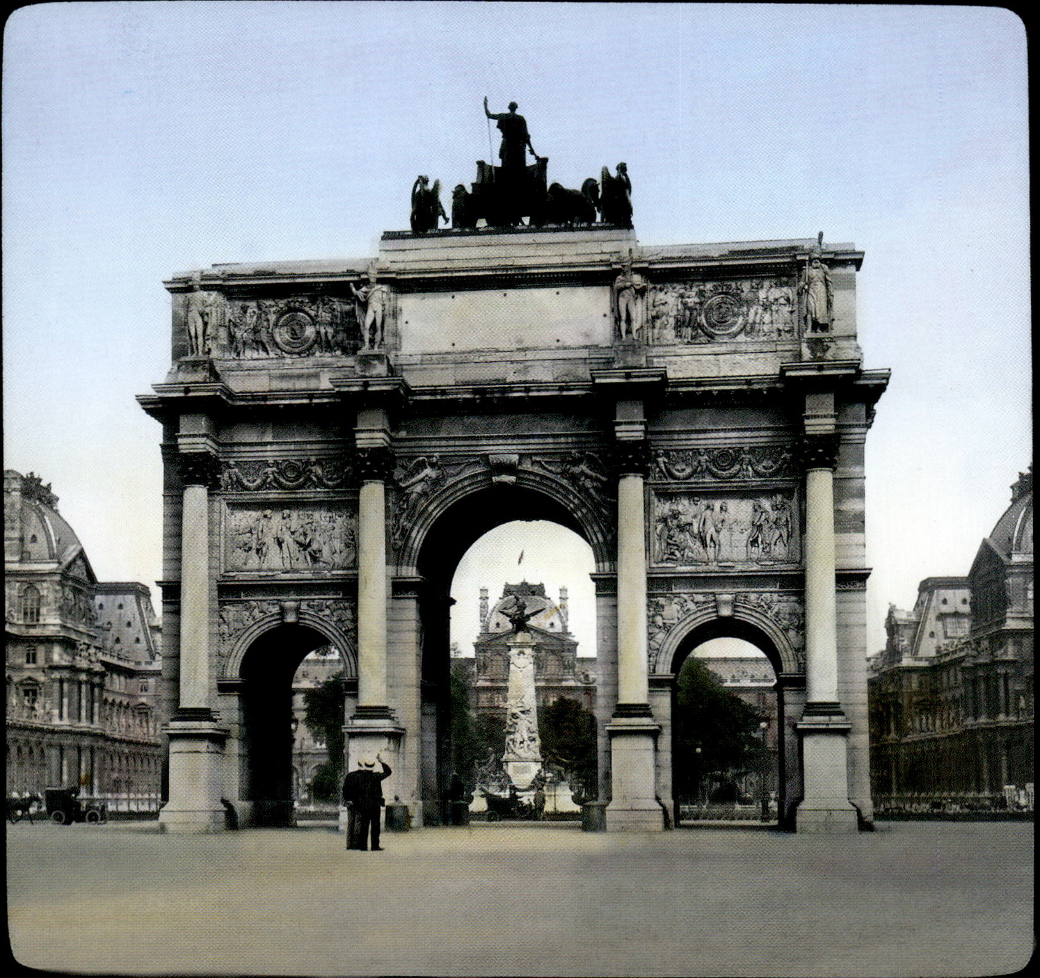

177–8 Arc de Triomphe du Carrousel, Place du Carrousel, Paris, France, 1920s

177–8 Der Arc de Triomphe du Carrousel, Place du Carrousel, Paris, Frankreich, 1920er Jahre

177–8 Arc de Triomphe du Carrousel, Place du Carrousel, Paris, France, années 1920

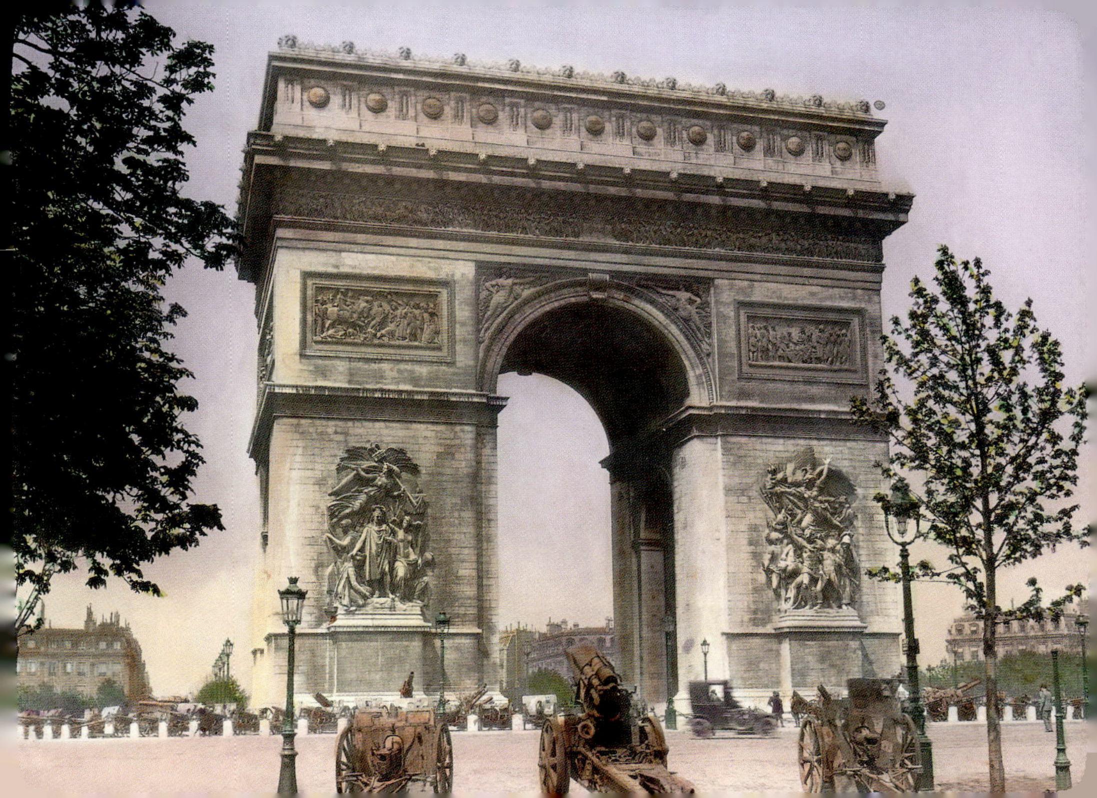

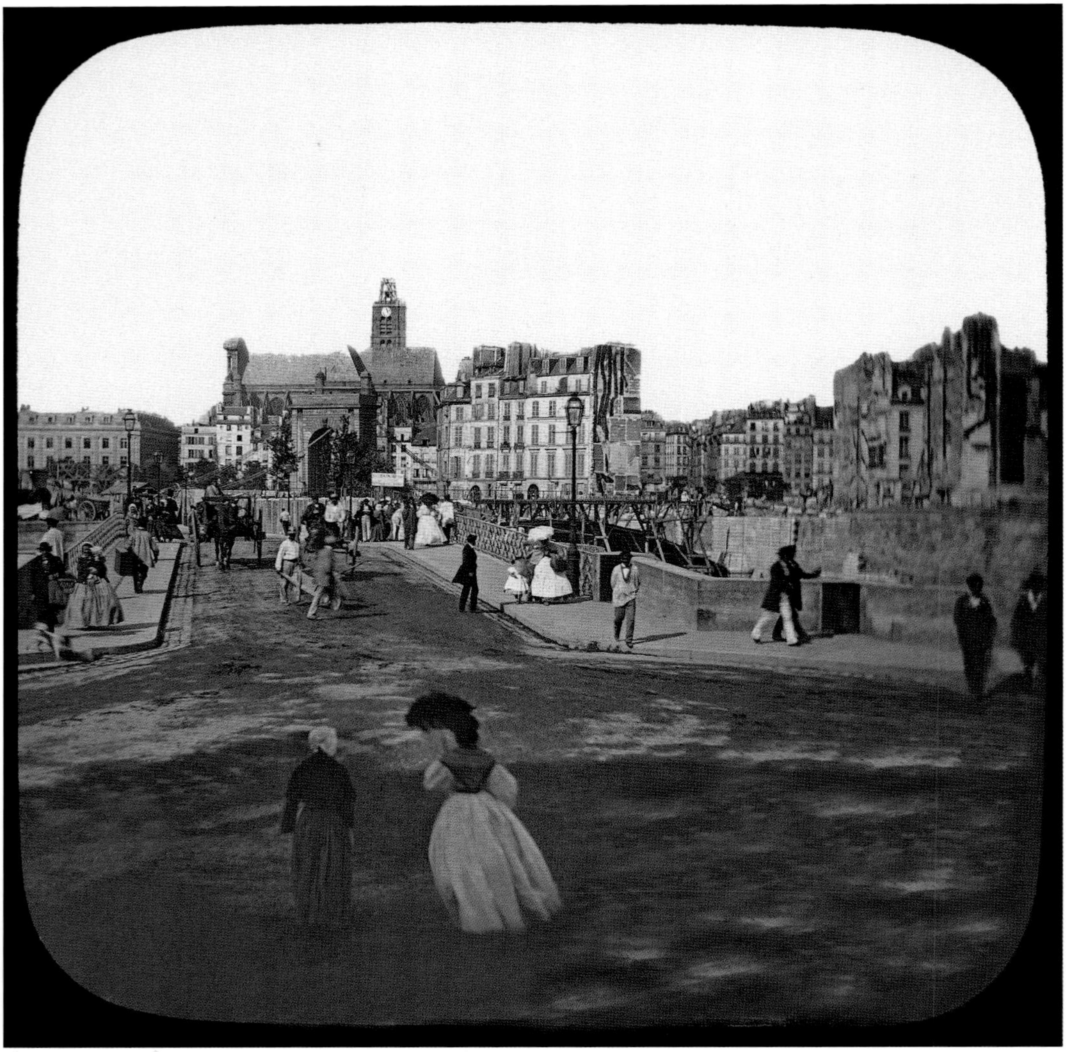

179 Pont de l'Archeveche, Paris, France, 1870s
180 Palais de la Femme, Exposition Universelle, Paris, France, 1900

179 Der Pont de l'Archevêché, Paris, Frankreich, 1870er Jahre
180 Der Palais de la Femme, Weltausstellung, Paris, Frankreich, 1900

179 Pont de l'Archevêché, Paris, France, années 1870
180 Palais de la Femme, Exposition Universelle, Paris, France, 1900

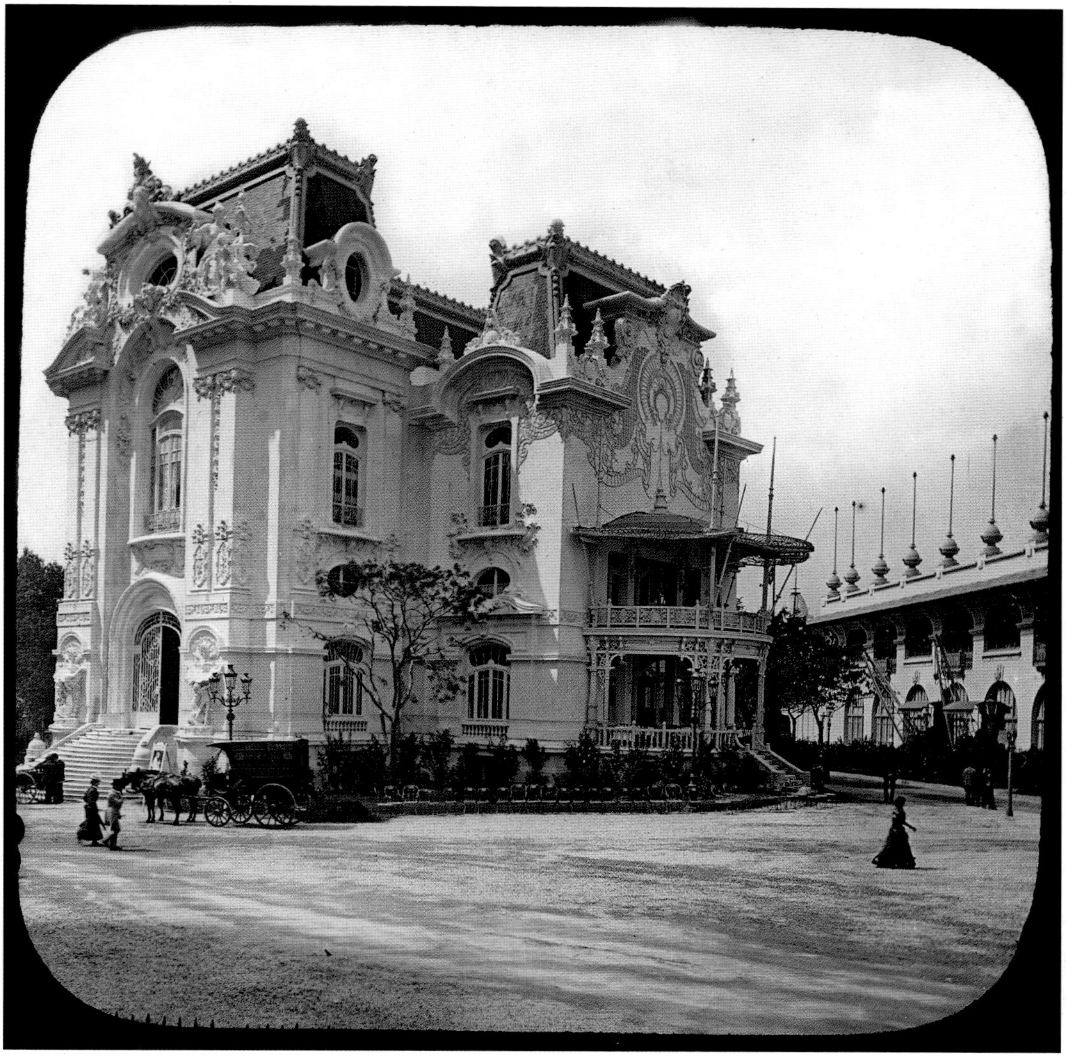

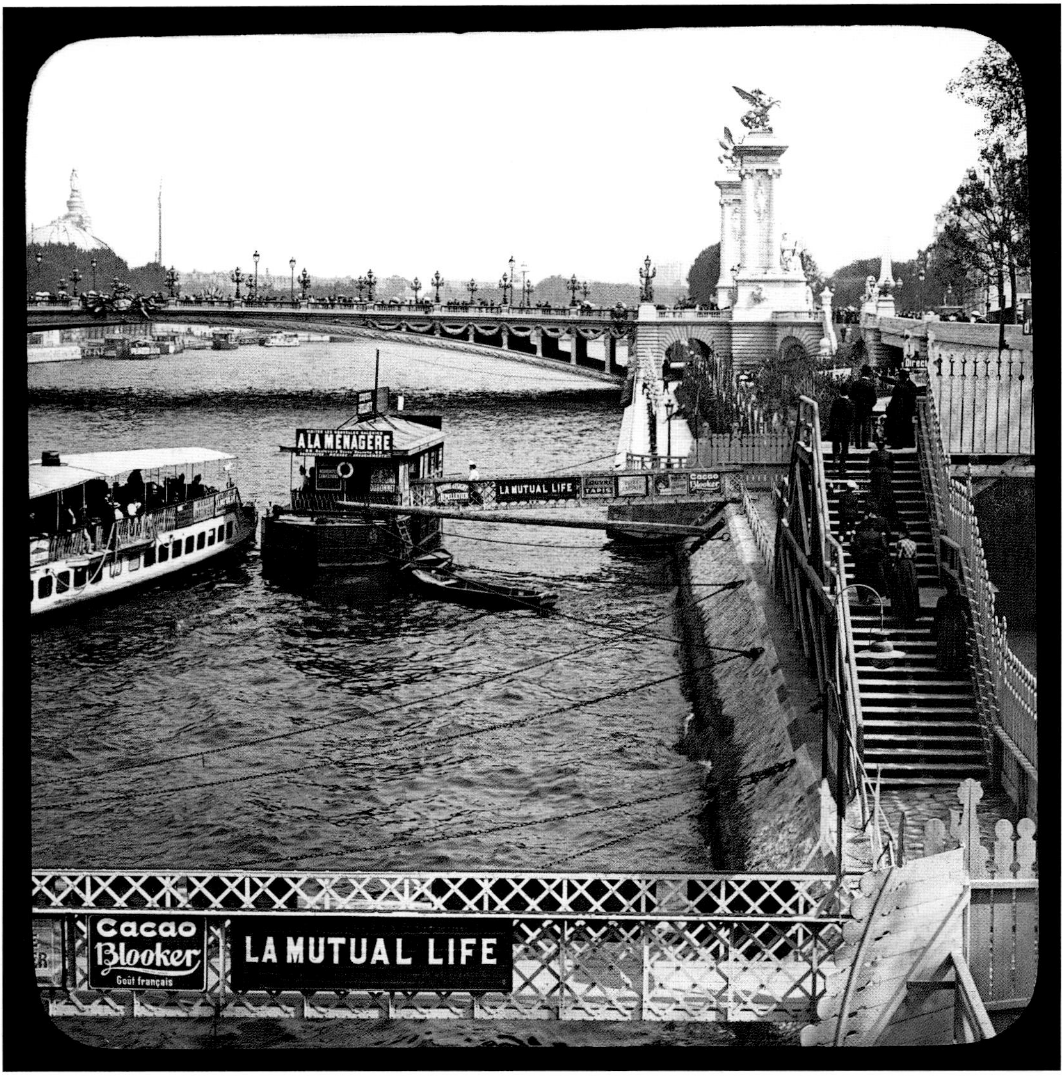

181 Ponte Alexandre III spanning the River Seine, Paris, c.1905
182 Entrance to Old Paris, 1890s

181 Der Pont Alexandre III, der die Seine überspannt, Paris, Frankreich, um 1905
182 Der Eingang ins Alte Paris, Paris, Frankreich, 1890er Jahre

181 Pont Alexandre III et la Seine, Paris, vers 1905
182 L'entrée du Vieux Paris, 1900

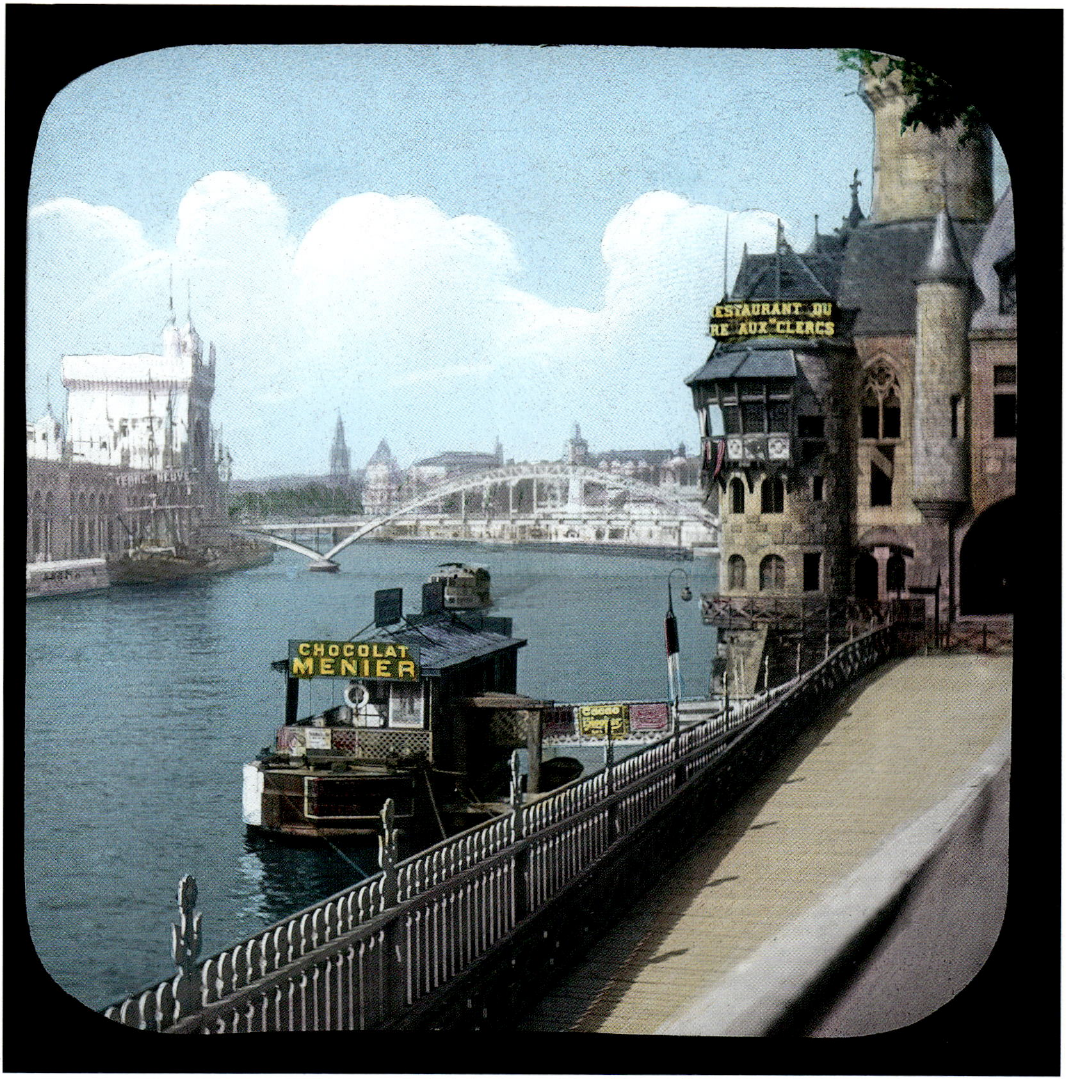
ESTAURANT DU
RE AUX CLERCS
CHOCOLAT
MENIER

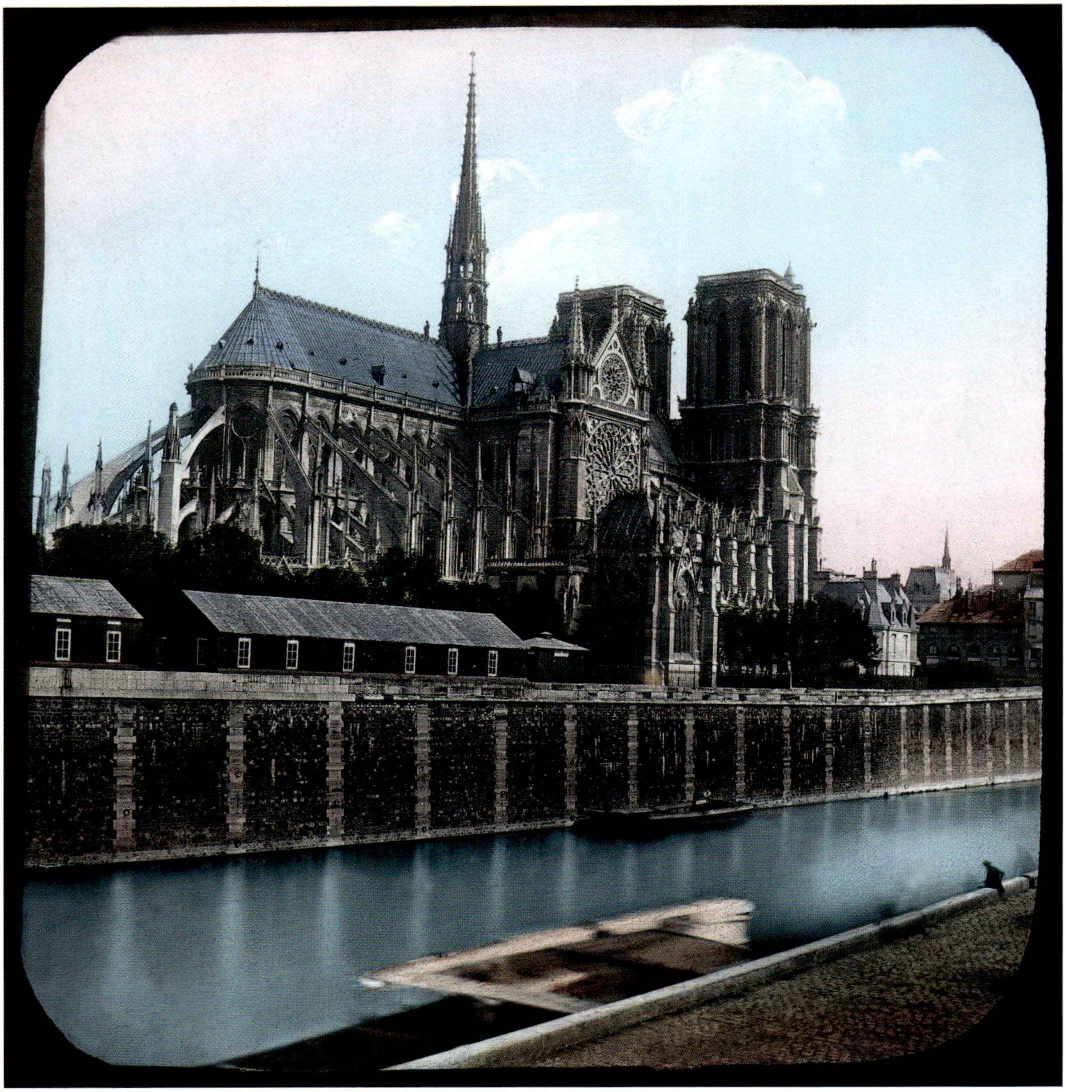

183 Notre Dame Cathedral, Paris, France, 1870s
184 Gateway to Château de Loches, Loire, France, 1880s

183 Die Kathedrale Notre Dame, Paris, Frankreich, 1870er Jahre
184 Das Eingangstor zum Château de Loches, Loire, Frankreich, 1880er Jahre

183 Cathédrale Notre-Dame de Paris, France, années 1870
184 Porte du château de Loches, Loire, France, années 1880

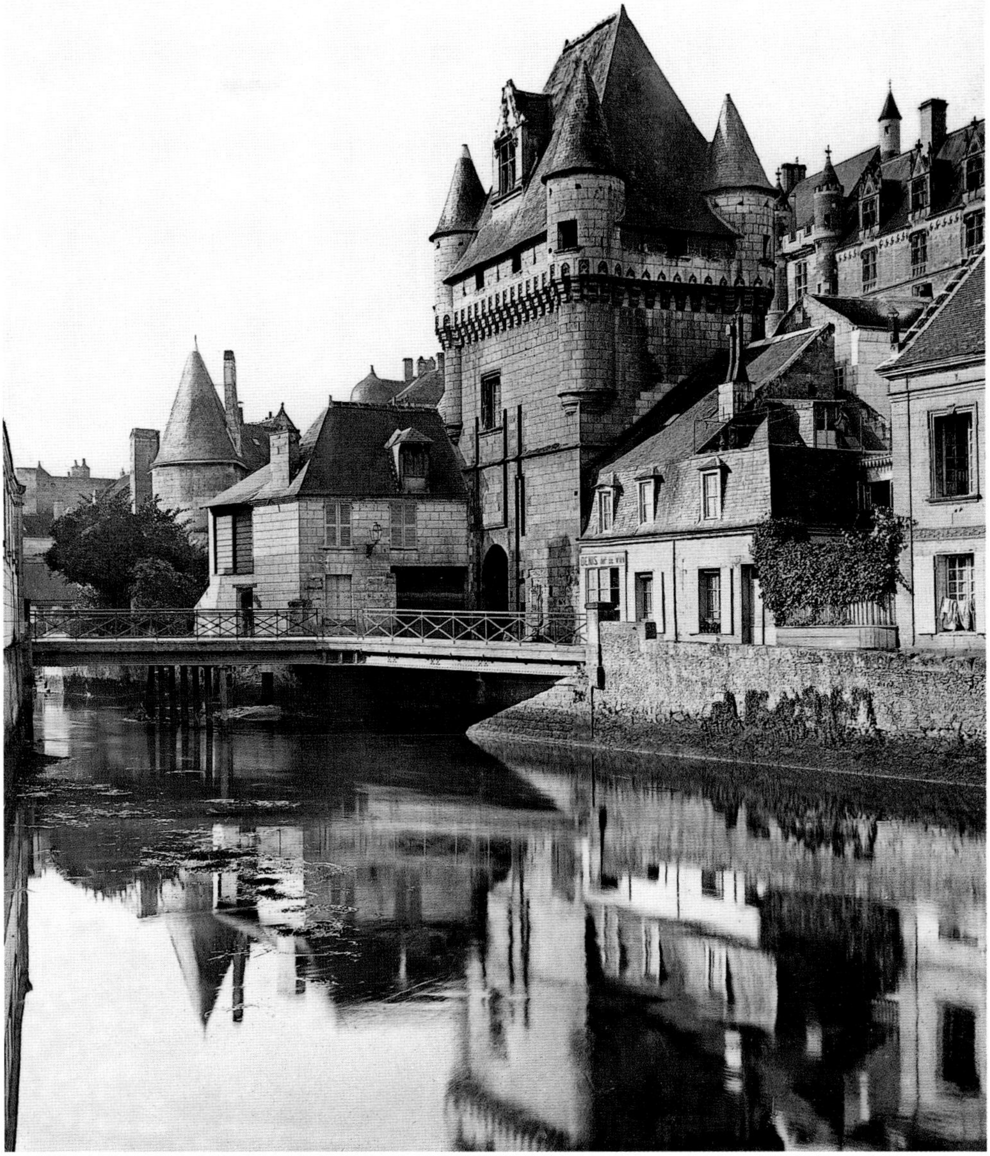

185 Grape pickers,
Champagne, France, 1870s

185 Weinlese,
Champagne, Frankreich,
1870er Jahre

185 Vendangeurs,
Champagne, France,
années 1870

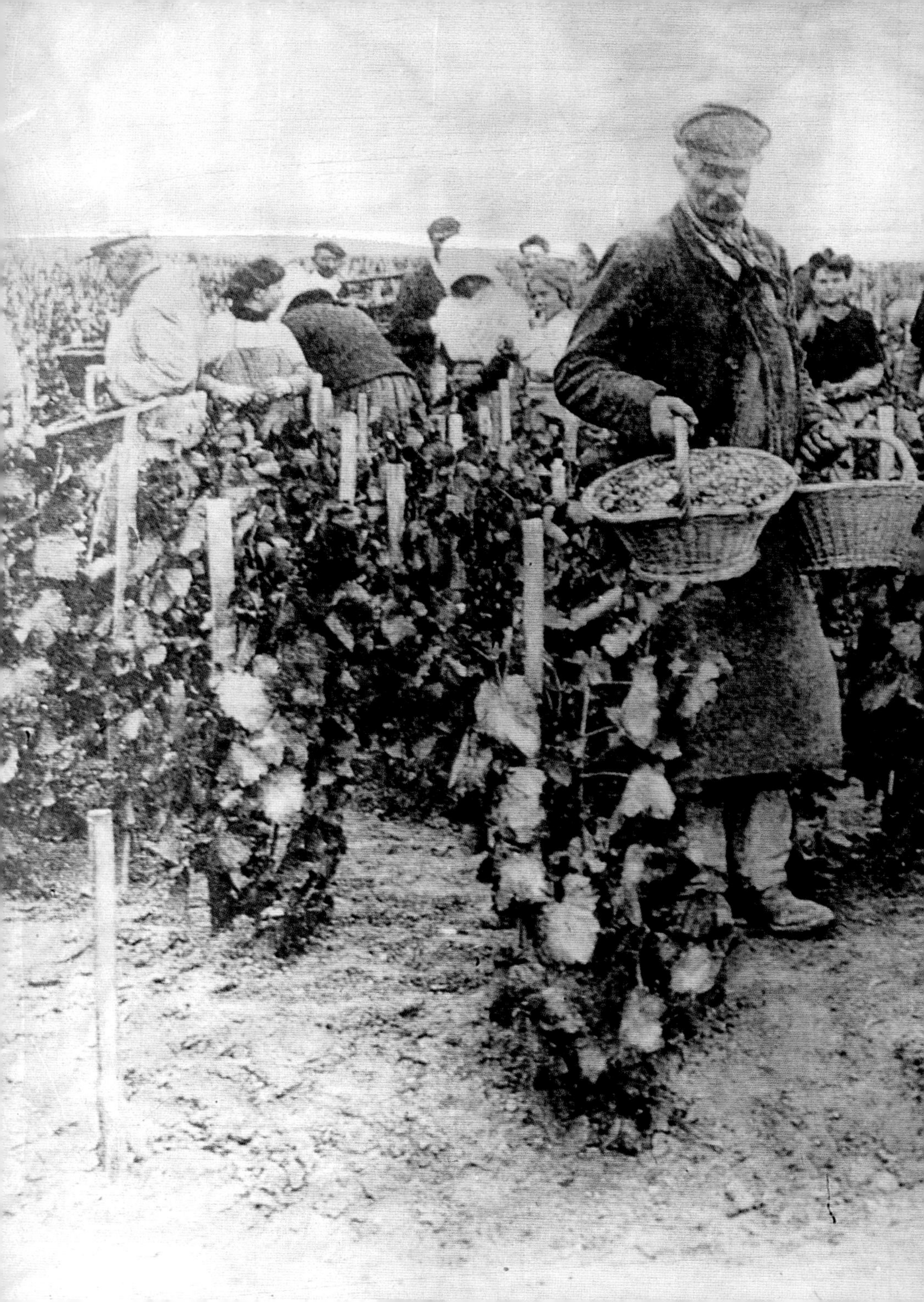

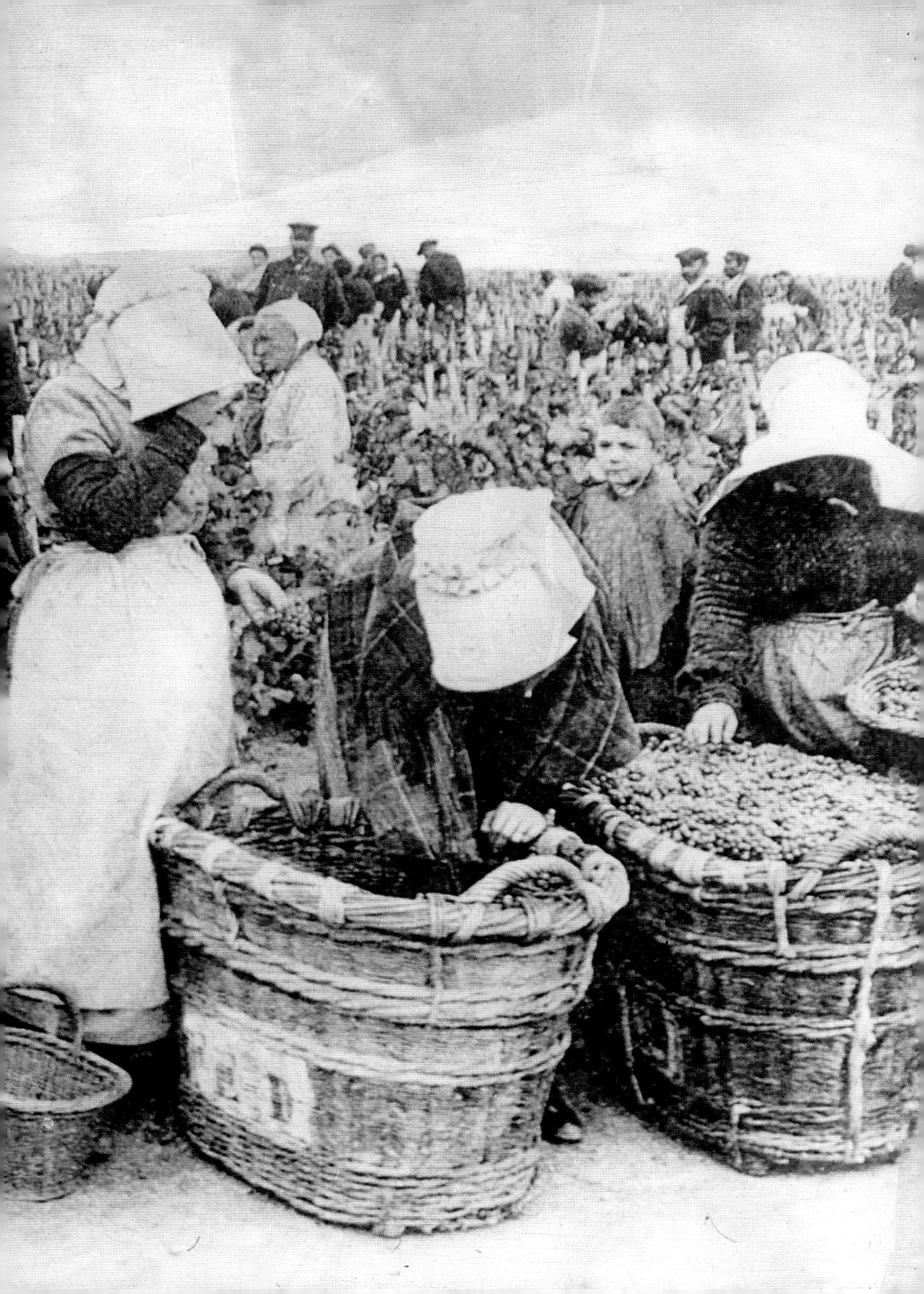

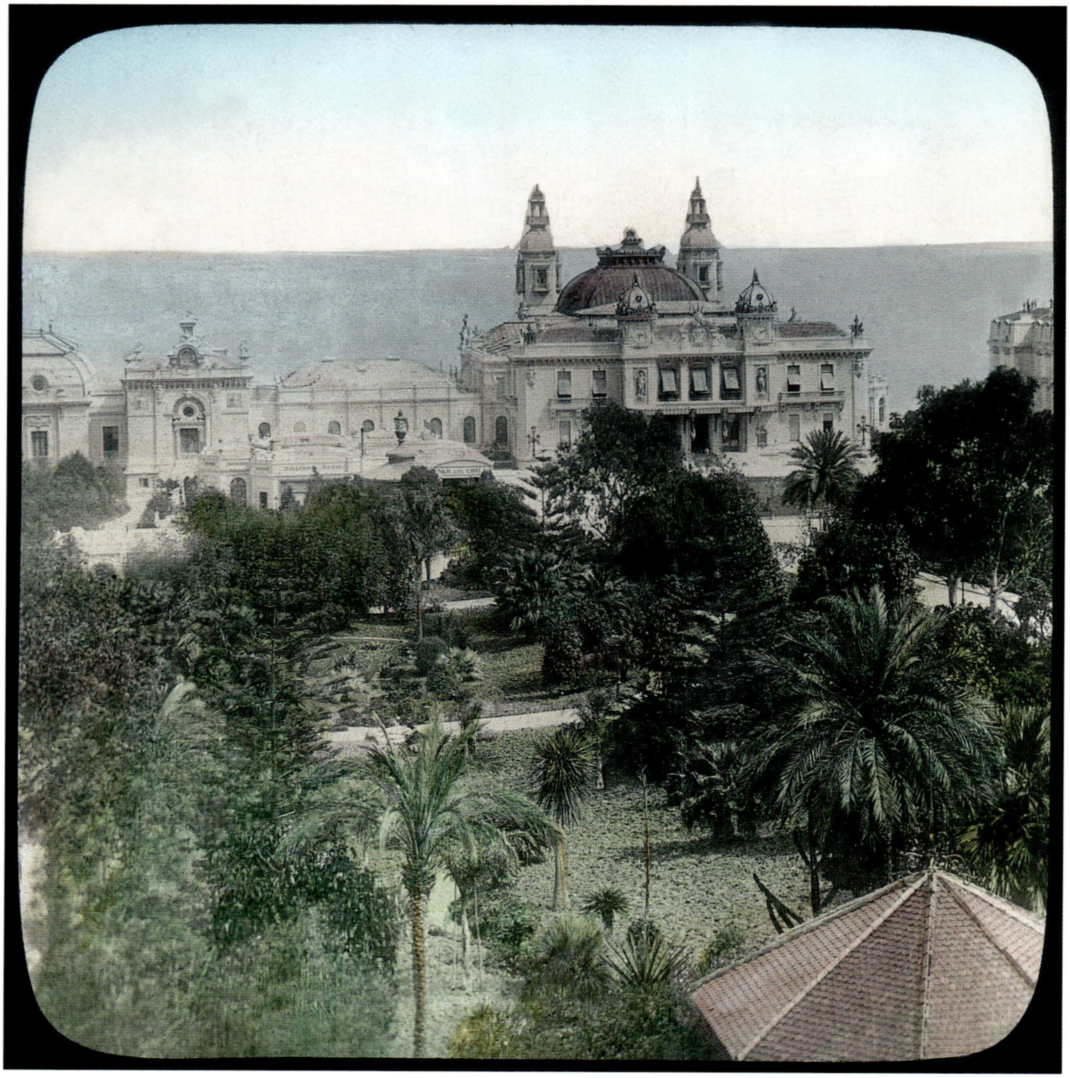

186 Monte Carlo casino and gardens, Monaco, Monte Carlo, 1880s
187 View of the Prince's Castle, Monte Carlo, Monaco, c.1900

186 Das Kasino und die Gärten von Monte Carlo, Monte Carlo, Monaco, 1880er Jahre
187 Blick auf den Fürstenpalast, Monte Carlo, Monaco, um 1900

186 Jardin et casino de Monte Carlo, Monaco, années 1880
187 Vue sur le palais princier, Monaco, vers 1900

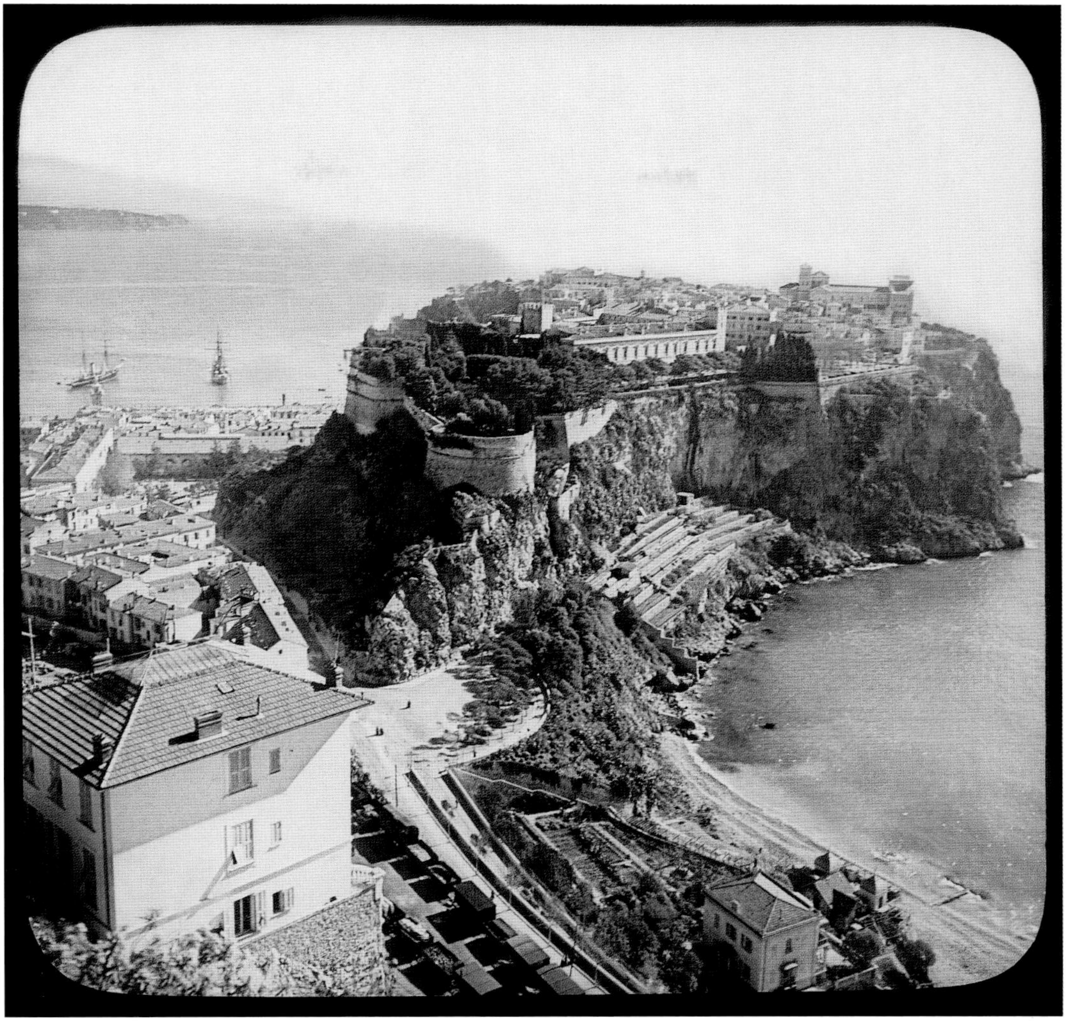

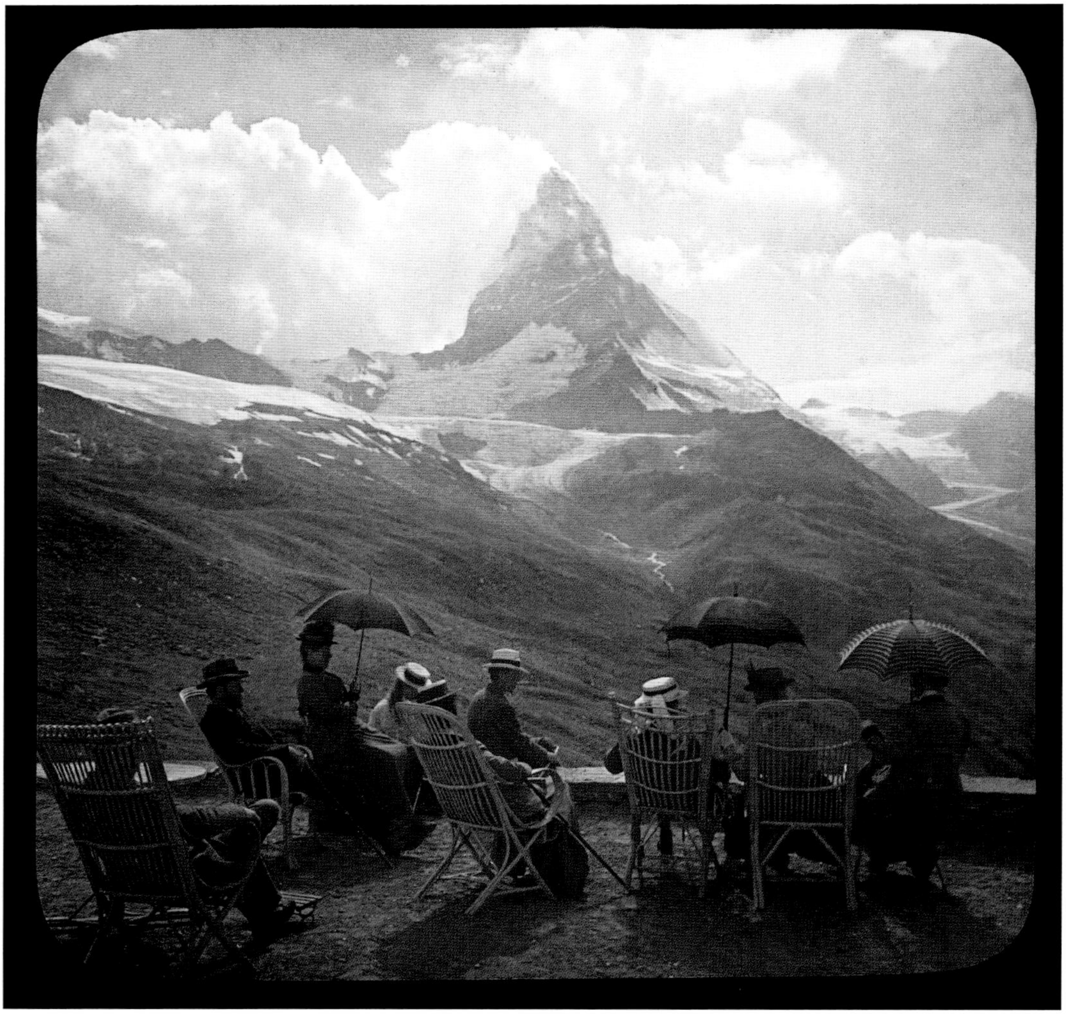

188 The Matterhorn, Switzerland, 1890s

188 Das Matterhorn, Schweiz, 1890er Jahre

188 Le Cervin, Suisse, années 1890

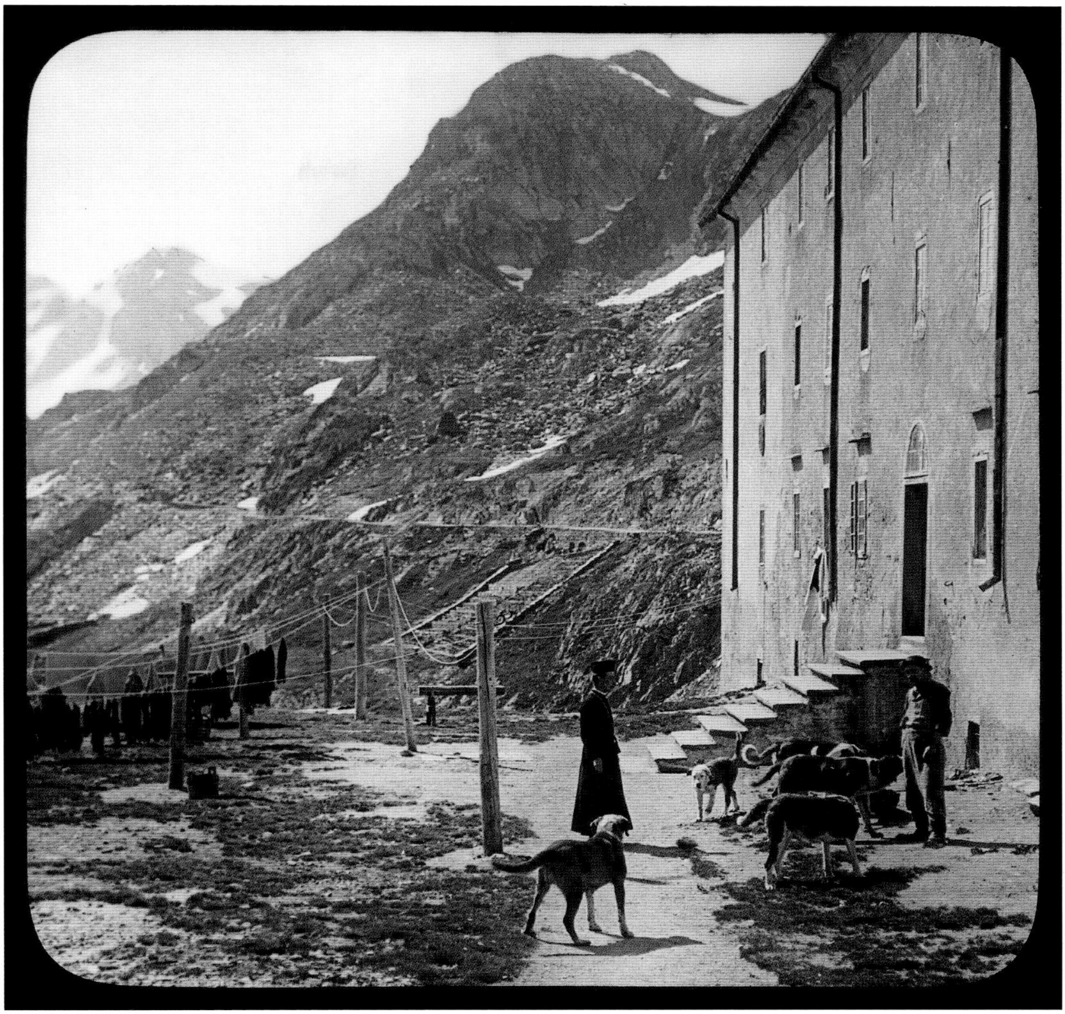

189 "The Pious Monks of St. Bernard", the Great St. Bernard Hospice in the Alps, Switzerland, c.1900

189 „Die frommen Mönche von St. Bernhard", das Hospiz auf dem Großen St. Bernhard in den Alpen, Schweiz, um 1900

189 « Les pieux moines de Saint-Bernard », hospice du Grand Saint-Bernard, Alpes suisses, vers 1900

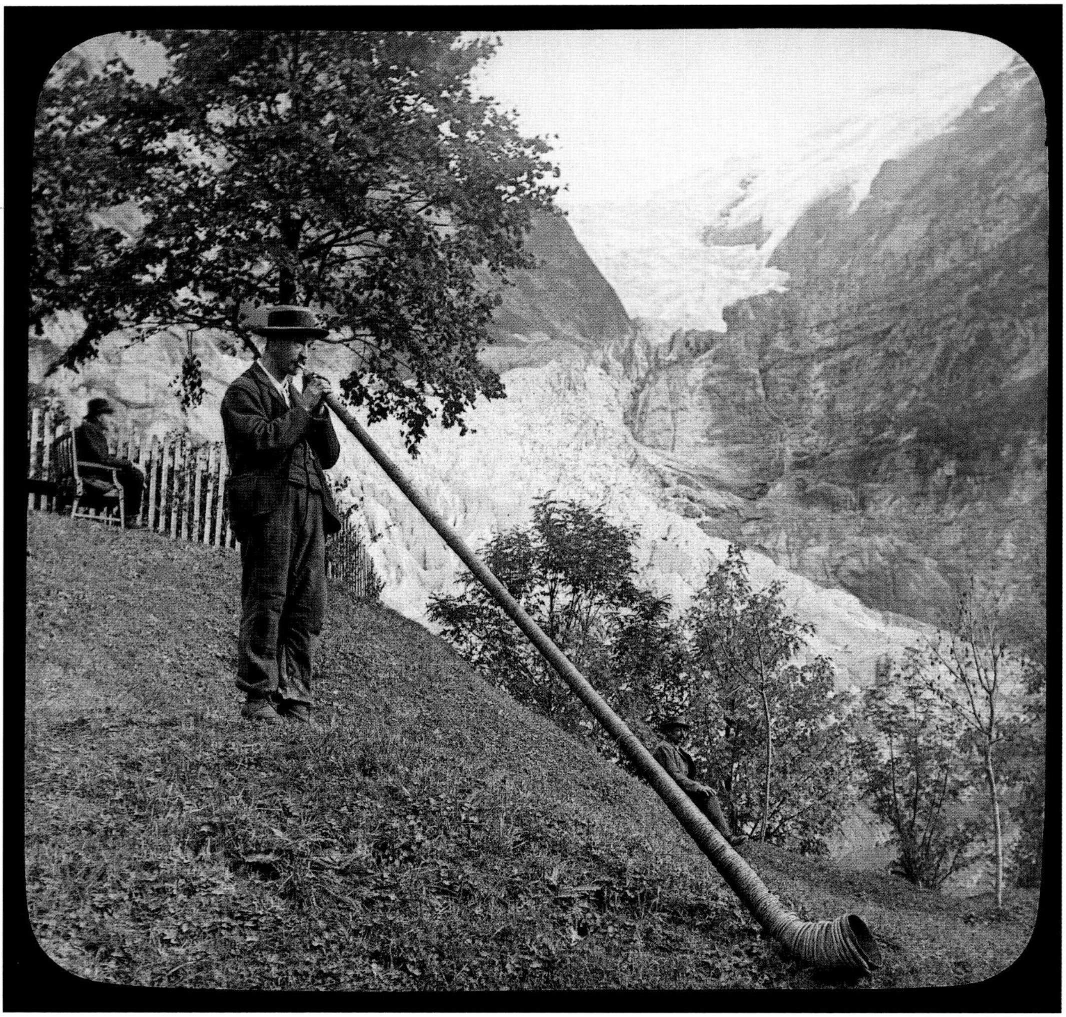

190 Blowing an alphorn, Grindelwald, Switzerland, 1880s

190 Alphornblasen, Grindelwald, Schweiz, 1880er Jahre

190 Cor alpin, Grindelwald, Suisse, années 1880

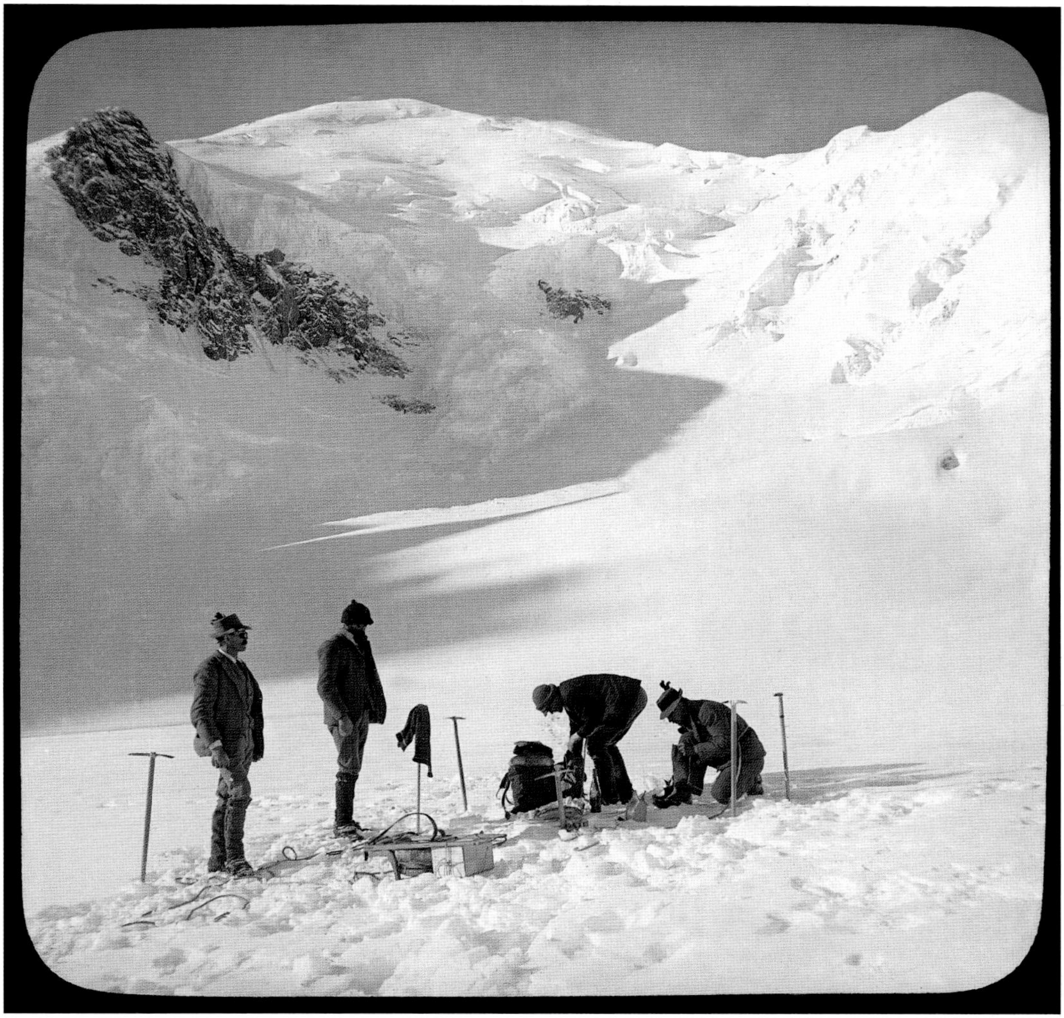

191 Resting on the Grand Plateau with Mont Blanc in the distance, Switzerland, c.1900

191 Verschnaufen auf dem Grand Plateau, im Hintergrund der Mont Blanc, Frankreich, um 1900

191 Repos sur le Grand Plateau avec, au fond, le Mont Blanc. France vers 1900

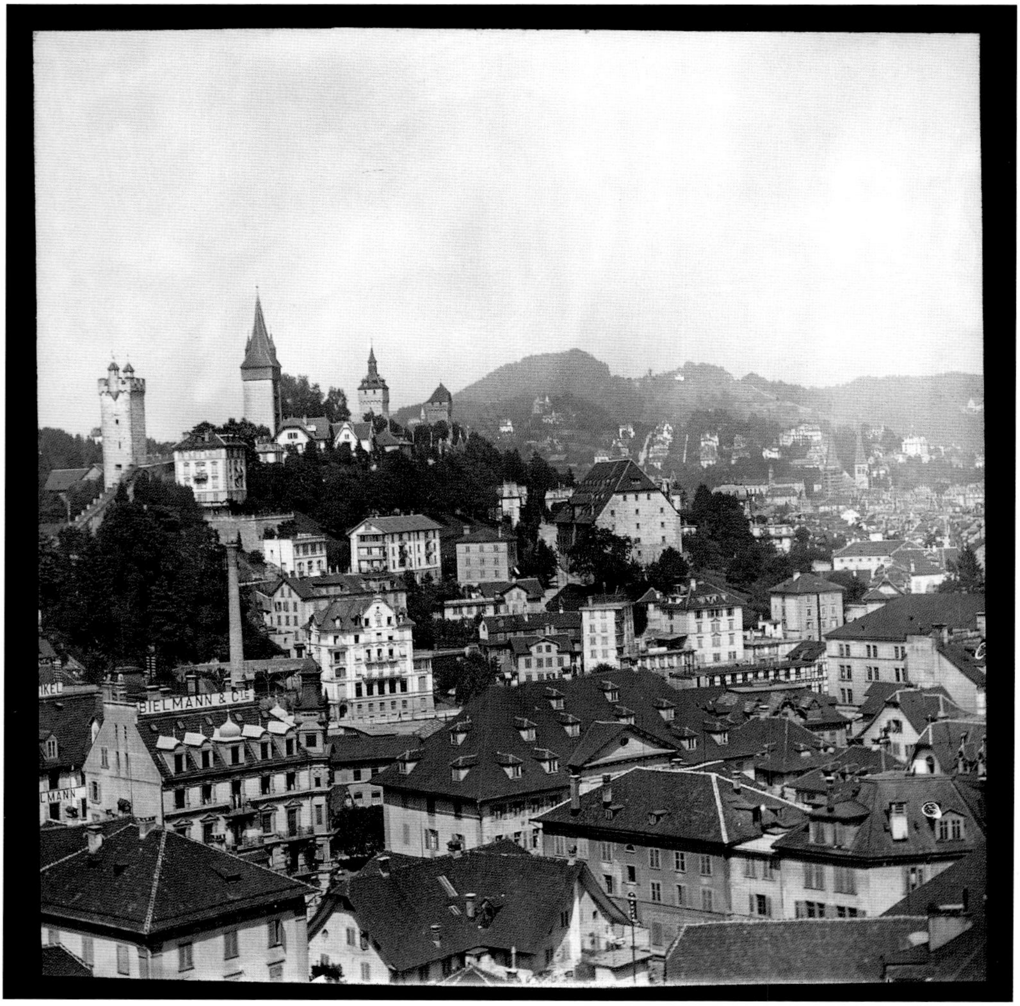

192 View of Lucerne, Switzerland, 1880s
193 Kapell-Brücke (Chapel Bridge), Lucerne, Switzerland, c.1900

192 Ansicht von Luzern, Schweiz, 1880er Jahre
193 Die Kapellbrücke, Luzern, Schweiz, um 1900

192 Vue de Lucerne, Suisse, années 1880
193 Kapell-Brücke (le pont de la chapelle) à Lucerne, Suisse, vers 1900

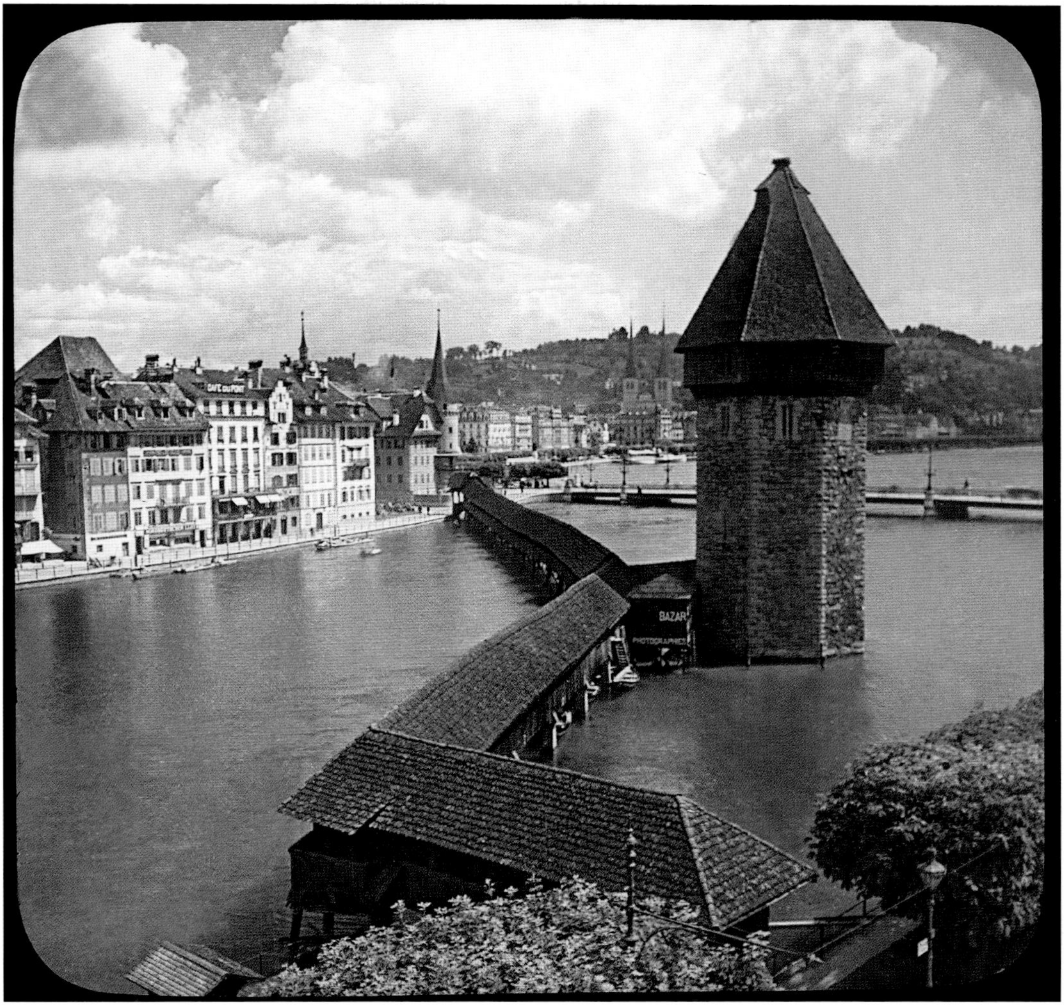
BAZAR

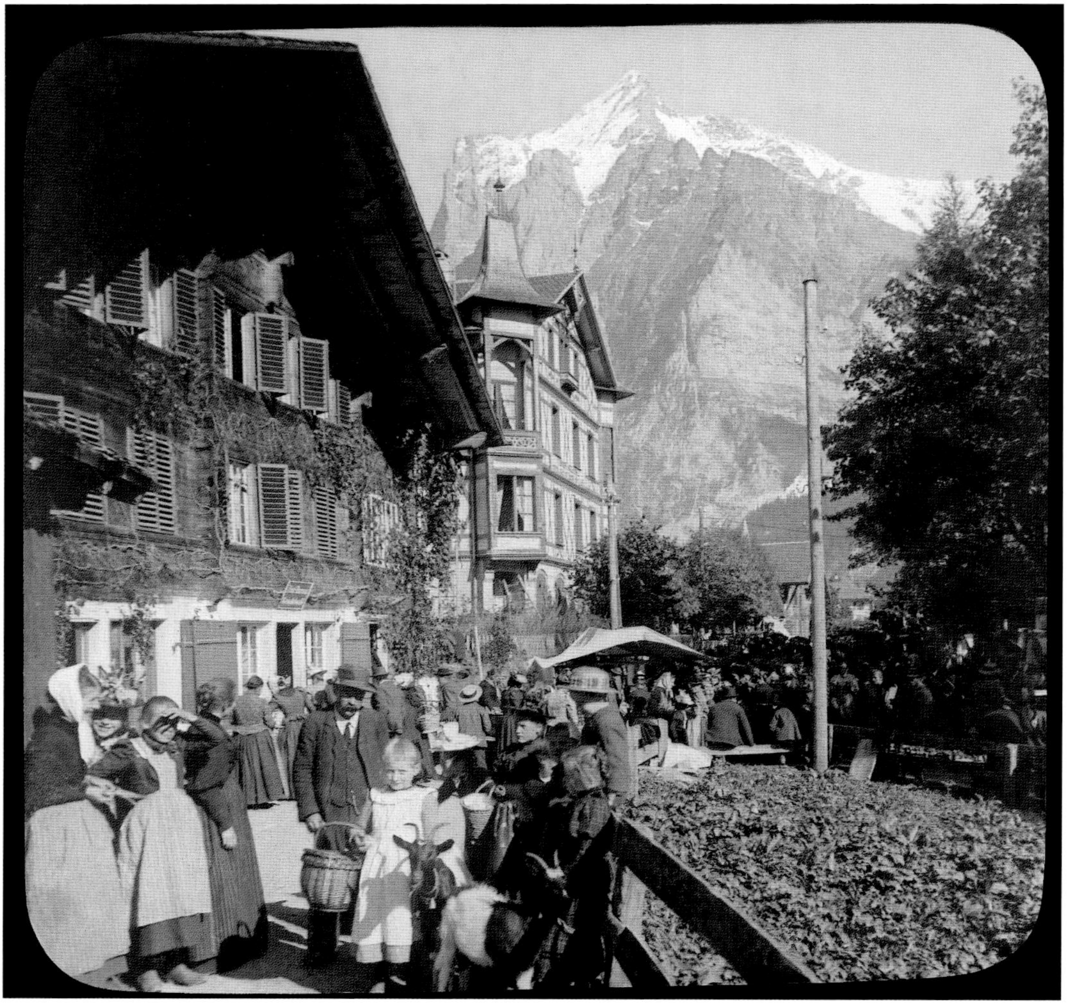

194 Market day in Grindelwald, Switzerland, c.1900
195 Gentleman on steps, Montreux, Switzerland, 1910s

194 Markttag in Grindelwald, Schweiz, um 1900
195 Eleganter Herr auf Treppenstufen, Montreux, Schweiz, 1910er Jahre

194 Jour de marché à Grindelwald, Suisse, vers 1900
195 Habitant de Montreux, Suisse, années 1910

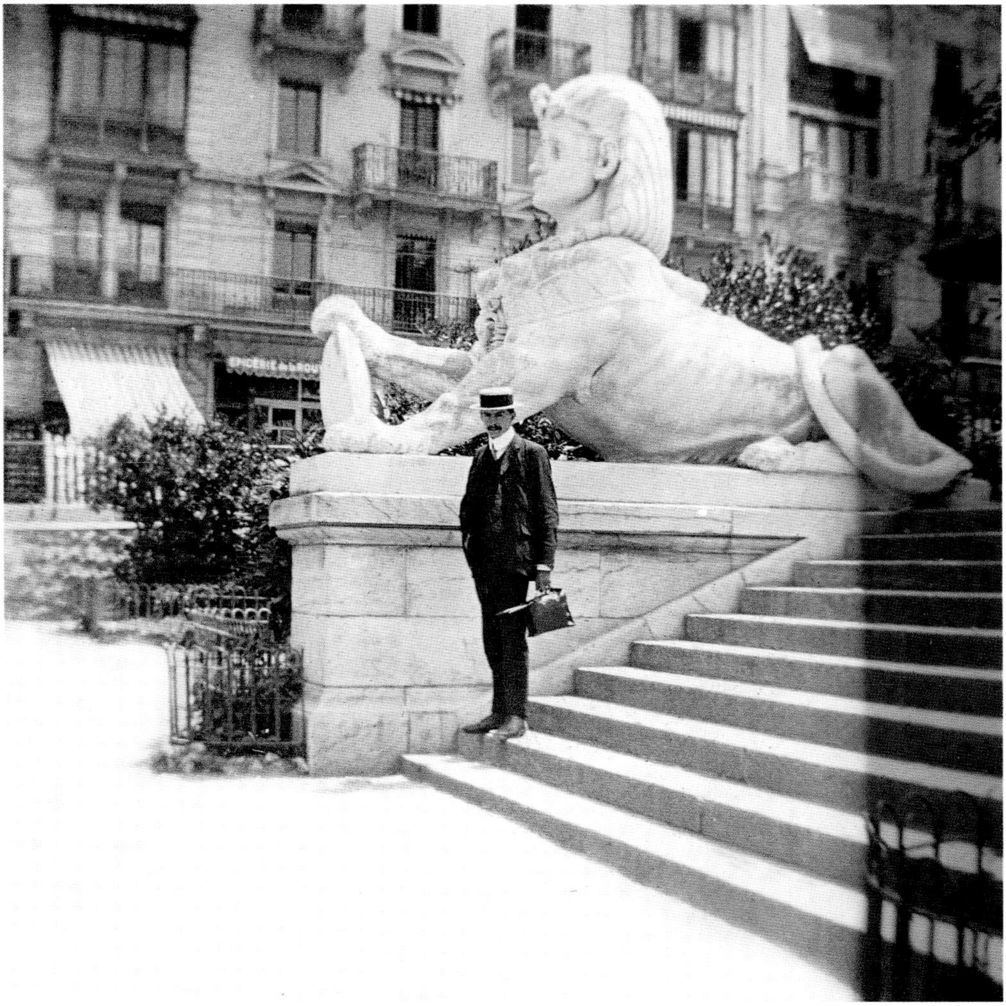

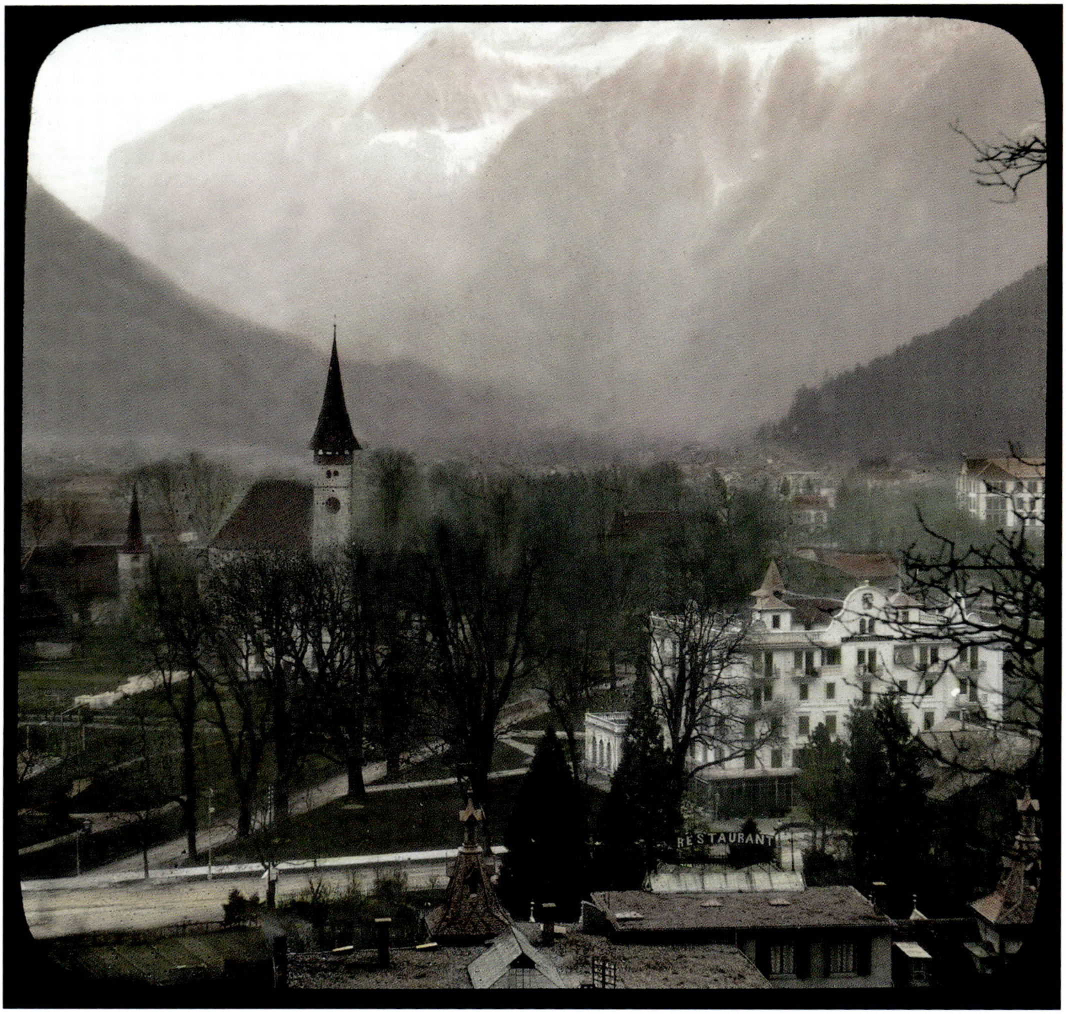

196 View of Interlaken, Switzerland, 1890s
197 Gornergrat Railway Station with views of the Matterhorn and Mont Blanc, Switzerland, 1928

196 Ansicht von Interlaken, Schweiz, 1890er Jahre
197 Bahnhof Gornergrat mit Blick auf das Matterhorn und den Mont Blanc, Schweiz, 1928

196 Vue sur Interlaken, Suisse, années 1890
197 Gare de Gornergrat. Au fond, le Cervin et le Mont Blanc, Suisse, 1928

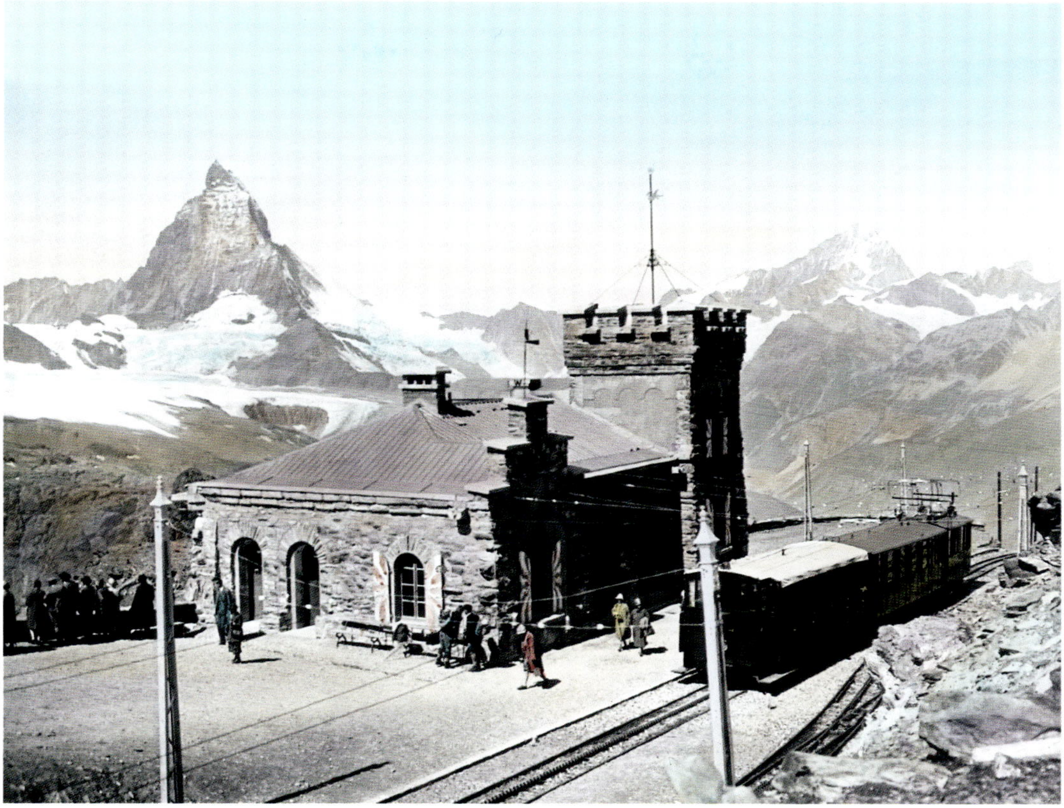

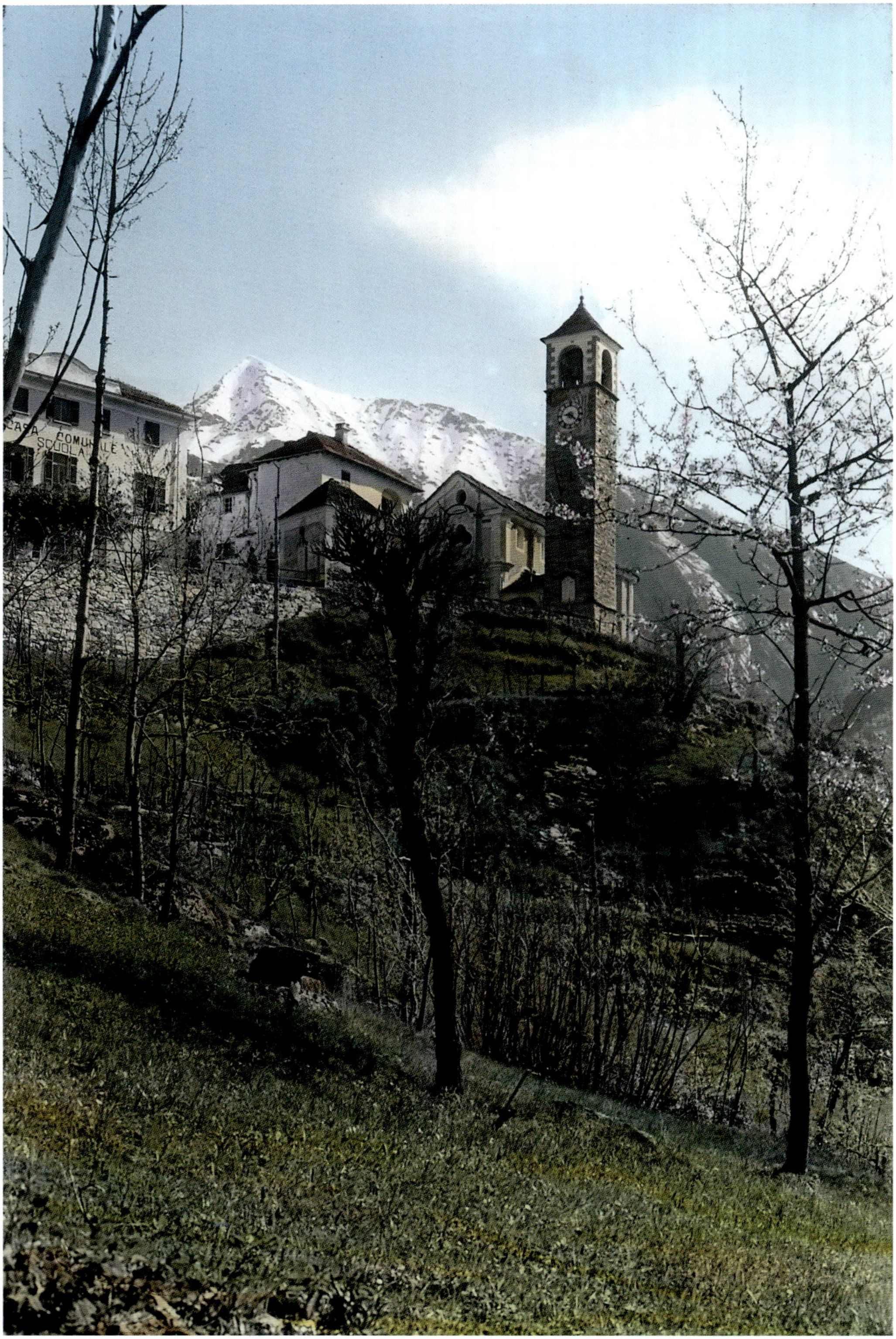
CASA COMUNALE
SCUOLA

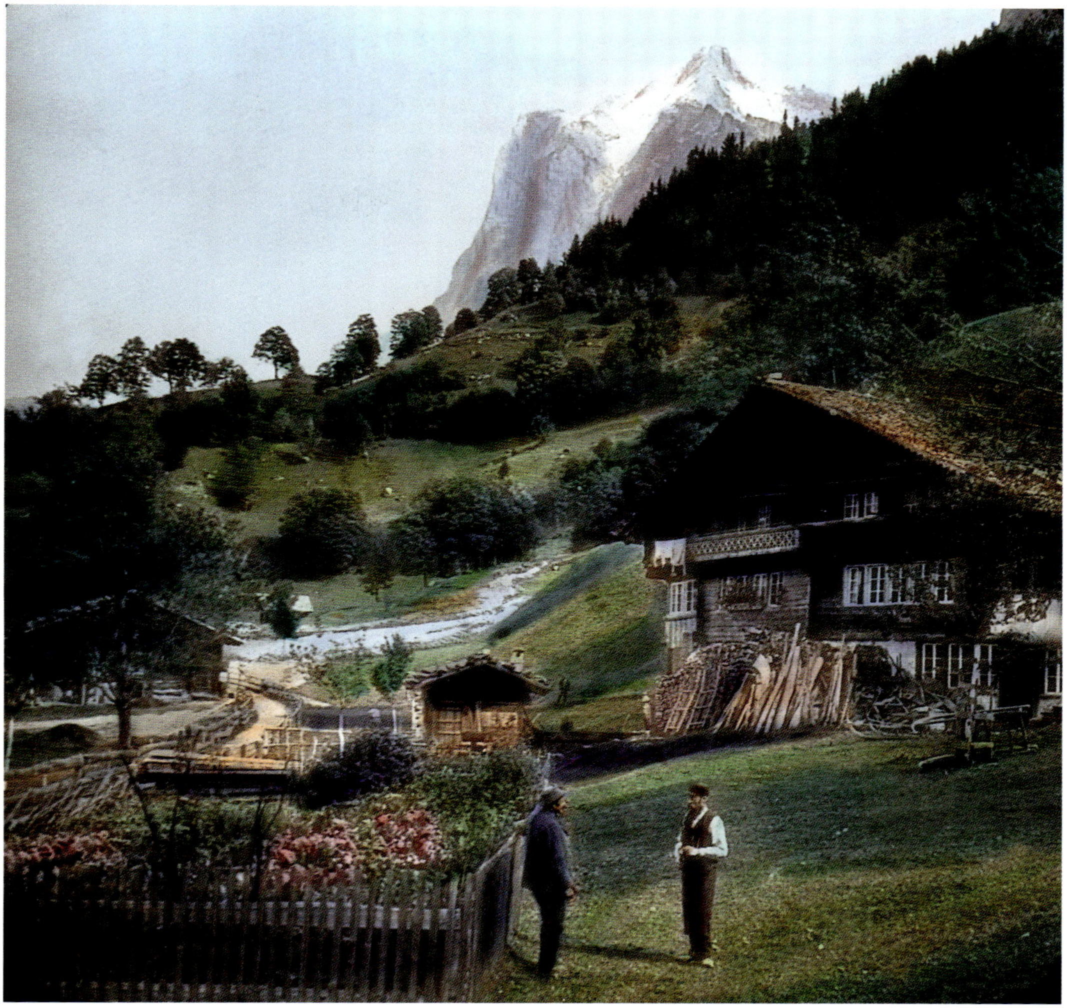

198 Mergoscia, near Lago di Vogorno, Switzerland, 1928
199 A Mountain Home in Switzerland, 1920s

198 Mergoscia, in der Nähe des Lago di Vogorno, Schweiz, 1928
199 Chalet in der Schweiz, 1920er Jahre

198 Mergoscia, près du lac de Vogorno, Suisse, 1928
199 Un chalet en Suisse, années 1920

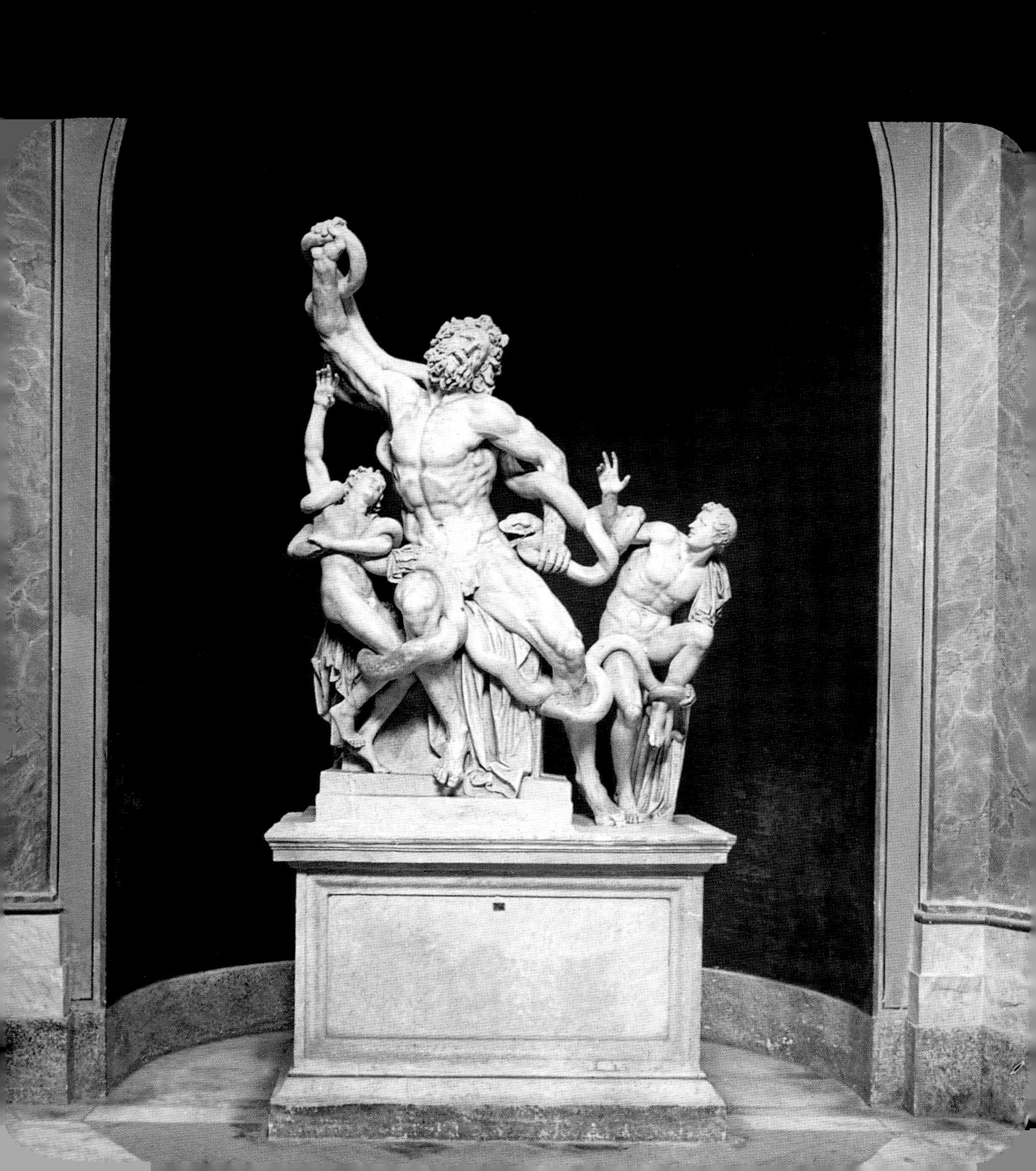

SOUTHERN EUROPE

SÜDEUROPA · EUROPE DU SUD

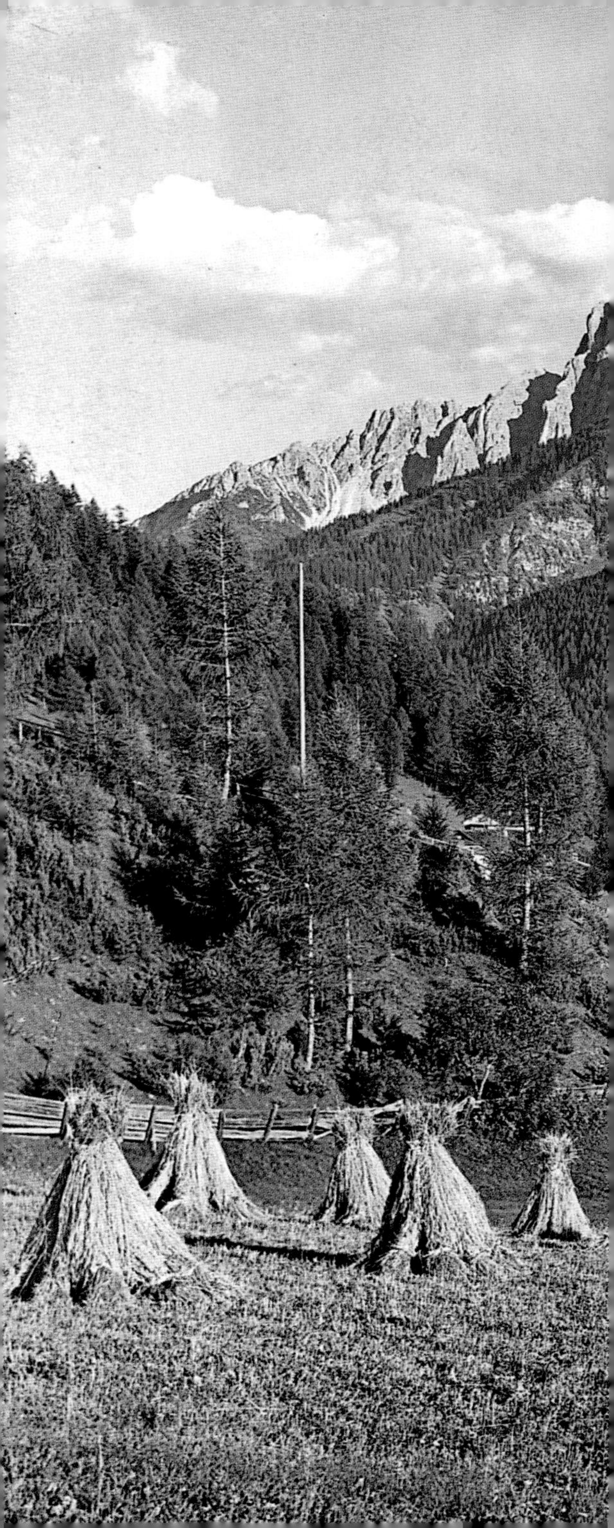

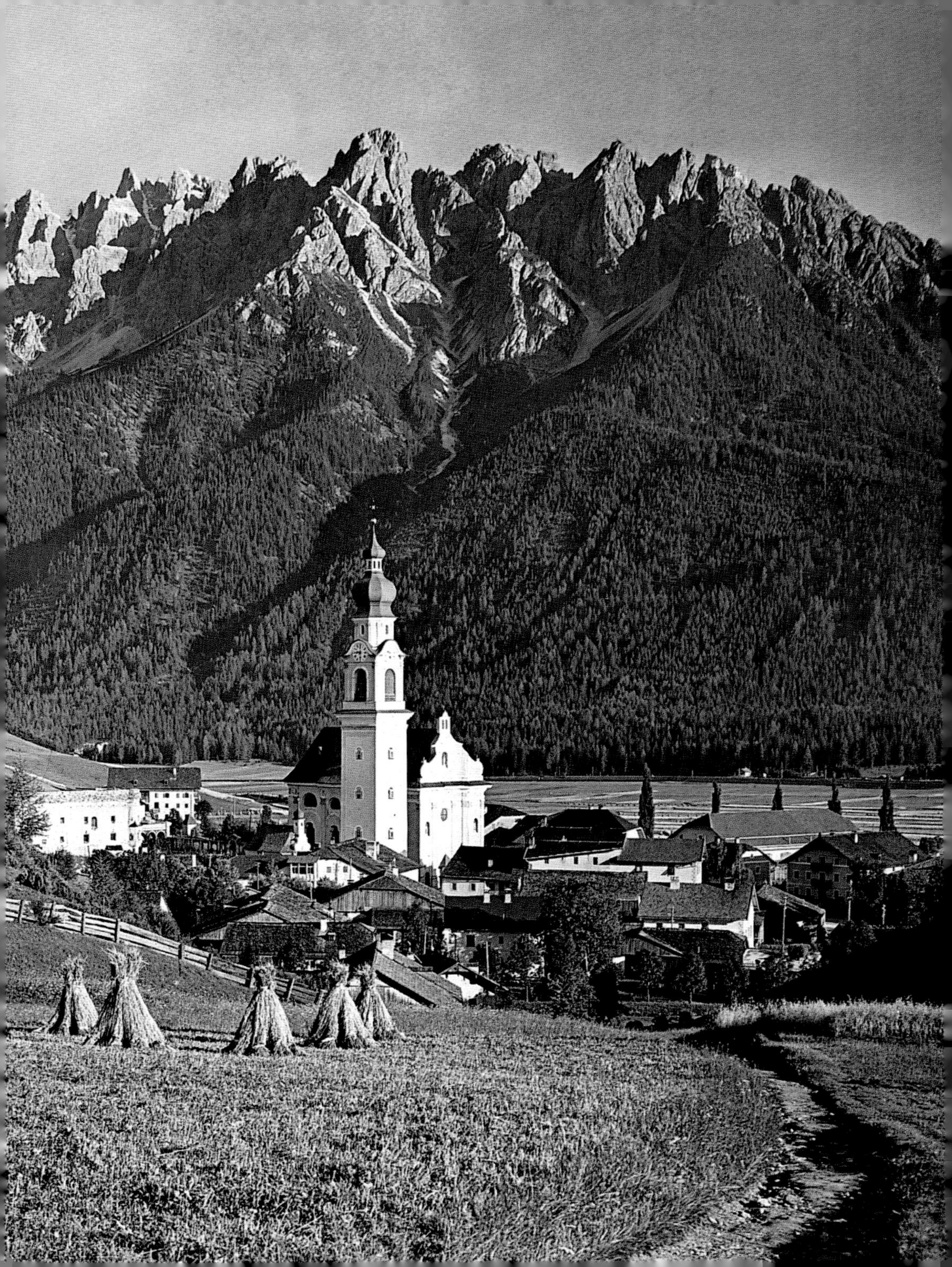

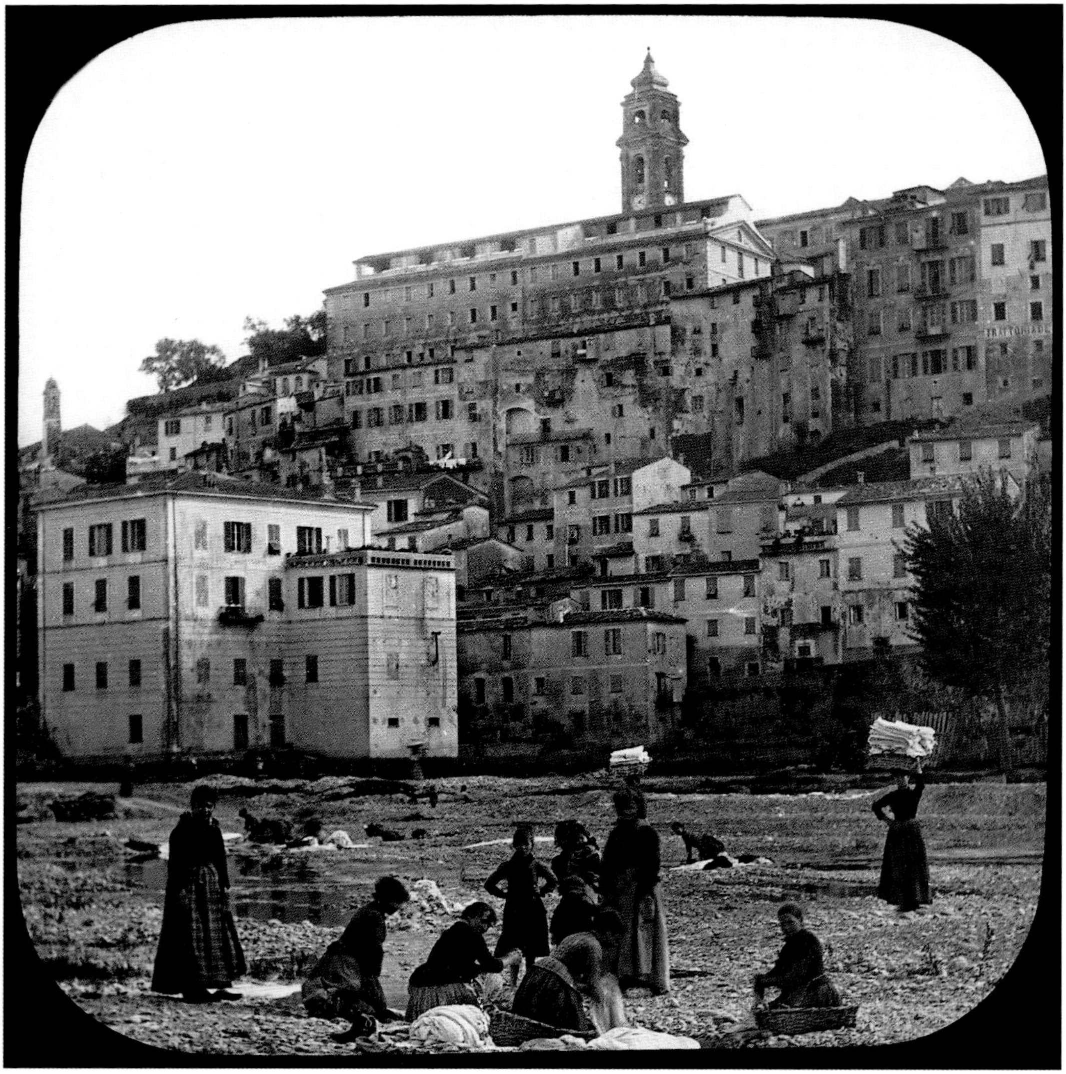

202 Women washing clothes along the river bed, Ventimiglia, Italy, 1880s
203 The Duomo (Cathedral), Milan, Italy, 1890s

202 Frauen waschen Wäsche entlang des Flussbetts, Ventimiglia, Italien, 1880er Jahre
203 Der Dom, Mailand, Italien, 1890er Jahre

202 Lavandières dans le lit d'une rivière, Ventimiglia, Italie, années 1880
203 Cathédrale de Milan, Italie, années 1890

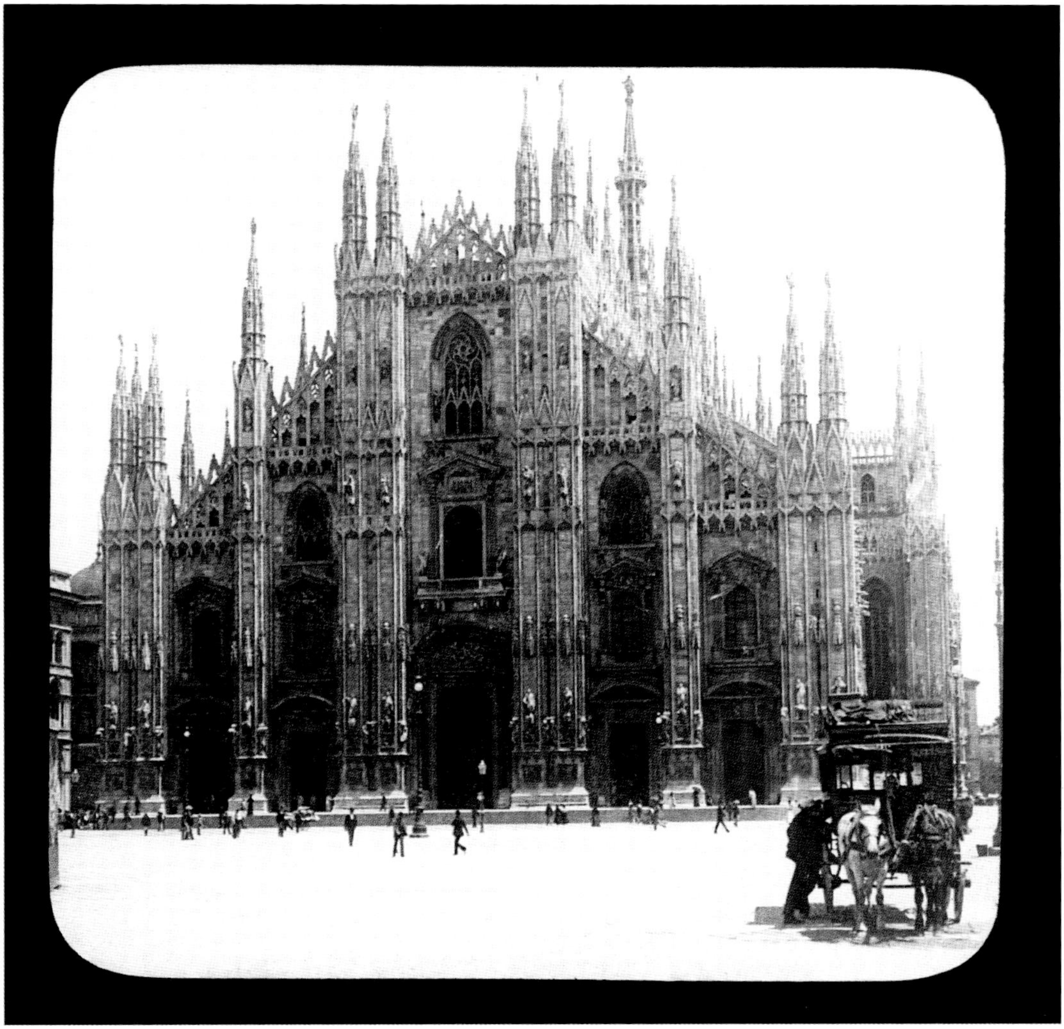

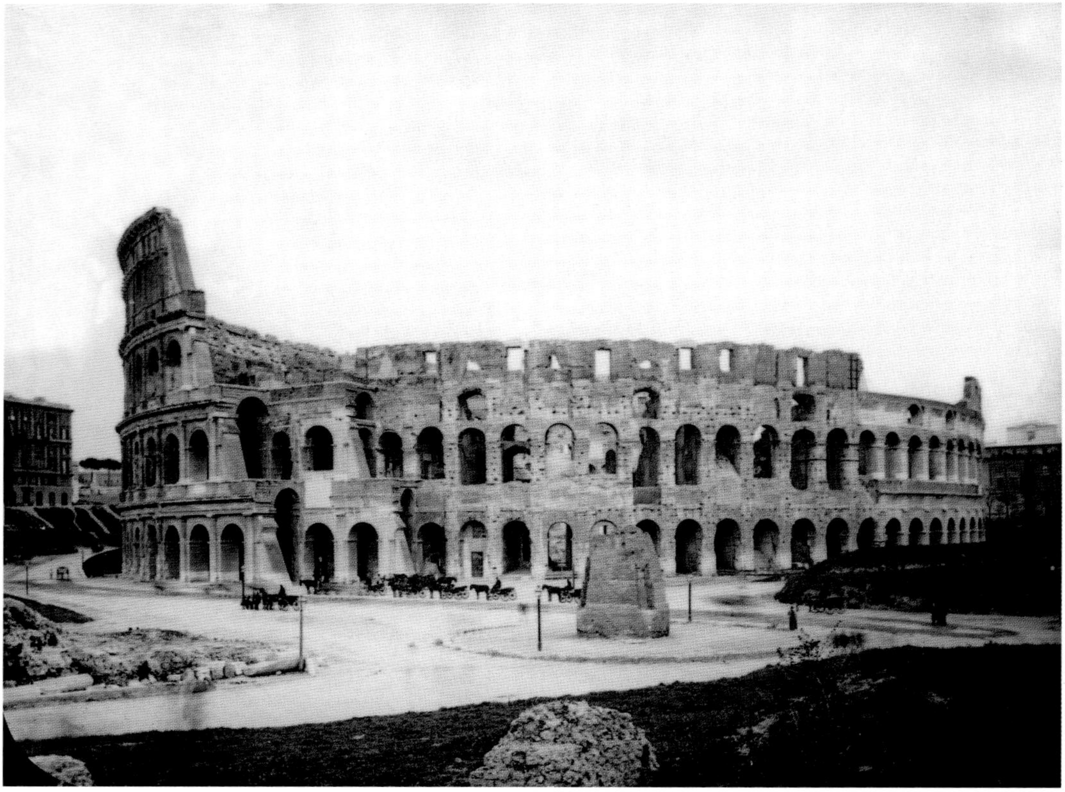

204 The Colosseum, Rome, 1880s
205 The Colosseum ("The King of Ruins"), Rome, Italy, c.1910

204 Das Kolosseum, Rom, Italien, 1880er Jahre
205 Das Kolosseum „Der König der Ruinen", Rom, Italien, um 1910

204 Le Colisée, Rome, années 1880
205 Le Colisée, Rome, Italie, vers 1910

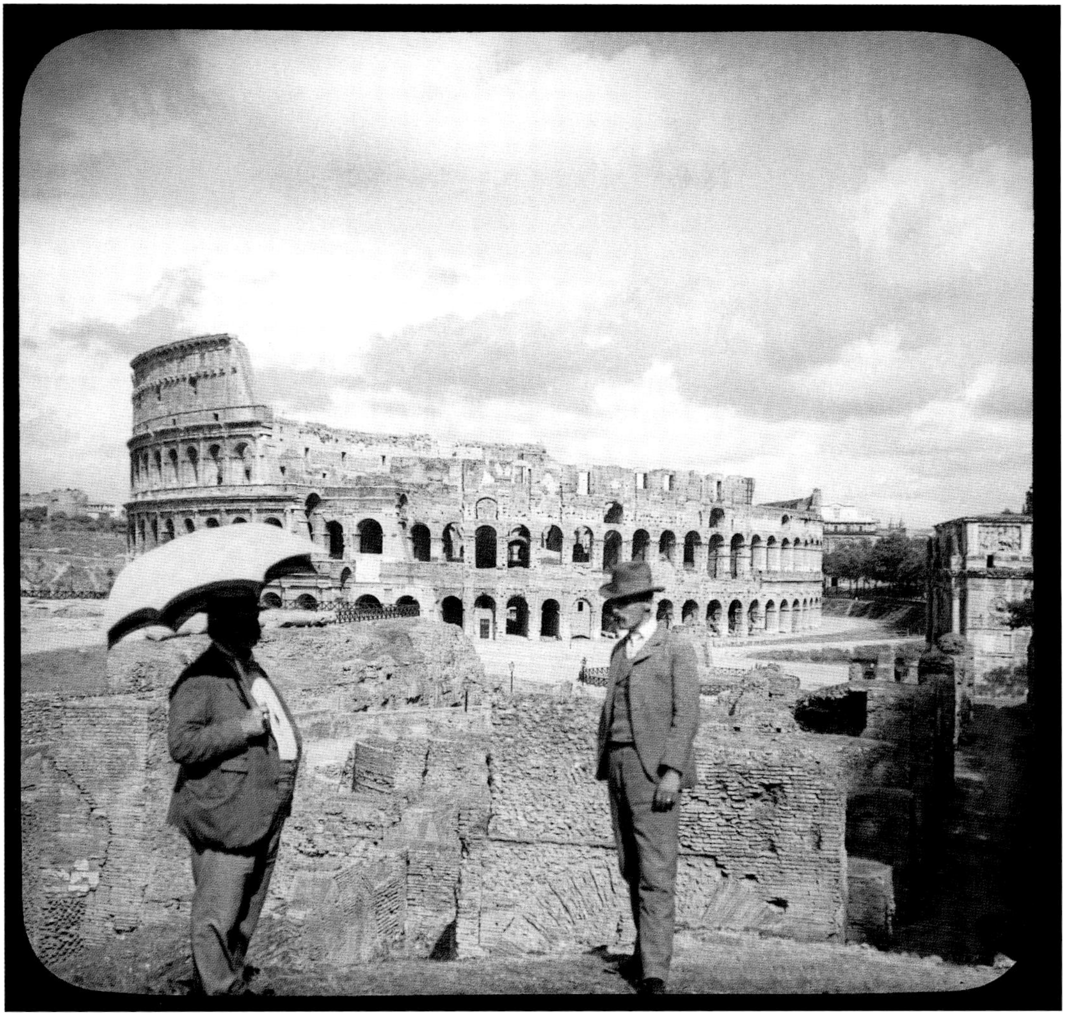

206 The Colosseum, Rome, Italy, 1890s, view from West

206 Das Kolosseum, Rom, Italien, 1890er Jahre, Ansicht von Westen

206 Le Colisée, Rome, Italie, années 1890, vu de l'ouest

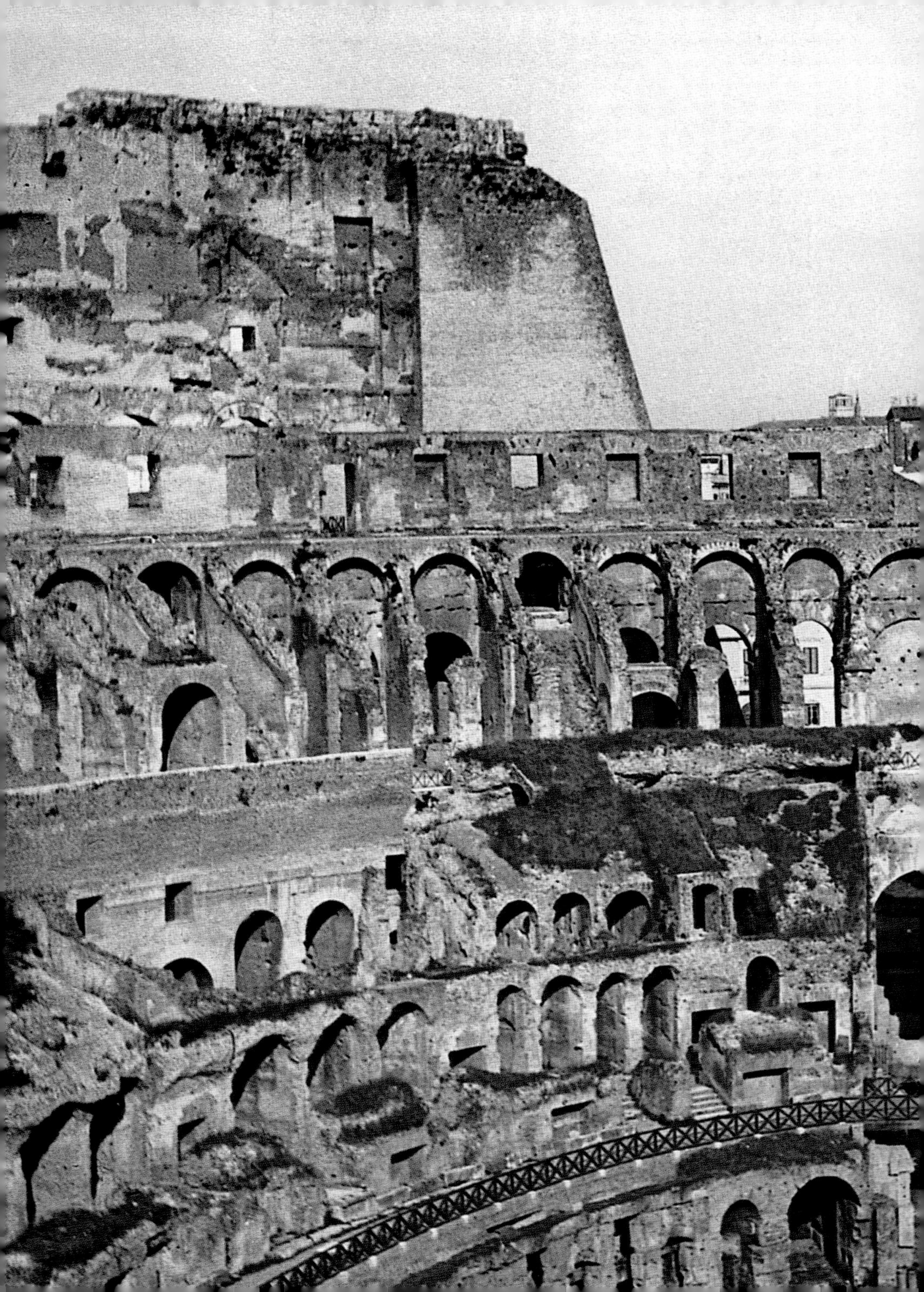

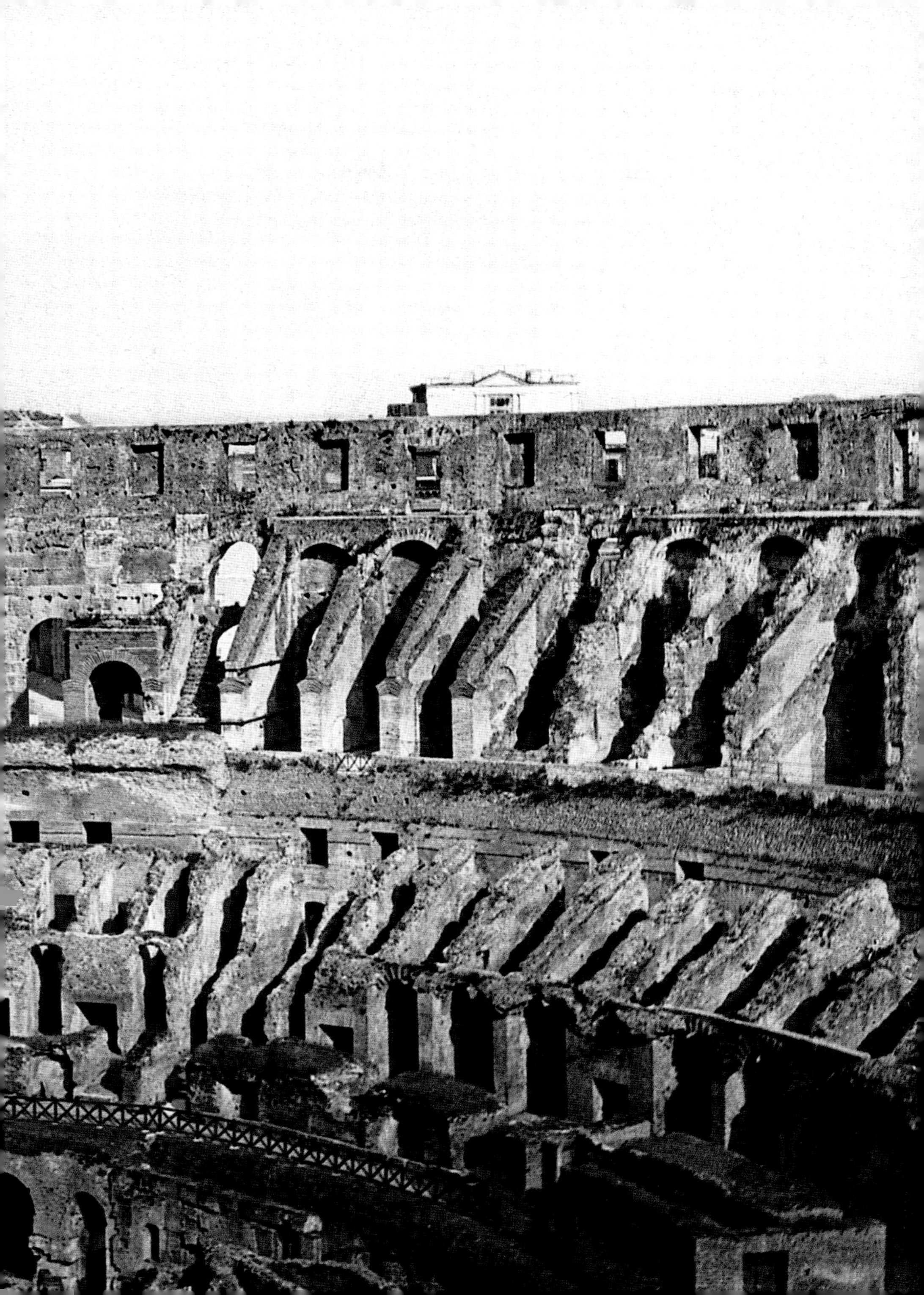

207 Trinità dei Monti church above the Spanish Steps, Rome, 1860s

207 Die Kirche Santa Trinità dei Monti oberhalb der Spanischen Treppe, Rom, Italien, 1860er Jahre

207 Église de la Trinité-des-Monts, en haut de l'escalier de la place d'Espagne, Rome, années 1860

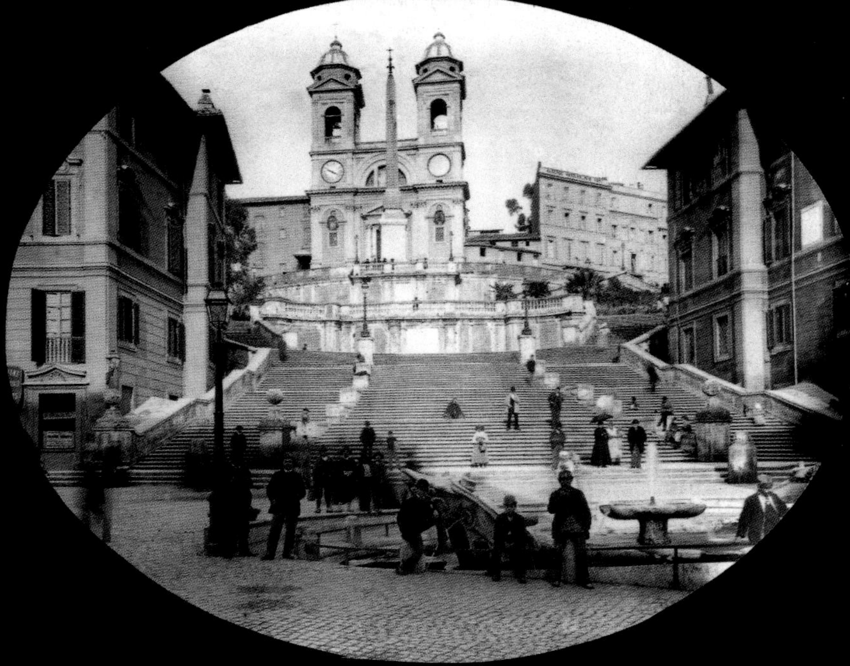

208 Fontana di Trevi (Trevi Fountain), Rome, 1860s

208 Fontana di Trevi (der Trevi-Brunnen), Rom, Italien, 1860er Jahre

208 Fontaine de Trevi, Rome, années 1860

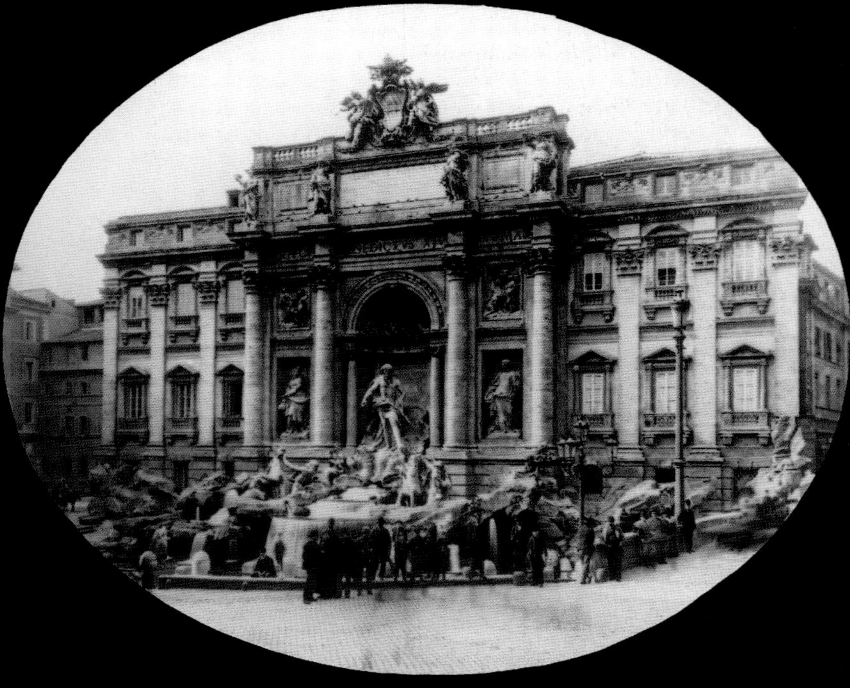

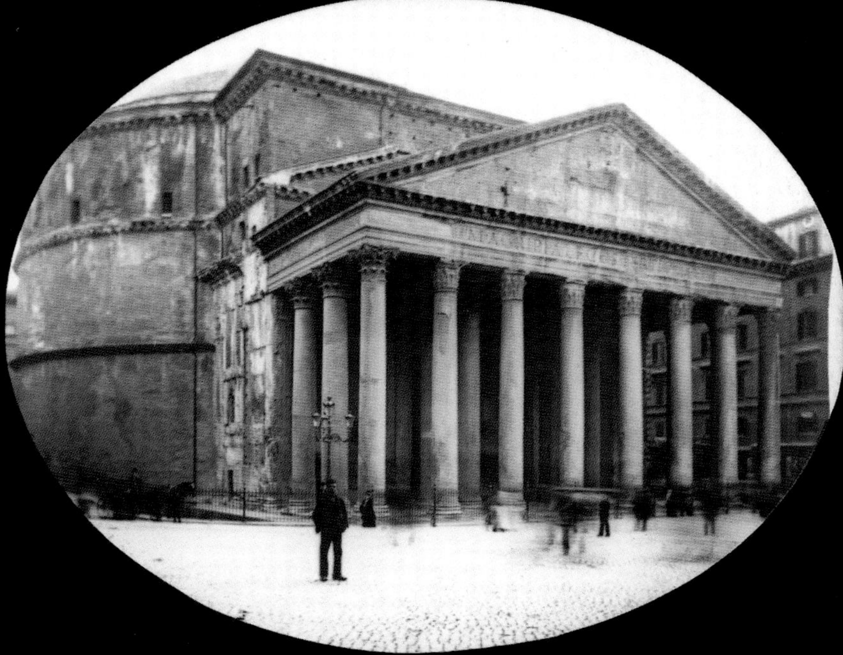

209 The Pantheon, Rome, 1860s

209 Das Pantheon, Rom, Italien, 1860er Jahre

209 Le Panthéon, Rome, années 1860

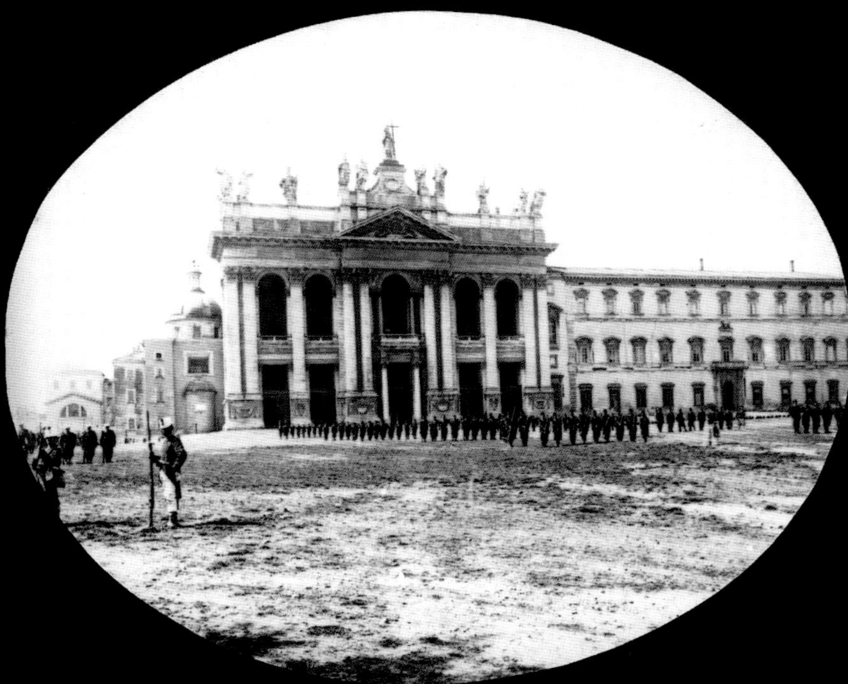

210 Basilica of St. John Lateran, Rome, 1860s

210 Basilika St. Johannes im Lateran, Rom, Italien, 1860er Jahre

210 Basilique Saint-Jean de Latran, Rome, années 1860

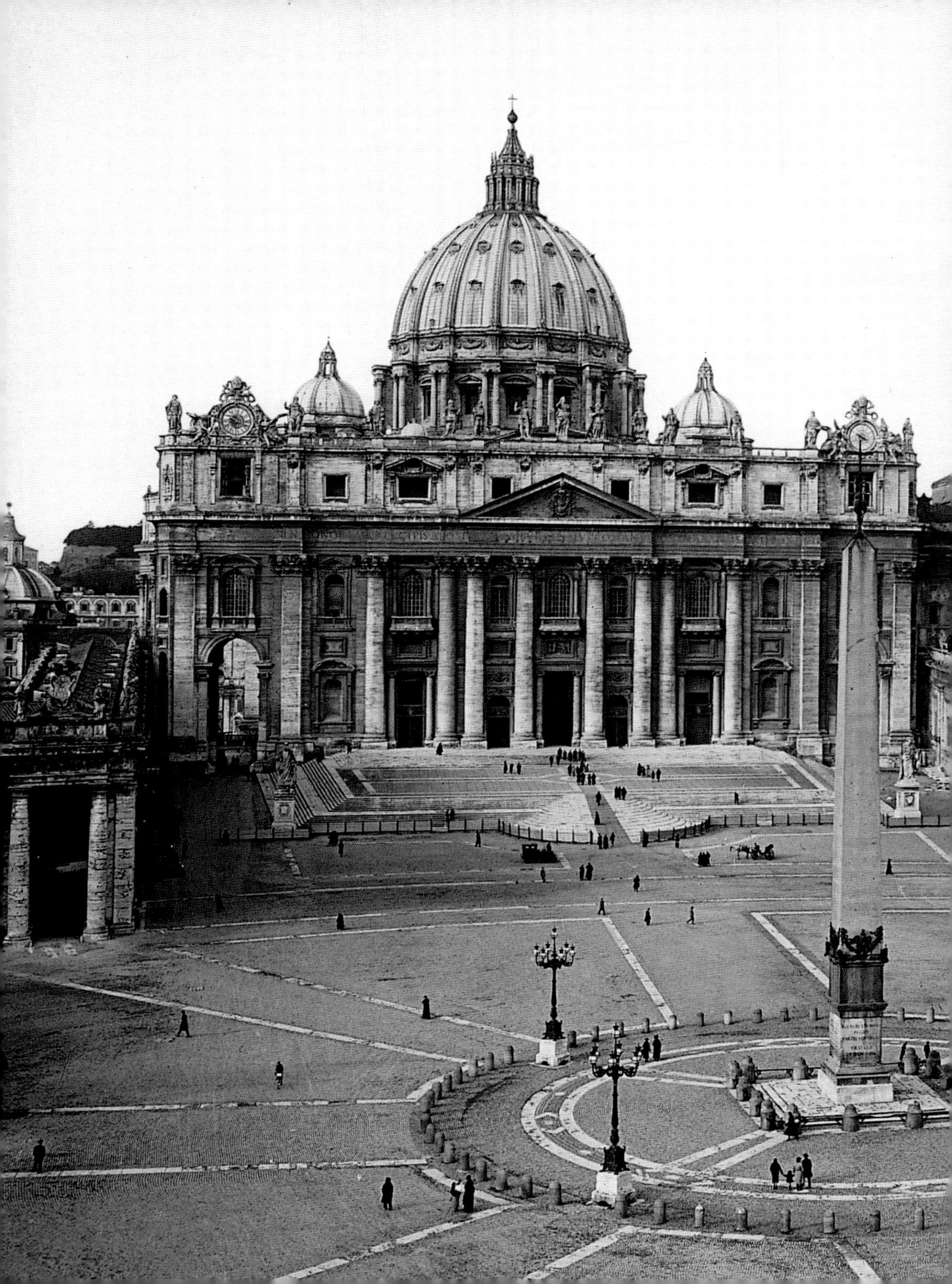

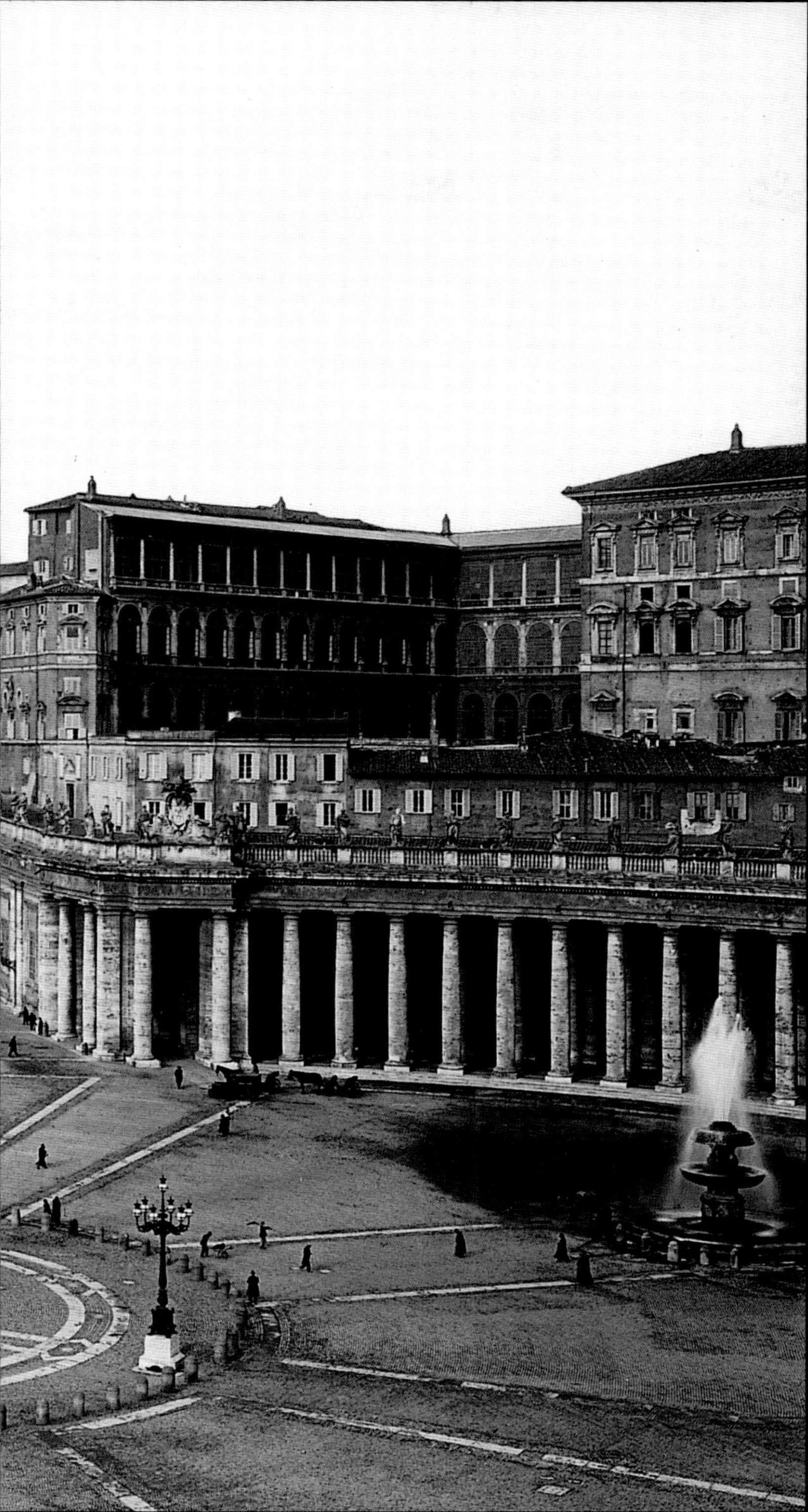

211 St. Peter's Basilica, The Vatican, Rome, Italy, 1925

211 Basilika St. Peter, Vatikan, Rom, Italien, 1925

211 Basilique Saint-Pierre, Le Vatican, Rome, Italie, 1925

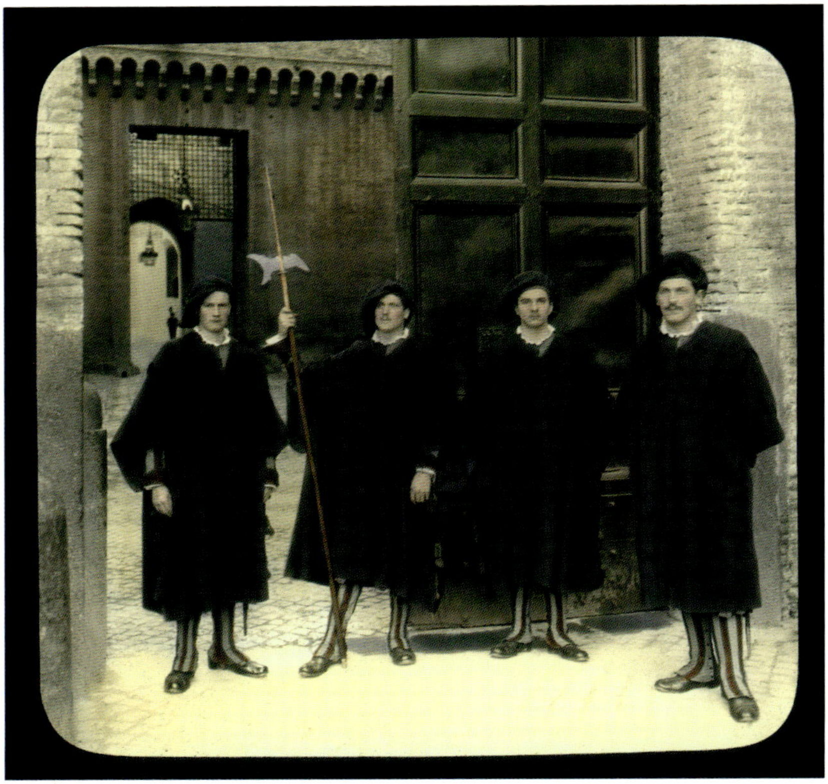

212 Swiss Guards at the Vatican, Rome, 1890s

212 Schweizer Gardisten im Vatikan, Rom, Italien, 1890er Jahre

212 Gardes suisses du Vatican, Rome, années 1890

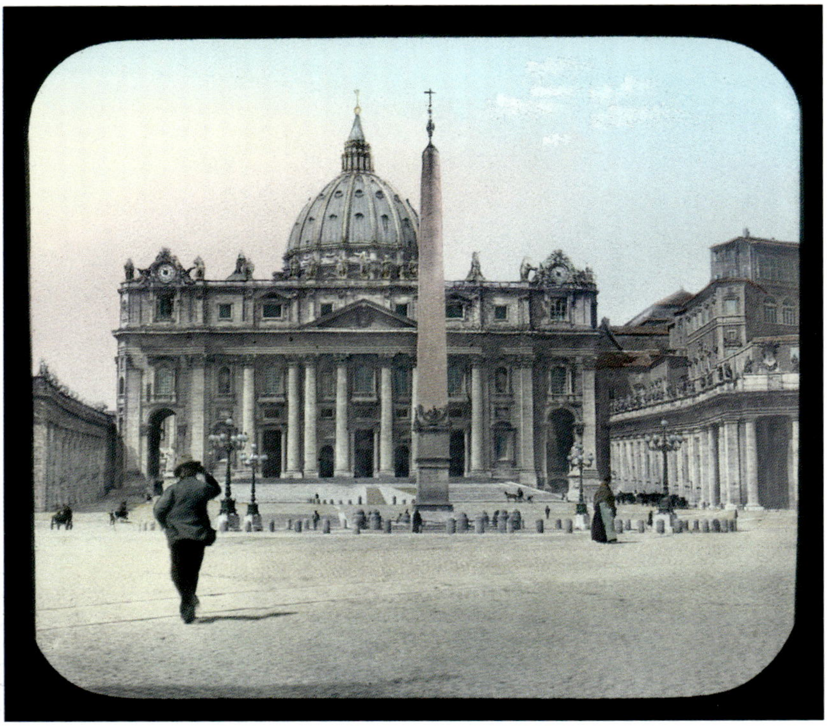

213 St. Peter's Square and Basilica (The Vatican), Rome, 1890s

213 Petersplatz und Basilika, Vatikan, Rom, Italien, 1890er Jahre

213 Place Saint-Pierre et la basilique (Le Vatican), Rome, années 1890

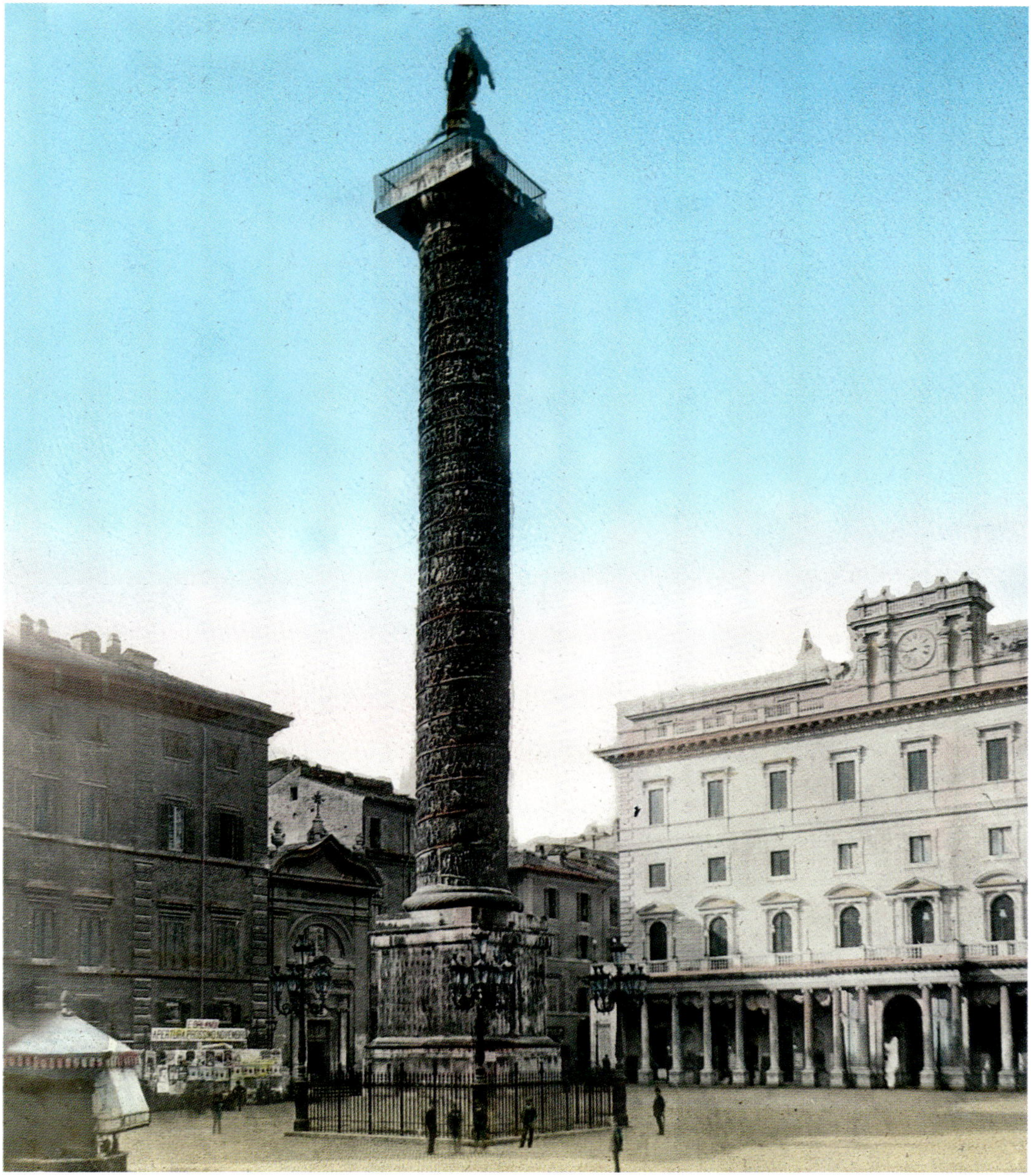

214 Trajan's Column, Piazza Colonna, Rome, Italy, 1890s

214 Die Trajanssäule, Piazza Colonna, Rom, Italien, 1890er Jahre

214 La colonne Trajane, piazza Colonna, Rome, Italie, années 1890

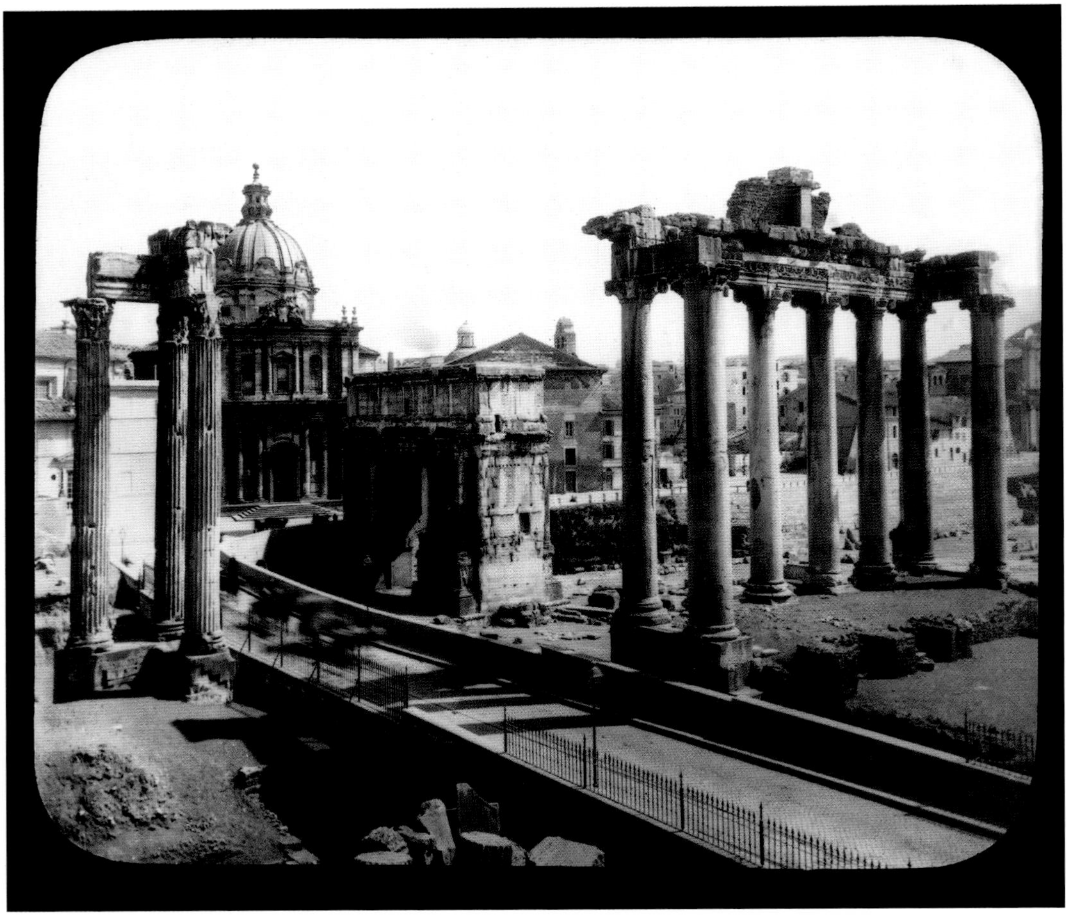

215 The Forum, Rome, 1880s
216 Catacombs of the Capuchin Monastery, Rome, 1880s

215 Forum Romanum, Rom, Italien, 1880er Jahre
216 Die Katakomben des Kapuzinerklosters, Rom, Italien, 1880er Jahre

215 Le Forum, Rome, années 1880
216 Catacombes du monastère des Capucins, Rome, années 1880

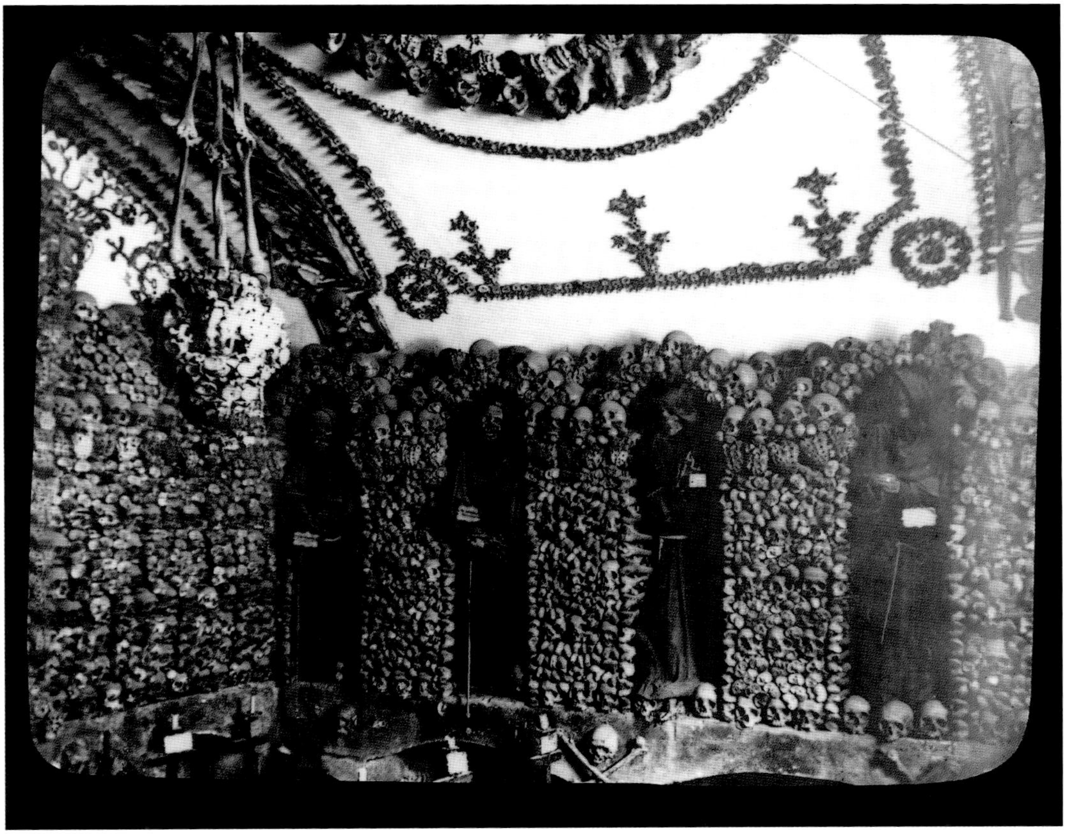

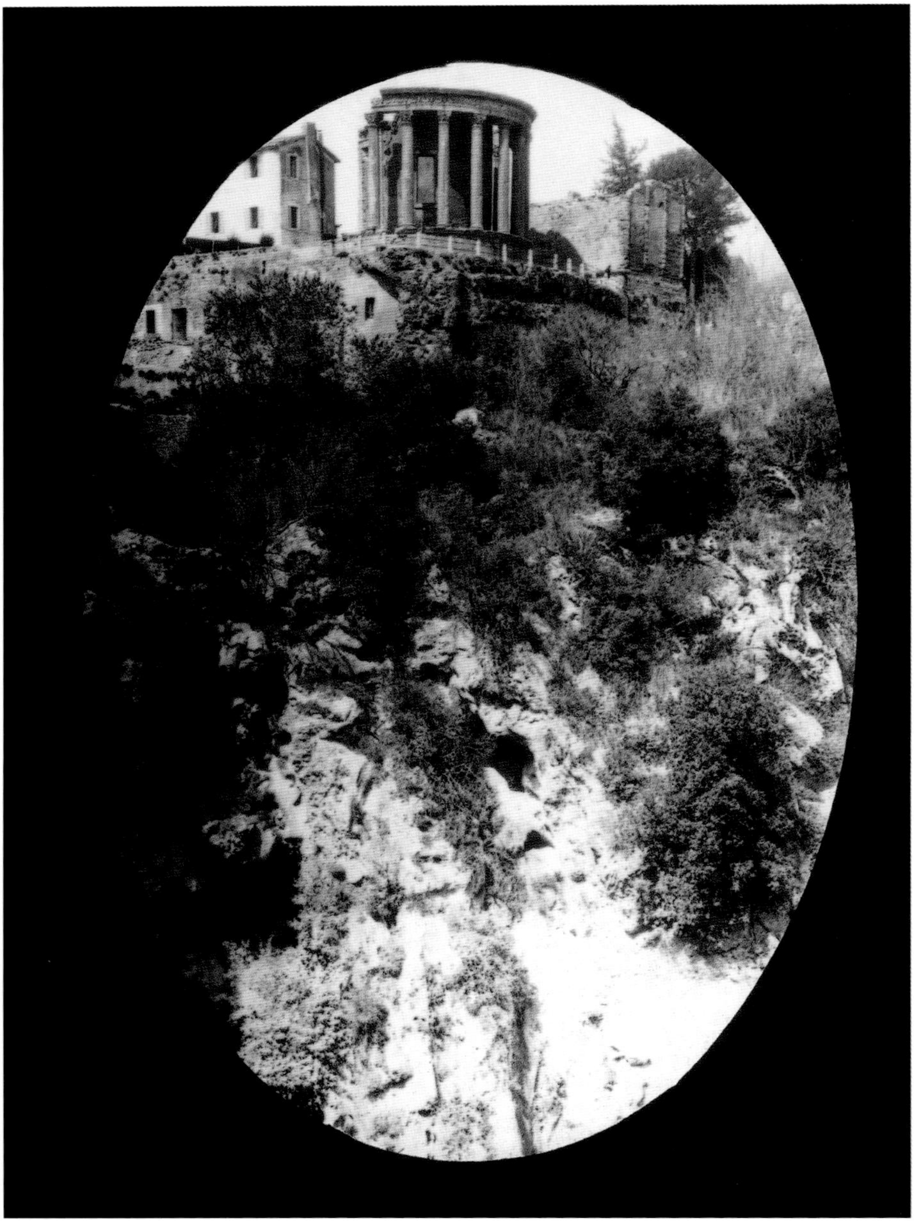

217 Temple of Vesta, Tivoli, Italy, 1880s
218 Tivoli, near Rome, Italy, 1880s

217 Tempel der Vesta, Tivoli, Italien, 1880er Jahre
218 Tivoli, nahe Rom, Italien, 1880er Jahre

217 Temple de Vesta, Tivoli, Italie, années 1880
218 Tivoli, près de Rome, Italie, années 1880

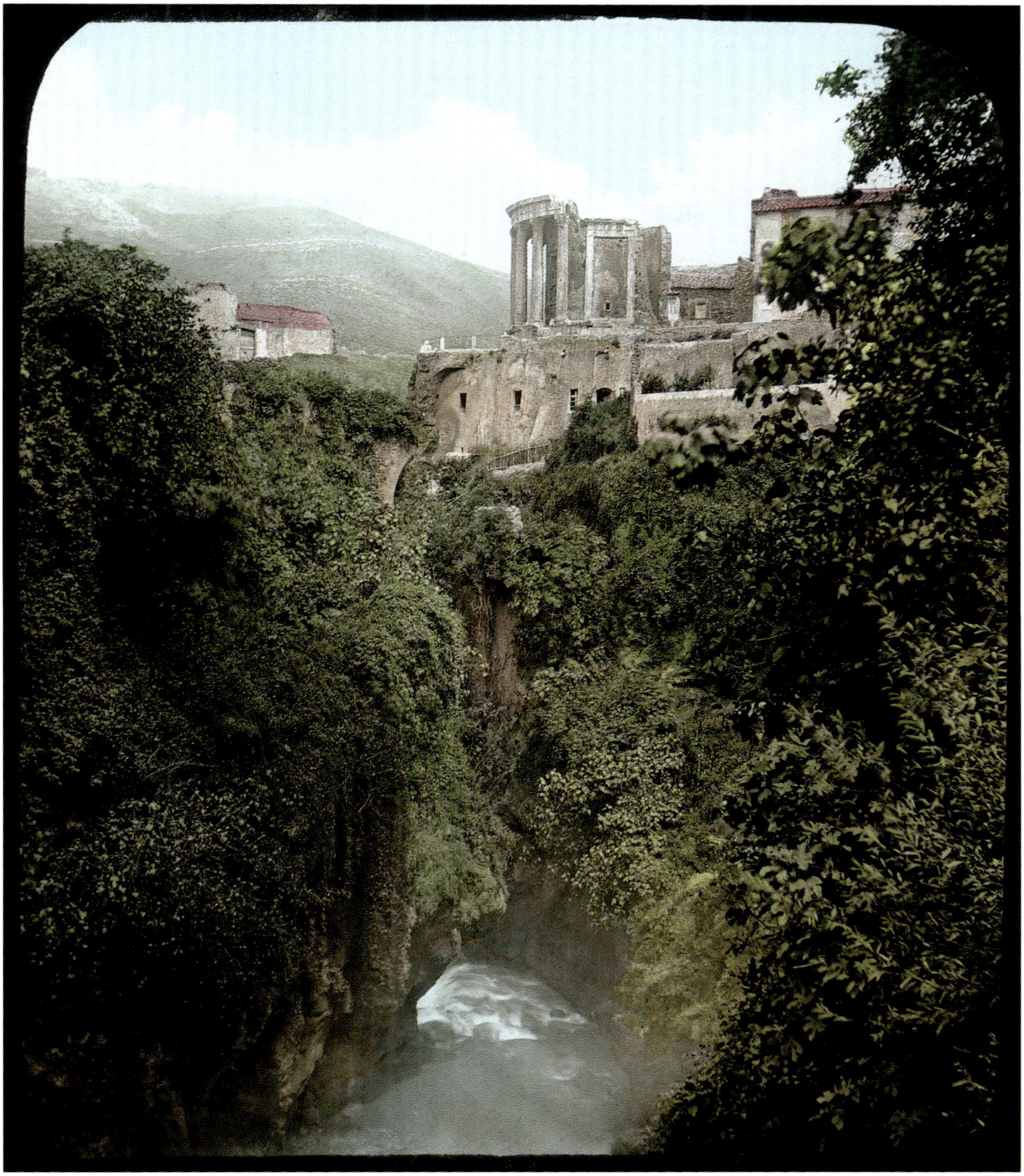

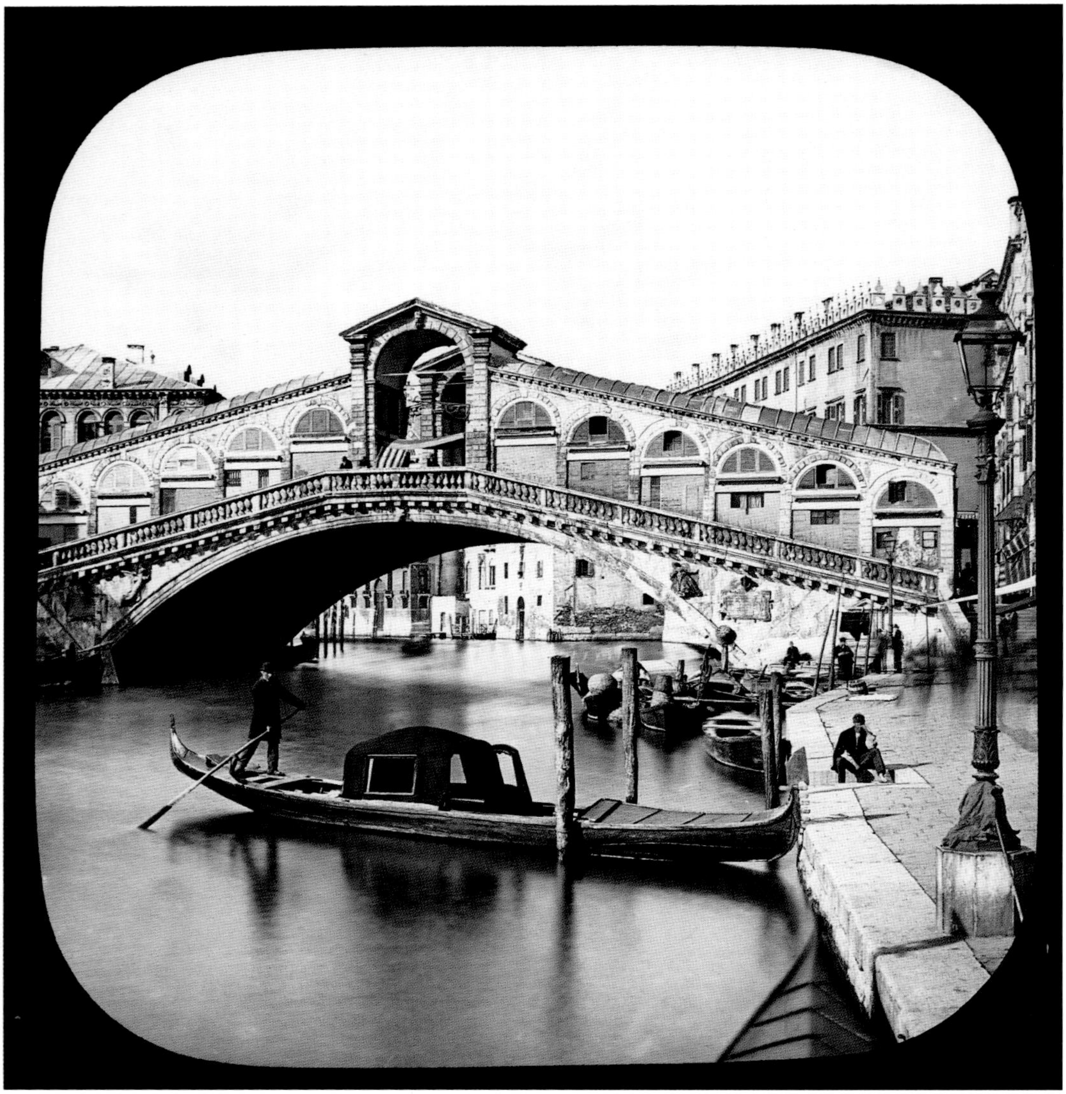

219 Ponte di Rialto (Rialto Bridge), Venice, Italy, 1910s
220 Ponte di Rialto (Rialto Bridge), Venice, Italy, 1900s

219 Ponte di Rialto (Rialtobrücke), Venedig, Italien, 1910er Jahre
220 Ponte di Rialto (Rialtobrücke), Venedig, Italien, 1900er Jahre

219 Pont du Rialto, Venise, Italie, années 1910
220 Pont du Rialto, Venise, Italie, années 1900

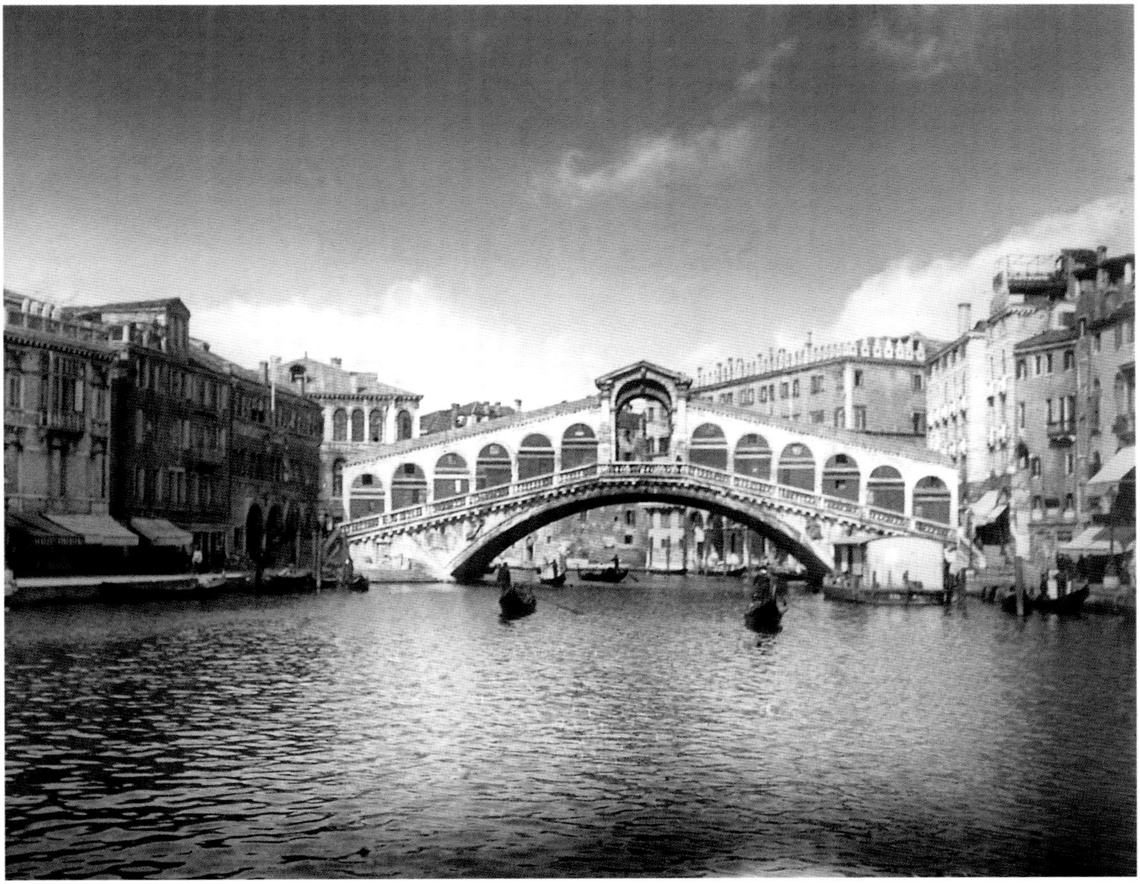

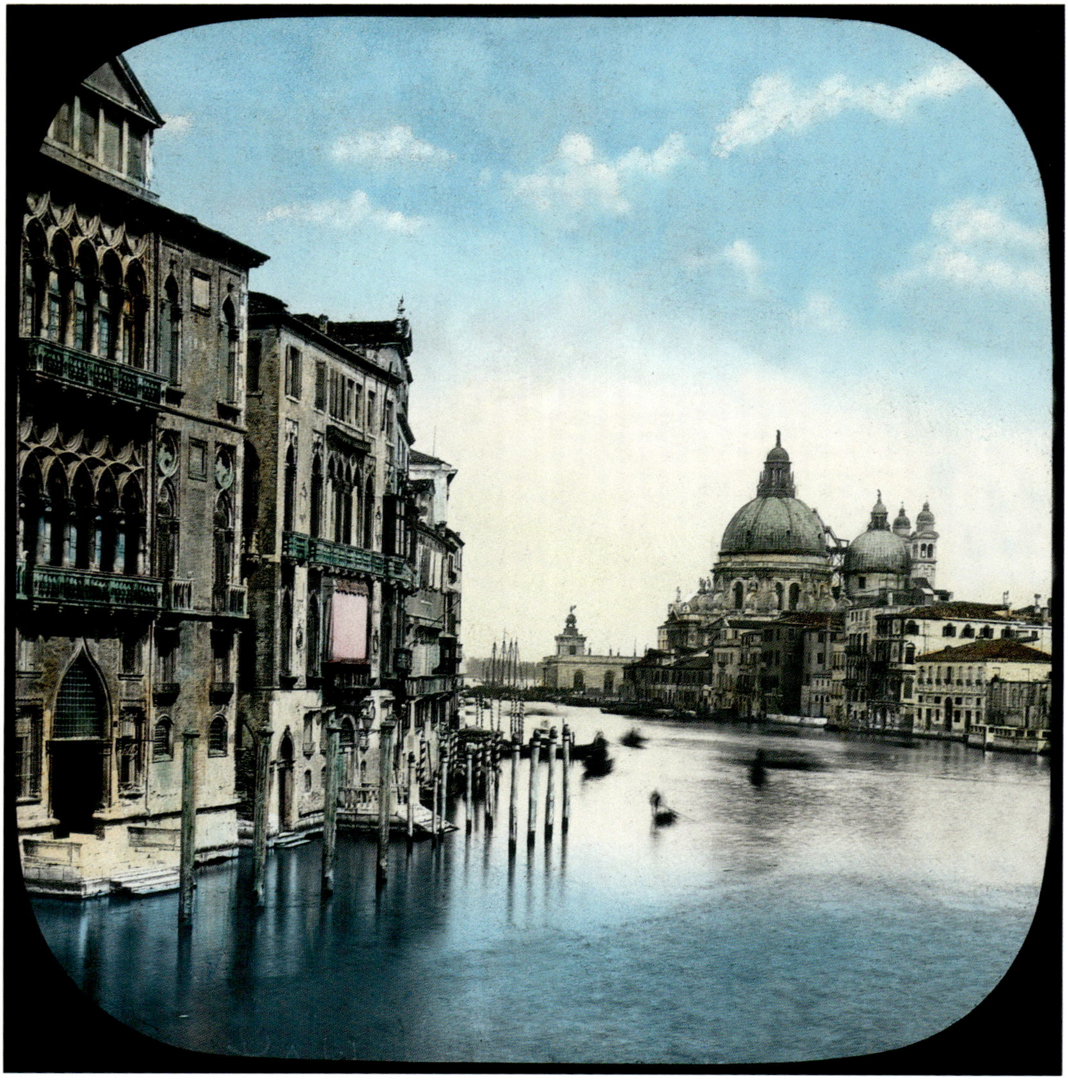

221 Basilica di Santa Maria della Salute (Basilica of St Mary of Health), Venice, Italy, 1880s
222 The Grand Canal, Venice, 1880s

221 Basilica di Santa Maria della Salute, Venedig, Italien, 1880er Jahre
222 Der Canal Grande, Venedig, Italien, 1880er Jahre

221 Basilique Santa Maria della Salute, Venise, Italie, années 1880
222 Le Grand Canal, Venise, années 1880

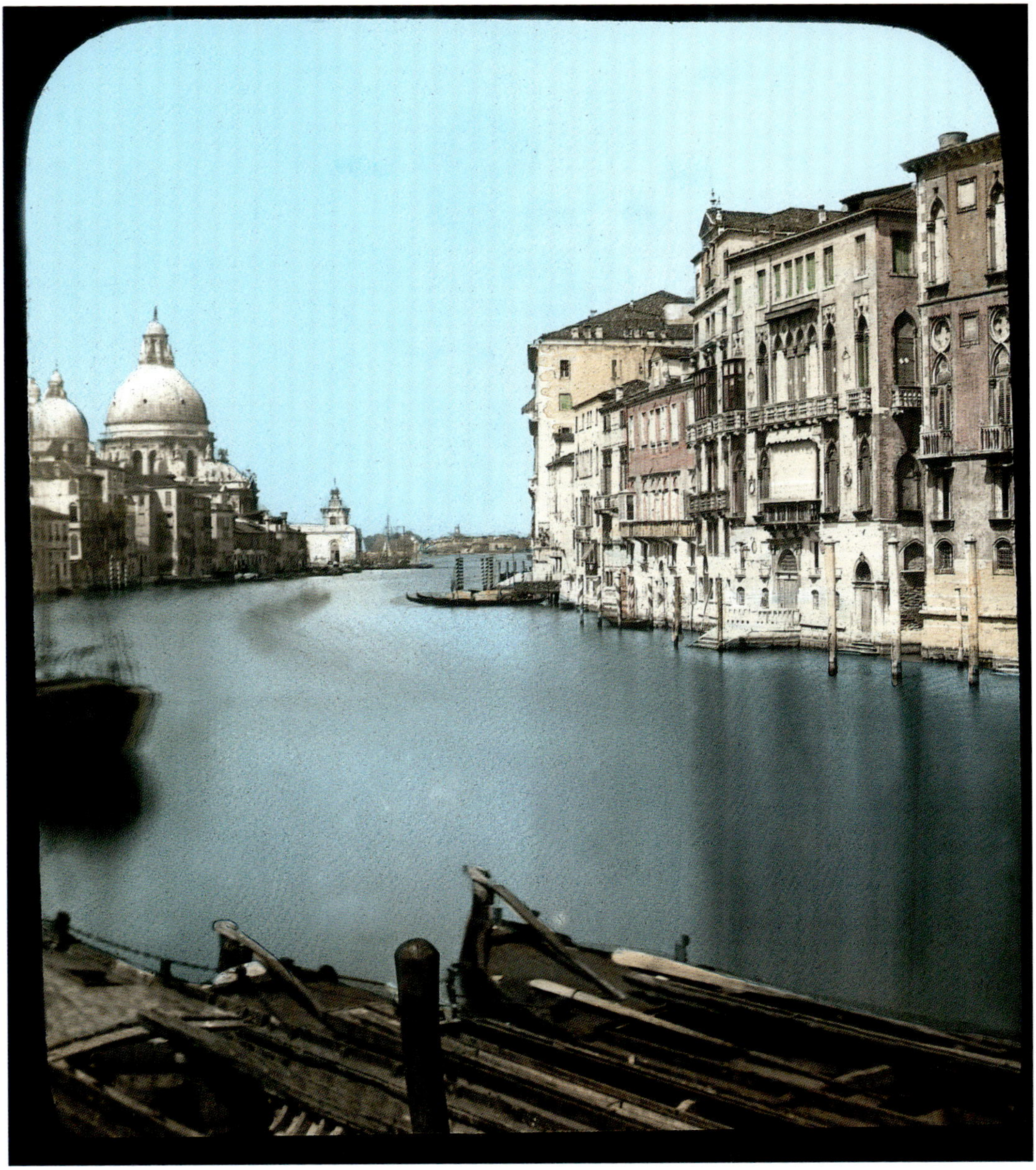

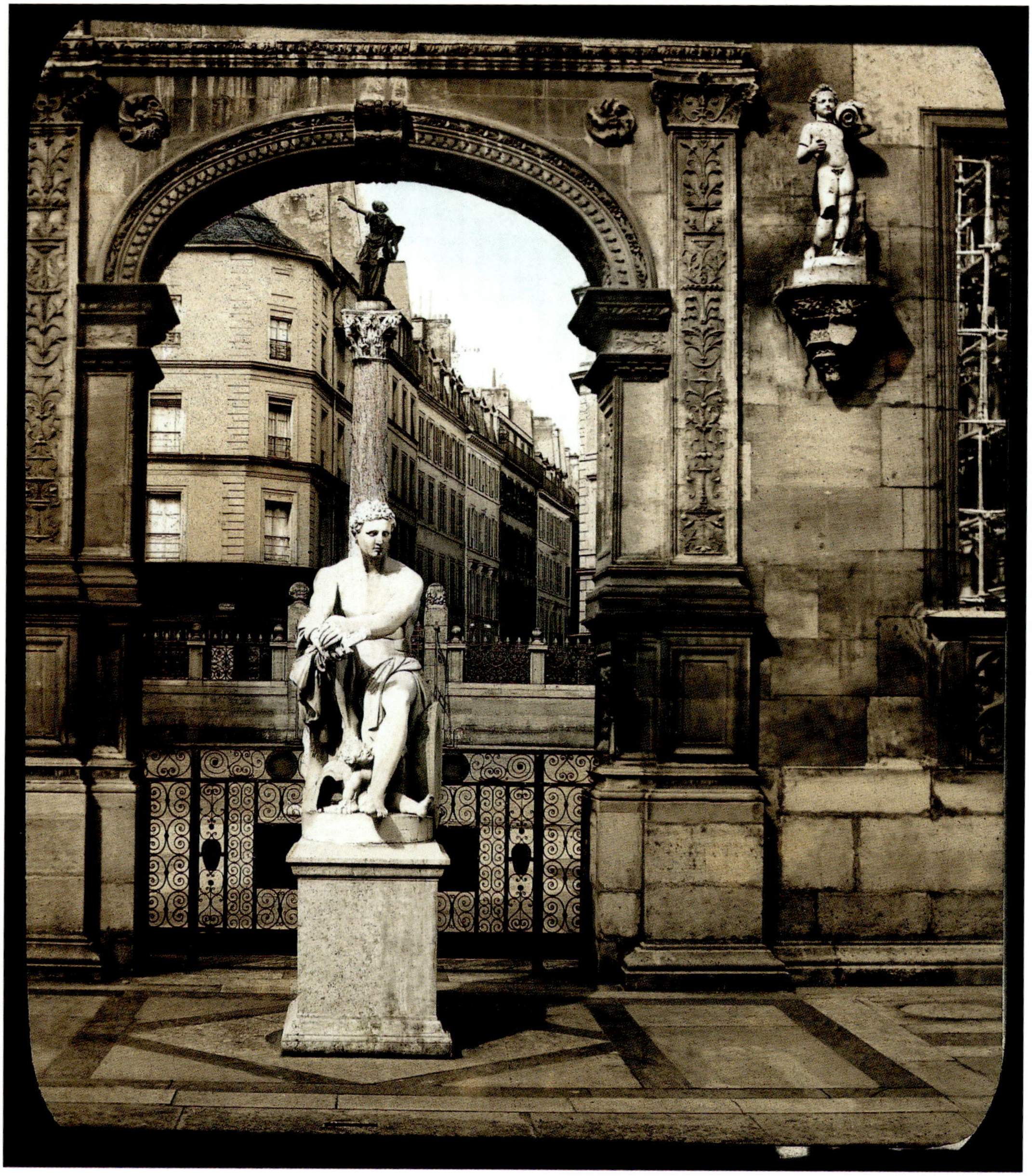

223 View of Venice, 1870s
224 View overlooking the district of San Marco, Venice, 1870s

223 Ansicht von Venedig, Italien, 1870er Jahre
224 Blick auf das Viertel San Marco, Venedig, Italien, 1870er Jahre

223 Vue de Venise, années 1870
224 Vue vers le quartier de Saint-Marc, Venise, années 1870

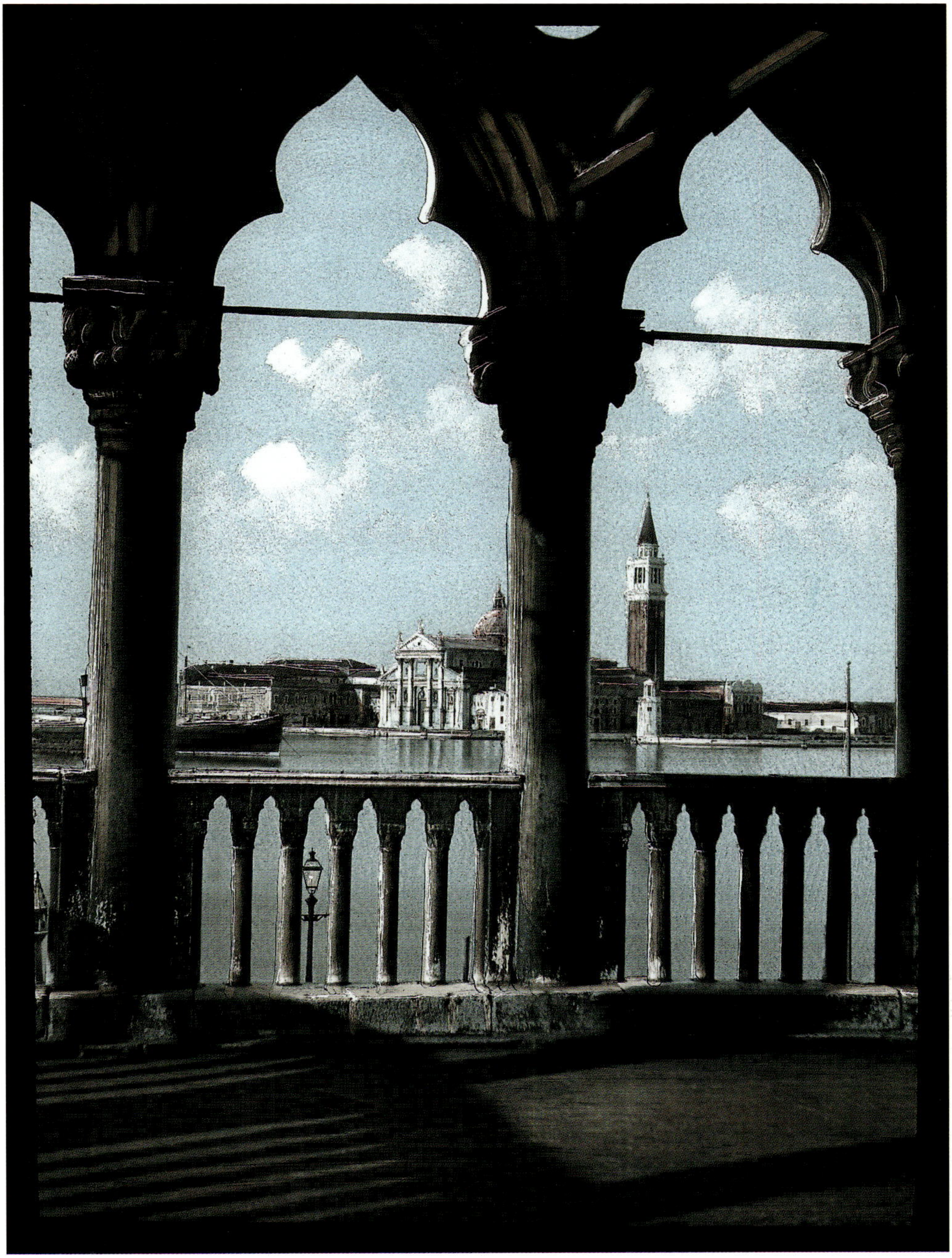

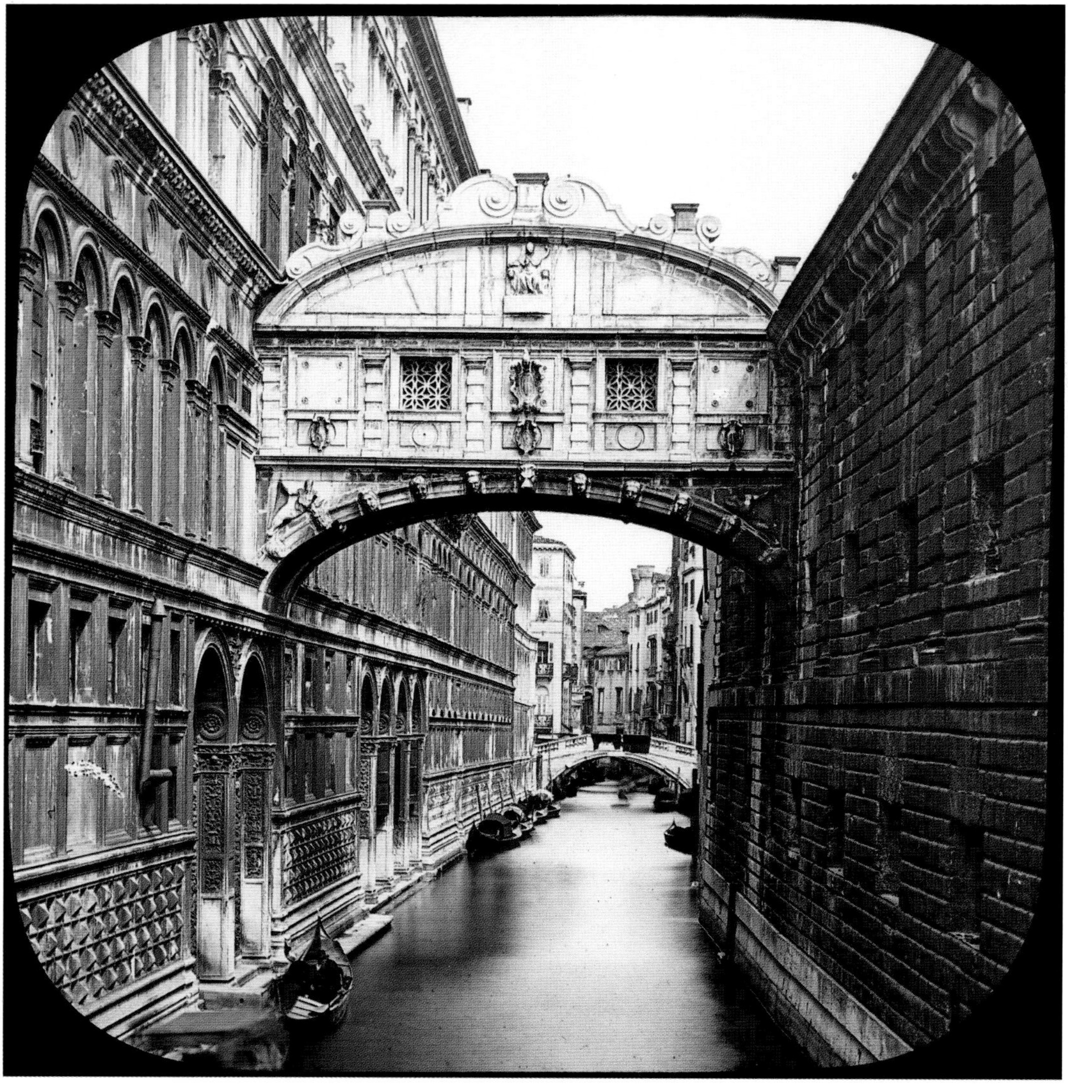

225 Ponte dei Sospiri (The Bridge of Sighs), Venice, Italy, 1880s
226 Palazzo Ducale (Palace of the Doges), Venice, Italy, 1880s

225 Ponte dei Sospiri (Seufzerbrücke), Venedig, Italien, 1880er Jahre
226 Der Palazzo Ducale (Dogenpalast), Venedig, Italien, 1880er Jahre

225 Pont des Soupirs, Venise, Italie, années 1880
226 Palais des Doges, Venise, Italie, années 1880

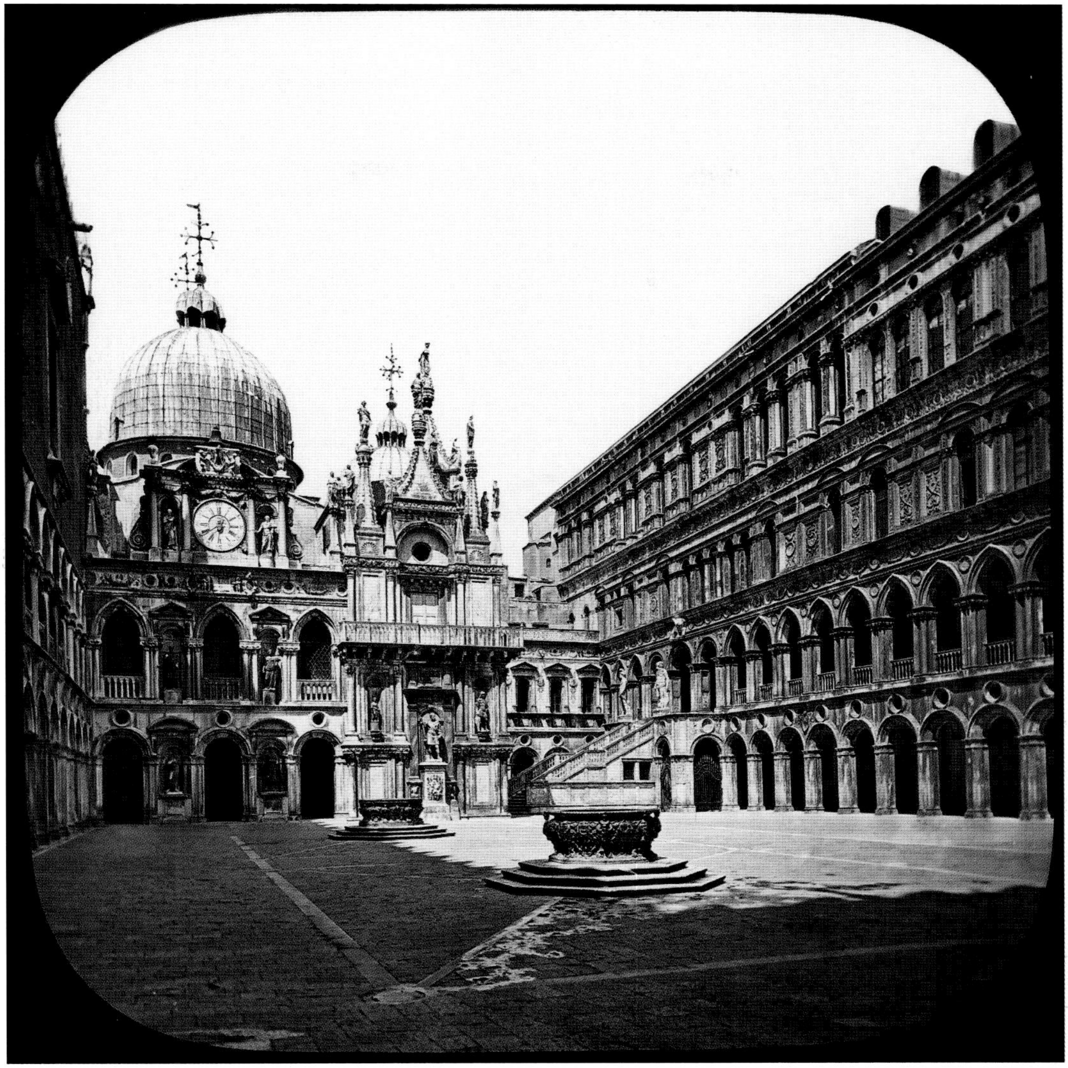

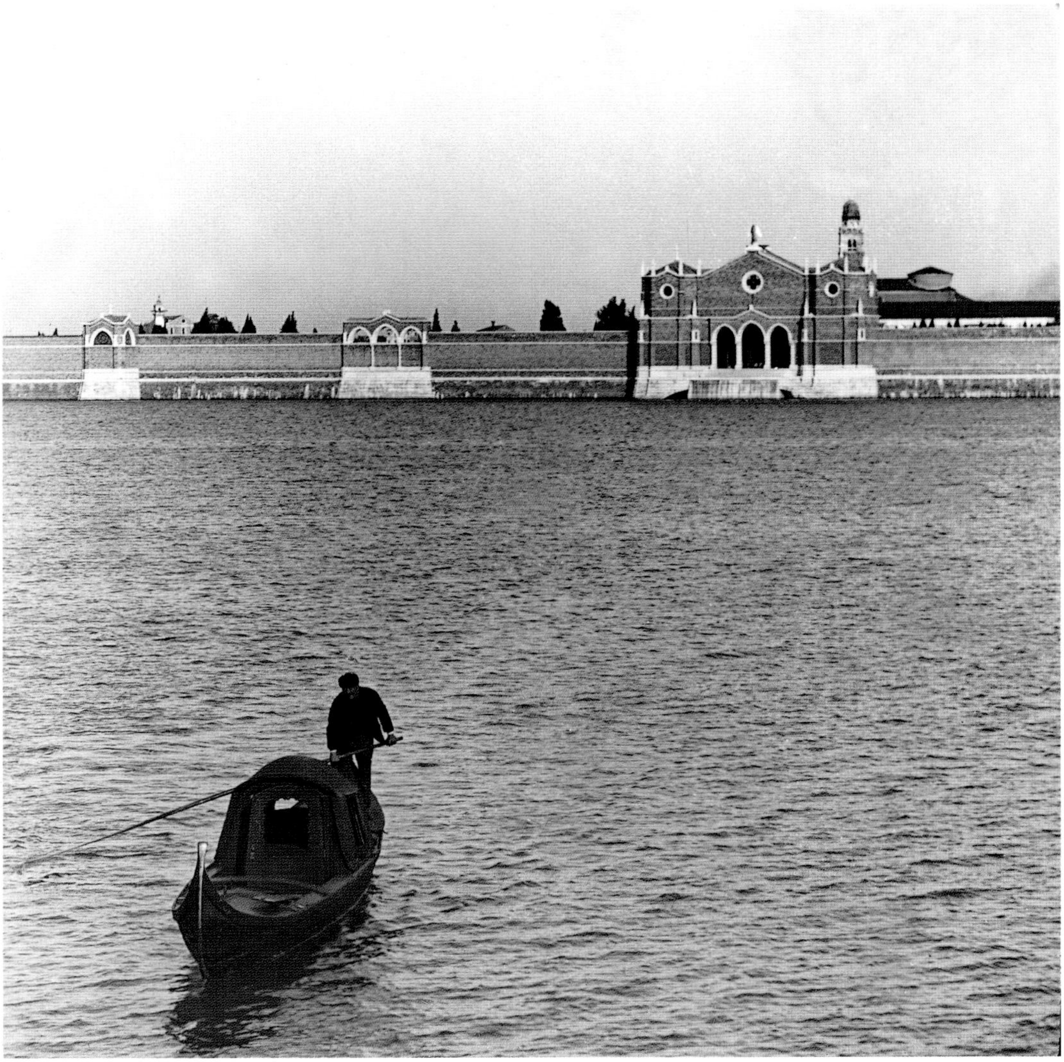

227 View of gondola and Isola di San Michele (Cemetery Island), Venice, Italy, 1880s

227 Ansicht einer Gondel und der Isola di San Michele (Friedhofsinsel), Venedig, Italien, 1880er Jahre

227 Une gondole et l'île San Michele (l'île-cimetière), Venise, Italie, années 1880

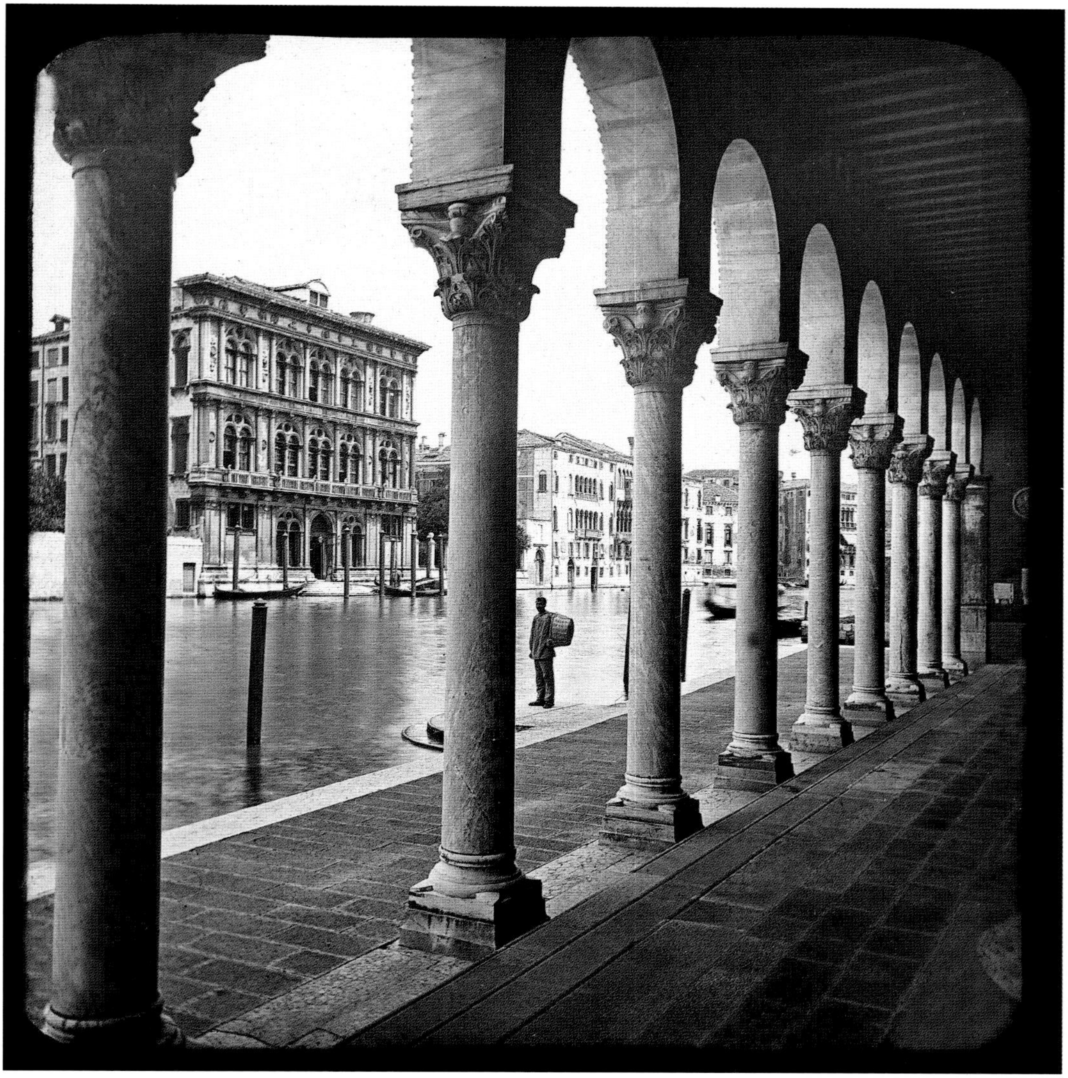

228 View of The Grand Canal from the Turkish Palace, Venice, Italy, 1880s

228 Blick auf den Canal Grande vom Türkischen Palast aus, Venedig, Italien, 1880er Jahre

228 Vue du Grand Canal depuis le palais des Turcs, Venise, Italie, années 1880

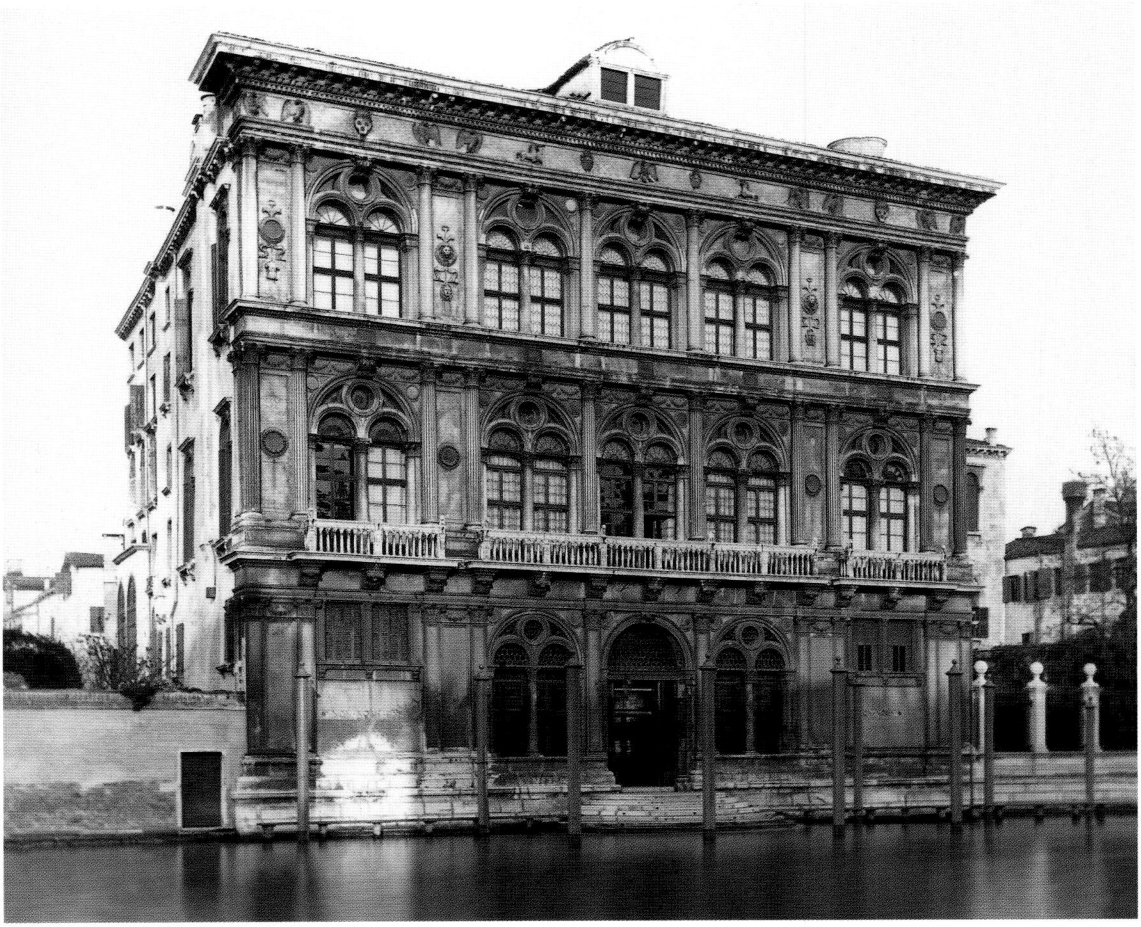

229 Palazzo Vendramin (Wagner's Palace) on The Grand Canal, Venice, Italy, 1880s

229 Der Palazzo Vendramin (Wagners Palast) am Canal Grande, Venedig, Italien, 1880er Jahre

229 Palazzo Vendramin (palais de Wagner) sur le Grand Canal, Venise, Italie, années 1880

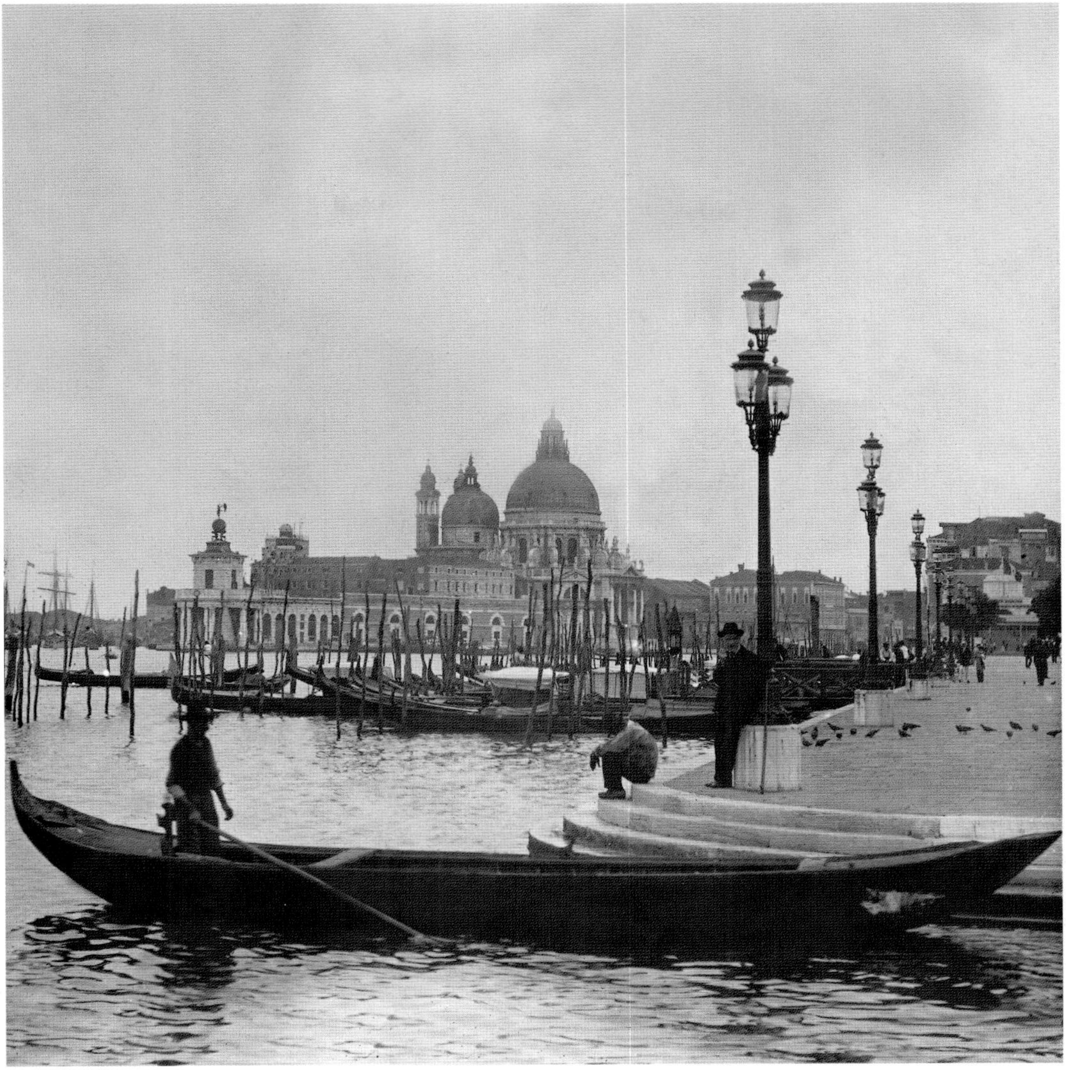

230 View of canal, Venice, 1910s

230 Ansicht des Canal Grande, Venedig, Italien, 1910er Jahre

230 Vue du canal, Venise, années 1910

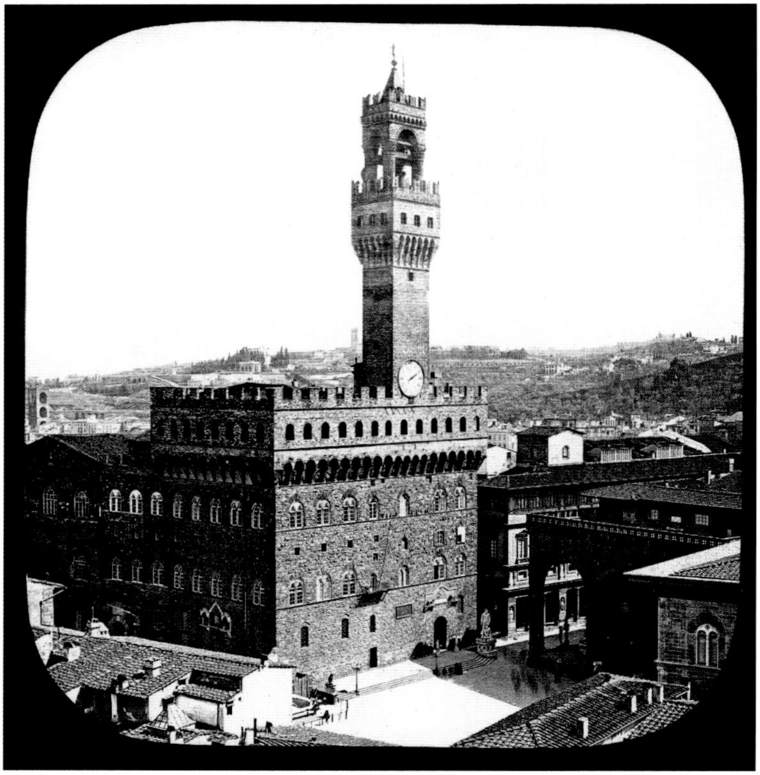

231 Palazzo Vecchio, Florence, Italy, 1870s

231 Der Palazzo Vecchio, Florenz, Italien, 1870er Jahre

231 Palazzo Vecchio, Florence, Italie, années 1870

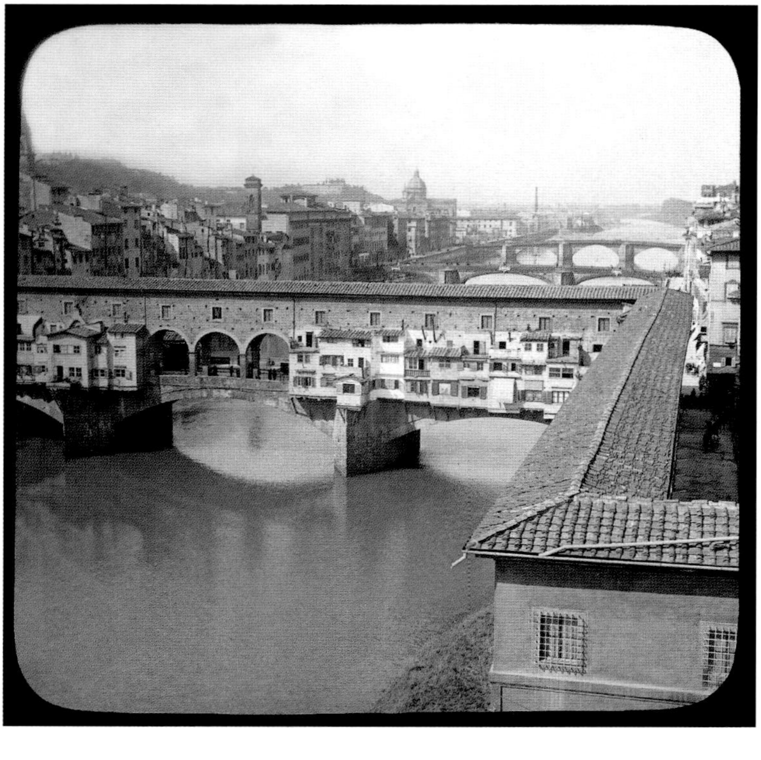

232 The Ponte Vecchio and the River Arno, Florence, Italy, 1890s

232 Ponte Vecchio und der Arno, Florenz, Italien, 1890er Jahre

232 Ponte Vecchio, Florence, Italie, années 1890

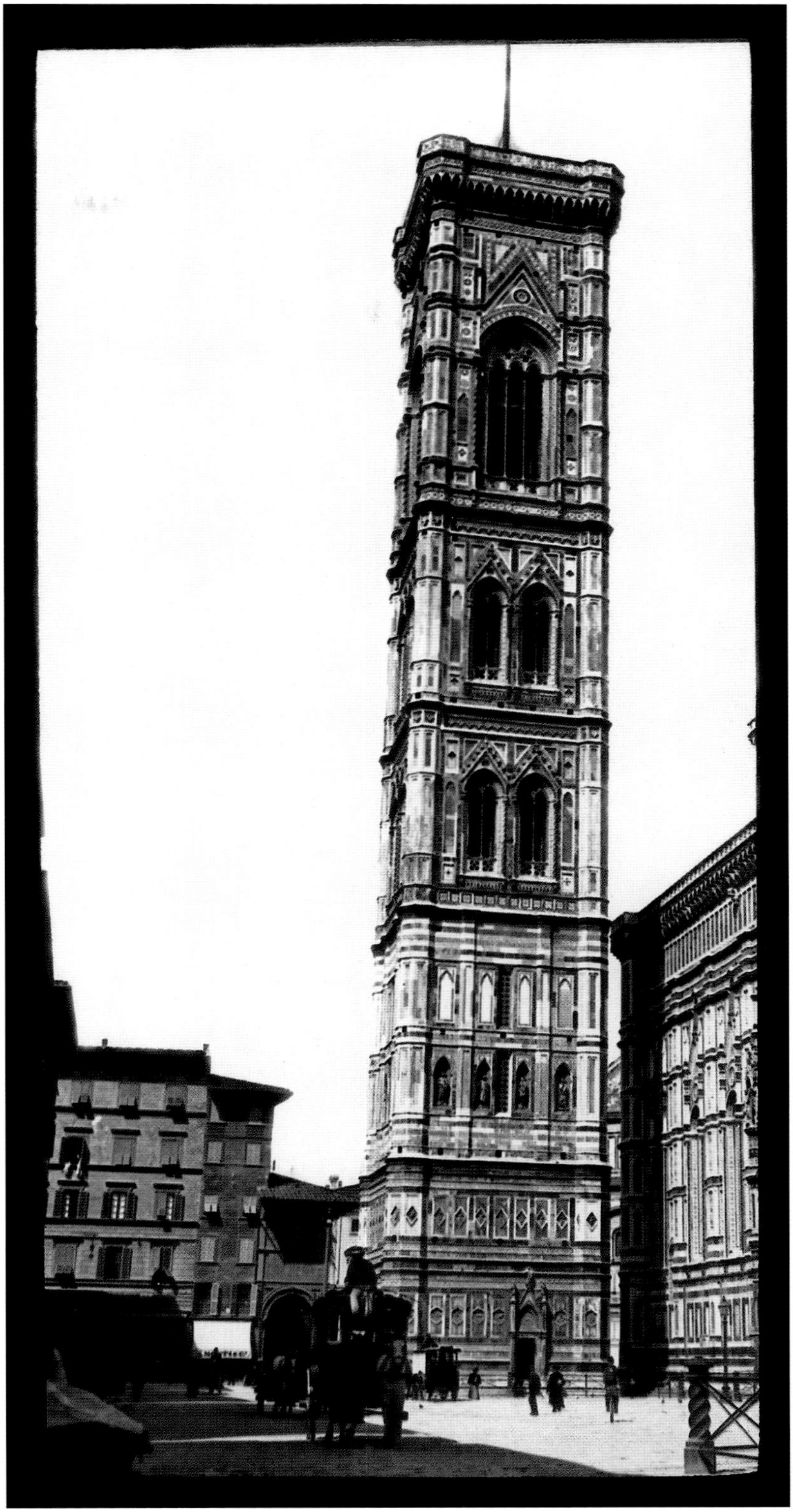

233 The Campanile,
Florence, Italy,
1870s

233 Der Campanile,
Florenz, Italien,
1870er Jahre

233 Le campanile,
Florence, Italie,
années 1870

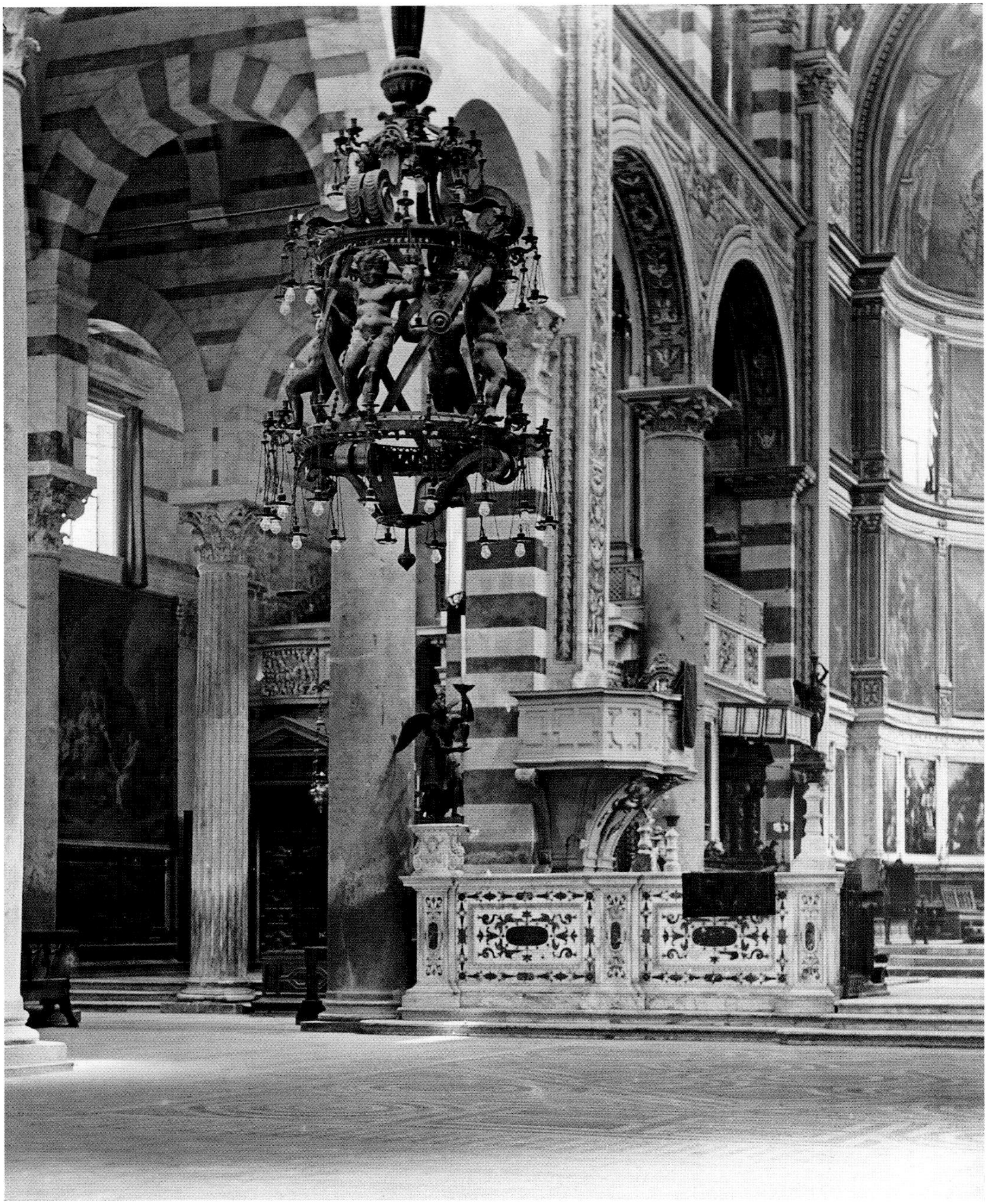

234 "The Lamp of Galileo" inside The Duomo (Cathedral), Pisa, Italy, 1890s
235 The Duomo (Cathedral), Florence, Italy, 1880s

234 „Der Leuchter Galileos" im Duomo (Dom), Pisa, Italien, 1890er Jahre
235 Der Duomo (Dom), Florenz, Italien, 1880er Jahre

234 Le « lustre de Galilée » dans le Duomo (cathédrale) de Pise, Italie, années 1890
235 Le Duomo (cathédrale) de Florence, Italie, années 1880

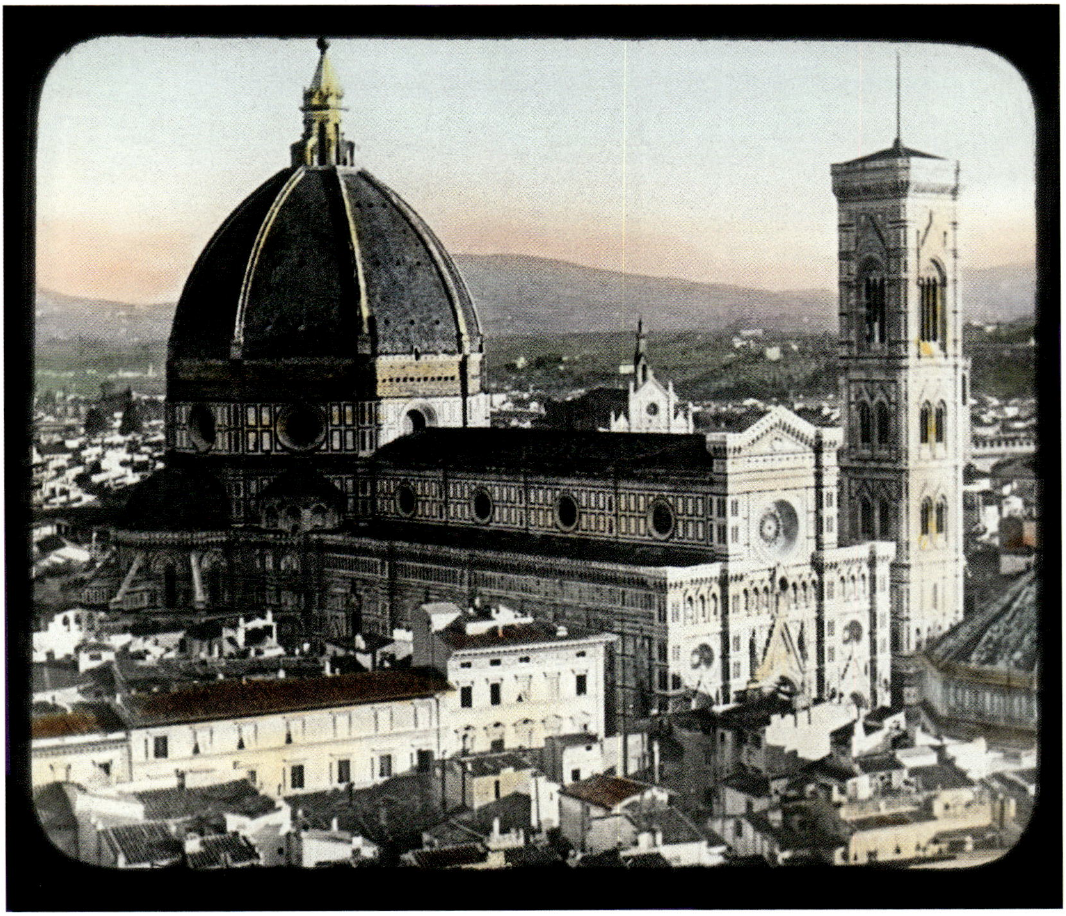

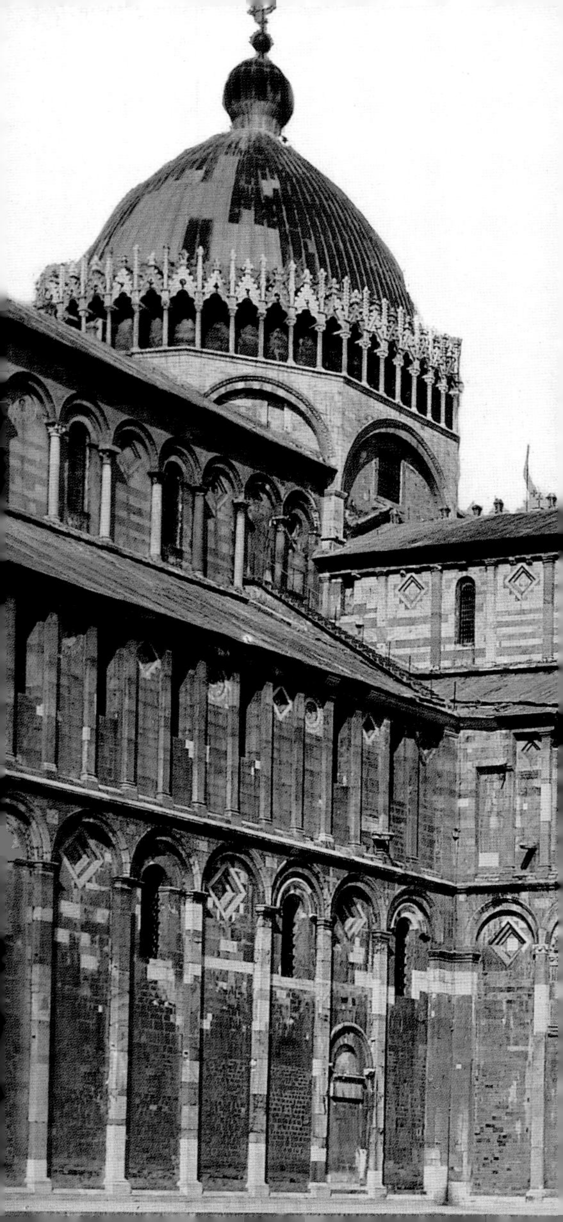

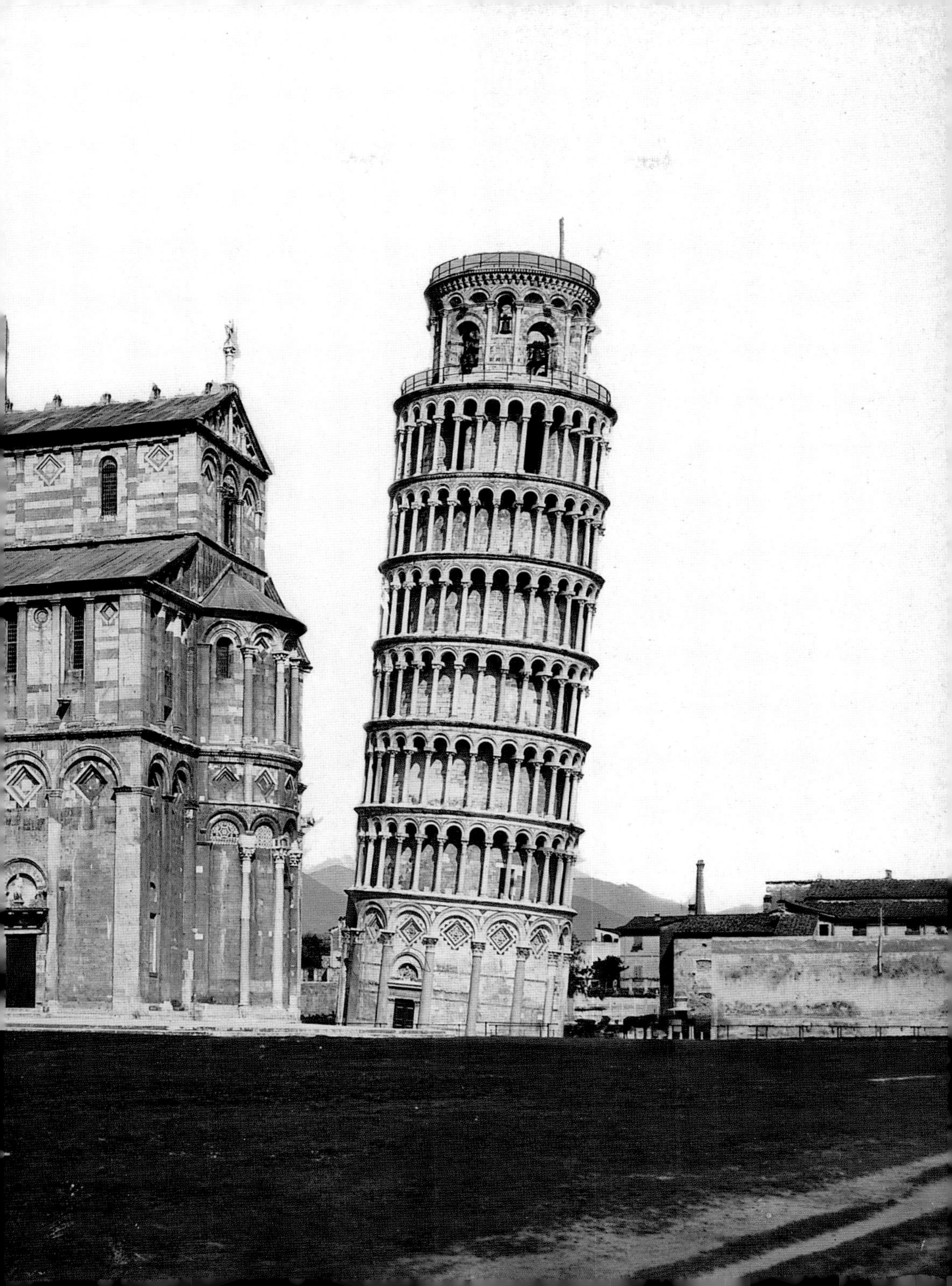

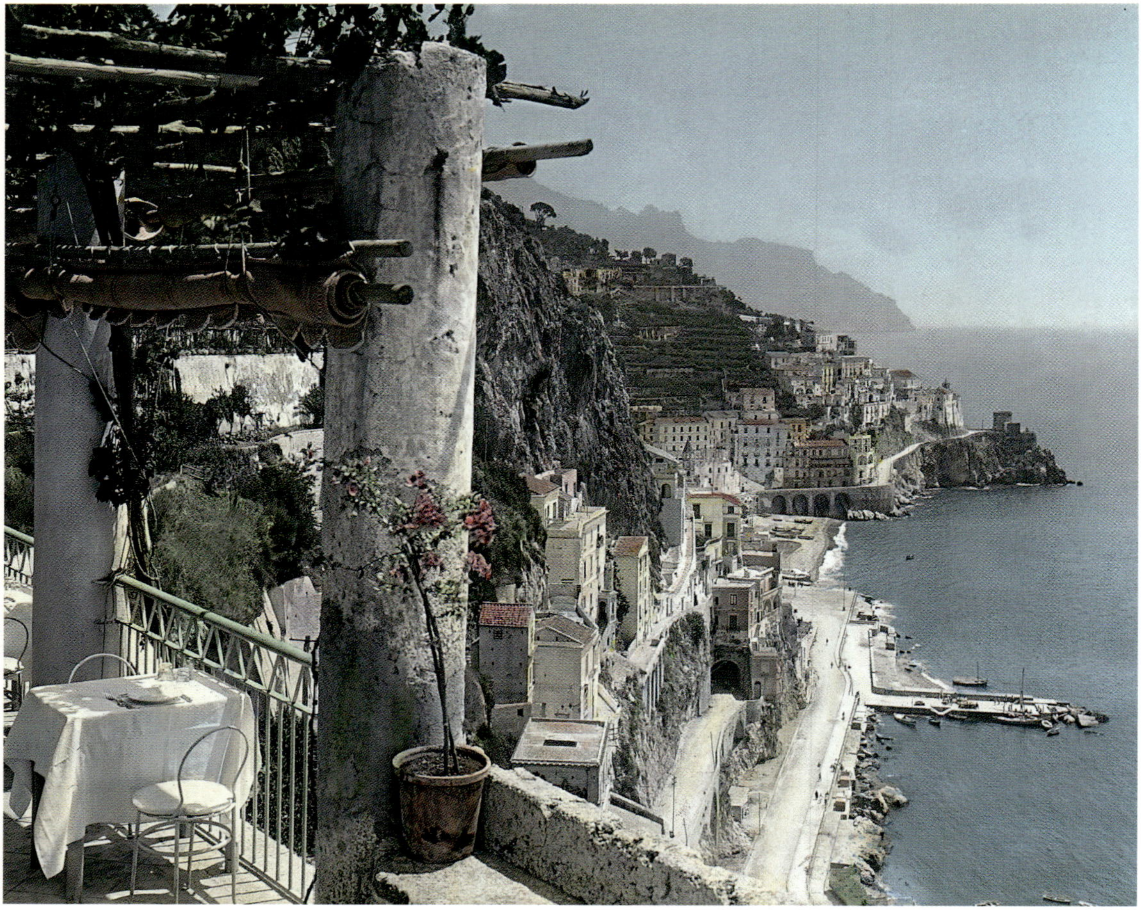

237 View from the Hotel Cappuccini-Convento, Amalfi, Italy, 1925
238 Castello Rezzonico, Lake Como, Italy, 1890s

237 Blick aus dem Hotel Cappuccini Convento, Amalfi, Italien, 1925
238 Castello Rezzonico, Comer See, Italien, 1890er Jahre

237 Vue depuis l'hôtel Cappuccini-Convento, Amalfi, Italie, 1925
238 Castello Rezzonico, lac de Come, Italie, années 1890

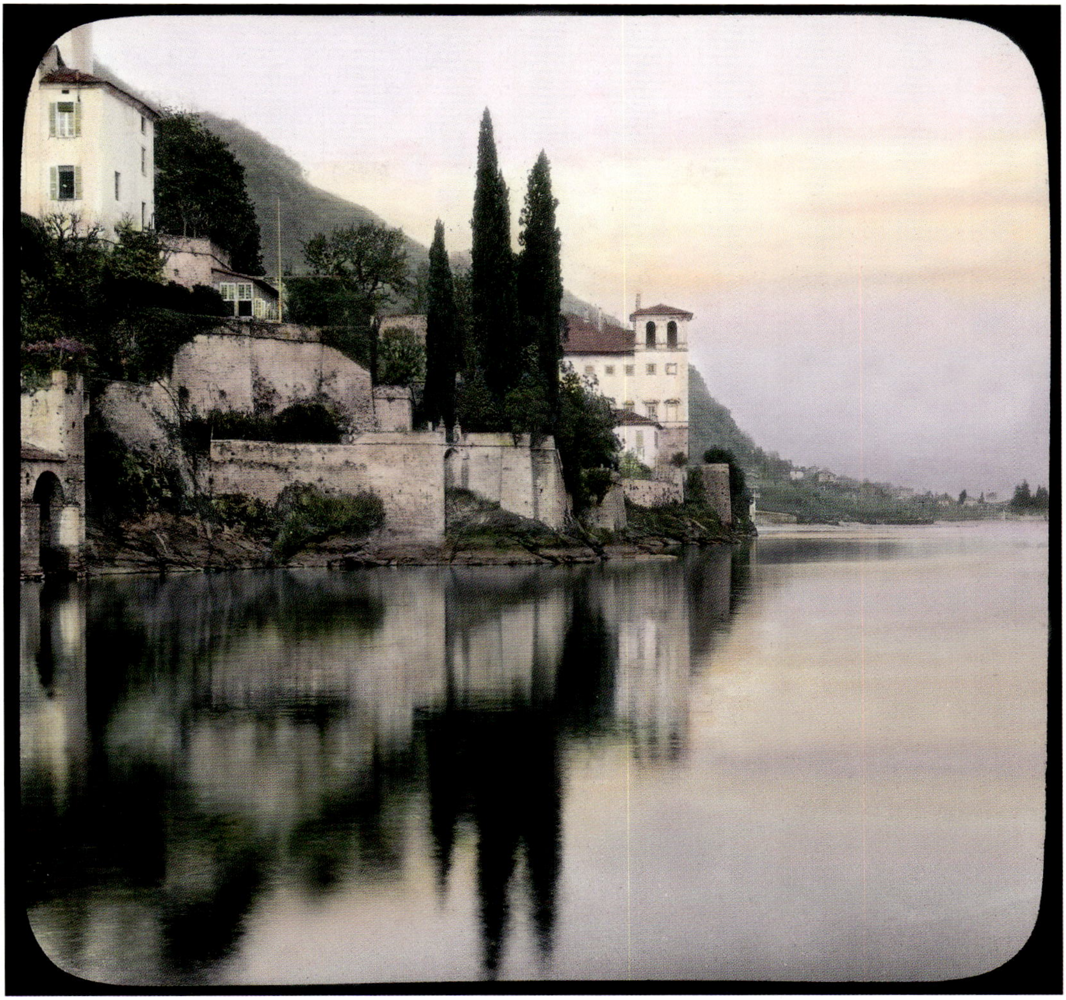

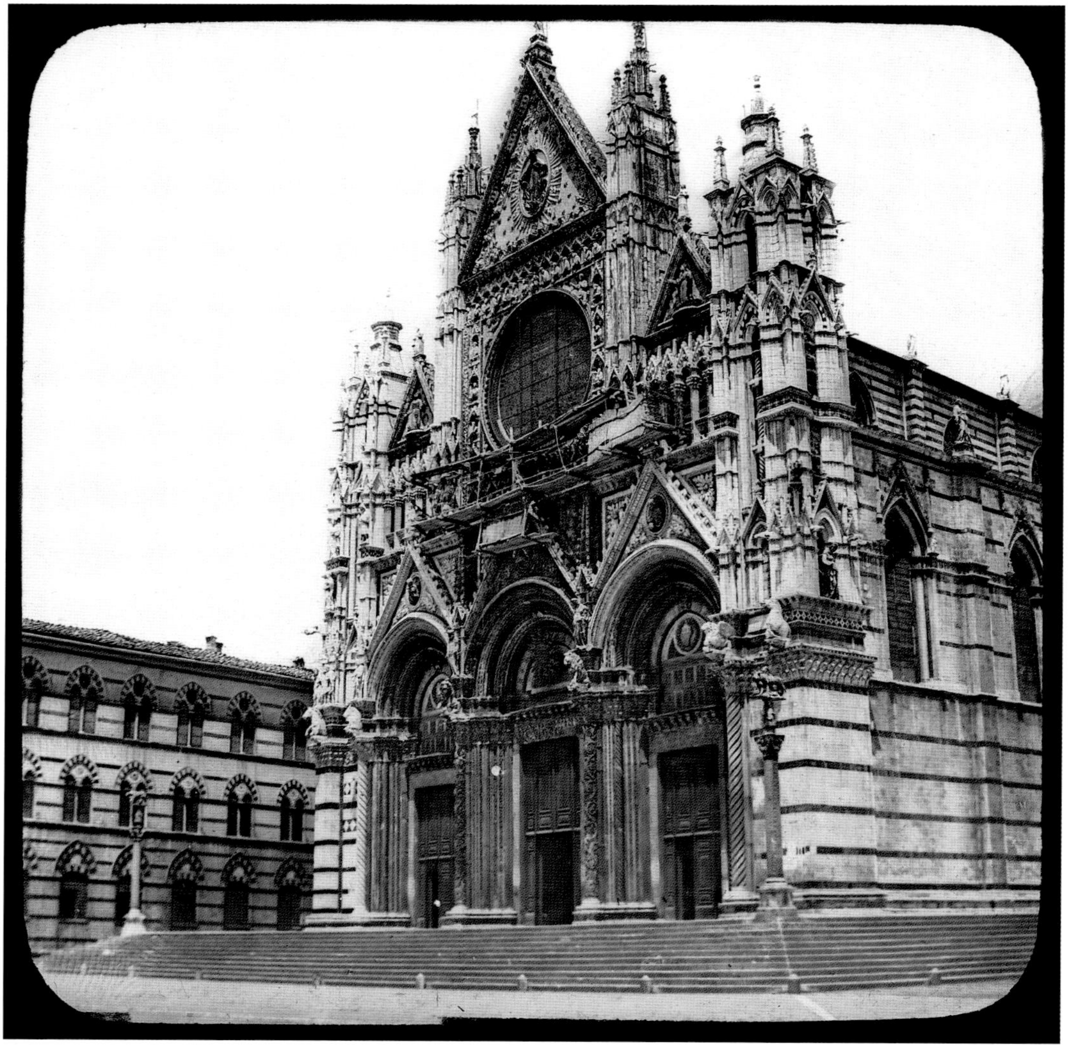

239 Cathedral, Siena, Italy, 1880s
240 Monks at Carthusian Monastery, Italy, 1880s

239 Der Dom, Siena, Italien, 1880er Jahre
240 Mönche eines Kartäuserklosters, Italien, 1880er Jahre

239 Cathédrale de Sienne, Italie, années 1880
240 Moines d'un monastère carthusien, Italie, années 1880

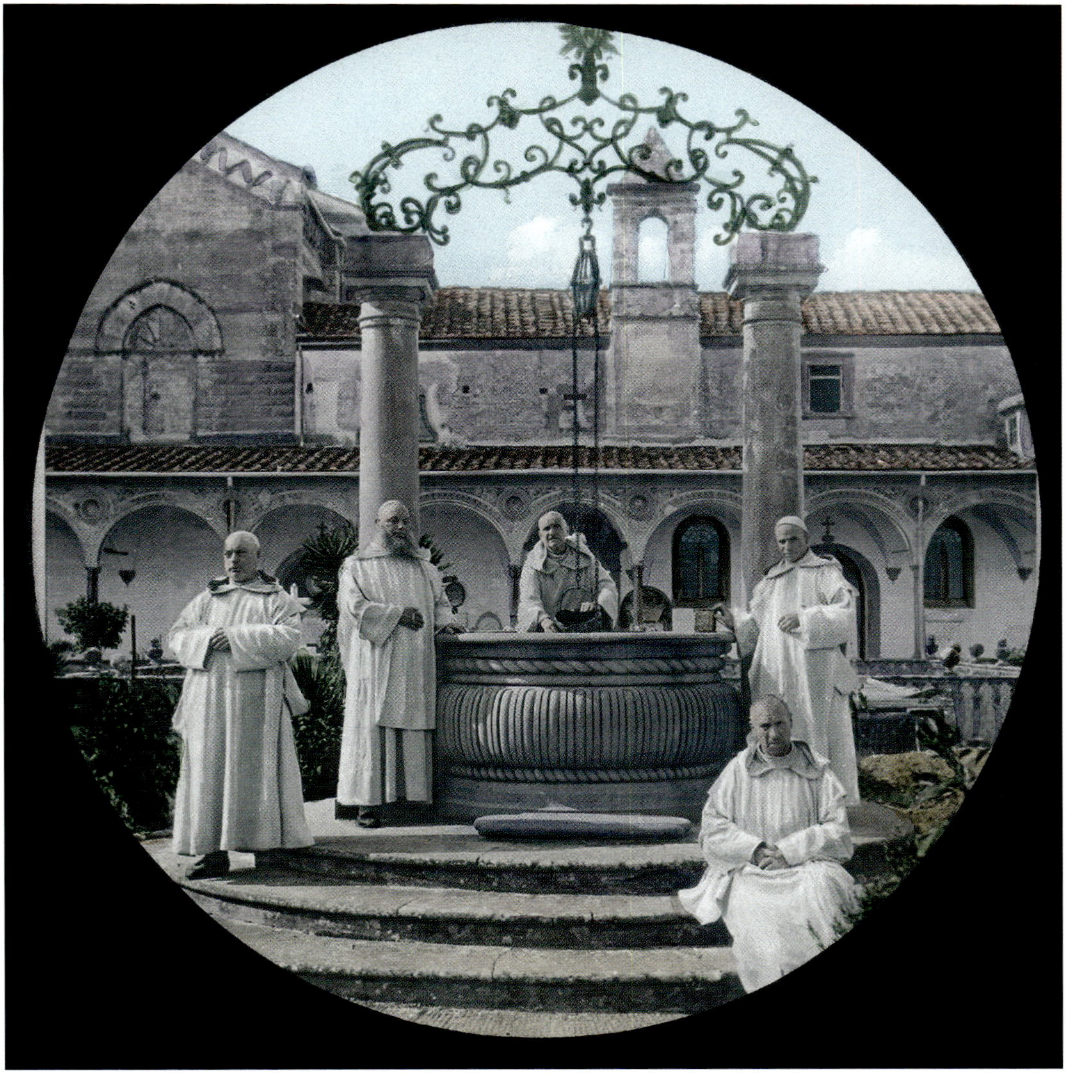

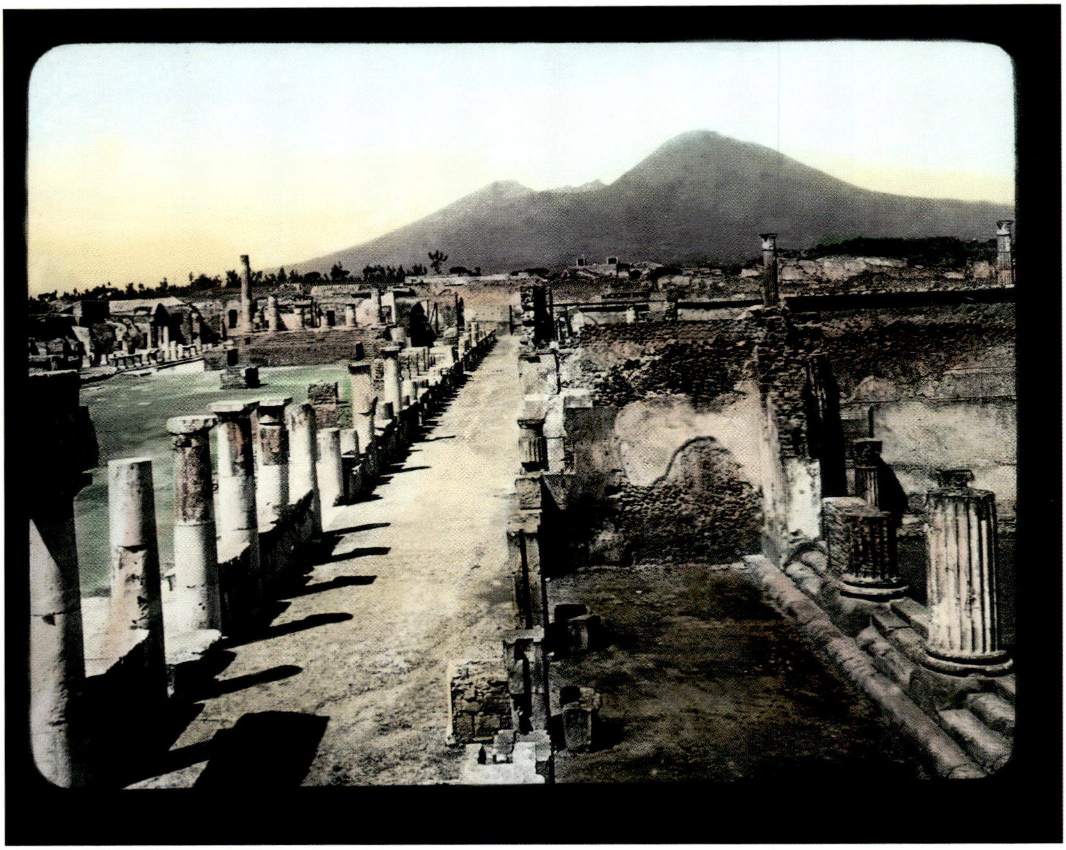

241 Pompeii with Mount Vesuvius, Italy, 1880s
242 The Ruins of Pompeii, Italy, 1880s

241 Pompeji und der Vesuv, Italien, 1880er Jahre
242 Die Ruinen von Pompeji, Italien, 1880er Jahre

241 Pompéi et le Vésuve, Italie, années 1880
242 Ruines de Pompéi, Italie, années 1880

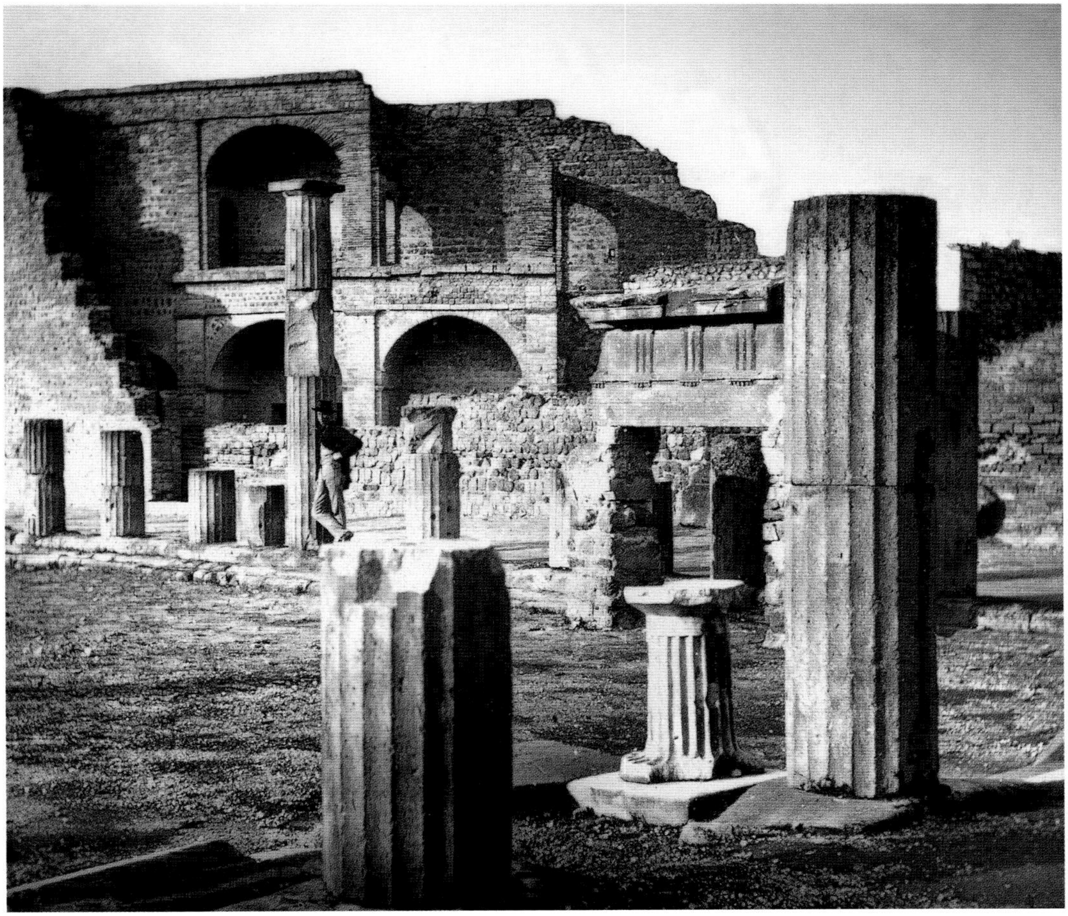

243 Temple of Venus, Pompeii, Italy, 1870s

243 Der Venustempel, Pompeji, Italien, 1870er Jahre

243 Temple de Vénus, Pompéi, Italie, années 1870

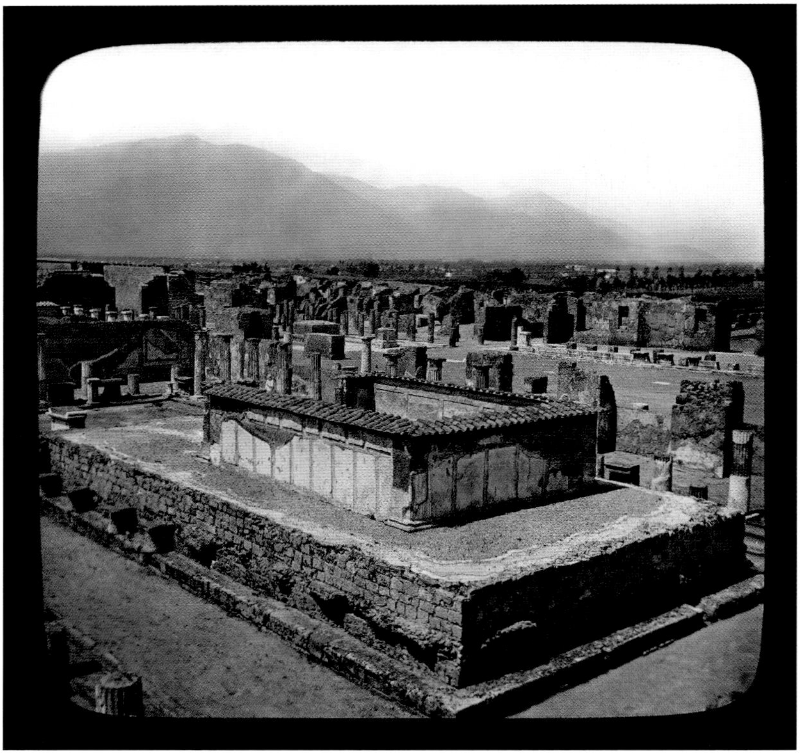

244 Cast of dog that died as a result of the eruption of Mt Vesuvius, Pompeii, Italy, 1880s

244 Abdruck eines Hundes, der durch den Ausbruch des Vesuvs umgekommen ist, Pompeji, Italien, 1880er Jahre

244 Moulage d'un chien victime de l'éruption du Vésuve, Pompéi, Italie, années 1880

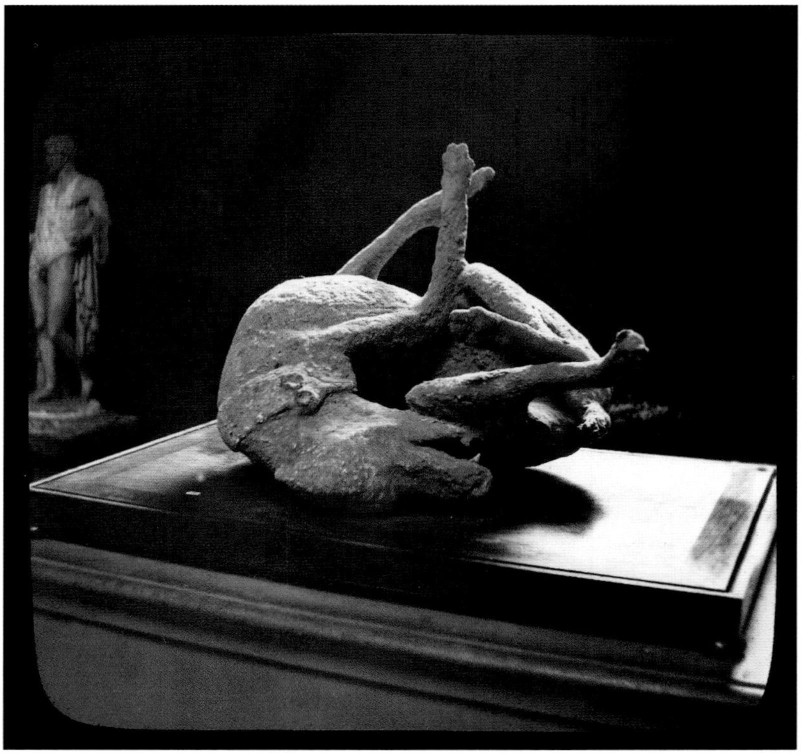

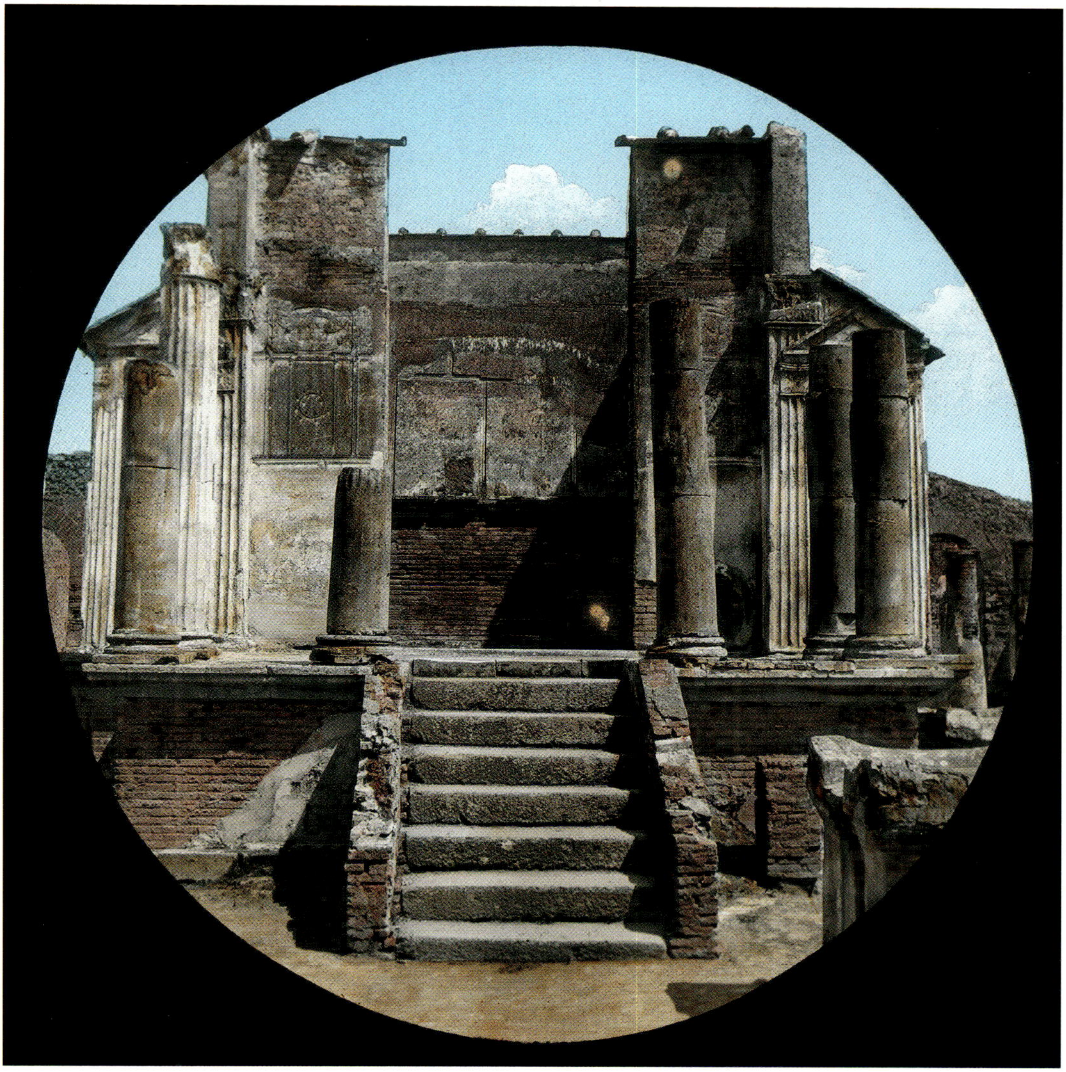

245 Temple of Venus, Pompeii, Italy, 1870s

245 Der Venustempel, Pompeji, Italien, 1870er Jahre

245 Temple de Vénus, Pompéi, Italie, années 1870

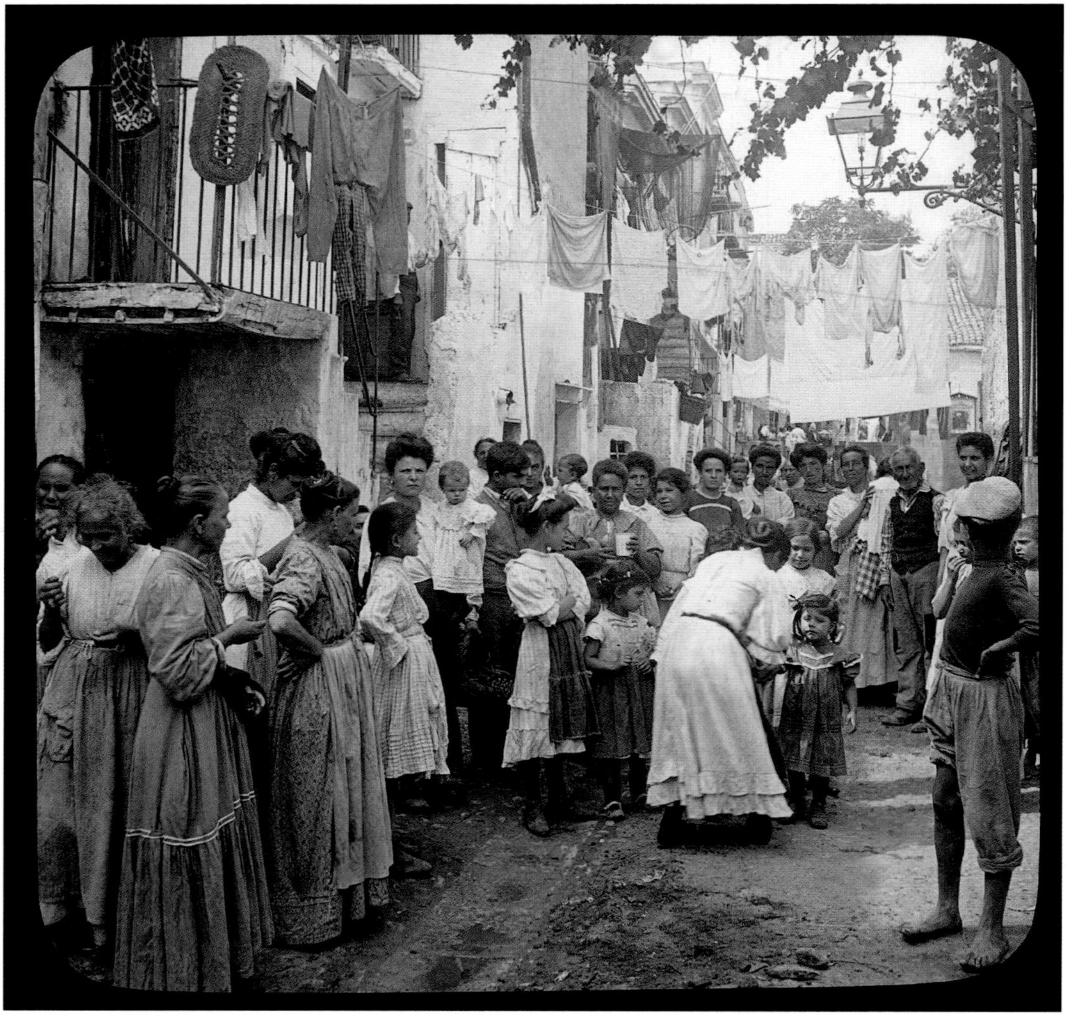

246 Street scene in tenement district, Palermo, Sicily, Italy, 1890s
247 A peasant in full costume, Messina, Sicily, Italy, 1890s

246 Straßenszene in einem Mietshausviertel, Palermo, Sizilien, Italien, 1890er Jahre
247 Bauer in kompletter Tracht, Messina, Sizilien, Italien, 1890er Jahre

246 Scène de rue dans un quartier populaire, Palerme, Sicile, Italie, années 1890
247 Paysan en costume, Messine, Sicile, Italie, années 1890

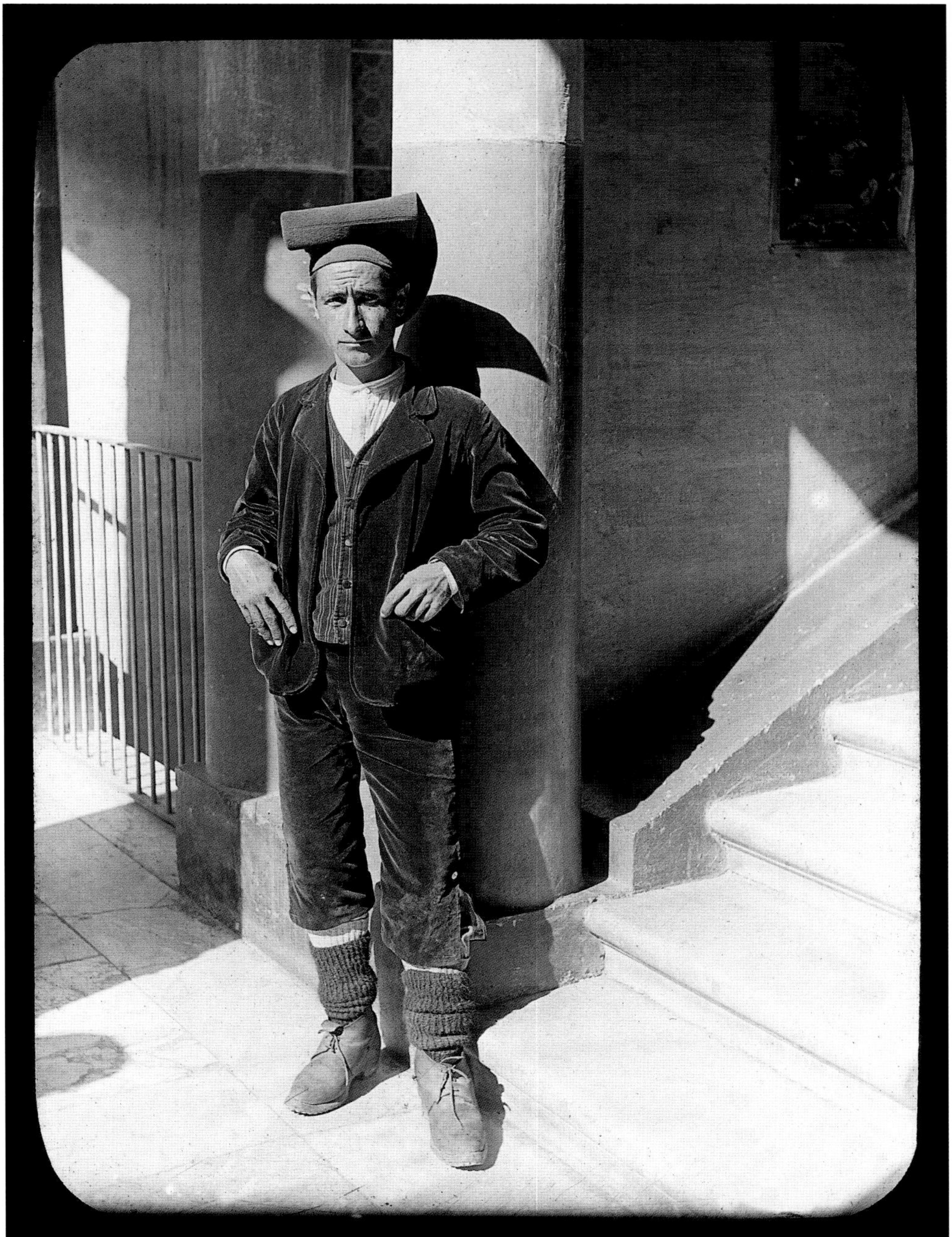

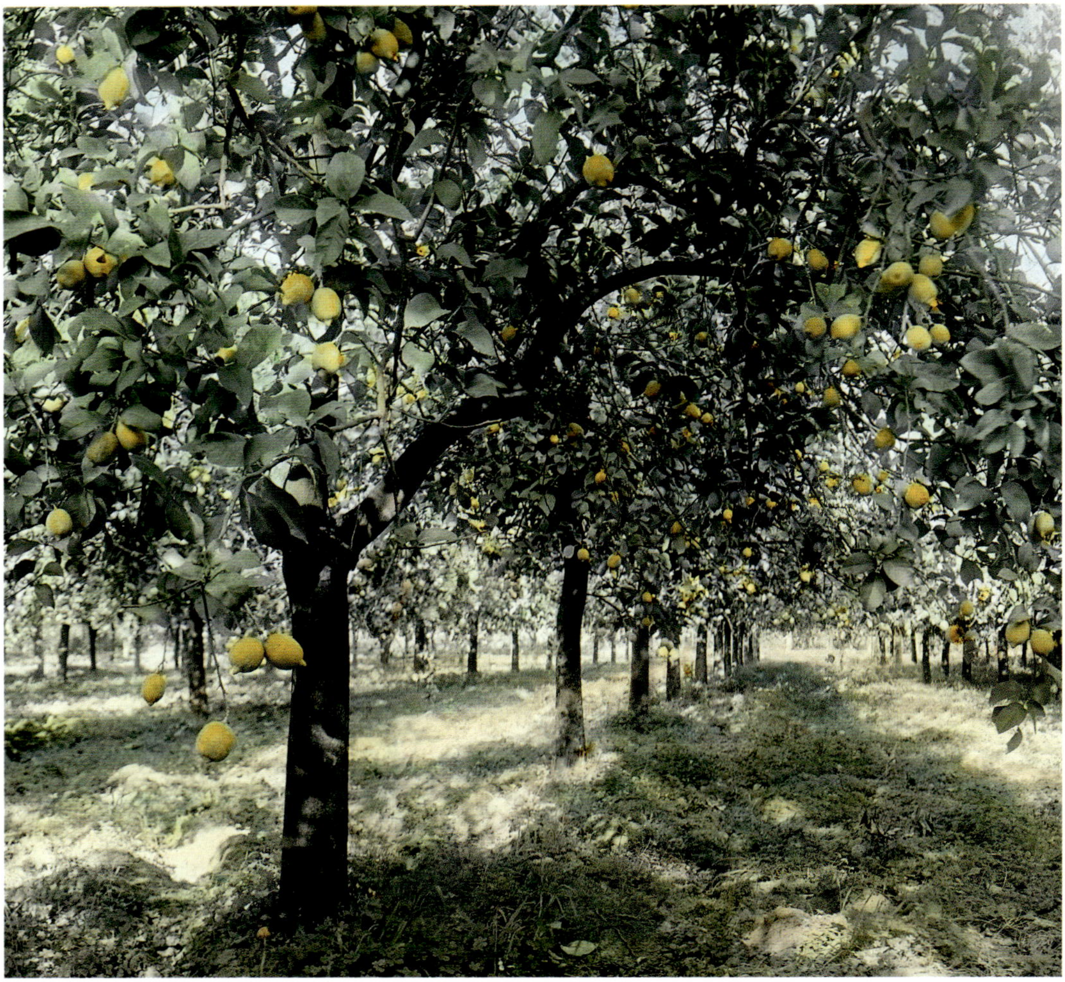

248 Lemon grove, near Calatabiano, Sicily, Italy, 1925

248 Zitronenhain, nahe Calatabiano, Sizilien, Italien, 1925

248 Citronniers près de Calatabiano, Sicile, Italie, 1925

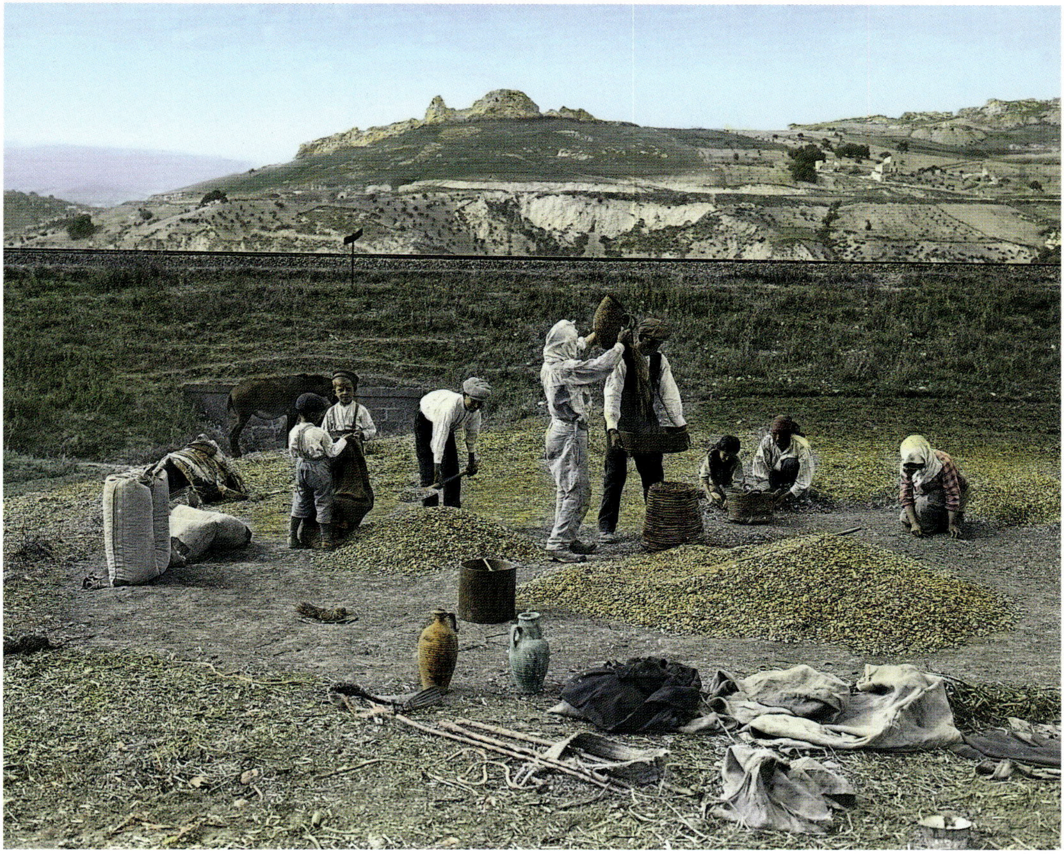

249 Men, women and small children cleaning and sacking castor beans, Girgenti, Sicily, Italy, 1925

249 Männer, Frauen und kleine Kinder beim Säubern und Einsacken von Rizinusbohnen, Agrigento, Sizilien, Italien, 1925

249 Homme, femmes et enfants remplissant des sacs de graines de ricin, Girgenti, Sicile, Italie, 1925

250 Horse and carriage, Palermo, Sicily, Italy, 1880s

250 Pferd und Kutsche, Palermo, Sizilien, Italien, 1880er Jahre

250 Cheval attelé, Palerme, Sicile, Italie, années 1880

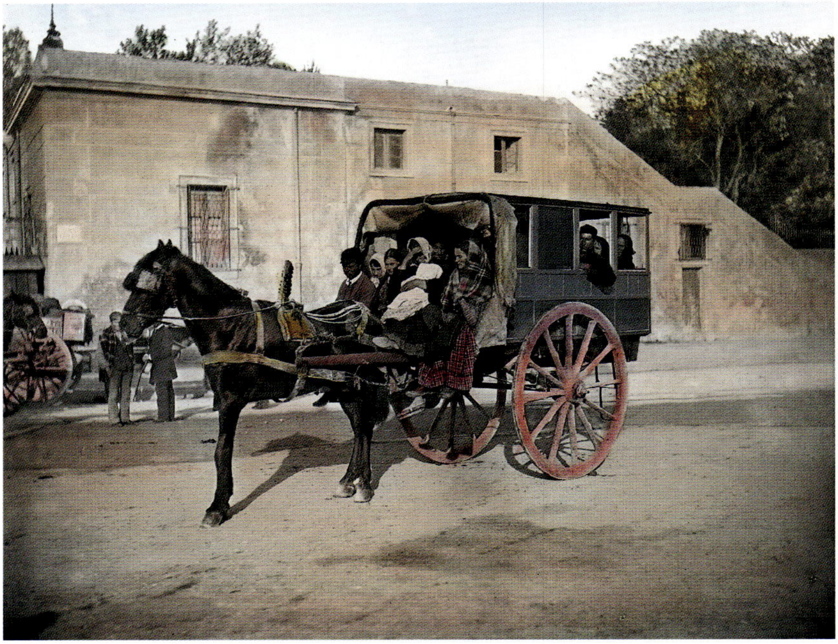

251 Boiling cork bark, Almoraima, Spain, 1910

251 Kochen von Korkrinde, Almoraima, Spanien, 1910

251 Ébullition d'écorces de chêne-liège, Almoraima, Espagne, 1910

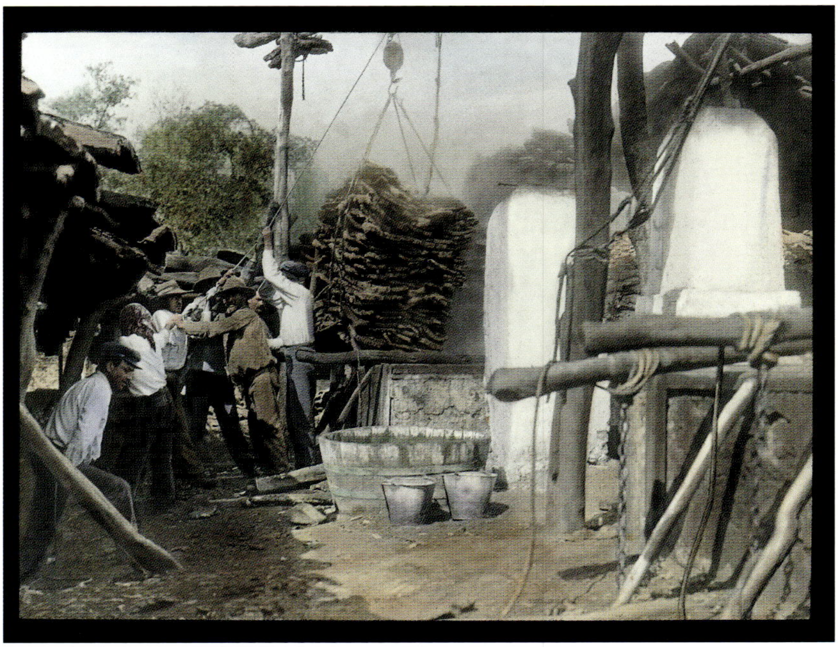

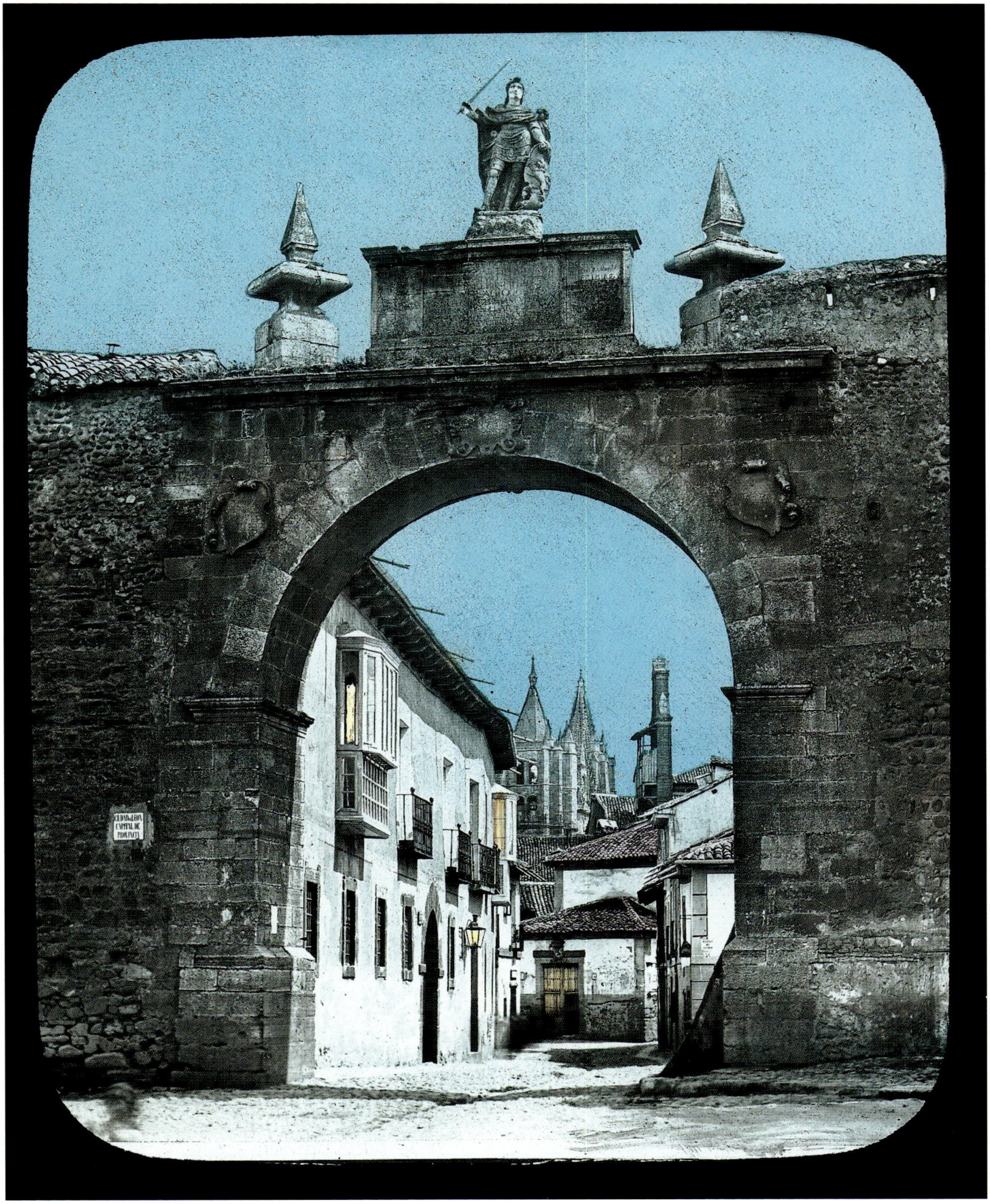

252 Town Gate, León, Spain, 1890s

252 Stadttor, León, Spanien, 1890er Jahre

252 Porte de la ville, León, Espagne, années 1890

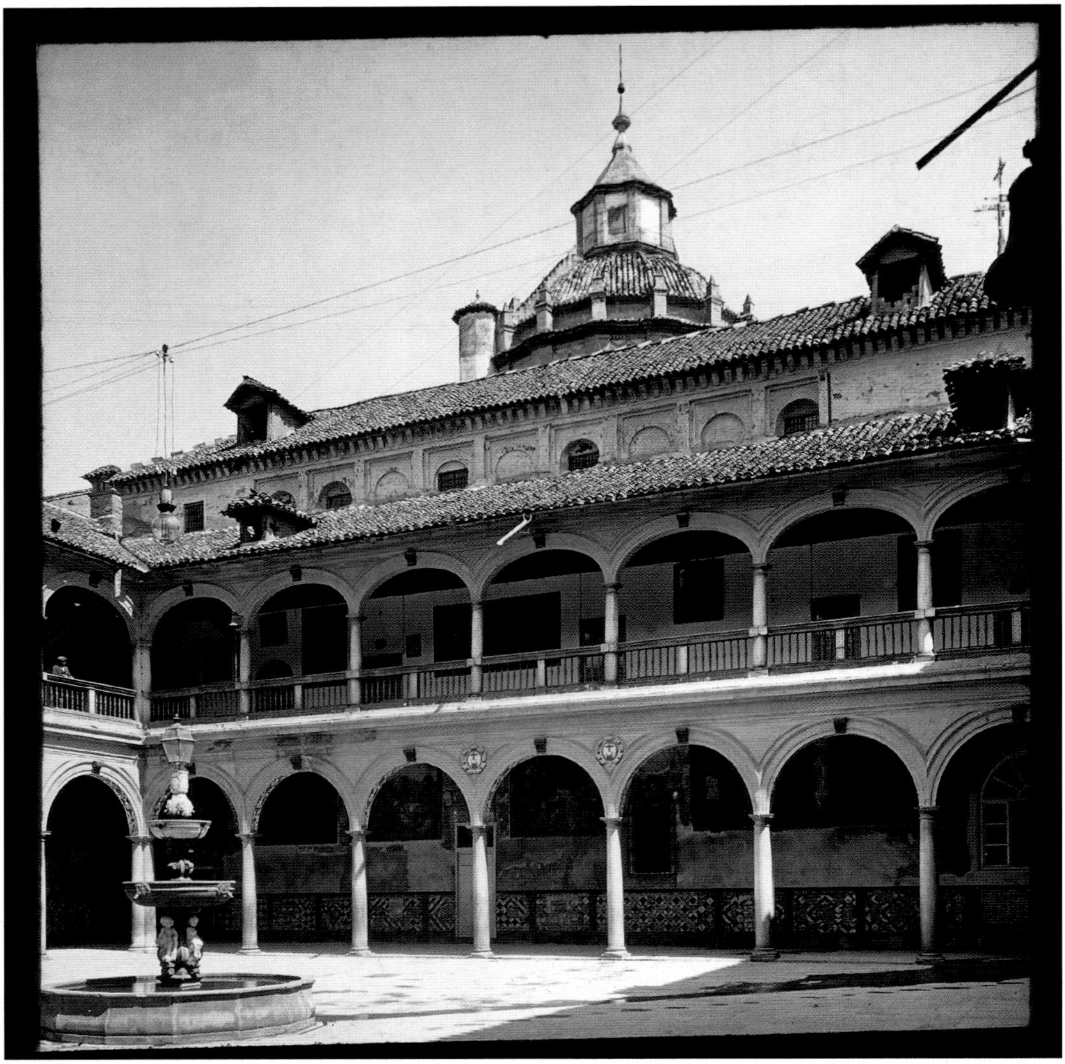

253 Cloisters of the Hospital San Juan de Dios, Granada, Spain, 1900s
254 Great Mosque (Mezquita) of Córdoba, Spain, 1870s

253 Kreuzgang des Hospitals San Juan de Dios, Granada, Spanien, 1900er Jahre
254 Die Große Moschee (Mezquita) von Córdoba, Spanien, 1870er Jahre

253 Cloître de l'hôpital San Juan de Dios, Grenade, Espagne, années 1900
254 Grande Mosquée (Mezquita) de Cordoue, Espagne, années 1870

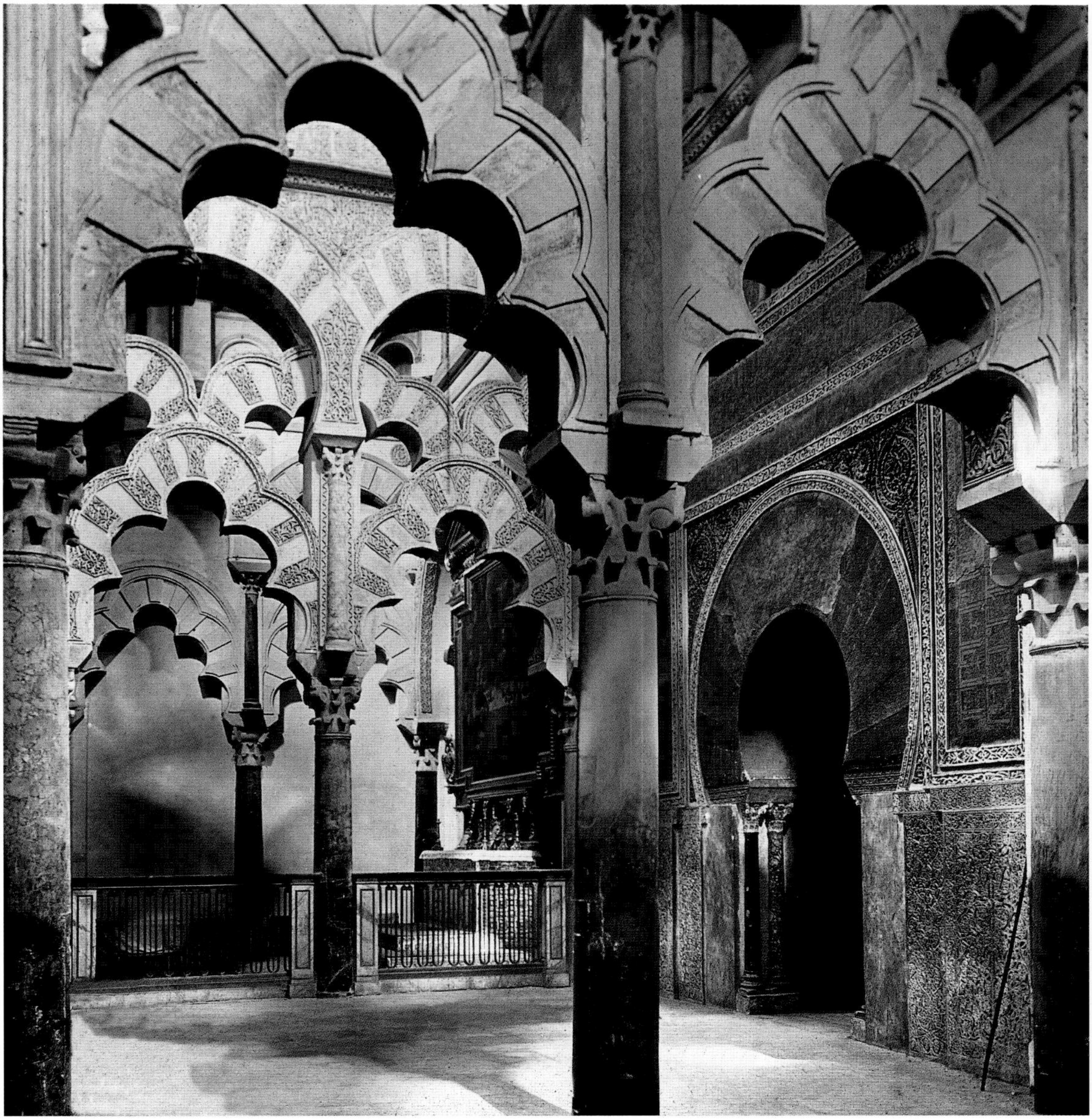

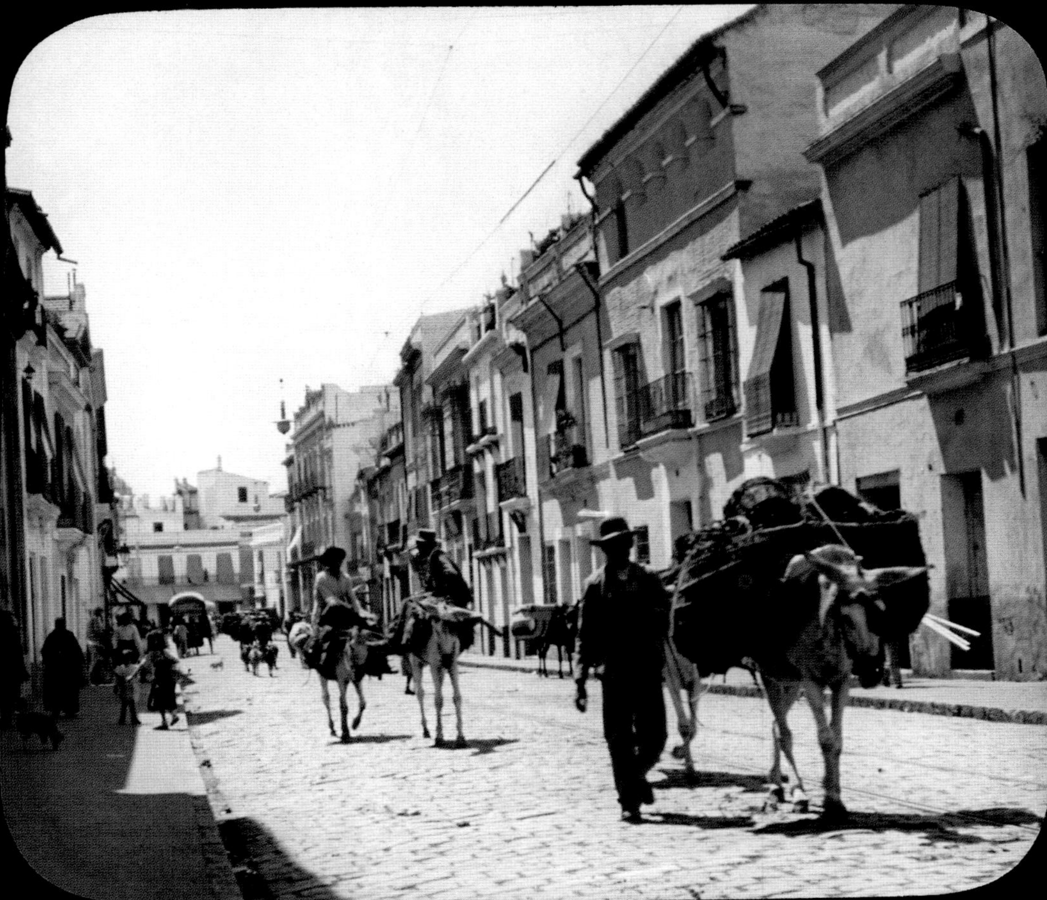

255 Street scene in Triana, Seville, Spain, 1910
256 Panoramic view of Madrid, Spain, 1880s

255 Straßenszene in Triana, Sevilla, Spanien, 1910
256 Panorama-Ansicht Madrids, Spanien, 1880er Jahre

255 Scène de rue à Triana, Séville, Espagne, 1910
256 Panorama sur Madrid, Espagne, années 1880

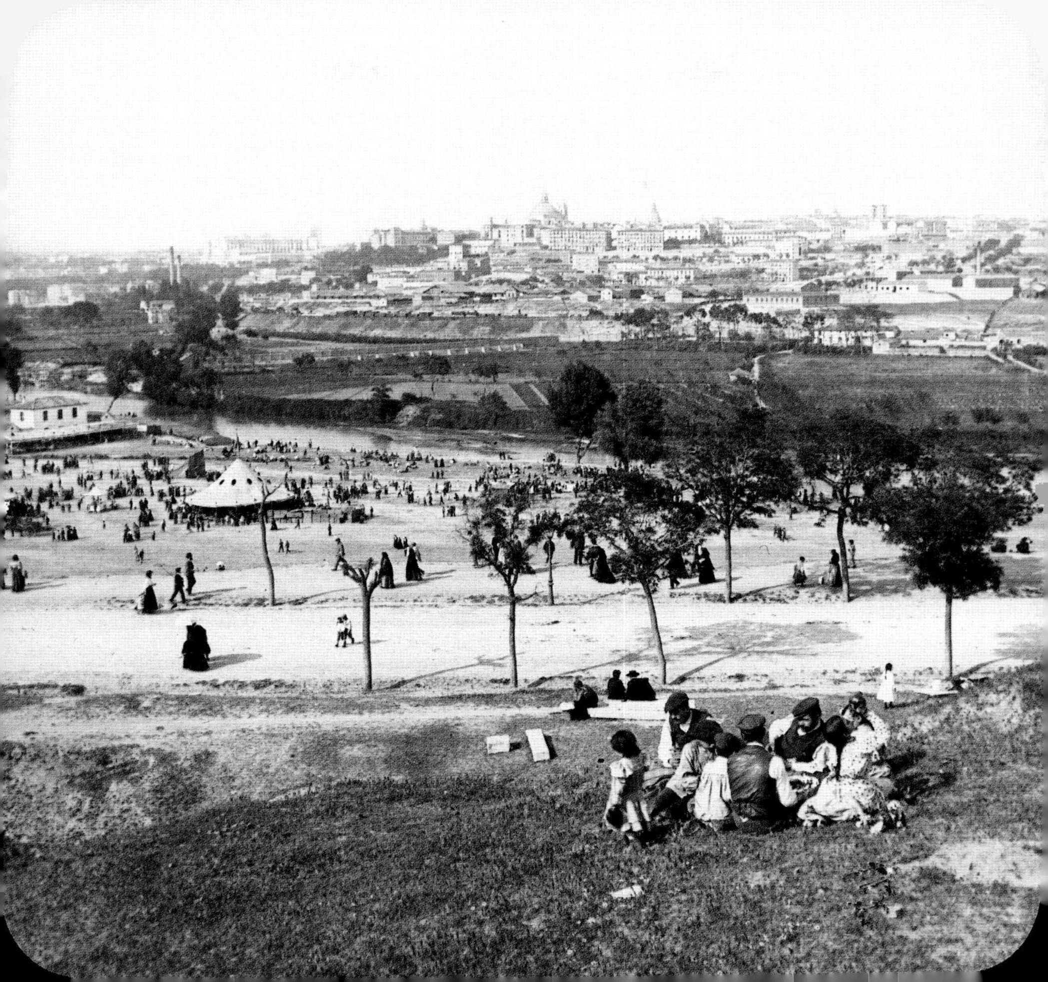

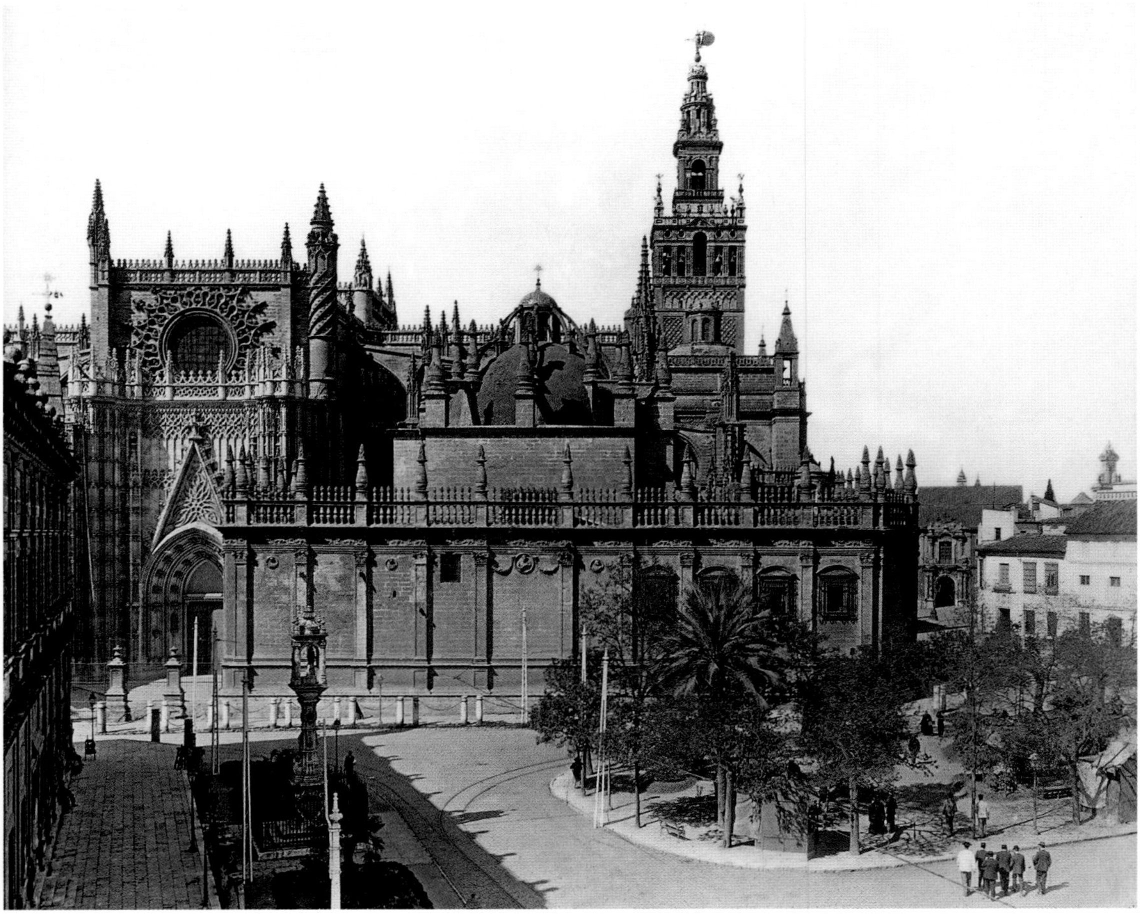

257 Plaza del Triumfo, Casa Lonja (left), the Cathedral and Puerta de San Cristóbal, Seville, Spain, 1910

257 Plaza del Triunfo, Casa Lonja (links), die Kathedrale und Puerta de San Cristóbal, Sevilla, Spanien, 1910

257 Plaza del Triunfo, Casa Lonja (à gauche), la cathédrale et Puerta de San Cristóbal, Séville, Espagne, 1910

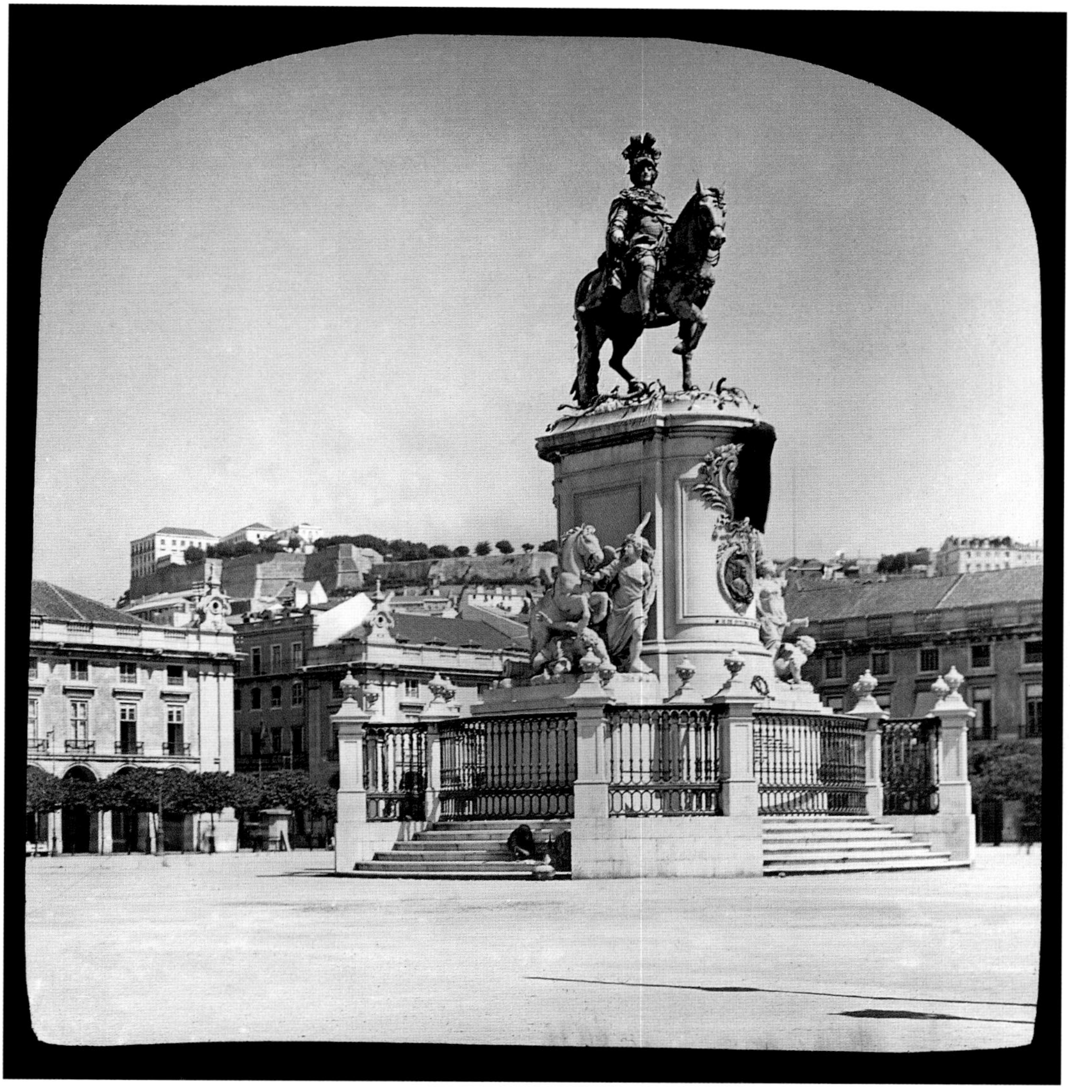

258 Praça do Comércio (Commerce Square), Lisbon, Portugal, c.1900

258 Praça do Comércio (Handelsplatz), Lissabon, Portugal, um 1900

258 Praça do Comércio (place du Commerce), Lisbonne, Portugal, vers 1900

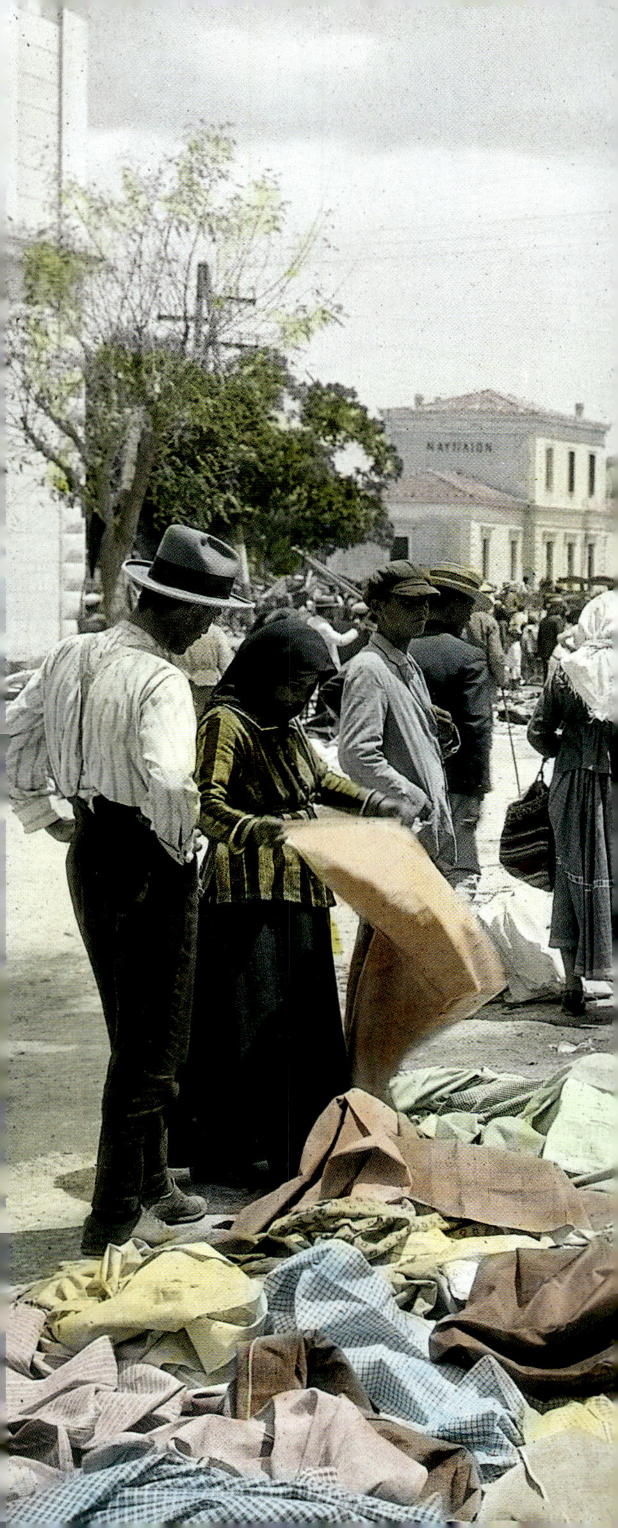
ΝΑΥΠΛΙΟΝ

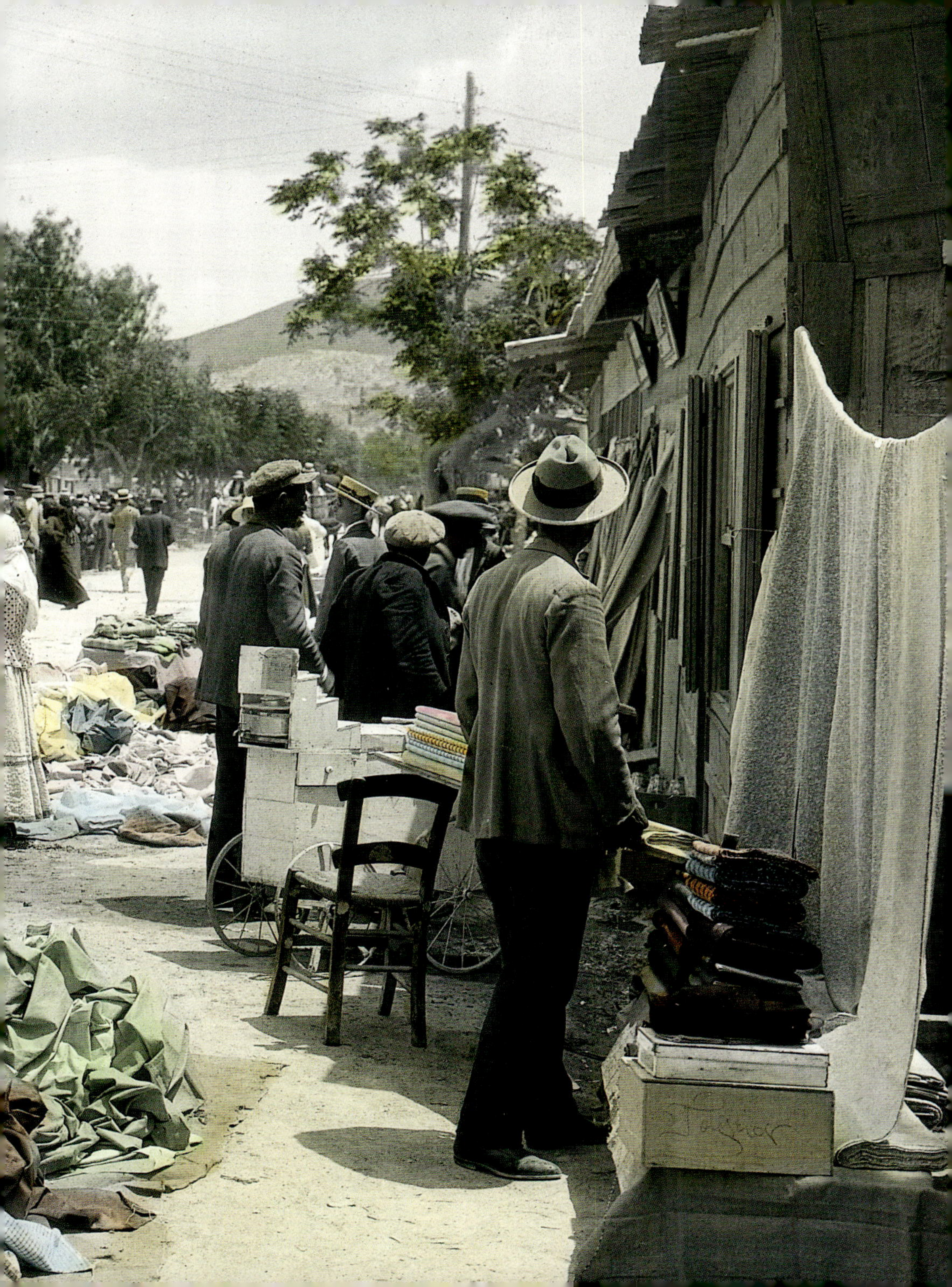

260 Grove of olives trees, near Makrades, Island of Corfu, Greece, 1926

260 Hain mit Olivenbäumen, nahe Makrades, Insel Korfu, Griechenland, 1926

260 Oliveraie près de Makradès, île de Corfou, Grèce, 1926

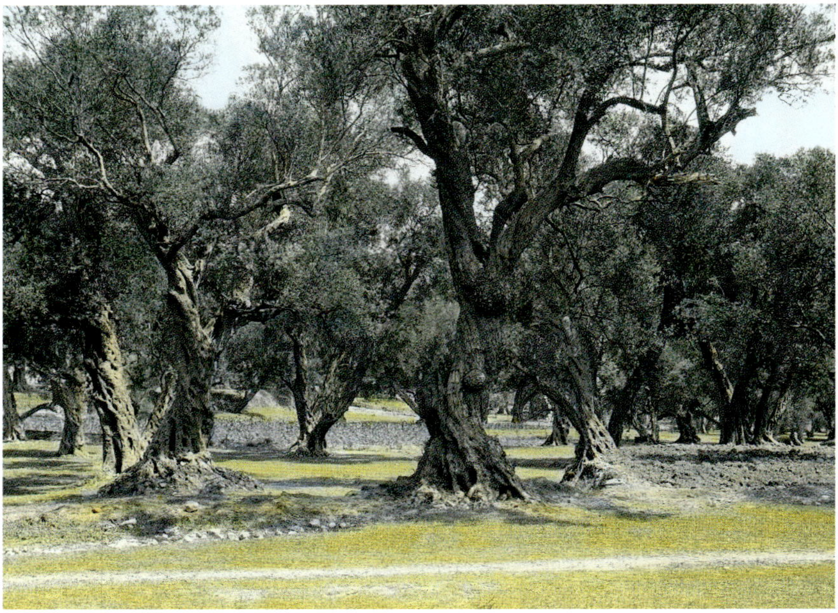

261 Farmyard, woman spinning wool and man milking a cow, near Kondokali, Corfu, Greece, 1926

261 Bauernhof, davor Frau, die Wolle spinnt, und Mann, der eine Kuh melkt, nahe Kondokali, Insel Korfu, Griechenland, 1926

261 Femme filant de la laine et homme trayant une vache dans une cour de ferme près de Kondokali, île de Corfou, Grèce, 1926

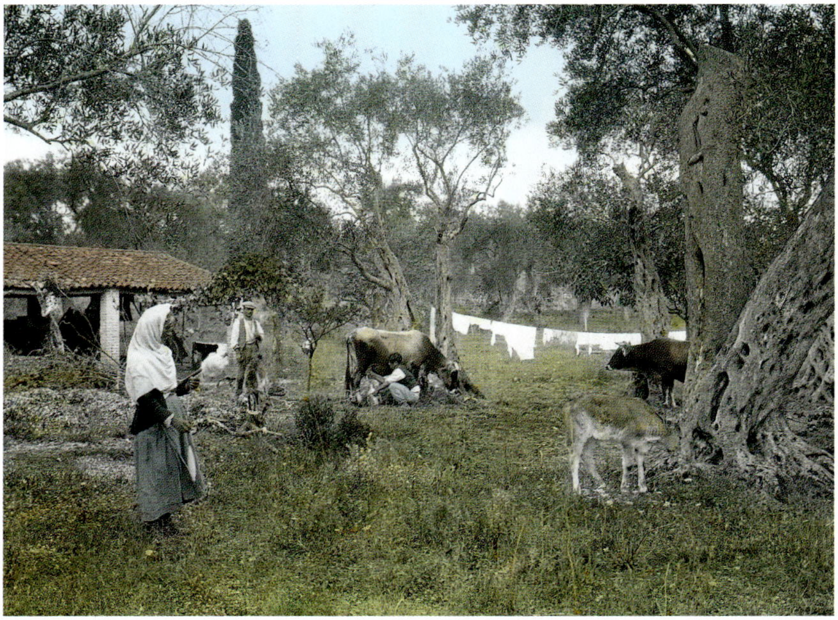

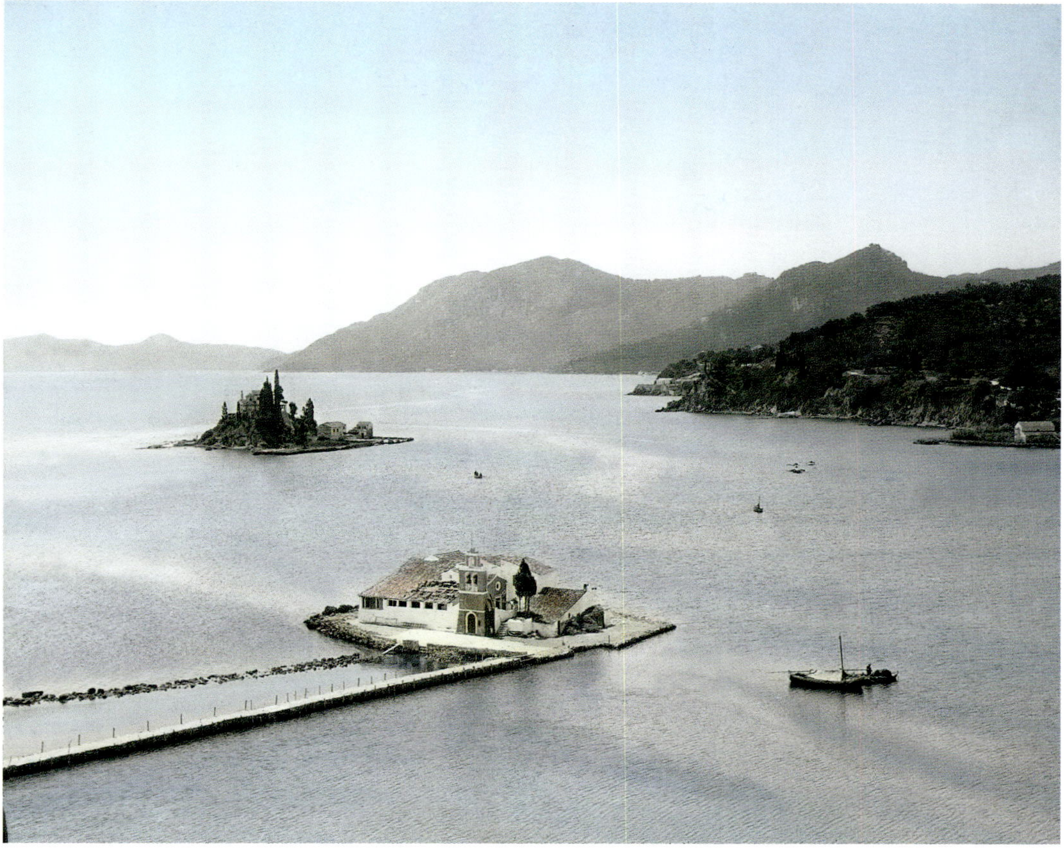

262 View from Kanoni on the Island of Corfu overlooking the Island of Pontikonisi (Mouse Island), Greece, 1926

262 Blick von Kanoni auf der Insel Korfu auf die Insel Pontikonisi (Mäuseinsel), Griechenland, 1926

262 Vue de Kanoni, sur la côte de Corfou, et de l'île de Pontikonissi (l'île de la souris), Grèce, 1926

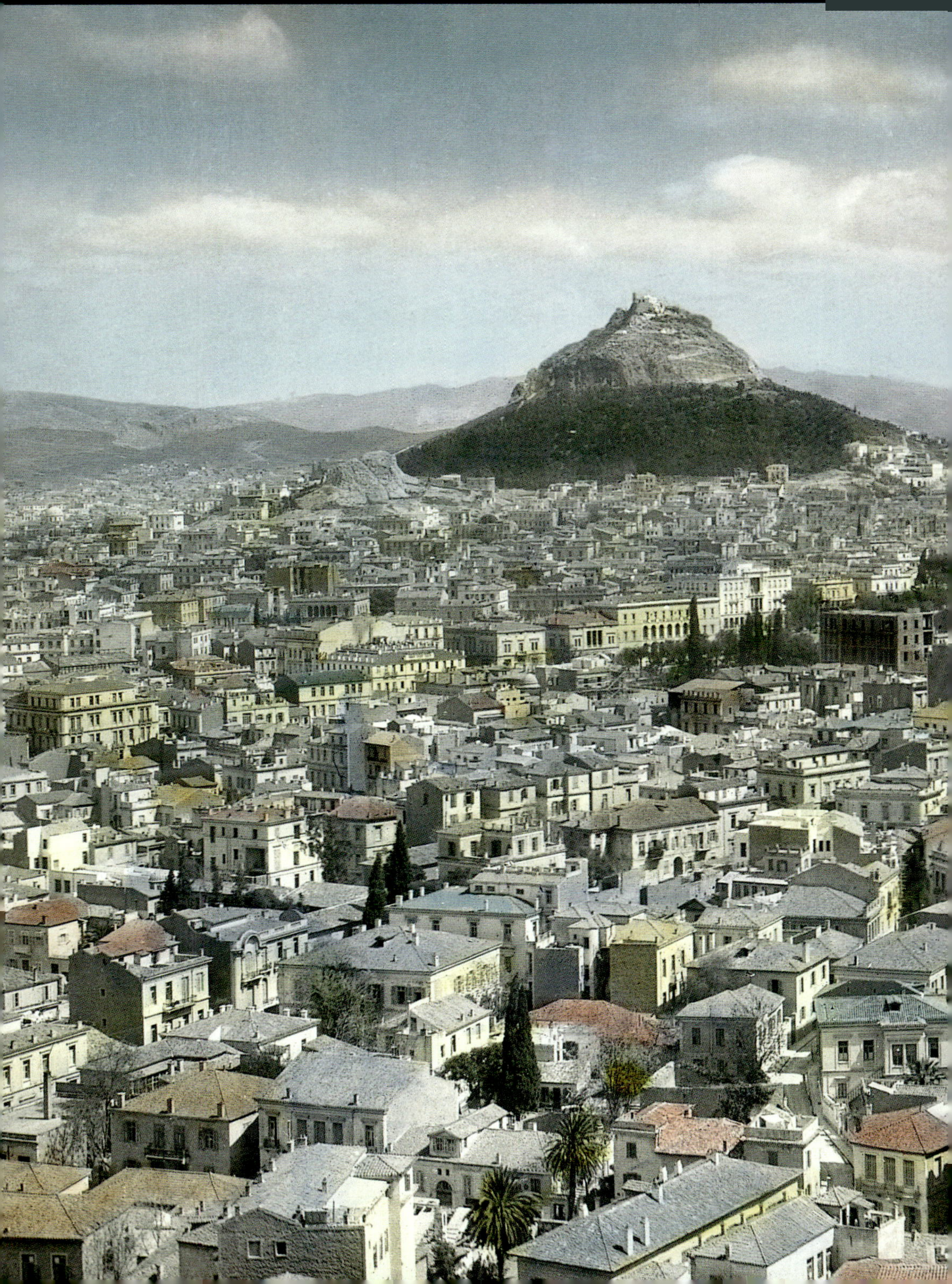

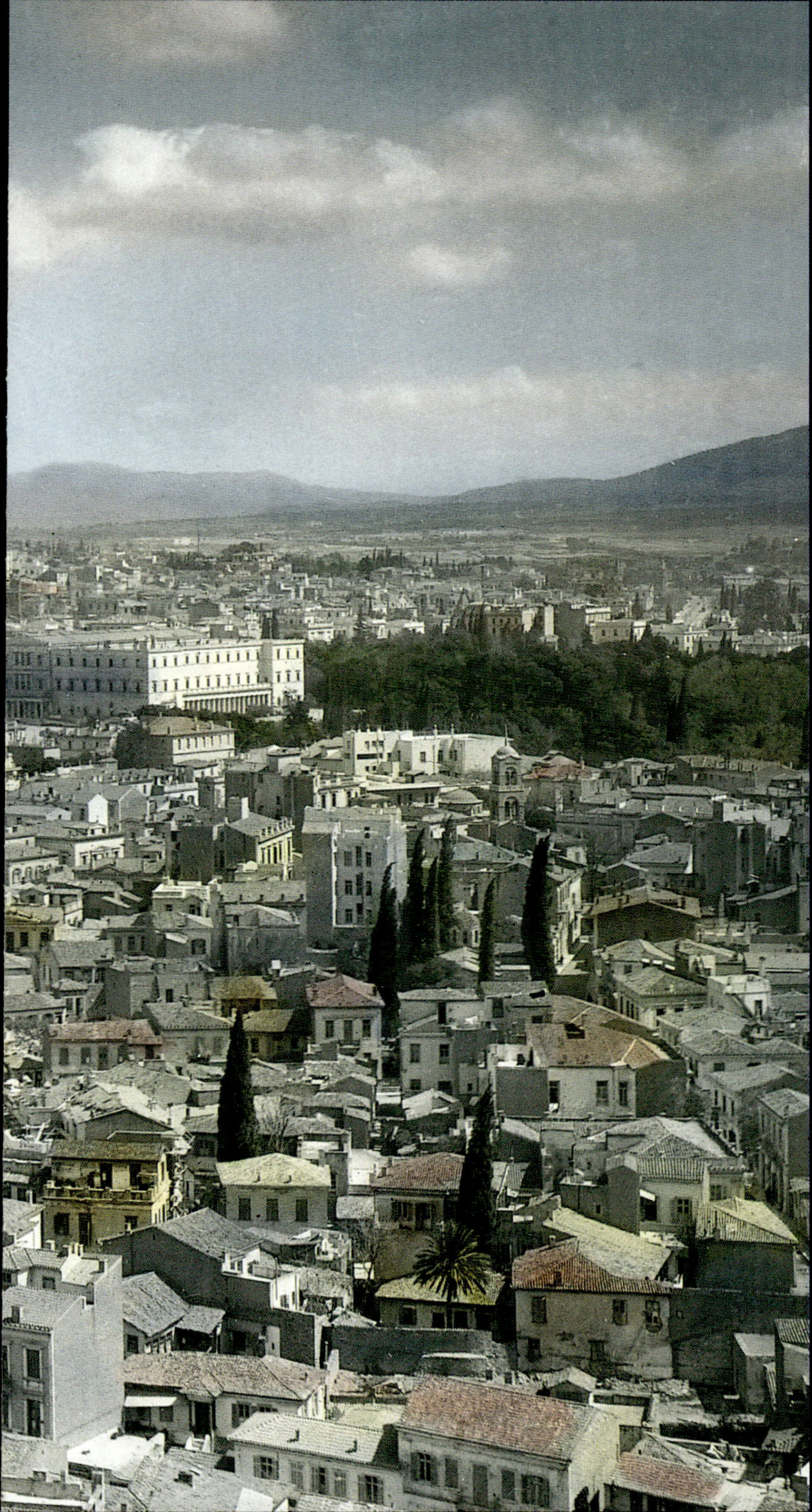

263 General view overlooking Athens (showing Northeast corner of the Acropolis, Modern City, Constitution Palace and Royal Garden), Greece, 1926

263 Gesamtansicht von Athen (sie zeigt die nordöstliche Ecke der Akropolis, die moderne Stadt, Stadtschloss und Schlossgarten), Griechenland, 1926

263 Vue générale sur Athènes (angle nord-est de l'Acropole, la ville moderne, le palais de la Constitution et le jardin royal), Grèce, 1926

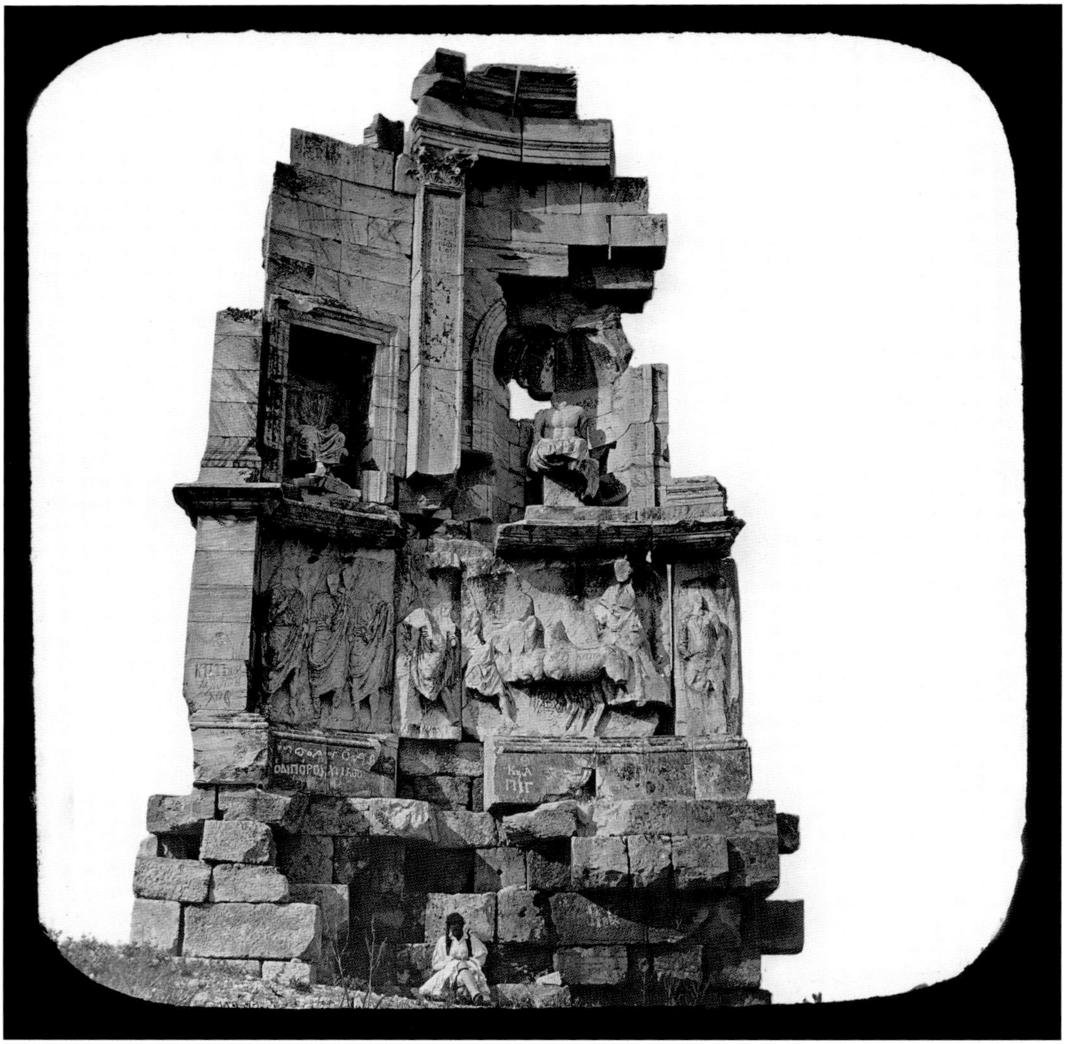

264 Ruins of the Philopappos Monument, Athens, Greece, 1870s

264 Die Ruinen des Philopapposdenkmals, Athen, Griechenland, 1870er Jahre

264 Ruines du monument Philopappos, Athènes, Grèce, années 1870

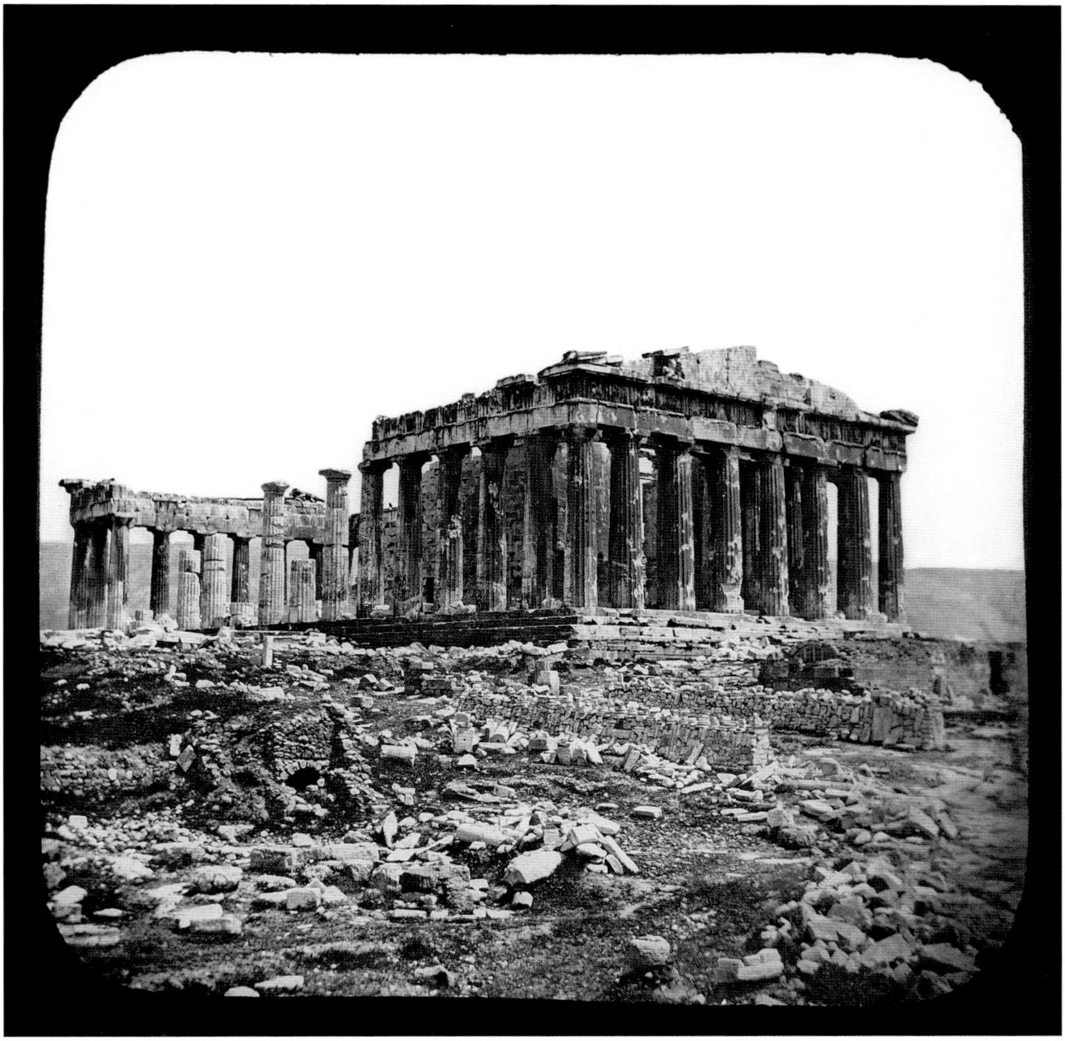

265 Ruins of the Parthenon, Acropolis, Athens, Greece, 1870s

265 Die Ruinen des Parthenon, Akropolis, Athen, Griechenland, 1870er Jahre

265 Ruines du Parthénon, l'Acropole, Athènes, Grèce, années 1870

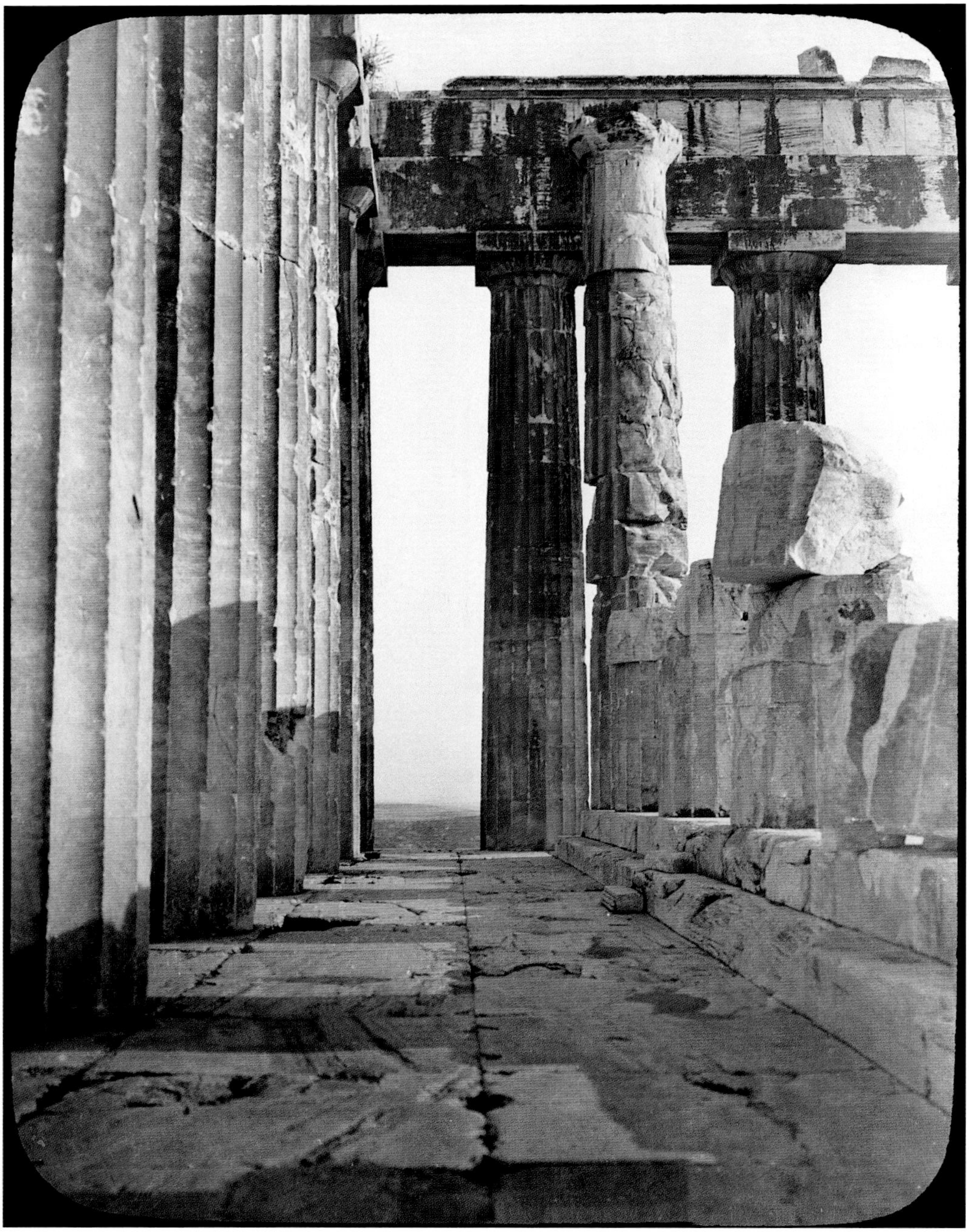

266 View of the Parthenon, The Acropolis, Athens, Greece, 1870s

266 Ansicht des Parthenon, Akropolis, Athen, Griechenland, 1870er Jahre

266 Vue du Parthénon, l'Acropole, Athènes, Grèce, années 1870

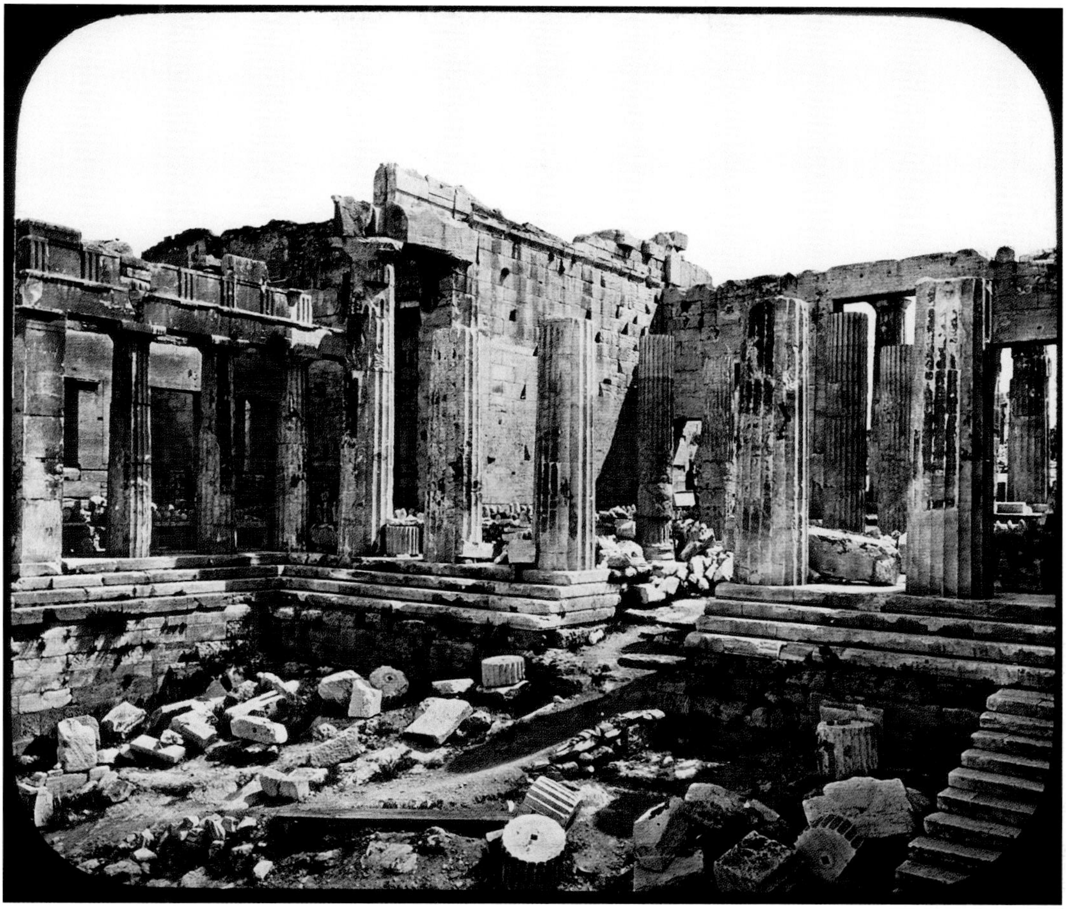

267 View of the Parthenon, The Acropolis, Athens, Greece, 1870s

267 Ansicht des Parthenon, Akropolis, Athen, Griechenland, 1870er Jahre

267 Vue du Parthénon, l'Acropole, Athènes, Grèce, années 1870

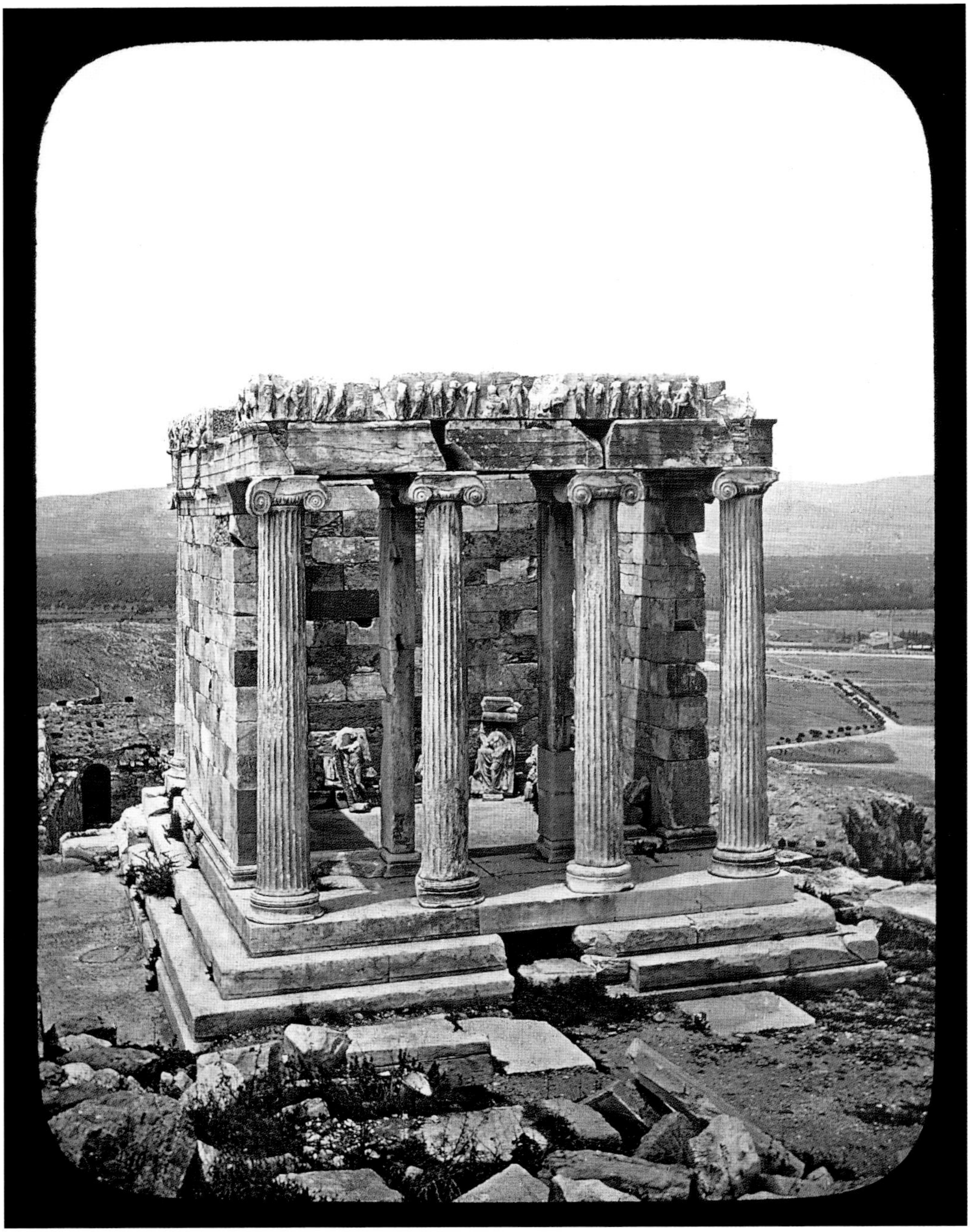

268 Temple of Victory (Temple of Athena Nike), Acropolis, Athens, Greece, 1870s

268 Der Siegestempel (Tempel der Athena Nike), Akropolis, Athen, Griechenland, 1870er Jahre

268 Temple de la Victoire (temple d'Athéna Niké), l'Acropole, Athènes, Grèce, années 1870

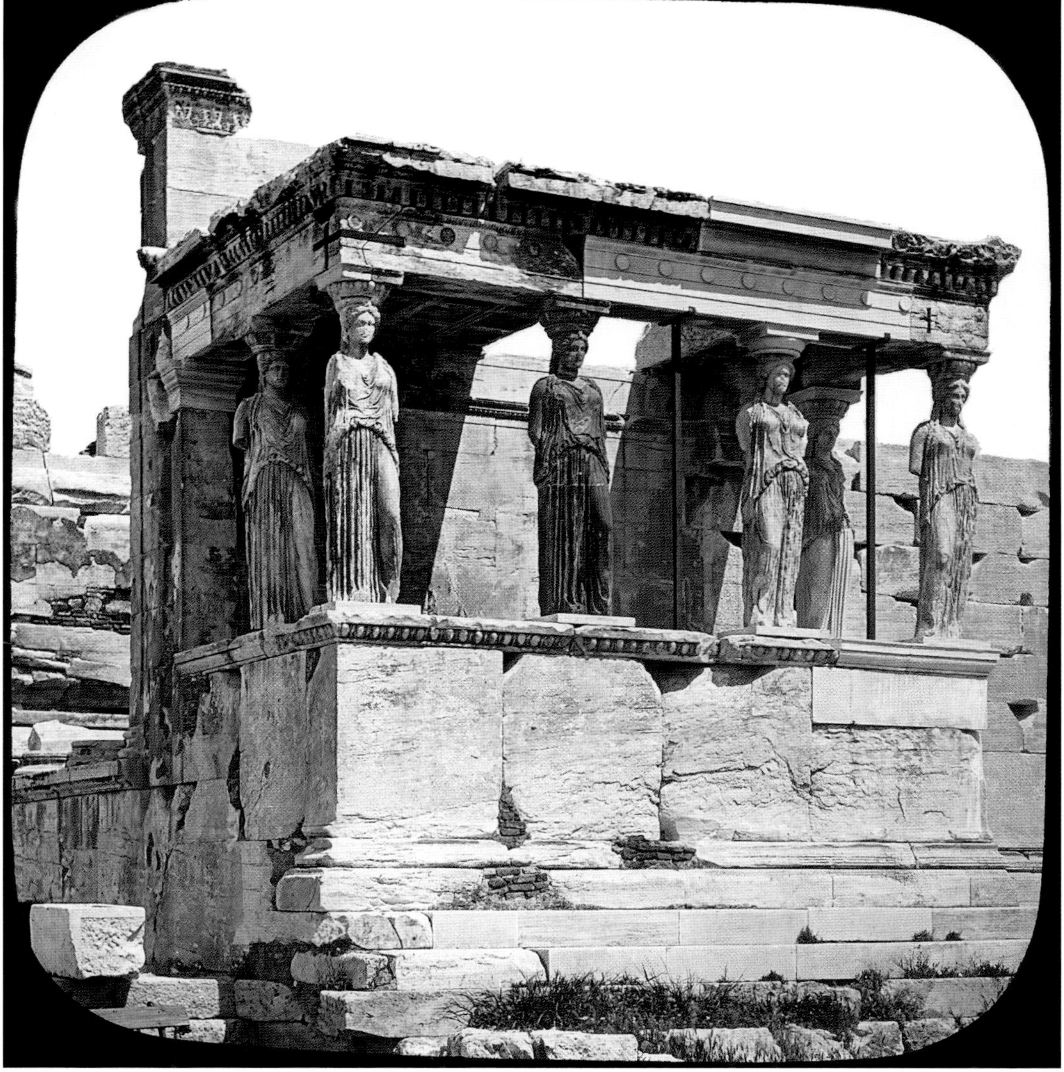

269 The Erechtheion, The Acropolis, Athens, Greece, 1870s

269 Das Erechtheion, Akropolis, Athen, Griechenland, 1870er Jahre

269 L'Érechthéion, l'Acropole, Athènes, Grèce, années 1870

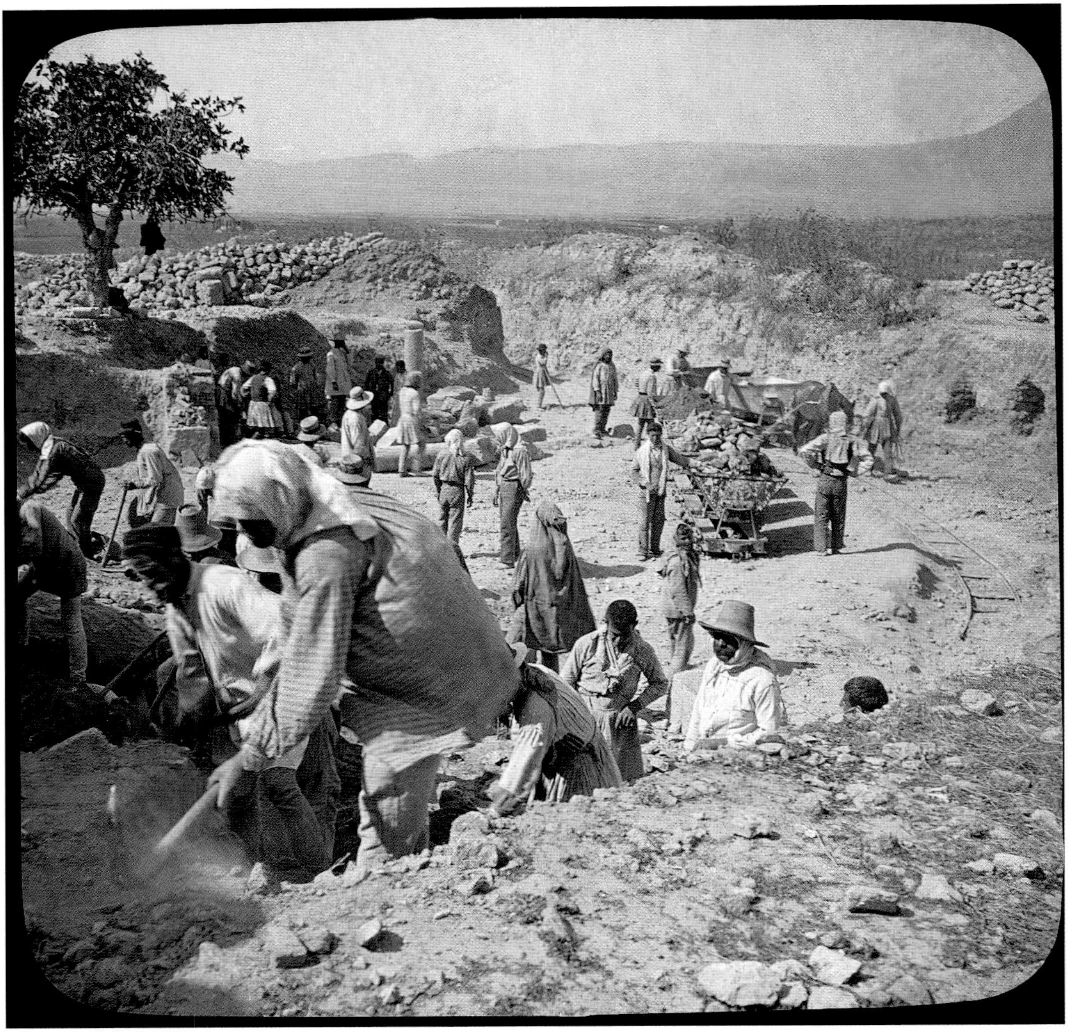

270 Excavators at work uncovering the ancient ruins of Old Corinth, Greece, 1890s

270 Ausgräber bei der Freilegung der antiken Ruinen des Alten Korinth, Griechenland, 1890er Jahre

270 Fouilles sur le site des ruines de la Corinthe antique, Grèce, années 1890

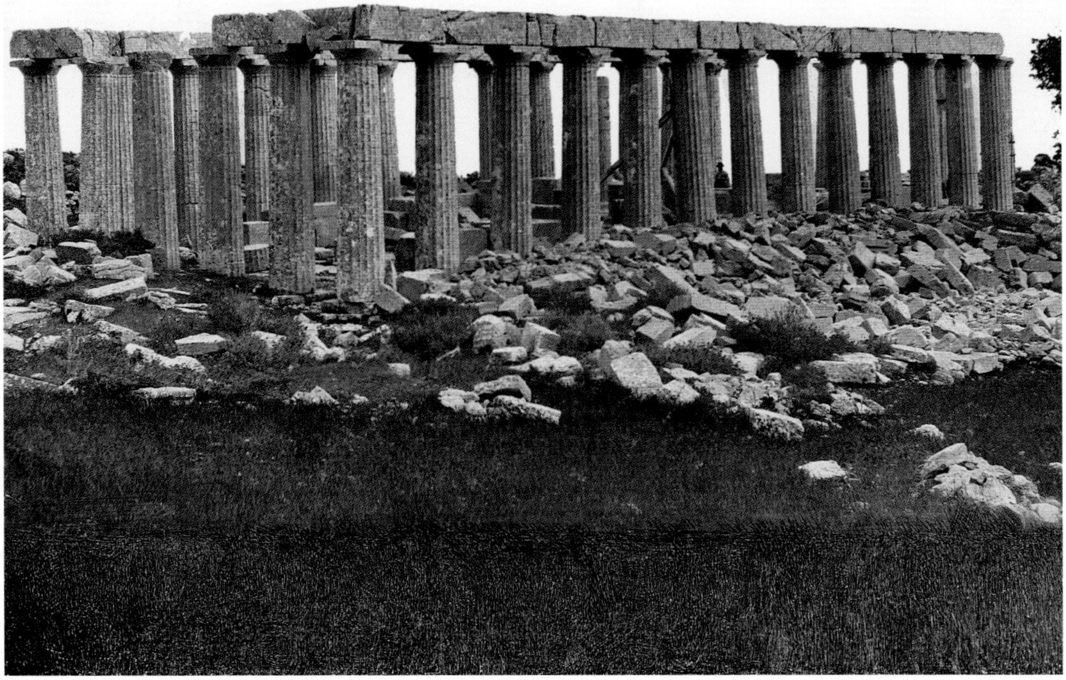

271 Temple of Apollo Epicurius, Bassae, Greece, 1880s

271 Der Tempel des Apollon Epikurios, Bassae, Griechenland, 1880er Jahre

271 Temple d'Apollon Épicure, Bassae, Grèce, années 1880

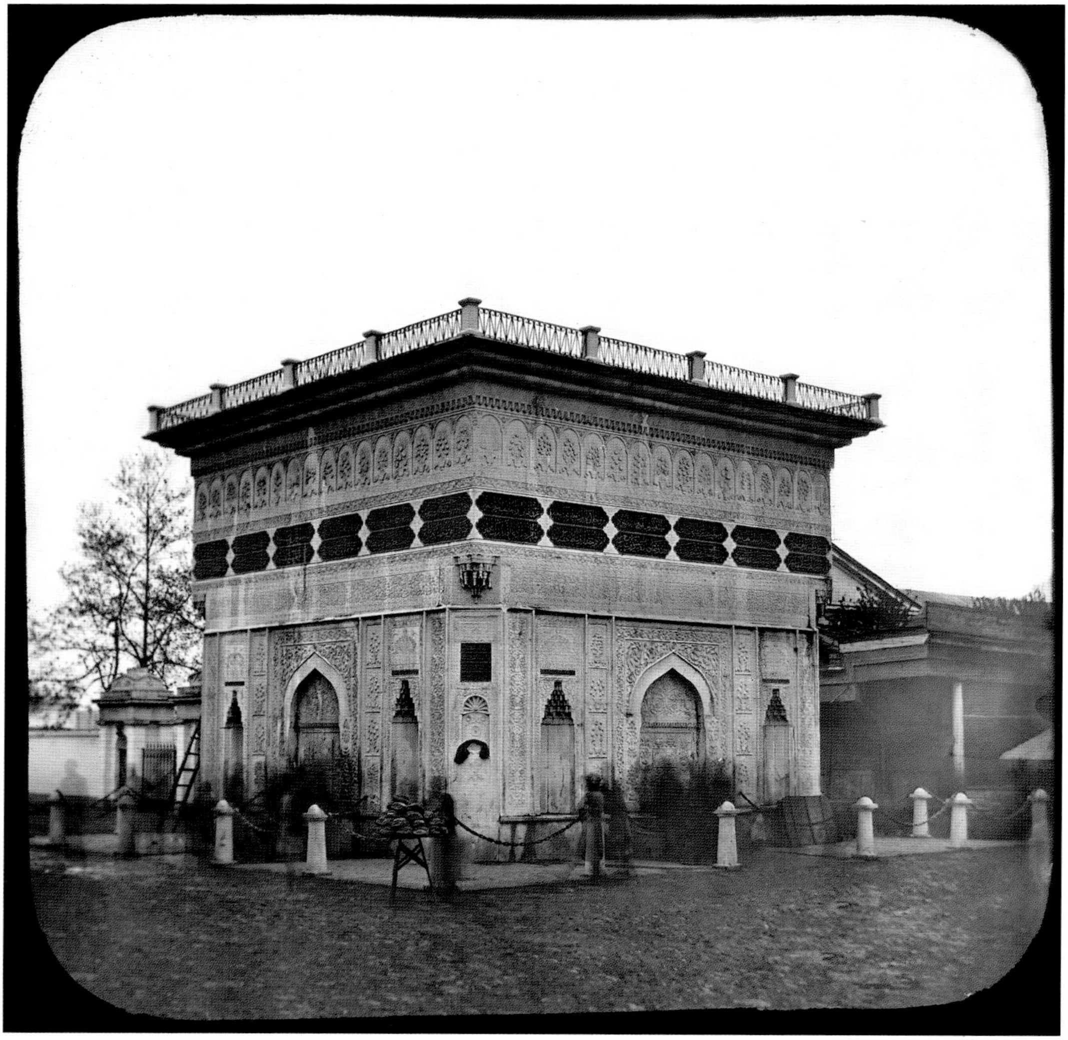

272 Fountain of Top Khani, Constantinople (now Istanbul), Turkey, 1860s

272 Der Tophane-Brunnen, Konstantinopel (heute Istanbul), Türkei, 1860er Jahre

272 Fontaine de Top Khani, Constantinople (auj. Istanbul), Turquie, années 1860

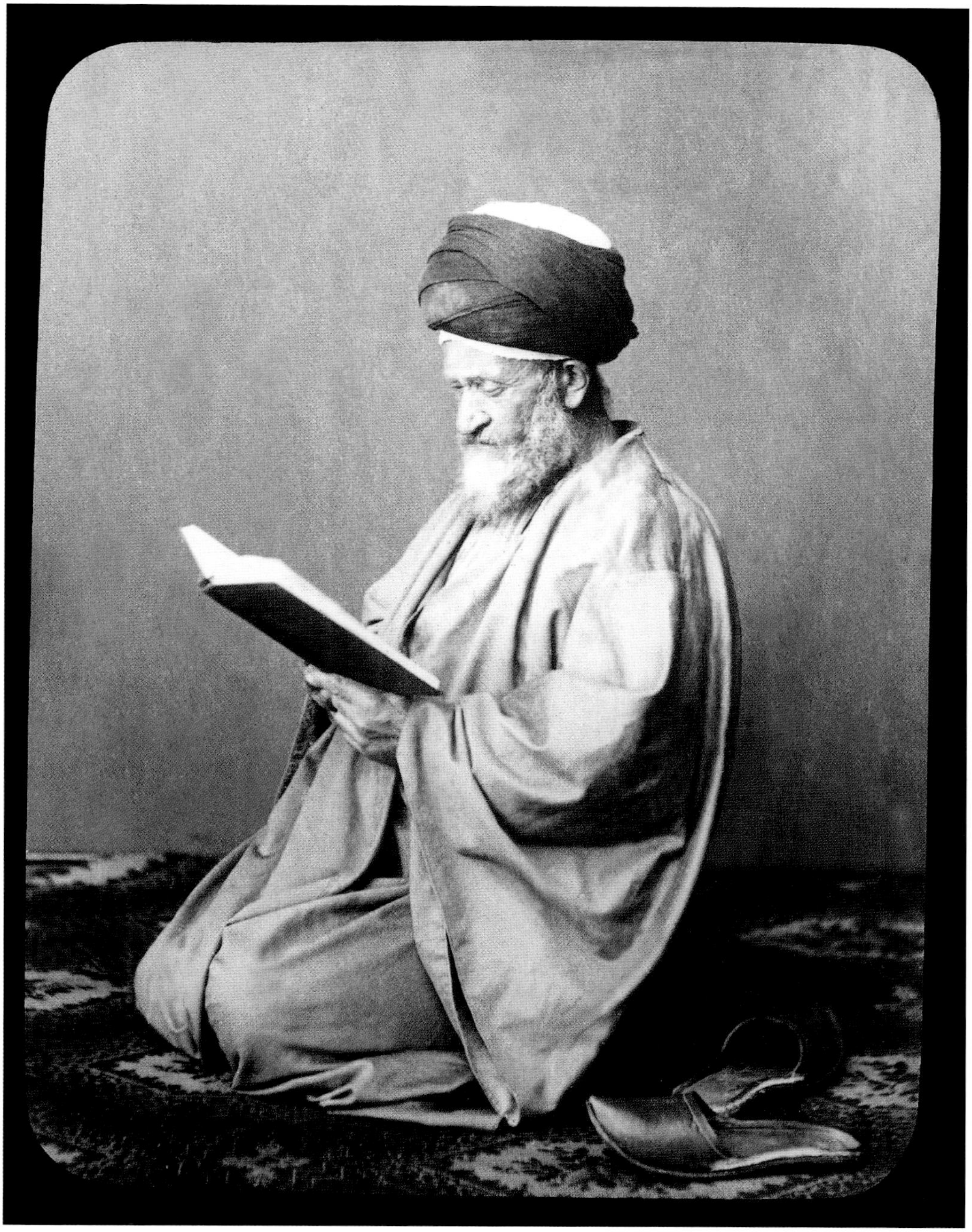

273 Iman at prayer, Constantinople (now Istanbul), Turkey, 1870s

273 Imam beim Gebet, Konstantinopel (heute Istanbul), Türkei, 1870er Jahre

273 Imam en prière, Constantinople (auj. Istanbul), Turquie, années 1870

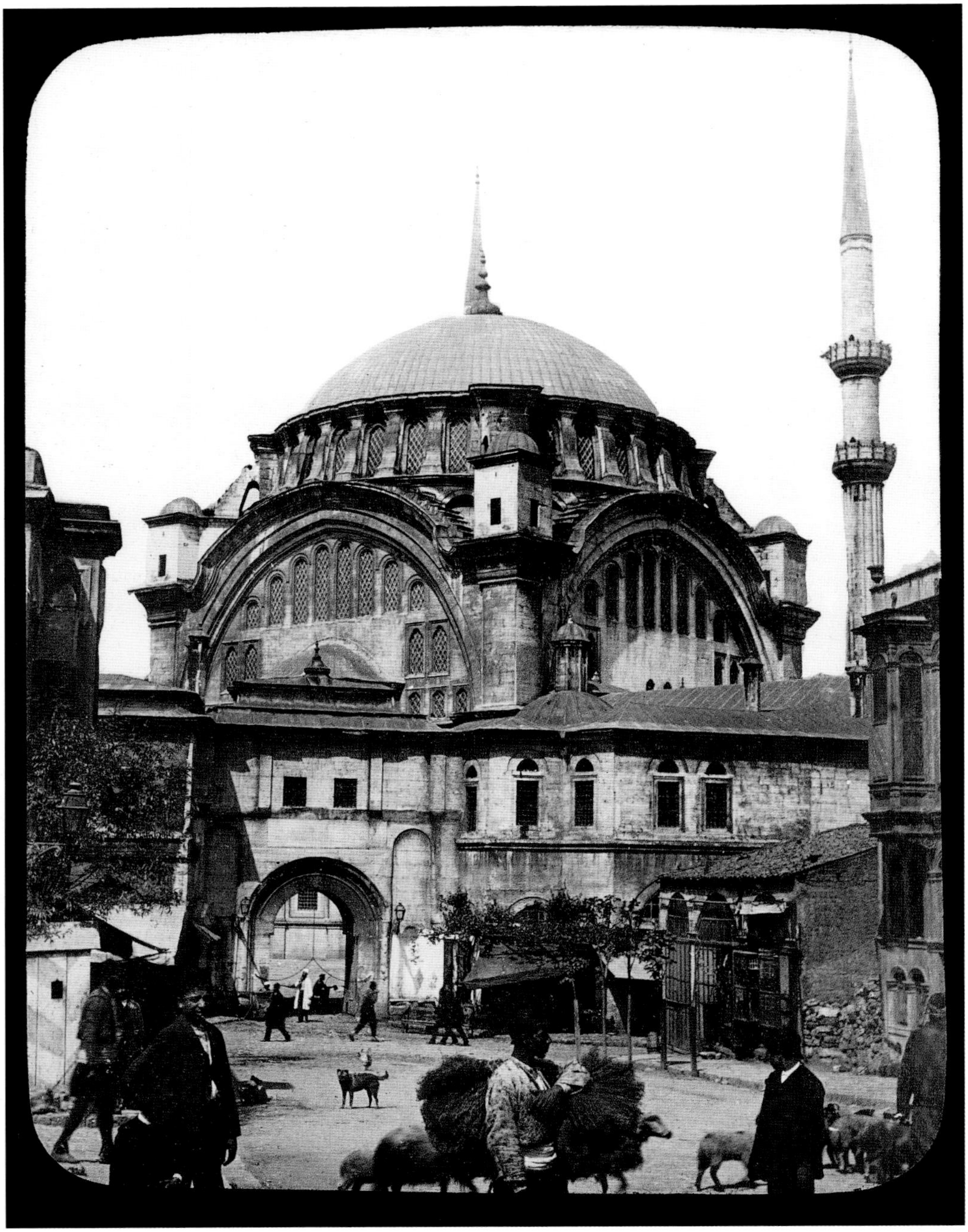

274 Mosque of Sultan Osman, Constantinople (now Istanbul), Turkey, 1890s

274 Die Sultan-Ahmed-Moschee, Konstantinopel (heute Istanbul), Türkei, 1890er Jahre

274 Mosquée du sultan Osman, Constantinople (auj. Istanbul), Turquie, années 1890

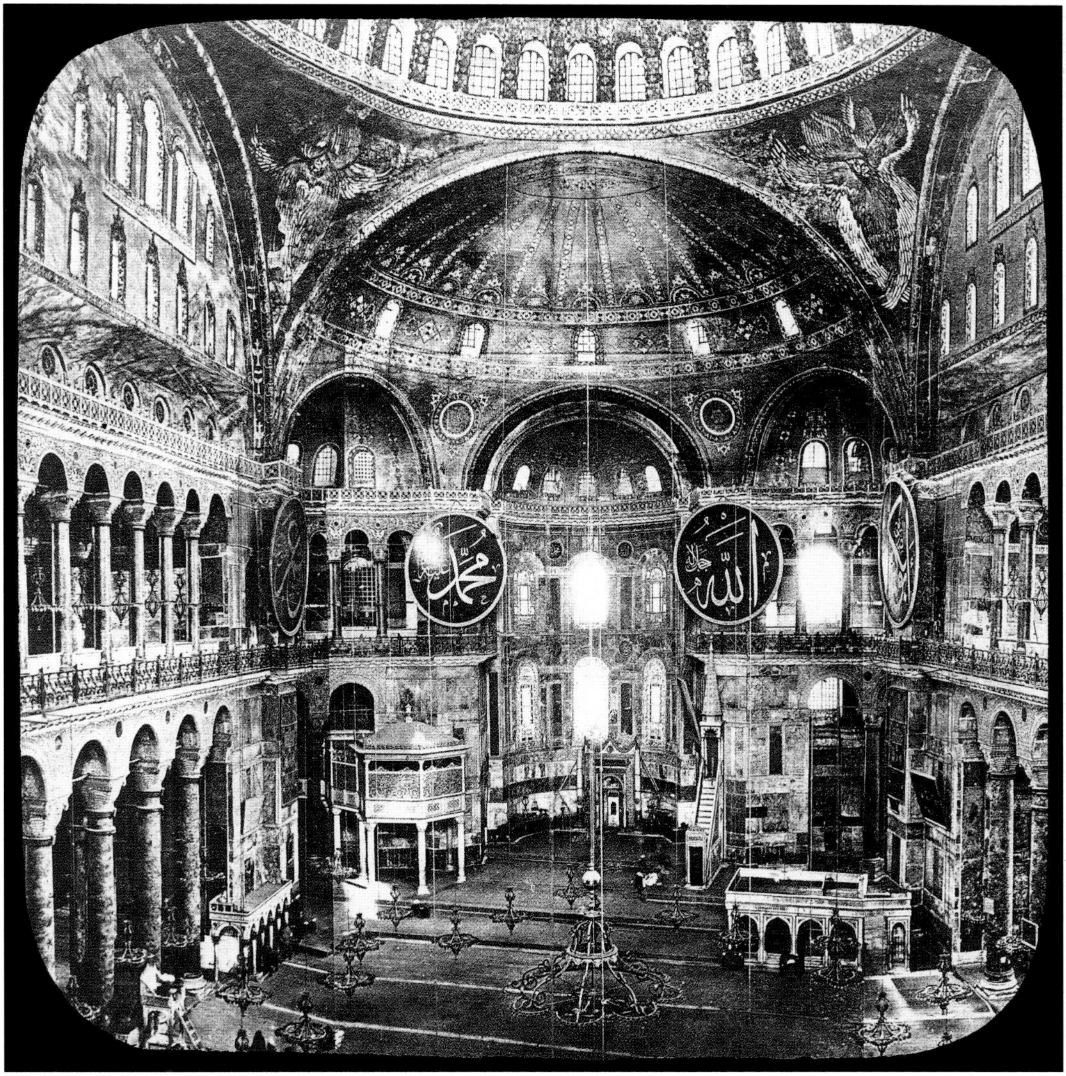

275 Interior of St. Sophia, Constantinople (now Istanbul), Turkey, 1880s

275 Innenraum der Hagia Sophia, Konstantinopel (heute Istanbul), Türkei, 1880er Jahre

275 Intérieur de St. Sophia, Constantinople (auj. Istanbul), Turquie, vers 1880

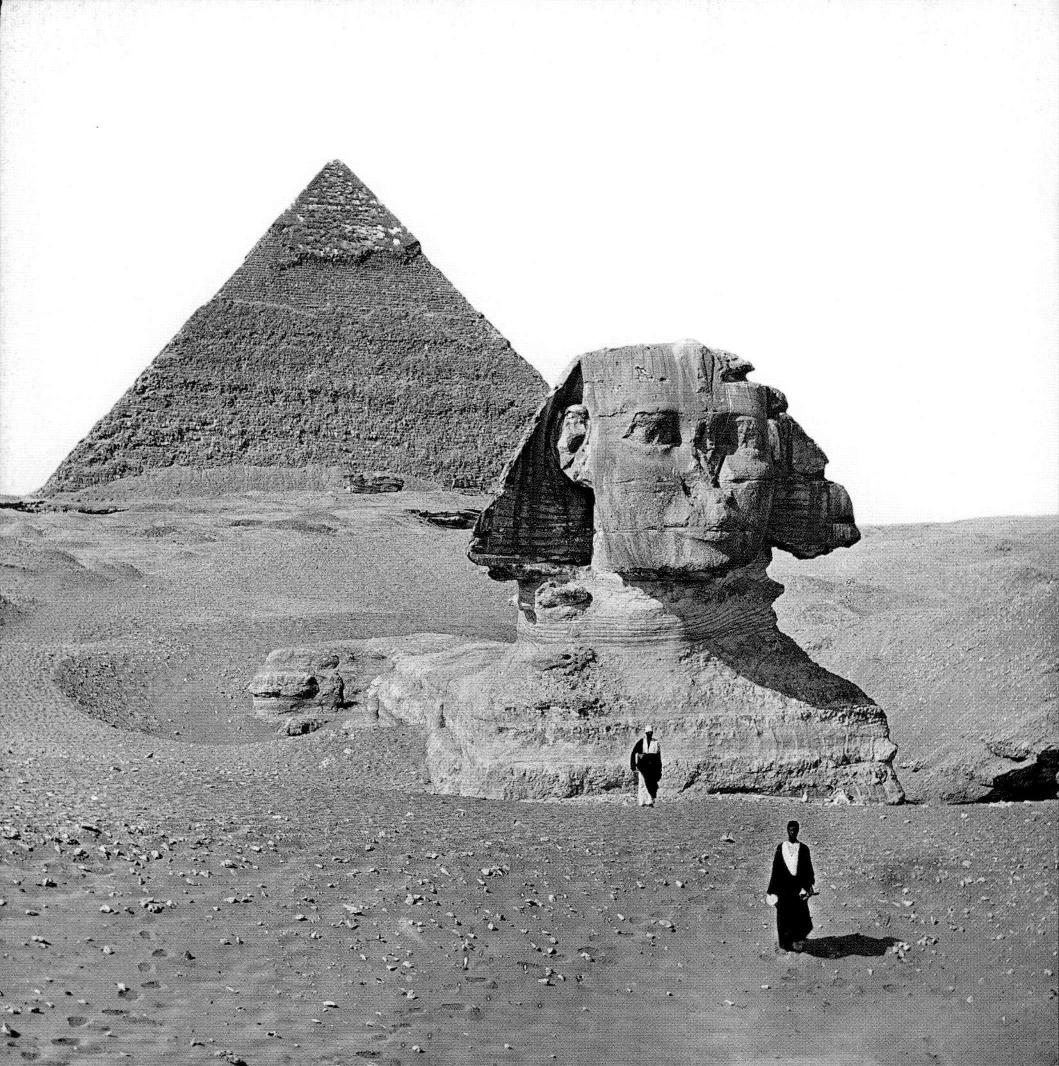

276 The Great Sphinx of Giza, Egypt, 1870s (before excavation)

276 Die Große Sphinx von Gizeh, Ägypten, 1870er Jahre (vor der Ausgrabung)

276 Le grand Sphinx de Gizeh, Égypte, années 1870

NORTHERN AFRICA

NORDAFRIKA · AFRIQUE DU NORD

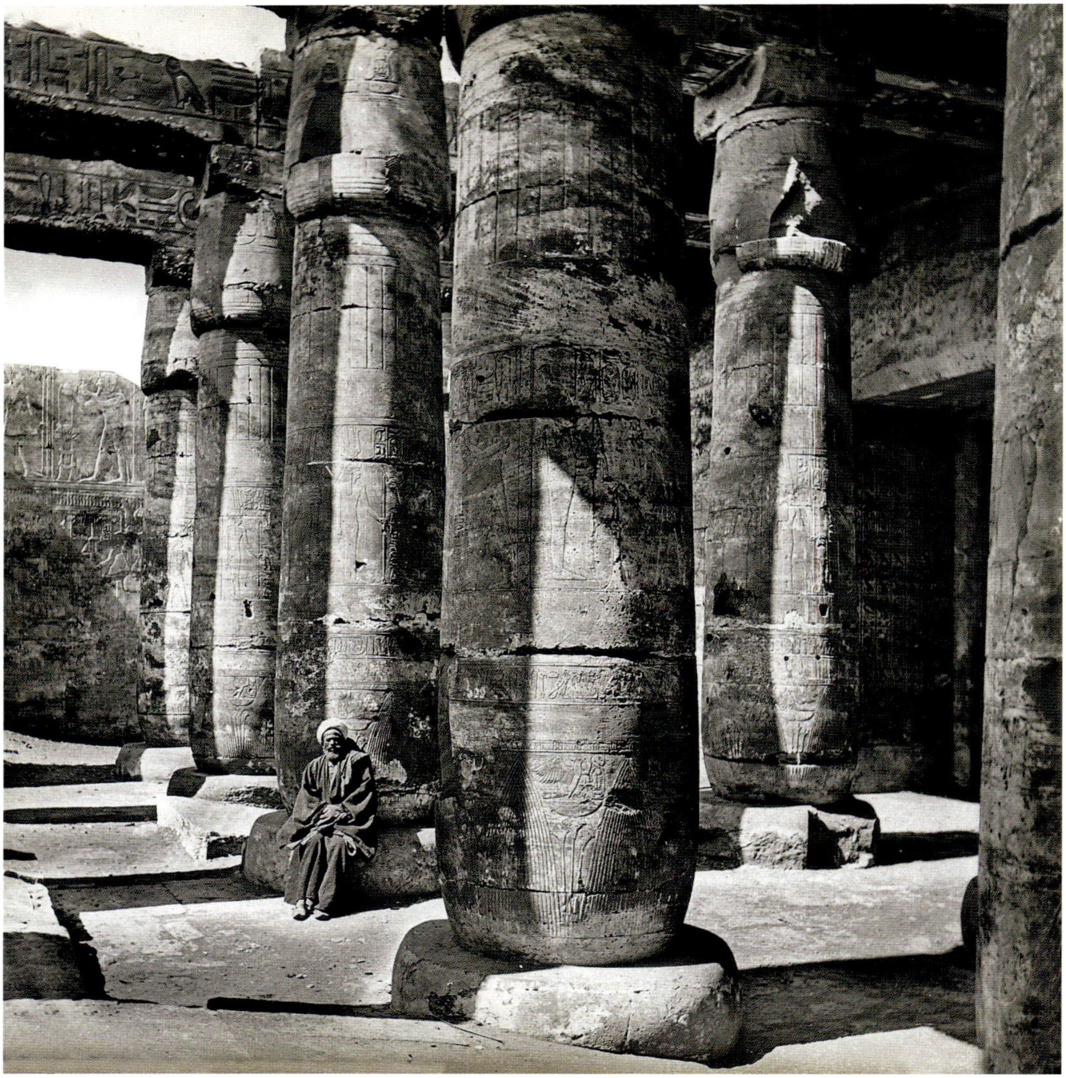

277 Colonnade at the Temple of Seti I, Abydos, Egypt, 1860s
278 Great Temple of Rameses II at Abu Simbel, Egypt, 1860s

277 Kolonnaden am Tempel Sethos' I., Abydos, Ägypten, 1860er Jahre
278 Der Große Tempel von Ramses II. in Abu Simbel, Ägypten, 1860er Jahre

277 Colonnades dans le temple de Séti Ier, Abydos, Égypte, années 1860
278 Grand temple de Ramsès II à Abou Simbel, Égypte, années 1860

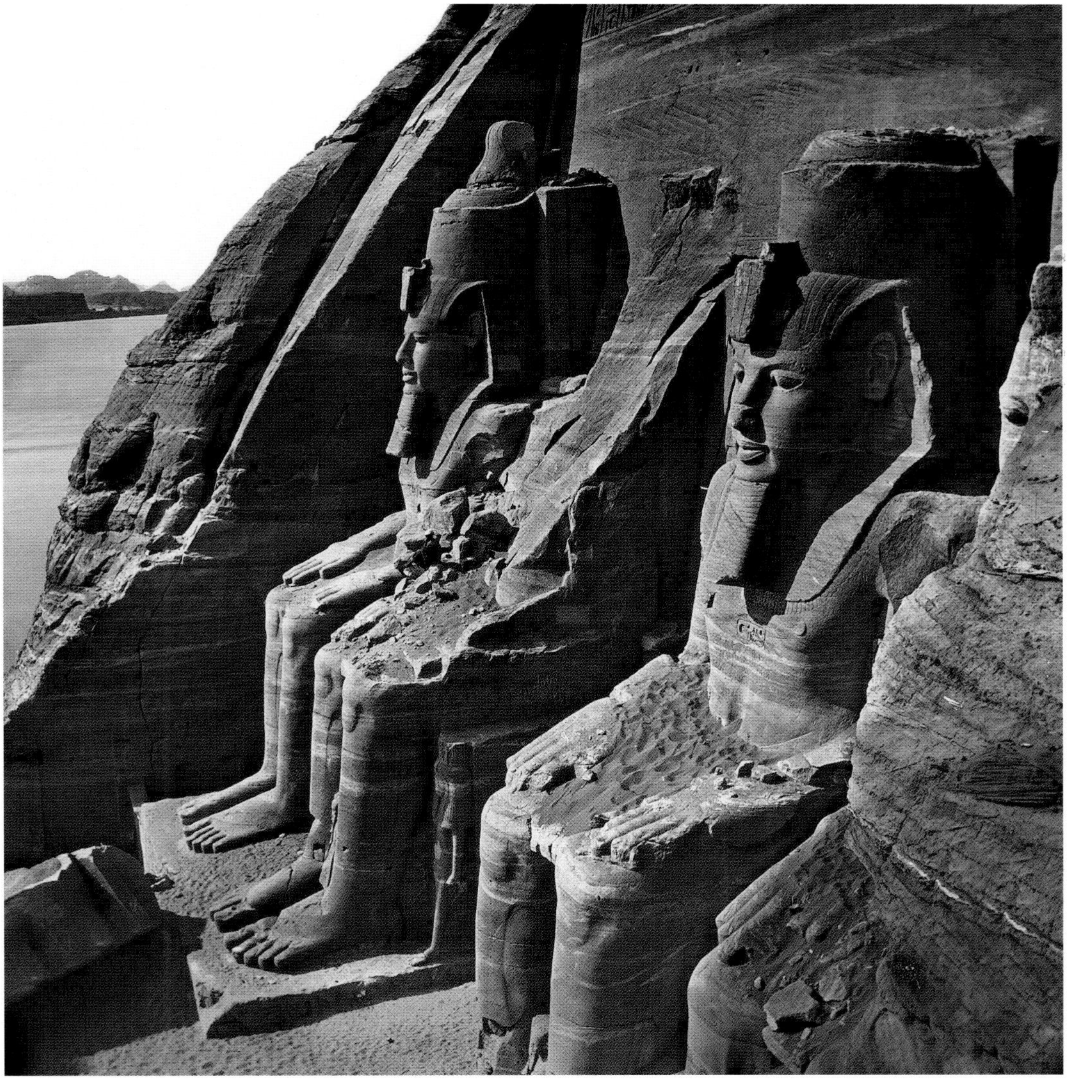

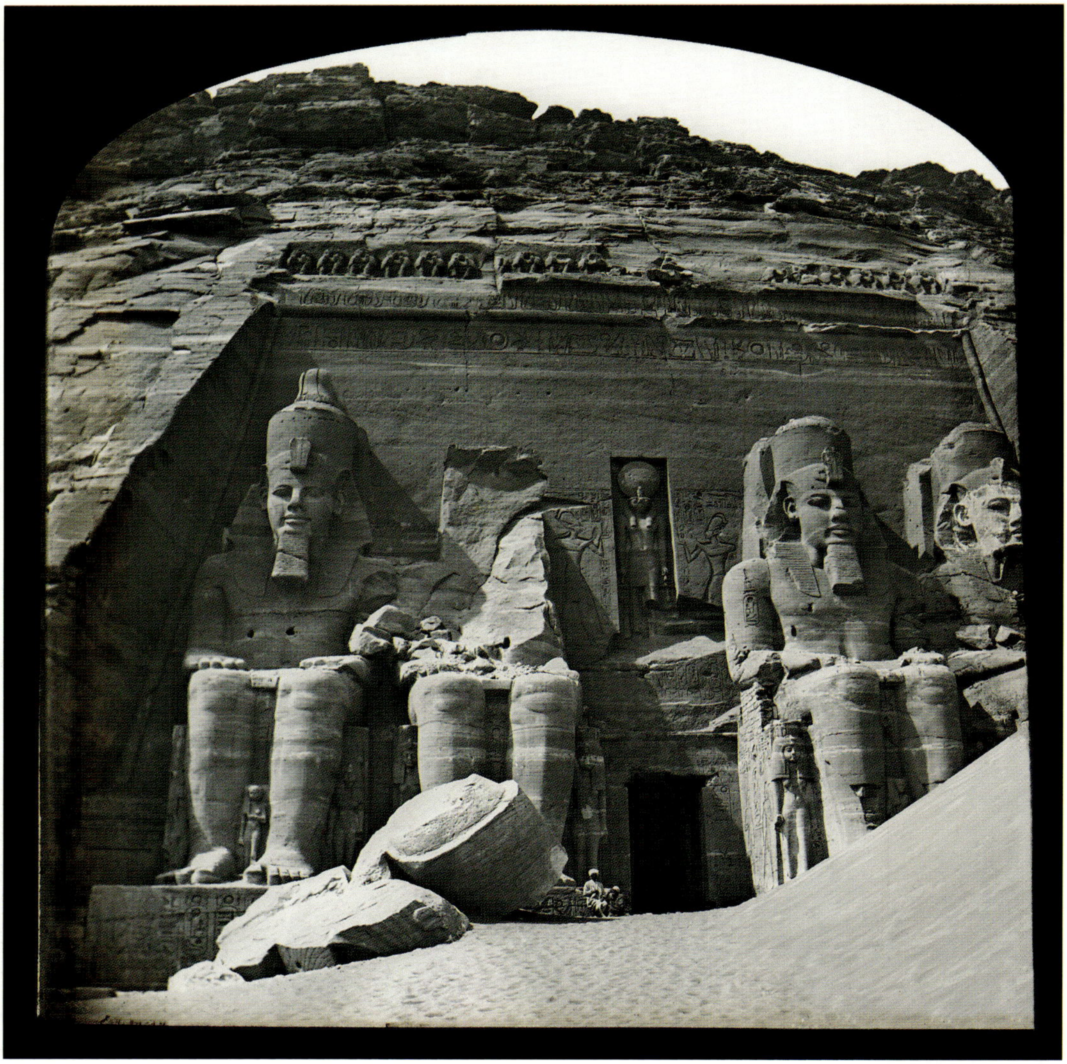

279 Great Temple of Rameses II at Abu Simbel, Egypt, 1860s

279 Der Große Tempel von Ramses II. in Abu Simbel, Ägypten, 1860er Jahre

279 Grand temple de Ramsès II à Abou Simbel, Égypte, années 1860

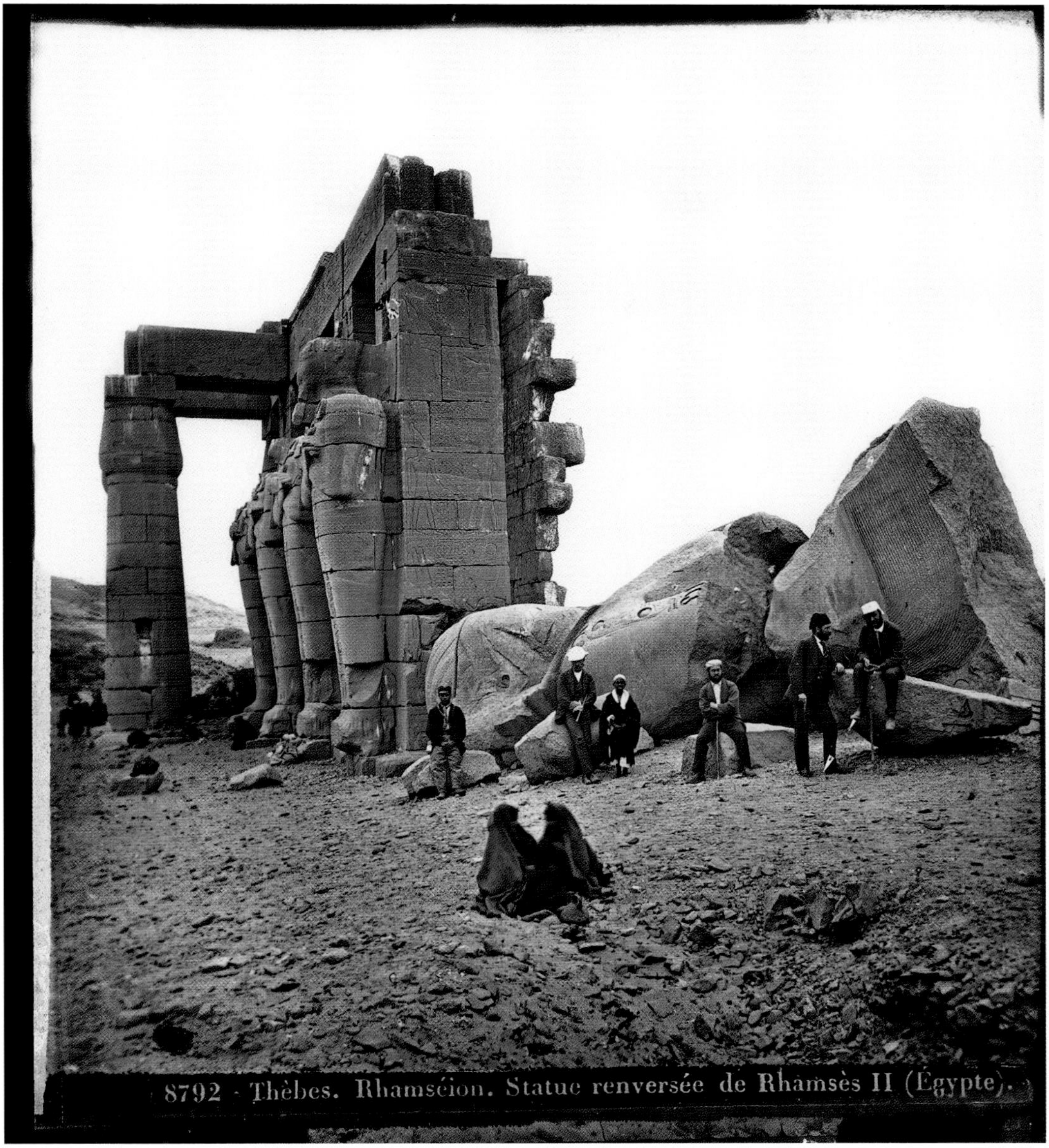

280 Ramesseum, the Mortuary Temple of Pharaoh Rameses II, Thebes, Egypt, 1860s

280 Das Ramesseum, Totentempel für Pharao Ramses II., Theben, Ägypten, 1860er Jahre

280 Le Ramesséum, temple funéraire du pharaon Ramsès II, Thèbes, Égypte, années 1860

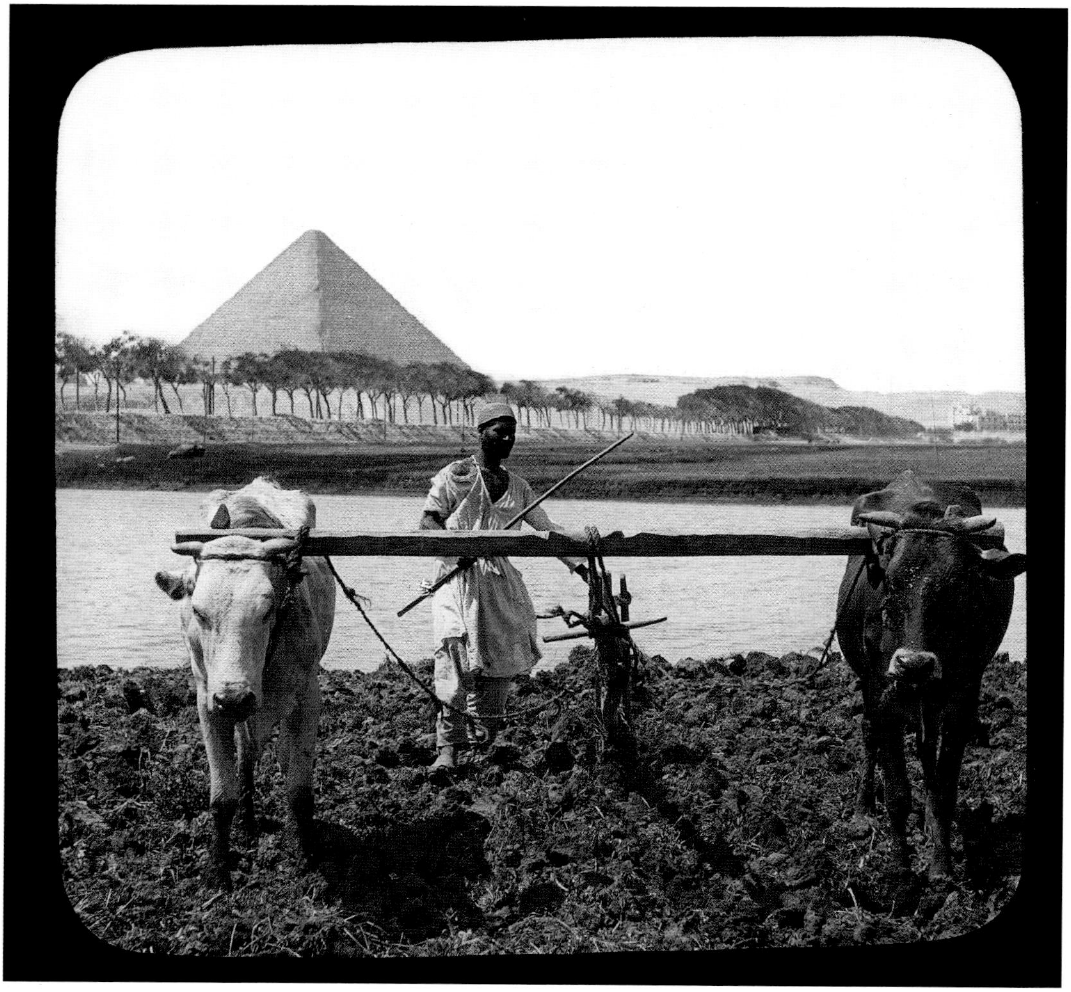

281 Tilling the Soil, Egypt, 1890s
282 Inundation (annual flood) of the Nile, Egypt, 1890s

281 Der Boden wird beackert, Ägypten, 1890er Jahre
282 Überschwemmung (jährliches Hochwasser) des Nils, Ägypten, 1890er Jahre

281 Labourage. Égypte, années 1890
282 Inondation (crue annuelle) du Nil, Égypte, années 1890

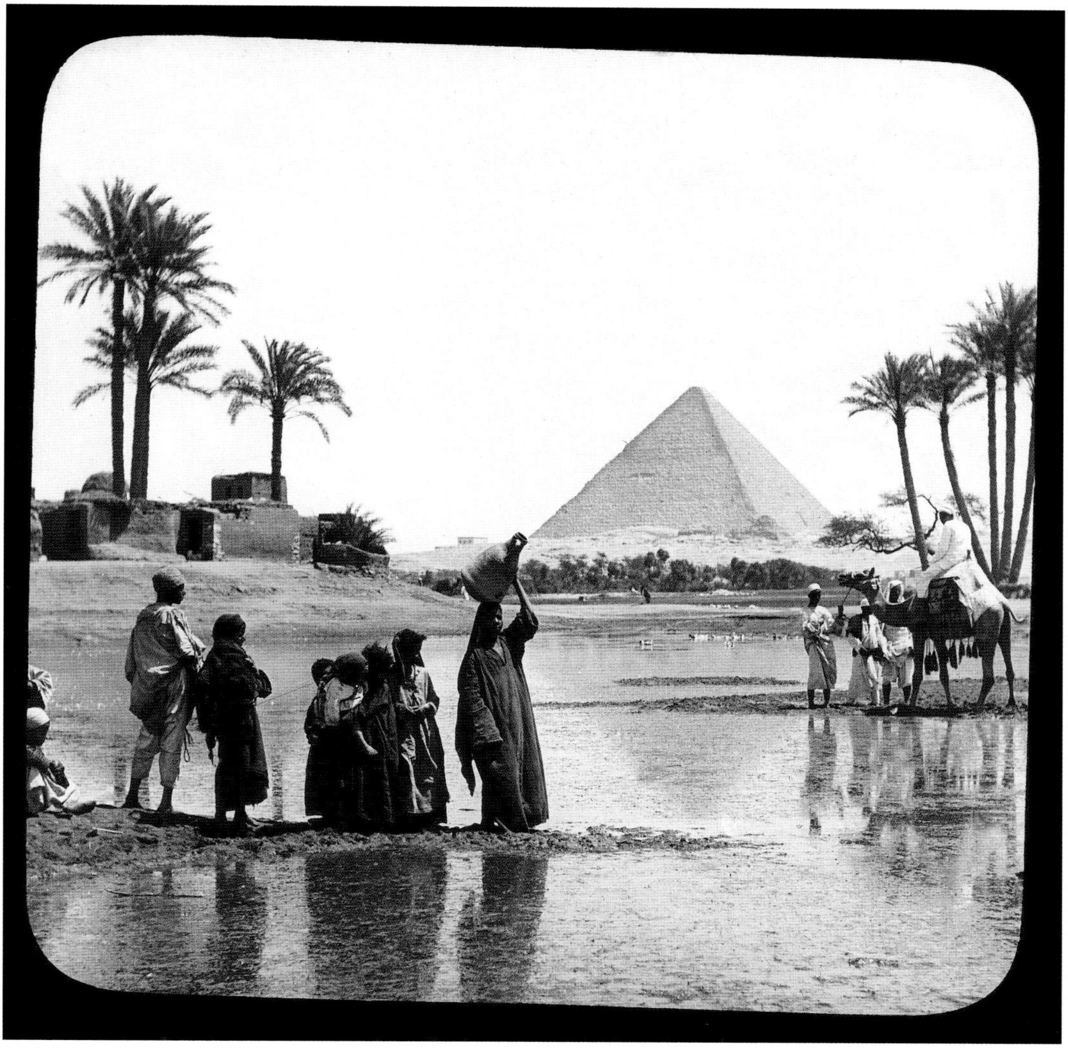

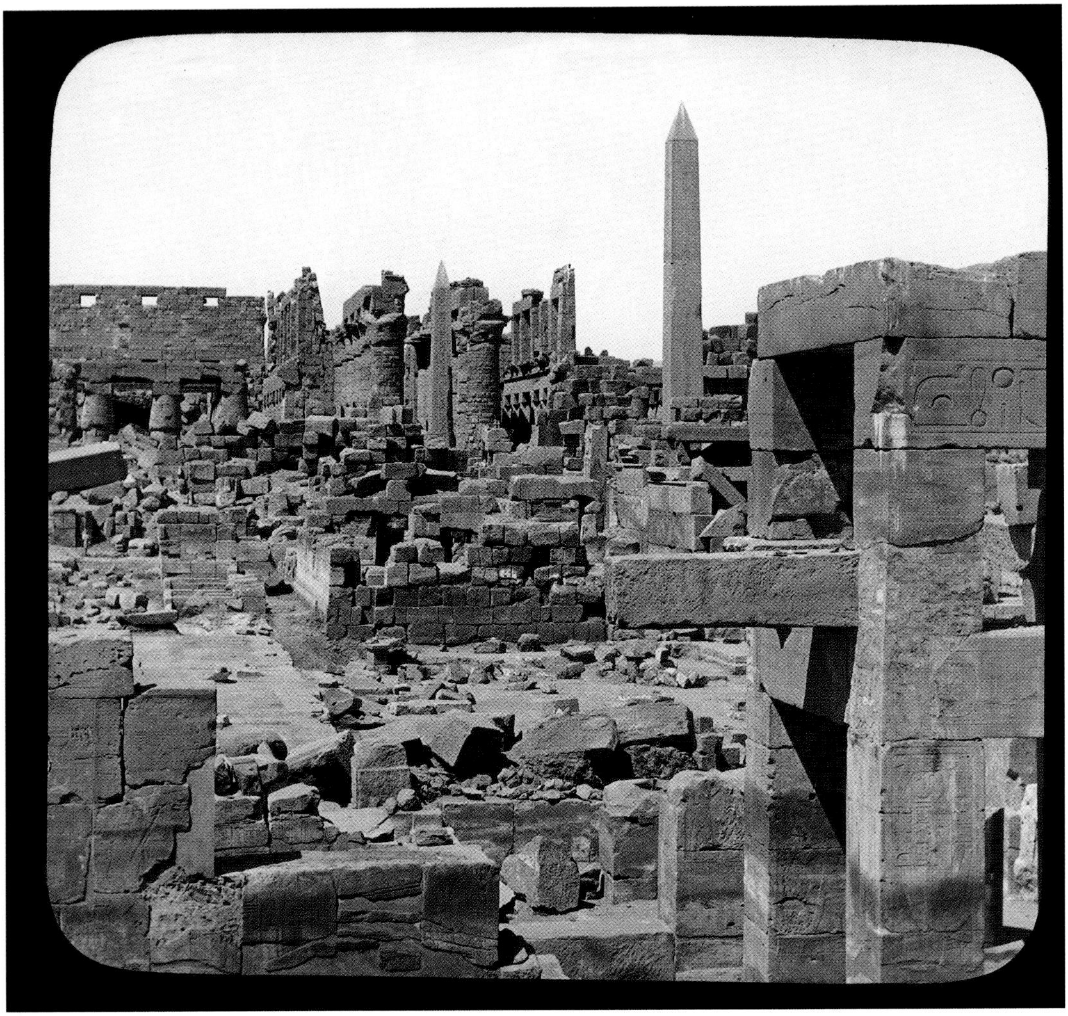

283 Ruins of Karnak, Egypt, 1880s
284 Ancient Ruins, Egypt, 1880s

283 Ruinen in Karnak, Ägypten, 1880er Jahre
284 Antike Ruinen, Ägypten, 1880er Jahre

283 Ruines de Karnak, Égypte, années 1880
284 Ruines anciennes, Égypte, années 1880

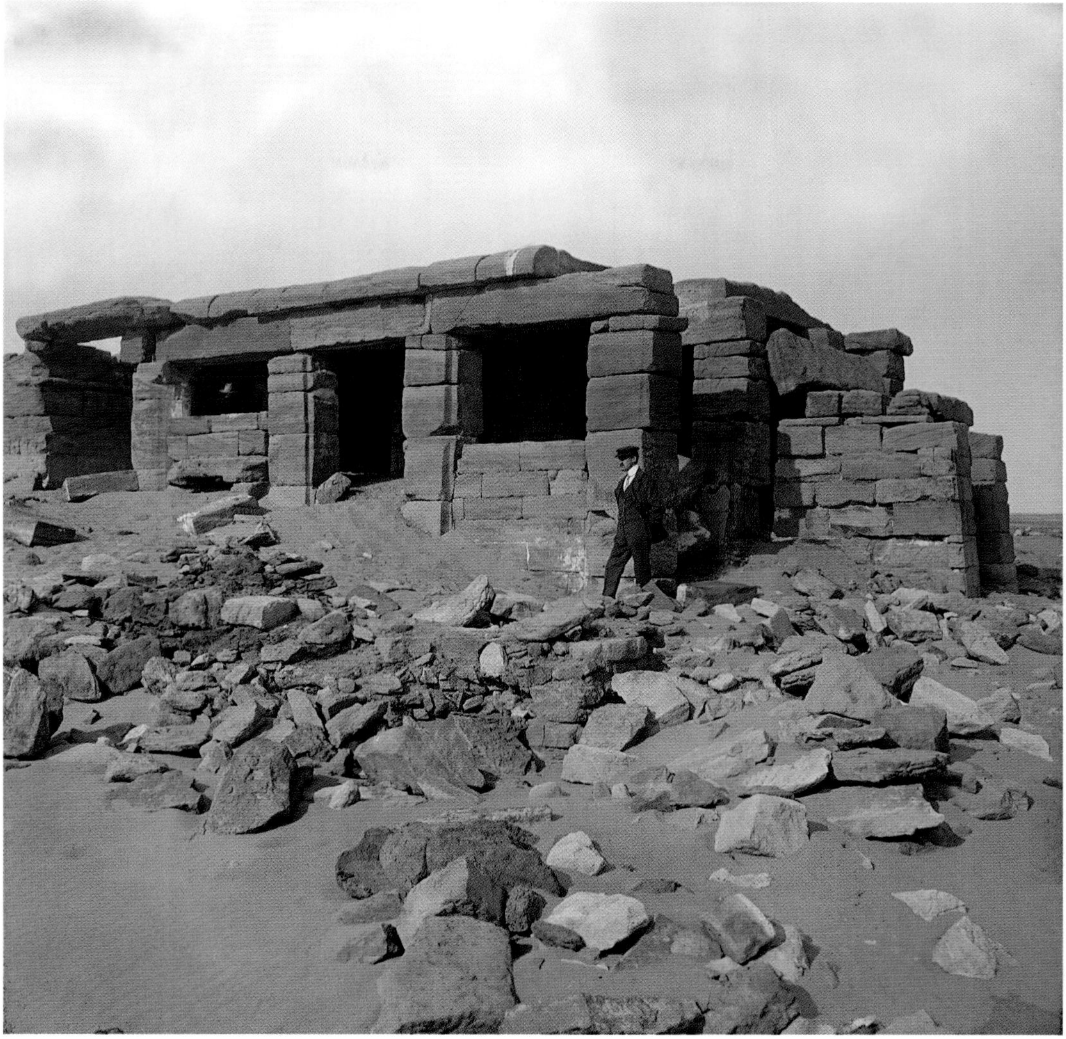

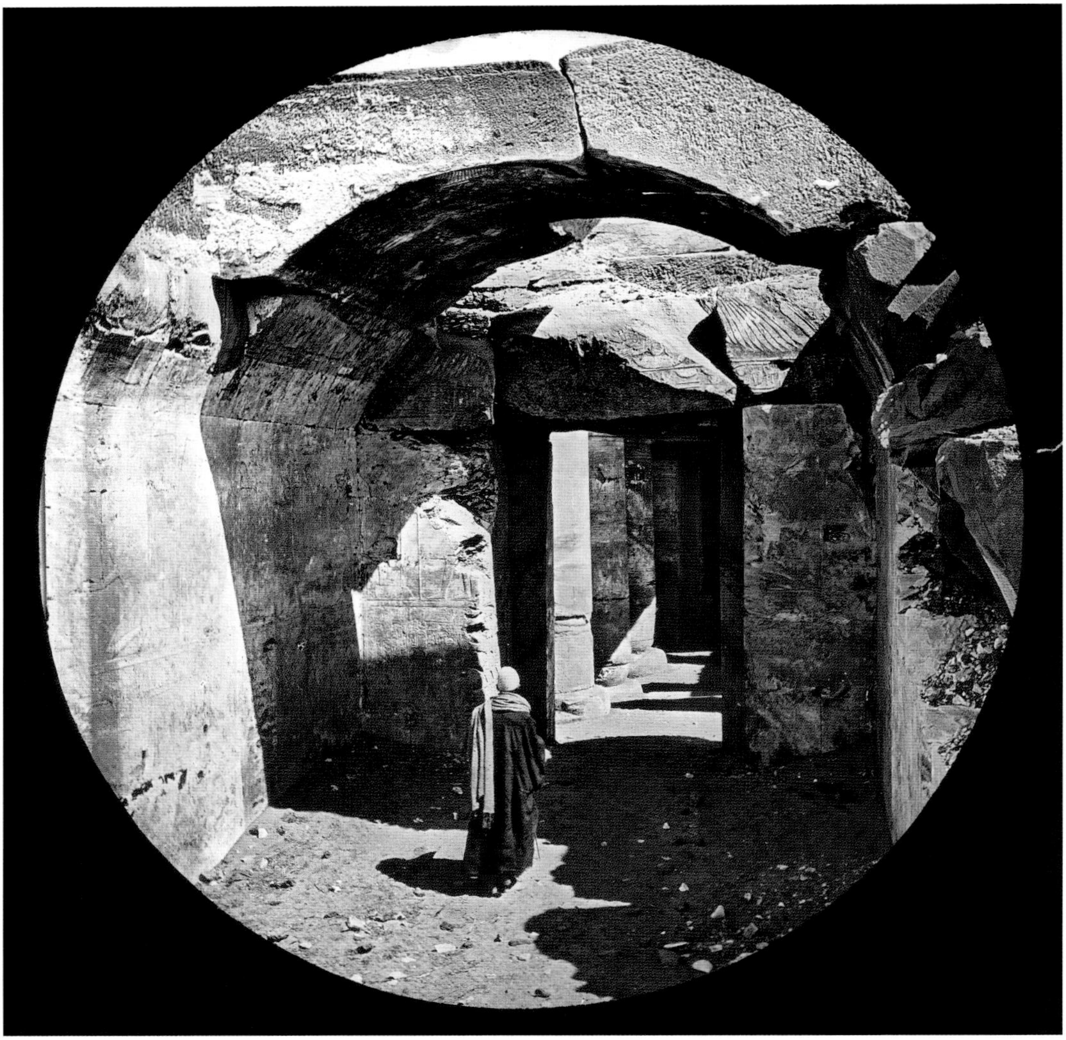

285 Ancient ruins, Egypt, 1860s
286 Sultan Hassan Mosque, Cairo, 1870s

285 Antike Ruinen, Ägypten, 1860er Jahre
286 Die Sultan-Hassan-Moschee, Kairo, Ägypten, 1870er Jahre

285 Ruines anciennes, Égypte, années 1860
286 Mosquée du sultan Hassan, Le Caire, années 1870

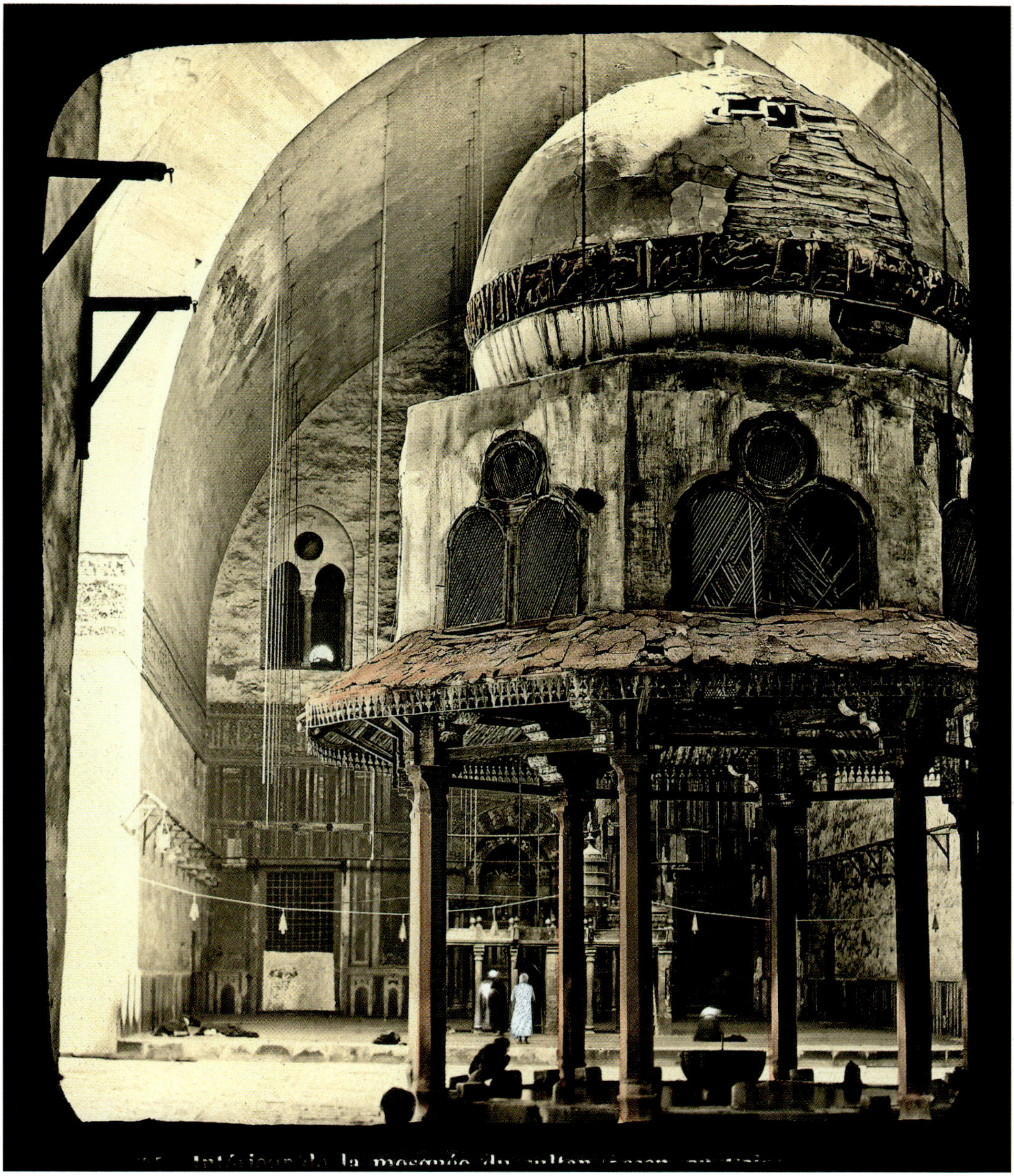

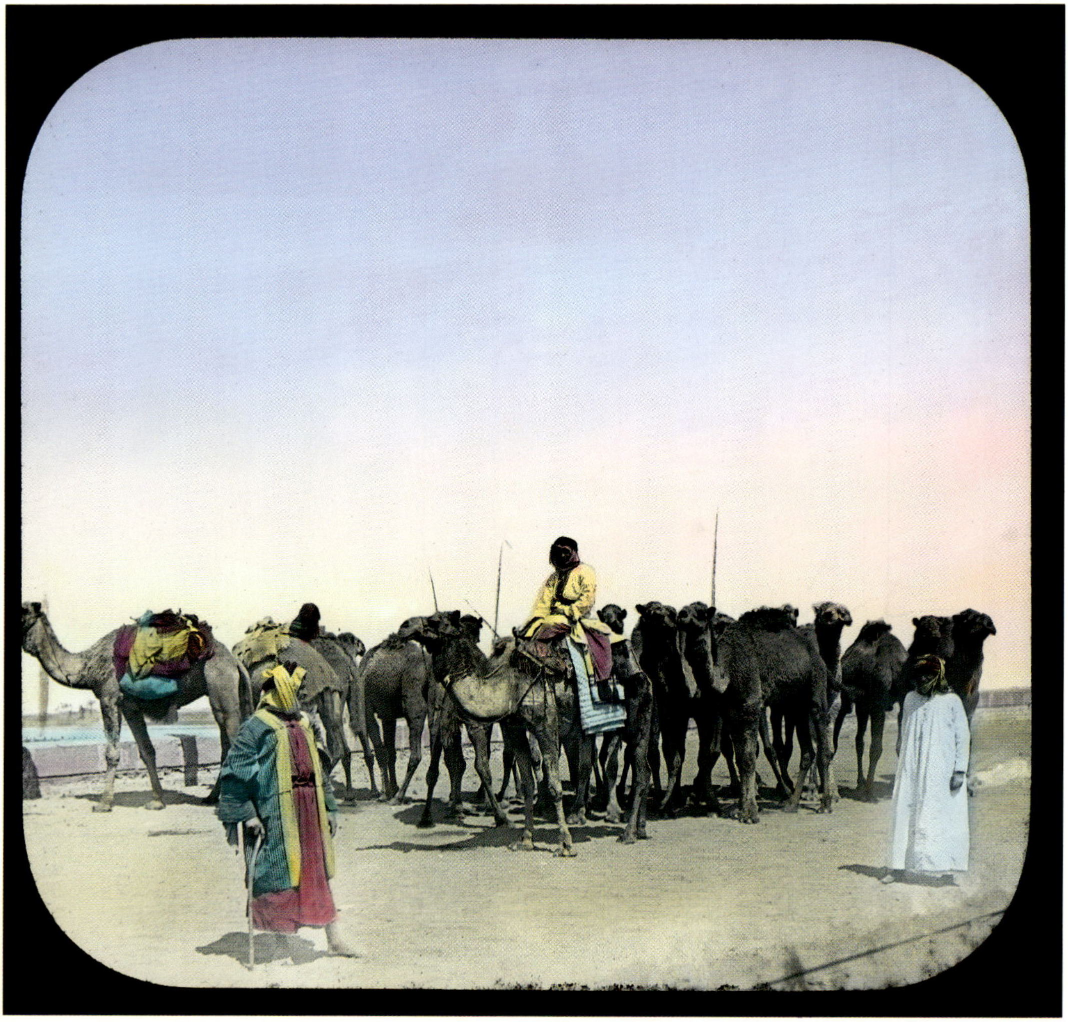

287 Camels and drivers, Cairo, Egypt, 1870s

287 Kamele und Treiber, Kairo, Ägypten, 1870er Jahre

287 Dromadaires et conducteurs, Le Caire, Égypte, années 1870

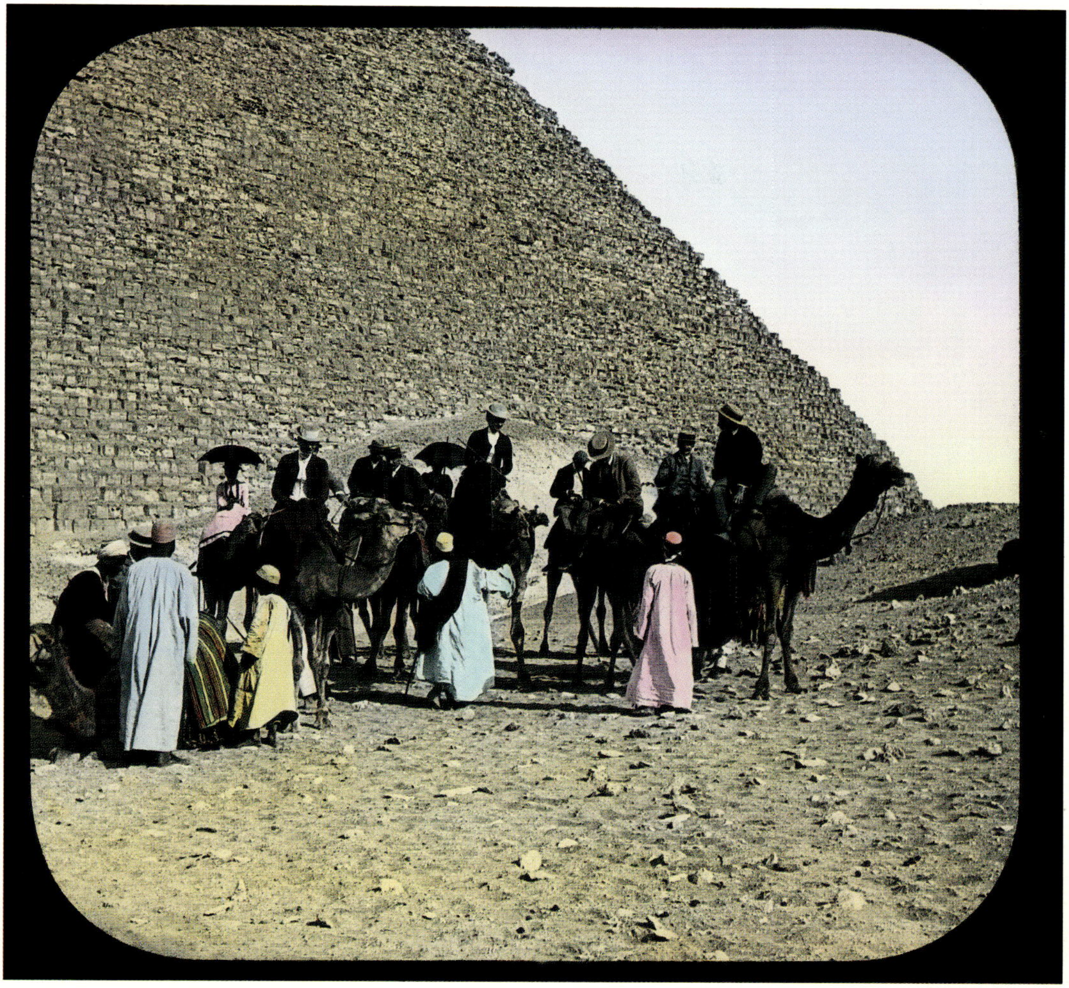

288 Tourists and guides, Pyramid of Cheops (The Great Pyramid of Giza), Egypt, 1870s

288 Touristen und Reiseführer, die Cheopspyramide (Die Große Pyramide von Gizeh), Ägypten, 1870er Jahre

288 Touristes et guides, pyramide de Chéops (Grande Pyramide de Gizeh), Égypte, années 1870

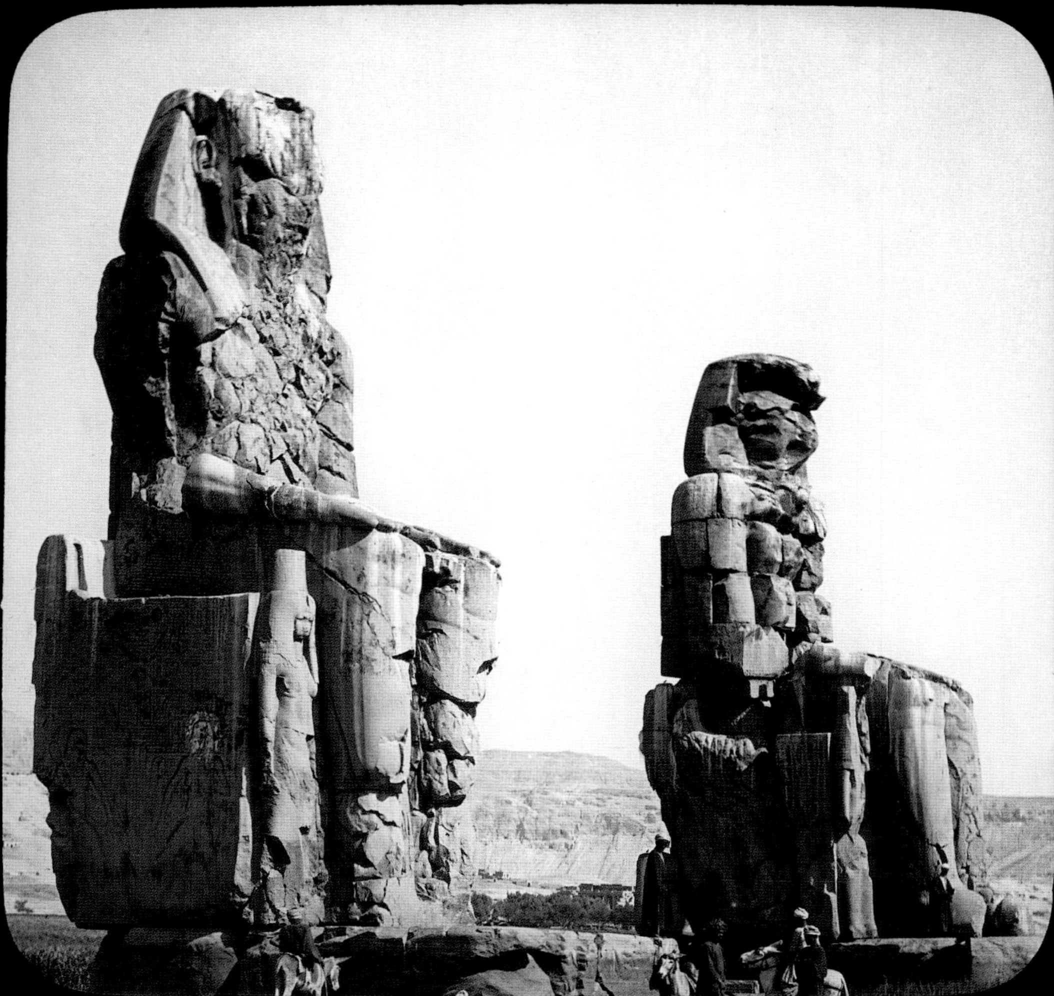

289 Colossi of Memnon, Thebes, Egypt, 1890s
290 Cleopatra's Needle, Alexandria, Egypt, 1870s

289 Die Memnonkolosse, Theben, Ägypten, 1890er Jahre
290 Kleopatras Nadel, Alexandria, Ägypten, 1870er Jahre

289 Colosses de Memnon, Thèbes, Égypte, années 1890
290 L'Aiguille de Cléopâtre, Alexandrie, Égypte, années 1870

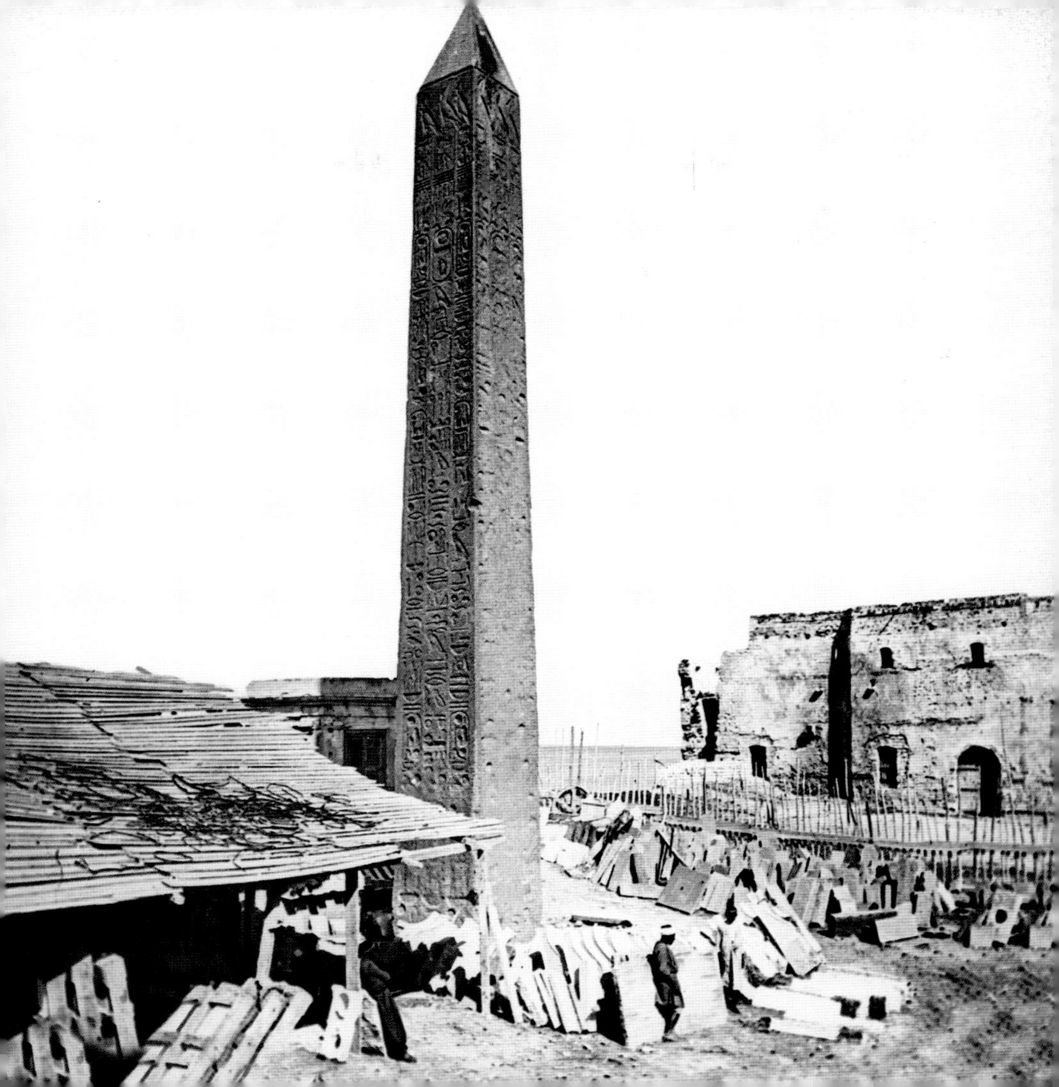

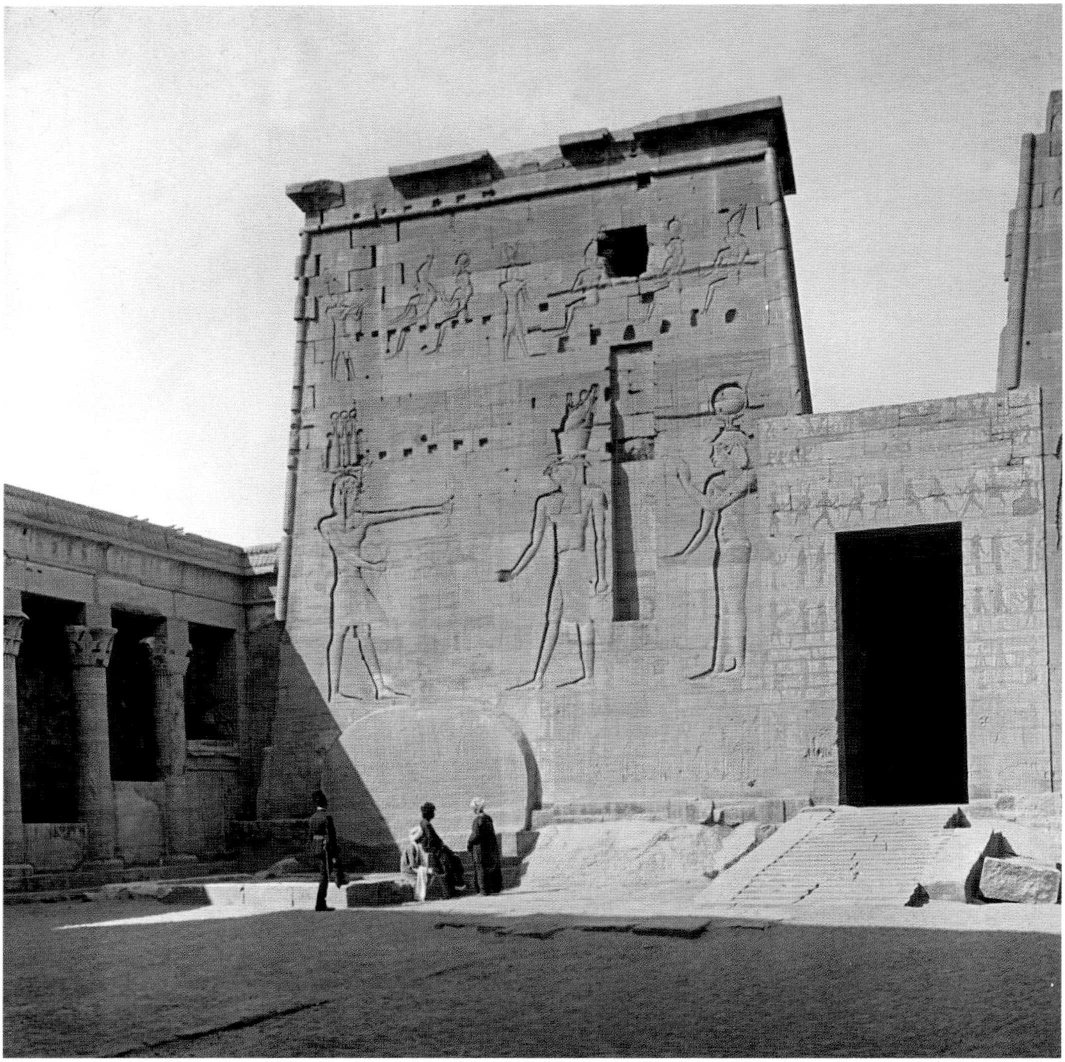

291 Trajan's Kiosk (Pharaoh's Bed), Philae Island, Egypt, 1880s
292 Temple of Isis, Philae Island, Egypt, 1880s

291 Der Trajan-Kiosk (Pharaos Bett), Insel Philae, Ägypten, 1880er Jahre
292 Der Isistempel, Insel Philae, Ägypten, 1880er Jahre

291 Kiosque de Trajan, île de Philae, Égypte, années 1880
292 Temple d'Isis, île de Philae, Égypte, années 1880

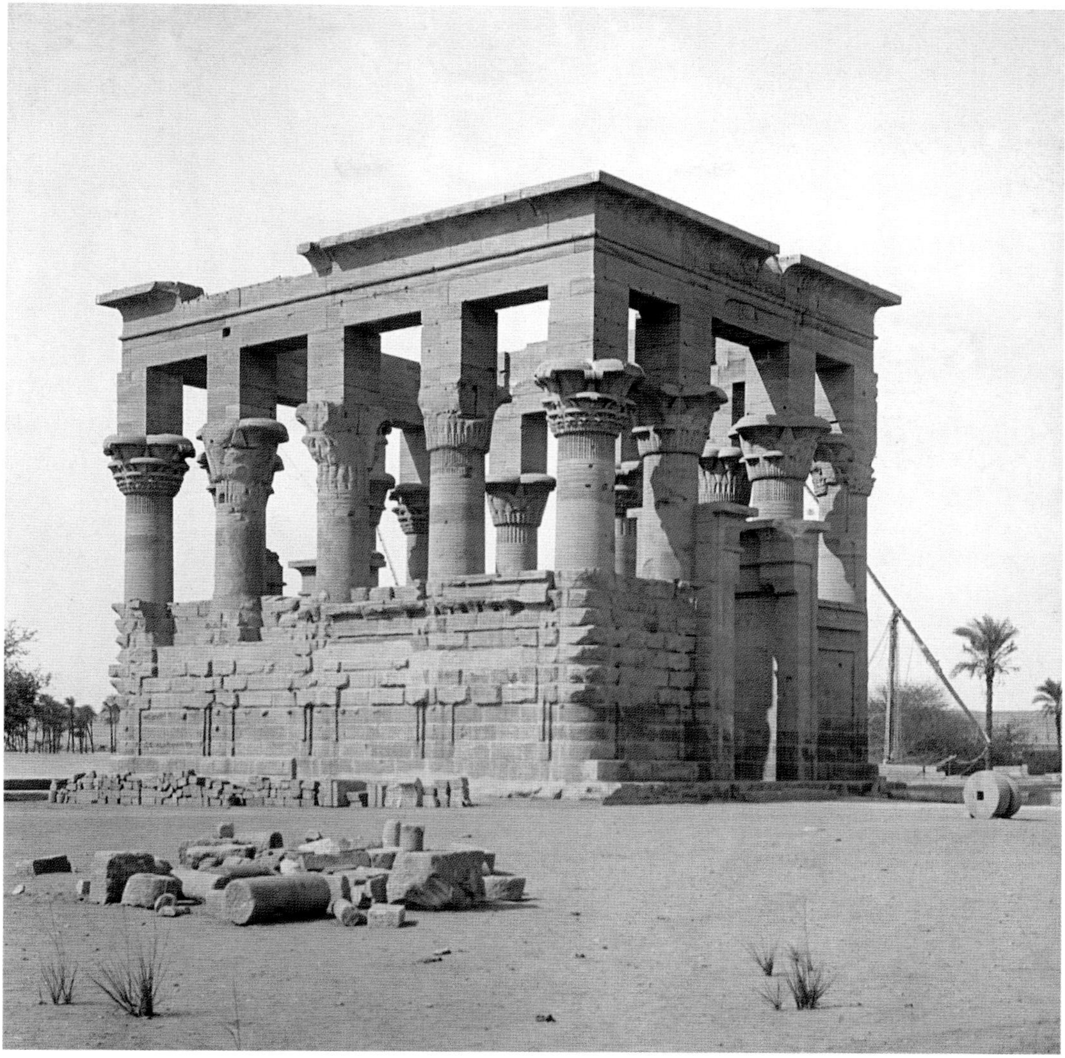

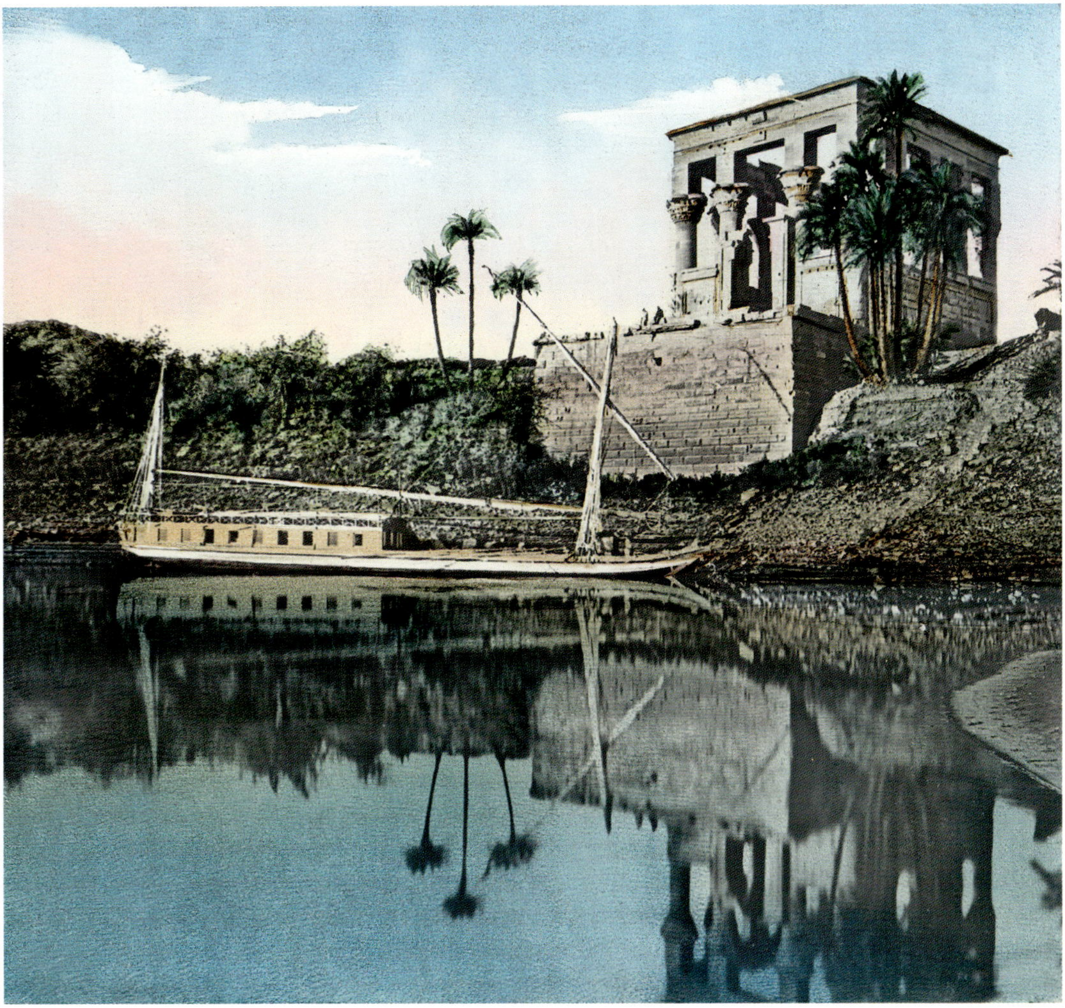

293 Pharaoh's Bed (Trajan's Kiosk) inside the Temple of Philae, Island of Philae, Egypt, 1870s

293 Pharaos Bett (Der Trajan-Kiosk) in der Tempelanlage von Philae, Insel Philae, Ägypten, 1870er Jahre

293 Kiosque de Trajan à l'intérieur du temple de Philae, île de Philae, Égypte, années 1870

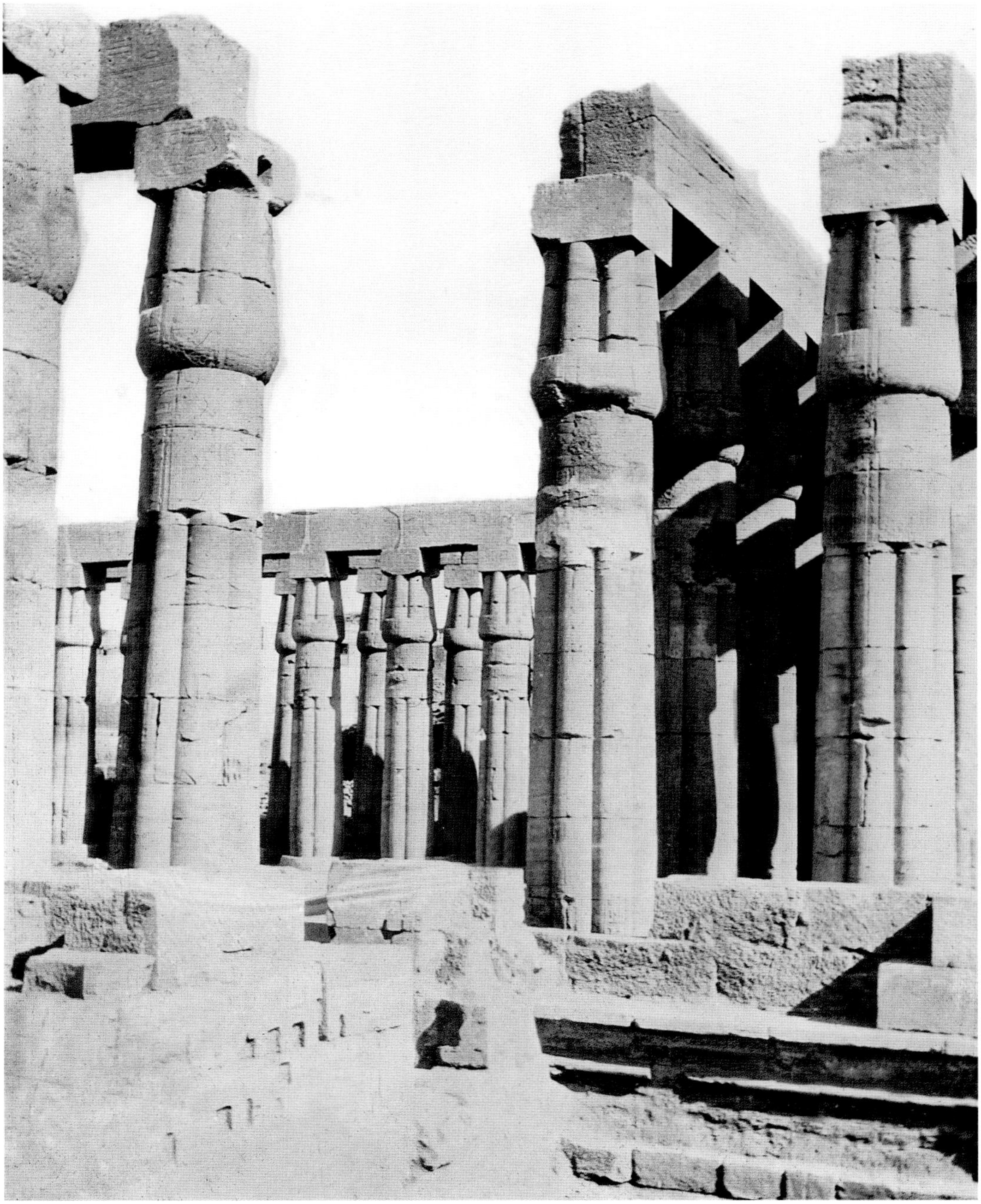

294 Columns of the Tomb of Horemheb, Saqqara, near Cairo, Egypt, 1870s

294 Säulen am Grab Haremhabs, Sakkara, nahe Kairo, Ägypten, 1870er Jahre

294 Colonnes de la tombe d'Horemheb, Saqqara, près du Caire, Égypte, années 1870

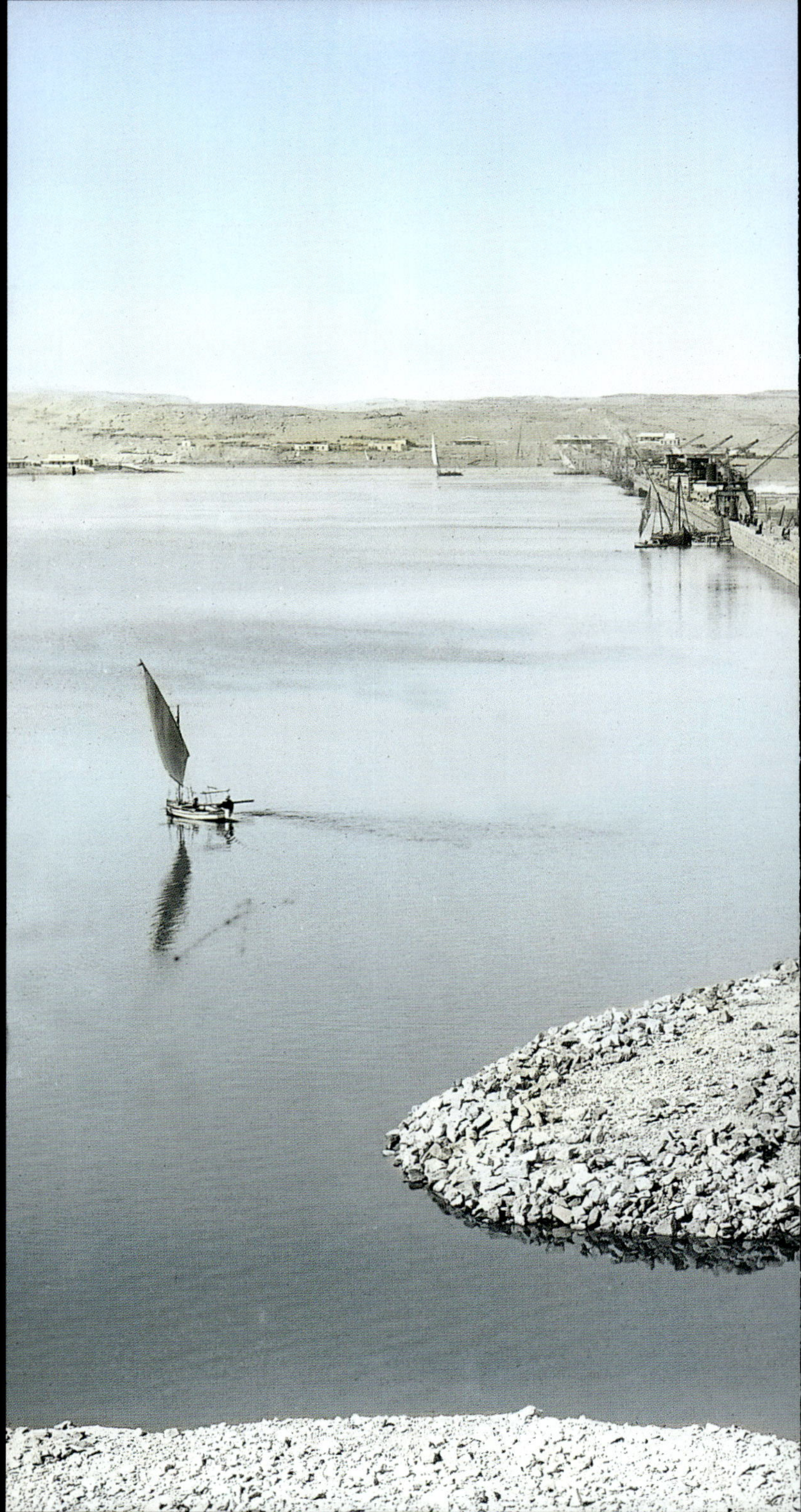

295 Dam and storage lake (from East End of Dam), Aswan, Egypt, 1920s

295 Staumauer und Stausee (vom östlichen Ende der Staumauer aus gesehen), Assuan, Ägypten, 1920er Jahre

295 Barrage et lac de retenue (de l'extrémité Est du lac), Assouan, Égypte, années 1920

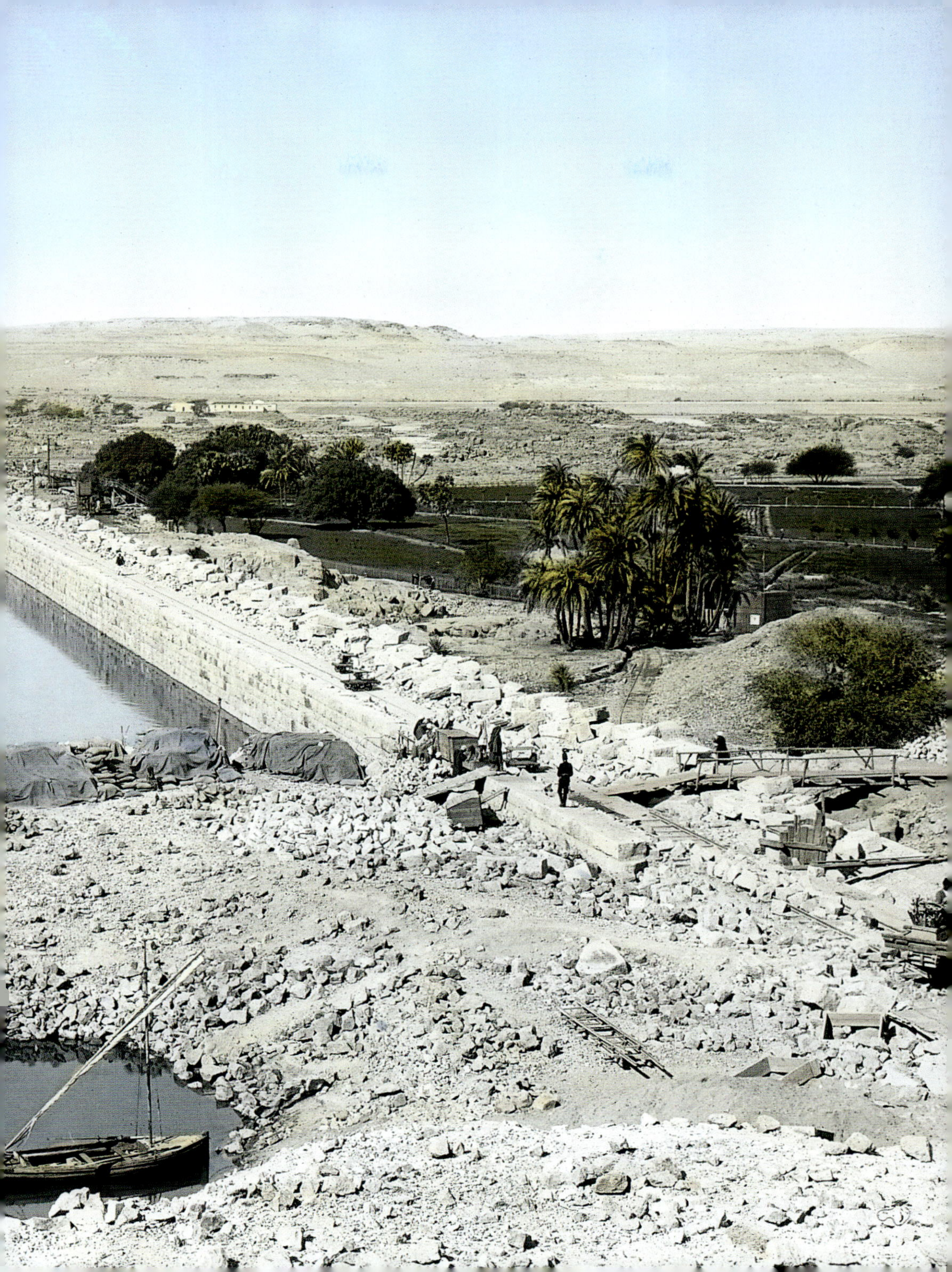

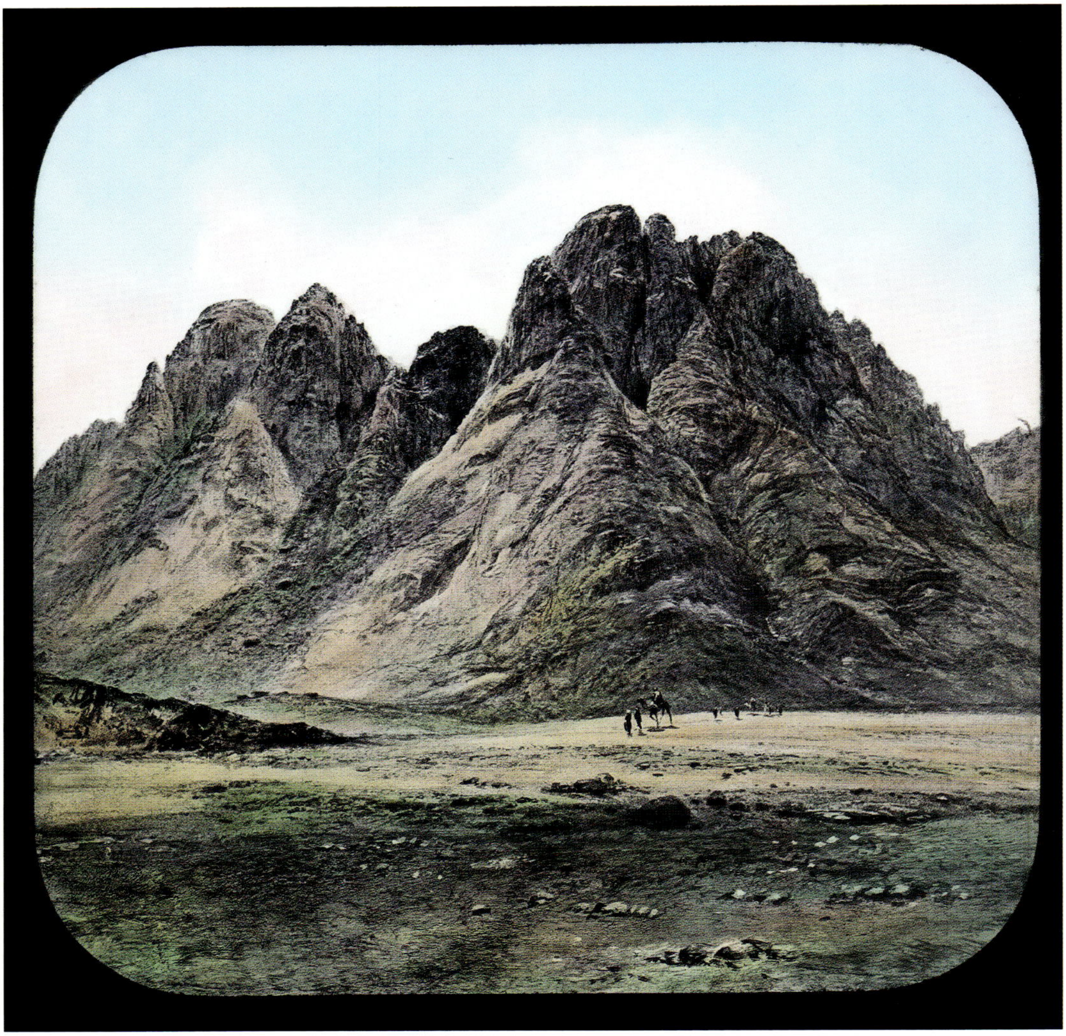

296 Mount Sinai, Egypt, 1880s
297 Bedouin elder (sheik), Egypt, 1860s

296 Der Berg Sinai, Ägypten, 1880er Jahre
297 Ein Beduinenältester (Scheich), Ägypten, 1860er Jahre

296 Mont Sinaï, Égypte, années 1880
297 Bédouin âgé (cheik), Égypte, années 1860

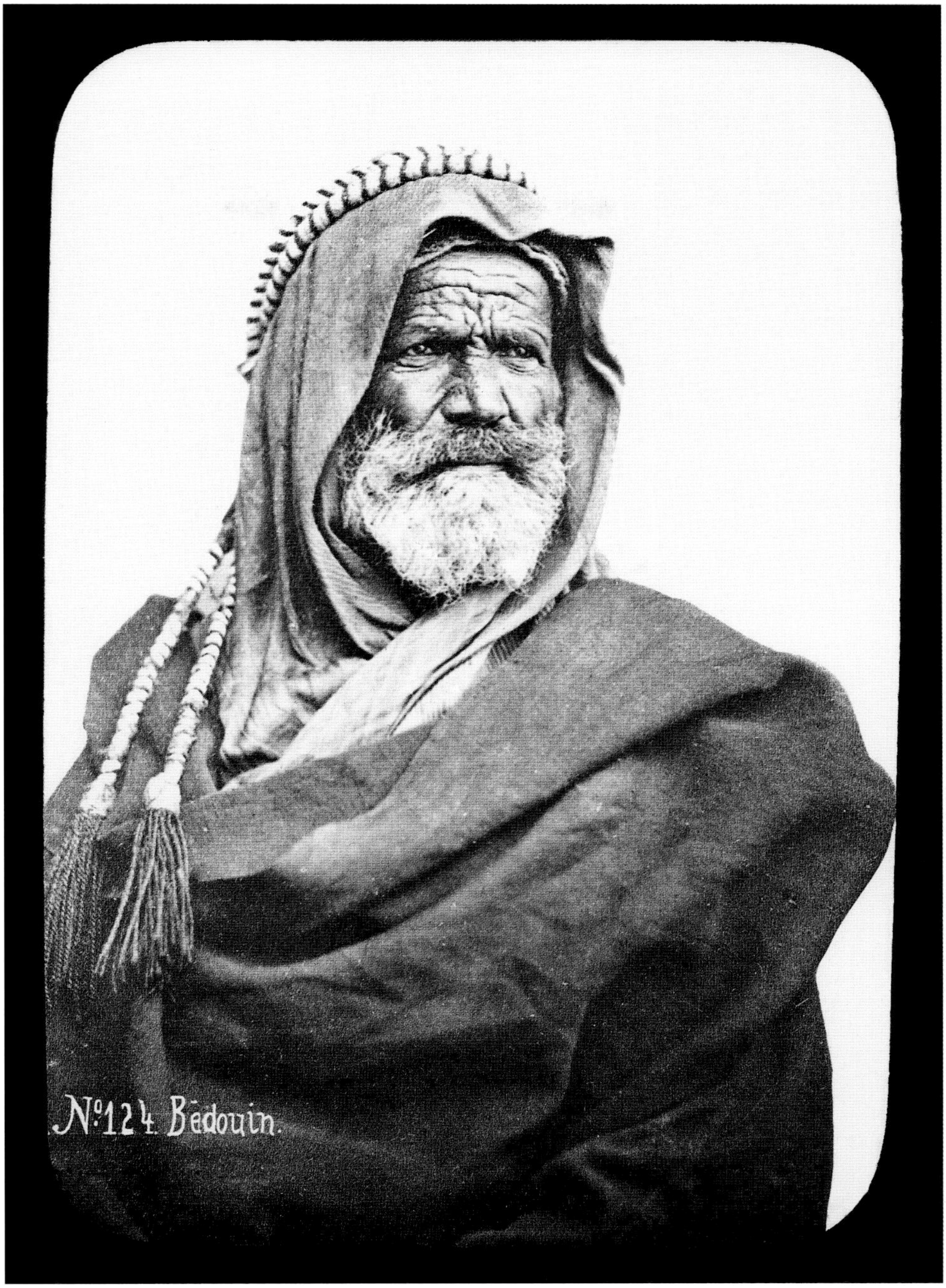
No. 124. Bédouin.

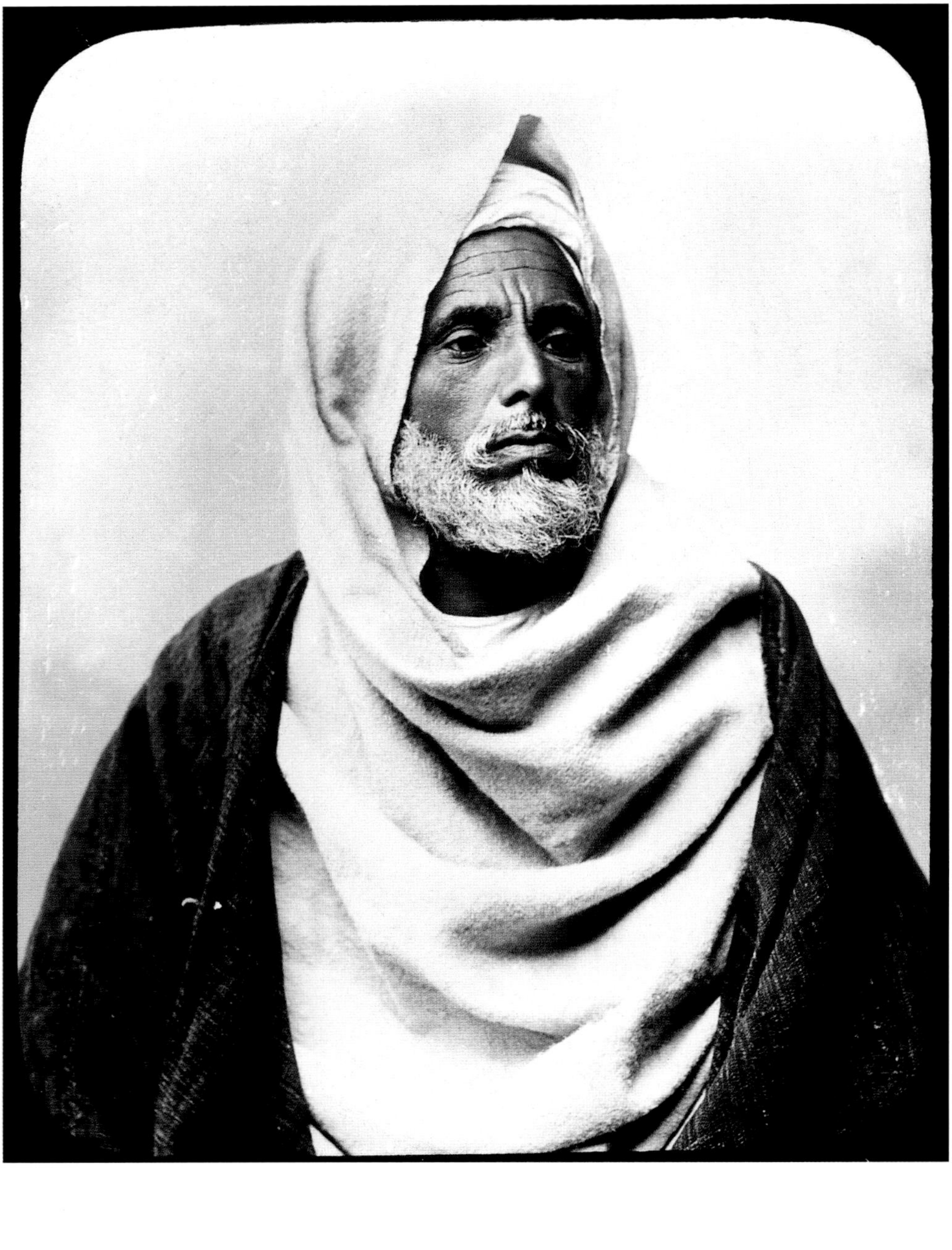

298 A bedouin, Egypt, 1860s
299 Woman pouring water into a bowl, Egypt, 1870s

298 Ein Beduine, Ägypten, 1860er Jahre
299 Eine Frau gießt Wasser in eine Schale, Ägypten, 1870er Jahre

298 Bédouin. Égypte, années 1860
299 Femme versant de l'eau, Égypte, années 1870

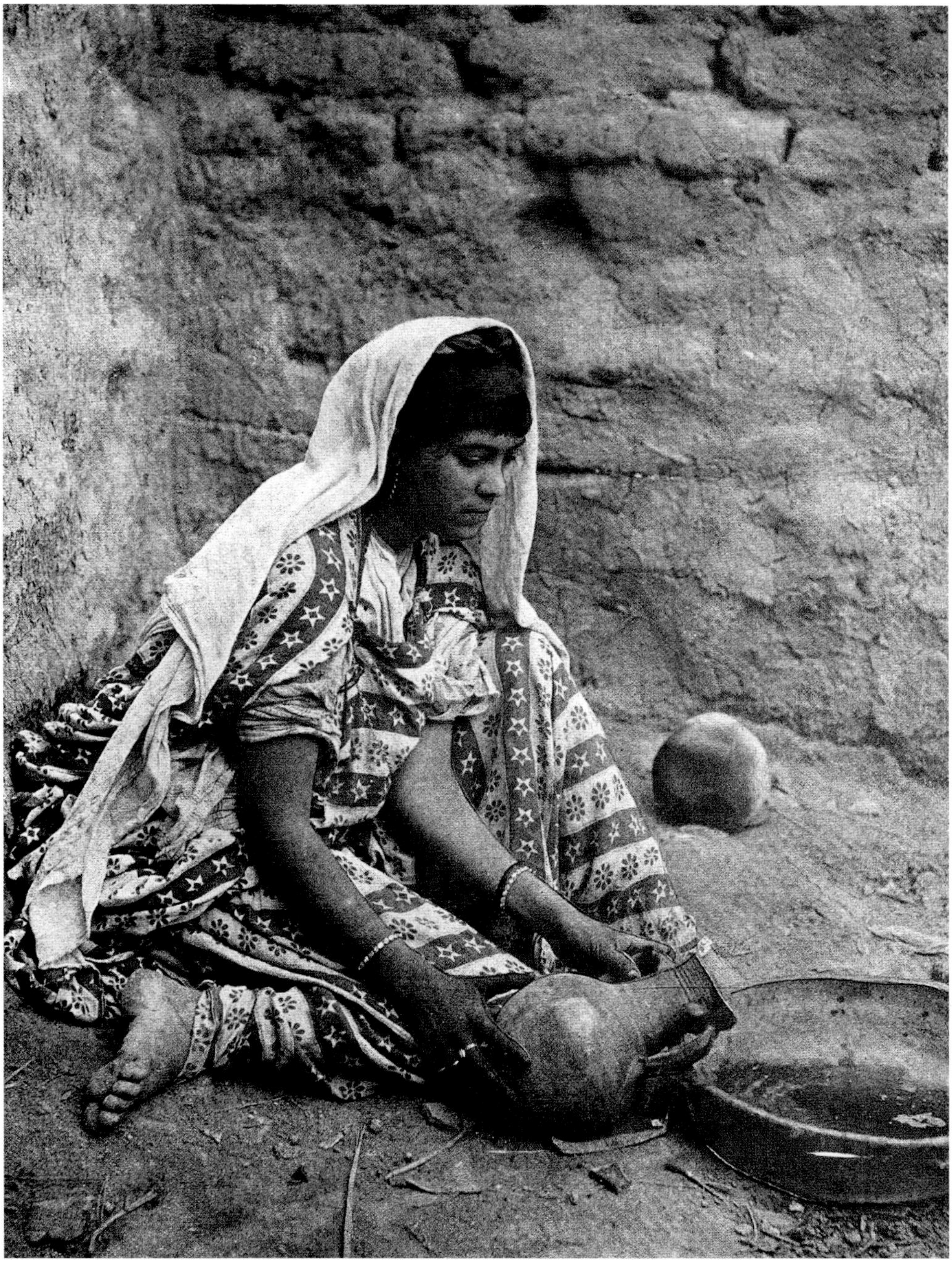

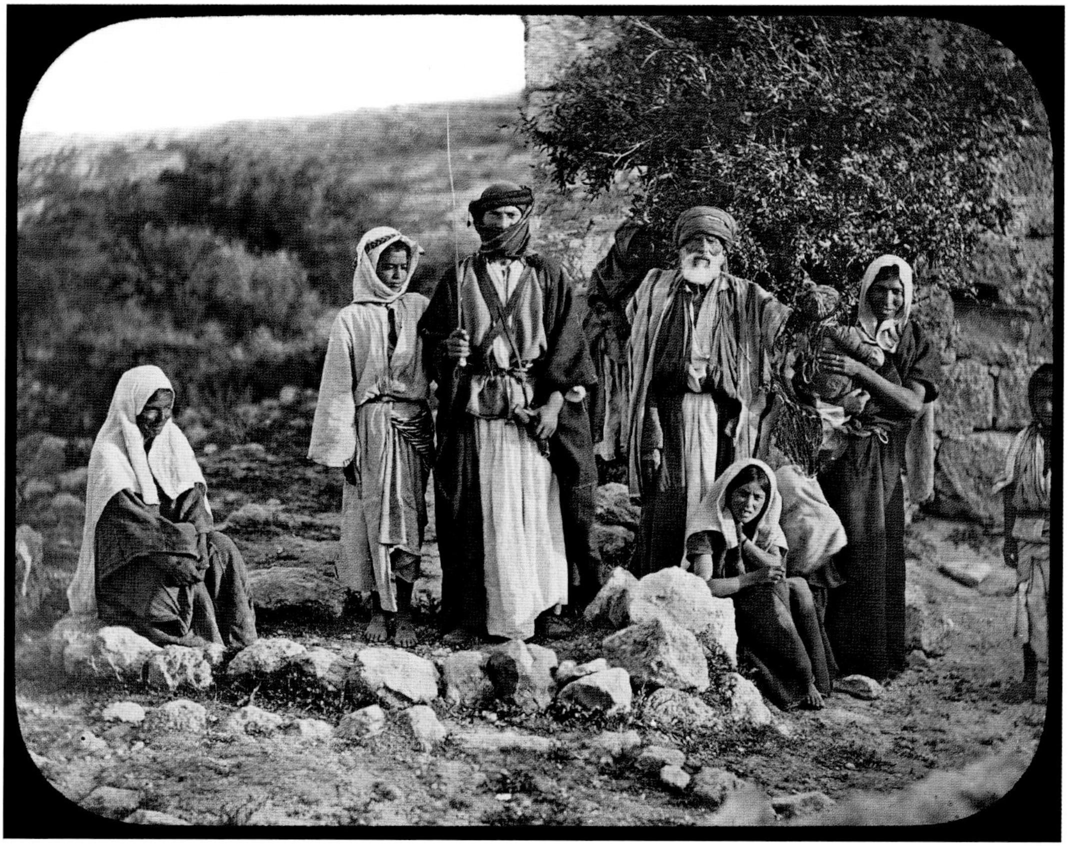

300 Family in traditional dress, North Africa, 1870s
301 Mosque, North Africa, 1870s

300 Eine Familie in traditionellen Gewändern, Nordafrika, 1870er Jahre
301 Moschee, Nordafrika, 1870er Jahre

300 Famille en vêtements traditionnels, Afrique du Nord, années 1870
301 Mosquée, Afrique du Nord, années 1870

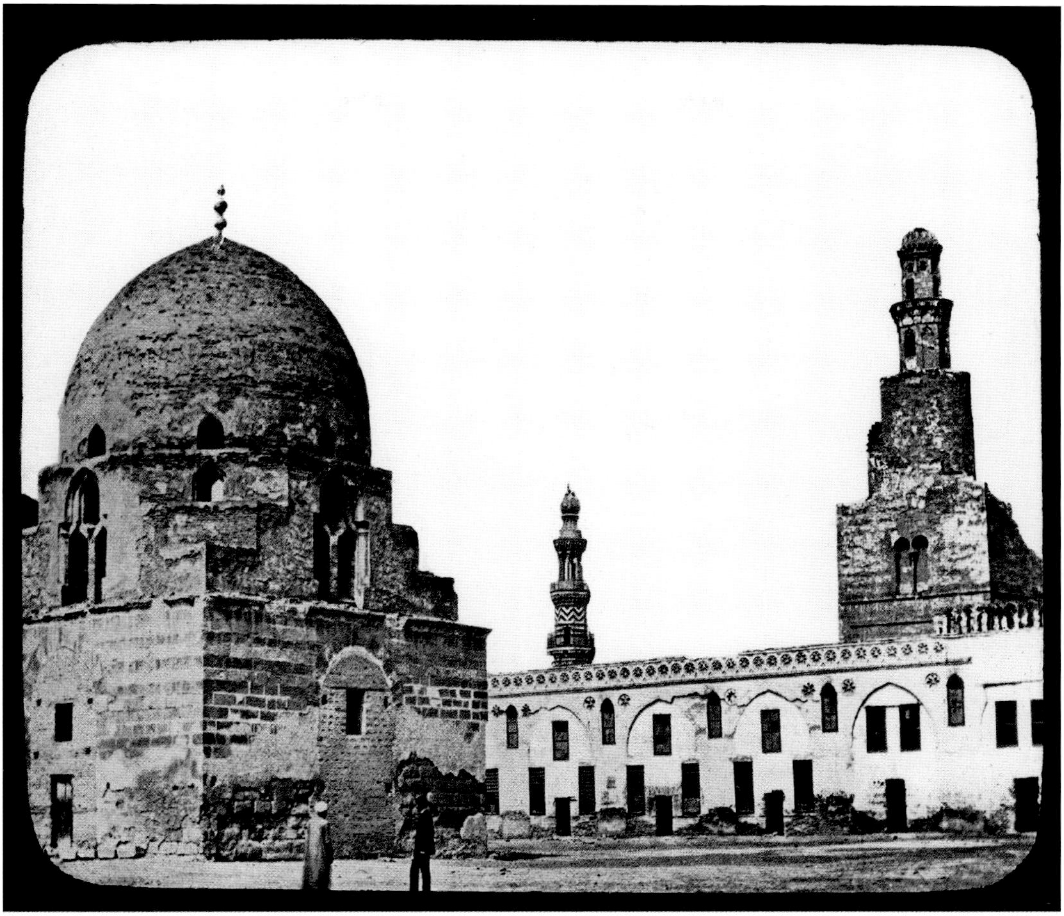

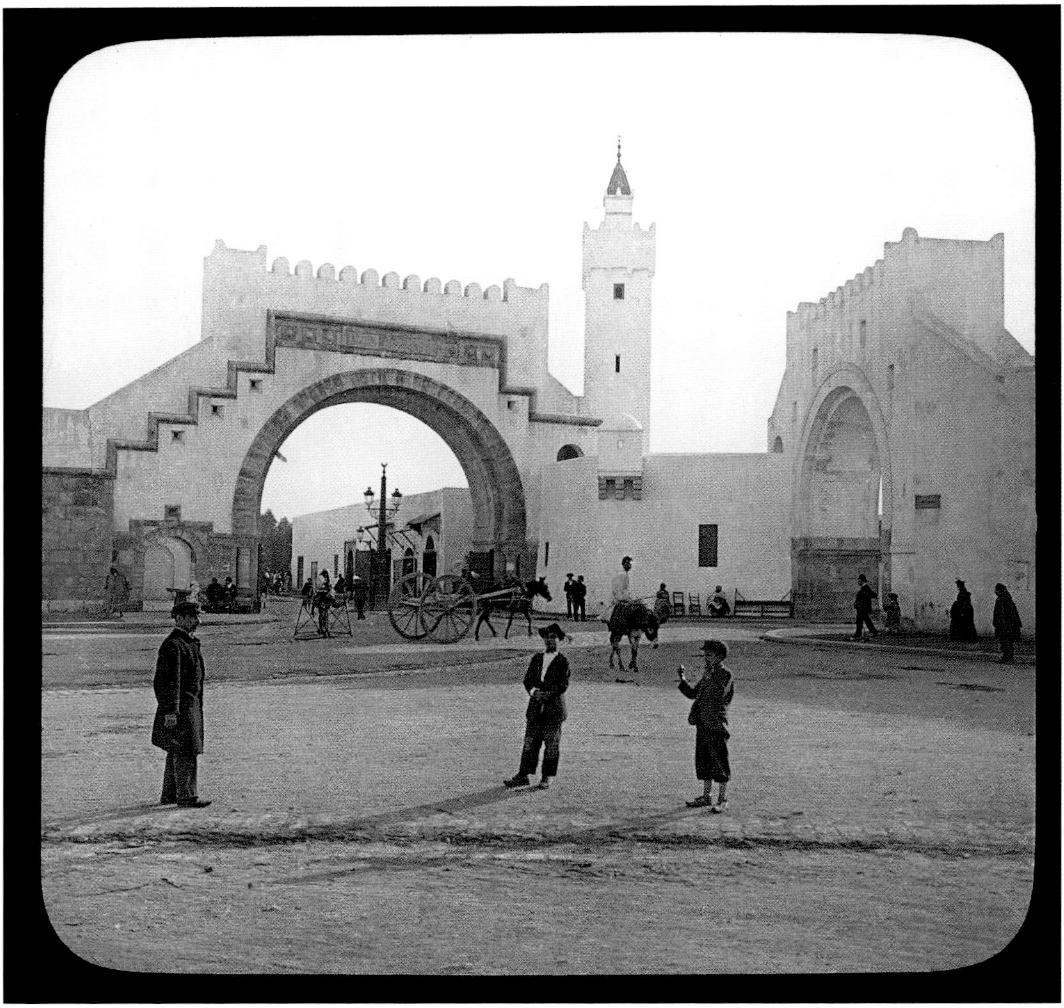

302 Gates in the Walls of Tunis, Tunisia, North Africa, 1890s

302 Tore in den Stadtmauern von Tunis, Tunesien, Nordafrika, 1890er Jahre

302 Portes de l'enceinte de Tunis, Tunisie, Afrique du Nord, années 1890

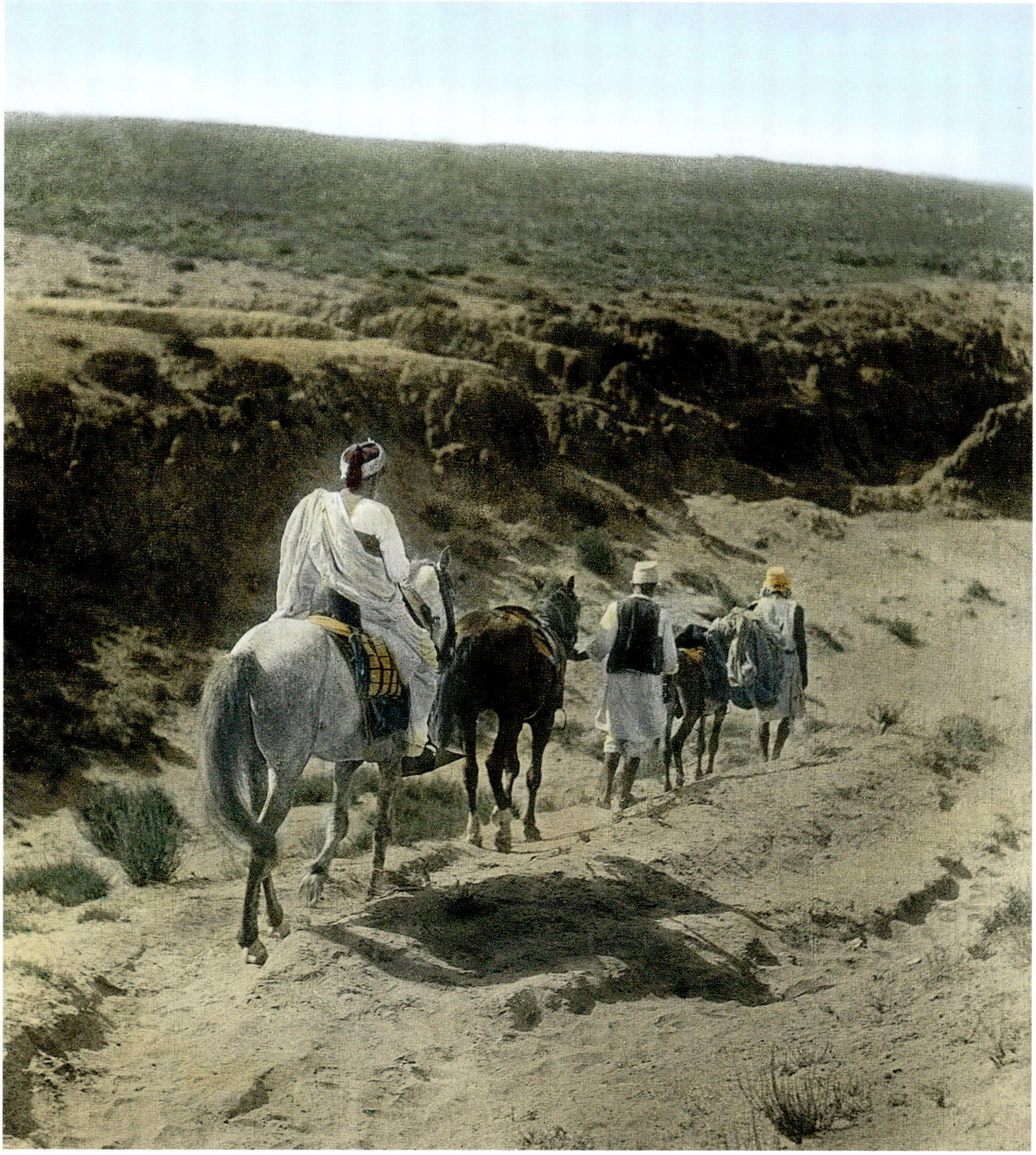

303 Travelling through a wadi in a plateau north of the Gharian Mountains, Libya, 1904

303 Reise durch einen Wadi auf einem Plateau nördlich des Ghariangebirges, Libyen, 1904

303 Voyage dans le lit d'un oued, sur un plateau au nord des montagnes près de Gharyan, Libye, 1904

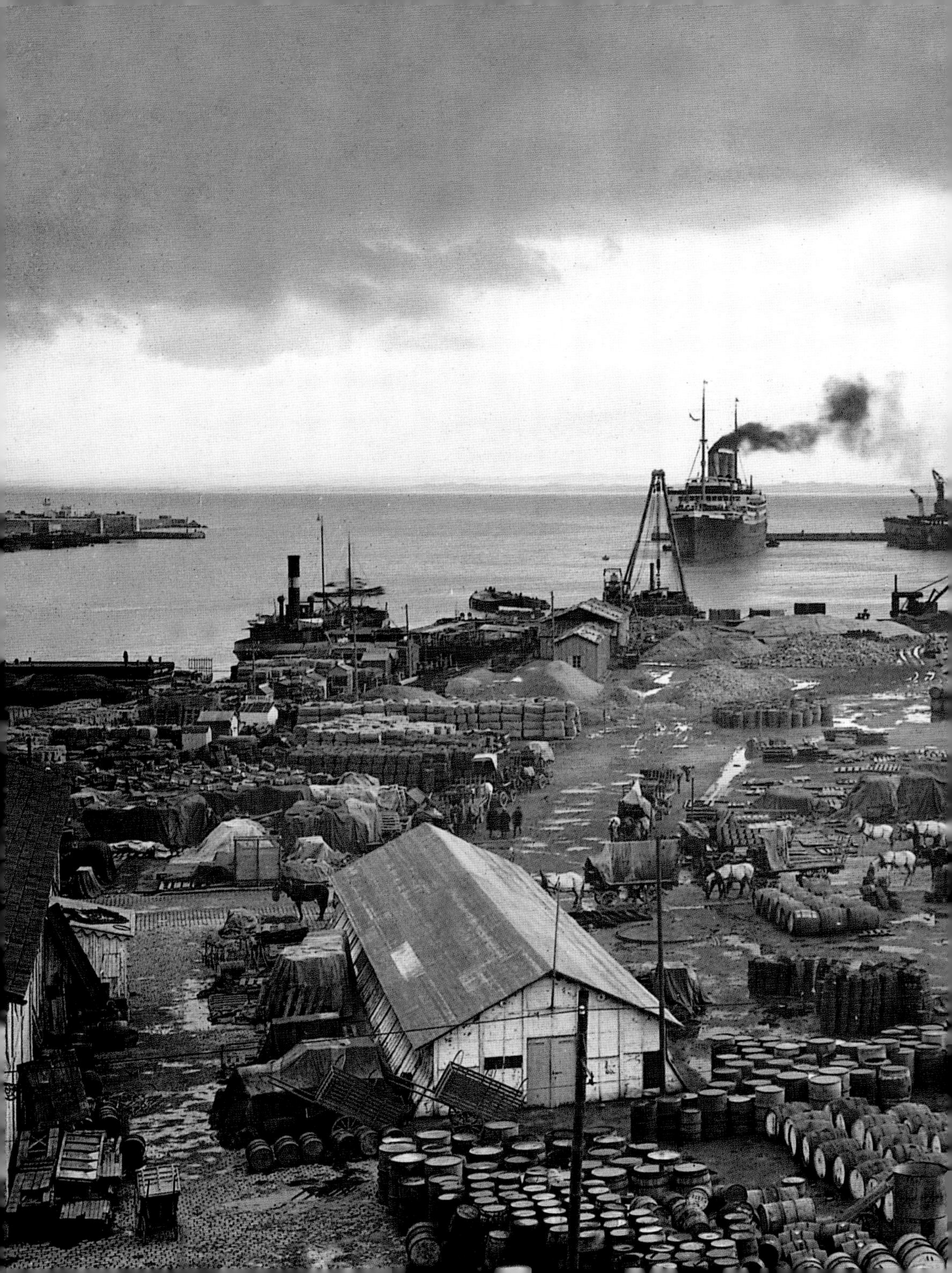

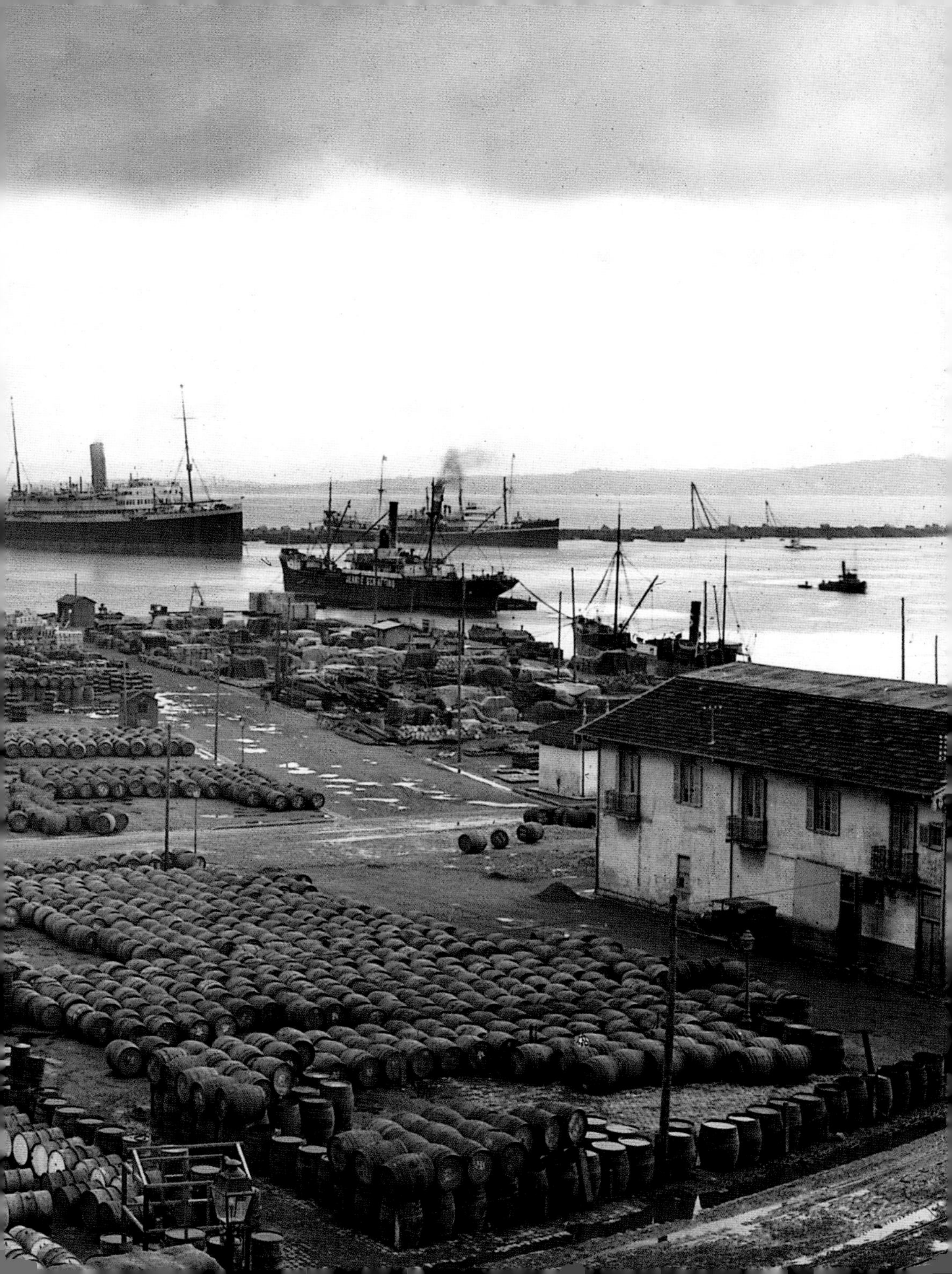

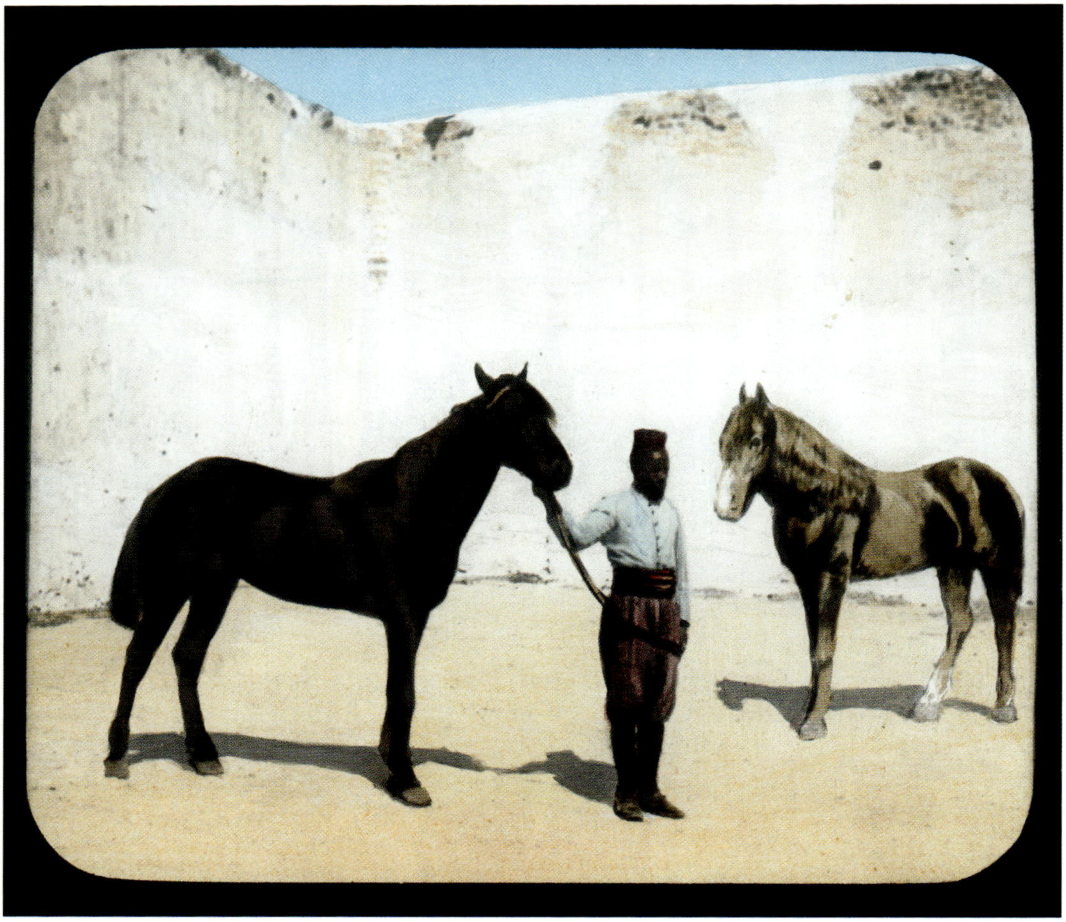

304 Barrels of olive oil on wharf and steamers in the harbour, Algiers, Algeria, 1924

304 Fässer mit Olivenöl am Kai und Dampfer im Hafen, Algier, Algerien, 1924

304 Tonneaux d'huile d'olive sur le quai et vapeurs dans le port, Algers, Algerie, 1924

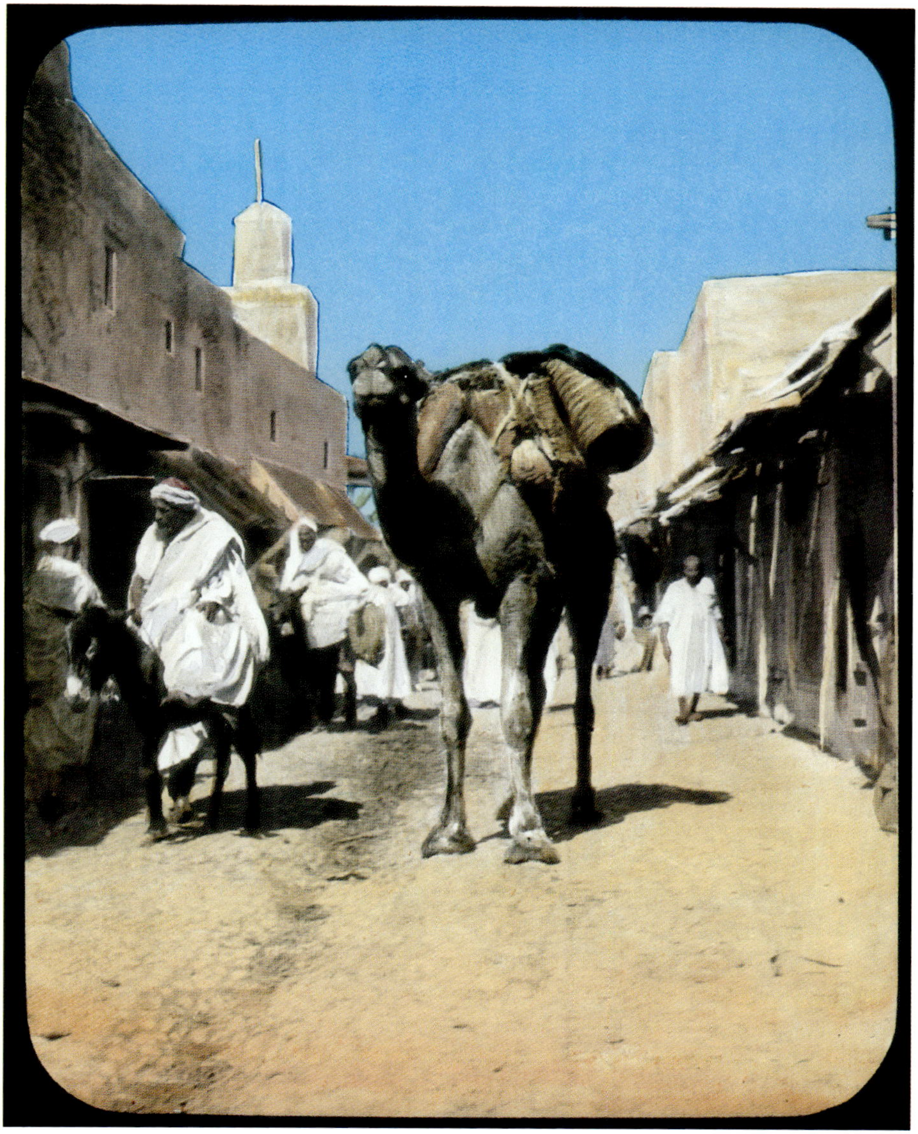

305 Man with two horses, Morocco, 1880s
306 Camel in street, Morocco, 1880s

305 Mann mit zwei Pferden, Marokko, 1880er Jahre
306 Kamel auf der Straße, Marokko, 1880er Jahre

305 Homme avec deux chevaux, Maroc, années 1880
306 Dromadaire en ville, Maroc, années 1880

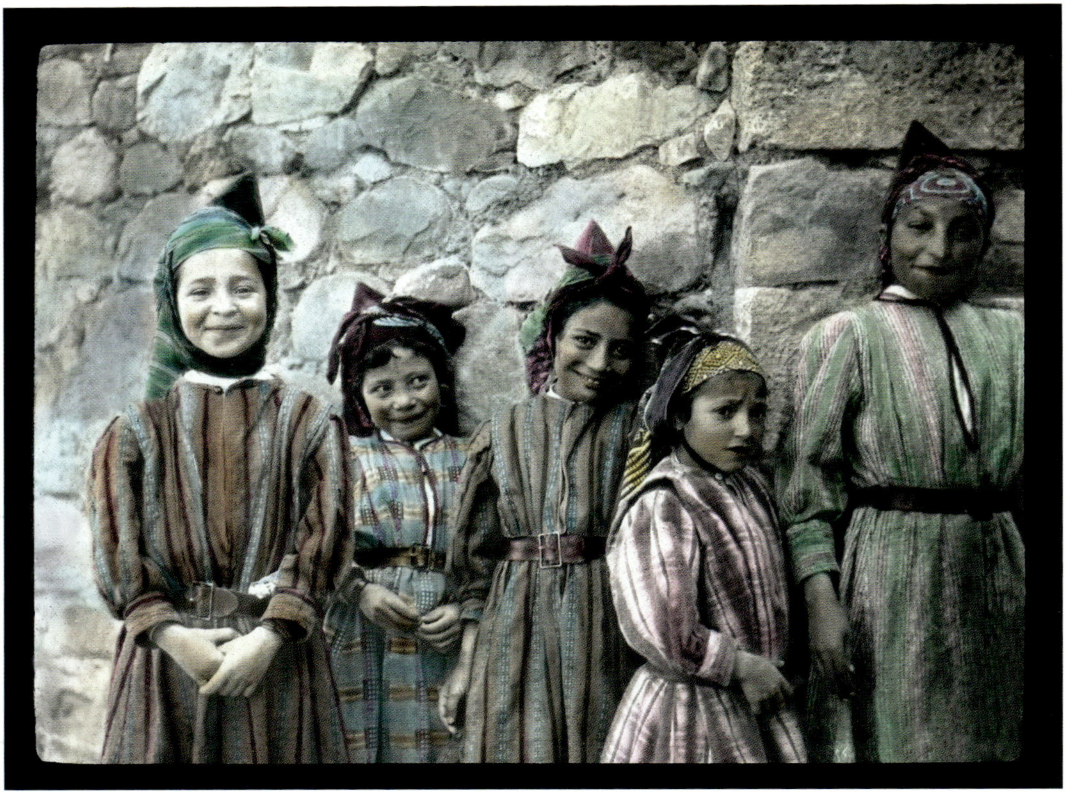

307 Group of young girls, North Africa, 1890s
308 Potter making pots on a wheel, Morocco, 1880s

307 Gruppe junger Mädchen, Nordafrika, 1890er Jahre
308 Ein Töpfer stellt Gefäße auf einer Töpferscheibe her, Marokko, 1880er Jahre

307 Groupe de fillettes, Afrique du Nord, années 1890
308 Potier au tour, Maroc, années 1880

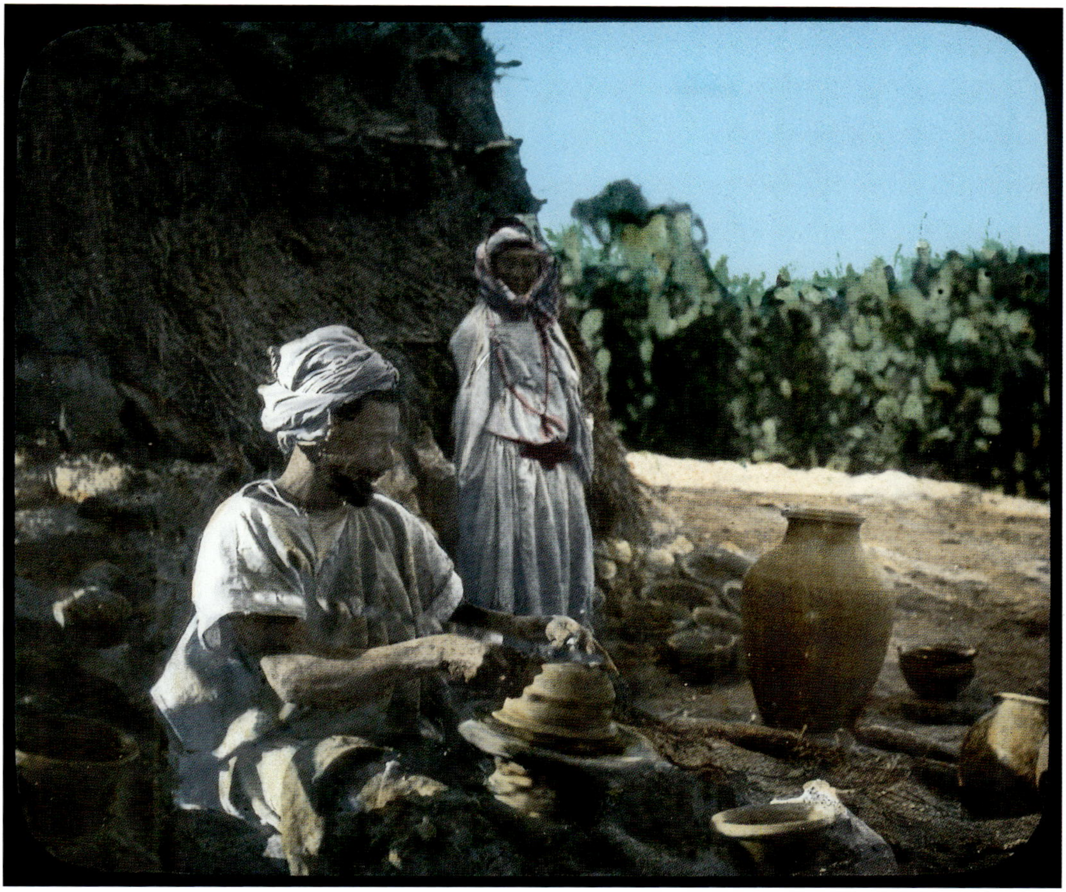

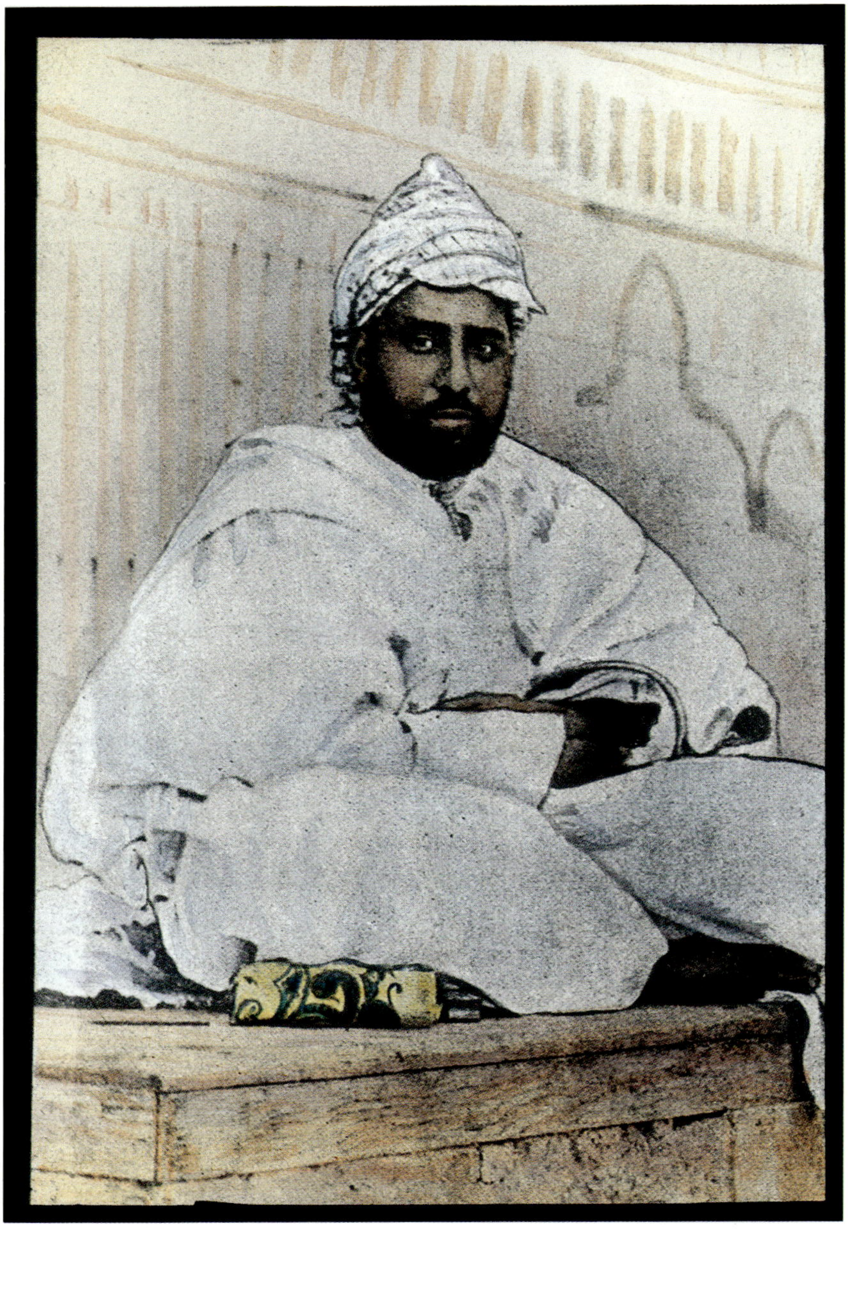

309 Man in traditional costume, Morocco, 1880s
310 Young woman in traditonal costume, Morocco, 1880s

309 Mann in traditioneller Kleidung, Marokko, 1880er Jahre
310 Junge Frau in traditioneller Tracht, Marokko, 1880er Jahre

309 Homme en costume traditionnel, Maroc, années 1880
310 Jeune femme en costume traditionnel, Maroc, années 1880

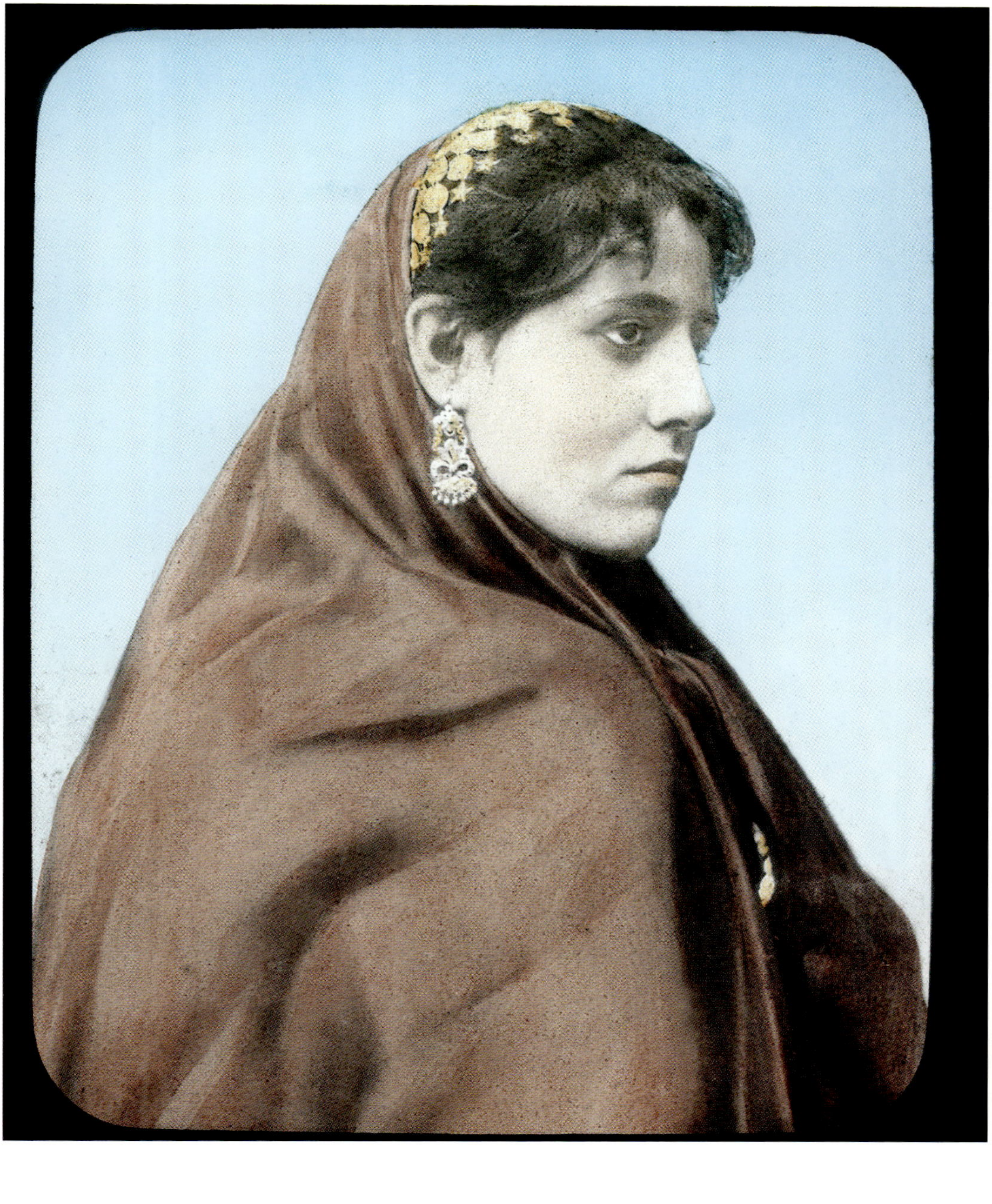

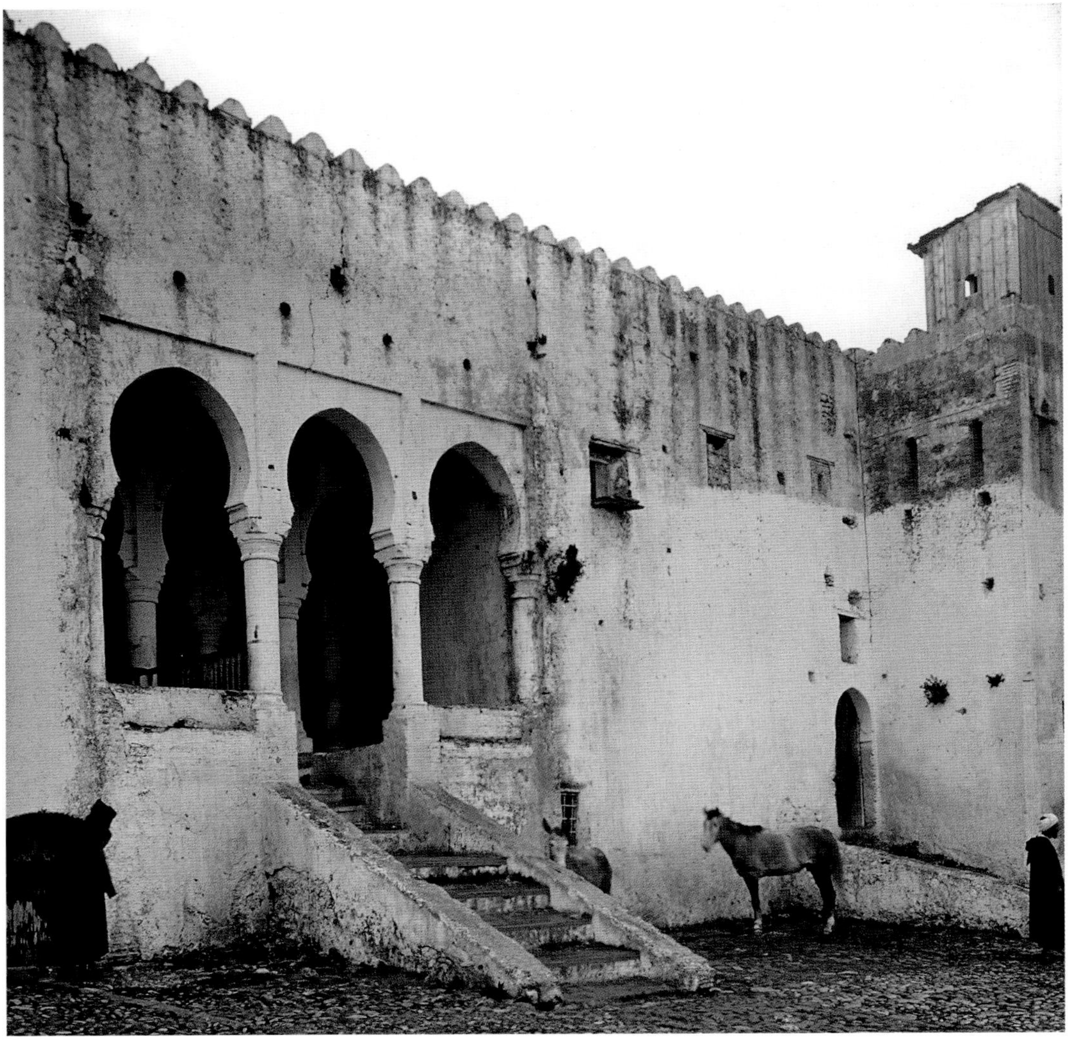

311 Prison and treasury, Tangiers, Morocco, 1870s

311 Gefängnis und Schatzkammer, Tanger, Marokko, 1870er Jahre

311 Prison et trésor, Tanger, Maroc, années 1870

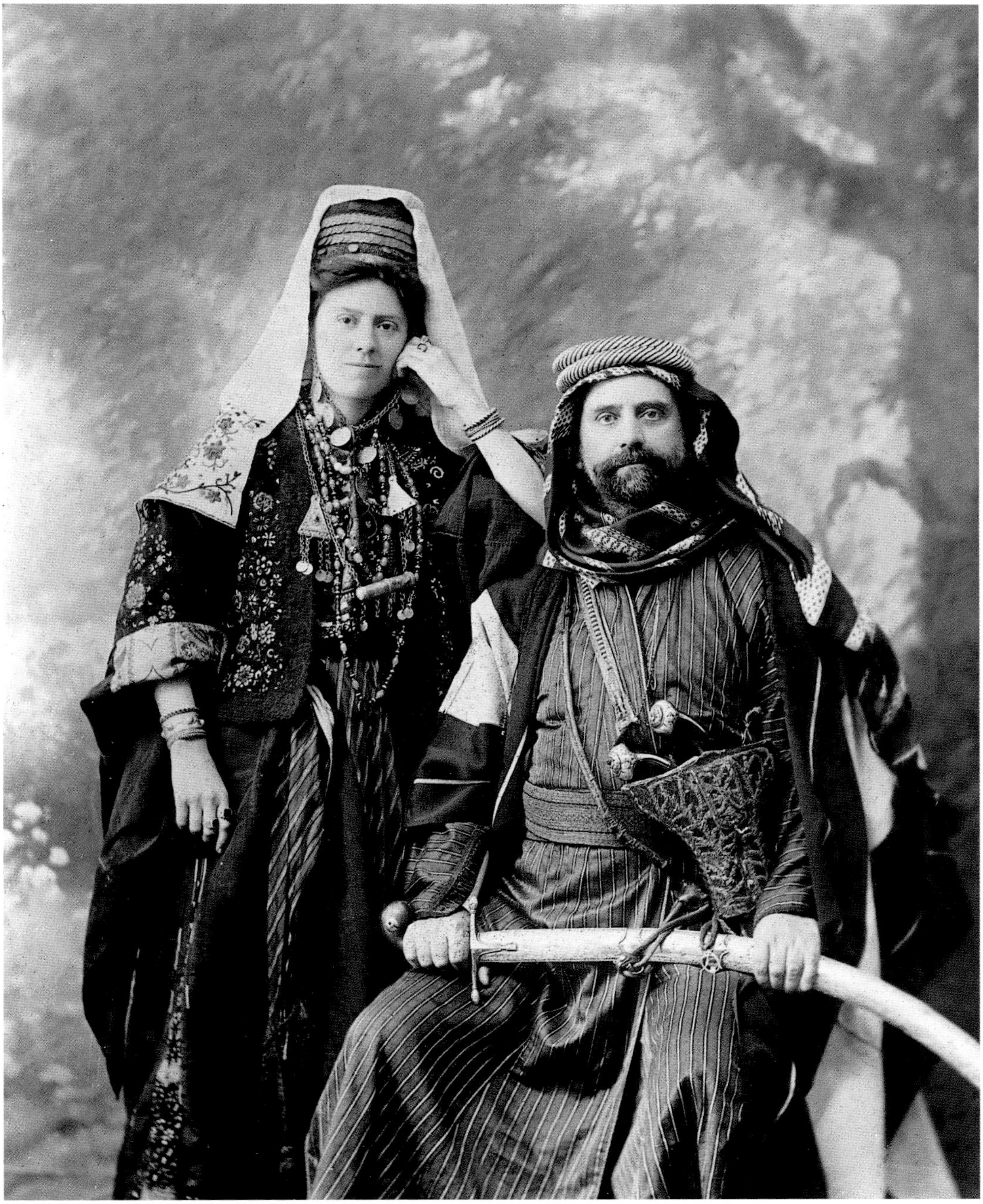

312 European couple in traditional Arab costume, Middle East/North Africa, 1870s

312 Europäisches Paar in traditioneller arabischer Kleidung, Naher Osten/ Nordafrika, 1870er Jahre

312 Couple d'européens en constume traditionnel arabe, Moyen-Orient/ Afrique du Nord, années 1870

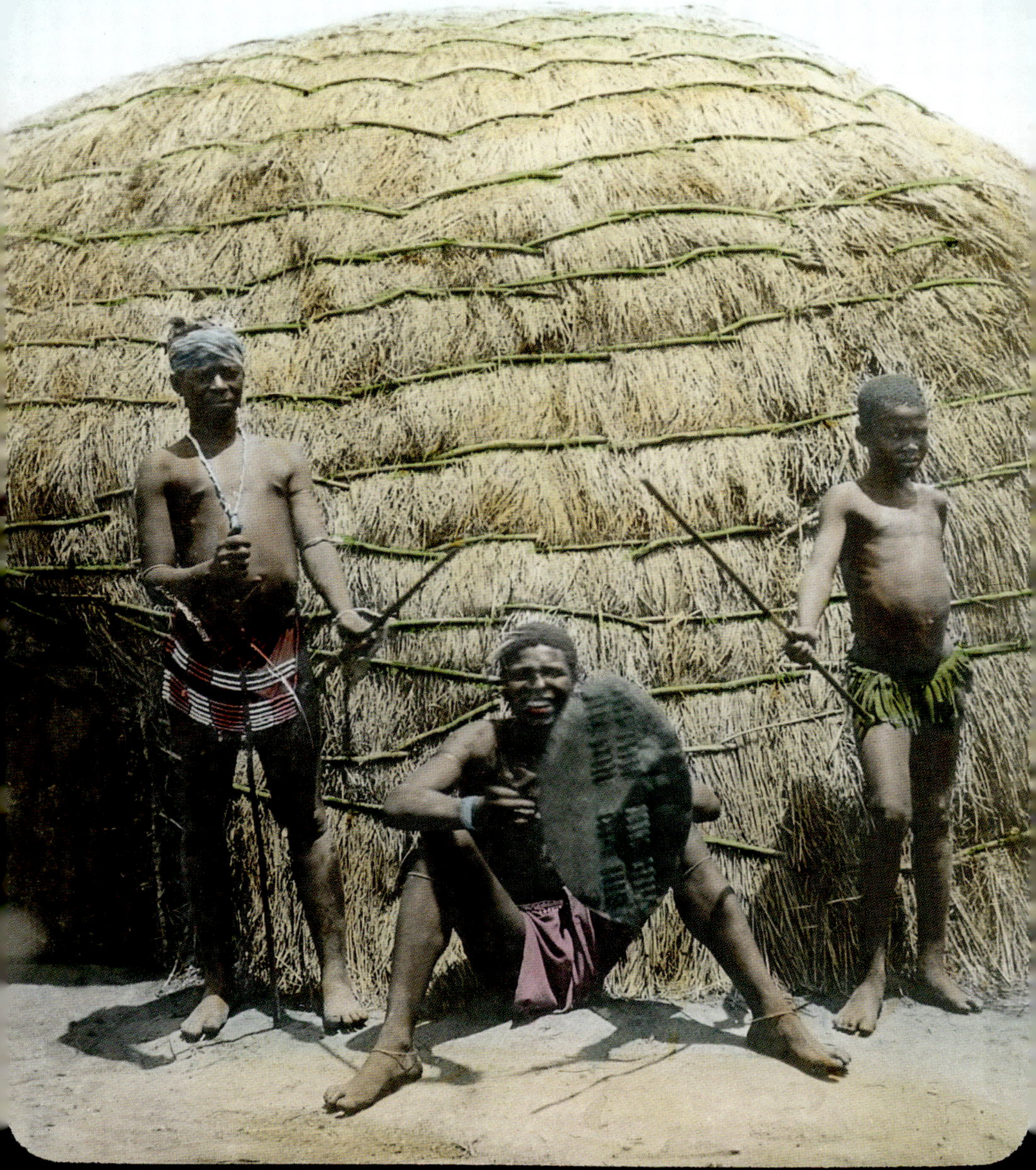

13 Karo tribesmen out-
de domed thatched hut,
thiopia, Africa 1890s

313 Angehörige des
Kara-Stamms vor
einer strohgedeckten
Rundhütte, Äthiopien,
Afrika, 1890er Jahre

313 Membres de la
tribu Karo devant une
hutte de chaume en
dôme, Éthiopie, Afrique,
années 1890

CENTRAL & EASTERN AFRICA

ZENTRAL- UND OSTAFRIKA ·

AFRIQUE CENTRALE ET DE L'EST

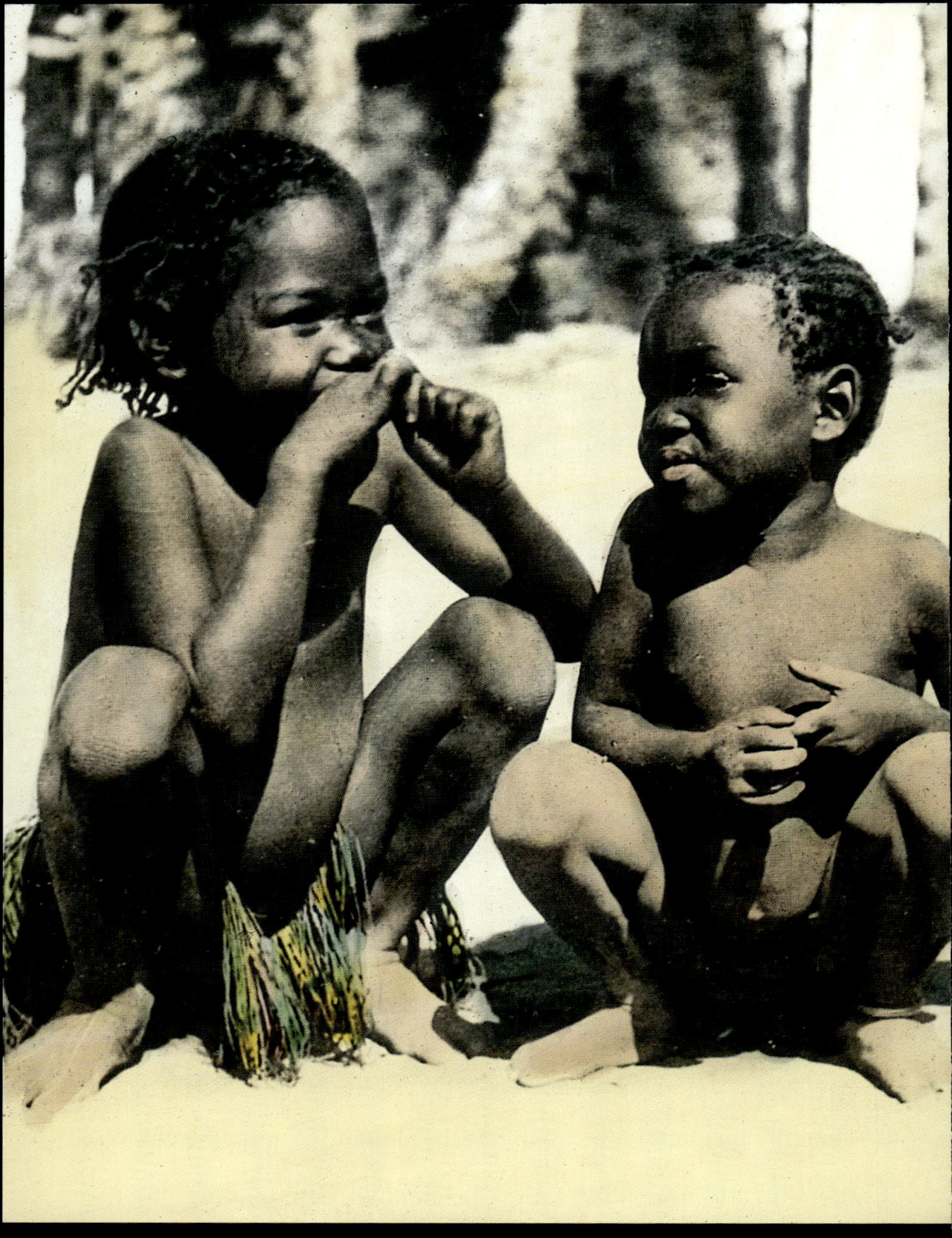

314 Moslem children,
Sudan, 1890s

314 Muslimische Kinder,
Sudan, 1890er Jahre

314 Enfants musulmans,
Soudan, années 1890

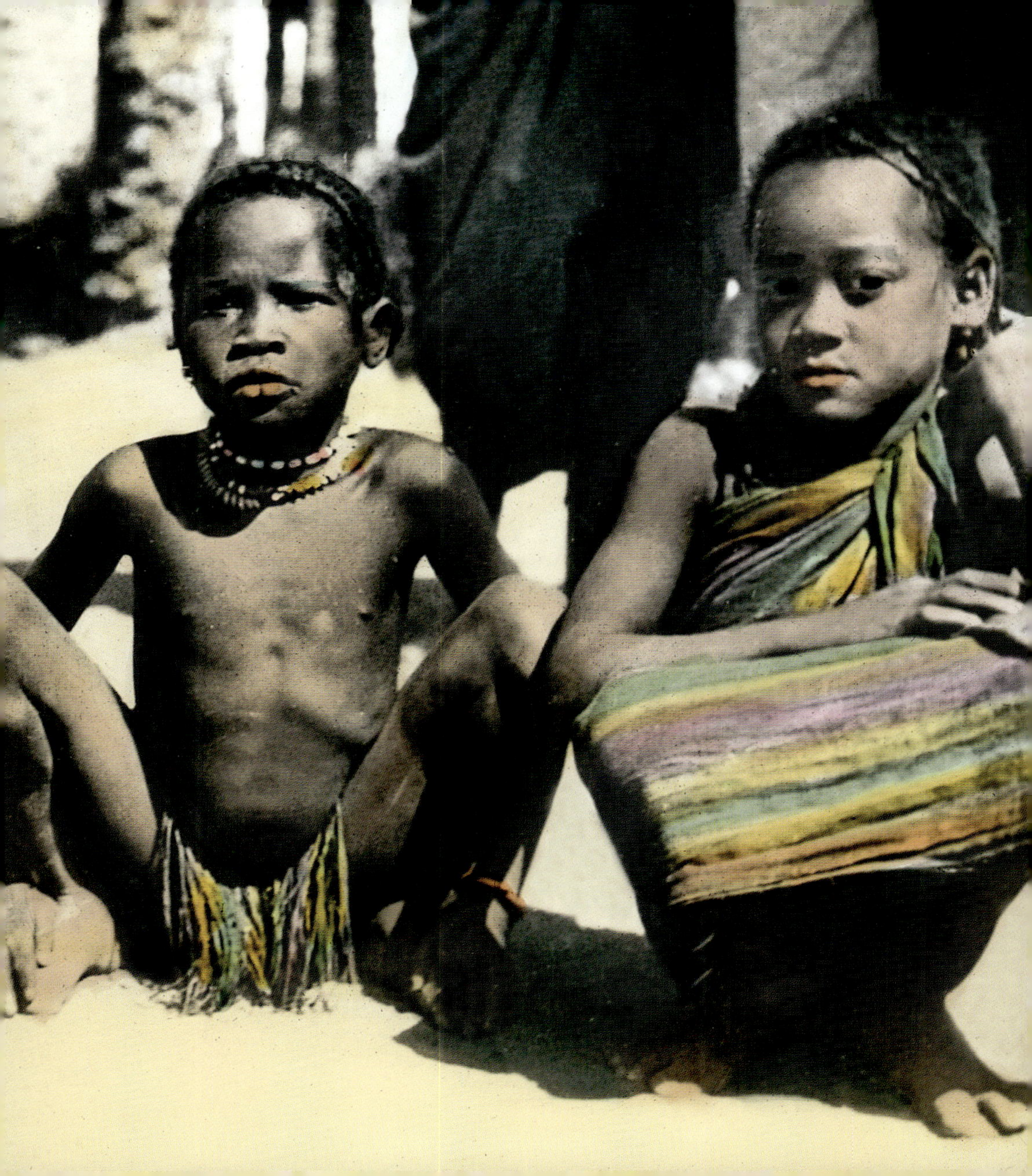

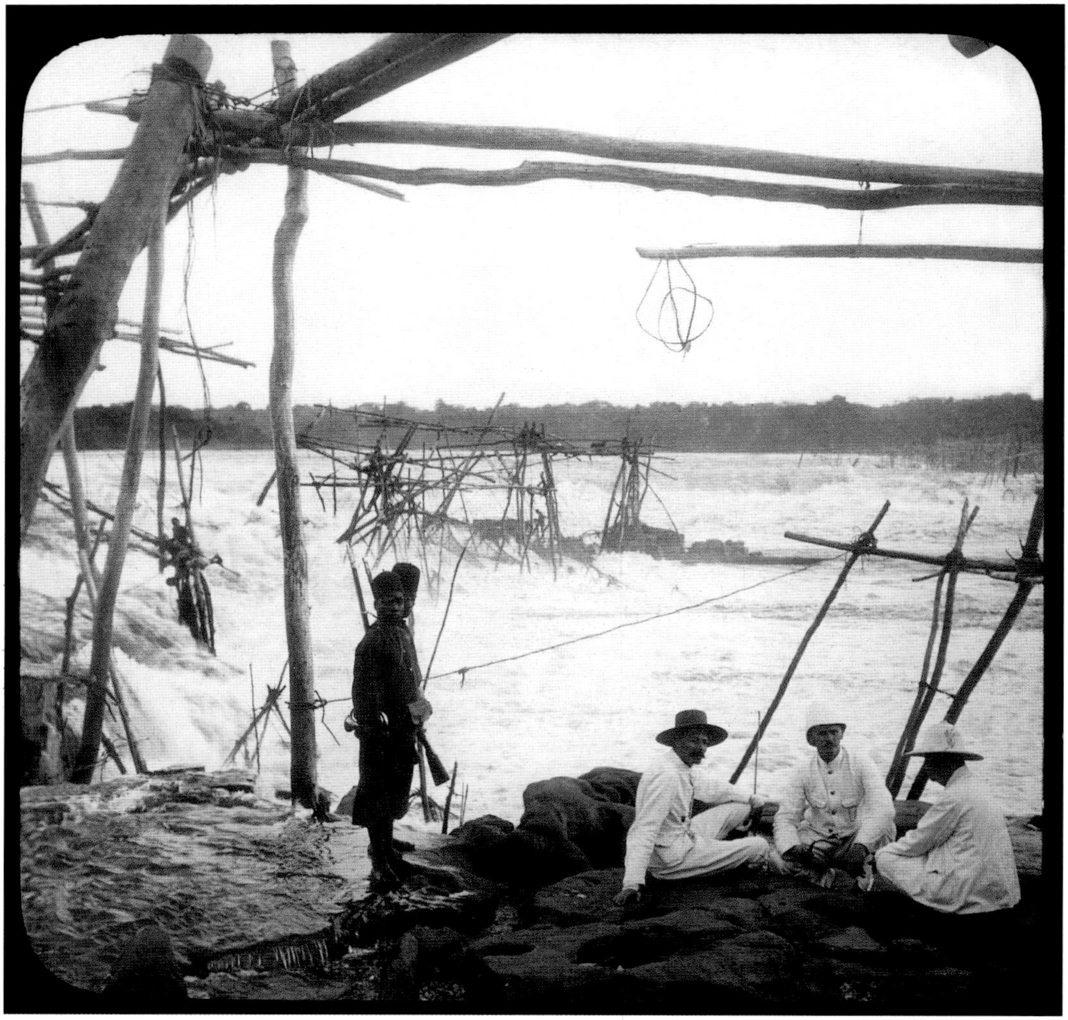

315 Fish traps at Stanley Falls (now Boyoma Falls), Congo (Democratic Republic of the Congo), Africa, 1880s

315 Fischreusen an den Stanleyfällen (heute Boyomafälle), Kongo (Demokratische Republik Kongo), Afrika, 1880er Jahre

315 Capture du poisson aux chutes Stanley (auj. chutes Boyoma), Congo (Rép. Démocratique du Congo), Afrique, années 1880

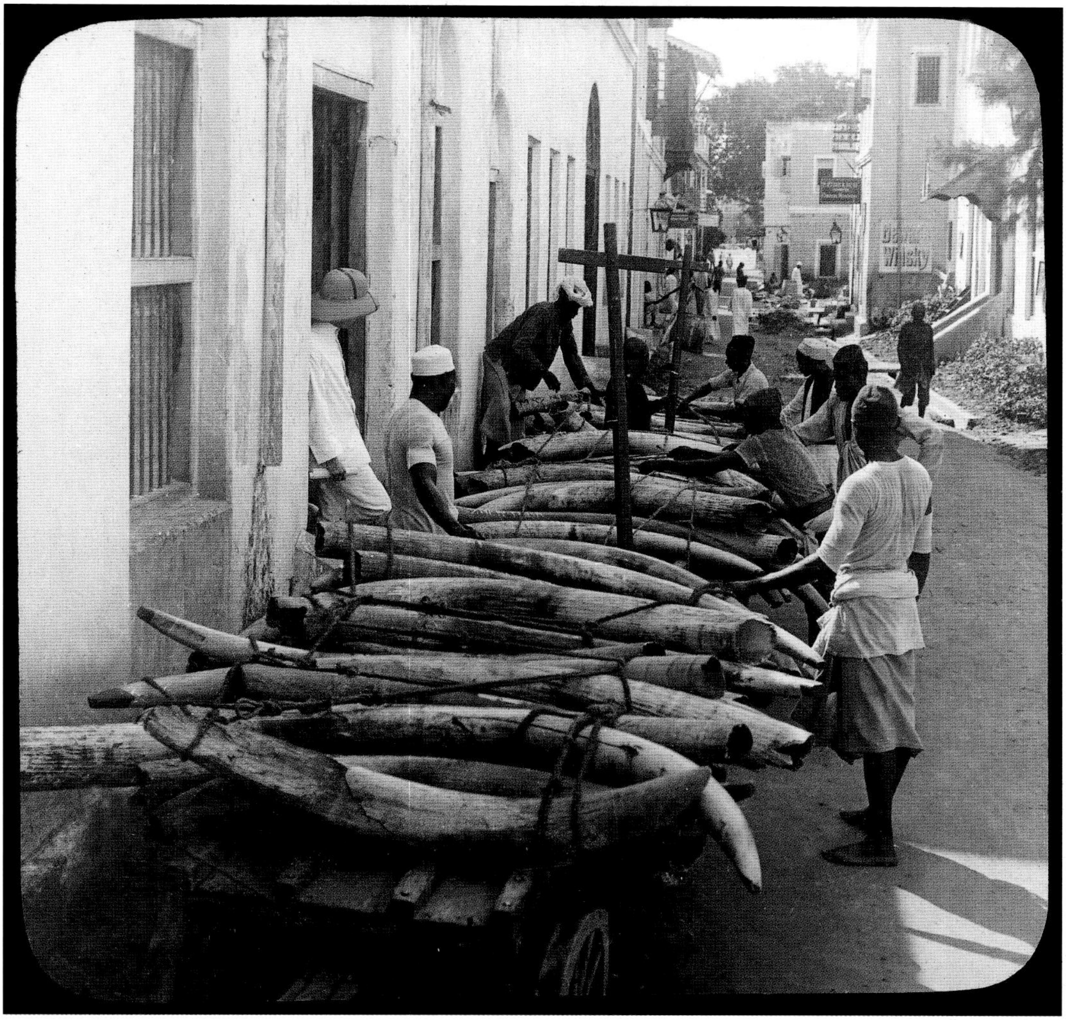

316 Ivory ready to ship, Mombasa, British East Africa (now Kenya), Africa 1890s

316 Elfenbein fertig zur Verschiffung, Mombasa, Britisch-Ostafrika (heute Kenia), Afrika, 1890er Jahre

316 Ivoire prêt à être livré, Mombasa, Colombie-Afrique de l'Est (auj. Kenya), Africa années 1890

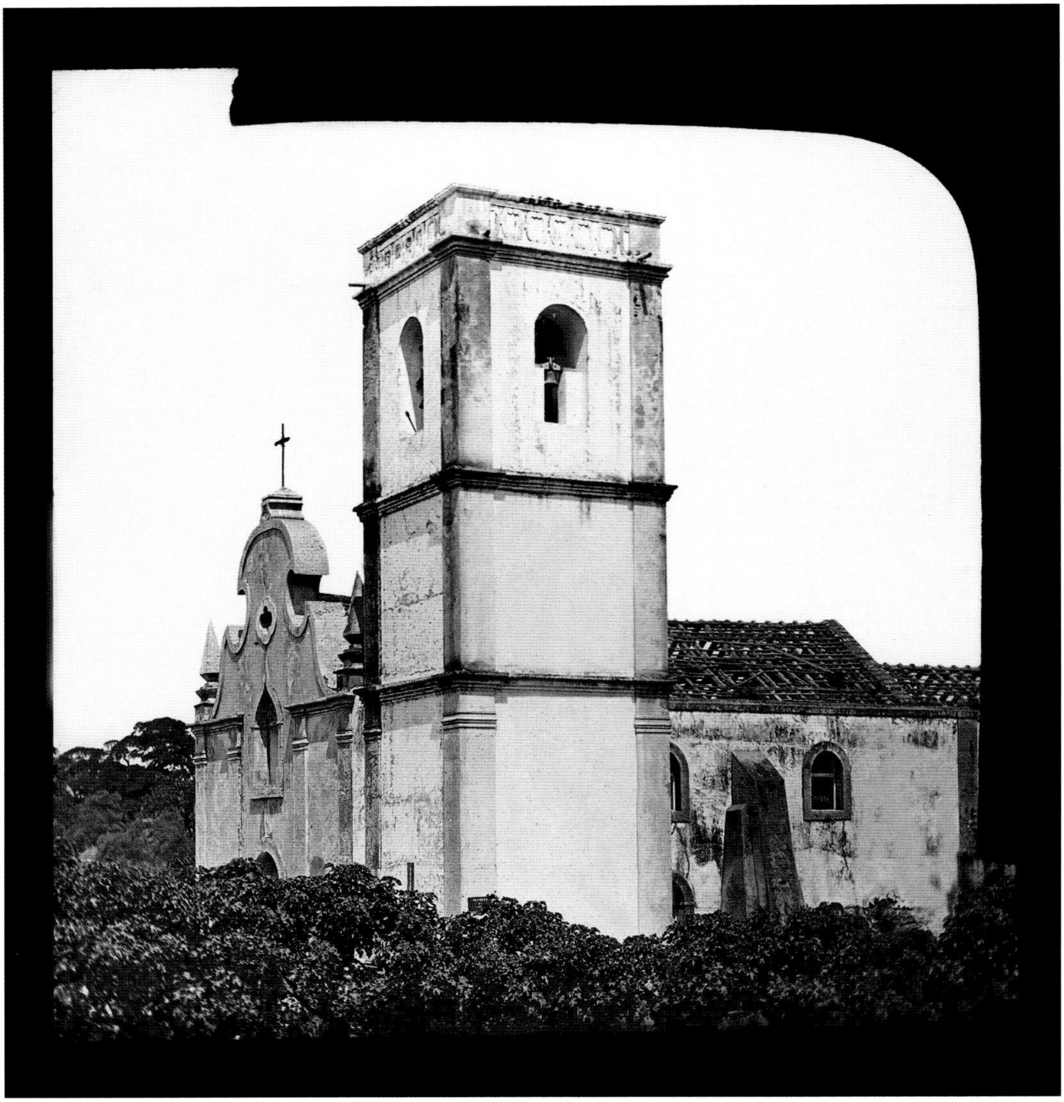

317 Burnt-out Portugese chapel, Inhambane, Mozambique, 1880s

317 Ausgebrannte portugiesische Kirche, Inhambane, Mosambik, 1880er Jahre

317 Chapelle portugaise brûlée, Inhambane, Mozambique, années 1880

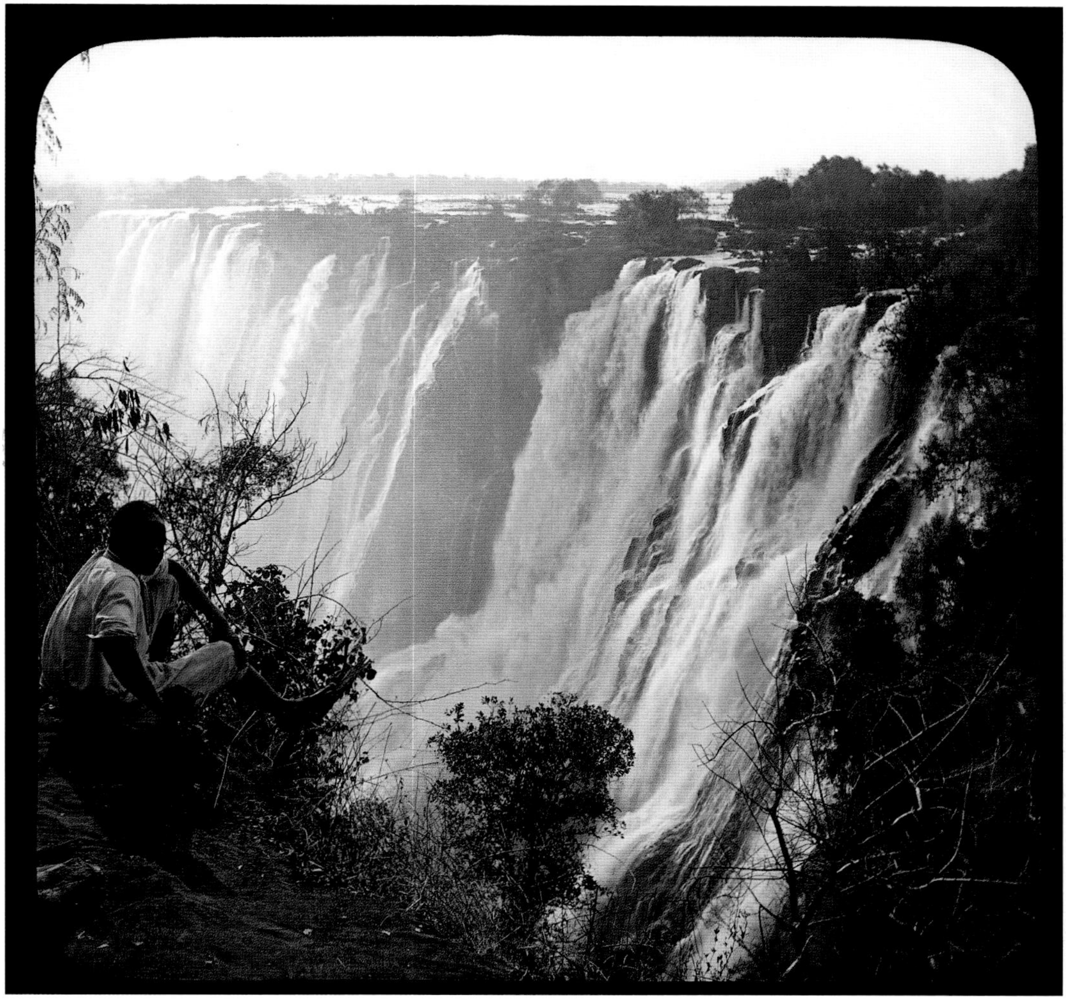

318 Victoria Falls, Rhodesia (now Zimbabwe), Africa, 1890s

318 Die Victoriafälle, Rhodesien (heute Simbabwe), Afrika, 1890er Jahre

318 Chutes Victoria, Rhodésie (auj. Zimbabwé), Afrique, années 1890

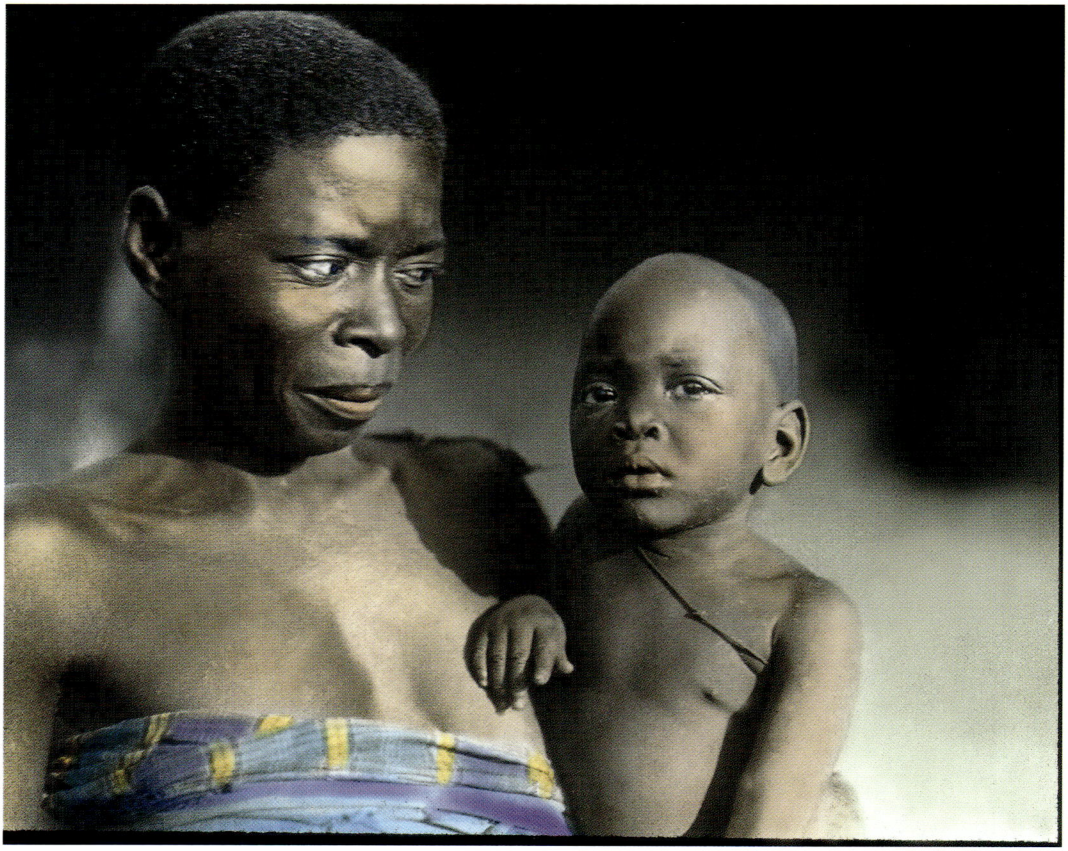

319 Mother and child, Africa, 1910s
320 Woman and baby, Africa, 1910s

319 Mutter und Kind, Afrika, 1910er Jahre
320 Mutter und Baby, Afrika, 1910er Jahre

319 Mère et son enfant, Afrique, années 1910
320 Femme et son bébé, Afrique, années 1910

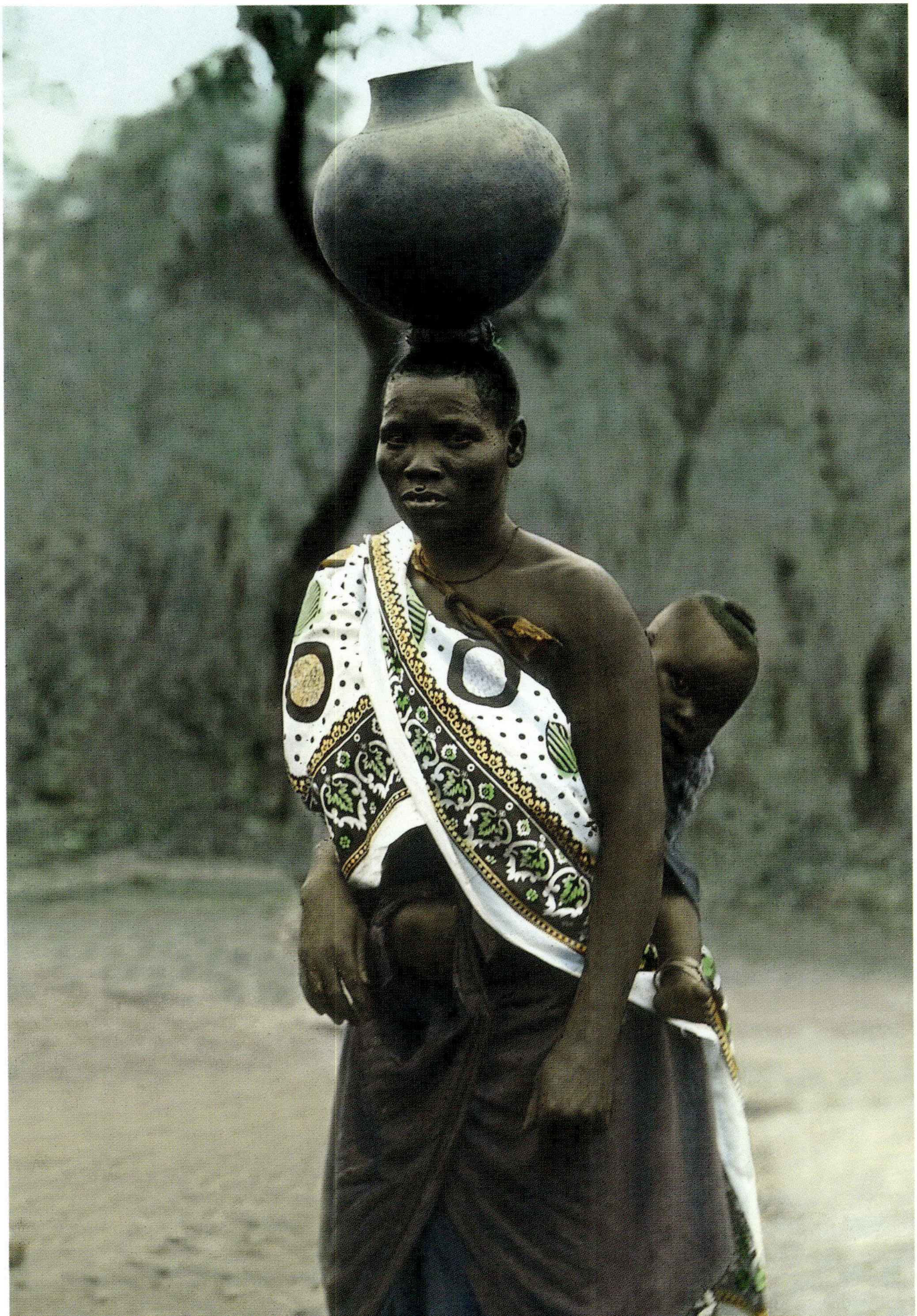

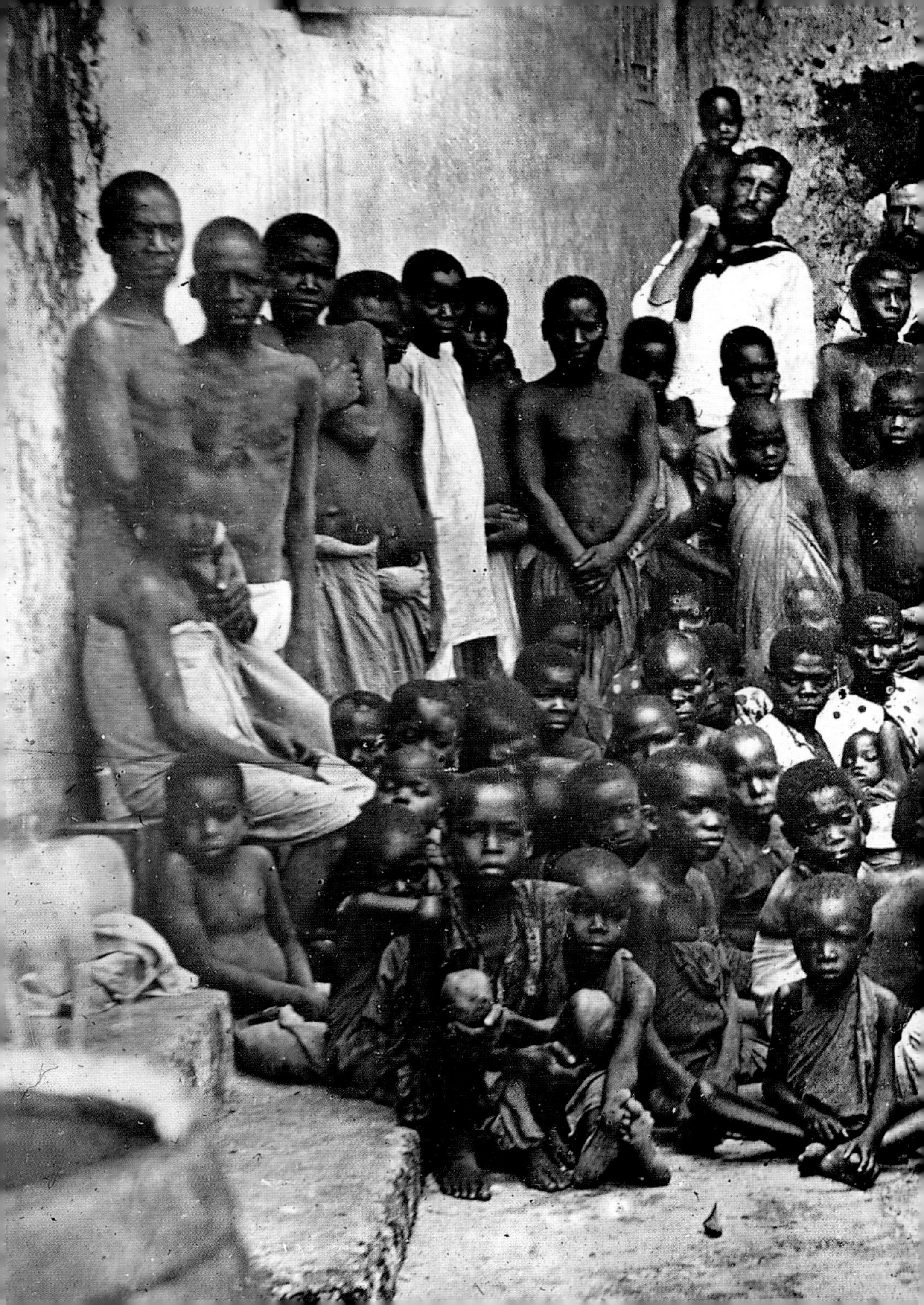

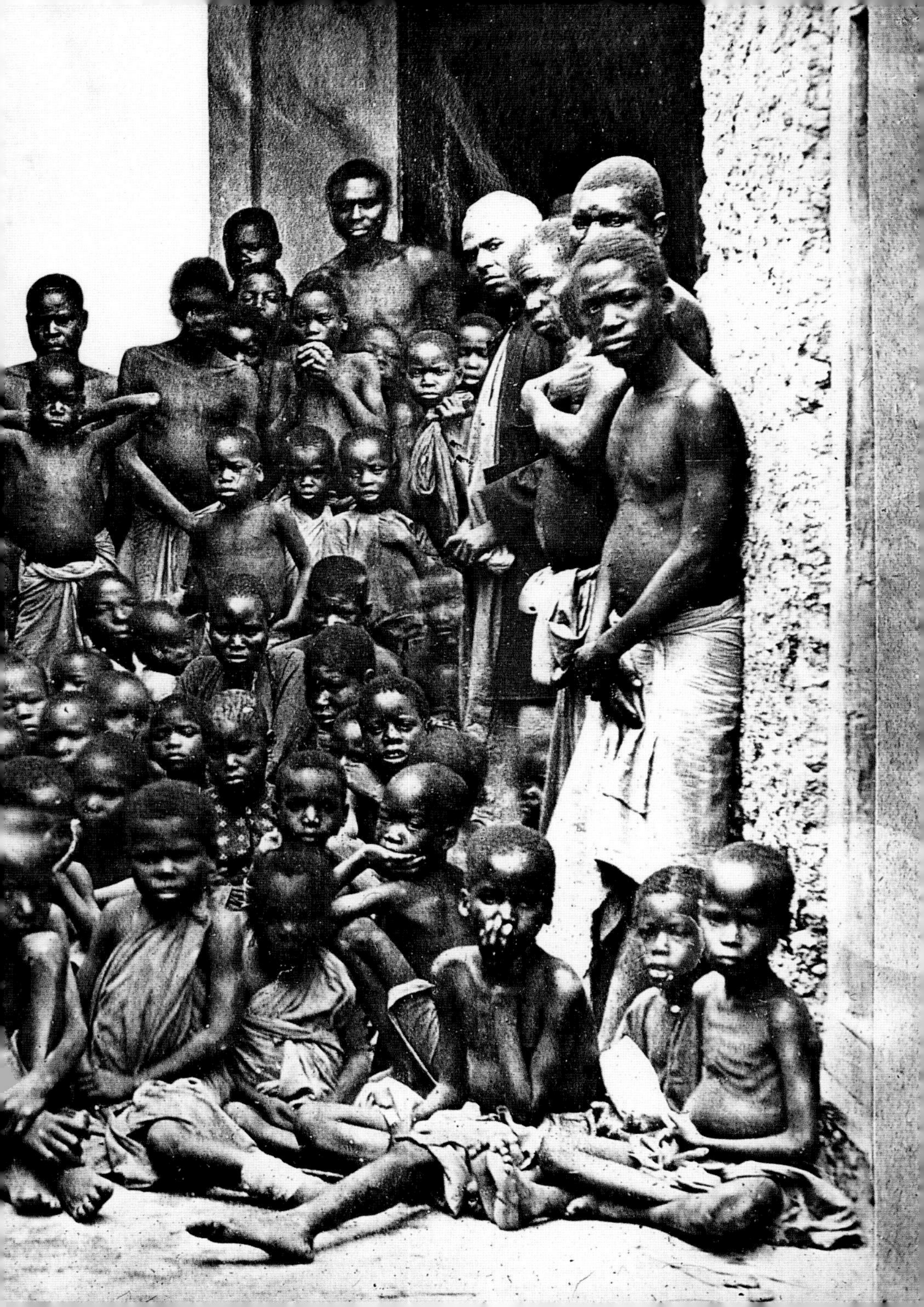

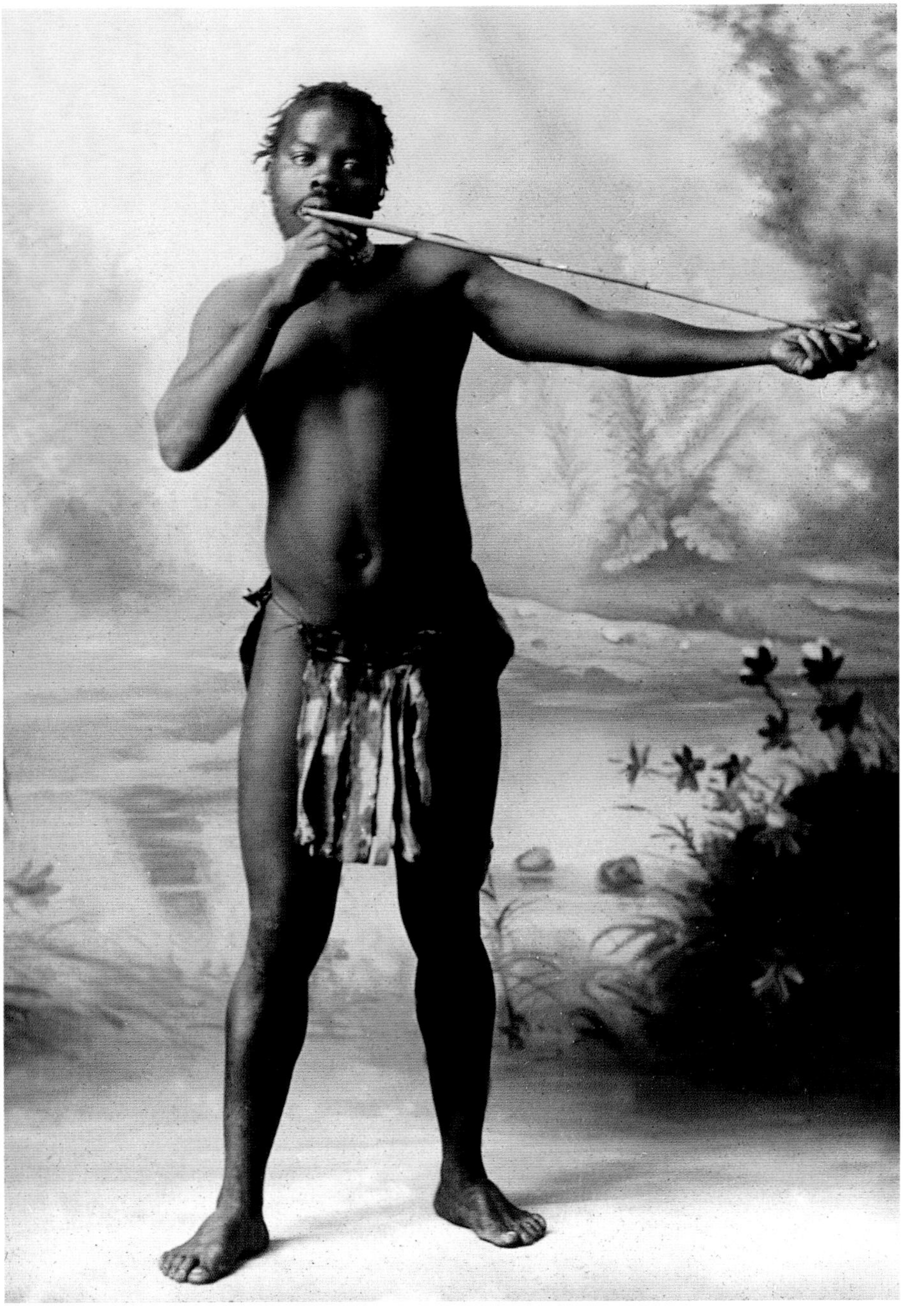

321 Group of rescued slaves, Africa, 1890s
322 Young man posing with blowpipe, Africa, 1900s

321 Gruppe befreiter Sklaven, Afrika, 1890er Jahre
322 Junger Mann posiert mit einem Blasrohr, Afrika, 1900er Jahre

321 Groupe d'esclaves libérés, Afrique, années 1890
322 Homme jeune posant avec une sarbacane, Afrique, années 1900

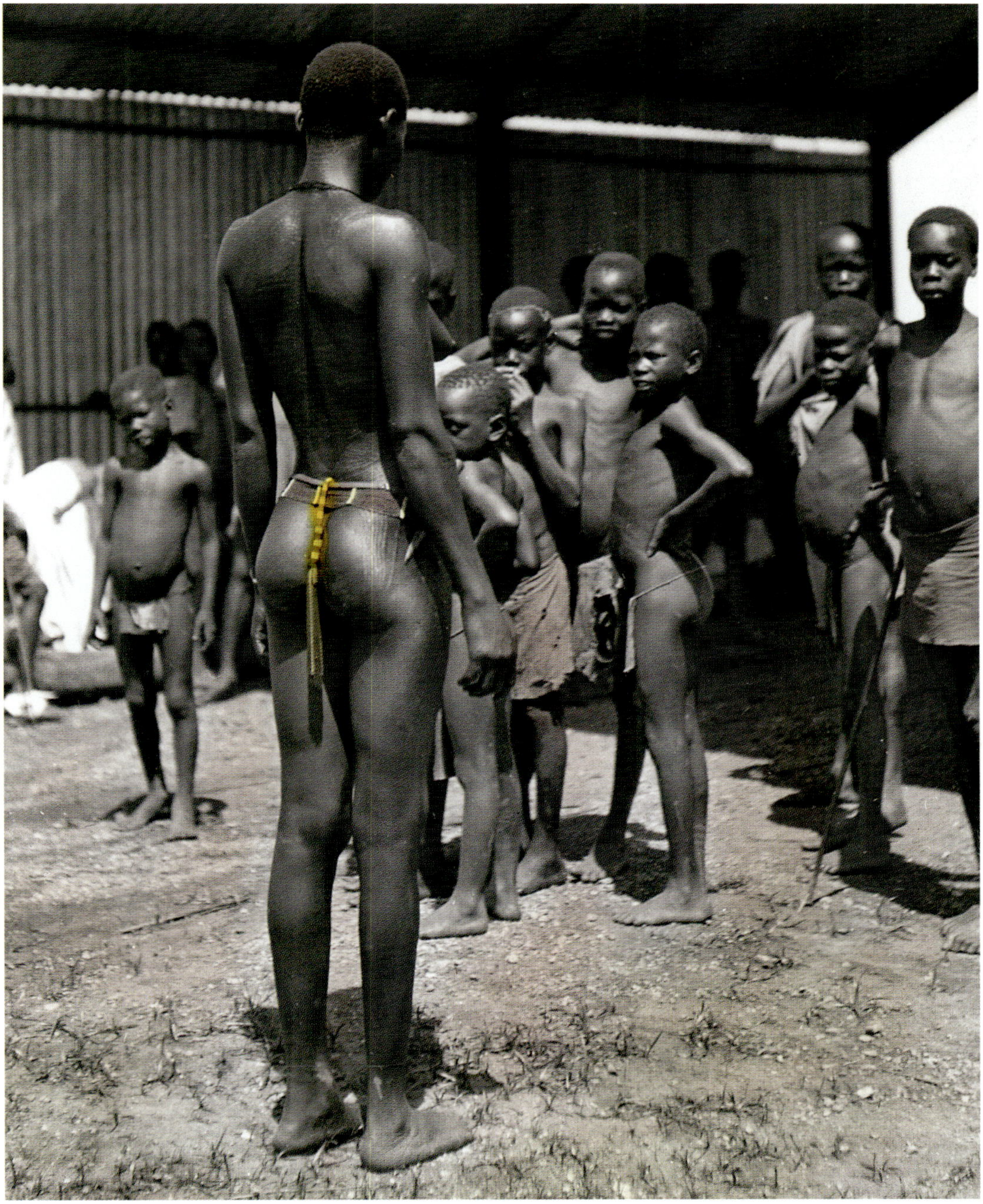

323 Married woman showing marriage tail, Nimuli, Uganda (now in Sudan), Africa, 1910s

323 Verheiratete Frau mit Heiratsschnur, Nimule, Uganda (heute im Sudan), Afrika, 1910er Jahre

323 Femme mariée portant la queue de mariage, Nimuli, Ouganda (auj. au Soudan), Afrique, années 1910

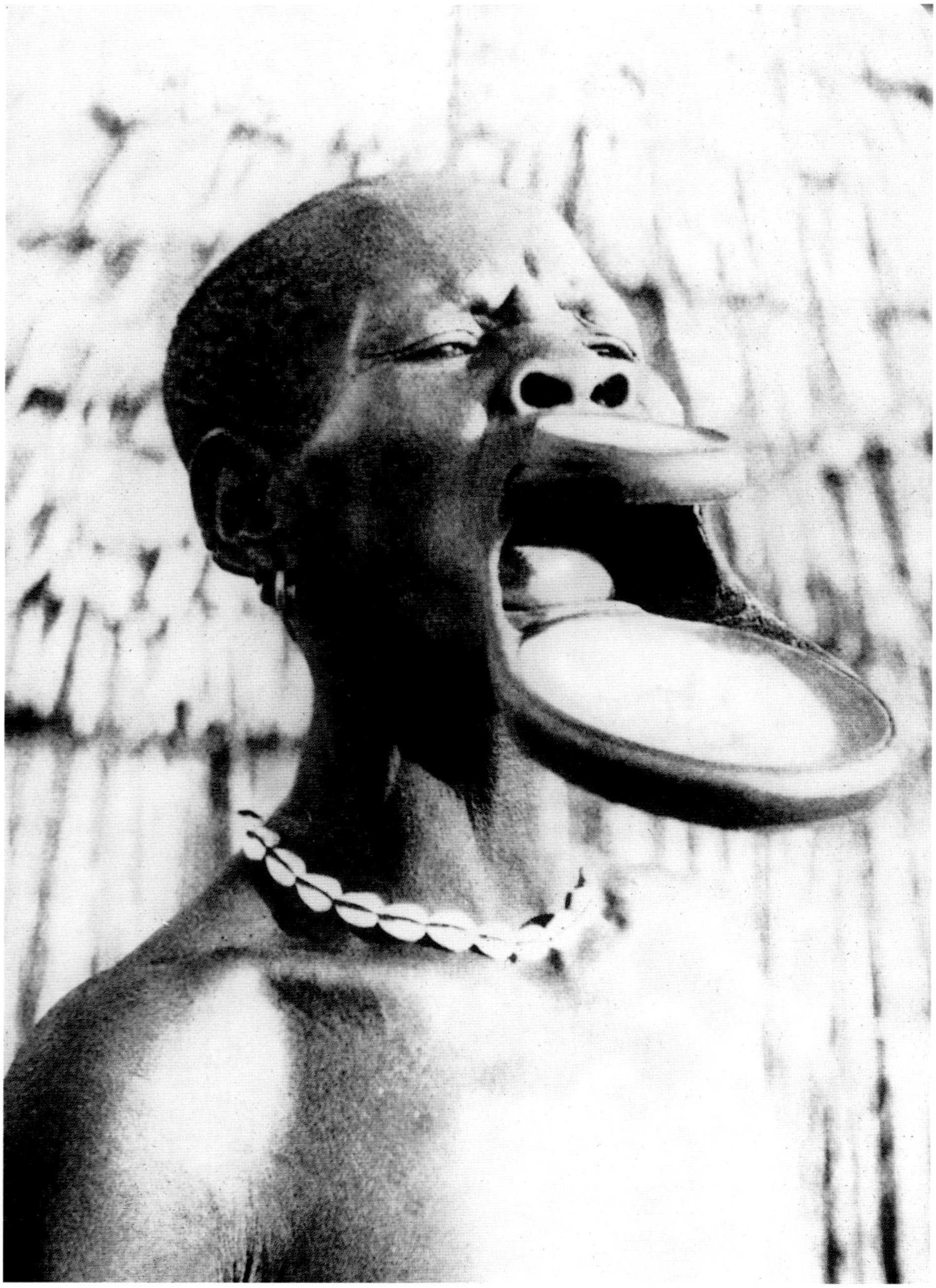

324 Mursi tribesman with lip plugs, Africa, 1880s

324 Angehöriger des Mursi-Stamms mit Lippentellern, Afrika, 1880er Jahre

324 Plateau labial d'un membre de la tribu Mursi, Éthiopie, Afrique, années 1880

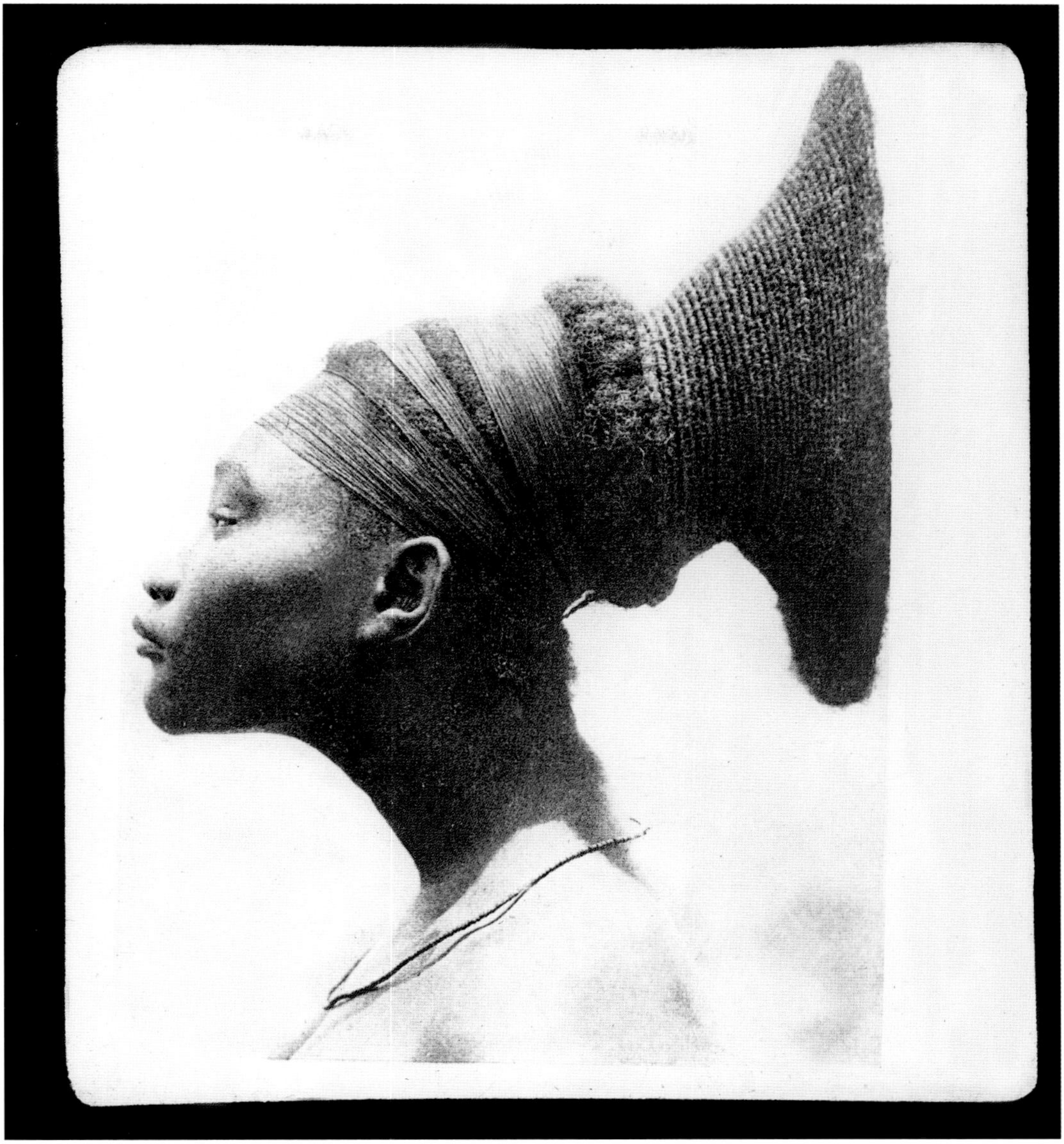

325 Mangbetu tribeswoman with ornate hair arrangement, Africa, 1880s

325 Angehörige des Mangbetu-Stamms mit schmuckvollem Haararrangement, Afrika, 1880er Jahre

325 Coiffure ornementale d'une femme de la tribu Mangbetu, Afrique, années 1880

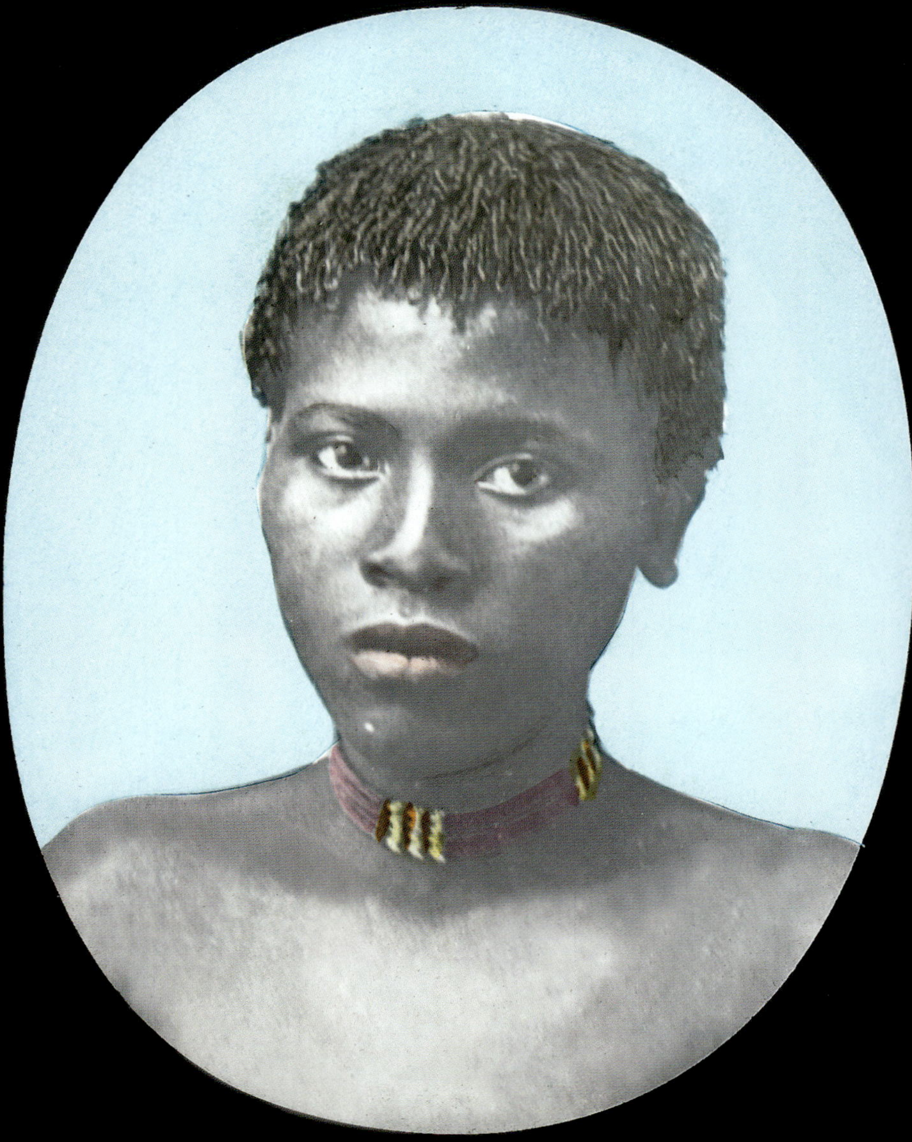

326 Young woman, South Africa, 1890s

326 Junge Frau, Südafrika, 1890er Jahre

326 Jeune femme, Afrique du Sud, années 1890

SOUTHERN AFRICA

SÜDAFRIKA · AFRIQUE DU SUD

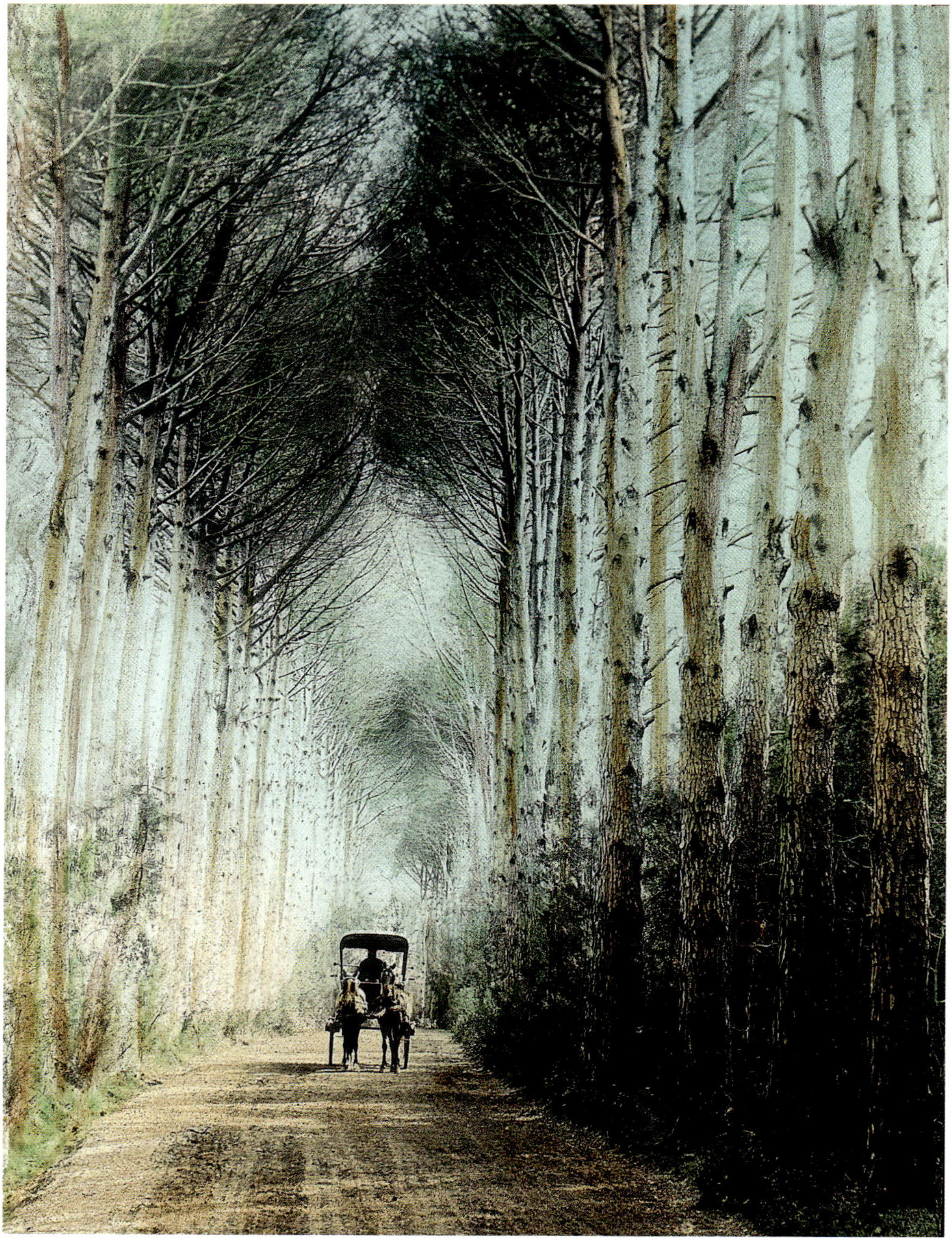

327 Fir Avenue, Cape Town, South Africa, 1890s
328 Boers "outspanning" (relaxing), South Africa, 1890s

327 Kiefer-Allee, Kapstadt, Südafrika, 1890er Jahre
328 Buren "spannen sich aus" (erholen sich), Südafrika, 1890er Jahre

327 Allée de pins, Le Cap, Afrique du Sud, années 1890
328 Boers au bivouac, Afrique du Sud, années 1890

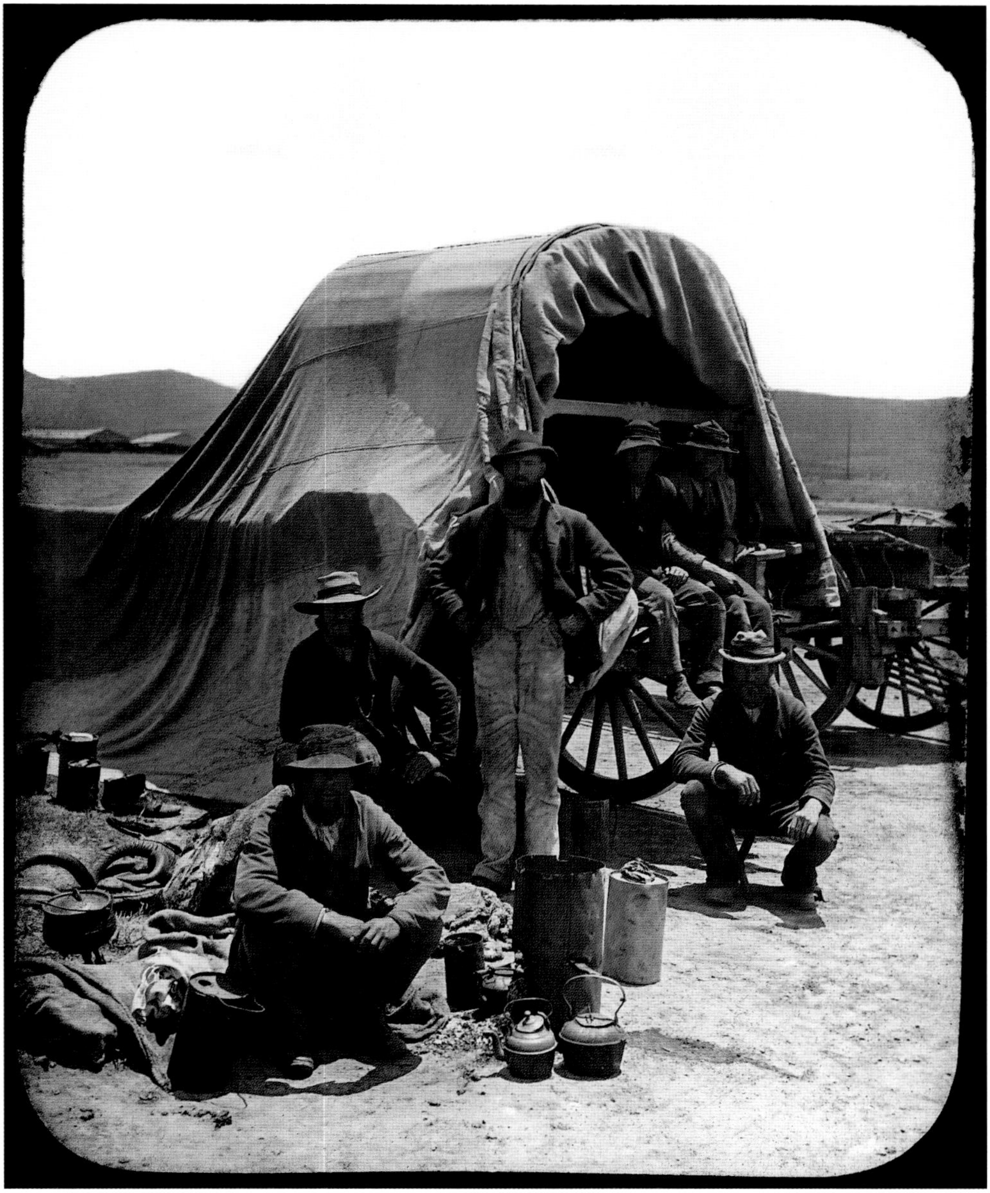

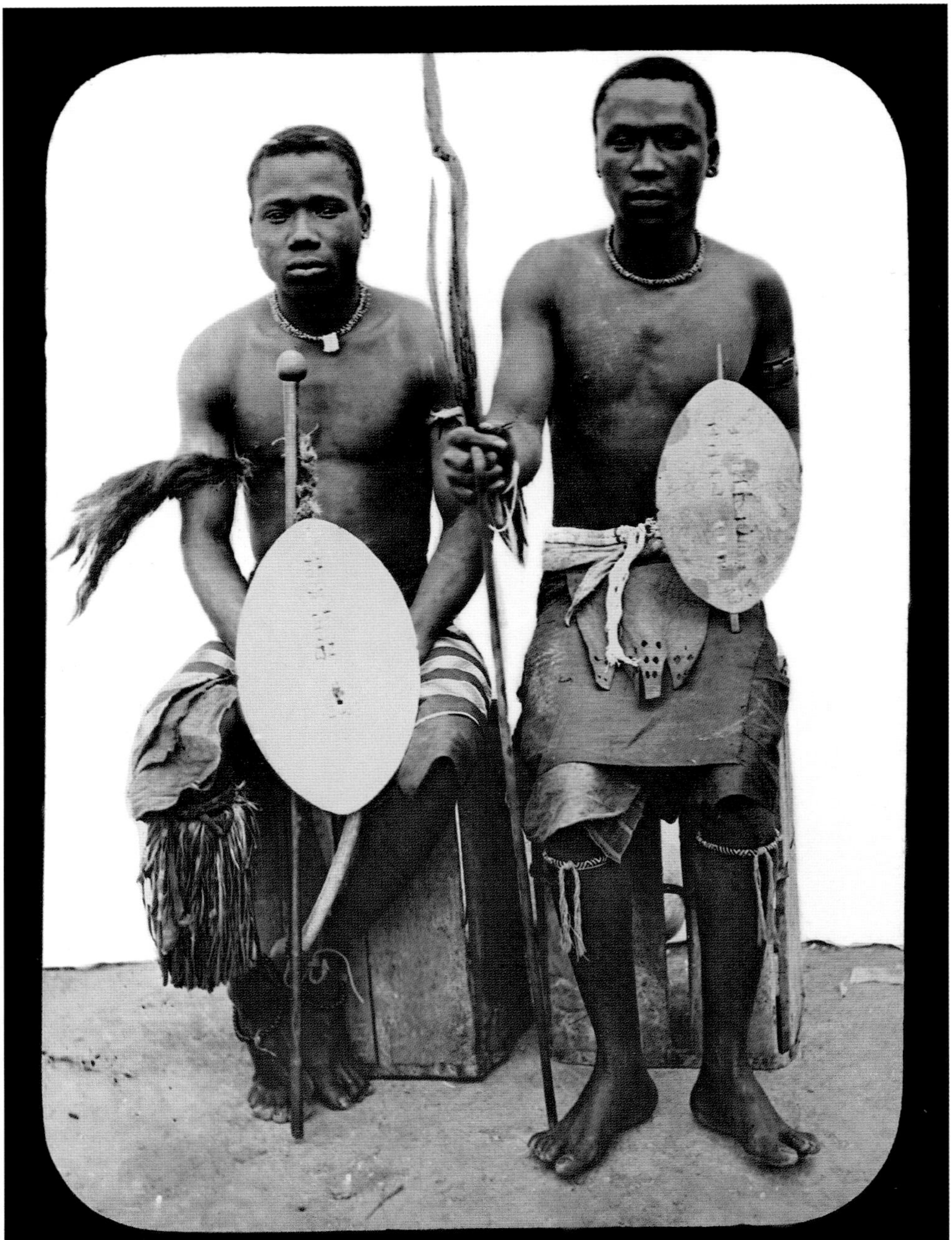

329 Tribesmen, South Africa, 1890s
330 Tribesman, South Africa, 1890s

329 Stammesangehörige, Südafrika, 1890er Jahre
330 Stammesangehöriger, Südafrika, 1890er Jahre

329 Membres d'une tribu d'Afrique du Sud, années 1890
330 Membre d'une tribu d'Afrique du Sud, années 1890

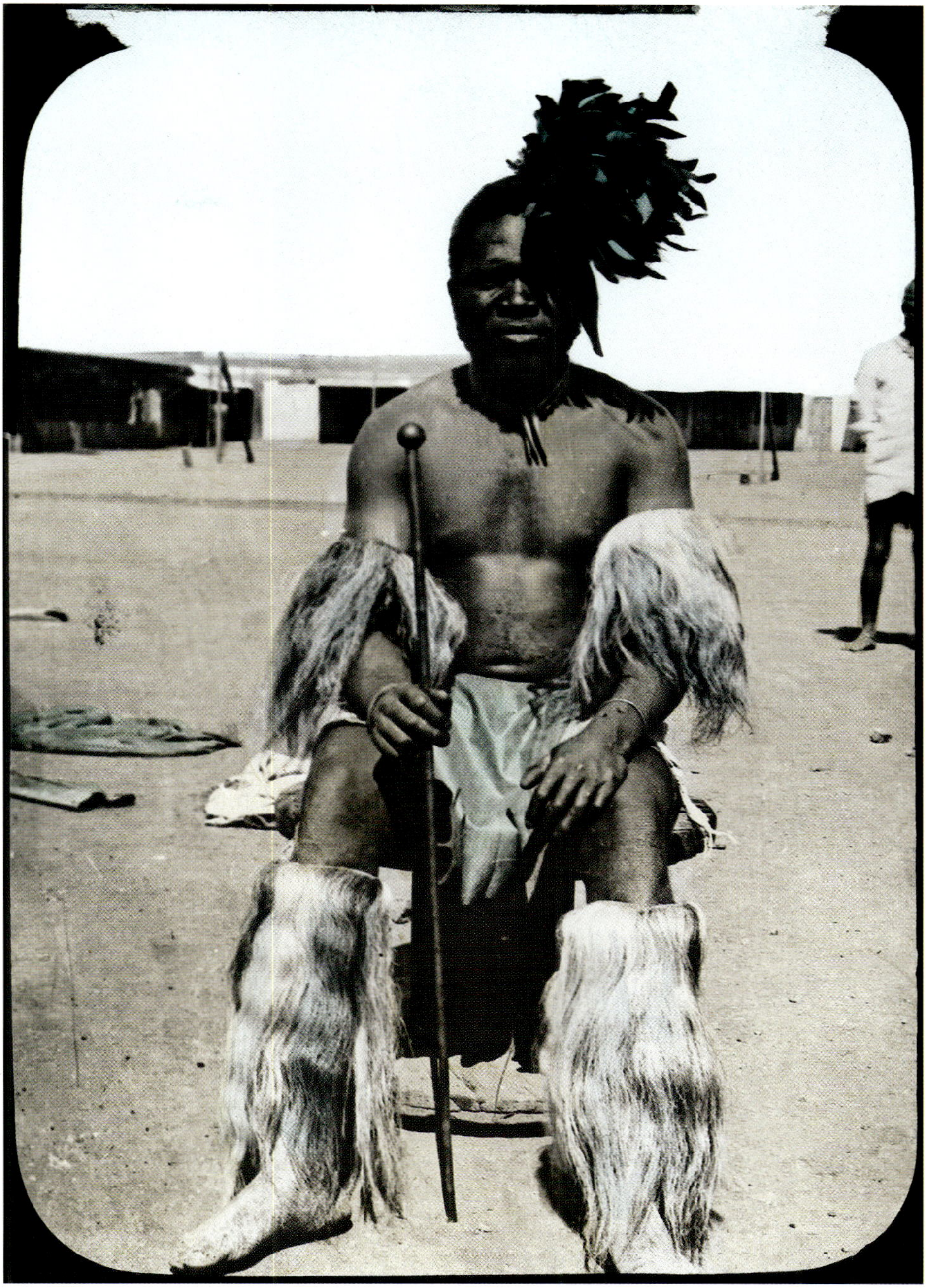

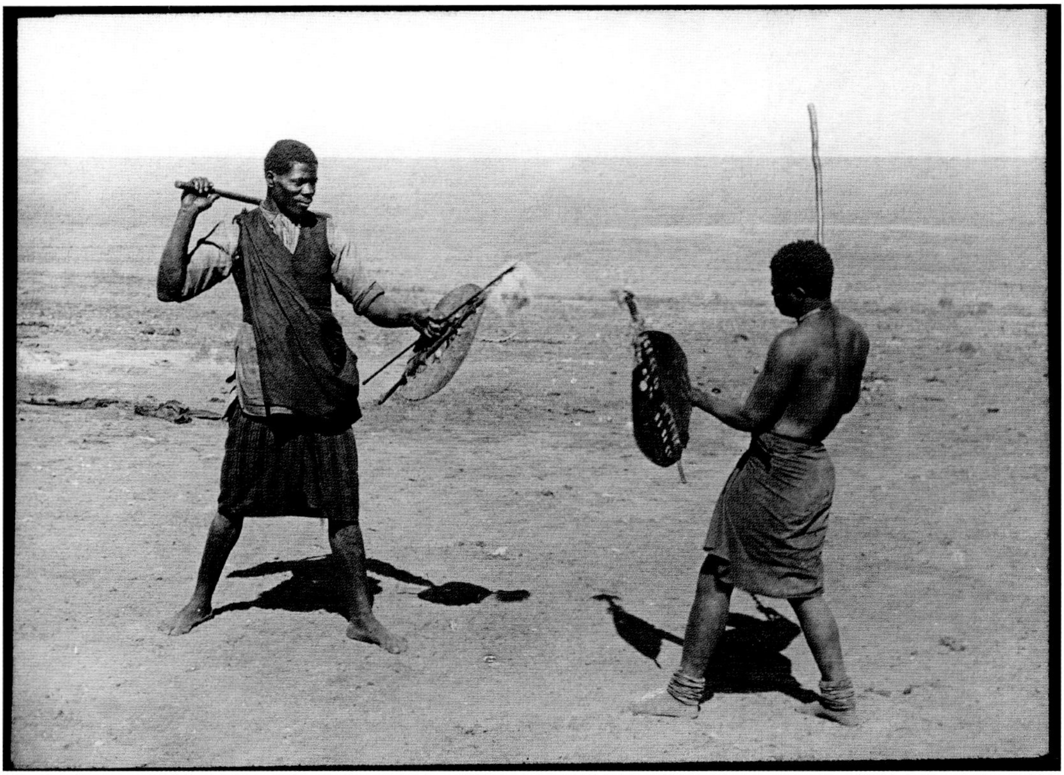

331 Warriors, South Africa, 1890s
332 Transports Crossing, The Vaal River at Viljoen's Drift, South Africa, 1890s

331 Krieger, Südafrika, 1890er Jahre
332 Übergangsstelle für Transporte, die Vaal bei Viljoensdrift, Südafrika, 1890er Jahre

331 Guerriers, Afrique du Sud, années 1890
332 Passage à gué de la rivière Vaal à Viljoen's Drift, Afrique du Sud, années 1890

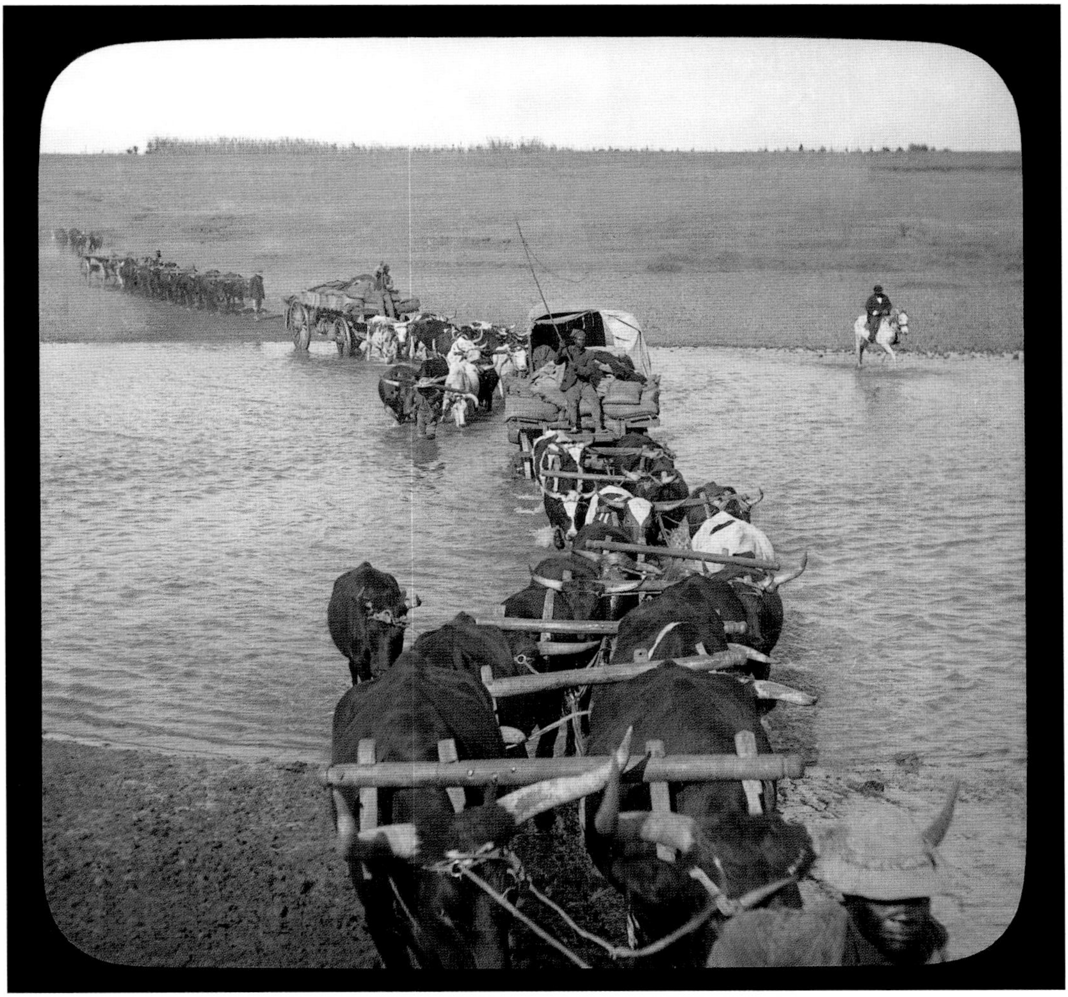

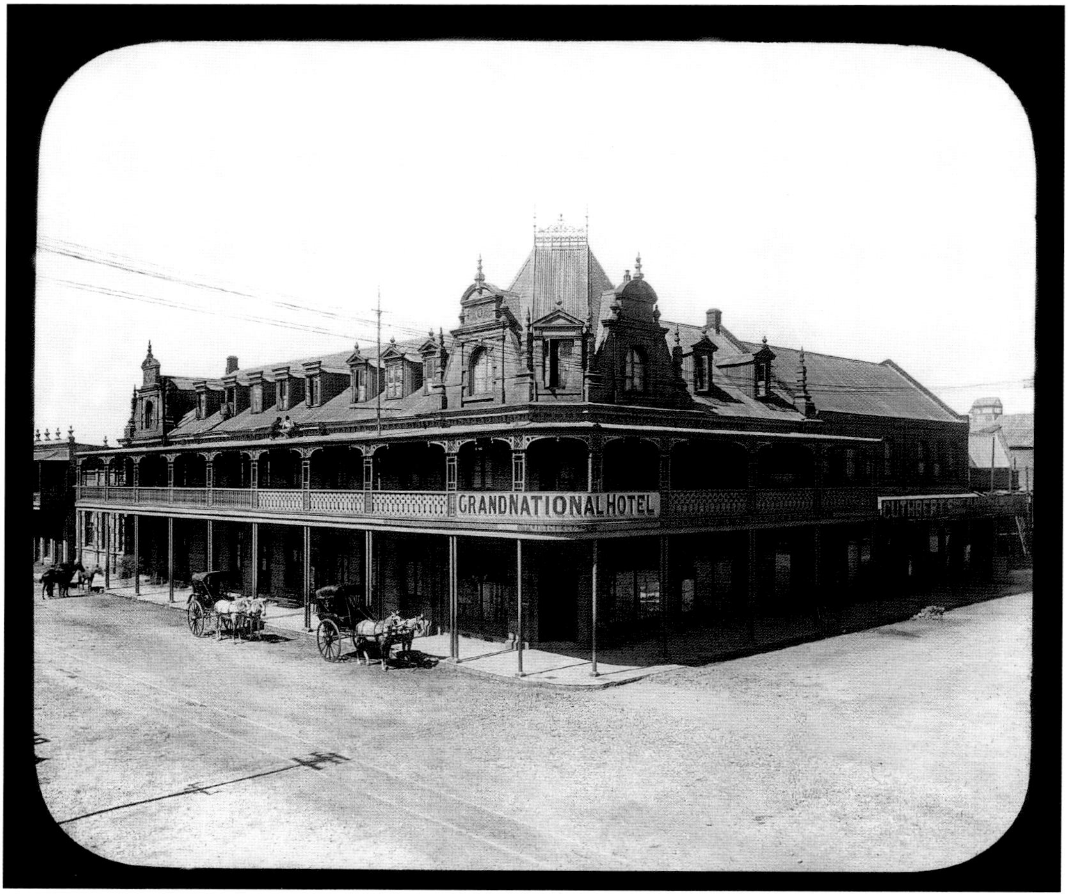

333 Grand National Hotel, Johannesburg, South Africa, 1890s
334 South African Light Horse Regiment, Cape Town, South Africa, 1900s

333 Das Grand-National-Hotel, Johannesburg, Südafrika, 1890er Jahre
334 Das Regiment der Südafrikanischen Leichten Kavallerie, Kapstadt, Südafrika, 1900er Jahre

333 Grand National Hotel, Johannesburg, Afrique du Sud, années 1890
334 Régiment de cavalerie légère, Le Cap, Afrique du Sud, années 1900

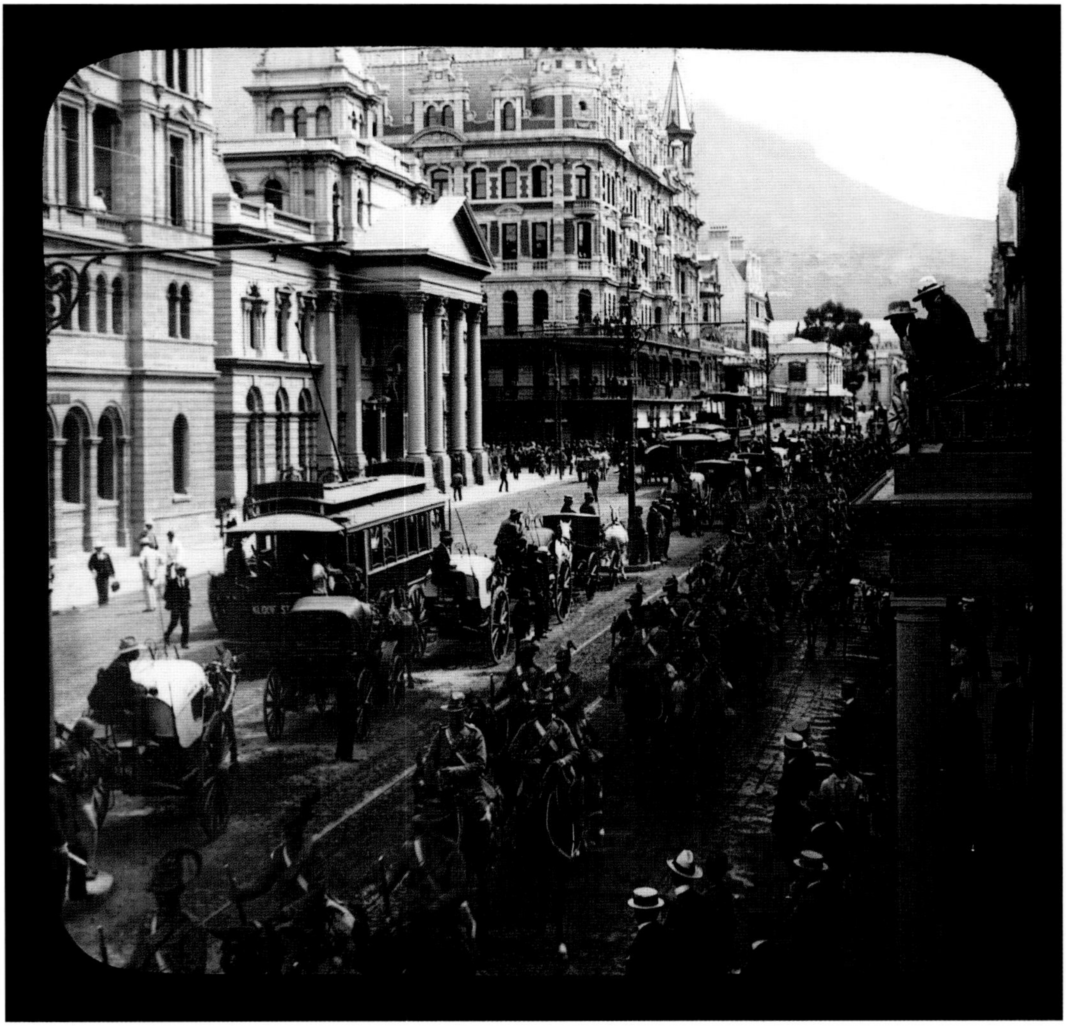

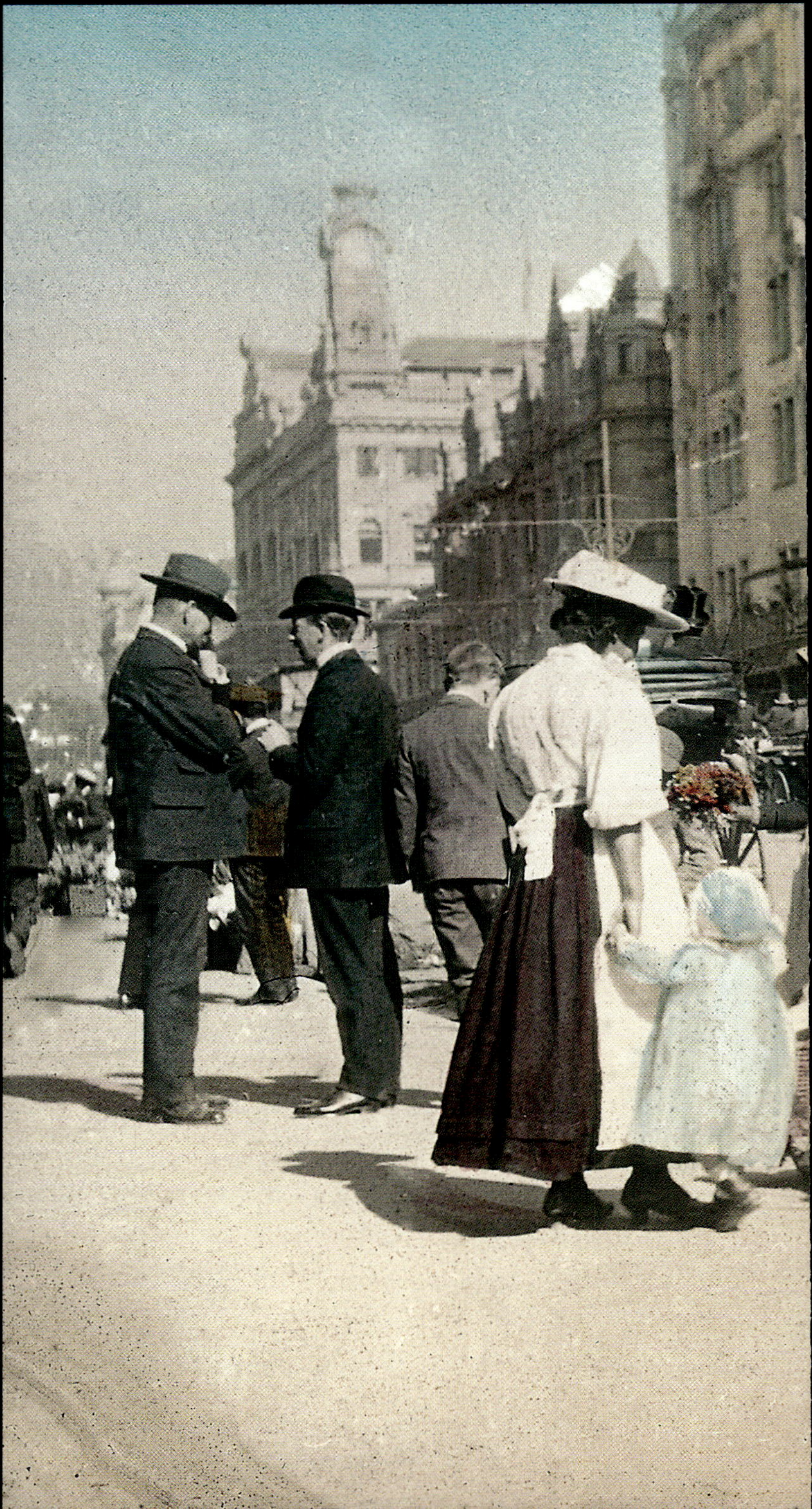

335 Flower sellers on Adderley Street, Cape Town, South Africa, 1900s

335 Blumenverkäufer in der Adderley Street, Kapstadt, 1900er Jahre

335 Fleuristes sur Adderley Street, Le Cap, Afrique du Sud, années 1900

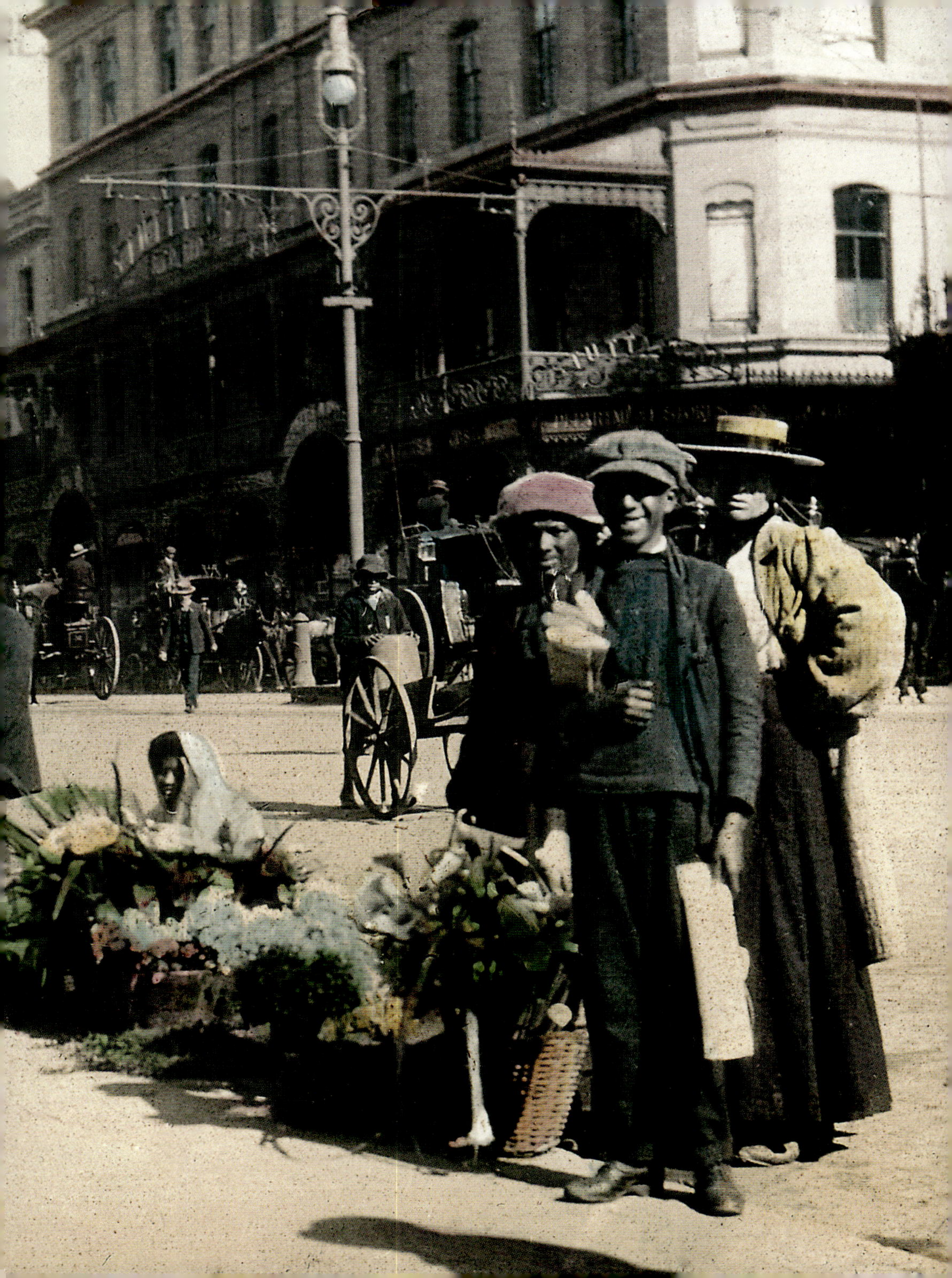

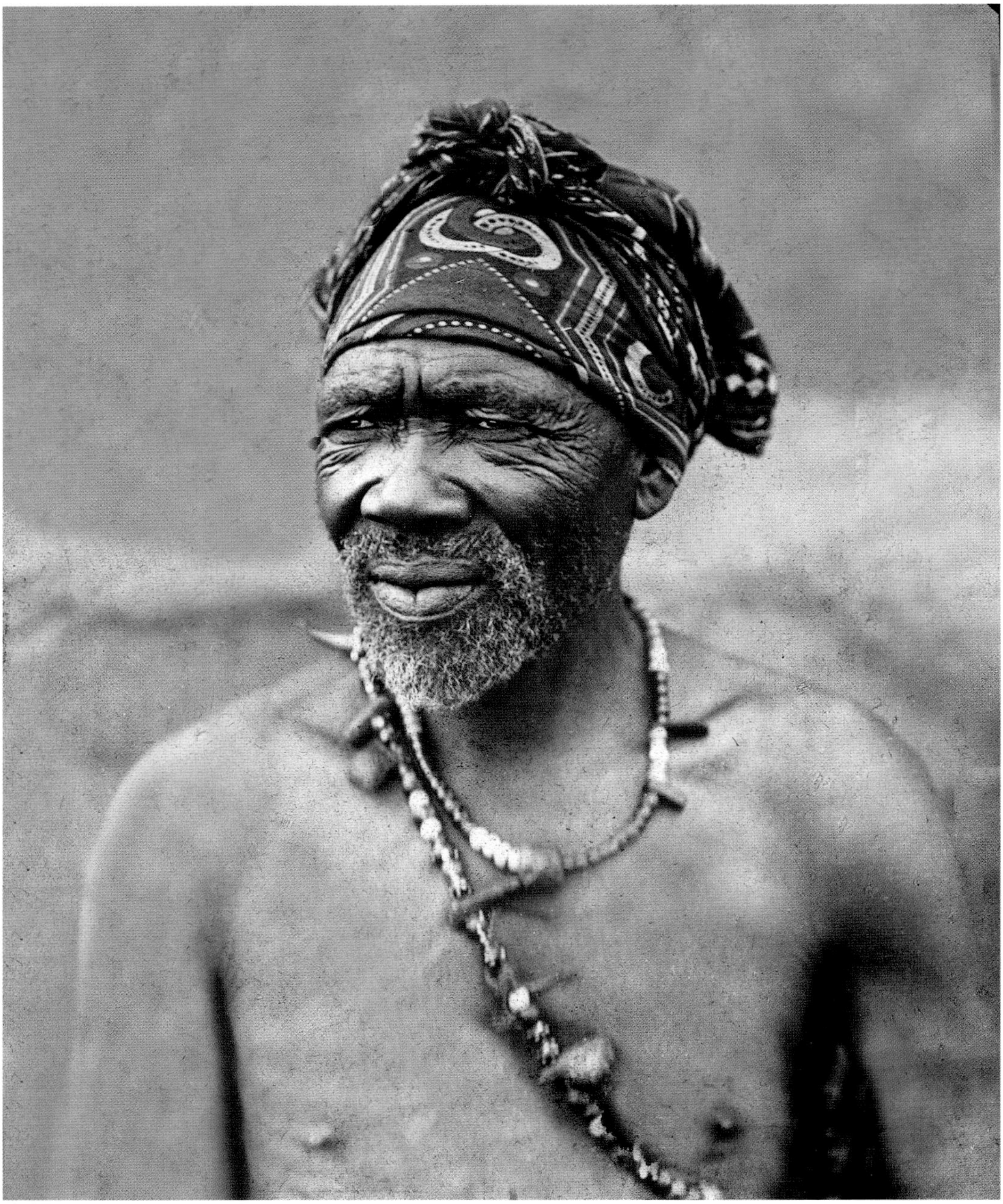

336 Medicine man, Africa, 1890s
337 Zulu girl, South Africa, 1900s

336 Medizinmann, Afrika, 1890er Jahre
337 Zulu-Mädchen, Südafrika, 1900er Jahre

336 Guérisseur, Afrique, années 1890
337 Jeune fille zoulou, Afrique du Sud, années 1900

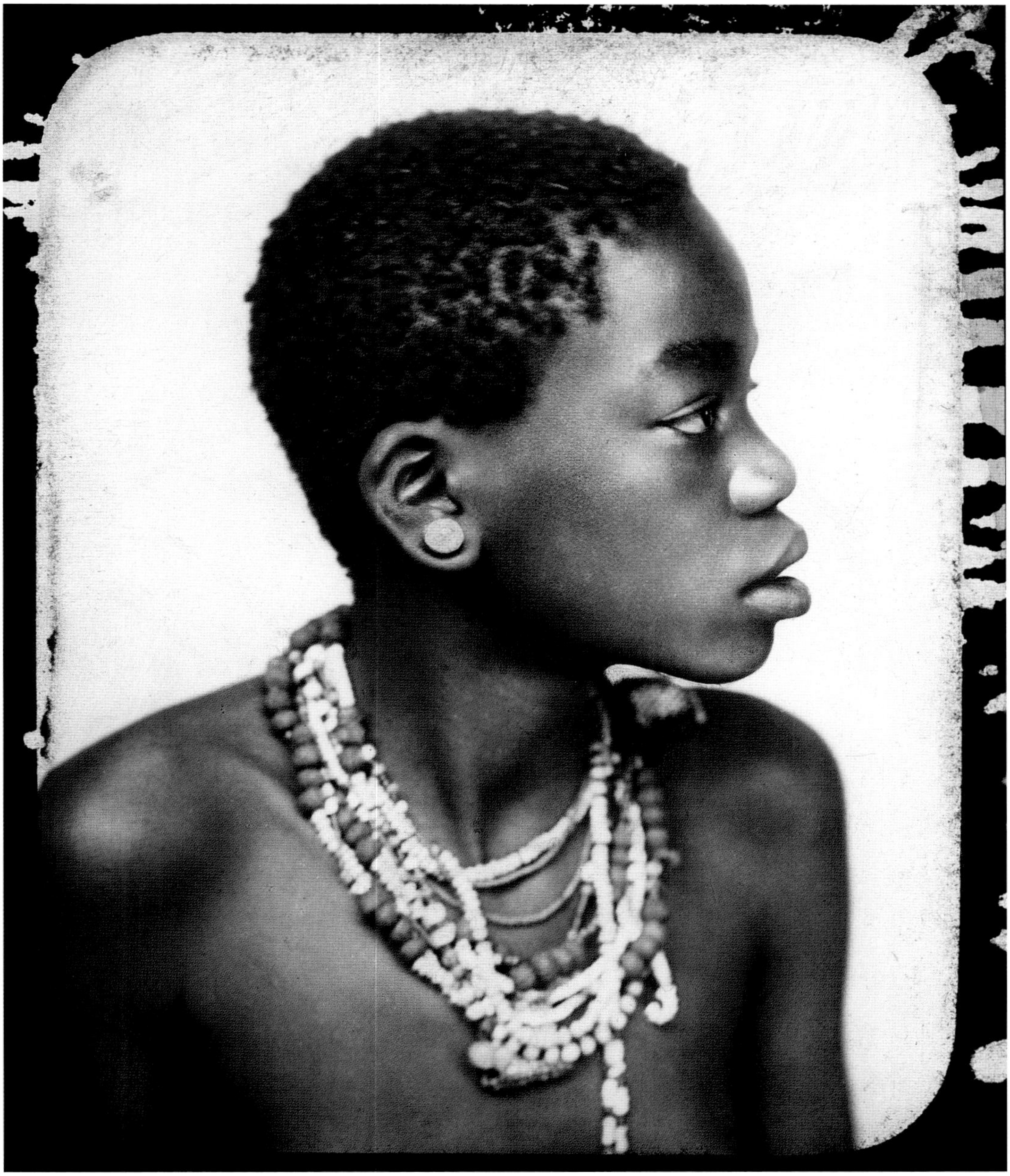

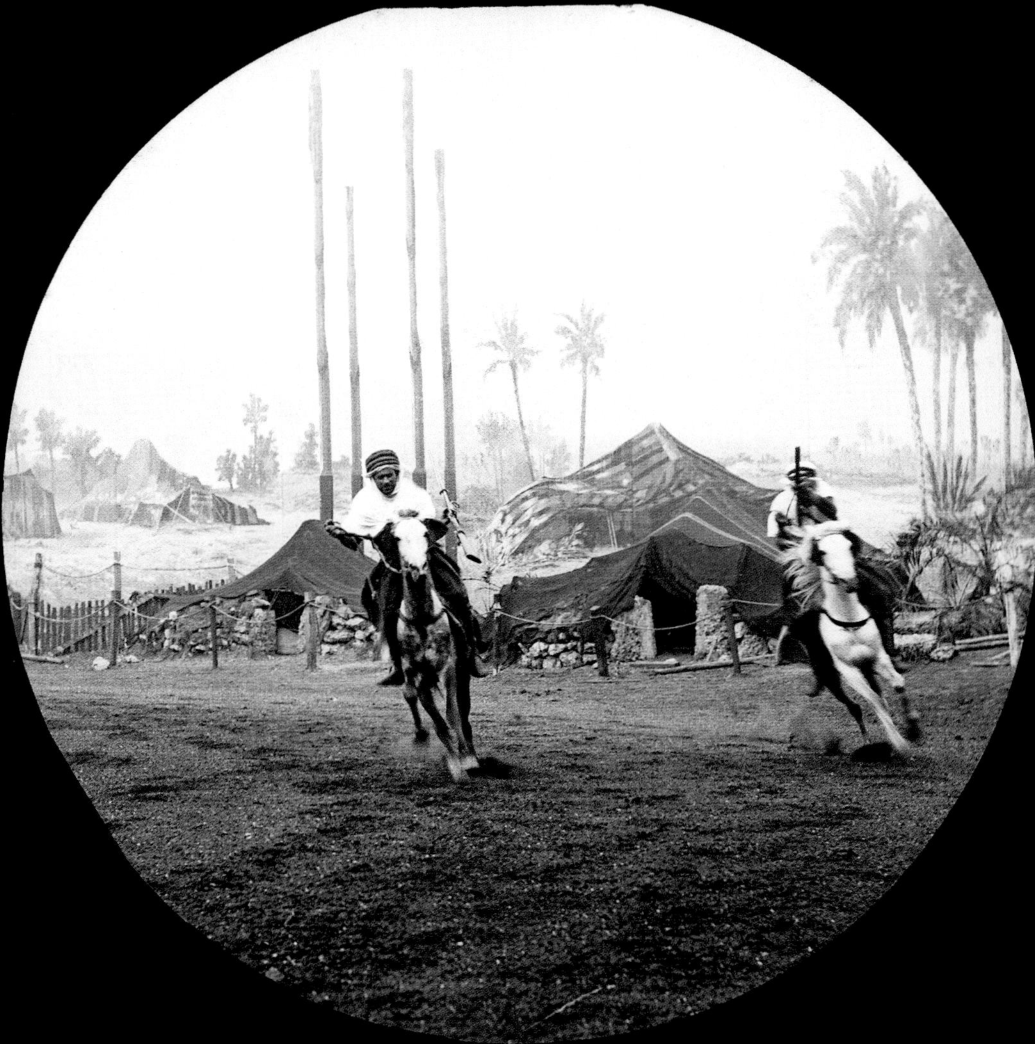

338 Arab horsemen racing, 1880s

338 Arabische Reiter beim Wettrennen, 1880er Jahre

338 Course de chevaux arabes, années 1880

THE MIDDLE EAST

NAHER OSTEN · MOYEN-ORIENT

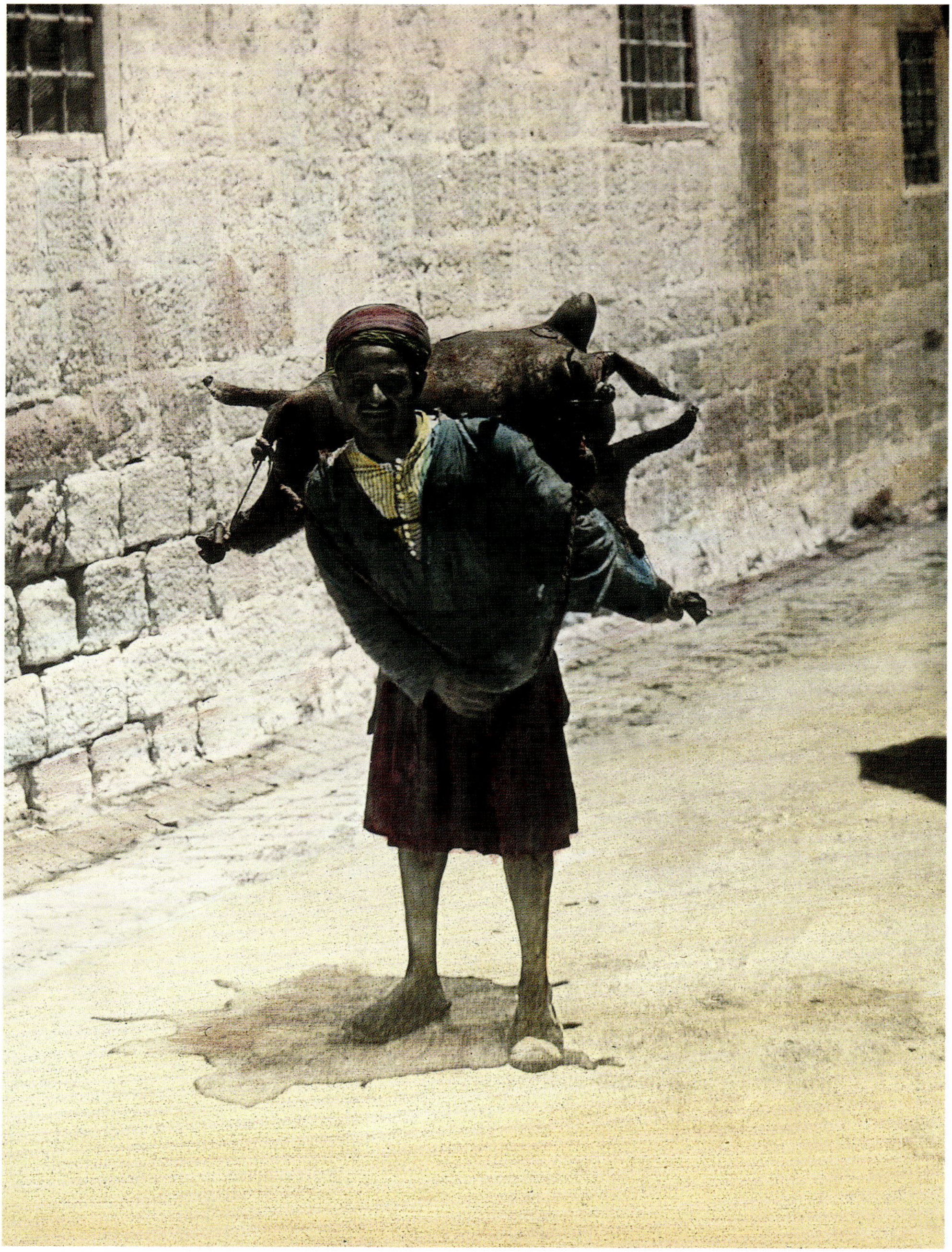

339 A water carrier, Jerusalem, Palestine (now Israel), 1890s

339 Ein Wasserträger, Jerusalem, Palästina (heute Israel), 1890er Jahre

339 Porteur d'eau, Jérusalem, Palestine (auj. Israël), années 1890

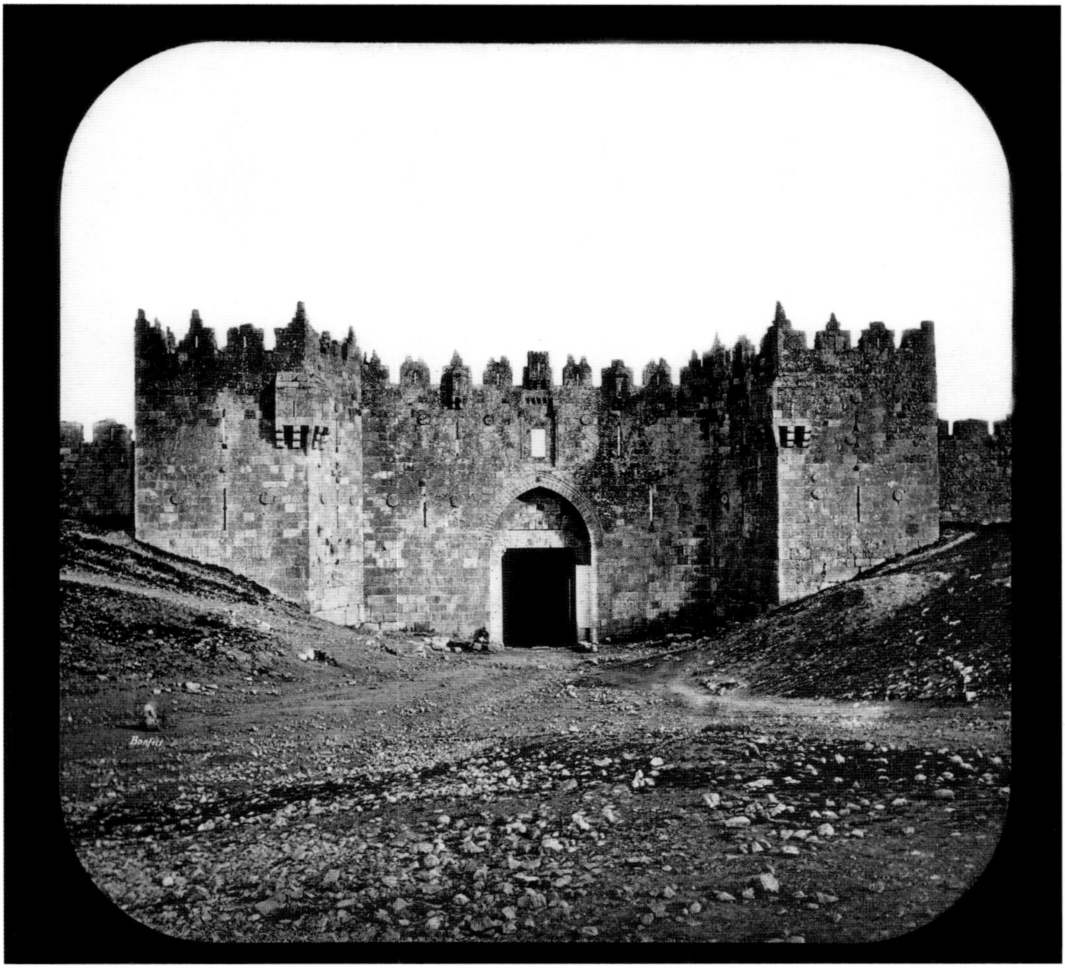

340 The Damascus Gate, Jerusalem, Palestine (now Israel), 1870s

340 Das Damaskustor, Jerusalem, Palästina (heute Israel), 1870er Jahre

340 La porte de Damas, Jérusalem, Palestine (auj. Israël), années 1870

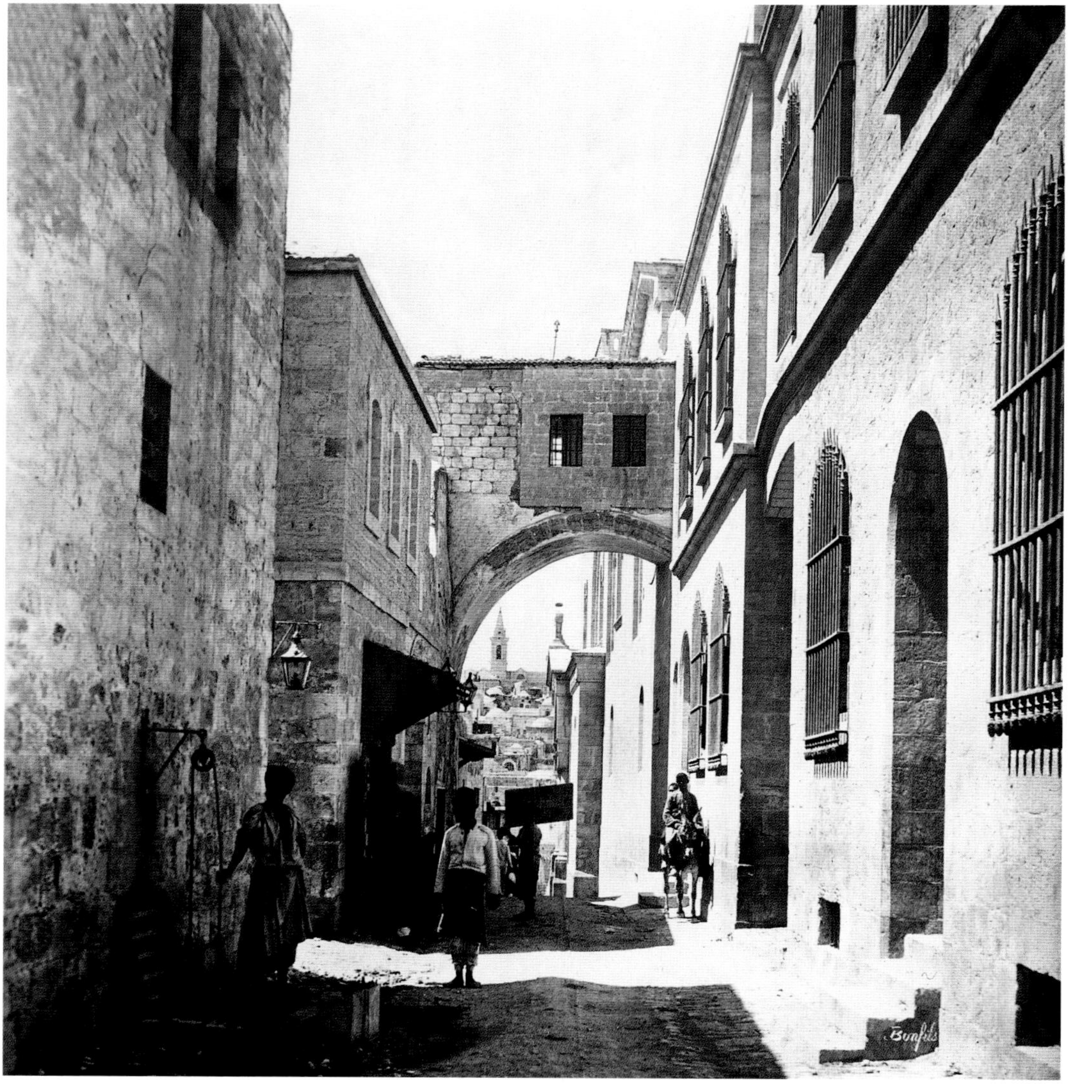

341 Ecce Homo Arch, Via Dolorosa, Jerusalem, Palestine (now Israel), 1890s

341 Der Ecce-Homo-Bogen, Via Dolorosa, Jerusalem, Palästina (heute Israel), 1890er Jahre

341 Arche "Ecce Homo", Via Dolorosa, Jérusalem, Palestine (auj. Israël), années 1890

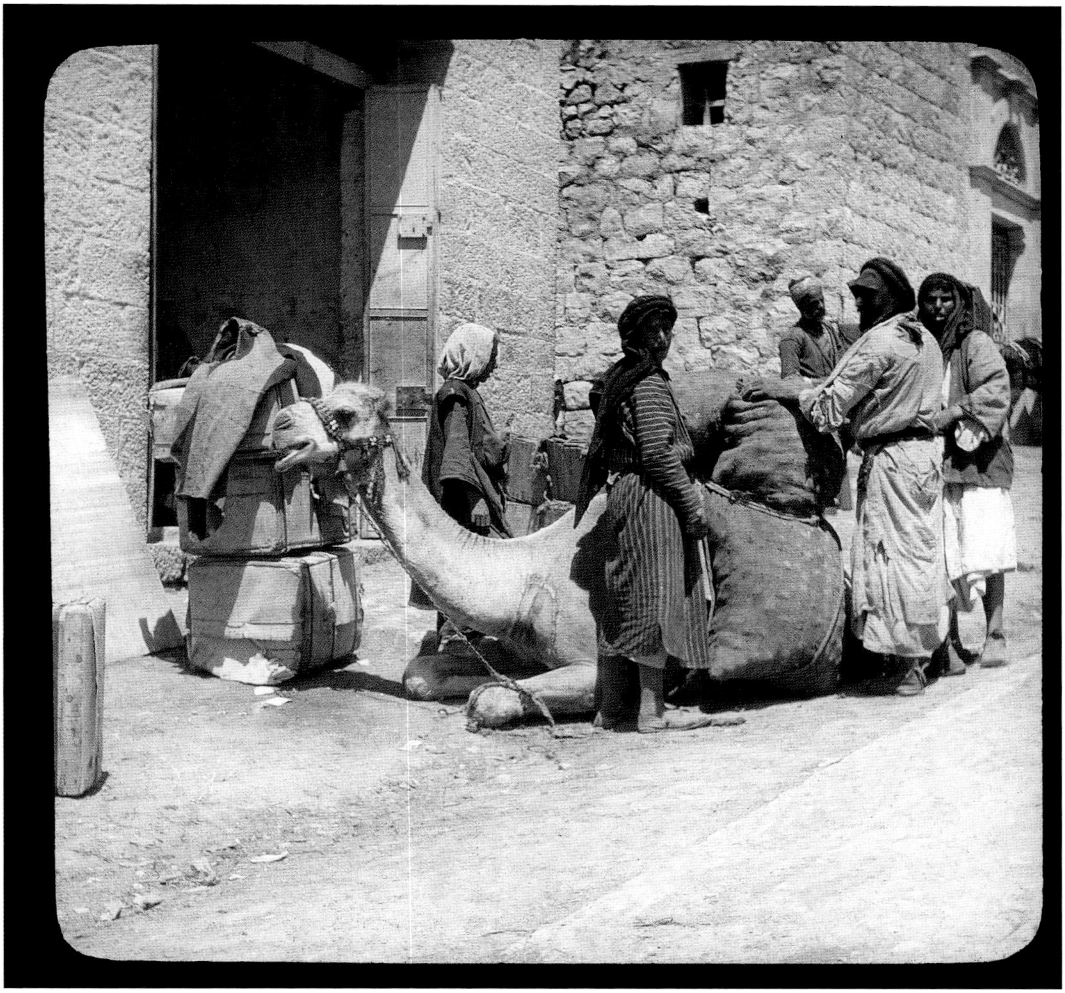

342 “Loading camels, The Holy Land”, Palestine, 1890s

342 „Das Beladen von Kamelen, Das Heilige Land“, Palästina, 1890er Jahre

342 Chargement d’un dromadaire, Terre Sainte, Palestine, années 1890

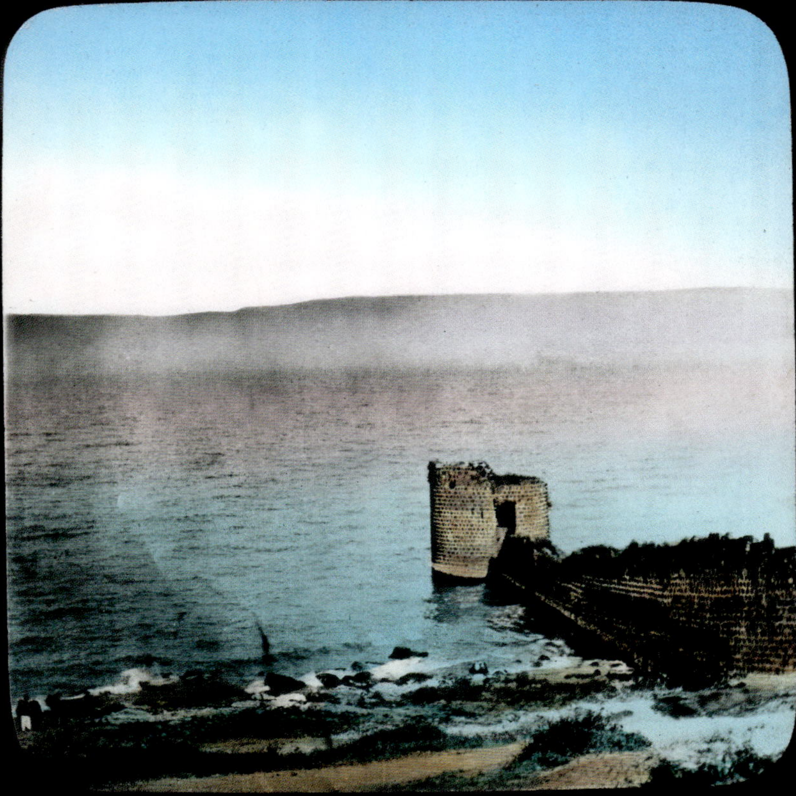

343 The Sea of Galilee, viewed from Tiberias, Palestine (now Israel), 1910s

343 Der See von Genezareth, von Tiberias aus gesehen, Palästina (heute Israel), 1910er Jahre

343 Mer de Galilée vue de Tibériade, Palestine (auj. Israël), années 1910

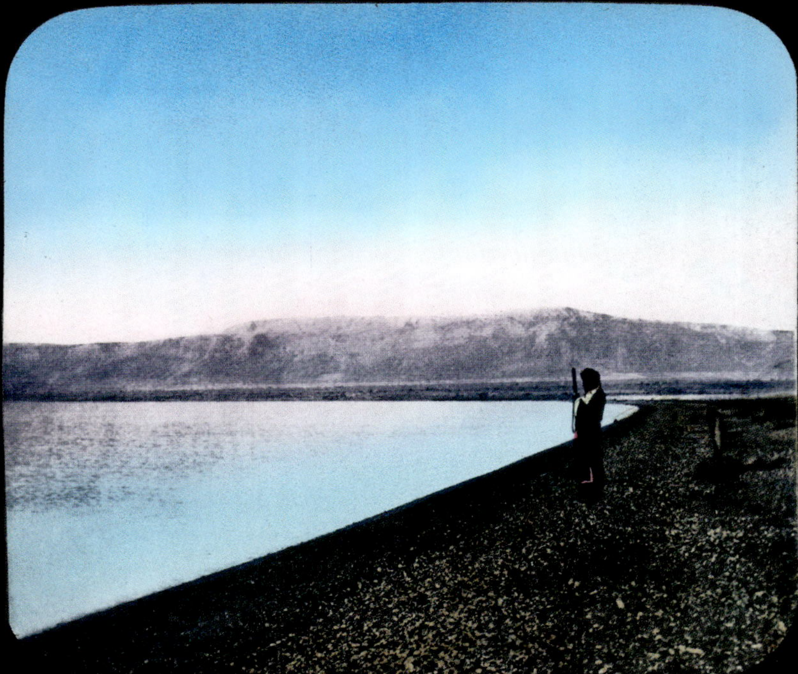

344 The Dead Sea, Palestine (now Israel), 1910s

344 Das Tote Meer, Palästina (heute Israel), 1910er Jahre

344 Mer Morte, Palestine (auj. Israël), années 1910

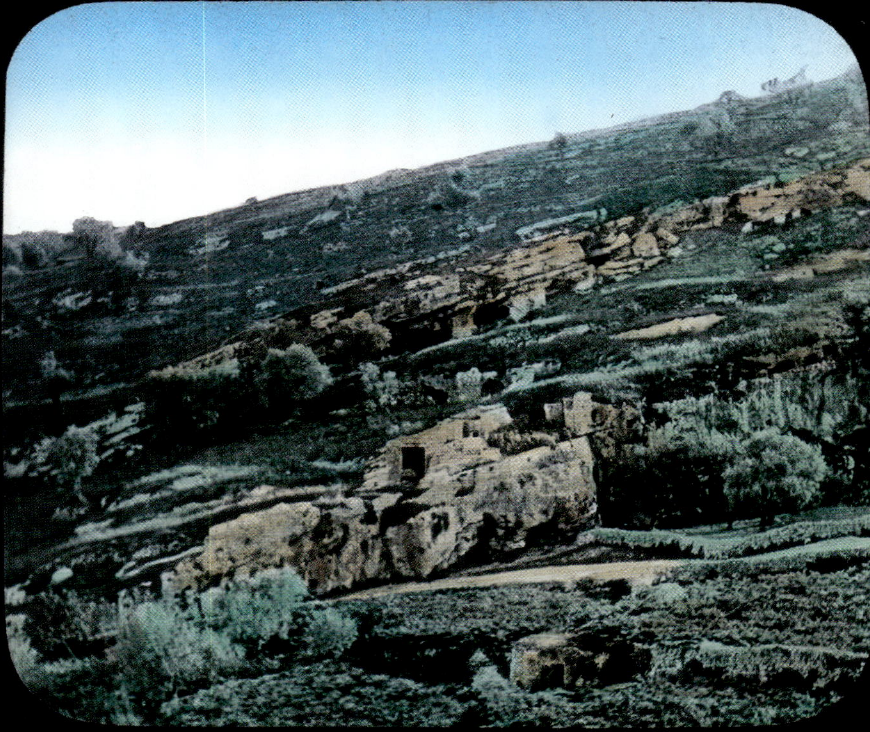

345 Aceldama (The Field of Blood), Jerusalem, Palestine (now Israel), 1910s

345 Acheldamach (Der Blutacker), Jerusalem, Palästina (heute Israel), 1910er Jahre

345 Aceldama (le champ du sang), Jérusalem, Palestine (auj. Israël), années 1910

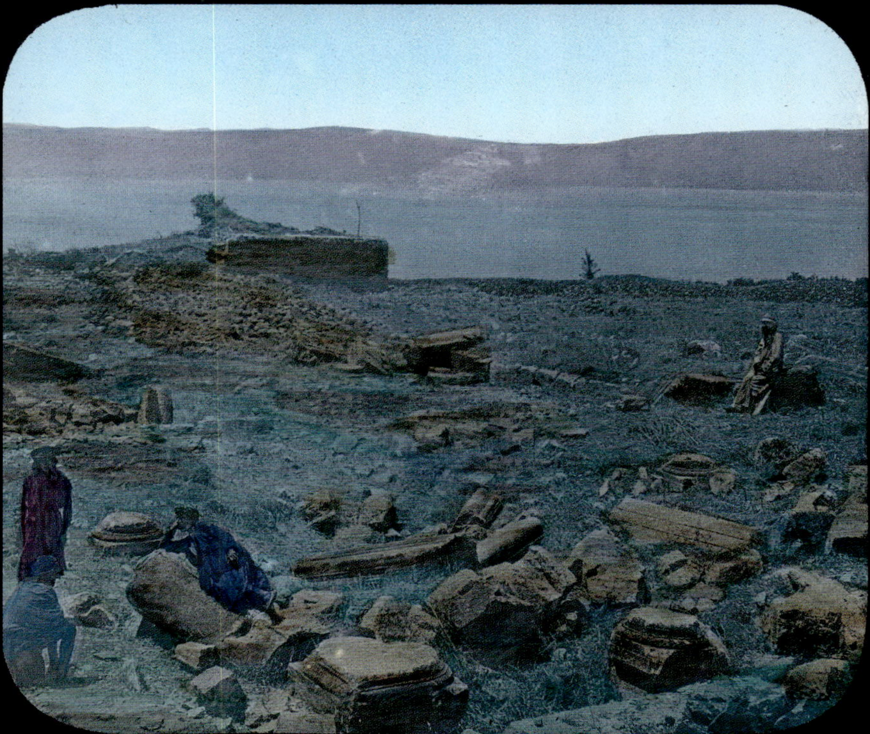

346 The Sea of Galilee, Palestine (now Israel), 1910s

346 Der See von Genezareth, Palästina (heute Israel), 1910er Jahre

346 Mer de Galilée, Palestine (auj. Israël), années 1910

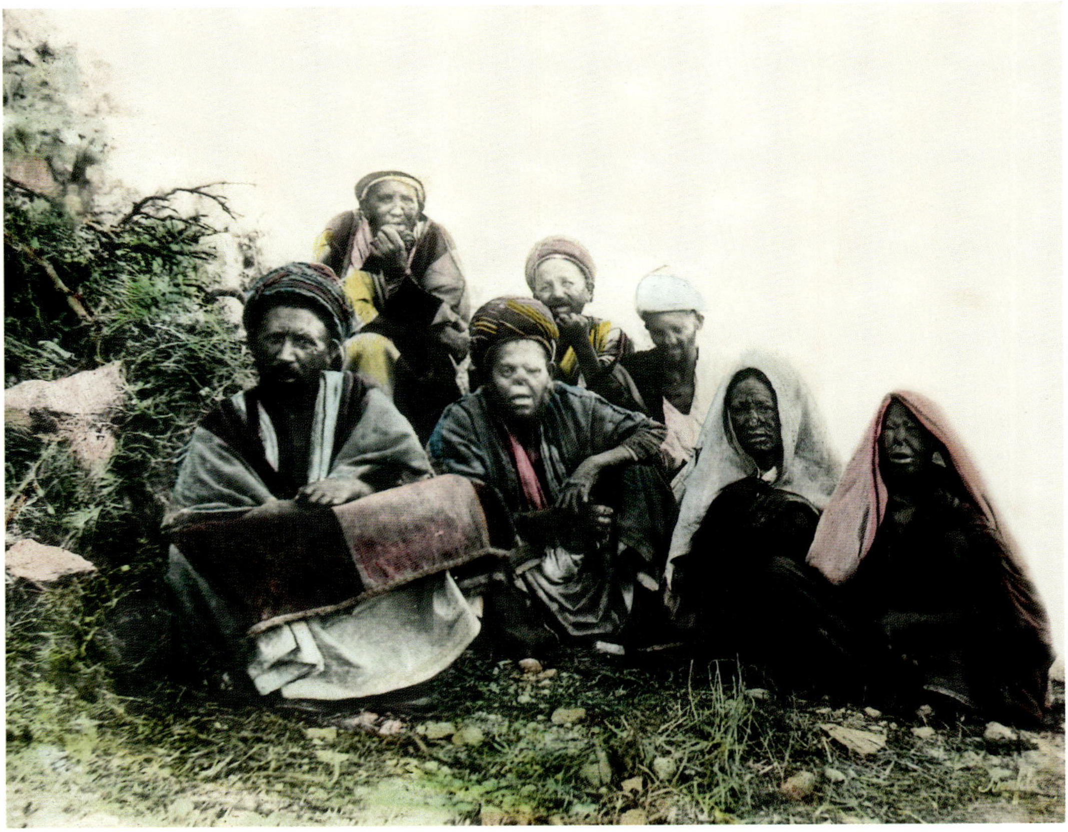

347 Group of lepers in Jerusalem, Palestine (now Israel), 1890s
348 Bedouin chiefs in Jericho, Palestine, 1890s

347 Gruppe von Leprakranken in Jerusalem, Palästina (heute Israel), 1890er Jahre
348 Beduinen-Häuptlinge in Jericho, Palästina, 1890er Jahre

347 Groupe de lépreux à Jérusalem, Palestine (auj. Israël), années 1890
348 Chefs bédouins à Jéricho, Palestine, années 1890

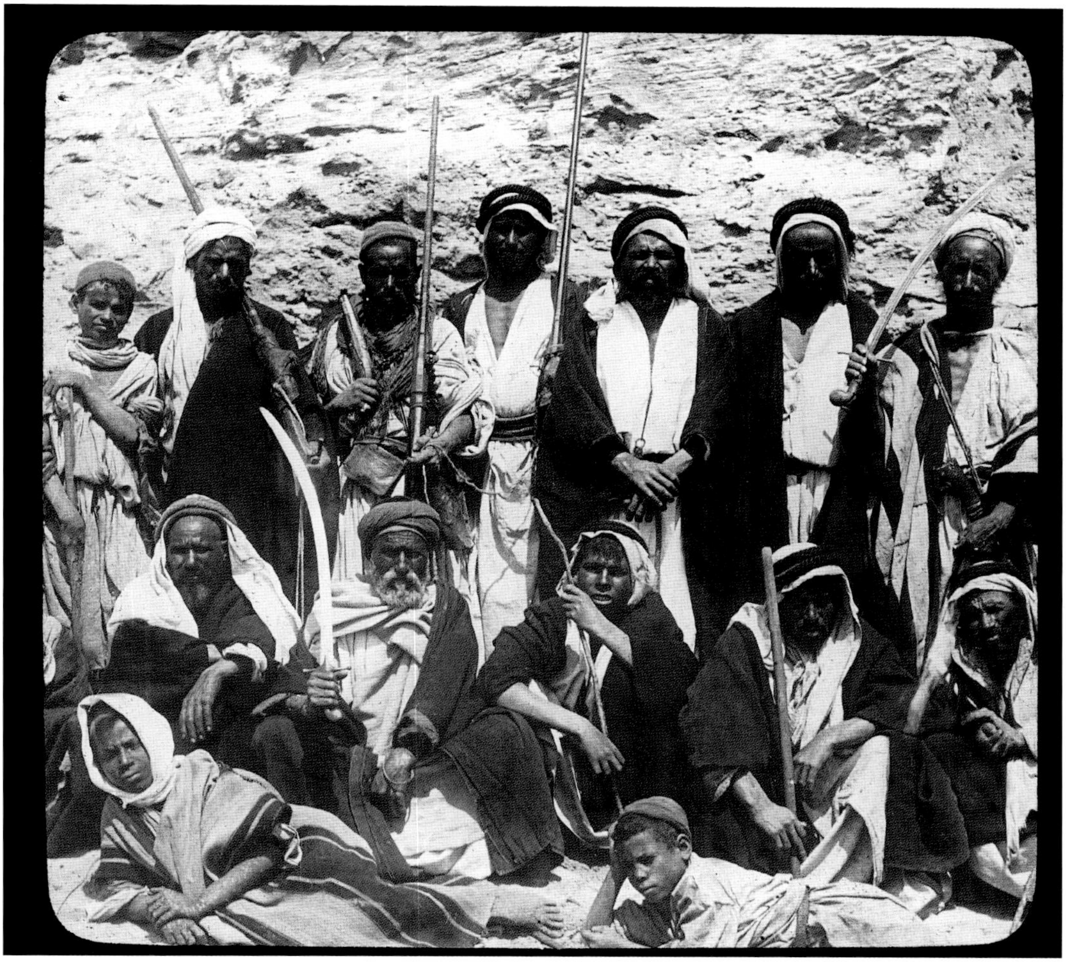

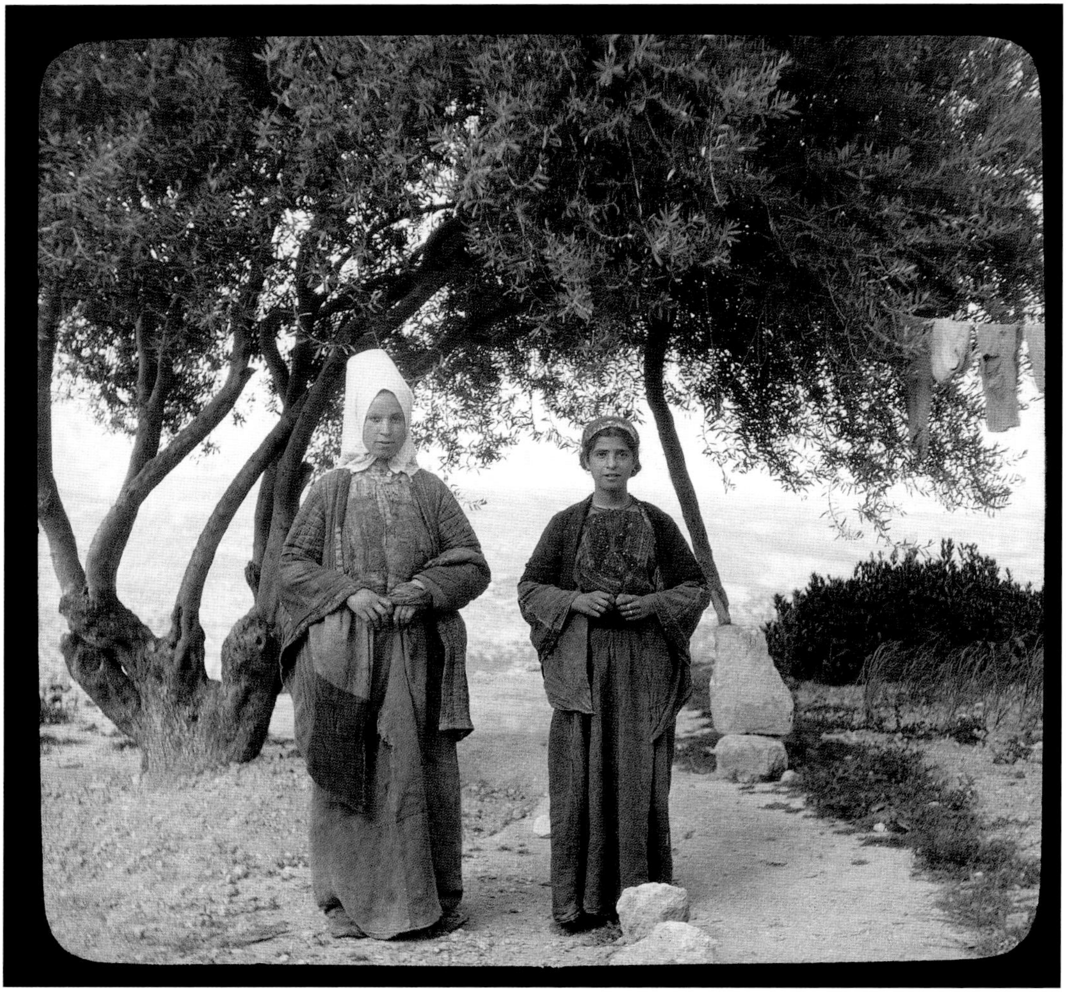

349 Girls in traditional costume, Bethlehem, Palestine, 1890s

349 Mädchen in traditioneller Kleidung, Bethlehem, Palästina, 1890er Jahre

349 Jeunes filles en costume traditionnel, Bethléhem, Palestine, années 1890

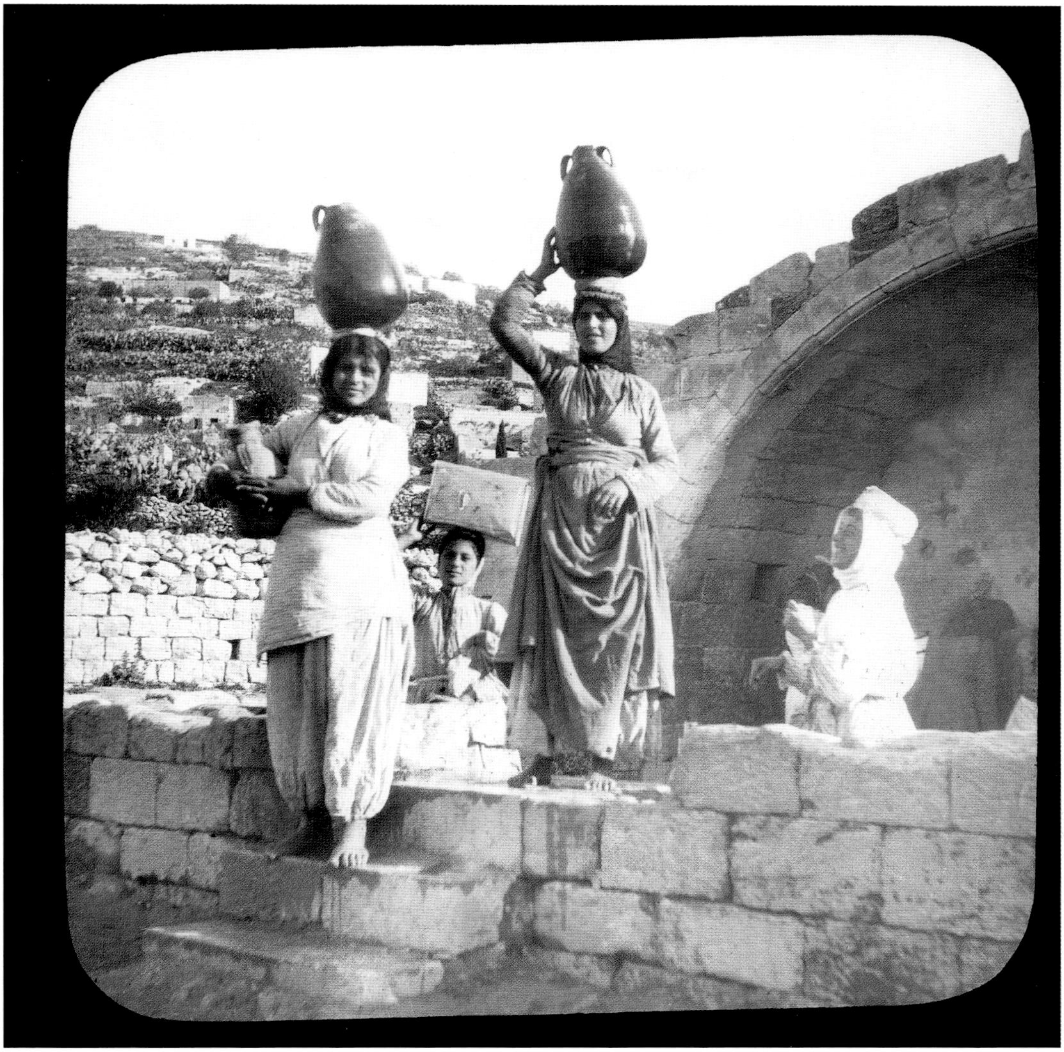

350 "Women with pitchers, The Holy Land", Palestine, 1890s

350 „Frauen mit Krügen, Das Heilige Land", Palästina, 1890er Jahre

350 Femmes portant des jarres, Terre Sainte, Palestine, années 1890

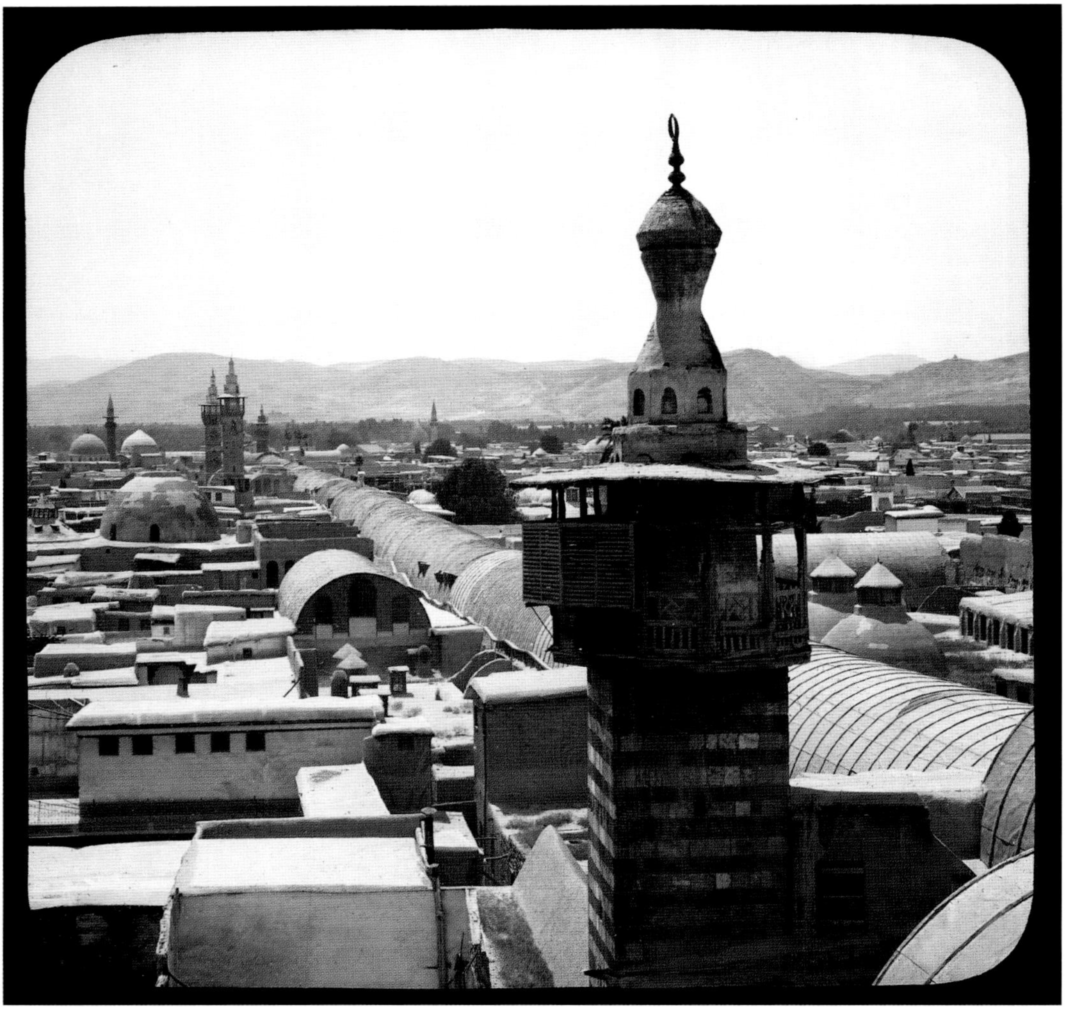

351 View over the roofs of Damascus, Syria, c.1900
352 Shoeing a buffalo, Tarsus, Syria, 1890s

351 Blick über die Dächer von Damaskus, Syrien, um 1900
352 Das Beschlagen eines Büffels, Tarsus, Syrien, 1890er Jahre

351 Vue des toits de Damas, Syrie, vers 1900
352 Ferrage d'un buffle à Tarsus, Syrie, années 1890

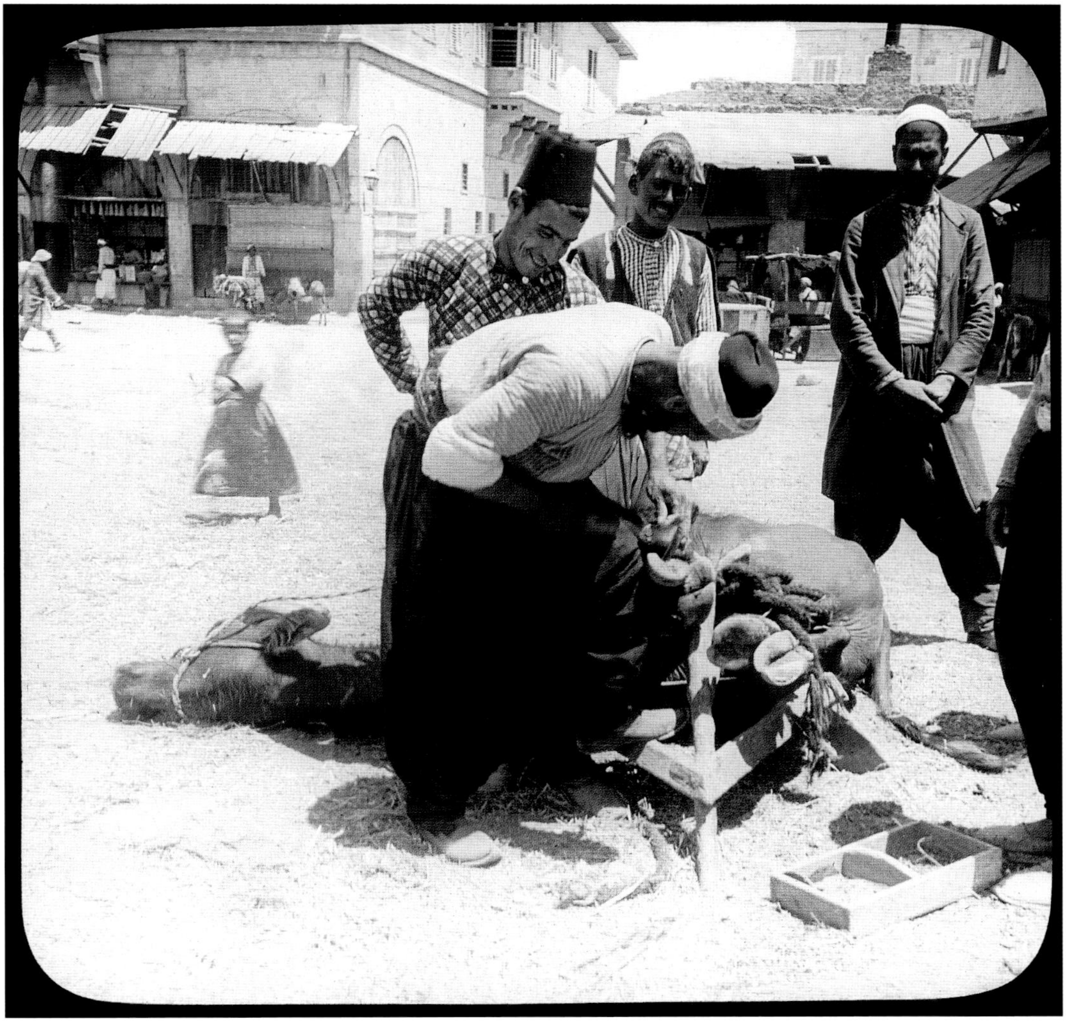

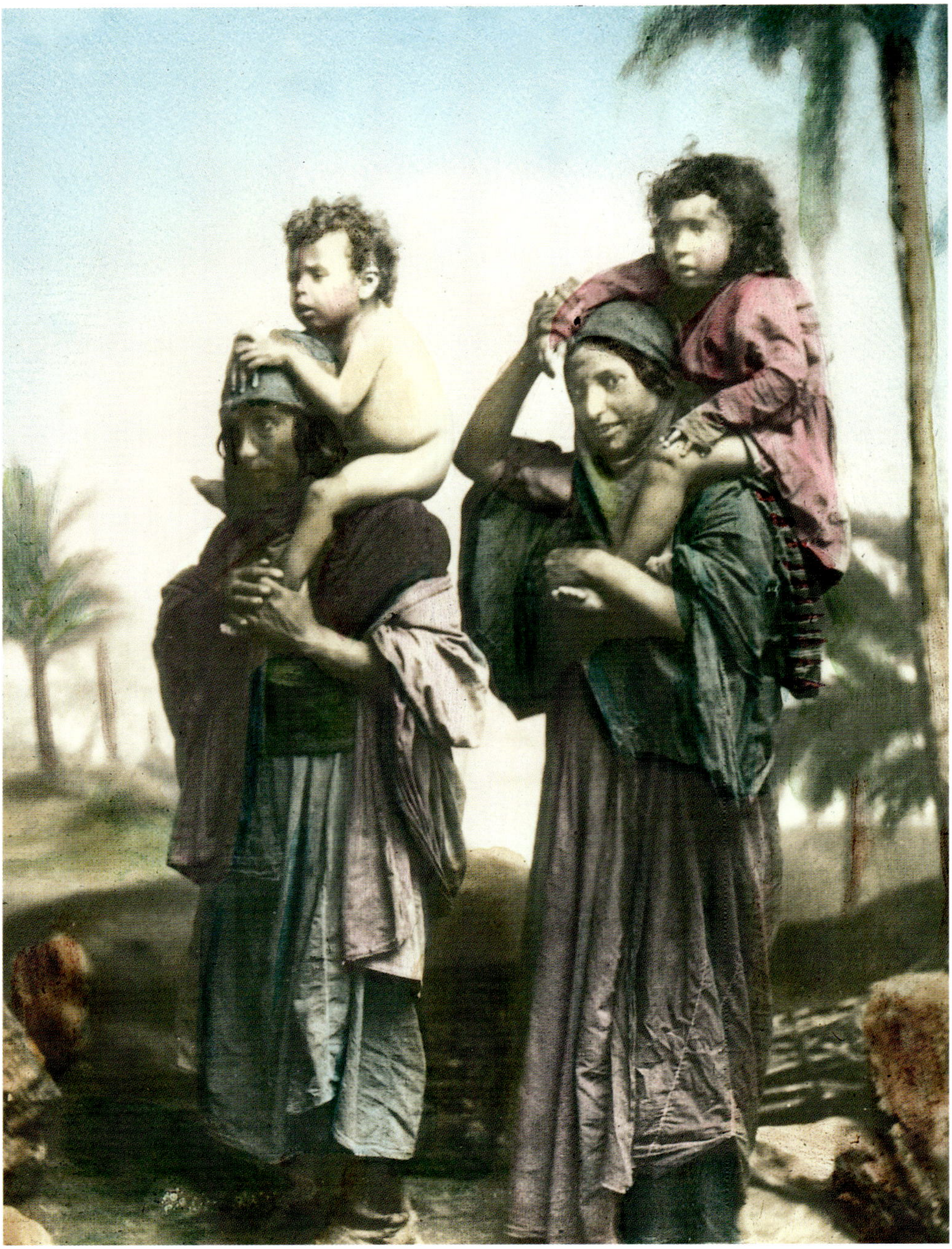

353 Bedouin women and children, Middle East, 1890s
354 Mirza Mohammed, Kurdish teacher and writer, 1890s

353 Beduinenfrauen und Kinder, Naher Osten, 1890er Jahre
354 Mirza Mohammed, kurdischer Lehrer und Autor, 1890er Jahre

353 Femmes et enfants bédouins, Moyen-Orient, années 1890
354 Mirza Mohammed, enseignant et écrivain kurde, années 1890

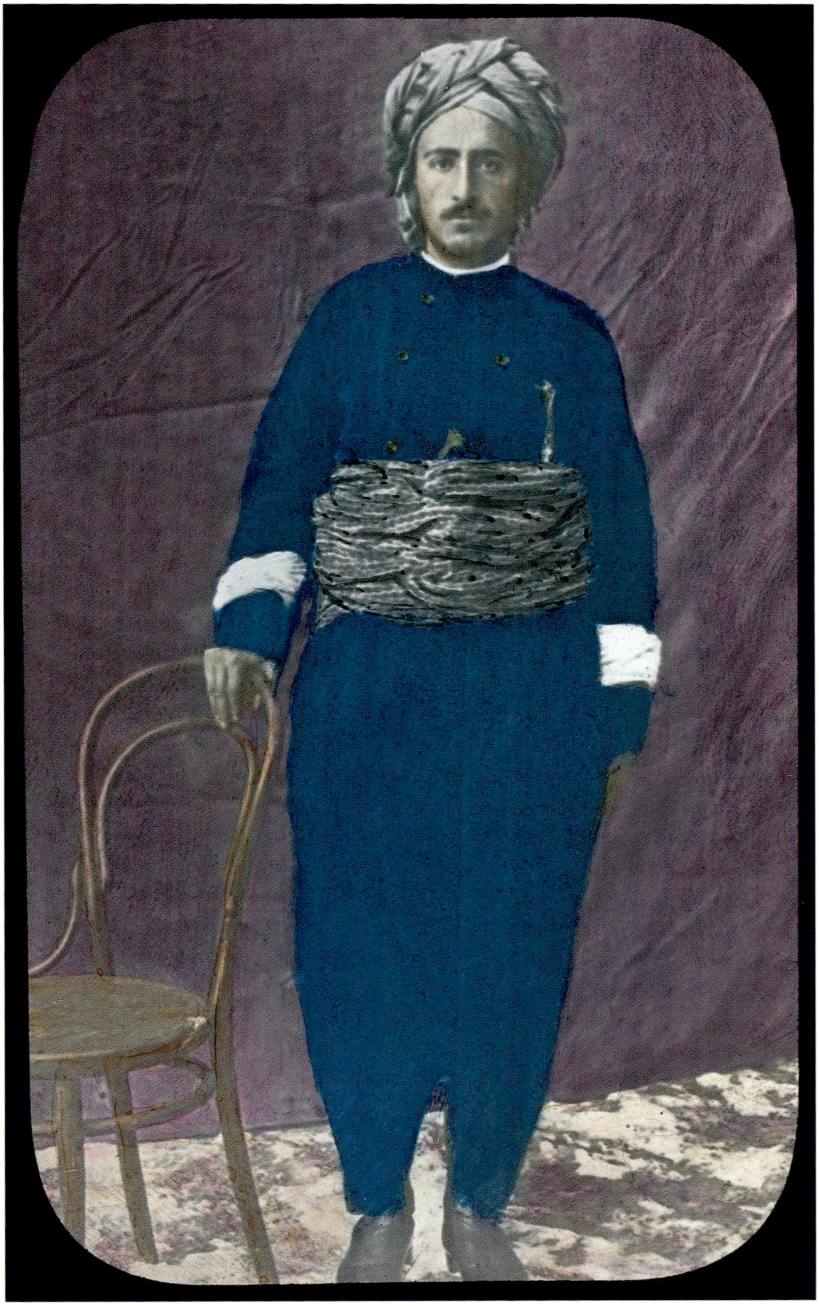

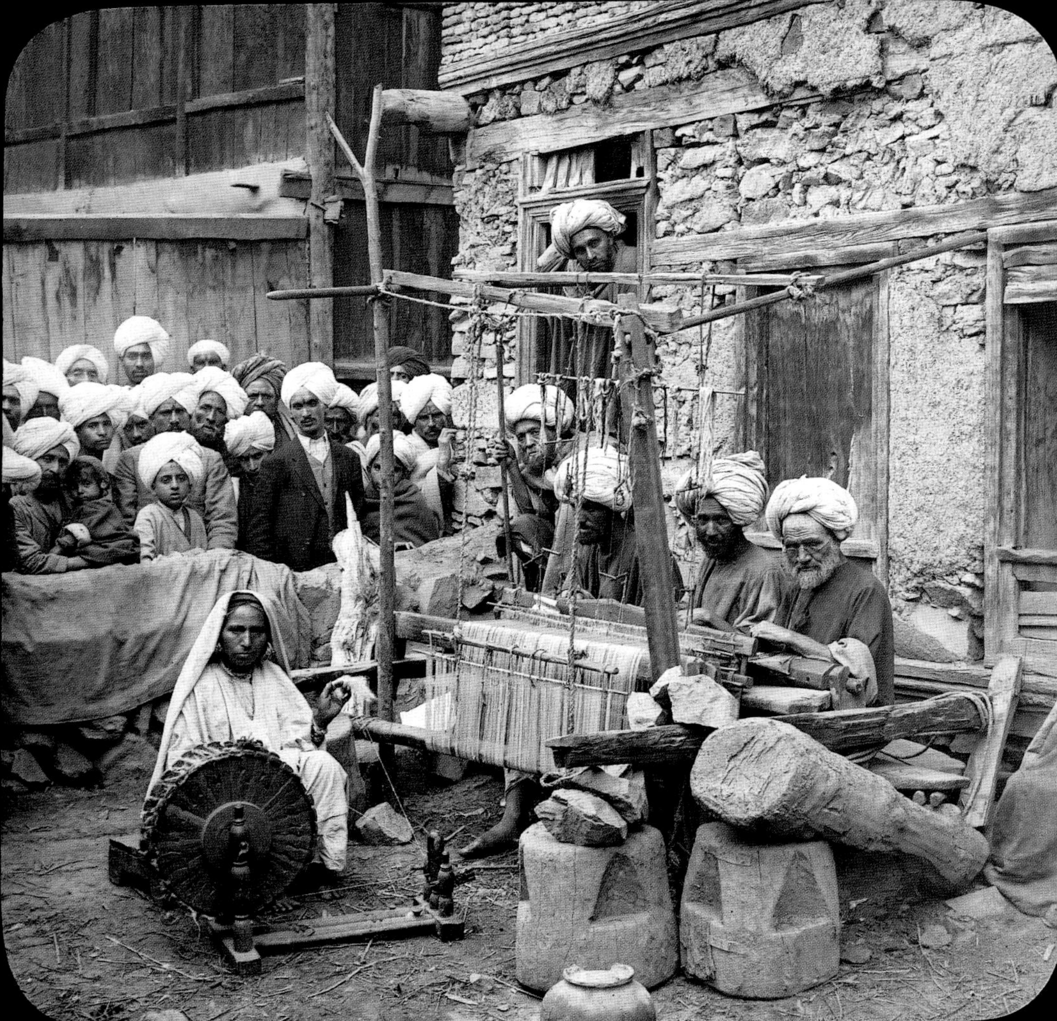

355 Spinning and weaving woollen shawls, Kashmir, 1880s

355 Spinnen und Weben von Wollschals, Kaschmir, 1880er Jahre

355 Filage et tissage des châles, Cachemire, années 1880

SOUTHERN ASIA

SÜDASIEN · ASIE DU SUD

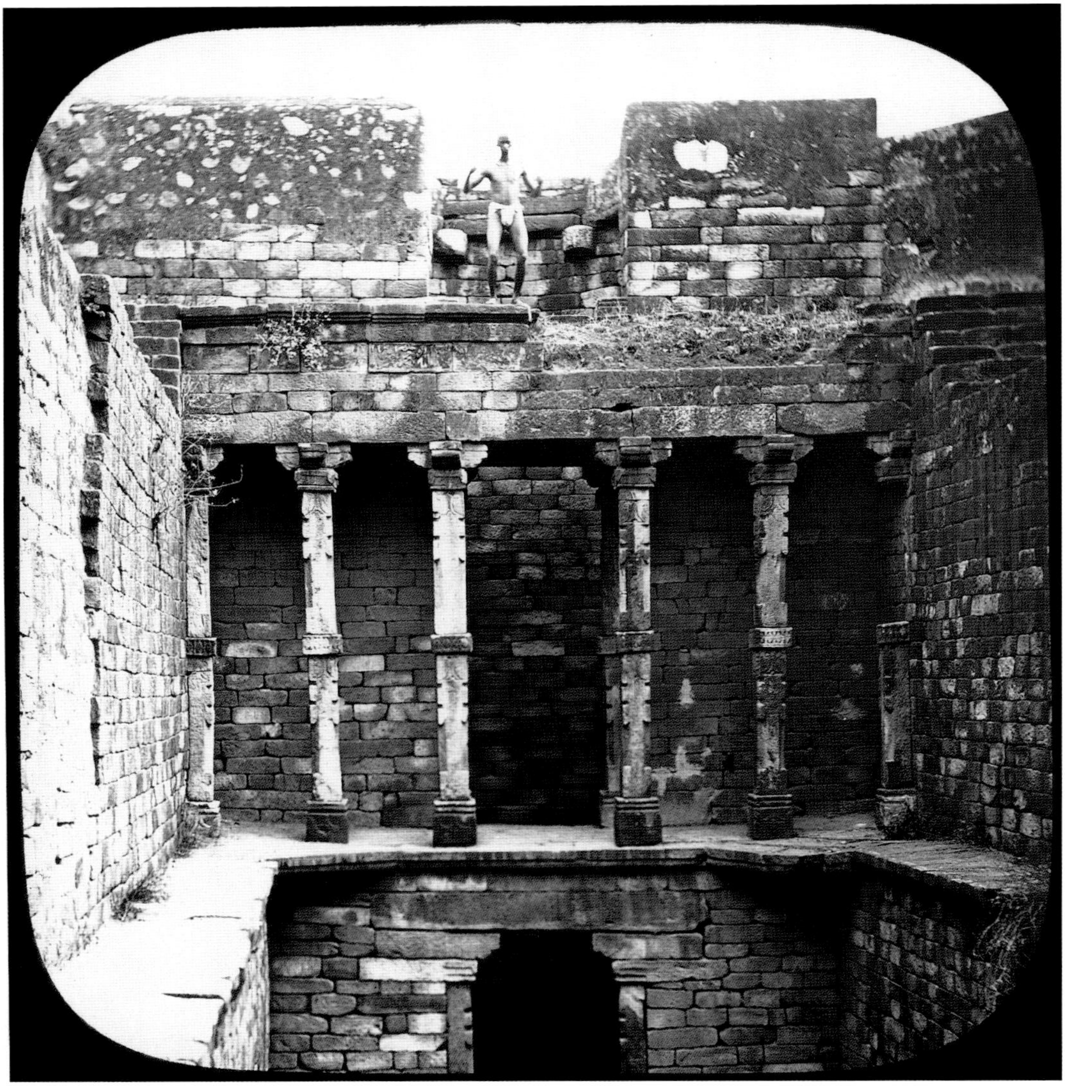

356 Diving Well at the Kootub, Delhi, India, 1870s, showing a man just about to take a plunge

356 Tauchbrunnen im Qutb-Komplex, Delhi, Indien, 1870er Jahre, abgebildet ist ein Mann kurz vor dem Sprung

356 Bassin-citerne à Kootub, Delhi, Inde, années 1870. Un homme s'apprête à plonger

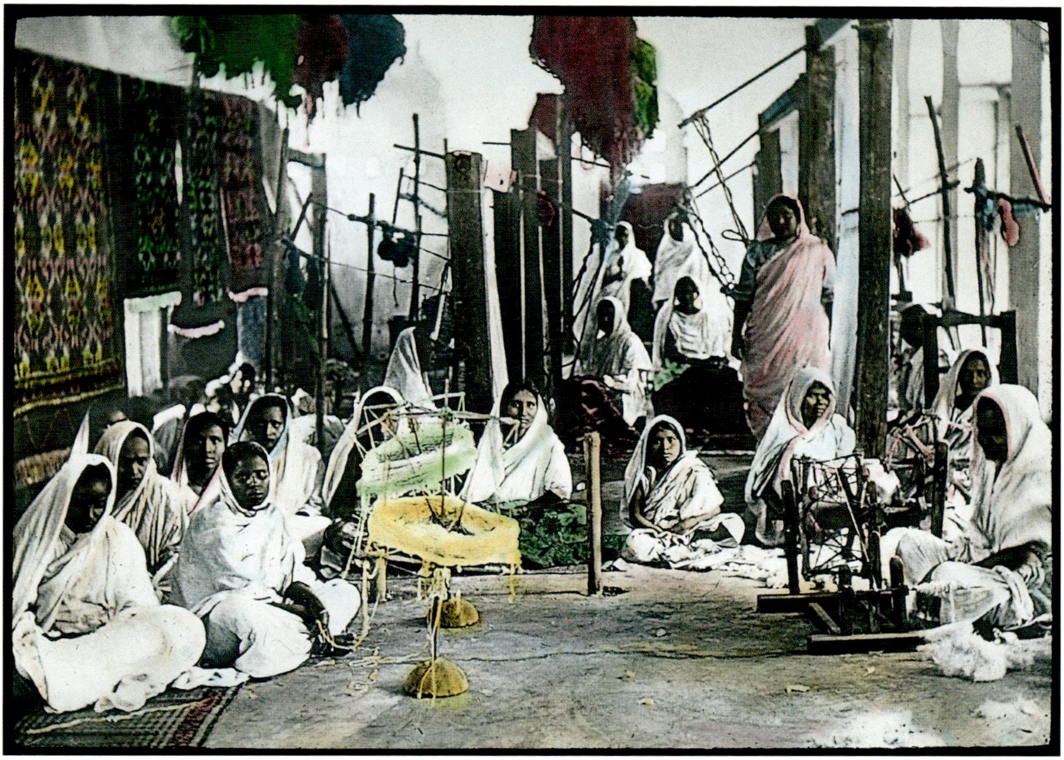

357 Carpet weaving, Baranagar, India, 1890s

357 Teppichweben, Baranagar, Indien, 1890er Jahre

357 Tissage de tapis, Baranagar, Inde, années 1890

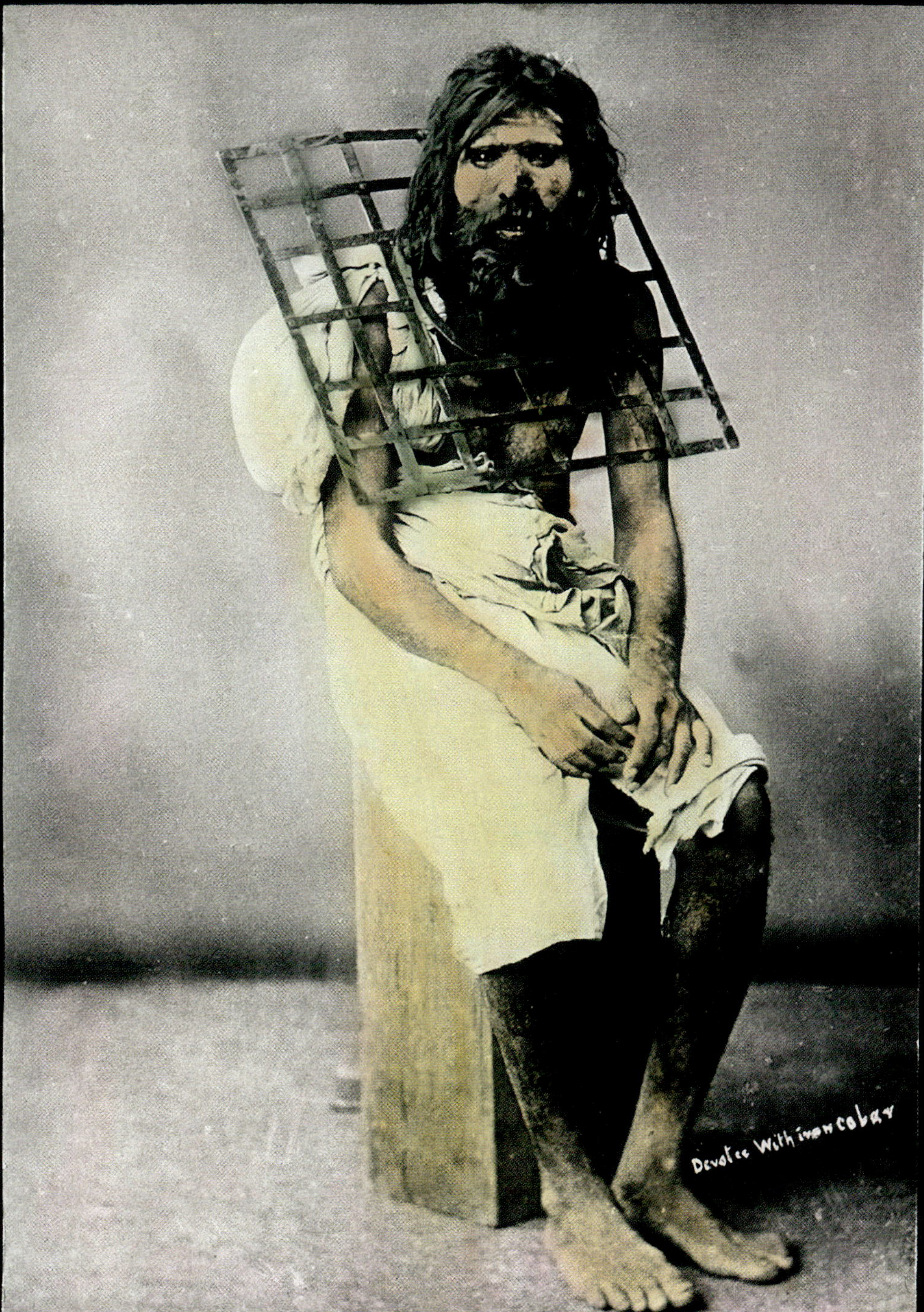

FAKIR WITH IRON COLLAR

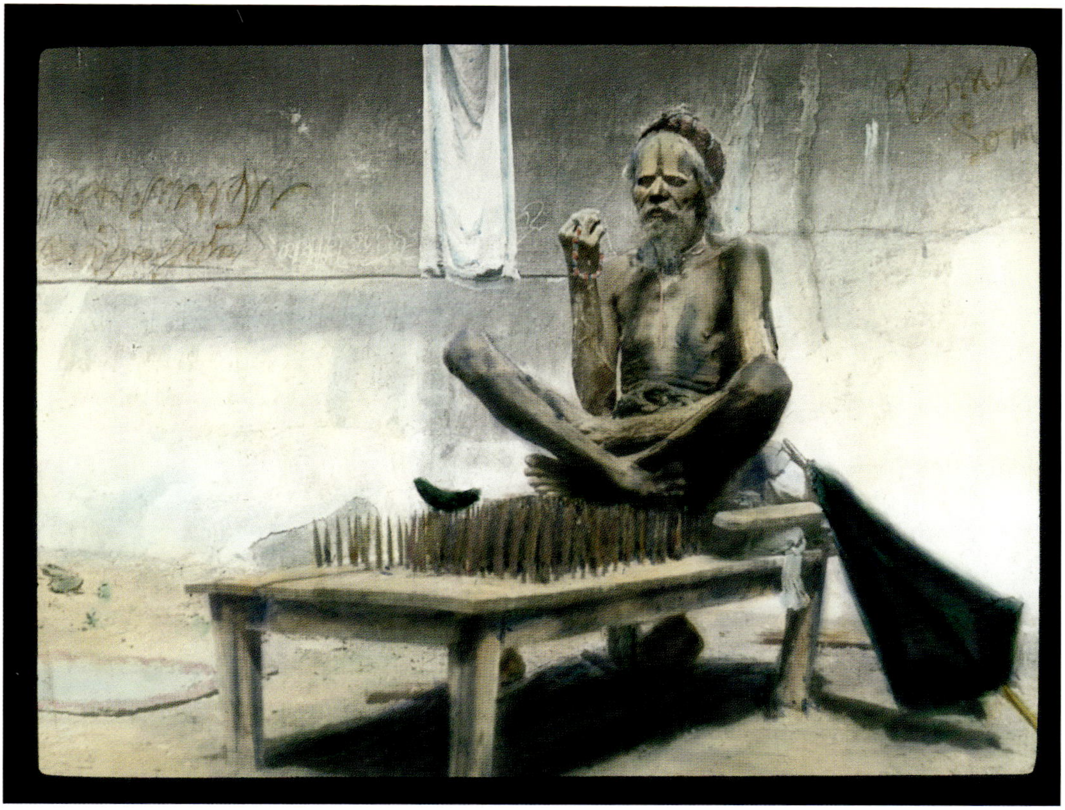

358 Fakir with iron collar, India, 1880s
359 Fakir on a bed of nails, India, 1880s

358 Fakir mit eiserner Halskrause, Indien, 1880er Jahre
359 Fakir auf einem Nagelbett, Indien, 1880er Jahre

358 Fakir avec un collier de fer, Inde, années 1880
359 Fakir sur une planche à clous, Inde, années 1880

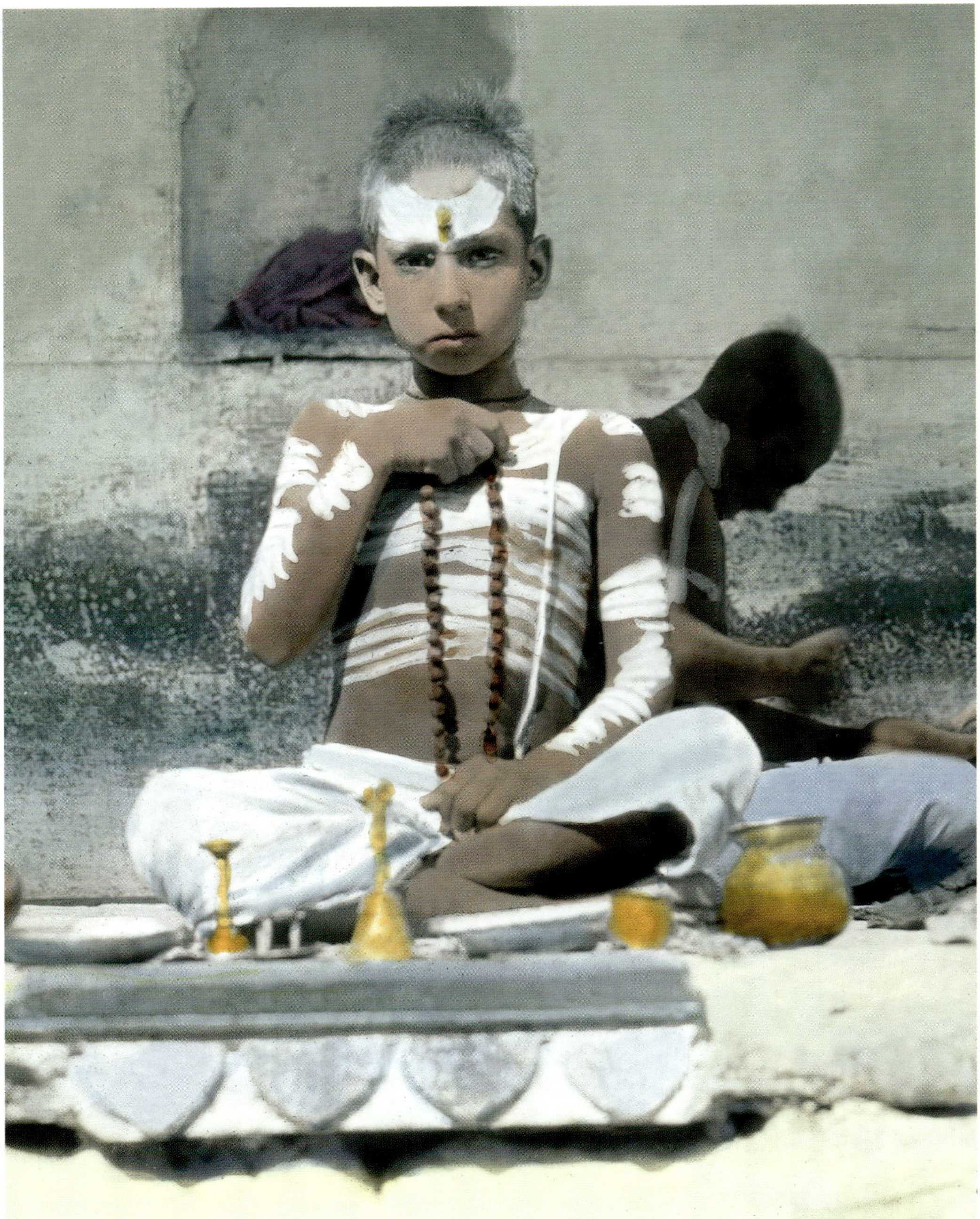

360 Boy learning to be a fakir, India, 1900s
361 A Fakir (Holy Man), India, 1880s

360 Ein Junge lernt, ein Fakir zu sein, Indien, 1900er Jahre
361 Ein Fakir (Heiliger Mann), Indien, 1880er Jahre

360 Apprenti fakir, Inde, années 1900
361 Fakir (homme saint), Inde, années 1880

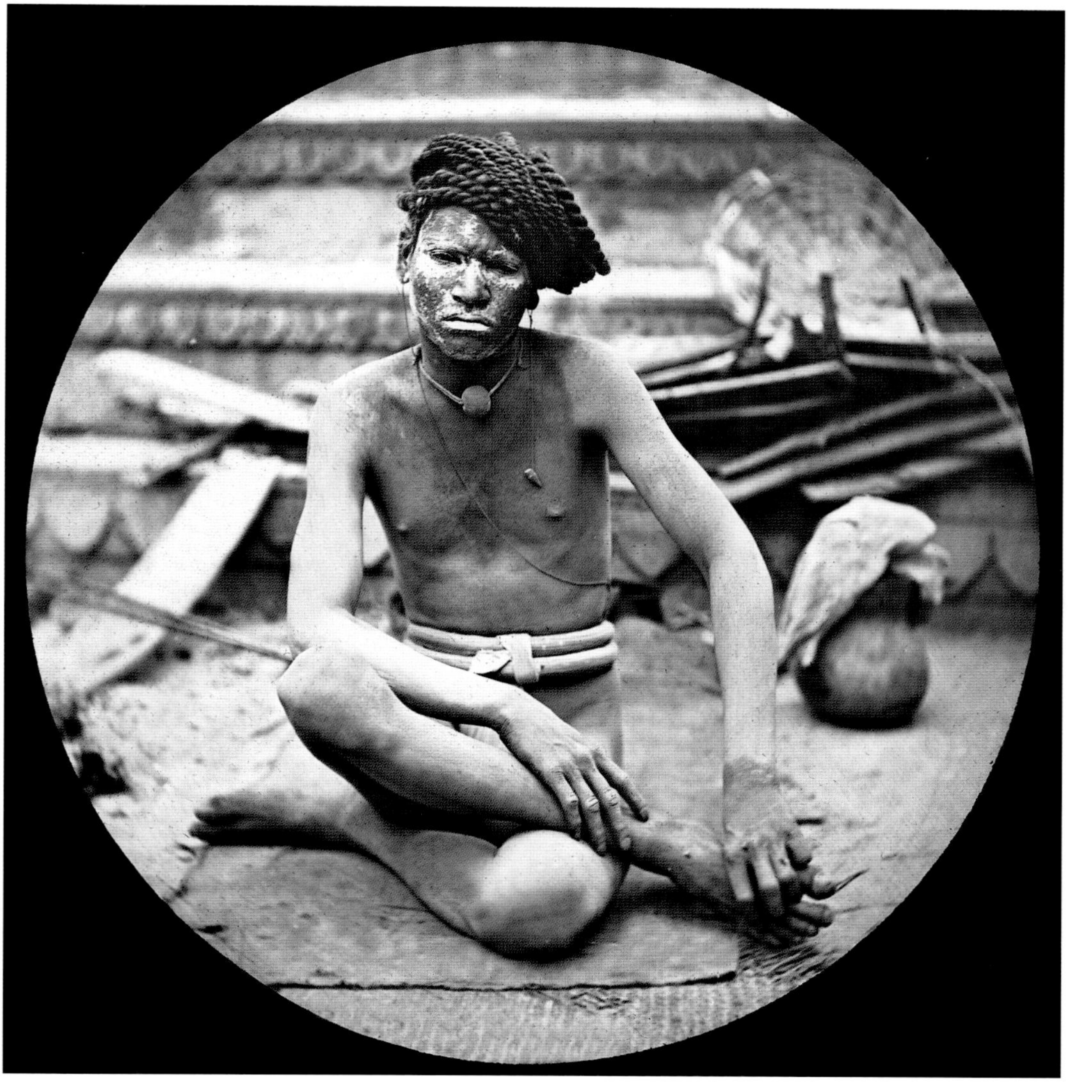

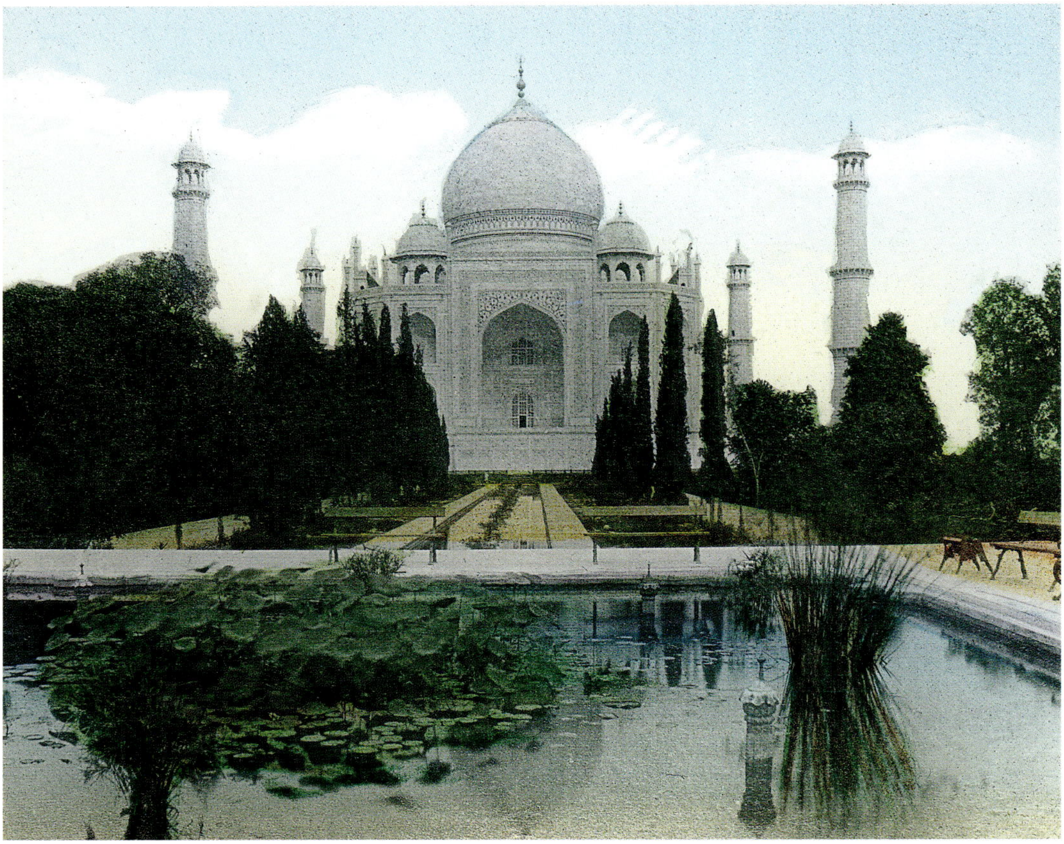

362 The Taj Mahal, Agra, India, 1880s
363 Front elevation of the Taj Mahal, India, 1880s

362 Der Taj Mahal, Agra, Indien, 1880er Jahre
363 Vorderansicht des Taj Mahal, Indien, 1880er Jahre

362 Le Taj Mahal, Agra, Inde, années 1880
363 Façade (élévation) du Taj Mahal, Inde, années 1880

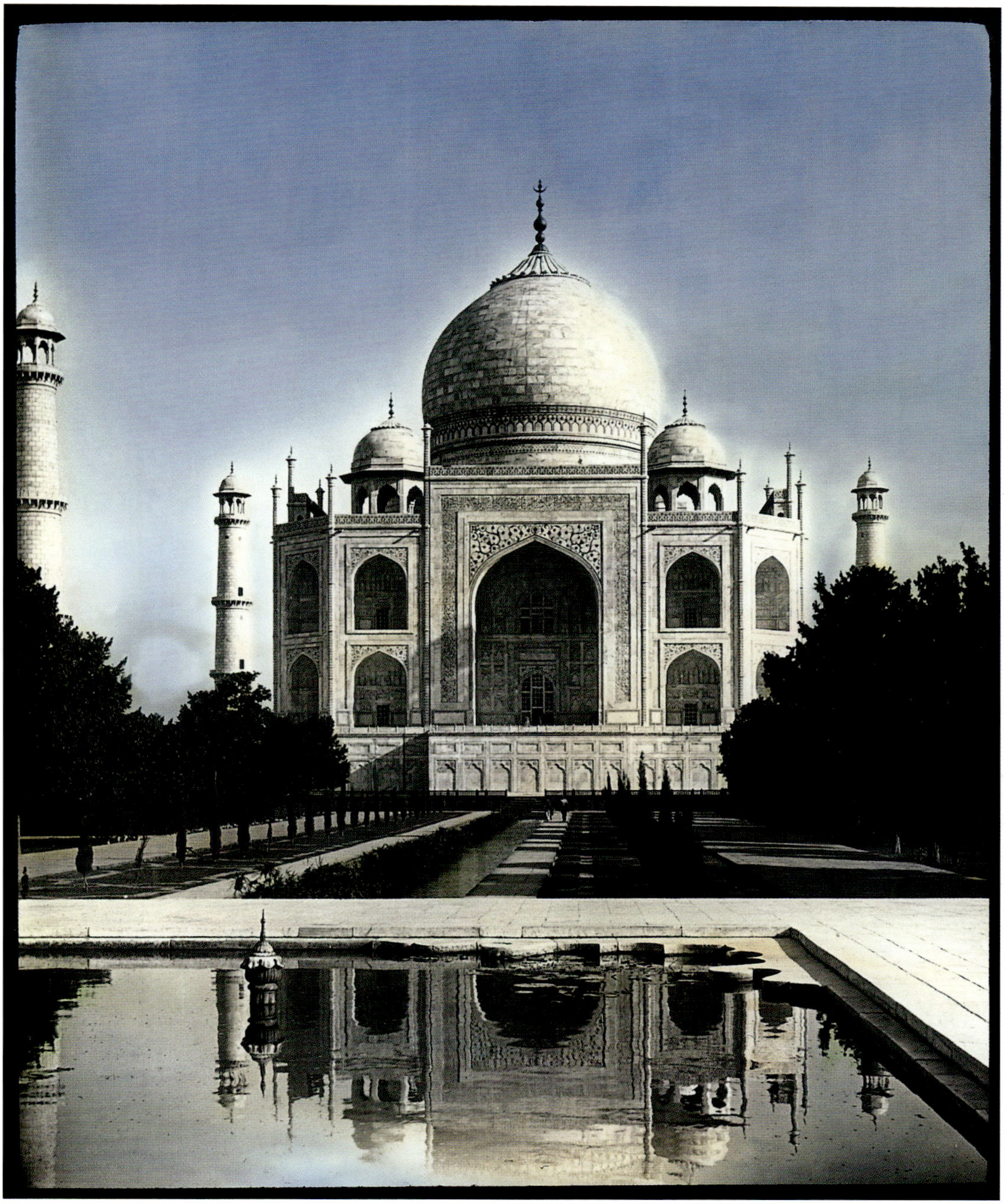

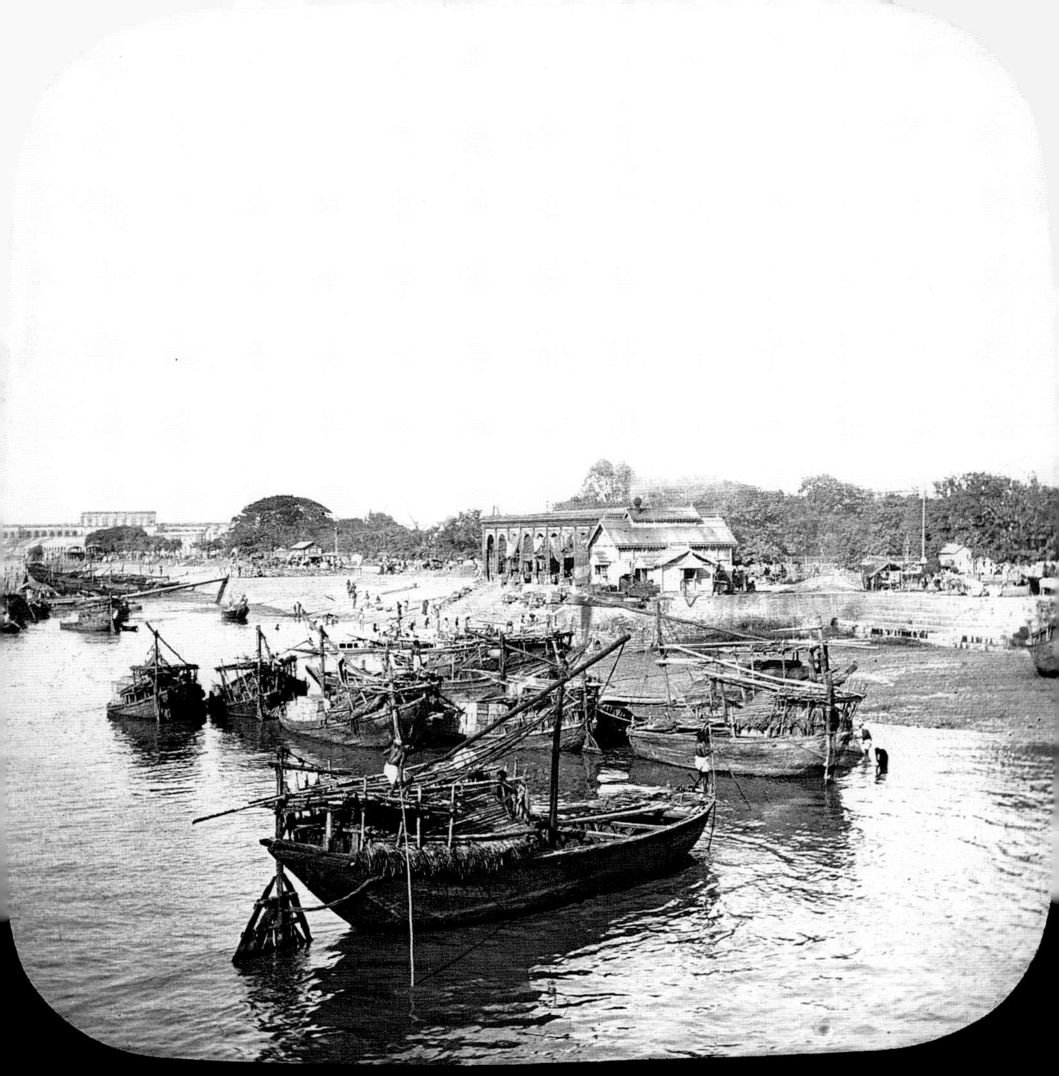

364 Boats on the Hugli River, Kolkata (Calcutta), 1900s
365 Bathing scene, Hugli River, Kolkata (Calcutta), 1890s

364 Boote auf dem Hugli-Fluss, Kolkata (Kalkutta), Indien, 1900er Jahre
365 Badeszene, Hugli-Fluss, Kolkata (Kalkutta), Indien, 1890er Jahre

364 Navire sur la rivière Hugli, Kolkata (Calcutta), Inde, années 1900
365 Ablutions dans la rivière Hugli, Kolkata (Calcutta), Inde, années 1890

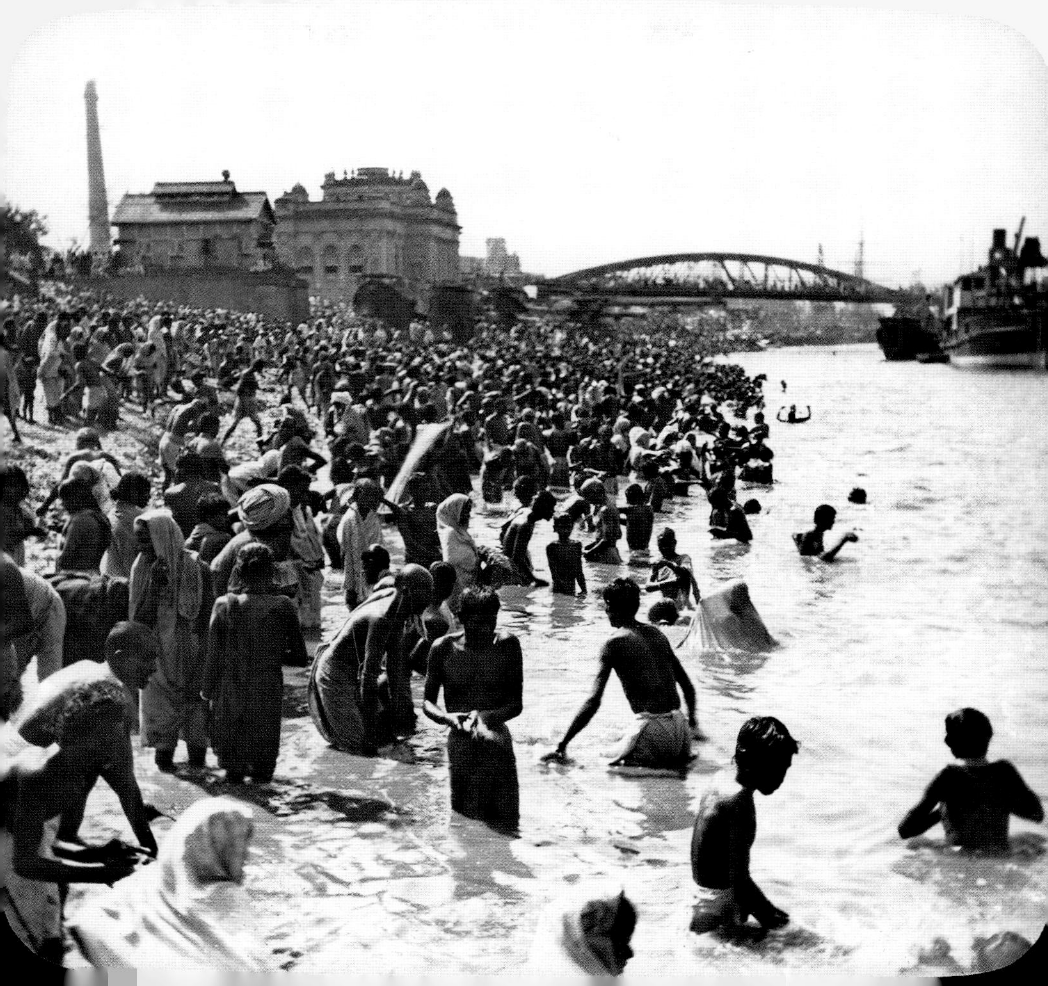

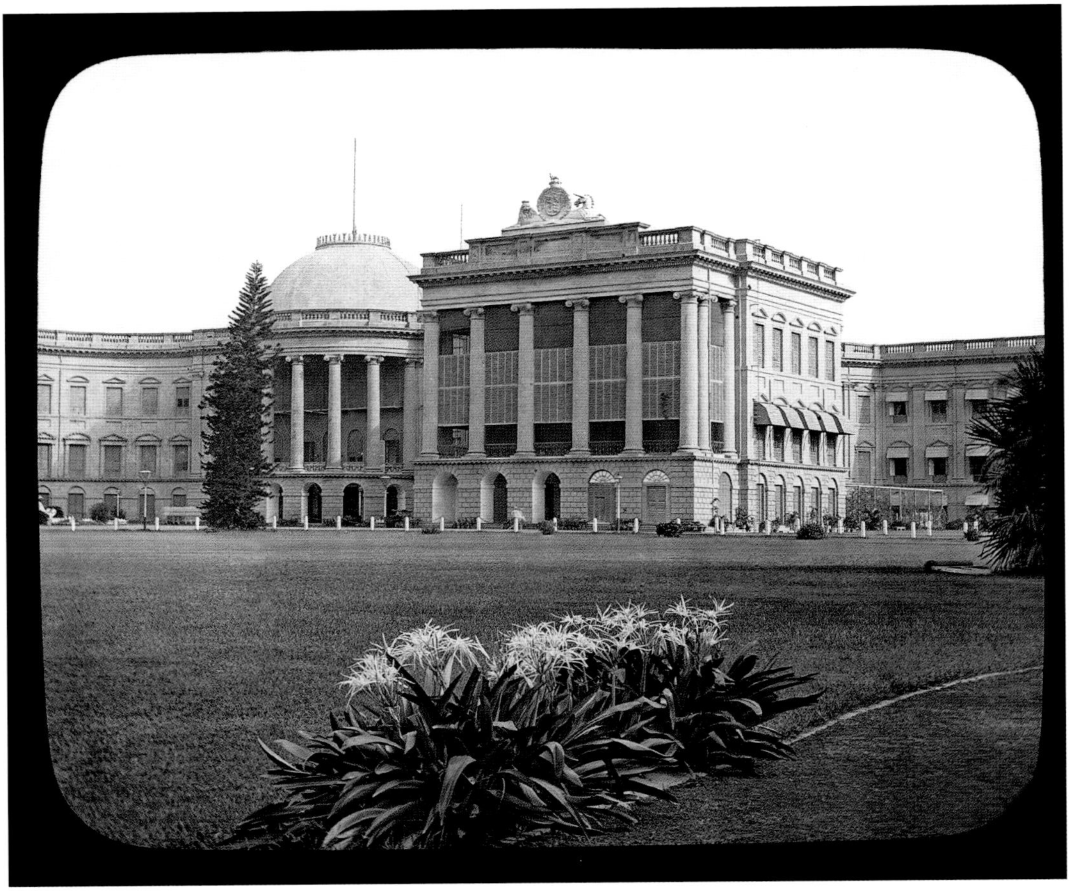

366 Government House, Calcutta (now Kolkata), India, c.1900
367 The Drawing Room of Government House, Calcutta (now Kolkata), India, c.1900

366 Das Government House, Kolkata (Kalkutta), Indien, um 1900
367 Der Salon im Government House, Kolkata (Kalkutta), Indien, um 1900

366 Palais du Gouvernement, Calcutta (auj. Kolkata), Inde, vers 1900
367 Salon du palais du Gouvernement, Calcutta (auj. Kolkata), Inde, vers 1900

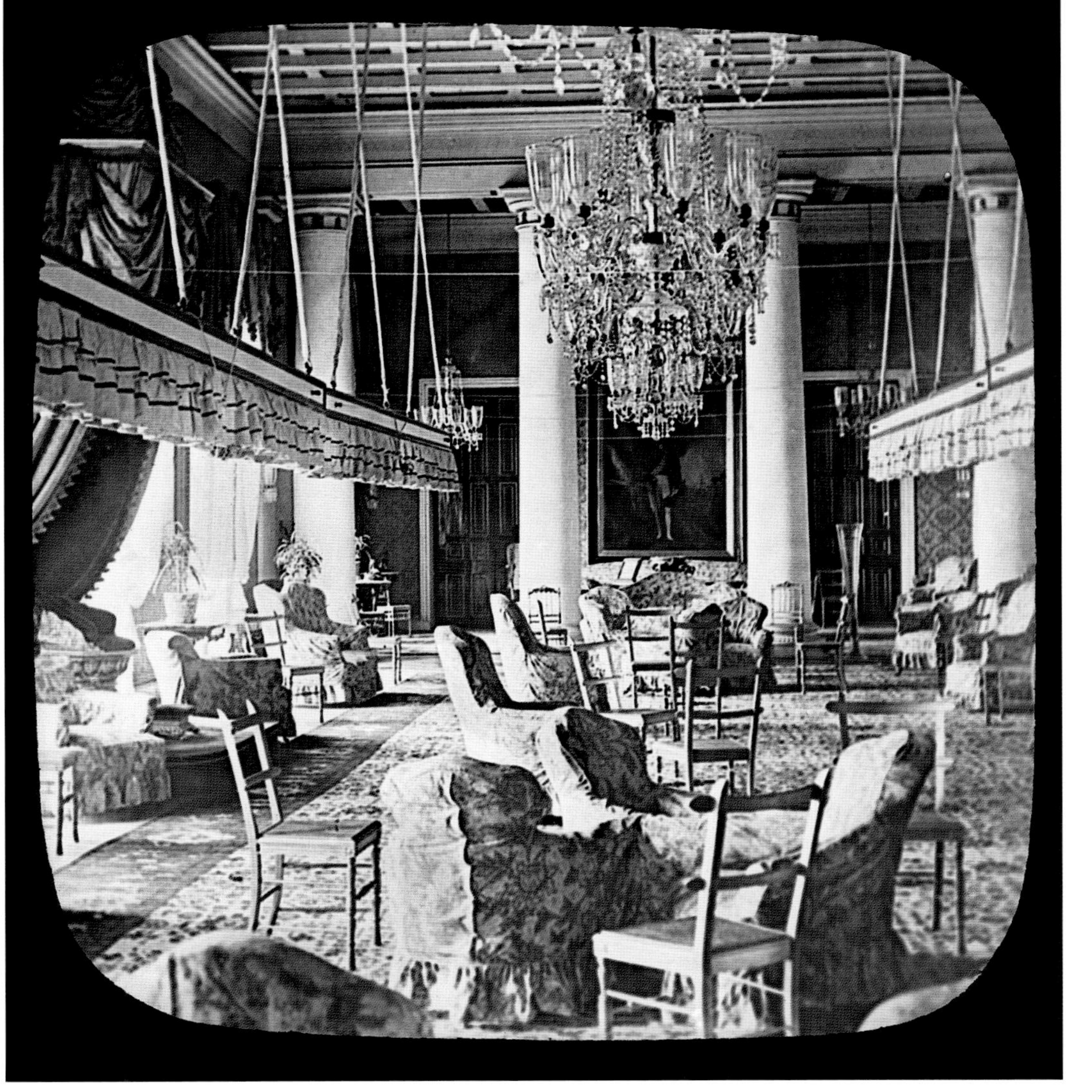

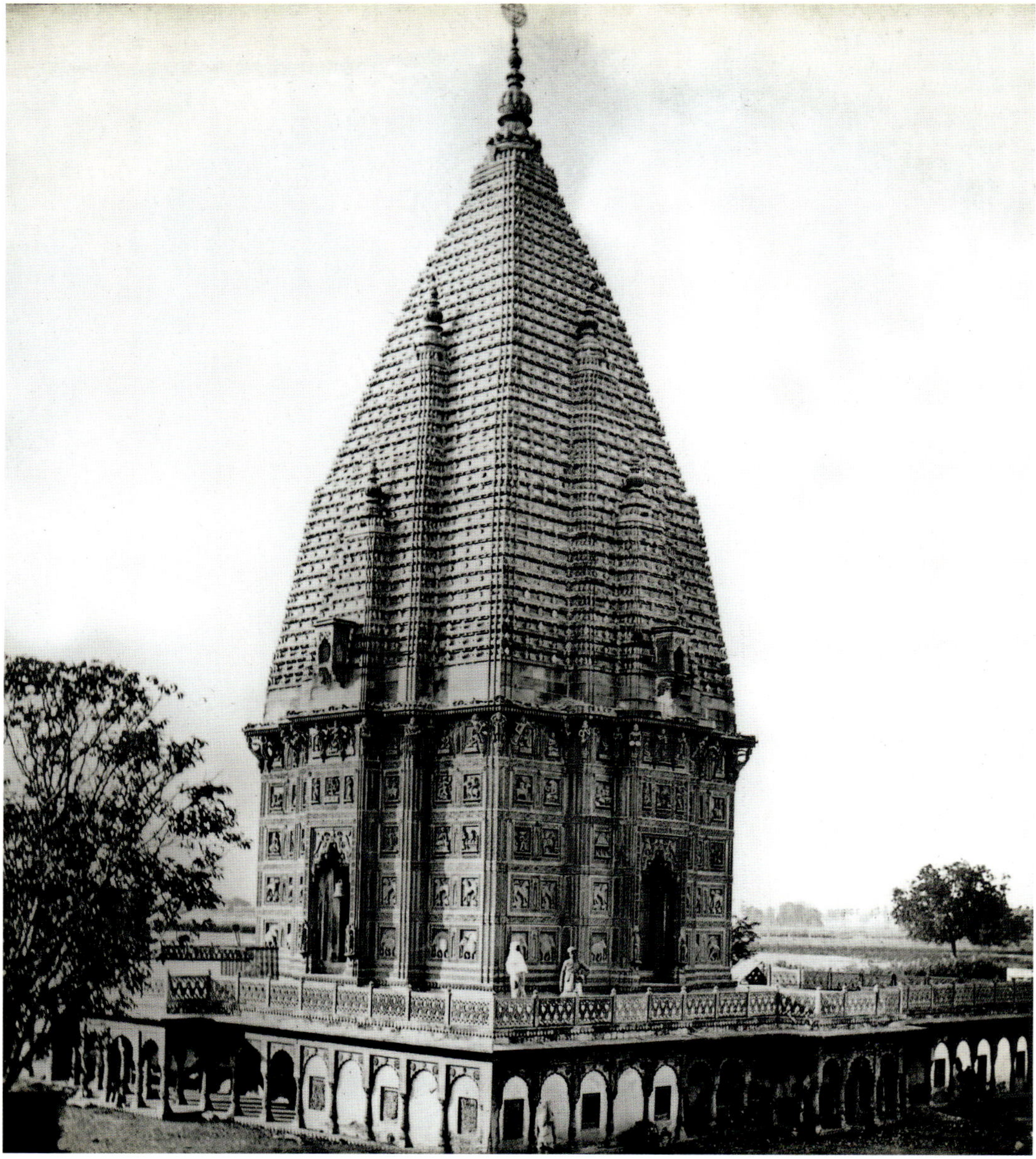

368 Sumeree Temple at Ramnagar, India , 1870s

368 Der Sumeree-Tempel in Ramnagar, Indien, 1870er Jahre

368 Temple à Ramnagar, Inde, années 1870

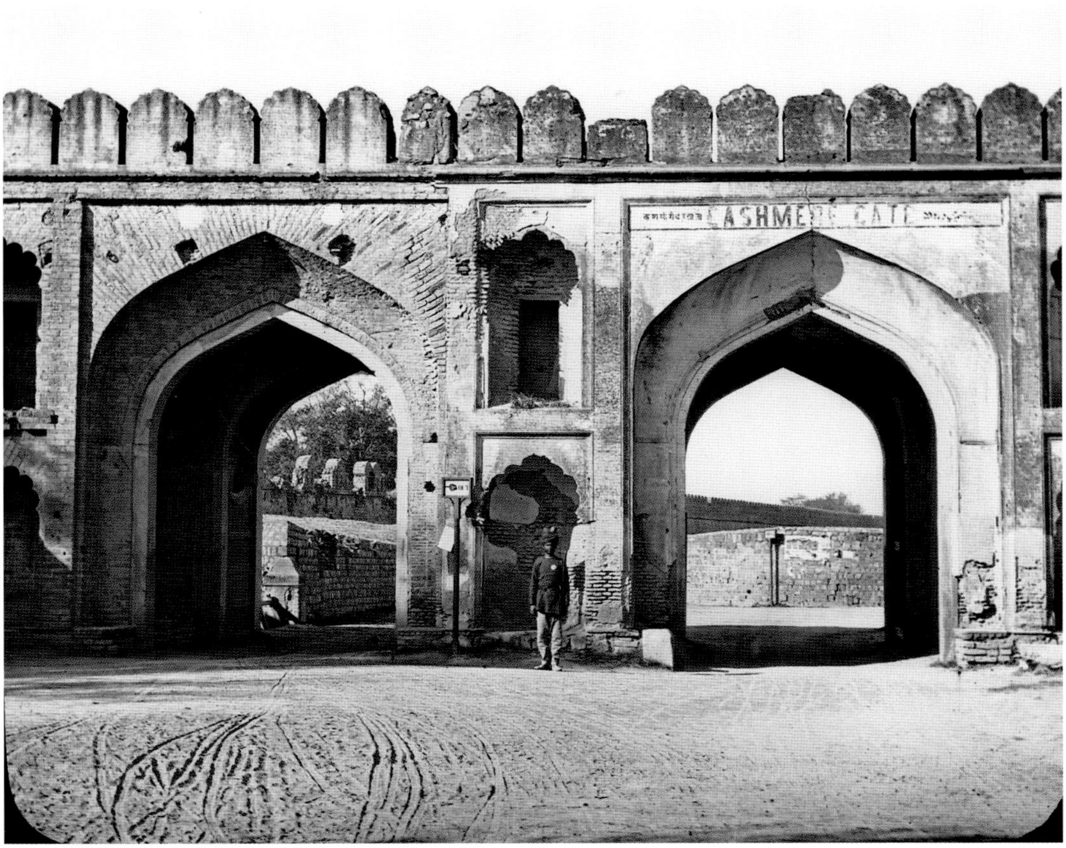

369 Kashmere Gate from inside City Walls, Delhi, 1870s

369 Das Kaschmirtor von innerhalb der Stadtmauern aus gesehen, Delhi, Indien, 1870er Jahre

369 La porte du Cachemire vue depuis l'intérieur du mur d'enceinte, Delhi, Inde, années 1870

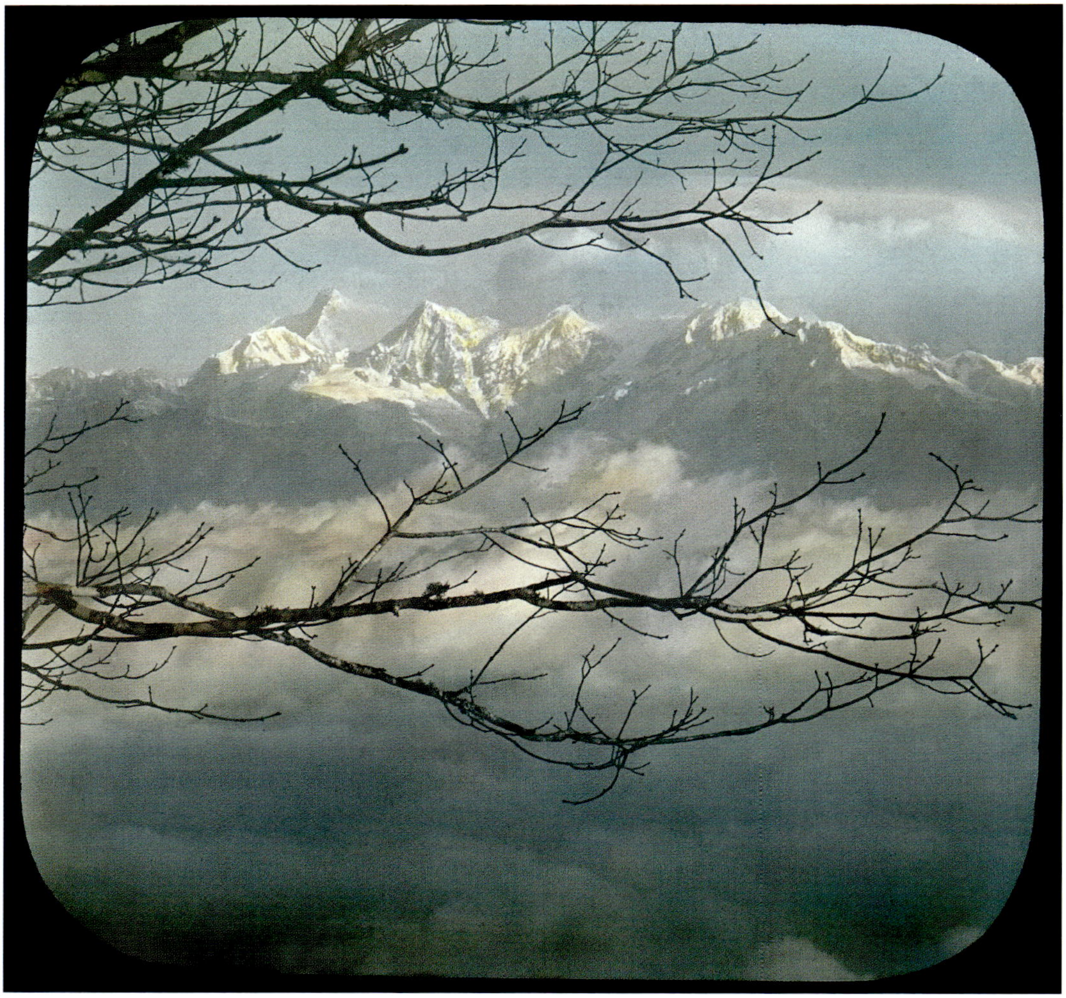

370 Sunrise on the Himalayas, Darjeeling, India, c.1900
371 Yaks in the Kashmir Valley, Kashmir, c.1900

370 Sonnenaufgang über dem Himalaya, Darjeeling, Indien, um 1900
371 Yaks im Kaschmir-Tal, Kaschmir, um 1900

370 Lever du soleil sur l'Himalaya, Darjeeling, Inde, vers 1900
371 Yaks dans la vallée du Cachemire, vers 1900

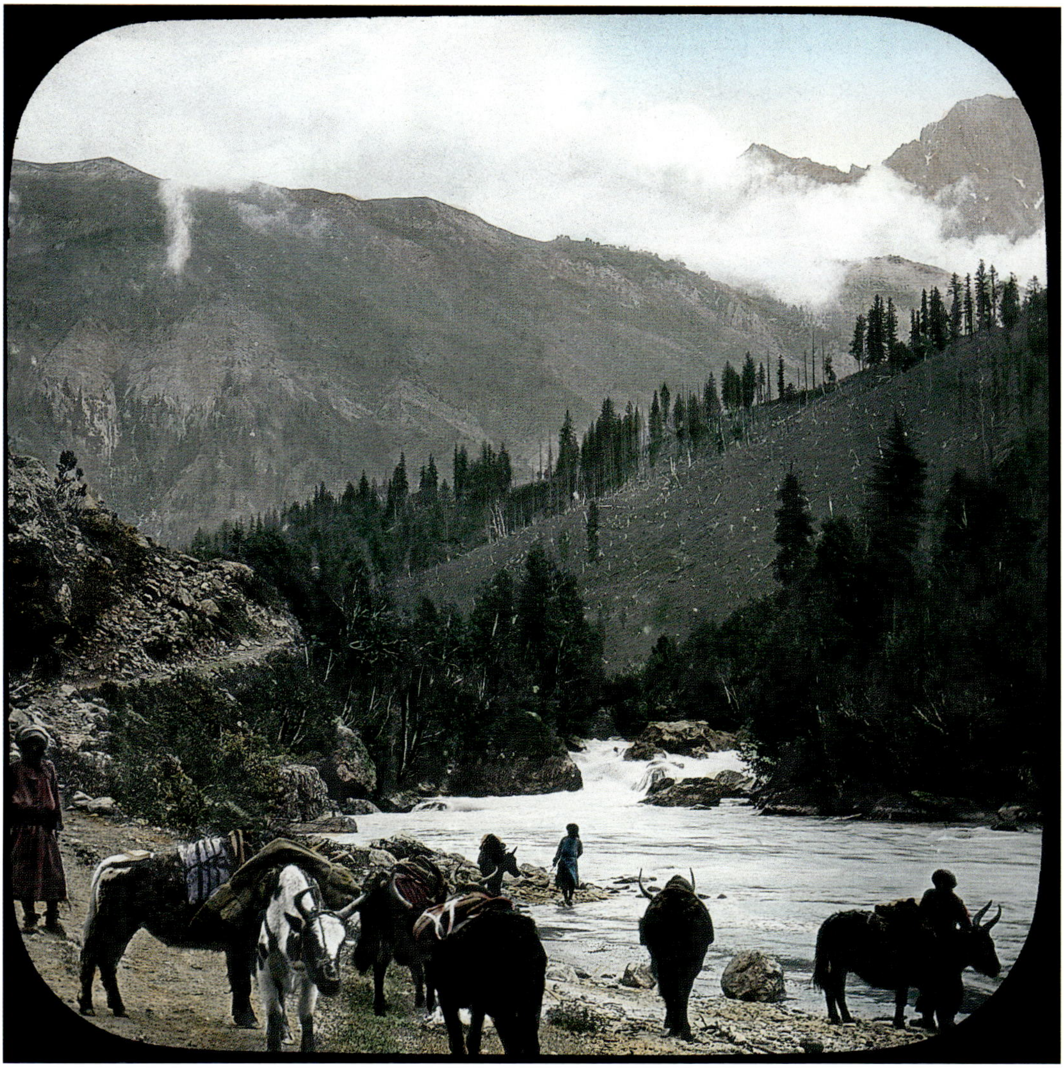

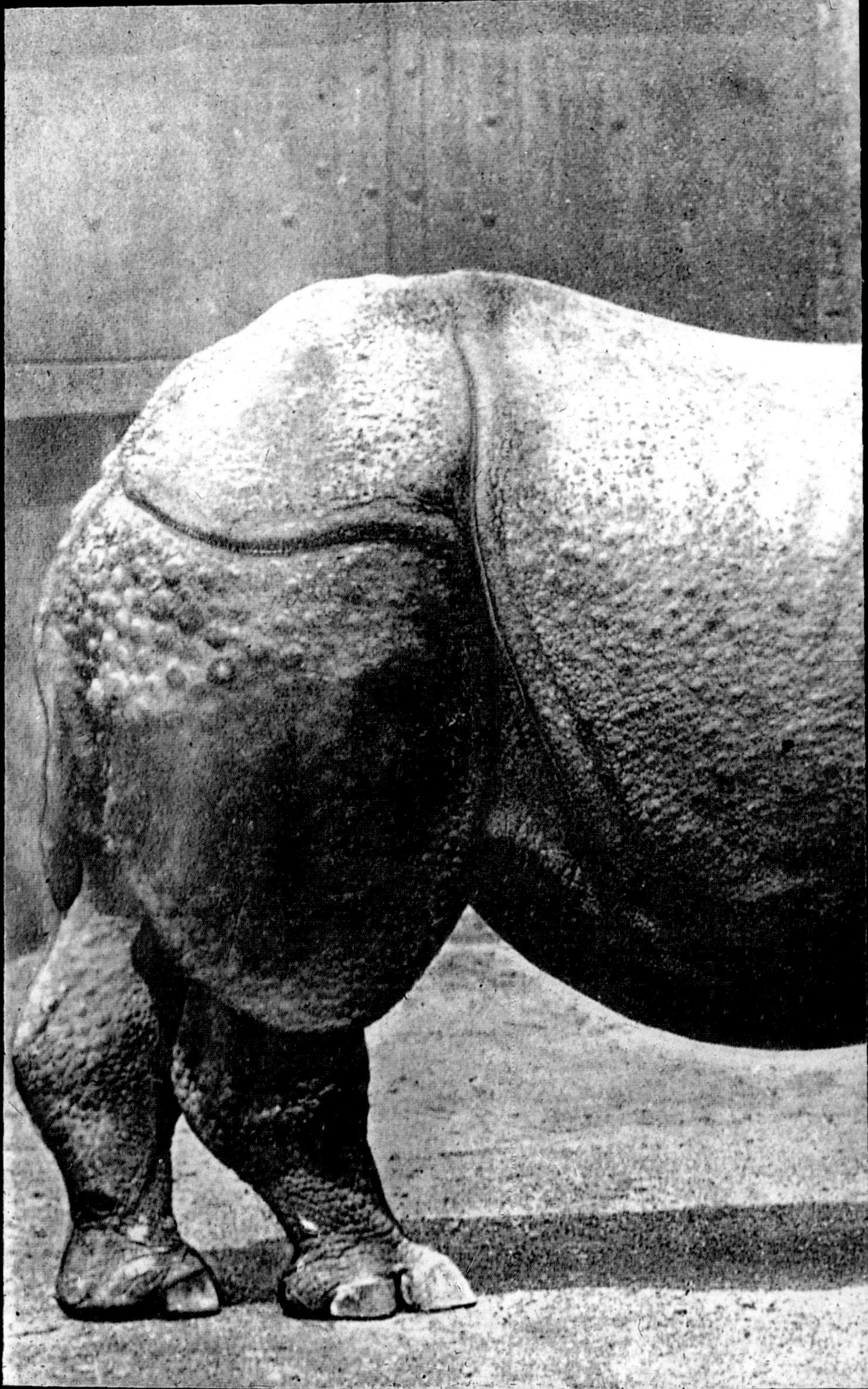

372 Rhinoceros,
India, 1870s

372 Rhinozeros,
Indien, 1870er Jahre

372 Rhinocéros,

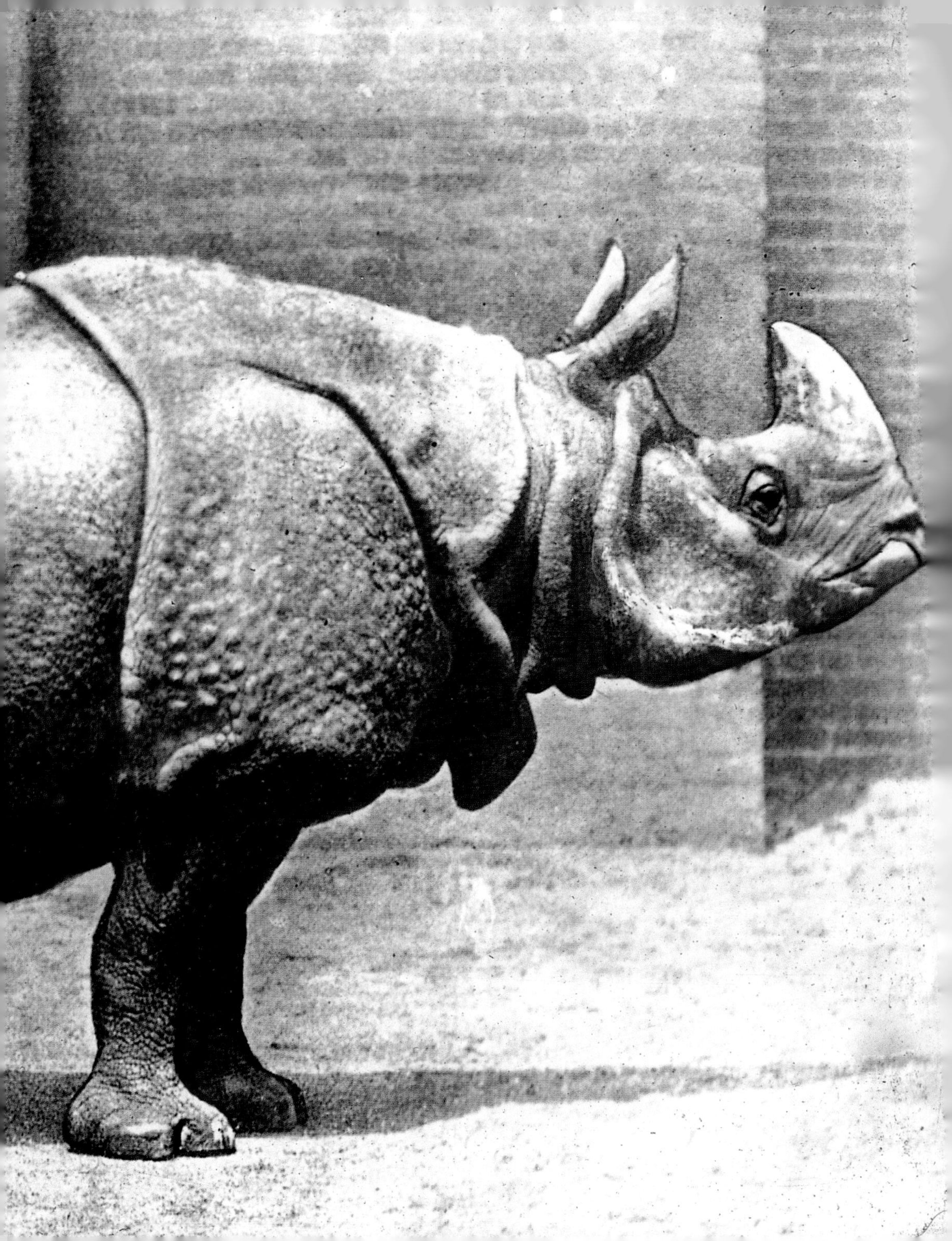

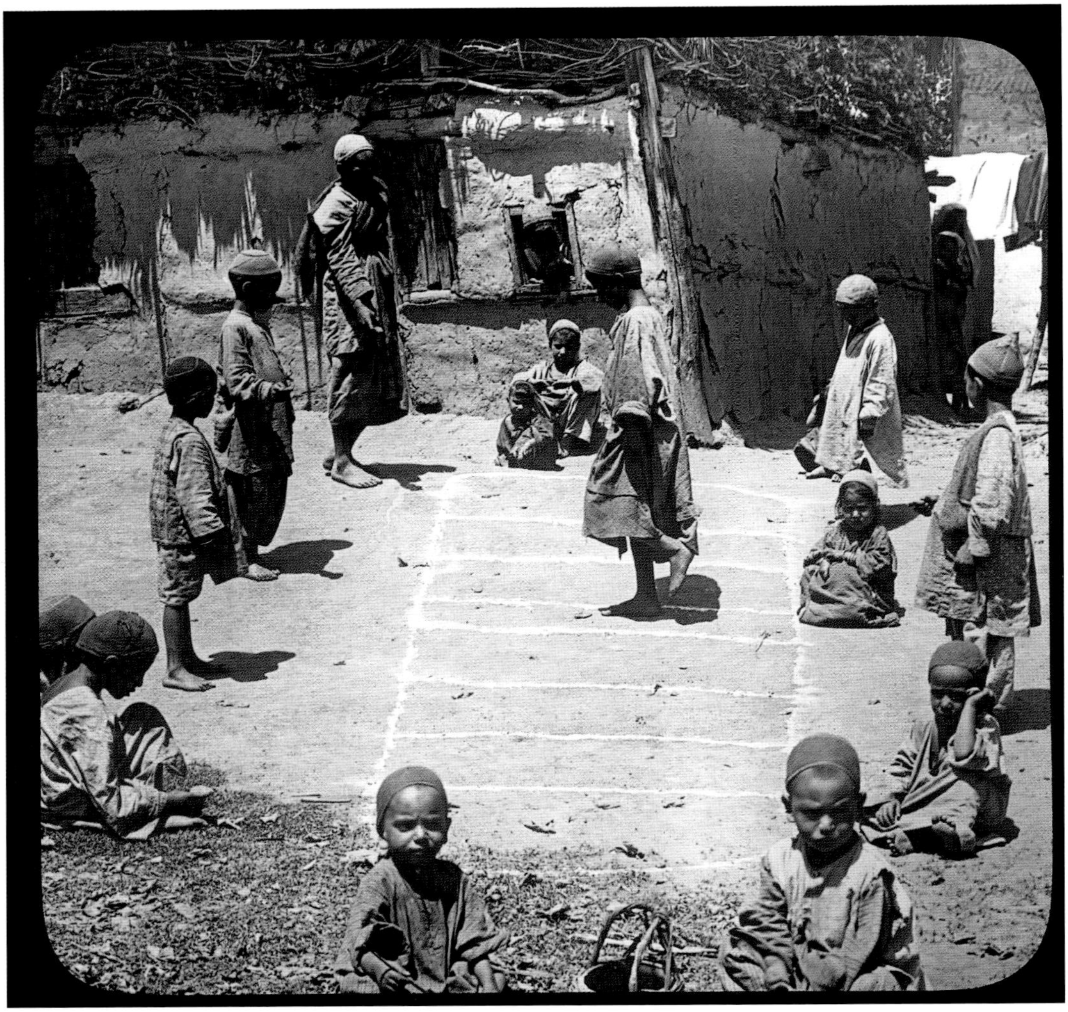

373 Children playing hopscotch, Kashmir, 1890s
374 Elephant at work, Ceylon (now Sri Lanka), 1870s

373 Kinder spielen Himmel und Hölle, Kaschmir, 1890er Jahre
374 Elefanten bei der Arbeit, Ceylon (heute Sri Lanka), 1870er Jahre

373 Enfants jouant à la marelle, Cachemire, années 1890
374 Éléphant au travail, Ceylan (auj. Sri Lanka), années 1870

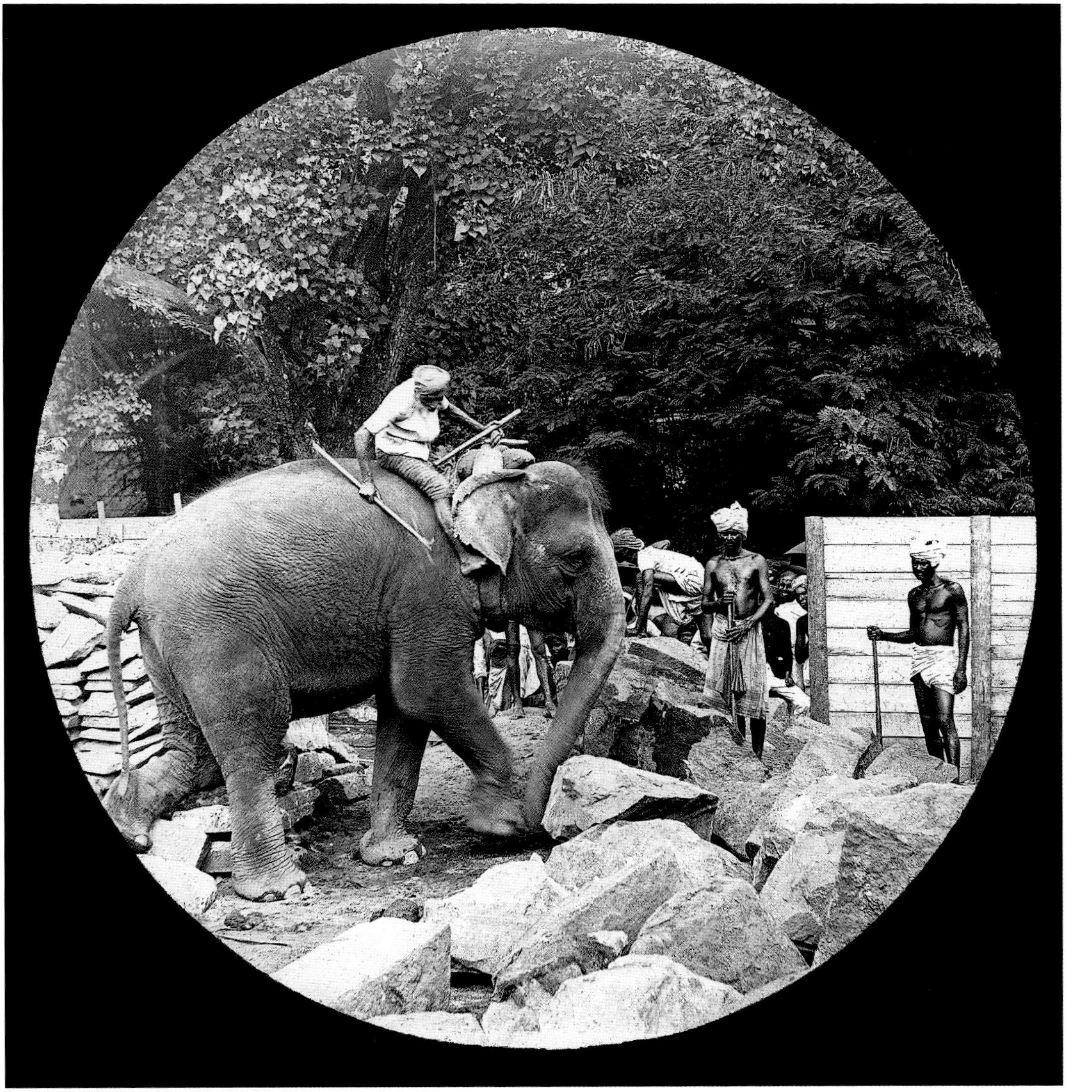

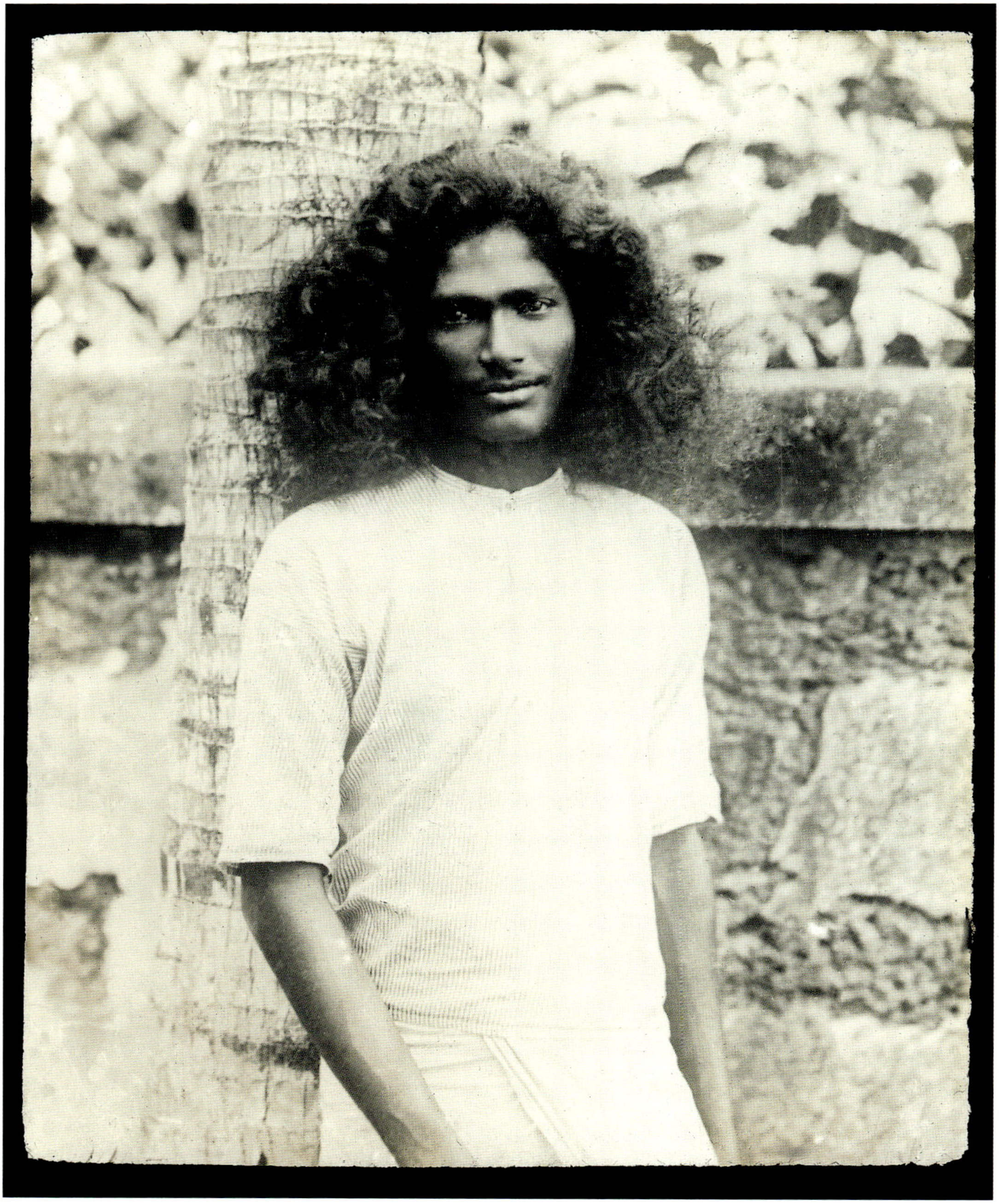

375 Young man, Ceylon (now Sri Lanka), 1910s
376 People walking along a beach, Ceylon (now Sri Lanka), 1920s

375 Junger Mann, Ceylon (heute Sri Lanka), 1910er Jahre
376 Spaziergänger am Strand, Ceylon (heute Sri Lanka), 1920er Jahre

375 Jeune homme, Ceylan (auj. Sri Lanka), années 1910
376 Promenade sur la plage, Ceylan (auj. Sri Lanka), années 1920

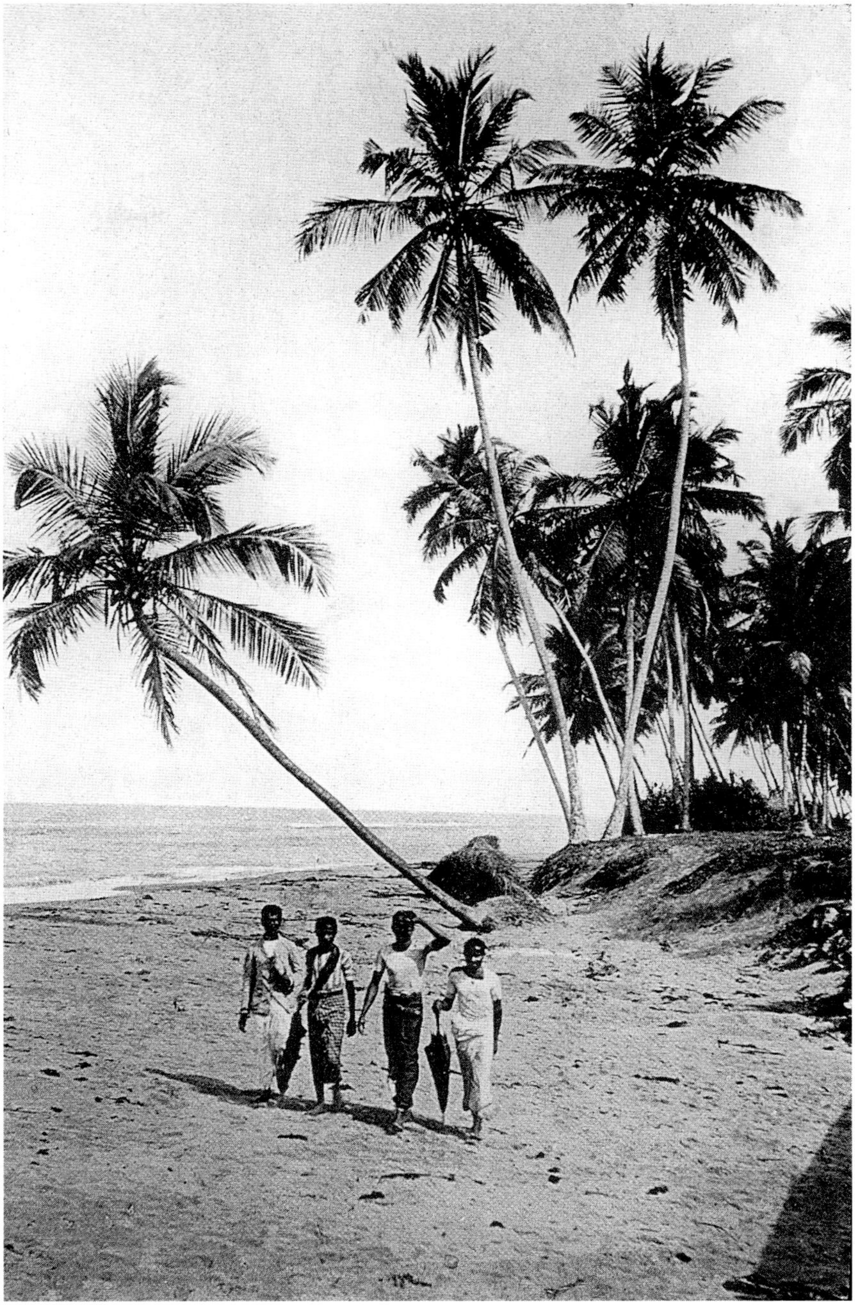

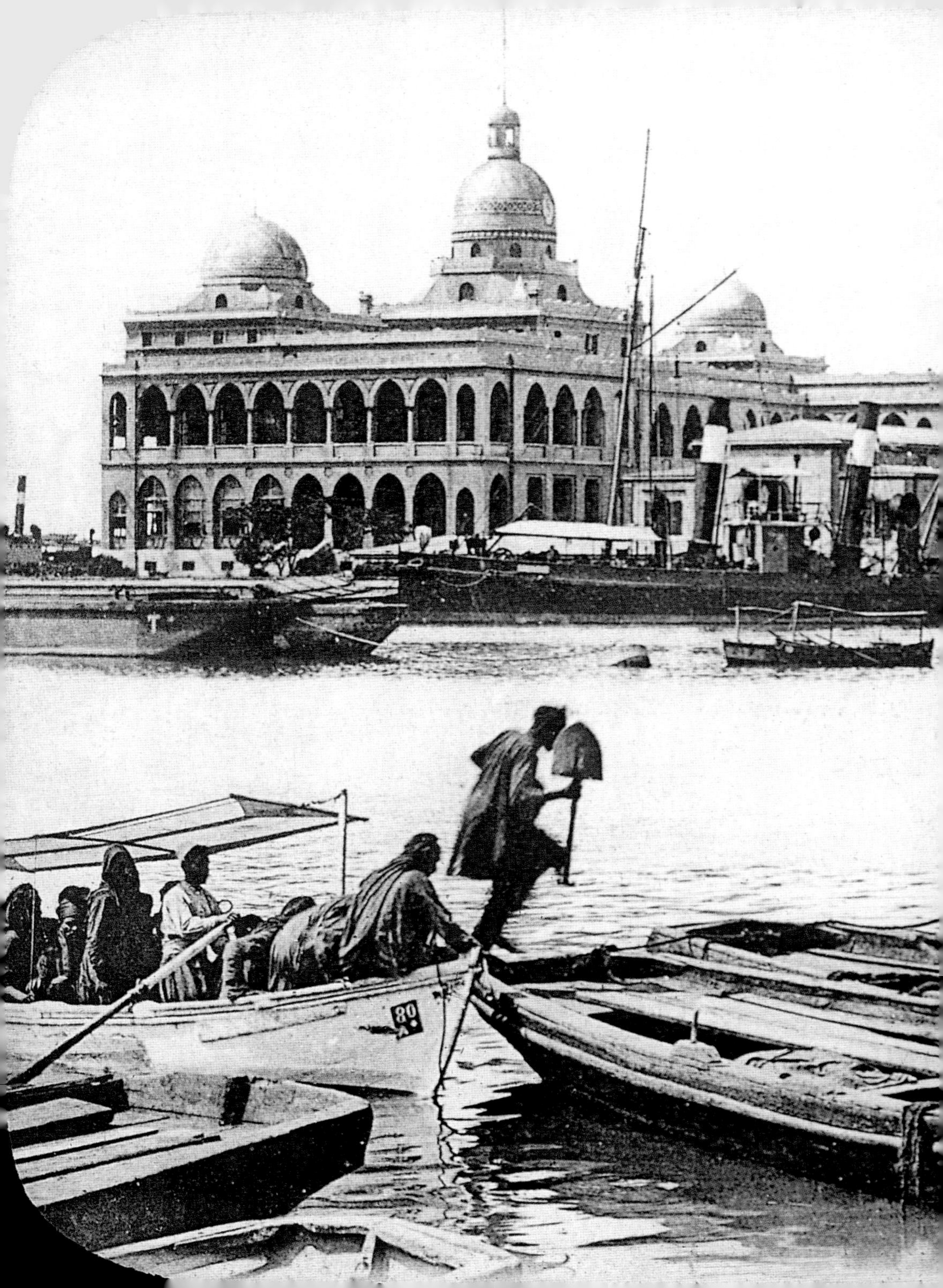
80

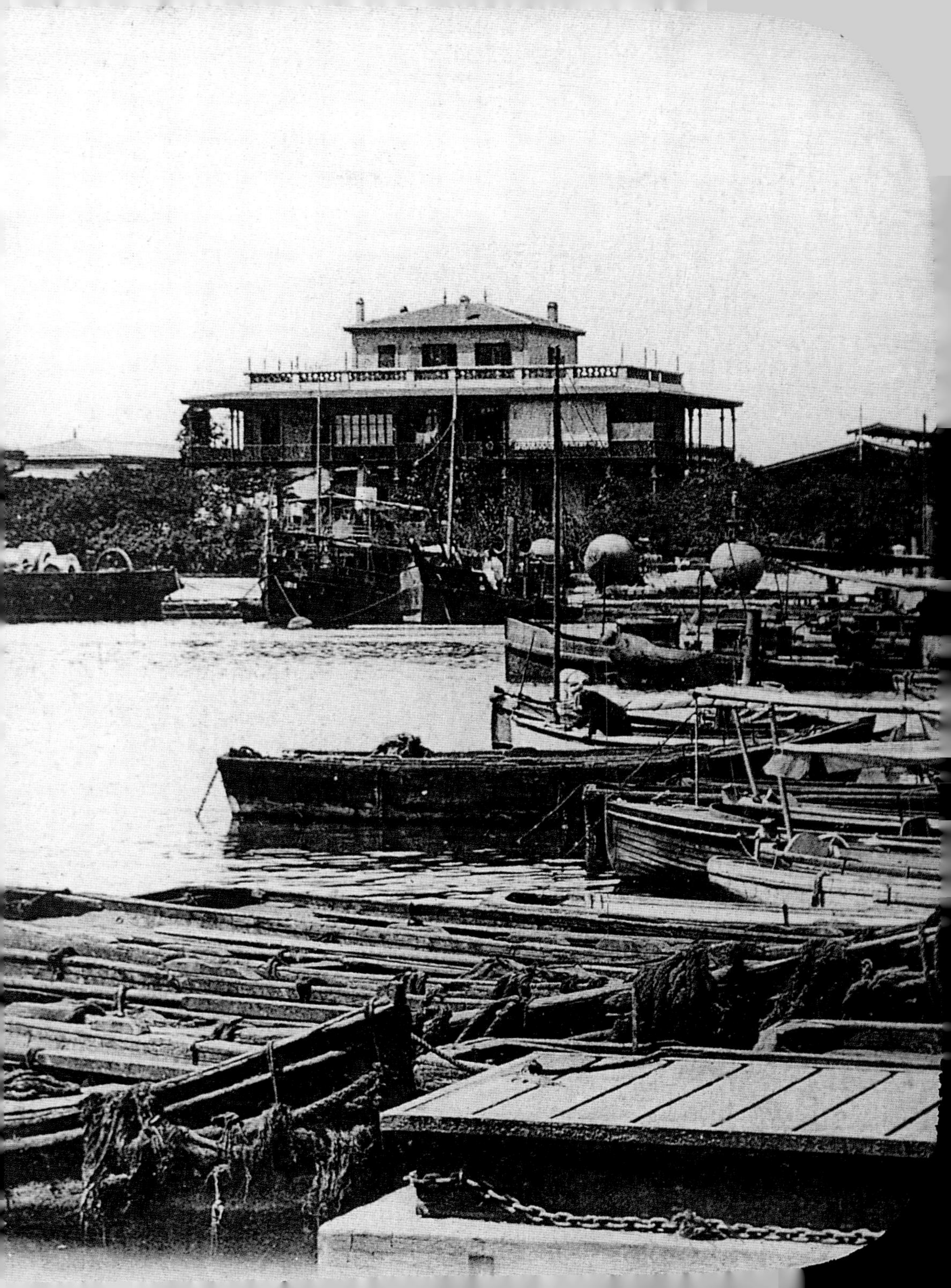

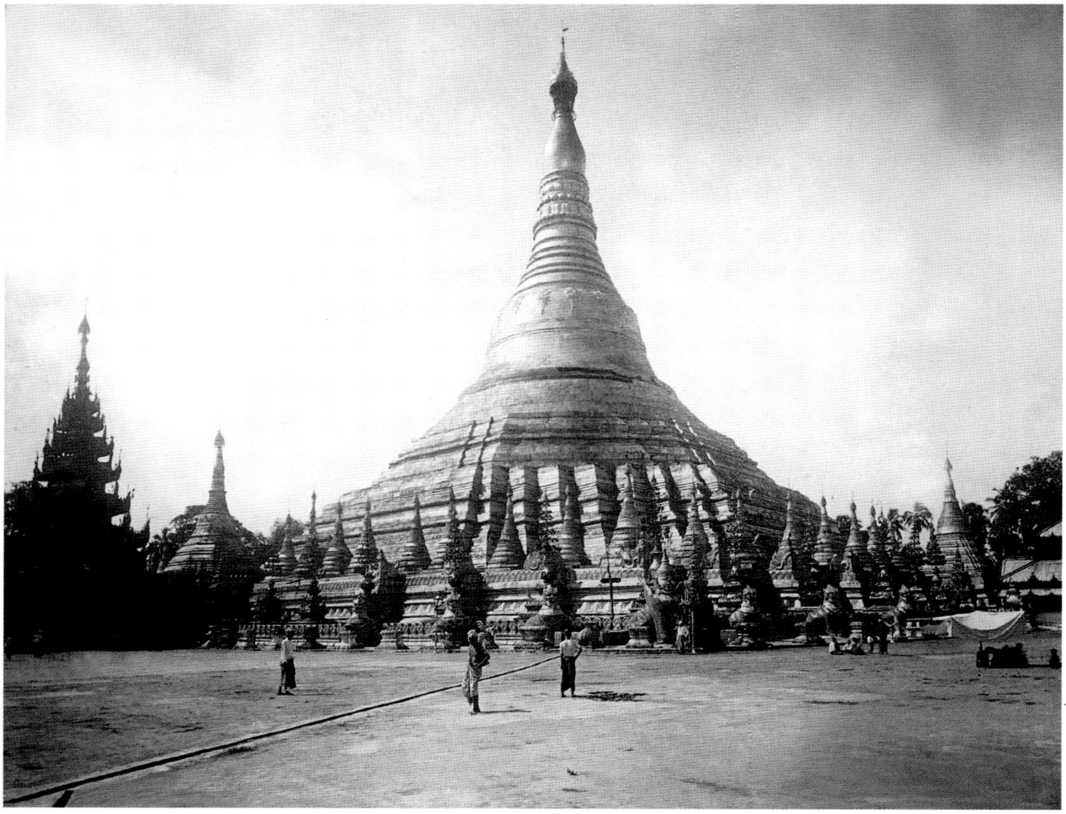

377 Yangon River,
Rangoon (now Yangon),
Burma (now Mynamar),
1900s

377 Der Yangon-Fluss,
Rangun (heute Yangon),
Birma (heute Myanmar),
1900er Jahre

377 Le fleuve Yangon à
Rangoon (auj. Yangon),
Birmanie (auj. Myanmar),
années 1900

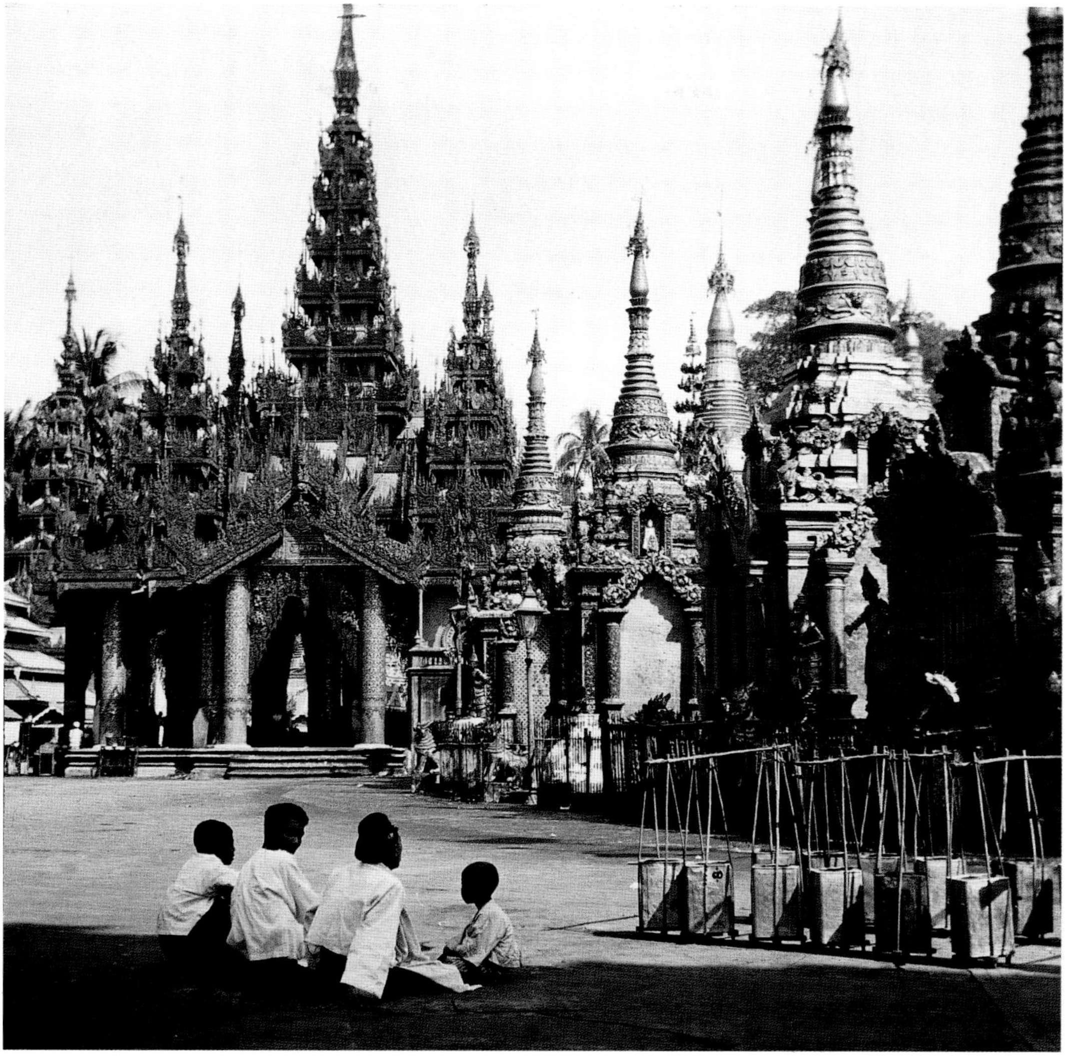

378–9 Shwedagon Pagoda, Rangoon (now Yangon), Burma (now Mynamar), 1900s

378–9 Die Shwedagon-Pagode, Rangun (heute Yangon), Birma (heute Myanmar), 1900er Jahre

378–9 Pagode Shwedagon, Rangoon (auj. Yangon), Birmanie (auj. Myanmar), années 1900

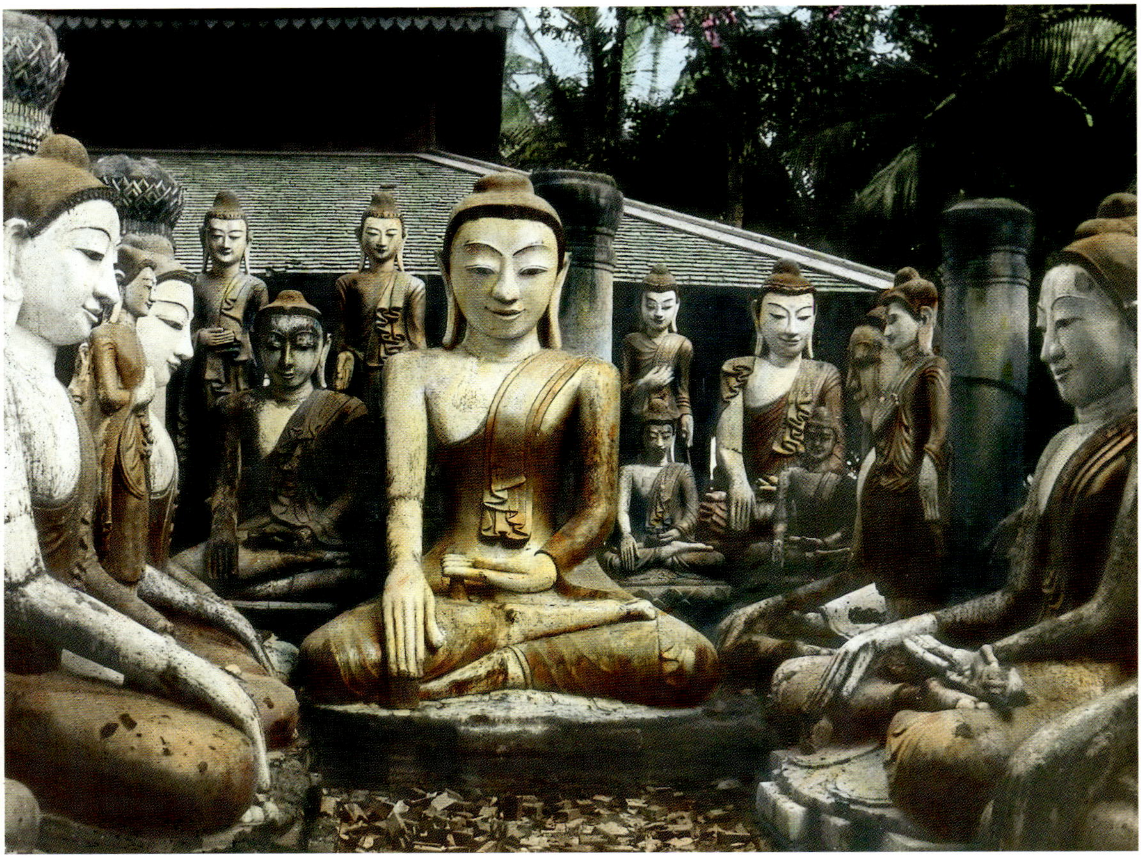

380 Buddhas, Mandalay, Burma (now Mynamar), 1900s
381 Street scene, Burma (now Mynamar), 1900s

380 Buddhas, Mandalay, Birma (heute Myanmar), 1900er Jahre
381 Straßenszene, Birma (heute Myanmar), 1900er Jahre

380 Bouddhas, Mandalay, Birmanie (auj. Myanmar), années 1900
381 Scène de rue, Birmanie (auj. Myanmar), années 1900

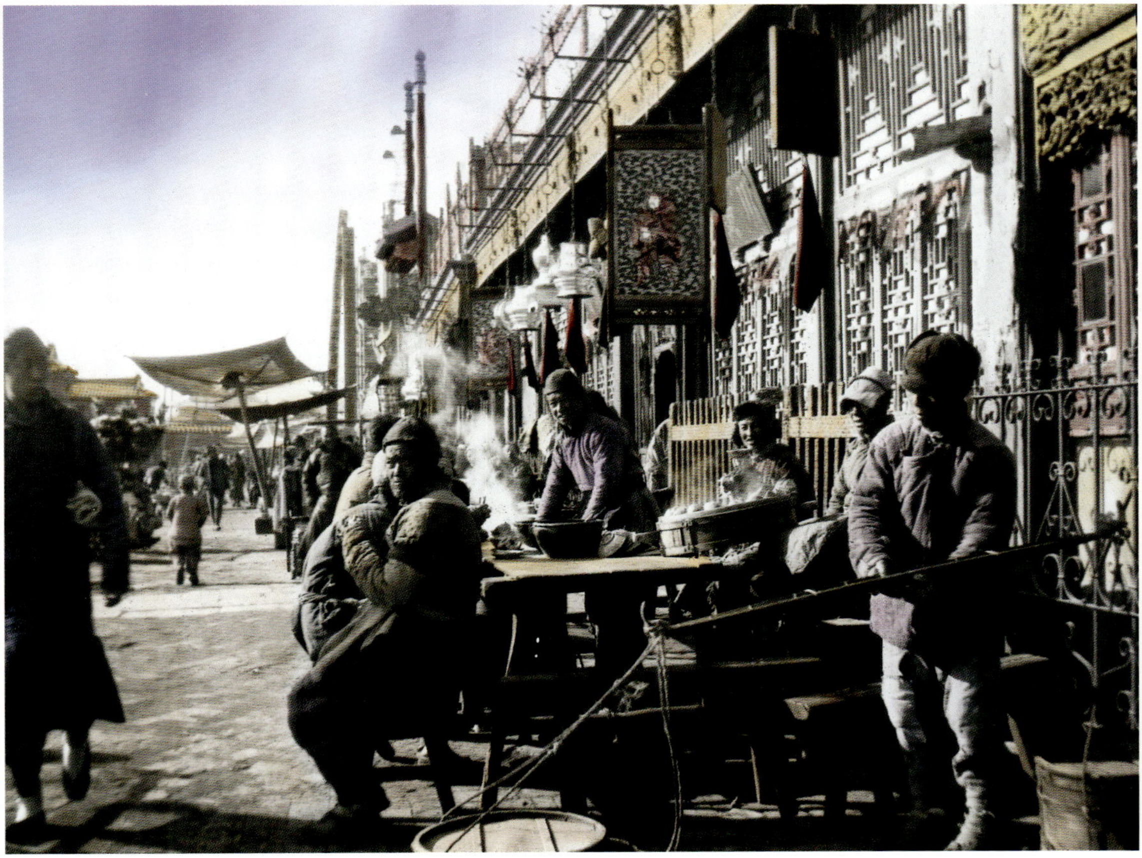

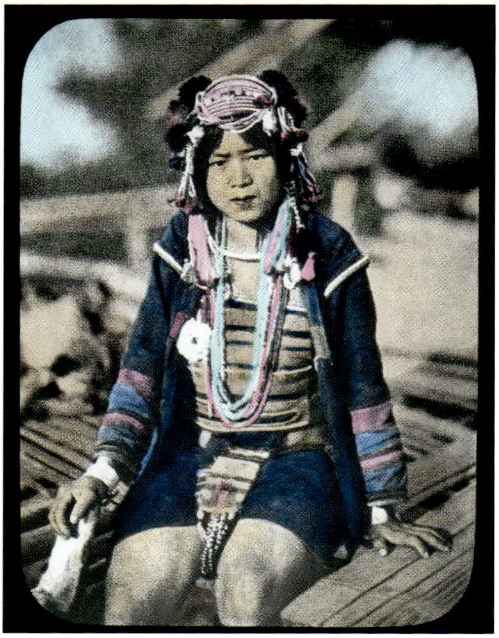

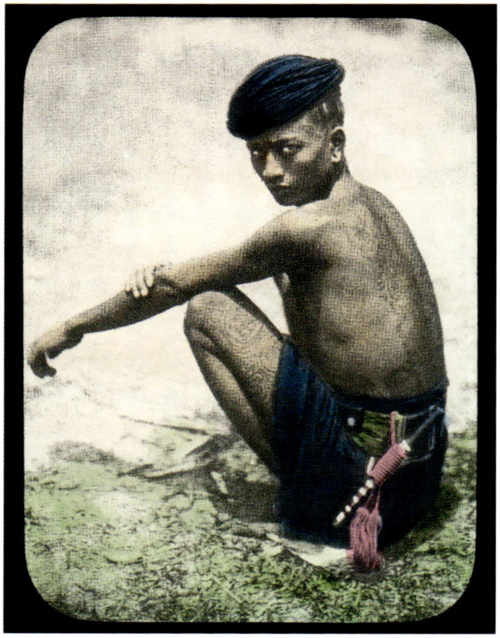

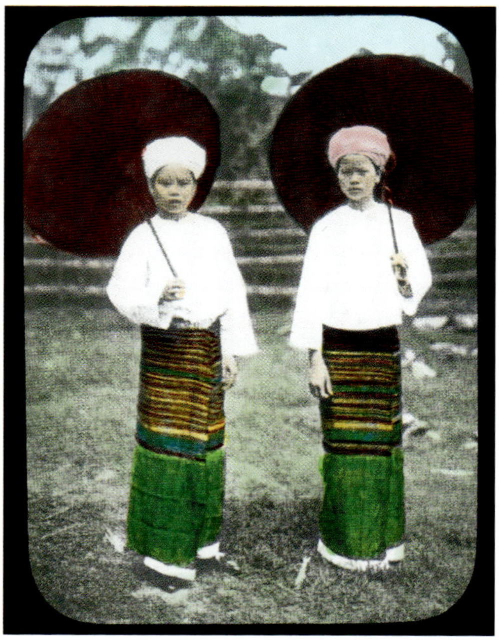

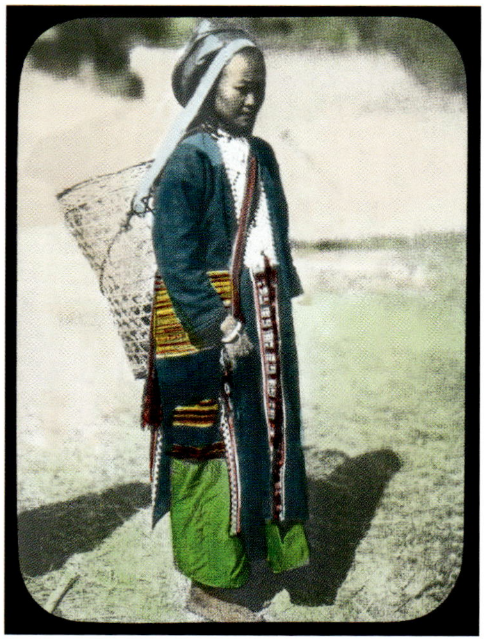

382–5 People wearing traditional costume, Burma (now Mynamar), 1890s

382–5 Menschen in traditioneller Tracht, Birma (heute Myanmar), 1890er Jahre

382–5 Les gens en costume traditionnel, Birmanie (auj. Myanmar), années 1890

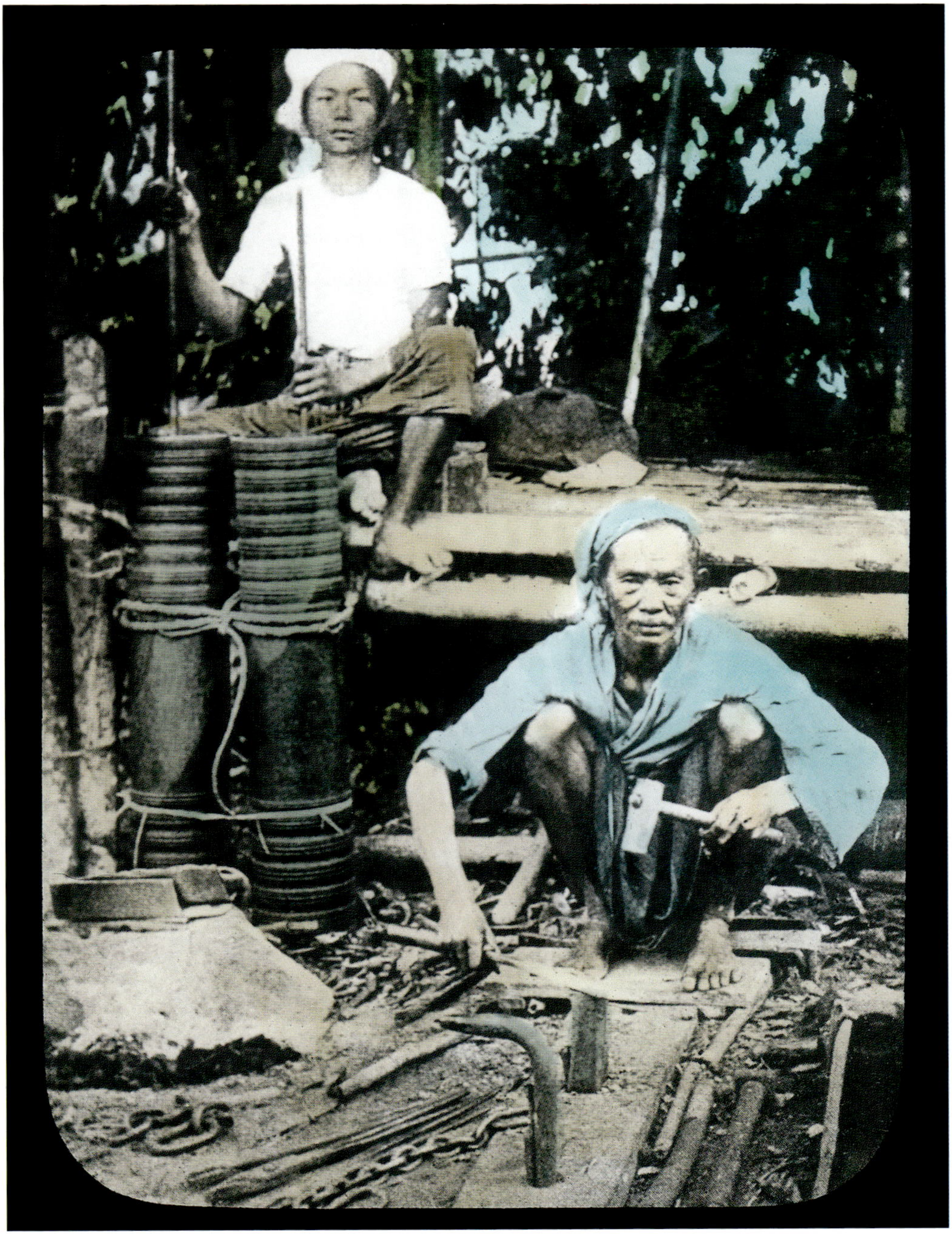

386 Men at work, Burma (now Mynamar), 1890s

386 Männer bei der Arbeit, Birma (heute Myanmar), 1890er Jahre

386 Ouvriers au travail, Birmanie (auj. Myanmar), années 1890

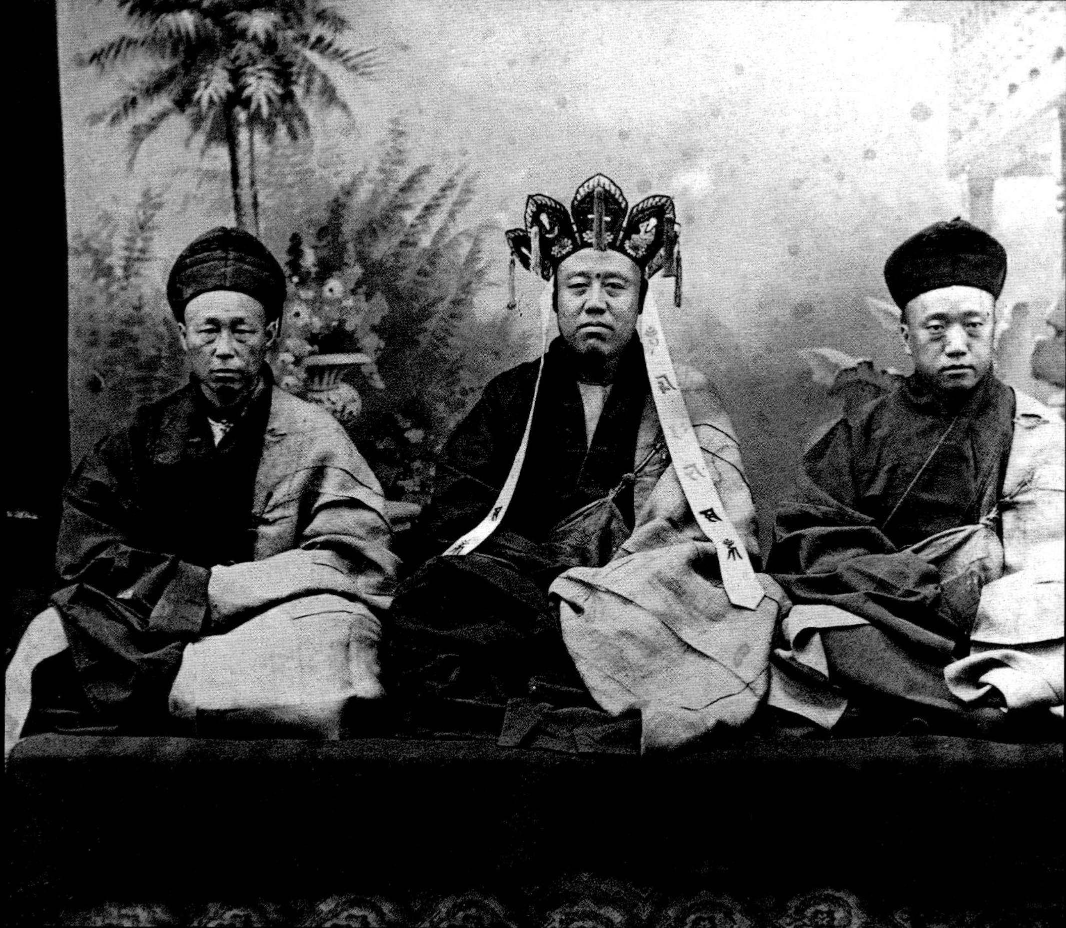

387 Taoist priests, China, 1880s

387 Taoistische Priester, China, 1880er Jahre

387 Prêtres taoïstes, Chine, années 1880

EASTERN ASIA

OSTASIEN · ASIE ORIENTALE

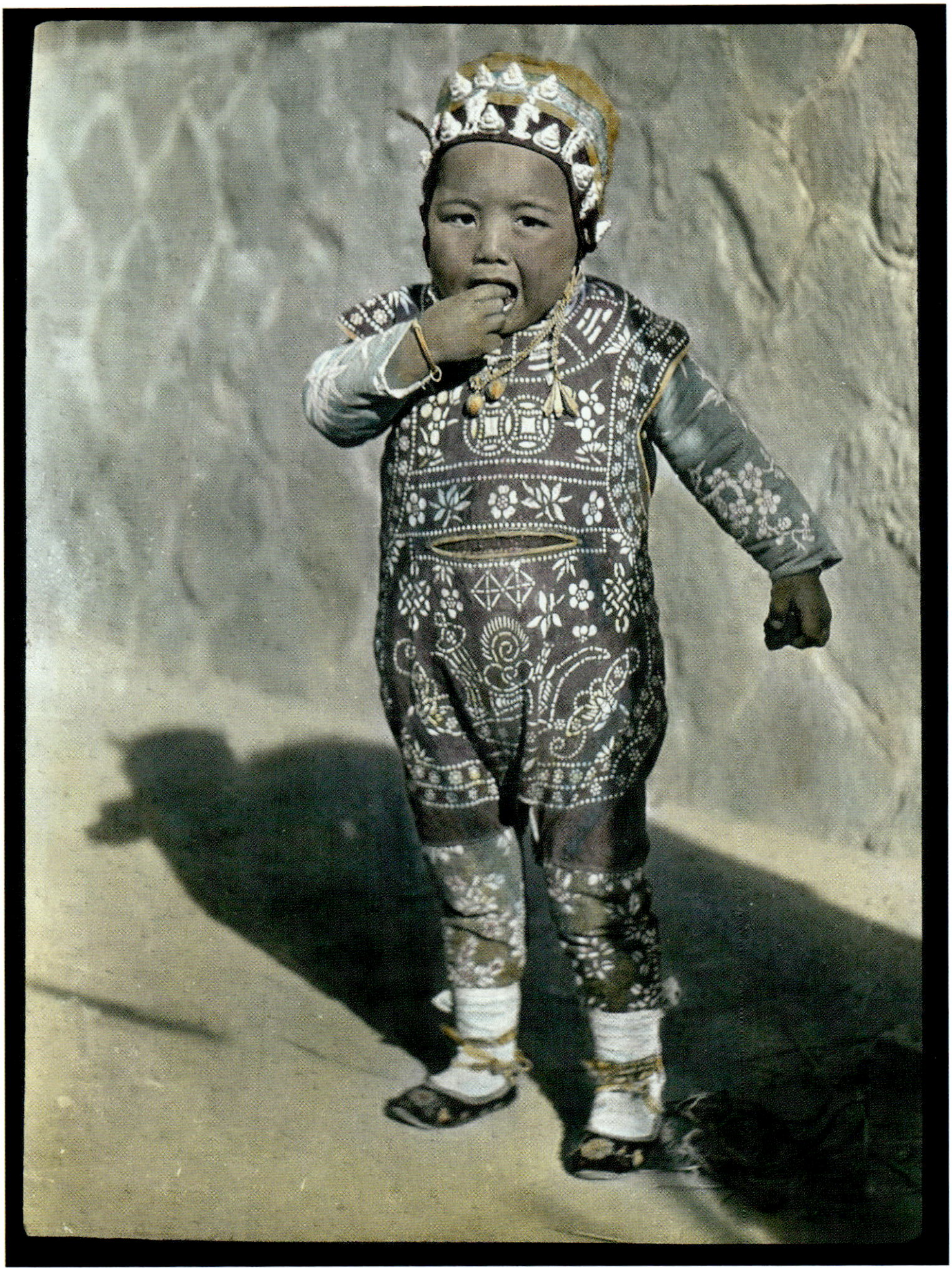

388 "Child with a sweet tooth", China, 1910s
389 Young girl with bound feet, China, 1910s

388 „Ein kleines Schleckermaul", China, 1910er Jahre
389 Ein kleines Mädchen mit gebundenen Füßen, China, 1910er Jahre

388 Enfant avec une sucrerie, Chine, années 1910
389 Jeune fille aux pieds bandés, Chine, années 1910

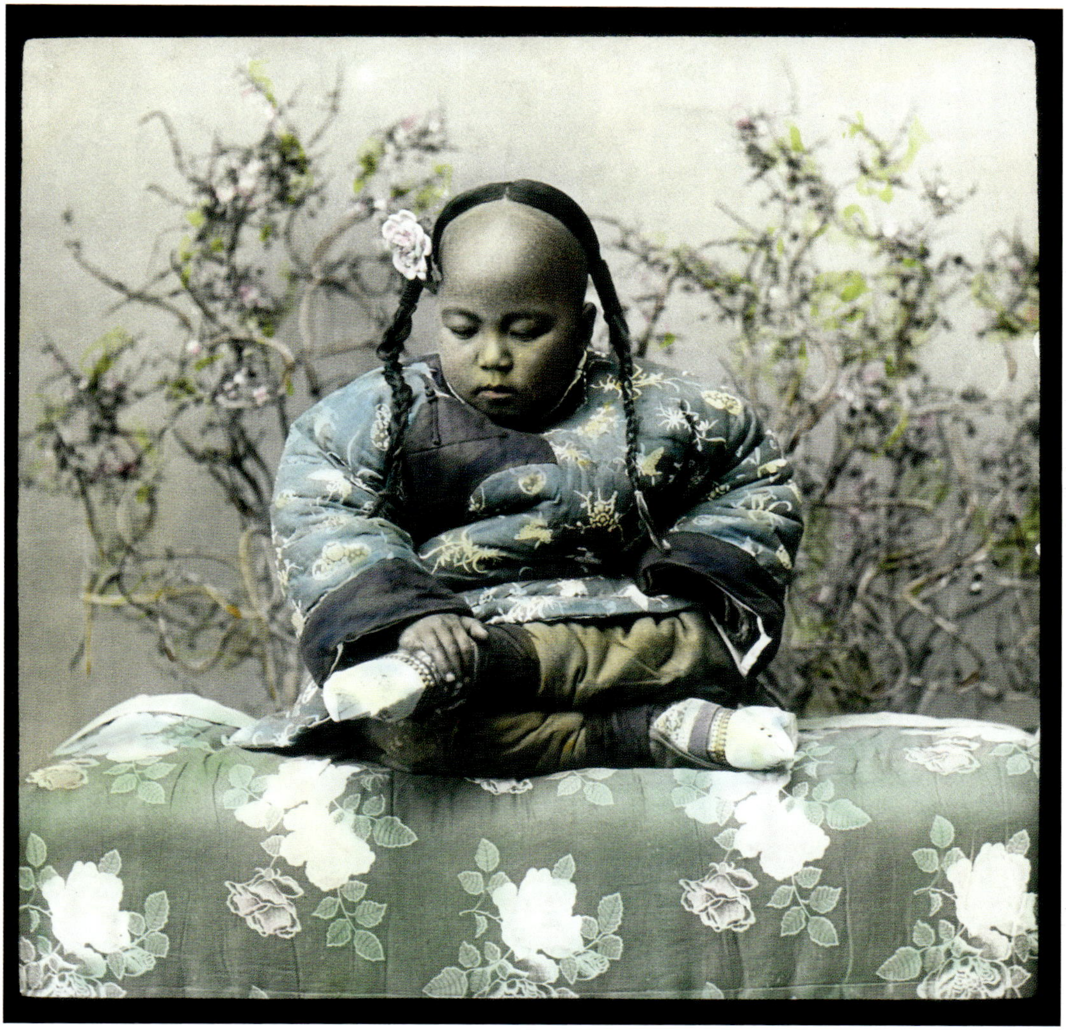

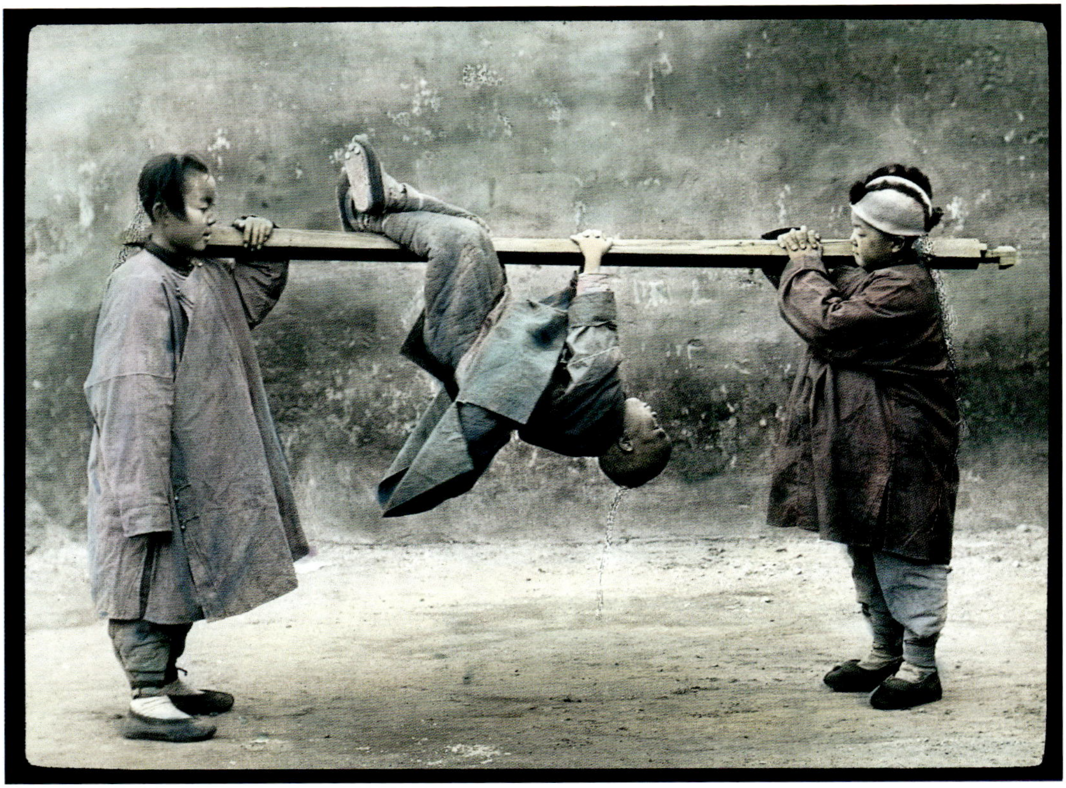

390 Boys playing, China, 1910s
391 "Newsboy", China, 1910s

390 Spielende Jungen, China, 1910er Jahre
391 „Zeitungsjunge", China, 1910er Jahre

390 Enfants en train de jouer, Chine, années 1910
391 Vendeur de journaux, Chine, années 1910

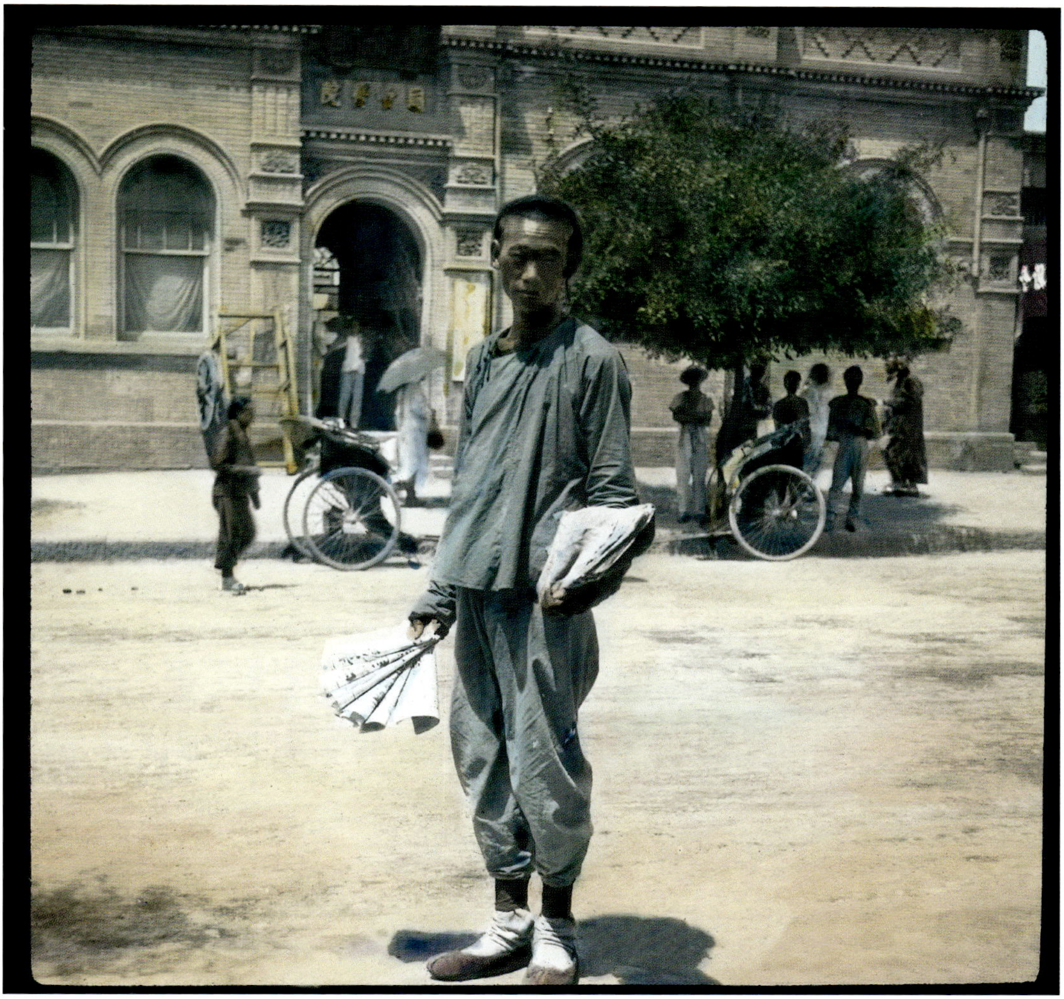

393 Packing tea,
China, 1880s

392 Teeziegel
werden in Papier
eingeschlagen,
China, 1880er Jahre

392 Emballage
de briques de thé,
Chine, années 1880

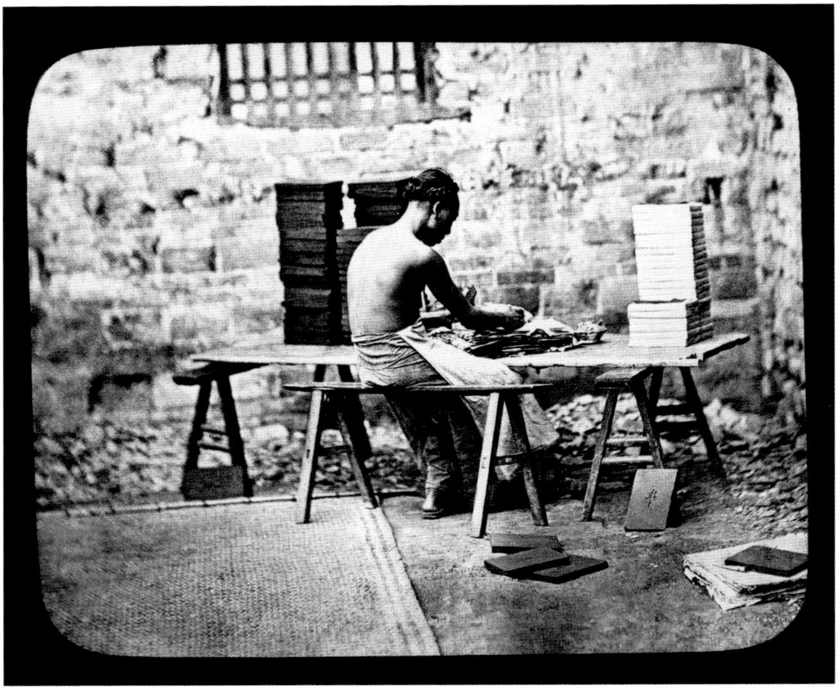

393 Packing tea,
China, 1880s

393 Tee wird
verpackt, China,
1880er Jahre

393 Emballage
du thé, Chine,
années 1880

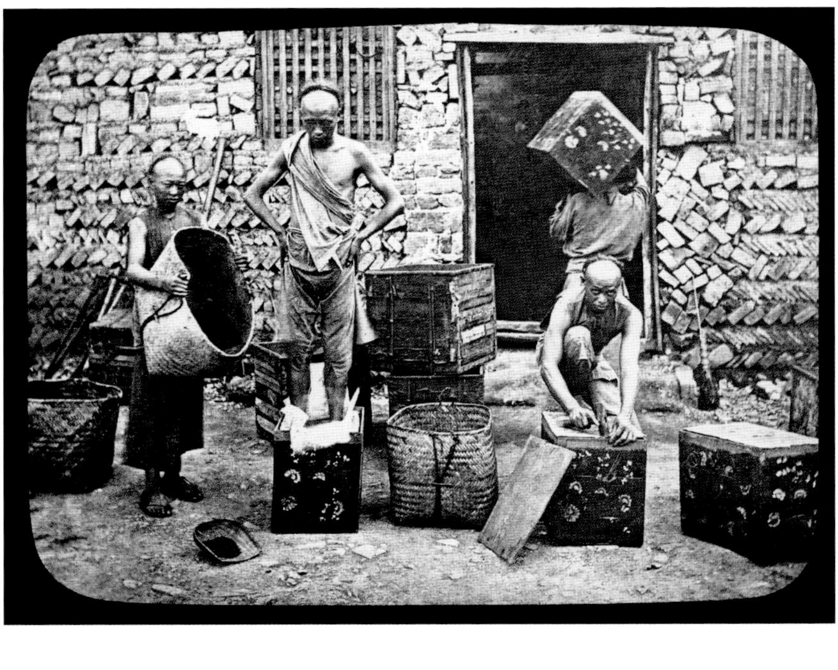

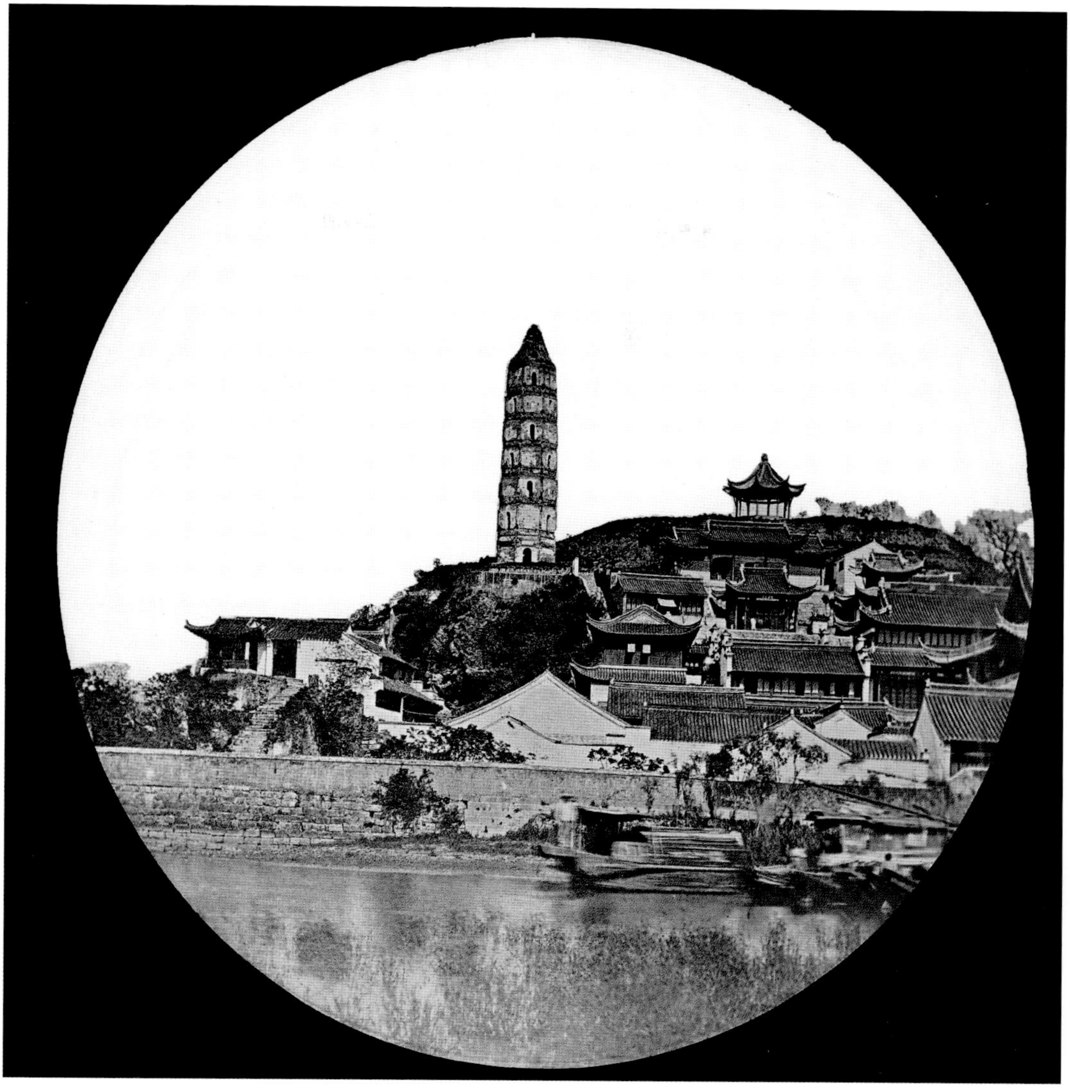

394 Yin-Shan (Silver Island) on the Yangtze River, China, 1870s
395 Great Wall of China at the Nankou Pass, China, 1900s

394 Yin-Shan (Silberinsel) im Jangtsekiang, China, 1870er Jahre
395 Die Chinesische Mauer am Nankou-Gebirgspass, China, 1900er Jahre

394 Yin-Shan (île d'argent) sur le fleuve Yangtzé, Chine, années 1870
395 Grande Muraille de Chine au col de Nankou, Chine, années 1900

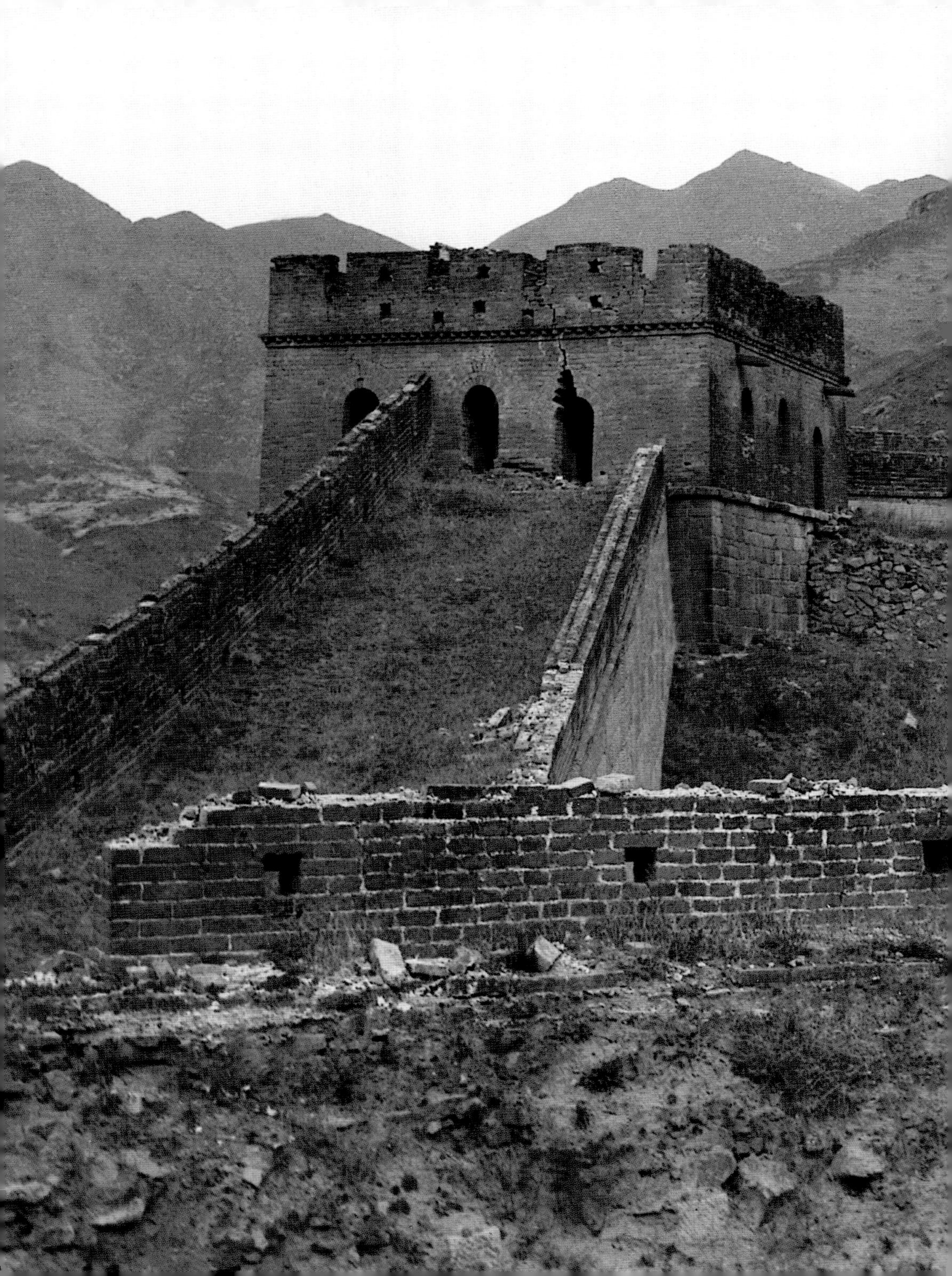

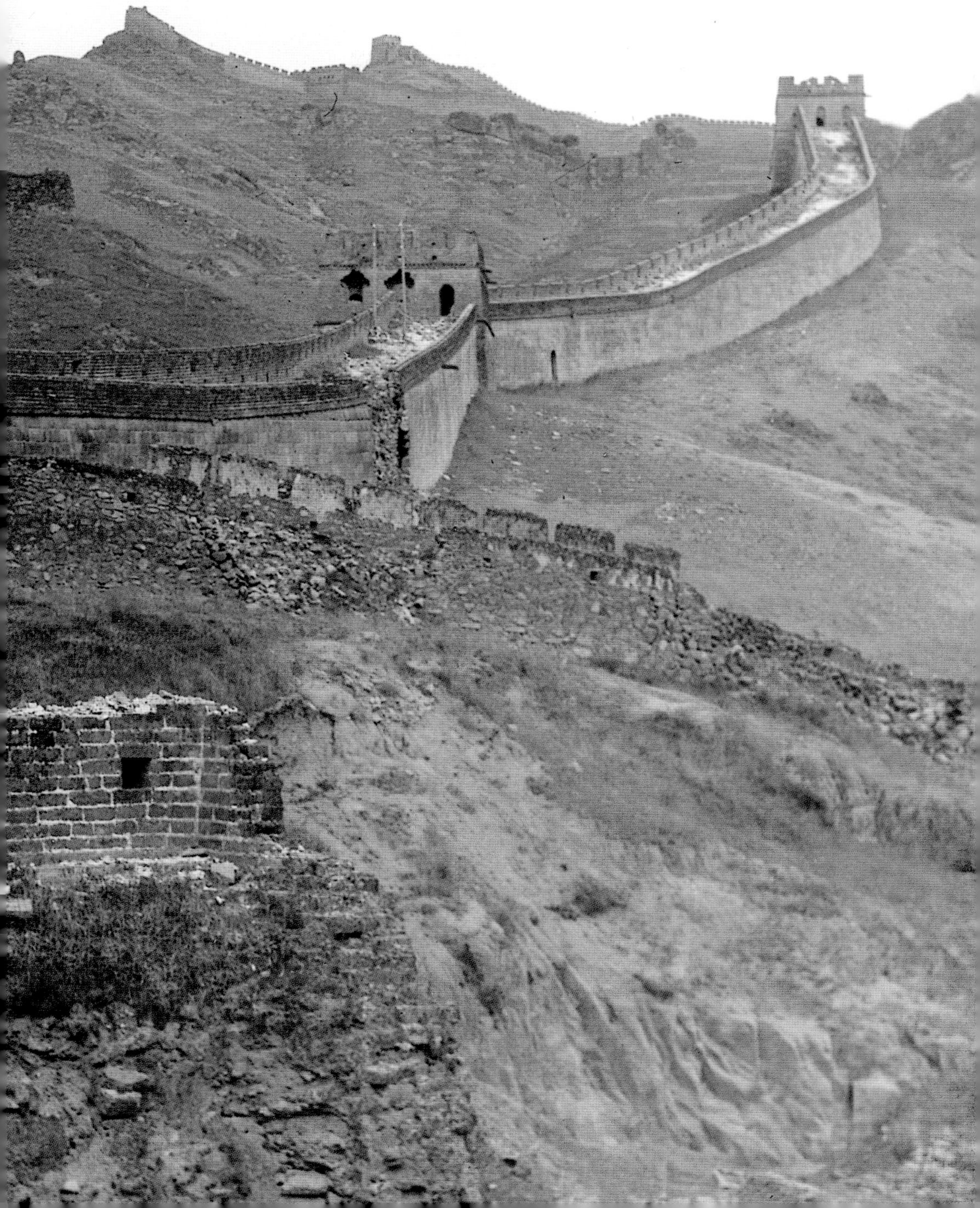

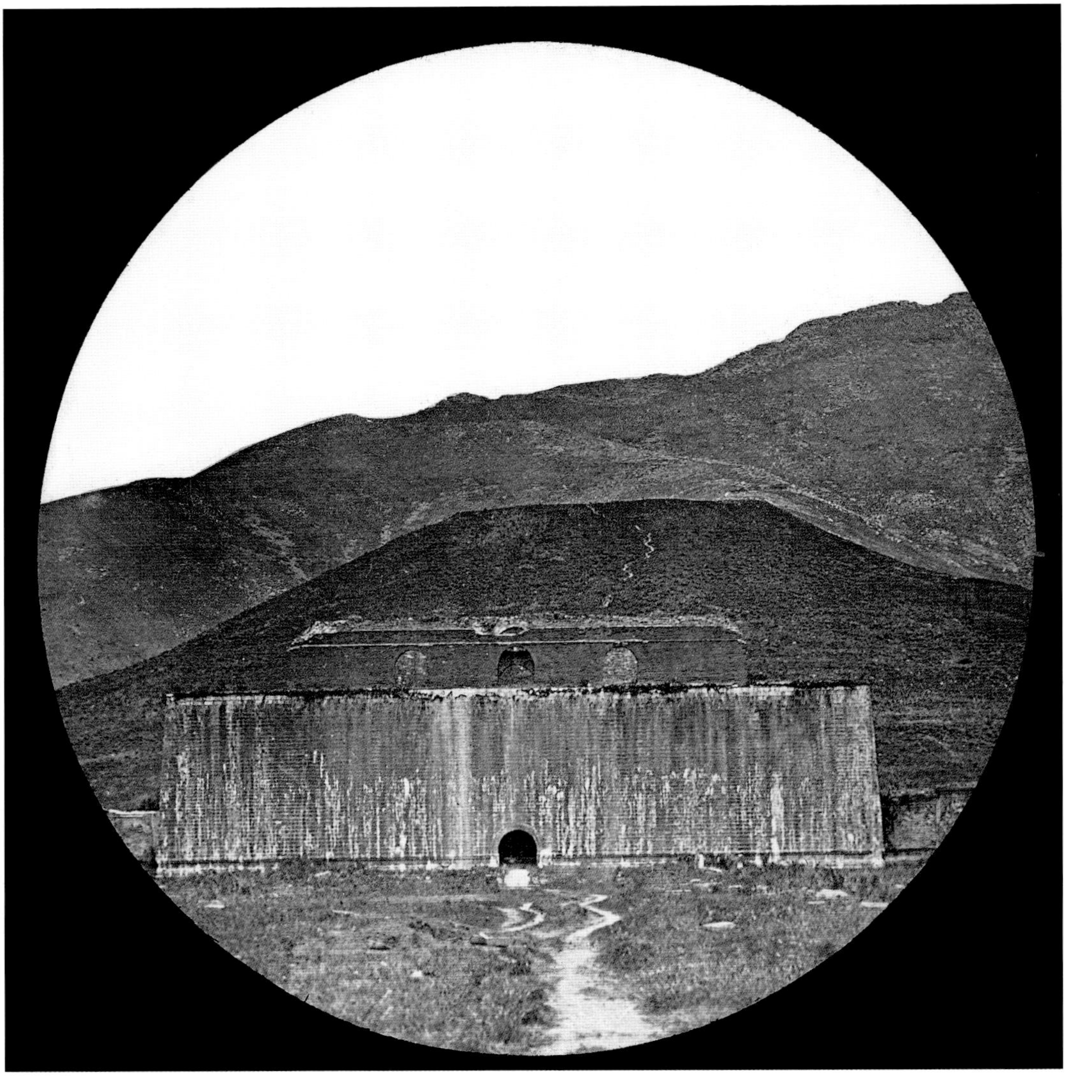

396 Tomb of Emperor Zhu Yuanzhang, Nanjing, China, 1870s

396 Das Grabmal von Kaiser Zhu Yuanzhang, Nanjing, China, 1870er Jahre

396 Tombe de l'empereur Zhu Yuanzhang, Nanjing, Chine, années 1870

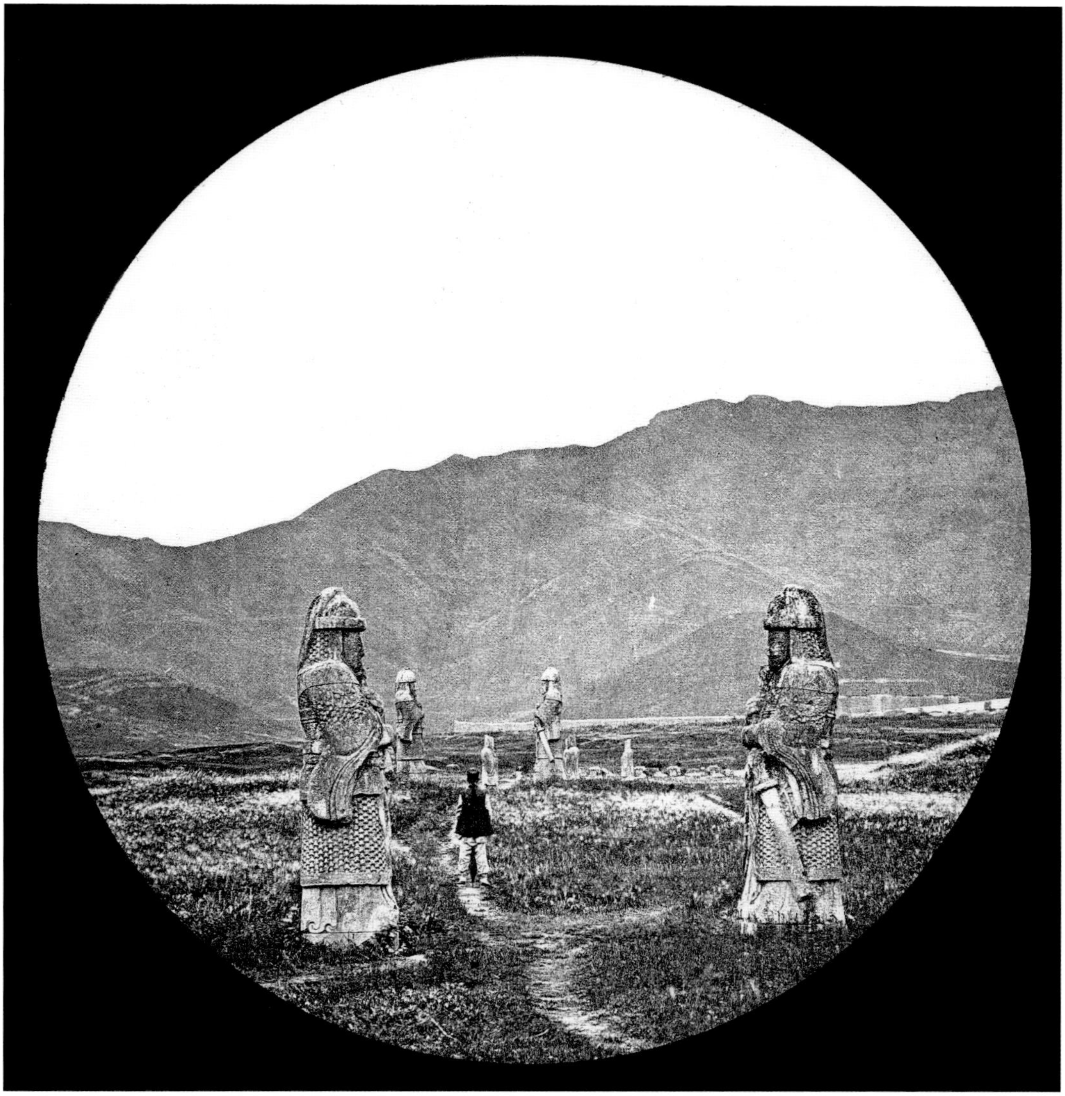

397 Avenue of Stone Warriors at the Tomb of Emperor Zhu Yuanzhang, Nanjing, China, 1870s

397 Weg der Steinkrieger am Grabmal von Kaiser Zhu Yuanzhang, Nanjing, China, 1870er Jahre

397 Allée des guerriers de pierre près de la tombe de l'empereur Zhu Yuanzhang, Nanjing, Chine, années 1870

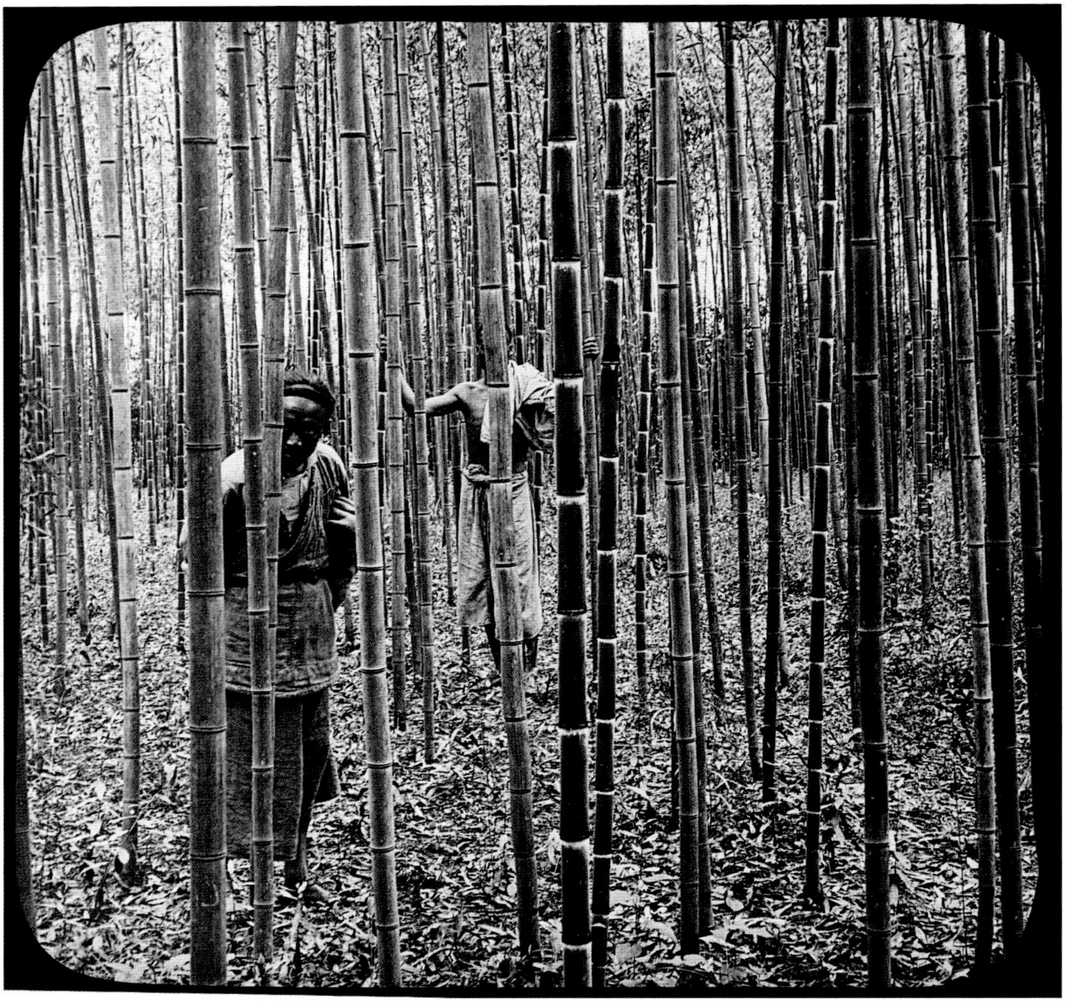

398 Bamboo plantation, Nanking (now Nanjing), China, 1910s
399 Pagoda at Hankow (now Wuhan), China, 1880s

398 Bambusplantage, Nanking (heute Nanjing), China, 1910er Jahre
399 Pagode in Hankow (heute Wuhan), China, 1880er Jahre

398 Bambouseraie, Nanking (auj. Nanjing), Chine, années 1910
399 Pagode à Hankow (auj. Wuhan), Chine, années 1880

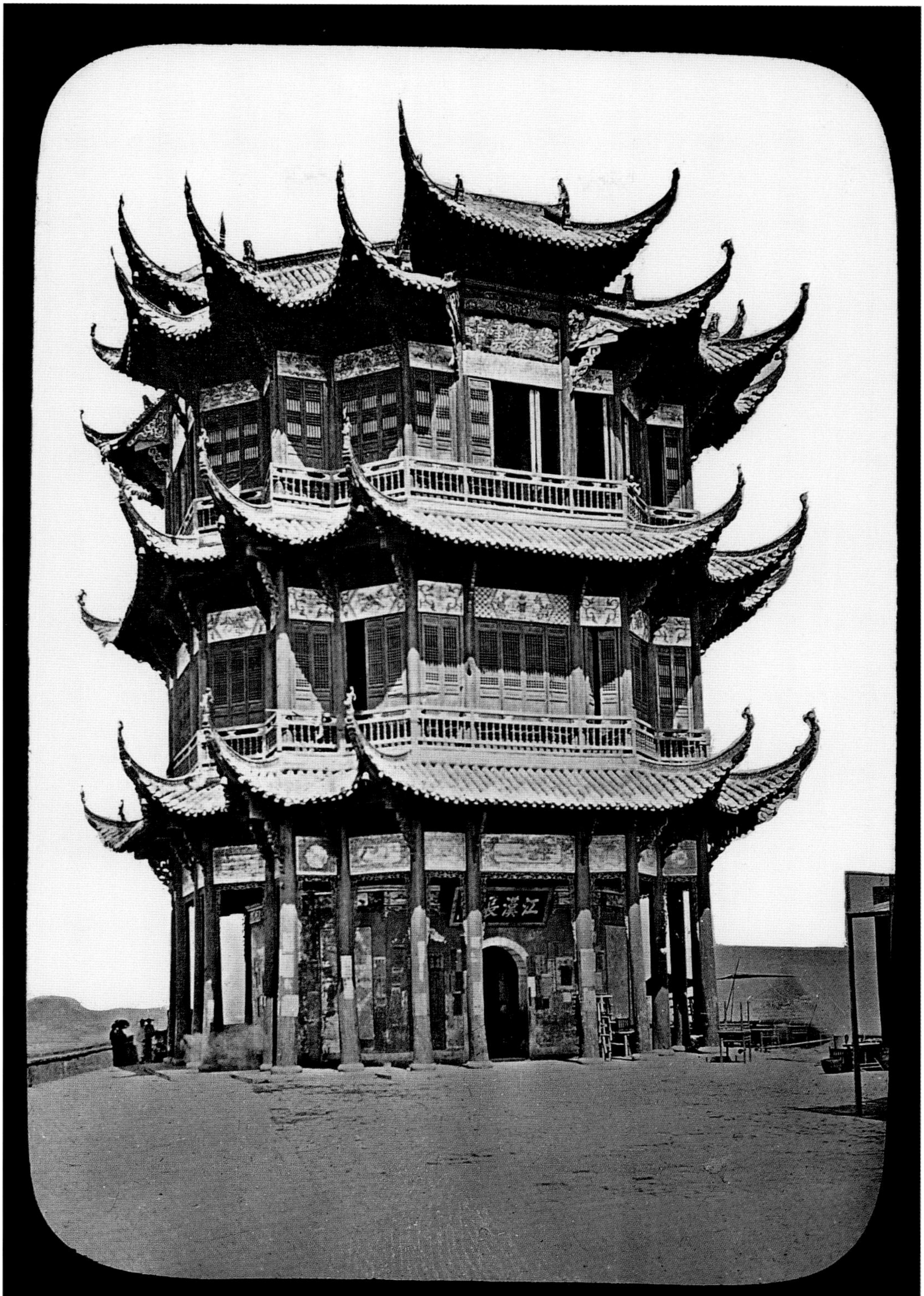

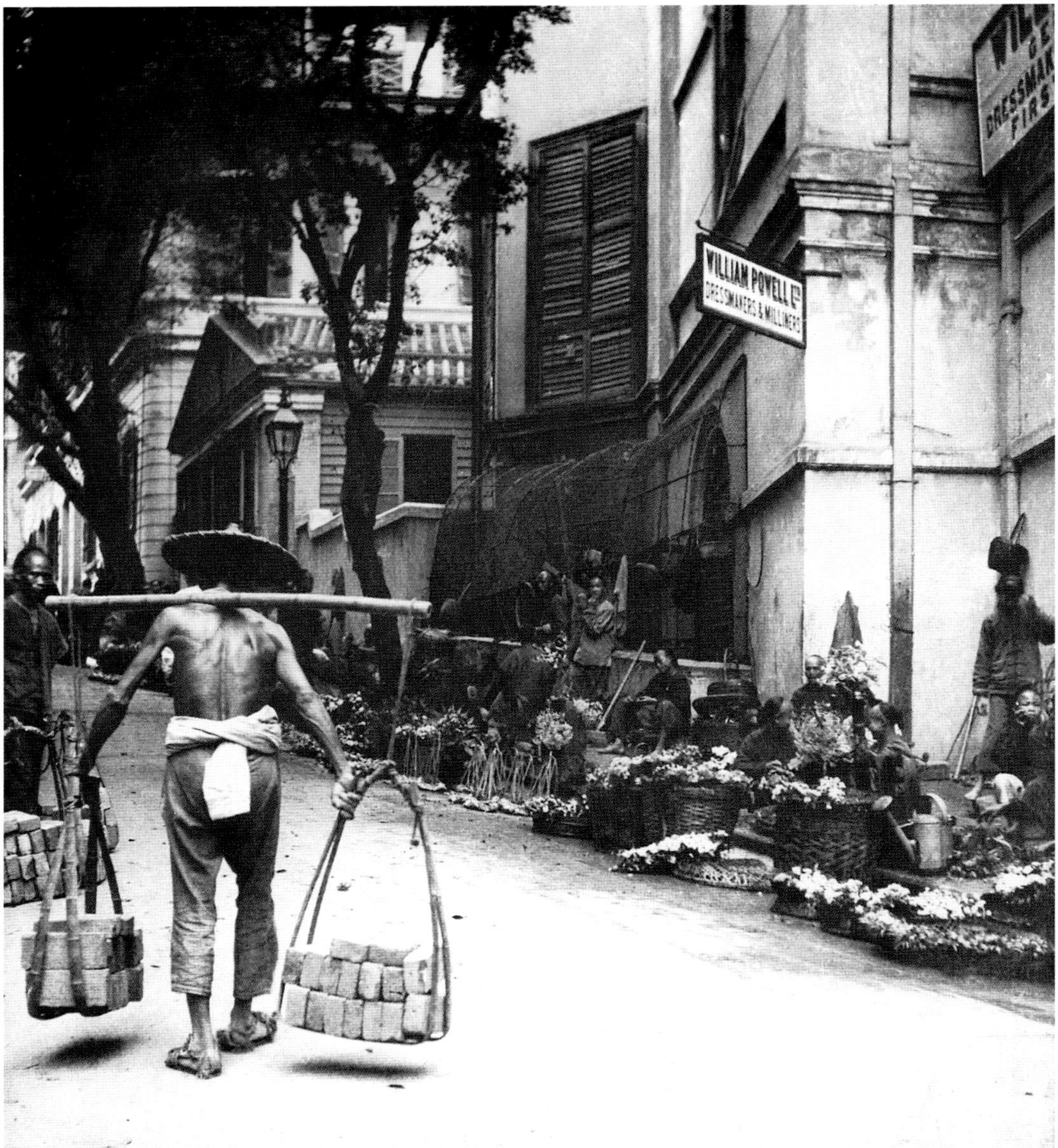

400 Man carrying bricks, China, 1900s
401 The Barber's Shop, China, 1900s
402 Jinriksha (two-wheeled carriage), China, 1900s

400 Ein Mann schleppt Ziegelsteine, China, 1900er Jahre
401 Der Herrenfriseur-salon, China, 1900er Jahre
402 Jinriksha (Rikscha), China, 1900er Jahre

400 Porteur de briques, Chine, années 1900
401 Boutique de barbier, Chine, années 1900
402 Jinriksha (pousse-pousse), Chine, années 1900

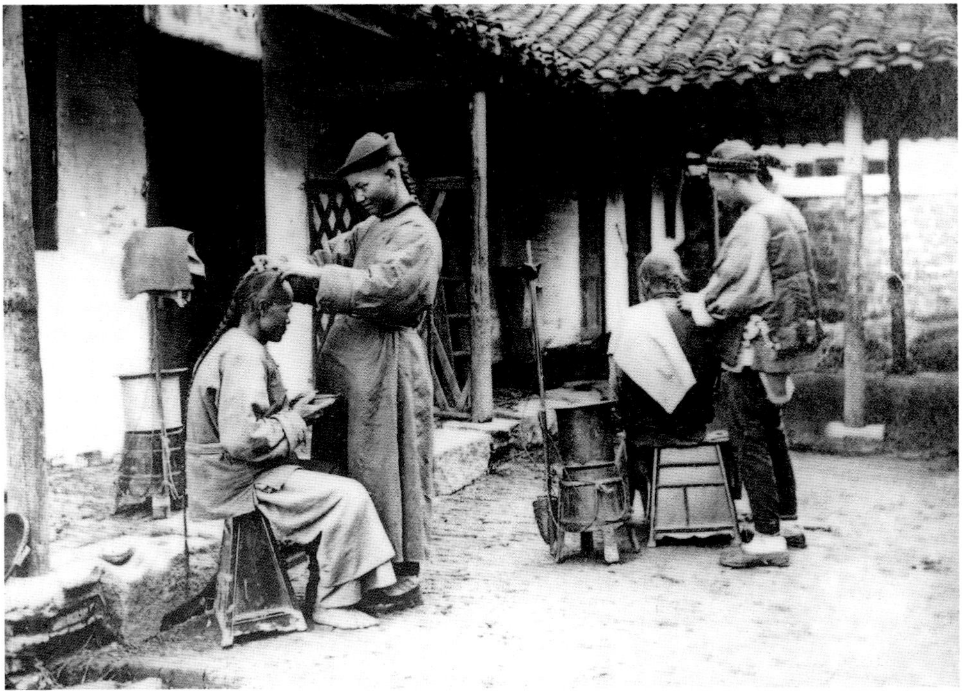

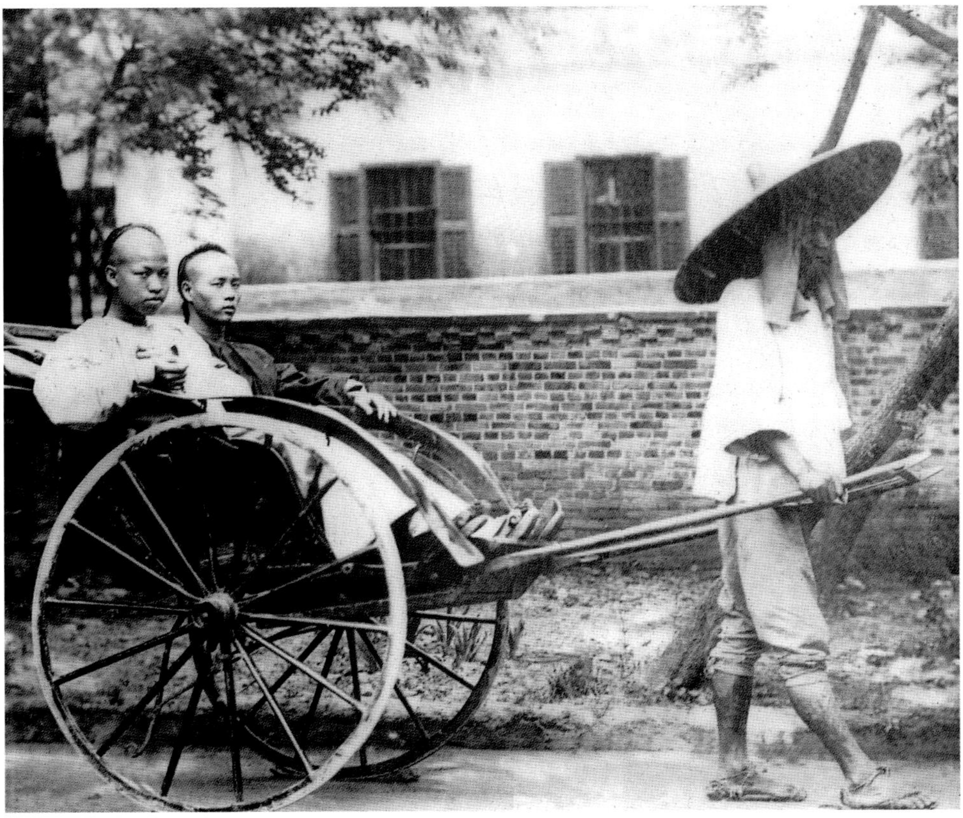

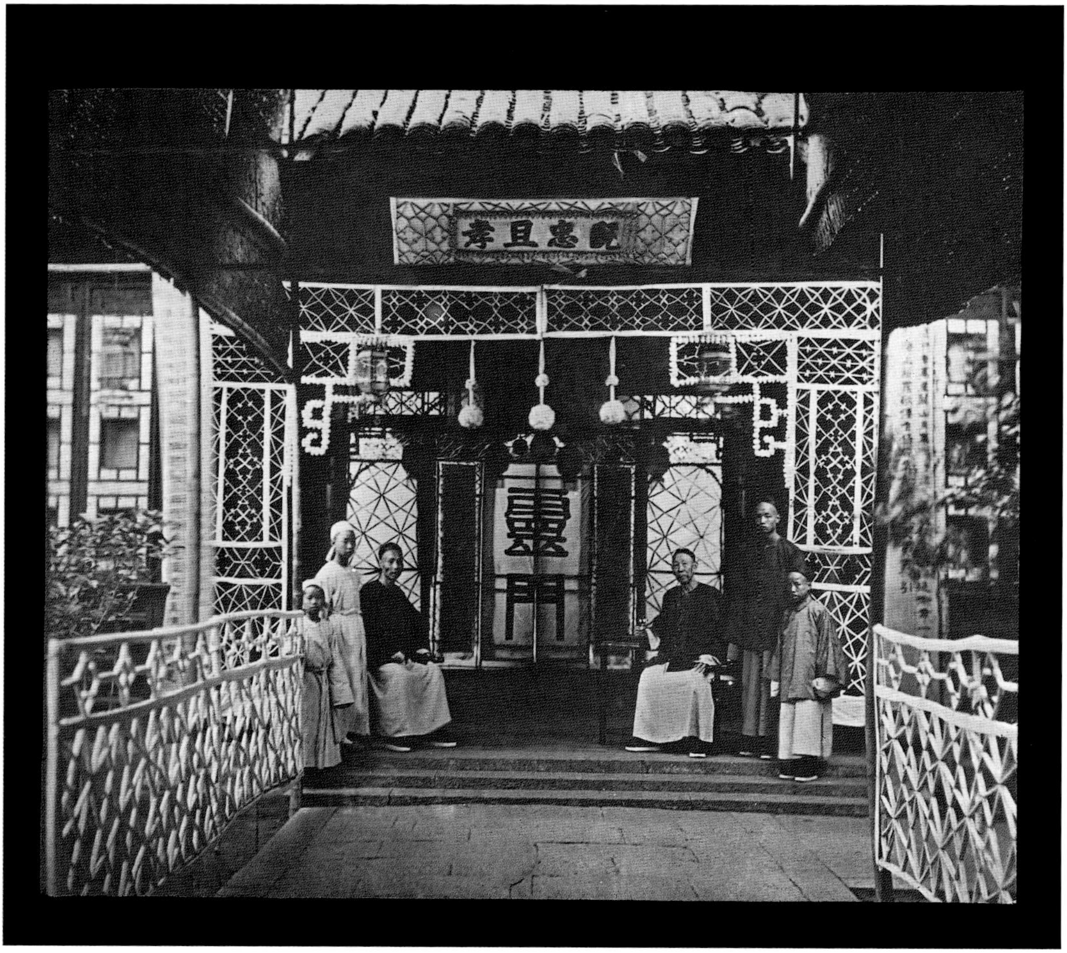

403 Entrance to house, China, 1880s
404 Mandarins (bureaucrats), China, 1880s

403 Hauseingang, China, 1880er Jahre
404 Mandarine (Beamte), China, 1880er Jahre

403 Entrée de maison, Chine, années 1880
404 Mandarins (bureaucrates), Chine, années 1880

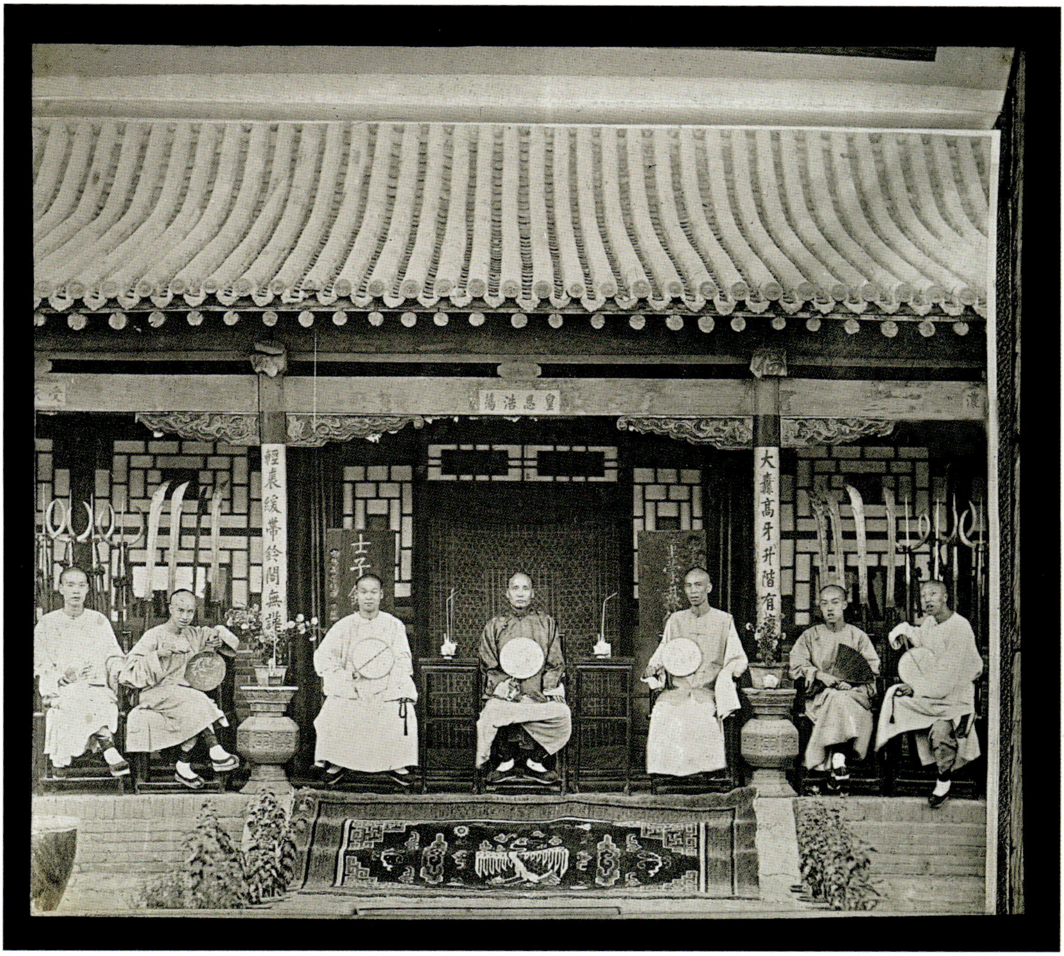
皇恩浩蕩
輕裘緩帶鈴閣無譁
大纛高牙幷階有

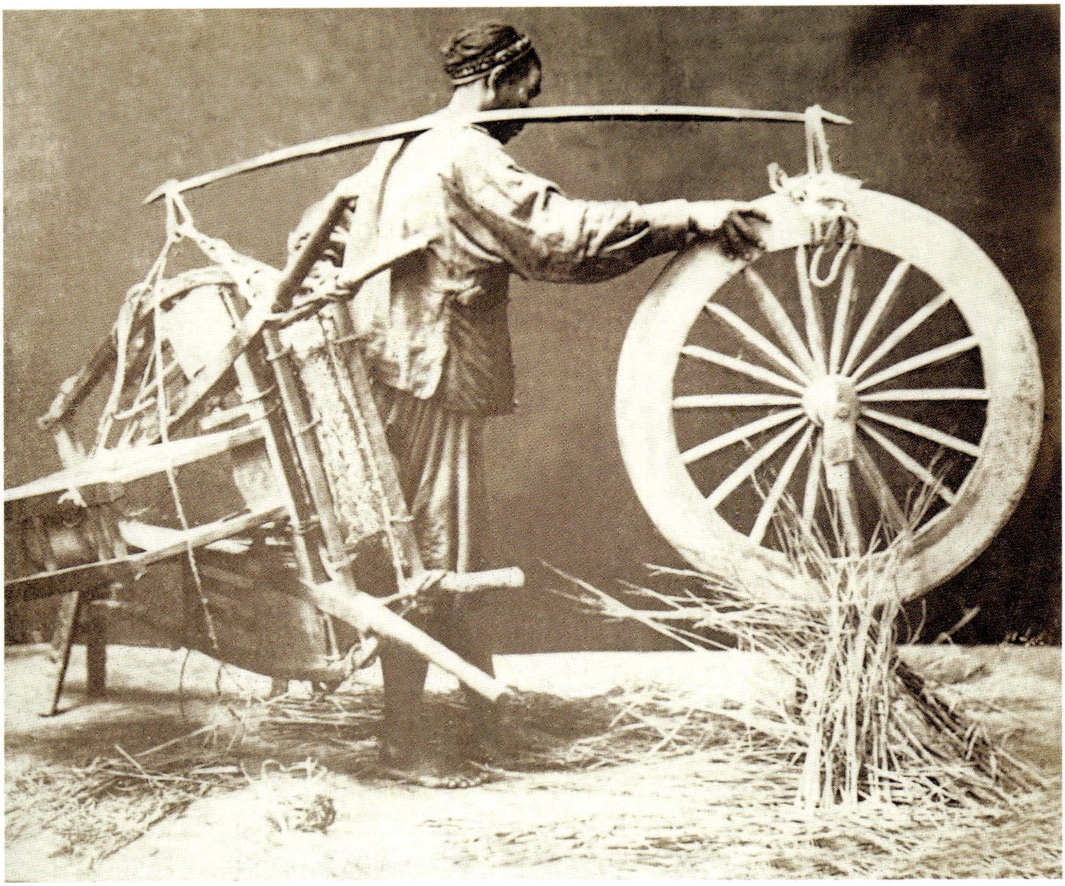

405 "Wheelbarrow", China, 1870s
406 Weaving loom, China, 1870s

405 „Schubkarre", China, 1870er Jahre
406 Webstuhl, China, 1870er Jahre

405 « Brouette », Chine, années 1870
406 Métier à tisser, Chine, années 1870

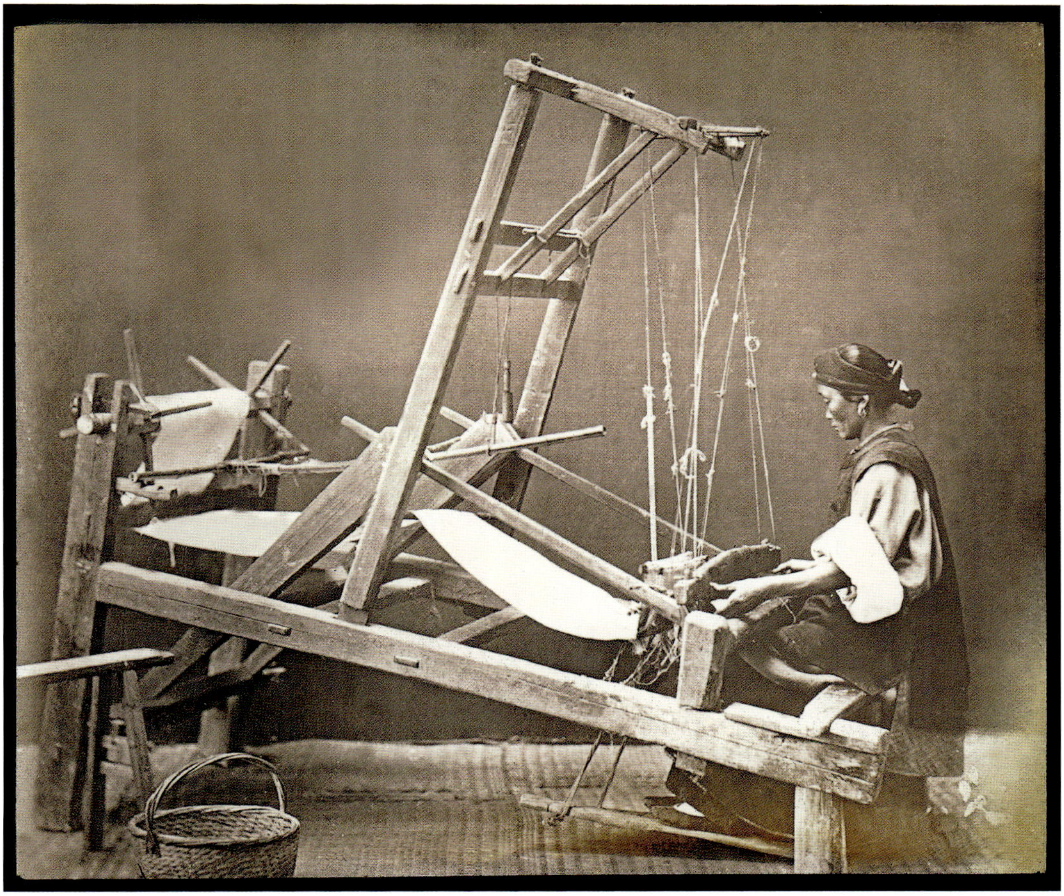

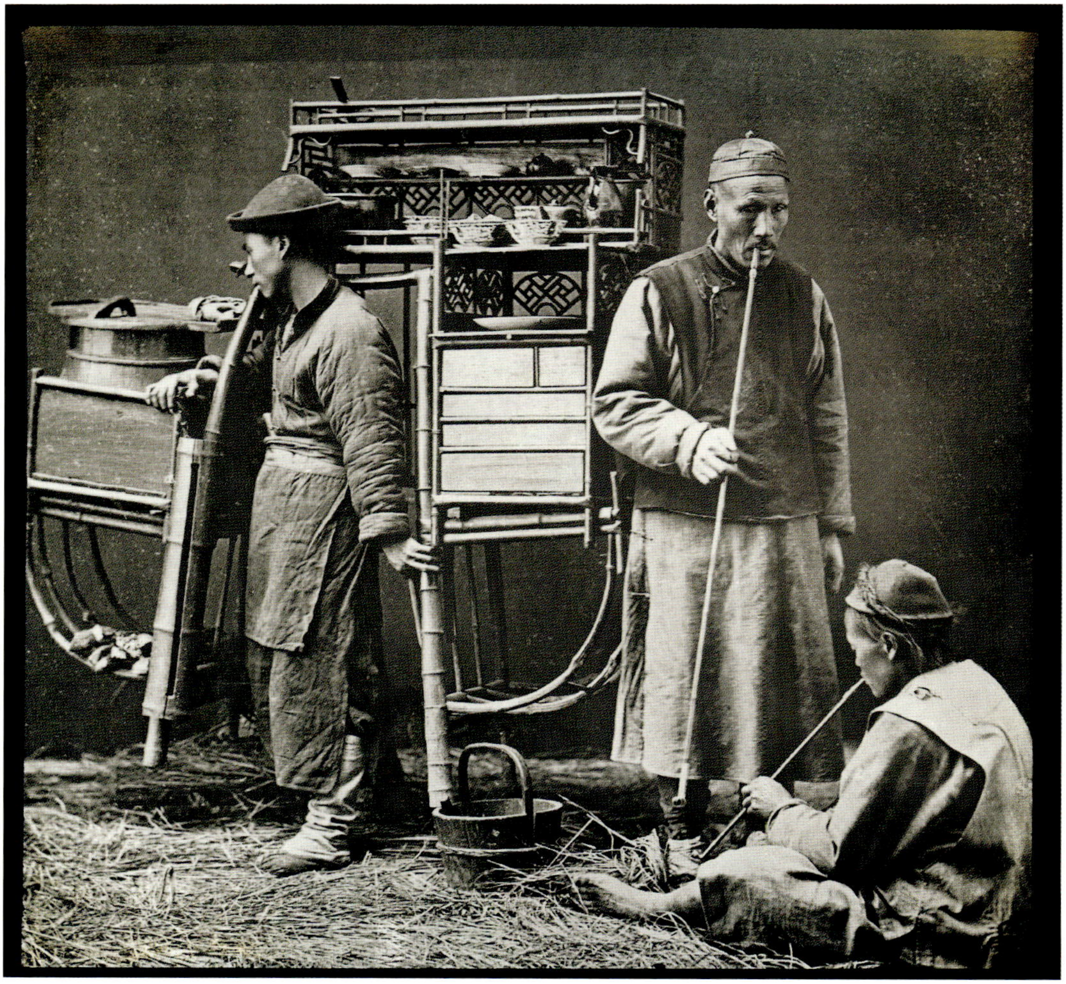

407 Travelling cookshop, China, 1870s
408 Children and teacher outside a school in Peking (now Beijing), China, 1900s

407 Transportable Garküche, China, 1870er Jahre
408 Kinder und Lehrer vor einer Schule in Peking (heute Beijing), China, 1900er Jahre

407 Cuisine portative, Chine, années 1870
408 Enfants et maîtresses devant l'école. Peking (auj. Pékin), Chine, années 1900

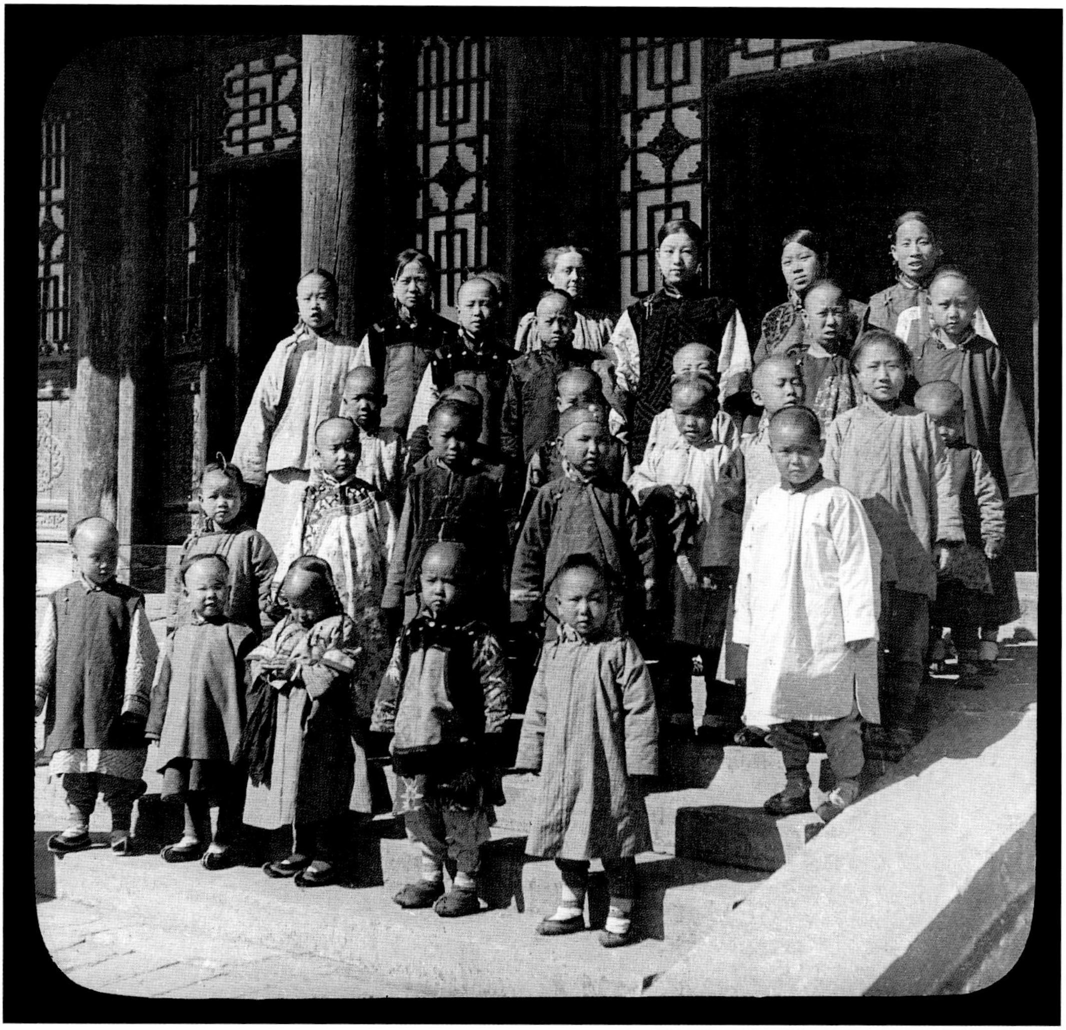

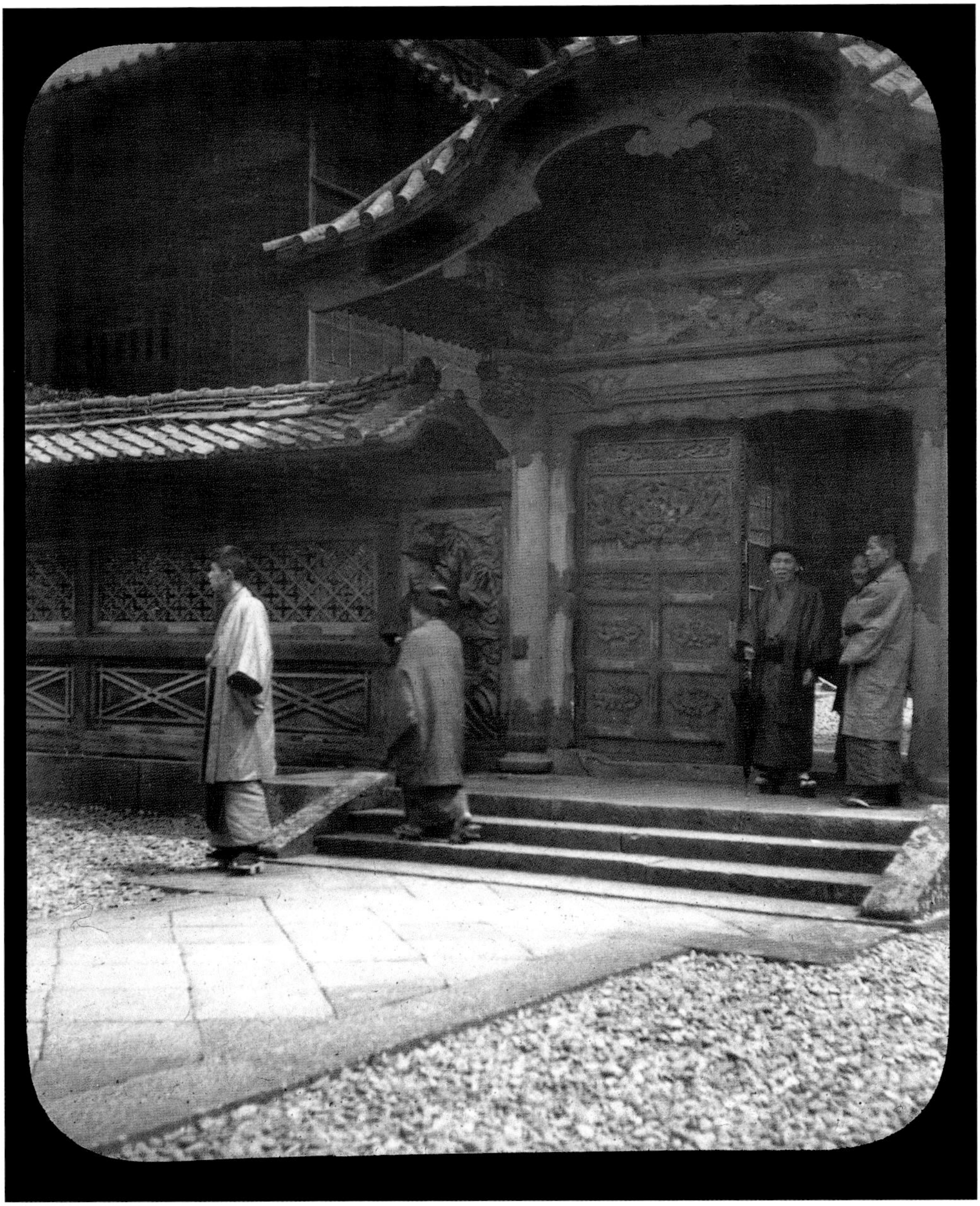

409 Temple, China, 1890s
410 Priest at a temple, China, 1890s

409 Tempel, China, 1890er Jahre
410 Priester in einem Tempel, China, 1890er Jahre

409 Temple, Chine, années 1890
410 Prêtre dans un temple, Chine, années 1890

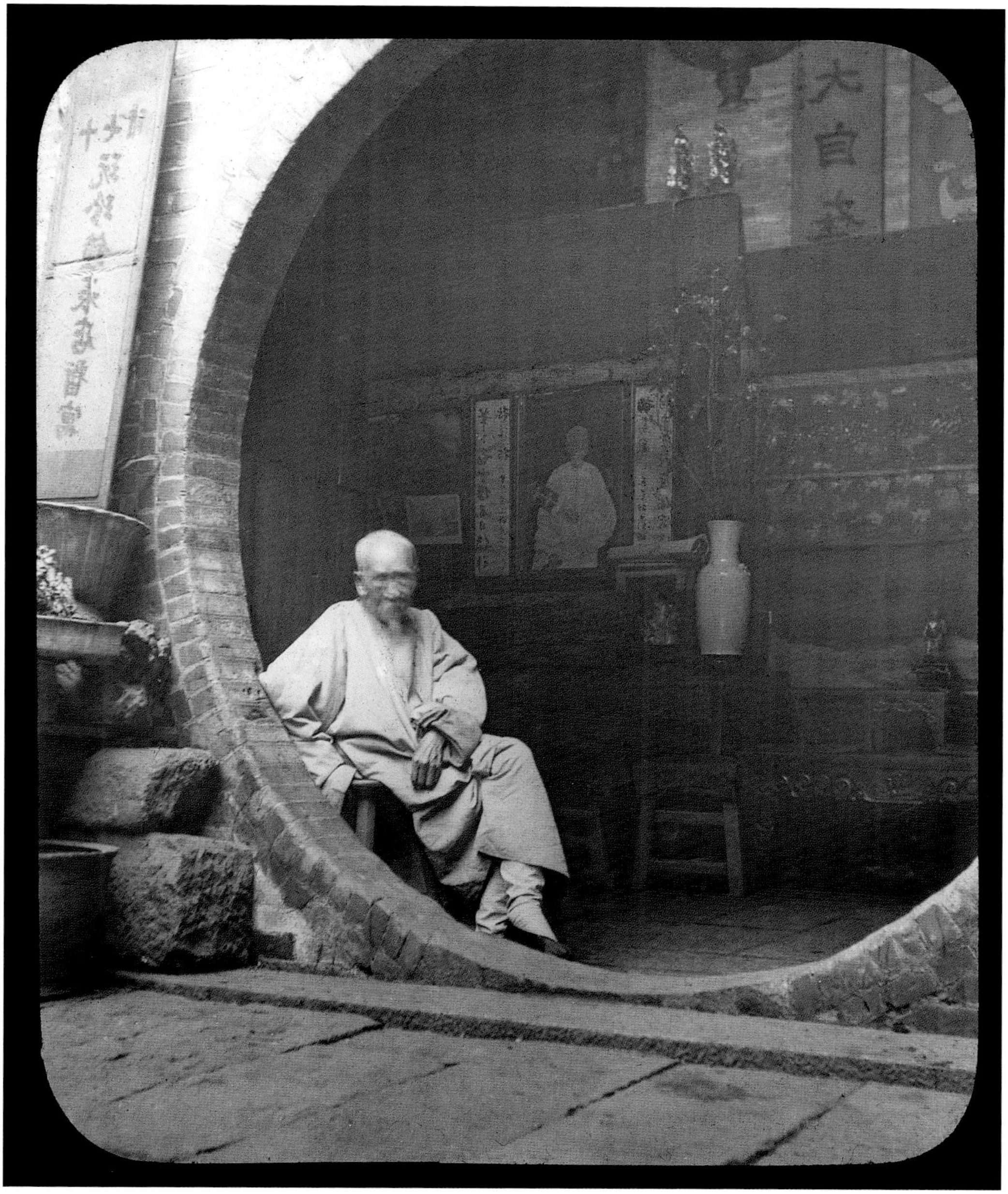

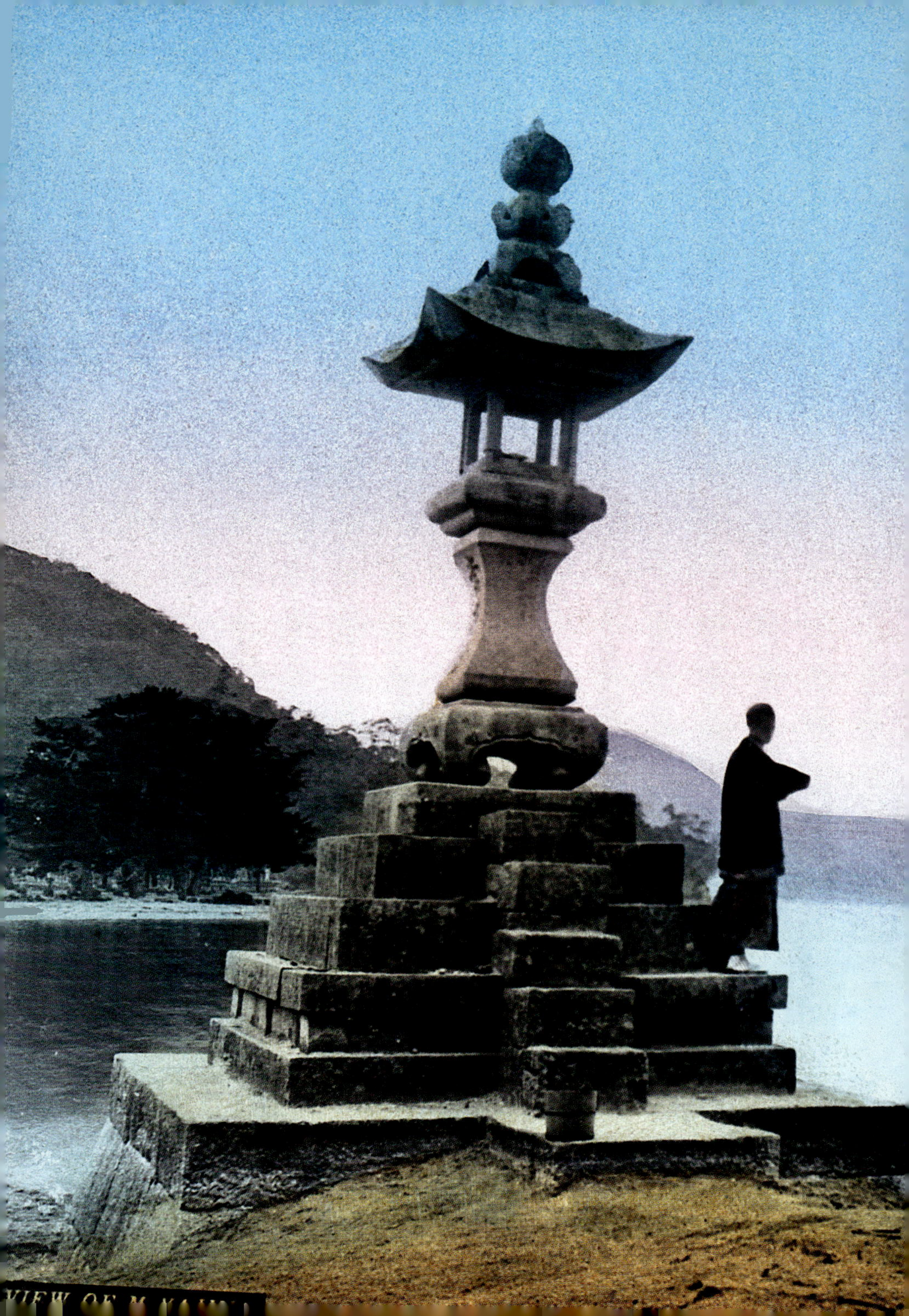
VIEW OF M

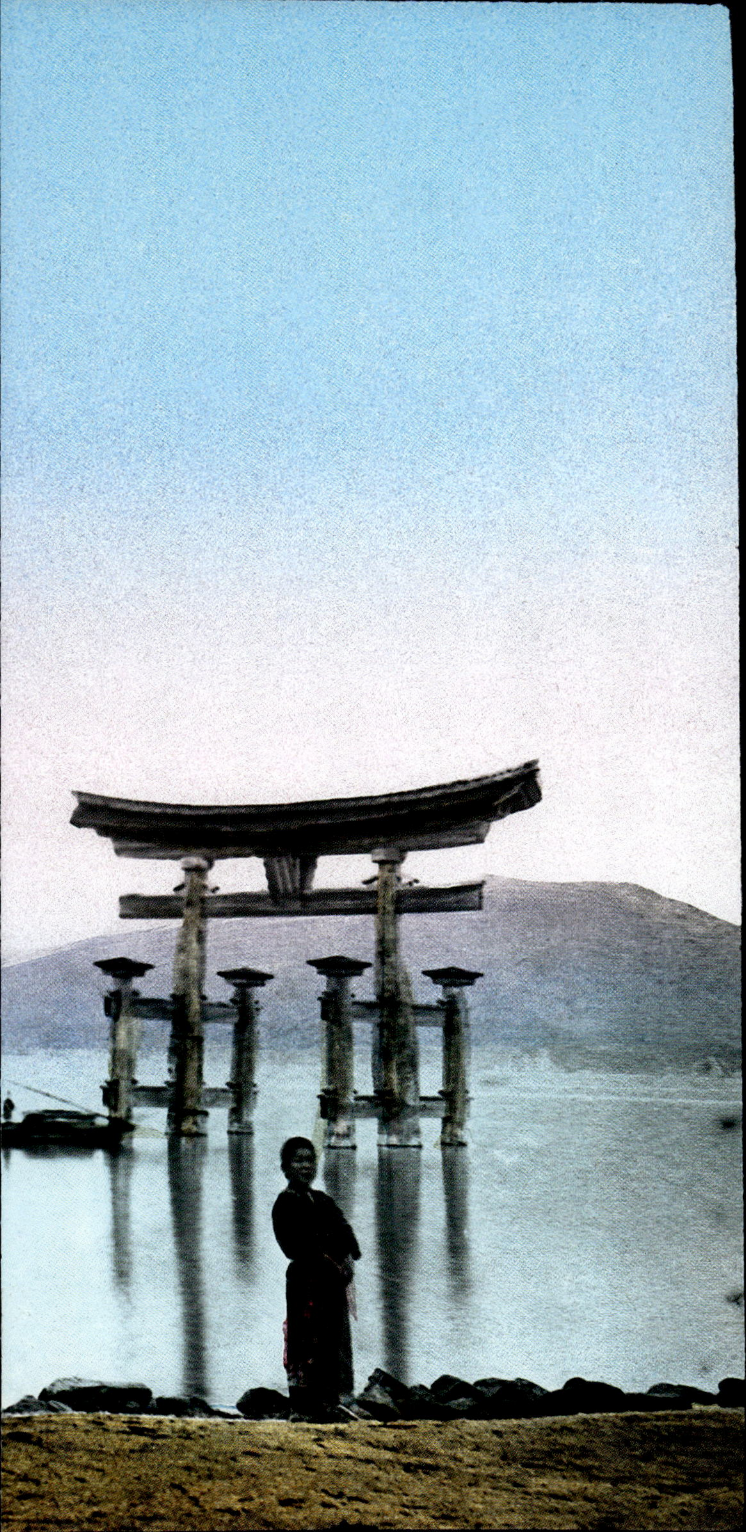

411 Shrine
at Miyajima
(Itsukushima),
Japan, 1890s

411 Schrein
auf Miyajima
(Itsukushima-
Schrein), Japan,
1890er Jahre

411 Sanctuaire
à Miyajima
(Itsukushima),
Japon, années 1890

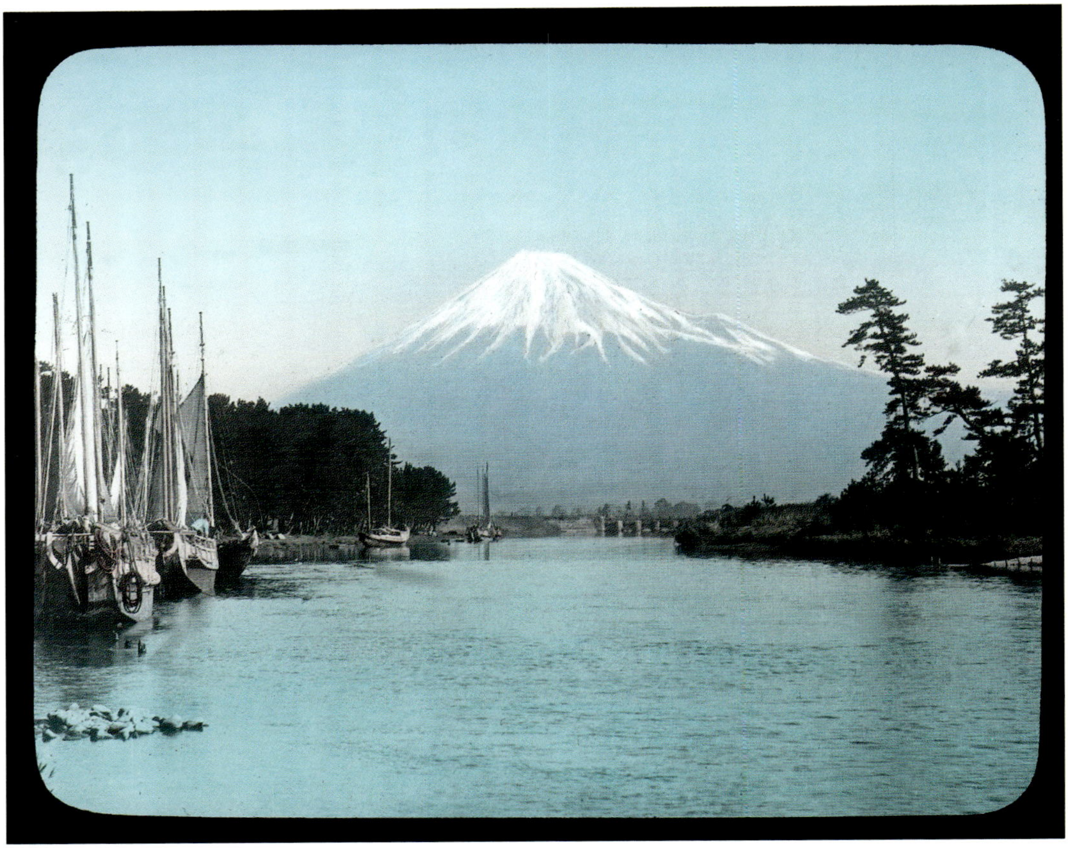

412 View of Mount Fuji (Fujiyama) from Tagono-ura, Japan, c.1900

412 Ansicht des Berges Fuji (Fujiyama) von Tagono-ura aus, Japan, um 1900

412 Vue du mont Fuji (Fujiyama) depuis Tagono-Ura, Japon, vers 1900

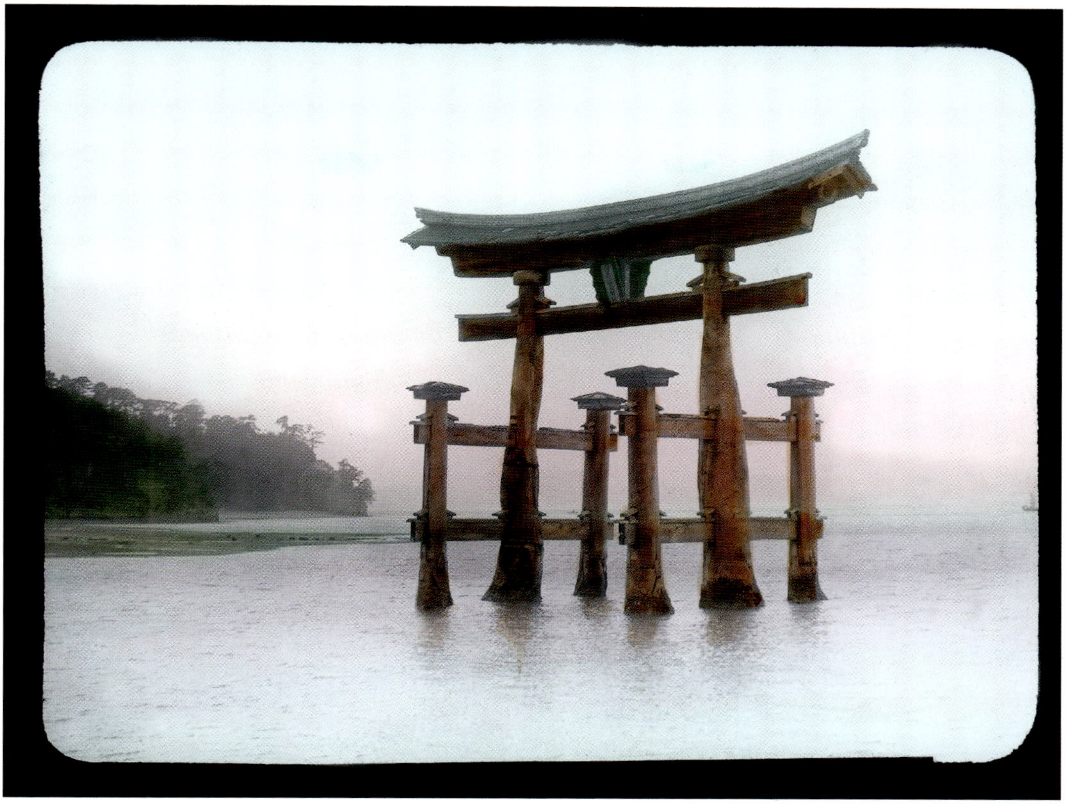

413 Torii Gate at Itsukushima Shrine in Miyajima, Japan, 1890s

413 Das Torii (Tor) des Itsukushima-Schreins auf Miyajima, Japan, 1890er Jahre

413 Porte Torii au sanctuaire d'Itsukushima à Miyajima, Japon, années 1890

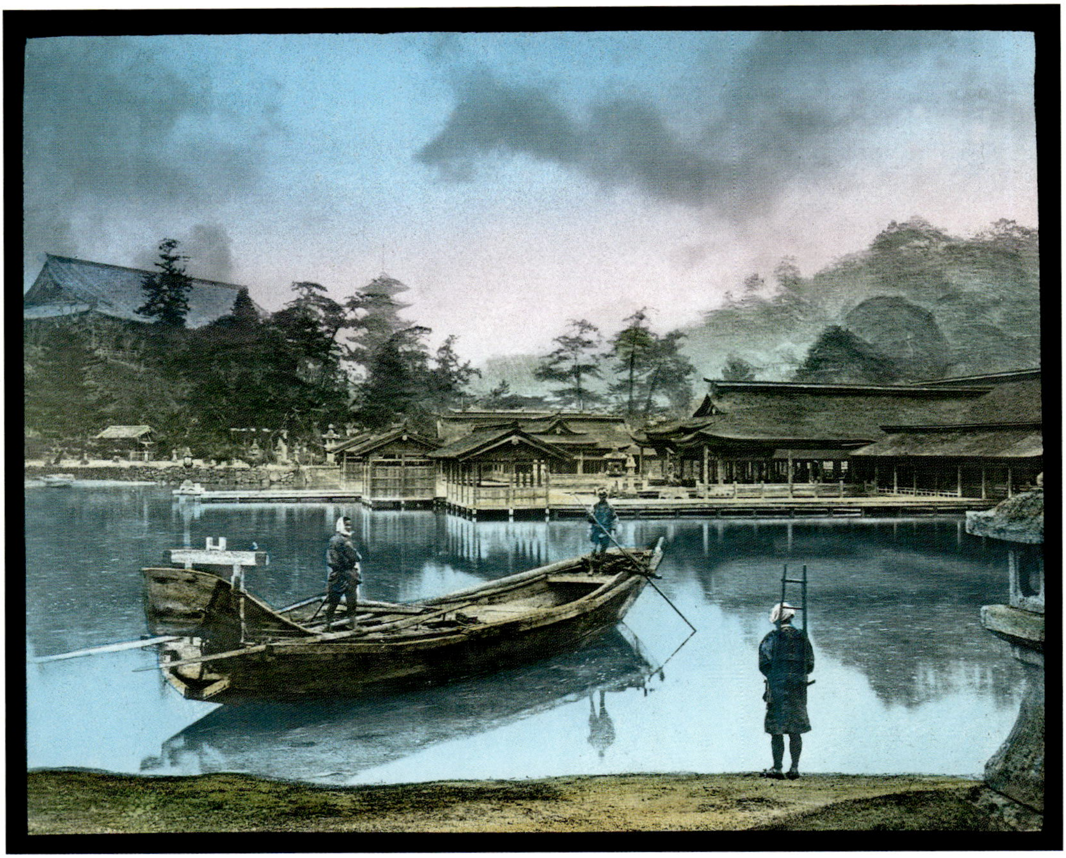

414 River-boat, Japan, 1890s
415 Harbour scene, Japan, 1890s

414 Flussschiff, Japan, 1890er Jahre
415 Hafenszene, Japan, 1890er Jahre

414 Embarcation fluviale, Japon, années 1890
415 Paysage portuaire, Japon, années 1890

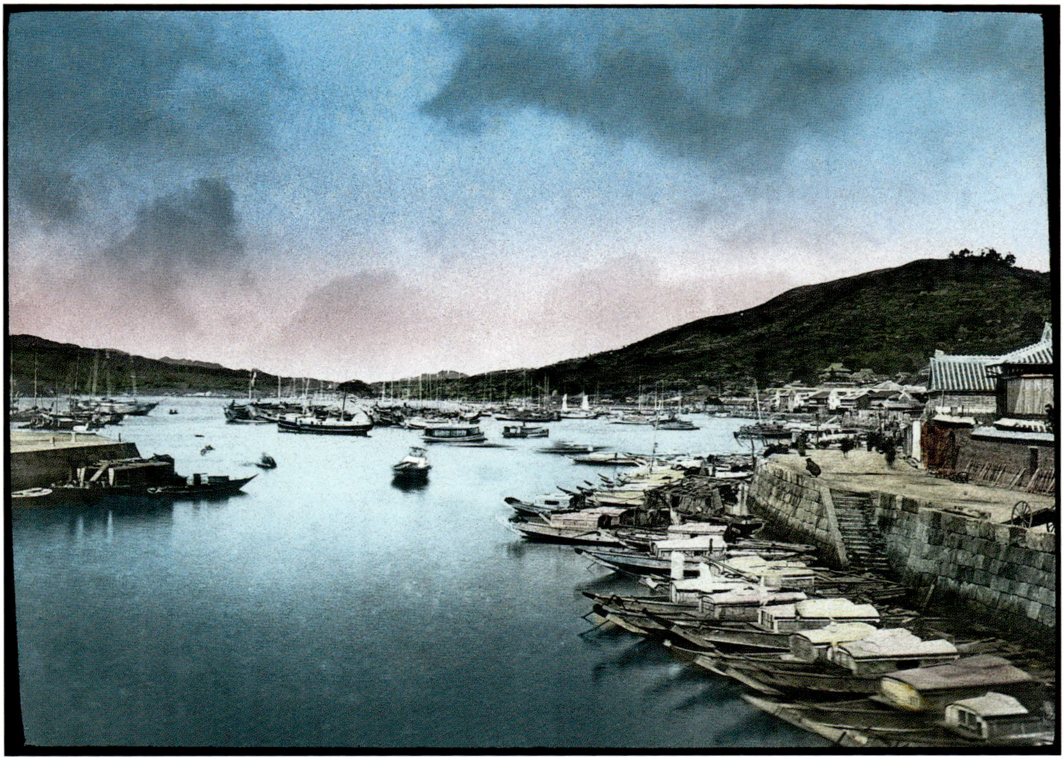

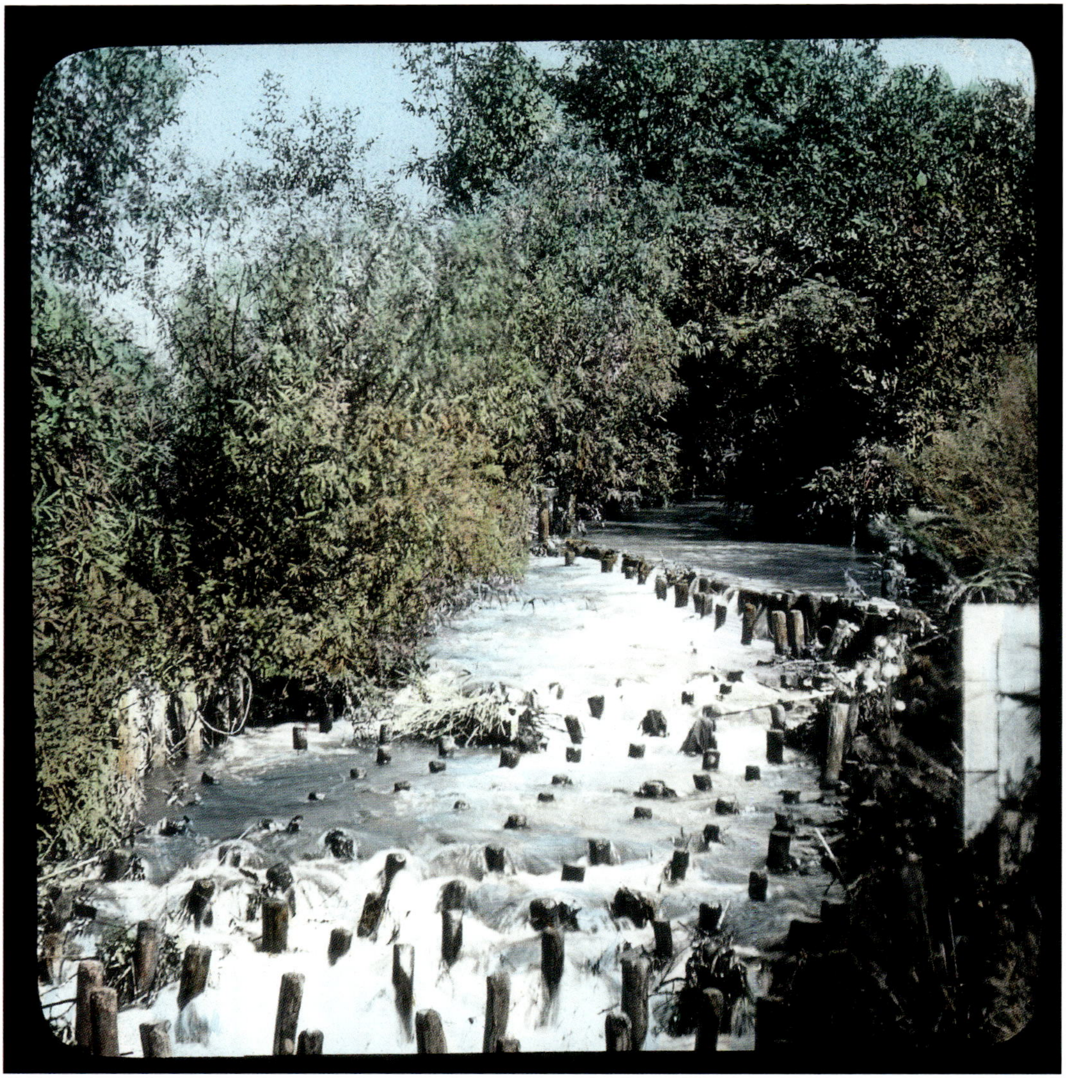

416 Sacred stream, Kyoto, 1890s
417 Ladies being carried in Yama-kago (mountain chairs), Japan, 1890s

416 Heiliger Bach, Kyoto, Japan, 1890er Jahre
417 Vornehme Frauen werden in Yama-kagos (Gebirgstragen) befördert, Japan, 1890er Jahre

416 Ruisseau sacré, Kyoto, années 1890
417 Femmes transportées dans des yama-kago (chaises de montagne), Japon, années 1890

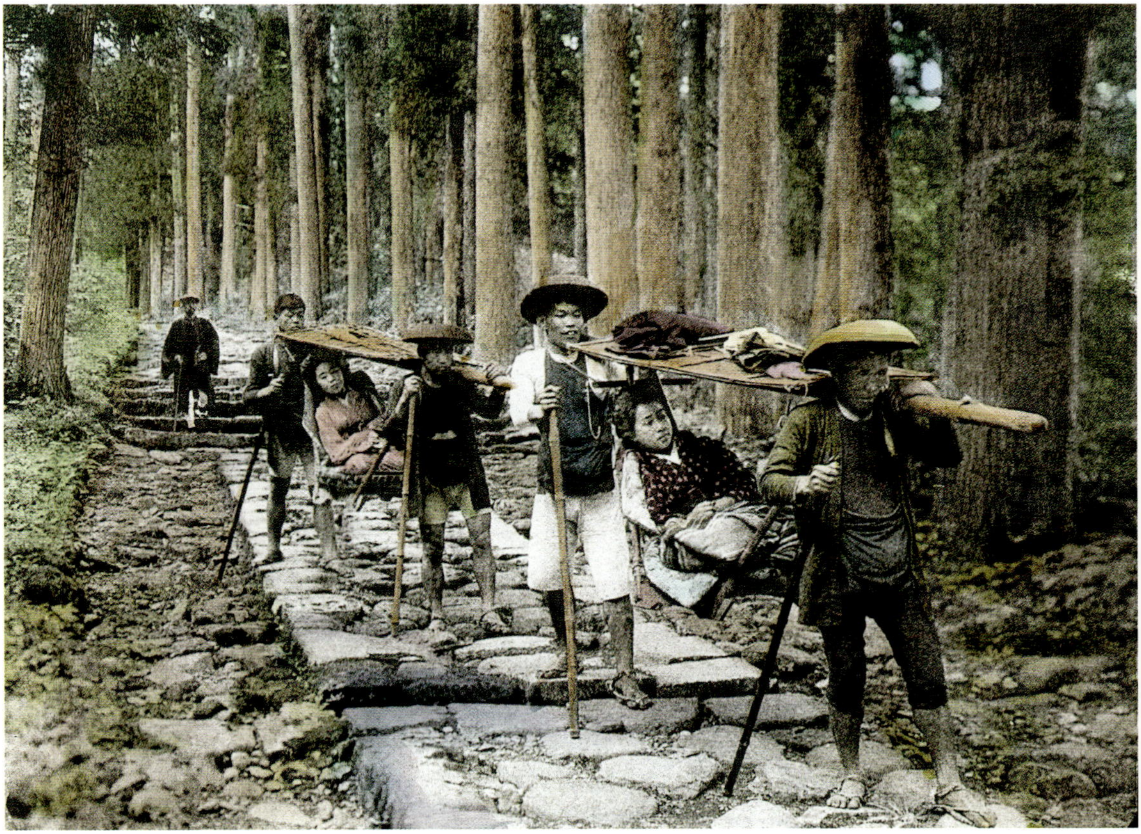

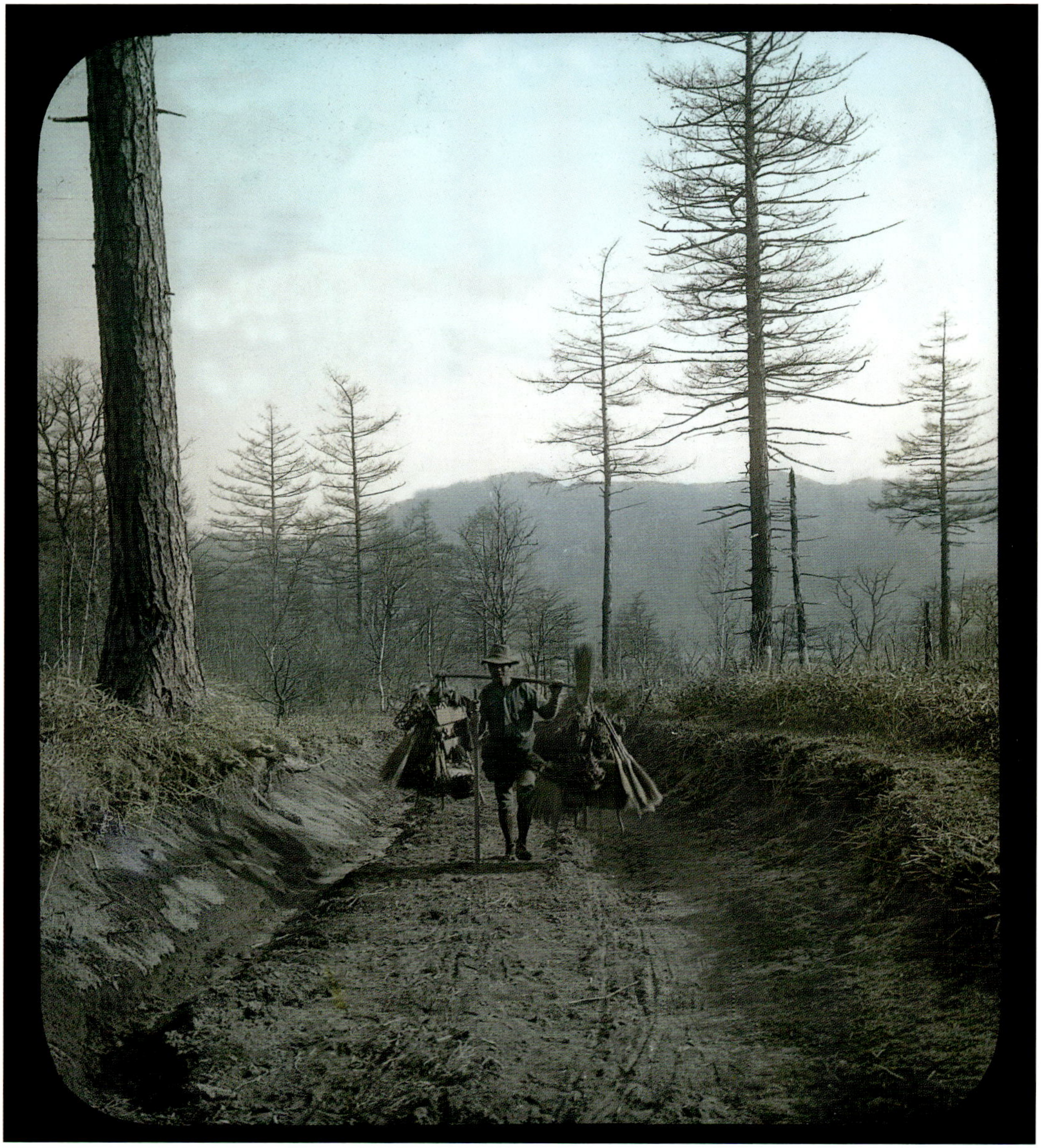

418 Peddlar carrying his wares, Japan, 1880s
419 A Chinese junk (traditional sailboat), Japan, 1880s

418 Ein Hausierer trägt seine Waren, Japan, 1880er Jahre
419 Chinesische Dschunke (traditionelles Segelschiff), Japan, 1880er Jahre

418 Colporteur transportant sa marchandise, Japon, années 1880
419 Jonque chinoise, Japon, années 1880

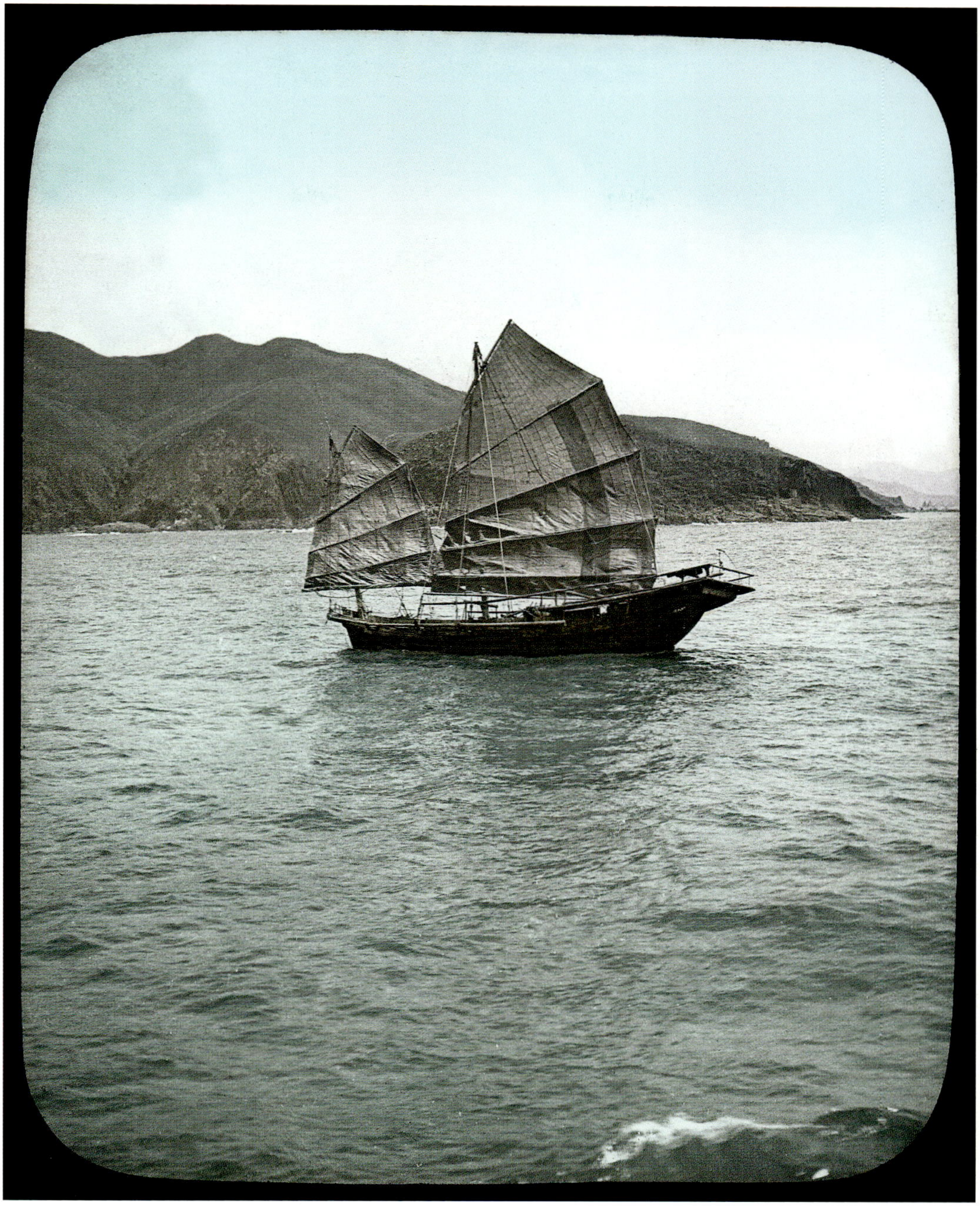

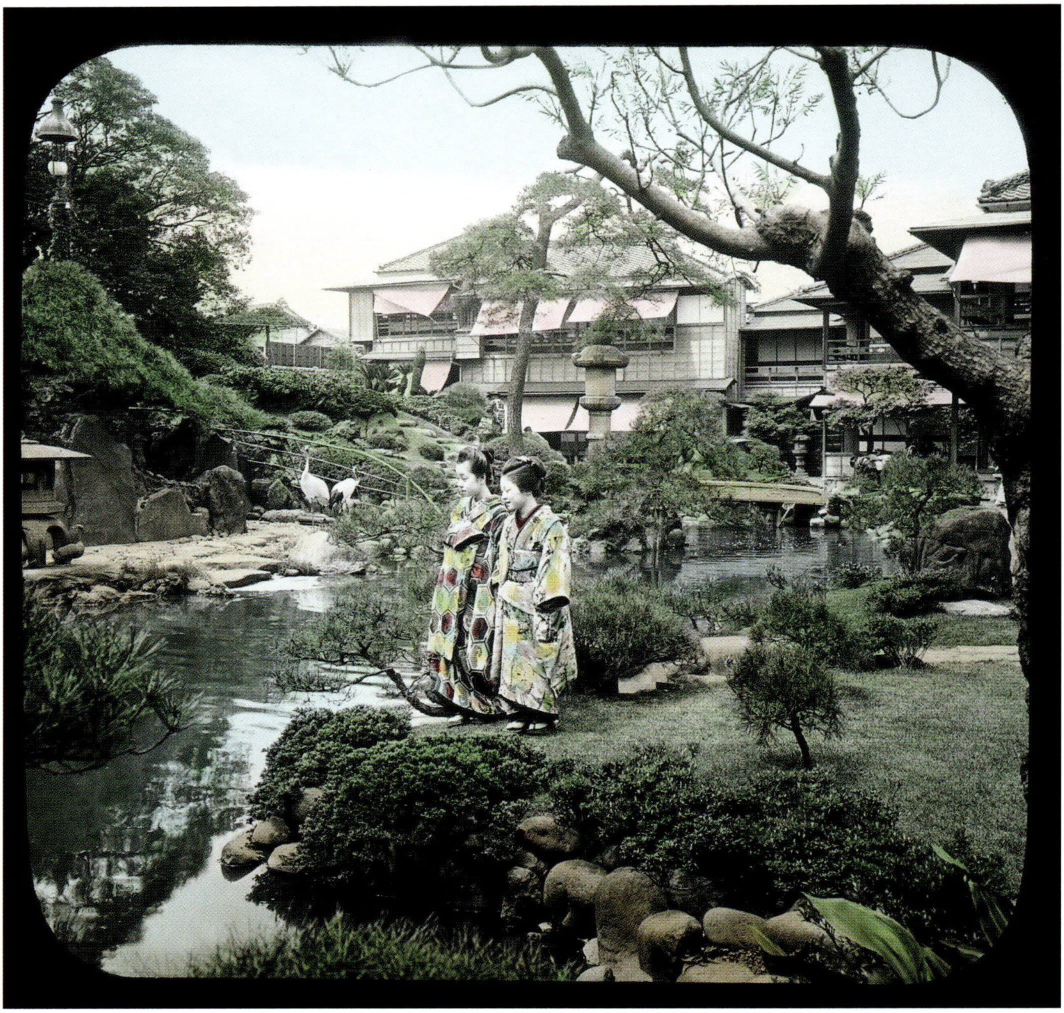

420 "An Idyllic Spot Where Little Japanese Maids Delight to Stroll", Japan, 1904

420 „Ein idyllischer Ort, an dem kleine japanische Mädchen gern lustwandeln", Japan, 1904

420 « Un lieu idyllique où les jeunes filles japonaises adorent se promener » – Japon, 1904

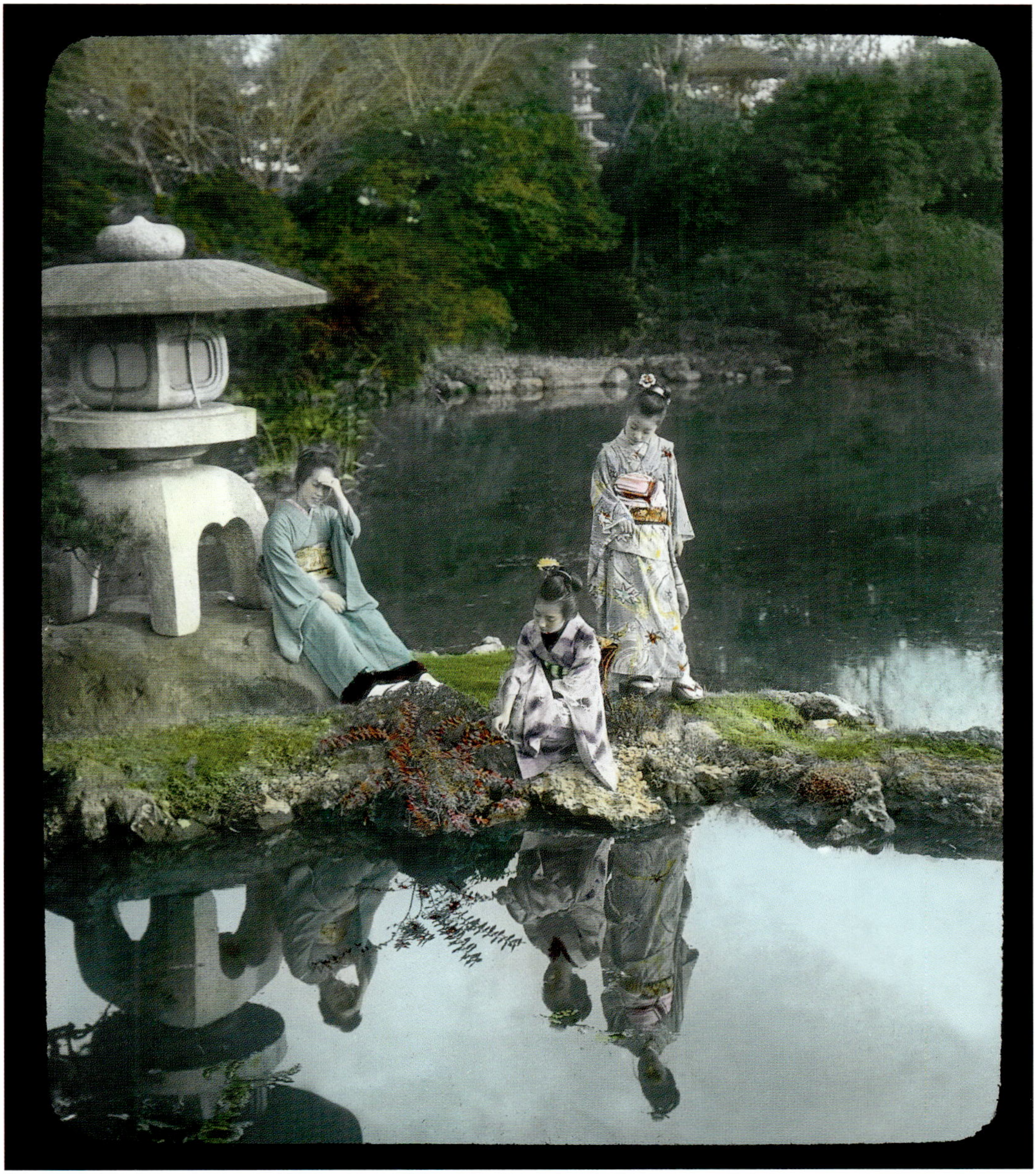

421 A stone lantern in the garden of the Fugetsu tea house, Shizuoka, Japan, 1890s

421 Eine Steinlaterne im Garten des Fugetsu-Teehauses, Shizuoka, Japan, 1890er Jahre

421 Lanterne de pierre dans la maison de thé Fugetsu, Shizuoka, Japon, années 1890

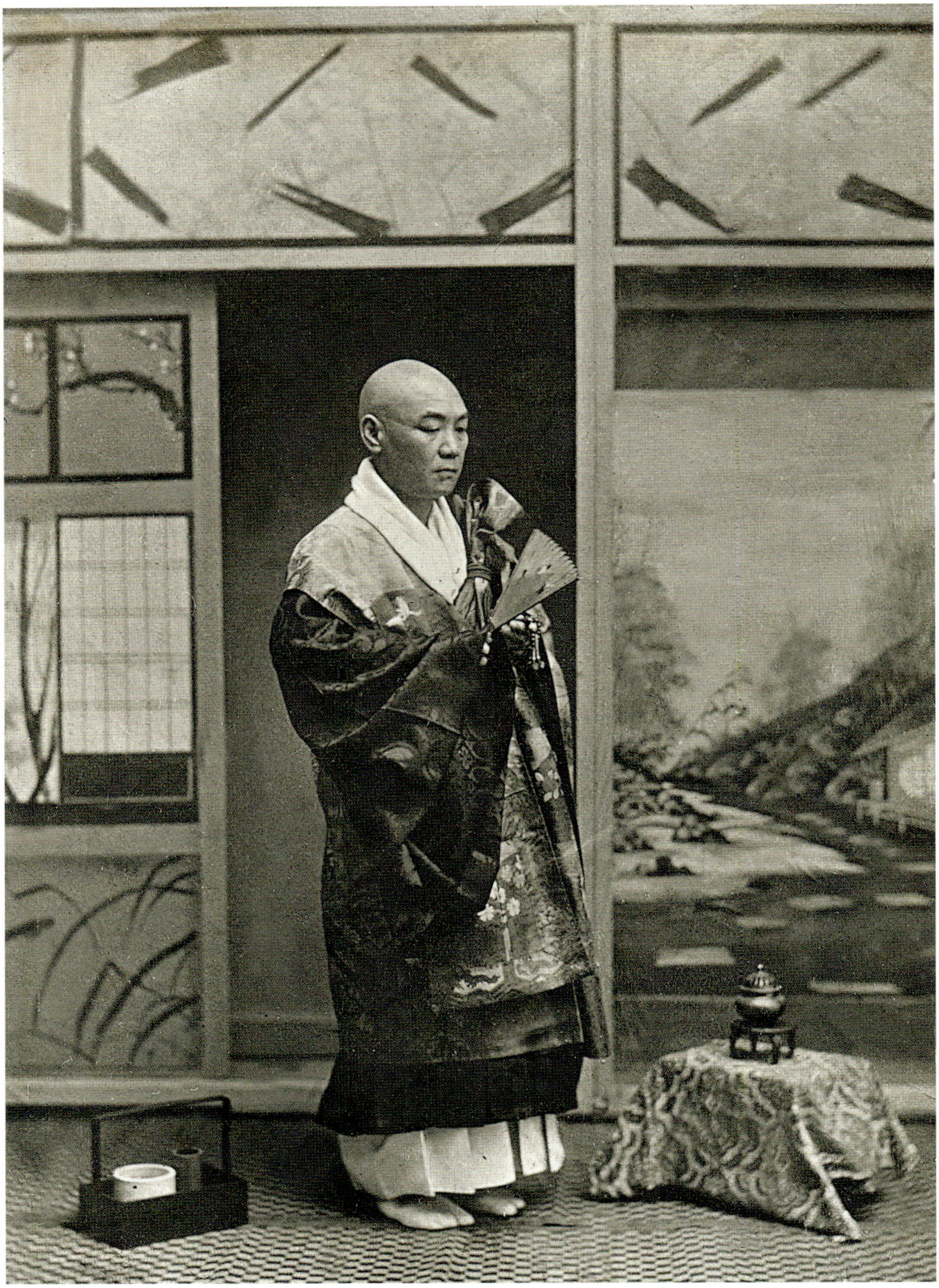

422 Buddhist priest, Japan, 1890s
423 Stone statues at Nikko, Japan, 1890s

422 Ein buddhistischer Priester, Japan, 1890er Jahre
423 Steinskulpturen in Nikko, Japan, 1890er Jahre

422 Prêtre bouddhiste, Japon, années 1890
423 Statues en pierre à Nikko, Japon, années 1890

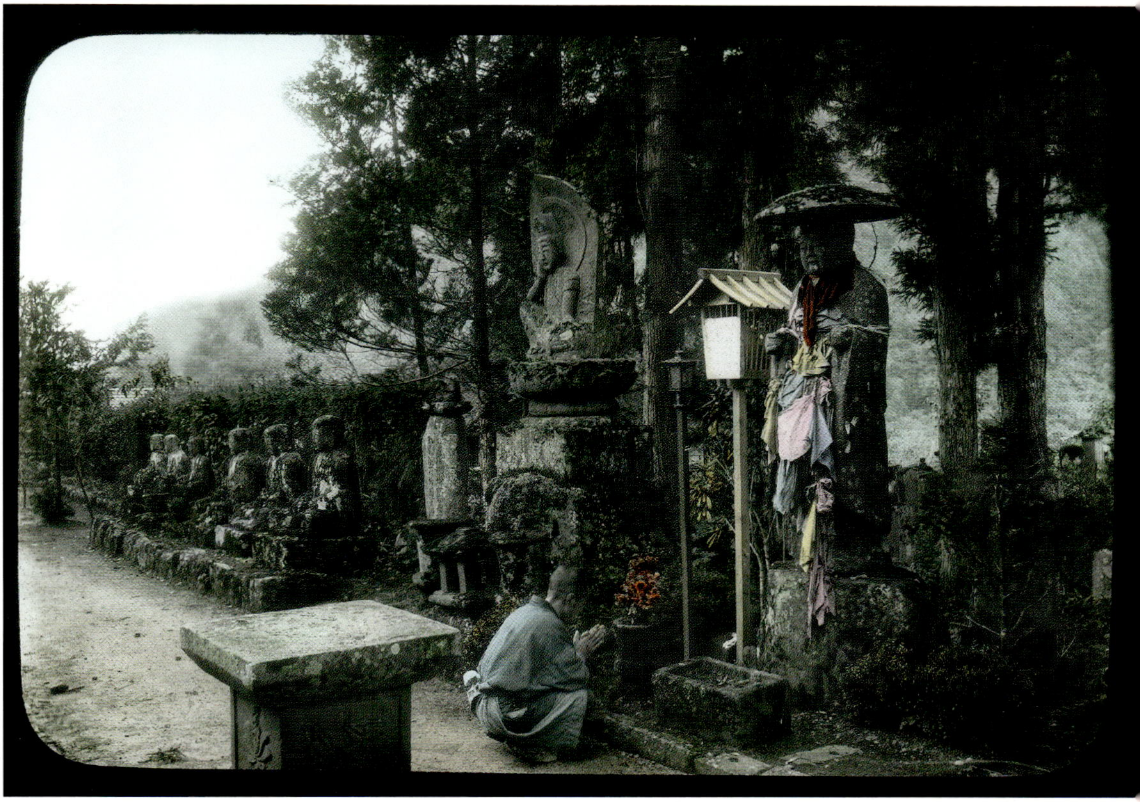

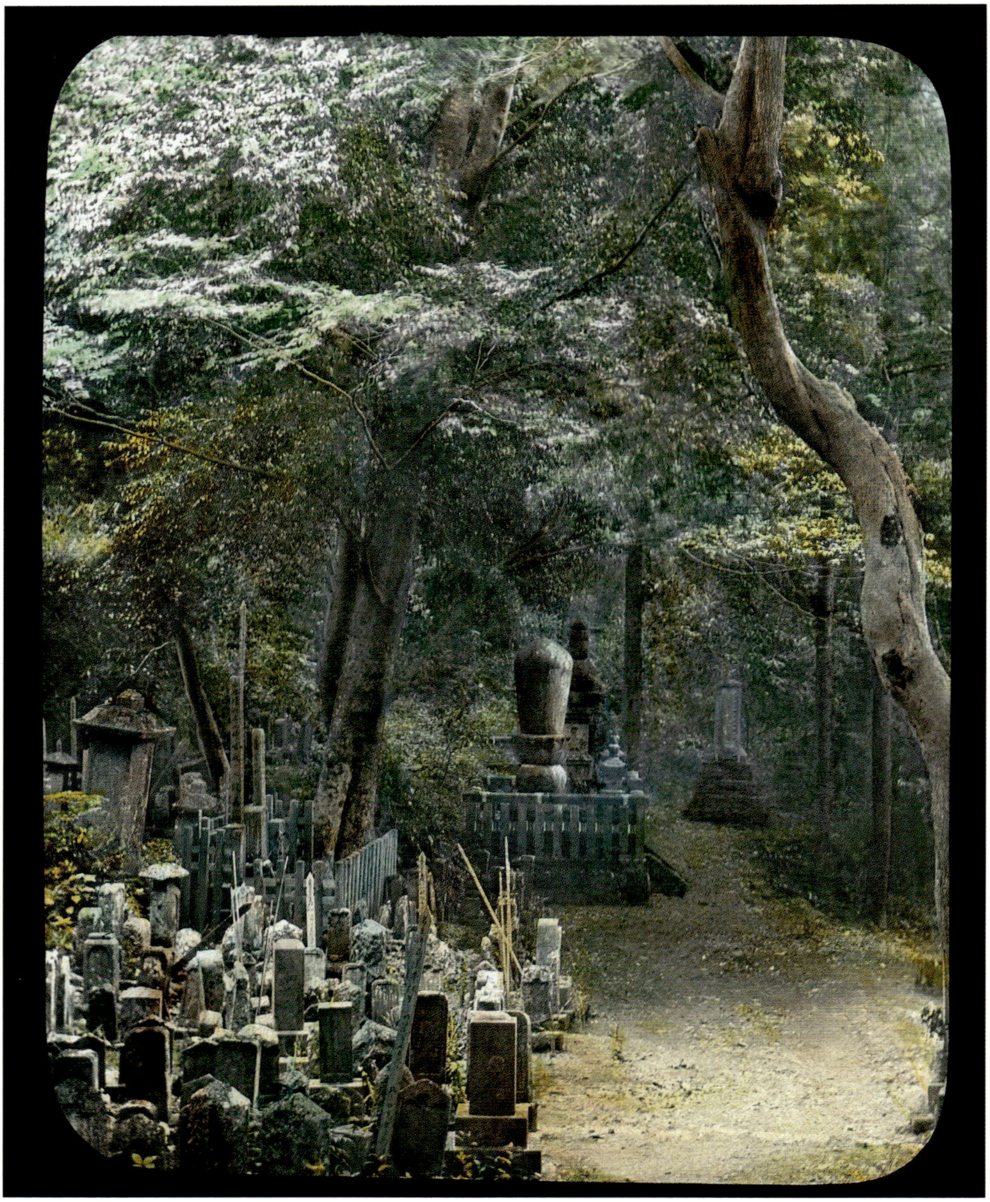

424 A village graveyard, Japan, 1890s
425 Tea house at Oyeno Park, Tokyo, 1890s

424 Ein Dorffriedhof, Japan, 1890er Jahre
425 Teehaus im Ueno-Park, Tokio, 1890er Jahre

424 Cimetière villageois, Japon, années 1890
425 Maison de thé dans le parc Oyeno, Tokyo, années 1890

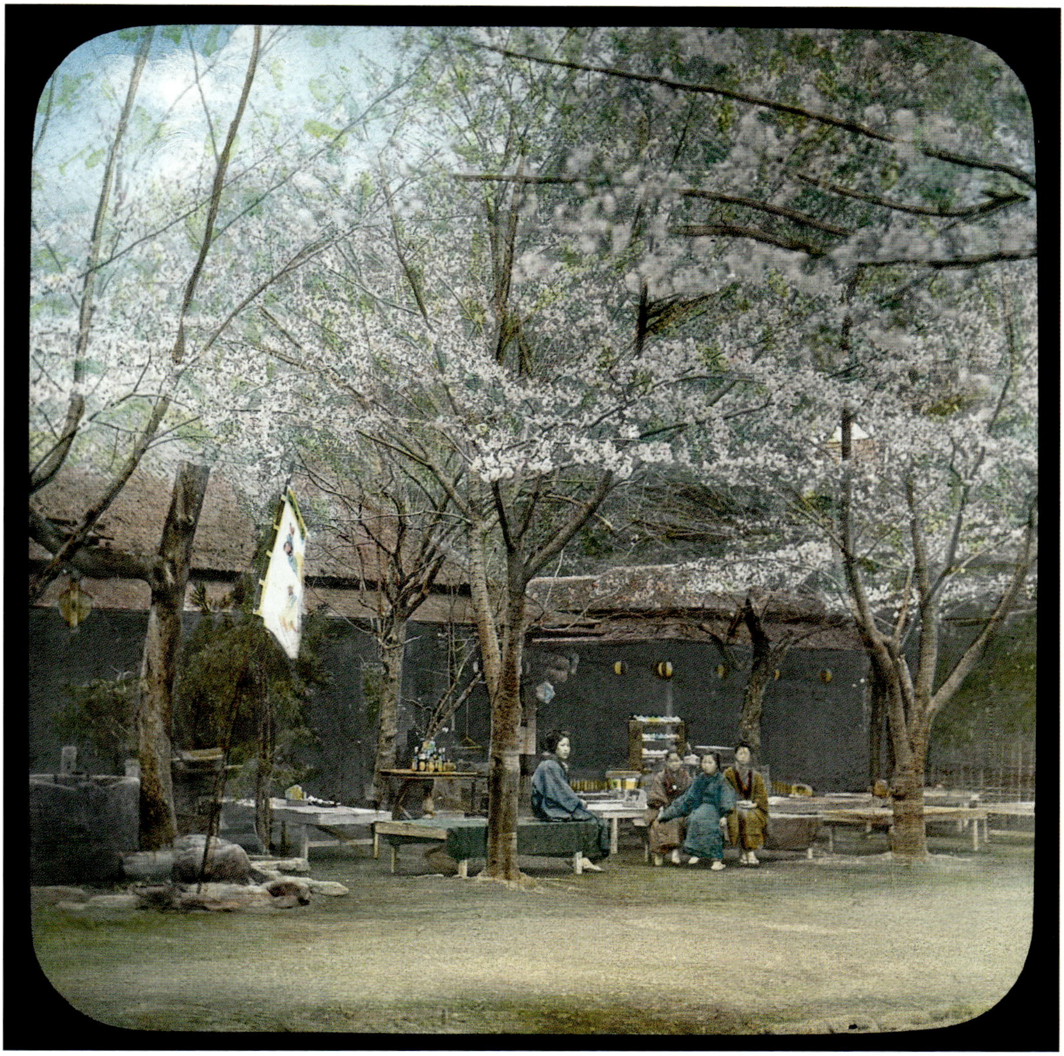

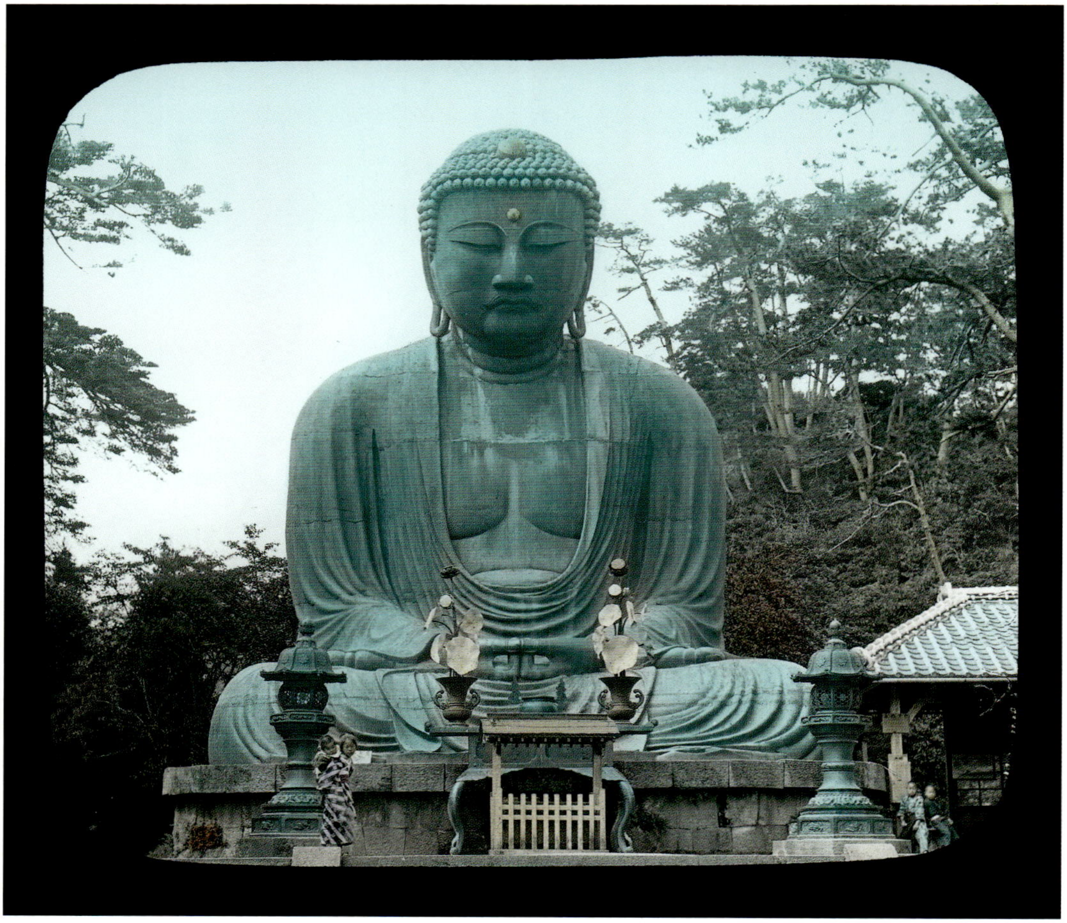

426 Daibutsu (Great Buddha) of Kamakura, Japan, c.1900
427 Hikone Castle, Hikone, Shiga Prefecture, Japan, c.1900

426 Der Daibutsu (Großer Buddha) von Kamakura, Japan, um 1900
427 Schloss Hikone, Hikone, Präfektur Shiga, Japan, um 1900

426 Daibutsu (Grand Bouddha) de Kamakura, Japon, vers 1900
427 Château de Hikone, préfecture de Shiga, Japon, vers 1900

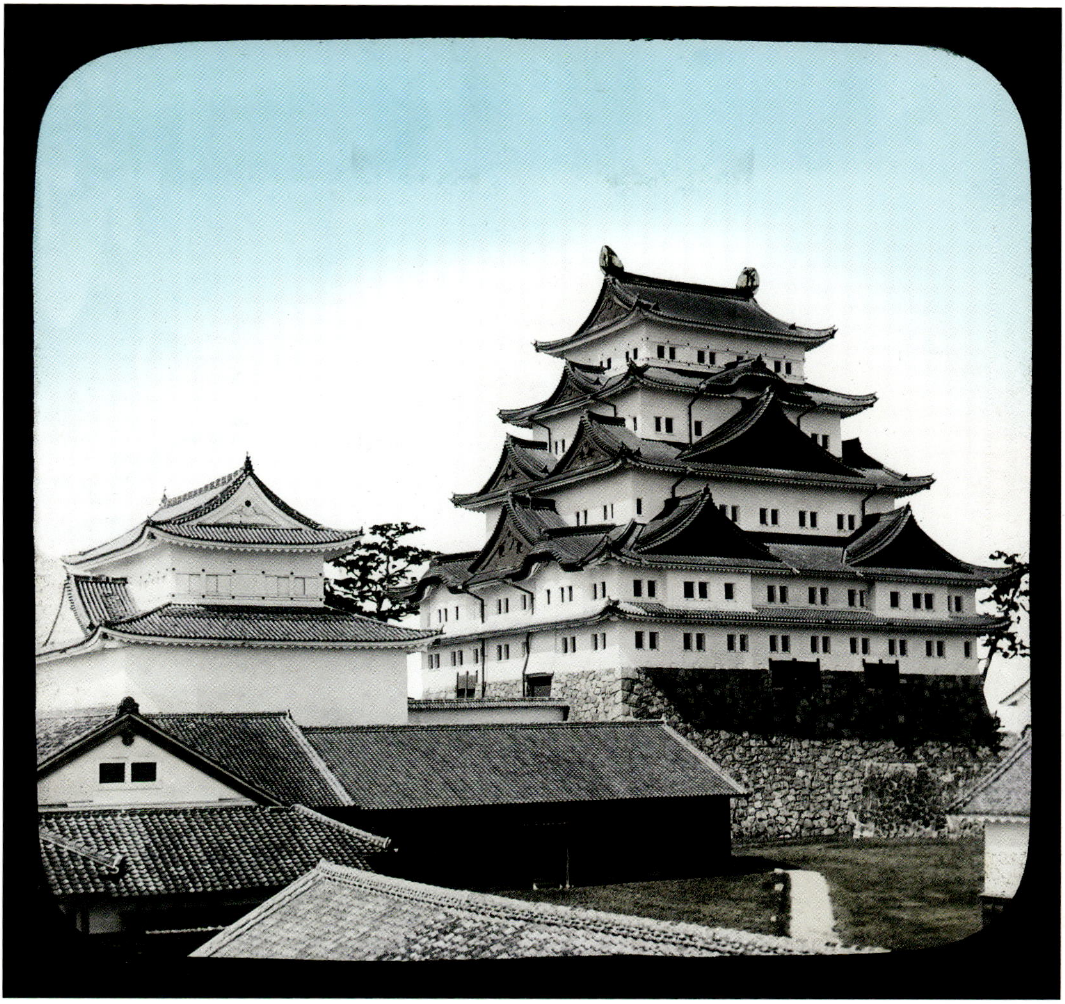

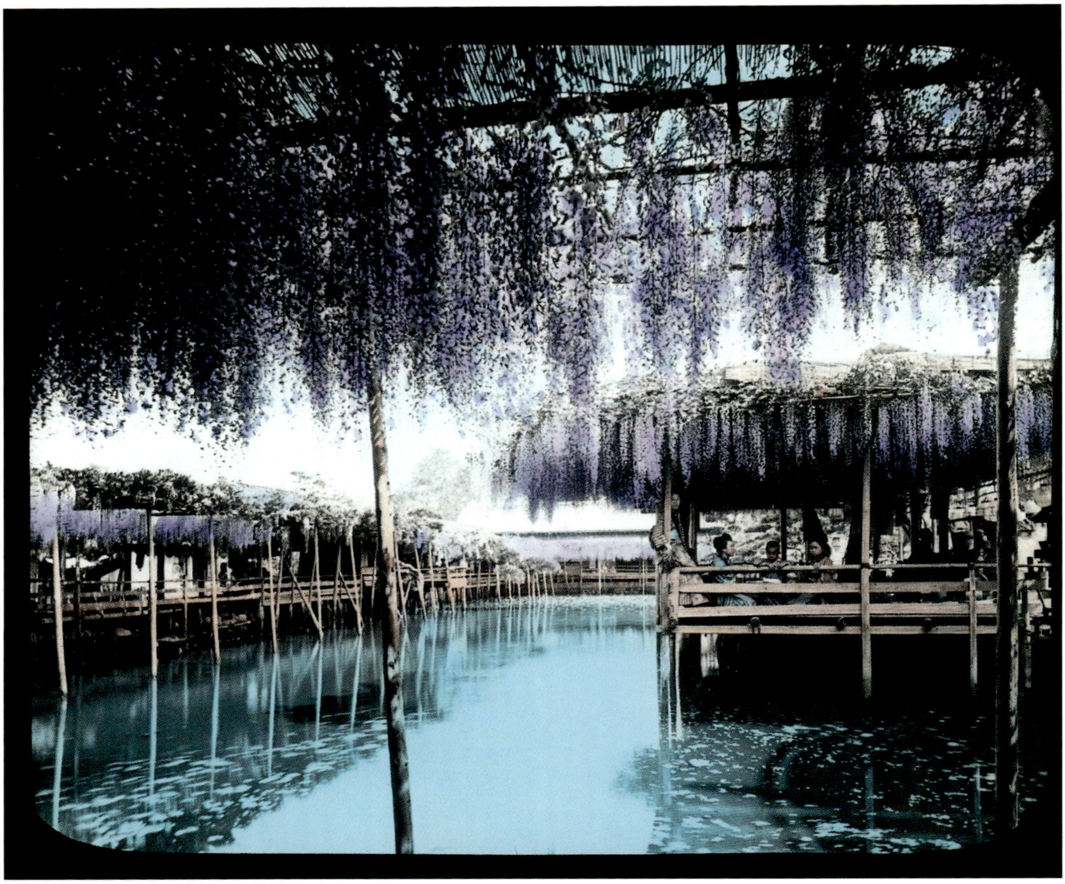

428 Wisteria blossoms in the gardens of the Kameido Tenjin Shrine, Tokyo, Japan, c.1900
429 "Banzai!!", Procession, Japan, 1890s

428 Glyzinienblüte in den Gärten des Kameido-Tenjin-Schreins, Tokio, Japan, um 1900
429 "Banzai!", Prozession, Japan, 1890er Jahre

428 Glycines en fleur dans les jardins du sanctuaire de Kameido Tenjin, Tokyo, Japon, vers 1900
429 « Banzaï ! », procession, Japon, années 1890

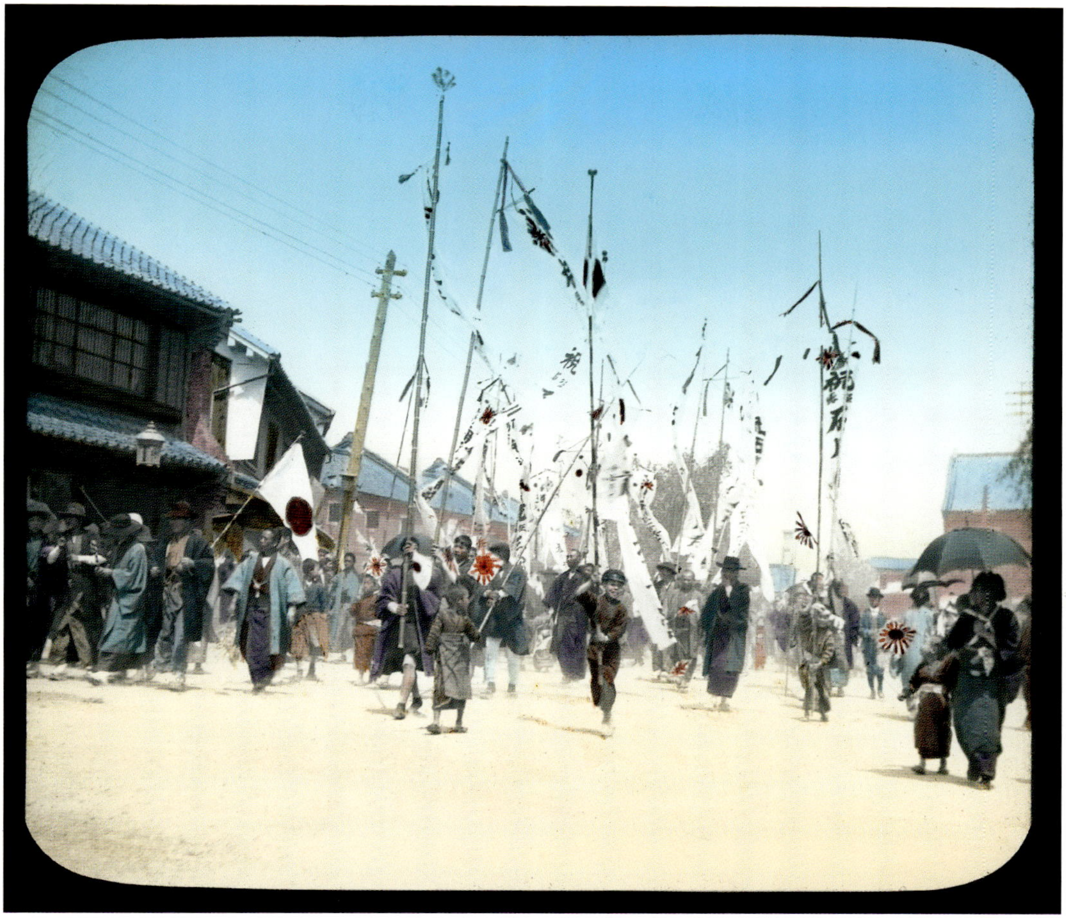

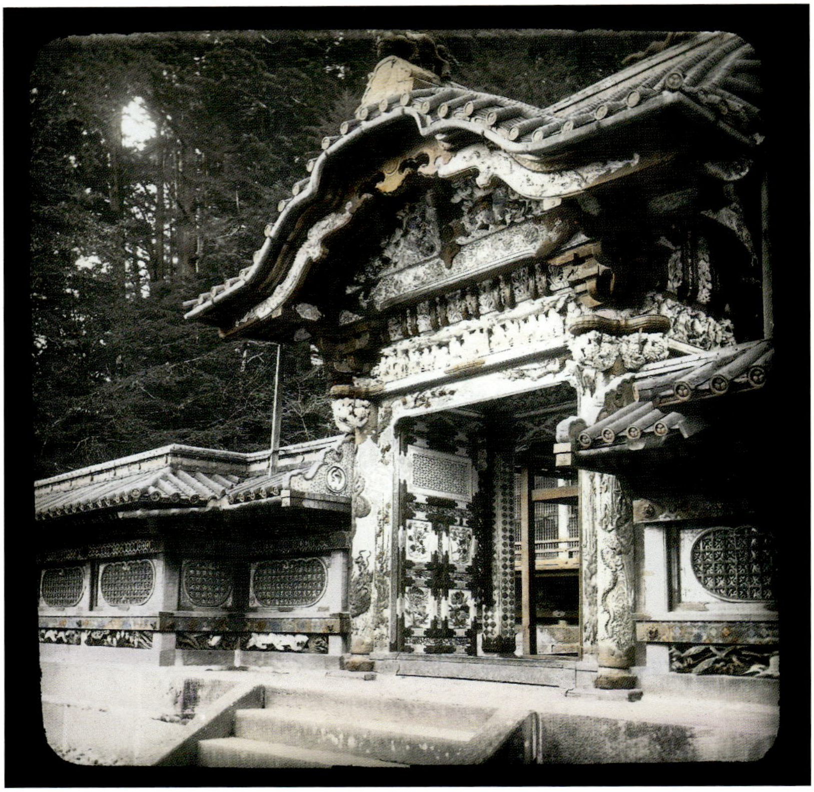

430 Karamon Gate at Toshogu Shrine, Nikko, 1890s

430 Das Karamon-Tor im Toshogu-Schrein, Nikko, Japan, 1890er Jahre

430 Porte Karamon au sanctuaire deToshogu, Nikko, années 1890

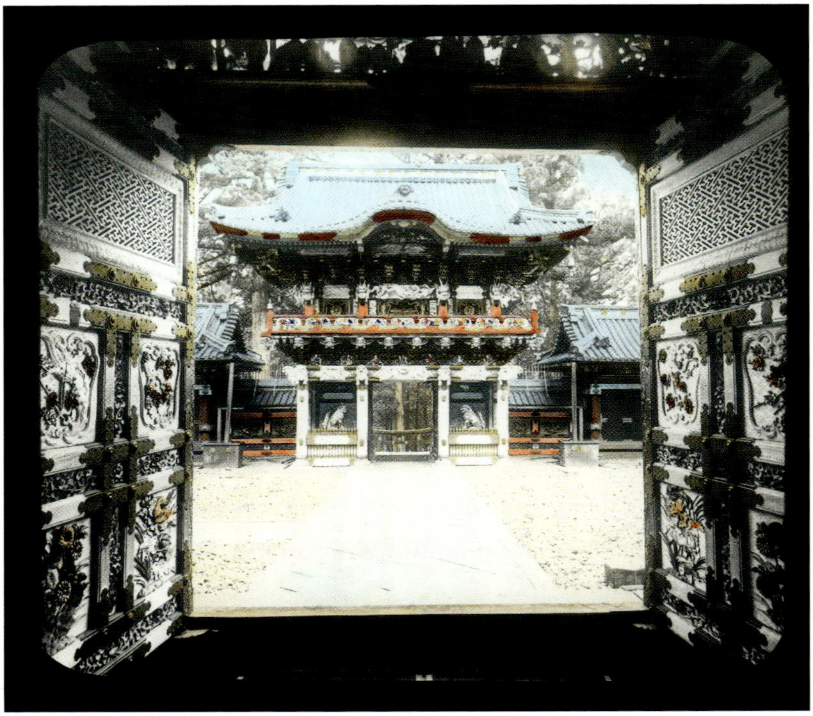

431 Yomeimon Gate at Nikko, Japan, 1890s

431 Das Yomeimon-Tor in Nikko, Japan, 1890er Jahre

431 Porte Yomeimon à Nikko, Japon, années 1890

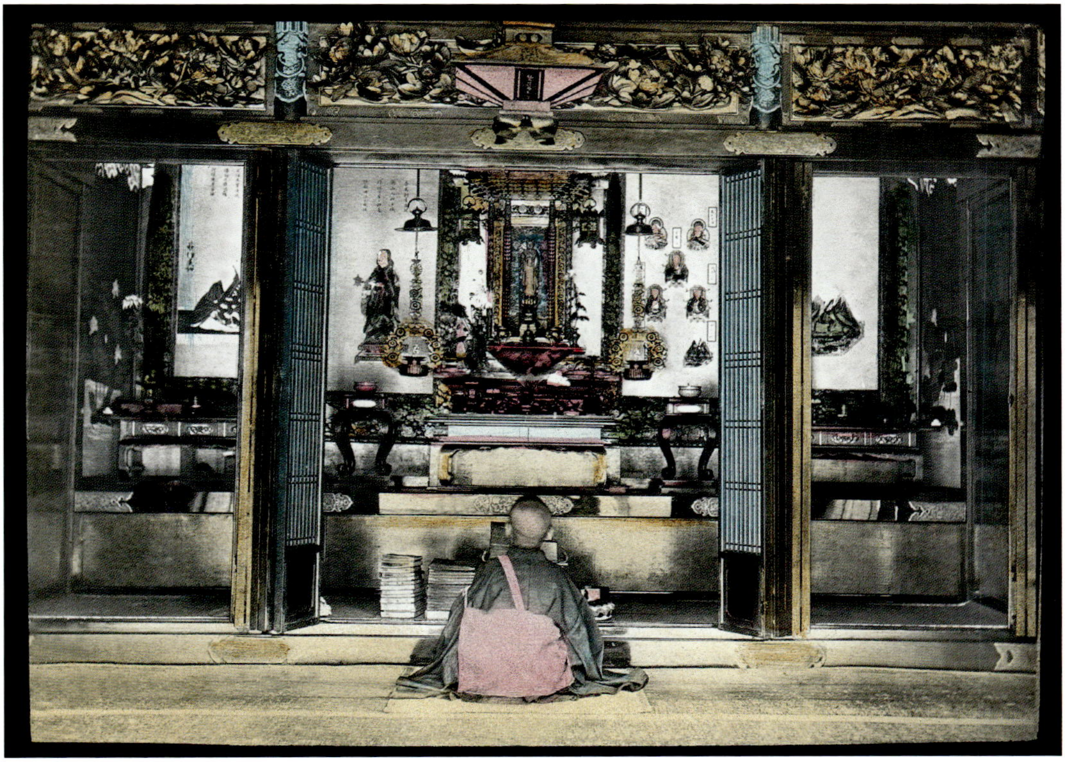

432 Monk praying at a temple, Japan, 1890s

432 Betender Mönch in einem Tempel, Japan, 1890er Jahre

432 Moine priant dans un temple, Japon, années 1890

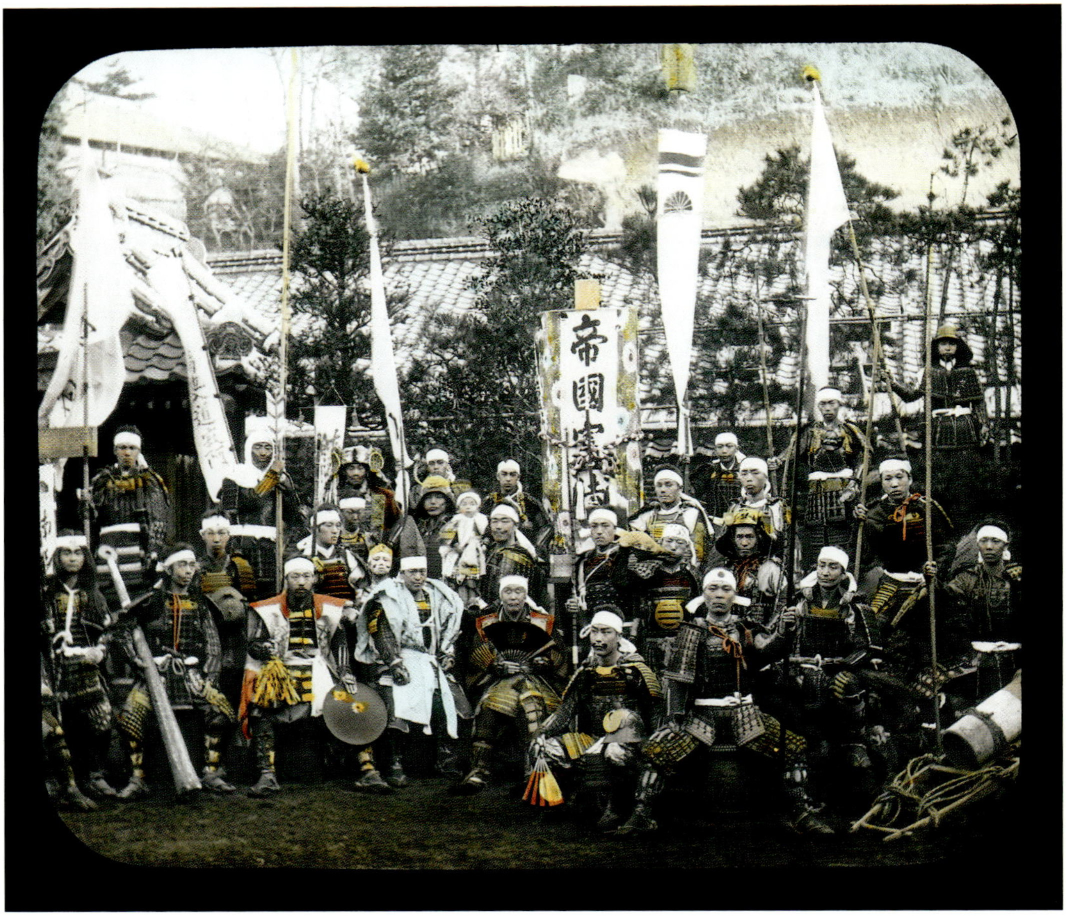

433 Japanese Samurai warriors, Japan, 1870s
434 Kendo fencing, Japan, 1870s

433 Japanische Samurai-Krieger, Japan, 1870er Jahre
434 Kendofechten, Japan, 1870er Jahre

433 Guerriers Samouraï, Japon, années 1870
434 Pratique du kendo, Japon, années 1870

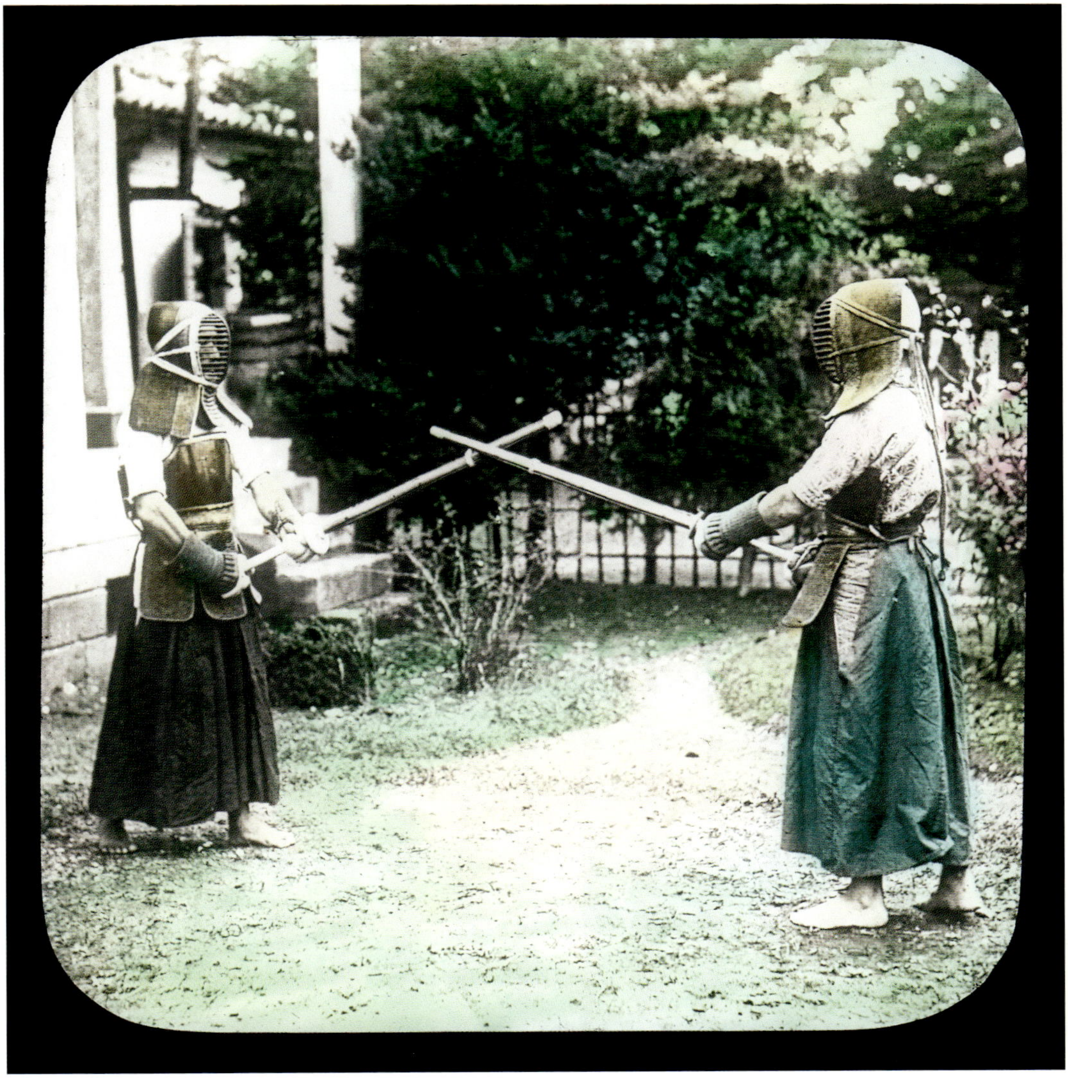

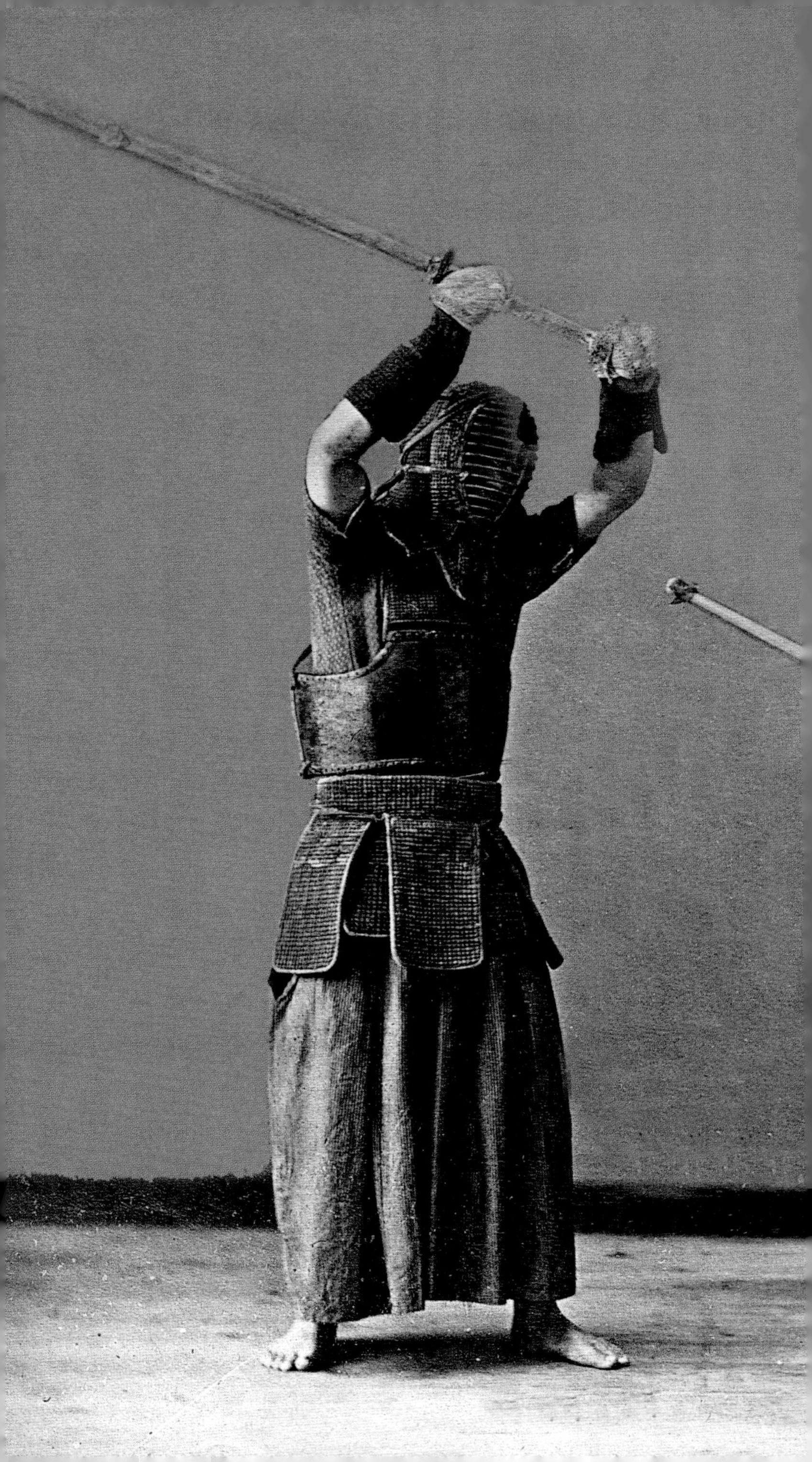

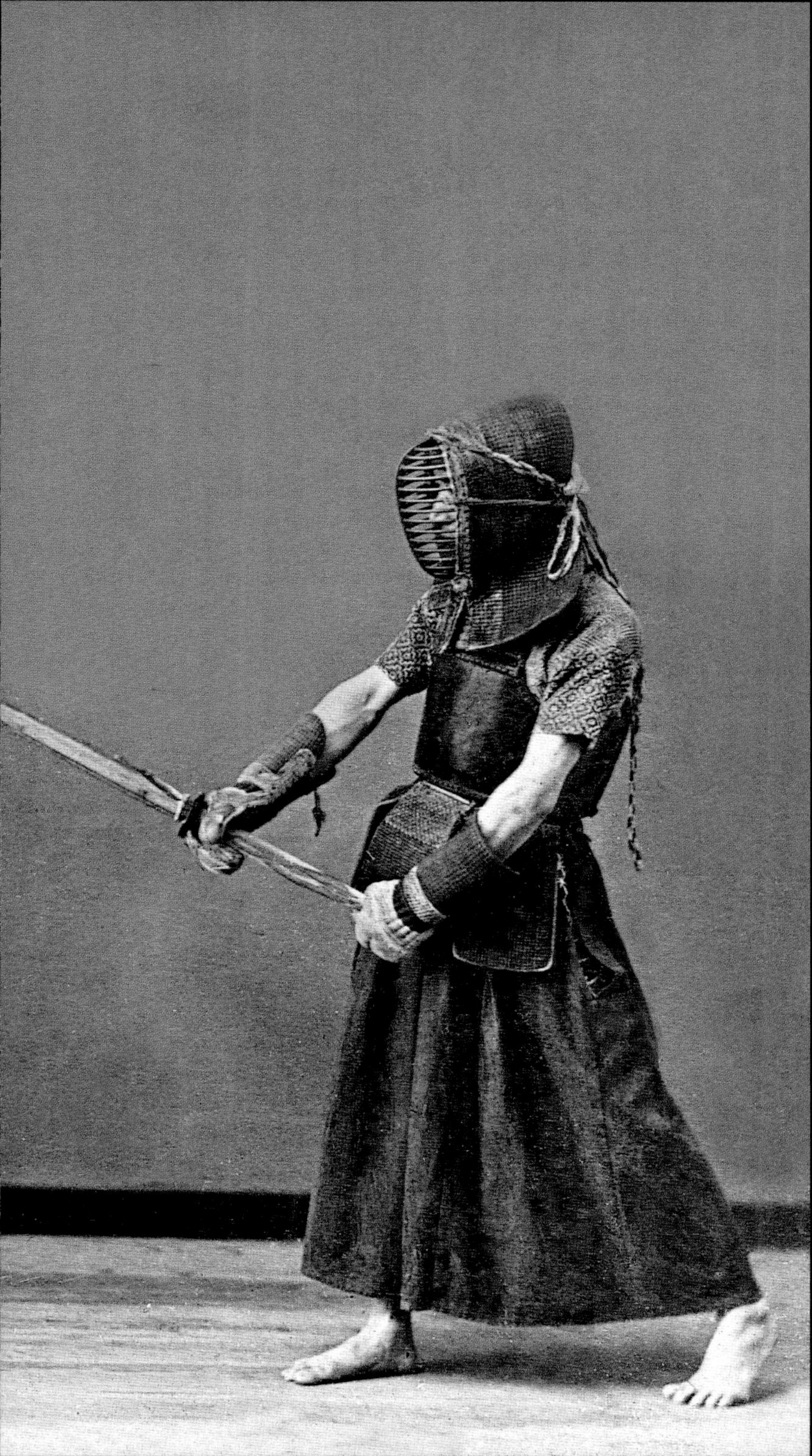

435 Kendo fencers, Japan, 1880s

435 Kendofechter, Japan, 1880er Jahre

435 Escrimeurs kendo, Japon, années 1880

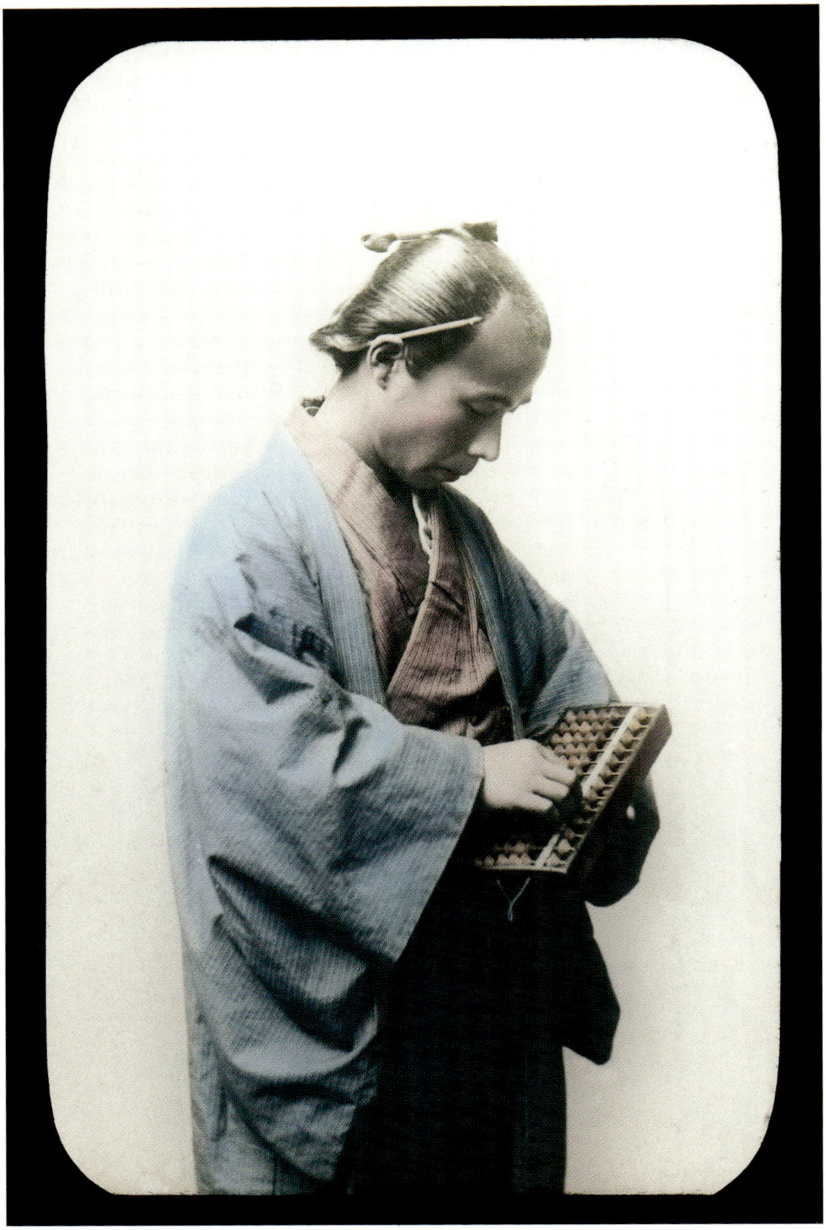

436 A merchant with an abacus, Japan, 1880s
437 Buddhist priest, Japan, 1890s

436 Ein Kaufmann mit einem Abakus, Japan, 1880er Jahre
437 Ein buddhistischer Priester, Japan, 1890er Jahre

436 Un marchand avec un boulier, Japon, années 1880
437 Prêtre bouddhiste, Japon, années 1890

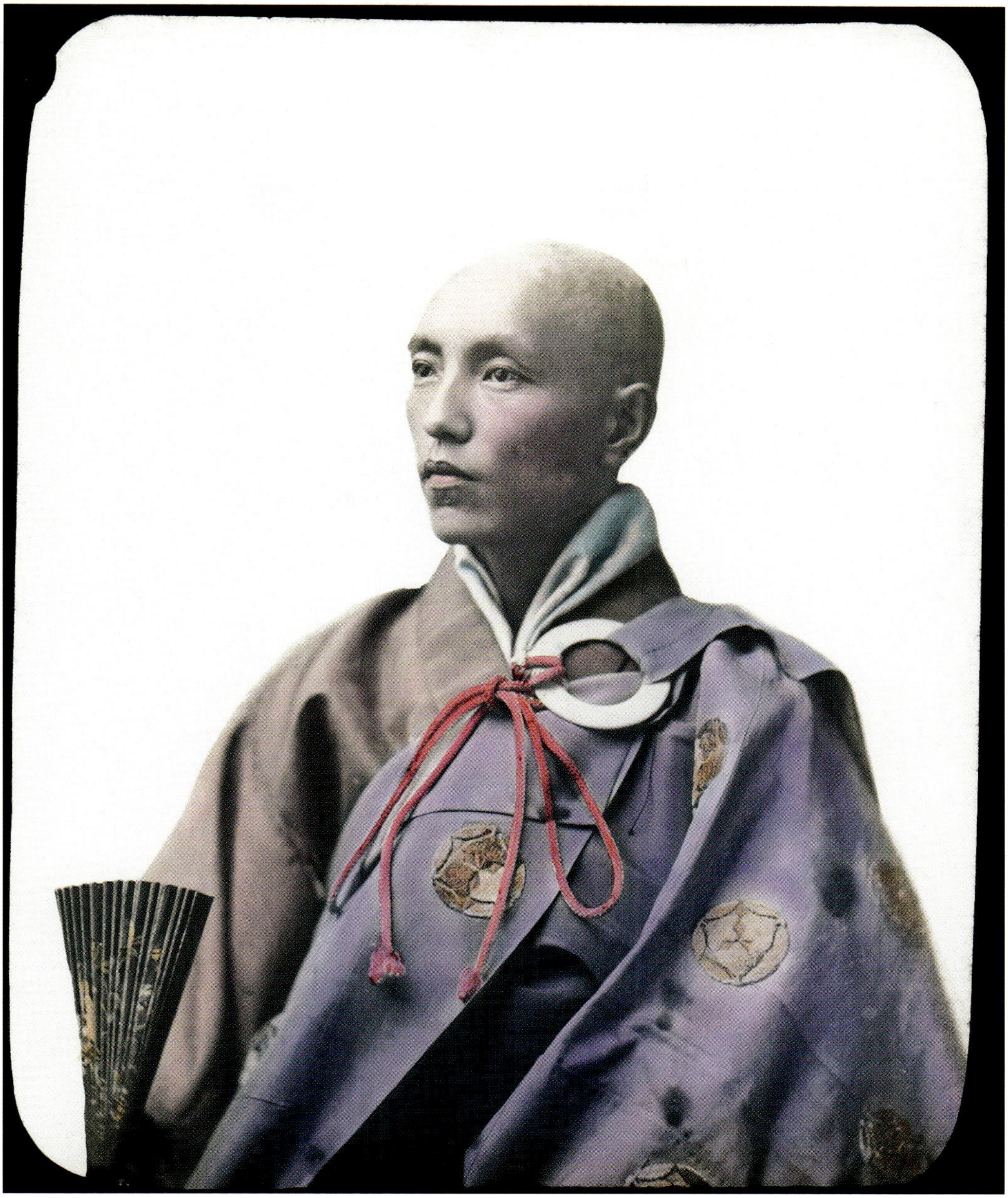

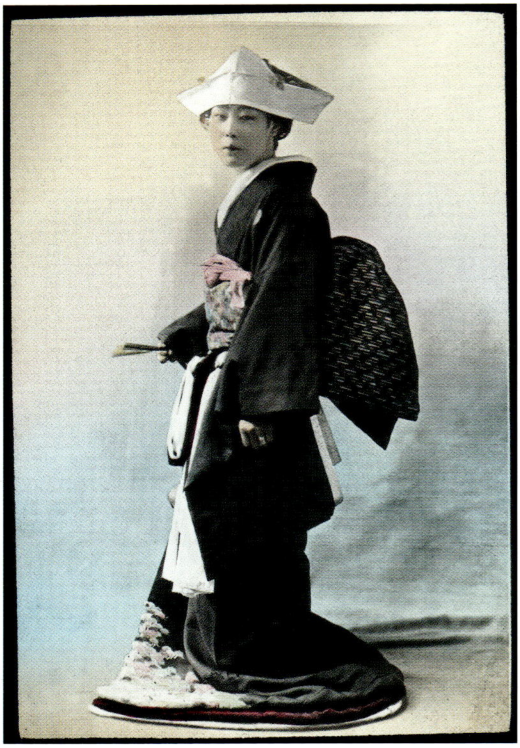
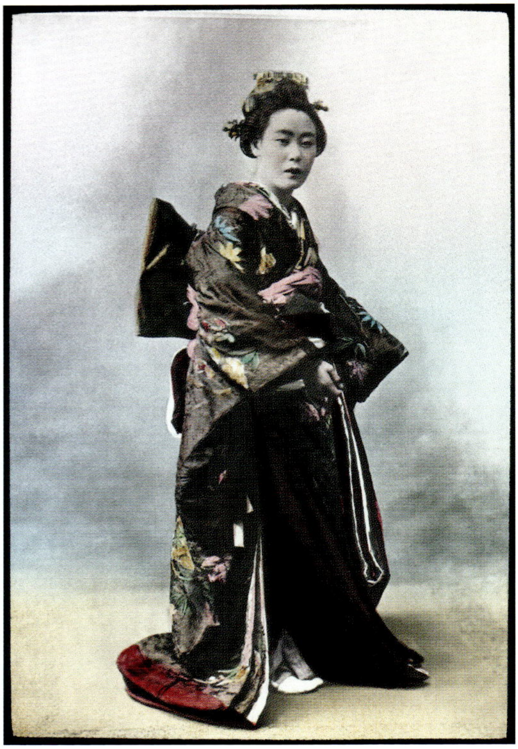
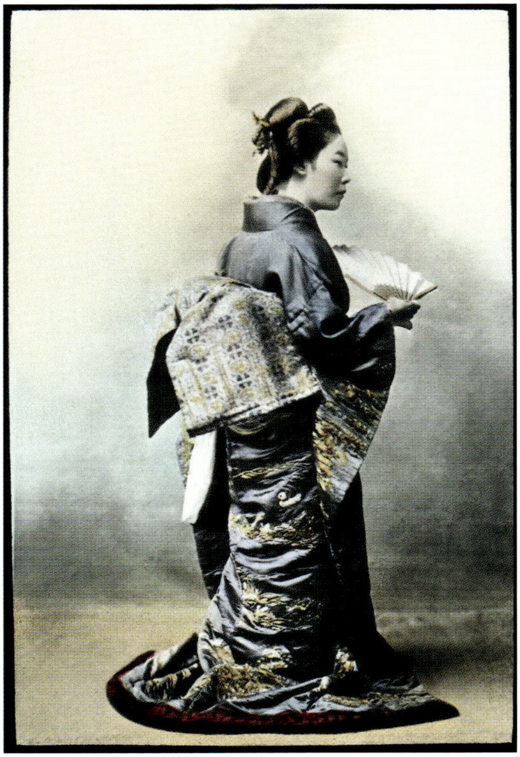
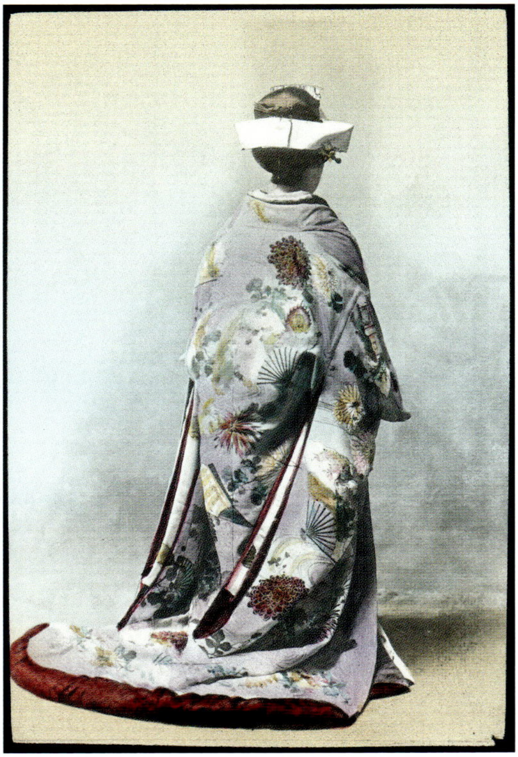

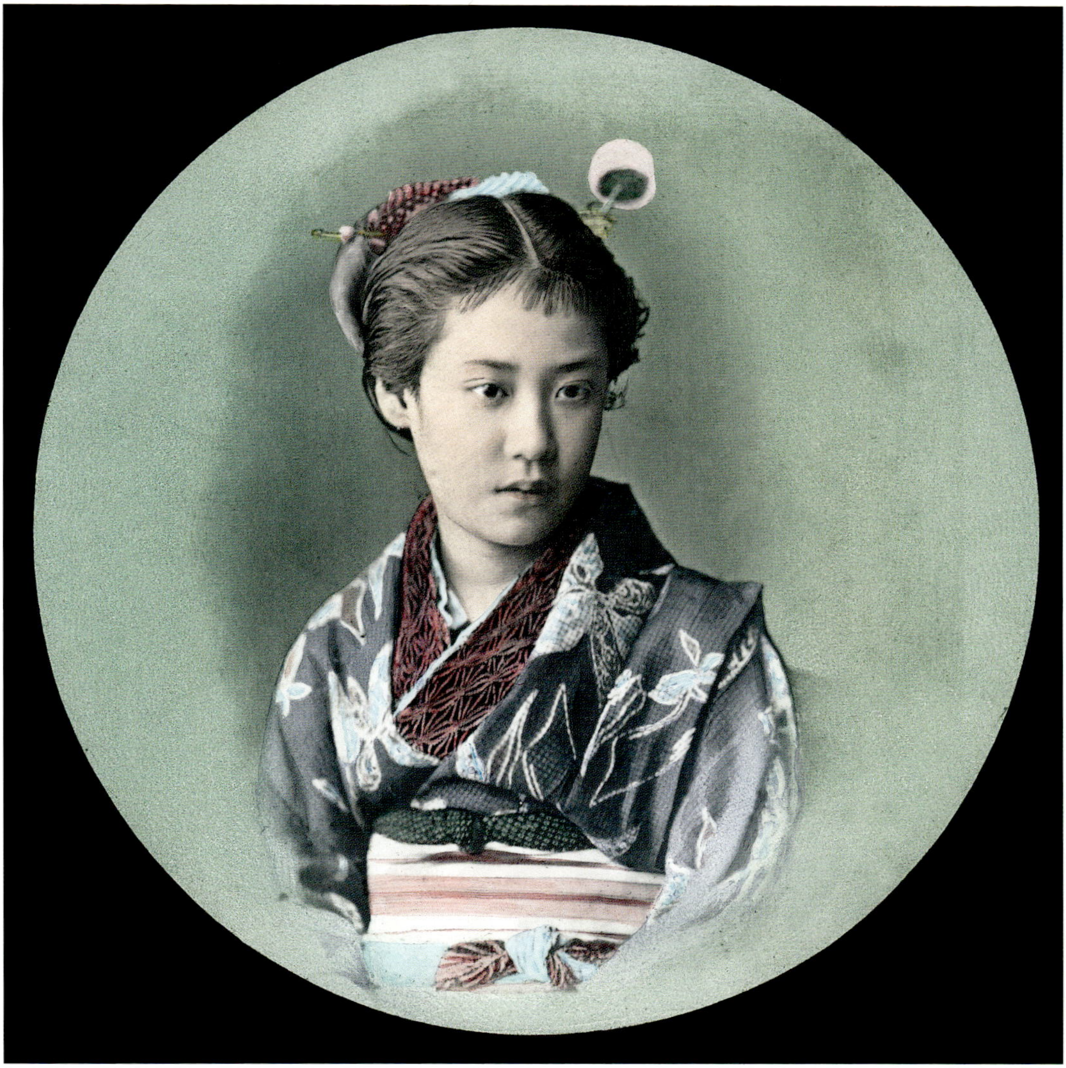

438–441 Woman wearing traditional kimono, Japan, 1870s
442 "Officer's Daughter" (believed to be a mixed race girl), Japan, 1880

438–441 Frauen in traditionellen Kimonos, Japan, 1870er Jahre
442 „Tochter des Offiziers" (vermutlich ein Mischlingsmädchen), Japan, 1880er Jahre

438–441 Femme vêtue du kimono traditionnel, Japon, années 1870
442 « Fille d'officier » (peut-être métissée), Japon, 1880

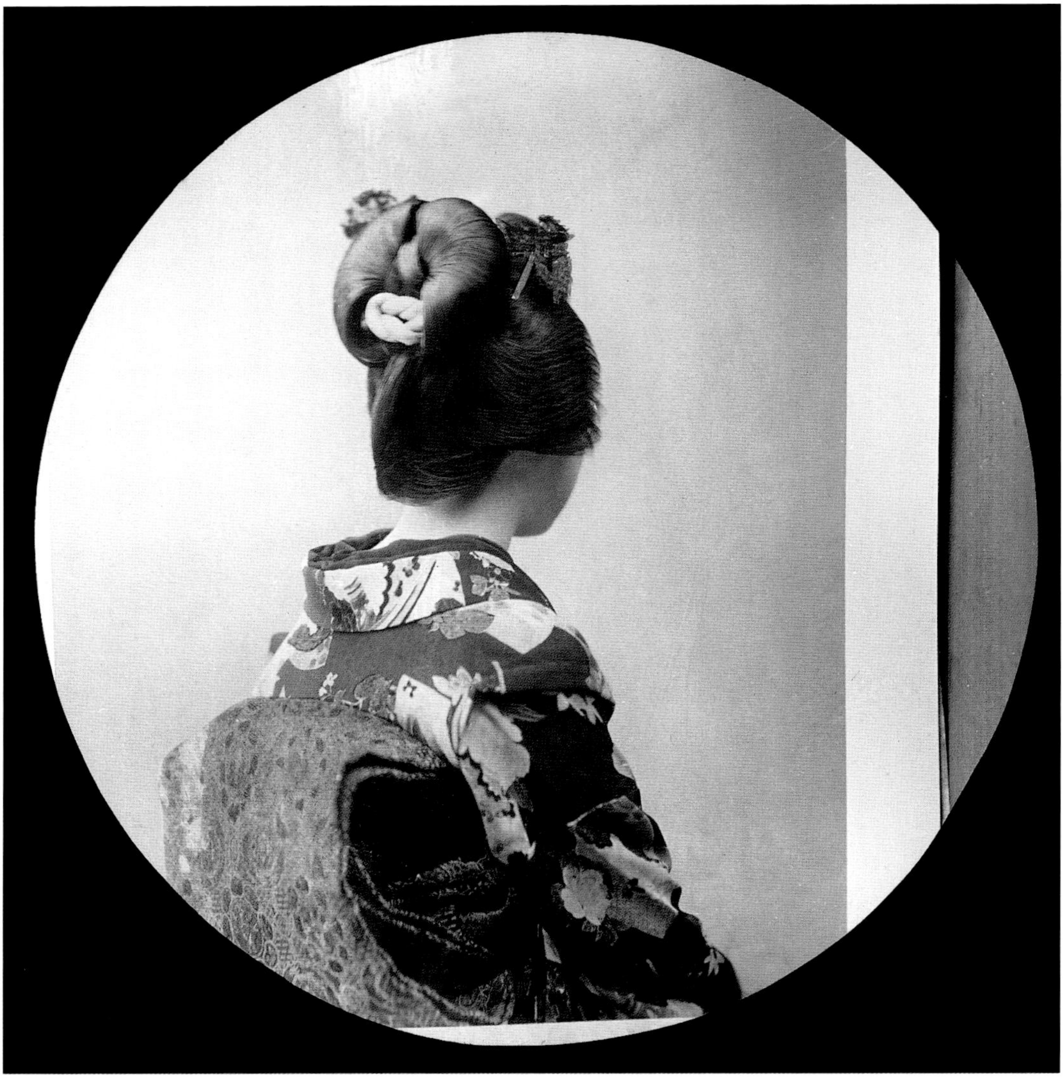

443 Woman's hairstyle, Japan, 1870s
444 Young woman playing musical instrument, Japan, 1870s

443 Frauenfrisur, Japan, 1870er Jahre
444 Junge Frau, die ein Musikinstrument spielt, Japan, 1870er Jahre

443 Coiffure féminine – Japon, années 1870
444 Jeune femme jouant du luth biwa, Japon, années 1870

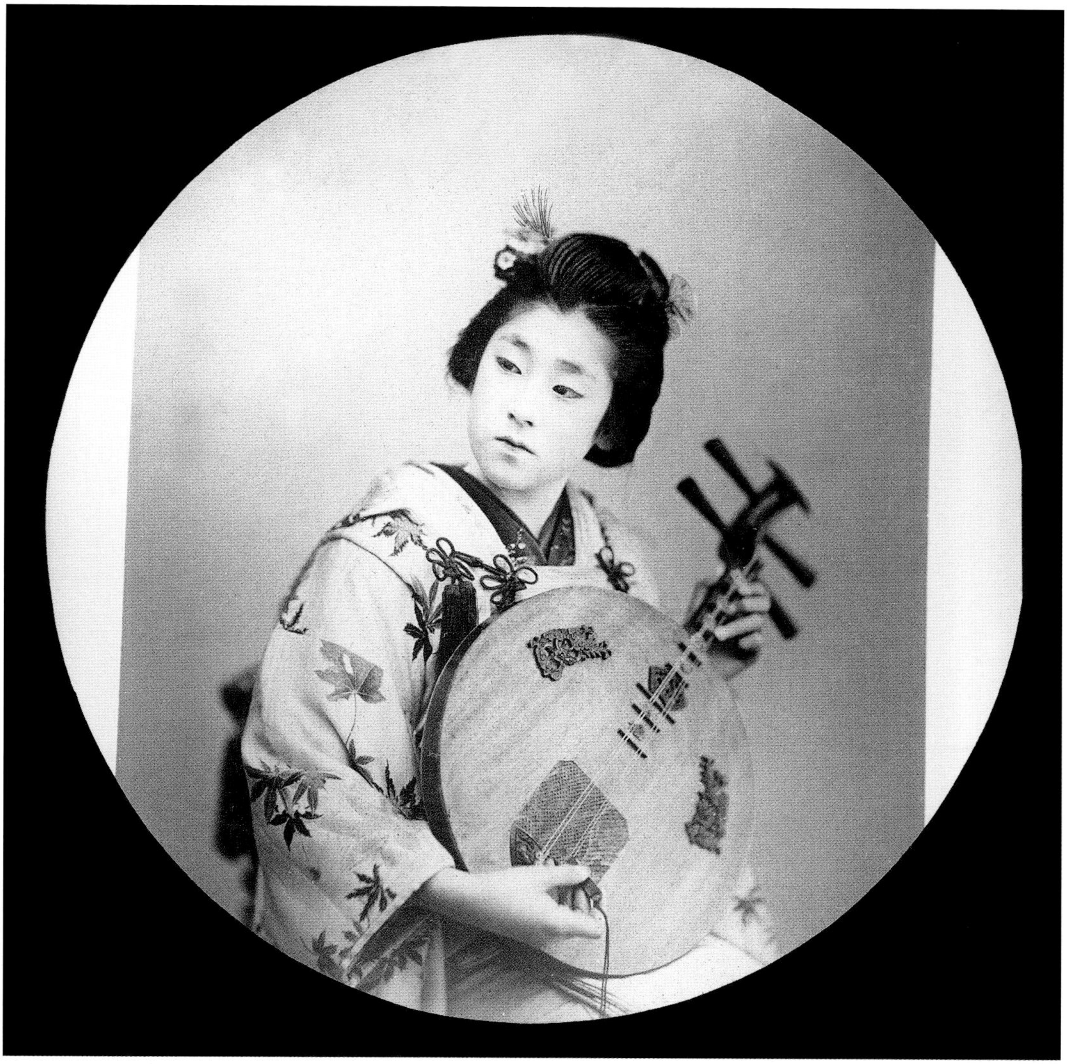

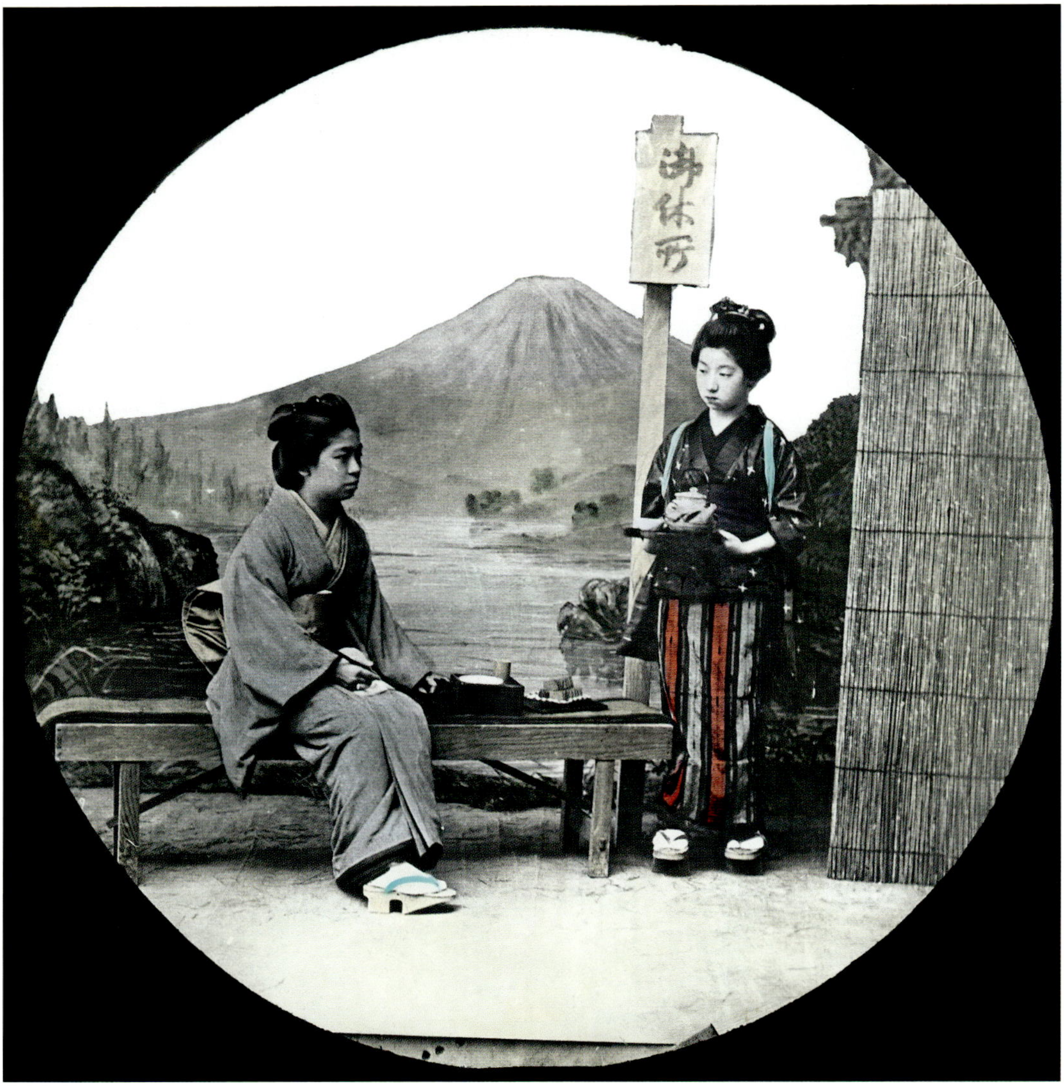

445 Young woman being served tea, Japan, 1870s
446 Hair preparation, Japan, 1870s

445 Einer jungen Frau wird Tee serviert, Japan, 1870er Jahre
446 Die Haare werden gemacht, Japan, 1870er Jahre

445 Jeune femme se faisant servir le thé, Japon, années 1870
446 Arrangement de la coiffure, Japon, années 1870

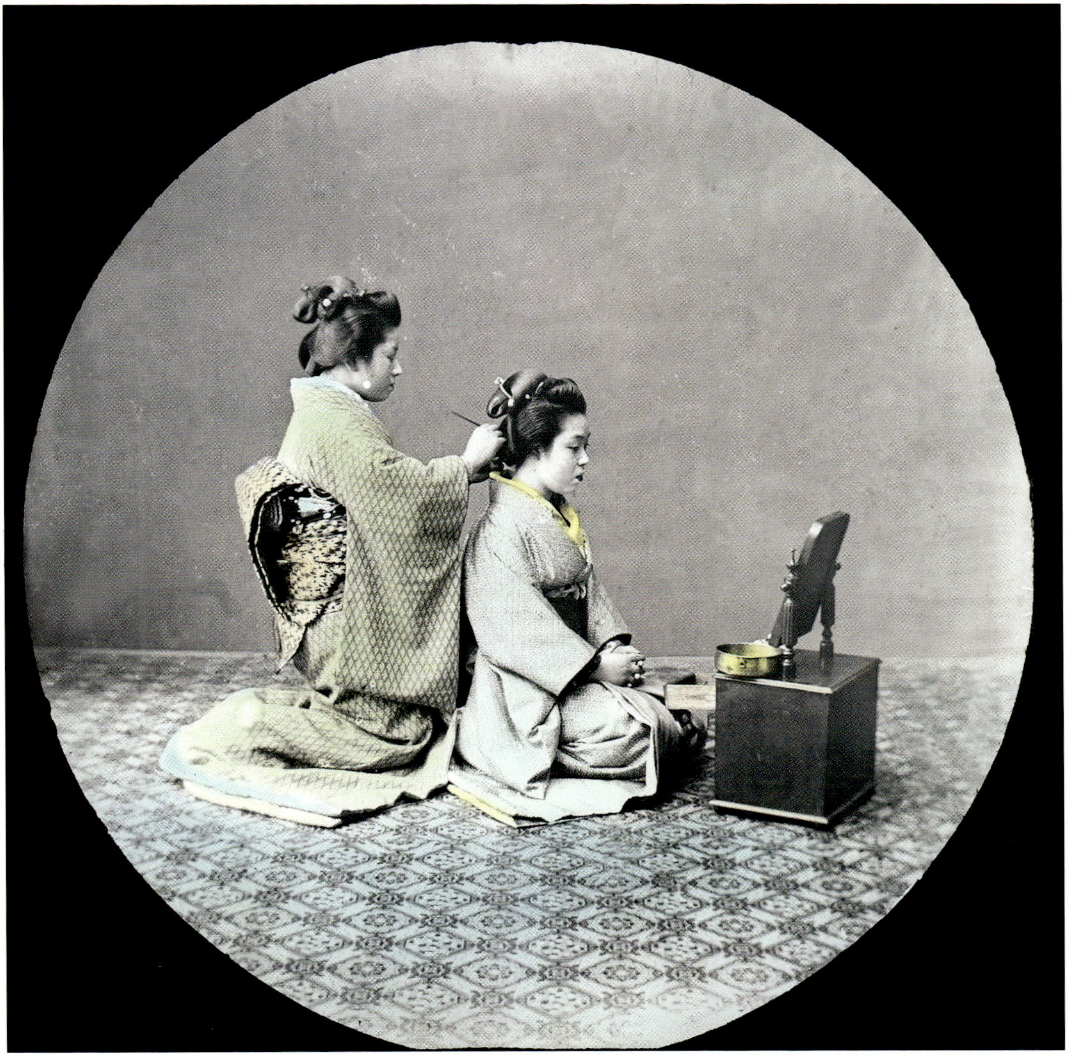

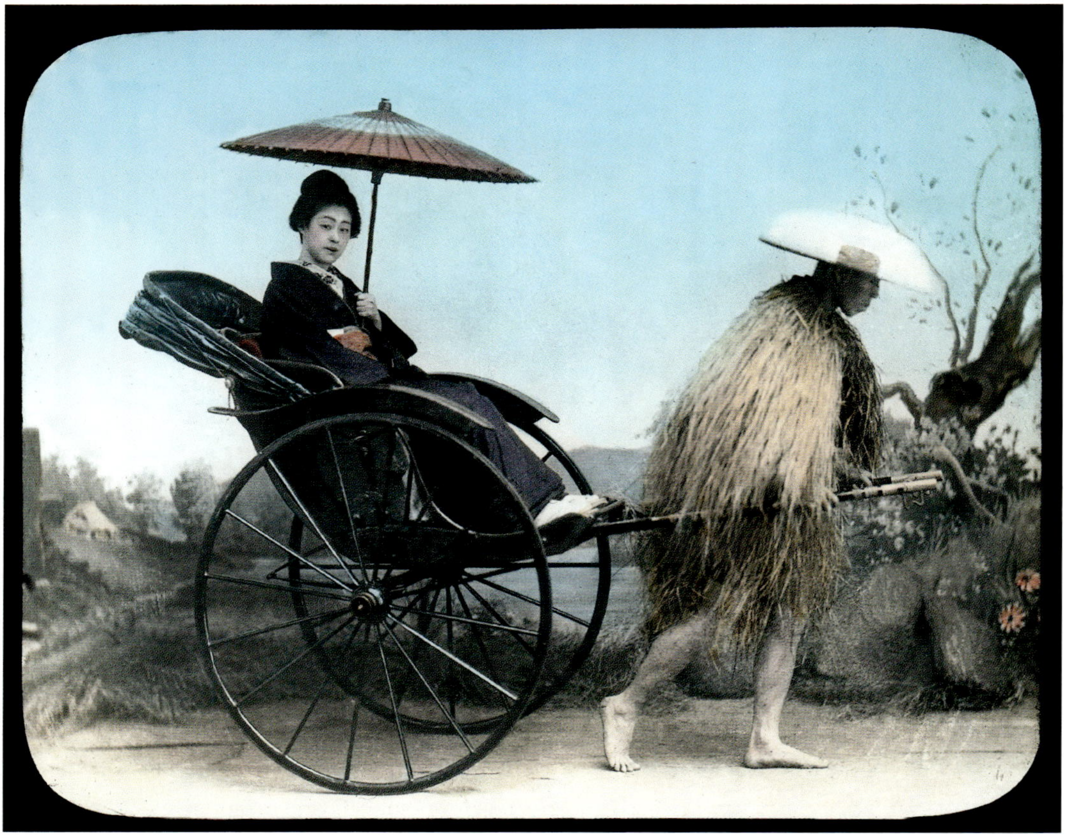

447 Jinrikisha (rickshaw) on a rainy day, Japan, 1870s
448 Outdoor costumes for wet weather, Japan, 1870s

447 Jinriksha (Rikscha) an einem regnerischen Tag, Japan, 1870er Jahre
448 Kleidung bei nassem Wetter, Japan, 1870er Jahre

447 Jinrikisha (pousse-pousse) par temps pluvieux, Japon, années 1870
448 La tenue lorsqu'il pleut, Japon, années 1870

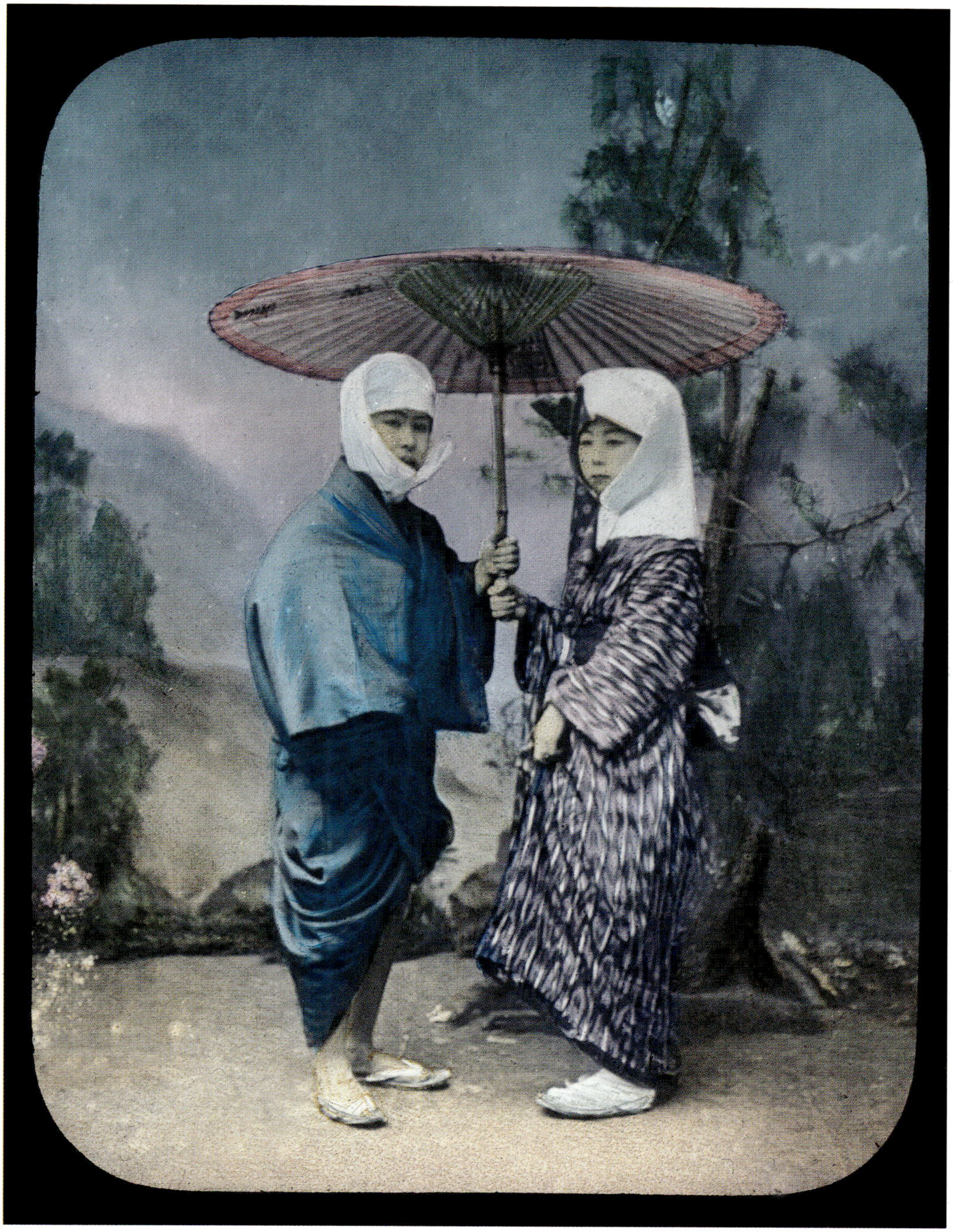

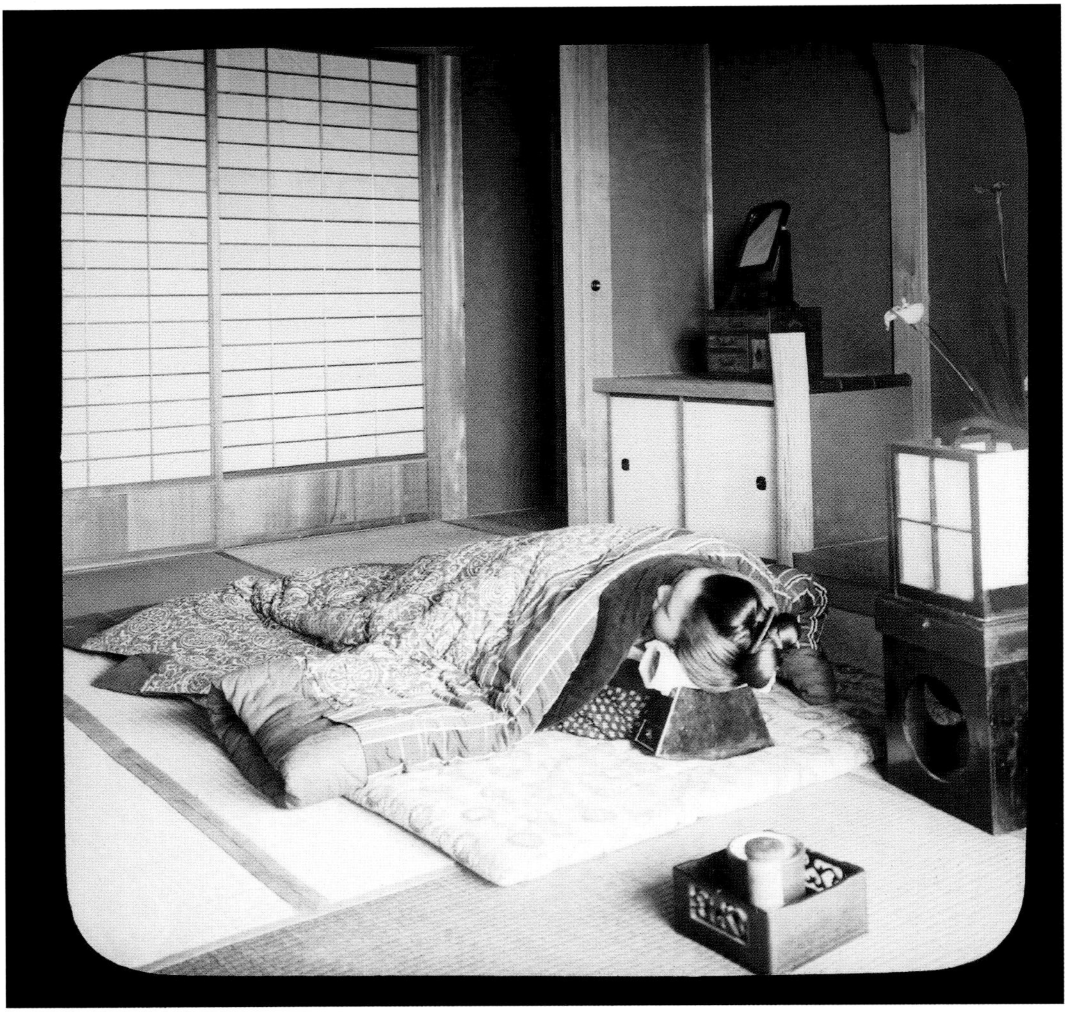

449 Japanese woman sleeping, showing traditional interior, Japan, 1880s
450 "A Beauty Beautifying", Japan, 1880s

449 Schlafende Japanerin in traditioneller Inneneinrichtung, Japan, 1880er Jahre
450 „Eine Schöne macht sich zurecht", Japan, 1880er Jahre

449 Chambre à coucher, Japon, années 1880
450 Soins de beauté, Japon, années 1880

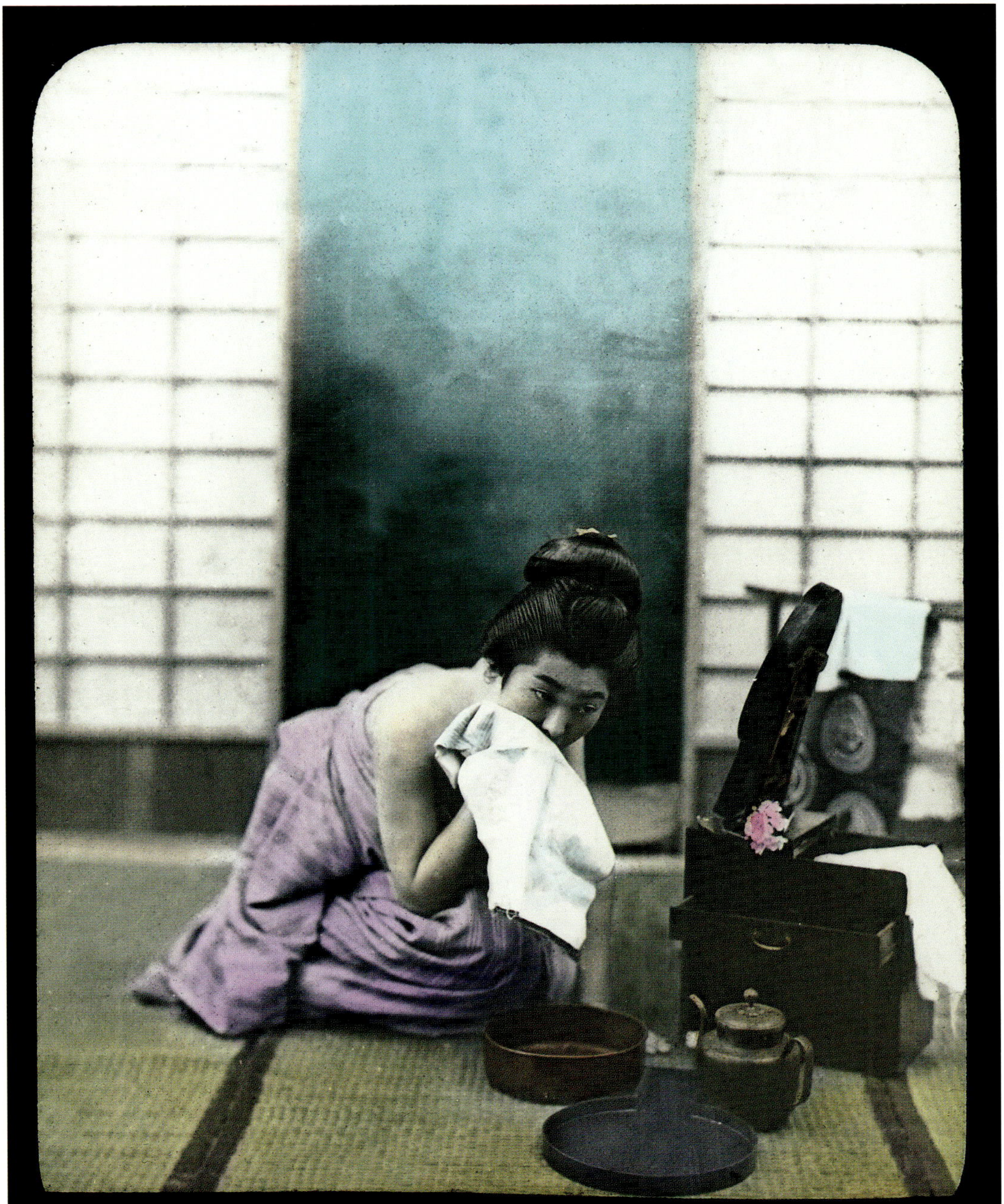

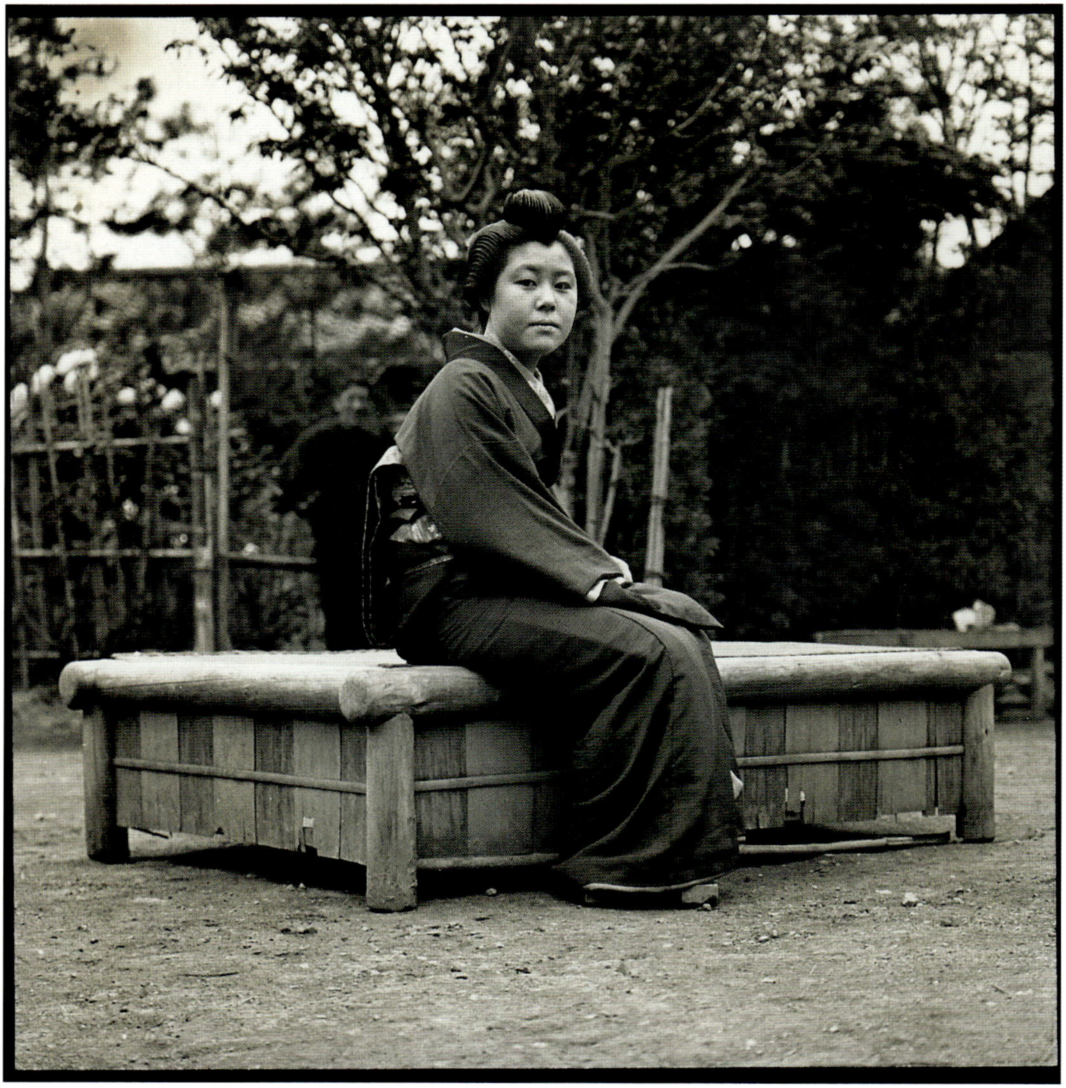

451 Young woman, Japan, 1900s
452 Singing girls, Japan, c.1900

451 Junge Frau, Japan, 1900er Jahre
452 Mädchen-Gesangsgruppe, Japan, um 1900

451 Jeune femme, Japon, années 1900
452 Chorale de jeunes filles, Japon, vers 1900

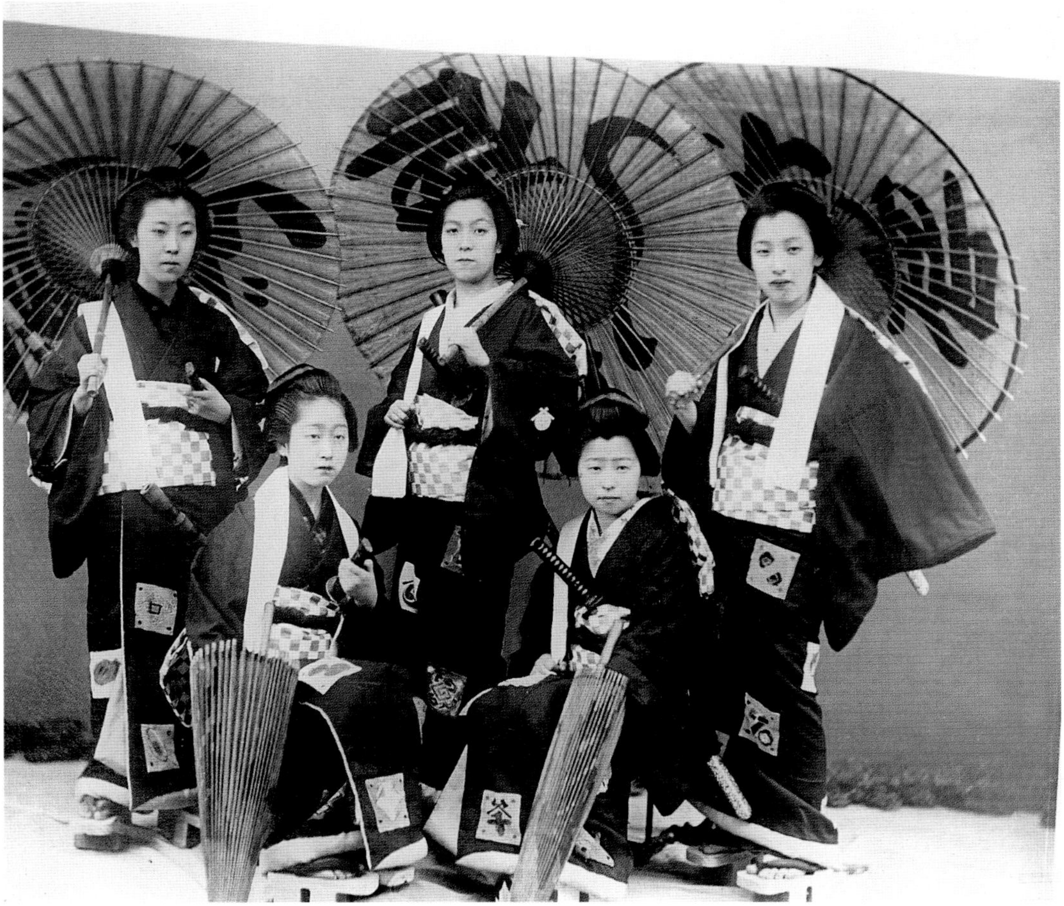

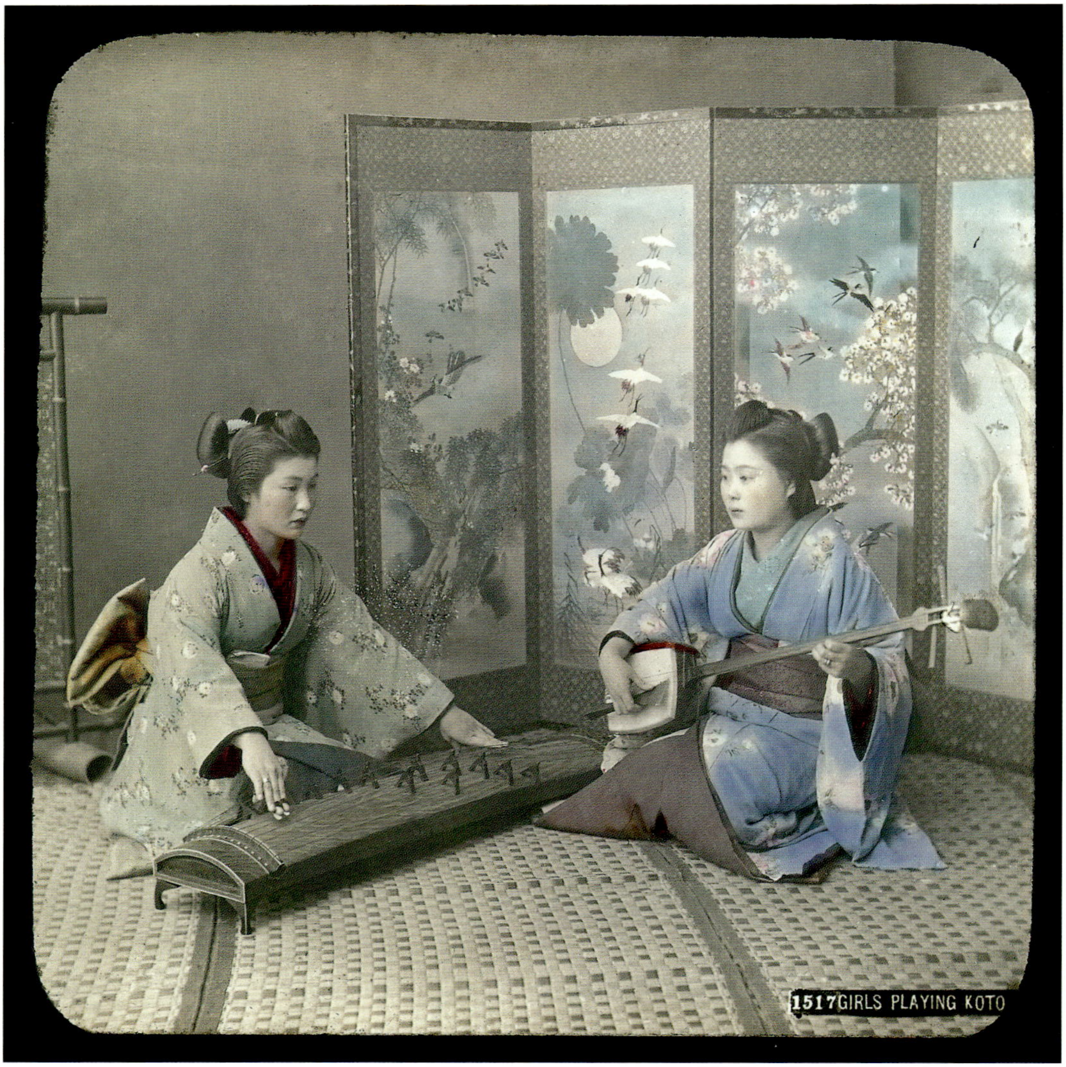

453 Girls playing koto, Japan, 1870s
454 Washing, Japan, 1880s

453 Mädchen spielen auf der Koto und der Shamisen, Japan, 1870er Jahre
454 Wäsche, Japan, 1880er Jahre

453 Jeunes filles jouant du koto et du shamisen - Japon, années 1870
454 Lessive. Japon, années 1880

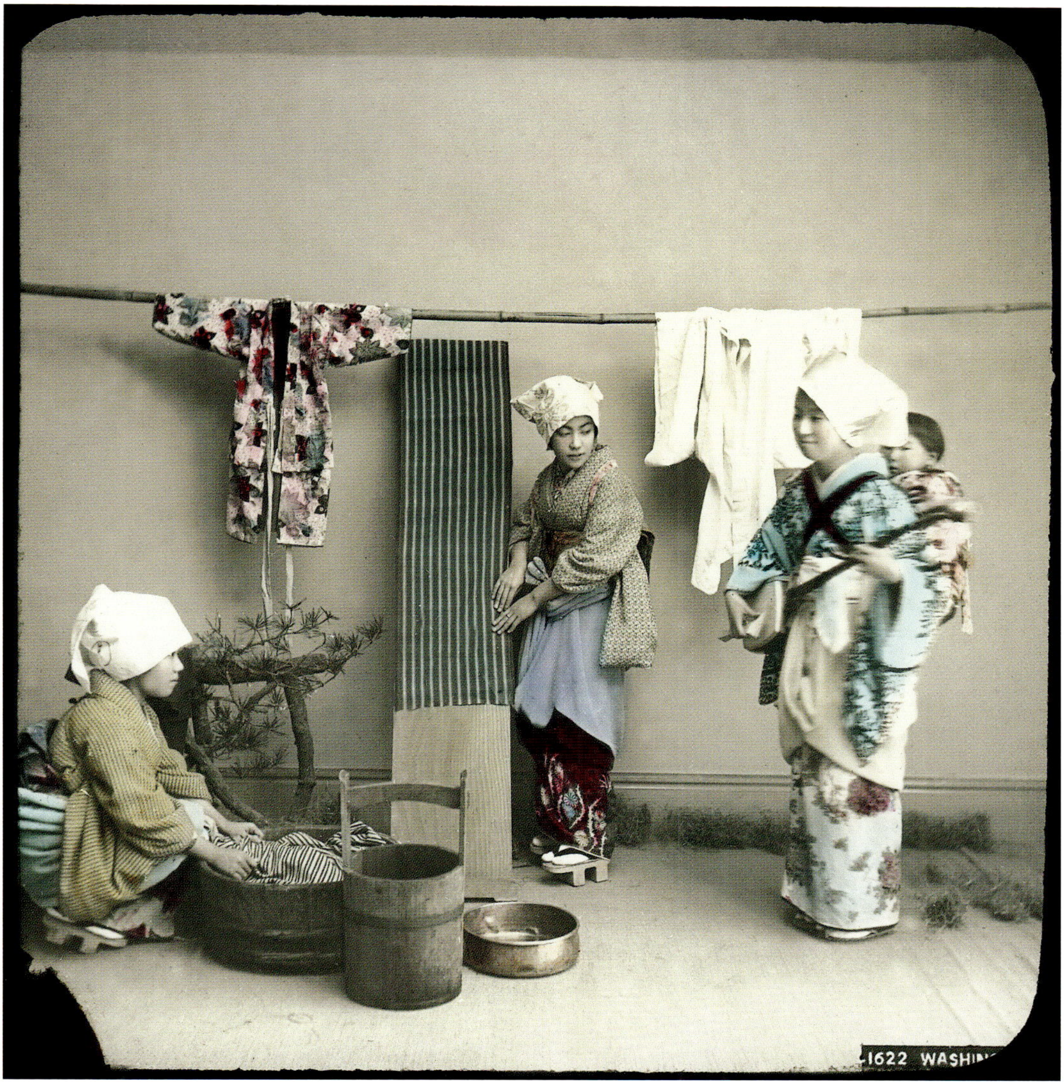
1622 WASHIN

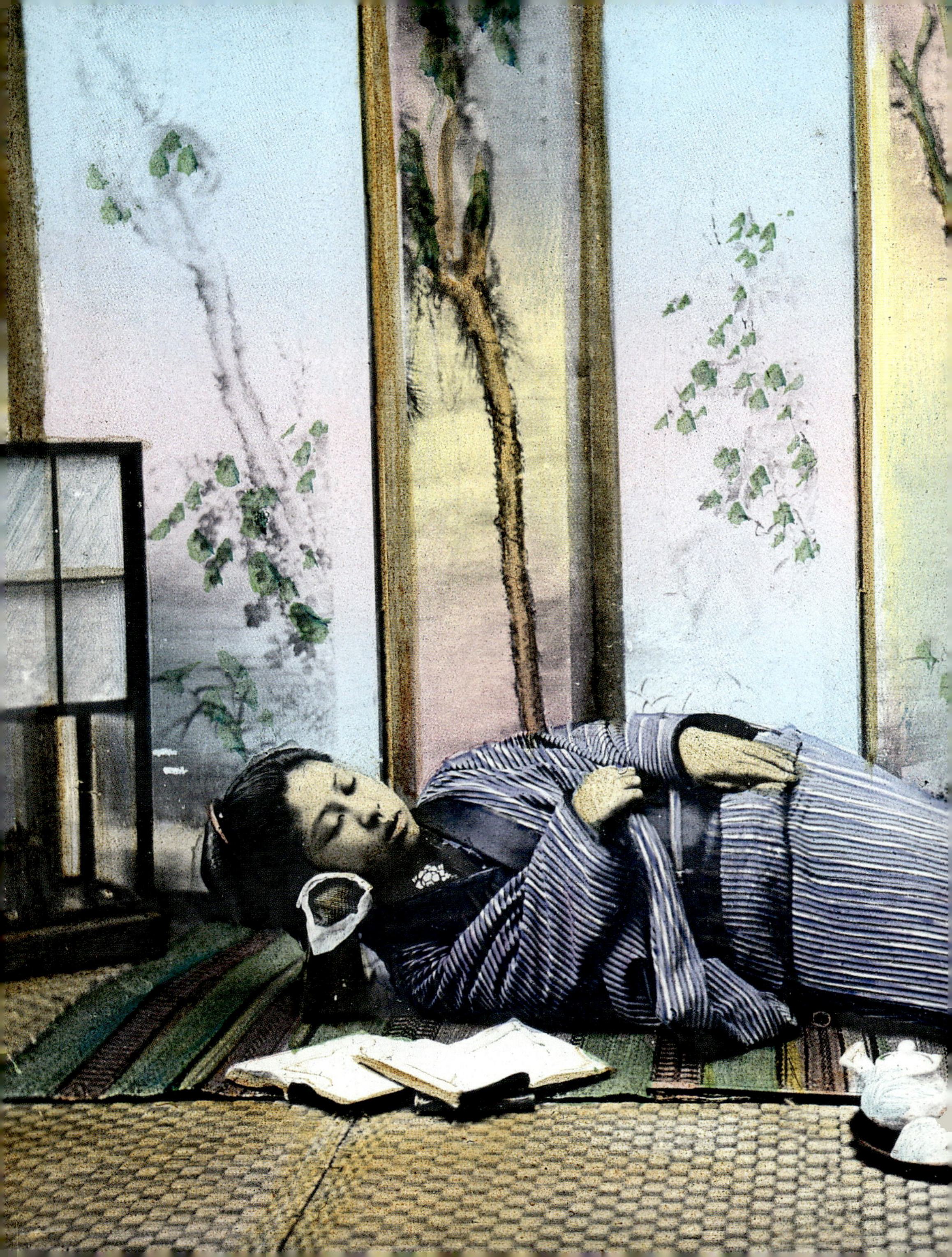

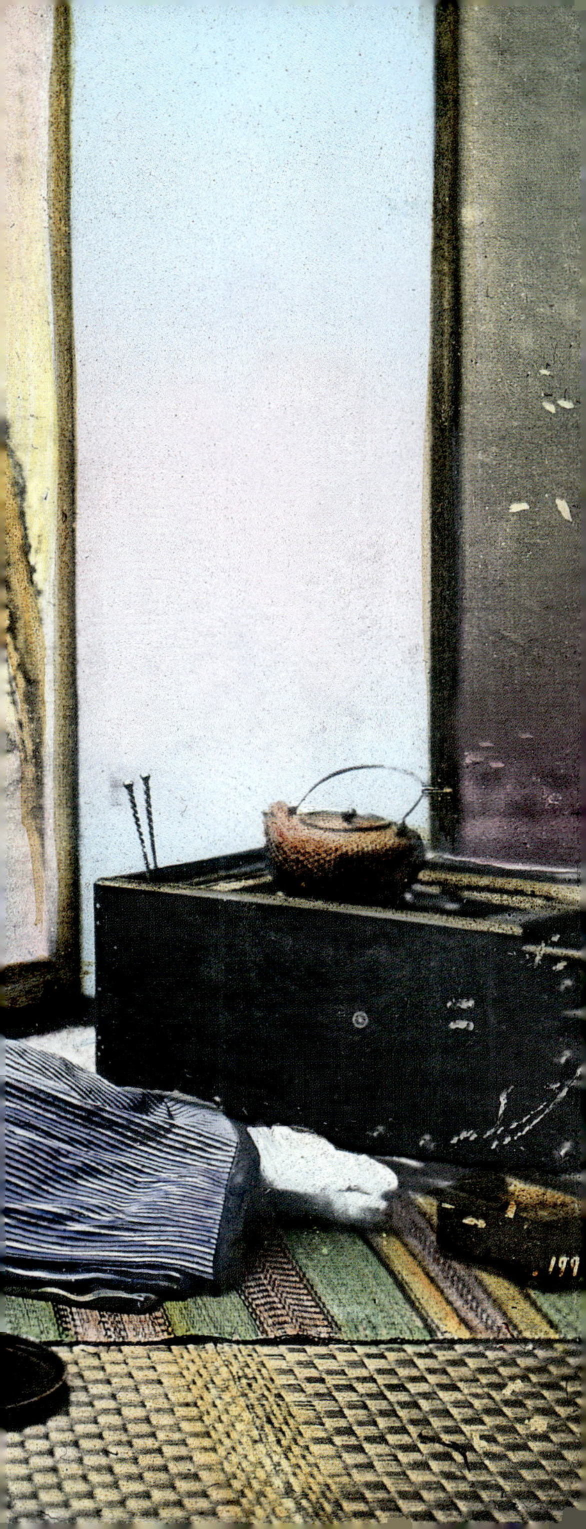

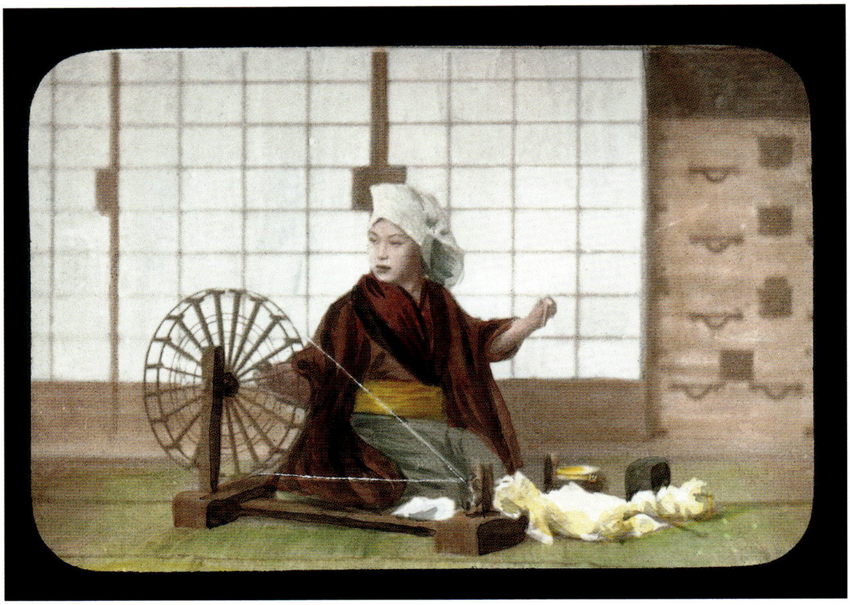

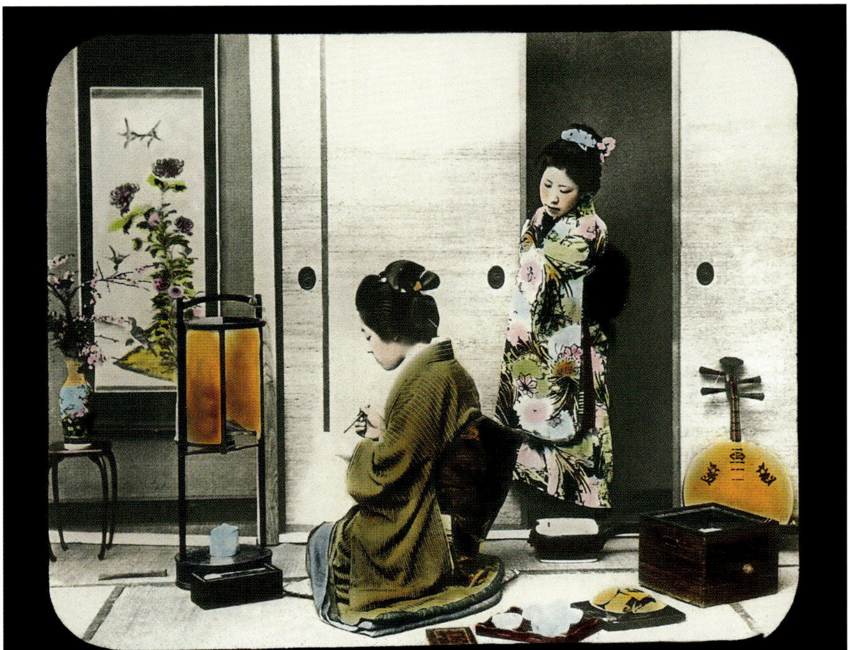

456 Woman spinning, Japan, 1870s
457 Woman writing a letter, Japan, 1890s

456 Frau beim Spinnen, Japan, 1870er Jahre
457 Frau beim Verfassen eines Briefes, Japan, 1890er Jahre

456 Fileuse, Japon, années 1870
457 Femme écrivant une lettre, Japon, années 1890

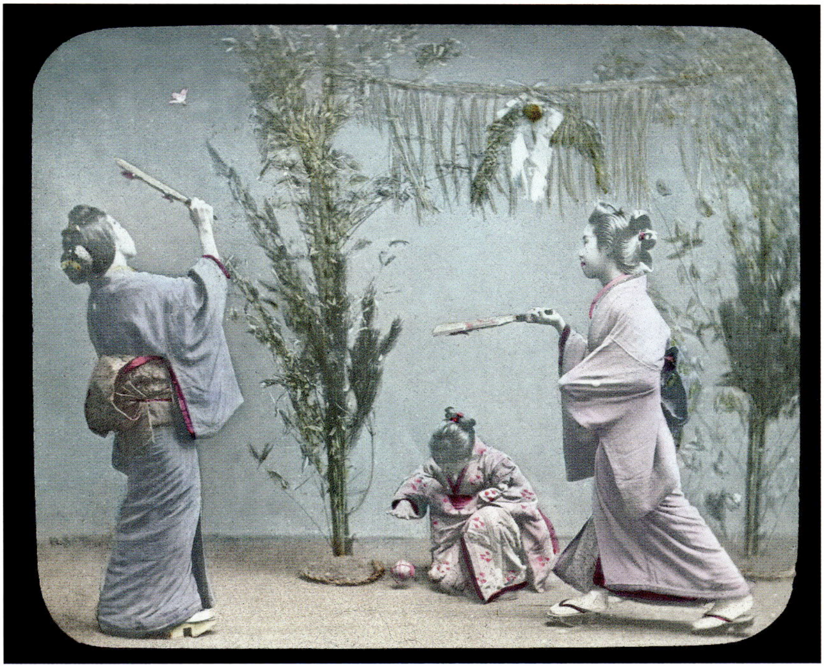

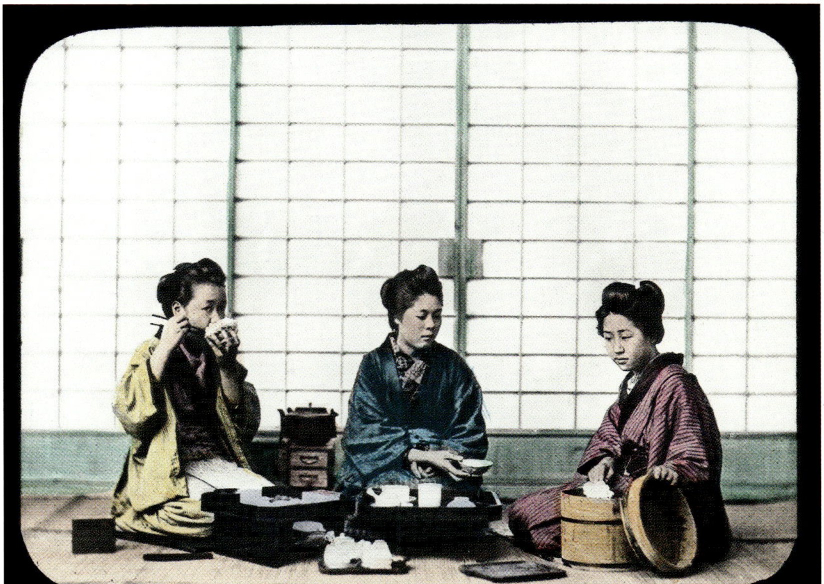

458 “Playing Battle-dore and Shuttle-cock”, Hane (New Year’s Game), Japan, 1870s
459 “Dinner”, Japan, 1870s

458 „Beim Federballspielen“, Hane (Neujahrsspiel), Japan, 1870er Jahre
459 „Das Mahl“, Japan, 1870er Jahre

458 « Volant et raquettes », Hane (jeu du nouvel’ an), Japon, années 1870
459 « Dîner », Japon, années 1870

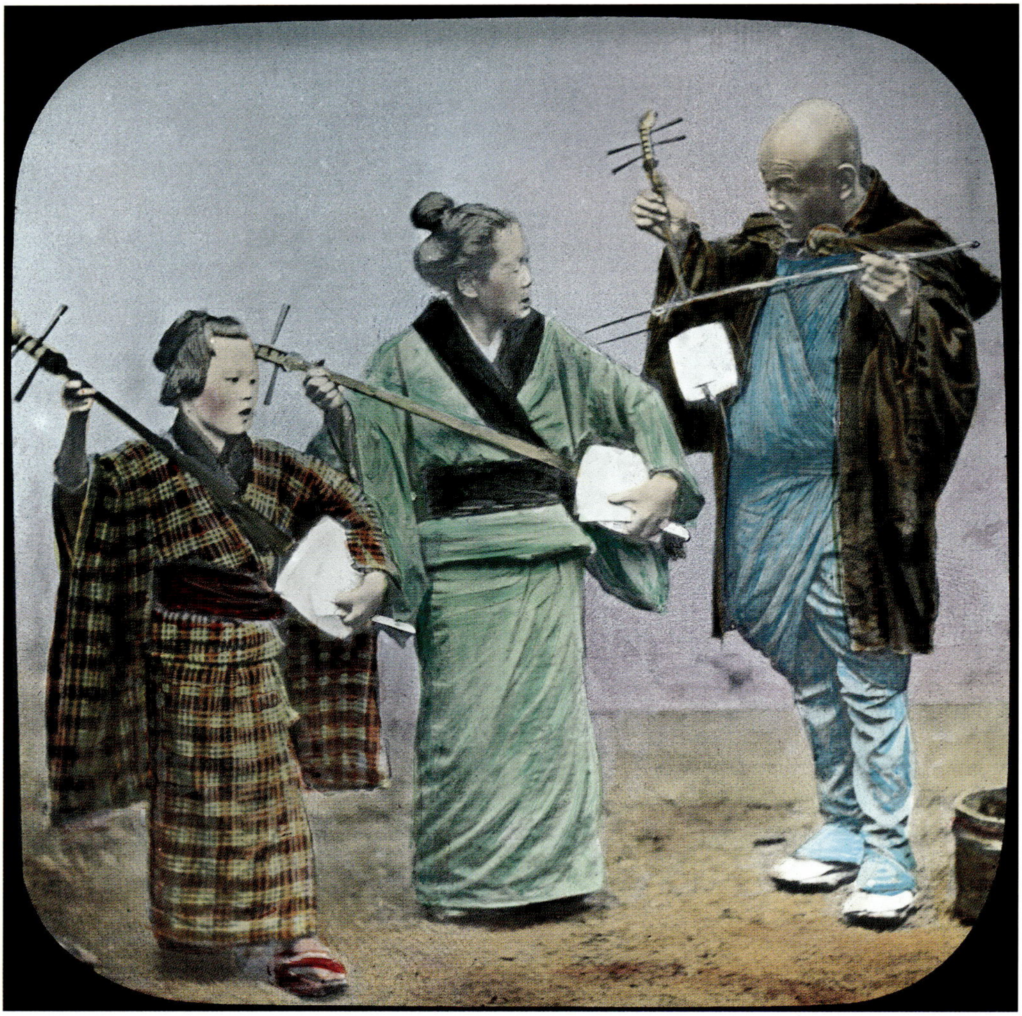

460 Streetplayers, Japan, 1880s
461 Moving home, Japan, 1880s

460 Straßenmusikanten, Japan, 1880er Jahre
461 Umzug, Japan, 1880er Jahre

460 Musiciens de rue, Japon, années 1880
461 Changement de domicile, Japon, années 1880

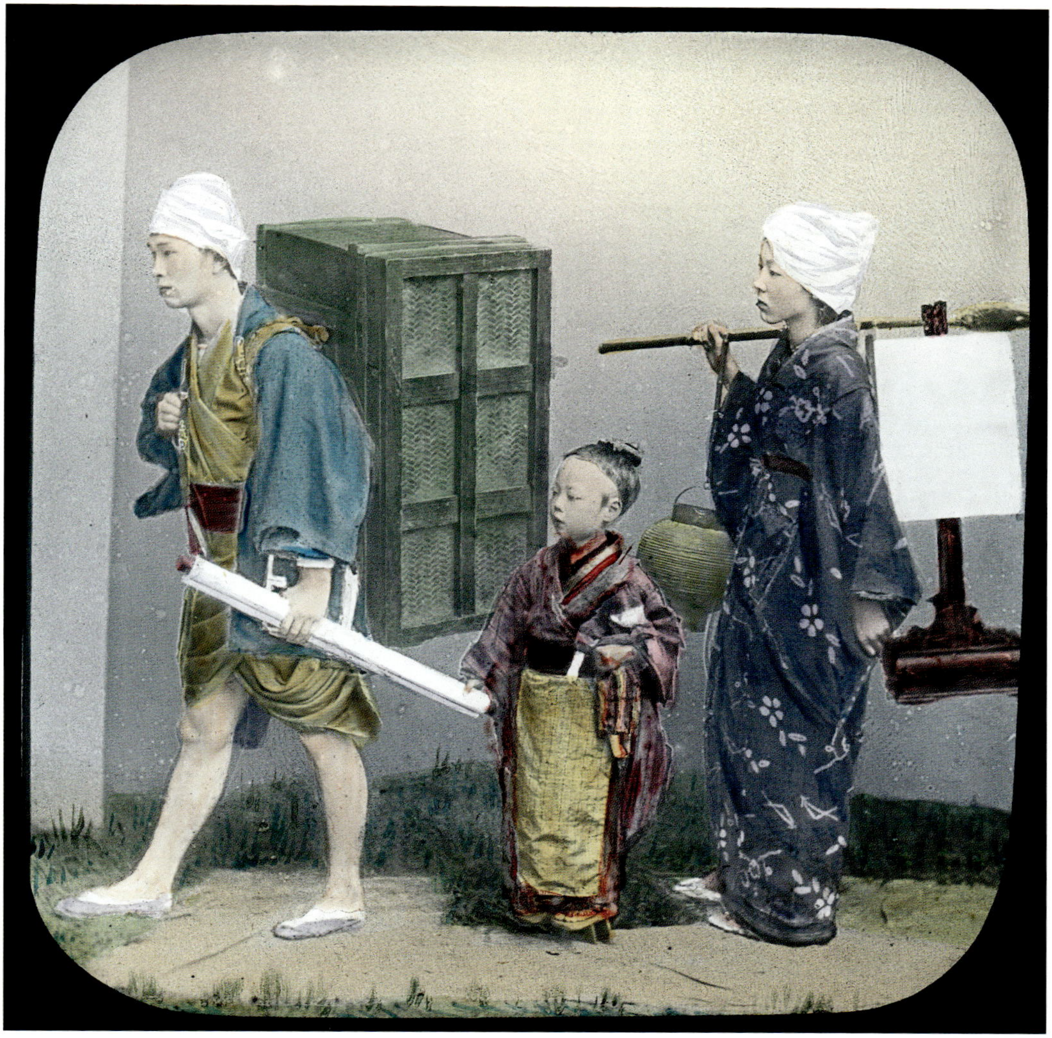

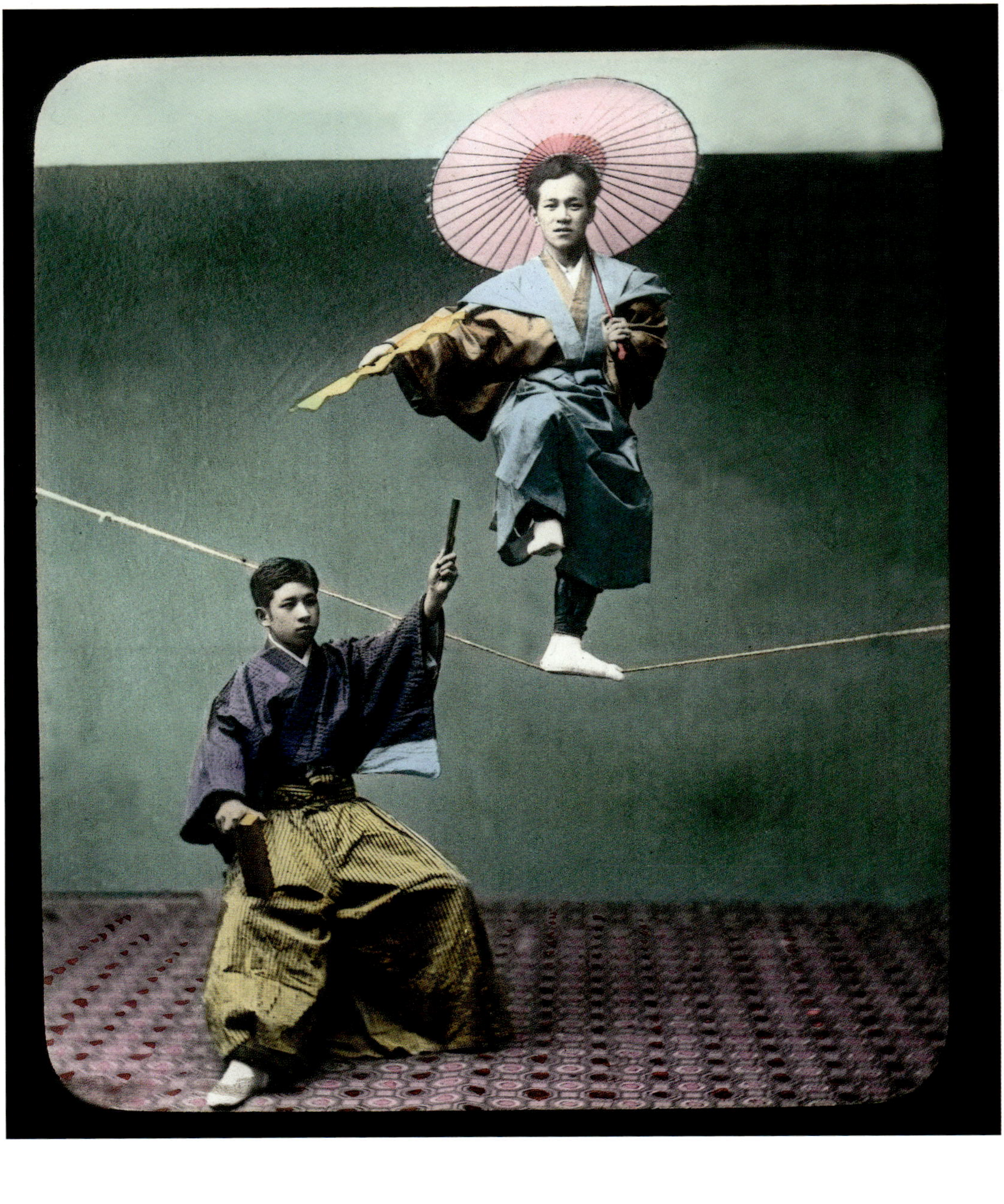

462 Tightrope walker, Japan, 1890s
463 Acrobats, Japan, 1890s

462 Seiltänzer, Japan, 1890er Jahre
463 Akrobaten, Japan, 1890er Jahre

462 Funambule, Japon, années 1890
463 Acrobates, Japon, années 1890

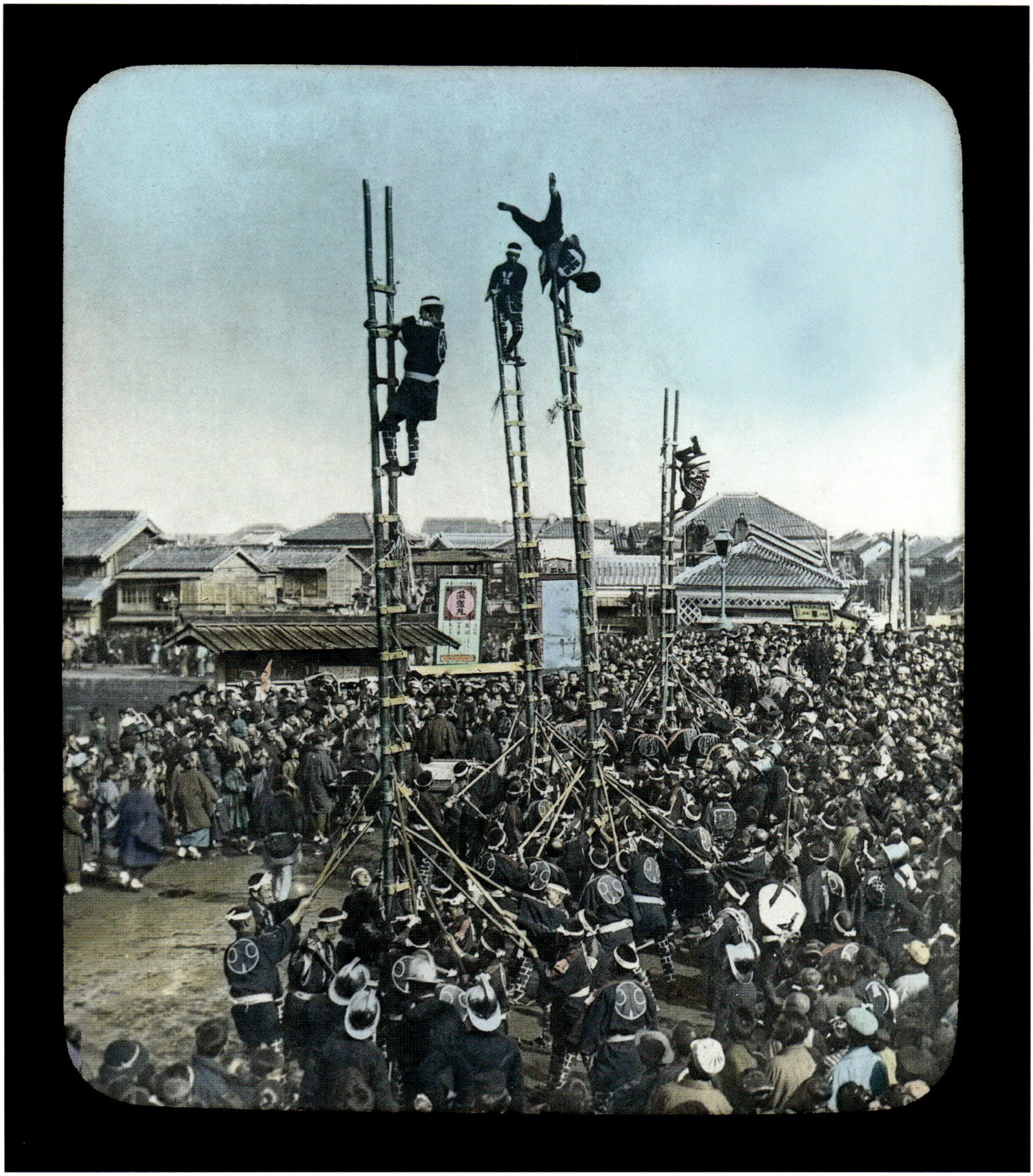

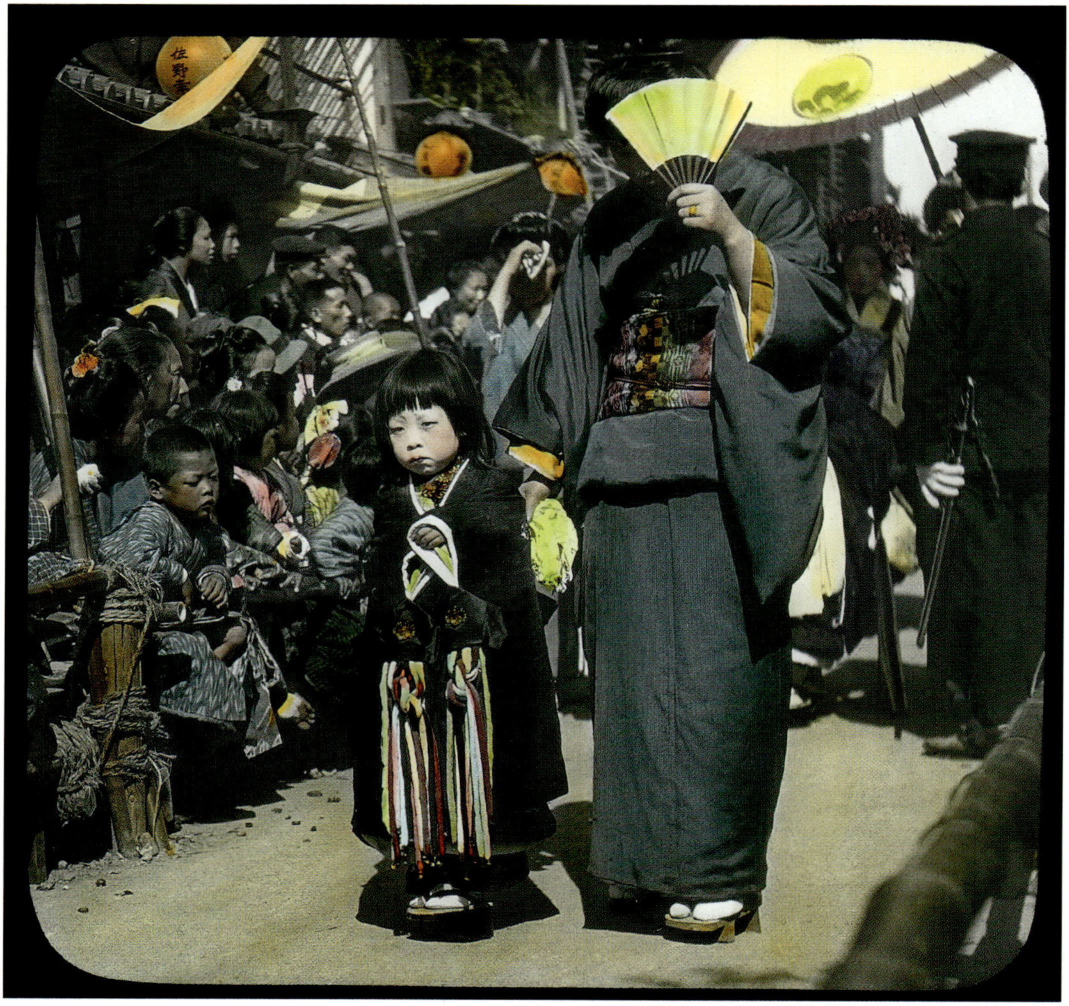

464 Procession with young girl, Japan, c.1900
465 Girl with doll, Japan, 1900s

464 Prozession mit kleinem Mädchen, Japan, um 1900
465 Mädchen mit Puppe, Japan, 1900er Jahre

464 Fillette lors d'une procession, Japon, vers 1900
465 Fillette avec une poupée, Japon, années 1900

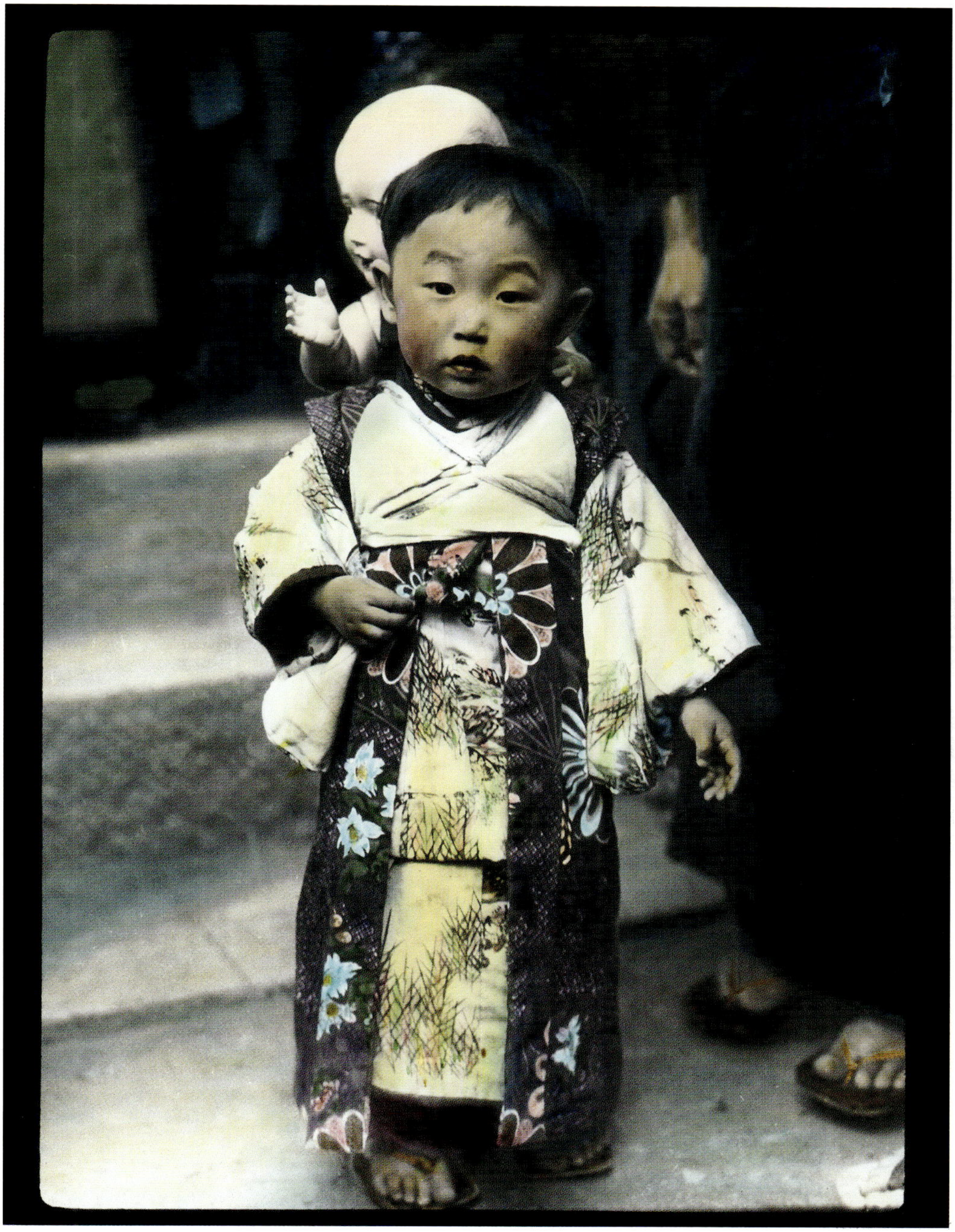

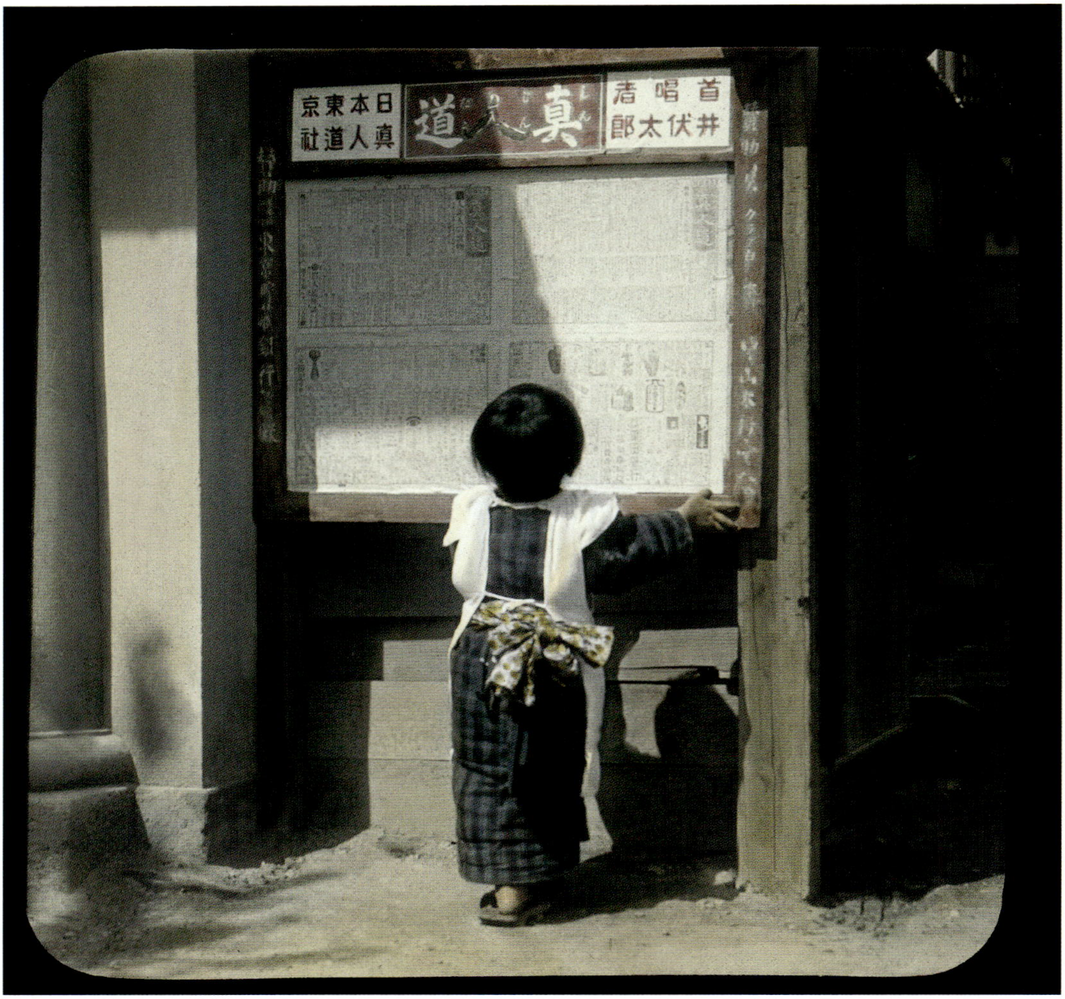

466 Child reading the war news, Tokyo, Japan, 1900s
467 Boy using a street water pump, Japan, 1910s

466 Kind liest die Kriegsnachrichten, Tokio, Japan, 1900er Jahre
467 Junge an einer Straßenwasserpumpe, Japan, 1910er Jahre

466 Enfant lisant les nouvelles de la guerre, Tokyo, Japon, années 1900
467 Enfant à une fontaine publique, Japon, années 1910

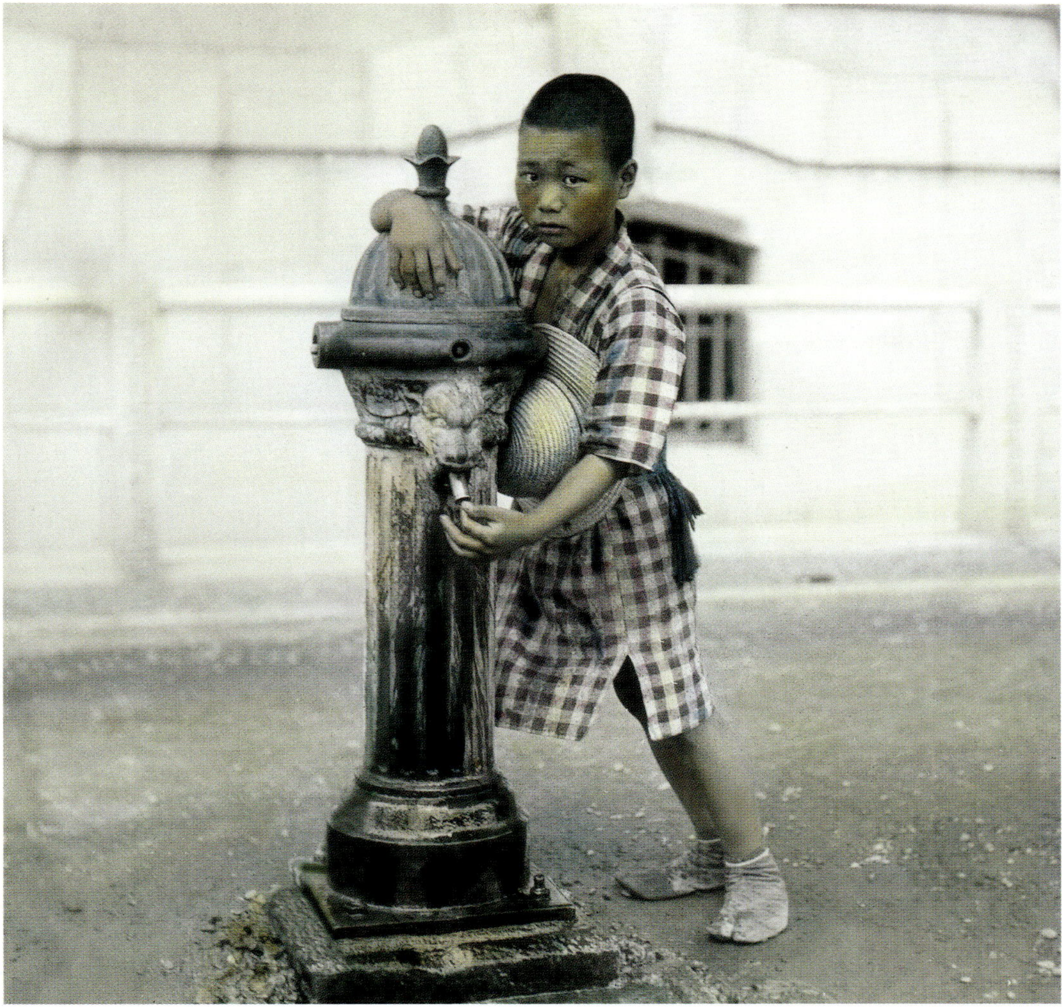

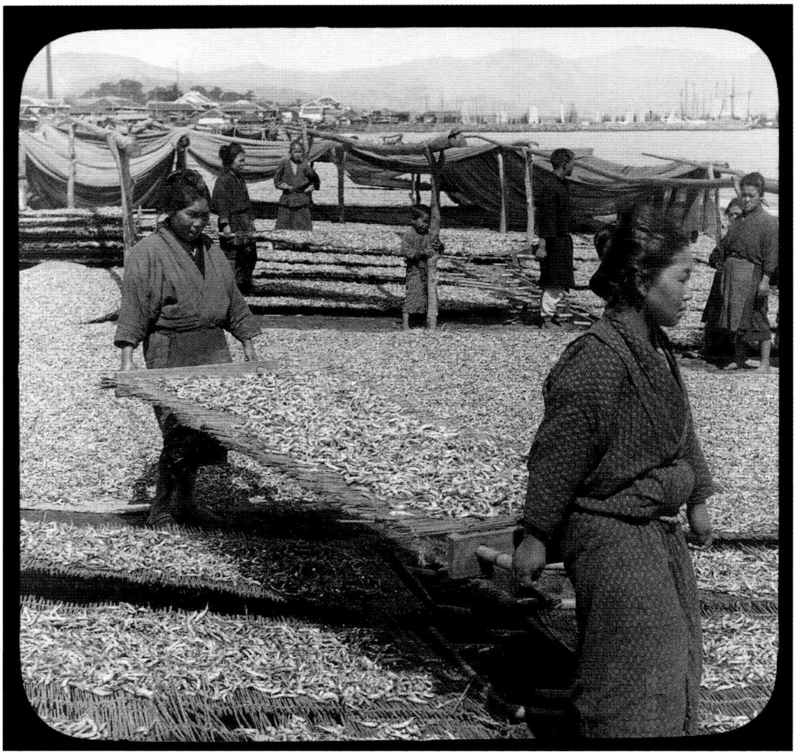

468 Drying sardines, Japan, c.1900

468 Trocknen von Sardinen, Japan, um 1900

468 Séchage des sardines, Japon, vers 1900

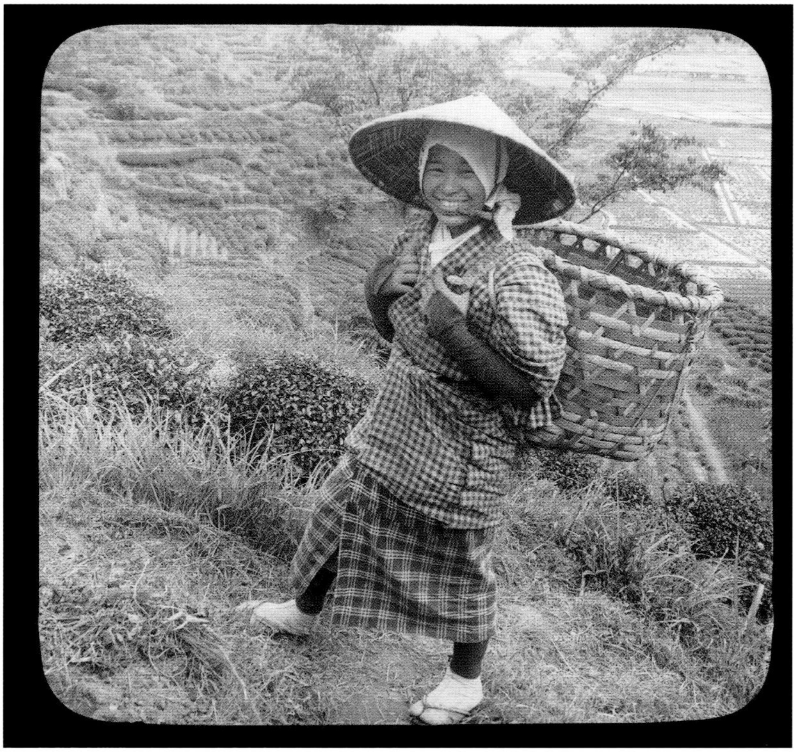

469 Woman gathering tea, Japan, c.1900

469 Frau beim Teesammeln, Japan, um 1900

469 Femme récoltant le thé, Japon, vers 1900

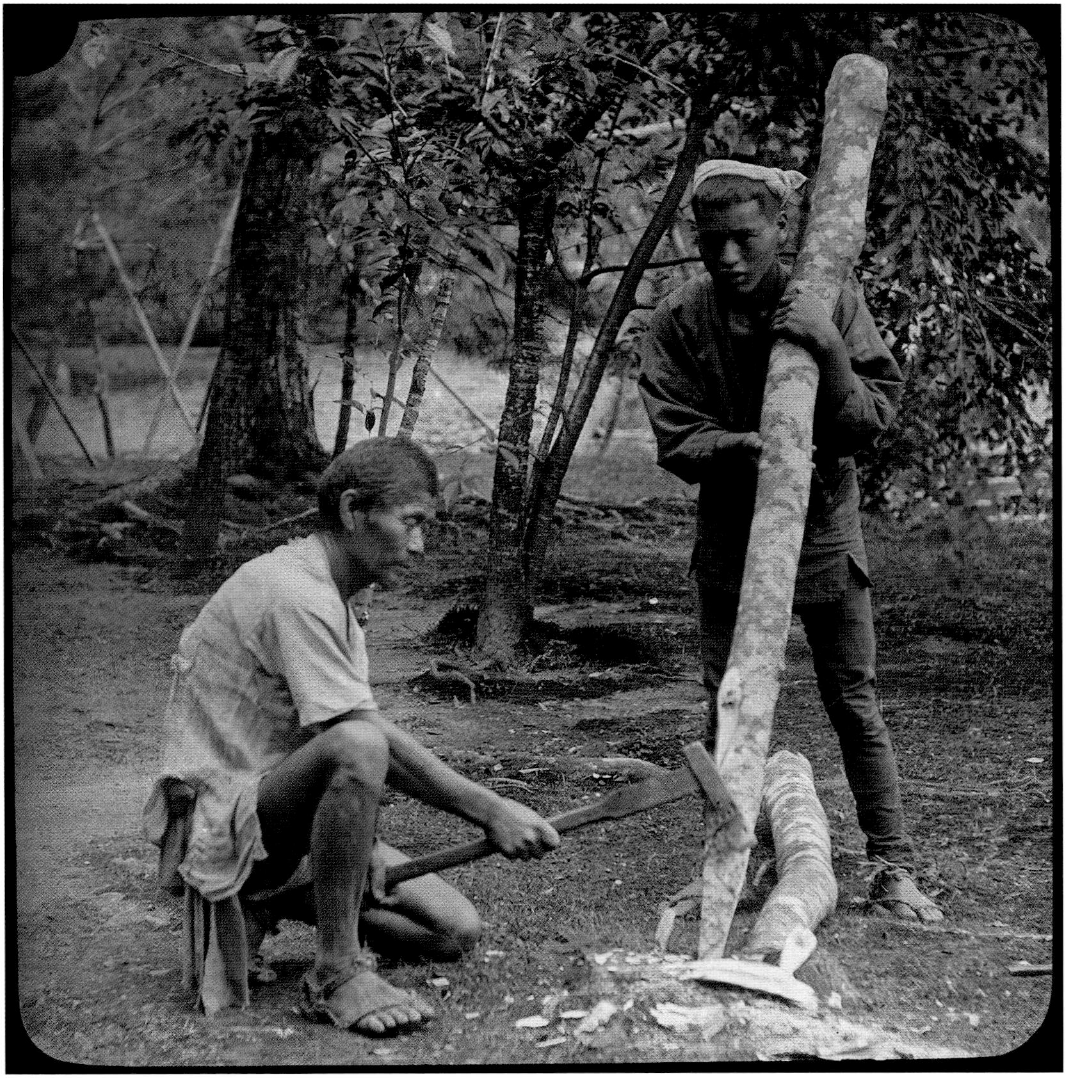

470 Woodmen, Japan, c.1900

470 Holzfäller, Japan, um 1900

470 Bûcheron, Japon, vers 1900

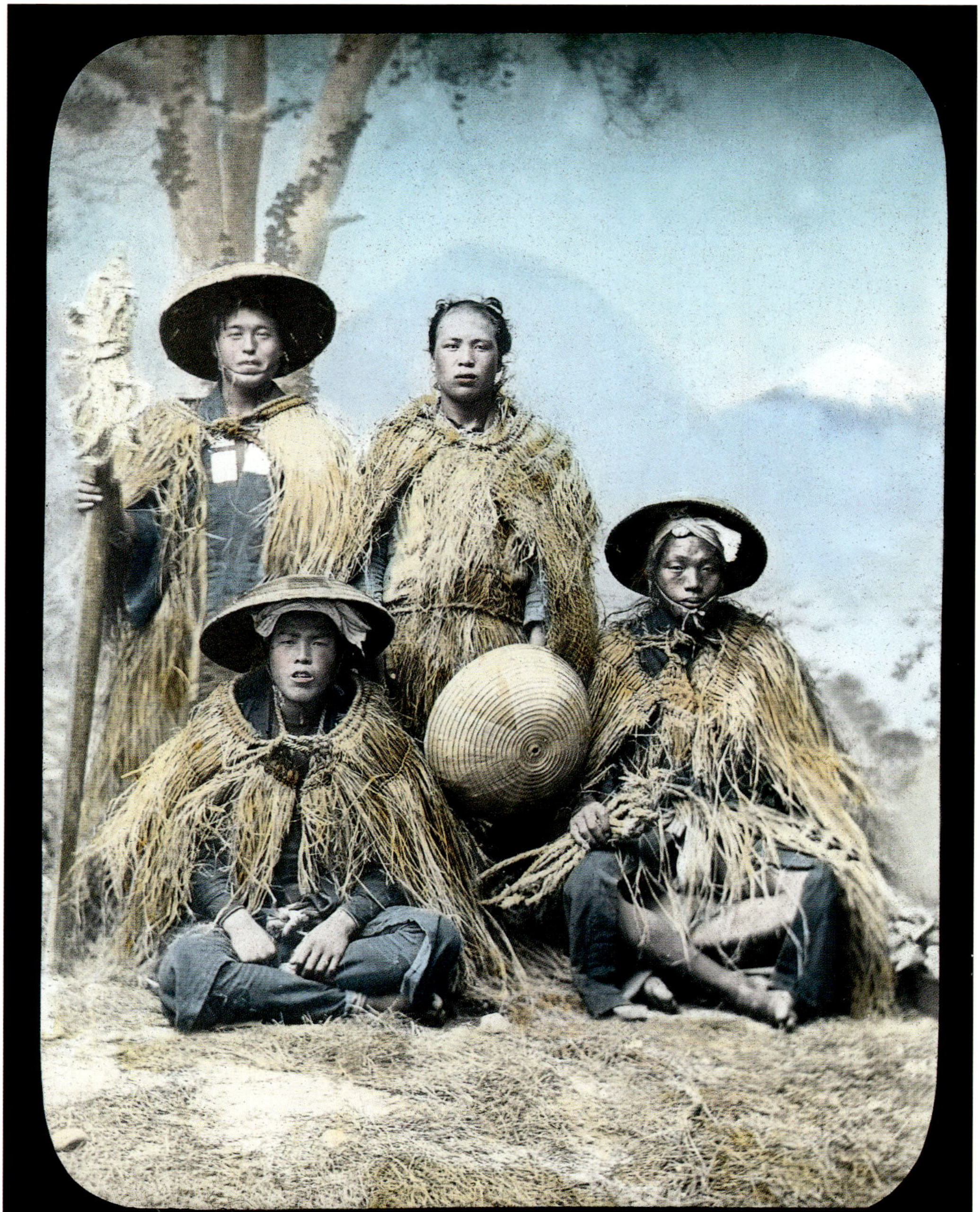

471 Farmers wearing mino (traditional raincoats made from straw), Japan, 1870s

471 Bauern mit Minos (traditionelle Regenumhänge aus Stroh), Japan, 1870er Jahre

471 Fermiers en mino (imperméable traditionnel en paille), Japon, années 1870

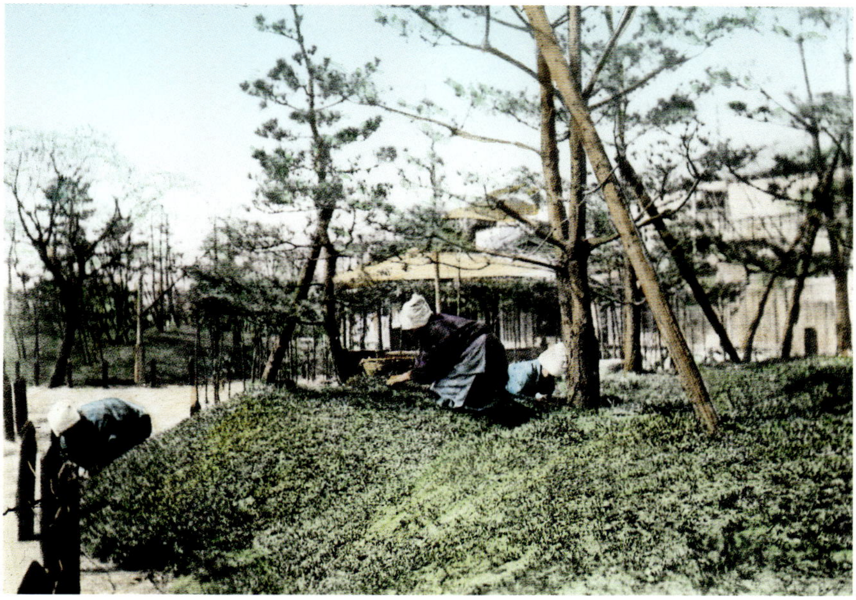

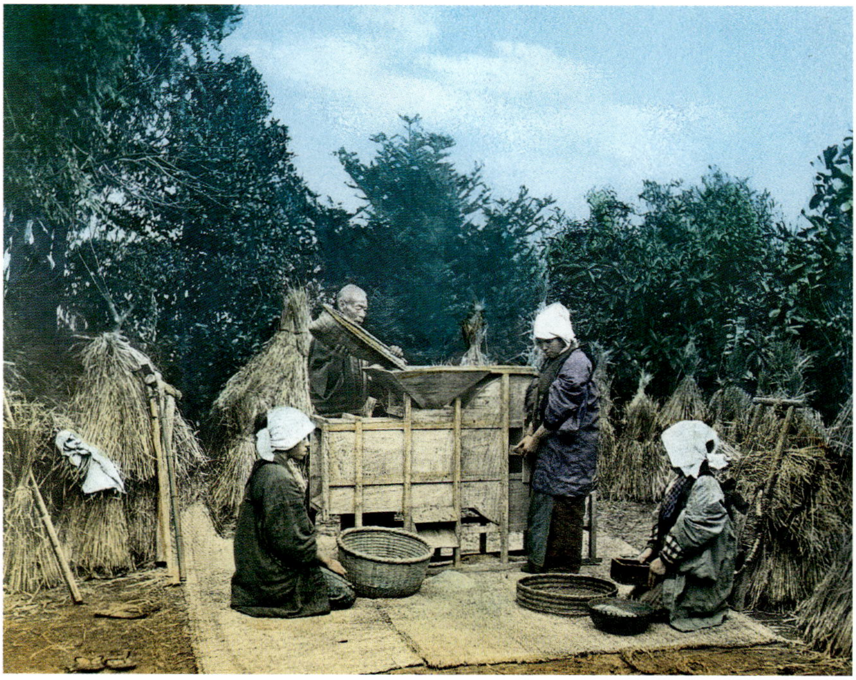

472 Women in traditional costume weeding gardens, Osaka, 1890s
473 Separating grain, Japan, 1890s

472 Frauen in traditioneller Kleidung beim Unkrautjäten, Osaka, 1890er Jahre
473 Korn wird getrennt, Japan, 1890er Jahre

472 Femme en costume traditionnel désherbant un jardin, Osaka, années 1890
473 Tri du grain, Japon, années 1890

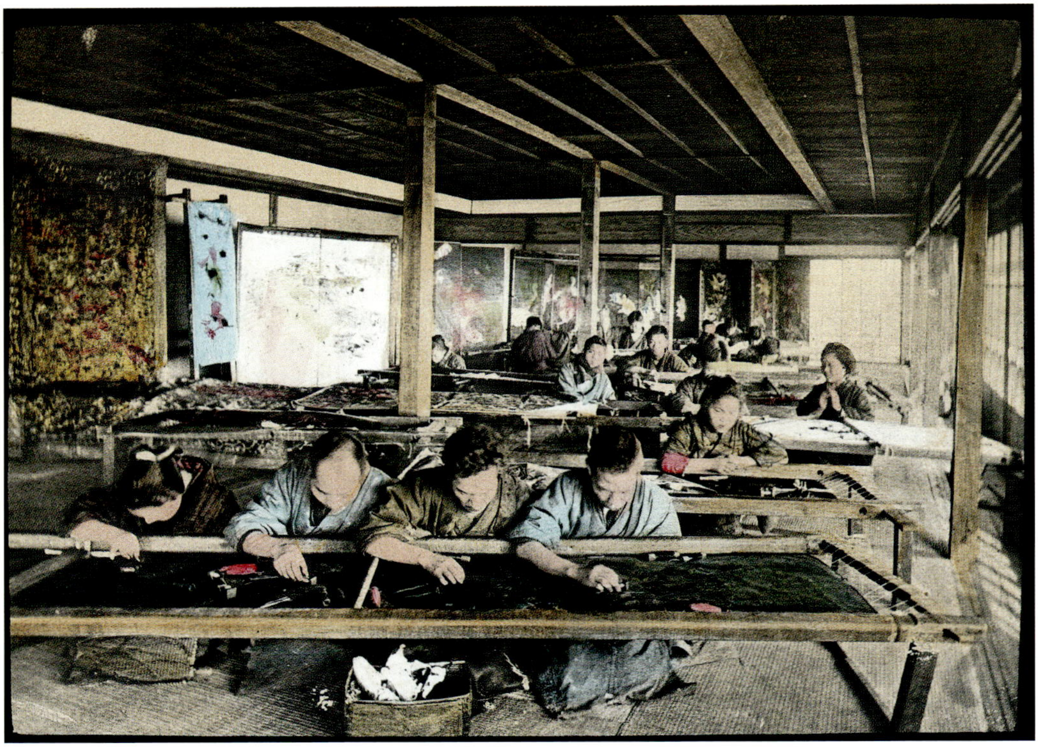

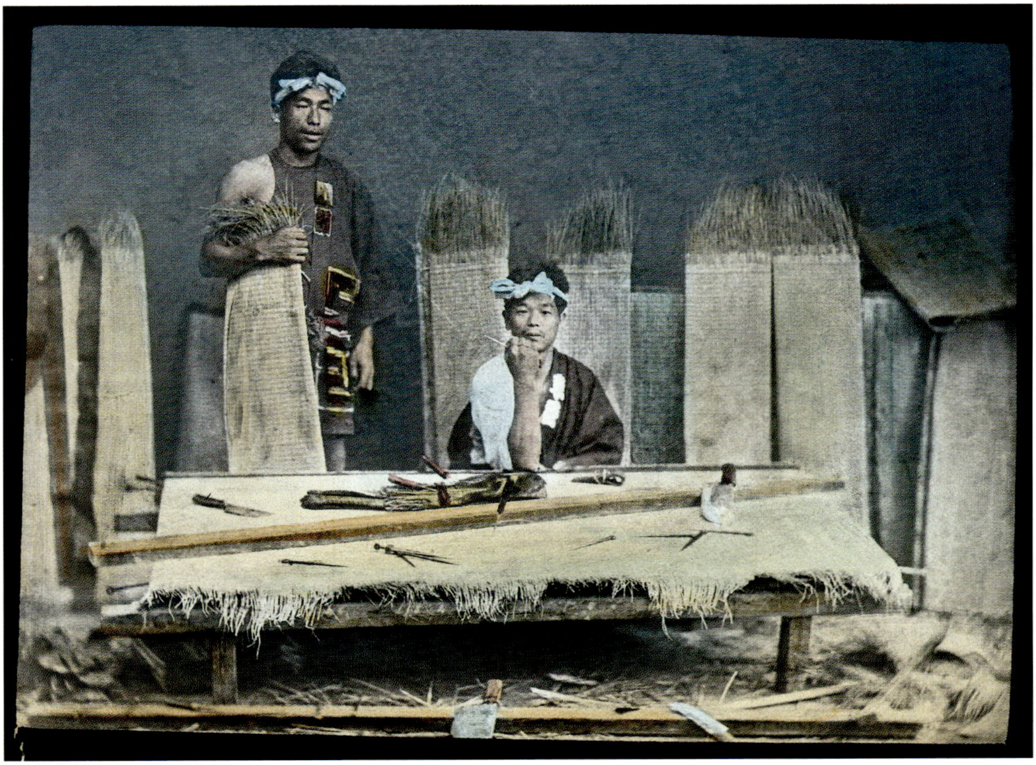

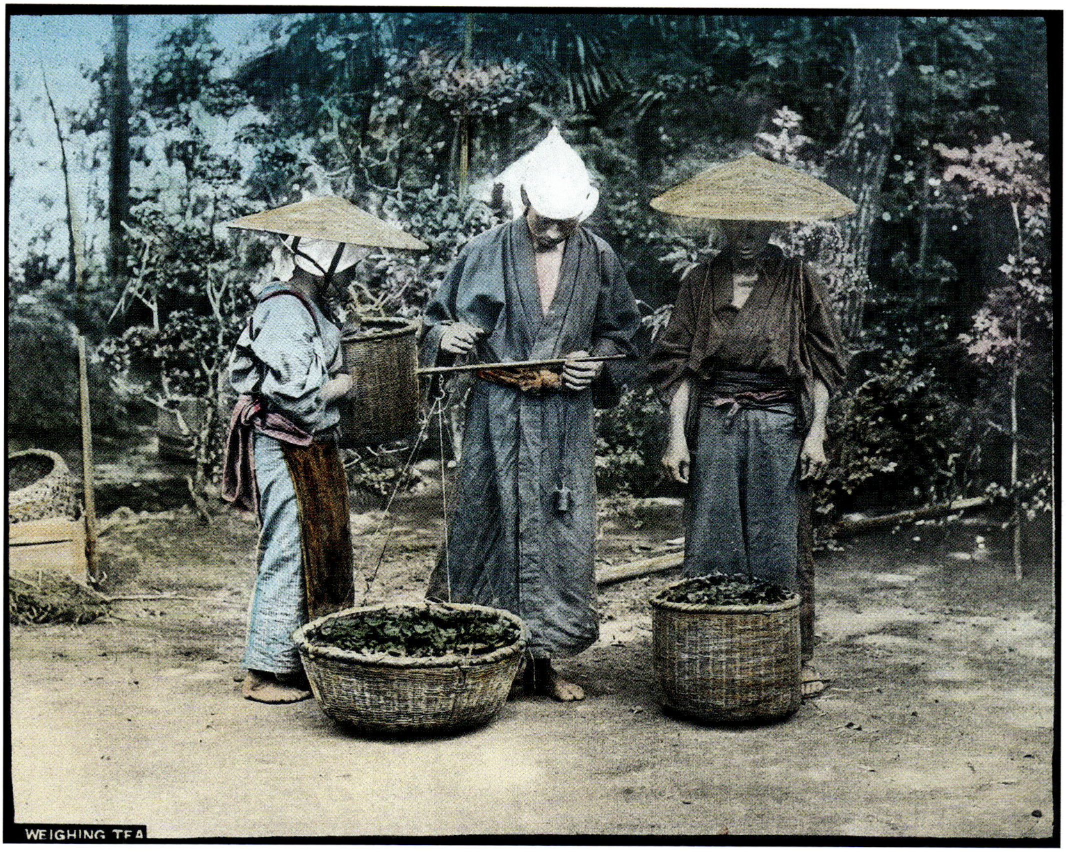

474 Embroidery workshop, Japan, 1890s
475 Mat makers, Japan, 1890s
476 Weighing tea, Japan, 1890s

474 Stickerei-Werkstätte, Japan, 1890er Jahre
475 Mattenmacher, Japan, 1890er Jahre
476 Tee wird abgewogen, Japan, 1890er Jahre

474 Atelier de broderie, Japon, années 1890
475 Fabricants de nattes, Japon, années 1890
476 Pesée du thé, Japon, années 1890

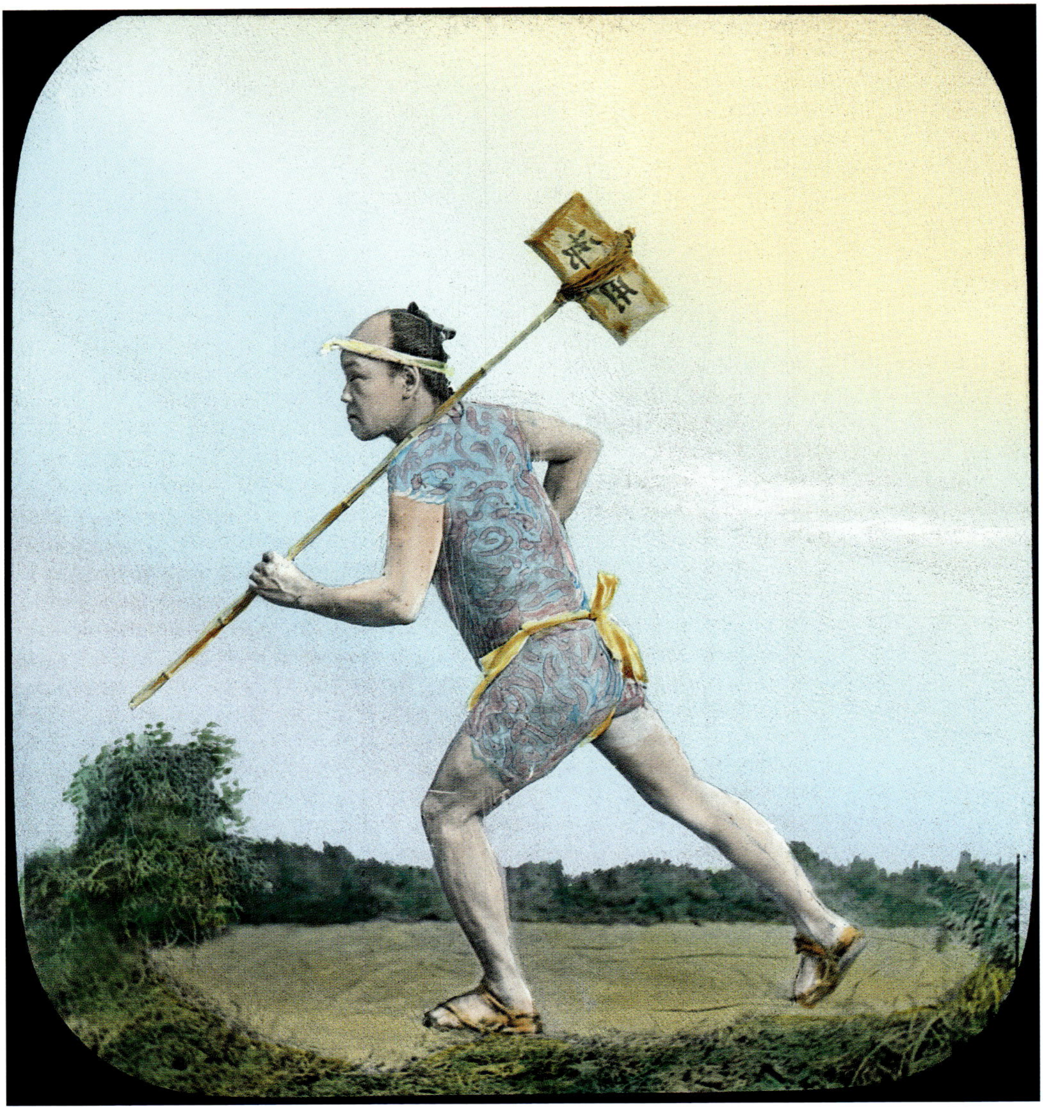

477 Tattooed postman, Japan, 1880s
478 "Hikeshu...", Japan, 1880s

477 Tätowierter Postbote, Japan, 1880er Jahre
478 „Hikeshu...“, Japan, 1880er Jahre

477 Postier tatoué, Japon, années 1880
478 « Hikeshu... », Japon, années 1880

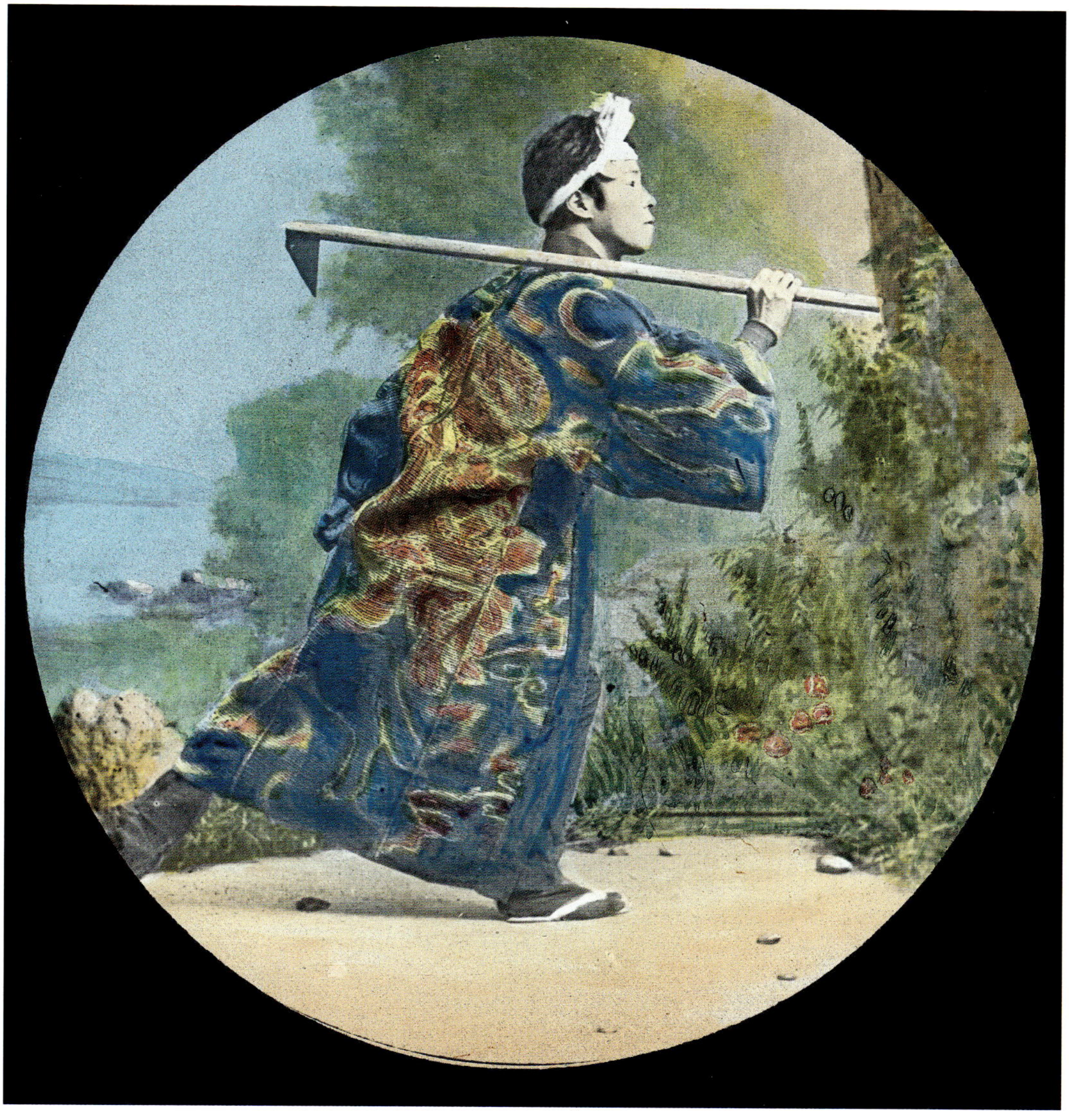

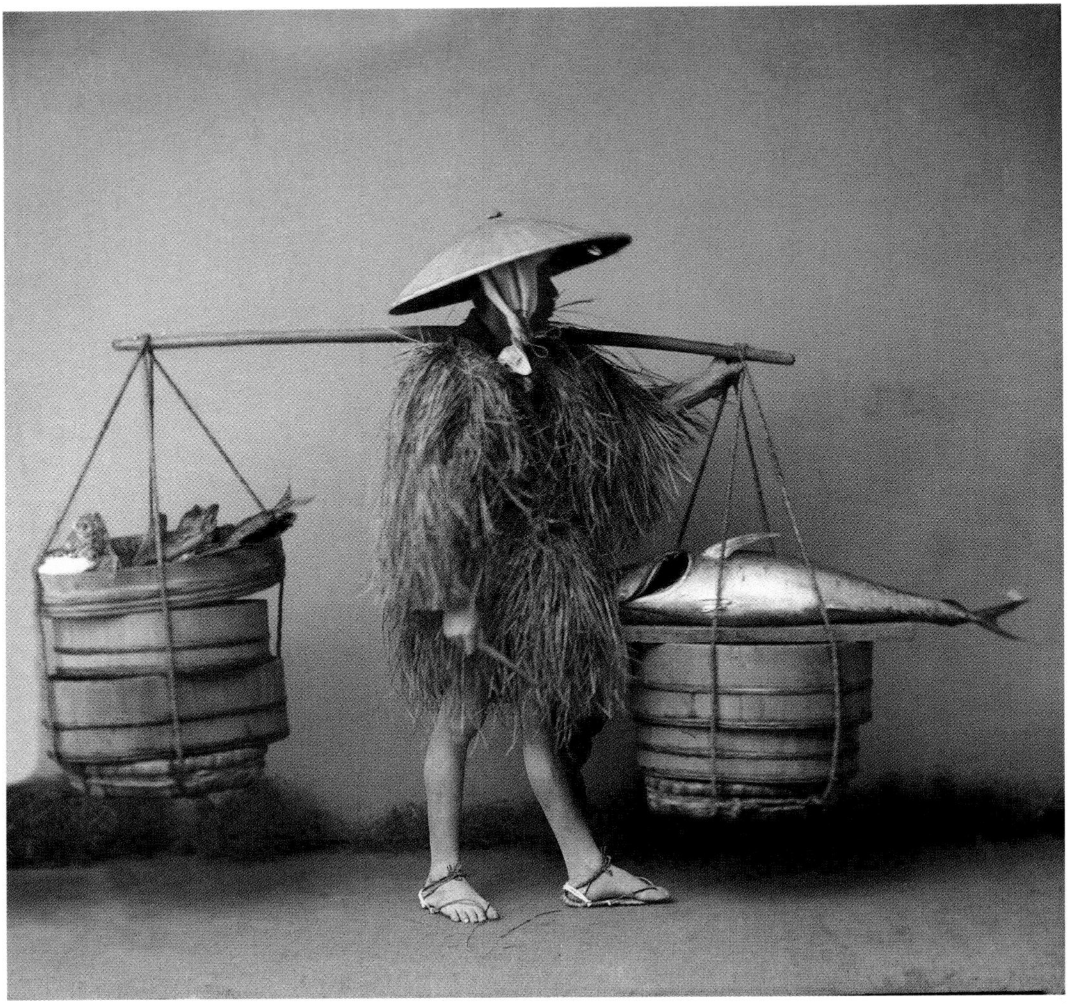

479 Fish seller, Japan, 1880s
480 Clam fisherman, Japan, 1880s

479 Fischverkäufer, Japan, 1880er Jahre
480 Ein Venusmuschel-Fischer, Japan, 1880er Jahre

479 Vendeur de poisson, Japon, années 1880
480 Pêcheur de palourdes, Japon, années 1880

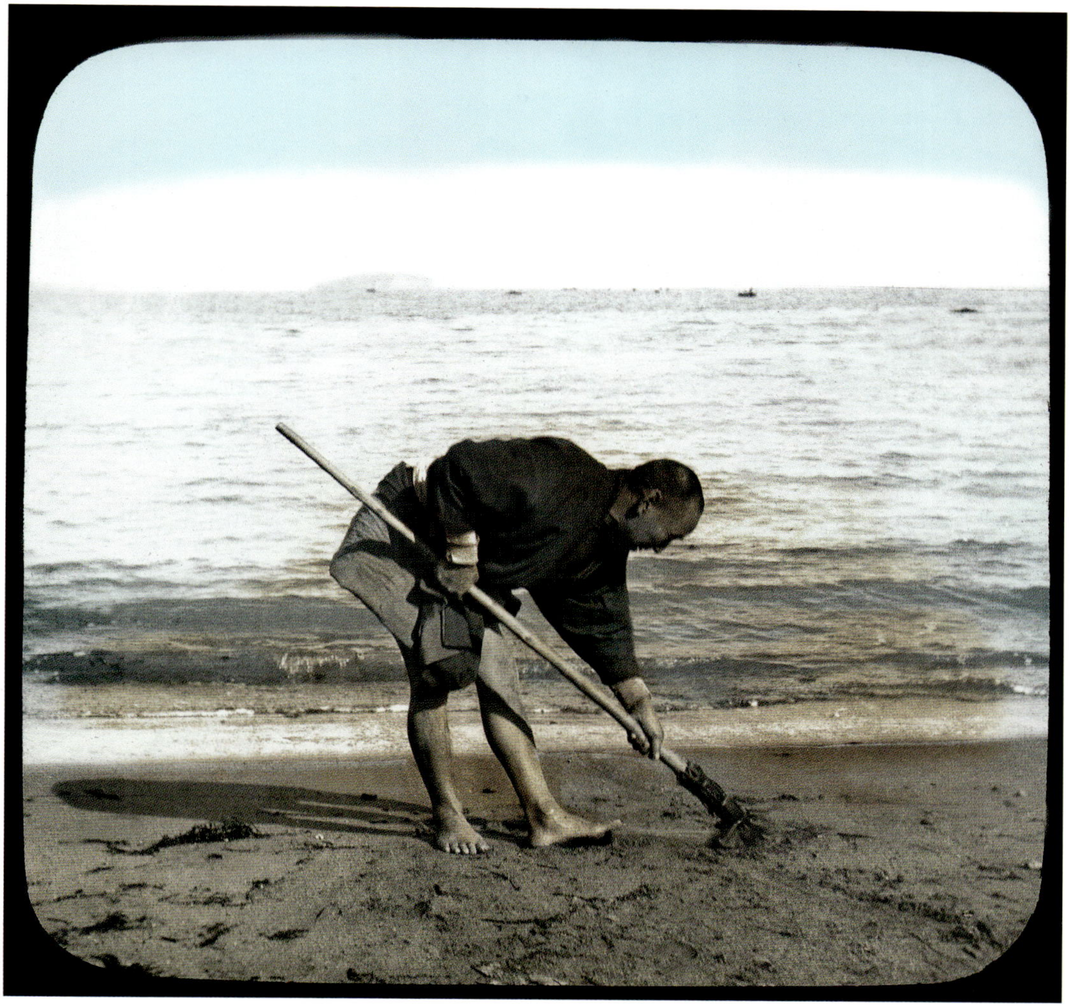

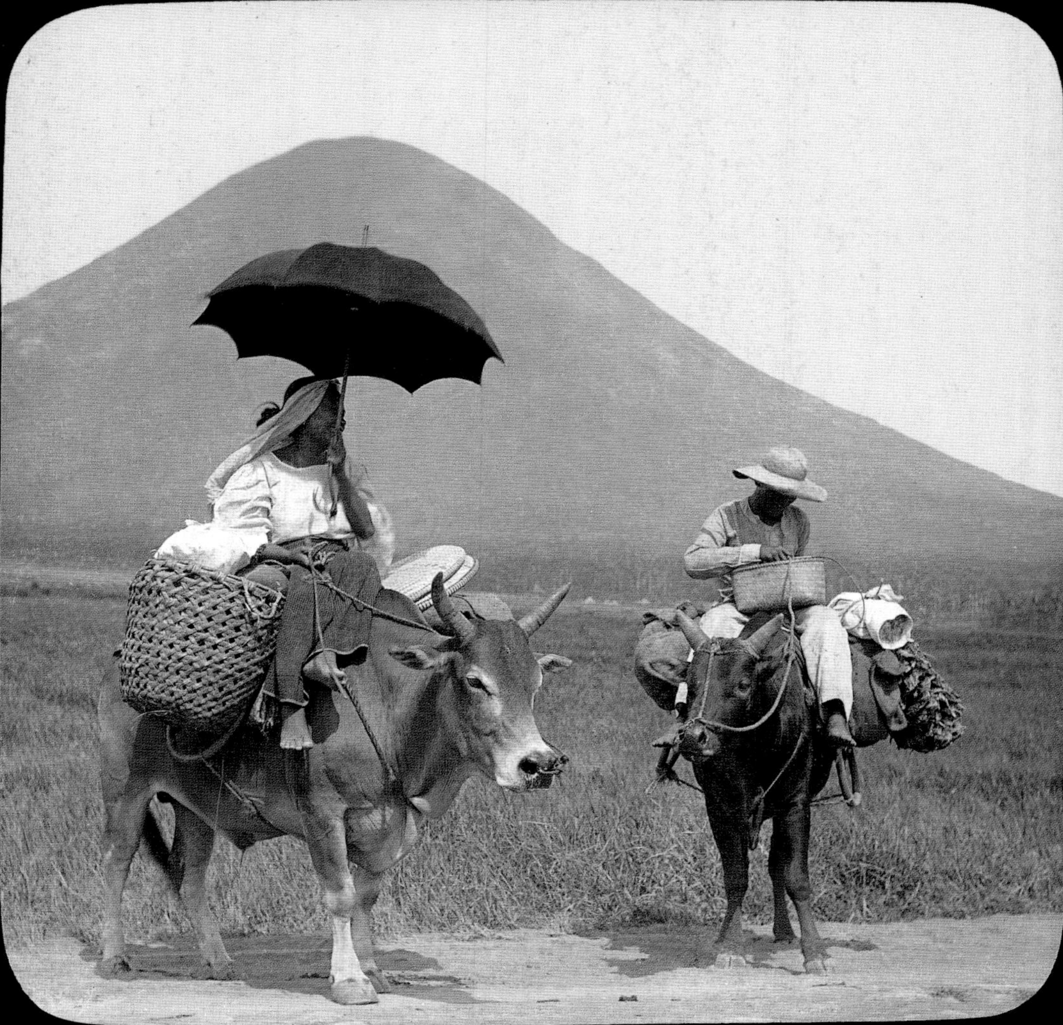

481 Cattle used as pack animals and for riding, Island of Luzon, Philippines, 1910s

481 Rinder, die als Pack- und Reittiere benutzt werden, Insel Luzon, Philippinen, 1910er Jahre

481 Bétail utilisé pour le bât et la monte, île de Luzon, Philippines, années 1910

SOUTH EAST ASIA

SÜDOSTASIEN · ASIE DU SUD-EST

482 Husking coconuts, Pagsanjan, Island of Luzon, Philippines, 1910s

482 Kokosnüsse werden geschält, Pagsanjan, Insel Luzon, Philippinen, 1910er Jahre

482 Épluchage des noix de coco, Pagsanjan, île de Luzon, Philippines, années 1910

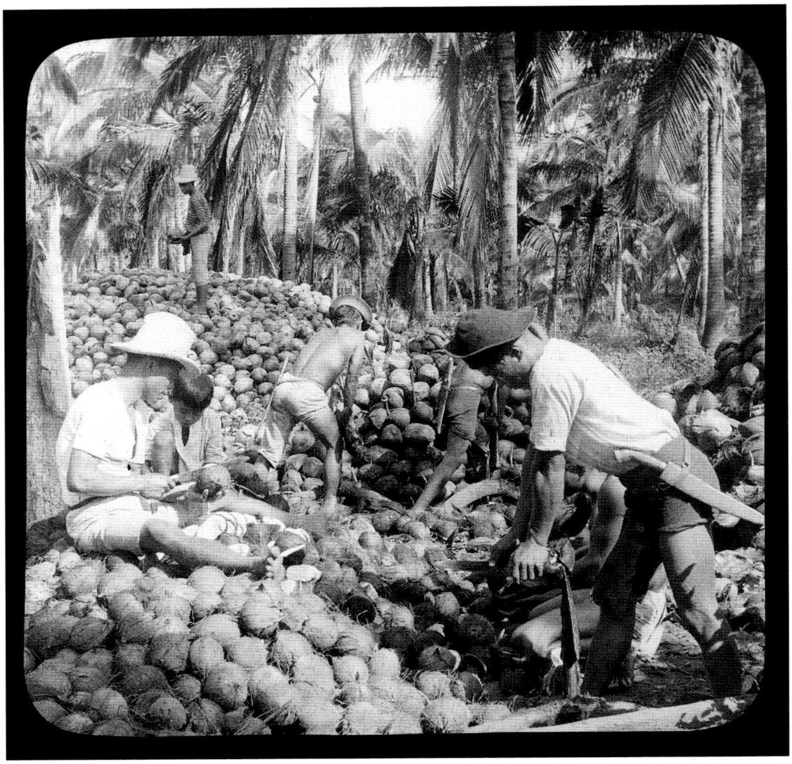

483 Sweet potatoes gathered by Igorrote girls, Philippines, 1910s

483 Igorroten-Mädchen sammeln Süßkartoffeln, Philippinen, 1910er Jahre

483 Patates douces ramassées par des jeunes filles Igorrote, Philippines, années 1910

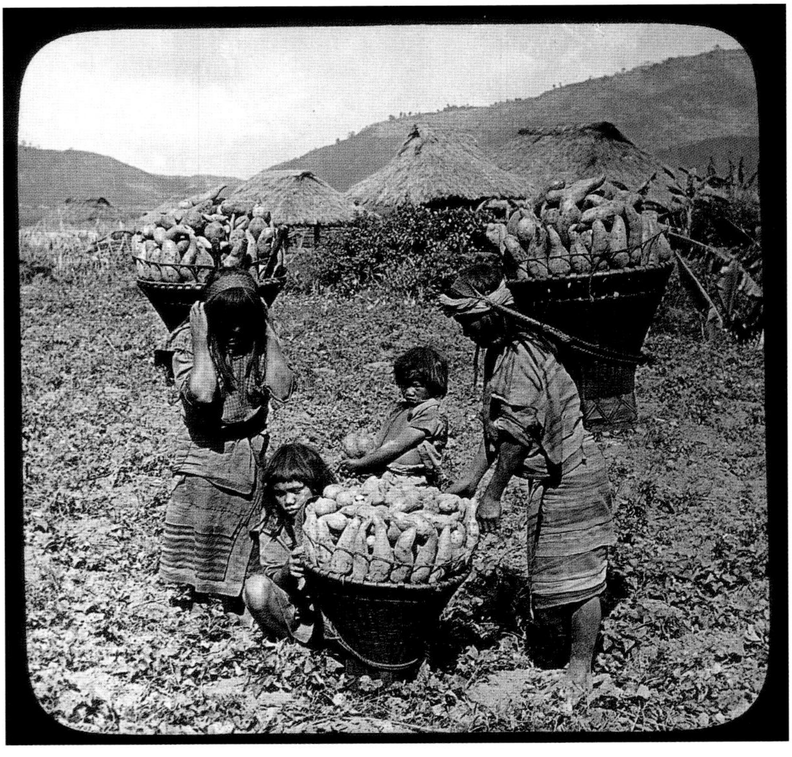

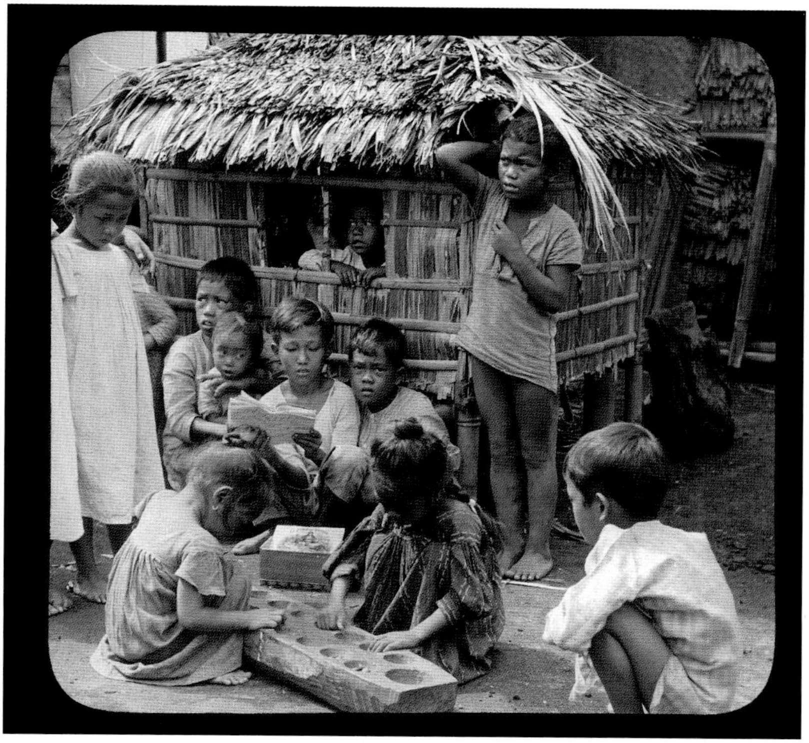

484 Children playing traditional "sungka" board game, Philippines, 1910s

484 Kinder spielen das traditionelle „Sungka"-Brettspiel, Philippinen, 1910er Jahre

484 Enfants jouant au « sungka », Philippines, années 1910

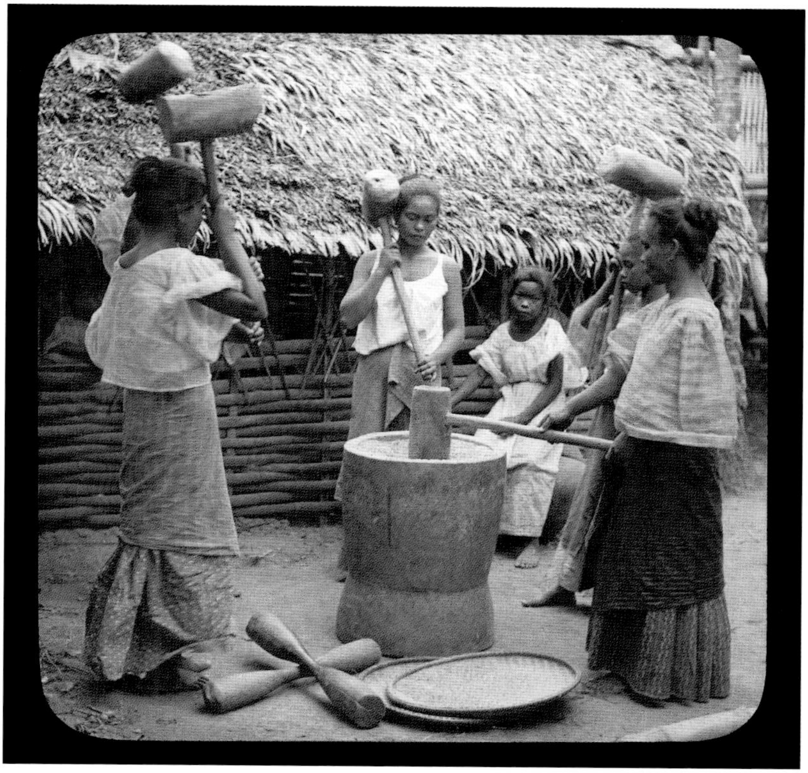

485 Hulling rice for breakfast, Island of Luzon, Philippines, 1910s

485 Der Reis fürs Frühstück wird enthülst, Insel von Luzon, Philippinen, 1910er Jahre

485 Pilage du riz pour le déjeuner, île de Luzon, Philippines, années 1910

486 Rice field and water buffalo, Luzon, Philippine Islands, 1910s

486 Reisfeld und Wasserbüffel, Insel Luzon, Philippinen, 1910er Jahre

486 Rizière et buffle d'eau, île de Luzon, Philippines, années 1910

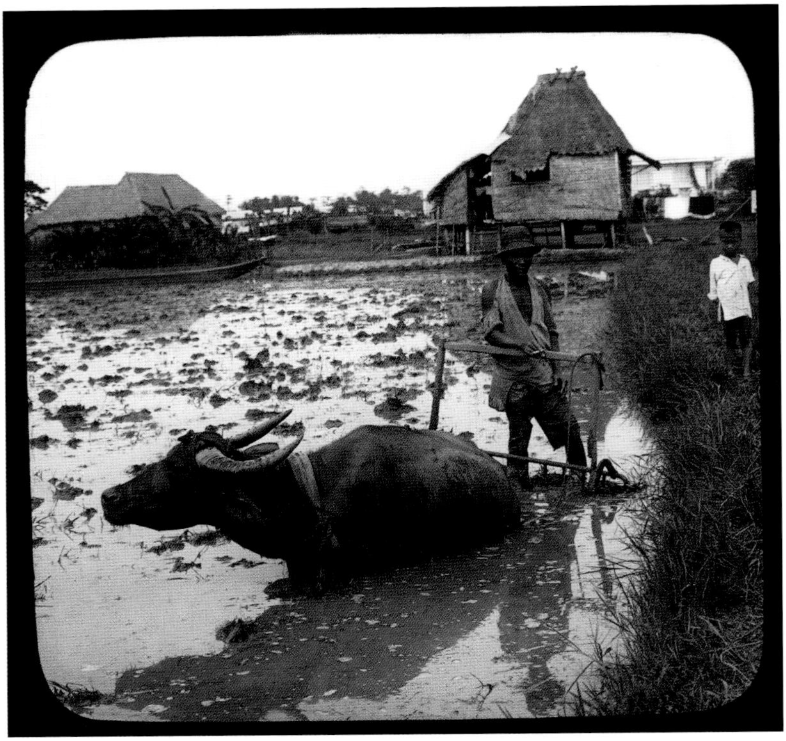

487 Farmers harrowing rice fields, near Manilla, Philippines, 1910s

487 Bauern eggen Reisfelder, nahe Manila, Philippinen, 1910 Jahre

487 Hersage d'une rizière près de Manille, Philippines, années 1910

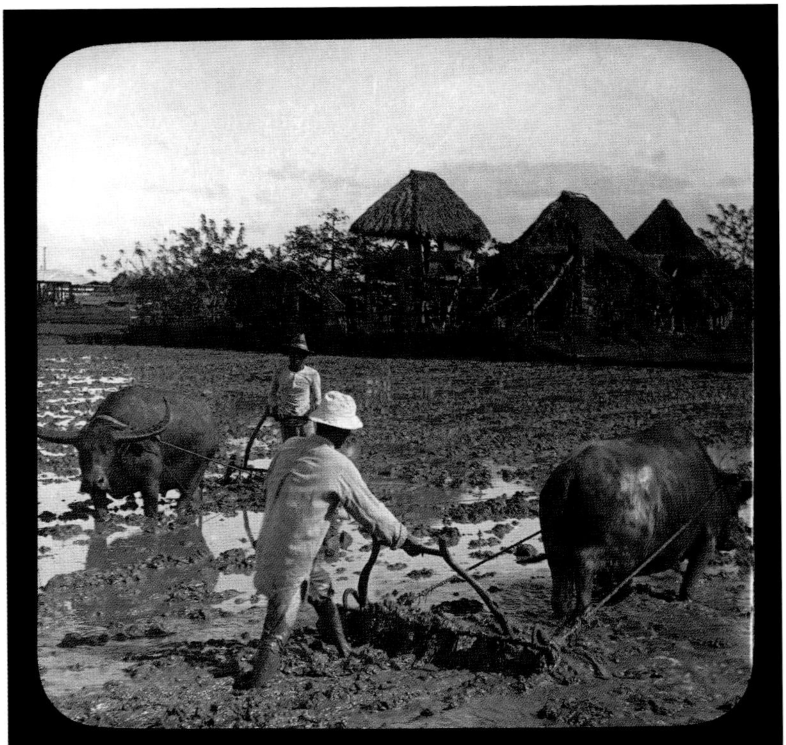

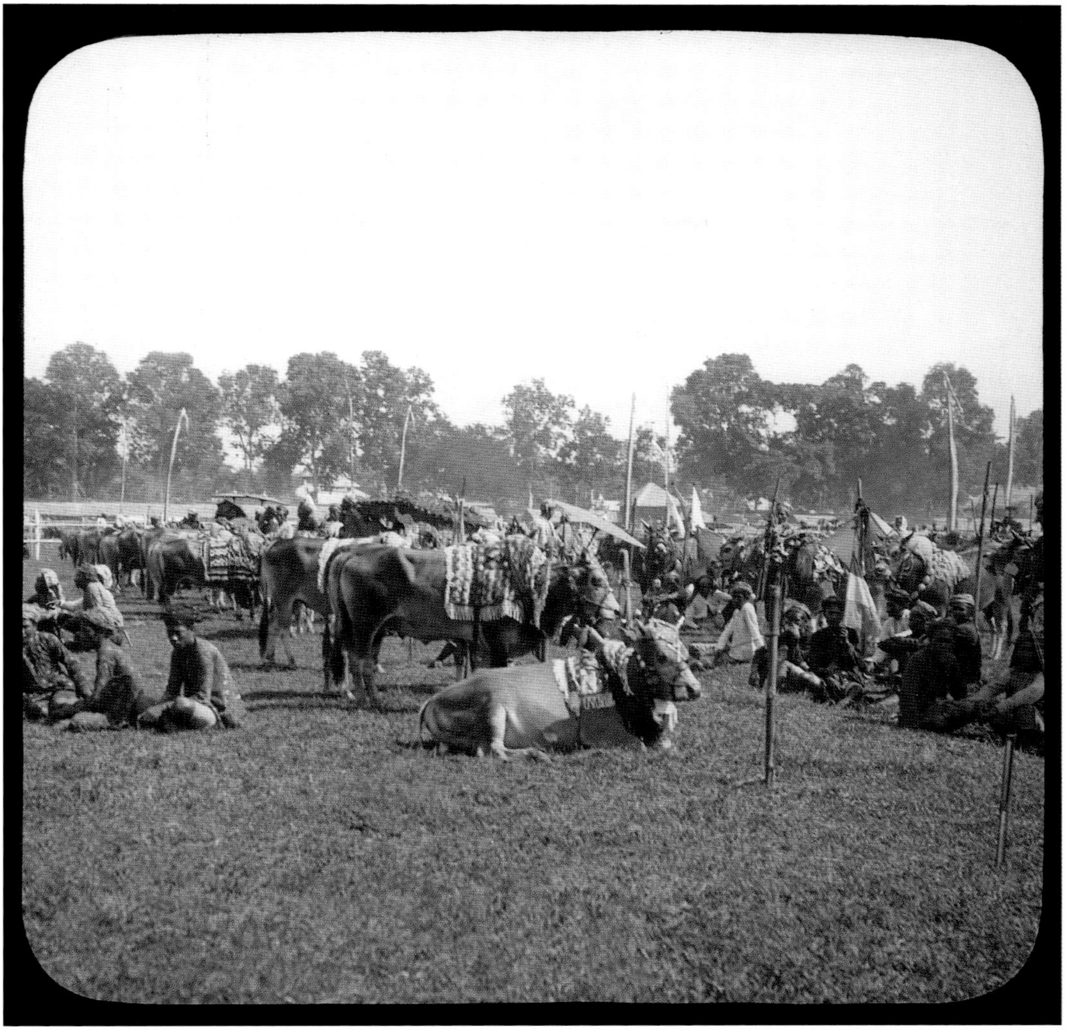

488 "Fancy Javanese Cattle at the Bull Races", Malang, Java, 1910s

488 „Fantasievoll geschmückte javanische Rinder bei den Bullenrennen", Malang, Java, 1910er Jahre

488 Bétail javanais paré, à la course de taureaux de Malang, Java, années 1910

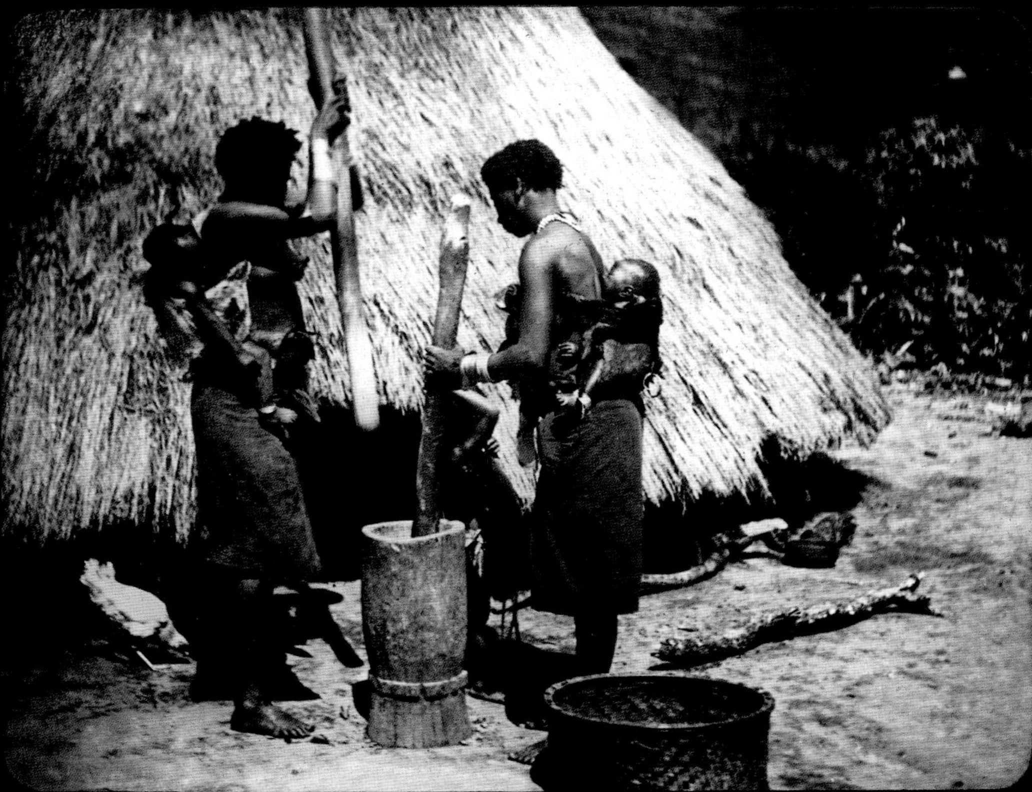

489 Pounding Corn,
South Sea Islands, c.1900

489 Getreidestampfen,
Südseeinseln, um 1900

489 Pilage du grain,
Océanie, vers 1900

OCEANIA

OZEANIEN · OCÉANIE

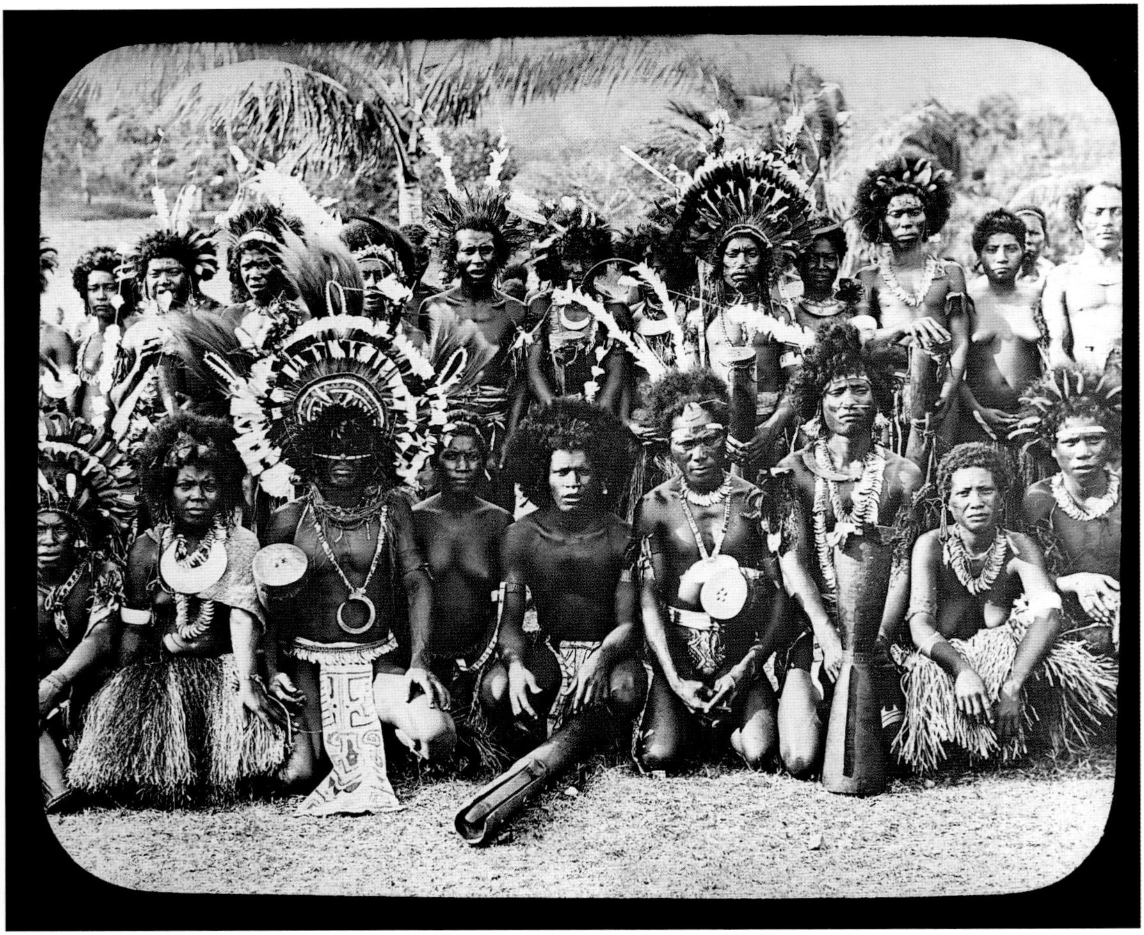

490 Tribal group, New Guinea, c.1900
491 Members of a Pygmy tribe, Papua New Guinea, 1890s

490 Eine Gruppe von Stammesangehörigen, Neuguinea, um 1900
491 Angehörige eines Pygmäen-Volks, Papua-Neuguinea, 1890er Jahre

490 Pilage du grain, Océanie, vers 1900
491 Tribu de pygmées, Papouasie Nouvelle-Guinée, années 1890

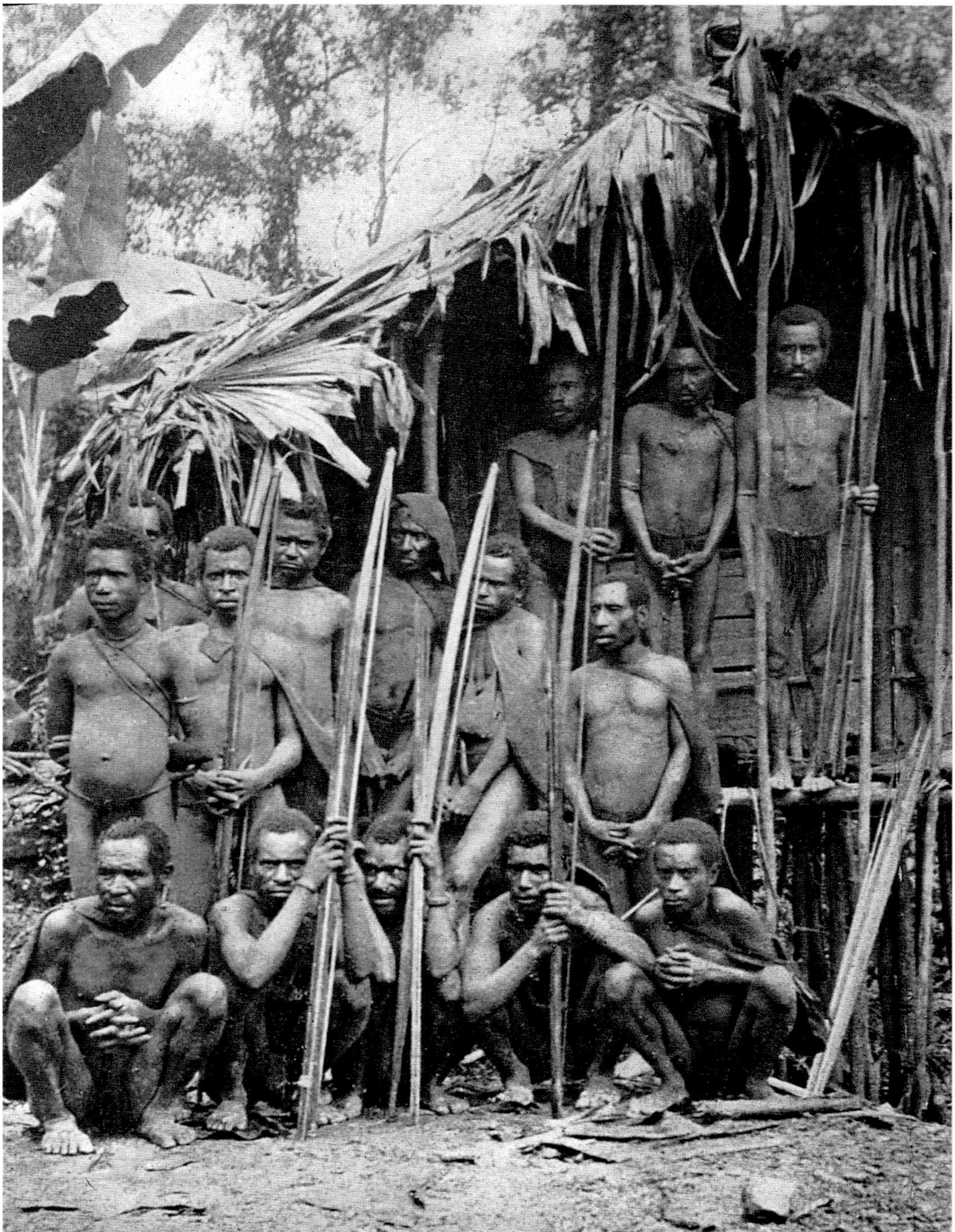

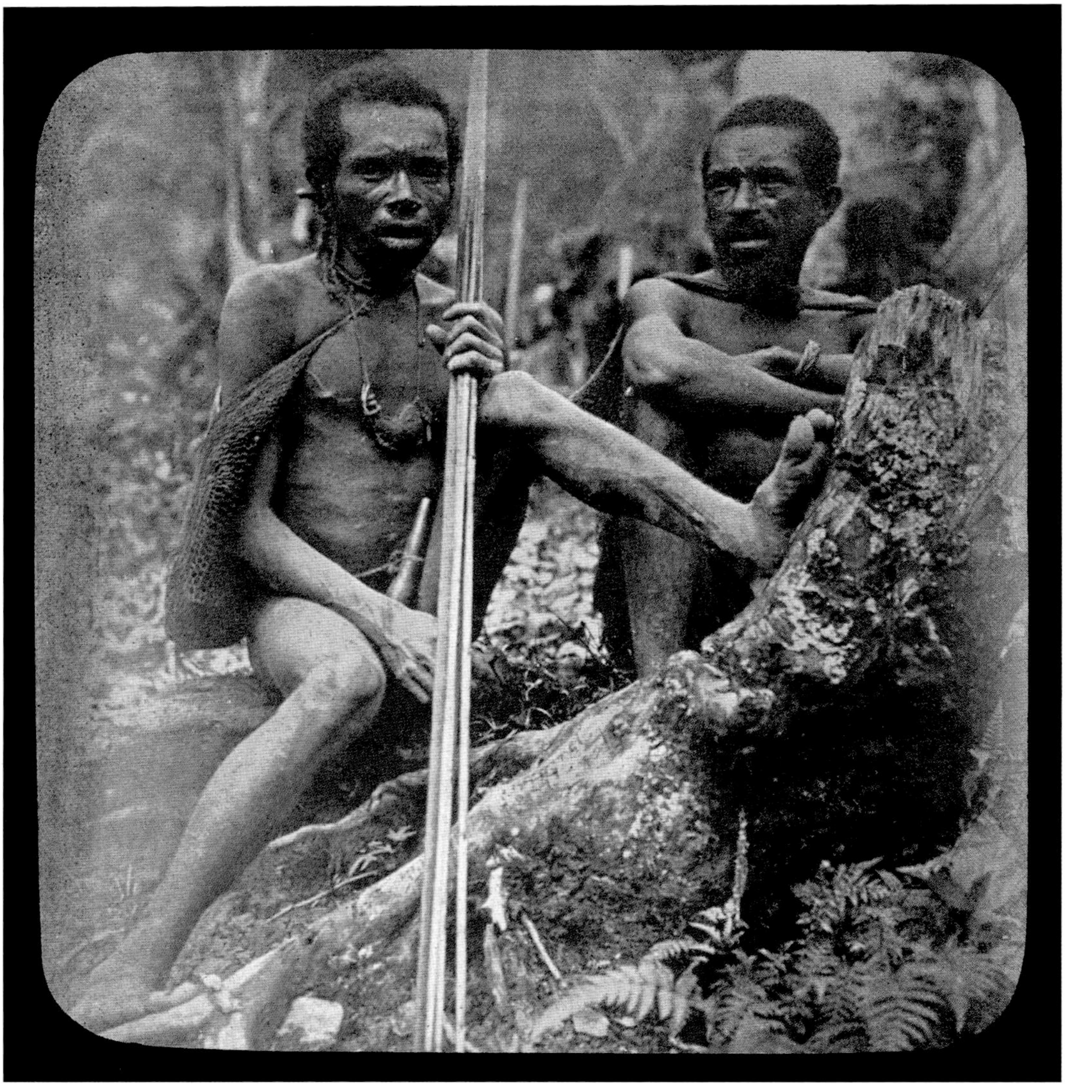

492 Two hunters of a Pygmy tribe, Papua New Guinea, 1890s

492 Zwei Jäger eines Pygmäen-Volks, Papua-Neuguinea, 1890er Jahre

492 Deux chasseurs pygmées, Papouasie Nouvelle-Guinée, années 1890

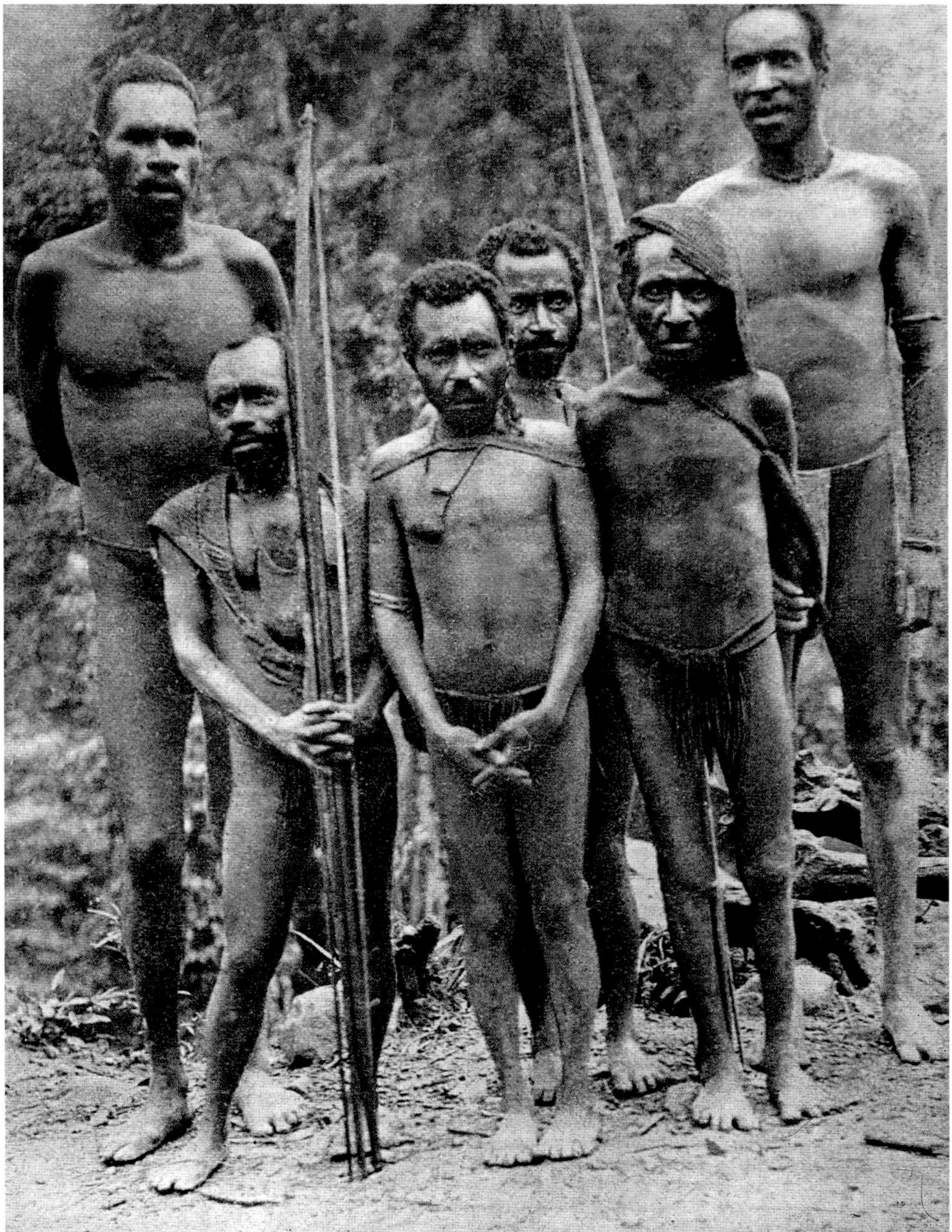

493 Four members of a Pygmy tribe with two other aboriginal tribesmen, Papua New Guinea, 1890s

493 Vier Angehörige eines Pygmäen-Volks mit zwei anderen Eingeborenen, Papua-Neuguinea, 1890er Jahre

493 Quatre pygmées avec deux membres d'une autre tribu aborigène, Papouasie Nouvelle-Guinée, années 1890

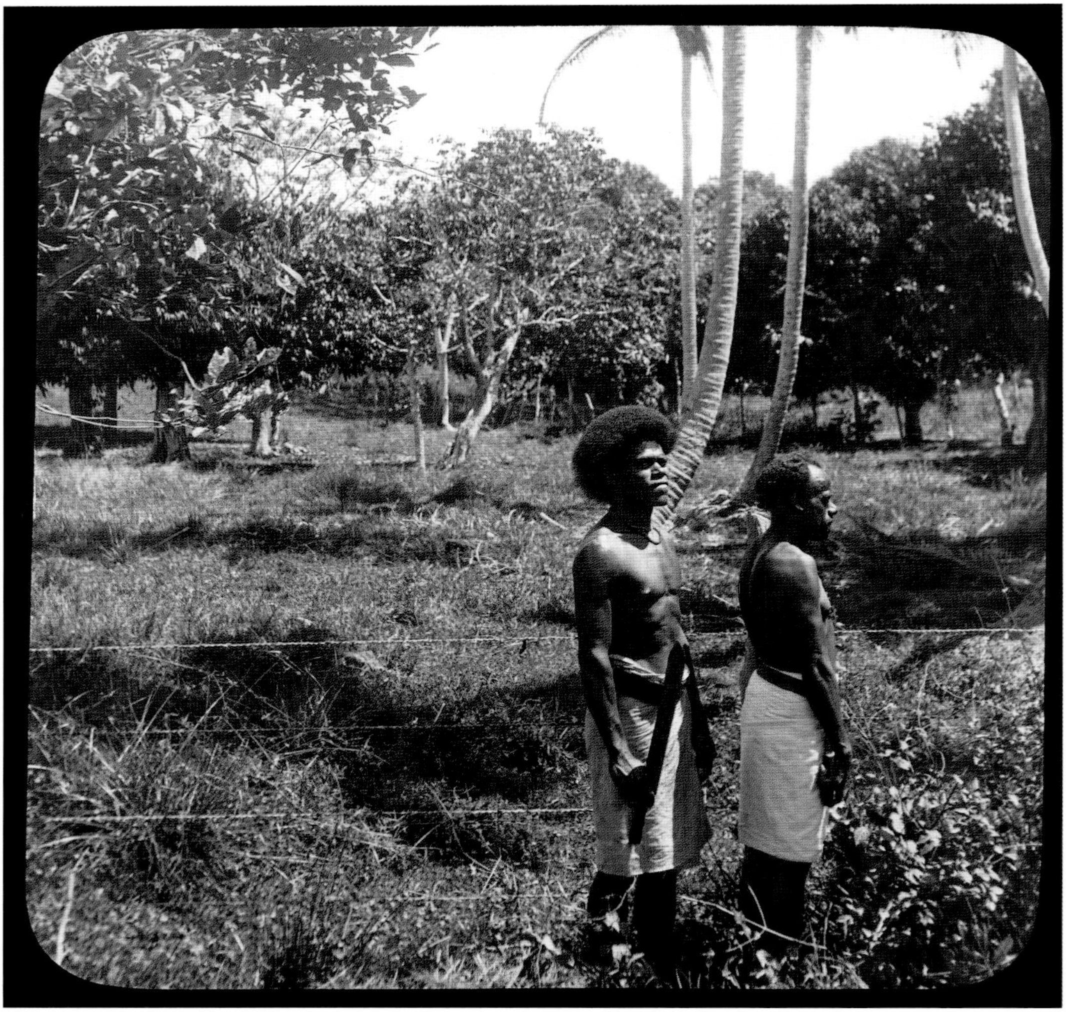

494 Young Fijian men, Suva, Viti Levu, Fiji Islands, 1900s
495 Aboriginal man, Australia, 1890s

494 Zwei junge Fidschianer, Suva, Viti Levu, Fidschi-Inseln, 1900er Jahre
495 Ureinwohner, Australien, 1890er Jahre

494 Jeunes Fidjiens, Suva, Viti Levu, îles Fidji, années 1900
495 Aborigène, Australie, années 1890

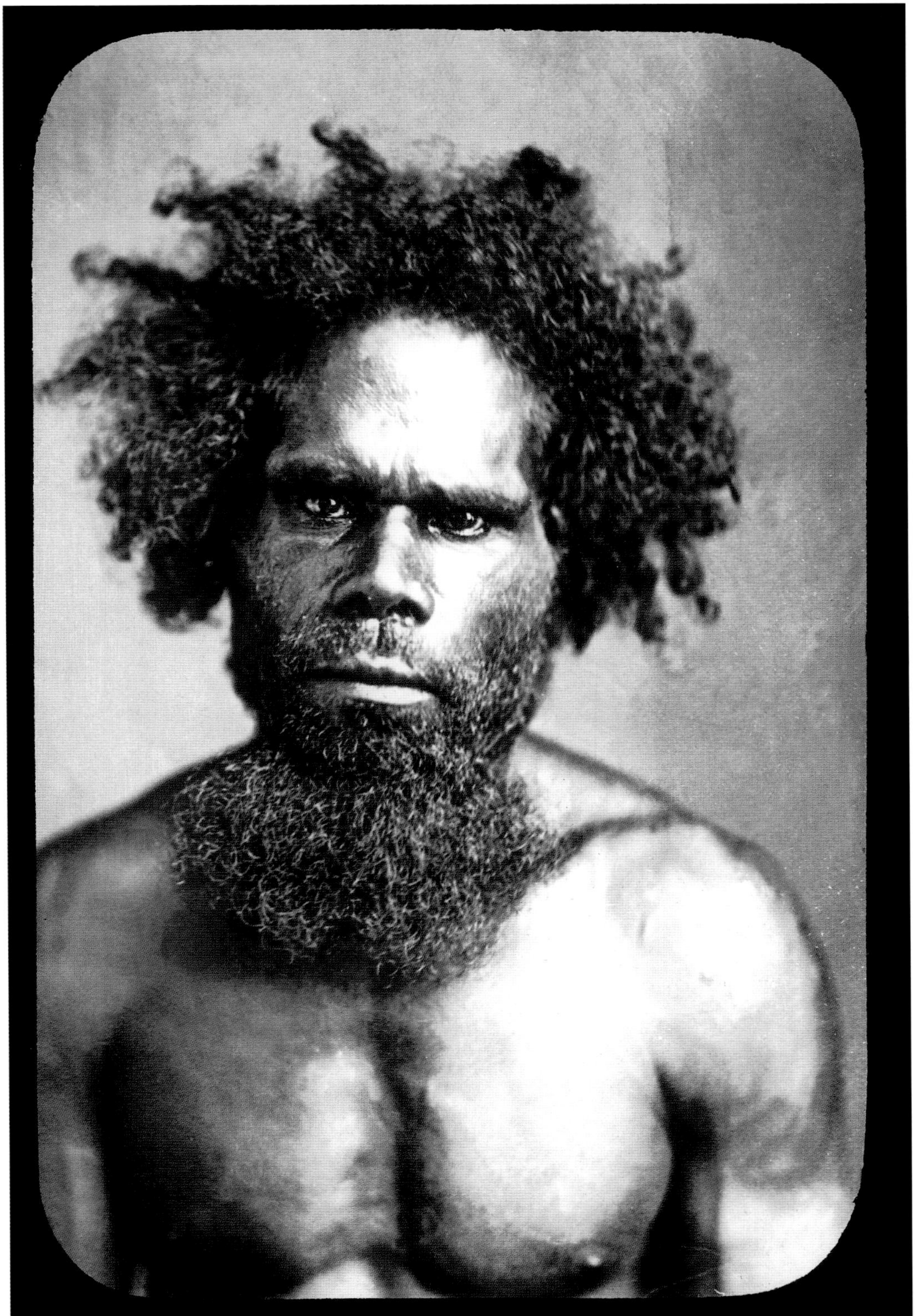

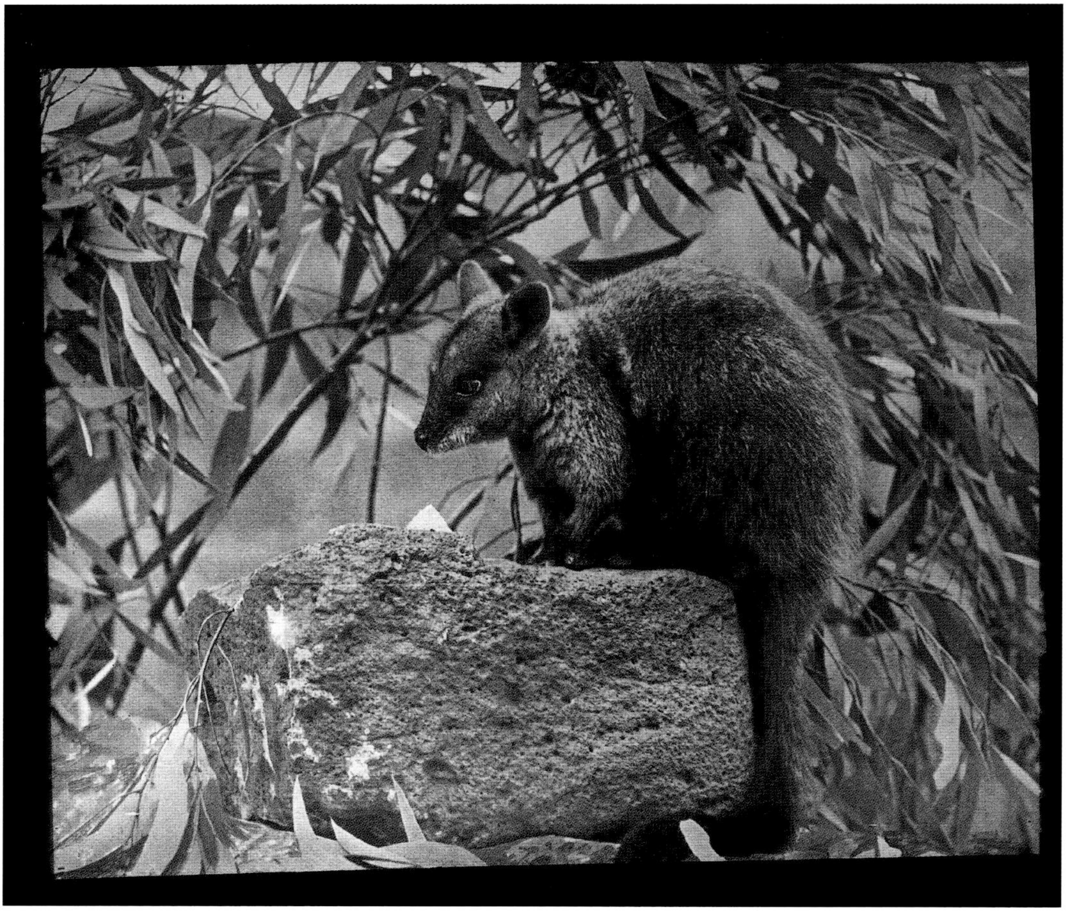

496 Rock wallaby,
Australia, 1910s
497 A boxing kangaroo
in the Zoo, Melbourne,
Australia, 1910s

496 Felskänguru,
Australien, 1910er Jahre
497 Ein boxendes
Känguru im Zoo,
Melbourne, Australien,
1910er Jahre

496 Rock-wallaby,
Australie, années 1910
497 Kangourou boxeur
dans le zoo de Melbourne,
Australie, années 1910

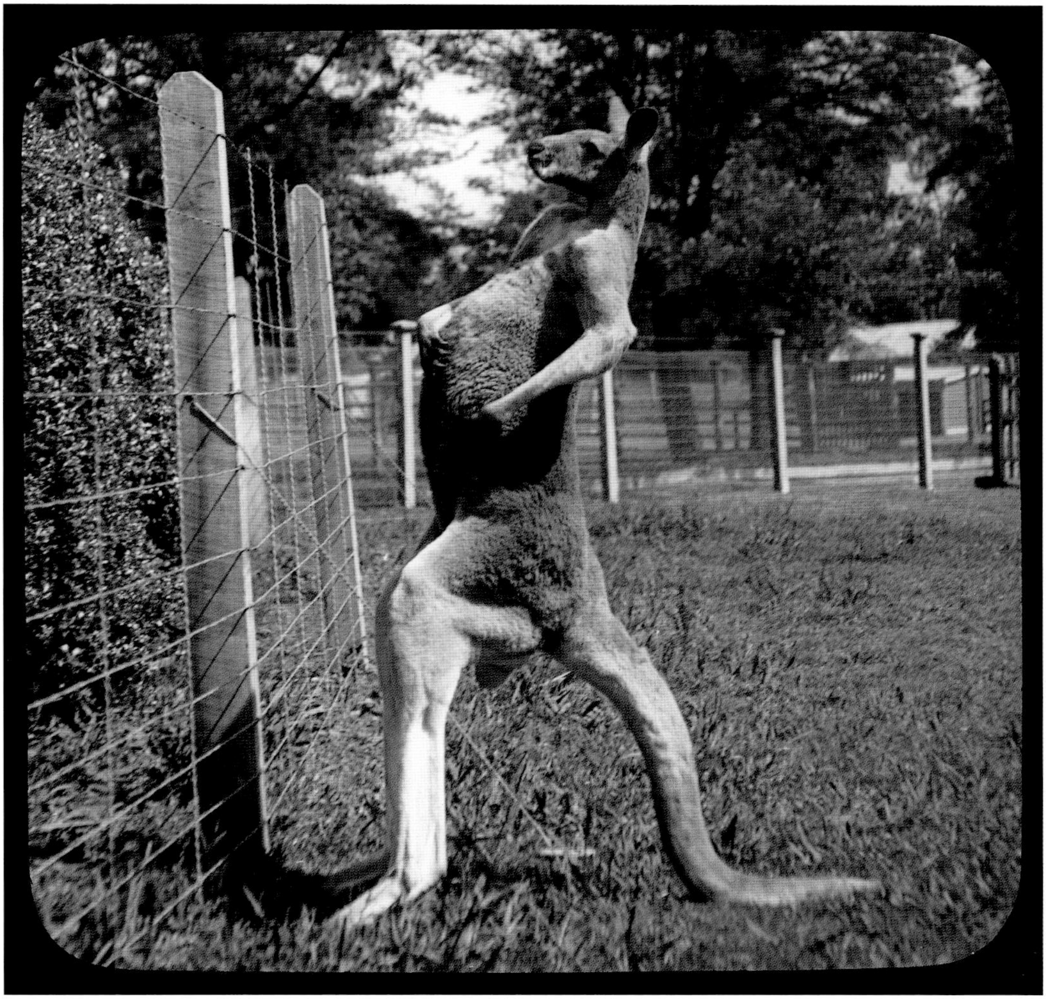

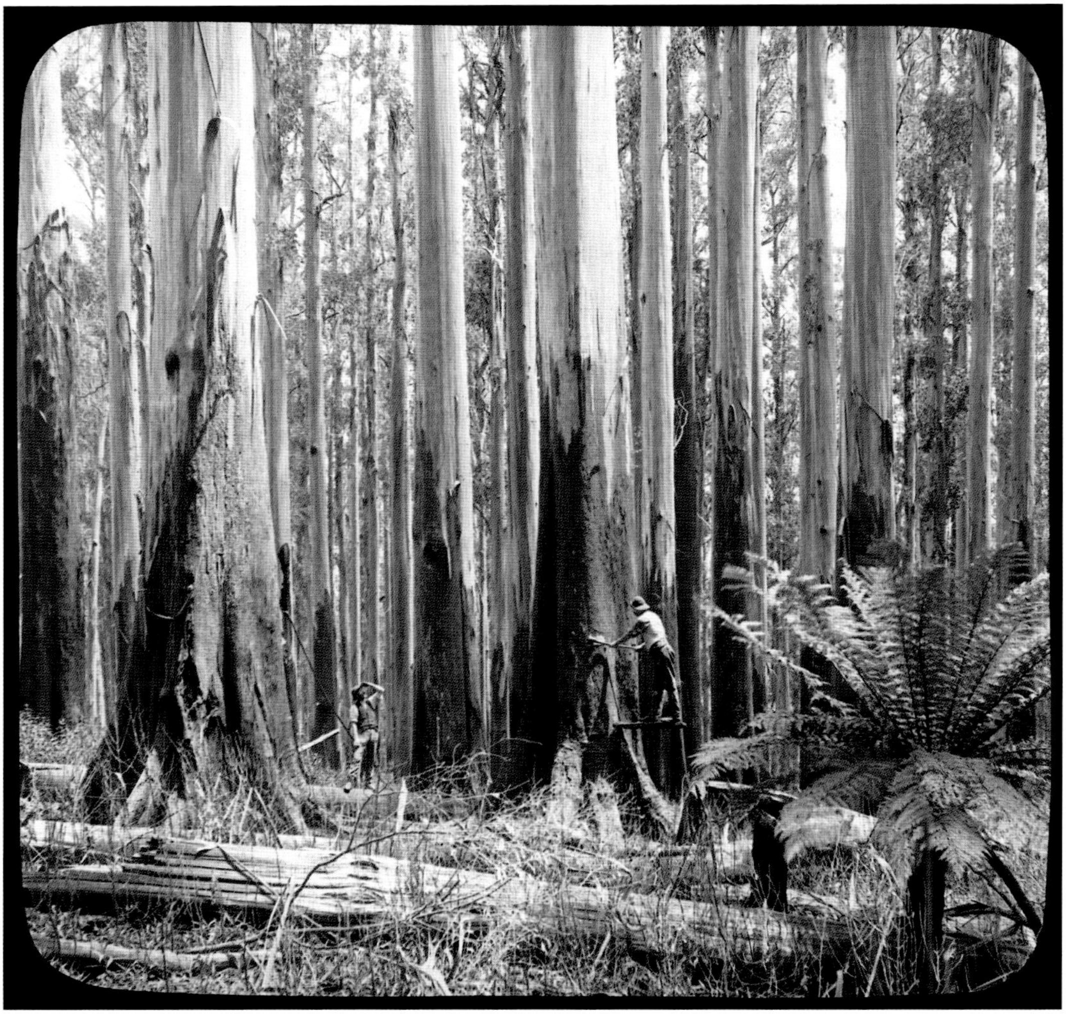

498 Giant eucalyptus trees (400 feet high), Victoria, Australia, c.1900
499 "Torpeder Smith" sitting outside his tent, Australia, 1890s

498 Riesen-Eukalyptus (120 Meter hoch), Victoria, Australien, um 1900
499 „Torpeder Smith" vor seinem Zelt, Australien, 1890er Jahre

498 Eucalyptus géants (120 mètres de haut), Victoria, Australie, vers 1900
499 "Torpeder Smith" devant sa tente, Australie, années 1890

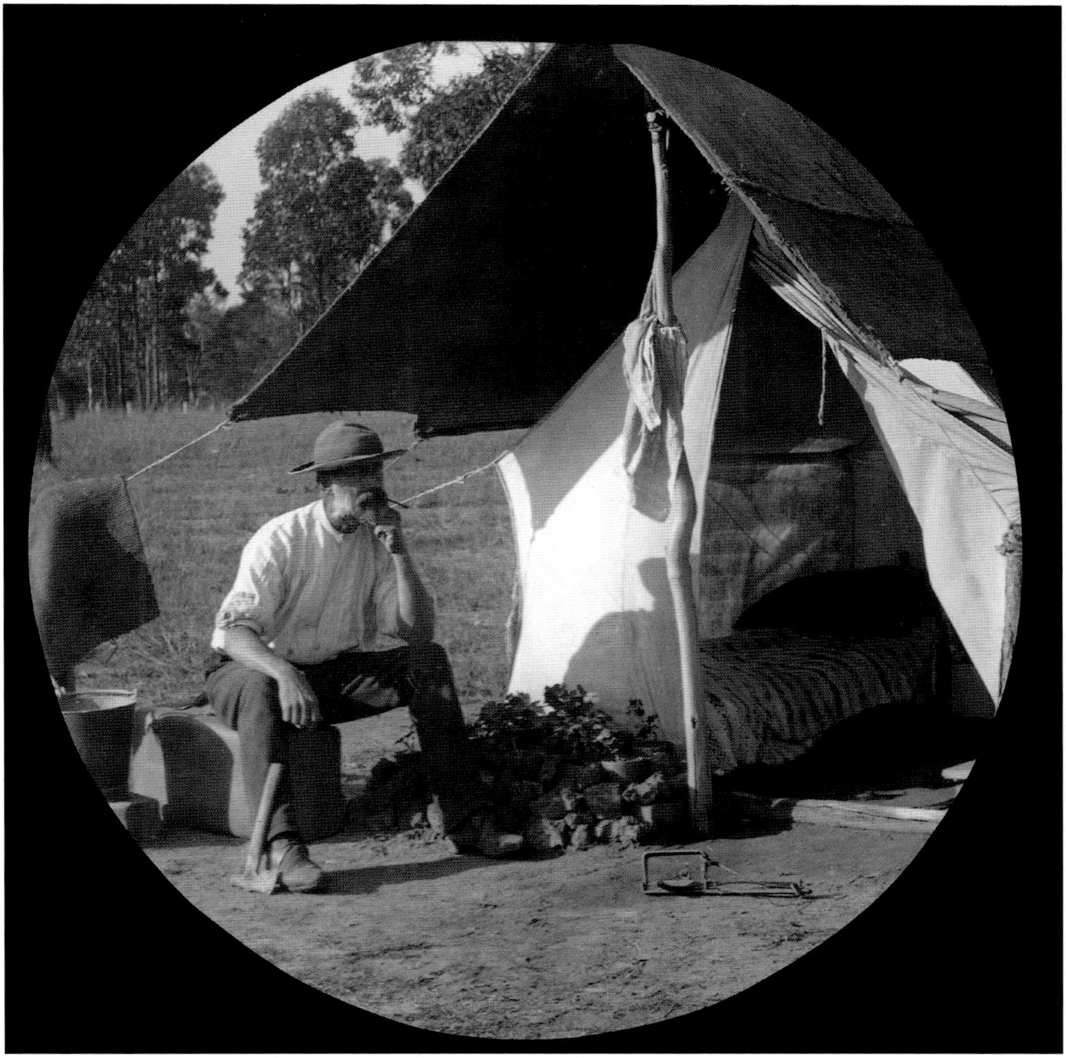

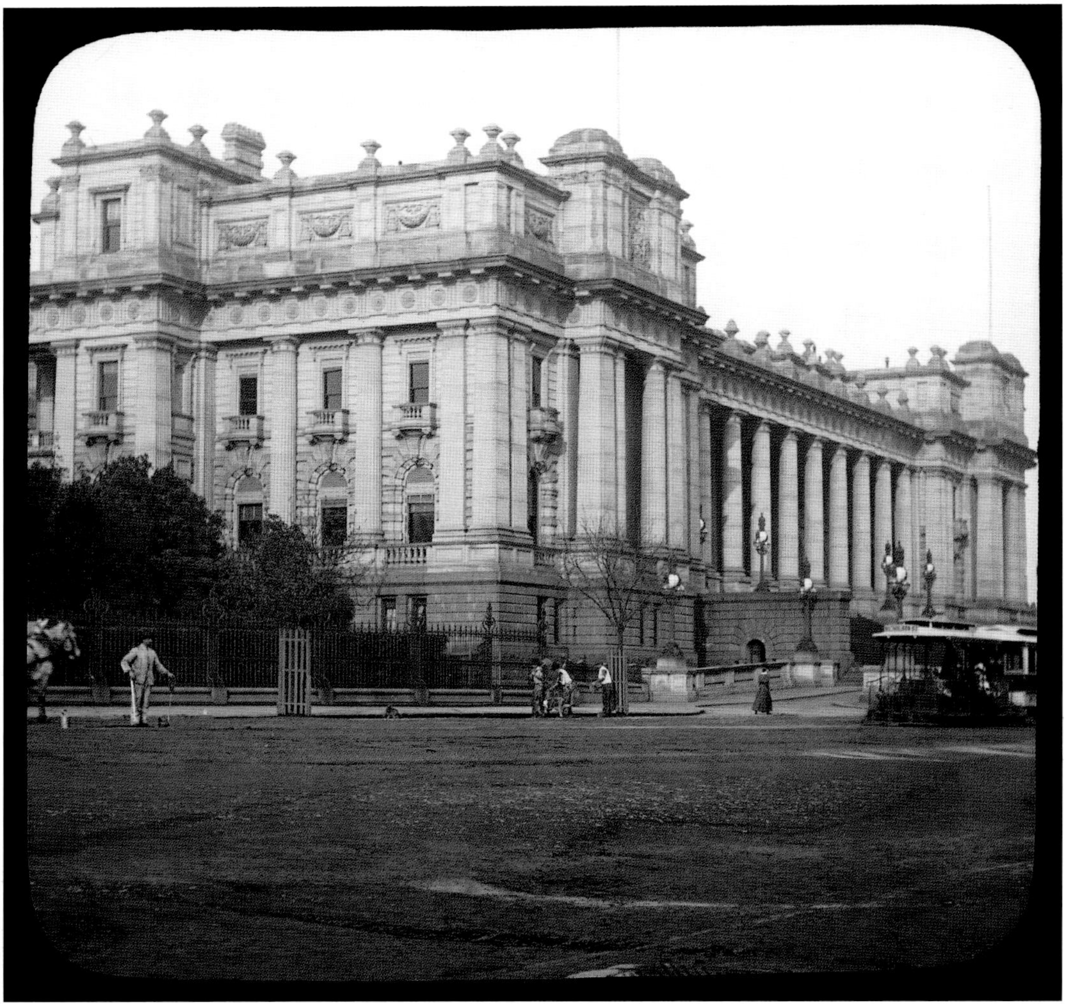

500 Federal Parliament Building, Melbourne, Australia, 1890s
501 Melbourne (Capital of Victoria), Australia, 1900s

500 Das Parlamentsgebäude, Melbourne, Australien, 1890er Jahre
501 Melbourne (Hauptstadt von Victoria), Australien, 1900er Jahre

500 Parlement fédéral, Melbourne, Australie, années 1890
501 Melbourne, capitale de l'État de Victoria. Australie, années 1900

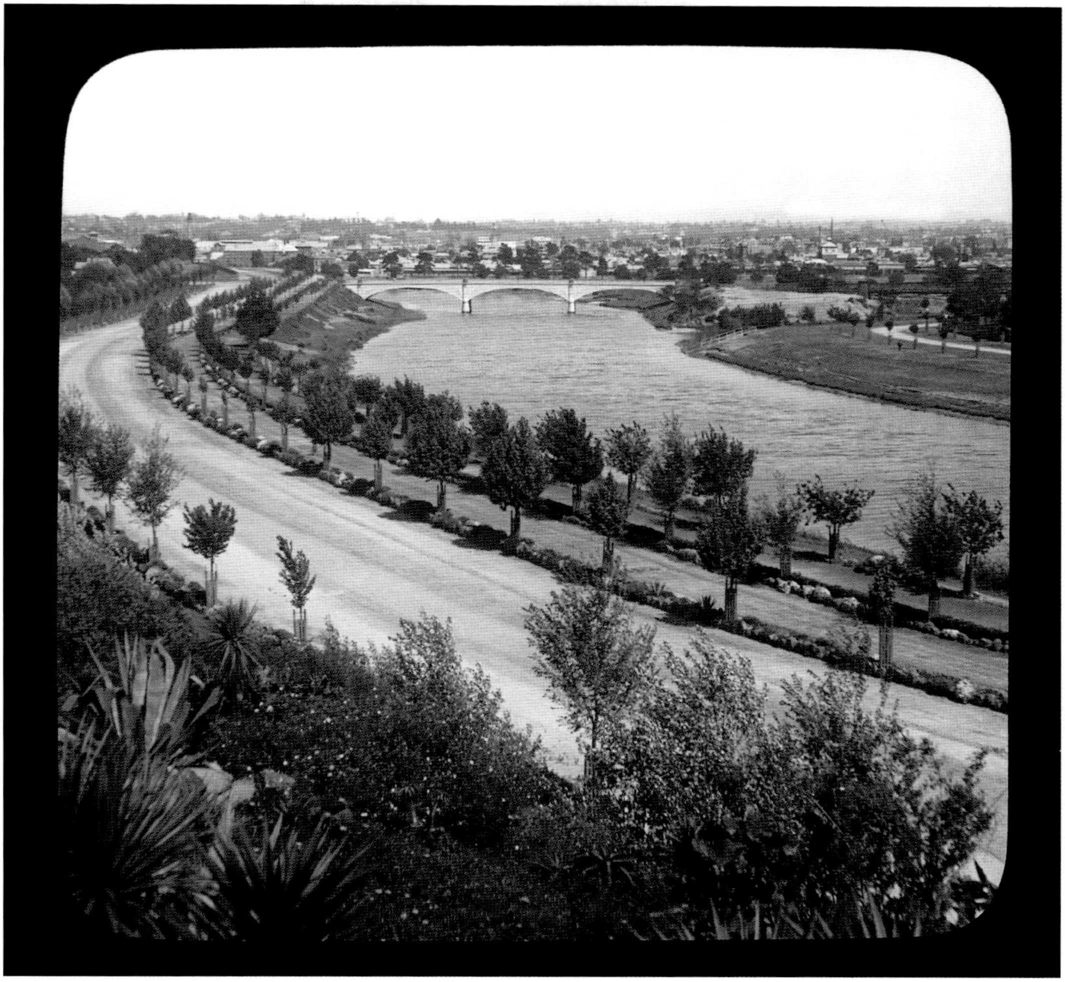

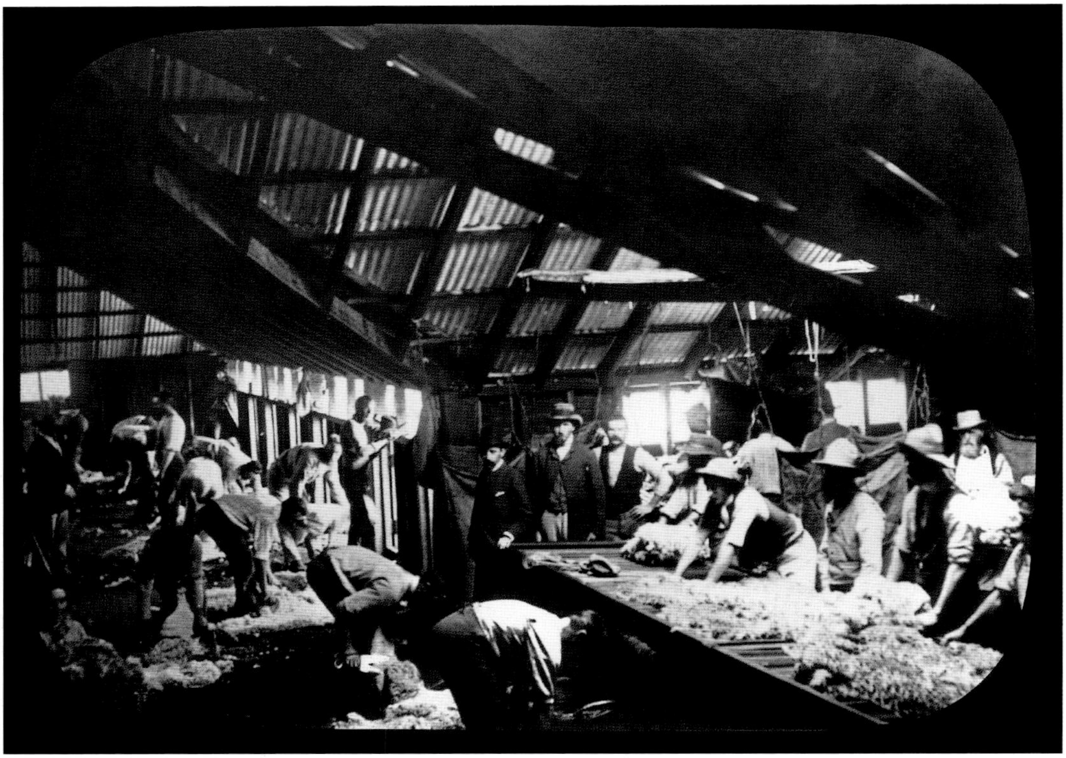

502 Wool sorting,
Australia, c.1900
503 Shearing sheep
with electric machinery,
Newmarket, Australia,
c.1900

502 Wollsortierung,
Australien, um 1900
503 Schafschur mit
elektrischen Maschinen,
Newmarket, Australien,
um 1900

502 Tri de la laine,
Australie, vers 1900
503 Tonte des moutons
avec des tondeuses
électriques, Newmarket,
Australie, vers 1900

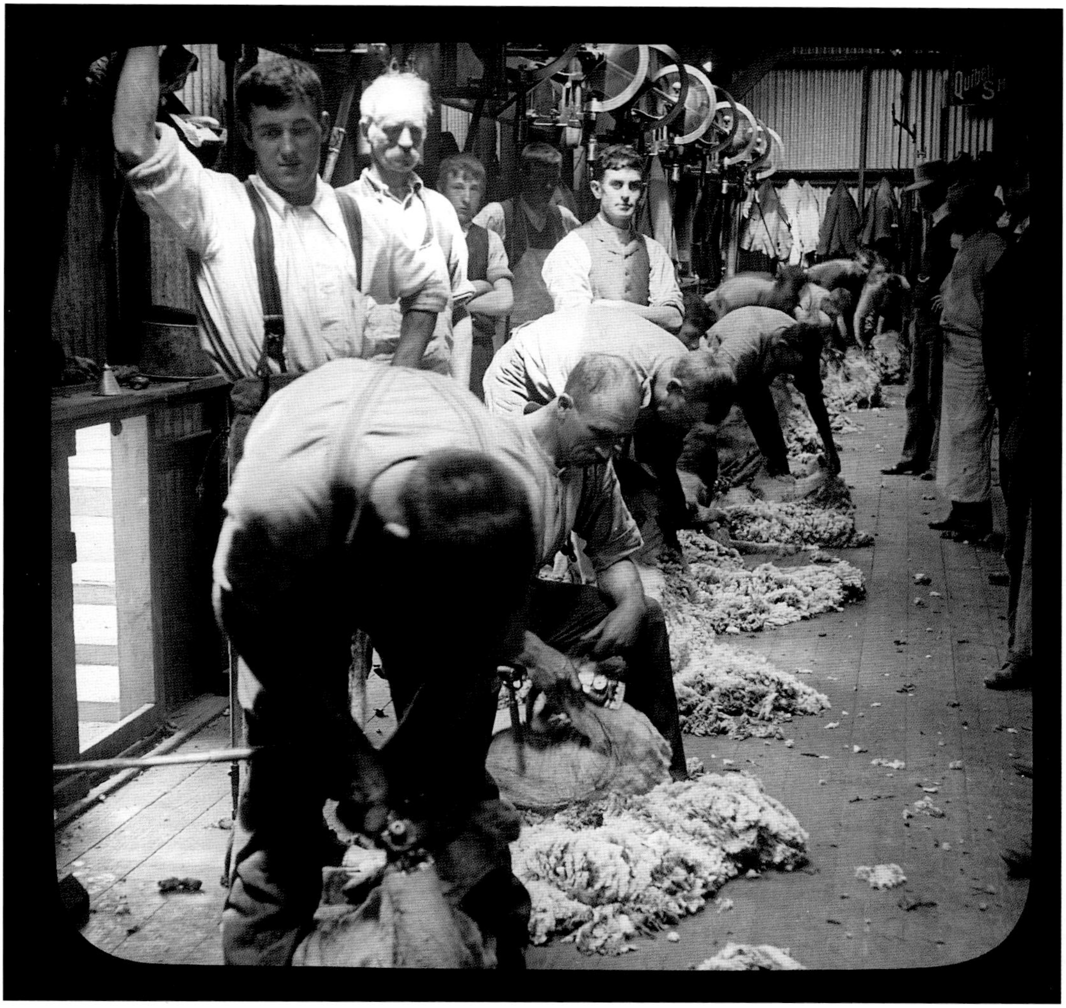

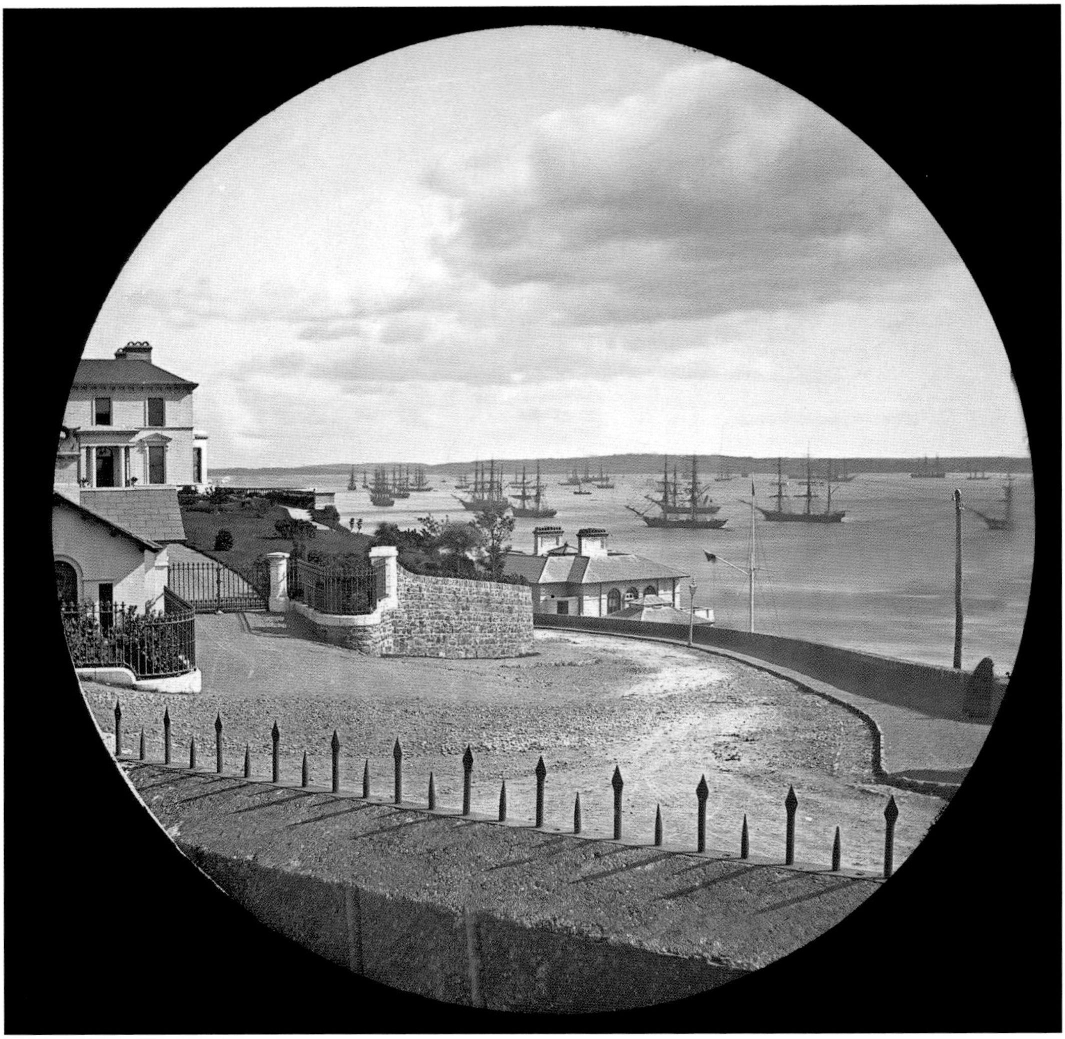

504 The Harbour, Queenstown, New Zealand, 1890s
505 Across Auckland Harbour from Northcote, New Zealand, 1900s

504 Der Hafen, Queenstown, Neuseeland, 1890er Jahre
505 Blick von Northcote auf den gegenüberliegenden Hafen von Auckland, Neuseeland, 1900er Jahre

504 Port de Queenstown, Nouvelle-Zélande, années 1890
505 Vue sur le port d'Auckland depuis Northcote, Nouvelle-Zélande, années 1900

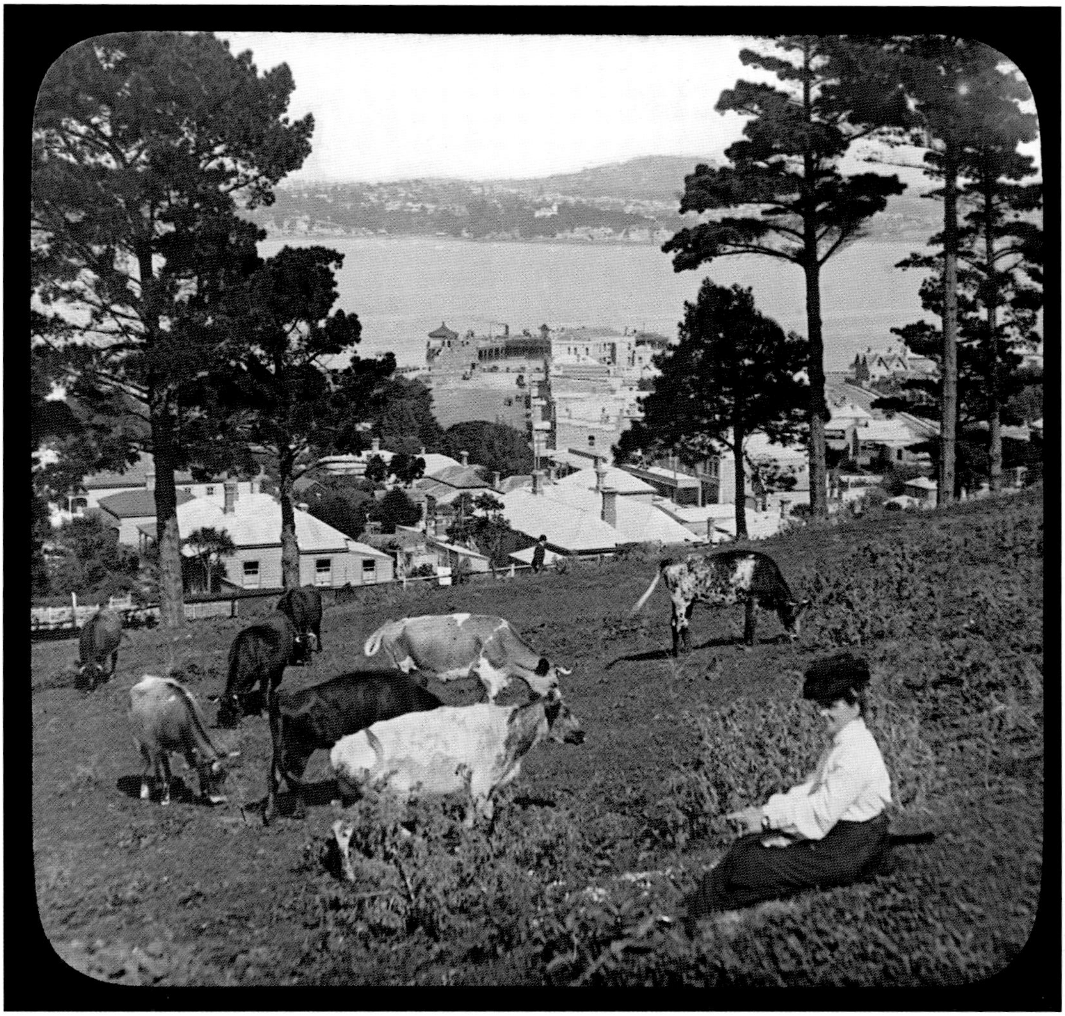

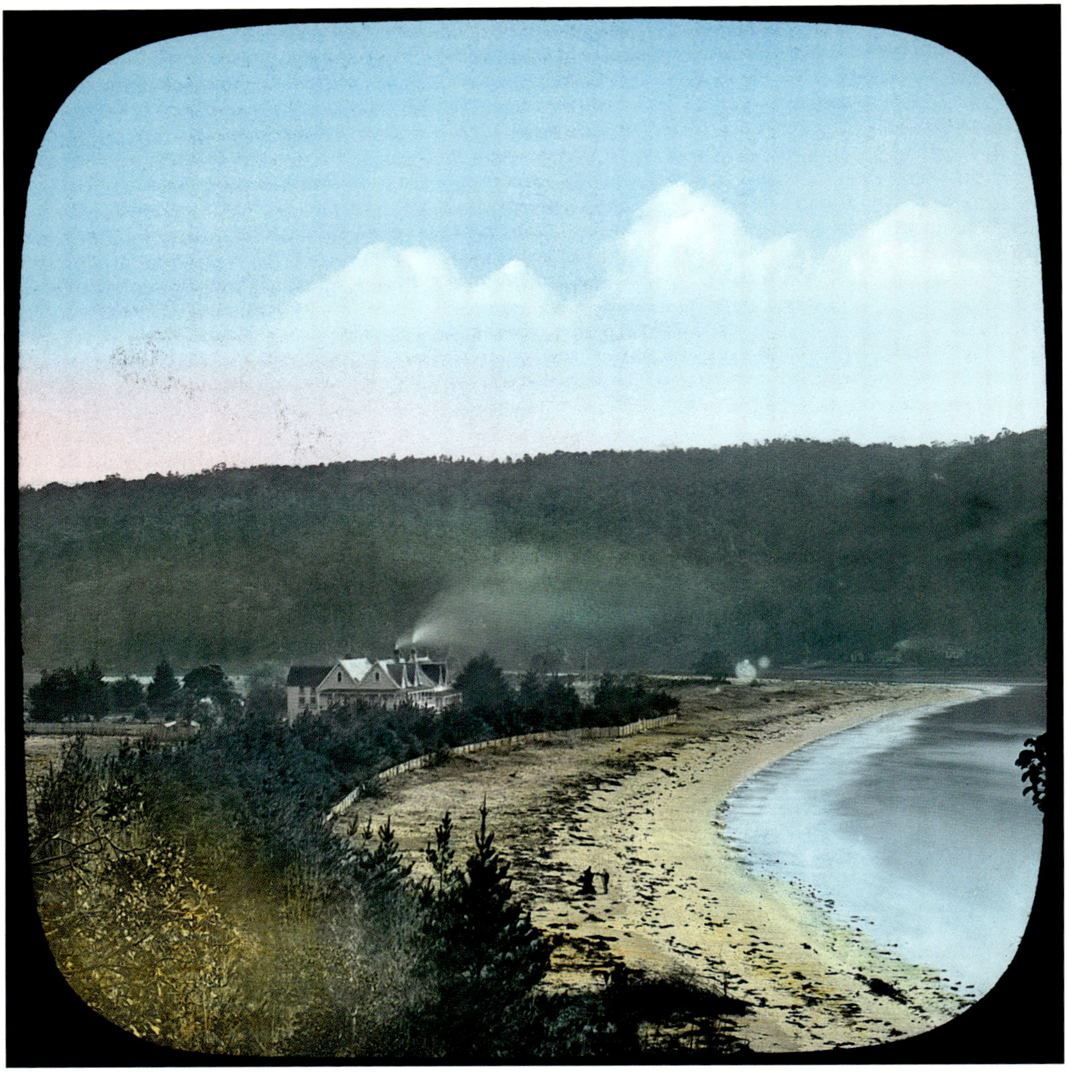

506 Waiwera Hotel and beach, Waiwera, North Auckland, New Zealand, 1890s
507 Samoan chiefs, Samoa, c.1900

506 Waiwera Hotel und Strand, Waiwera, North Auckland, Neuseeland, 1890er Jahre
507 Samoanische Häuptlinge, Samoa, um 1900

506 L'hôtel Waiwera et la plage, Waiwera, au nord d'Auckland, Nouvelle-Zélande, années 1890
507 Chefs samoans, Samoa, vers 1900

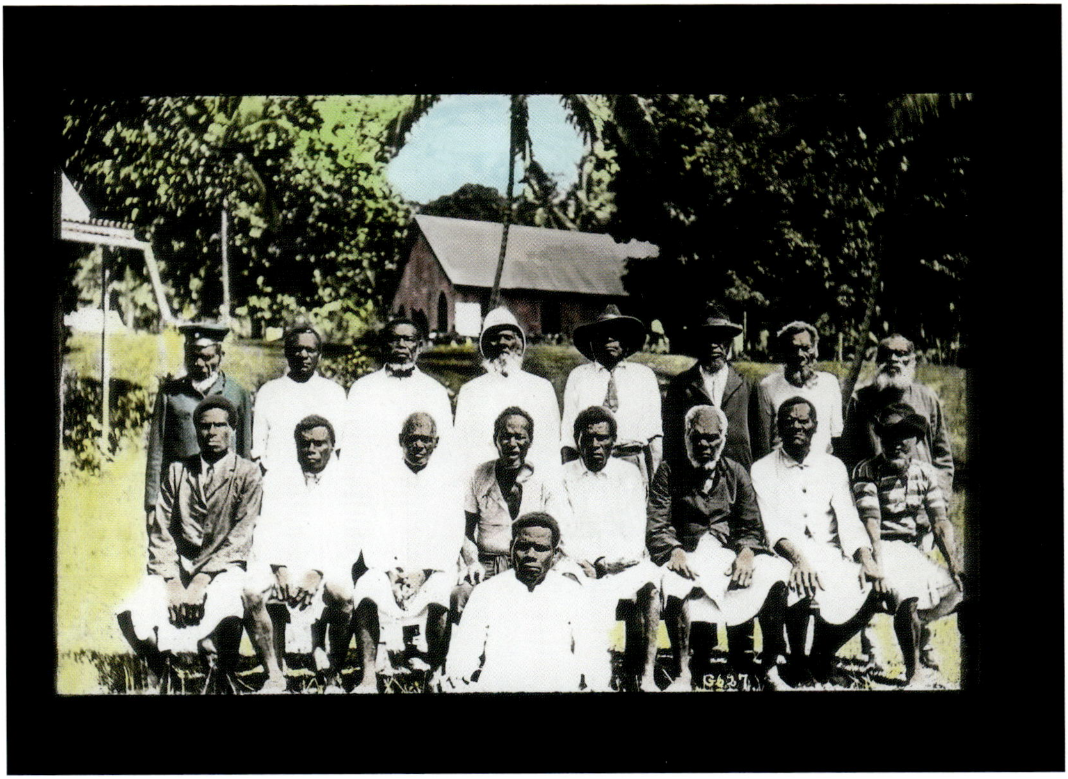

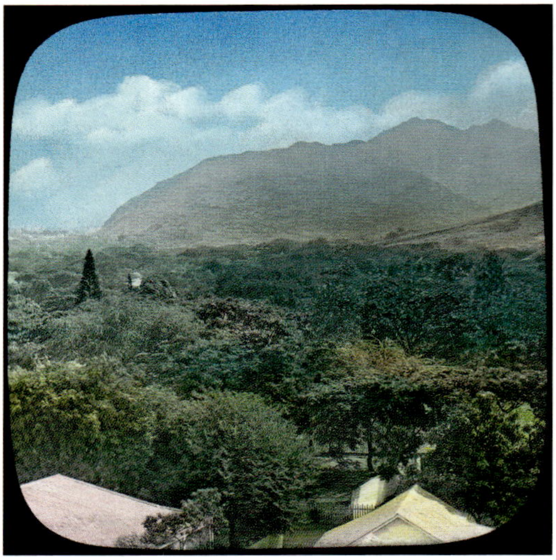
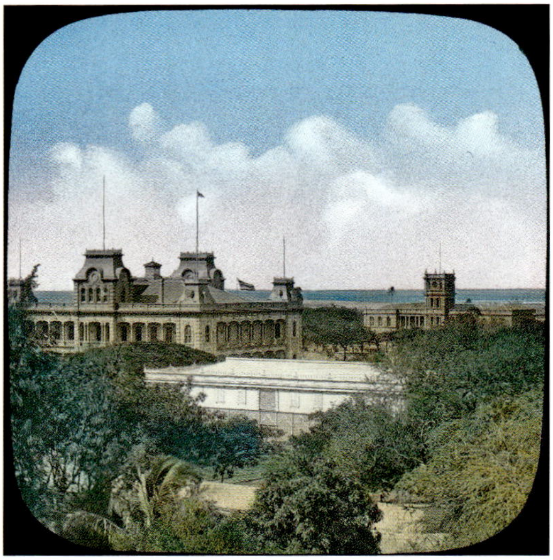
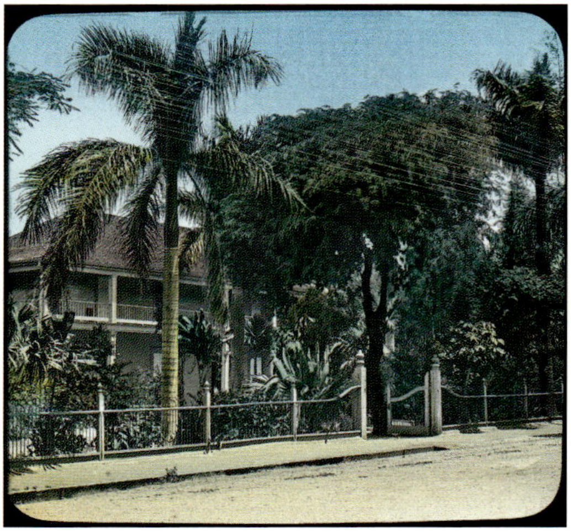
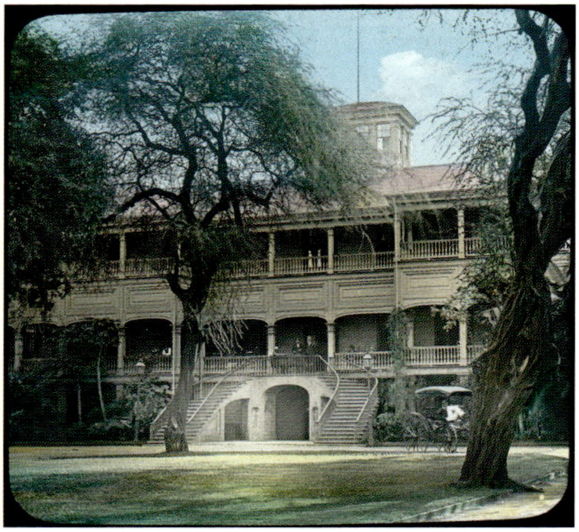

508 View from Tower Hotel, Hawaii, 1890s
510 Iolani Palace, Honolulu, Hawaii, 1890s
509 Trees on Honolulu, Hawaii, 1890s

508 Blick vom Tower Hotel aus, Hawaii, 1890er Jahre
509 Der Iolani-Palast, Honolulu, Hawaii, 1890er Jahre
510 Bäume in Honolulu, Hawaii, 1890er Jahre

508 Vue du Tower Hotel, Hawaii, années 1890
509 Iolani Palace, Honolulu, Hawaii, années 1890
510 Arbres à Honolulu, Hawaii, années 1890

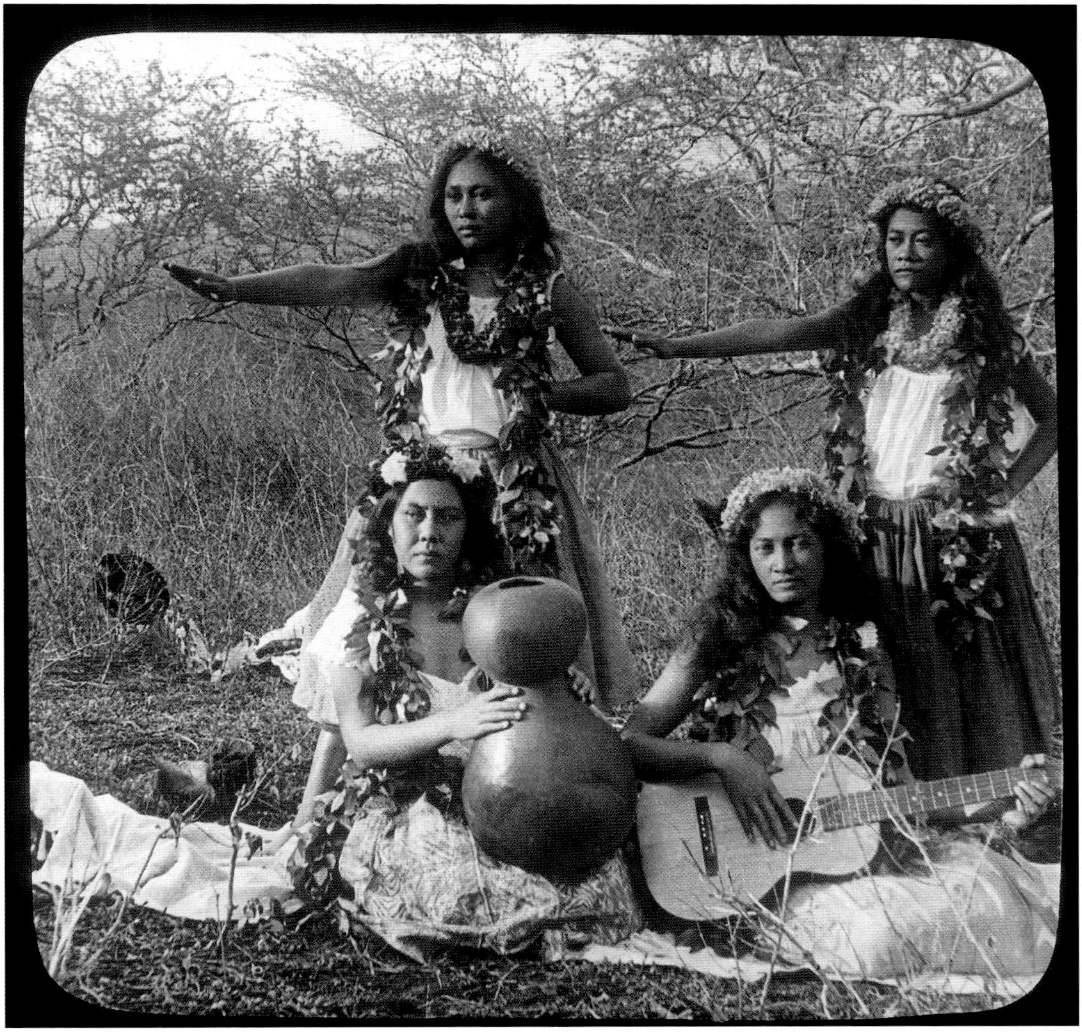

511 Hotel in Honolulu, Hawaii, 1890s
512 "Pretty Hula Girls", Honolulu, Hawaii, 1900s

511 Hotel in Honolulu, Hawaii, 1890er Jahre
512 „Hübsche Hula-Mädchen", Honolulu, Hawaii, 1900er Jahre

511 Hôtel à Honolulu, Hawaii, années 1890
512 "Jolies jeunes filles Hula", Honolulu, Hawaii, années 1900

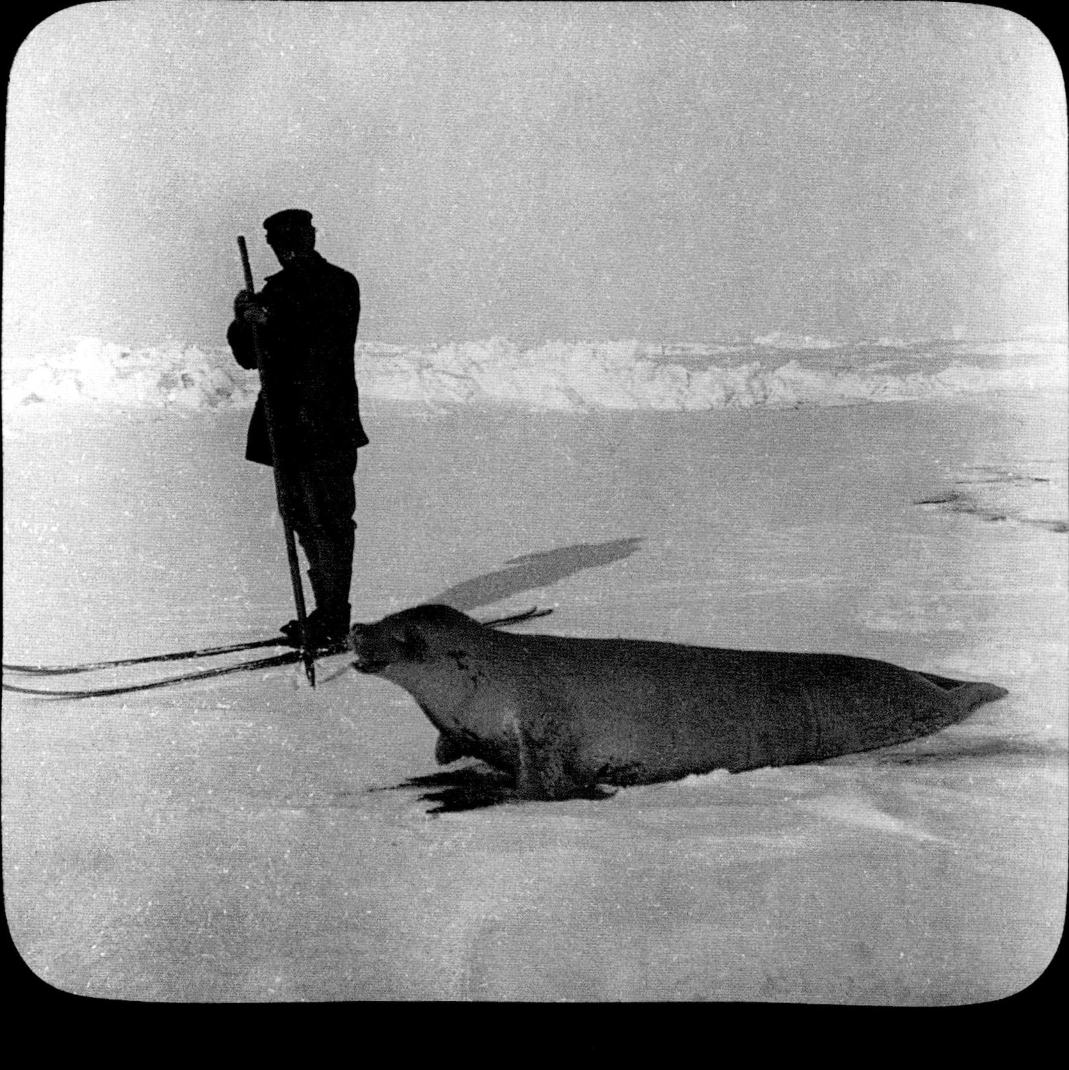

513 Commander Adrien de Gerlache hunting seals on skis, Antarctica, 1897–99

513 Kapitän Adrien de Gerlache jagt auf Skiern Robben, Antarktis, 1897–1899

513 Le commandant Adrien de Gerlache chasse le phoque à ski, Antarctique, 1897–99

ANTARCTICA

ANTARKTIS · ANTARCTIQUE

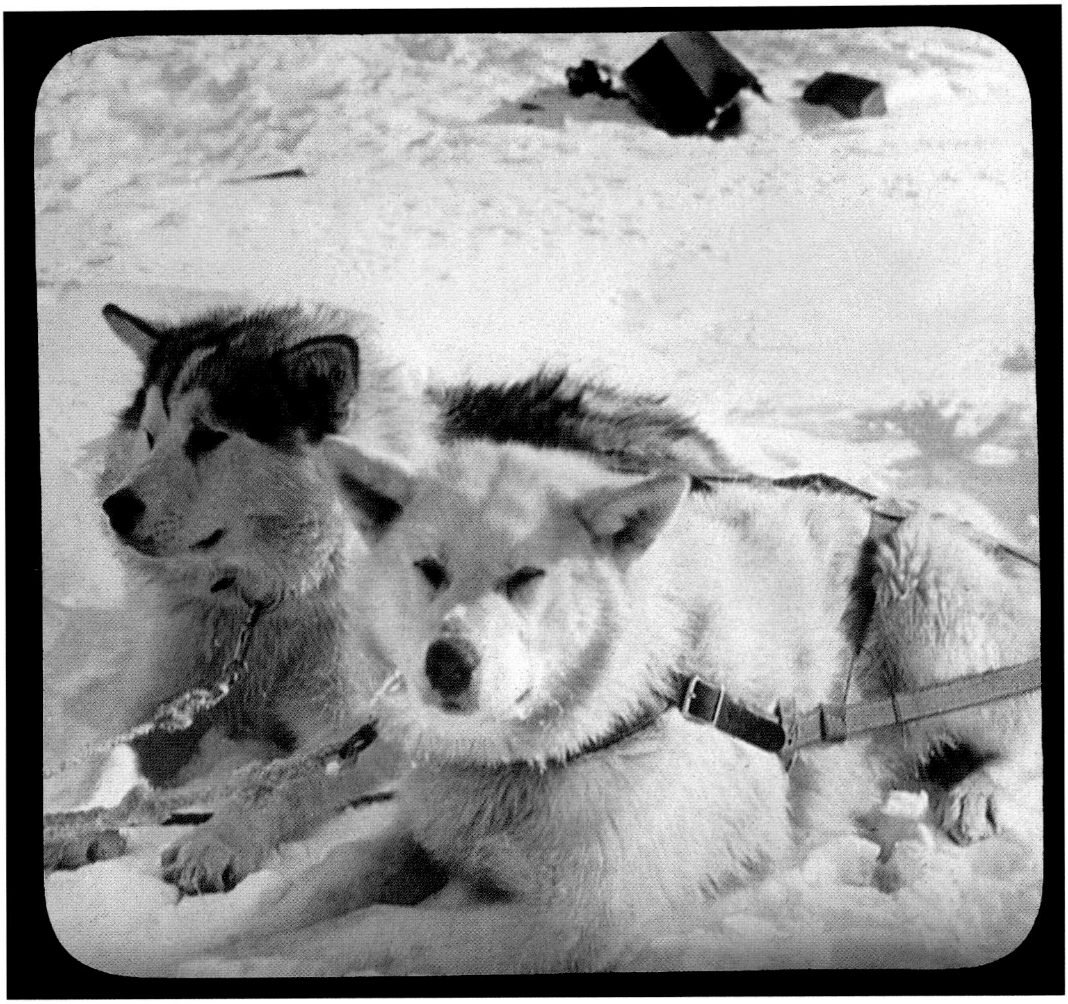

514 Huskies at rest, Antarctica, 1897–99
515 "What the Antarctica Explorer Wears", Antarctica, 1897–99

514 Huskies ruhen sich aus, Antarktis, 1897–1899
515 „Was der Antarktisforscher trägt", Antarktis, 1897–1899

514 Chiens husky au repos, Antarctique, 1897–99
515 « La tenue de l'explorateur polaire », Antarctique, 1897–99

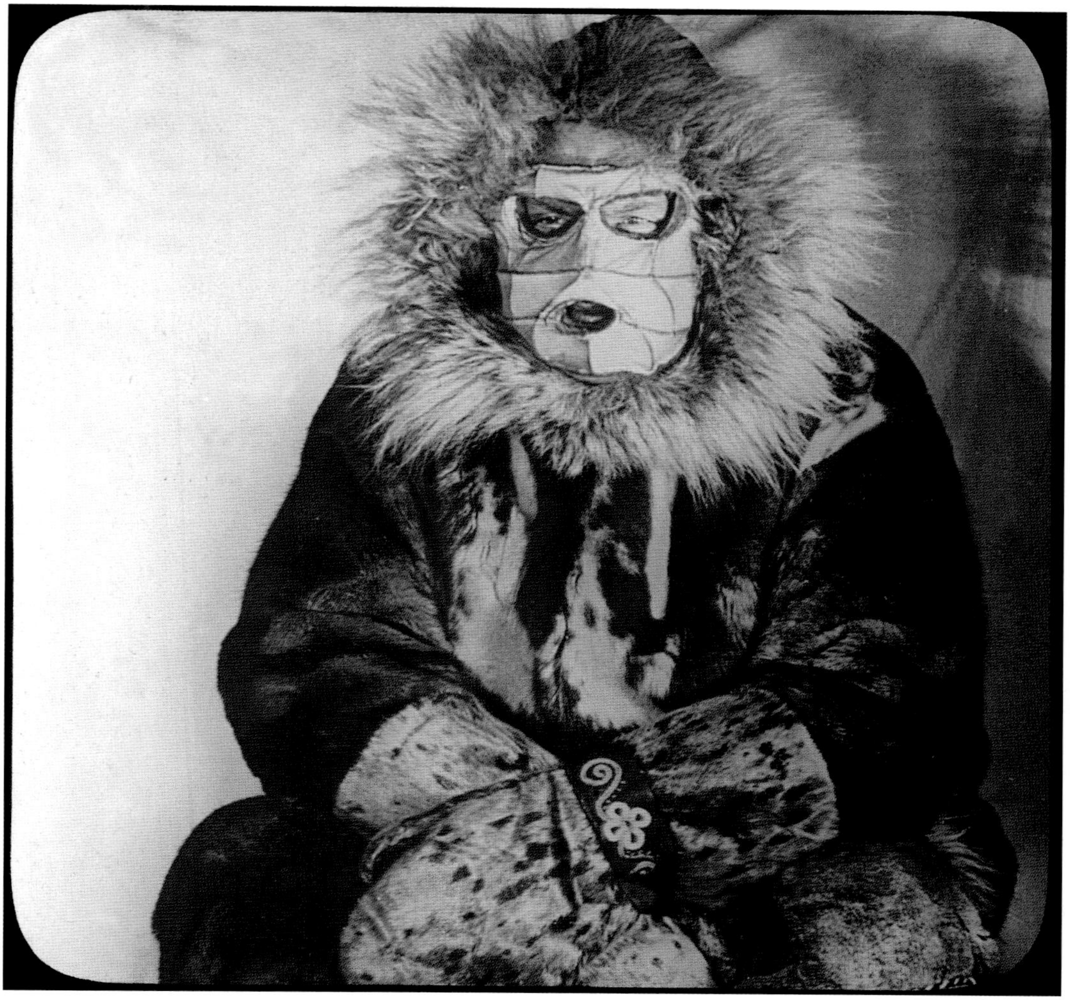

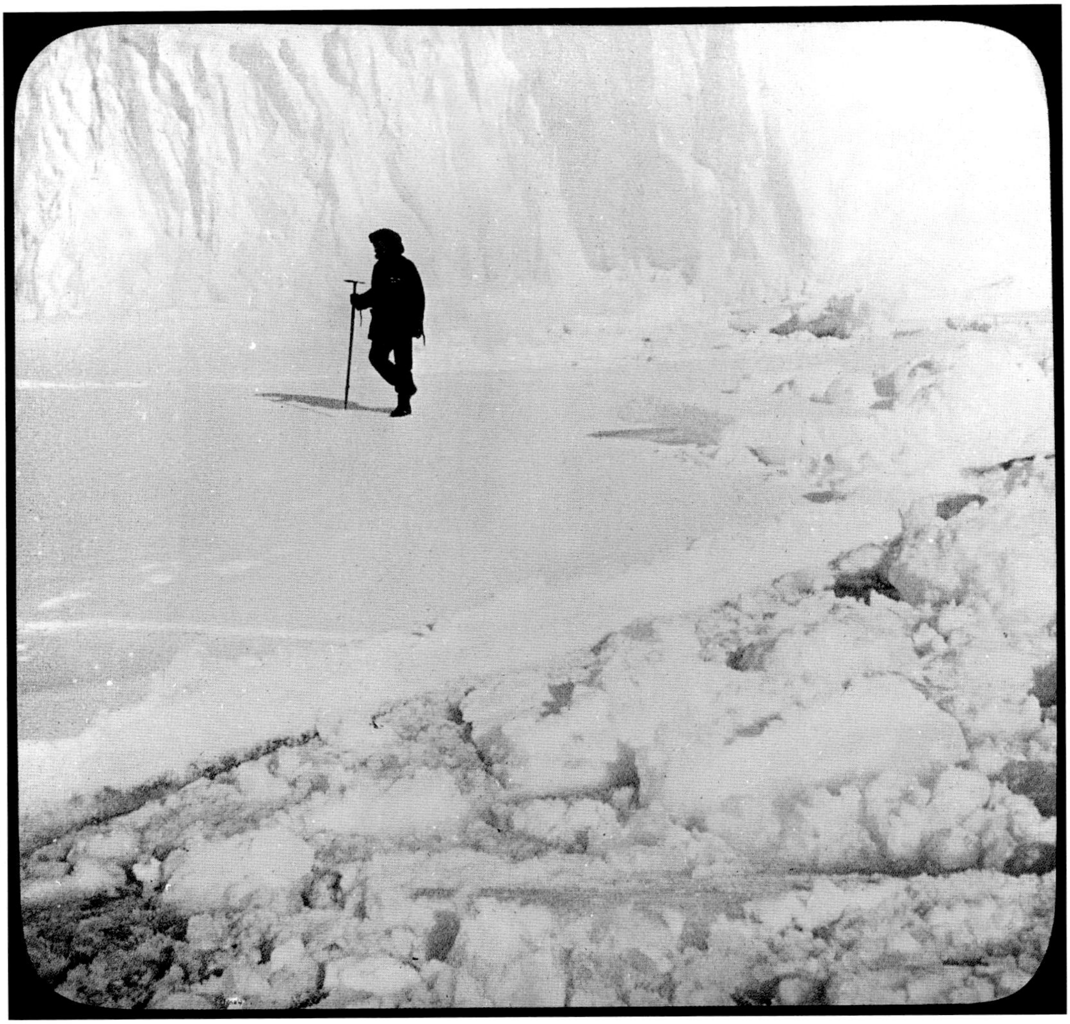

516 The explorer, Roald Amundsen inspecting ice field, Southern Ocean, c.1910
517 A crack in the ice, Antarctica, 1897–99

516 Der Forscher, Roald Amundsen untersucht ein Eisfeld, Südlicher Ozean, um 1910
517 Eine Spalte im Eis, Antarktis, 1897–1899

516 L'explorateur Roald Amundsen inspecte un champ de glace, océan Antarctique, vers 1910
517 Crevasse dans la glace, Antarctique, 1897–99

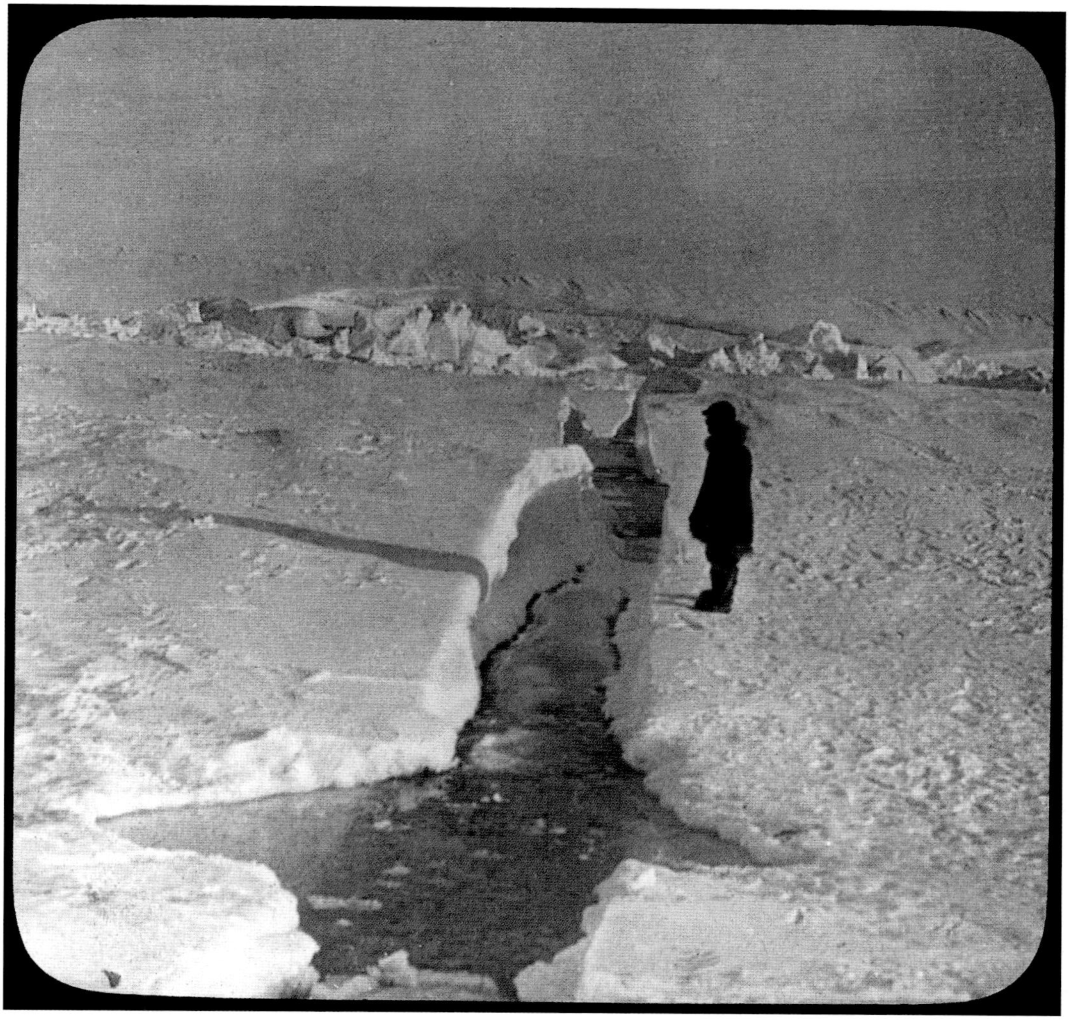

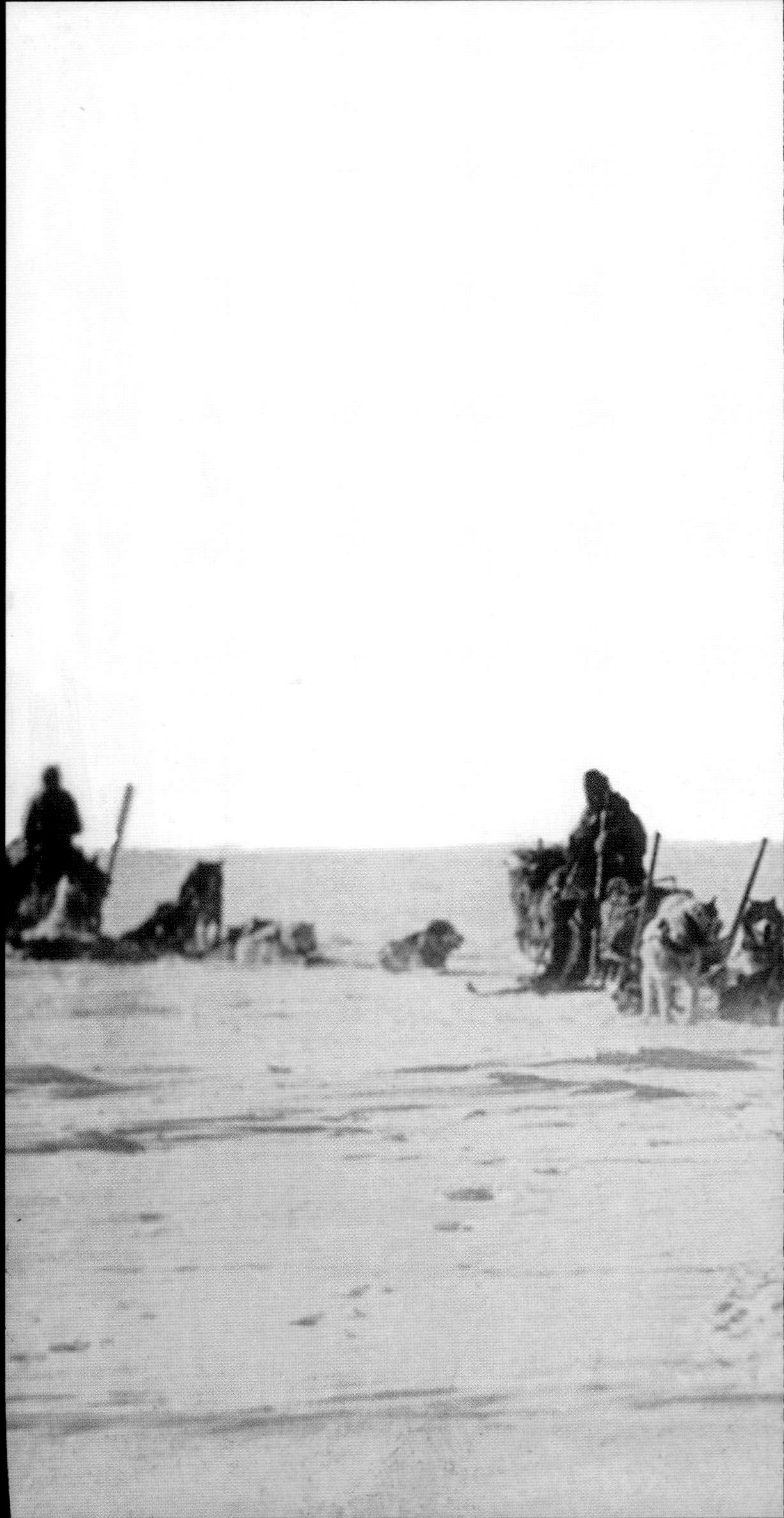

518 Sledging supplies, Antarctica, 1897–99

518 Nachschub auf Schlitten, Antarktis, 1897–1899

518 Ravitaillement en traîneaux, Antarctique, 1897–99

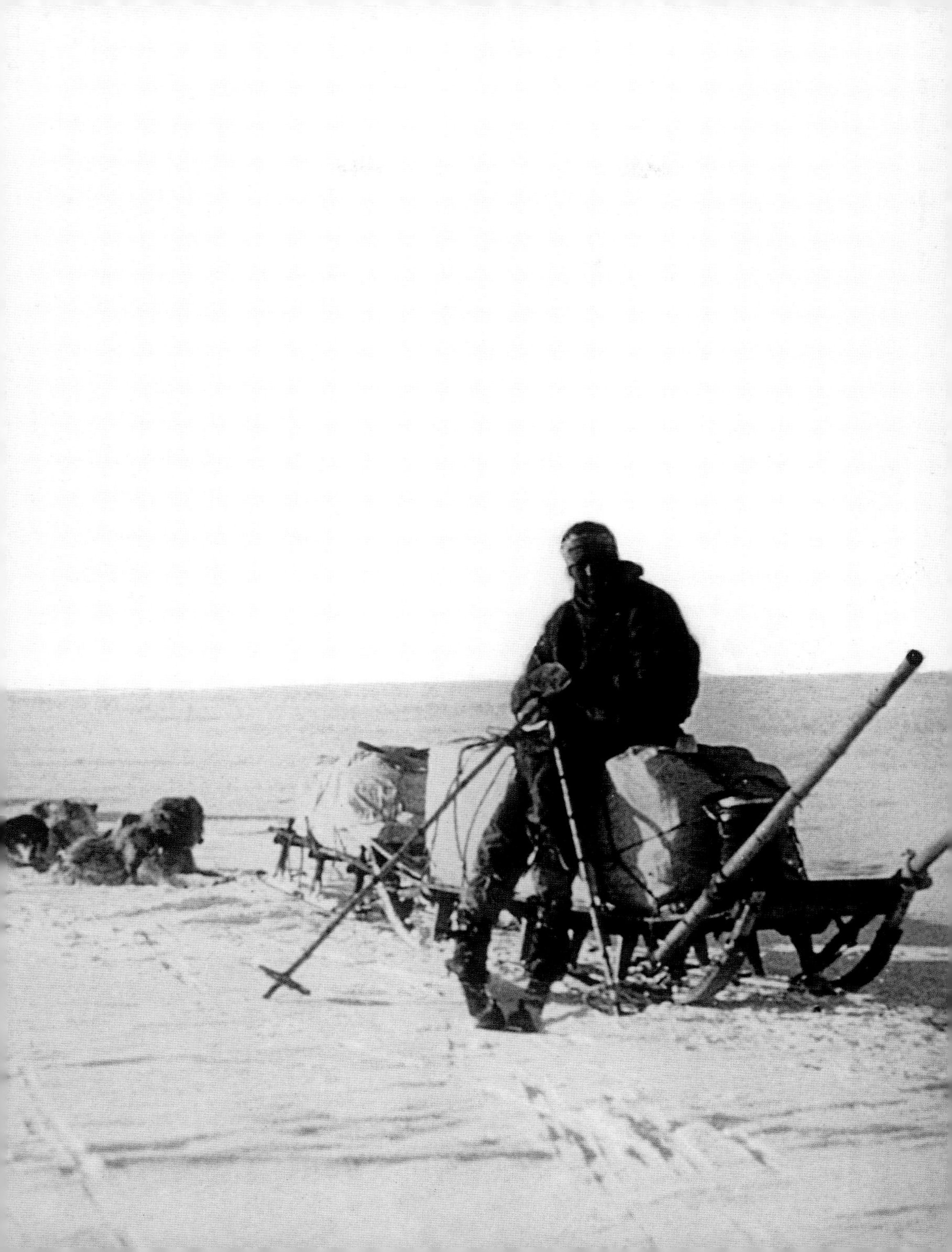

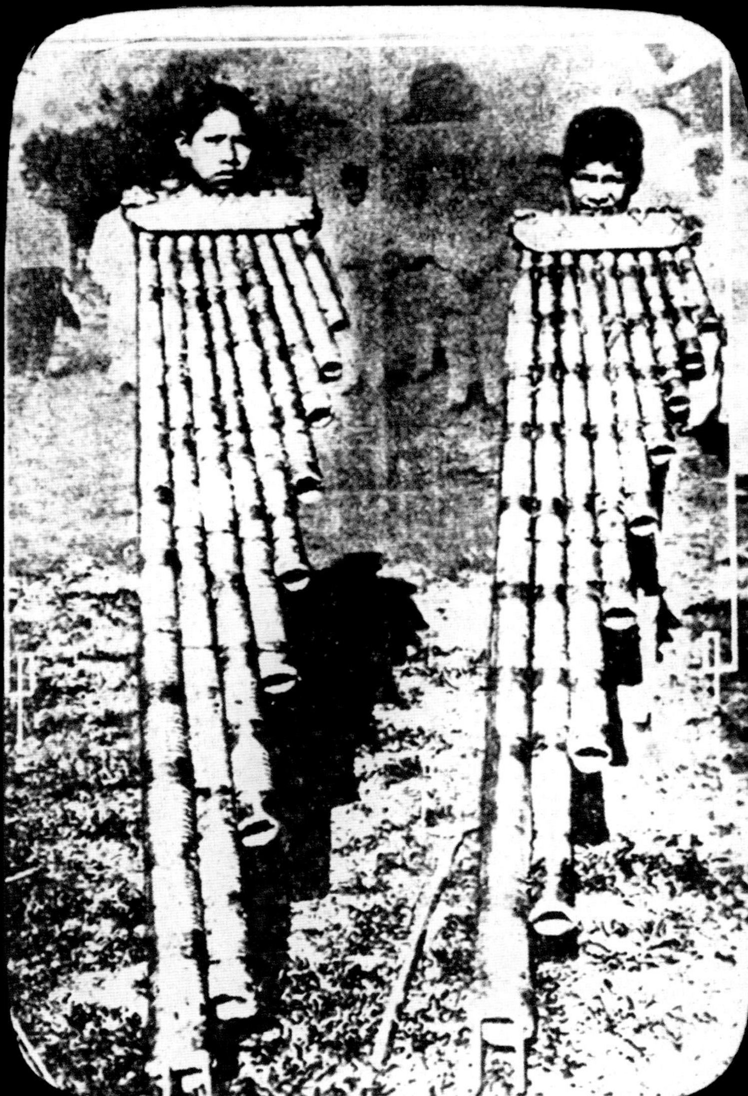

SOUTH AMERICA

SÜDAMERIKA · AMÉRIQUE DU SUD

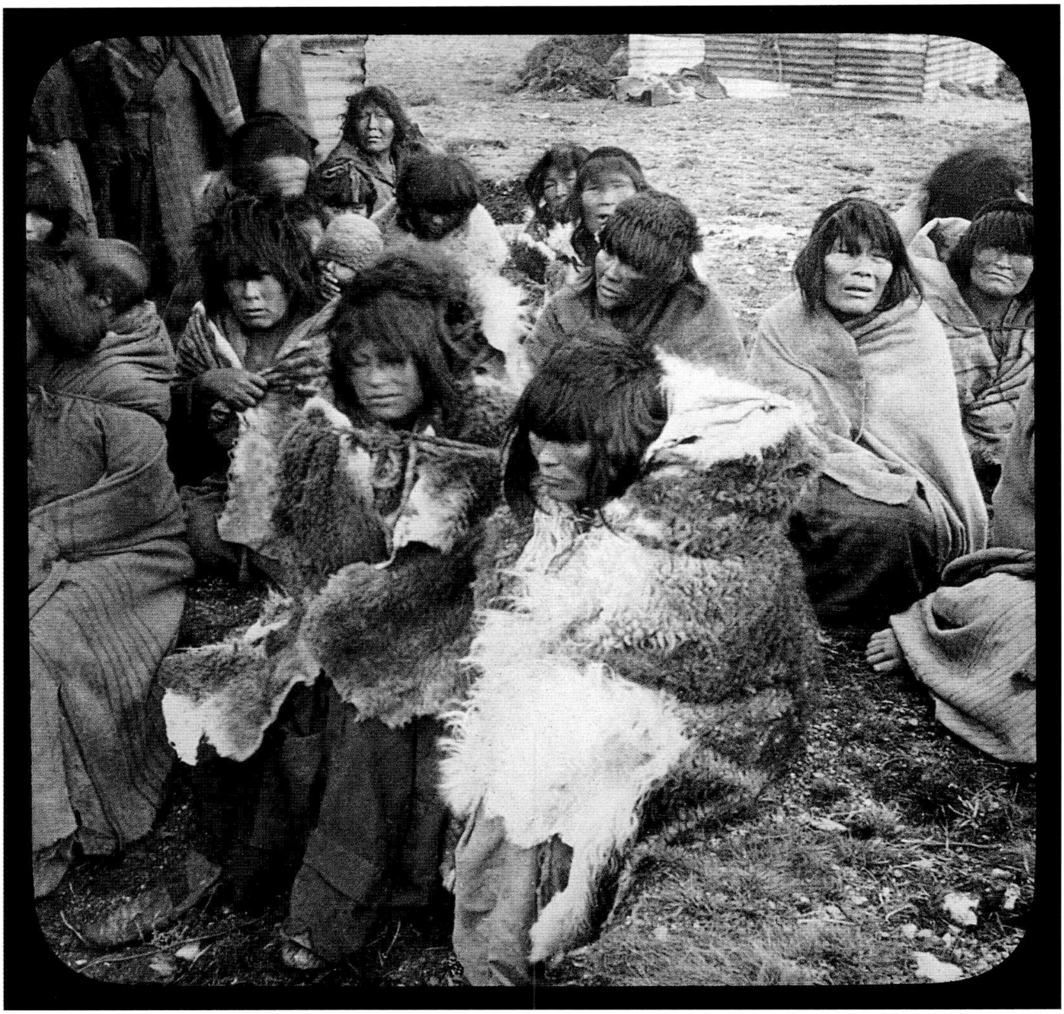

520 Indians on the Strait of Magellan near Punta Arenas, Chile, 1900s

520 Indianer an der Magellanstraße nahe Punta Arenas, Chile, 1900er Jahre

520 Indiens du détroit de Magellan, près de Punta Arenas, Chili, années 1900

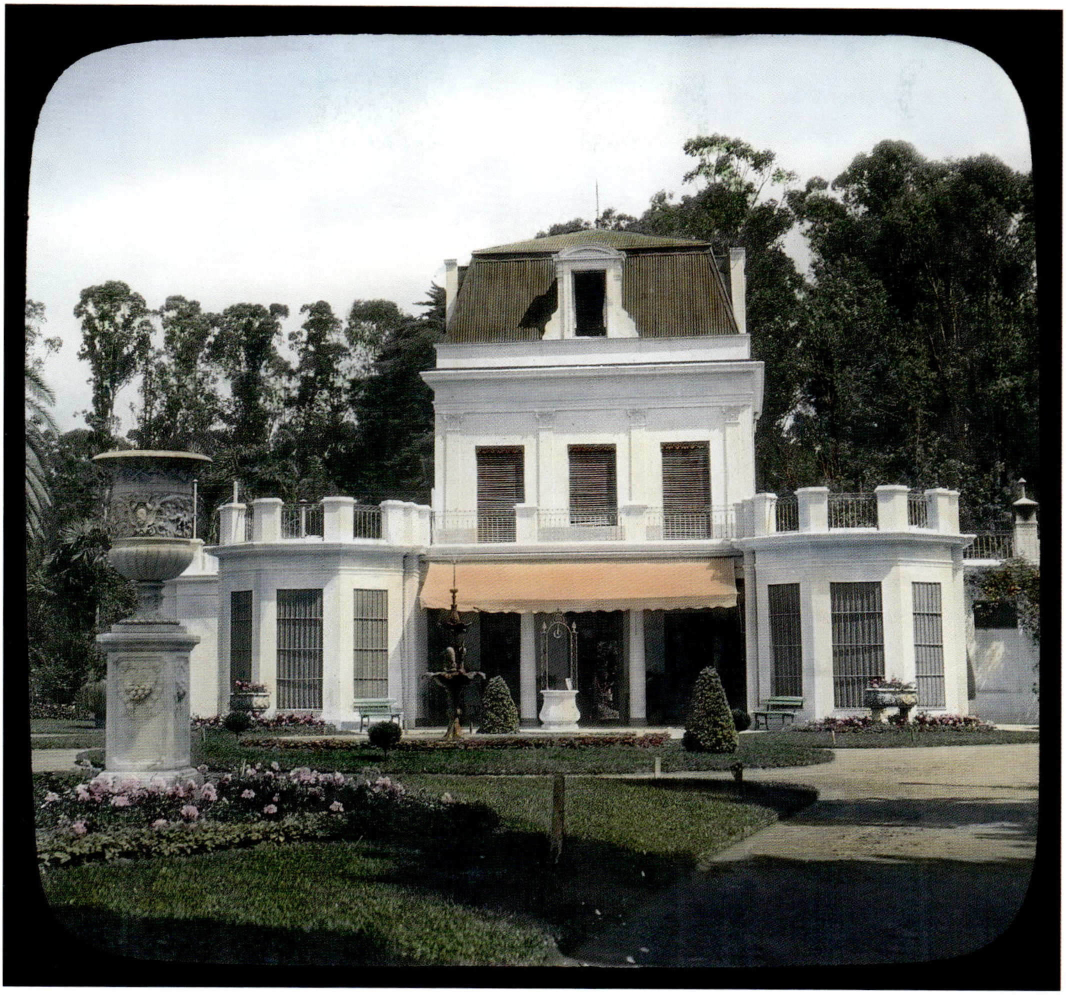

523 House and garden in Estancia, near Buenos Aires, Argentina, 1910s

523 Haus und Garten in einer Estancia,, nahe Buenos Aires, Argentinien, 1910er Jahre

523 Maison et jardin d'une Estancia près de Buenos Aires, Argentine, années 1910

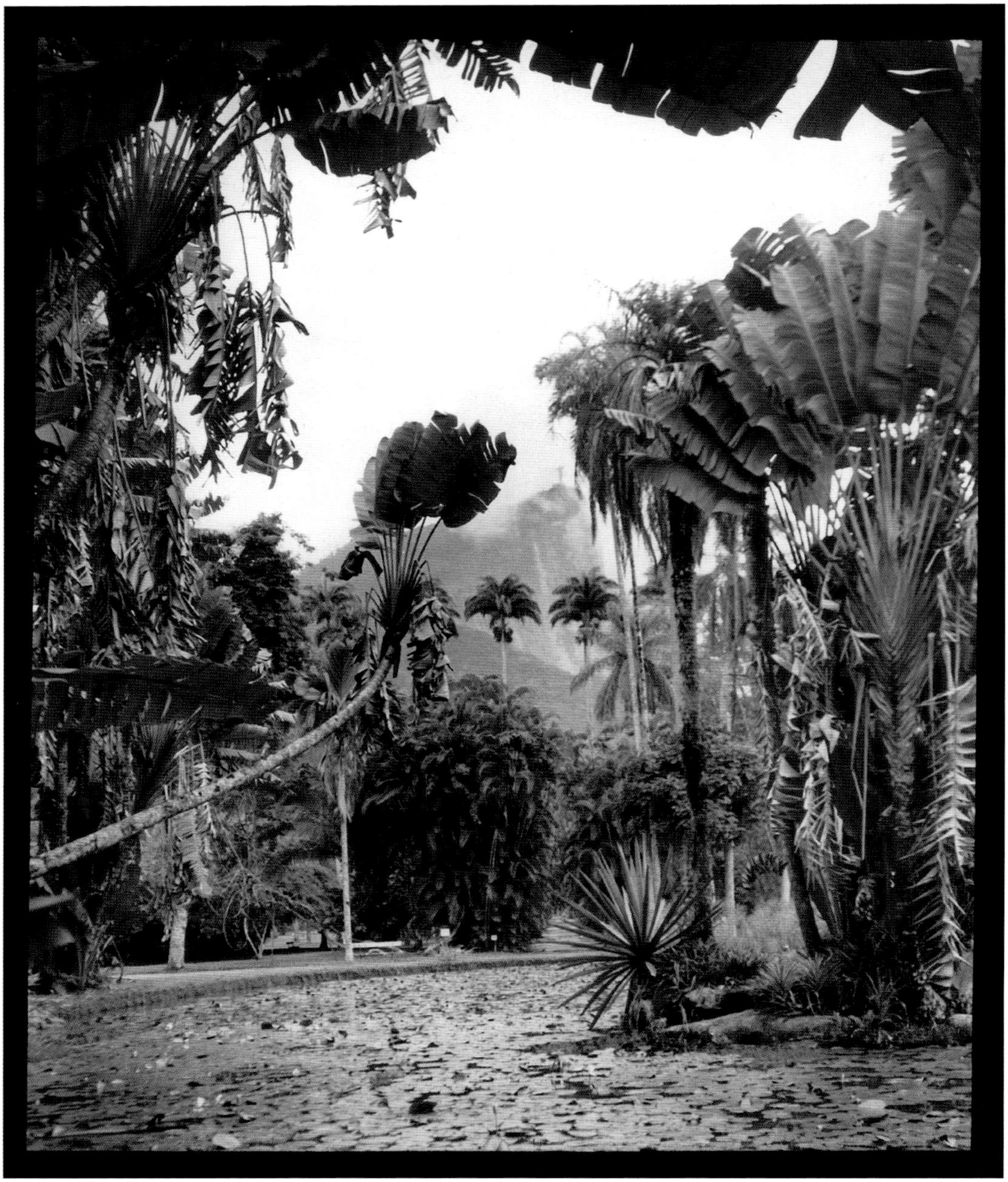

524 Botanical Gardens, in the background Corcovado with statue of "Christ the Redeemer", Rio de Janeiro, Brazil, c.1930

524 Botanischer Garten, im Hintergrund der Corcovado mit der Statue „Christus der Erlöser", Rio de Janeiro, Brasilien, um 1930

524 Jardin botanique, À l'arrière-plan, le Corcovado avec la statue du Christ Rédempteur, Rio de Janeiro, Brésil, vers 1930

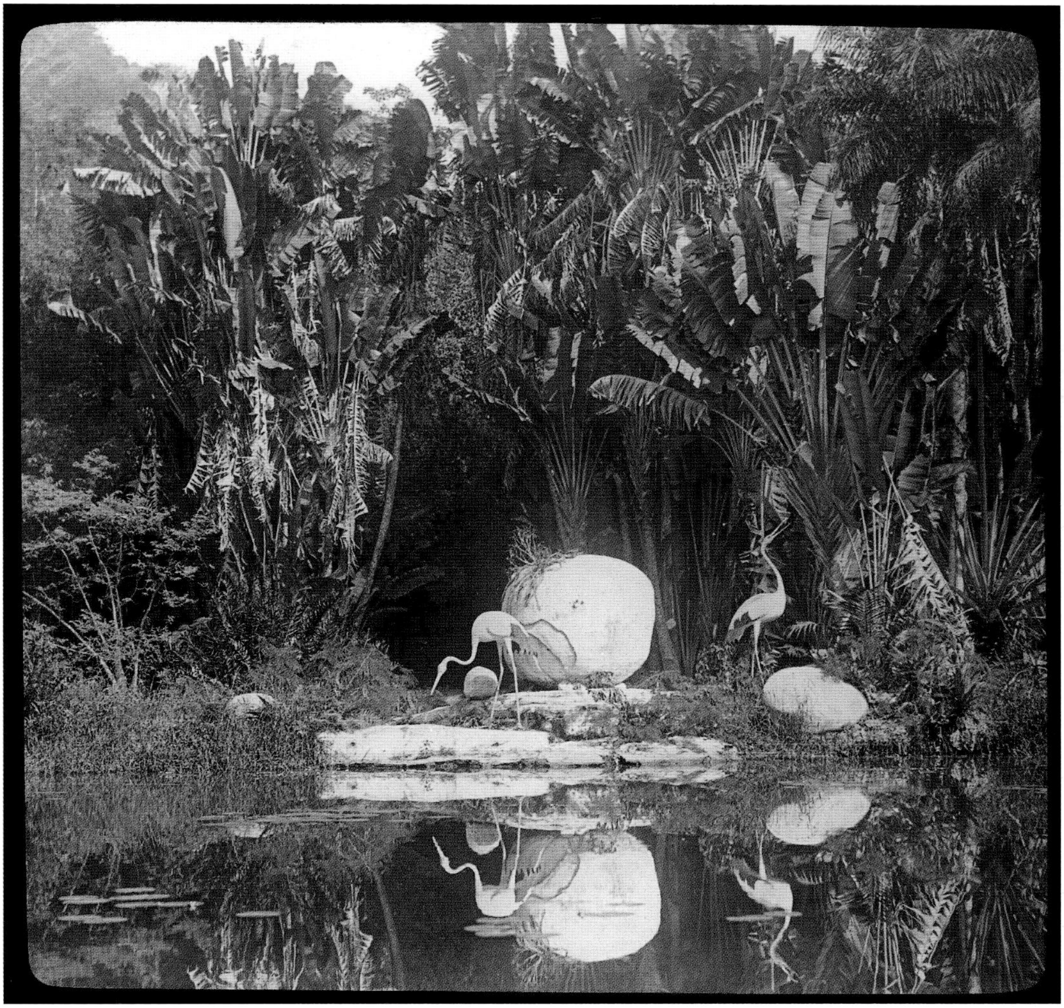

525 Botanical Gardens, Rio de Janeiro, Brazil, c.1930

525 Botanischer Garten, Rio de Janeiro, Brasilien, um 1930

525 Jardin botanique, Rio de Janeiro, Brésil, vers 1930

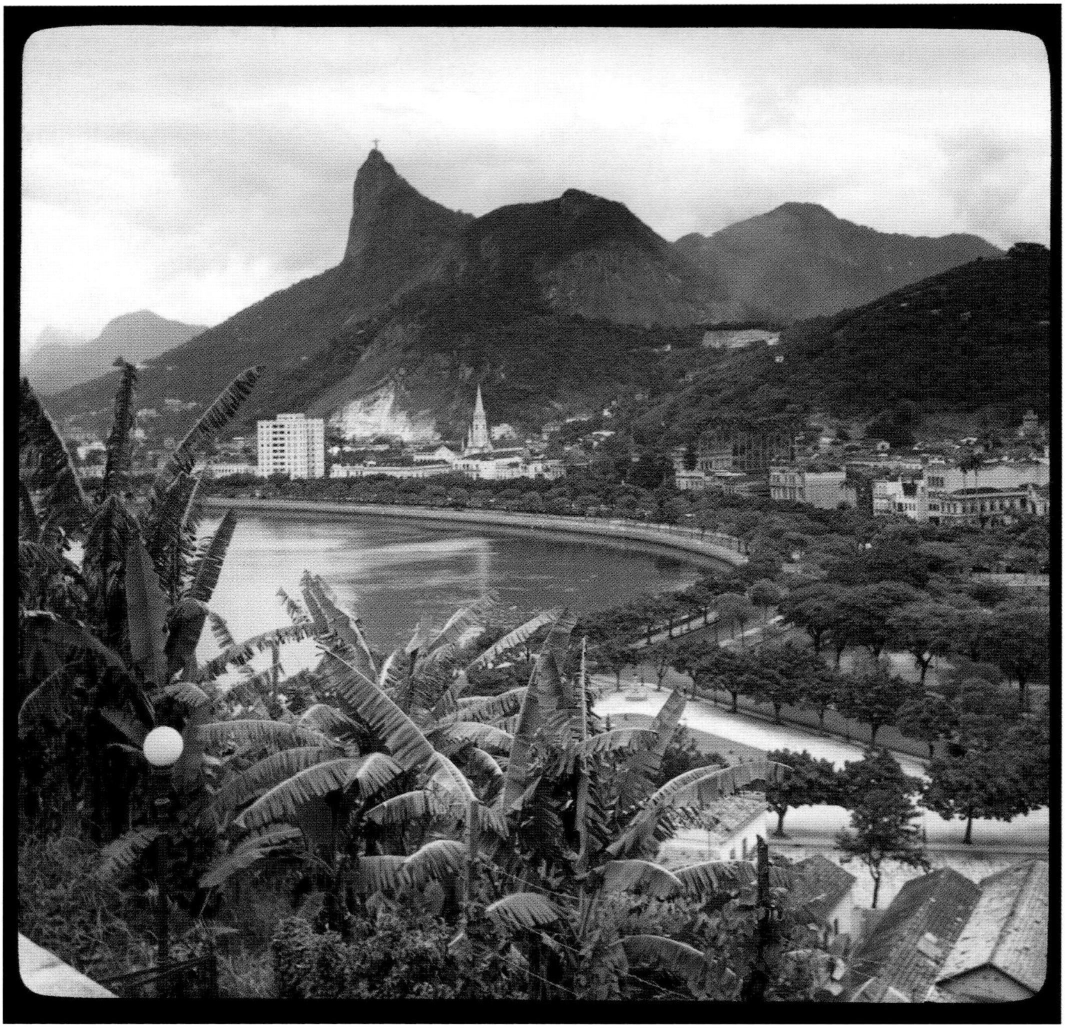

526 The Bay of Botofogo with Corcovado in the distance, Rio de Janeiro, Brazil, c.1930

526 Die Bucht von Botafogo mit dem Corcovado in der Ferne, Rio de Janeiro, Brasilien, um 1930

526 Baie de Botofogo avec, au loin, le Corcovado. Rio de Janeiro, Brésil, vers 1930

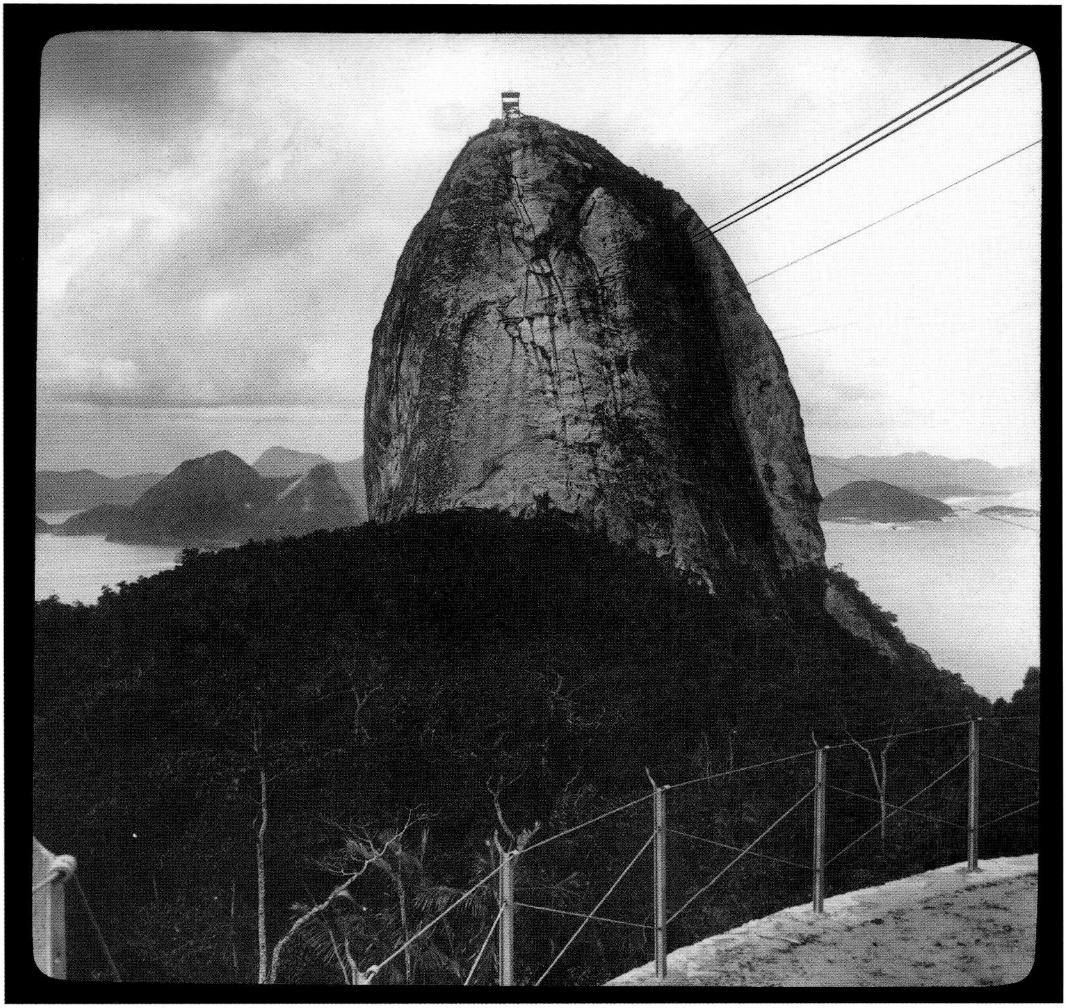

527 Looking towards Sugar Loaf Mountain from the first station, Rio de Janeiro, Brazil, 1920s

527 Blick auf den Zuckerhut von der ersten Station aus, Rio de Janeiro, Brasilien, 1920er Jahre

527 Vue sur le Pain de sucre depuis la première station, Rio de Janeiro, Brésil, années 1920

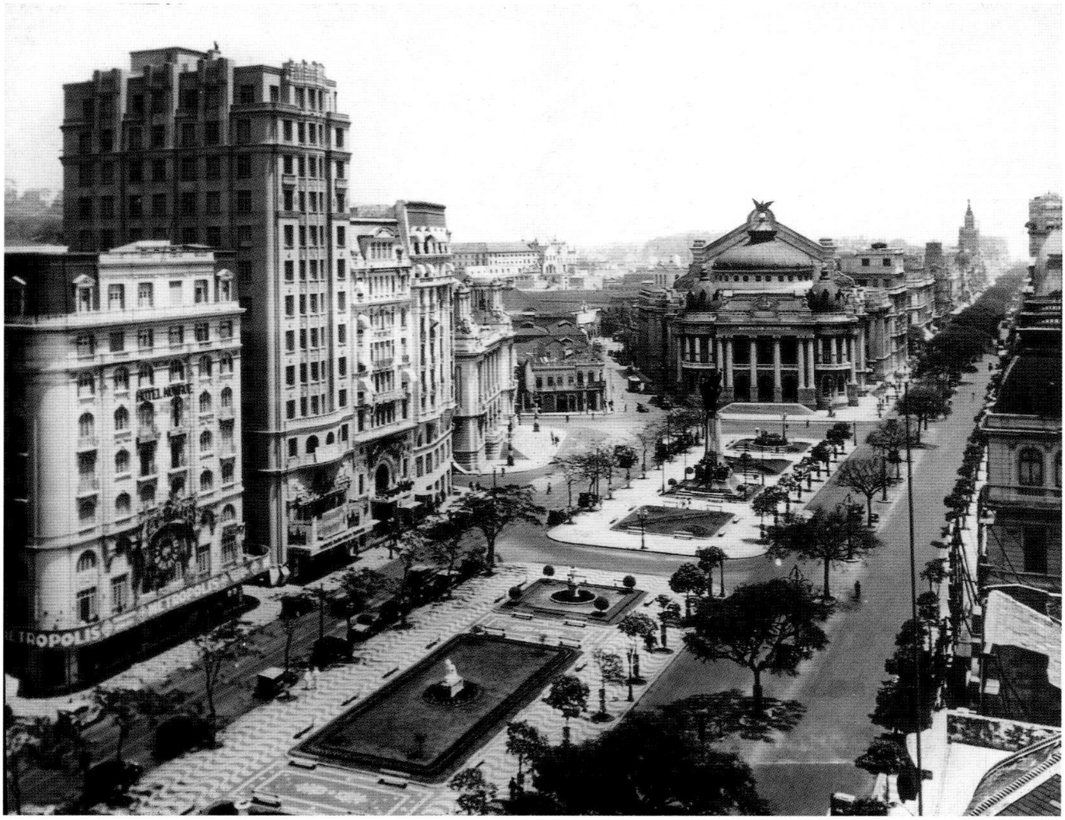

528 Municipal Theatre and (to the right) the Avenida Rio Branco, Rio de Janeiro, Brazil, 1920s

528 Das Stadttheater und (rechts davon) die Avenida Rio Branco, Rio de Janeiro, Brasilien, 1920er Jahre

528 Théâtre municipal et à droite, l'avenida Rio Branco, Rio de Janeiro, Brésil, années 1920

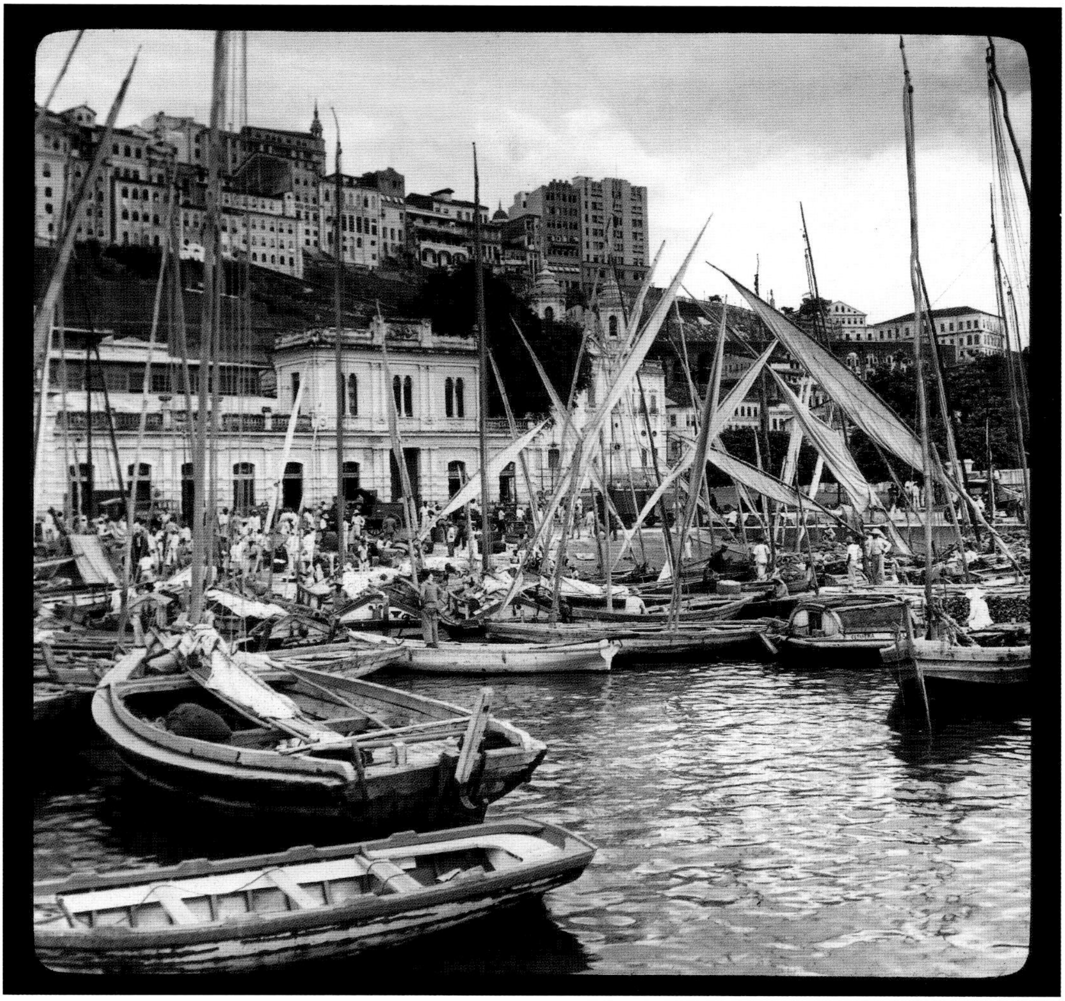

529 Inner harbour and marketplace, Bahia, Brazil, 1920s

529 Innenhafen und Marktplatz, Bahia, Brasilien, 1920er Jahre

529 Port intérieur et place du marché, Bahia, Brésil, années 1920

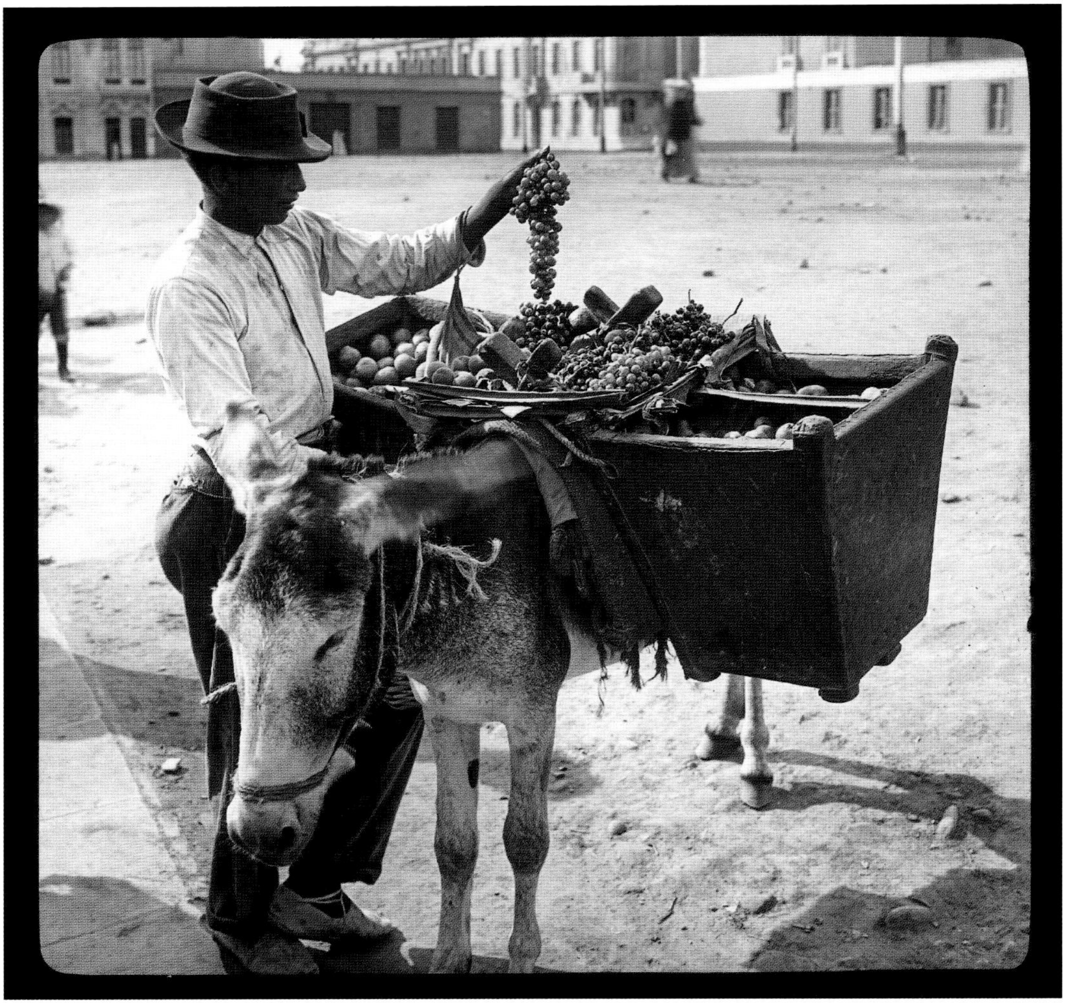

530 Street vendor, Lima, Peru, 1910s
531 Cathedral, Lima, Peru, 1910s

530 Straßenhändler, Lima, Peru, 1910er Jahre
531 Die Kathedrale, Lima, Peru, 1910er Jahre

530 Vendeur ambulant, Lima, Pérou, années 1910
531 Cathédrale de Lima, Pérou, années 1910

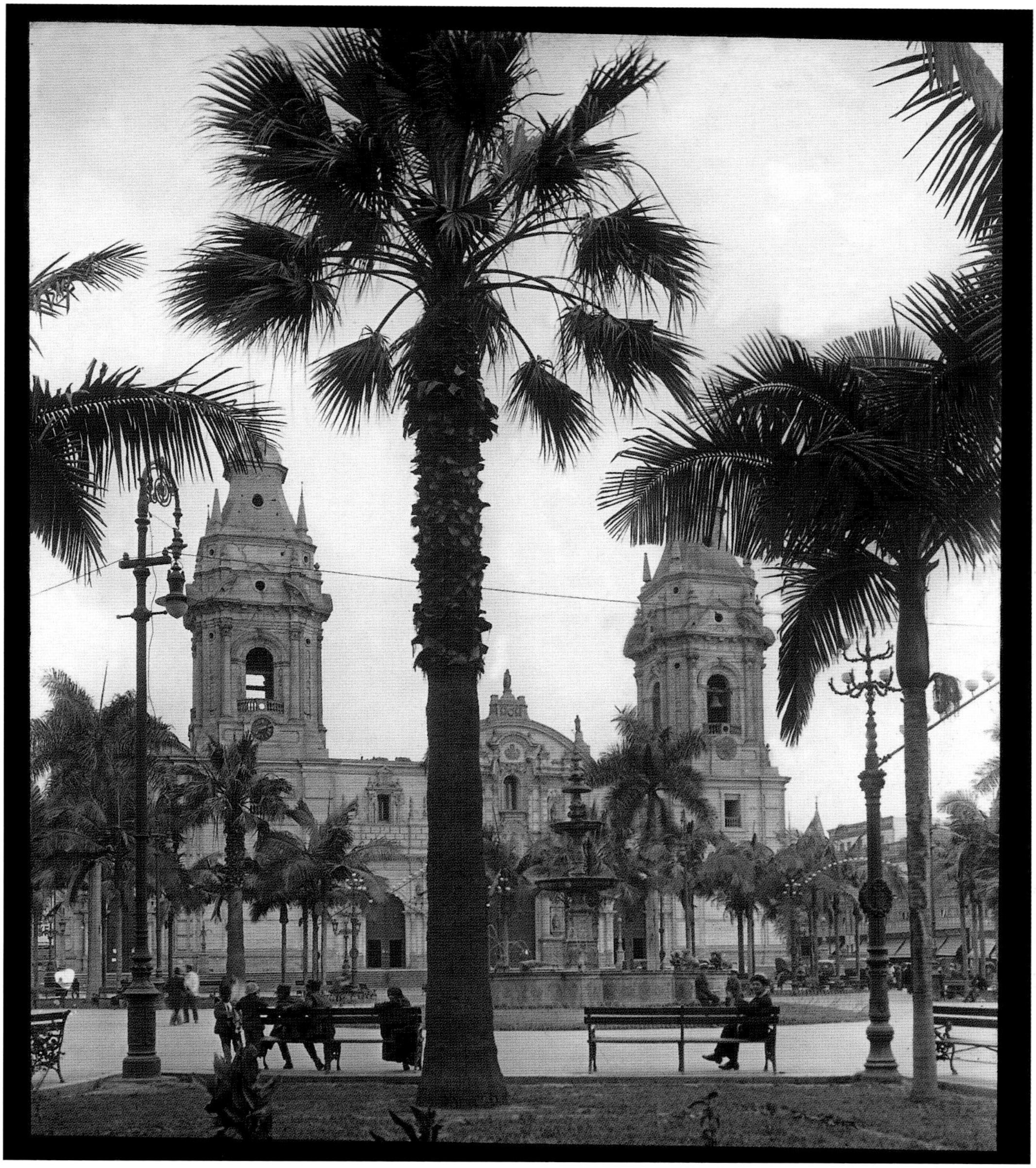

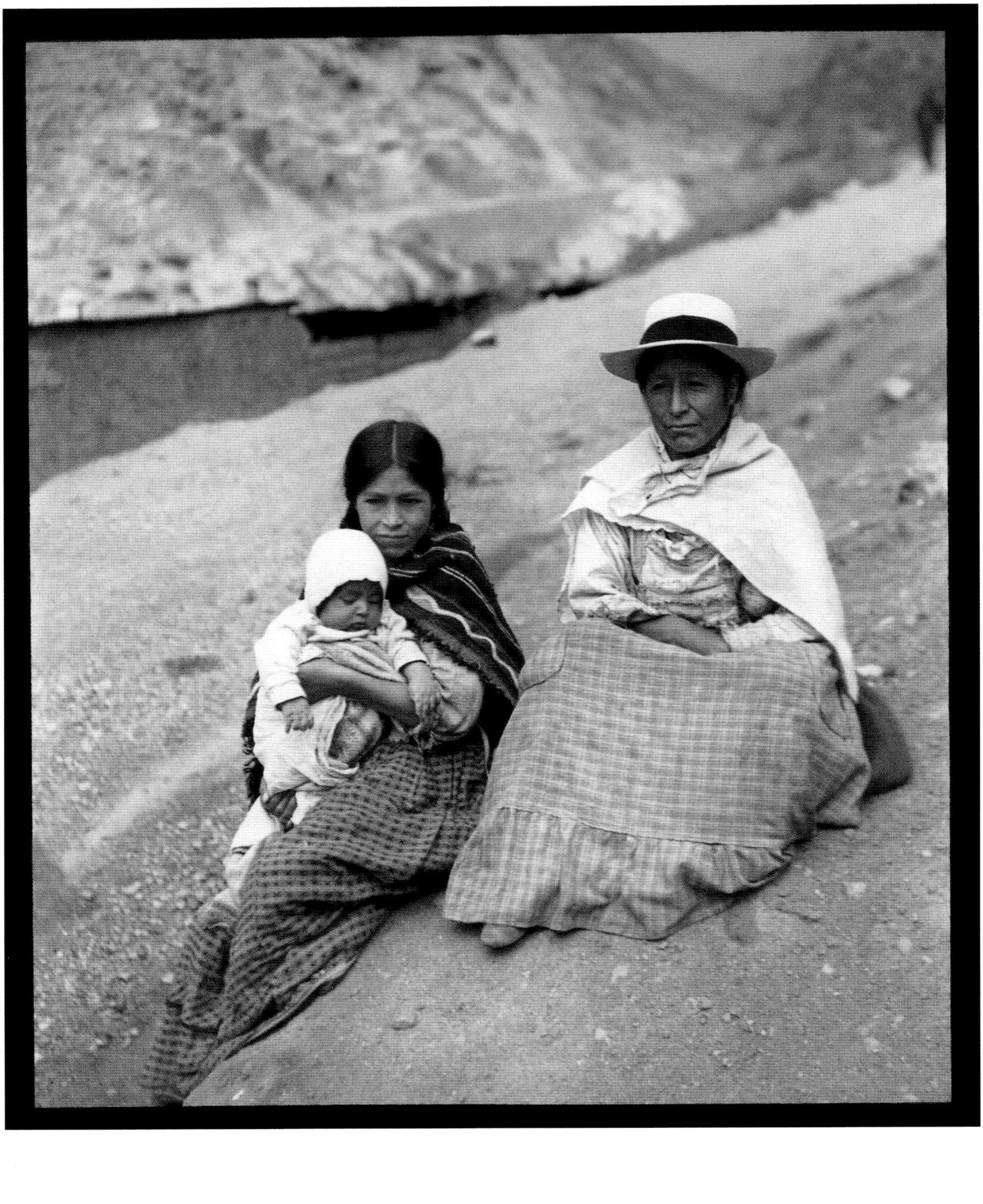

532 A Chola Indian mother and her baby, and its grandmother, Peru, 1920s

532 Eine Chola und ihr Baby sowie die Großmutter, Peru, 1920er Jahre

532 Mère andine Chola, son bébé et la grand mère, Pérou, années 1920

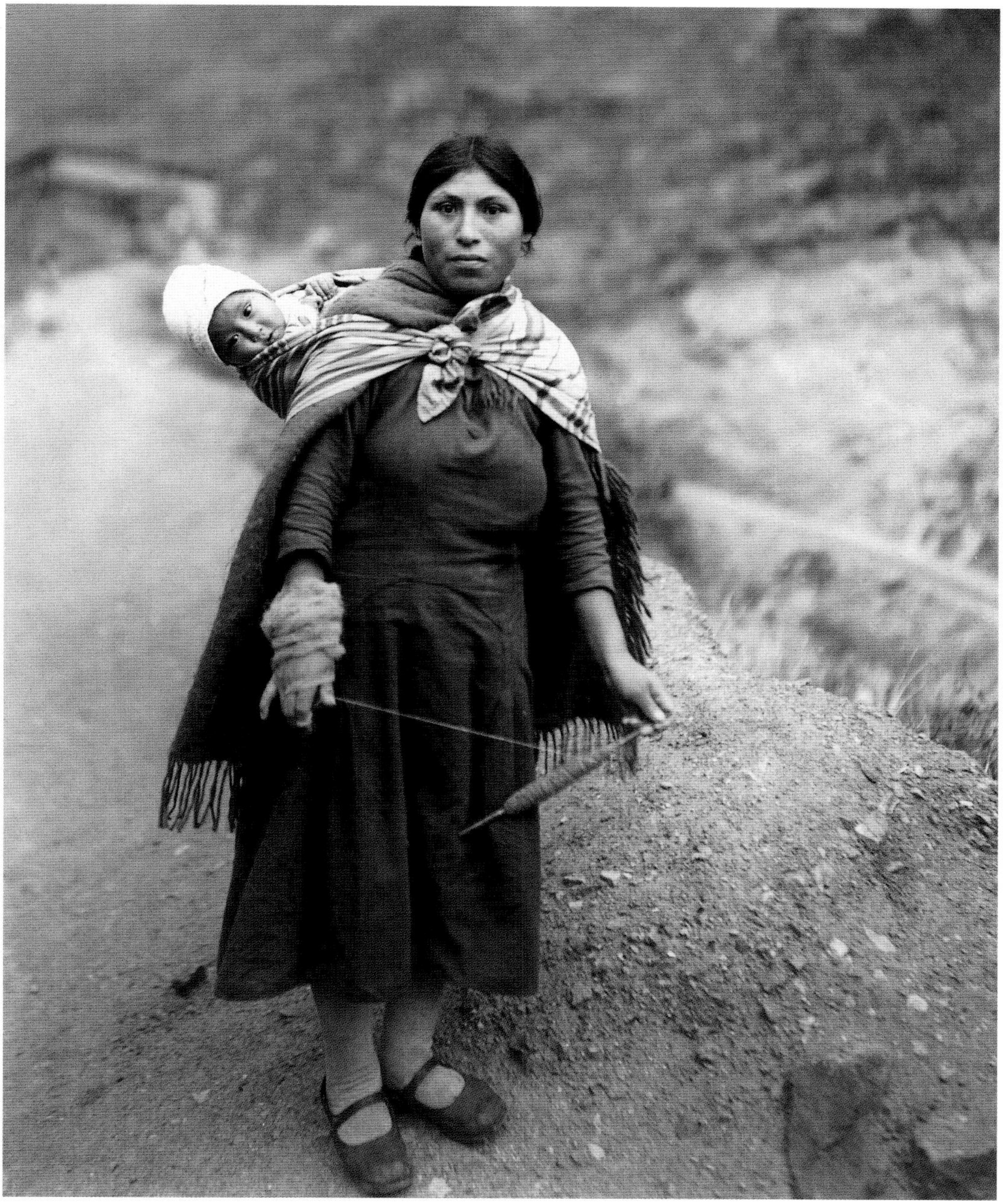

533 A Chola mother out for a walk with her baby and spinning vicuña wool, near Tamboraque Mines, Peru, 1920s

533 Eine Chola geht mit ihrem Baby spazieren und spinnt dabei Vicuña-Wolle, nahe der Minen von Tamboraque, Peru, 1920er Jahre

533 Mère Chola avec son bébé, et une quenouille pour filer la laine de vigogne. Près de la mine Tamboraque, Pérou, années 1920

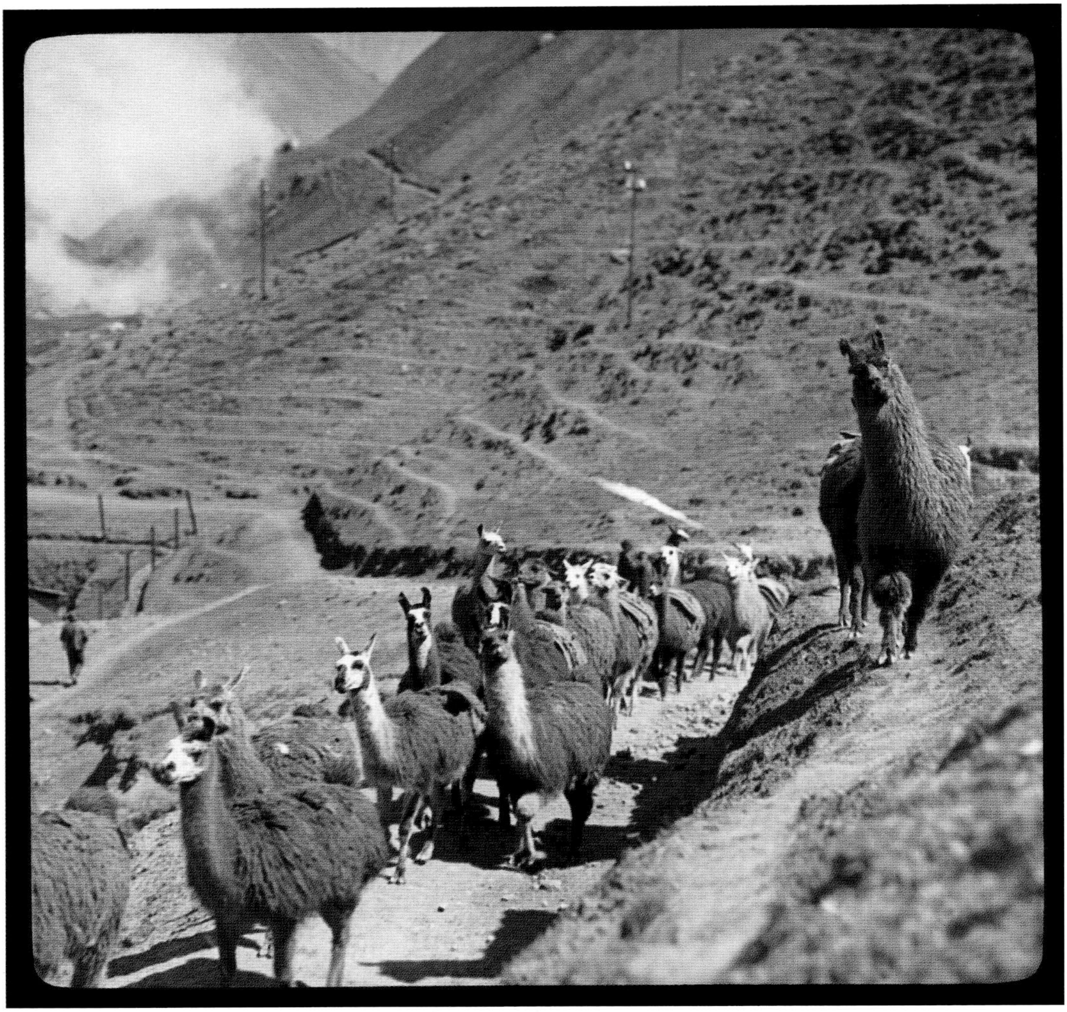

534 Llama pack train in the Andes, Peru, 1900s
535 Child slave, Arequipa, Peru, 1900s

534 Eine Herde Lamas in den Anden, Peru, 1900er Jahre
535 Kindersklave, Arequipa, Peru, 1900er Jahre

534 Troupeau de lamas dans les Andes, Pérou, années 1900
535 Enfant exploité, Arequipa, Pérou, années 1900

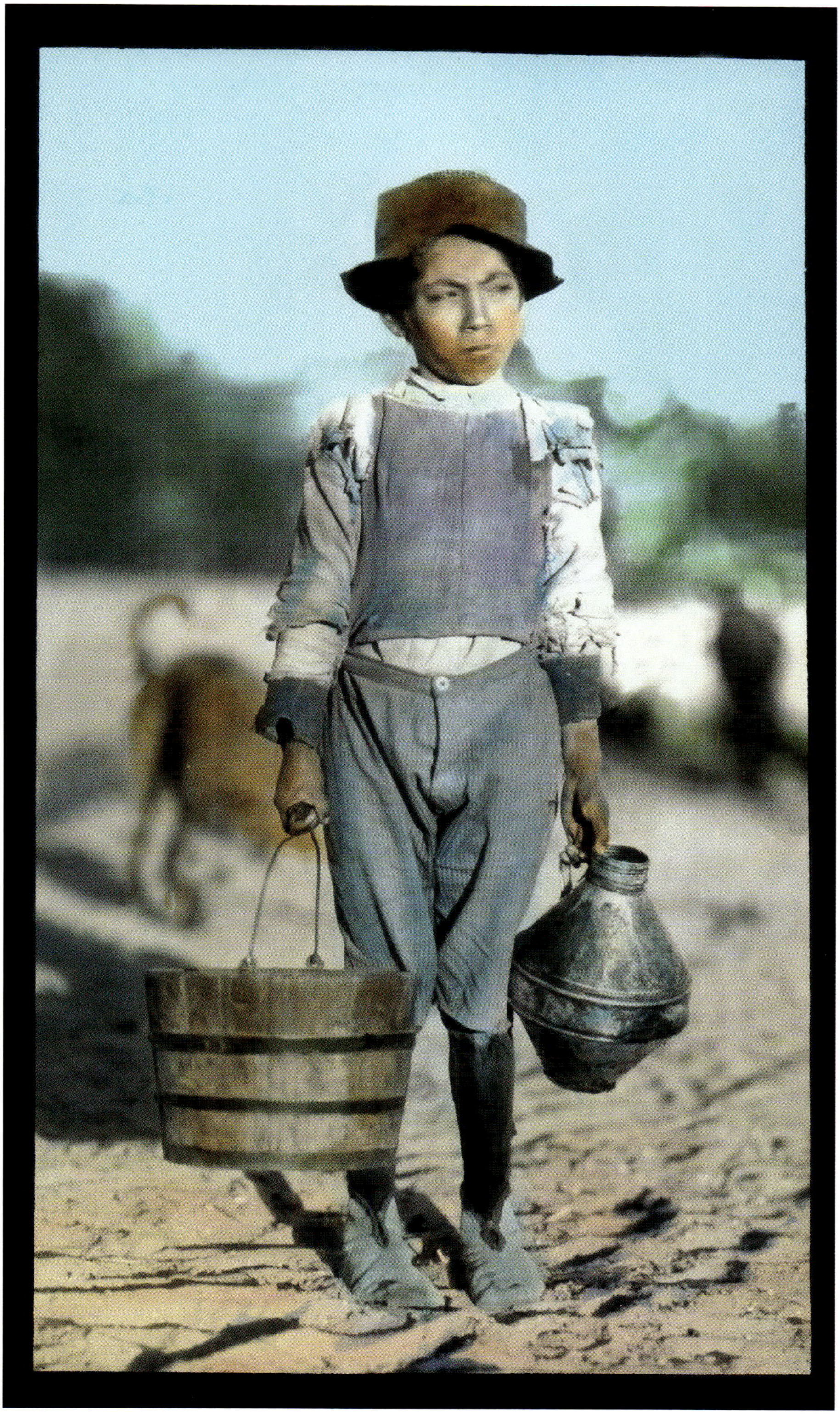

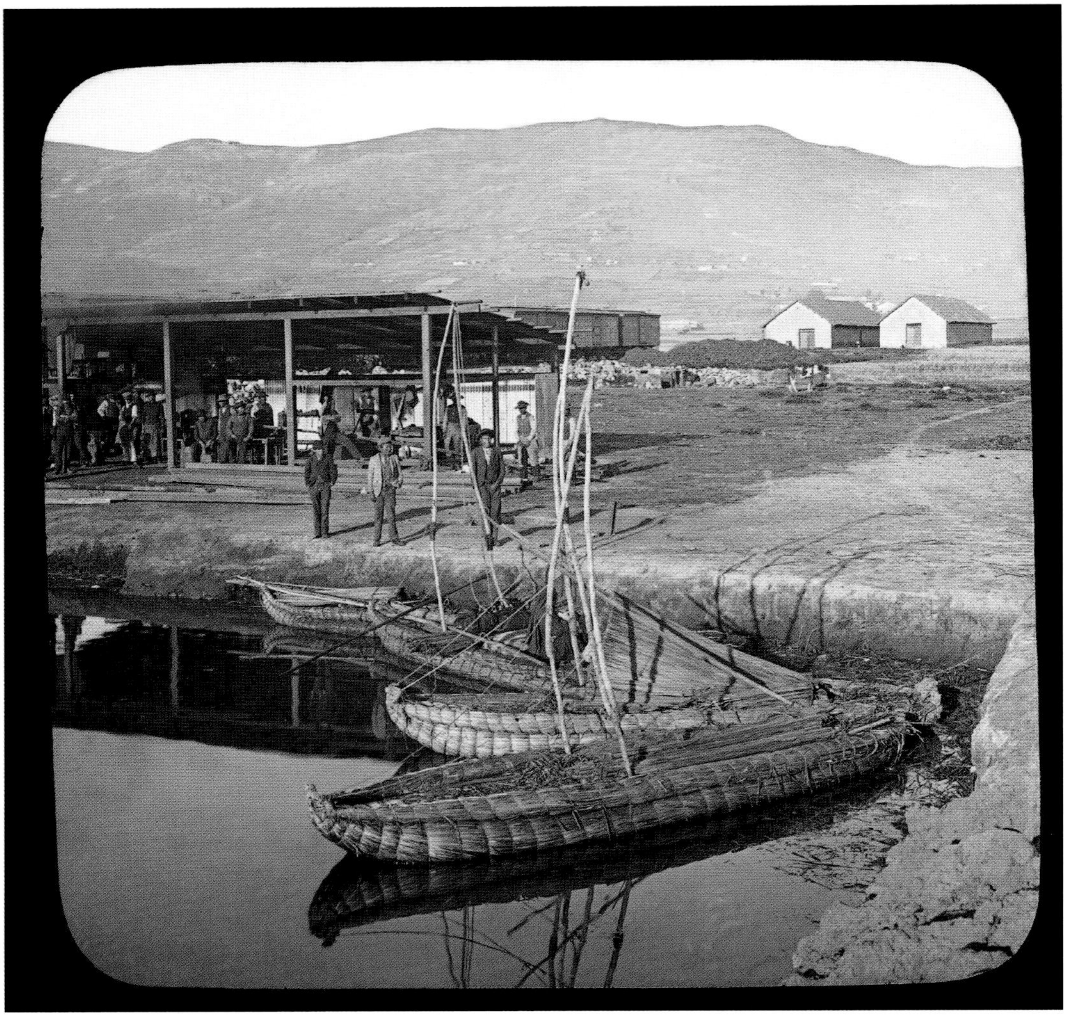

536 Straw boats on Lake Titicaca, Peru, 1890s
537 The Cofa Bridge on the Oroya Railway, Peru, 1890s

536 Strohboote auf dem Titicacasee, Peru, 1890er Jahre
537 Die Cofa-Brücke der Eisenbahnlinie nach La Oroya, Peru, 1890er Jahre

536 Embarcations en paille sur le lac Titicaca, Pérou, années 1890
537 Viaduc de Cofa sur la ligne de chemin de fer d'Oroya, Pérou, années 1890

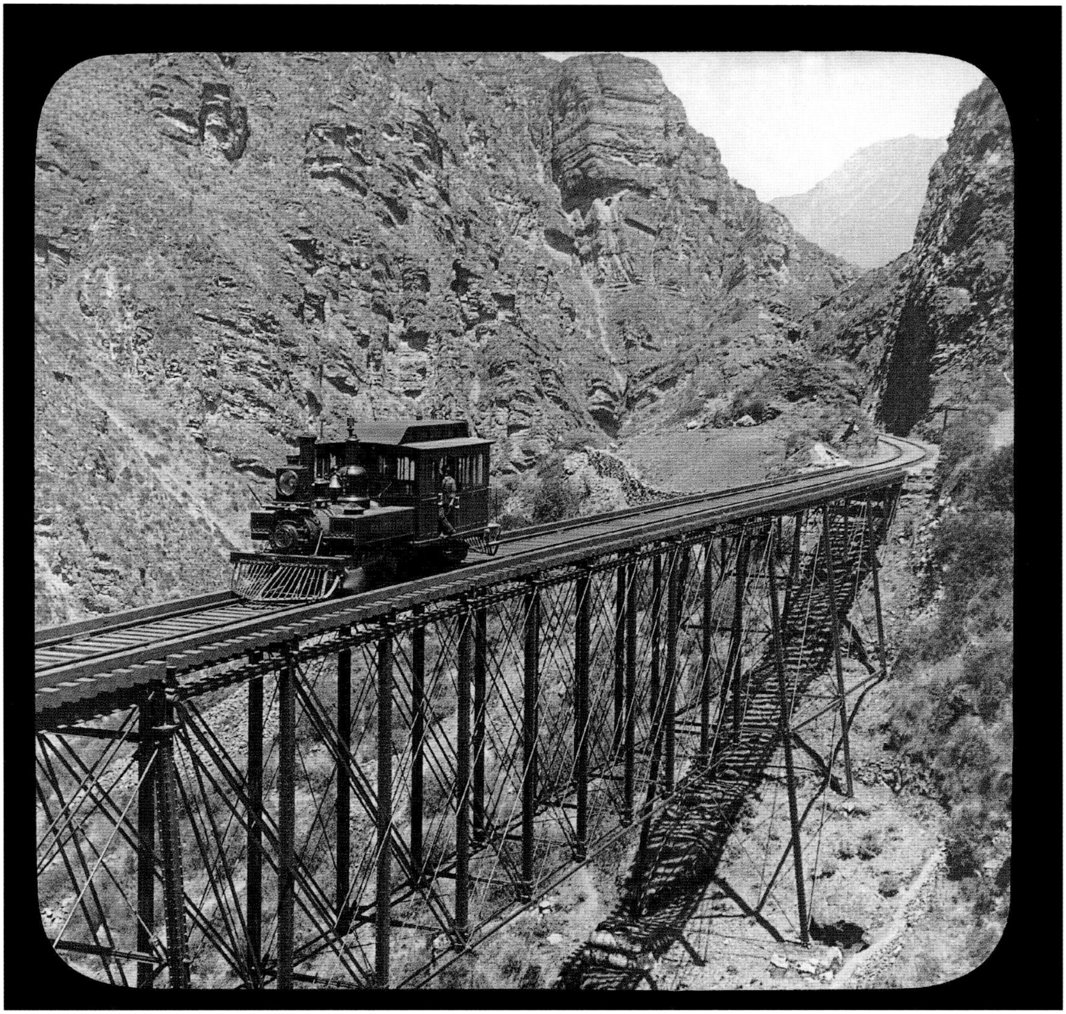

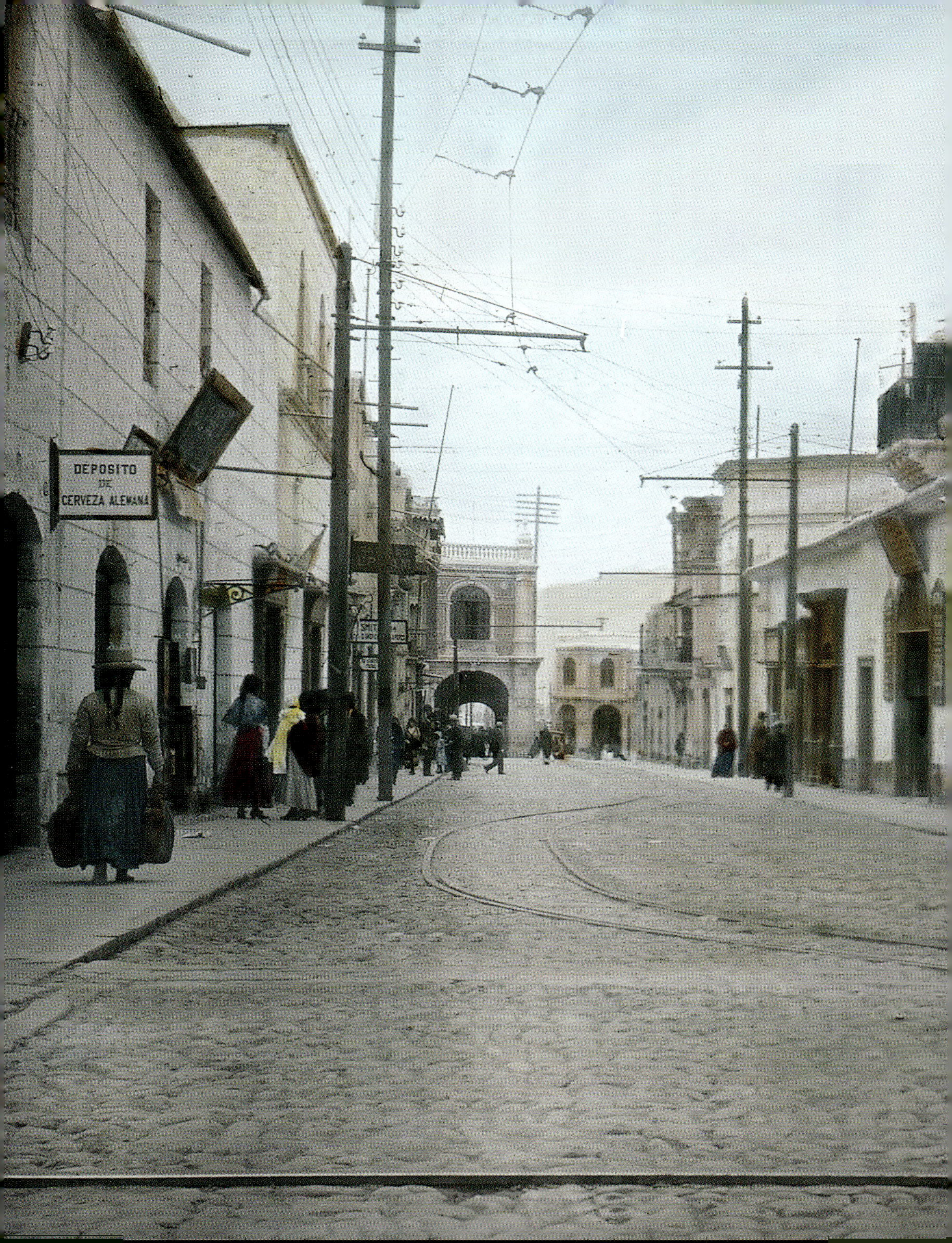
DEPOSITO
DE
CERVEZA ALEMANA

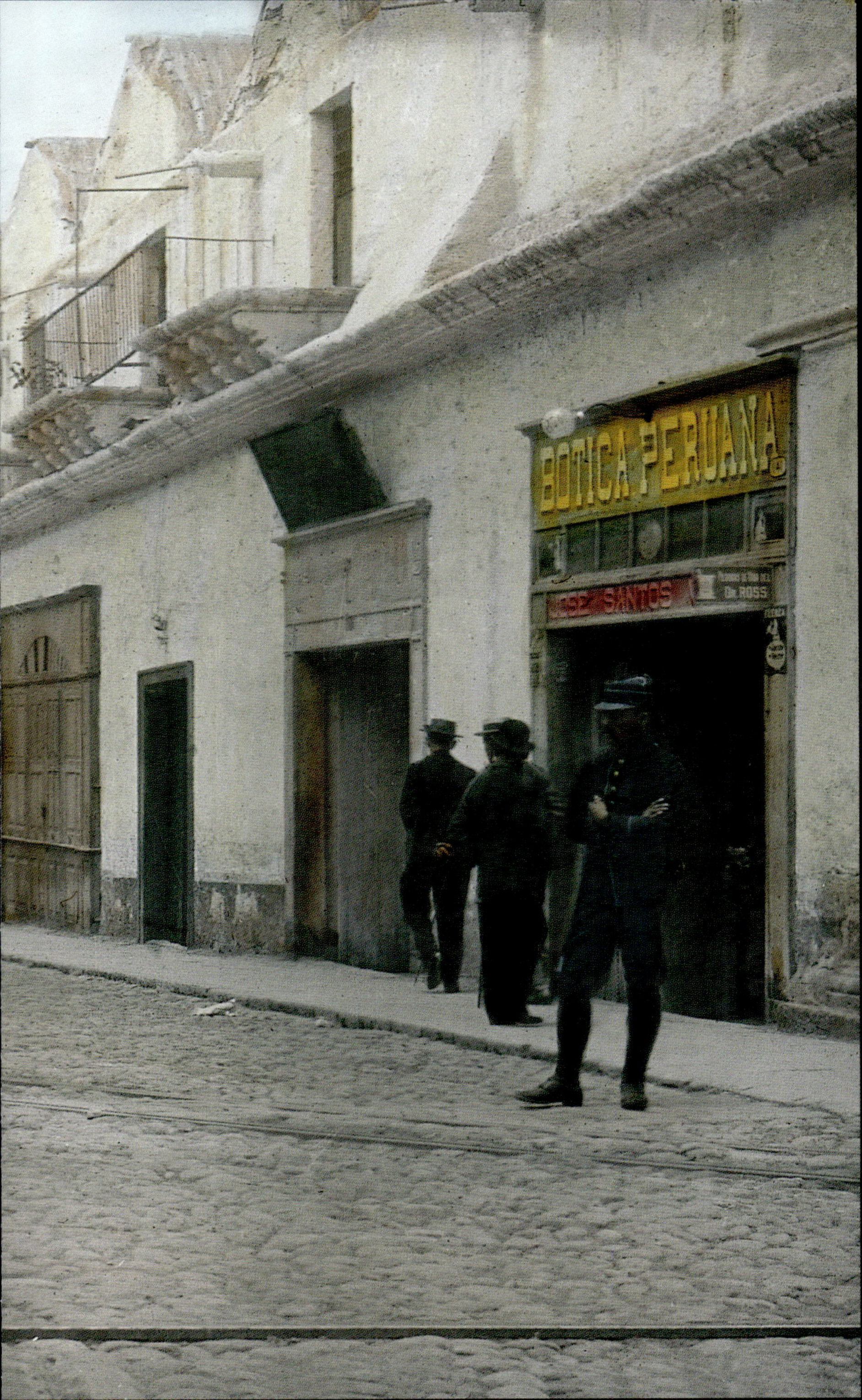

538 Street scene, Arequipa, Peru, 1900s

538 Straßenszene, Arequipa, Peru, 1900er Jahre

538 Rue d'Arequipa, Pérou, années 1900

539 Ice-crested Chimborazo mountain (20,498 feet from road to Quito), Ecuador, c.1900

539 Der mit Eis bedeckte Chimborazo (6.268 Meter, von der Straße nach Quito aus gesehen), Ecuador, um 1900

539 Le volcan Chimborazo enneigé (6 268 m.) vu depuis la route de Quito. Équateur, vers 1900

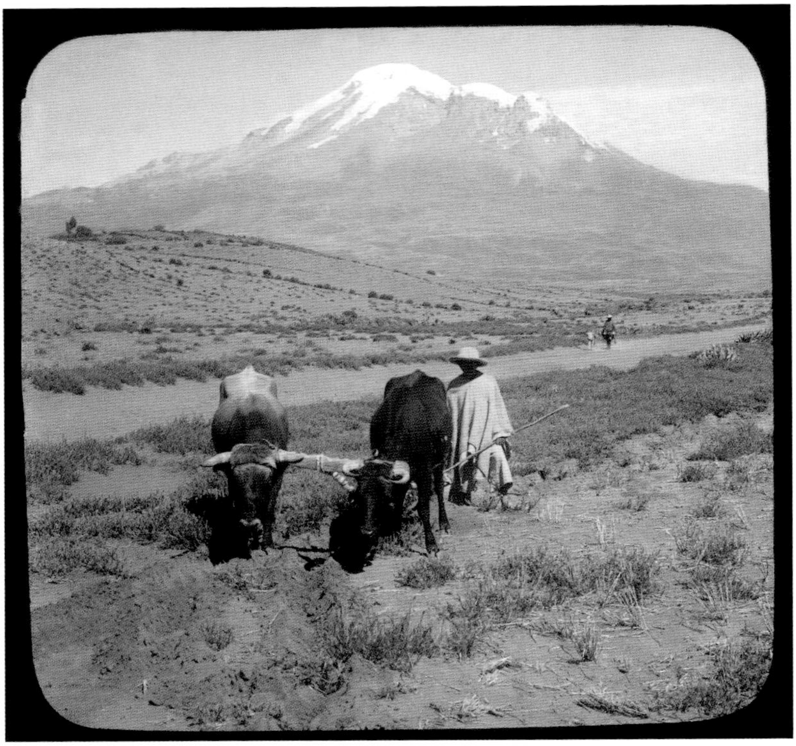

540 Schoolroom full of boys at Guayaquil, Ecuador, 1910s

540 Ein Schulraum voller Jungen in Guayaquil, Ecuador, 1910er Jahre

540 Salle de l'école de garçons de Guayaquil, Équateur, années 1910

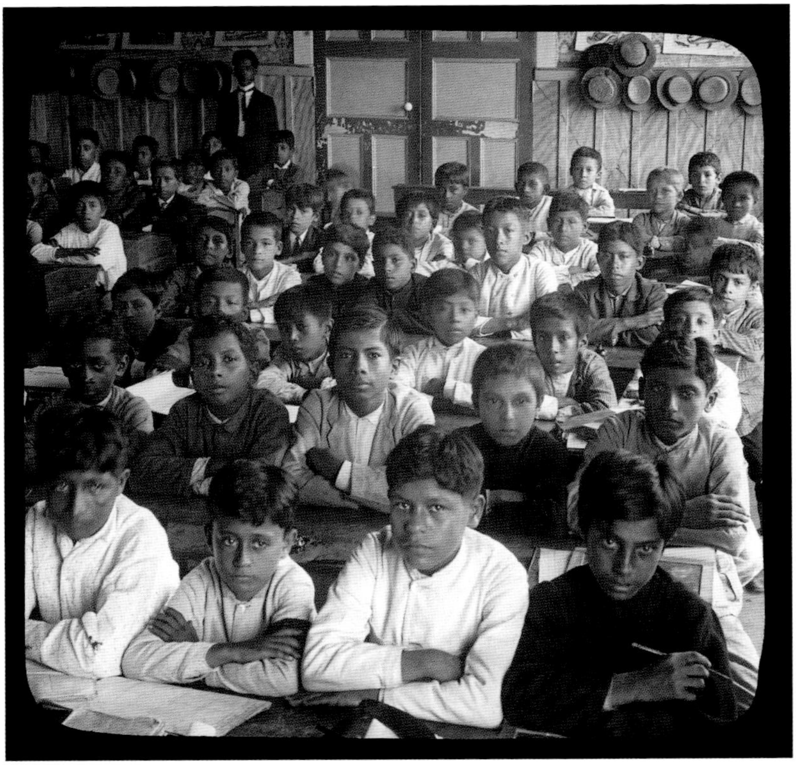

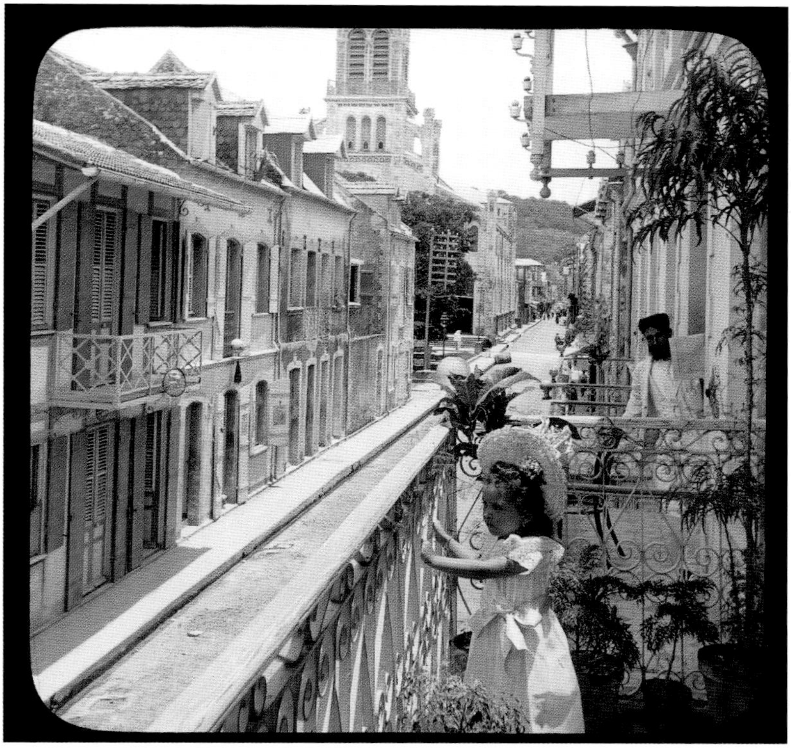

541 Charming Spanish Maiden on Balcony, Guayaquil, Ecuador, 1920

541 Bezauberndes spanisches Mädchen auf einem Balkon, Guayaquil, Ecuador, 1920

541 Charmante fillette espagnole au balcon, Guayaquil, Équateur, 1920

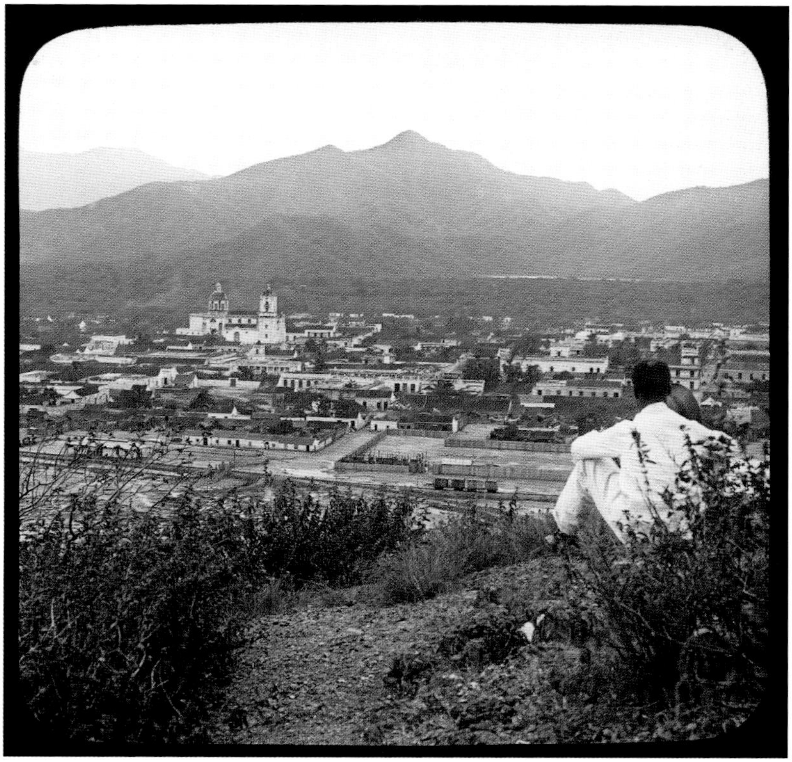

542 Santa Marta (centre of the banana industry), Colombia, 1920s

542 Santa Marta (Zentrum der Bananen-Industrie), Kolumbien, 1920er Jahre

542 Santa Marta (centre de l'industrie bananière), Colombie, années 1920

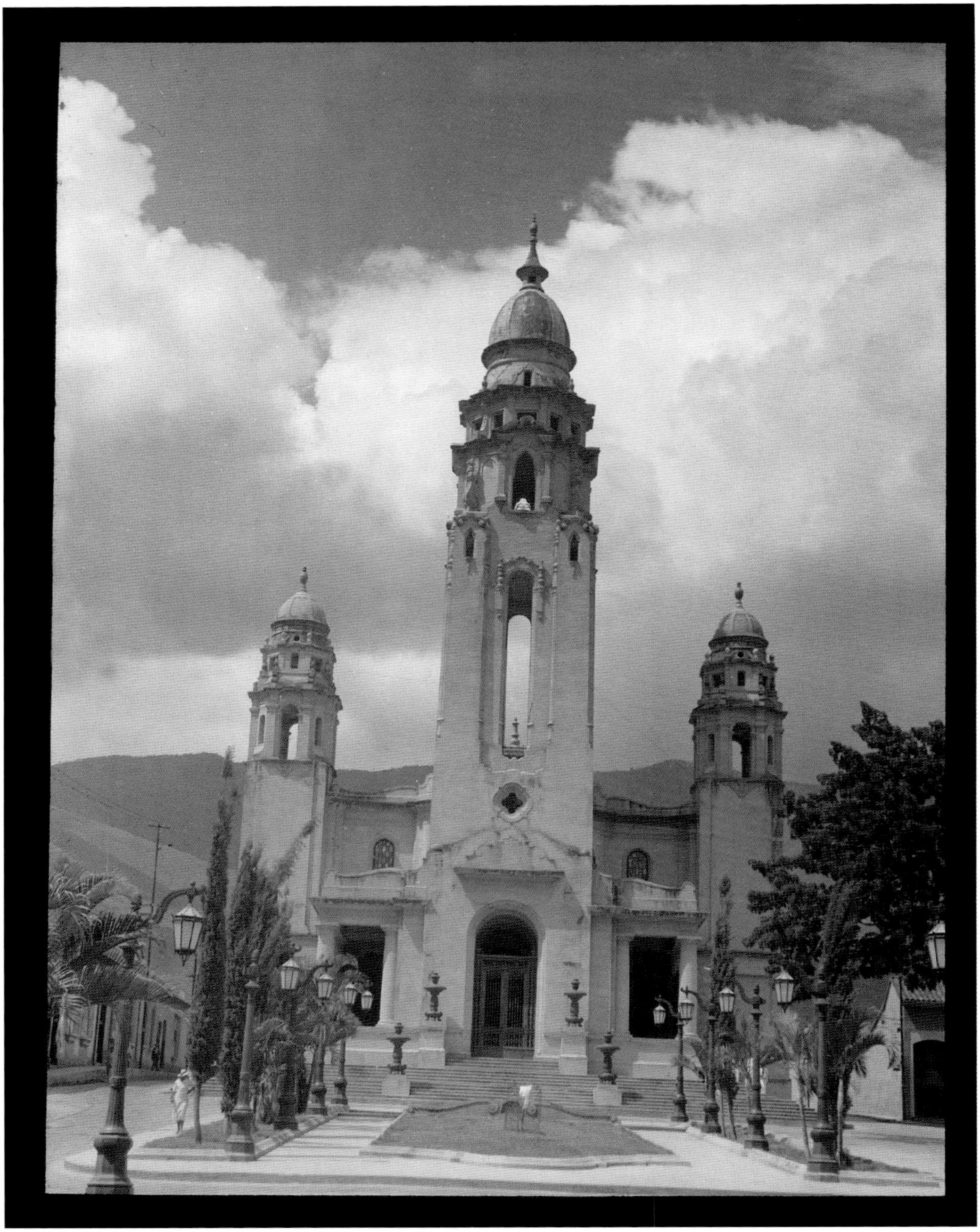

543 The Panthéon, Caracas, Venezuela, 1920s
544 Delivering bread, Caracas, Venezuela, 1880s

543 Das Pantheon, Caracas, Venezuela, 1920er Jahre
544 Die Anlieferung von Brot, Caracas, Venezuela, 1880er Jahre

543 Le Panthéon, Caracas, Vénézuéla, années 1920
544 Livraison du pain, Caracas, Vénézuéla, années 1880

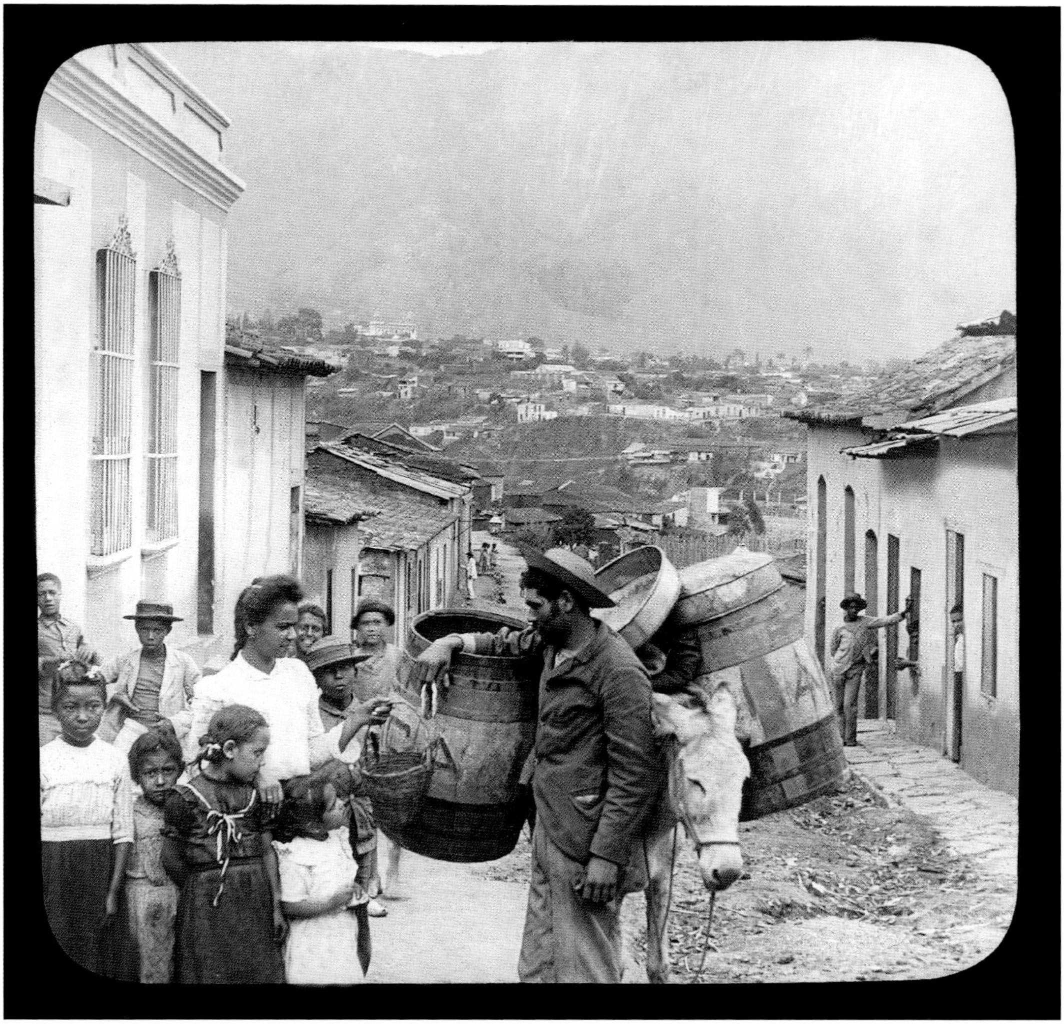

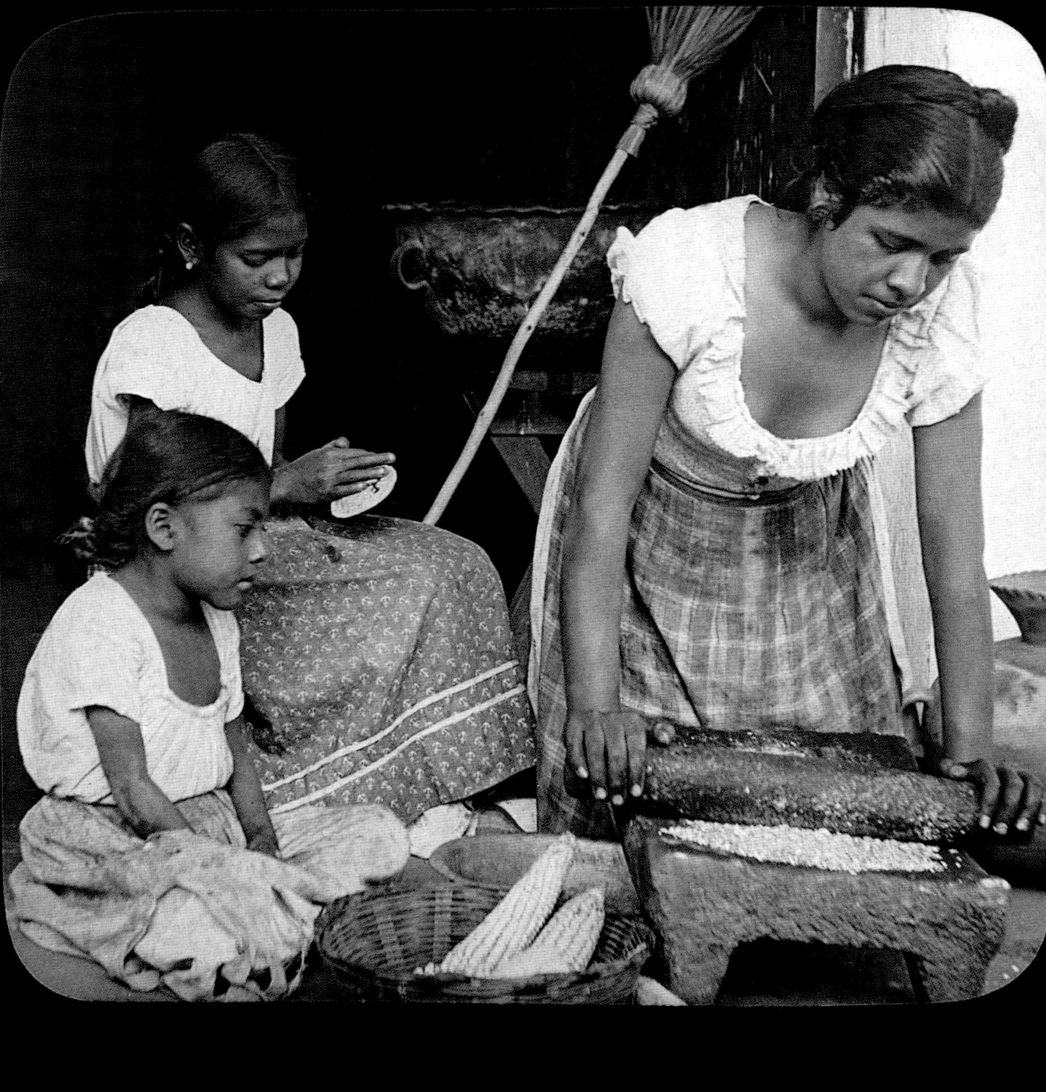

545 Tortilla making, El Salvador, 1900s

545 Die Zubereitung einer Tortilla, El Salvador, 1900er Jahre

545 Préparation de tortillas. Salvador, années 1900

CENTRAL AMERICA

MITTELAMERIKA · AMÉRIQUE CENTRALE

546 Dwellings built for French settlers, Colon, Panama, c.1900

546 Unterkünfte für französische Siedler, Colón, Panama, um 1900

546 Demeure de colons français à Colon, Panama, vers 1900

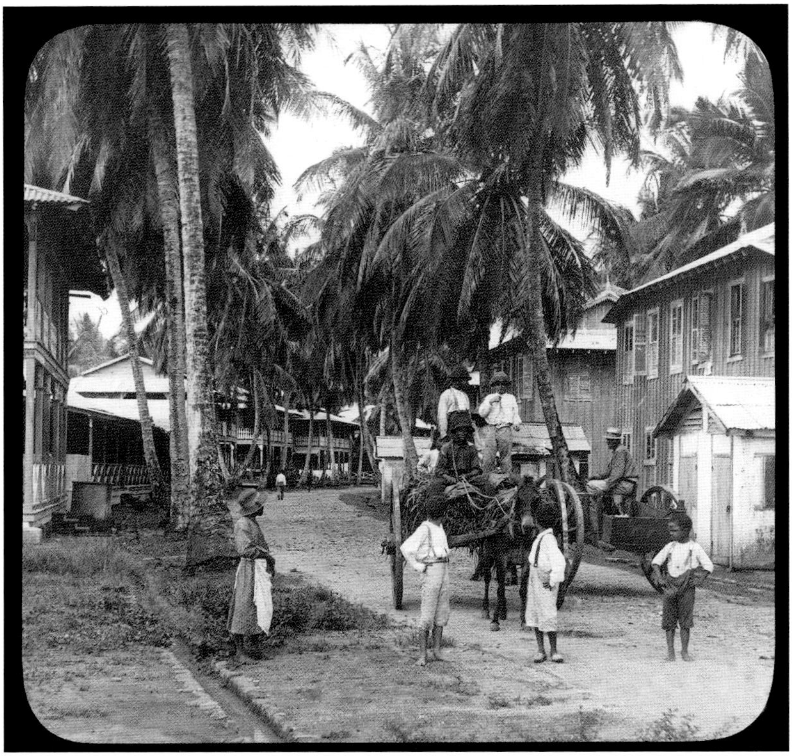

547 The Beach Market in Panama City, Panama, c.1900

547 Der Strandmarkt in Panama-Stadt, Panama, um 1900

547 Marché de la plage Panama City, Panama, vers 1900

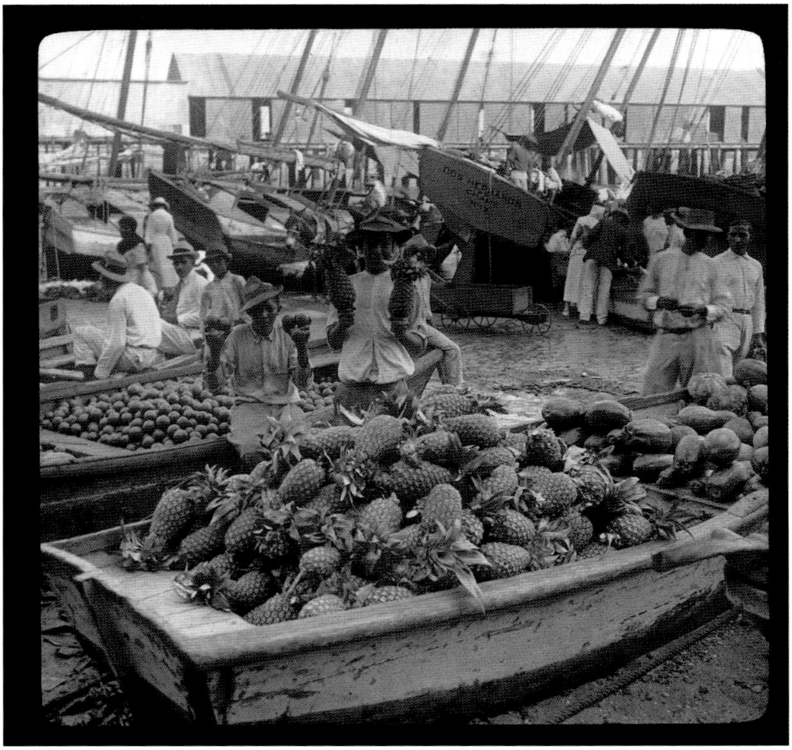

548 Children
carrying bananas,
Central America,
c.1900

548 Kinder
tragen Bananen,
Mittelamerika,
um 1900

548 Enfants
transportant des
bananes, Amérique
Centrale, vers 1900

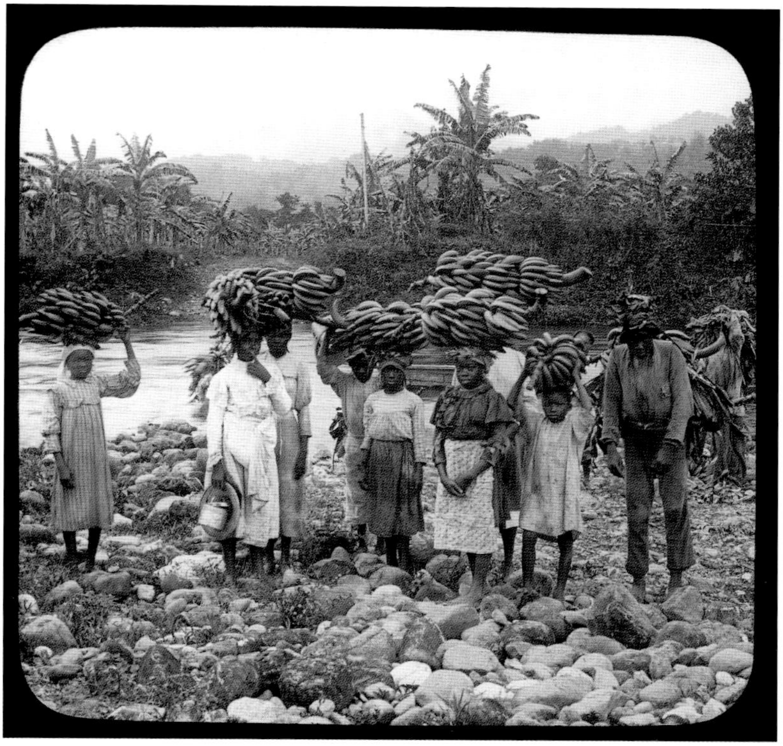

549 Harvesting
bananas, Costa Rica,
c.1900

549 Bananenernte,
Costa Rica, um 1900

549 Récolte des
bananes, Costa Rica,
vers 1900

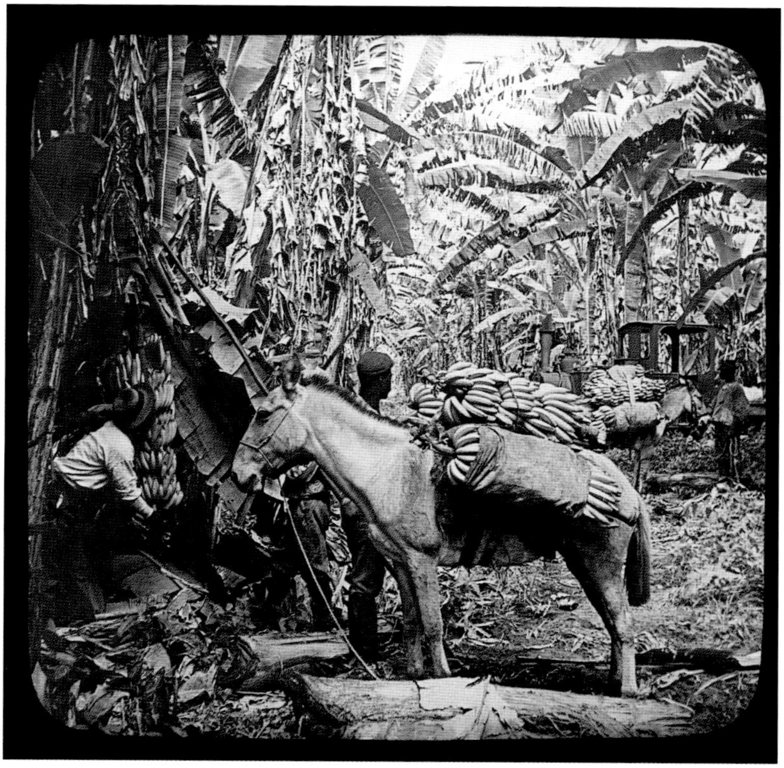

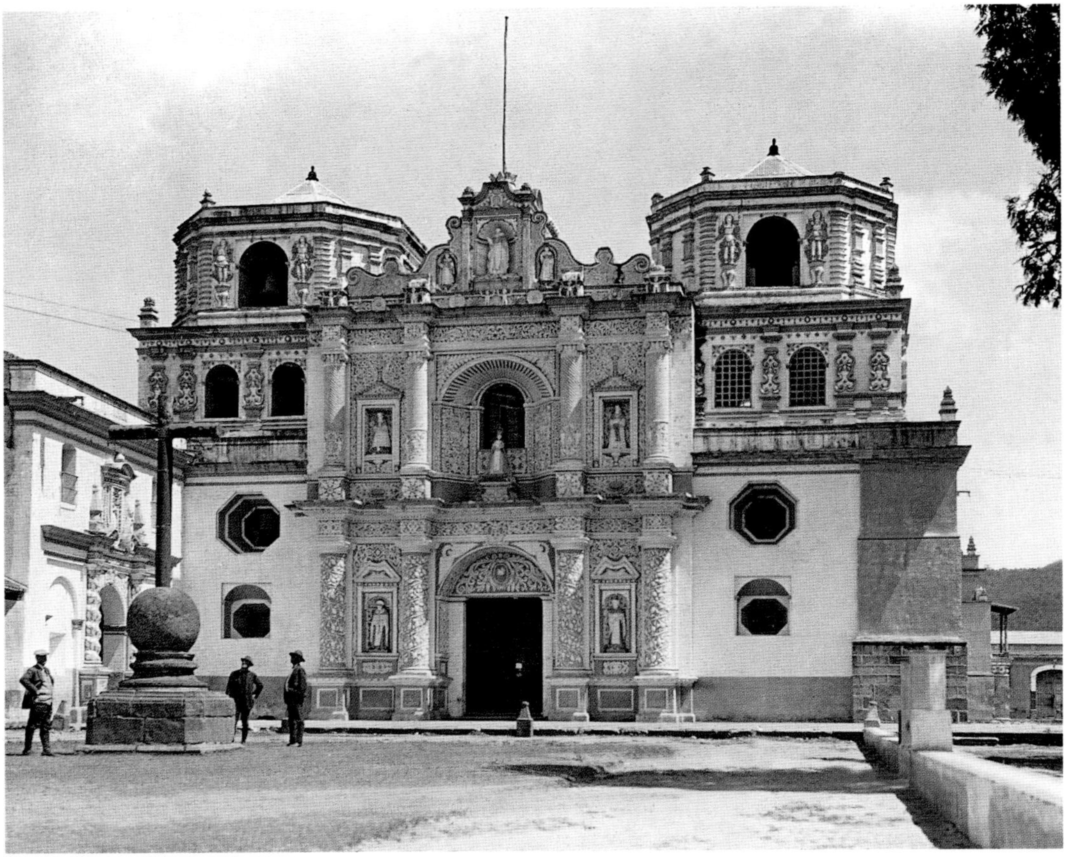

550 Nuestra Señora de la Merced church, Antigua, Guatemala, 1925
551 Escuintla and the twin volcanoes of Fuego and Acatenango, Guatemala, 1910s

550 Die Kirche Nuestra Señora de la Merced, Antigua, Guatemala, 1925
551 Escuintla und die Zwillingsvulkane Fuego und Acatenango, Guatemala, 1910er Jahre

550 Église Nuestra Señora de la Merced, Antigua, Guatemala, 1925
551 Escuintla et les volcans jumeaux de Fuego et Acatenango, Guatemala, années 1910

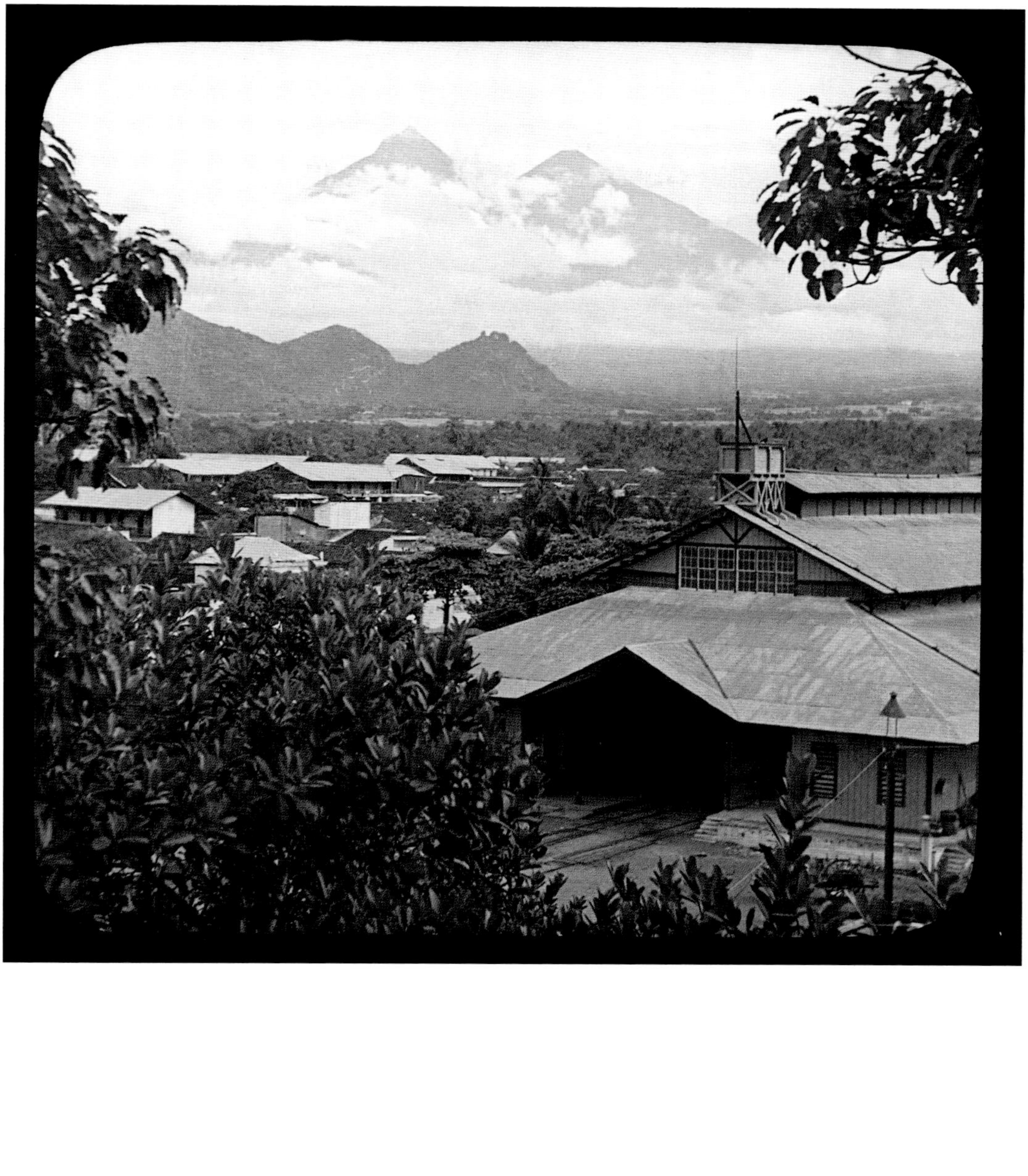

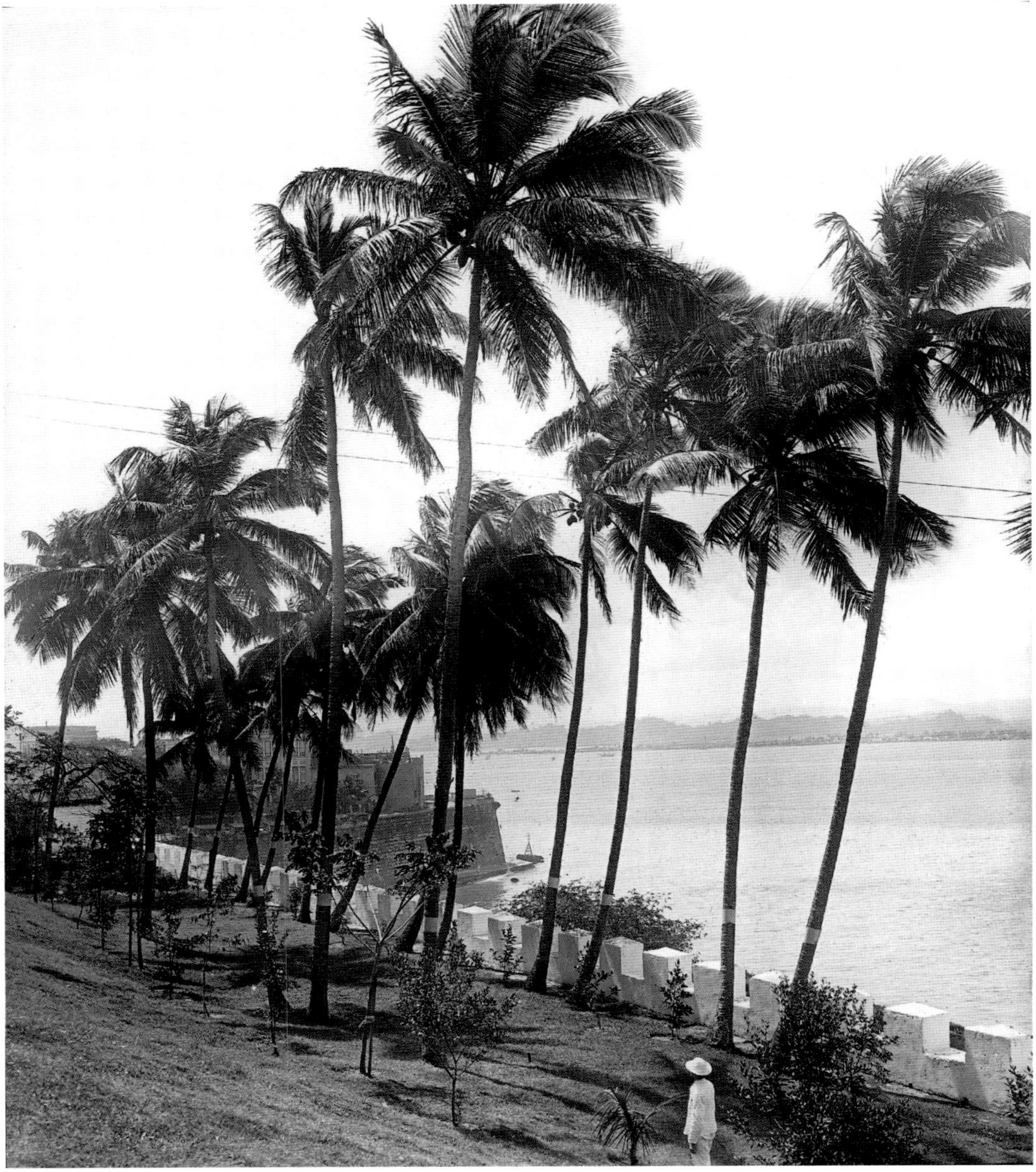

552 Grounds of the Military Governor's Residence, Casa Blanca, San Juan, Puerto Rico, 1910s

552 Parkanlagen der Residenz des Militärgouverneurs, Casa Blanca, San Juan, Puerto Rico, 1910er Jahre

552 Domaine de la résidence du Gouverneur militaire, Casa Blanca, San Juan, Porto-Rico, années 1910

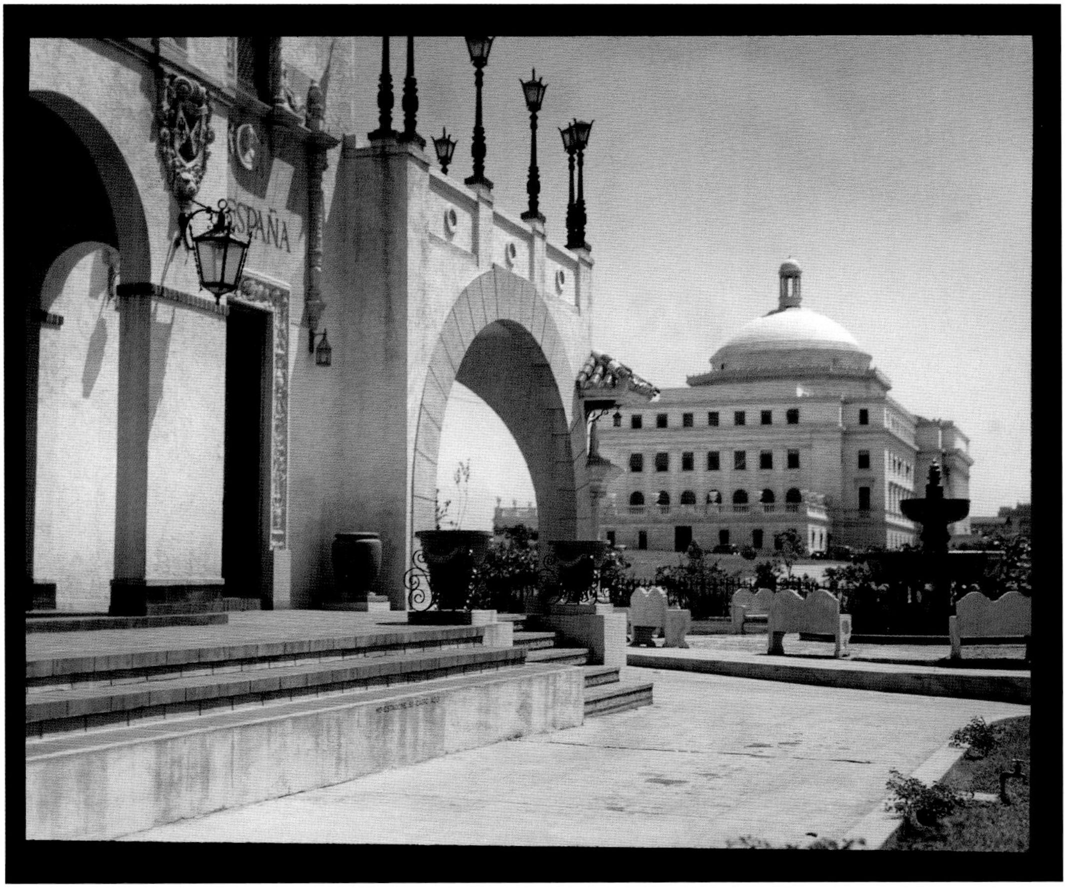

553 The Capitol Building and the Casa de España casino, San Juan, Puerto Rico, 1910s

553 Das Kapitol und das Kasino Casa de España, San Juan, Puerto Rico, 1910er Jahre

553 Le Capitole et le casino Casa de España, San Juan, Porto-Rico, années 1910

554 A Village in Central America, 1910s

554 Ein Dorf in Mittelamerika, 1910er Jahre

554 Village en Amérique Centrale, années 1910

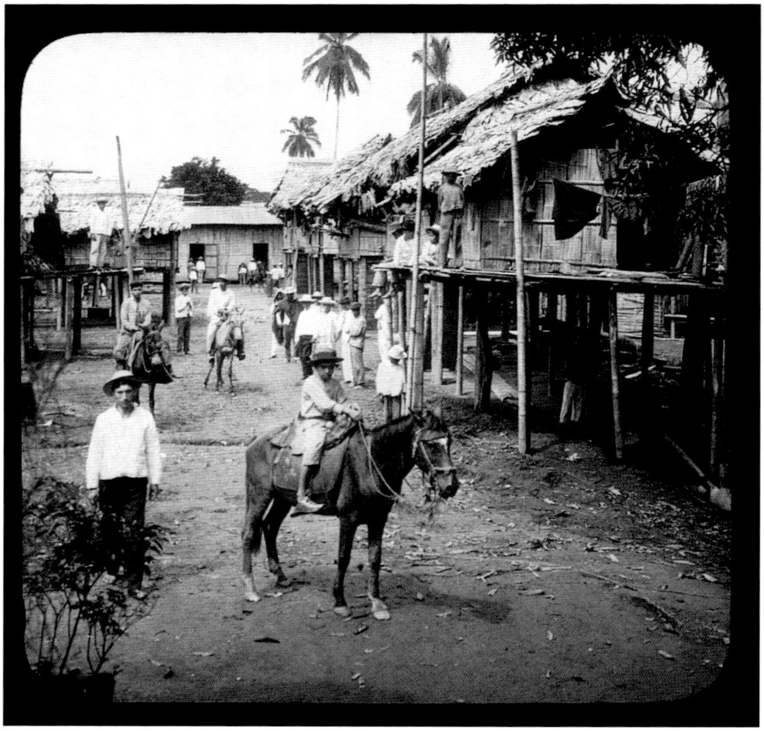

555 Sorting grapefruit, Puerto Rico, 1900s

555 Sortieren von Grapefruits, Puerto Rico, 1900er Jahre

555 Tri des pamplemousses, Porto-Rico, années 1900

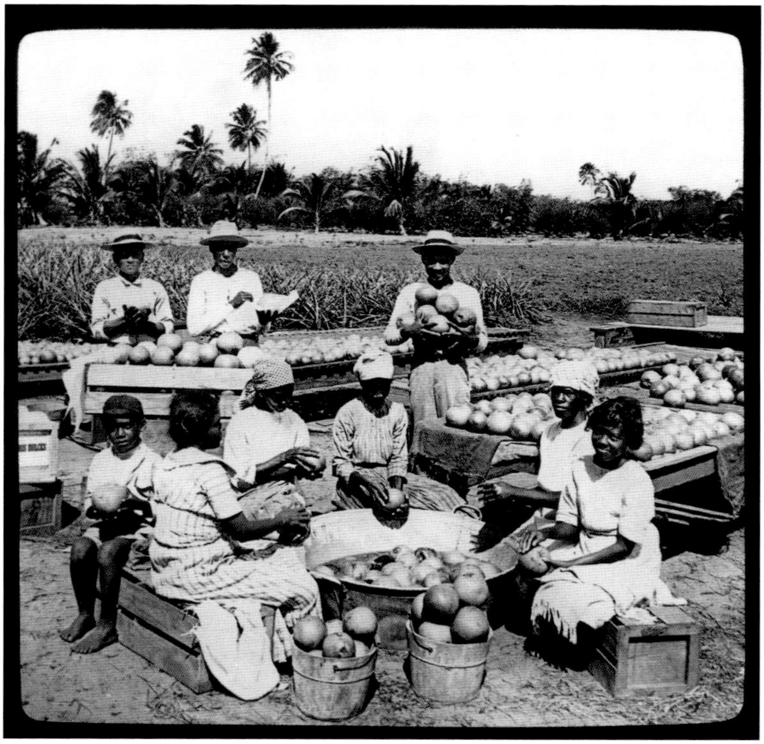

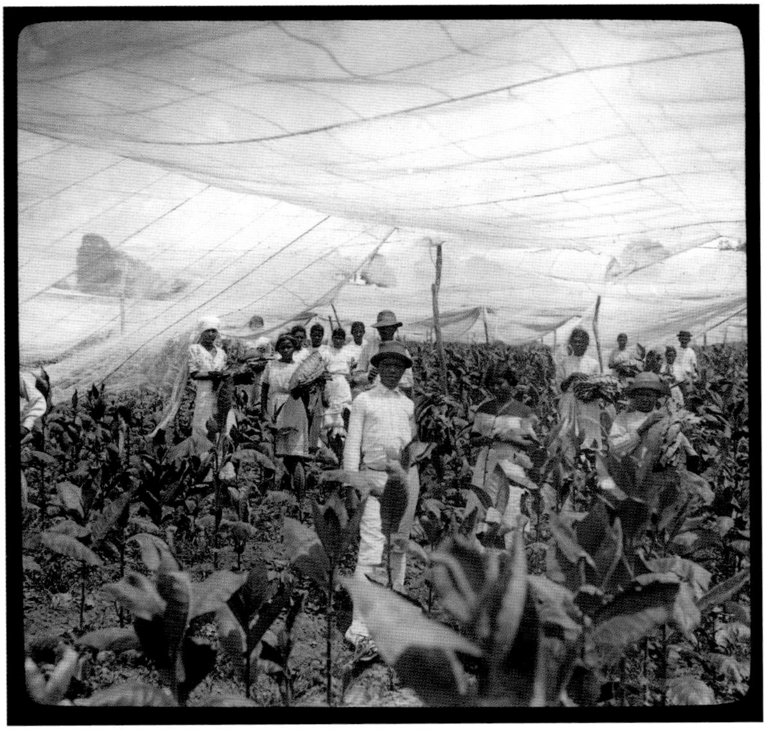

556 Growing tobbaco under cheesecloth to produce the finest leaves for the final wrapping of cigars, Puerto Rico, 1910s

556 Tabakanbau unter Schleiernesseln zur Herstellung der feinsten Blätter für die Deckblätter von Zigarren, Puerto Rico, 1910er Jahre

556 Culture du tabac sous du crépon afin de produire les feuilles les plus fines pour la cape des cigares, Porto-Rico, années 1910

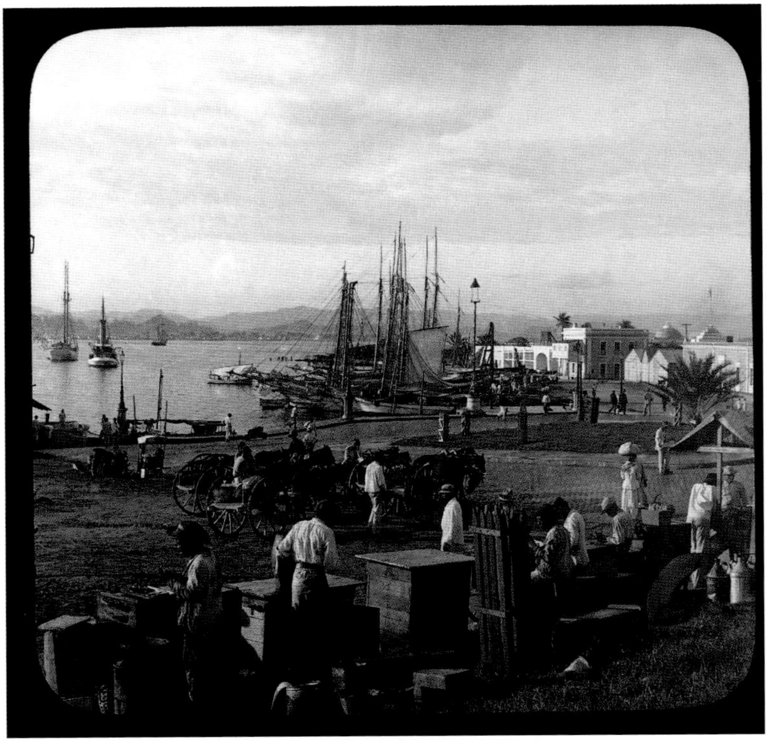

557 Overlooking the harbour, San Juan, Puerto Rico, 1900s

557 Hafenansicht, San Juan, Puerto Rico, 1900er Jahre

557 Vue du port de San Juan, Porto-Rico, années 1900

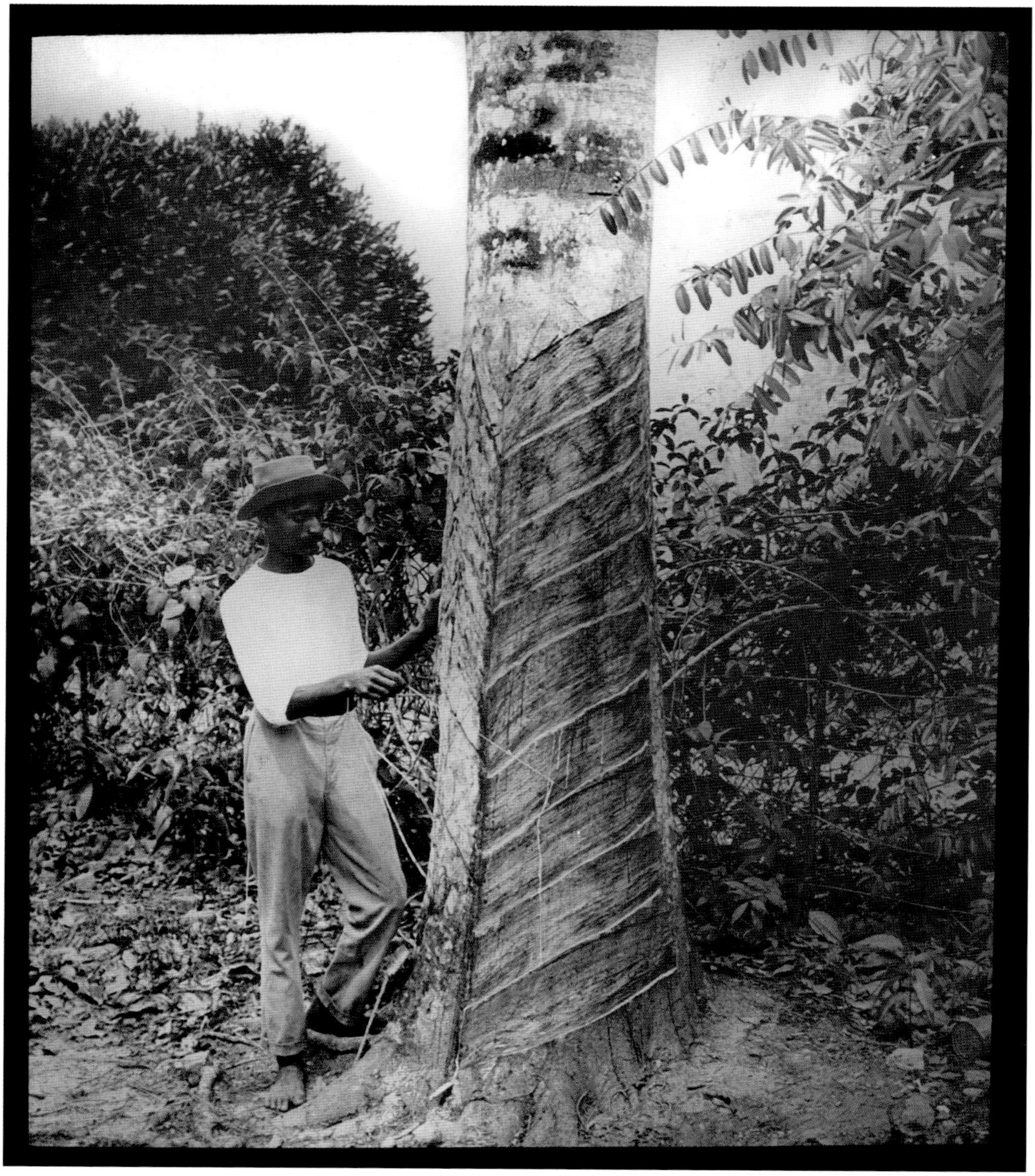

558 Rubber tree, showing the incisions from which the gum runs into a cup at the bottom of the tree, Trinidad, c.1900

558 Kautschukbaum, bei dem die Einschnitte sichtbar sind, aus denen der Kautschuk in ein Gefäß am Fuß des Baumes fließt, Trinidad, um 1900

558 Arbre à caoutchouc, Trinidad, vers 1900. Les saignées d'où le latex coule jusqu'au gobelet, au pied de l'arbre, sont visibles

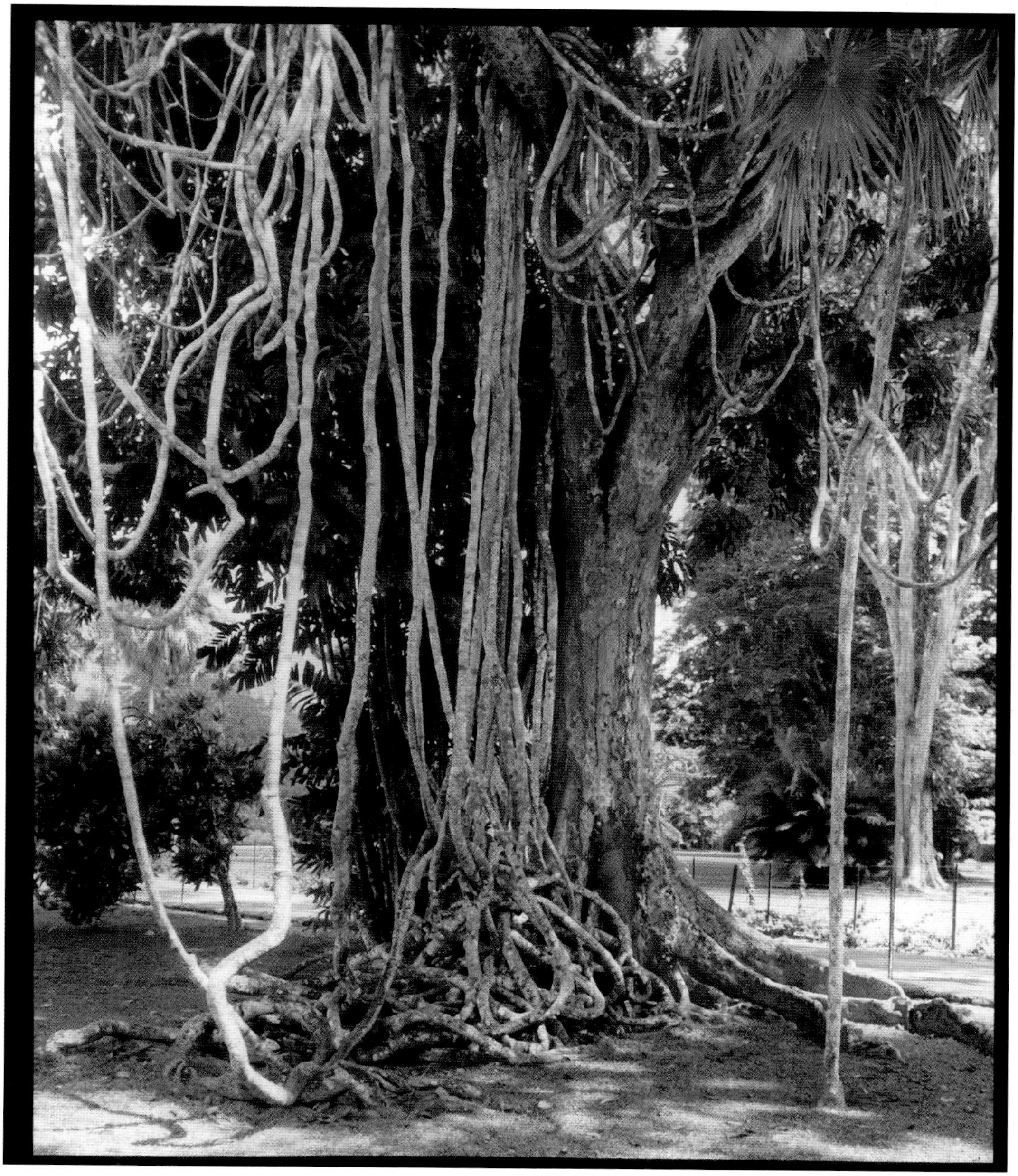

559 Cable-like llanas growing around the trunk of a large cottonwood tree (ceiba), Botanical Gardens, Port-au-Spain, Trinidad, c.1900

559 Kabelartige Lianen wachsen um den Stamm eines großen Baumwollbaums (Ceiba), Botanischer Garten, Port of Spain, Trinidad, um 1900

559 Lianes poussant autour du tronc d'un grand cotonnier (ceiba), Jardin botanique, Port d'Espagne, Trinidad, vers 1900

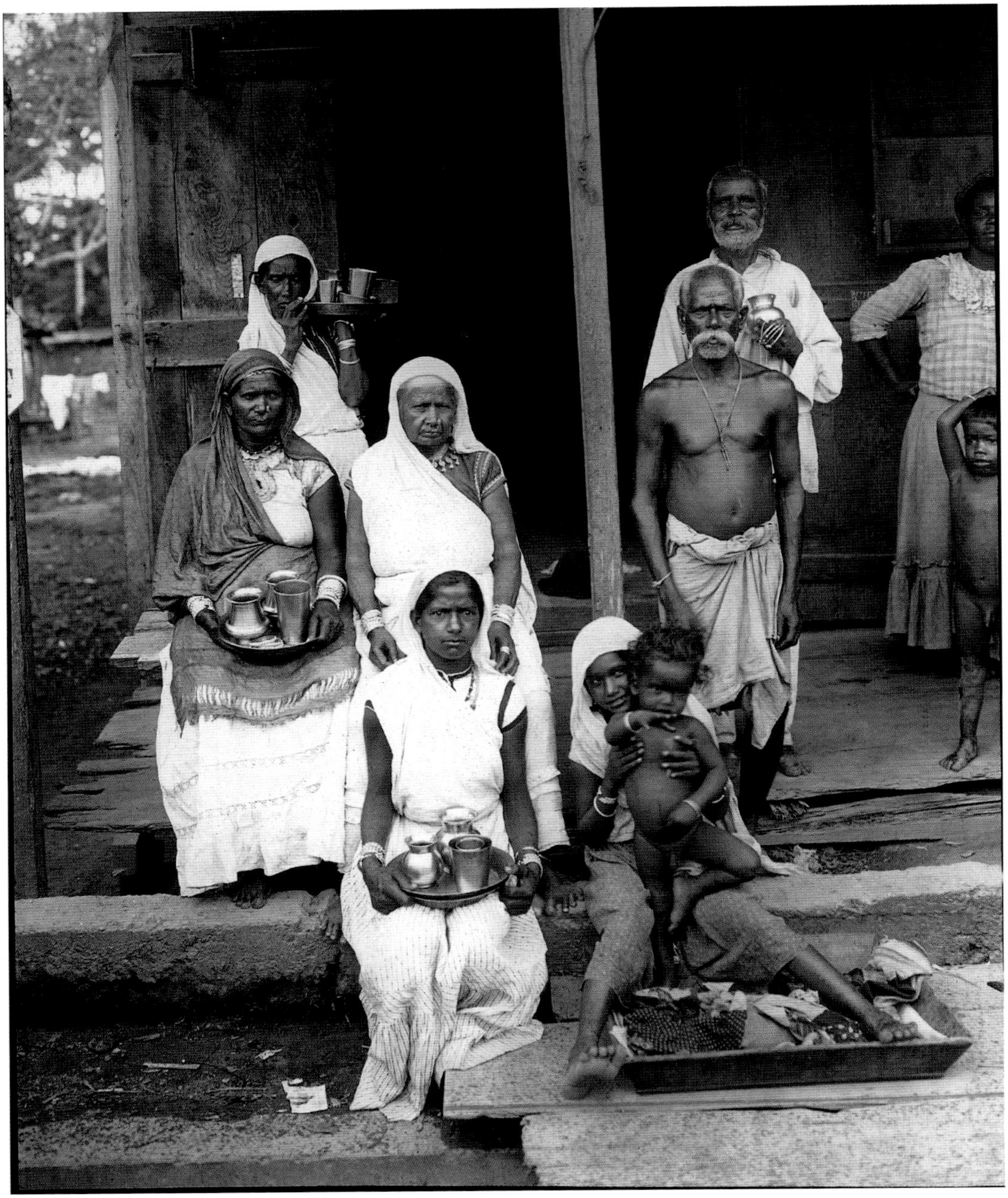

560 Hindu family,
Port-au-Spain, Trinidad,
1900s, during the East
Indian Famines many
thousands of Hindus were
"imported" to work on
the plantations

560 Hindu-Familie,
Port of Spain, Trinidad,
1900er Jahre. Während der
Hungersnöte in Ostindien
wurden viele tausende
Hindus „importiert", zu
arbeiten

560 Famille hindoue,
Port d'Espagne, Trinidad,
années 1900. Pendant
la famine dans l'est de
l'Inde, des milliers d'hin-
dous furent « importés »
pour travailler

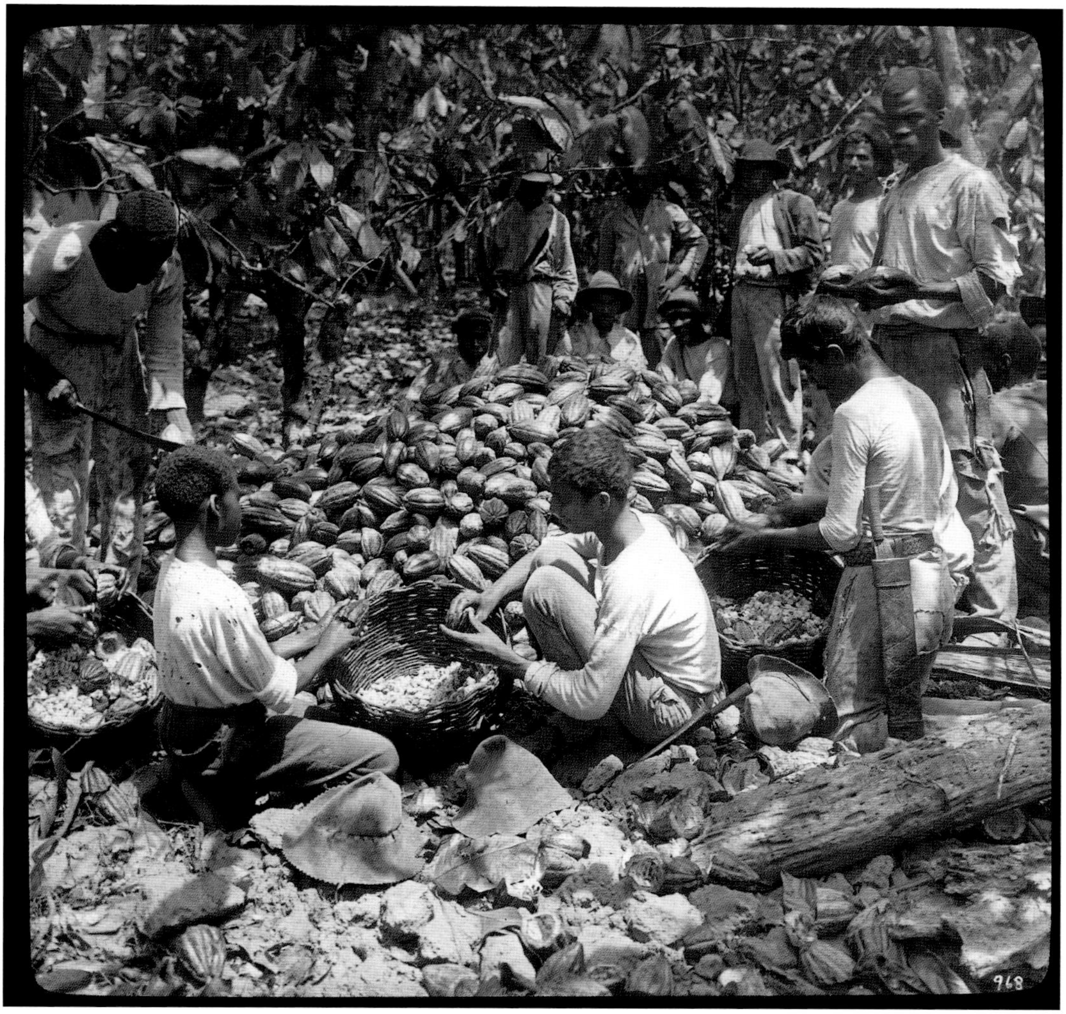

561 Husking cocoa, Trinidad, 1900s

561 Die Enthülsung von Kakaobohnen, Trinidad, 1900er Jahre

561 Épluchage des cocos, Trinidad, années 1900

562 Coffee pickers at work, Guadeloupe, Carribean, 1900s

562 Kaffeepflücker bei der Arbeit, Guadeloupe, Karibik, 1900er Jahre

562 Cueillette du café, Guadeloupe, Antilles, années 1900

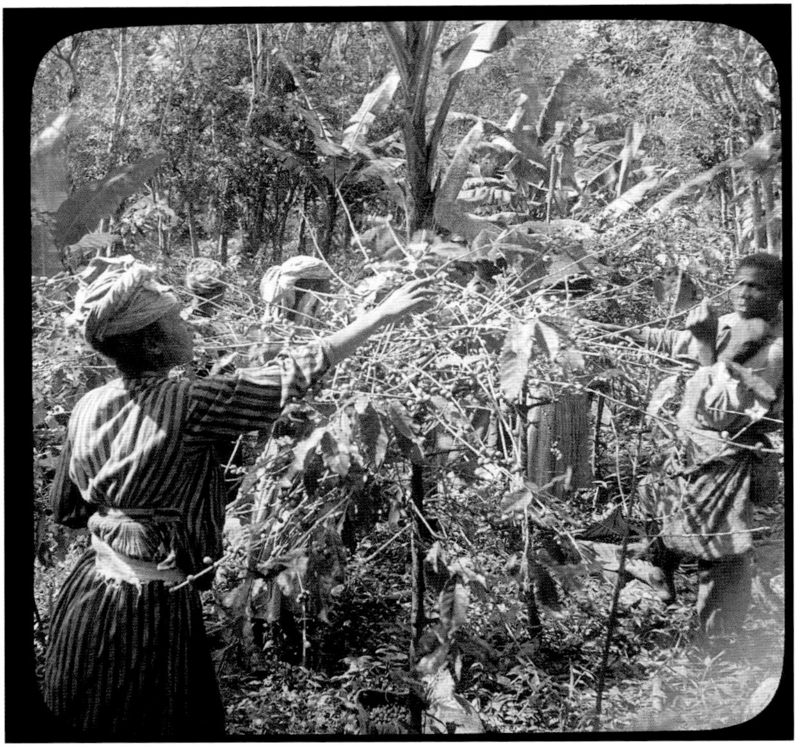

563 Woman selling fruit and vegetables in the marketplace, Kingston, Jamaica, 1900s

563 Eine Frau verkauft Obst und Gemüse auf dem Marktplatz, Kingston, Jamaika, 1900er Jahre

563 Vendeuse de fruits et légumes sur la place du marché de Kingston, Jamaïque, années 1900

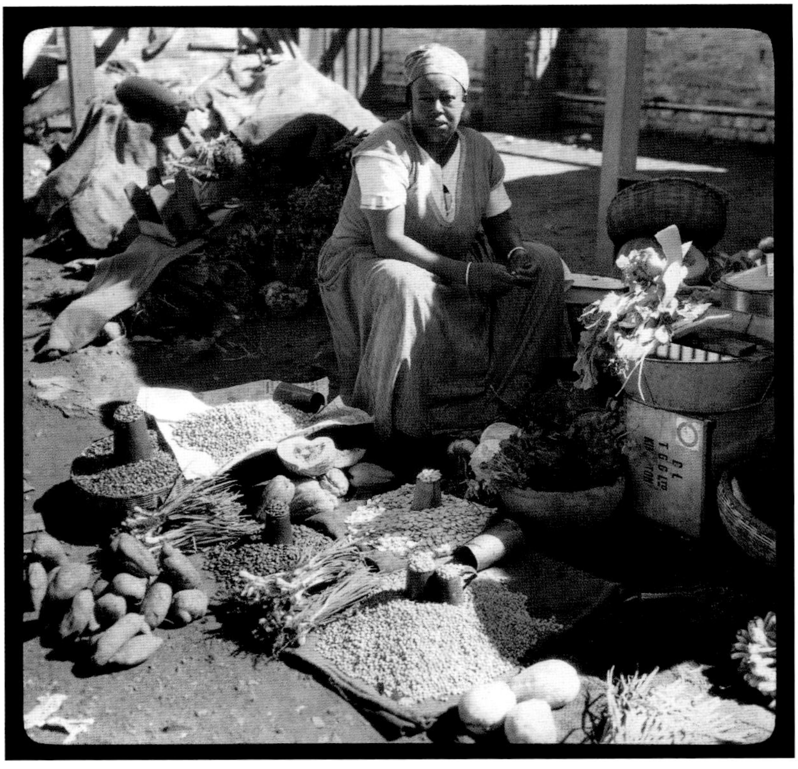

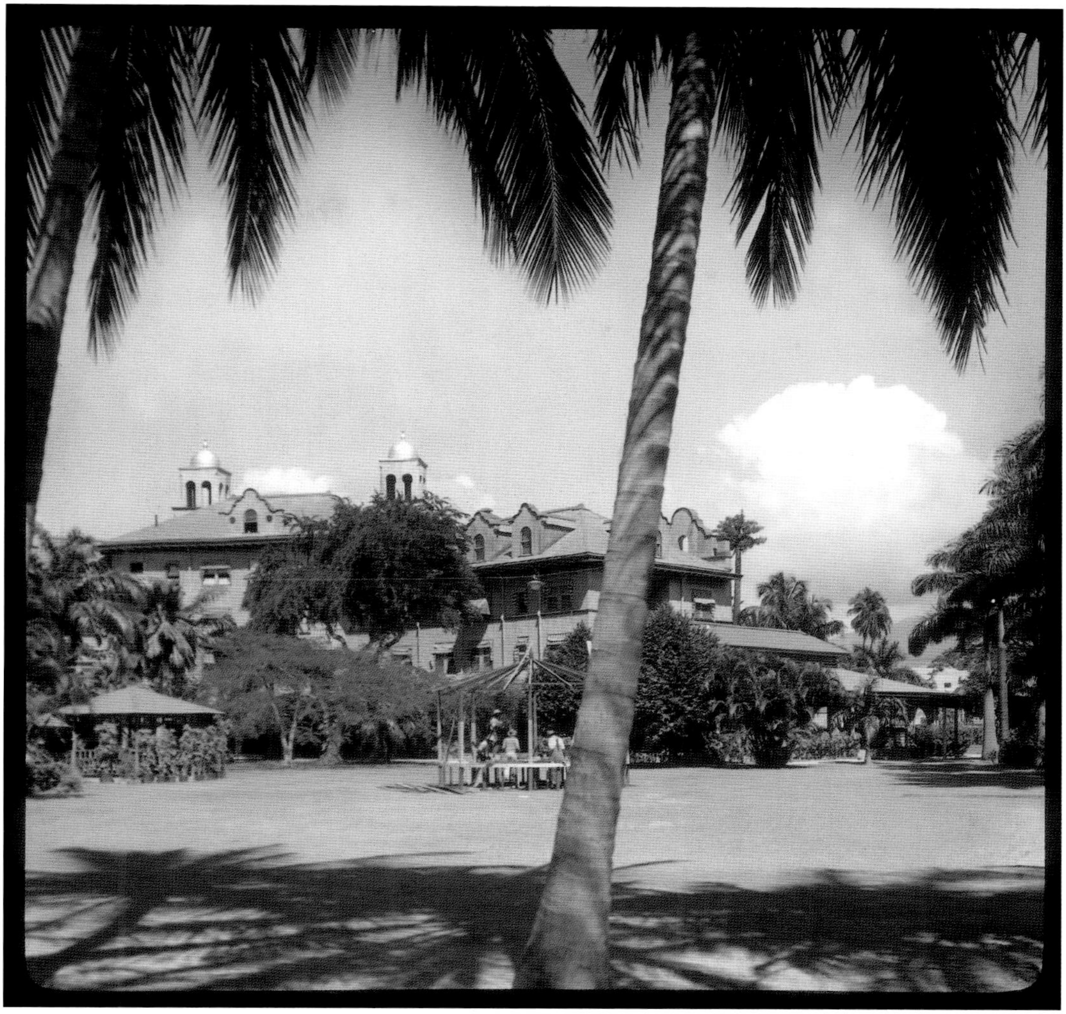

564 The grounds of Myrtle Bank Hotel, Kingston, Jamaica, 1910s

564 Die Parkanlagen des Myrtle-Bank-Hotels, Kingston, Jamaika, 1910er Jahre

564 Domaine du Myrtle Bank Hotel, Kingston, Jamaïque, années 1910

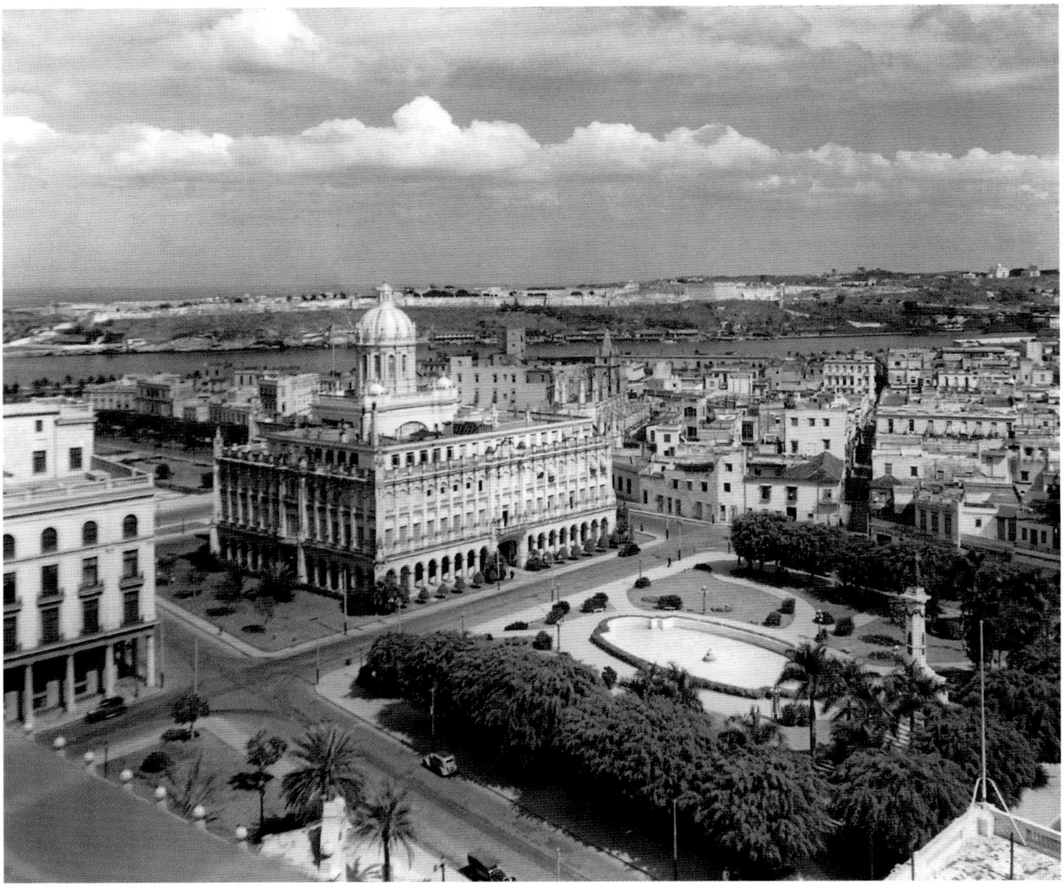

565 View of the Presidential Palace, Havana, Cuba, c.1930
566 Catedral de San Cristóbal, Havana, Cuba, 1910s

565 Ansicht des Präsidentenpalasts, Havanna, Kuba, um 1930
566 Die Kathedrale San Cristóbal, Havanna, Kuba, 1910er Jahre

565 Vue du palais présidentiel, La Havane, Cuba, vers 1930
566 Cathédrale San Cristóbal, La Havane, Cuba, années 1910

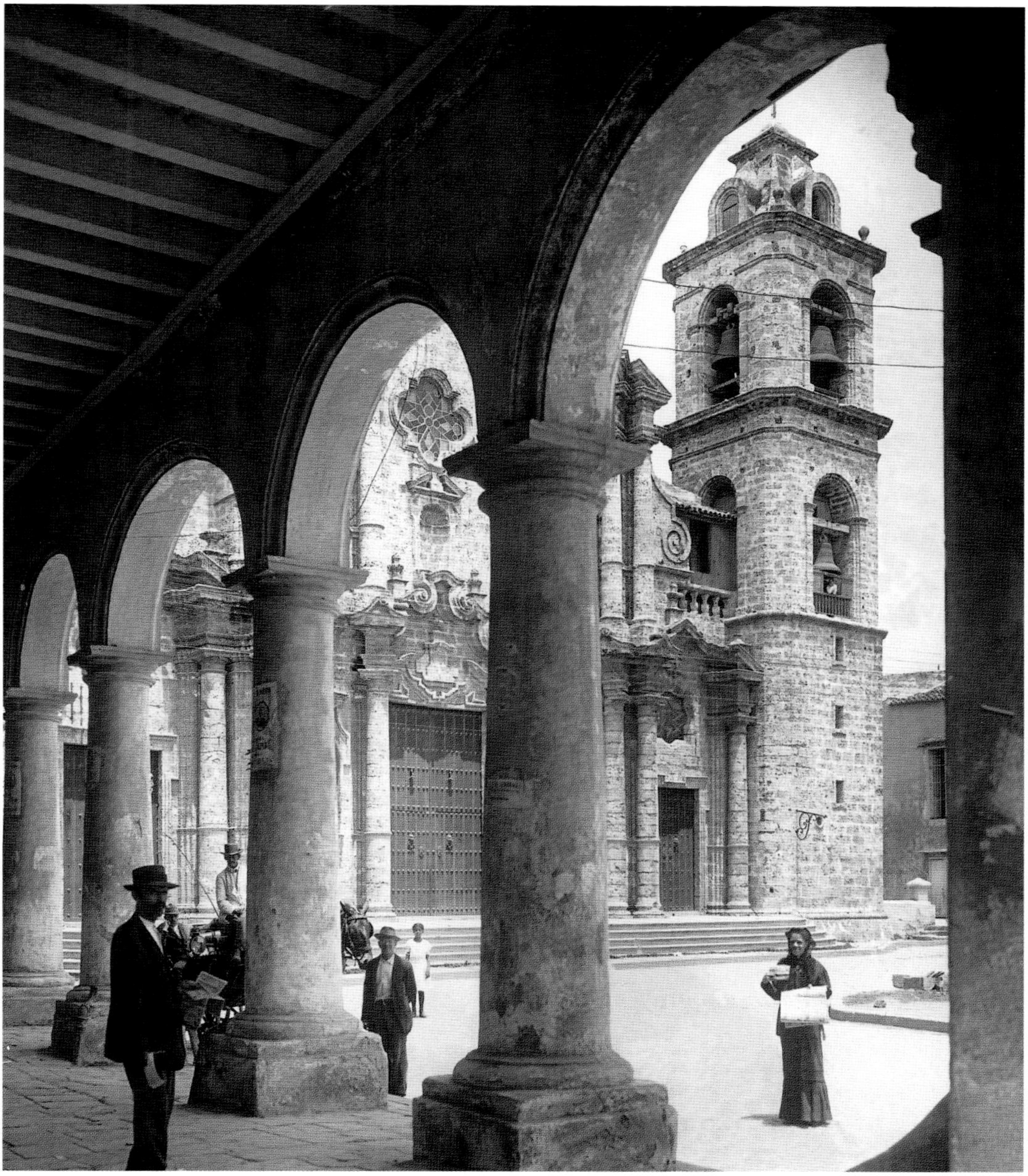

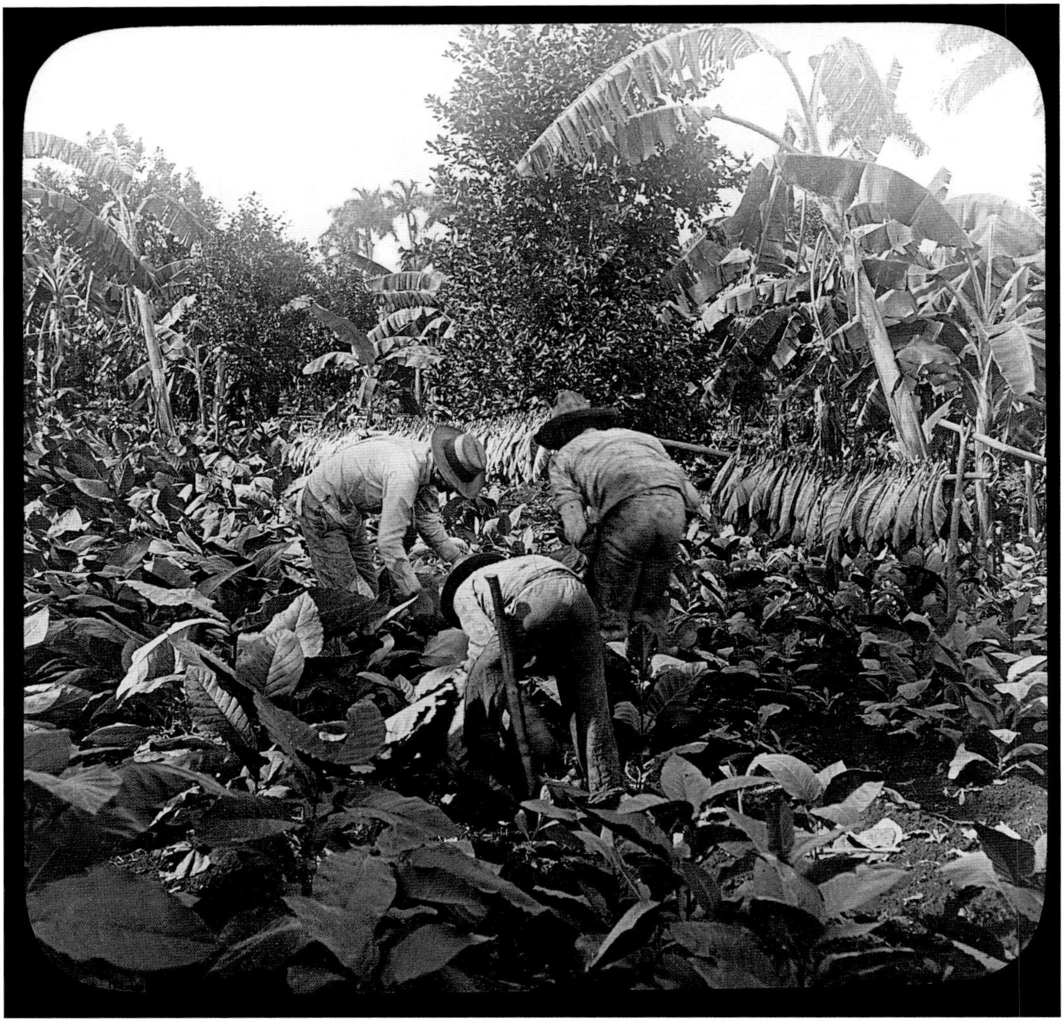

567 Cutting tobacco, Province of Havana, Cuba, 1910s
568 Coffee from Puerto Rico being off-loaded onto Havana Wharf, Cuba, 1910s

567 Tabakschneiden, Provinz Havanna, Kuba, 1910er Jahre
568 Kaffee aus Puerto Rico wird an den Kais von Havanna ausgeladen, Kuba, 1910er Jahre

567 Coupe du tabac, Province de La Havane, Cuba, années 1910
568 Café de Porto-Rico déchargé sur le quai de La Havane, Cuba, années 1910

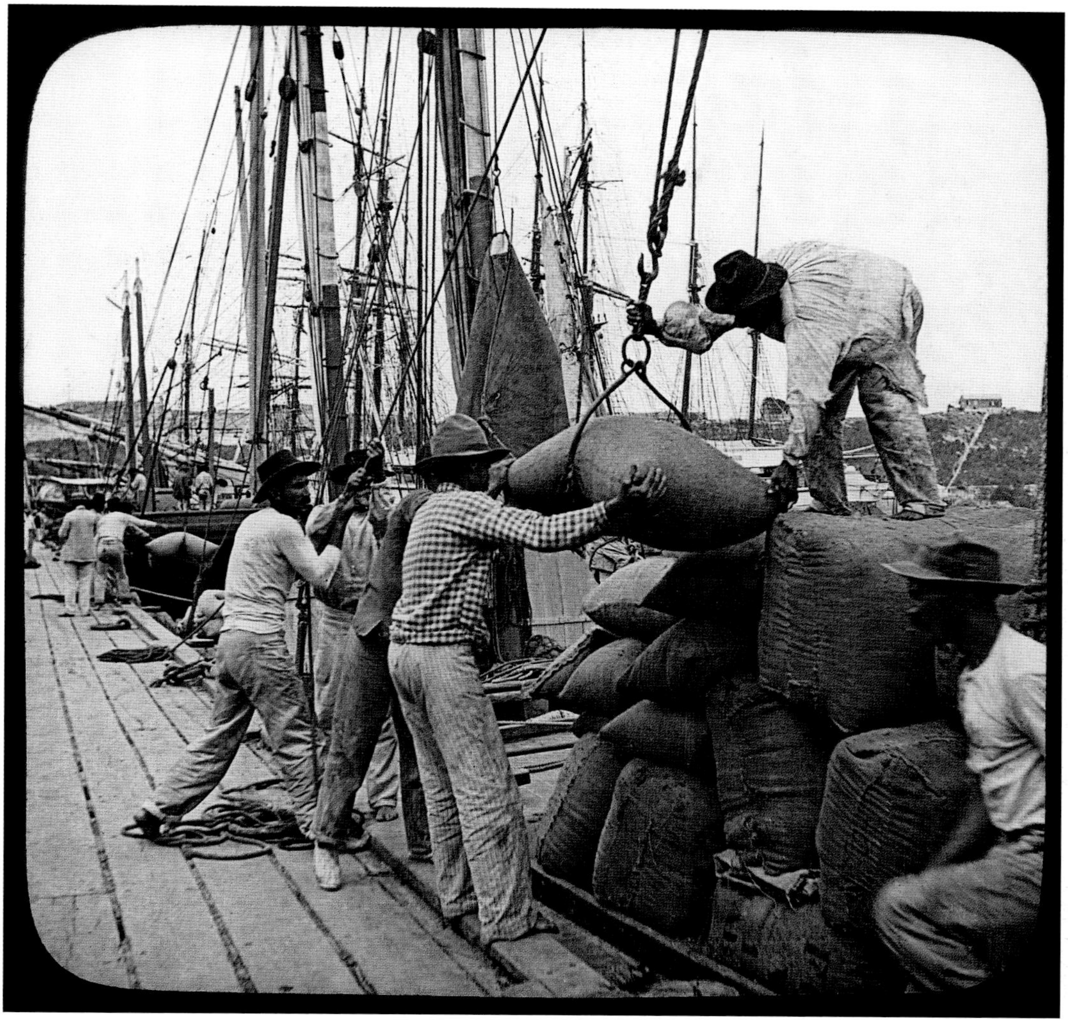

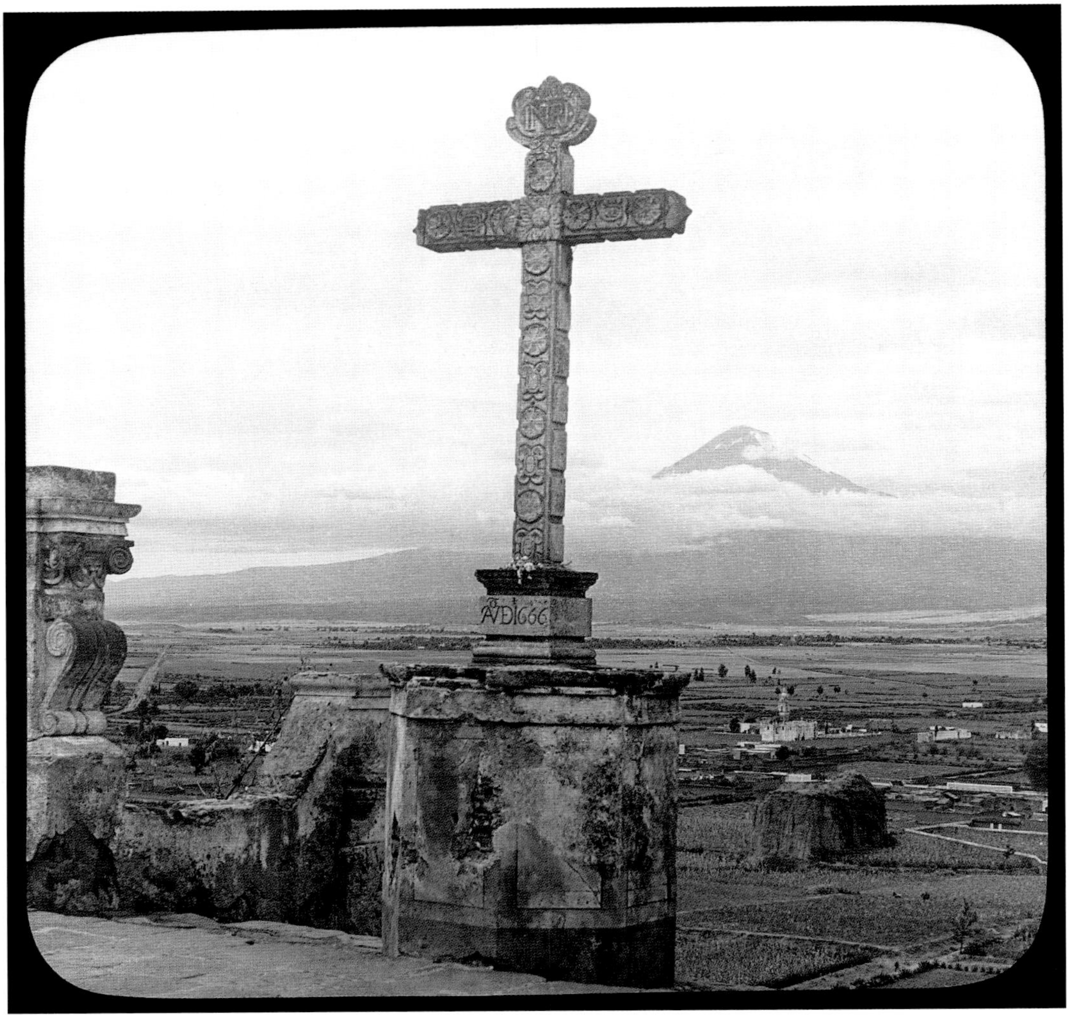

569 The Sacred Shrine and "Old Popocatapeti", Cholula, Mexico, 1900s

569 Der Heilige Schrein und der „Alte Popocatépetl", Cholula, Mexiko, 1900er Jahre

569 Un calvaire et le « vieux Popocatépetl », Cholula, Mexique, années 1900

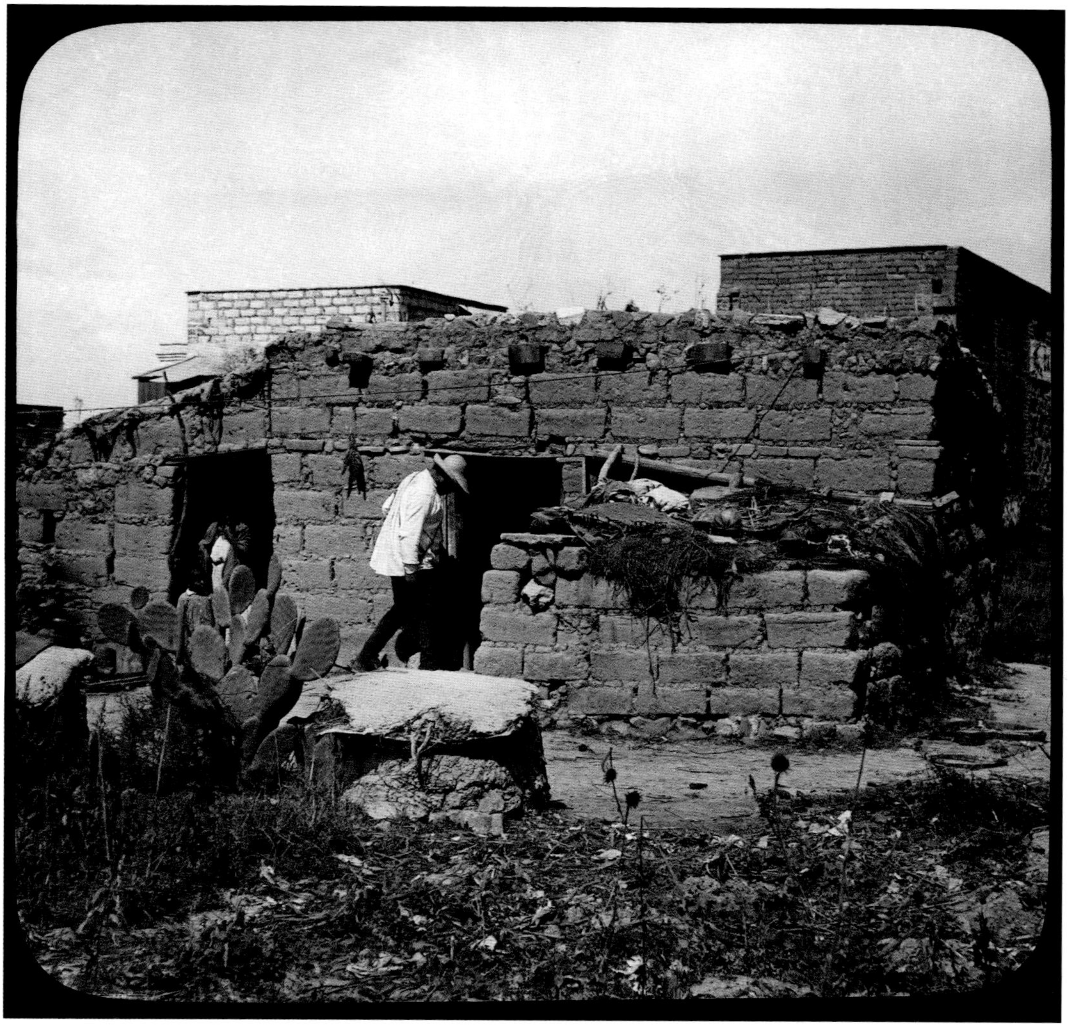

570 An Adobe hut (a home of the Peon), Mexico City, Mexico, 1900s

570 Adobe-Lehmhütte (das Zuhause eines Peons, Tagelöhner), Mexiko-Stadt, Mexiko, 1900er Jahre

570 Hutte en pisé (habitation d'un péon), Mexico, Mexique, années 1900

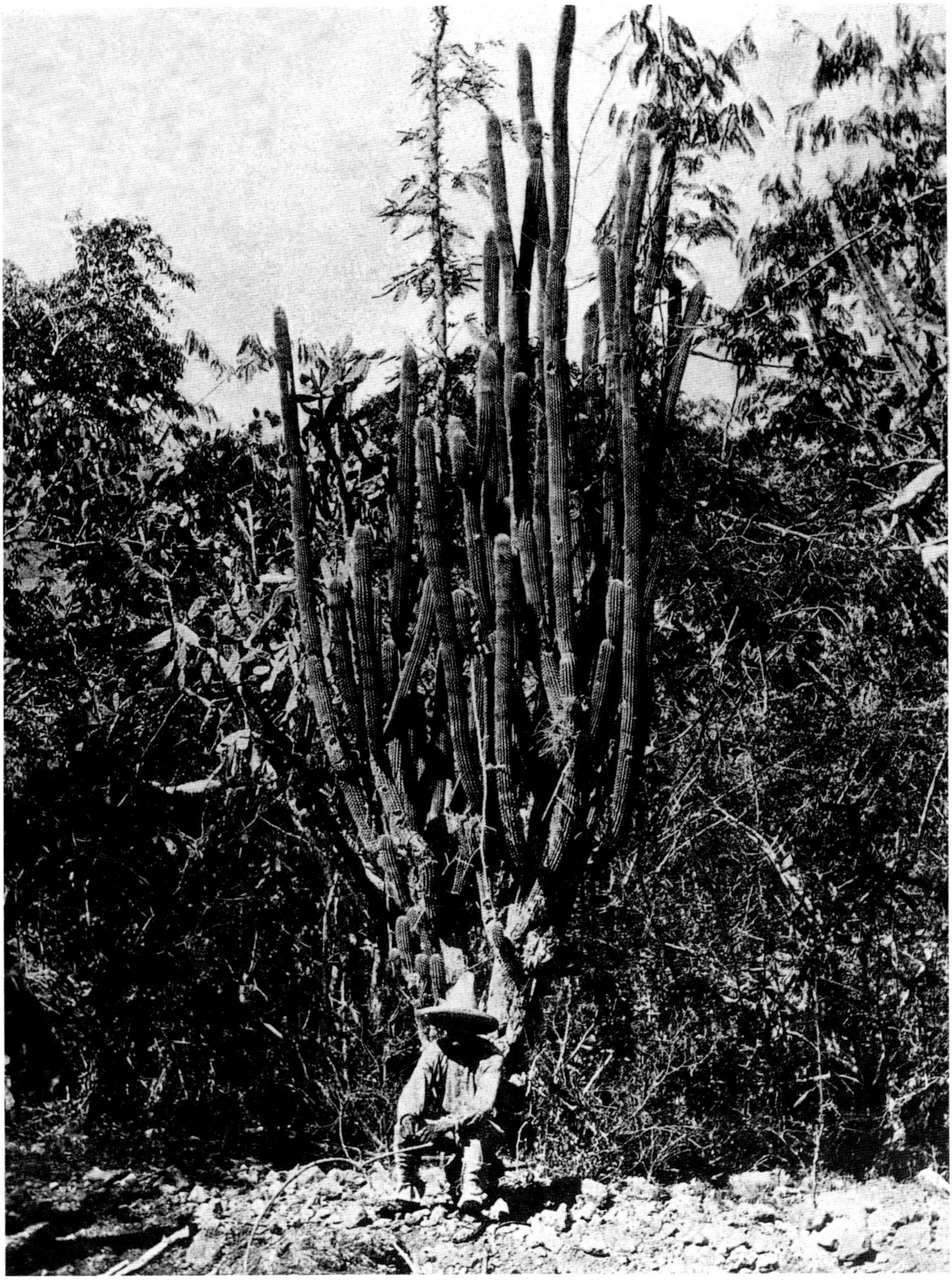

571 Tropical thorn forest, Mexico, 1900s
572 El Chival rubber planter, Palenque, Mexico, 1904

571 Tropischer Dornwald, Mexiko, 1900er Jahre
572 El Chival, Kautschukpflanzer, Palenque, Mexiko, 1904

571 Forêt d'épineux, Mexique, années 1900
572 El Chival, planteur d'hévéas, Palenque, Mexique, 1904

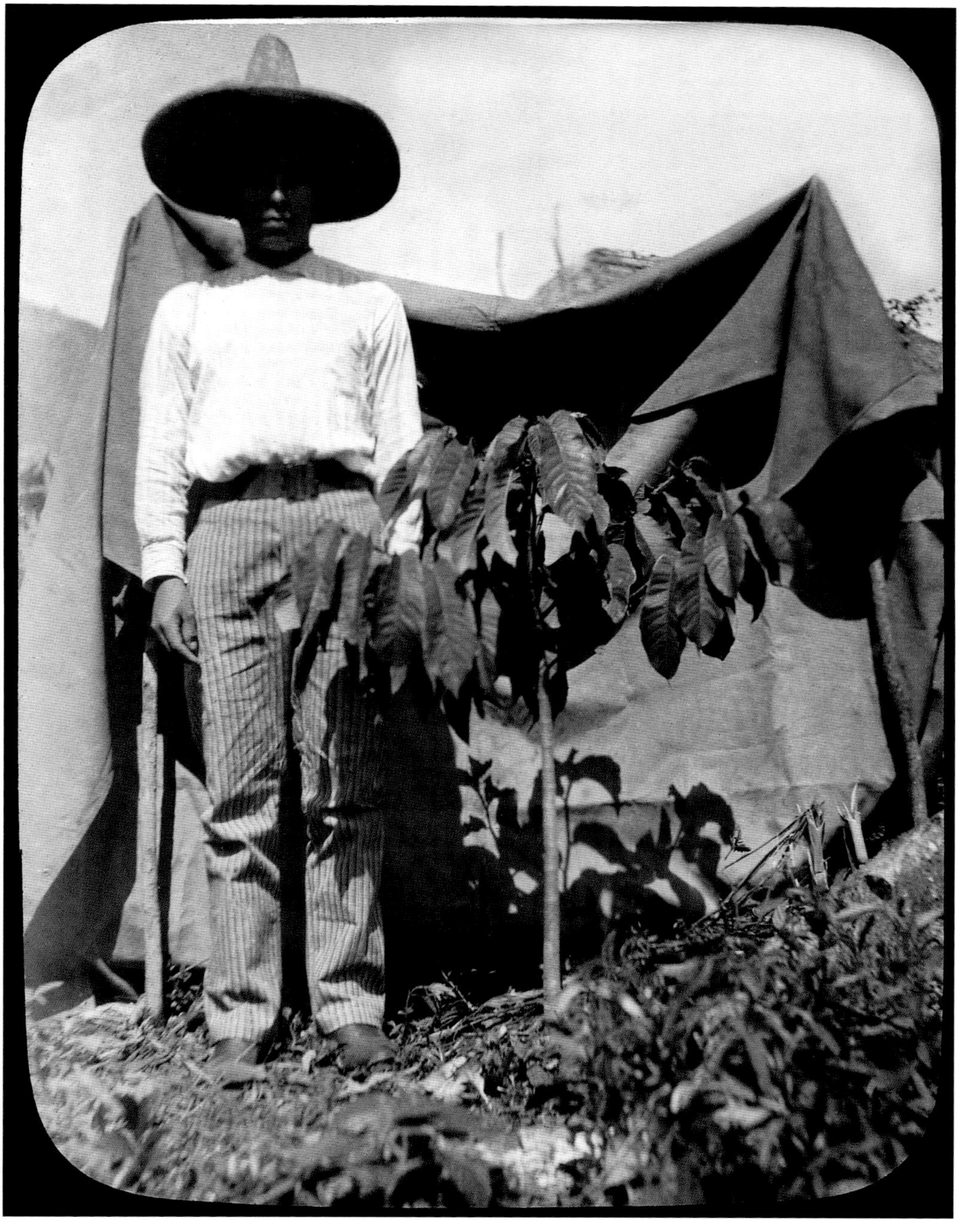

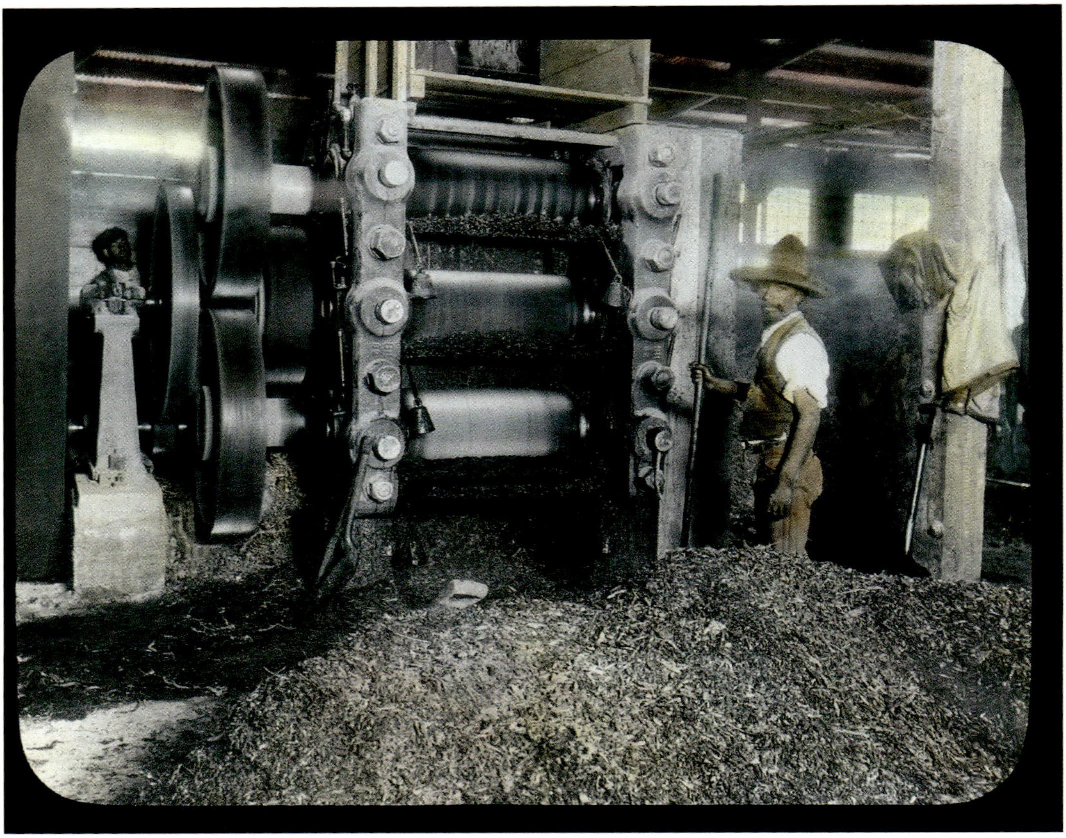

573 Pile of crushed quayule (a natural source of latex rubber) with crushing rollers, Coahuila, Mexico, 1910s

573 Haufen mit von Walzen zerdrückten Guayulen (eine natürliche Quelle für Latex), Coahuila, Mexiko, 1910er Jahre

573 Guayule (une source naturelle de latex) écrasé par des rouleaux, Coahuila, Mexique, années 1910

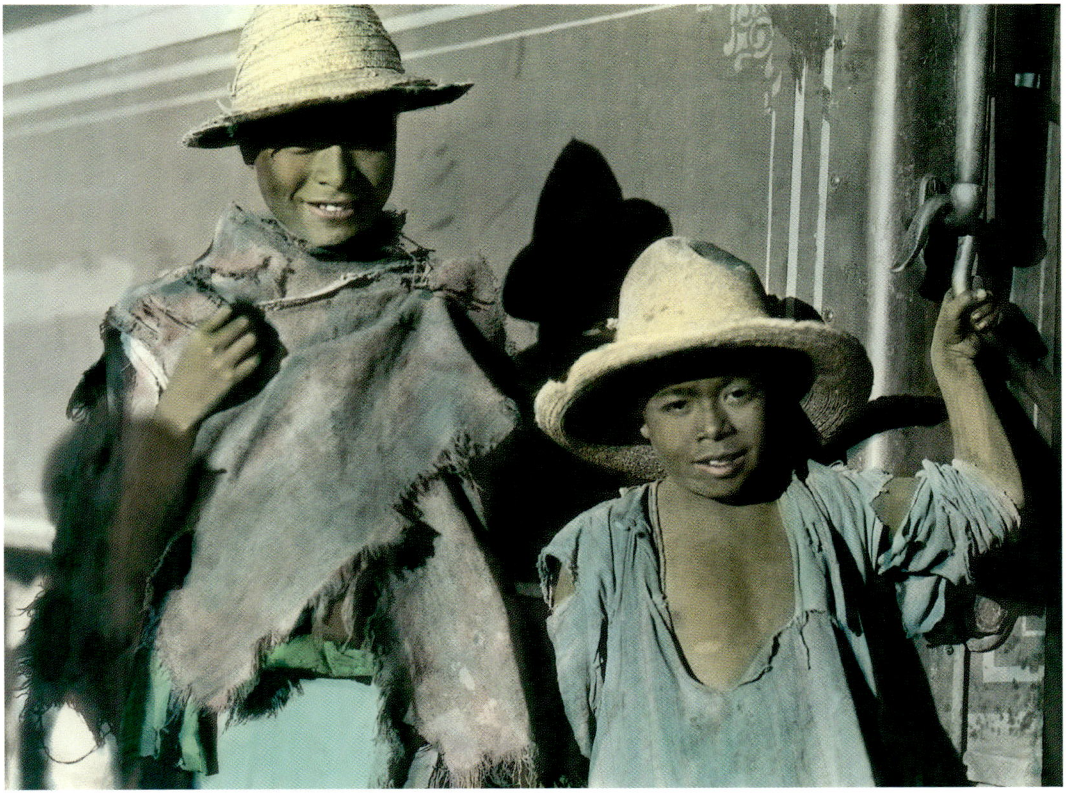

574 Boys dressed in rags, Mexico, 1910s

574 Mit Lumpen bekleidete Jungen, Mexiko, 1910er Jahre

574 Garçons vêtus de haillons, Mexique, années 1910

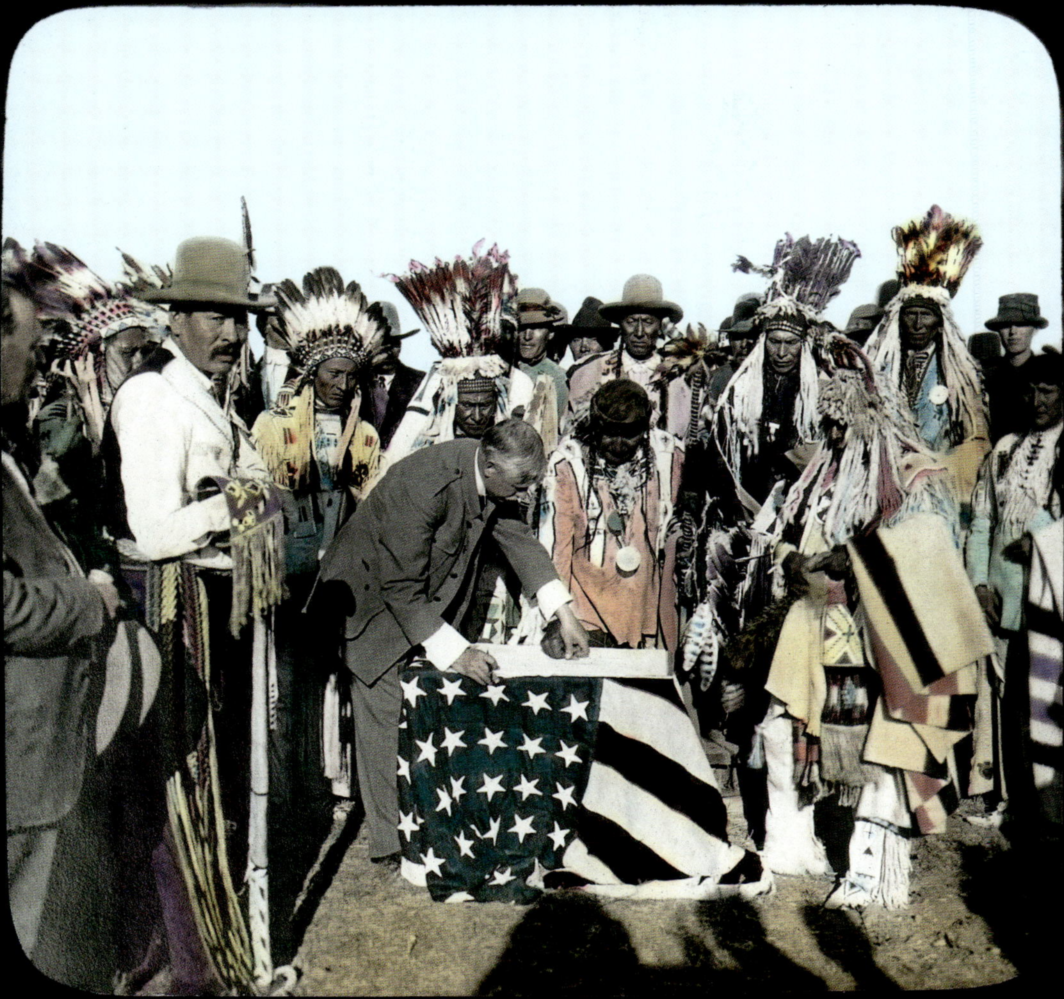

575 "Saluting the Flag", USA, 1890s

575 „Die Flagge wird gegrüßt", USA, 1890er Jahre

575 « Salut au drapeau », USA, années 1890

UNITED STATES OF AMERICA

VEREINIGTE STAATEN VON AMERIKA ·
ÉTATS-UNIS D'AMÉRIQUE

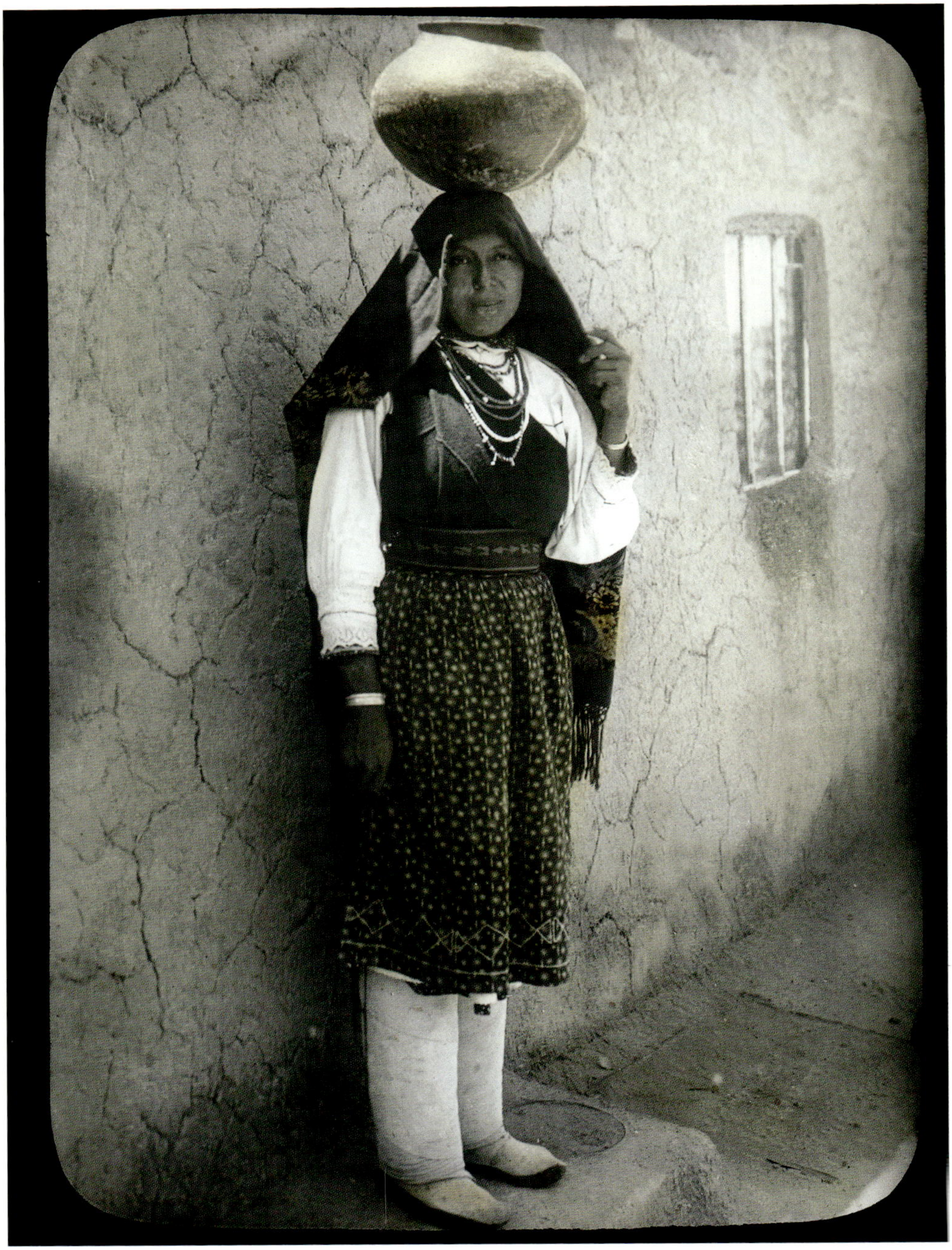

576 Woman of the Isleta Pueblo, New Mexico, USA, 1900s

576 Bewohnerin des Isleta-Pueblos, New Mexico, USA, 1900er Jahre

576 Habitante d'Isleta Pueblo, Nouveau-Mexique, USA, années 1900

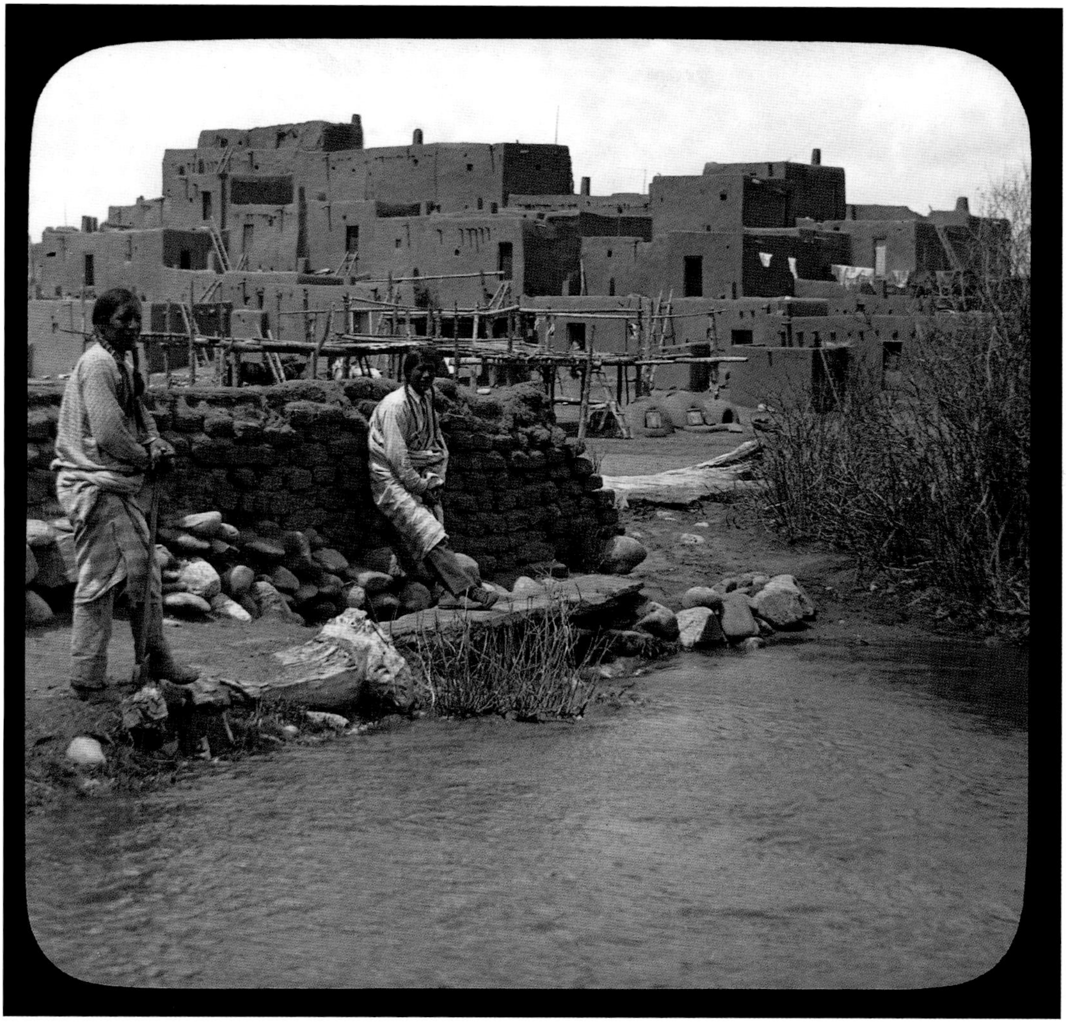

577 Pueblo of Taos Indians, Taos, New Mexico, USA, 1900s

577 Pueblo der Taos-Indianer, Taos, New Mexico, USA, 1900er Jahre

577 Pueblo d'indiens Taos, Taos, Nouveau-Mexique, USA, années 1900

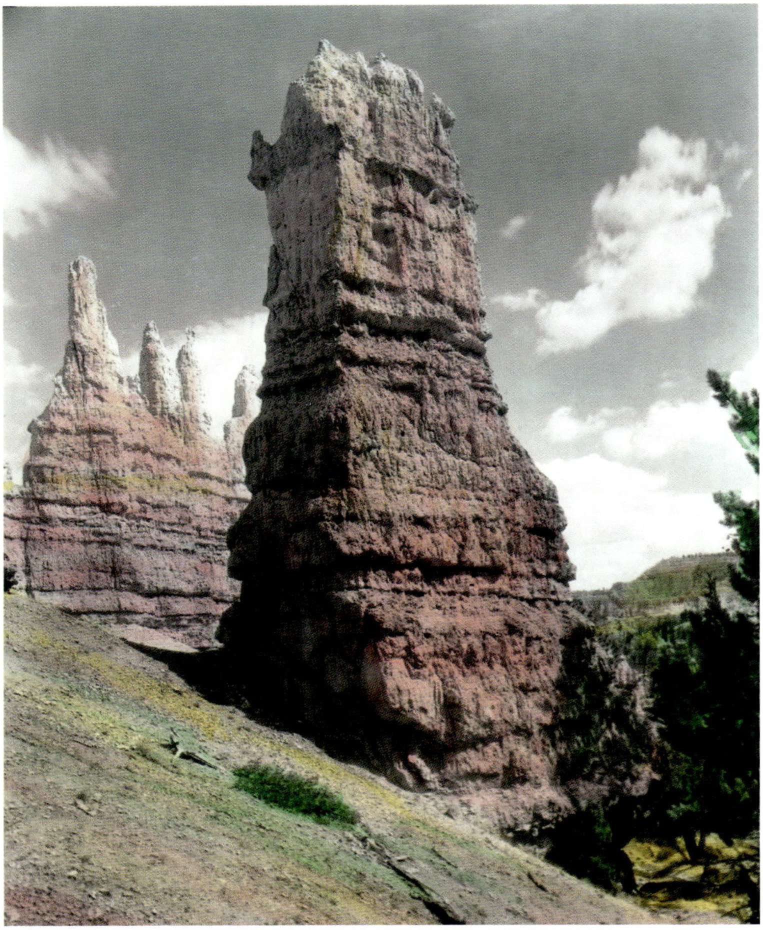

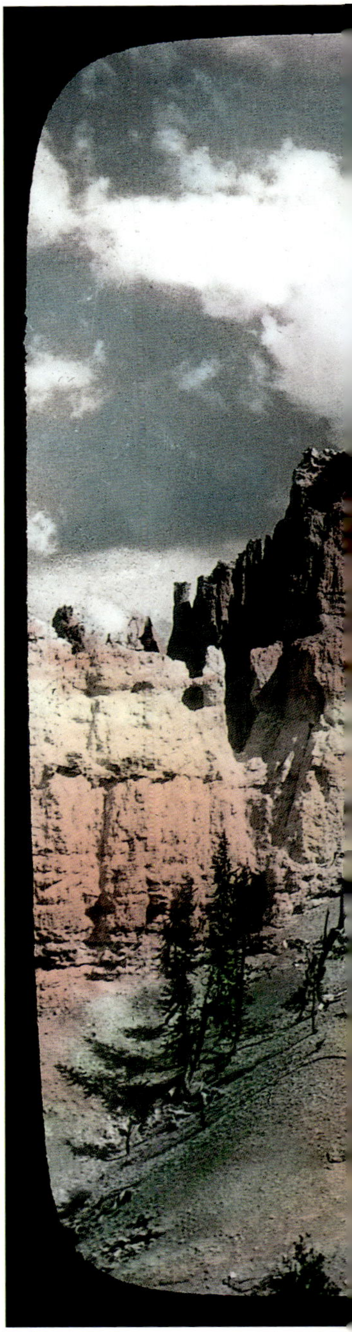

578–9 Chinese Pagoda and The Cathedral, Bryce Canyon National Park, Utah, USA, 1900s

578–9 Chinesische Pagode und Die Kathedrale, Bryce-Canyon-Nationalpark, Utah, USA, 1900er Jahre

578–9 La Pagode chinoise et La Cathédrale, Bryce Canyon National Park, Utah, USA, années 1900

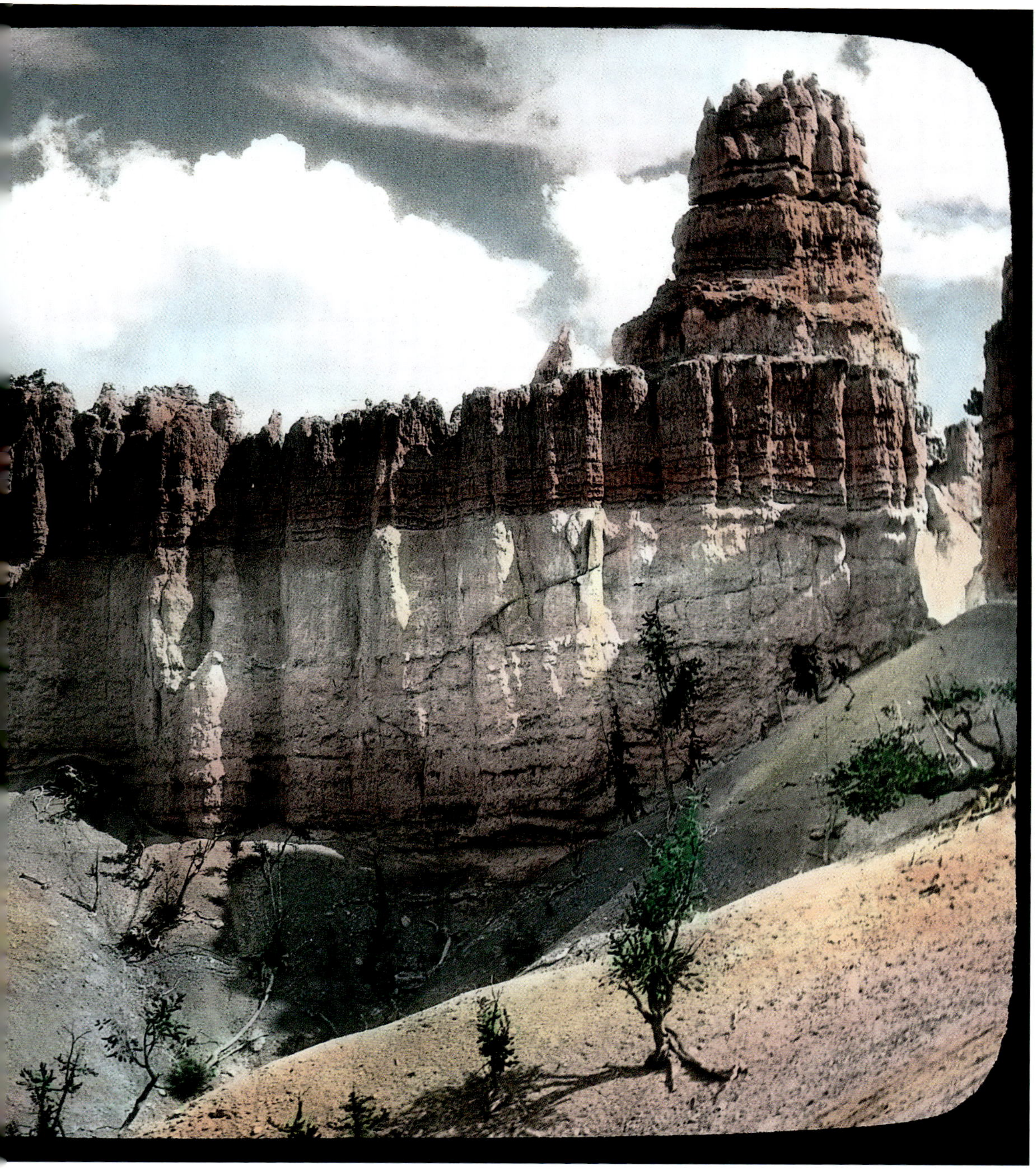

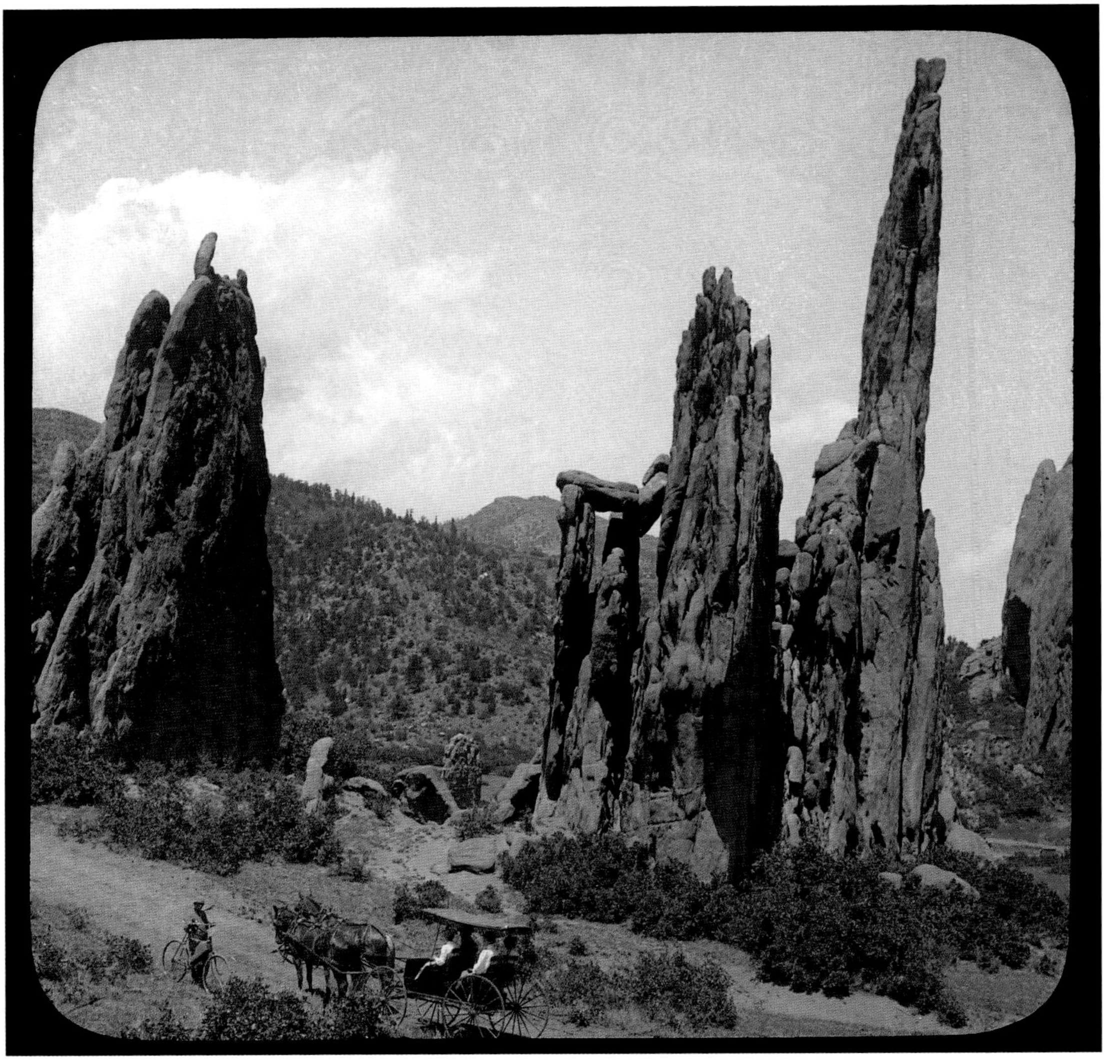

580 Cathedral Spires, Garden of the Gods, near Colorado Springs, Colorado, USA, 1900s

580 Kathedralenhelme, Garden of the Gods, nahe Colorado Springs, Colorado, USA, 1900er Jahre

580 Les Flèches de la cathédrale, le Jardin des Dieux, près de Colorado Springs, Colorado, USA, années 1900

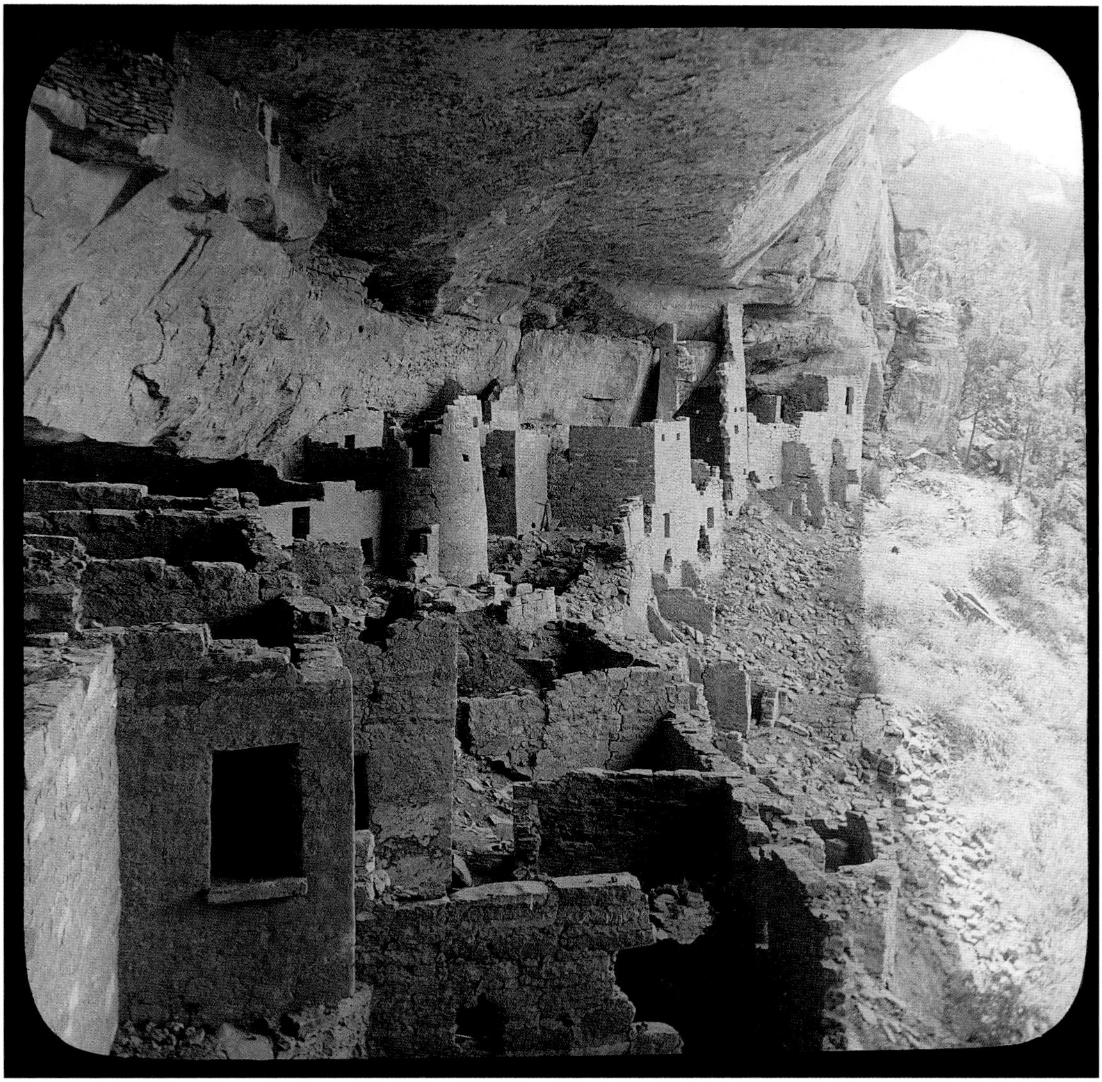

581 Cliff Dwellers' Palace, Mesa Verde, Colorado, USA, 1900s

581 Die Felsnischensiedlung Cliff Palace, Mesa-Verde-Nationalpark, Colorado, USA, 1900er Jahre

581 Habitations à Cliff Palace, Mesa Verde, Colorado, USA, années 1900

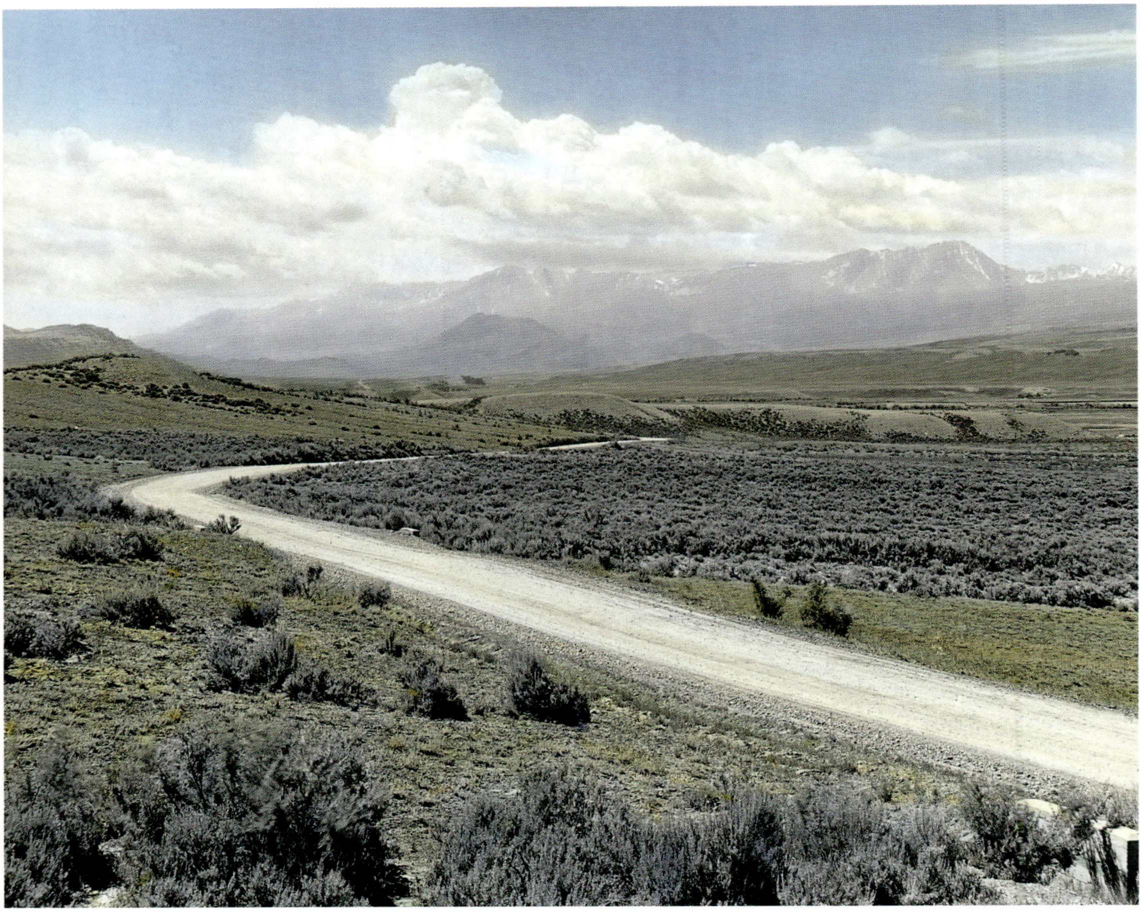

582 Sagebrush in Middle Park with Park Range in distance (view Southwest from Kremmling), Colorado, USA, 1929

582 Salbeisträucher im Middle Park, in der Ferne die Park Range (Südwestansicht von Kremmling aus), Colorado, USA, 1929

582 Buissons de sauge à Middle Park et, au fond, Park Range (vue au sud-ouest de Kremmling), Colorado, USA, 1929

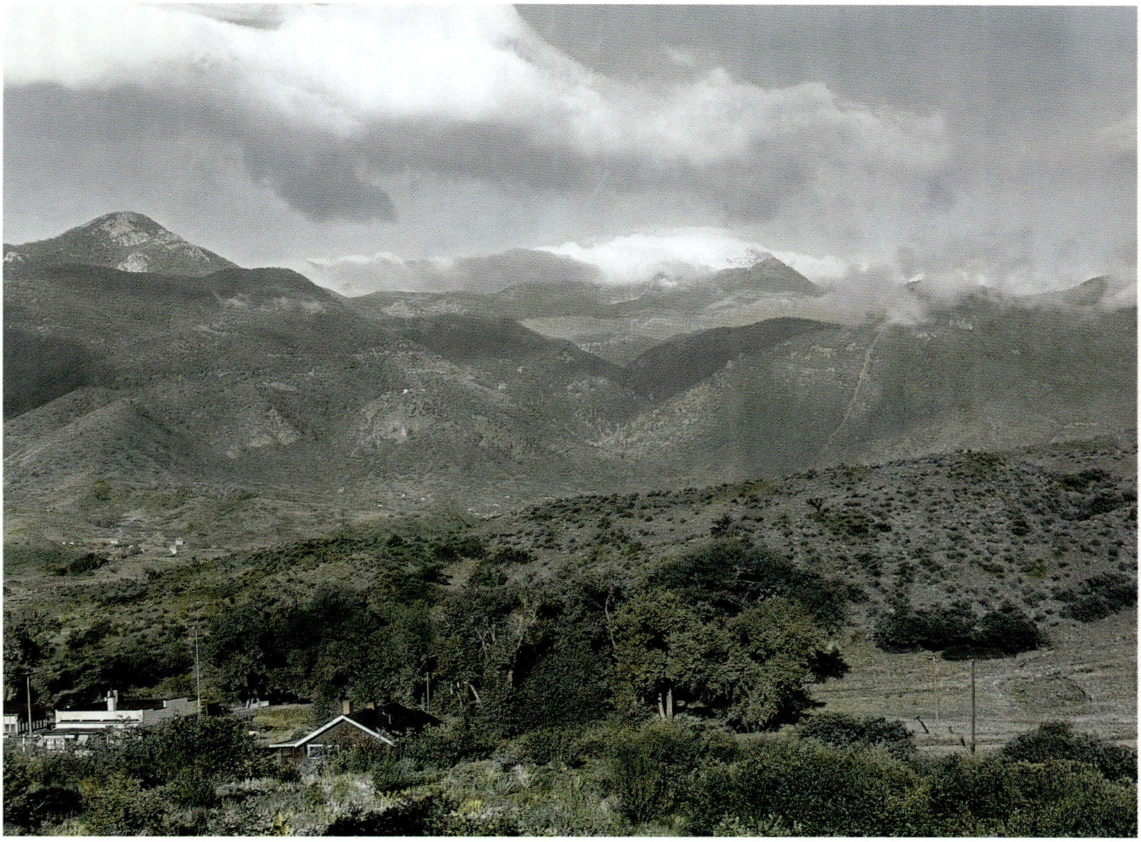

583 Rocky Mountains, Colorado Springs, Colorado, USA, 1927

583 Rocky Mountains, Colorado Springs, Colorado, USA, 1927

583 Montagnes Rocheuses, Colorado Springs, Colorado, USA, 1927

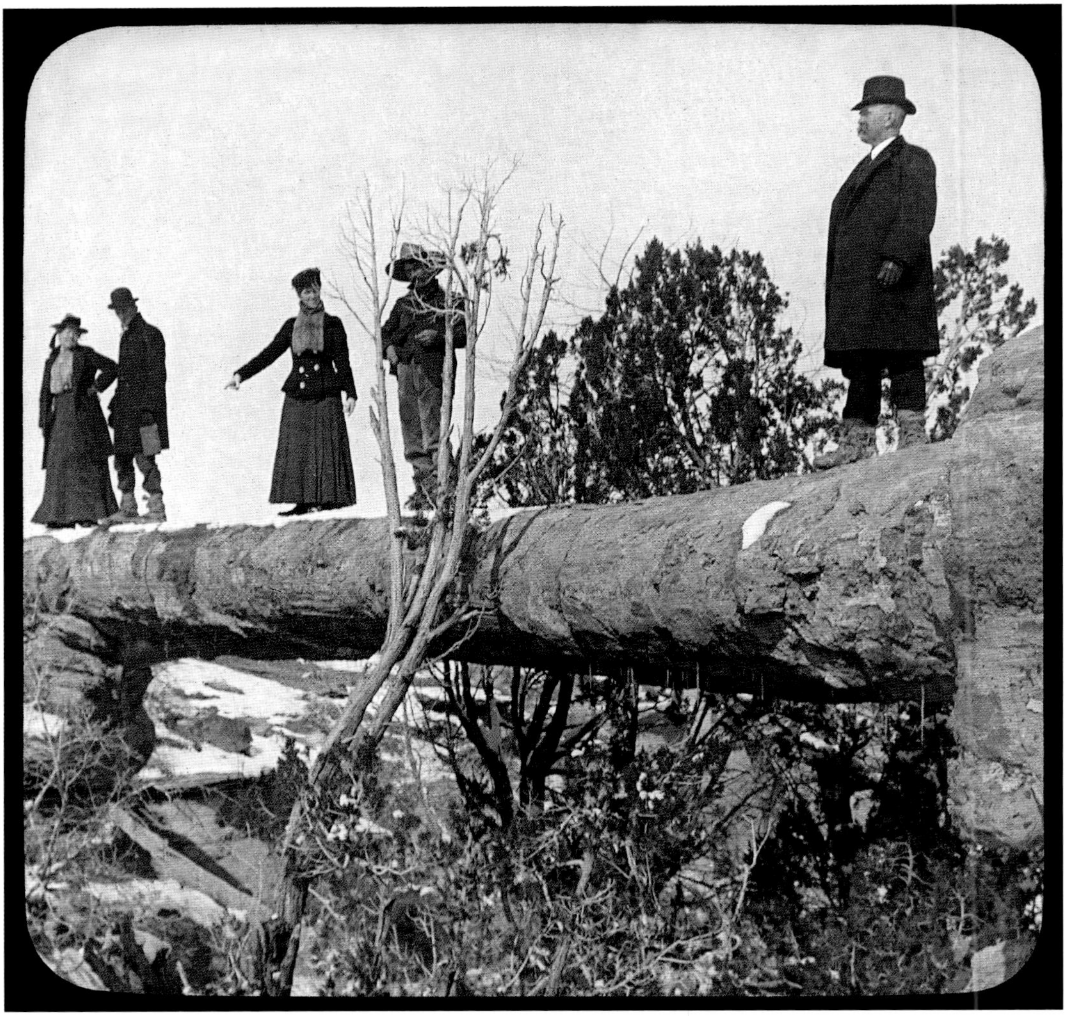

584 Log bridge, Petrified Forest, Arizona, USA, 1910s
585 Oil field, Bakersfield, California, 1910s

584 Baumstammbrücke, Petrified-Forest-Nationalpark, Arizona, USA, 1910er Jahre
585 Ölfeld, Bakersfield, Kalifornien, 1910er Jahre

584 Rondin servant de pont. Forêt Pétrifiée, Arizona, USA, années 1910
585 Champ pétrolifère, Bakersfield, Californie, années 1910

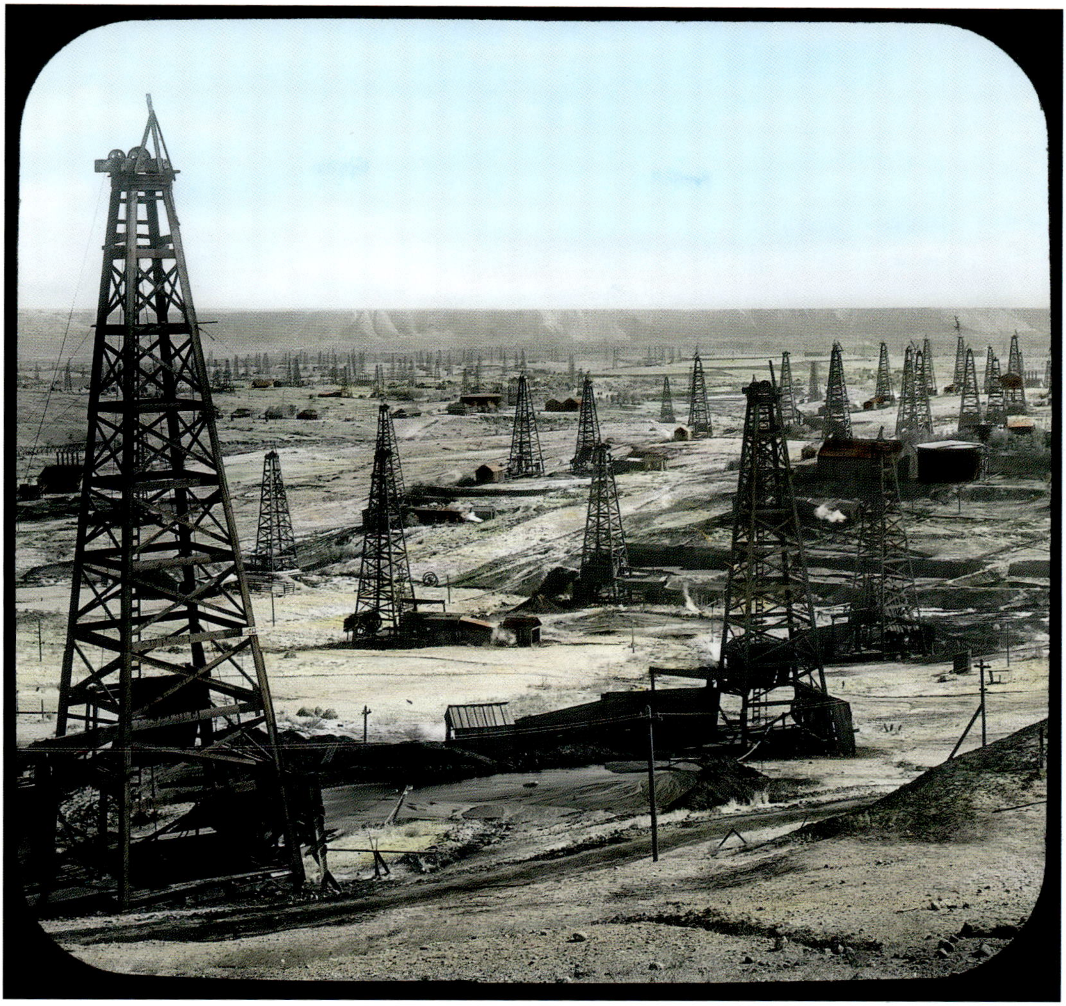

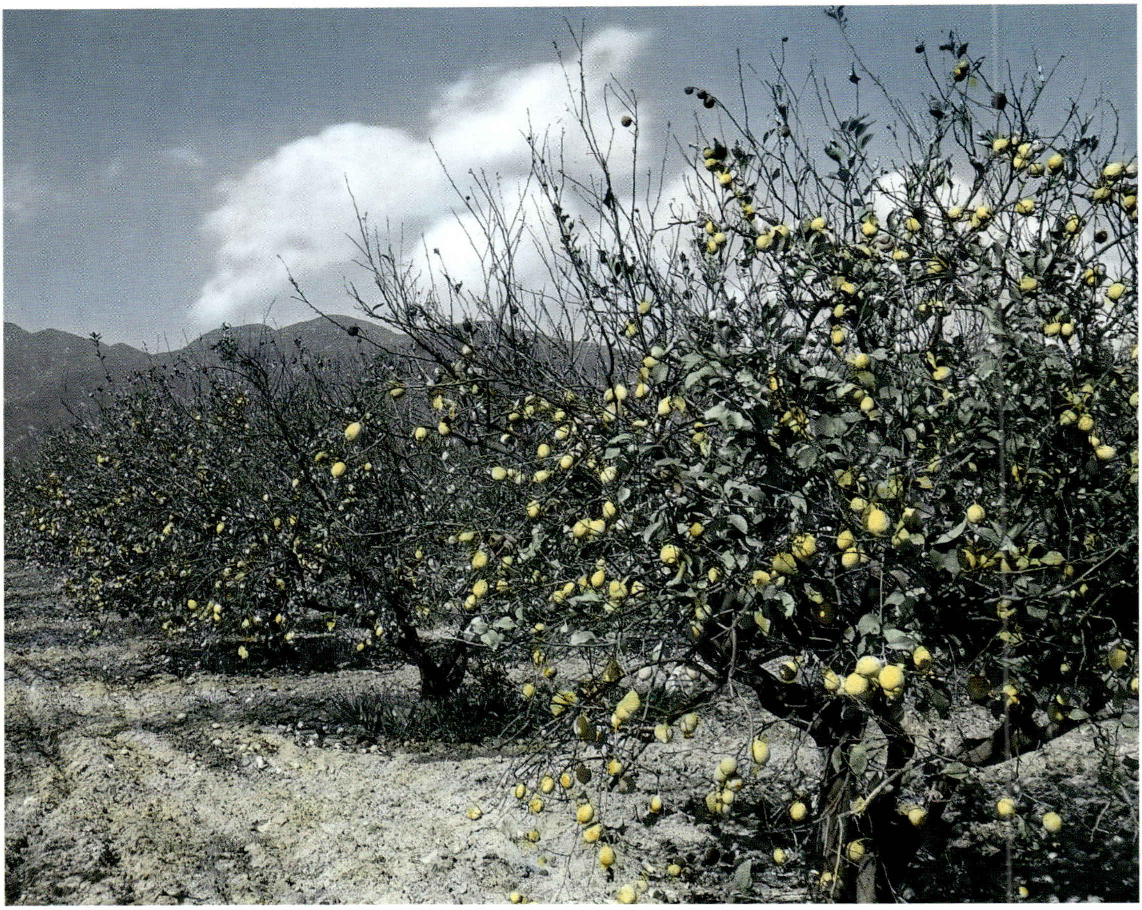

586 Lemon crop ruined by frost in the foothills of Southern California, USA, 1920s

586 Vom Frost ruinierte Zitronenbäume an den Gebirgsausläufern Südkaliforniens, USA, 1920er Jahre

586 Citronniers tués par le gel dans les collines au sud de la Californie, USA, années 1920

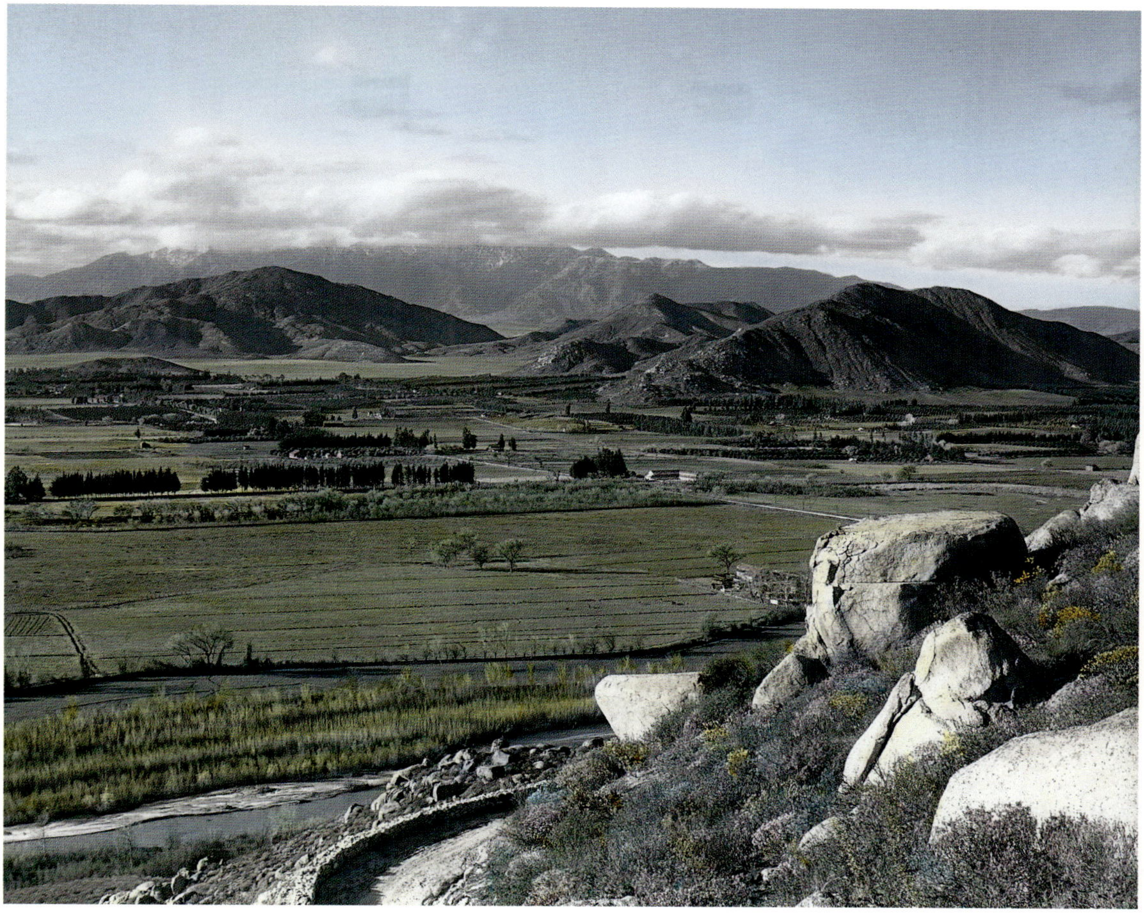

587 Santa Ana Valley with Jurupa Mountains and San Gabriel Mountains in the distance, California, 1906

587 Das Santa-Ana-Tal mit den Jurupa Mountains und San Gabriel Mountains in der Ferne, Kalifornien, 1906

587 Vallée de Santa Ana, la montagne Jurupa et au loin, la montagne San Gabriel, Californie, 1906

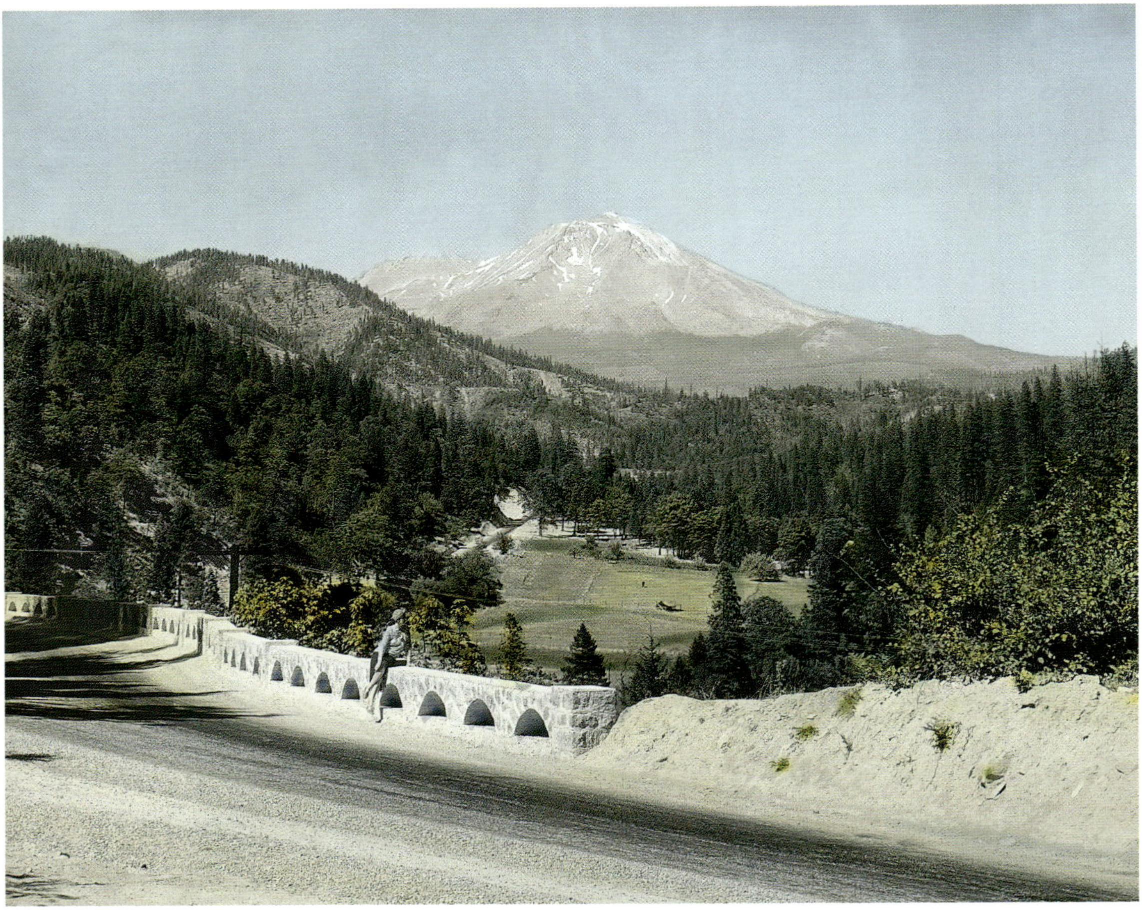

588 Mount Shasta and Shastina, California, USA, 1929
589 Mission of San Juan Capistrano, California, USA, c.1900

588 Der Mount Shasta und der Mount Shastina, Kalifornien, USA, 1929
589 Die Missionsstation von San Juan Capistrano, Kalifornien, USA, um 1900

588 Montagnes Shasta et Shastina, Californie, USA, 1929
589 Mission de San Juan Capistrano, Californie, USA, vers 1900

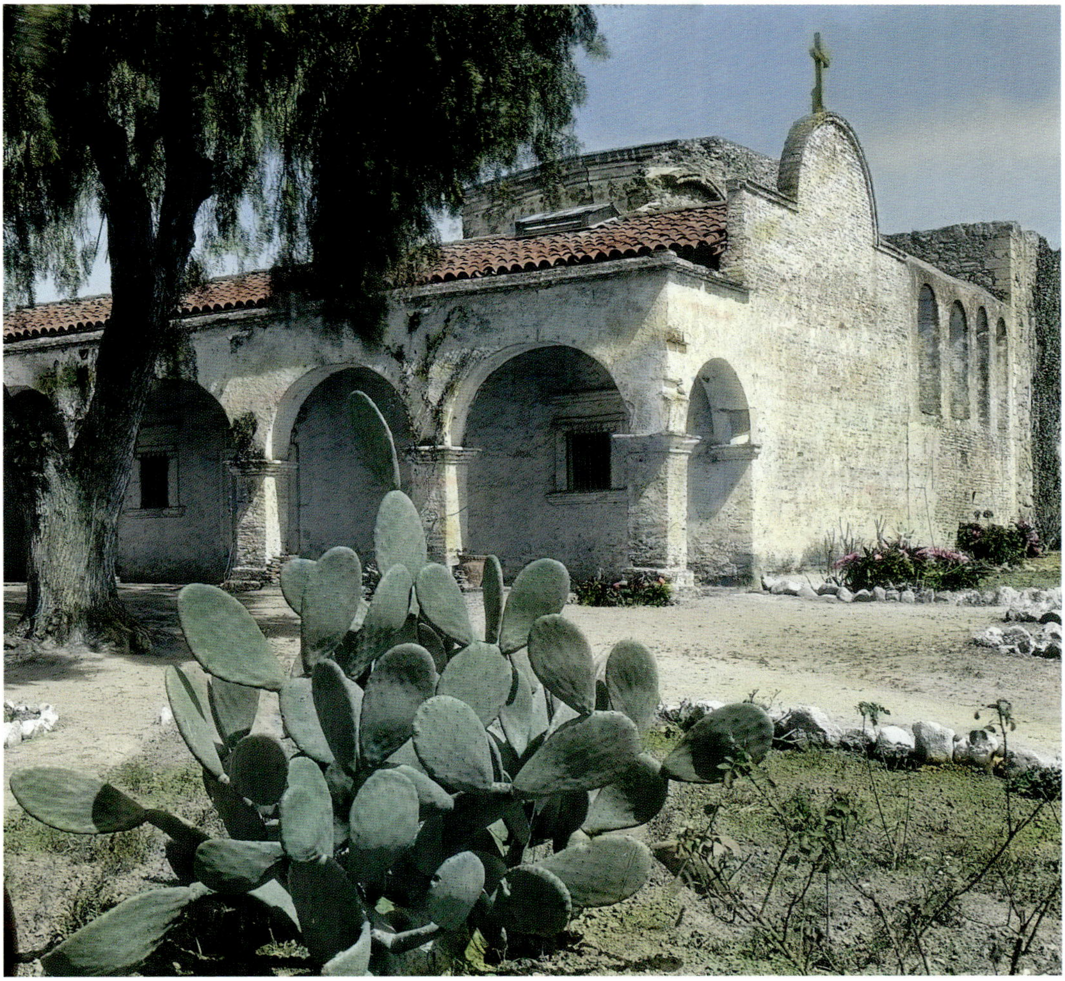

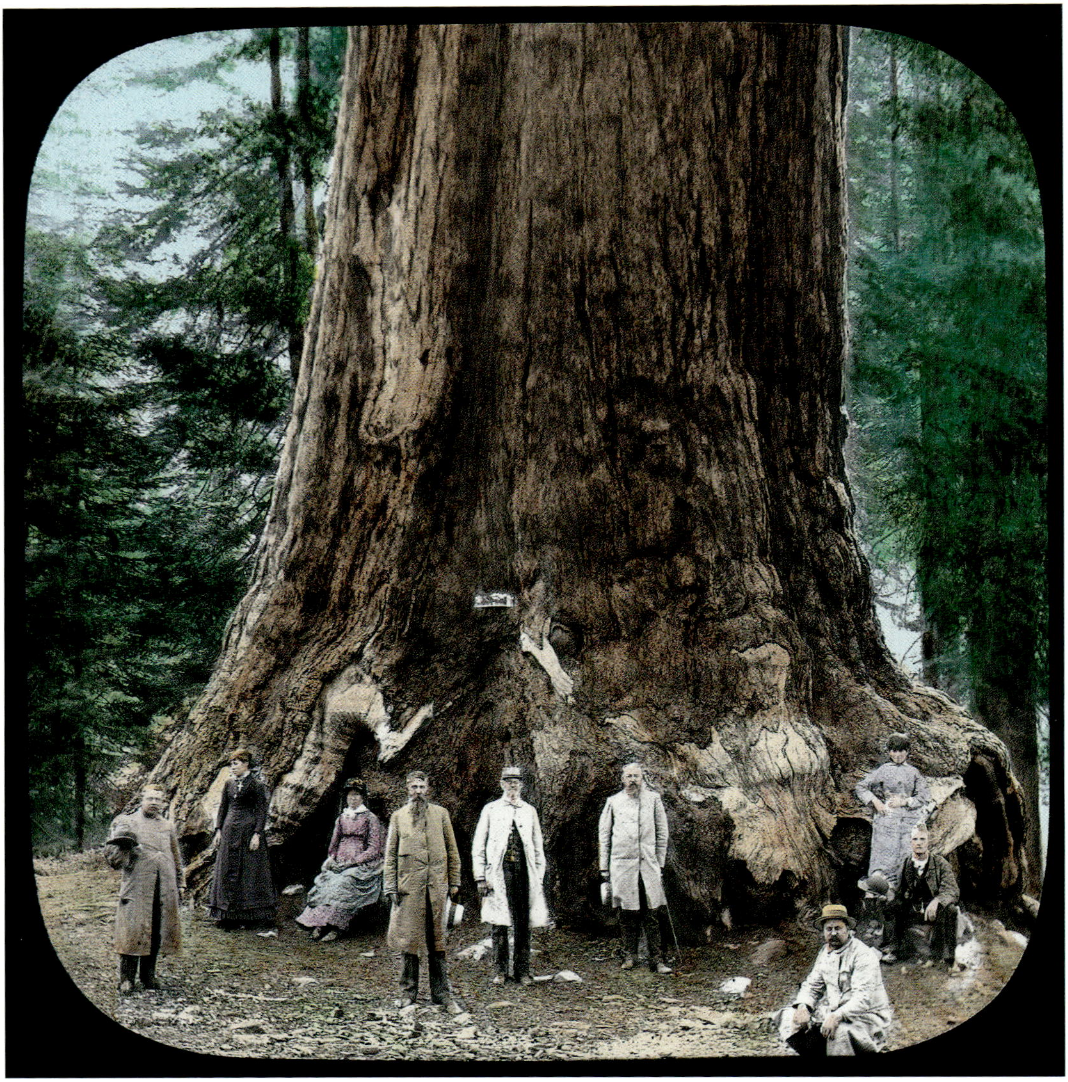

590 Giant redwood tree, Sequoia, California, 1890s

590 Riesenmammutbaum, Sequoia, Kalifornien, 1890er Jahre

590 Séquoias géants, Sequoia, Californie, années 1890

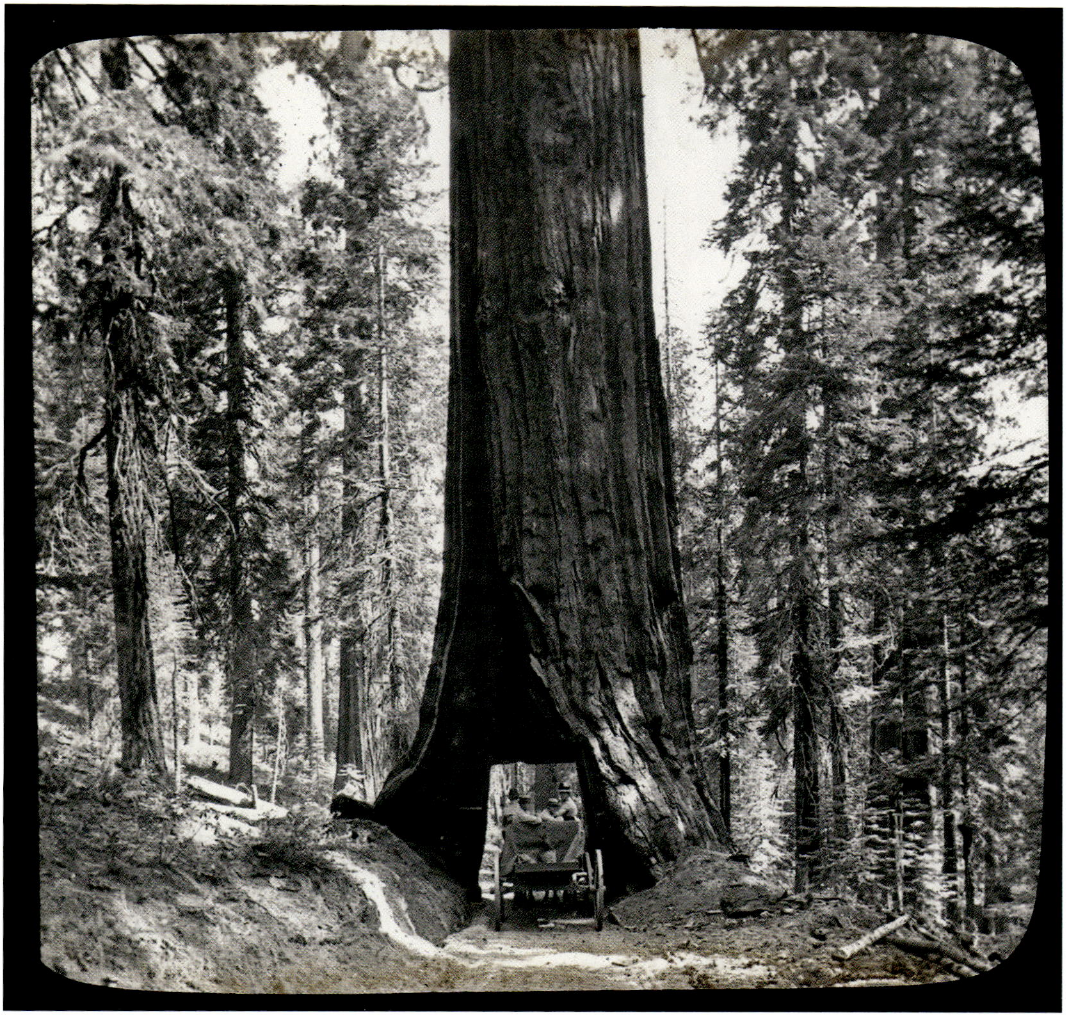

591 Tunnel Tree, Mariposa Grove, Wawona, Yosemite National Park, California, USA, 1890s

591 Tunnelbaum, Mariposa Grove, Wawona, Yosemite-Nationalpark, Kalifornien, USA, 1890er Jahre

591 Arbre-tunnel, Mariposa Grove, Wawona, Yosemite National Park, Californie, USA, années 1890

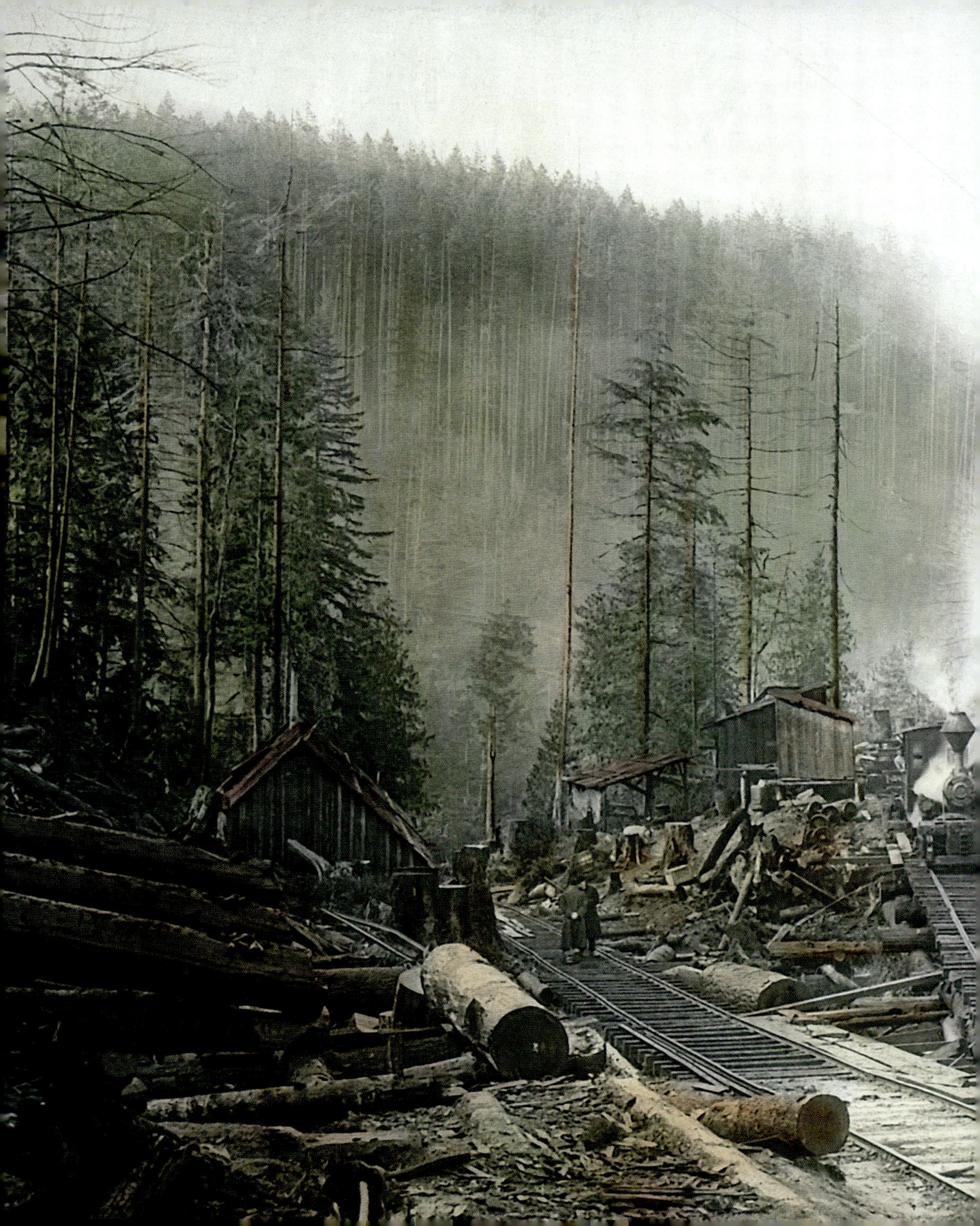

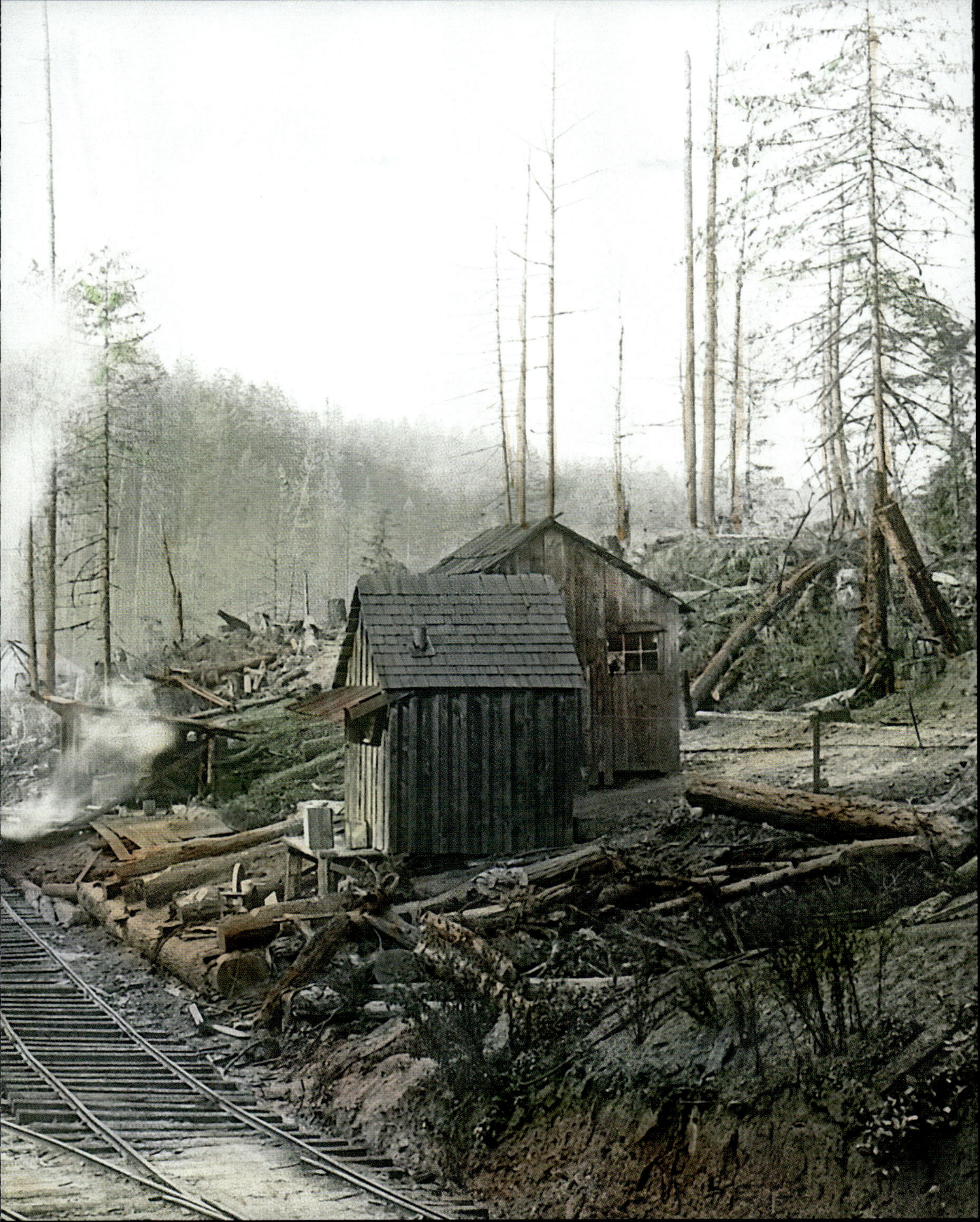

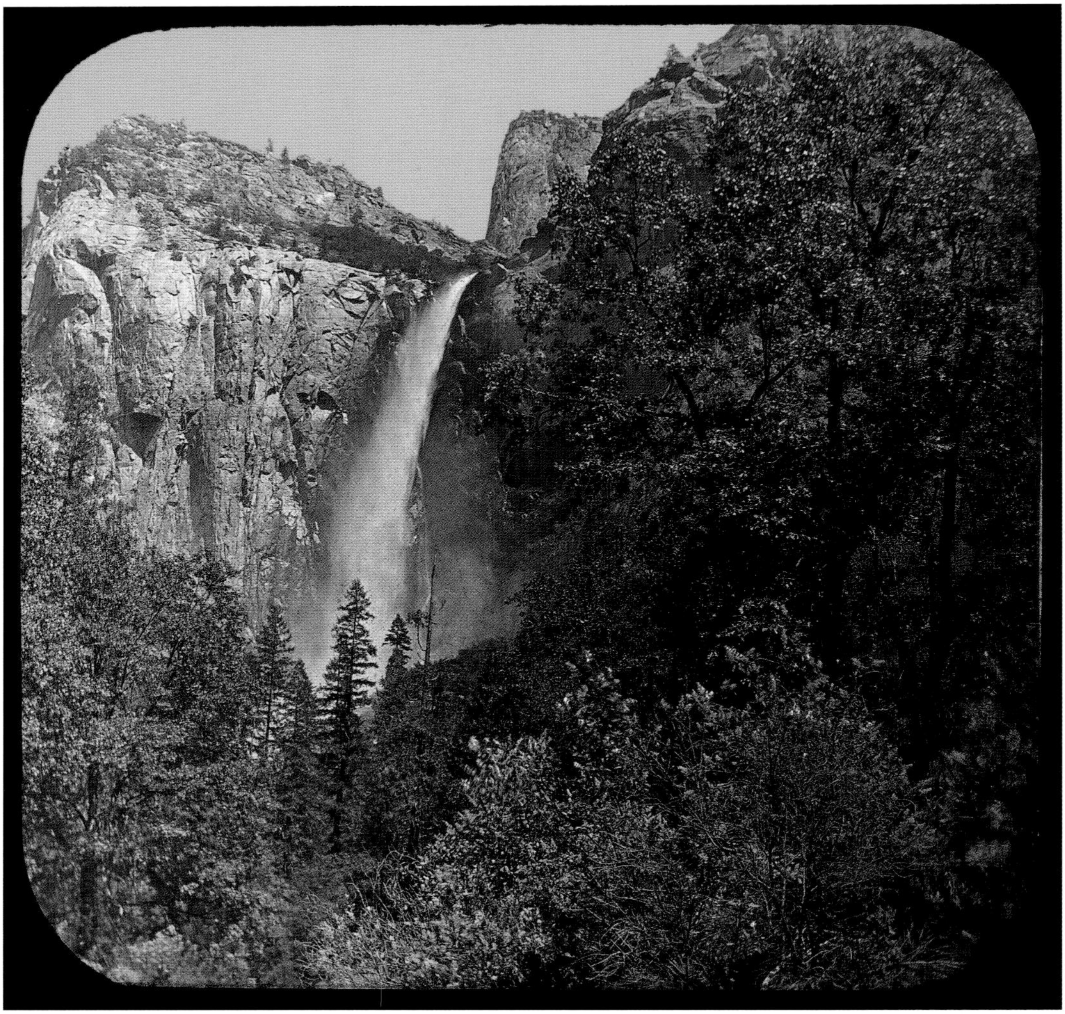

592 A frontier lumbering town, USA, 1900s
593 Bridal Veil Falls, Yosemite National Park, USA, 1890s

592 Eine Holzfällerstadt direkt am Wald, USA, 1900er Jahre
593 Der Bridal-Veil-Wasserfall, Yosemite-Nationalpark, Kalifornien, USA, 1890er Jahre

592 Bourg en lisière de forêt, USA, années 1900
593 Chute du voile de la mariée, Yosemite National Park, USA, années 1890

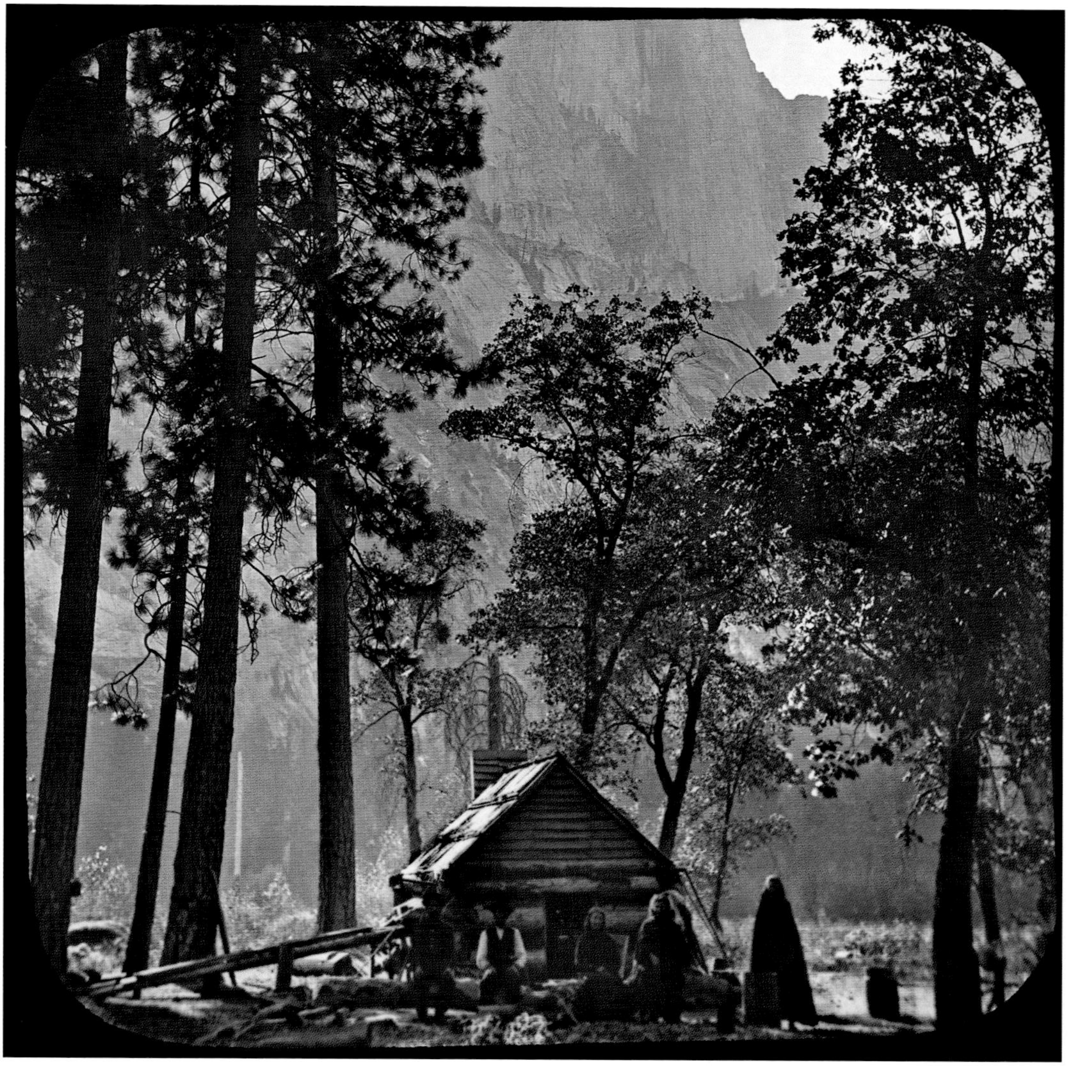

594 First House, Yosemite Valley, California, USA, 1890s

594 Das Erste Haus, Yosemite-Tal, Kalifornien, USA, 1890er Jahre

594 La première maison, Yosemite Valley, Californie, USA, années 1890

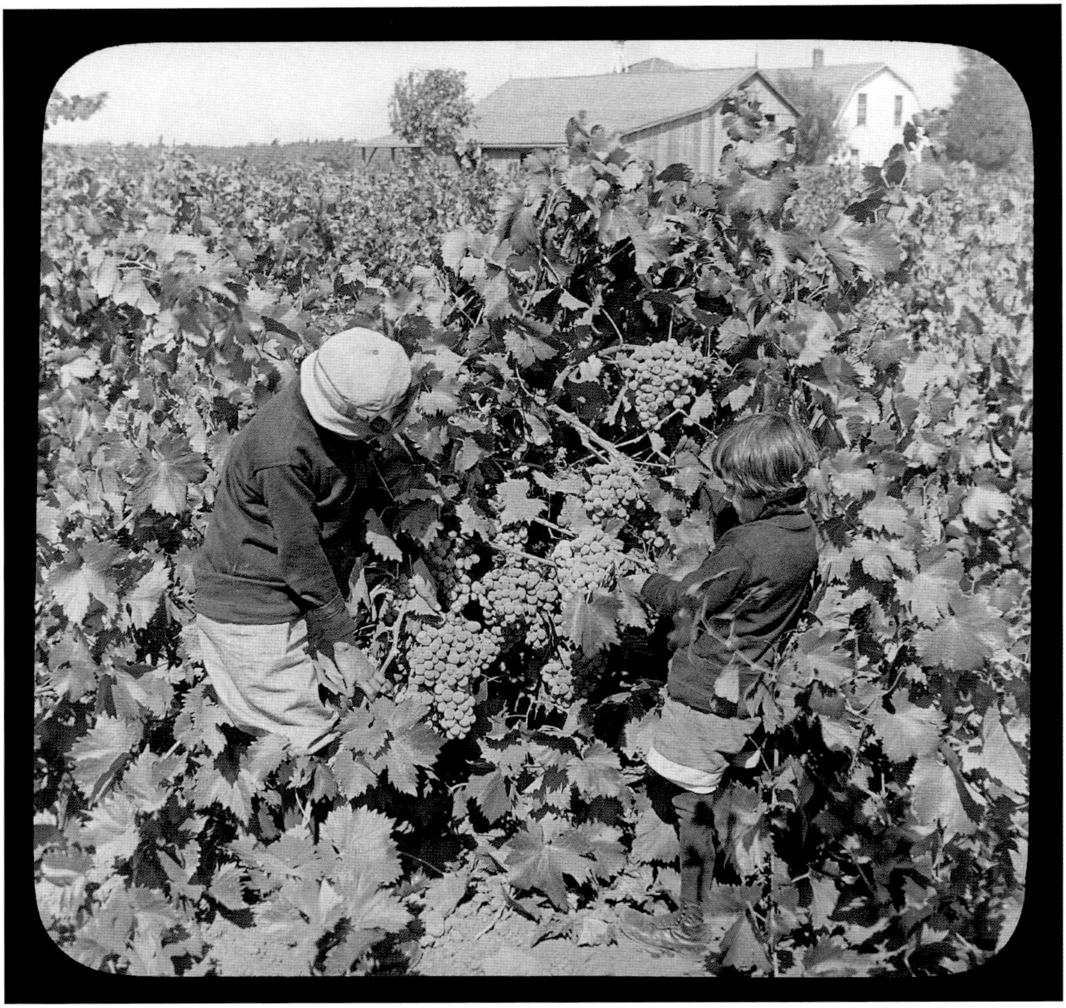

595 Tokay grapes growing in a Californian vineyard, Acampo, California, USA, 1920s
596 A desert scene, USA, 1900s

595 Kalifornischer Weinberg mit Trauben für Tokajer, Acampo, Kalifornien, USA, 1920er Jahre
596 Eine Wüstenlandschaft, USA, 1900er Jahre

595 Vignoble pour la production de Tokay, Acampo, Californie, USA, années 1920
596 Paysage dans le désert, USA, années 1900

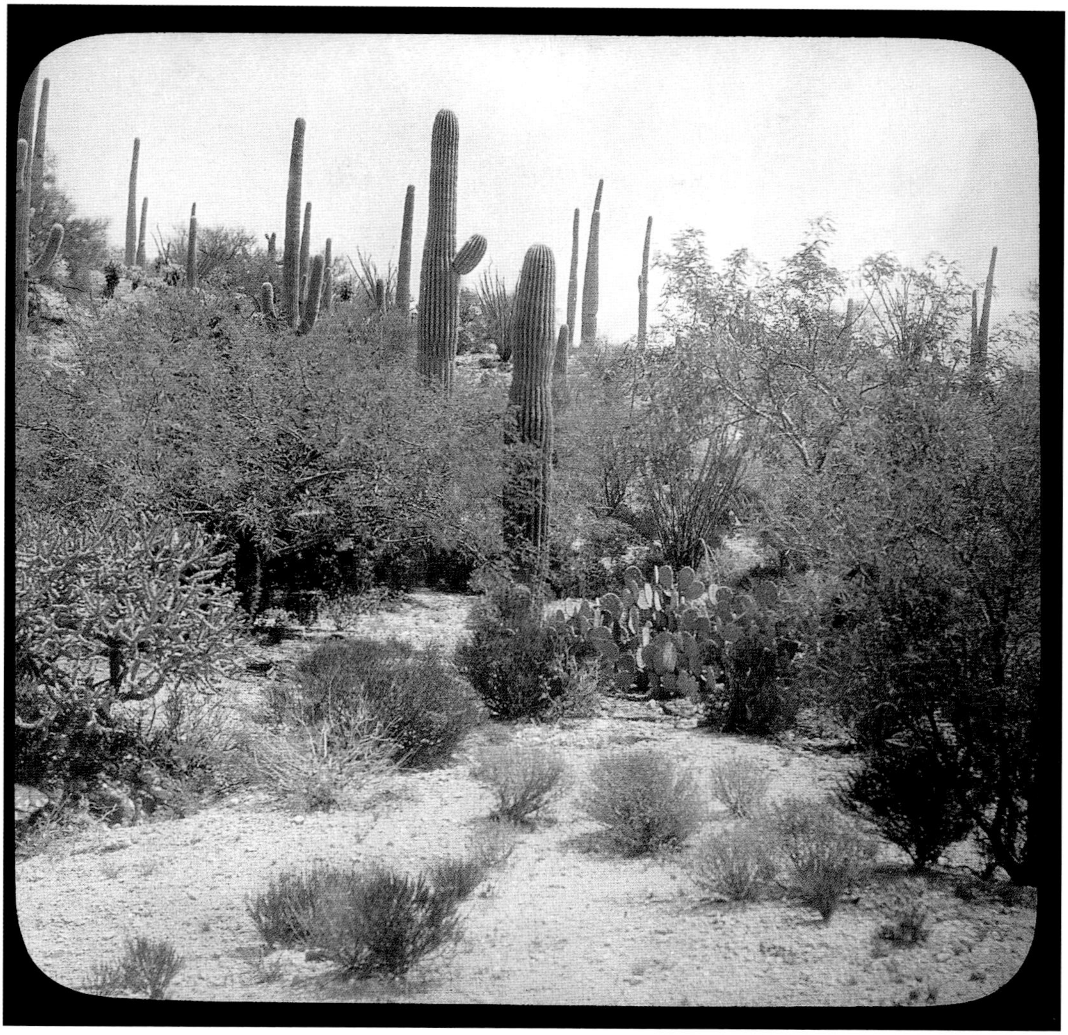

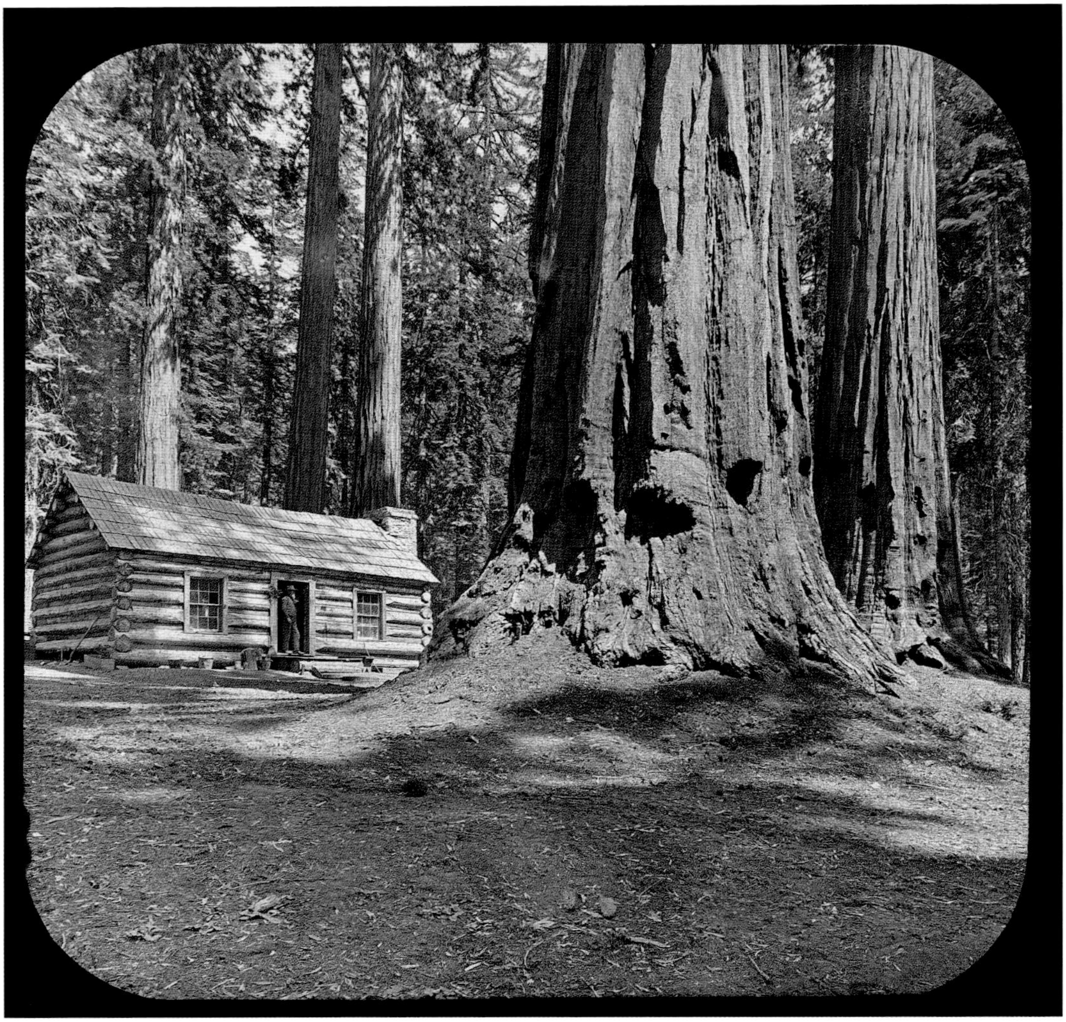

597 The Cabin, Big Trees, California, 1900s
598 Round the Camp Fire, North America, 1890s

597 Die Hütte, Große Bäume, Kalifornien, 1900er Jahre
598 Am Lagerfeuer, Nordamerika, 1890er Jahre

597 La cabane, grands arbres, Californie, années 1900
598 Autour du feu de camp, Amérique du Nord, années 1890

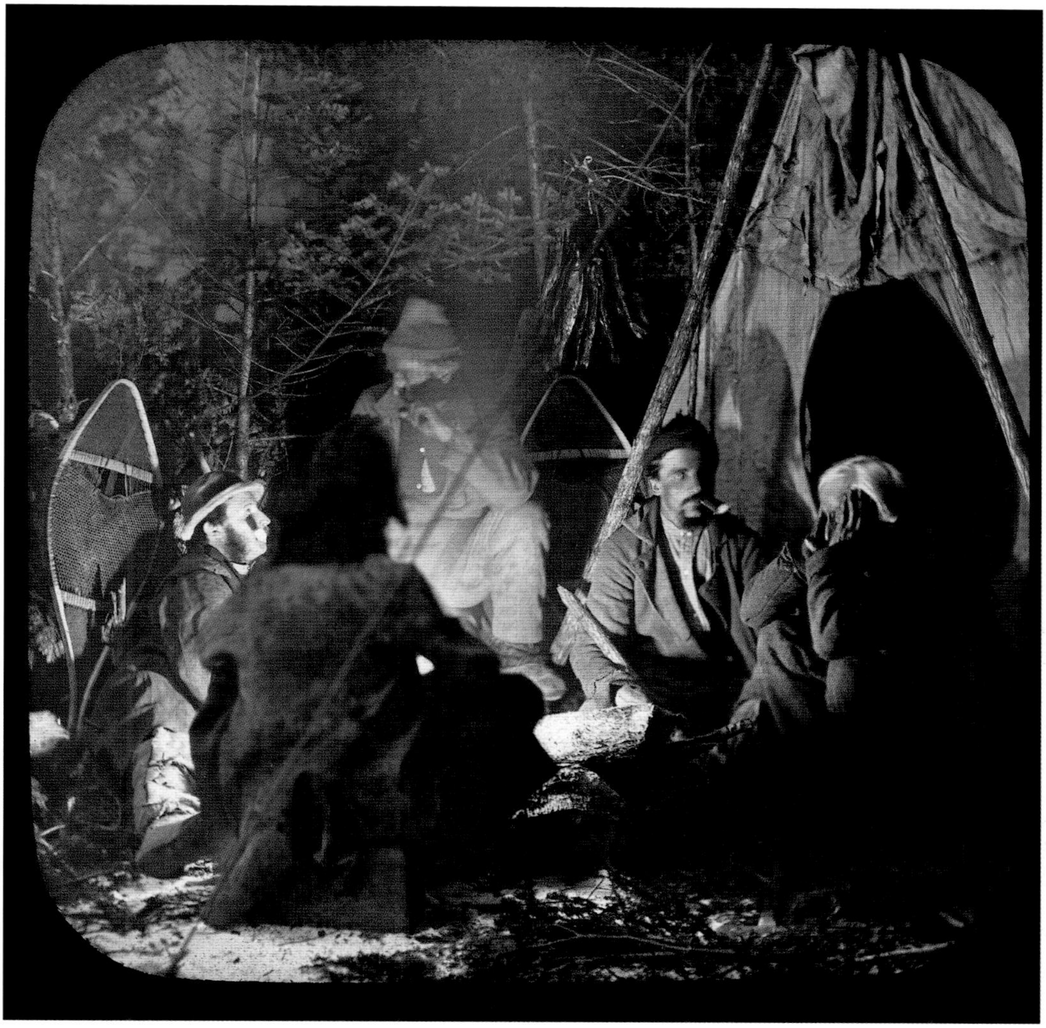

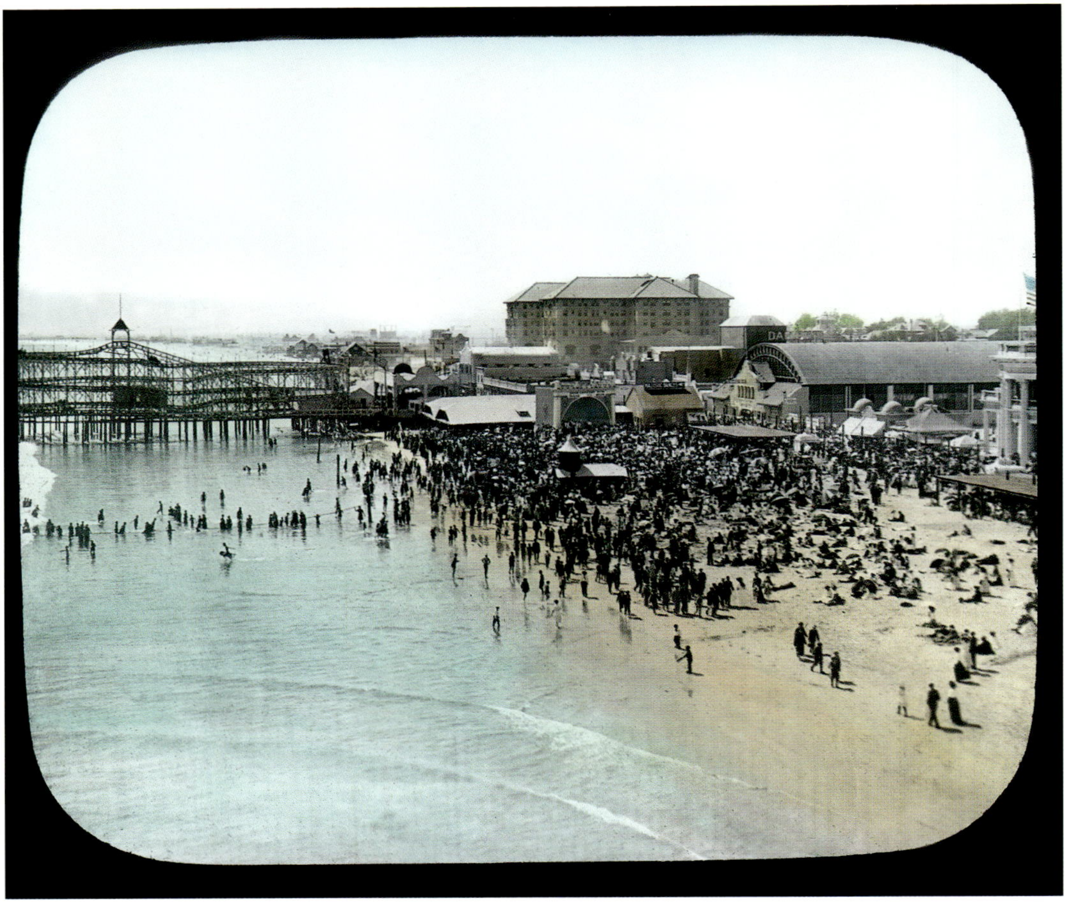

599 The Strand, Long Beach, California, USA, c.1902

599 The Strand, Long Beach, Kalifornien, USA, um 1902

599 The Strand, Long Beach, Californie, USA, vers 1902

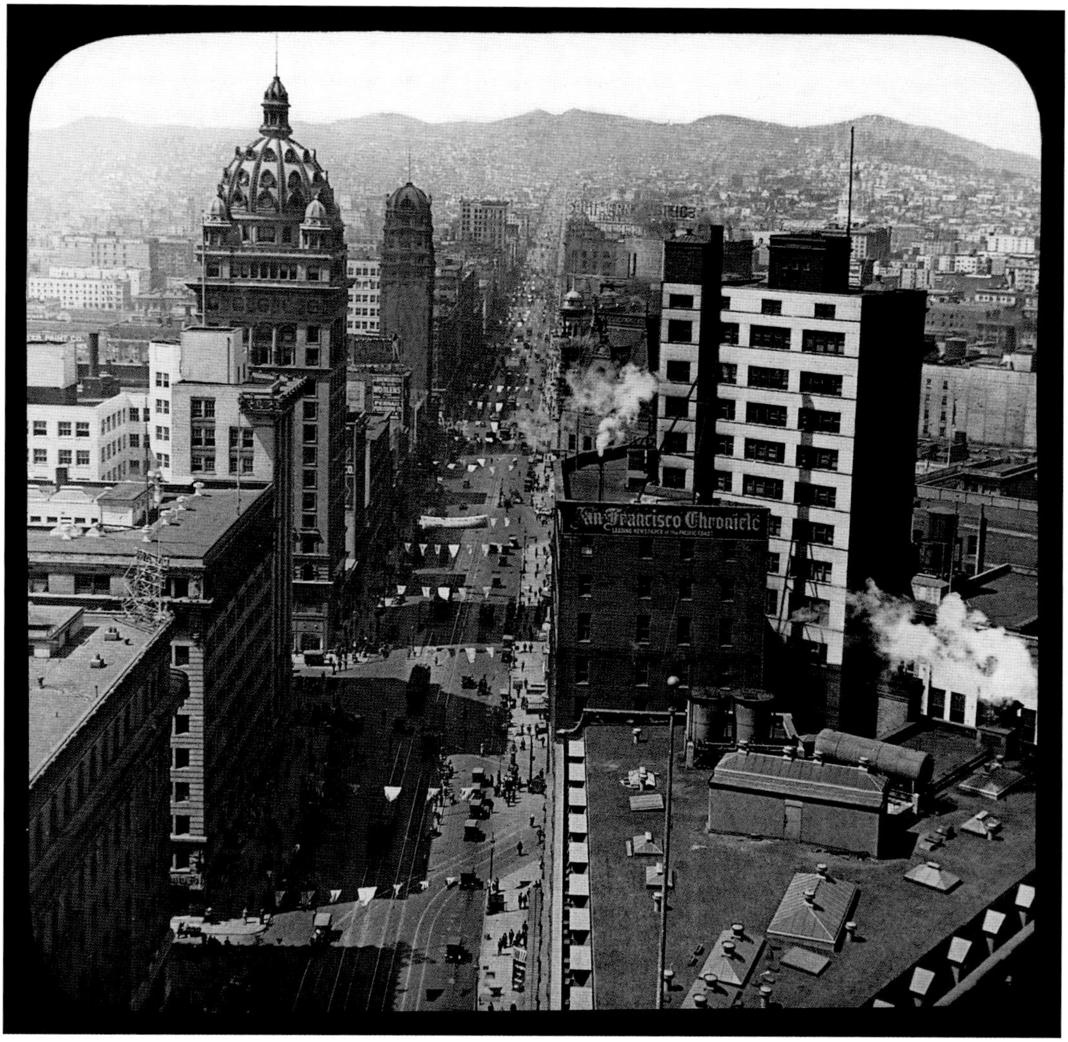

600 Market Street, with Twin Peaks in the distance, San Francisco, USA, 1900s

600 Die Market Street, im Hintergrund die Twin Peaks, San Francisco, USA, 1900er Jahre

600 Market Street et les collines de Twin Peaks, San Francisco, USA, années 1900

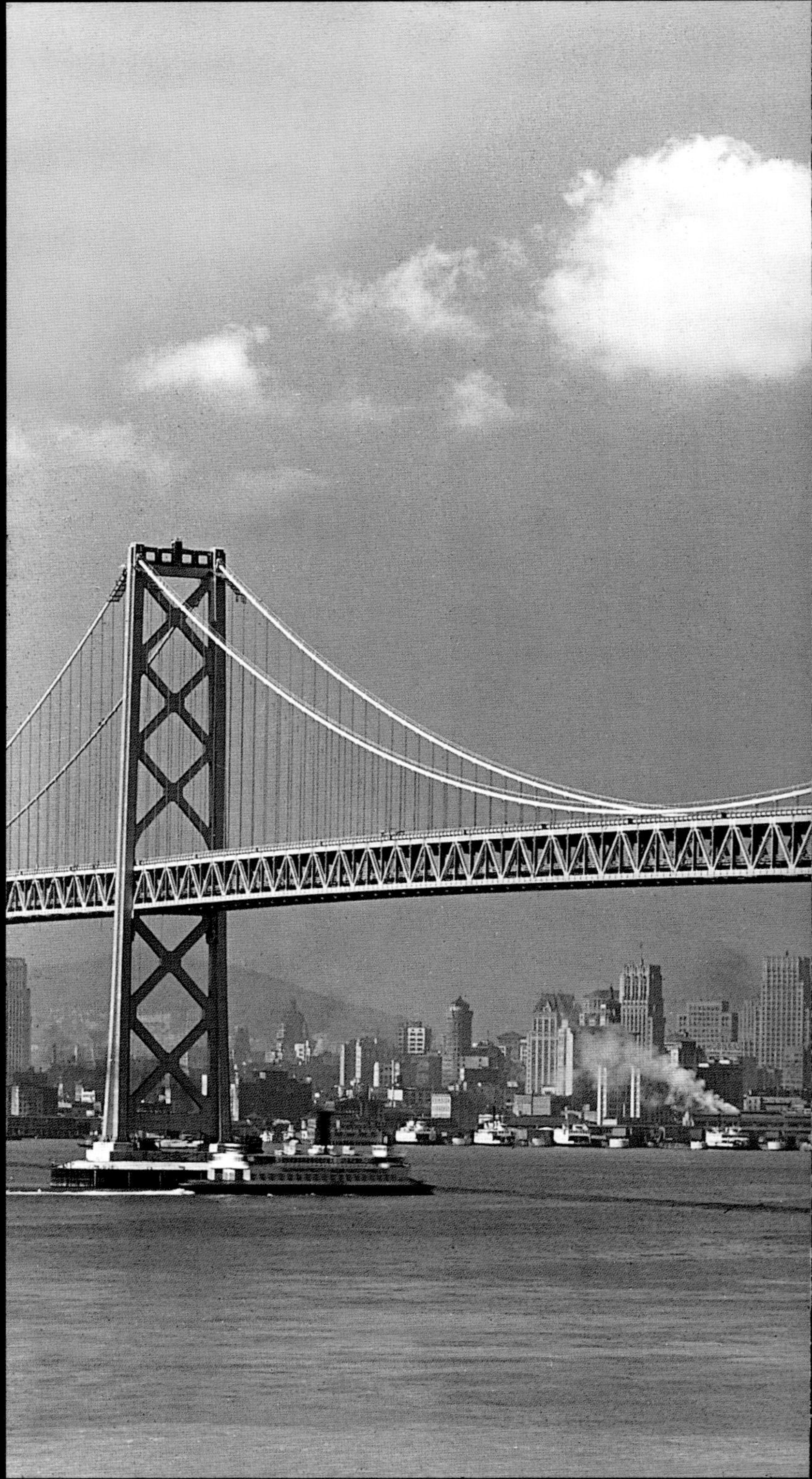

601 Golden
Gate Bridge, San
Francisco, c.1937

601 Die Golden-
Gate-Brücke, San
Francisco, um 1937

601 Pont du Golden
Gate, San Francisco,
vers 1937

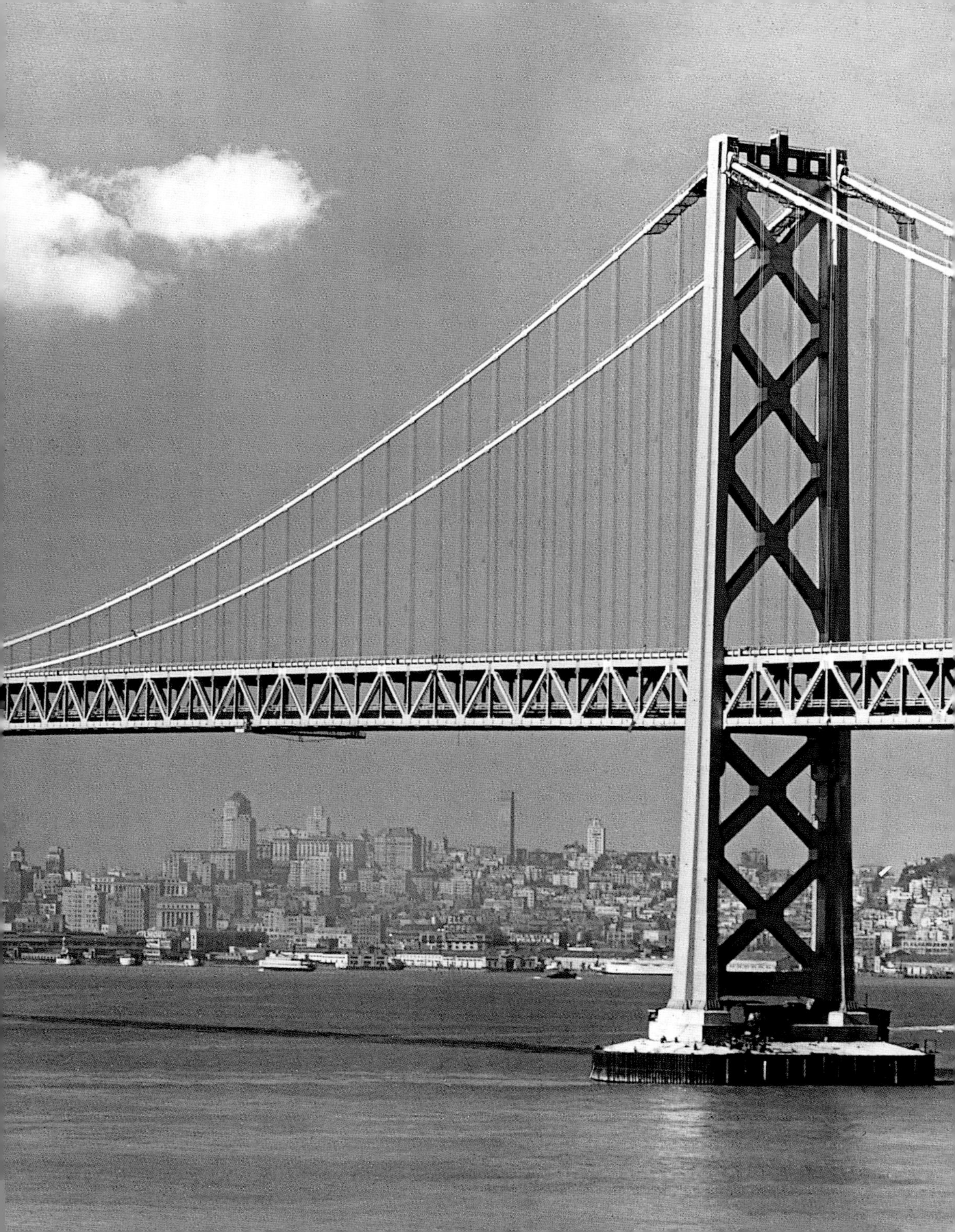

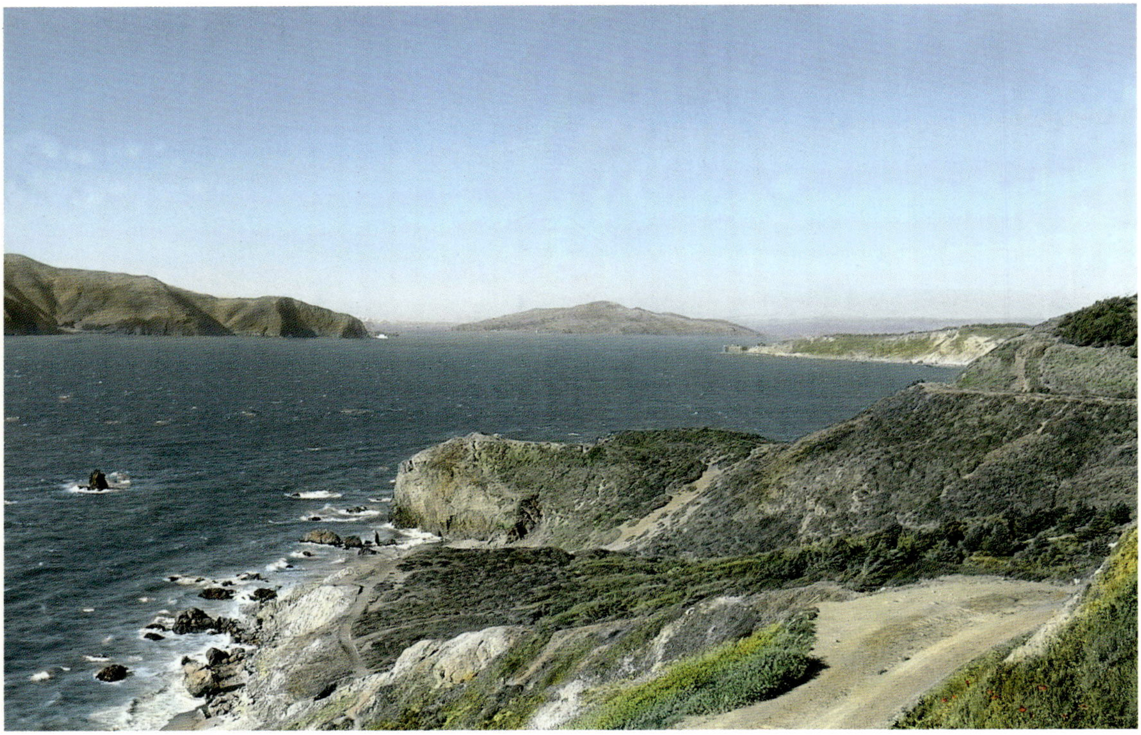

602 Golden Gate from Land's End with Angel Island in distance, San Francisco, California, USA, 1929

602 Das Golden Gate von Land's End aus gesehen, im Hintergrund Angel Island, San Francisco, Kalifornien, USA, 1929

602 Vue du Golden Gate depuis Land's End, et Angel Island au fond, San Francisco, Californie, USA, 1929

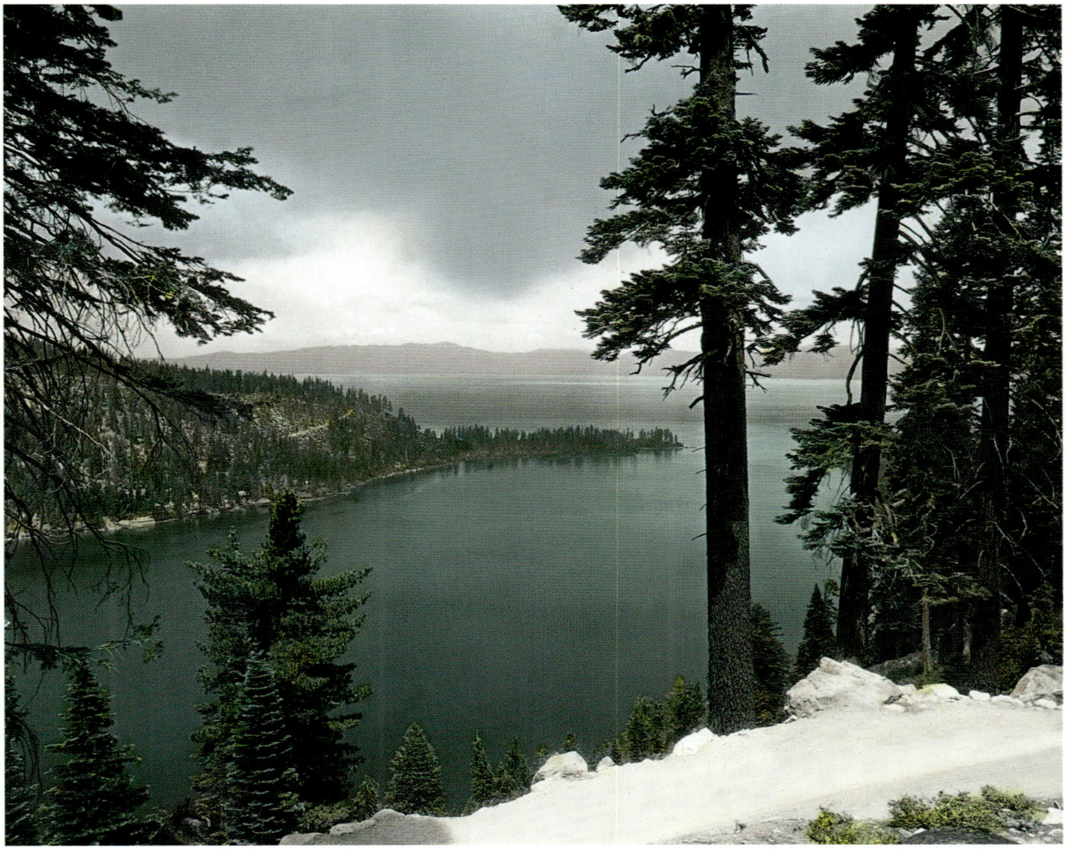

603 Emerald Bay, Lake Tahoe (view from Tioga Road), California, USA, c.1920

603 Die Emerald Bay, Lake Tahoe (Ansicht von der Tioga Road), Kalifornien, USA, um 1920

603 La baie d'Émeraude, lac Tahoe vu de Tioga Road, Californie, USA, vers 1920

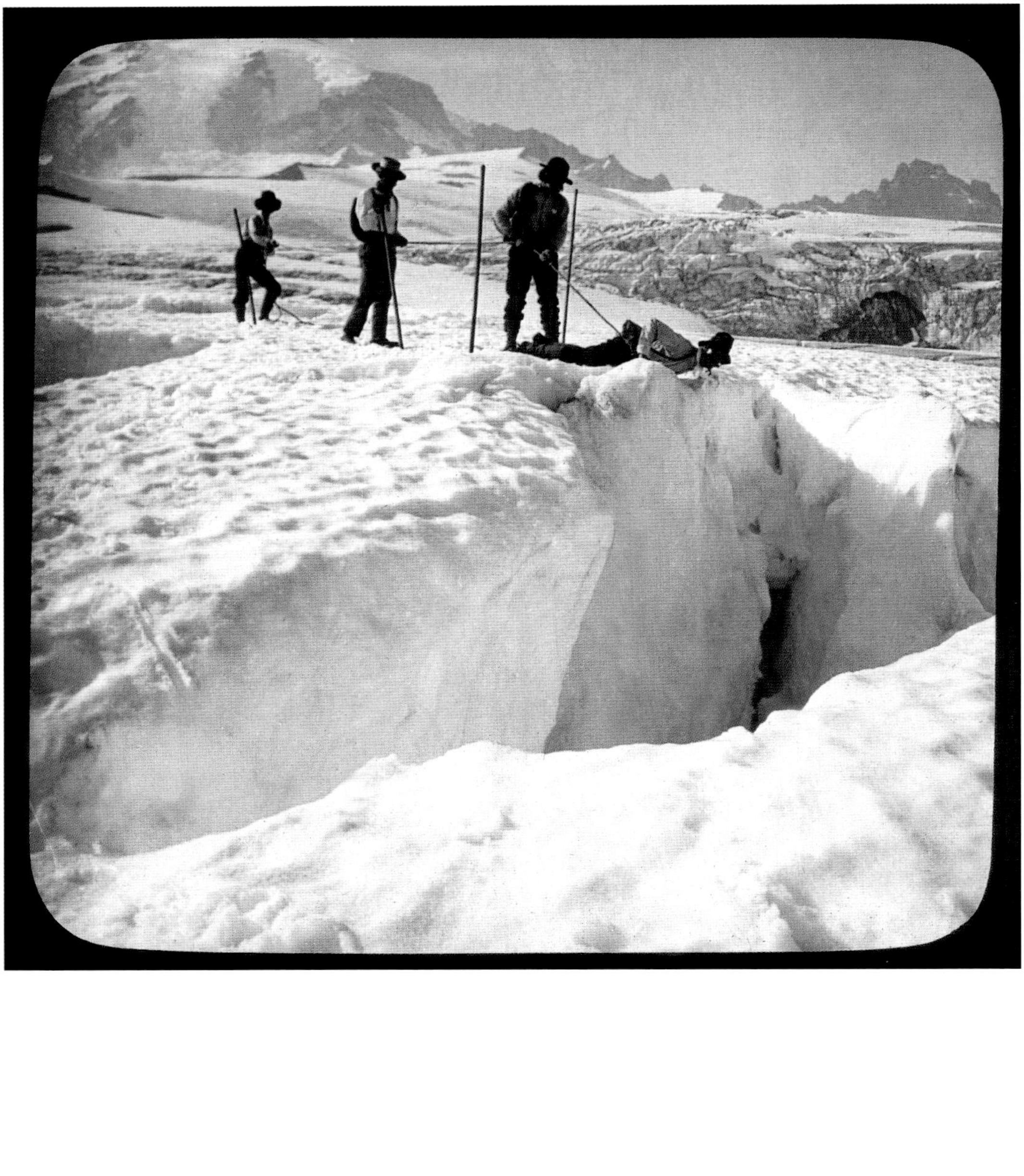

604 Deep crevasse on the Paradise Glacier, Rainer National Park, Washington, USA, 1890s

604 Tiefe Spalte auf dem Paradise-Gletscher, Mount-Rainier-Nationalpark, Washington, USA, 1890er Jahre

604 Profonde crevasse dans le glacier Paradise, Rainier National Park, Washington, USA, années 1890

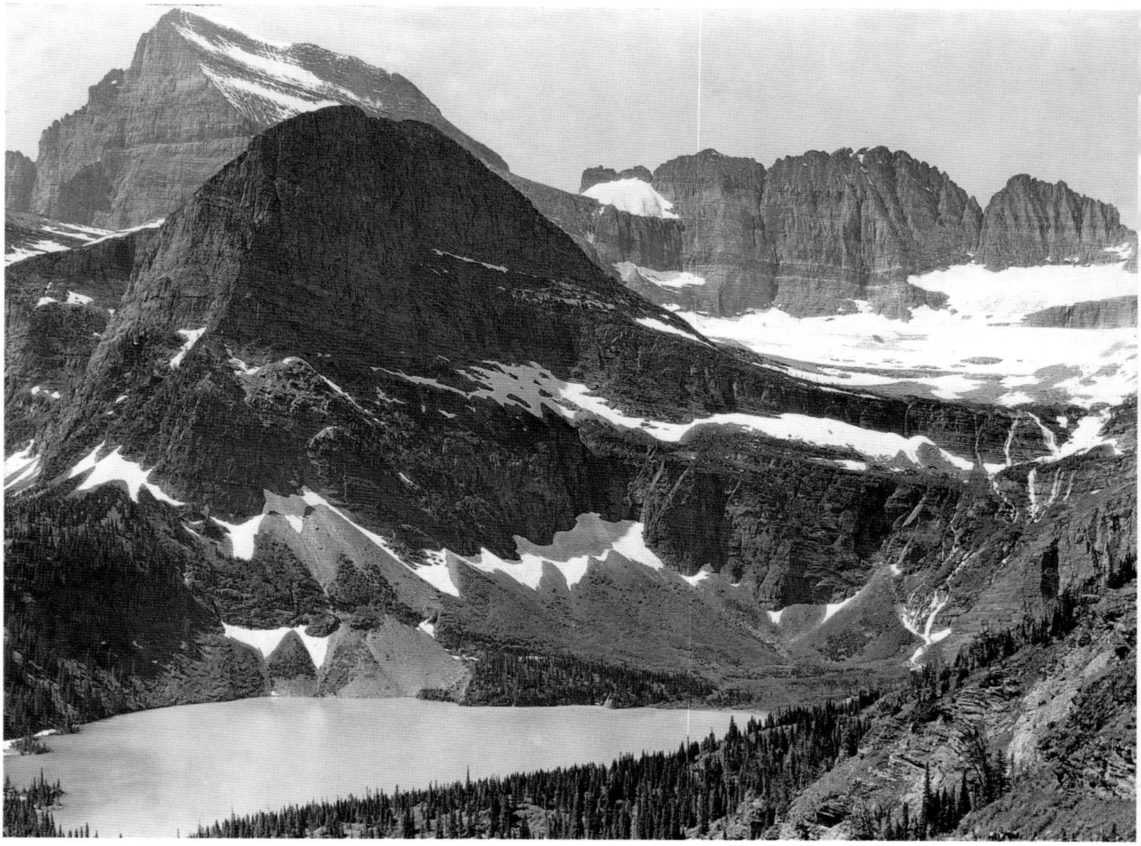

605 Grinnell Lake and Glacier, Mount Gould and Garden Wall, Glacier National Park, Montana, USA, c.1920

605 Der Grinnell-See und -Gletscher, Mount Gould und Garden Wall, Glacier-Nationalpark, Montana, USA, um 1920

605 Lac et glacier Grinnell, le mont Gould et Garden Wall, Glacier National Park, Montana, USA, vers 1920

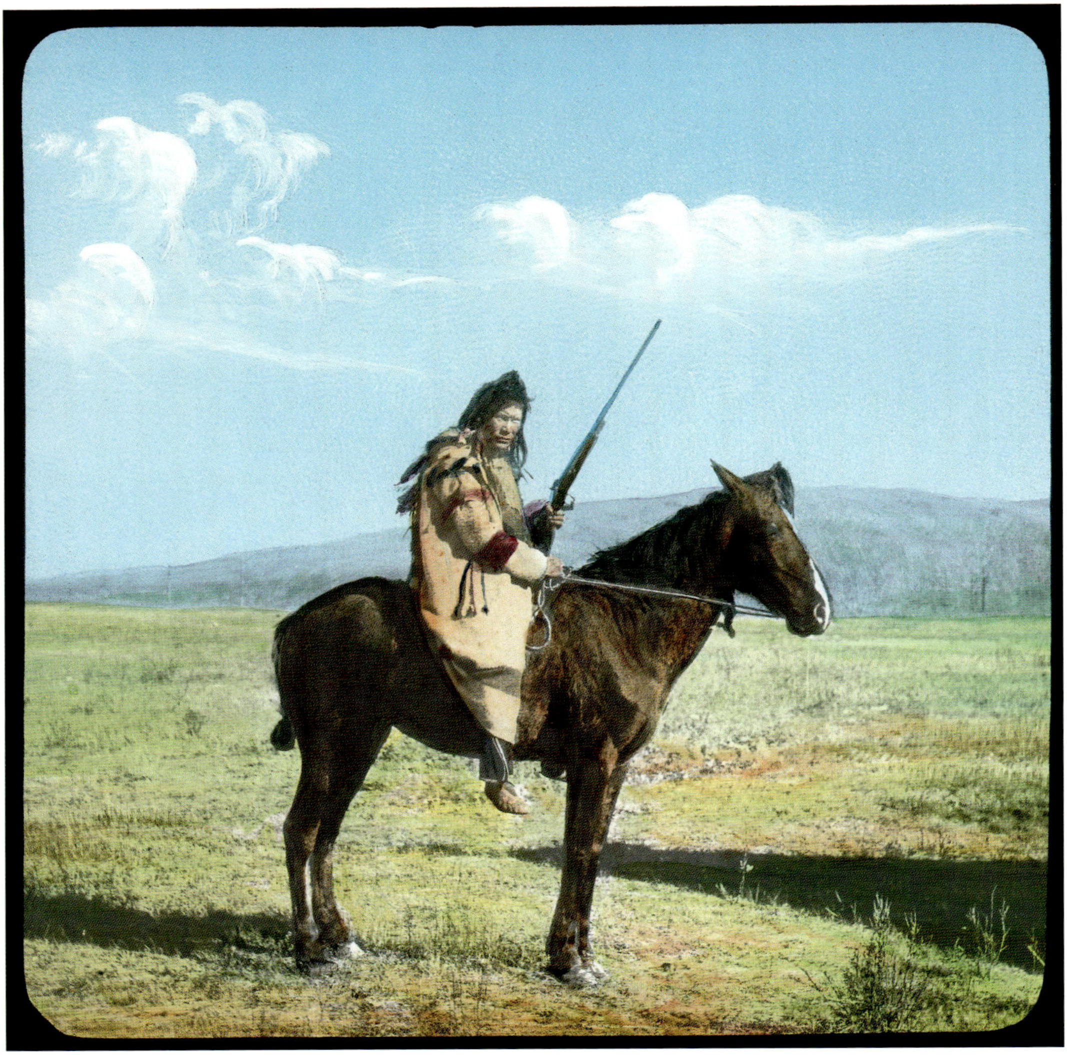

606 Native American on horse, USA, 1890s
607 Many Glacier Hotel, Glacier National Park, Montana, USA, c.1915, with bear grass in the foreground

606 Indianer auf einem Pferd, USA, 1890er Jahre
607 Das Many-Glacier-Hotel, Glacier-Nationalpark, Montana, USA, um 1915, im Vordergrund Bärengras

606 Amérindien à cheval, USA, années 1890
607 Many Glacier Hotel, Glacier National Park, Montana, USA, vers 1915 ; herbe d'ours au premier plan

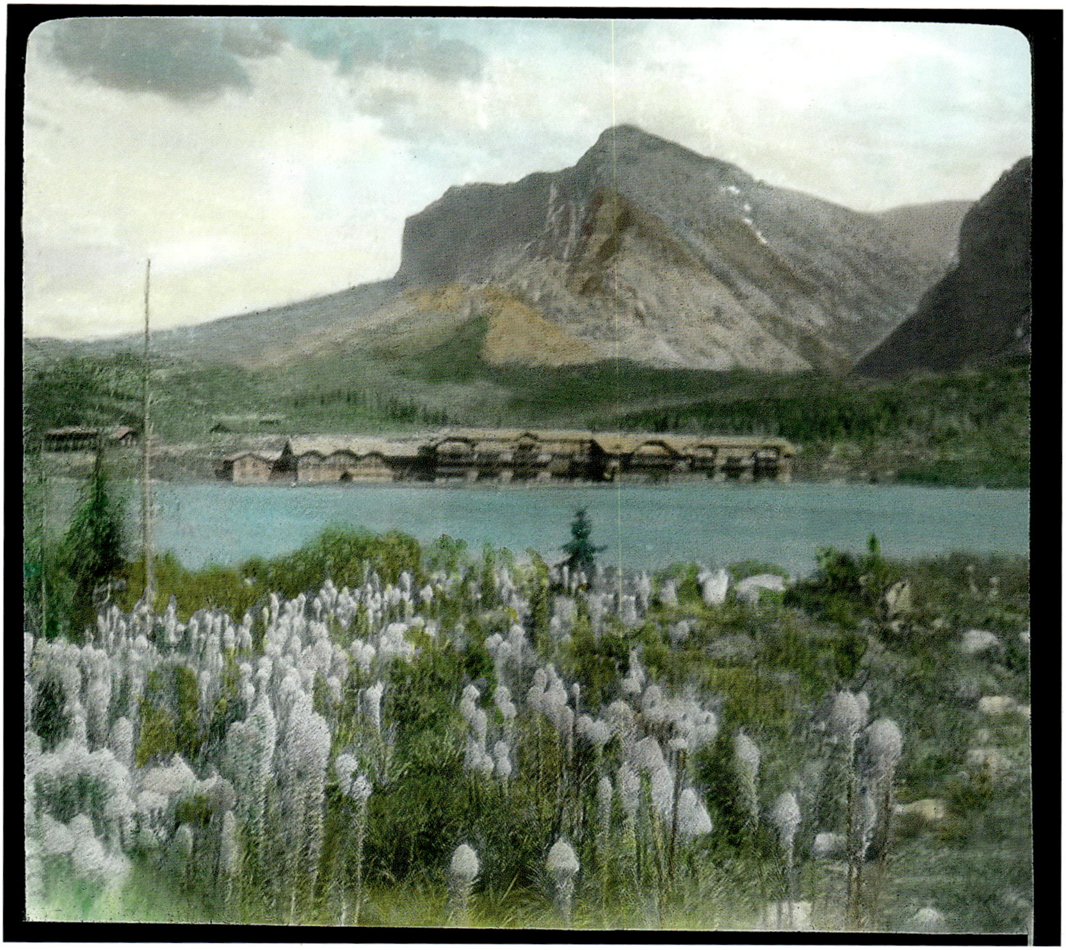

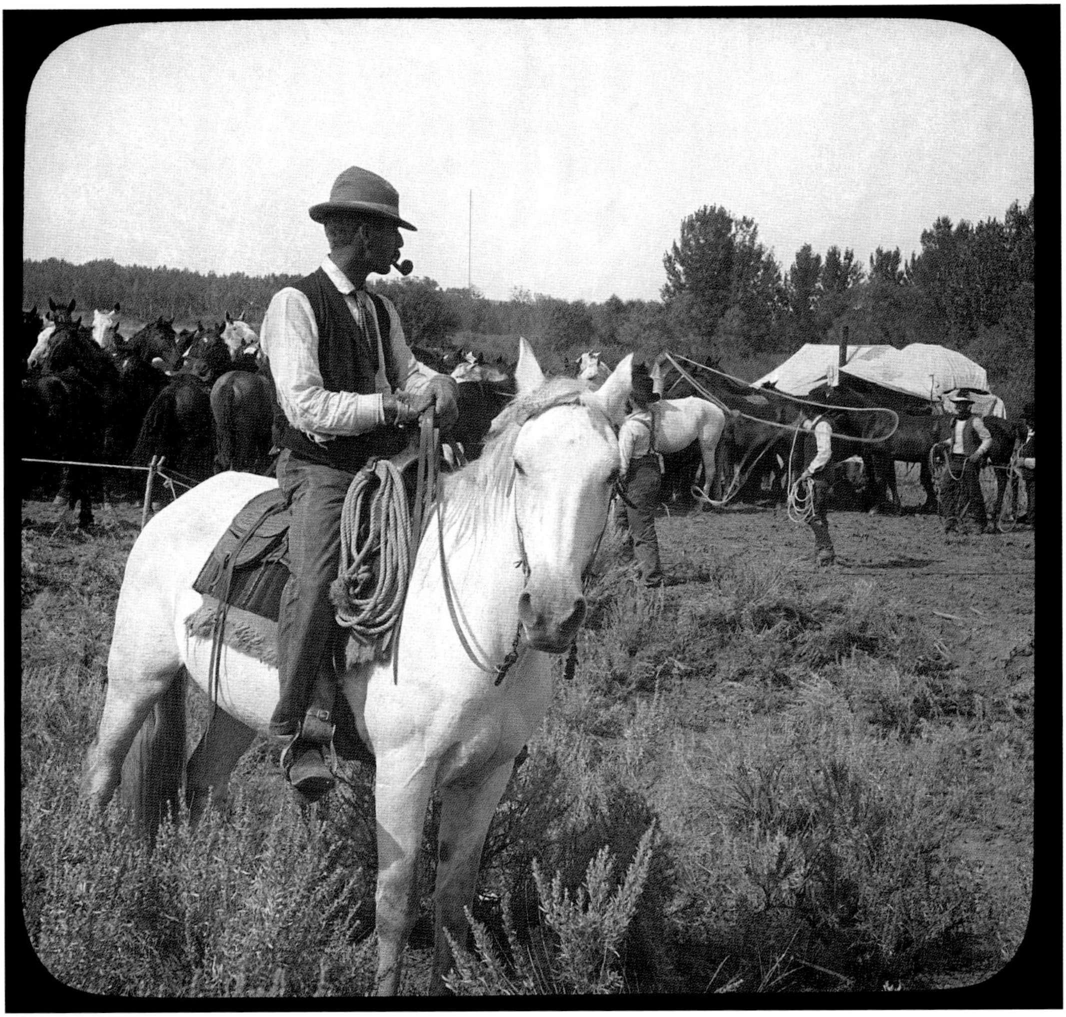

608 Cowboys, Bronco Corral and Camps, Montana, USA, c.1900
609 Harvest time in Middle West, America, 1900s

608 Cowboys, Pferch mit halbwilden Pferden und Lager, Montana, USA, um 1900
609 Erntezeit im Mittleren Westen, Amerika, 1900er Jahre

608 Cowboys, corral et camps de chevaux sauvage, Montana, USA, vers 1900
609 Temps des moissons dans le Middle West, Amérique, années 1900

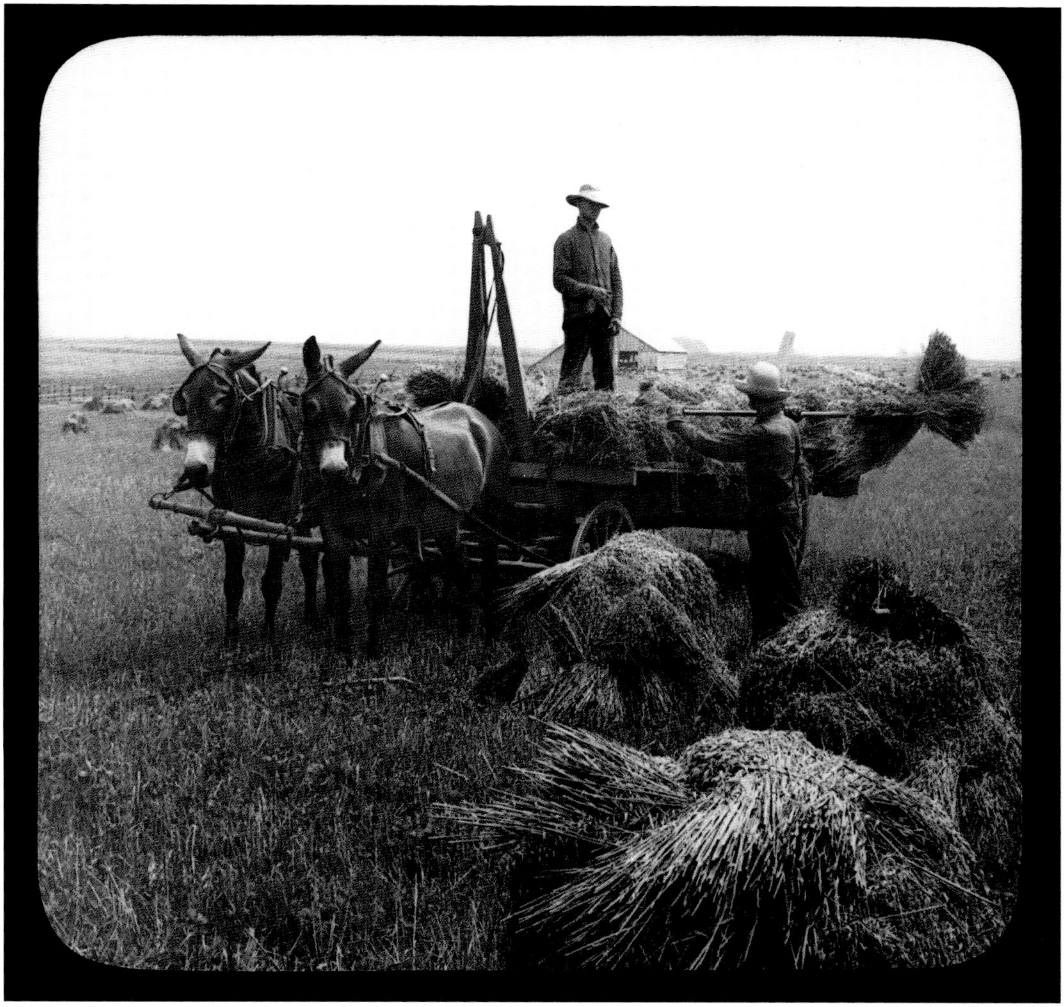

610 "Old Faithful" geyser, Yellowstone National Park, Wyoming, 1900s

610 Der Geysir „Old Faithful", Yellowstone-Nationalpark, Wyoming, 1900er Jahre

610 Geyser du "Vieux Fidèle", Yellowstone National Park, Wyoming, années 1900

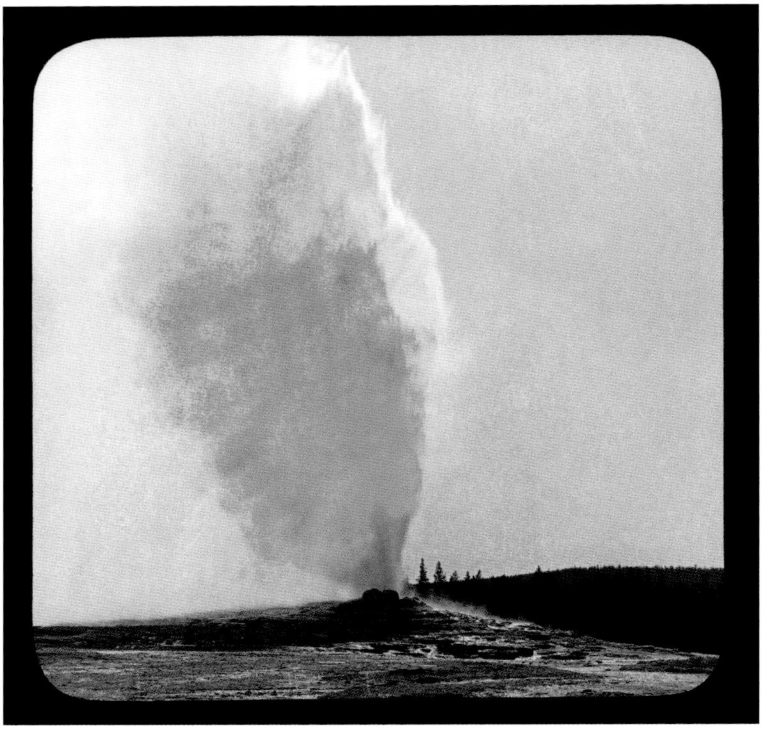

611 Rapids of the Canyon, Yosemite National Park, Wawona (CA), USA, 1900s

611 Stromschnellen im Canyon, Yosemite-Nationalpark, Wawona (Kalifornien), USA, 1900er Jahre

611 Rapides dans le canyon, Yosemite National Park, Wawona (CA), USA, années 1900

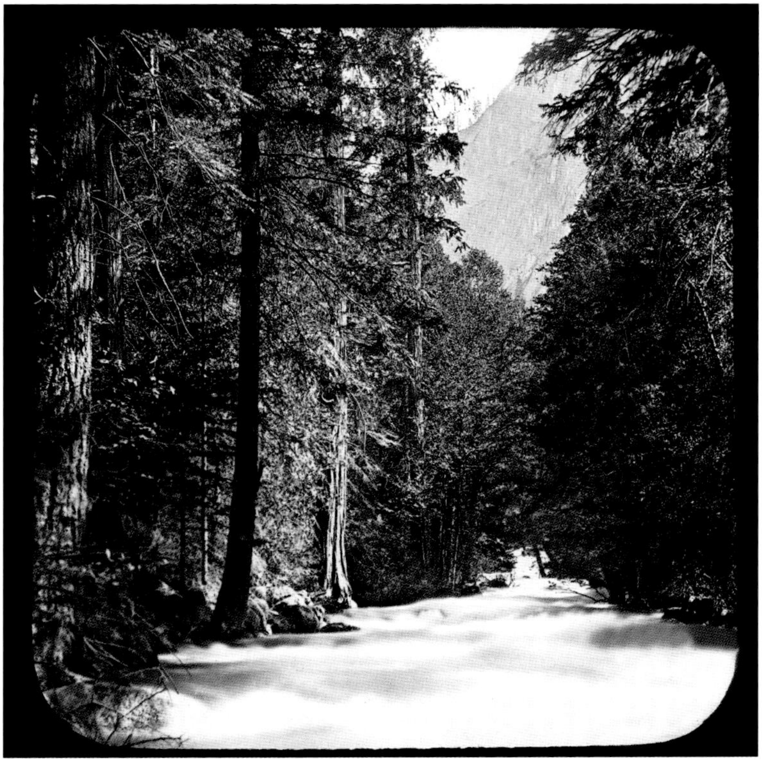

612 Castle Geyser, Upper Basin, Yellowstone National Park, Wyoming USA, 1900s

612 Der Castle-Geysir, Oberes Geysirbecken, Yellowstone-Nationalpark, Wyoming, USA, 1900er Jahre

612 Geyser du Château, bassin supérieur, Yellowstone National Park, Wyoming USA, années 1900

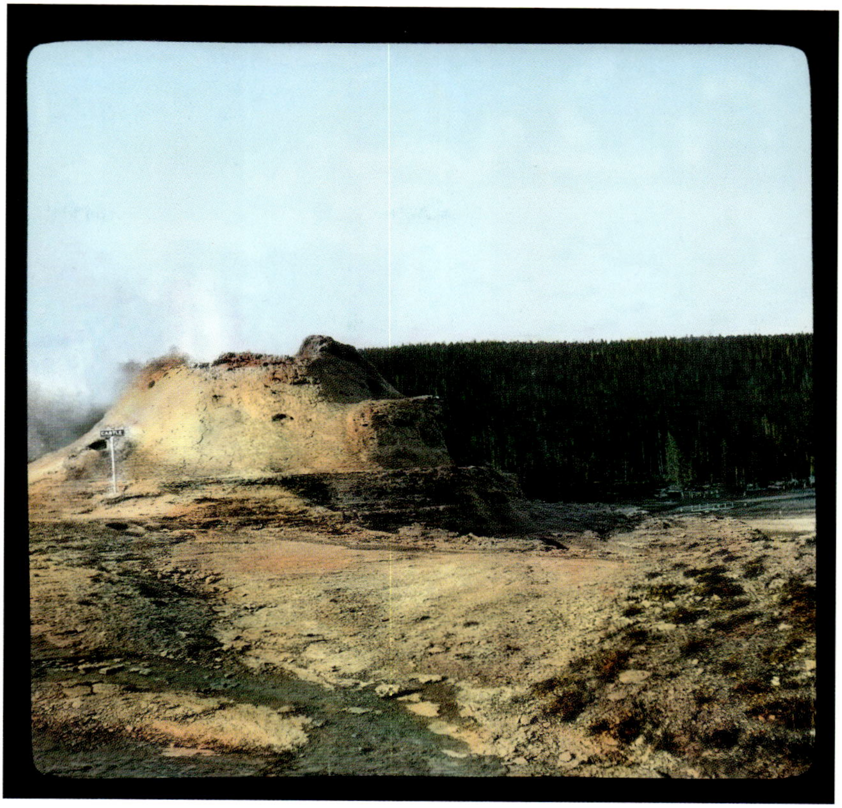

613 Riverside Geyser, Upper Basin, Yellowstone National Park, Wyoming, USA, 1900s

613 Der Riverside-Geysir, Oberes Geysirbecken, Yellowstone-Nationalpark, Wyoming, USA, 1900er Jahre

613 Geyser du bord de l'eau, bassin supérieur, Yellowstone National Park, Wyoming, USA, années 1900

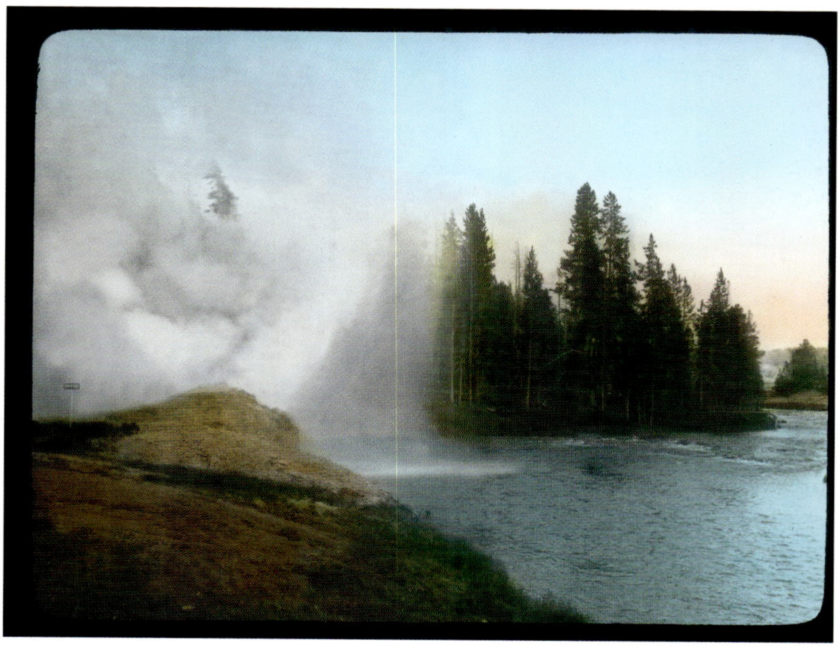

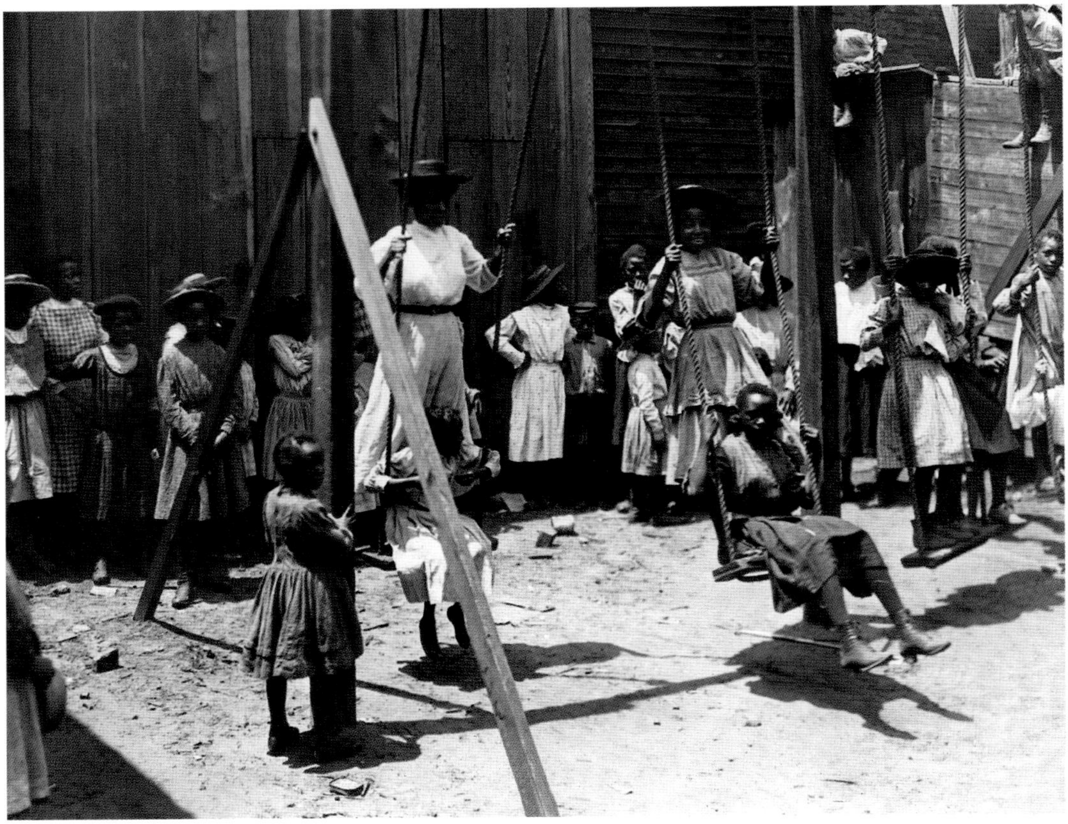

614 “Playground movement for Negro Children”, USA, 1920s
615 “A June Carnival, Dancing Around the Daisy Pole”, USA, c.1900

614 „Die Bewegung ‚Spielplatz für Negerkinder‘“, USA, 1920er Jahre
615 “Karneval im Juni, Tanz um den Sonnenbaum”, USA, um 1900

614 “Le mouvement Cour de récré pour les enfants noirs”, USA, années 1920
615 “Carnaval de juin, danse autour du mât à marguerites”, USA, vers 1900

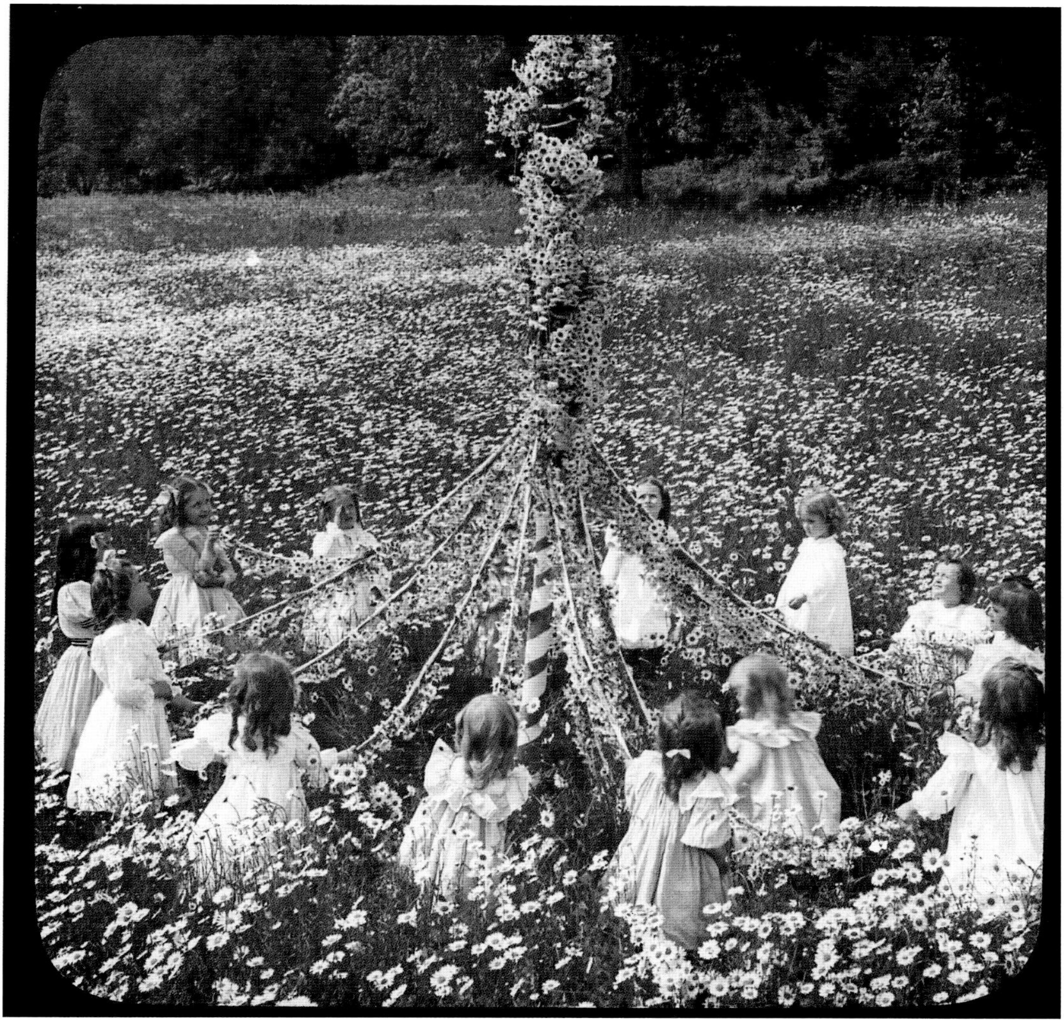

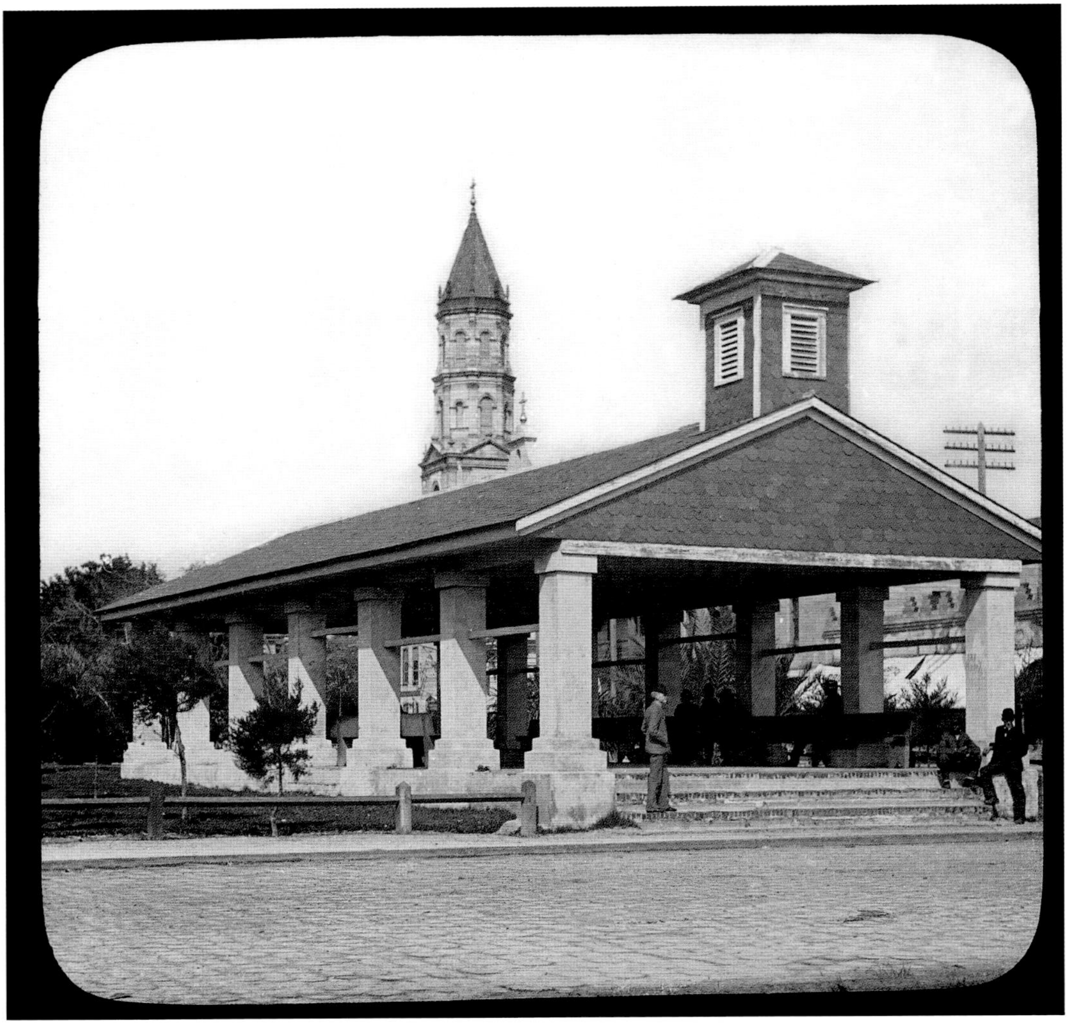

616 Old Slave Market, St. Augustine, Florida, USA, 1910s
617 "Battle with a Wounded 'Gator", Palm Beach, Florida, USA, c.1900

616 Der Alte Sklavenmarkt, St. Augustine, Florida, USA, 1910er Jahre
617 "Kampf mit einem verwundeten Alligator", Palm Beach, Florida, USA, um 1900

616 Ancien marché aux esclaves, St. Augustine, Floride, USA, années 1910
617 "Confrontation avec un alligator blessé", Palm Beach, Floride, USA, vers 1900

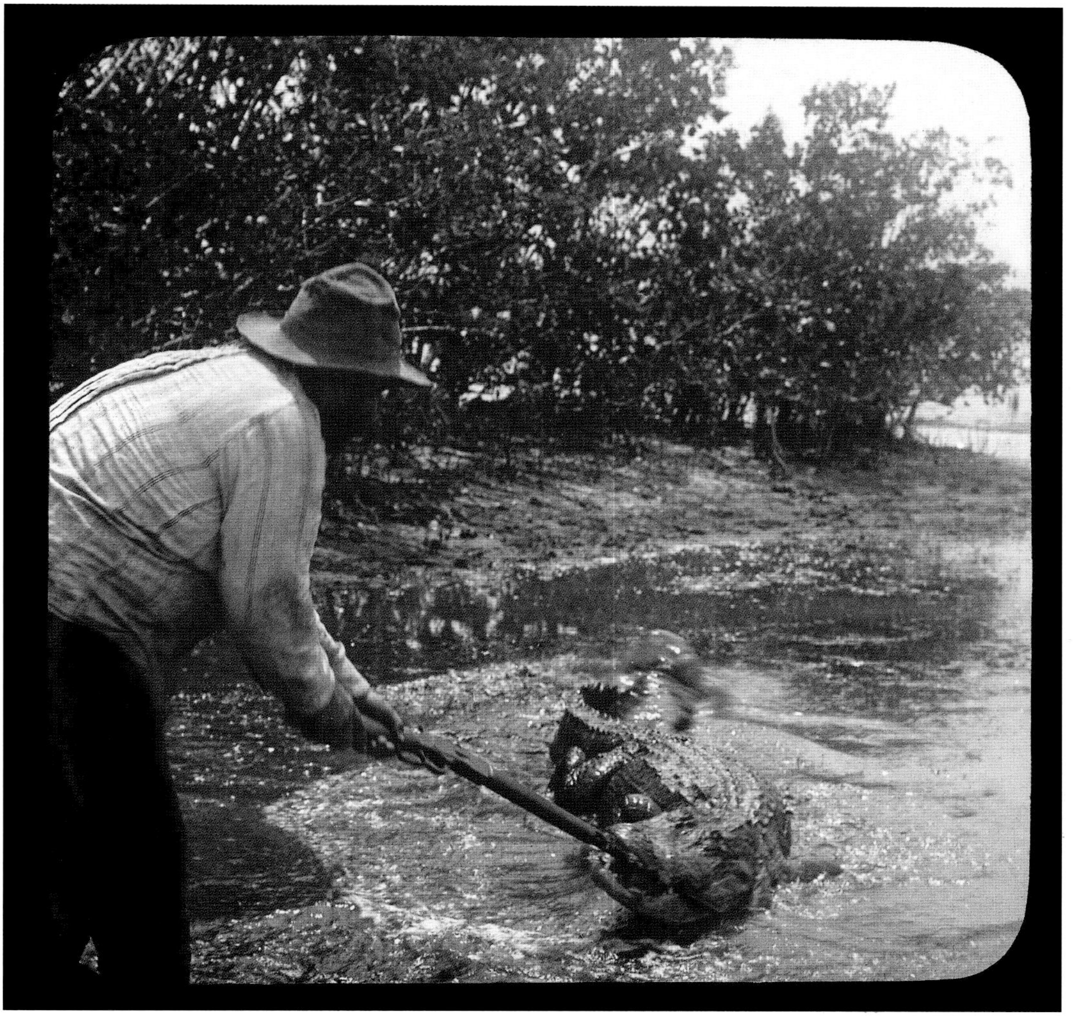

618 Child cotton pickers, Missouri, USA, 1890s

618 Kinder beim Baumwollpflücken, Missouri, USA, 1890er Jahre

618 Enfants cueilleurs de coton, Missouri, USA, années 1890

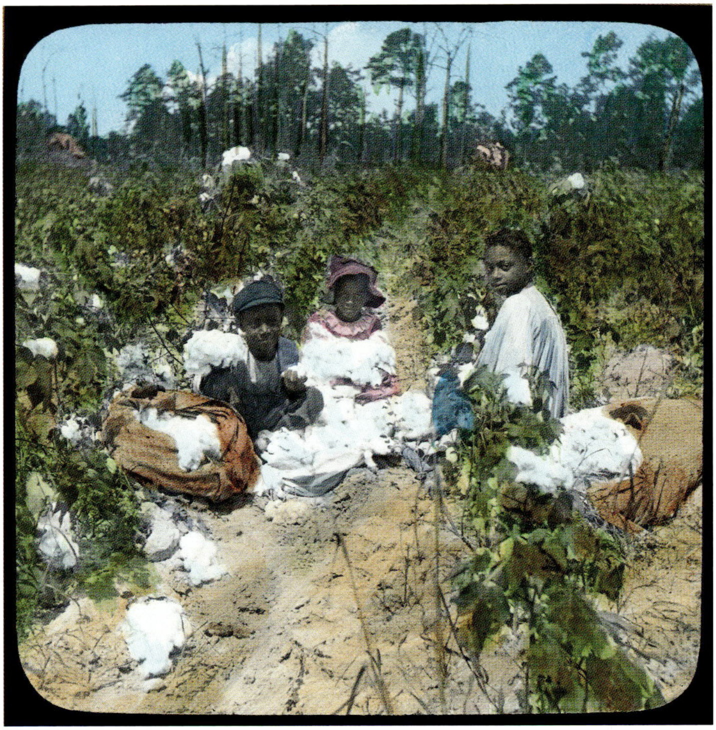

619 Girl cotton picker, Missouri, USA, 1890s

619 Mädchen beim Baumwollpflücken, Missouri, USA, 1890er Jahre

619 Jeune cueilleuse de coton, Missouri, USA, années 1890

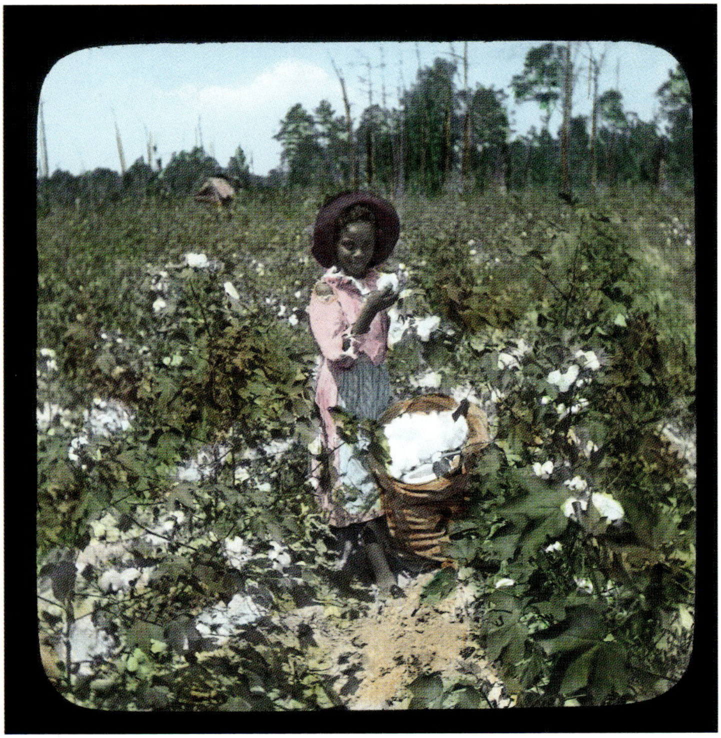

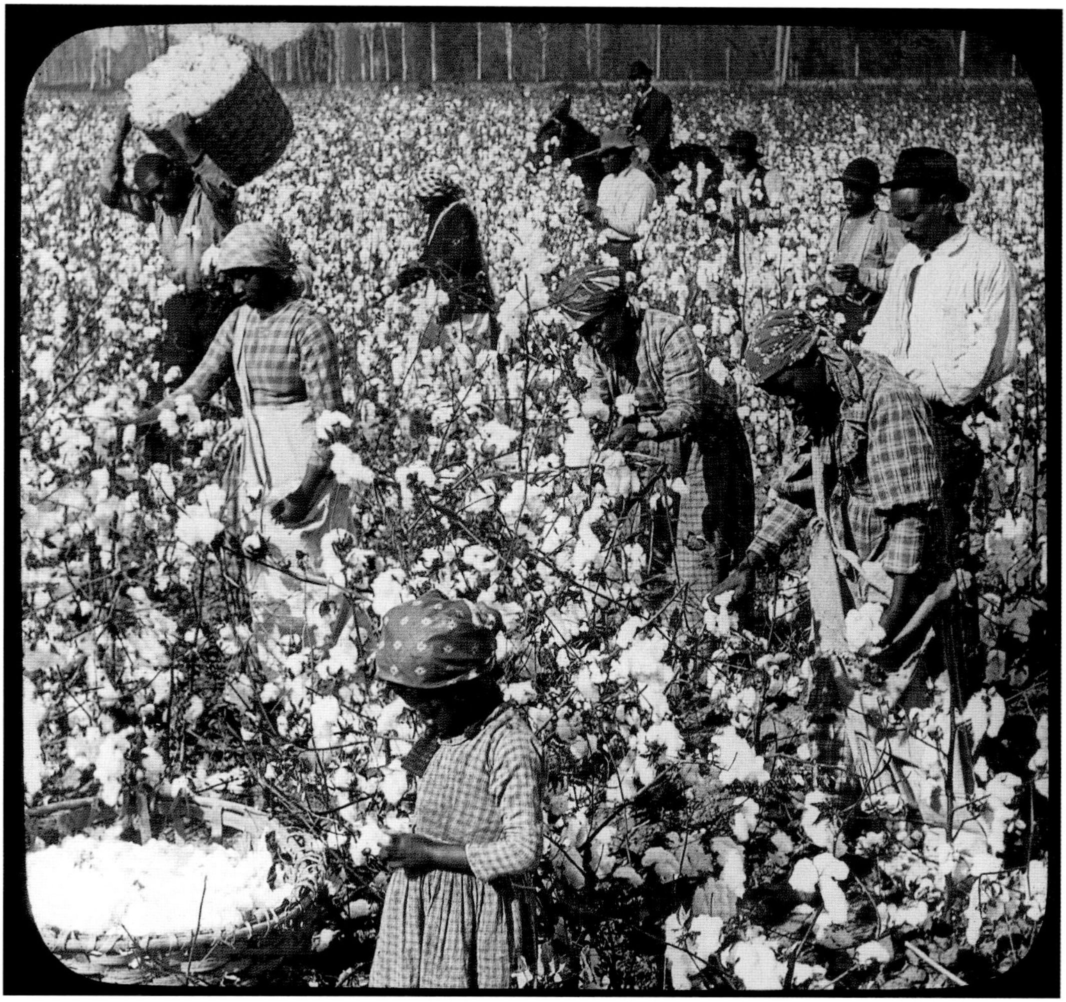

620 Plantation scene, Georgia, USA, 1900s

620 Baumwollplantage, Georgia, USA, 1900er Jahre

620 Plantation de coton, Géorgie, USA, années 1900

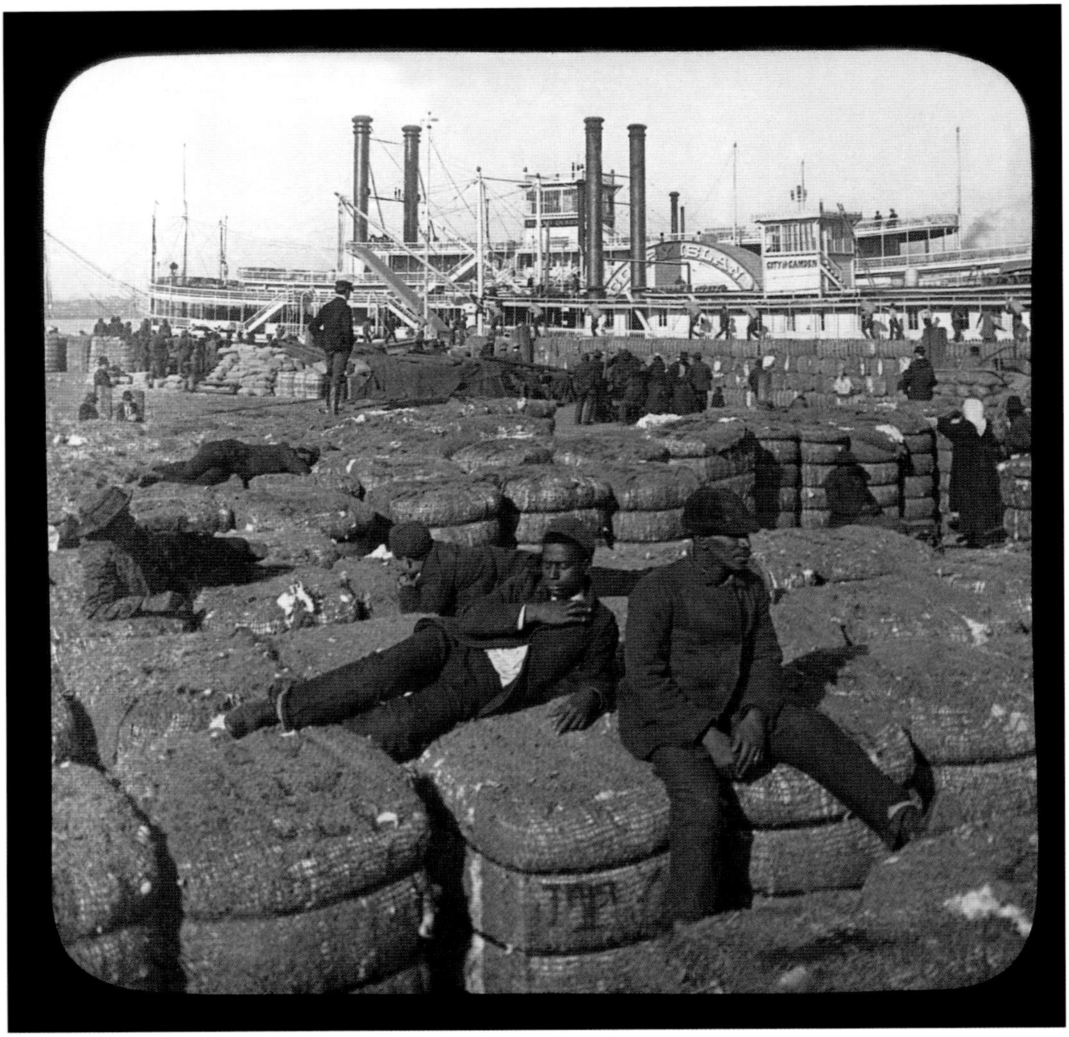

621 "Cotton! Cotton! Cotton!", workers resting on bundles of cotton on a Levee, New Orleans, Louisiana, USA, 1900s

621 "Baumwolle! Baumwolle! Baumwolle!", Arbeiter ruhen sich auf Baumwollballen auf einem Damm aus, New Orleans, Louisiana, USA, 1900er Jahre

621 "Coton ! Coton ! Coton !" Ouvriers se reposant sur des ballots de coton, sur une digue à La Nouvelle-Orléans, Louisiane, USA, années 1900

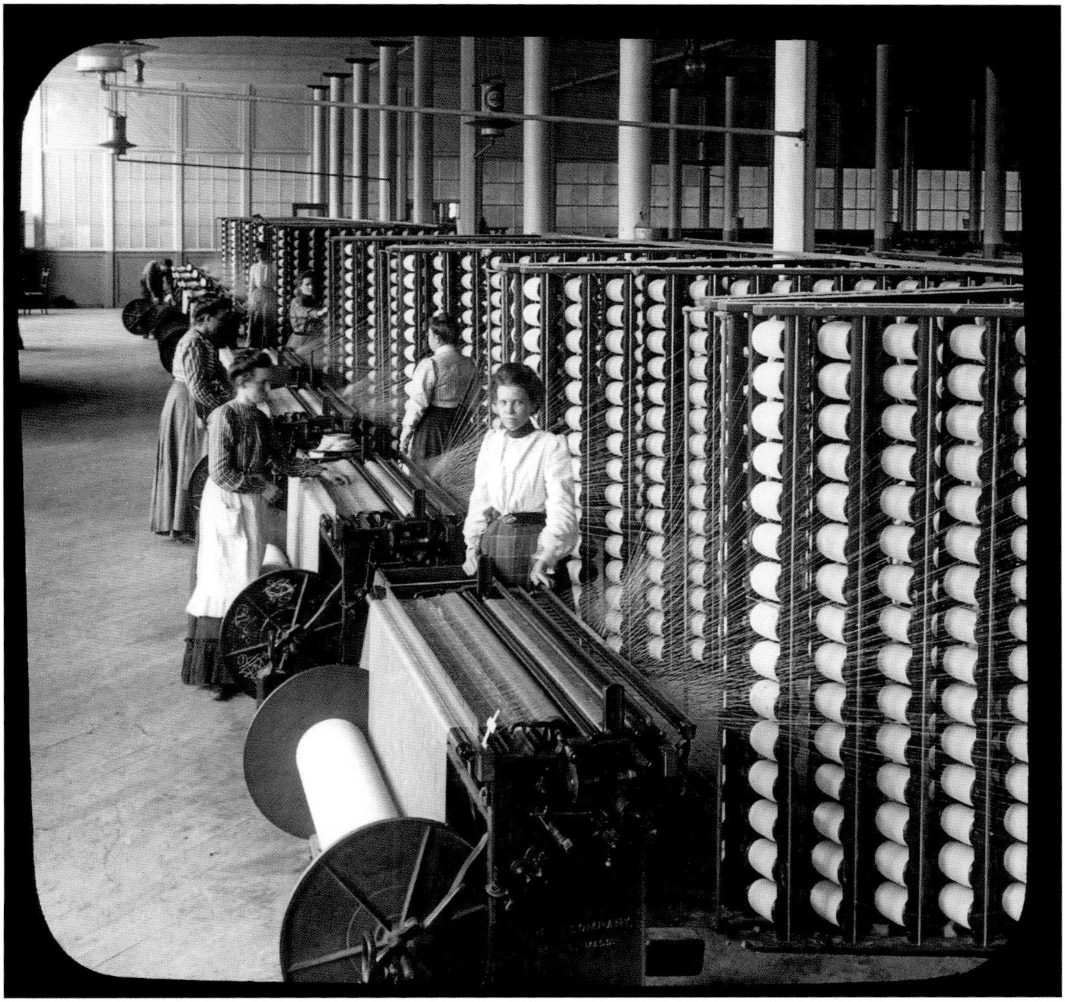

622 Warping room at the Olympian Cotton Mills, Columbia, South Carolina, USA, c.1900

622 Schärerei der Olympian Cotton Mills, Columbia, South Carolina, USA, um 1900

622 Salle d'ourdissage à l'Olympian Cotton Mills, Columbia, Caroline du Sud, USA, vers 1900

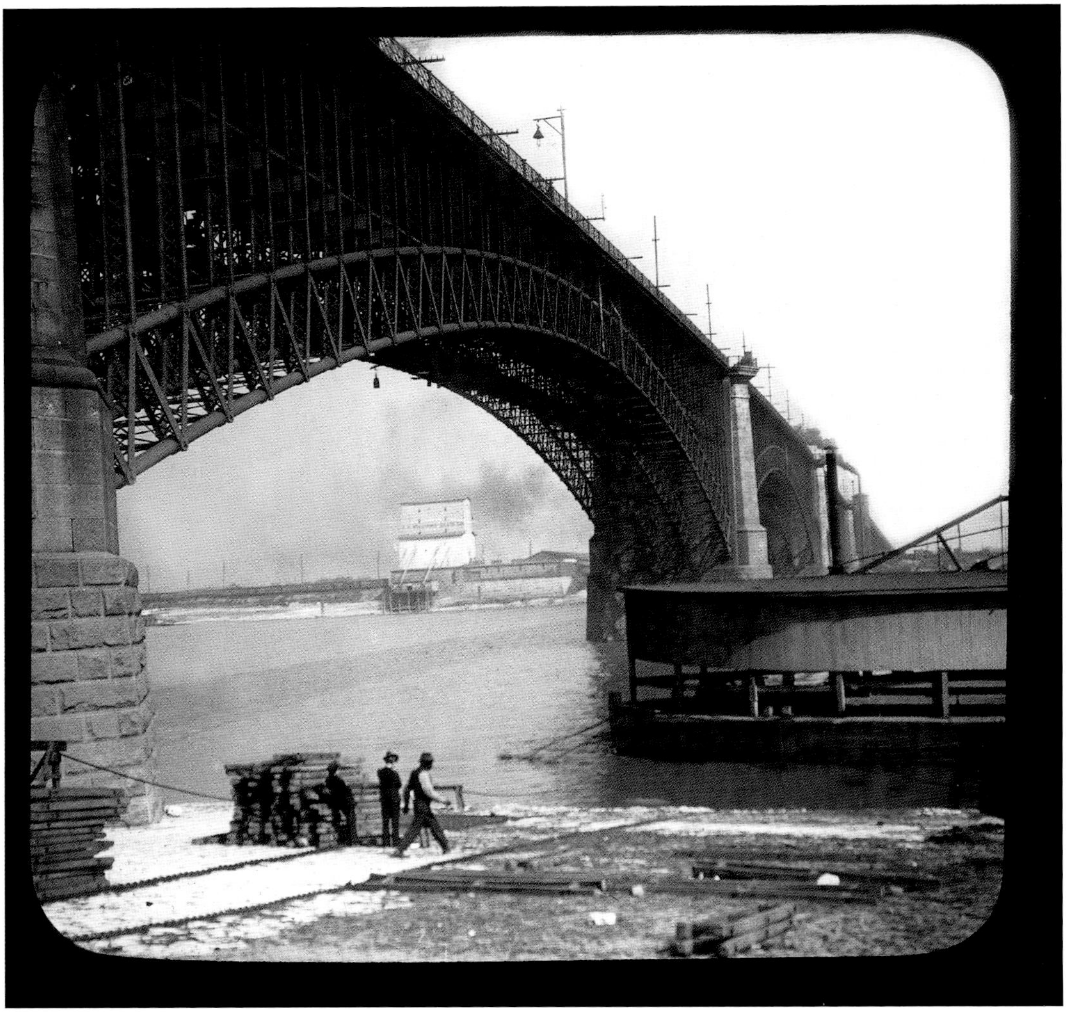

623 Eads Bridge spanning the Mississippi River, St. Louis, USA, 1890s

623 Die Eads-Brücke, die den Mississippi überspannt, St. Louis, USA, 1890er Jahre

623 Pont Eads franchissant le Mississippi, St. Louis, USA, années 1890

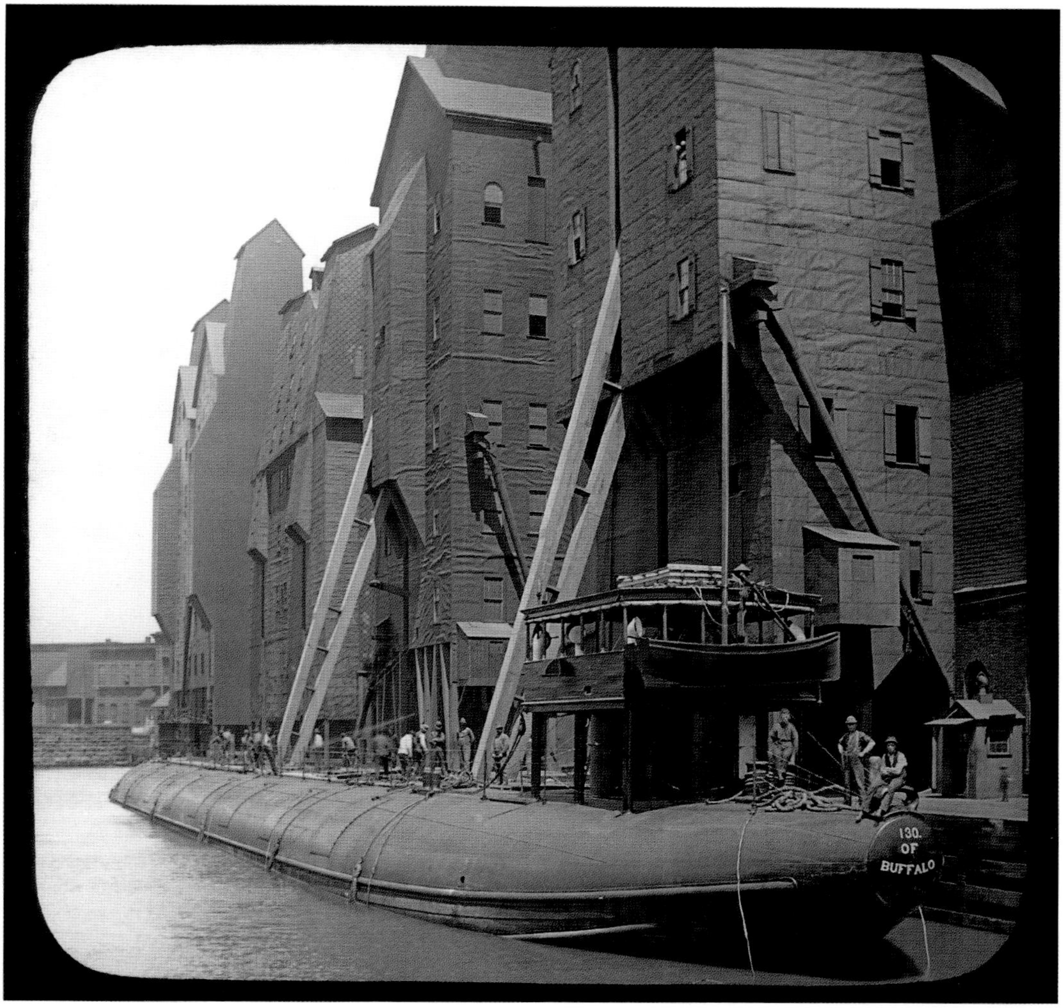

624 Loading a whaleback ship at the grain elevators of Chicago, Illinois, USA, 1895

624 Ein Whaleback-Schiff (Walrücken) wird an den Getreidespeichern von Chicago beladen, Illinois, USA, 1895

624 Chargement d'un navire de type whaleback, "dos de baleine", aux élévateurs à grain de Chicago, Illinois, USA, 1895

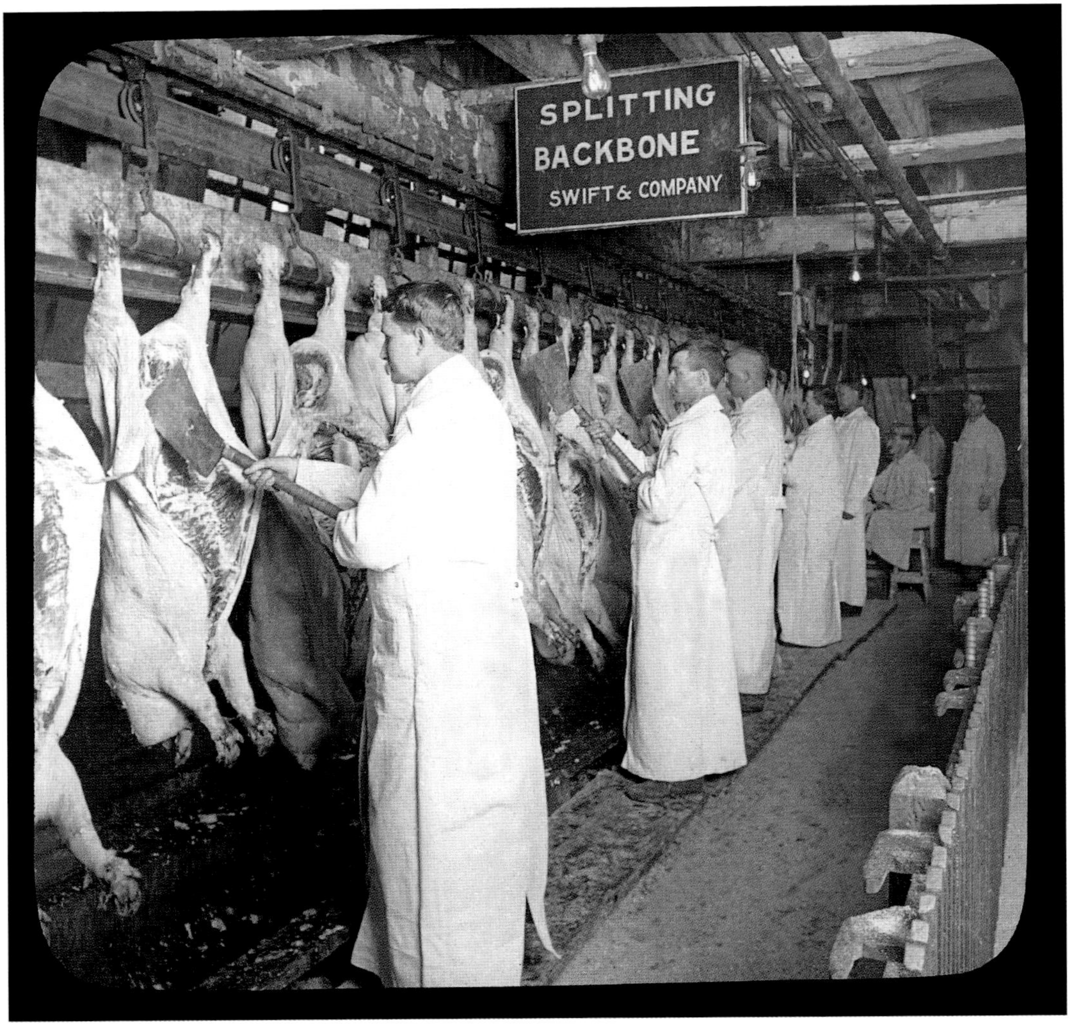

625 Splitting backbones and inspection of hogs, Swift & Co. (meatpackers), Chicago, Illinois, c.1900

625 Zerlegen und Beschau von Schweinerücken, Swift & Co. (Fleischpacker), Chicago, Illinois, um 1900

625 Fente des échines et inspection des porcs aux abattoirs Swift & Co. à Chicago, Illinois, vers 1900

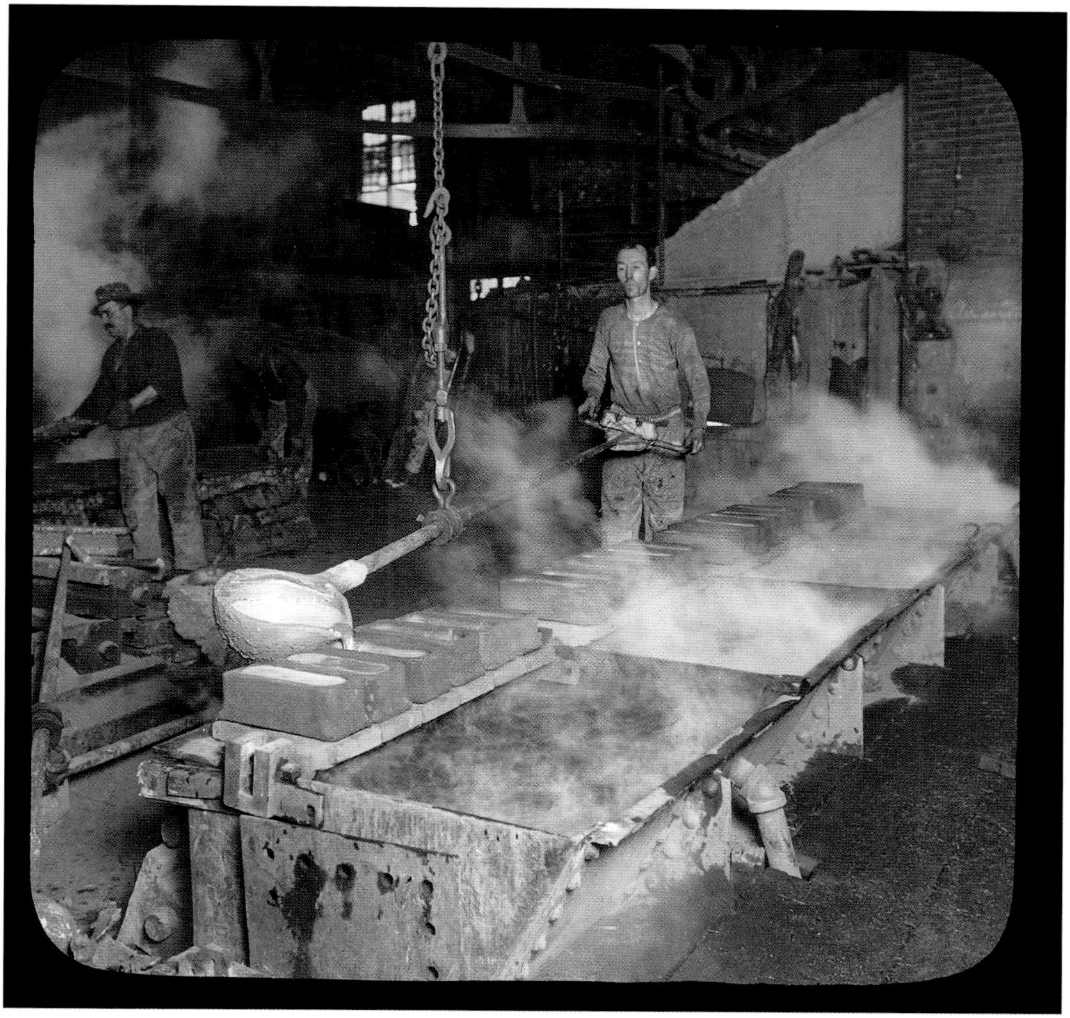

626 Pouring molten copper into ingot moulds, Calumet, Michigan, USA, c.1900

626 Geschmolzenes Kupfer wird in Barrenkokillen gegossen, Calumet, Michigan, USA, um 1900

626 Coulée du cuivre dans les moules à lingot, Calumet, Michigan, USA, vers 1900

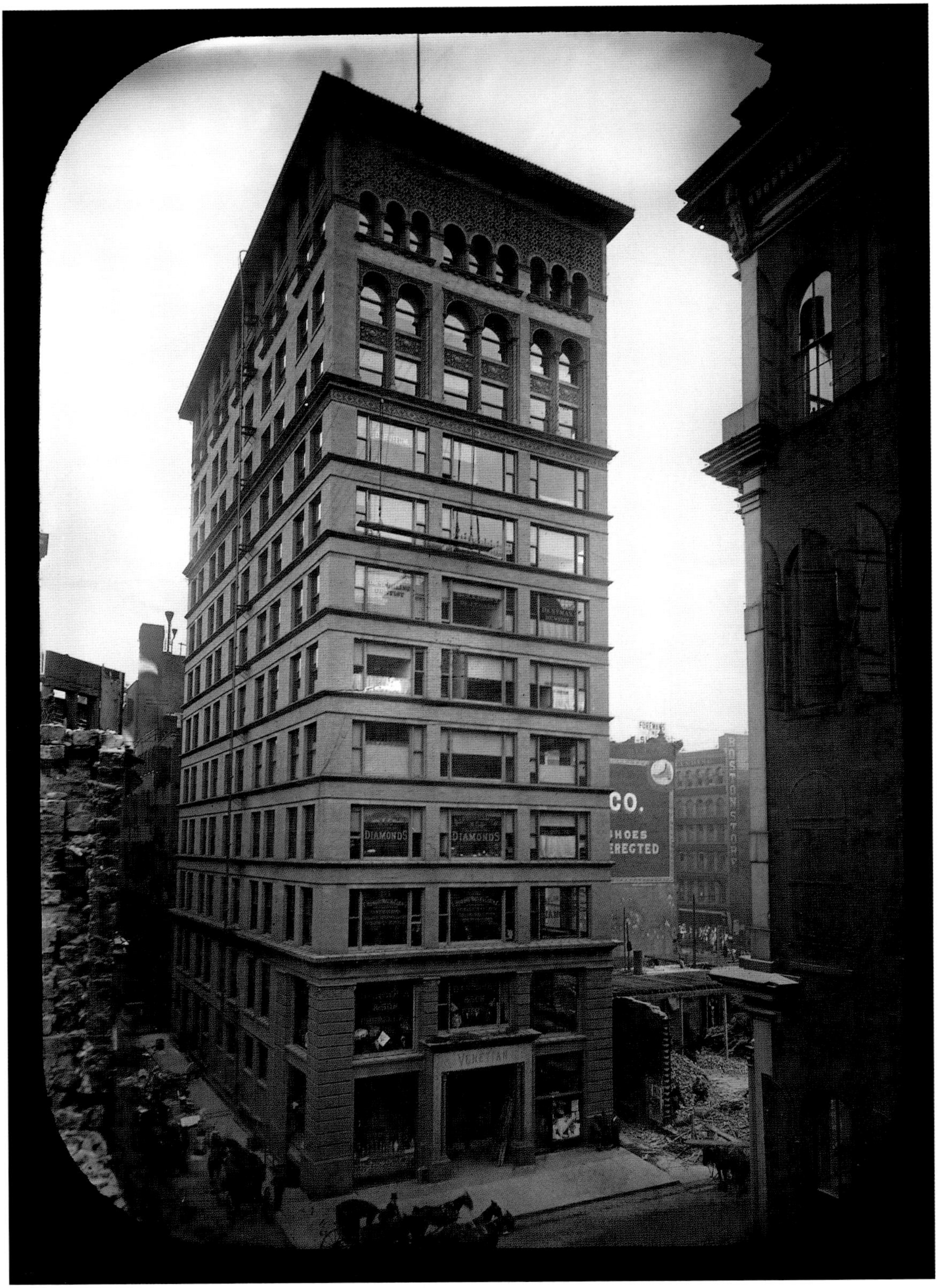
DIAMONDS
DIAMONDS
VENETIAN
CO.
SHOES
ERECTED

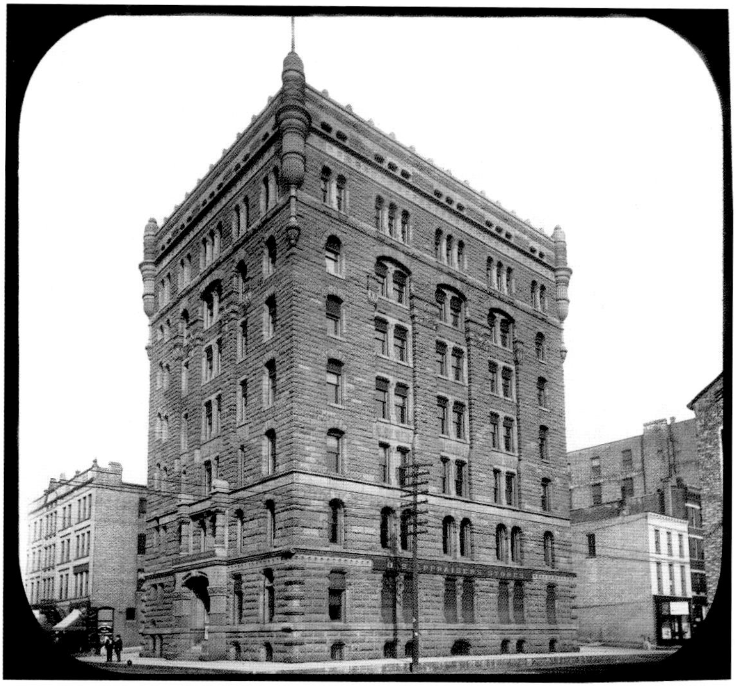

627 Venetian Building, Chicago, USA, 1890s

627 Das Venetian Building, Chicago, USA, 1890er Jahre

627 L'immeuble Venetian, Chicago, USA, années 1890

628 U.S. Appraisers Warehouse, Chicago, USA, 1890s

628 Das U.S. Appraisers Warehouse, Chicago, USA, 1890er Jahre

628 Entrepôts U.S. Appraisers, Chicago, USA, années 1890v

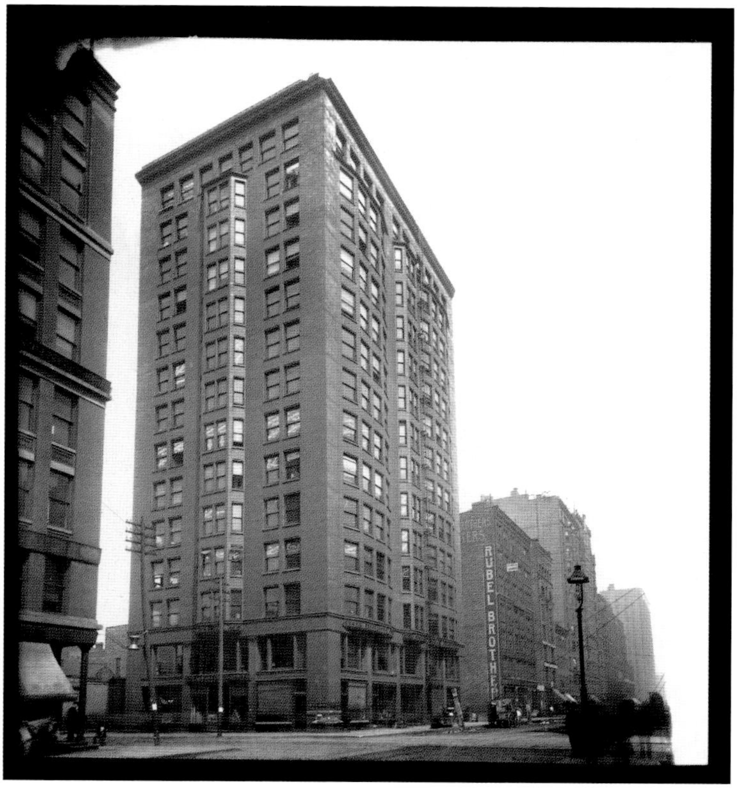

629 Pontiac Building, Chicago, USA, 1890s

629 Das Pontiac Building, Chicago, USA, 1890er Jahre

629 Immeuble Pontiac, Chicago, USA, années 1890

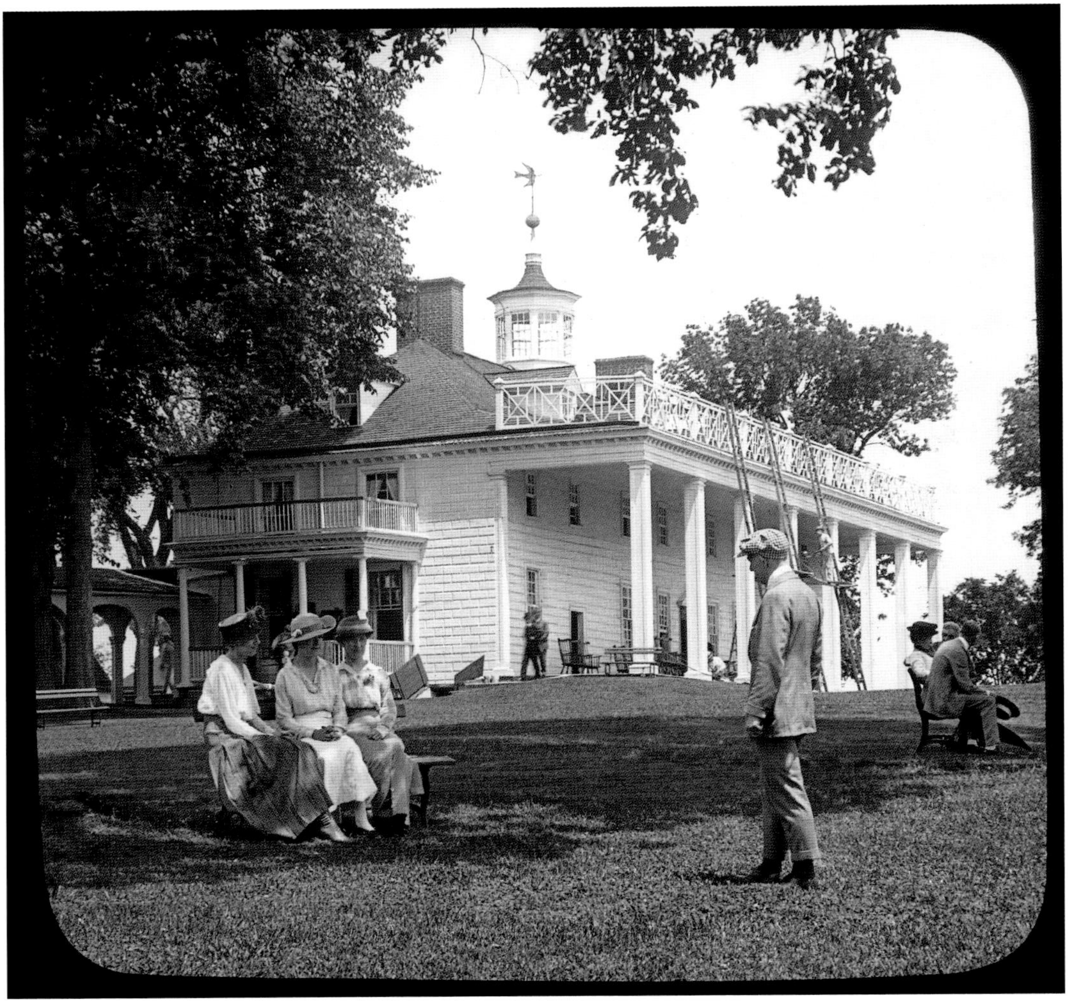

630 Mount Vernon (home of the first President of the United States, George Washington) near Alexandria, Virginia, 1910s

630 Mount Vernon (Landsitz des ersten Präsidenten der Vereinigten Staaten, George Washington) nahe Alexandria, Virginia, 1910er Jahre

630 Mount Vernon. Résidence du premier président des USA, George Washington, près d'Alexandria, Virginie, années 1910

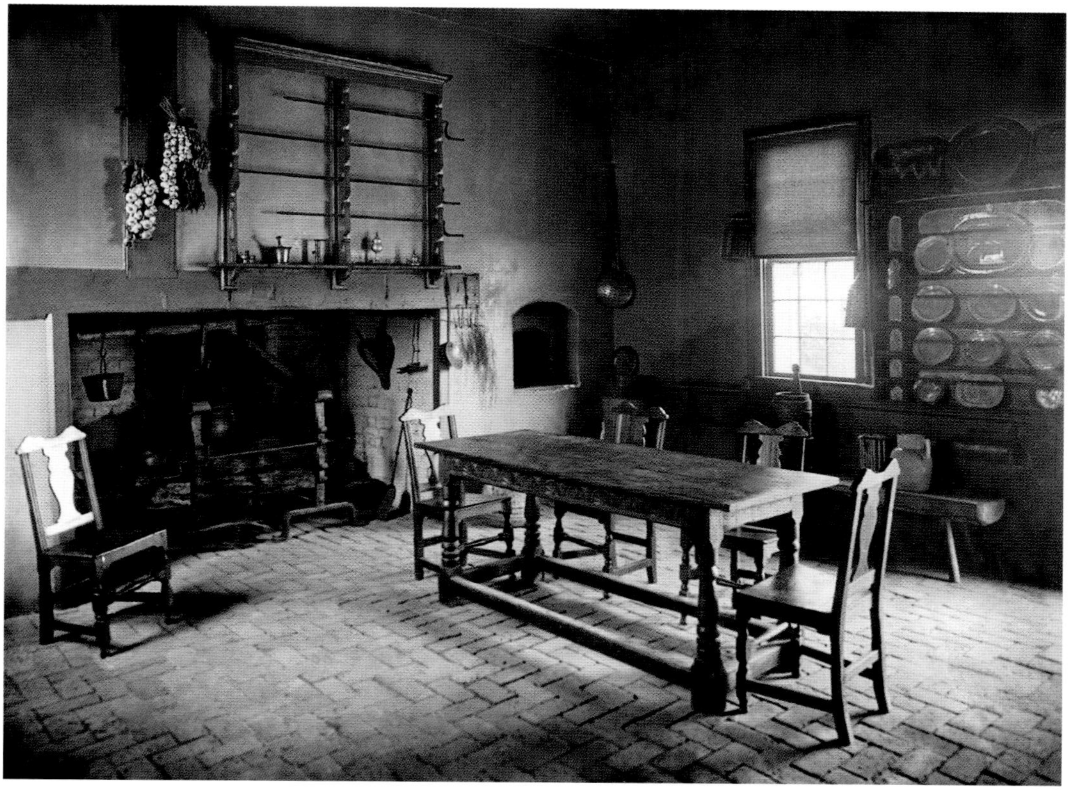

631 Interior of kitchen, Mount Vernon (home of George Washington), Virginia, USA, c.1910

631 Die Küche, Mount Vernon (Landsitz George Washingtons), Virginia, USA, um 1910

631 La cuisine de Mount Vernon, résidence de George Washington, Virginie, USA, vers 1910

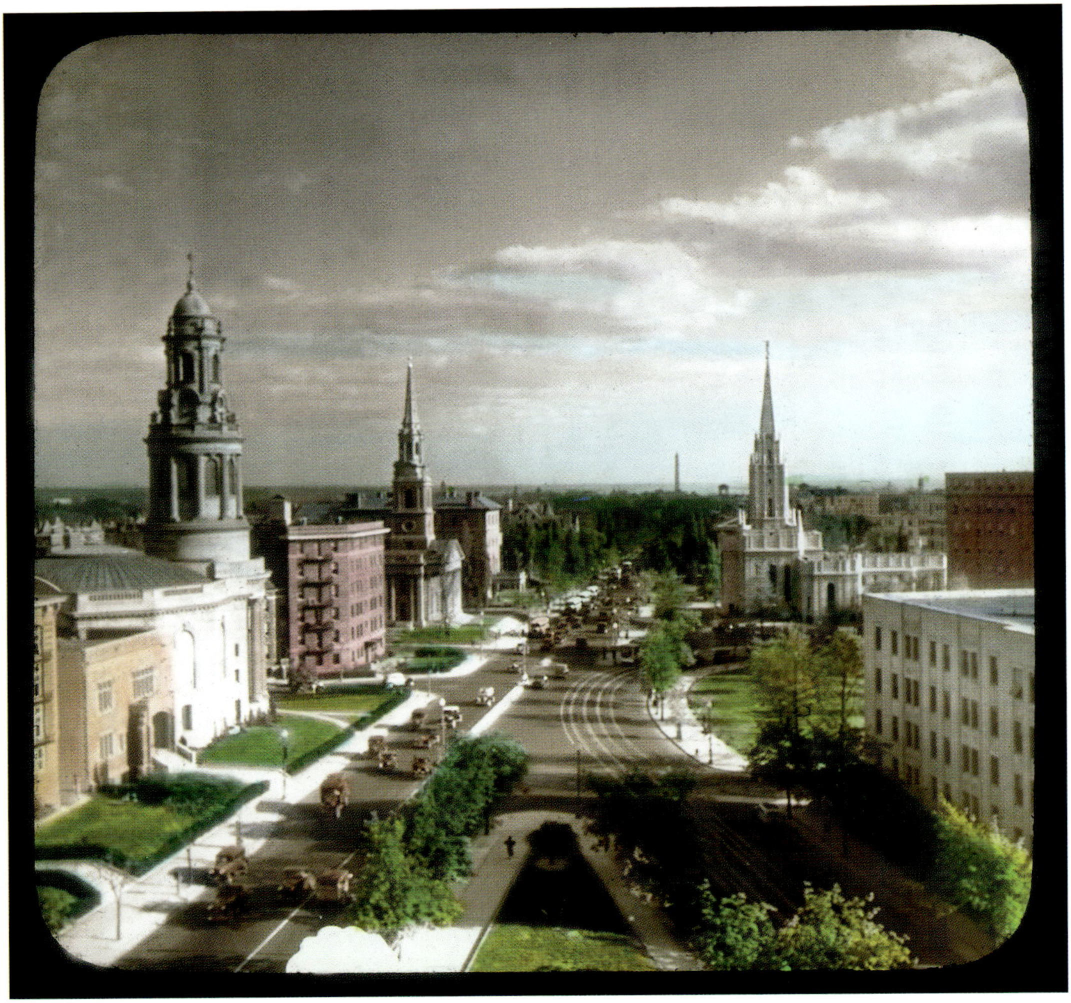

632 “The Street of the World”, Sixteenth Street, Washington D.C., USA, c.1900

632 “Die Straße der Welt”, die Sixteenth Street, Washington D.C., USA, um 1900

632 “La rue du Monde”, Seizième rue, Washington D.C., USA, vers 1900

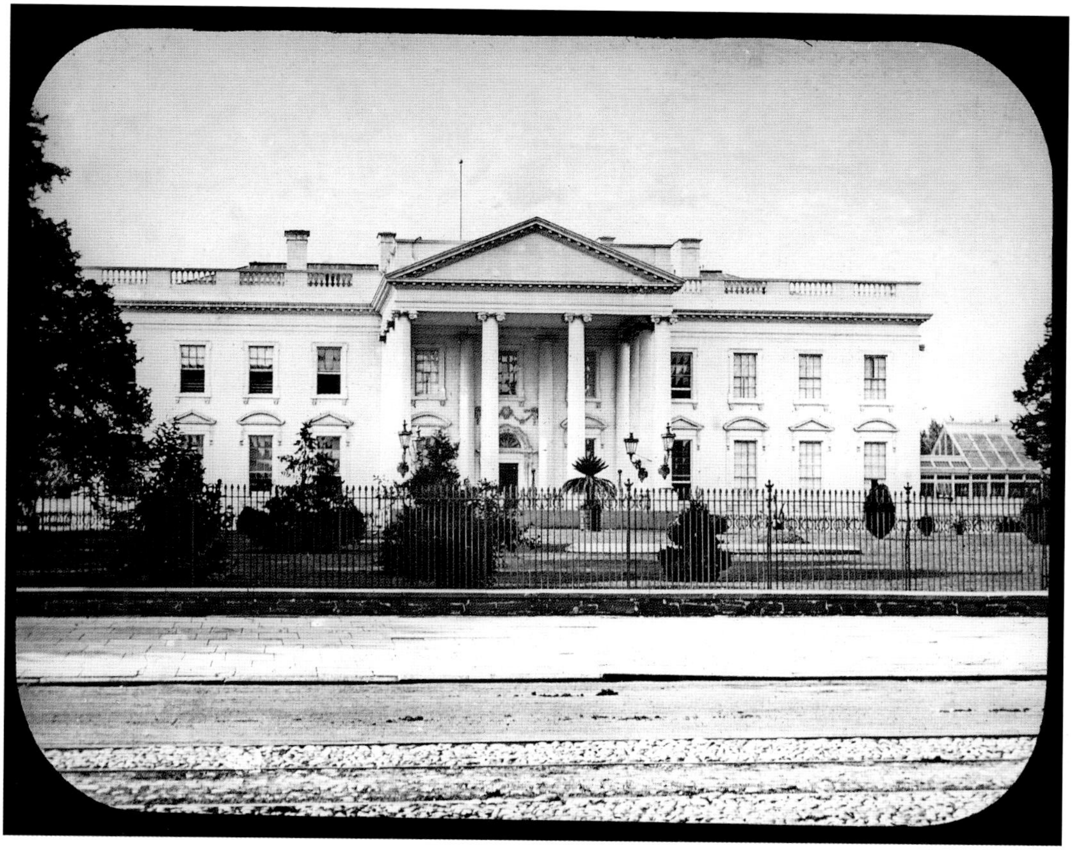

633 The White House, Washington D.C., USA, 1880s

633 Das Weiße Haus, Washington D.C., USA, 1880er Jahre

633 La Maison Blanche, Washington D.C., USA, années 1880

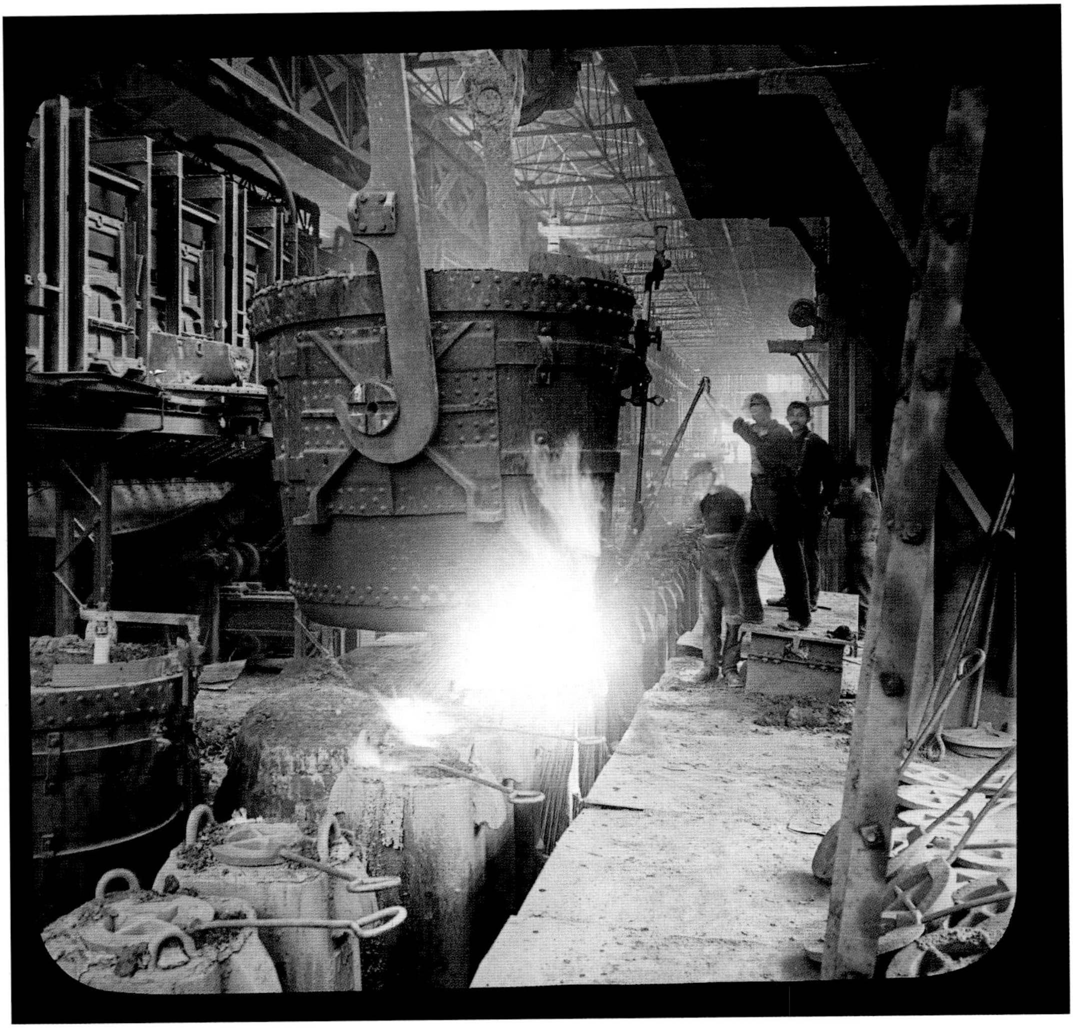

634 Filling moulds with steel, Pittsburgh, Pennsylvania, USA, c.1900

634 Befüllen von Kokillen mit Stahl,, Pittsburgh, Pennsylvania, USA, um 1900

634 Coulée d'acier dans les moules, Pittsburgh, Pennsylvanie, USA, vers 1900

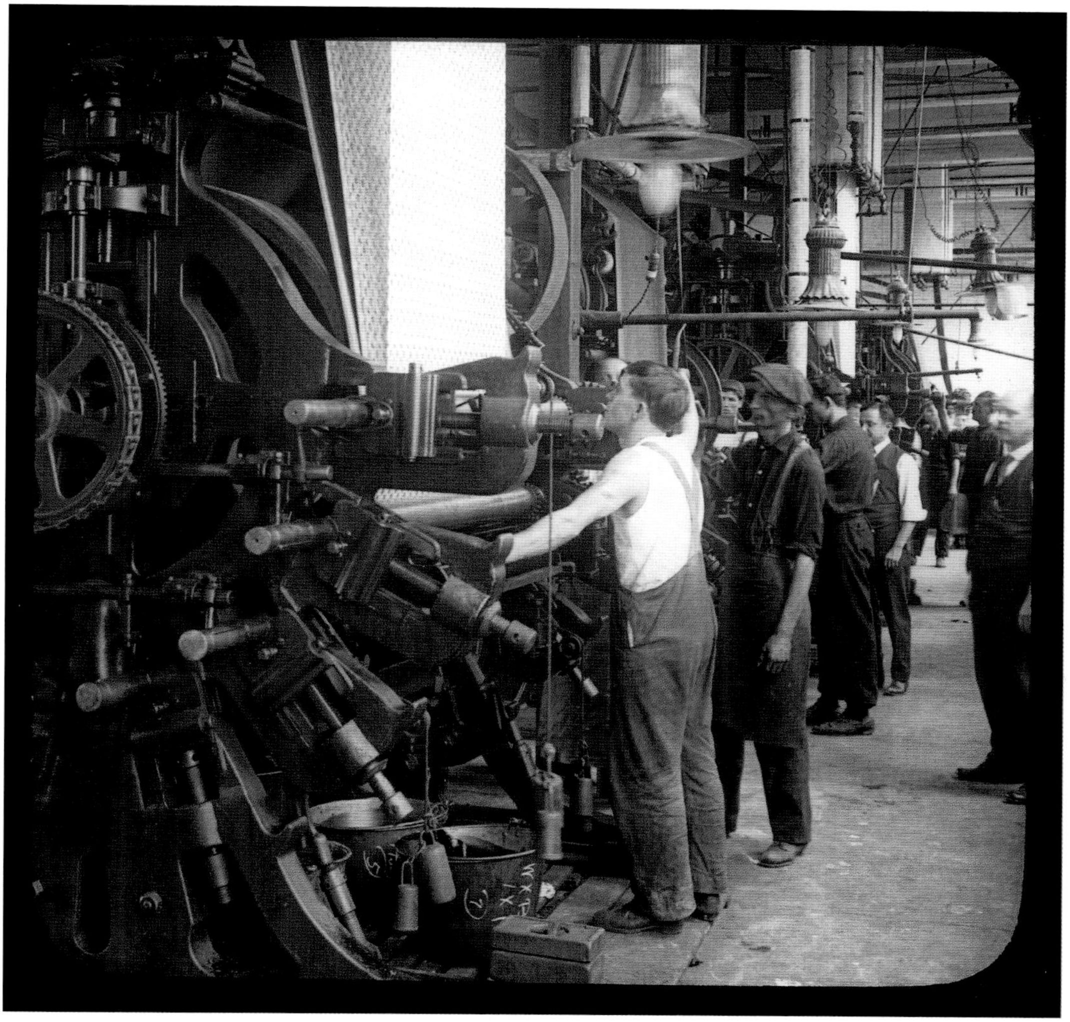

635 Printing colour designs on silk cloth (ten colours at once), Paterson, New Jersey, USA, c.1900

635 Bedruckung von Seidenstoff mit Farbmustern (zehn Farben zugleich), Paterson, New Jersey, USA, um 1900

635 Impression en couleur (dix à la fois) sur de l'étoffe en soie, Paterson, New Jersey, USA, vers 1900

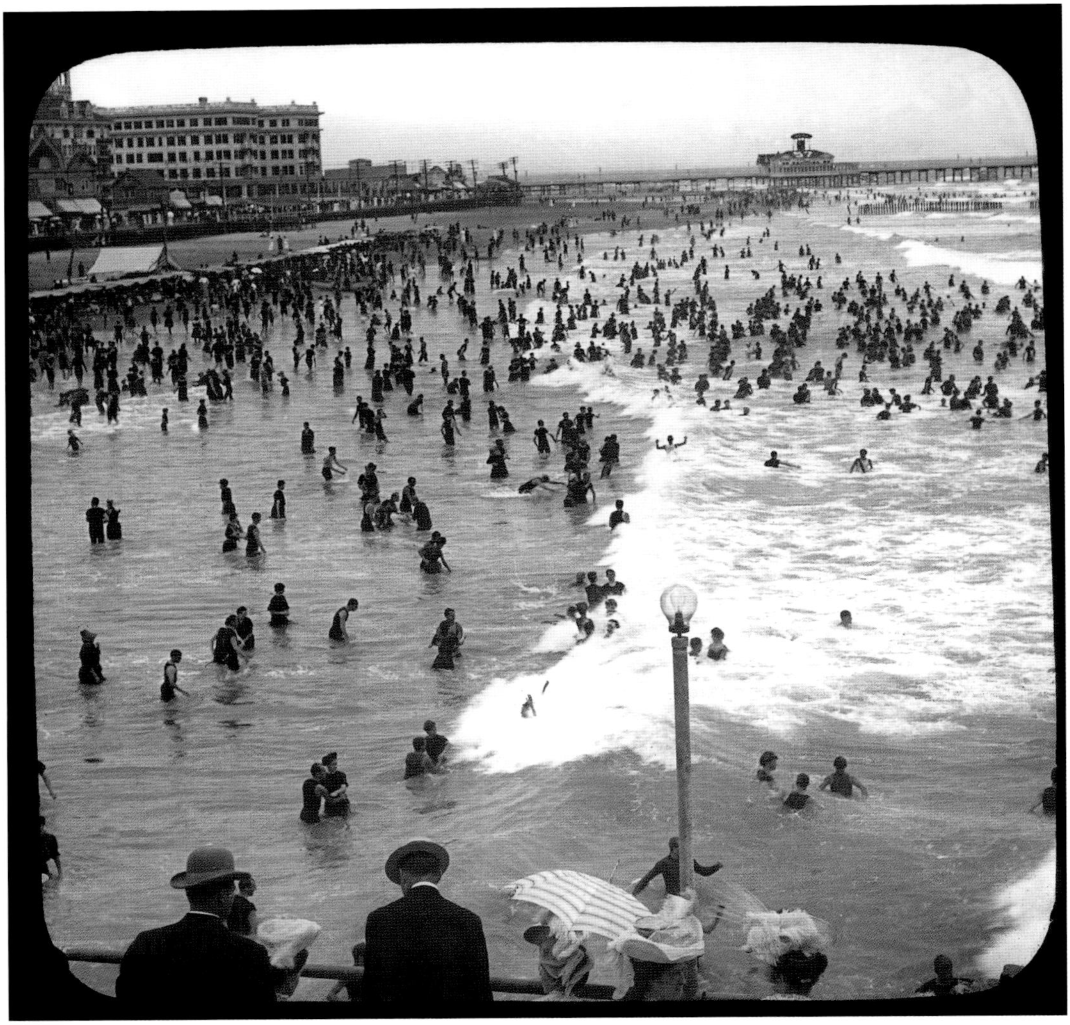

636 Life on the ocean wave, Atlantic City, New Jersey, USA, 1900s
637 Bronx Park, New York City, USA, c.1900

636 Wellenbaden, Atlantic City, New Jersey, USA, 1900er Jahre
637 Der Bronx Park, New York City, USA, um 1900

636 Portés par la vague, Atlantic City, New Jersey, USA, années 1900
637 Bronx Park, New York City, USA, vers 1900

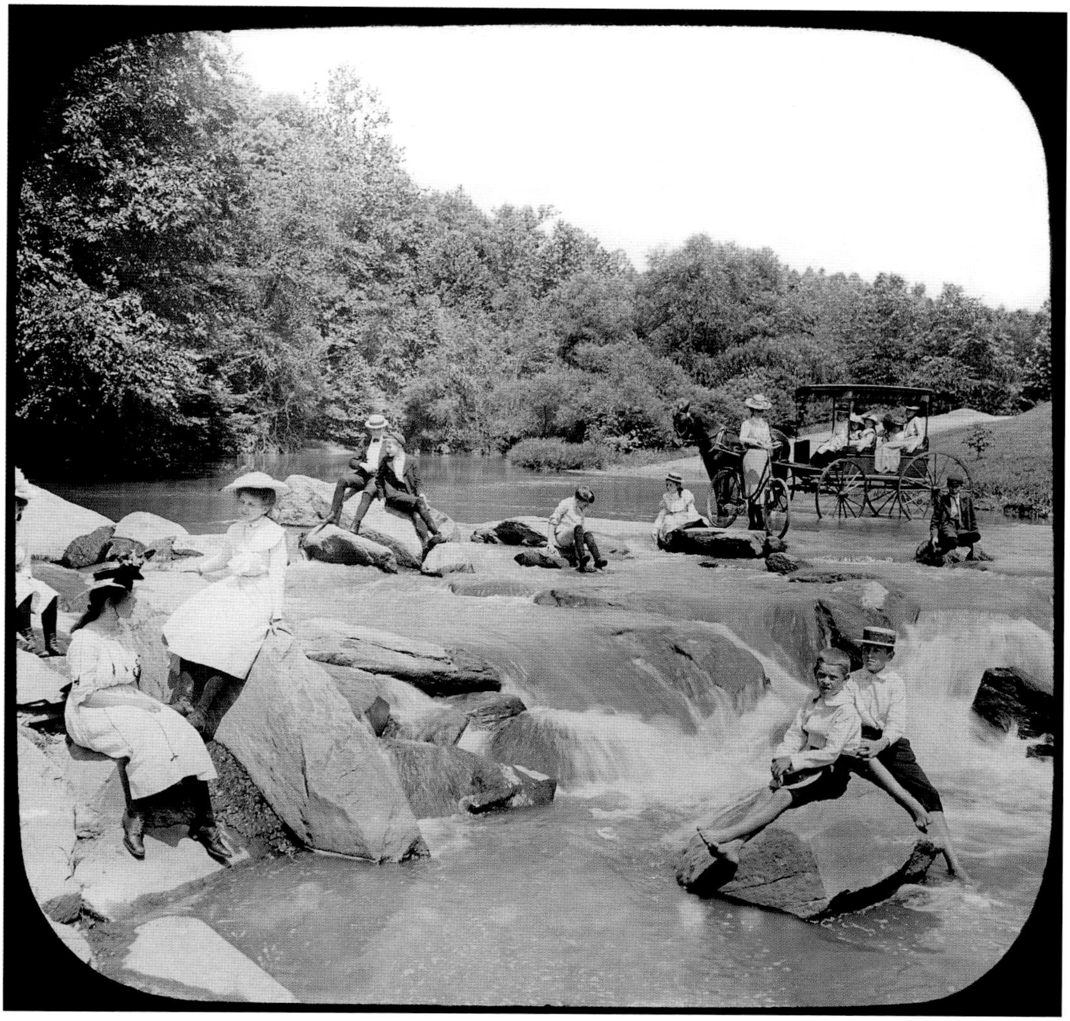

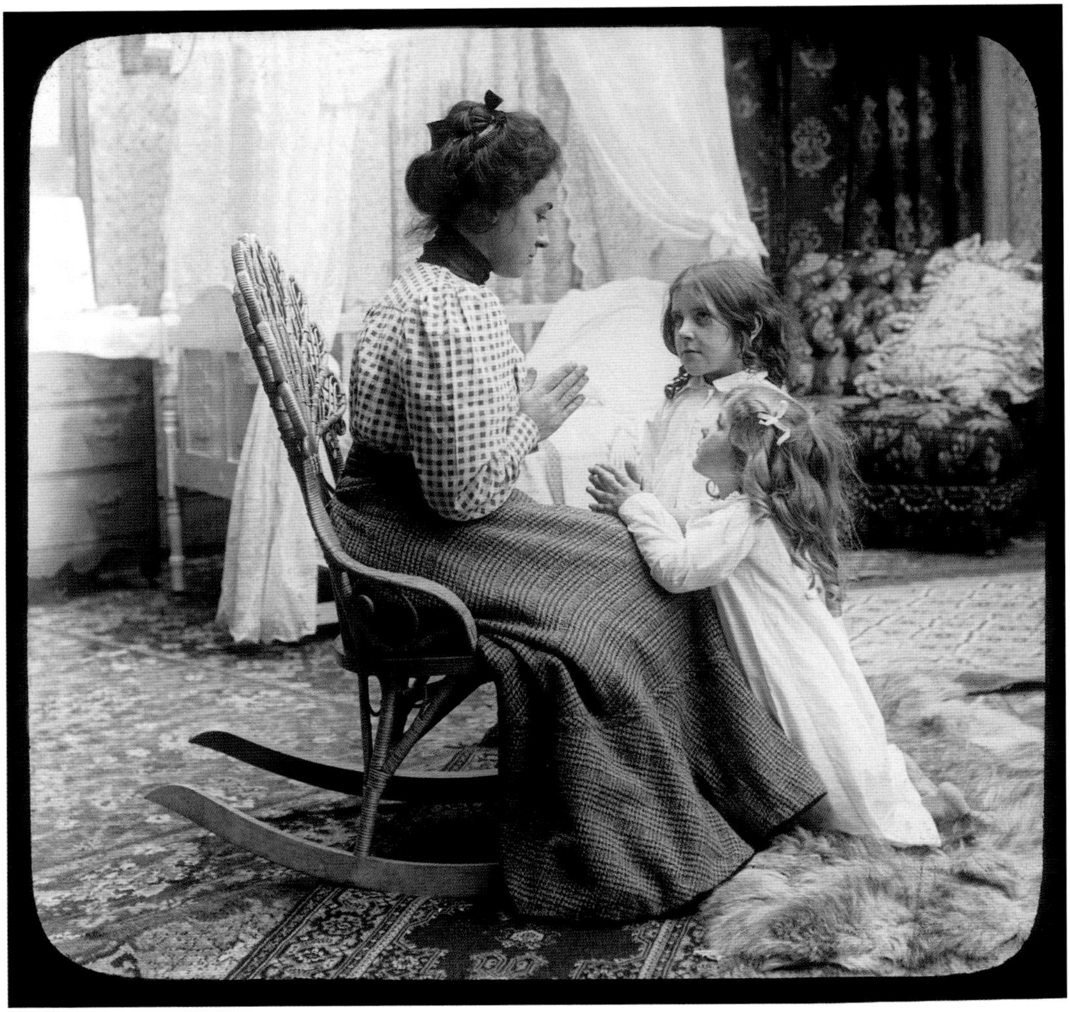

638 Mother and children, USA, 1890s
639 Sisters playing with dolls, USA, 1890s

638 Mutter und Kinder, USA, 1890er Jahre
639 Schwestern spielen mit Puppen, USA, 1890er Jahre

638 Femme et enfants, USA, années 1890
639 Sœurs jouant à la poupée, USA, années 1890

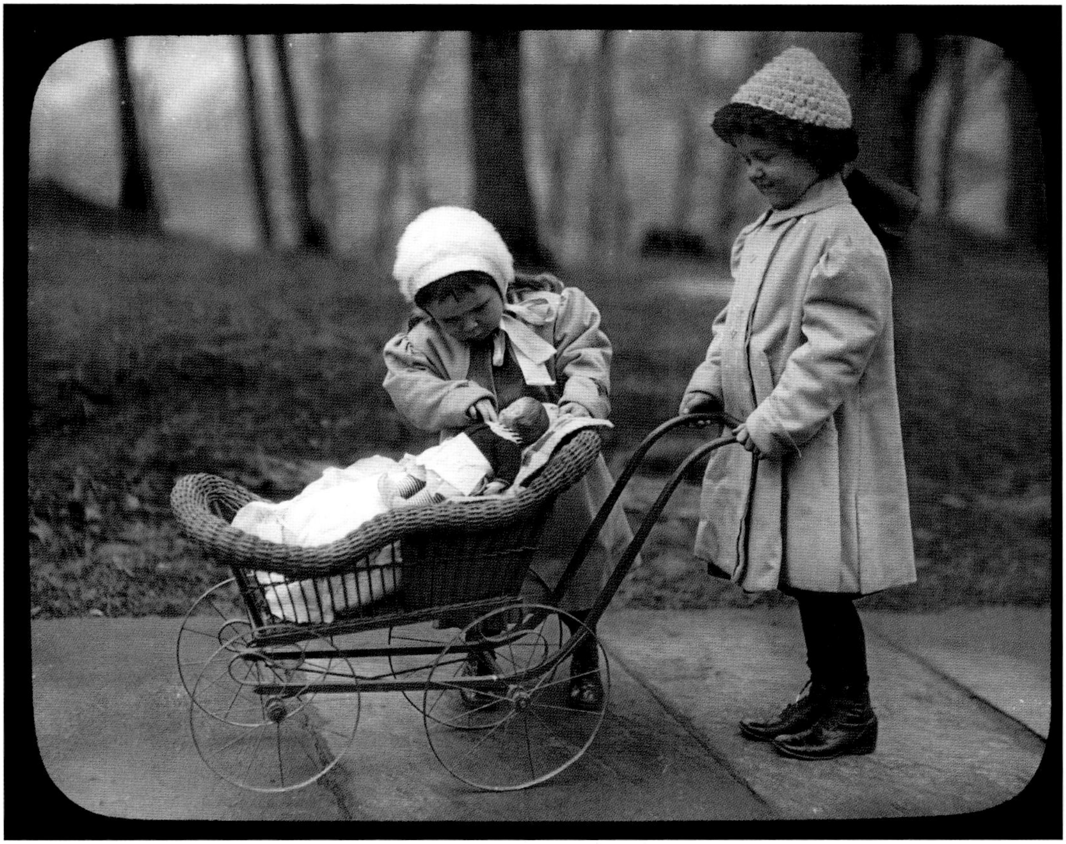

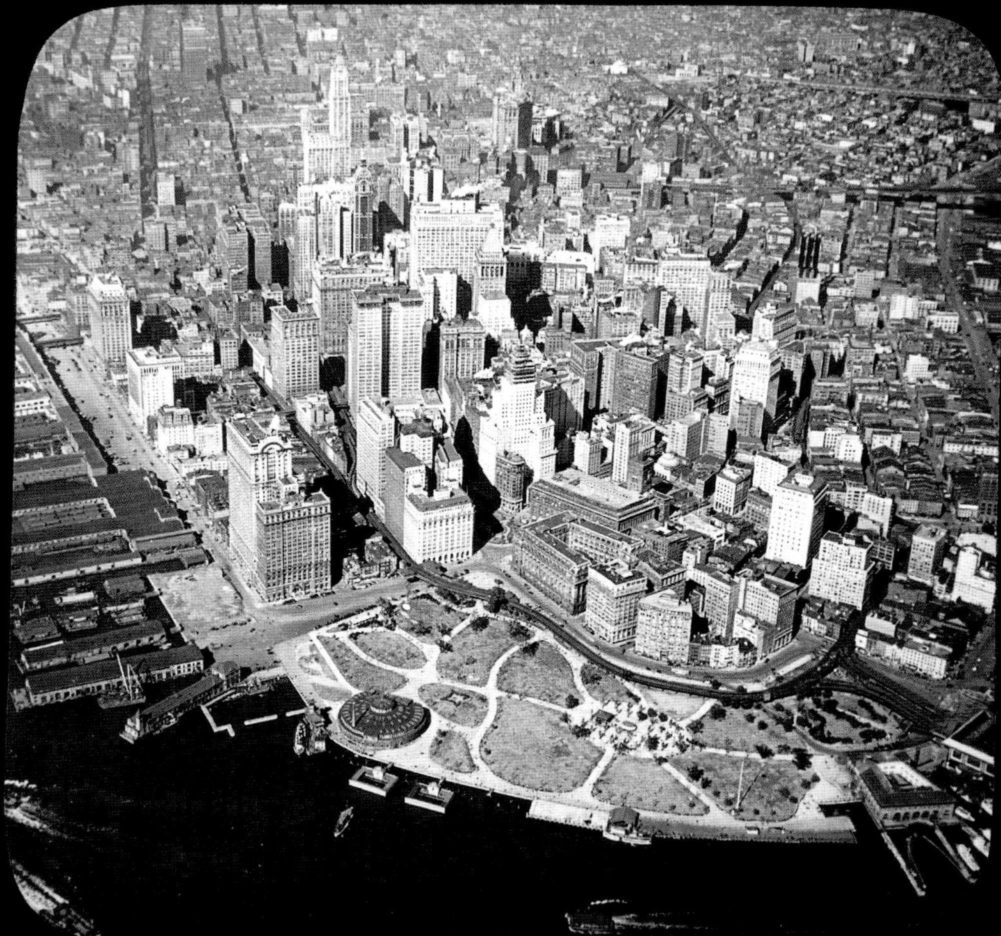

640 Aerial view of lower New York City, USA, 1920s

640 Luftbildaufnahme von Lower New York City, USA, 1920er Jahre

640 Vue aérienne de Lower New York City, USA, années 1920

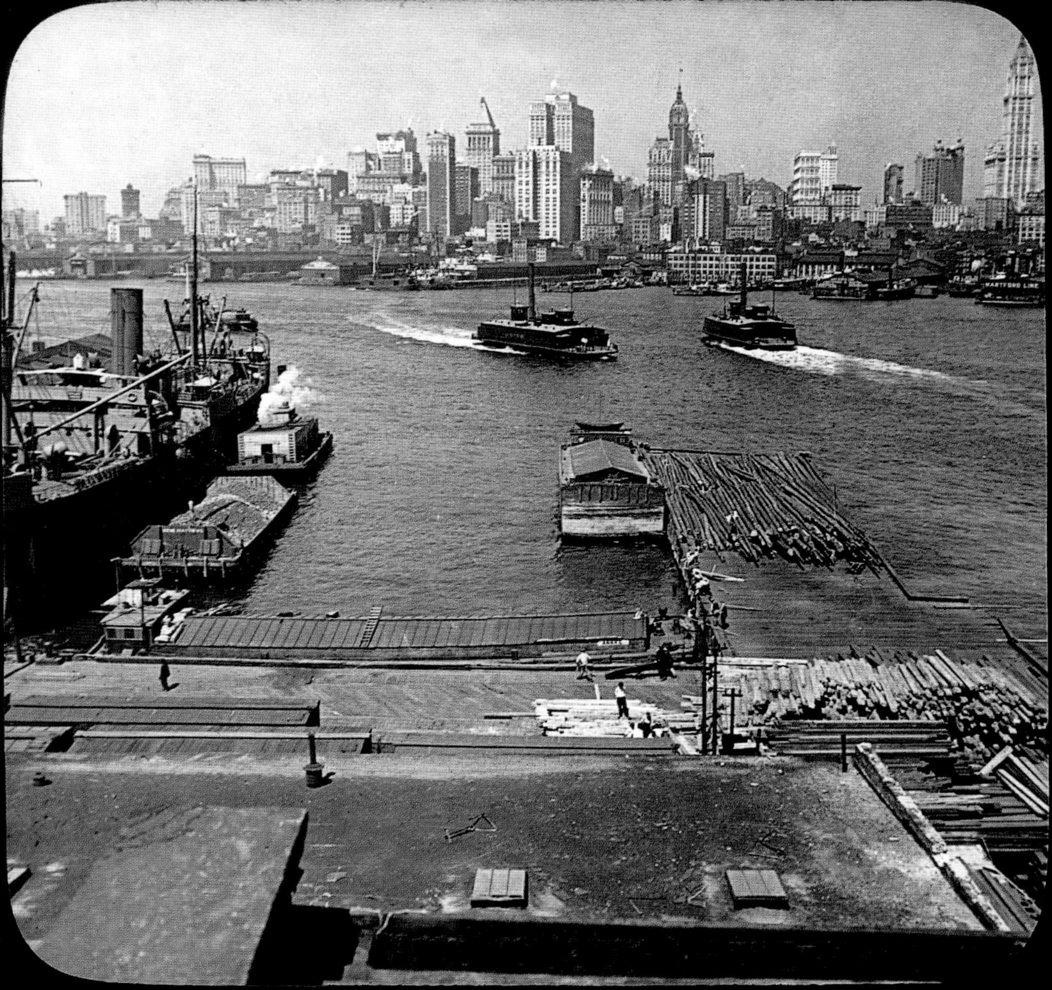

541 Overlooking New
ork City from Brooklyn
ide with steamers at the
lock, New York, USA,
900s

641 Blick auf New
York City von Brooklyn
aus, Dampfer an den
Stegen, New York, USA,
1900er Jahre

641 Panorama de New
York depuis les docks
de Brooklyn, avec le
va-et-vient des bateaux
à vapeur, New York, USA,

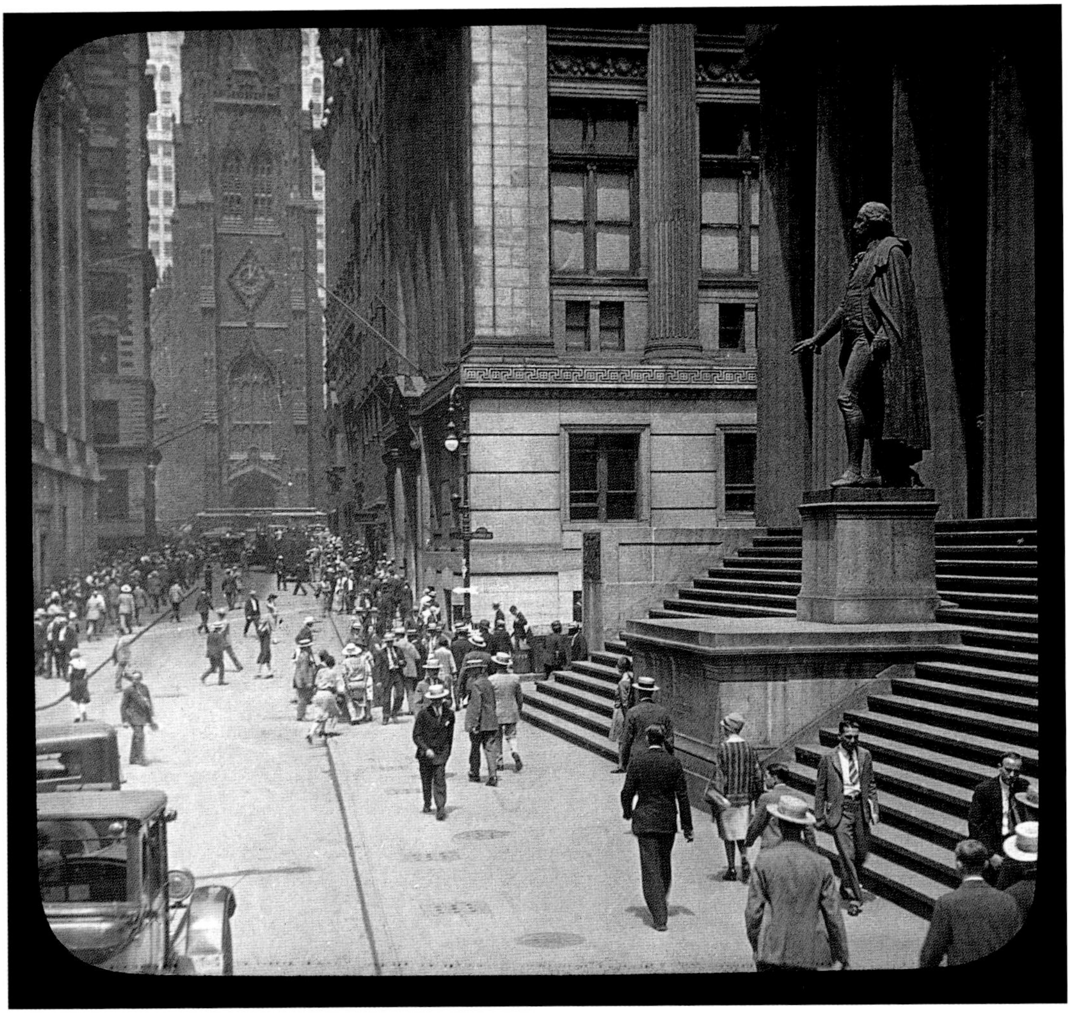

642 Wall Street, New York City, USA, 1910s
643 Looking North on Broadway from the Empire State Building, New York City, USA, 1900s

642 Wall Street, New York City, USA, 1910er Jahre
643 Blick von Norden auf den Broadway vom Empire State Building aus, New York City, USA, 1900er Jahre

642 Wall Street, New York City, USA, années 1910
643 Vue sur Broadway vers le nord, depuis l'Empire State Building, New York City, USA, années 1900

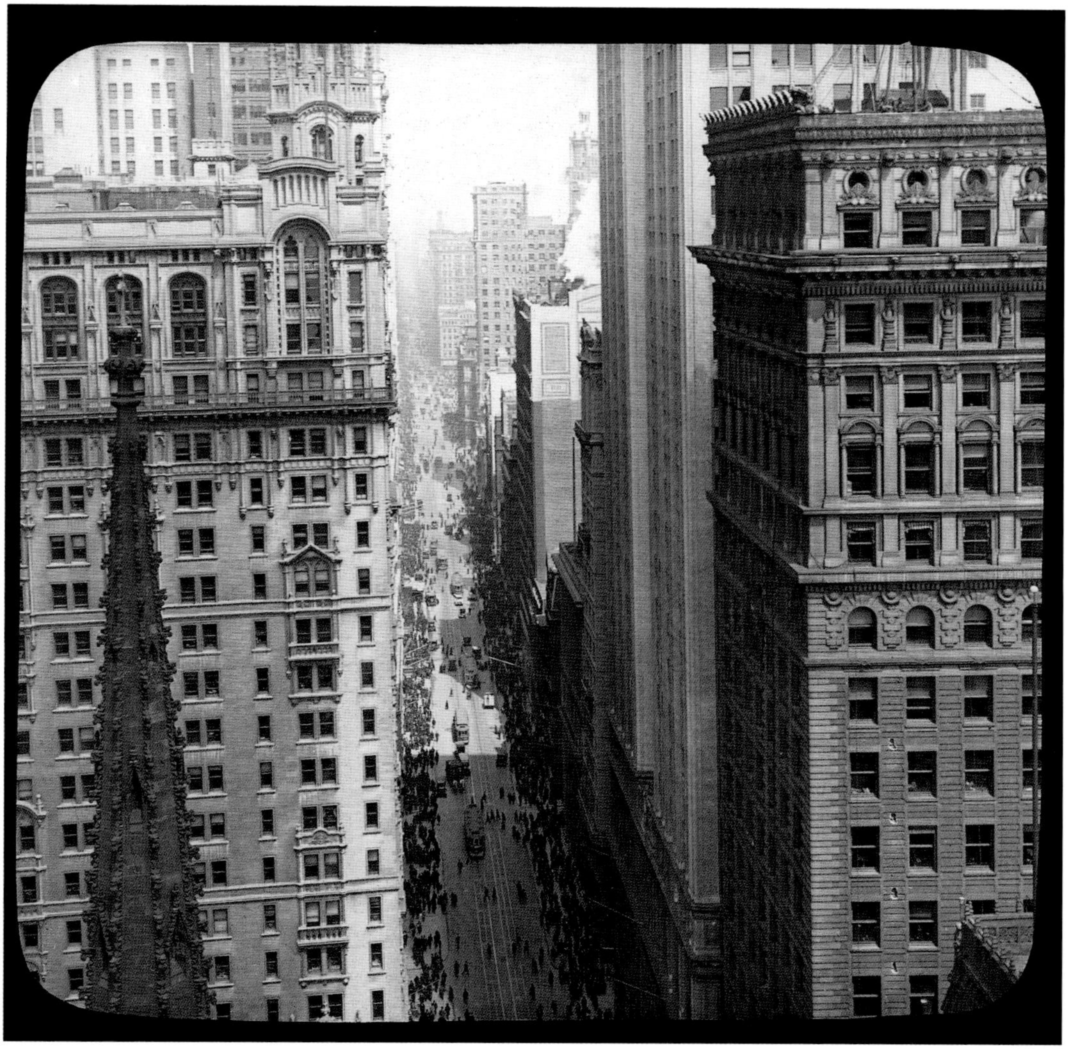

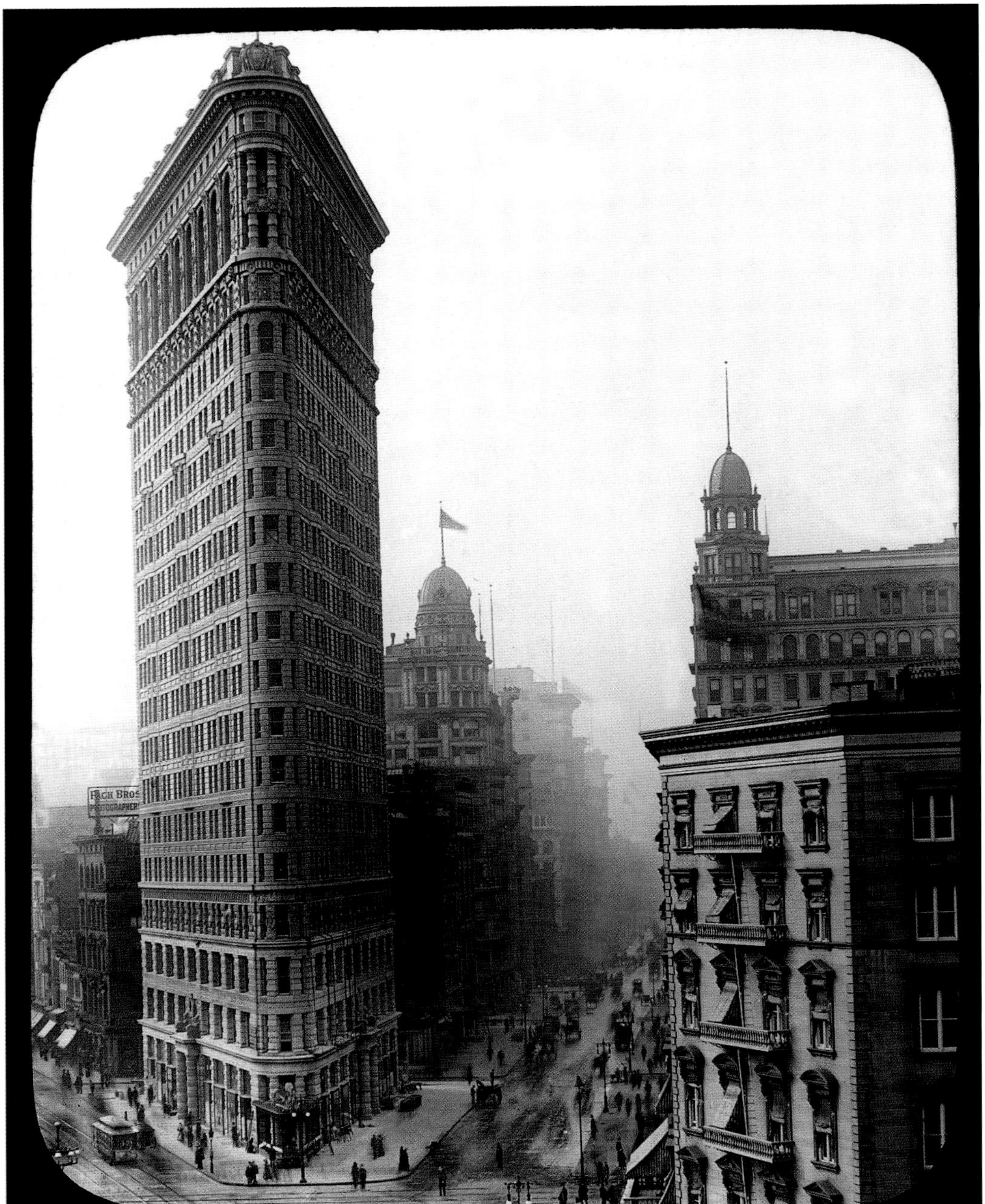

644 The Fuller Building (The Flatiron Building), New York City, c.1903
645 The Empire State Building, New York City, 1930s

644 Das Fuller Building (Das Flatiron Building), New York City, um 1903
645 Das Empire State Building, New York City, 1930er Jahre

644 Fuller Building (« l'immeuble en fer à repasser »), New York City, vers 1903
645 Empire State Building, New York City, années 1930

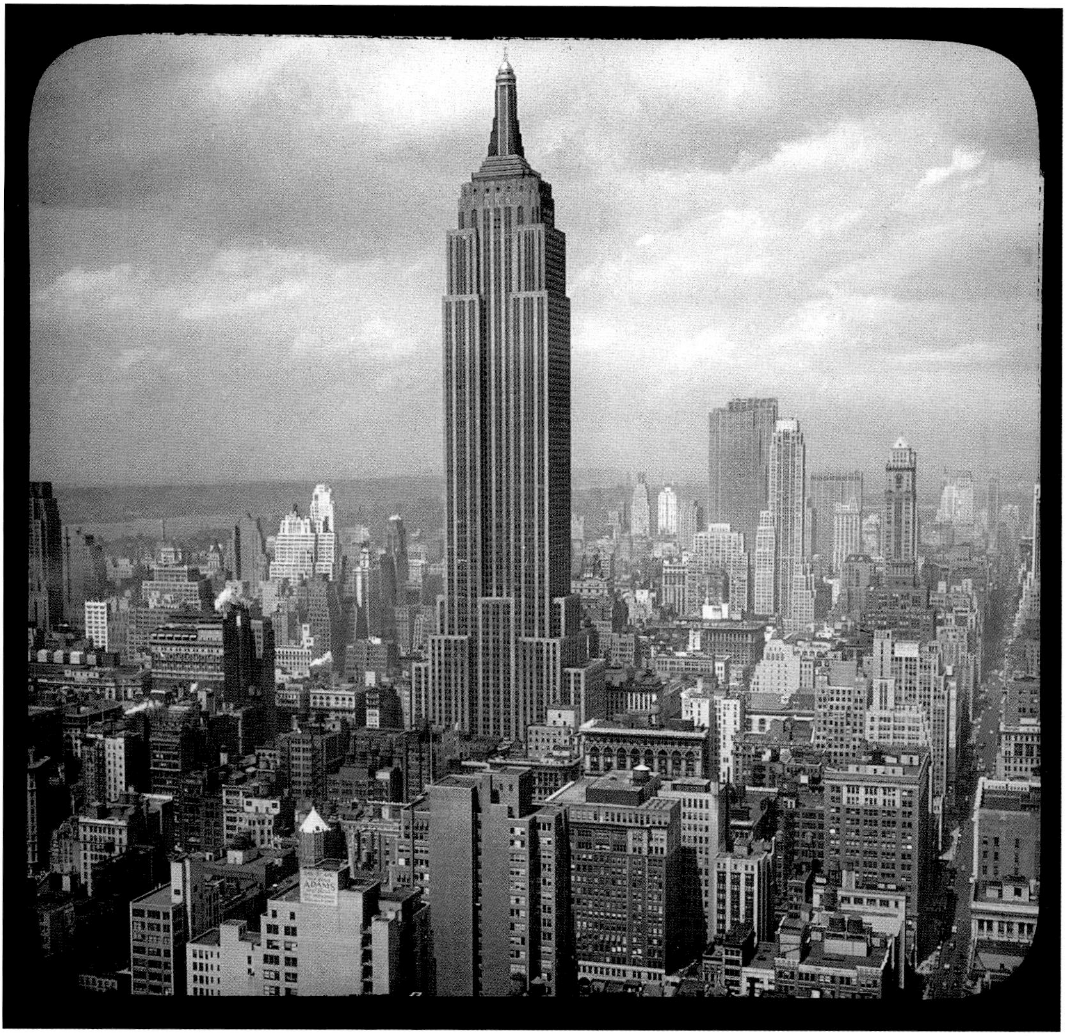
ADAMS

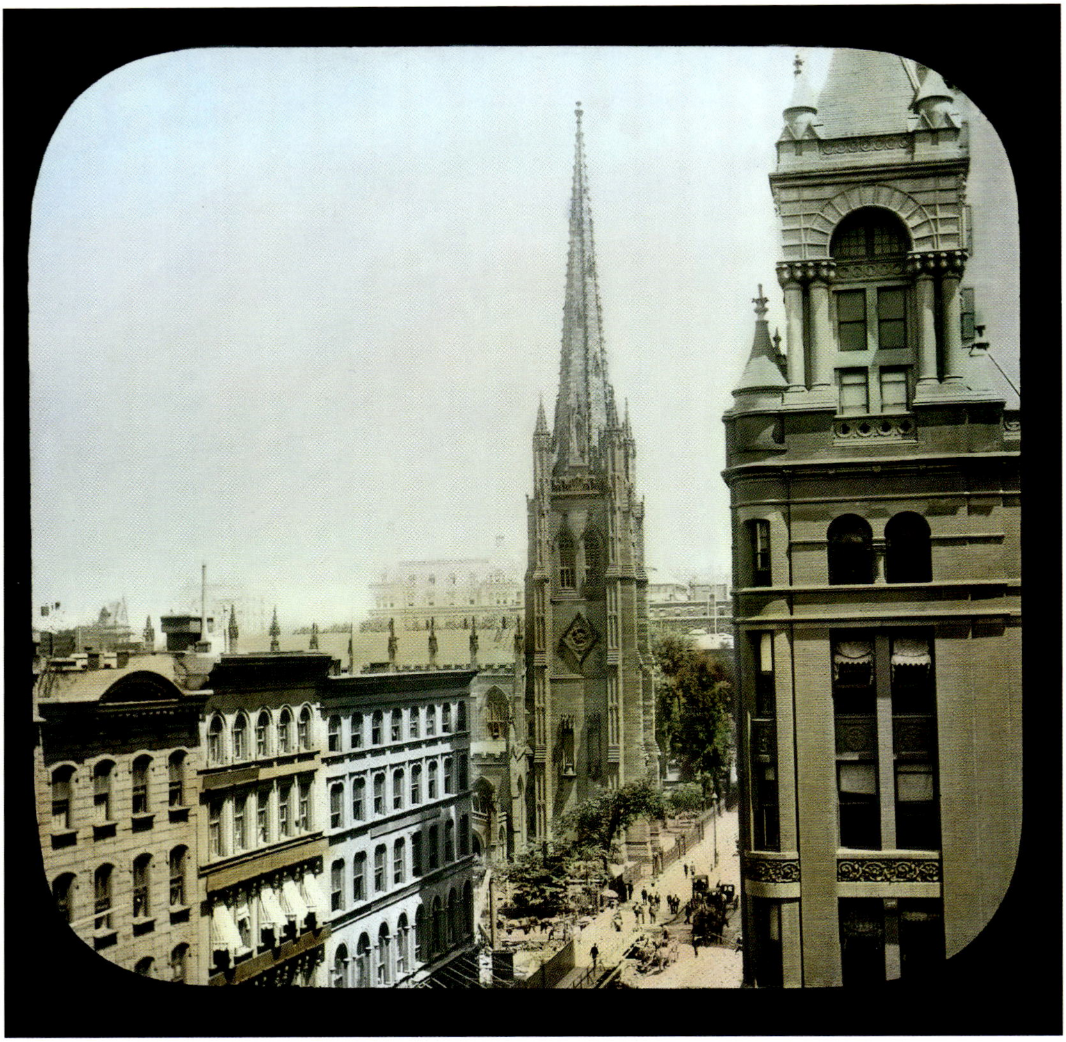

646 Trinity Church on Wall Street, New York City, 1900
647 City Hall, New York City, USA, 1880s

646 Die Trinity Church auf der Wall Street, New York City, 1900er Jahre
647 Das Rathaus, New York City, USA, 1880er Jahre

646 Église de la Trinité sur Wall Street, New York City, 1900
647 Hôtel de Ville, New York City, USA, années 1880

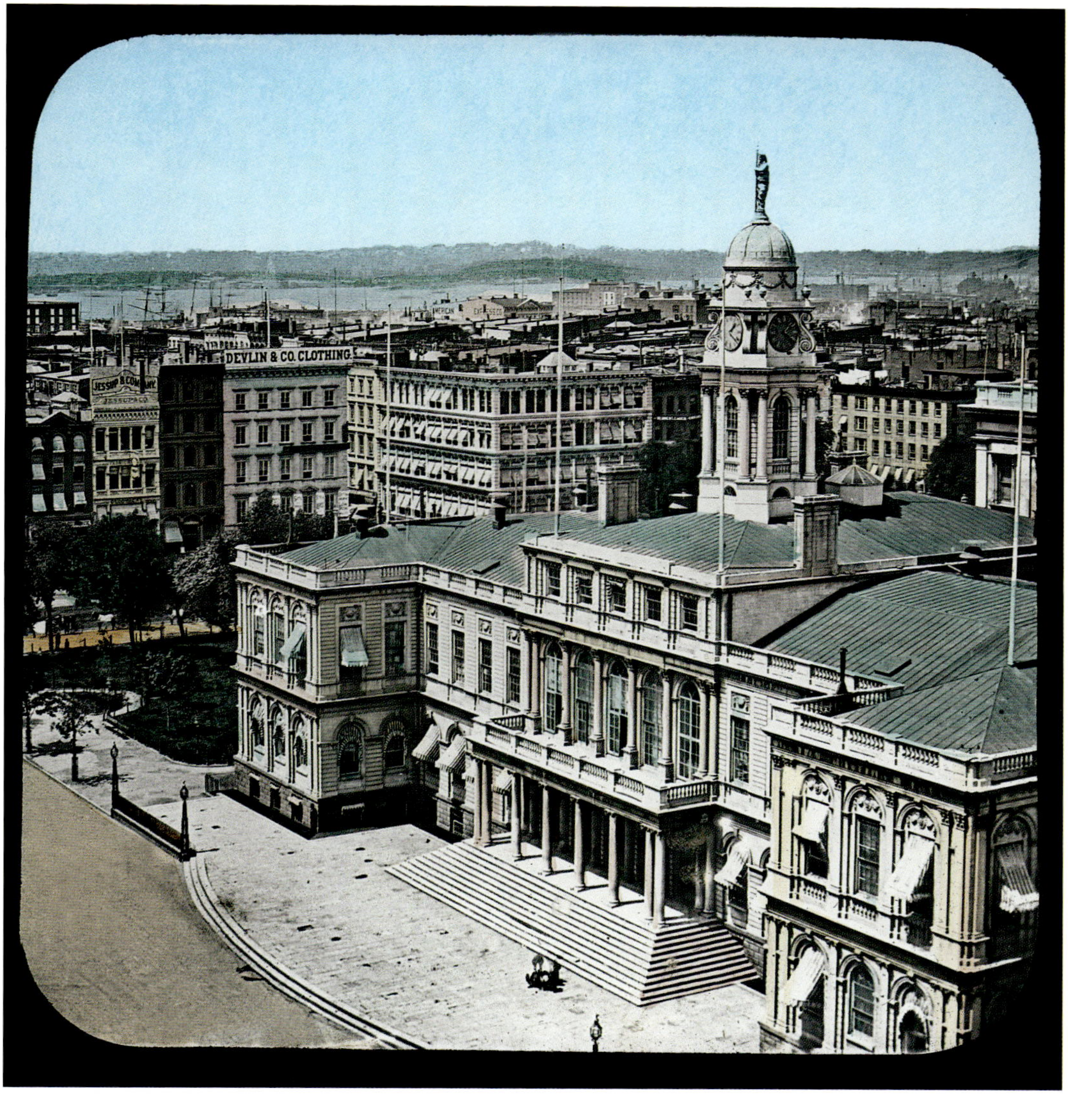
DEVLIN & CO. CLOTHING.

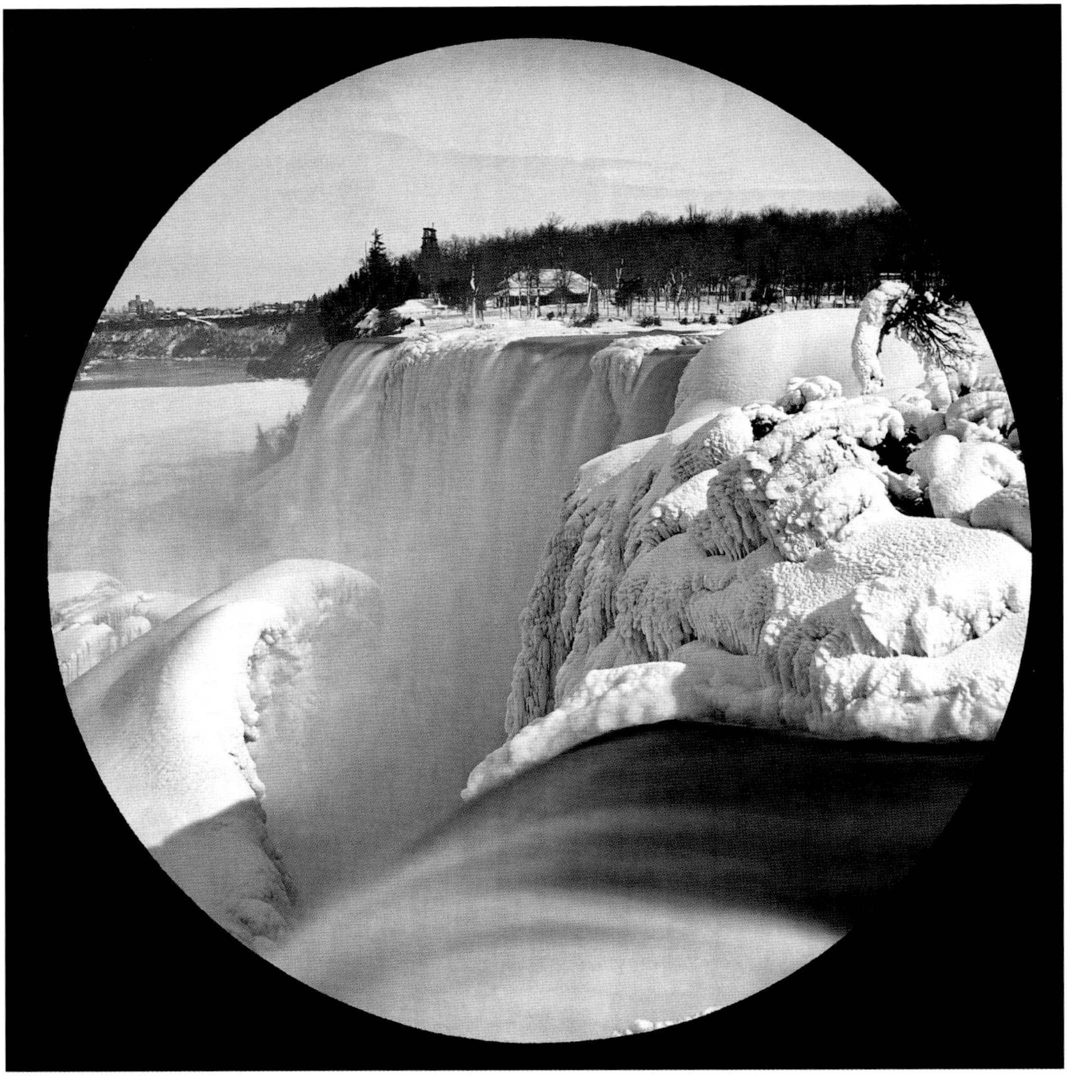

648 Winter view of American falls from Hog's Back, Niagara Falls, New York, 1870s

648 Die American Falls im Winter von Hog's Back aus gesehen, Niagara Falls, New York, 1870er Jahre

648 Les chutes américaines en hiver, vues depuis Hog's Back, chutes du Niagara, New York, années 1870

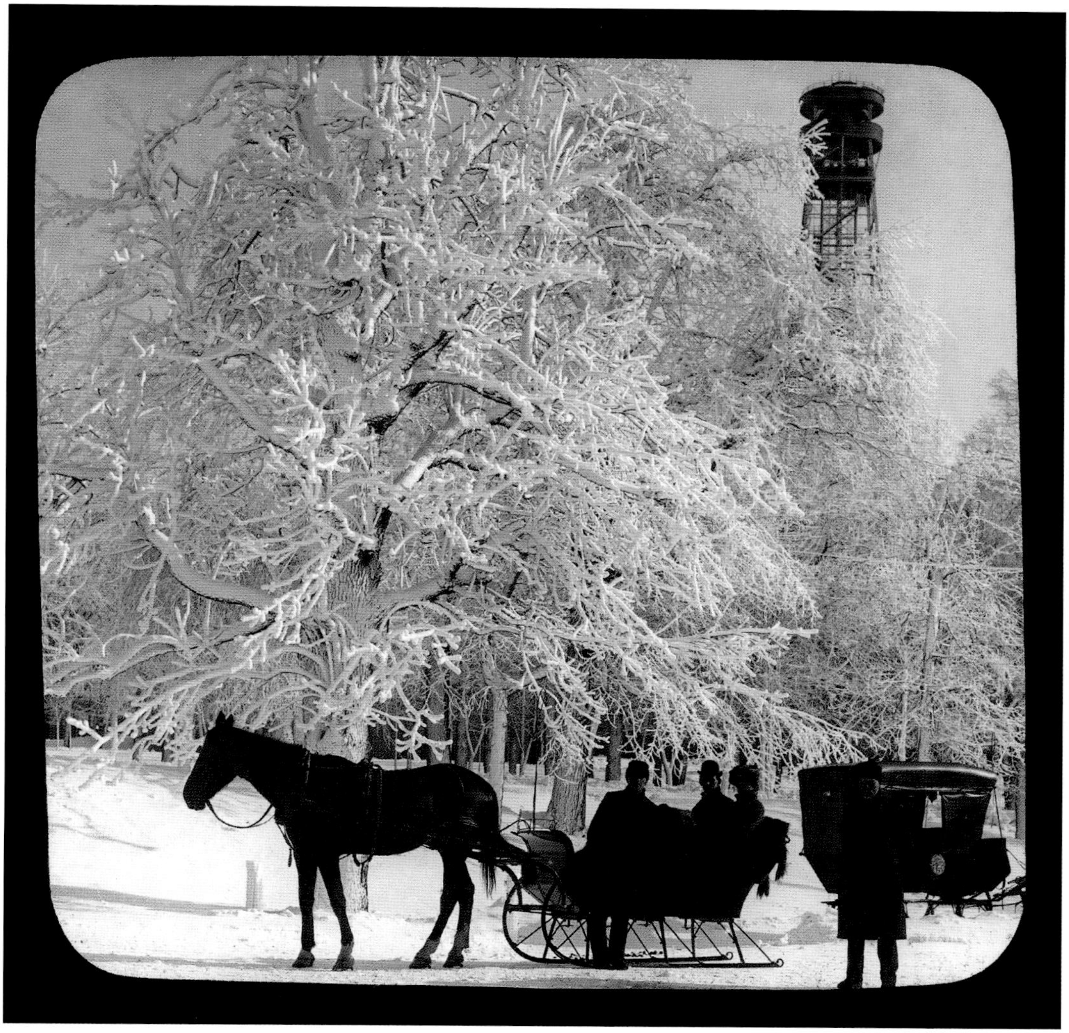

649 A forest of crystal, Prospect Park, Niagara Falls, New York, USA, 1910s

649 Ein Wald aus Kristall, Prospect Park, Niagara Falls, New York, USA, 1910er Jahre

649 Une forêt de cristal, Prospect Park, chutes du Niagara, New York, USA, années 1910

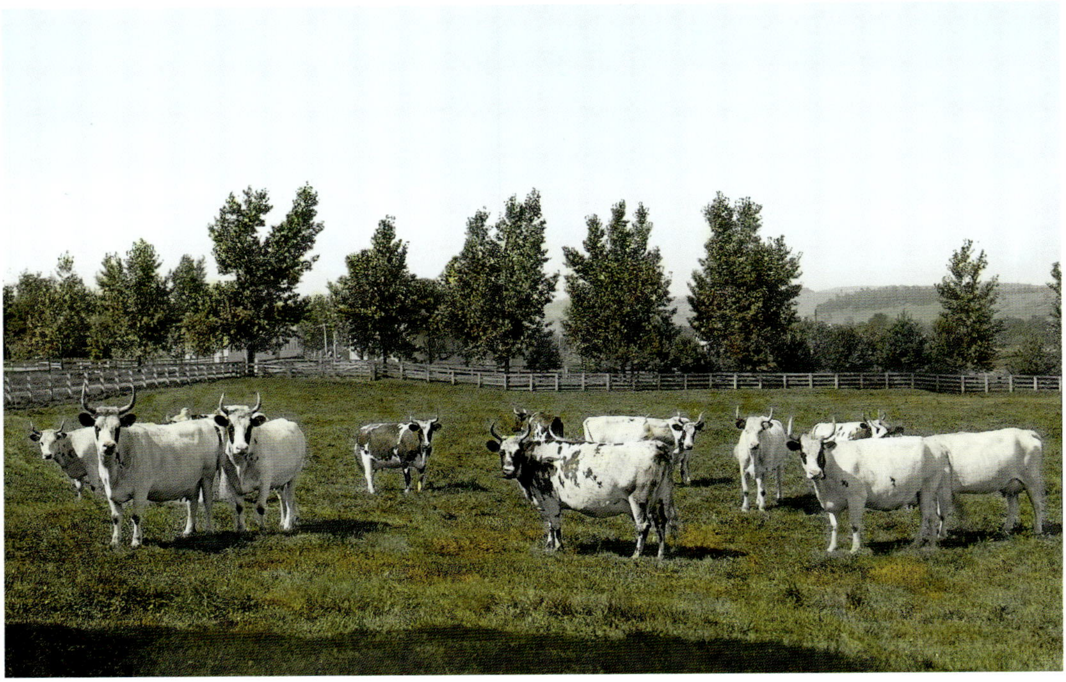

650 Pure-bred Ayreshire dairy cattle in pasture, near Copperstown, New York, USA, 1924

650 Reinrassige Ayreshire-Kühe auf einer Weide, nahe Copperstown, New York, USA, 1924

650 Vaches de pure race Ayreshire au pâturage près de Copperstown, New York, USA, 1924

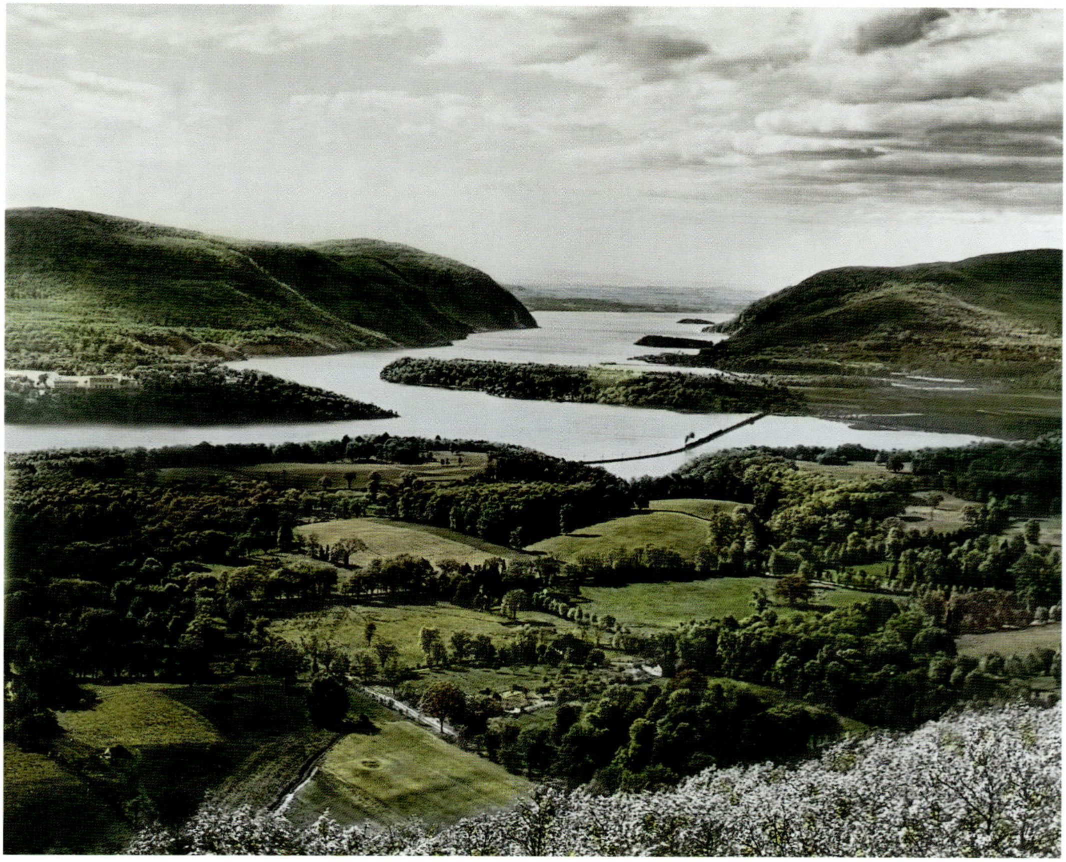

651 Hudson River (panorama of Hudson Valley from near Sugar Loaf Mountain), New York, USA, c.1900

651 Der Hudson (Panorama-Ansicht des Hudson-Tals nahe des Sugar Loaf Mountain), New York, USA, um 1900

651 Fleuve Hudson. Panorama de la vallée de l'Hudson près des monts Sugar Loaf, New York, USA, vers 1900

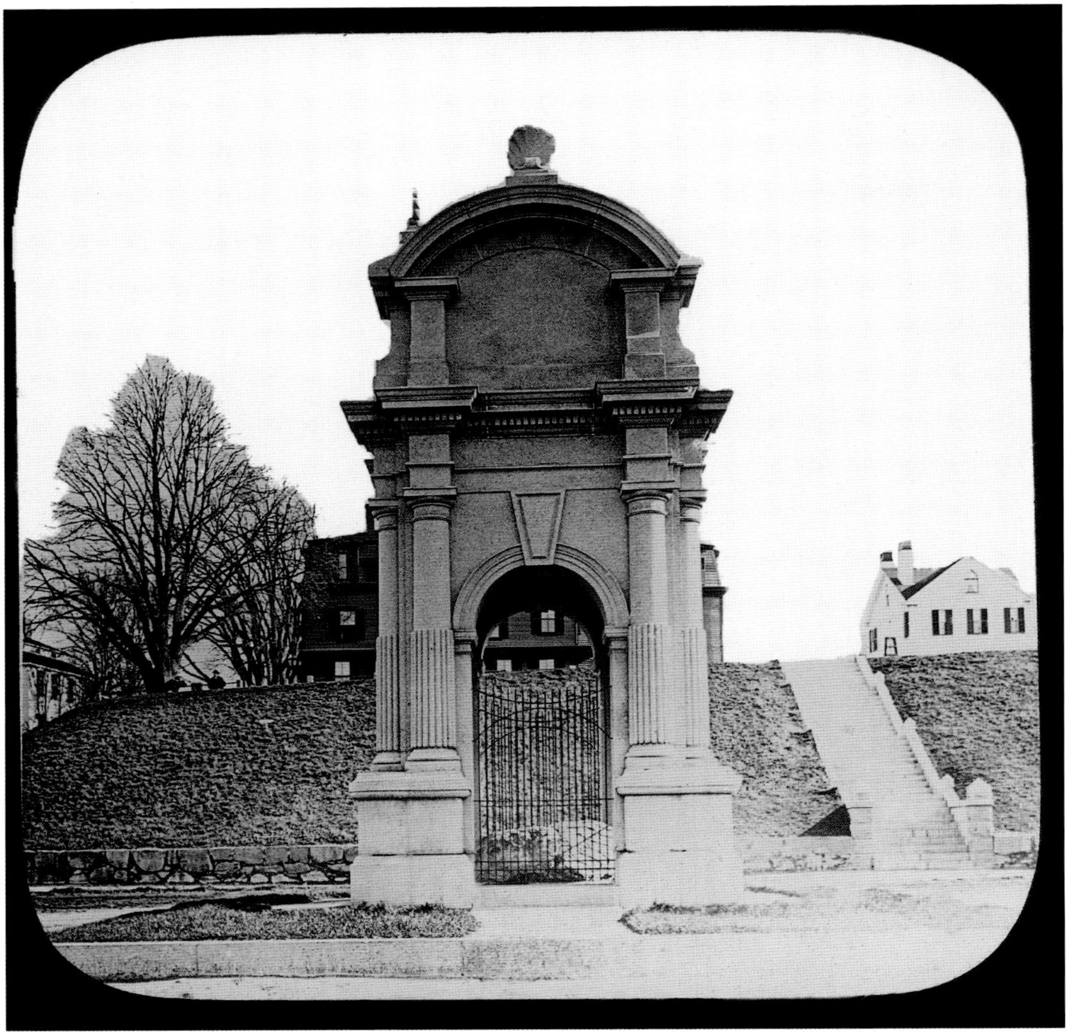

652 Plymouth Rock, Massachusetts, USA, 1880s

652 Plymouth Rock, Massachussetts, USA, 1880er Jahre

652 Plymouth Rock, Massachusetts, USA, années 1880

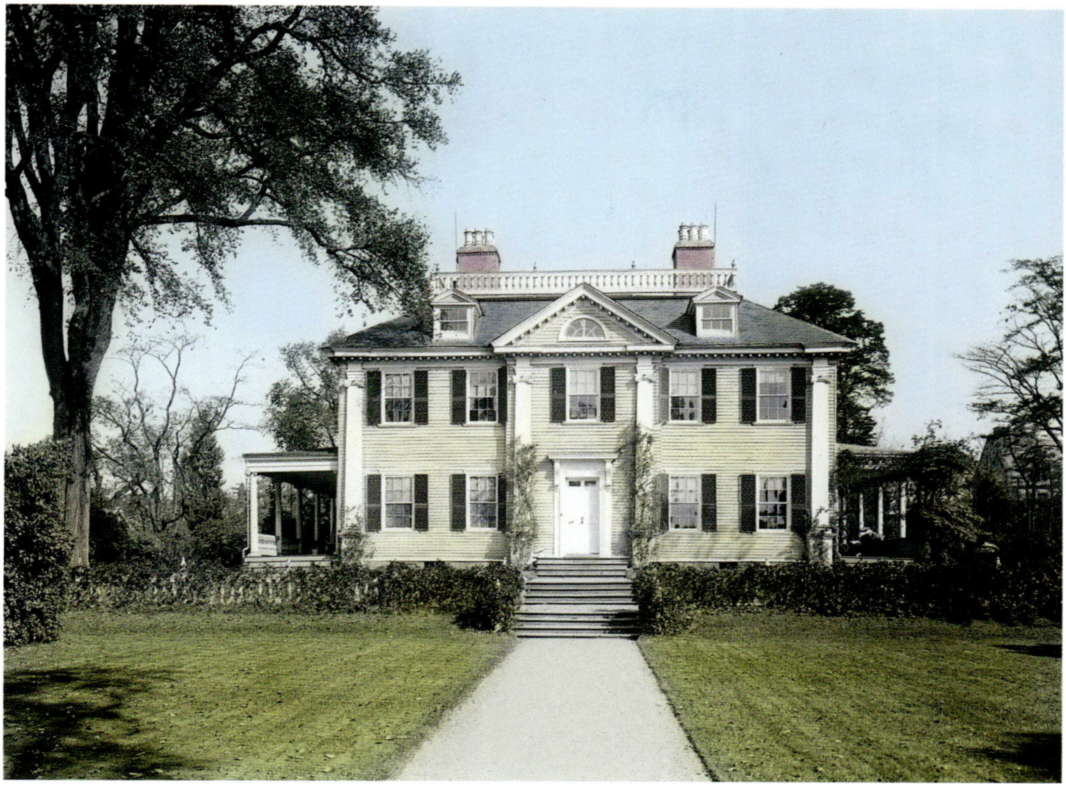

653 Craigie House (home of Henry Wadsworth Longfellow and previously Washington's Headquarters, built 1759), Cambridge, Massachusetts, USA, 1911

653 Craigie House (Anwesen von Henry Wadsworth Longfellow, davor Washingtons Hauptquartier, erbaut 1759), Cambridge, Massachussetts, USA, 1911

653 Craigie House (résidence de Henry Wadsworth Longfellow et le quartier général de Washington, édifié en 1759). Cambridge, Massachusetts, USA, 1911

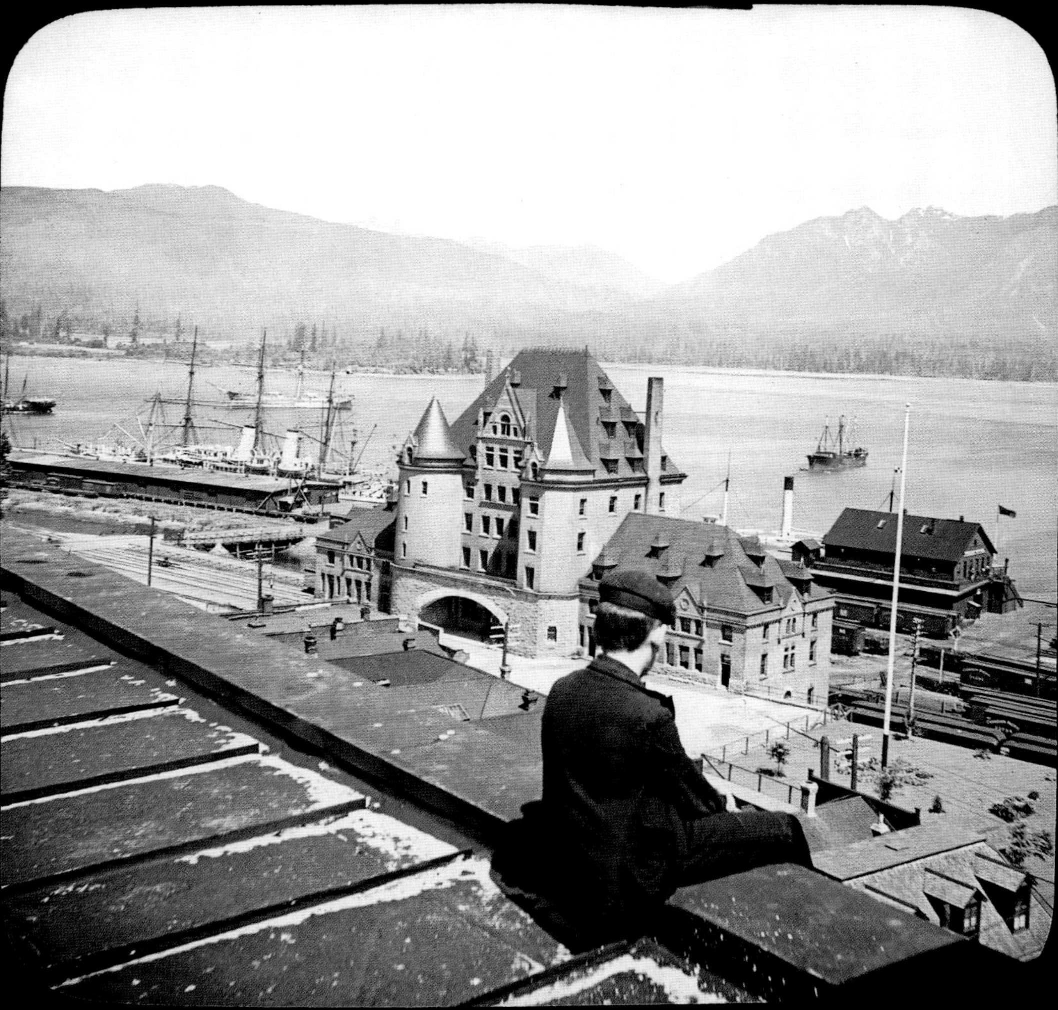

654 Western Terminus
of Canadian Pacific,
Vancouver, British
Columbia, Canada, 1890s

654 Westliche Endstation
der Canadian Pacific,
Vancouver, British
Columbia, Kanada,
1890er Jahre

654 Terminus ouest
de la Canadian Pacific,
Vancouver, Colombie-
Britannique, Canada,
années 1890

CANADA

KANADA · CANADA

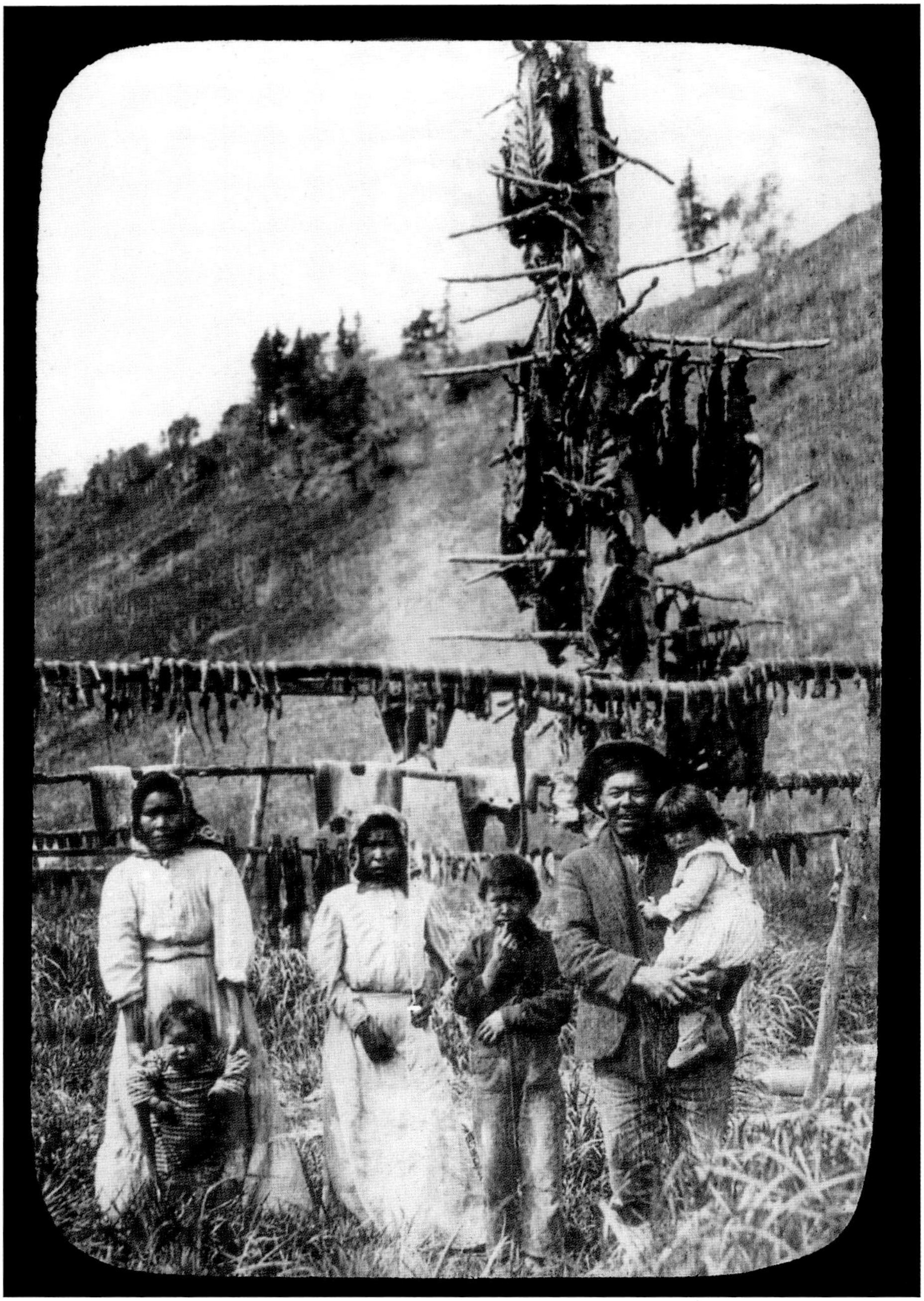

655 Drying fish on the Yukon River, Canada, 1880s
656 Iroquois Indians, Tercentenary Pageant, Quebec, Canada, 1903

655 Trocknen von Fisch am Yukon, Kanada, 1880er Jahre
656 Irokesen, Dreihundertjahrfeier, Quebec, Kanada, 1903

655 Séchage du poisson près du fleuve Yukon, Canada, années 1880
656 Indiens Iroquois, festivités du tricentenaire, Québec, Canada, 1903

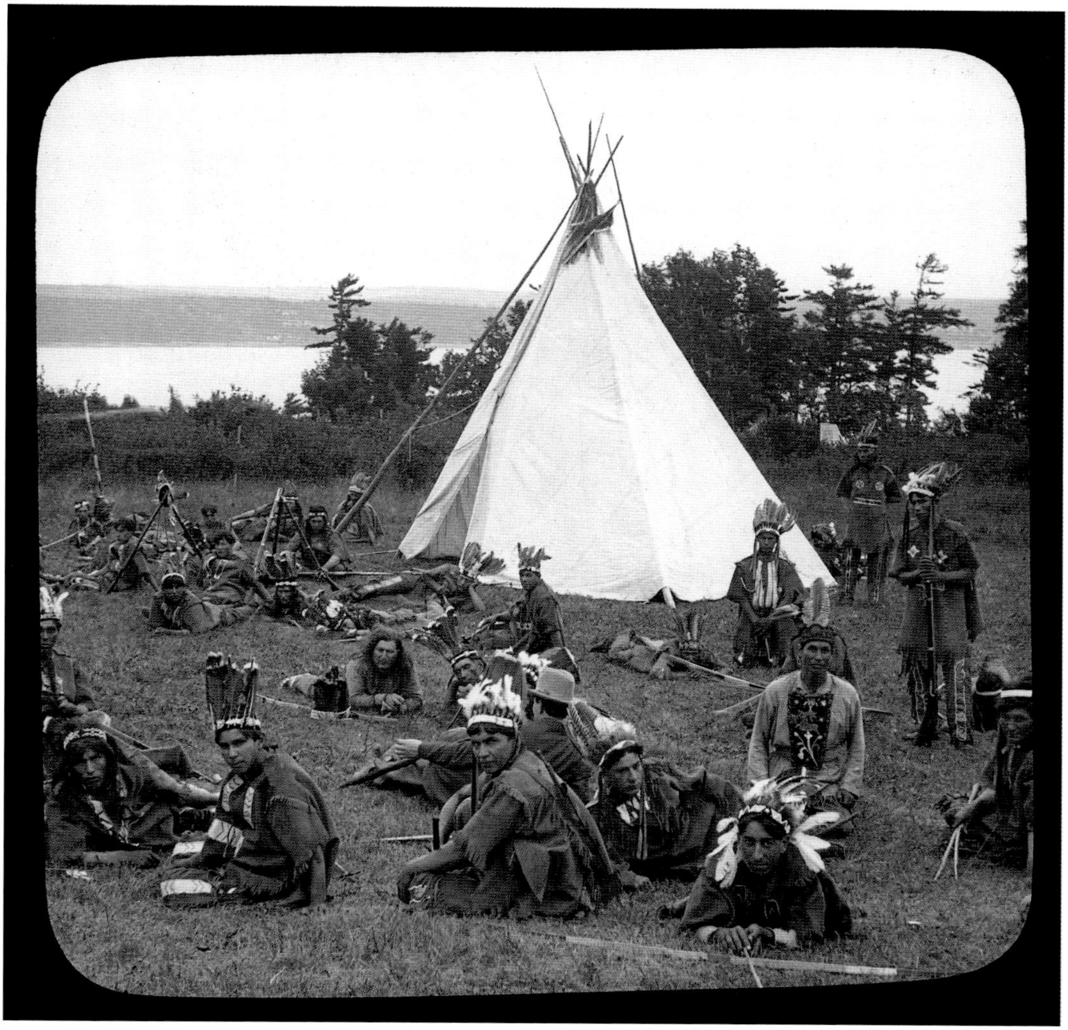

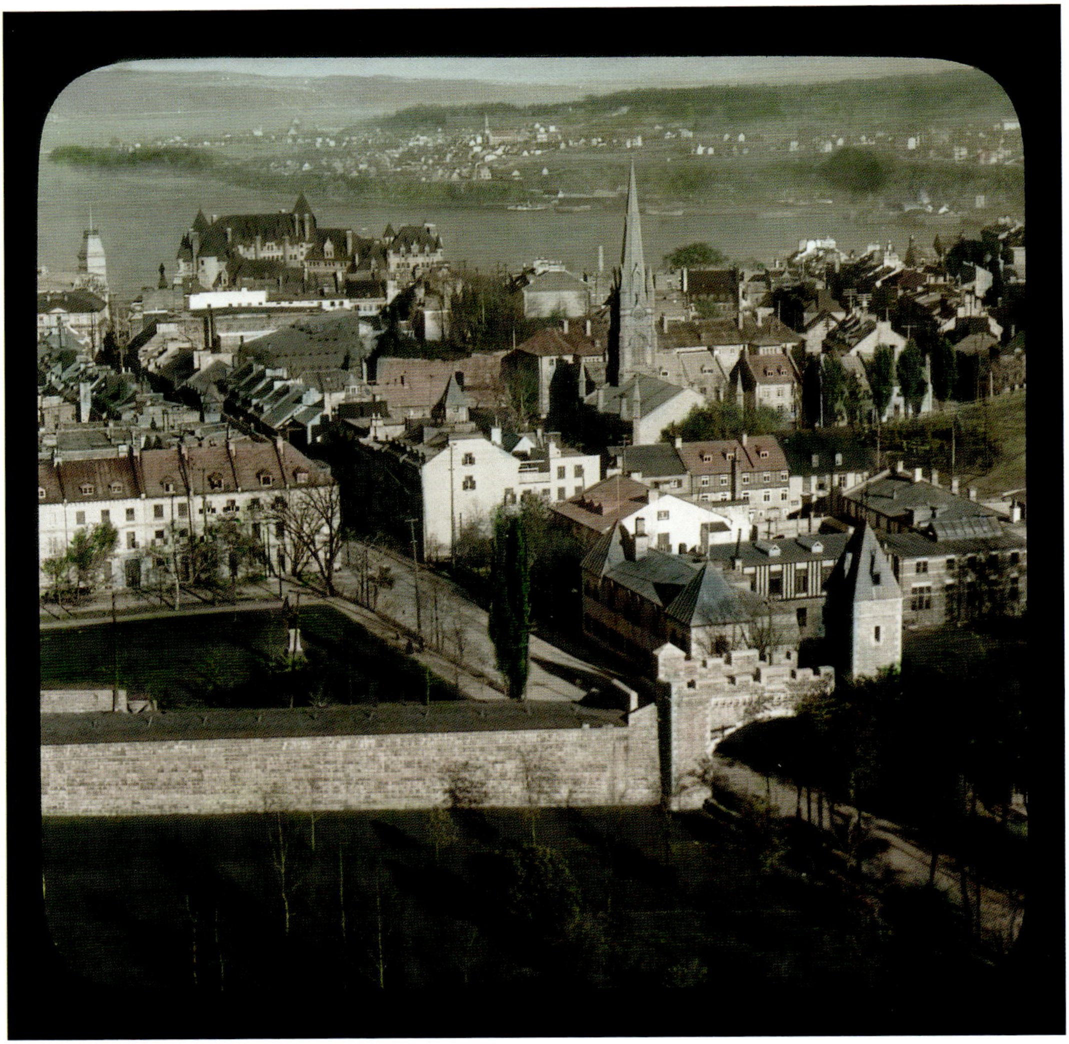

657 View of Quebec City from the Tower of the Parliament Building and looking across the St. Lawrence River to Levis, Quebec City, Canada, 1890s

657 Ansicht Quebecs vom Turm des Parlamentsgebäudes aus mit Blick über den Sankt-Lorenzstrom auf Levis, Quebec, Kanada, 1890er Jahre

657 Vue sur la ville de Québec depuis la tour du Parlement, sur le fleuve Saint-Laurent et au loin, Lévis. Canada, années 1890

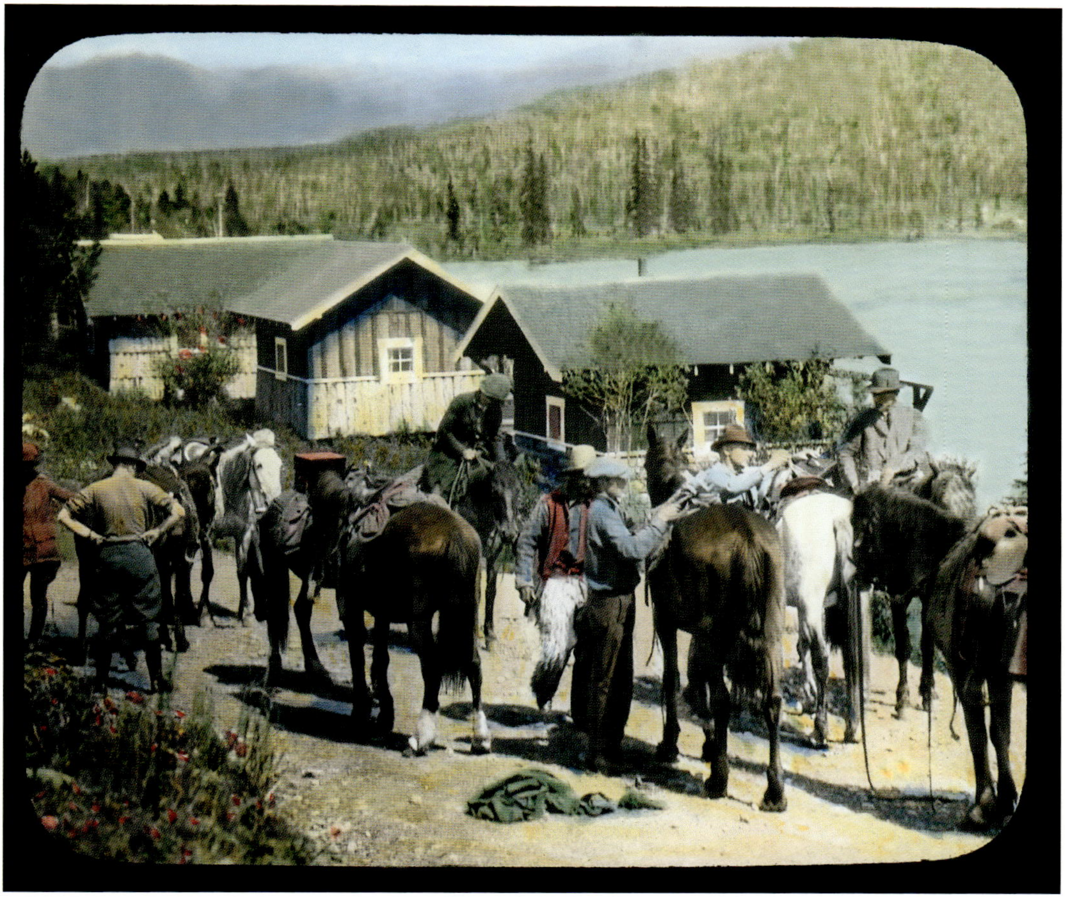

658 Pack train in the Rockies, Canada, 1890s

658 Packtierkolonne in den Rockies, Kanada, 1890er Jahre

658 Convoi de bêtes de somme dans les Rocheuses, Canada, années 1890

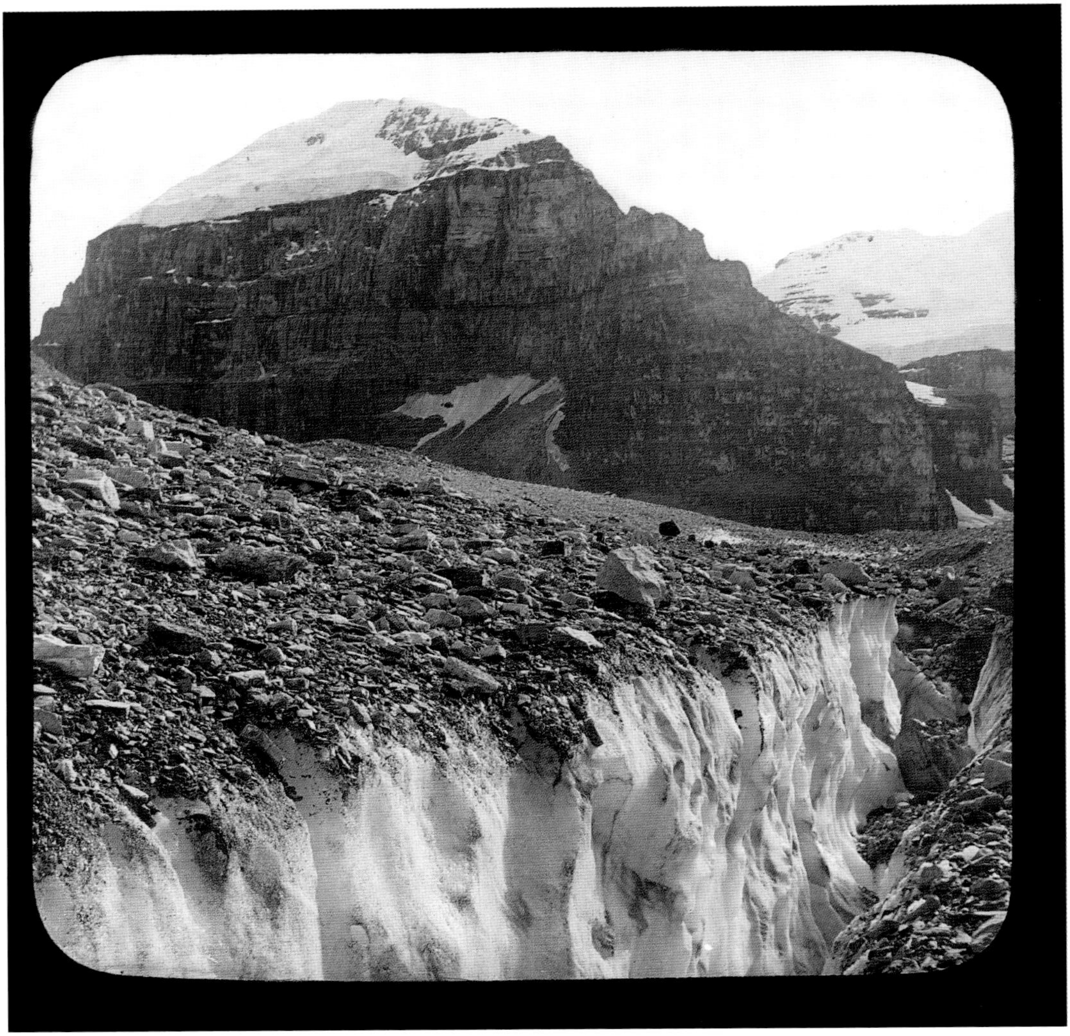

659 Crevasse in Victoria Glacier above Lake Louise, Alberta, Canada, 1890s

659 Spalte auf dem Victoria-Gletscher oberhalb des Lake Louise, Alberta, Kanada, 1890er Jahre

659 Crevasse sur le glacier Victoria, au-dessus du lac Louise, Alberta, Canada, années 1890

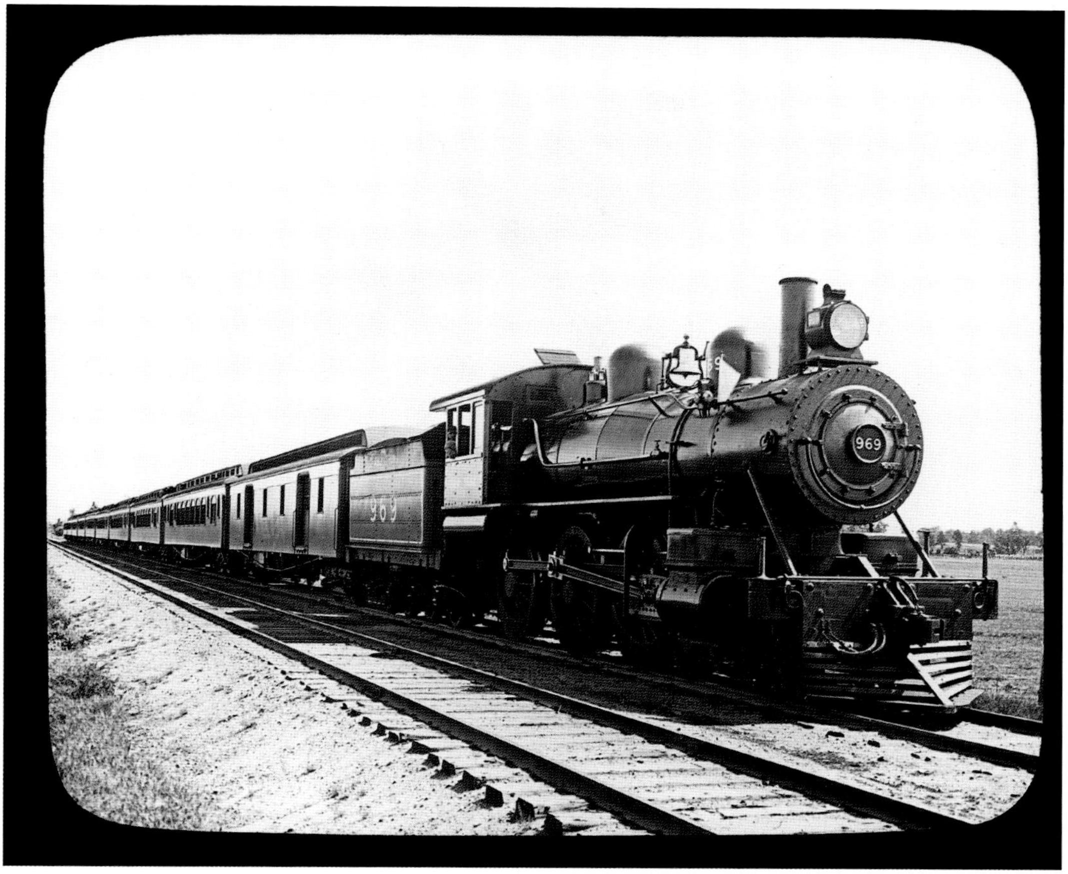

660 Standard passenger train, Grand Trunk Railway System, Canada, c.1900

660 Standard-Personenzug der Grand Trunk Railway, Kanada, um 1900

660 Train de passager de la compagnie du Grand Tronc, Canada, vers 1900

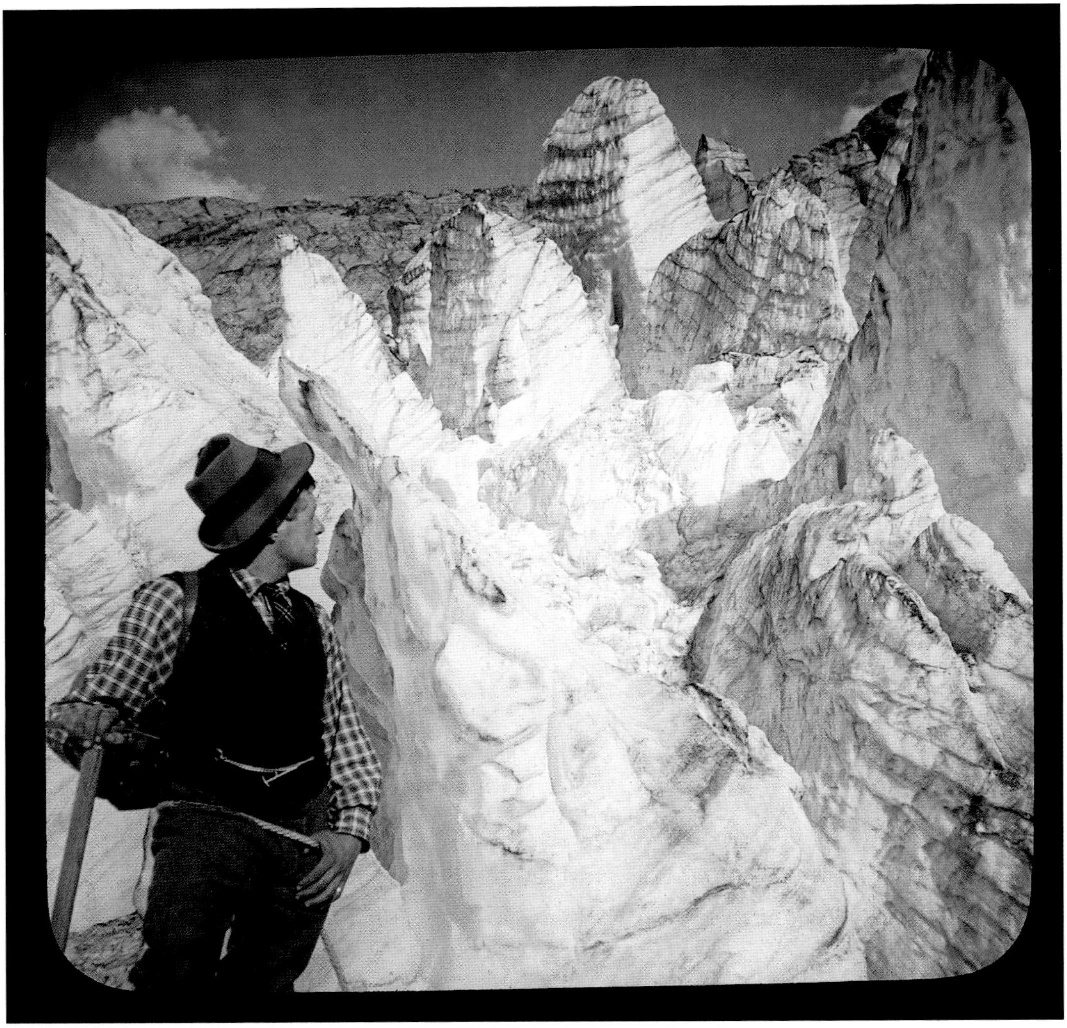

661 Ice peaks of the Illecillewaet Glacier, British Columbia, Canada, 1890s

661 Eisspitzen am Illecillewaet-Gletscher, British Columbia, Kanada, 1890er Jahre

661 Pics de glace du glacier Illecillewaet, Colombie-Britannique, Canada, années 1890

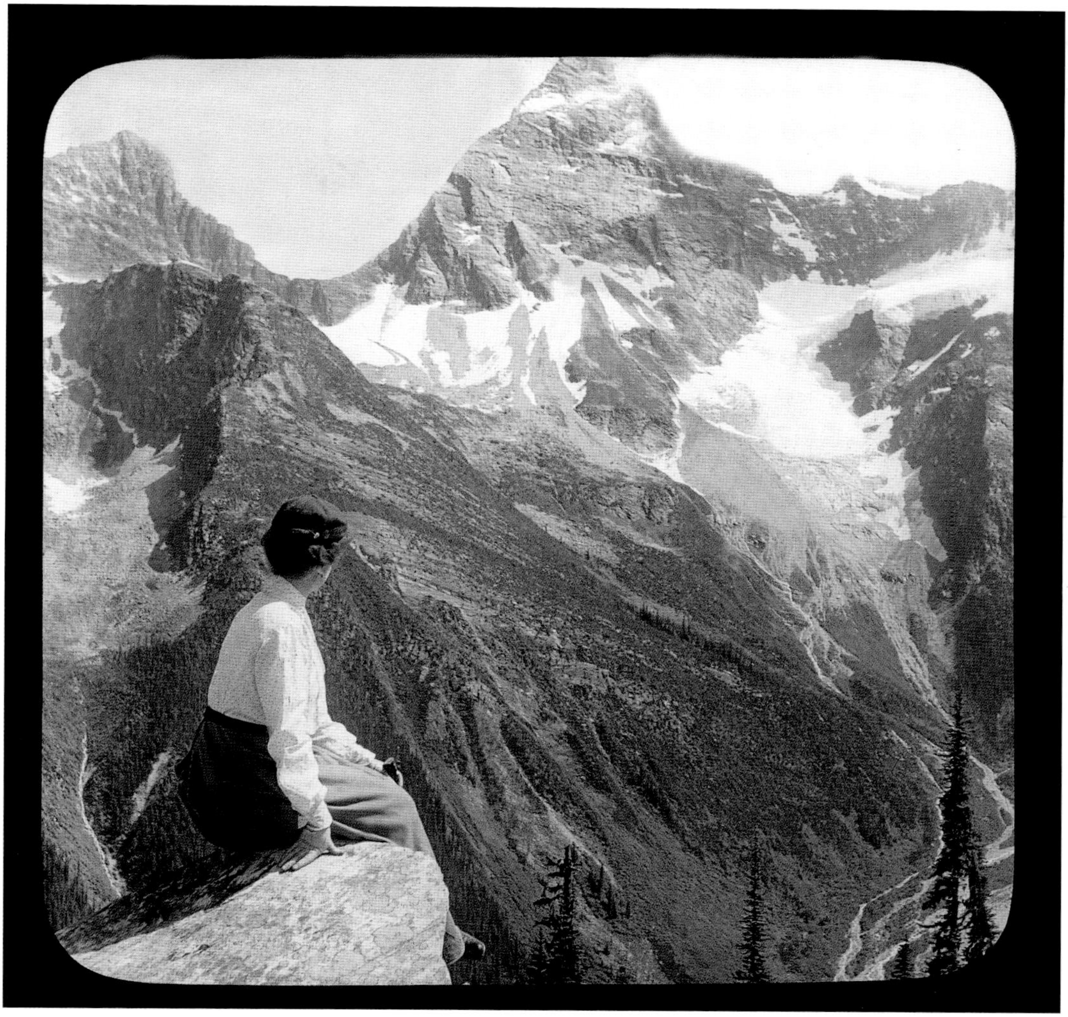

662 Mount Sir Donald (The Matterhorn of the North American Alps), British Columbia, Canada, 1890s

662 Mount Sir Donald (das Matterhorn der Nordamerikanischen Alpen), British Columbia, Kanada, 1890er Jahre

662 Mont Sir Donald (le Cervin des "Alpes" nord-américaines), Colombie-Britannique, Canada, années 1890

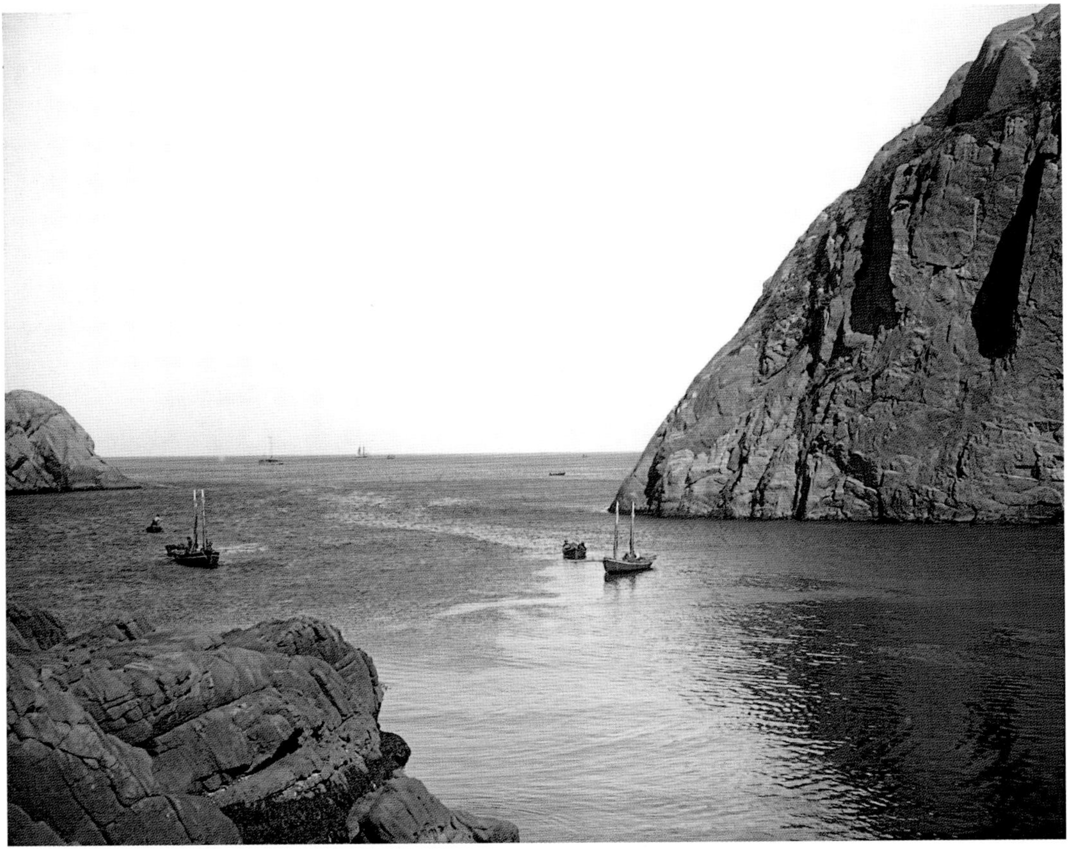

663 Fishing boats in Quidi Vidi Inlet, Newfoundland, 1911

663 Fischerboote in der Bucht von Quidi Vidi, Neufundland, 1911

663 Bateaux de pêche dans la crique de Quidi Vidi, Terre-Neuve, 1911

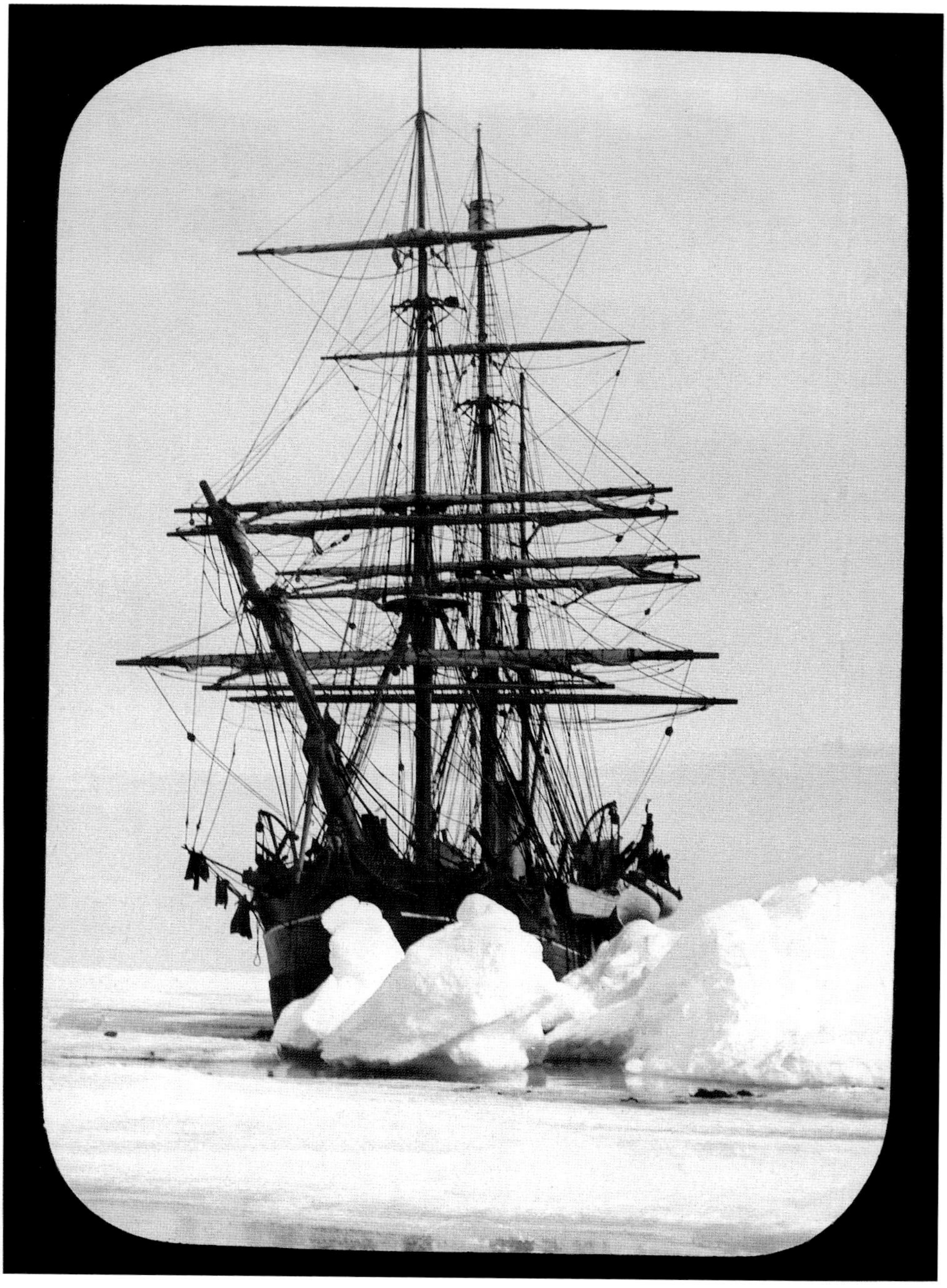

664 Ship surrounded by ice off Cape Hooper, North West Territories, Canada, 1880s

664 Von Eis eingeschlossenes Schiff vor Cape Hooper, Nordwest-Territorien, Kanada, 1880er Jahre

664 Navire pris par la glace, Cape Hooper, Territoires du Nord-Ouest, Canada, années 1880

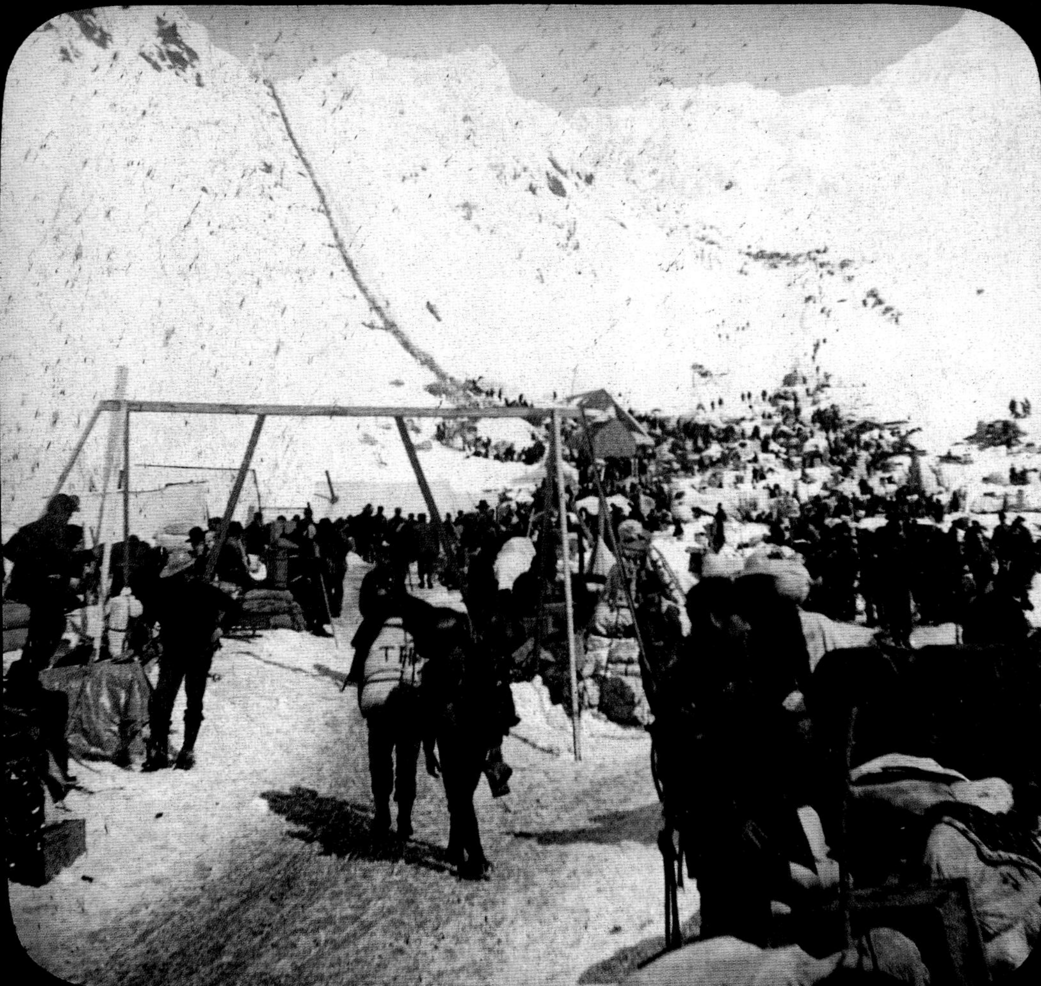

665 "The Golden Stair and Peterson's Trail", Chilkoot Pass, Alaska, c.1897

665 „Die goldene Treppe und Peterson's Spur", Chilkoot-Pass, Alaska, um 1897

665 "L'escalier de l'or" et la piste de Peterson, col du Chilkoot, Alaska, vers 1897

Note sur la datation de diapositives photographiques de lanternes magiques

Bon nombre de diapositives présentées dans cette publication n'ont été initialement datées et nous leur avons donc attribuées des dates approximatives, ce qui semble beaucoup plus facile que cela ne l'était réellement. Nous étions cependant extrêmement chanceux d'avoir Lester Smith, le fondateur de la Société de la Lanterne Magique, qui nous a gentillement offert son aide pour cela, et nous a donné beaucoup de conseils précieux sur les indices à rechercher en terme de datation. Il y a un certain nombre d'indicateurs qui sont utiles, par exemple, si les personnages représentés sur les diapositives apparaissent comme flous, vaporeux, cela indique de longues vitesses d'obturation et suggère donc une date de début des années 1860 ou 1870 ; alors que si les images sont d'une netteté certaine et sont soigneusement teintées-main, cela indique souvent une date environnant les années 1880. Si toutefois, la teinte-main est plutôt approximative et grossière, il est alors plus probable que cela indique une date environnant les années 1890, étant donné que des kits de coloration amateur devenaient dès lors disponibles durant cette décennie. Des diapositives datant des années 1900 et au-delà peuvent être datées par le biais des modes de transport (par exemple, les omnibus à chevaux par rapport aux véhicules automobiles), de la mode vestimentaire ou de l'architecture qu'elles illustrent. Un autre mode de datation que nous avons trouvé est d'utiliser les étiquettes des fabricants qui, parfois, sont encore sur les diapositives - si le nom du fabricant est connu, il est alors souvent possible de déterminer les années au cours desquelles elles ont été utilisées, ce qui peut aider à considérablement réduire les délais. Bien-sûr tout cela signifie que la datation des diapositives photographiques de lanternes magiques est souvent plus un art qu'une science ; et nous espérons donc que les lecteurs comprendront que lorsqu'une diapositive n'a pas une année bien précise indiquée dans la légende l'accompagnant mais plutôt une dizaine d'années (par exemple les années 1890 ou 1920) qui lui sont assignées, la méthode ci-dessus a été utilisée.

Acknowledgements

This publication has been a wonderful personal journey of discovery into the world of the magic lantern. Firstly, I would like to offer immense thanks to Imad Douglas, Mark Fairman and all the rest of the team at DL Imaging for their incredible scanning and retouching work, Mark Thomson for his excellent graphic design solution and Rob Payne for his tireless implementation of the book's layout and his utter dedication to the project, Isabel Wilkinson for her good natured help with image organisation and co-ordination, James Ryan for his wonderfully insightful text that brought a fresh perspective to the subject, Quintin Colville for the excellence of his copy-editing, Zoë Fawcett for her help with production, Bernard Jolivalt and Klaus Kramp for their translations, and Nicolas Lissajoux for his speedy but exacting proofreading. I would also like to express my incredible gratitude to Lester Smith and "Professor" Mervyn Heard for their advice on the dating of slides and also their encouragement. And lastly, my dear husband, Peter, also deserves my heartfelt thanks for his enthusiasm, support and perceptive insights... Thank you all for making this book happen!

Published by Fiell Publishing Limited
www.fiell.com

A catalogue record for this book is available from the British Library

ISBN 978-1-906863-07-4

Project Concept: Charlotte & Peter Fiell
Text: Charlotte Fiell
Additional text: James R. Ryan
Design: Mark Thomson Design
(Mark Thomson and Rob Payne)
Repro: DL Imaging
Production: Zoë Fawcett
German translation: Klaus Kramp
French translation: Bernard Jolivalt

Printed in China

ALASKA

ALASKA · ALASKA

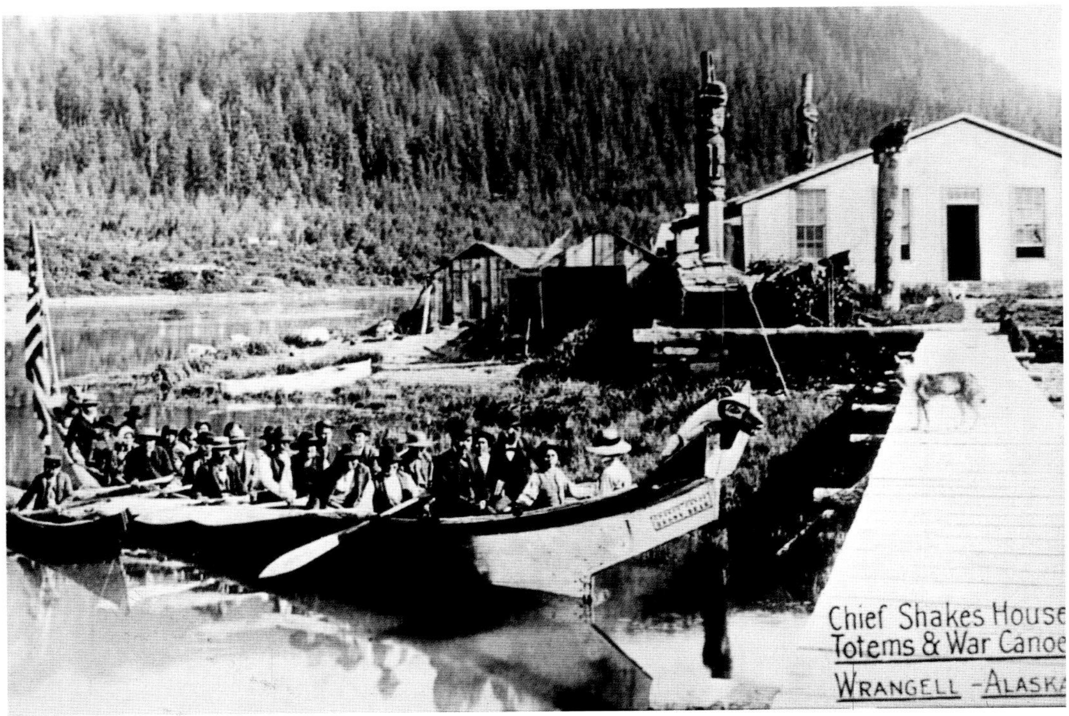

666 Chief Shakes House, Totems and War Canoes, Wrangell, Alaska, 1915
667 Alaska, 1915

666 Chief Shakes House, Totems and War Canoes, Wrangell, Alaska, 1915
667 Alaska, 1915

666 Maisons sur l'île Chief Shakes, totems et canoës de guerre, Wrangell, Alaska, 1915
667 Alaska, 1915

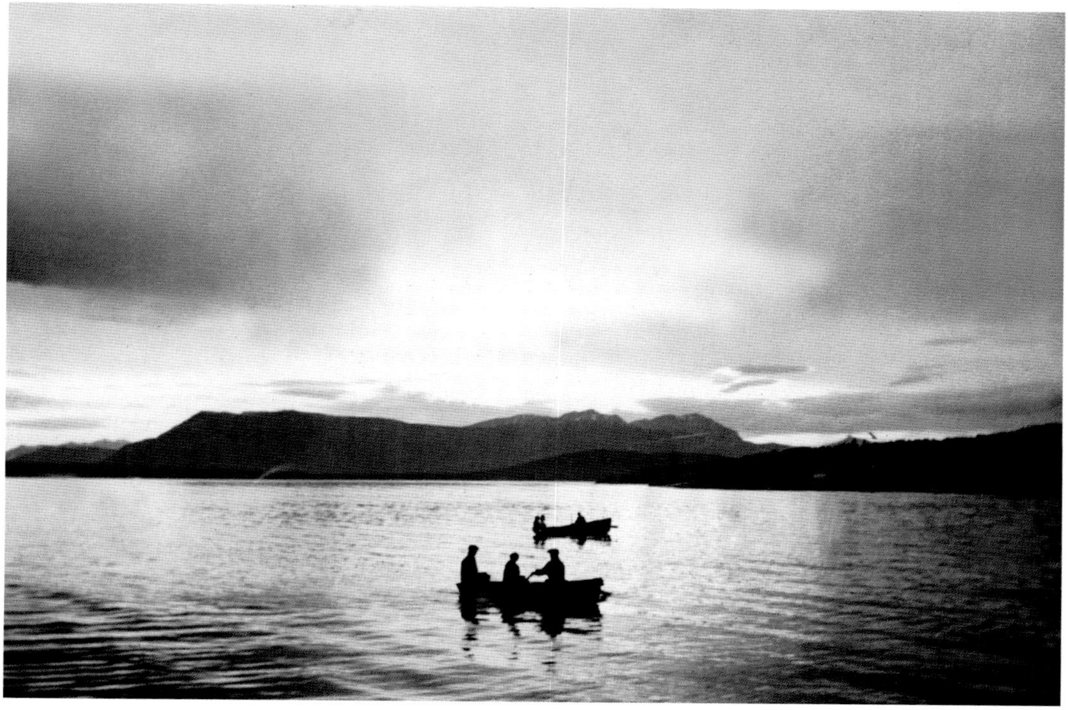

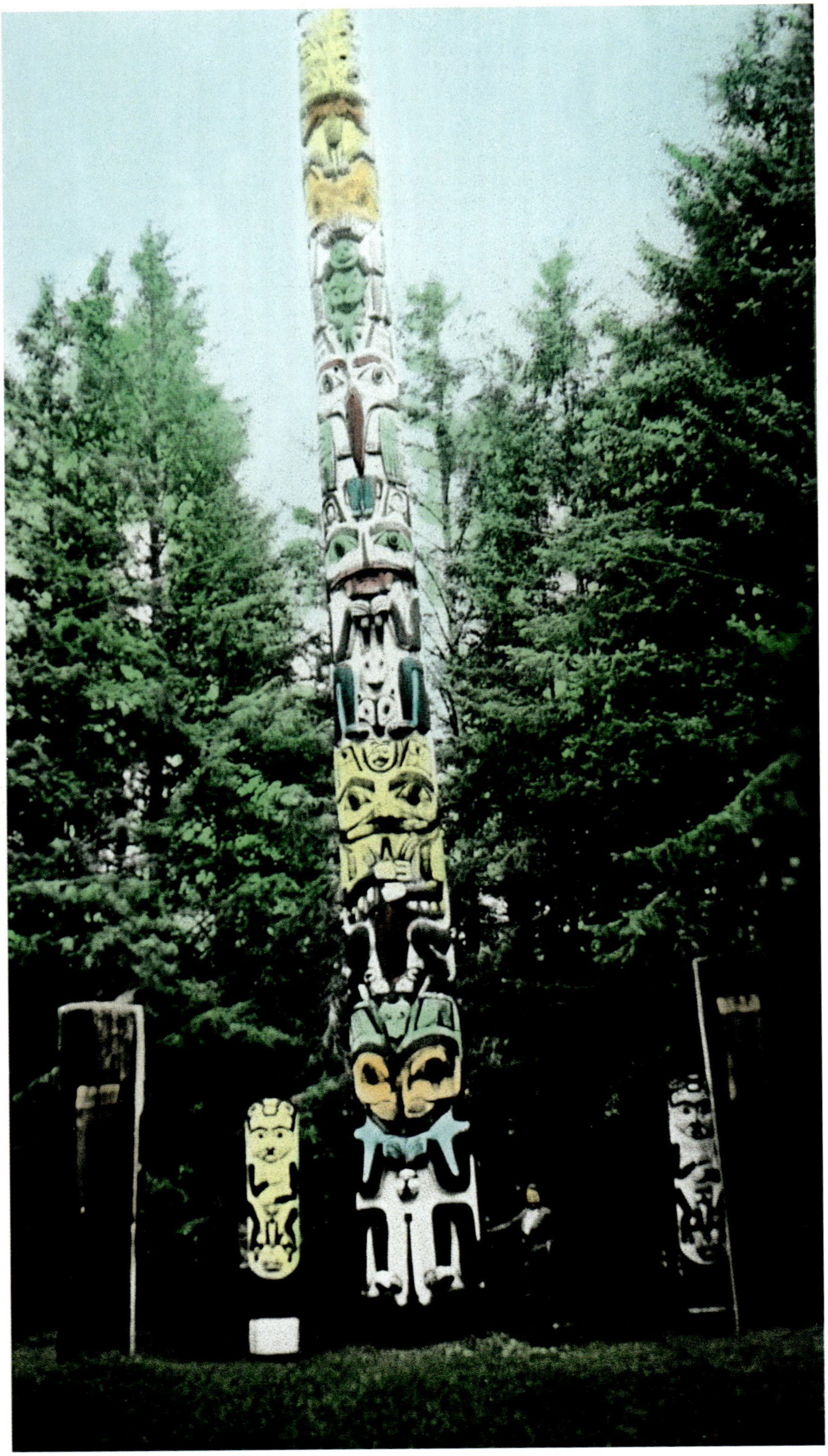

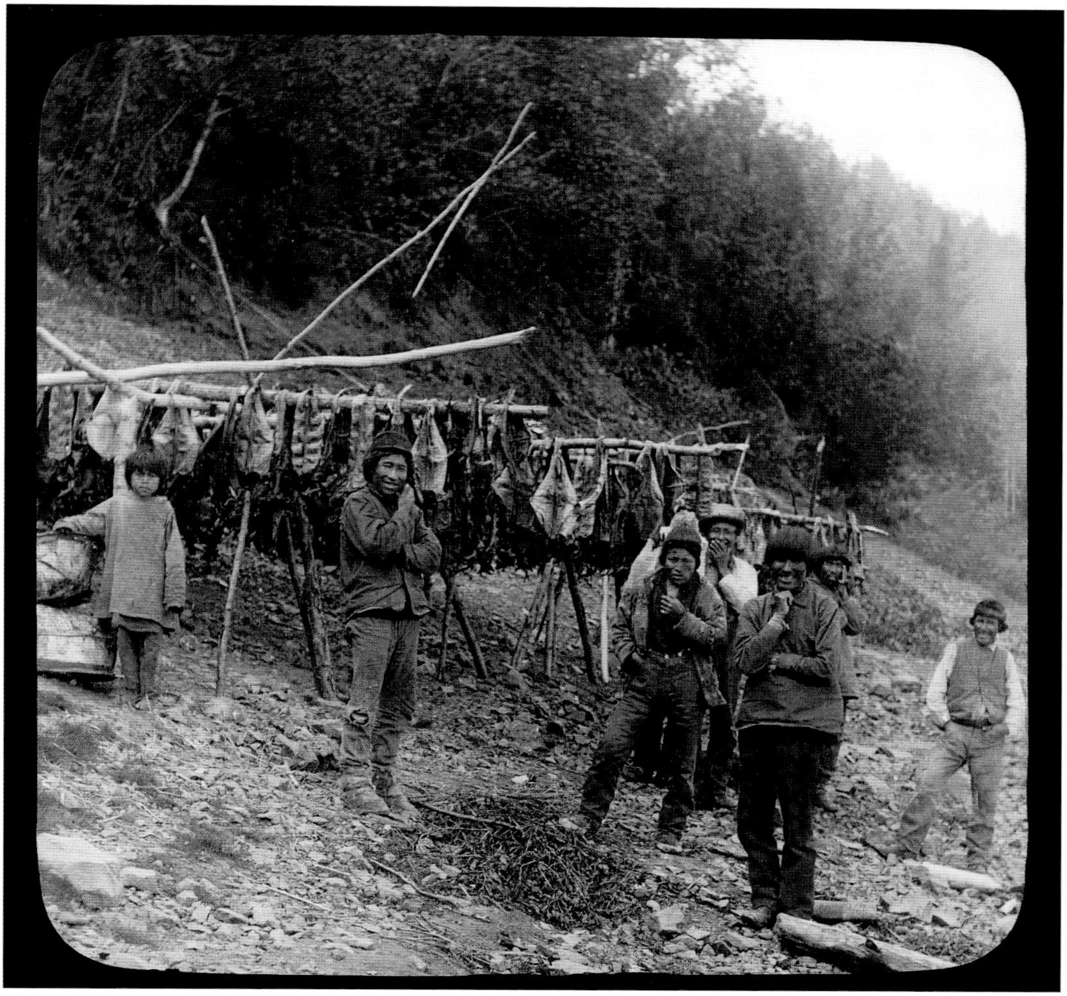

668 Totem pole, Alaska, 1915
669 Drying fish on the Yukon River, Alaska, 1880s

668 Totempfahl, Alaska, 1915
669 Trocknen von Fisch am Yukon, Alaska, 1880er Jahre

668 Totem, Alaska, 1915
669 Séchage du poisson au bord du fleuve Yukon, Alaska, années 1880

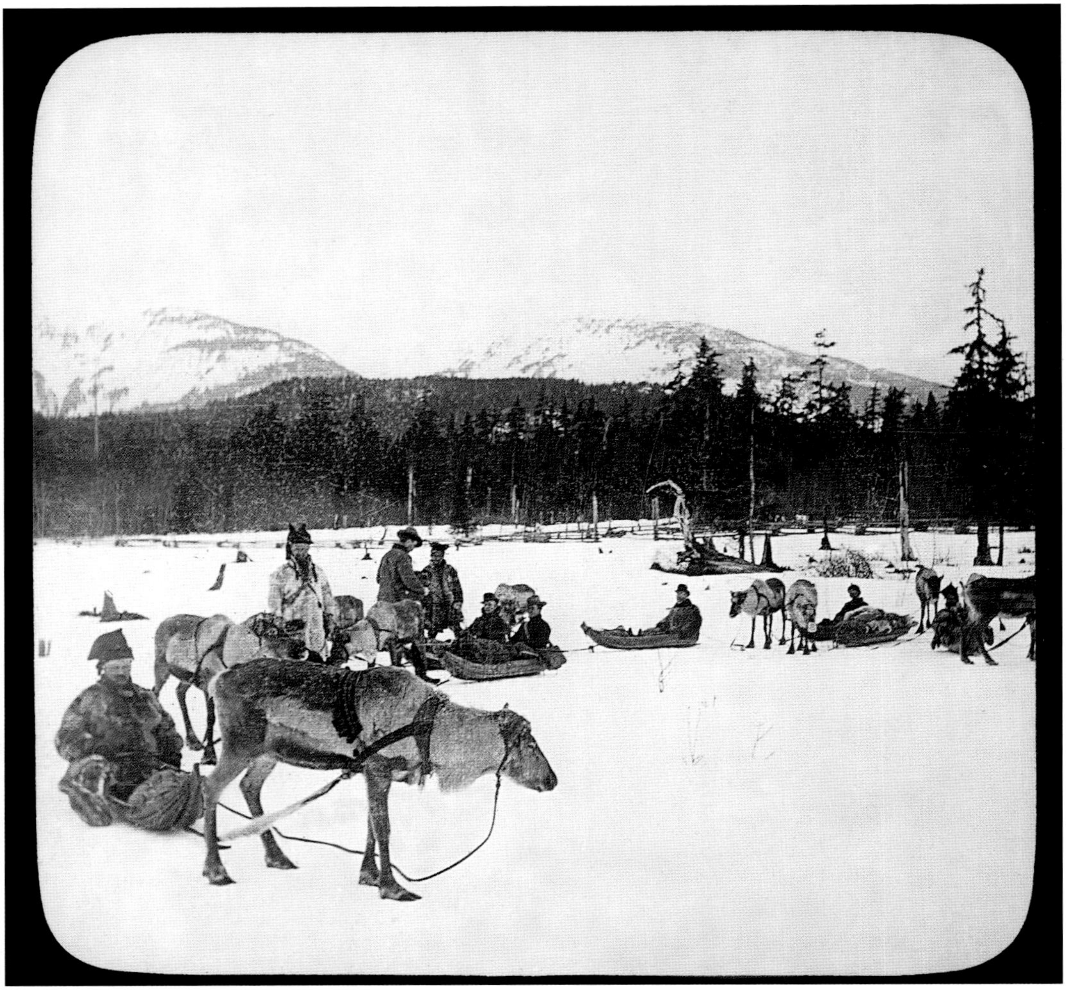

670 Reindeer and sleds, Haines, Alaska, 1890s
671 "The Loose Leader", Team of Sled Dogs, Alaska, 1915

670 Rentiere und Schlitten, Haines, Alaska, 1890er Jahre
671 "The Loose Leader", Schlittenhundegespann, Alaska, 1915

670 Rennes et traîneaux, Haines, Alaska, années 1890
671 "Le chef de meute en tête". Attelage de chiens de traîneau, Alaska, 1915

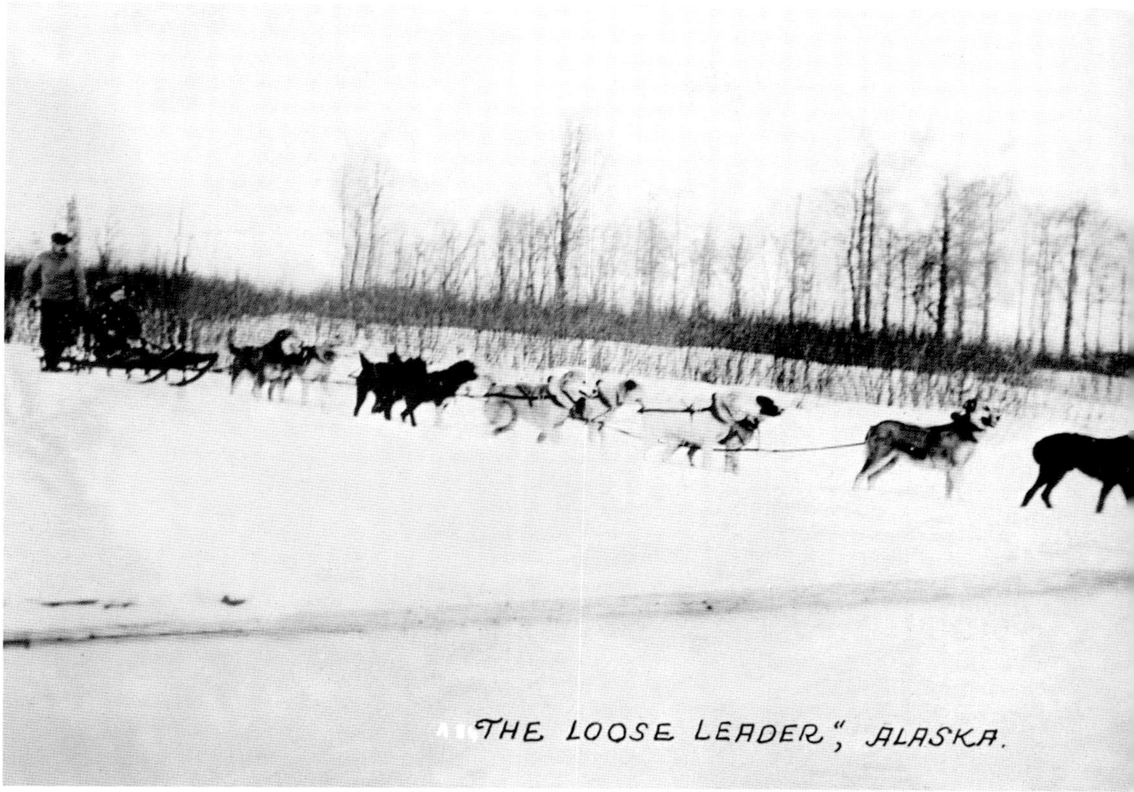
"THE LOOSE LEADER", ALASKA.

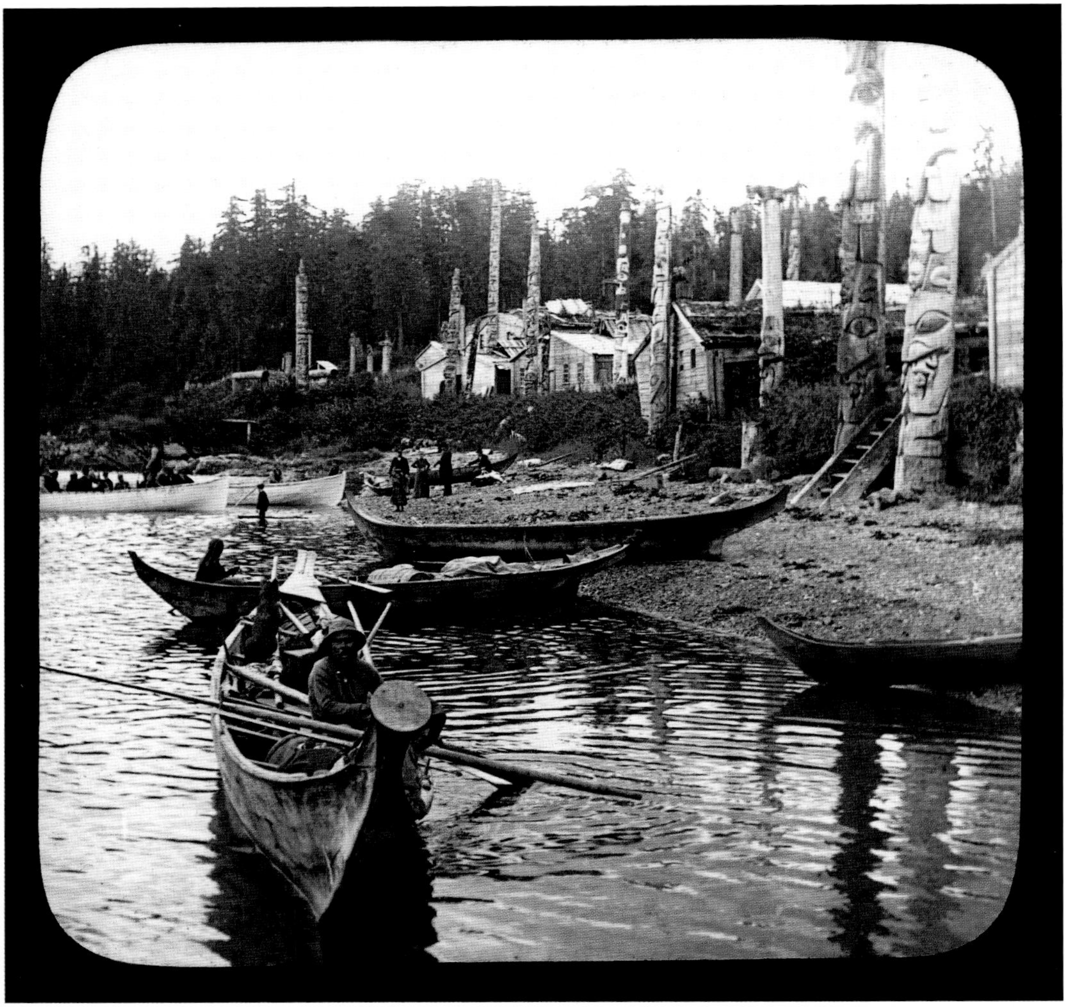

672 Kasaan Village, Alaska, 1890s
673 Inuit paddlers with canoes, Alaska, 1890s

672 Das Dorf Kasaan, Alaska, 1890er Jahre
673 Inuit-Paddler in ihren Kanus, Alaska, 1890er Jahre

672 Le village de Kasaan, Alaska, années 1890
673 Inuits à bord de leur kayak, Alaska, années 1890

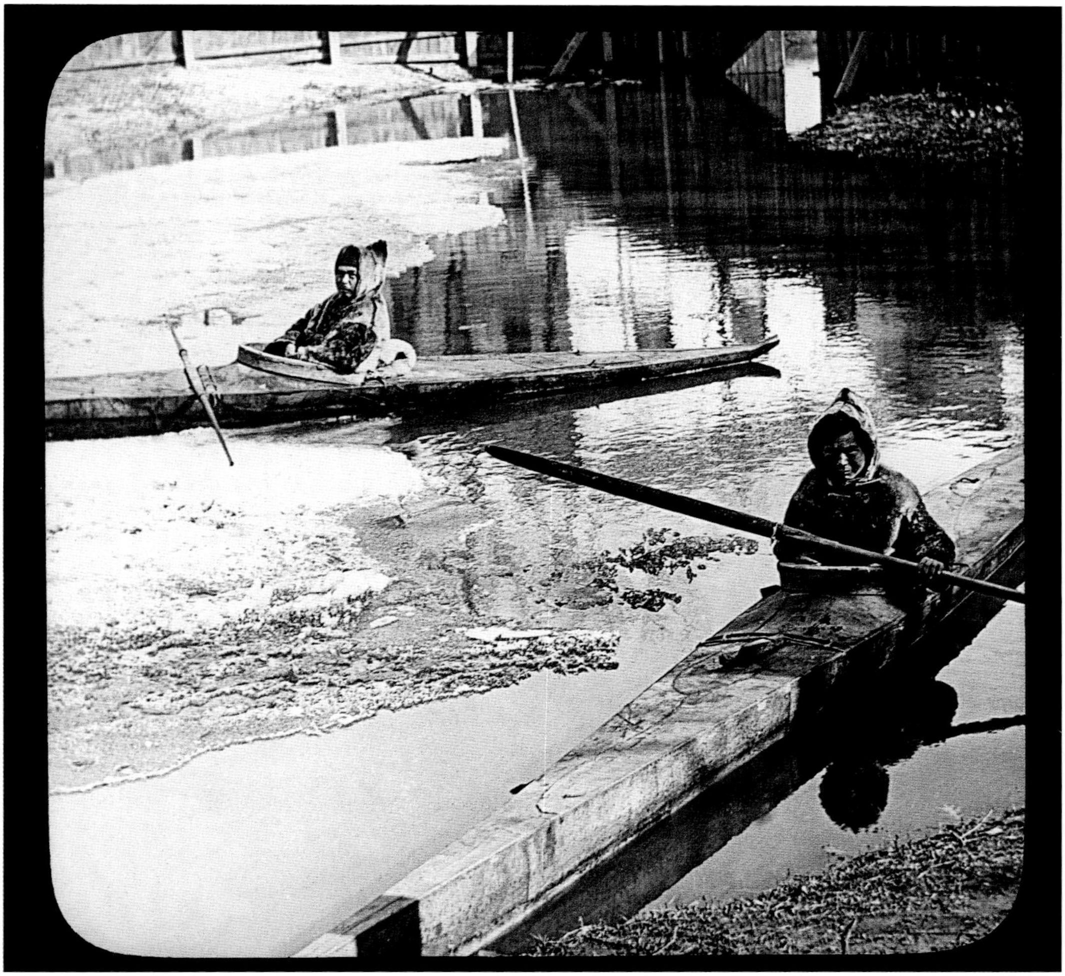

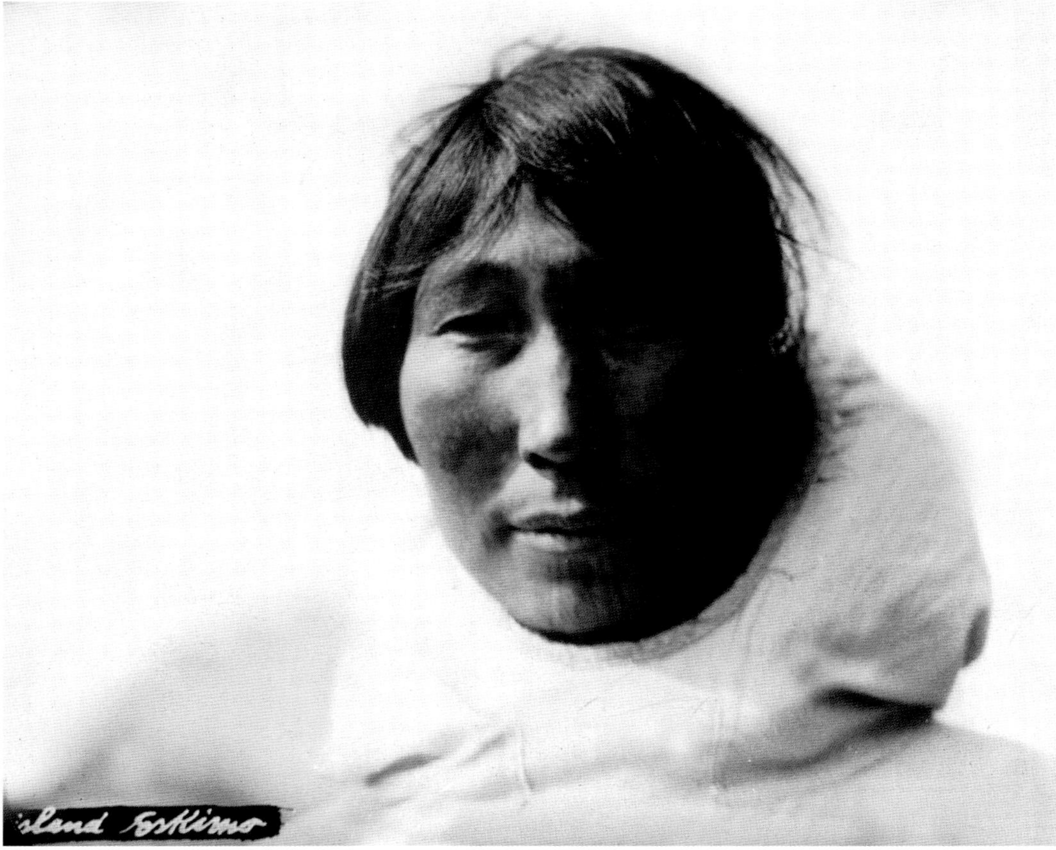

674 "Island Eskimo", Inuit man, Alaska, 1915

674 „Island Eskimo", ein männlicher Inuit, Alaska, 1915

674 « Island Eskimo », Homme Inuit, Alaska, 1915

Key to Lantern Slide Manufacturers

Note on the Dating of Photographic Magic Lantern Slides

Many of the slides shown in this publication were initially undated and so we therefore assigned approximate dates to them, which sounds much easier than it actually was. We were, however, extremely lucky to have Lester Smith, the founder of the Magic Lantern Society, kindly offer to help us with this, and he gave us much invaluable advice on what clues to look for in terms of dating. There are a number of different indicators that are useful, for example if the people portrayed in the slides appear as wispy blurs it indicates long shutter speeds and therefore suggests an early date of 1860s or 1870s, while if the images have a certain crispness and are also painstakingly hand-tinted it often implies a date of around 1880s. If, however, the hand-tinting is rather crude and blotchy then a date of 1890s is more probable, as it was during this decade that amateur tinting kits became available. Slides from around the 1900s and onwards can be dated through the modes of transport (e.g. horse-drawn omnibuses versus motor cars), clothing fashions or architecture depicted in them. Another way of dating we found useful was through the manufacturers' labels that sometimes remained on the slides – if a manufacturer's name is known then it is often possible to find out the years they were in business, which can help narrow the time-frame down considerably. Of course, this all means that the dating of photographic magic lantern slides is often more an art than a science, and we hope, therefore, that readers will understand that if a slide does not have a specific year showing in the accompanying caption, but instead has a decade (e.g. 1890s or 1920s) assigned to it, then the above methodology was used.

Informationen zu der Datierung der Fotografien in „Photographic Magic Lantern"

Viele der Dias, die wir in diesem Buch veröffentlicht haben, waren ursprünglich undatiert und wurden deshalb mit wahrscheinlichen Daten versehen, was sehr plausibel klingt, aber eigentlich eine schwere Arbeit war. Dabei waren wir sehr froh, den Gründer des Vereins „Magic Lantern", Herr Lester Smith, an unserer Seite zu haben, der uns bei der Suche nach wichtigen Aufschlüssen über die Datierung der Dias mit seinem unschätzbaren Rat und Wissen half.

Es gibt eine wesentliche Anzahl von Indikatoren, die sich bei der Fotodatierung als hilfreich erwiesen. Ein Beispiel dafür sind die Porträts von etwas dünn und verschwommen erscheinenden Menschen, die auf eine längere Belichtungszeit der Kamera hinweisen. Dies gibt uns Aufschluss darüber, dass die Aufnahmen zu einem sehr frühen Zeitpunkt um die 1860er oder 1870er Jahre entstanden sind. Bei schärferen mit Hand gefärbten Fotografien handelt es sich um Aufnahmen der 1880er Jahre.

Dabei gibt es aber auch Exemplare, deren Handfärbungen etwas grober und fleckiger erscheinen. Diese Aufnahmen sind wahrscheinlich in den 1890er Jahren entstanden, da zu diesem Zeitpunkt entsprechende Amateurausrüstung auf den Markt kam. Dias der 1900er Jahre und den darauf folgenden Jahren können aufgrund der Bauart von Fahrzeugen (z.B. mit Pferden bespannte Omnibusse sowie Motorräder), Art der Kleidung sowie Architektur bestimmt werden.

Eine andere Art und Weise, die uns wesentlich bei der Datierung half, waren die Herstellerbeschriftungen, die in einigen Fällen an den Dias zu finden waren – kennt man den Namen des Herstellers, so ist es meist auch möglich herauszufinden, in welchen Jahren dieser tätig war. Dies war sehr hilfreich, um den wahrscheinlichen Zeitrahmen der Entstehungszeit eines Dias wesentlich einzugrenzen.

Natürlich bedeutet dies auch, dass die Datierung der „Magic Lantern"-Dias mehr eine Kunst ist, als eine Wissenschaft. Wir hoffen daher, dass die Leser verstehen werden, dass unsere Fotos keine Auskunft über genaue Daten treffen können. Stattdessen kann der Leser in der dazugehörigen Bildunterschrift herausfinden, in welchem Jahrzehnt (z.B. in den 1890er oder 1920er Jahren) das entsprechende Foto entstand. Dabei haben wir die oben genannte Methodik angewandt.